FIFTH EDITION

# Children's Thinking

## Cognitive Development and Individual Differences

**David F. Bjorklund**
*Florida Atlantic University*

WADSWORTH
CENGAGE Learning™

Australia • Brazil • Japan • Korea • Mexico • Singapore • Spain • United Kingdom • United States

**WADSWORTH**
CENGAGE Learning

**Children's Thinking: Cognitive Development and Individual Differences, Fifth Edition**
David F. Bjorklund

Acquisitions Editor: Jaime Perkins

Associate Development Editor: Nic Albert

Assistant Editor: Philip Hovanessian

Editorial Assistant: Jessica Alderman

Marketing Manager: Jessica Egbert

Executive Marketing Communications Manager: Talia Wise

Art Director: Vernon Boes

Manufacturing Director: Marcia Locke

Manufacturing Buyer: Betsy Donaghey

Rights Acquisition Director: Bob Kauser

Rights Acquisition Specialist, Text: Roberta Broyer

Rights Acquisition Specialist, Image: Roberta Broyer

Content Project Management: PreMediaGlobal

Production Service: PreMediaGlobal

Cover Designer: Andy Norris

Cover Image: Aurora Open/Myles McGuinness/ Getty Images

Production House/Compositor: PreMediaGlobal

For product information and technology assistance, contact us at **Cengage Learning Customer & Sales Support, 1-800-354-9706**

For permission to use material from this text or product, submit all requests online at **www.cengage.com/permissions** Further permissions questions can be emailed to **permissionrequest@cengage.com**

Library of Congress Control Number: 2010939528

ISBN-13: 978-1-111-34605-8

ISBN-10: 1-111-34605-4

**Wadsworth**
20 Davis Drive
Belmont, CA 94002
USA

Cengage Learning is a leading provider of customized learning solutions with office locations around the globe, including Singapore, the United Kingdom, Australia, Mexico, Brazil and Japan. Locate your local office at **international.cengage.com/region**

Cengage Learning products are represented in Canada by Nelson Education, Ltd.

For your course and learning solutions, visit **www.cengage.com**.

Purchase any of our products at your local college store or at our preferred online store **www.cengagebrain.com**.

**Instructors:** Please visit **login.cengage.com** and log in to access instructor-specific resources.

Printed in the United States of America
1 2 3 4 5 6 7 14 13 12 11 10

# BRIEF CONTENTS

PREFACE xiii

**Chapter 1**   An Introduction to Cognitive Development   1

**Chapter 2**   Biological Bases of Cognitive Development   31

**Chapter 3**   The Social Construction of Mind: Sociocultural Perspectives on Cognitive Development   74

**Chapter 4**   Infant Perception and Cognition   100

**Chapter 5**   Thinking in Symbols: The Development of Representation   154

**Chapter 6**   The Development of Folk Knowledge   196

**Chapter 7**   Learning to Think on Their Own: Executive Function, Strategies, and Problem Solving   248

**Chapter 8**   Memory Development   301

**Chapter 9**   Language Development   348

**Chapter 10**   Social Cognition   398

**Chapter 11**   Schooling and Cognition   442

**Chapter 12**   Approaches to the Study of Intelligence   492

**Chapter 13**   Origins, Modification, and Stability of Intellectual Differences   530

GLOSSARY  576

REFERENCES  585

CREDITS  645

AUTHOR INDEX  648

SUBJECT INDEX  661

# CONTENTS

PREFACE  xiii

## Chapter 1  An Introduction to Cognitive Development  1

Basic Concepts in Cognitive Development  3
  Cognition  3
  Development  4
  Developmental Function and Individual Differences  6
Five "Truths" of Cognitive Development  7
  Cognitive Development Proceeds as a Result of the Dynamic and
    Reciprocal Transaction of Internal and External Factors  8
  Cognitive Development Is Constructed Within a Social Context  16
  Cognitive Development Involves Both Stability and Plasticity over
    Time  18
  Box 1-1: *The Adaptive Nature of Cognitive Immaturity*  19
  Cognitive Development Involves Changes in the Way Information
    Is Represented  22
  Children Develop Increasing Intentional Control over Their Behavior
    and Cognition  24
  Cognitive Development Involves Changes in Both Domain-General and
    Domain-Specific Abilities  25
Goals of Cognitive Developmentalists  28
Summary  28
Key Terms and Concepts  29
Suggested Readings  30

## Chapter 2  Biological Bases of Cognitive Development  31

Evolution and Cognitive Development  34
  Evolutionary Theory  34
  Evolutionary Developmental Psychology  35
Models of Gene-Environment Interaction  38
  The Developmental Systems Approach  40
  The Genotype → Environment Theory  47
The Development of the Brain  51
  Box 2-1: *The Evolution of the Human Brain*  53
  Neuronal Development  54
  How Do Young Brains Get Hooked Up?  59
  The Development of the Neocortex  62
  The Brain's Plasticity  65

Developmental Biology and Cognitive Development   69

Summary   70

Key Terms and Concepts   72

Suggested Readings   72

**Chapter 3   The Social Construction of Mind: Sociocultural Perspectives on Cognitive Development   74**

The Role of Culture in Cognitive Development   78
   Tools of Intellectual Adaptation   78
   The Social Origins of Early Cognitive Competencies   81
   The Zone of Proximal Development   84
   Apprenticeship in Thinking and Guided Participation   86
   Sociohistorical Influences   92
   Assessing Cognitive Development from a Sociocultural Perspective   93

Implications for Education   94

Sociocultural Theory and Cognitive Development   97

Summary   97

Key Terms and Concepts   98

Suggested Readings   98

**Chapter 4   Infant Perception and Cognition   100**

Basic Perceptual Abilities of Young Infants   102

Some Methodologies Used to Assess Infant Perception   103
   "This Sucks": Using Infant Sucking to Provide Insight into Infant
      Perception   103
   Visual Preference Paradigm   104
   Habituation/Dishabituation Paradigm   105

The Development of Visual Perception   106
   Vision in the Newborn   107
   The Development of Visual Preferences   108
   The Development of Face Processing   113

Auditory Development   118
   Box 4-1: *The Development of Infants' "Specialization" for Processing
      Faces*   119
   Speech Perception   120
   Music Perception   122

Combining Senses   124
   Intermodal Integration   124
   Intermodal Matching   125
   The Intersensory Redundancy Hypothesis   127

How Do We Know What Babies Know? The Violation-of-Expectation
Method   128

Core Knowledge  129
   Object Representation  131
   Early Number Concepts  143
   Arguments Against Core Knowledge  146
Category Representation  147
   How Is Categorization Measured?  147
   The Structure of Infants' Categories  148
What Is Infant Cognition Made Of?  150
Summary  151
Key Terms and Concepts  153
Suggested Readings  153

## Chapter 5  Thinking in Symbols: The Development of Representation  154

Learning to Use Symbols  155
   Young Children's Interpretation of Pictures and Models  156
   The Appearance/Reality Distinction  159
Piaget's Theory  160
   Some Assumptions of Piaget's Theory  161
   Stages of Development  165
   Box 5-1: *Culture and Symbolic Development*  179
   The State of Piaget's Theory Today  181
Everyday Expressions of the Symbolic Function  183
   Symbolic Play  183
   Distinguishing Between Fantasy and Reality  185
Fuzzy-Trace Theory  188
   Assumptions of Fuzzy-Trace Theory  189
   Developmental Differences  191
The Symbolic Species  192
Summary  192
Key Terms and Concepts  195
Suggested Readings  195

## Chapter 6  The Development of Folk Knowledge  196

Theory Theories of Cognitive Development  198
Folk Psychology: Developing a Theory of Mind  199
   Basic Social-Cognitive Skills Underlying Theory of Mind  200
   The Development of Mind Reading  203
   Box 6-1: *Do False-Belief Tasks Overestimate Children's Theory of Mind? Solving True-Belief Tasks*  208
   Theory of Mind, Evolved Modules, and Autism  213
   Extending Theory of Mind  215
   Some Final Reflections on Theory of Mind  219

Box 6-2: *Do Chimpanzees Have a Theory of Mind?* 219

Folk Biology: Understanding the Biological World 221
Is It Alive? 221
What Young Children Know and Don't Know about Biology 222
Where Do Babies Come From? 224

Folk Physics: Understanding the Physical World 225
The Development of Spatial Cognition 226
Object-Oriented Play and Tool Use 234
The Relationship between Tool Use and Object-Oriented Play 240
Children's Understanding of Time 241
Some Final Reflections on Children's Understanding of the
Physical World 245

Summary 245

Key Terms and Concepts 246

Suggested Readings 246

## Chapter 7    Learning to Think on Their Own: Executive Function, Strategies, and Problem Solving    248

Assumptions of Information-Processing Approaches 249

The Development of Basic-Level Processes: Executive Function 251
Speed of Processing 252
Memory Span and Working Memory 254
Attention 258
Learning How Not to Respond: Inhibition and Resistance to
Interference 260
Cognitive Flexibility 263
Some Final Thoughts on Executive Function 264

The Development of Strategies 265
Increases in Strategy Use, Improvements in Performance 265
Box 7-1: *Executive Functioning and Brain Development* 266
Utilization Deficiencies 268
How Do Children's Strategies Develop? Siegler's Adaptive Strategy
Choice Model 270
The Development of Memory Strategies 272
Factors that Influence Children's Strategy Use and Effectiveness 275
Culture and Strategies 284
Strategies in the Classroom 285

Learning to Solve Problems 286
The Development of Problem Solving 287
Reasoning 290

Summary 298

Key Terms and Concepts 299

Suggested Readings 300

## Chapter 8    Memory Development    301

Representation of Knowledge    303

Memory Development in Infancy    305
  Preference for Novelty as an Indication of Memory    305
  Kicking Up Their Heels    306
  Deferred Imitation as a Measure of Memory    310
  Neurological Basis of Infant Memory    313

Infantile Amnesia    314
  Why Can't We Remember Events from Infancy and Early
    Childhood?    315
  Infantile Amnesia and Hypnotic Age Regression    317

Implicit Memory    318

The Development of Event Memory    320
  Script-Based Memory    321
  The Role of Parents in "Teaching" Children to Remember    323

Children as Eyewitnesses    326
  Age Differences in Children's Eyewitness Memories    327
  Age Differences in Suggestibility    333
  Some Final Thoughts on Children as Eyewitnesses    339
  Box 8-1: *Assessing Children's Memories in Real-Life Settings*    340

Remembering to Remember    341

Consistency and Stability of Memory    343
  Is "Memory" a Domain-General Faculty or a Set of Domain-Specific
    Abilities?    343
  How Stable Is Memory Performance over Time?    344

Summary    346

Key Terms and Concepts    347

Suggested Readings    347

## Chapter 9    Language Development    348

  Box 9-1: *Is Language Unique to Humans? Can Apes "Talk"?*    350

What Is Language?    351

Describing Children's Language Development    352
  Phonological Development    353
  Morphological Development    356
  Syntactic Development    358
  Semantic Development    361
  Pragmatics    365
  Speech Registers: The Case of Black English    366

Some Theoretical Perspectives of Language Development    371
  Nativist Perspectives on Language Development    373
  Box 9-2: *The "Less Is More" Hypothesis*    381
  Social-Interactionist Perspectives of Language Development    382

Bilingualism and Second-Language Learning   388
Gender Differences in Language Acquisition   390
Language and Thought   391
Summary   394
Key Terms and Concepts   396
Suggested Readings   396

**Chapter 10    Social Cognition   398**

Social Learning   401
  Forms of Social Learning   403
  Age Differences in Social Learning   405
  Social Learning in Chimpanzees   412
  Box 10-1: *Mirror Neurons: The Foundation of Social Learning?*   415
Social Cognitive Theory   416
  Factors Involved in Observational Learning   417
  The Development of Self-Efficacy   418
Social Information Processing   421
The Development of a Concept of Self   424
Cognitive Bases of Gender Identity   427
  Gender Constancy   428
  Gender Schemas   431
  Gender Knowledge and Sex-Typed Behavior: Possible
    Predispositions   436
  Children's Theories of Gender   438
How "Special" Is Social Cognition?   439
Summary   439
Key Terms and Concepts   441
Suggested Readings   441

**Chapter 11    Schooling and Cognition   442**

The Development of Reading Skills   444
  A Brief Overview of Learning to Read   444
  Emergent Literacy   445
  Cognitive Development and Reading   447
  How to Teach Children to Read   453
  Sex Differences in Reading and Verbal Abilities   455
Children's Number and Arithmetic Concepts   459
  Conservation of Number   460
  Learning to Count   461
  Children's Arithmetic Concepts   463
  Math Disability   470
  Box 11-1: *The (Math) Games Children Play*   471

Cultural Differences in Mathematics   472
Sex Differences in Mathematical Ability   475

Schooling and Cognitive Development   480
Schooling Versus Age Effects on Intelligence   481
The Effect of Schooling on IQ   482
The Costs and Benefits of Academic Preschools   484

Evolutionary Educational Psychology   485
Principles of Evolutionary Educational Psychology   486
Physical Activity   488

Summary   489

Key Terms and Concepts   491

Suggested Readings   491

## Chapter 12   Approaches to the Study of Intelligence   492

The Psychometric Approach to the Study of Intelligence   494
Factors of Intelligence   495
IQ Tests   497

Information-Processing Approaches to the Study
of Intelligence   506
Basic-Level Processes   507
Higher-Level Cognitive Abilities   509

Sternberg's Triarchic Theory of Intelligence   514
The Contextual Subtheory, or Practical Intelligence   514
The Experiential Subtheory, or Creative Intelligence   516
The Componential Subtheory, or Analytic Intelligence   517

Gardner's Theory of Multiple Intelligences   519
Box 12-1: *The Triarchic Theory Goes to School*   520
Criteria of an Intelligence   523
Multiple Intelligences and Education   525
Assessment of Gardner's Theory   526

Summary   527

Key Terms and Concepts   529

Suggested Readings   529

## Chapter 13   Origins, Modification, and Stability of Intellectual Differences   530

A Transactional Approach to the Study of Intelligence   532

Behavioral Genetics and the Heritability of Intelligence   536
The Concept of Heritability   536
Elementary Cognitive Tasks and Intelligence   538
Familial Studies of Intelligence   540
The Role of the Environment in Behavioral Genetics Analyses   542
How Seriously Should We Take Heritability Studies of IQ?   545

Experience and Intelligence   546
    Establishing Intellectual Competence   546
    Modification and Maintenance of Intellectual Functioning   553
    How Modifiable Is Human Intelligence?   563
The Stability of Intelligence   563
    Defining Stability   563
    Predicting Later Intelligence from Tests in Infancy   564
    The Stability of IQ Scores During Childhood   569
    Patterns of IQ Change During Childhood   570
    Box 13-1: *Are People Getting Smarter? The Flynn Effect*   572
Summary   574
Key Terms and Concepts   575
Suggested Readings   575


GLOSSARY   576
REFERENCES   585
CREDITS   645
AUTHOR INDEX   648
SUBJECT INDEX   661

# PREFACE

Cognitive development continues to be a dynamic field. Theories and research findings from a variety of areas combine to produce a picture of a developing child who is born prepared to make some sense of the world, but whose mind is also shaped by forces in the physical and social environment. This theme, of the continuous transaction between an embodied child embedded in a social world, continues to serve as the focus of the fifth edition. In addition, themes prominent in the previous editions have even greater emphasis in the fifth, reflecting, I believe, how the science of cognitive development has changed over recent years. First, there is a greater recognition of the dynamical nature of development. As in the fifth edition, dynamical systems approaches are discussed in some detail in the introductory chapter, explaining concepts such as *self-organization*, *emergence*, and the concept of *dynamic systems* itself. My intention is that this explicit treatment of dynamic systems up front will help students better understand discussions based on these concepts that follow in later chapters.

This edition also extends a trend begun in earlier editions of including more research from cognitive developmental neuroscience. There has been a "biologizing" of cognitive development in recent years, and this is most reflected in research looking at how the brains of infants and children change over time and are associated with different patterns of cognitive functioning. I firmly believe that "mind" is a state of brain, and, although knowing what's happening in the brain will not, by itself, tell us what we, as psychologists, need to know, it is an essential ingredient in understanding cognitive development. However, having a developmental theory of the brain does not obviate having a developmental theory of the mind. Our job is to develop an understanding of how children's thinking changes over time and how such changes affect how children function in their world, and knowing something about the biology of thinking can help us achieve this goal although it is not the goal itself.

Related to this biologizing of development is an increased interest in evolutionary thinking—how selective pressures in our ancient past may influence how children develop today. I have been a proponent of the emerging field of *evolutionary developmental psychology* and believe that such a perspective has much to offer the field of cognitive development. This perspective is outlined in Chapter 2 in the *Biological Bases of Cognitive Development*, and found, where appropriate, in various chapters in the book.

Throughout this book I attempt to present cognitive development not as a series of separate accomplishments (e.g., memory, language, theory of mind, executive function), but as a process that involves the dynamic interaction between an active organism with a changing environment. As such, I strive to integrate biological (e.g., genetics, brain functioning) with sociocultural and evolutionary factors to describe and explain human cognitive development. Where appropriate, I contrast human cognitive development with those of our close genetic relatives (e.g., chimpanzees) to develop an appreciation of how unique human thinking is (or is not, depending on what cognitive abilities great apes possess).

This book is still unique in that it deals with both the typical patterns of change in thinking observed over time (cognitive development) and individual differences in children's thinking in infancy, childhood, and adolescence. Children use their developing cognition to solve problems, and many of those problems are related to acquiring the skills necessary for success in a highly technological world. Research and theory in cognitive development should do more than inform researchers: they should also provide insights, both for parents and teachers, into how best to deal with children. Although this new edition is in no way a "how to" book for educating children, I describe research that has implications for education, making it useful for students training to be teachers as well as psychologists.

Several pedagogical features from the earlier editions are retained here. These include a glossary that includes all the key terms at the end of the book, and the "Key Terms and Concepts" and "Suggested Readings" sections at the end of each chapter. I provide a brief paragraph about each suggested reading to explain why each particular paper or book is worth perusing. The Suggested Readings section is expanded in this edition, providing a category of "Scholarly Works," as well as a category "Reading for Personal Interests," which includes books and articles written for an educated lay audience.

As in previous editions, the 5th edition provides up-to-date research and theory on cognitive development appropriate for graduate and upper-level undergraduate students. However, I aimed to make the book more "reader friendly" and accessible throughout, reducing discussion of some topics while adding topics that may be of more inherent interest to a broader range of students. Each chapter starts with a vignette illustrating some concept or phenomenon discussed in the chapter, easing students into the chapter. I have also added one or more boxed items to most chapters, based on one of the themes of the book.

Perhaps the most obvious change in the 5th edition is a reduction of chapters from 16 (plus an Epilogue) to 13 (without an Epilogue). The change in the number of chapters is accompanied by a reorganization of chapters, plus the inclusion of new chapters in addition to the deletion of several others. Gone from the 5th edition are the chapters titled *Piaget's Theory*, *Information-Processing Approaches*, *Spatial Cognition*, and *Problem Solving and Reasoning*. Most of the content in these former chapters are included in other chapters in the 5th edition. For example, Piaget's theory is still covered in substantial detail in the new chapter titled *The Development of Representation*, and information-processing approaches and problem solving and reasoning are integrated in the chapters titled *Memory Development* and *Learning to Think on Their Own: Executive Function, Strategies, and Problem Solving*. The remaining chapters of the 4th edition are all included in the 5th (with some subtle differences, see *Chapter-by-Chapter Examination of Organizational Changes between 4th and 5th Editions*), with the addition of a new chapter, *The Development of Folk Knowledge*, which examines children's intuitive understanding of the major domains of their world. In this chapter, I discuss the development of folk psychology (such as theory of mind), folk physics (including much of the material that was formerly covered in the *Spatial Cognition* chapter from the 4th edition), and new material on folk biology. As in previous editions, the last three chapters deal primarily with issues of individual differences in children's thinking, specifically schooling and cognition (Chapter 11), approaches to the study of intelligence (Chapter 12), and the origins, modification, and stability of intellectual differences (Chapter 13). I believe this new organization provides a better-integrated view of the contemporary science of cognitive development, while still presenting the classic research and theories that have made the discipline what it is today. The following details specific chapter-by-chapter changes to the 5th edition:

# CHAPTER-BY-CHAPTER EXAMINATION OF ORGANIZATIONAL CHANGES BETWEEN 4TH AND 5TH EDITIONS

All chapters in the 5th edition have been substantially revised, including the latest research and ideas pertaining to cognitive development. There are many new tables and figures, sometimes replacing older research discussed in previous editions. Here I discuss what I see as major organizational changes (and stabilities) between the 4th and 5th editions of *Children's Thinking*.

## Chapter 1: An Introduction to Cognitive Development

The major change in this introductory chapter involves removing a major section titled "Some Issues in Cognitive Development" and replacing it with one titled "Five 'Truths' of Cognitive Development." I've also eliminated the section from the 4th edition titled "Changes that Occur in Cognitive Development." Some of the "issues" and "changes" of the 4th edition and the "truths" of the 5th edition are the same (for example, discussions of the dynamical nature of development, stability and plasticity in development, domain-general and domain-specific abilities, the importance of studying changes in representation and intentional control), but there are some differences. Gone is an in-depth discussion of stages of development (e.g., continuity vs. discontinuity of developmental change) and added is a section titled "Cognitive Development is Constructed within a Social Context." The changes represent a streamlining of important content found in both the 4th and 5th editions, but also the addition or highlighting of new concepts reflecting how cognitive development is practiced today.

## Chapter 2: Biological Bases of Cognitive Development

The organization of this chapter has remained essentially the same between the two editions. The opening section on "Evolution and Cognitive Development" has been reorganized, eliminating the sections on "Evolutionary Psychology" and "Selectionist Theories of Cognitive and Brain Development," and replaced with a section titled "Evolutionary Developmental Psychology," which looks more specifically at evolutionary theory as it applies to cognitive development. The remaining major sections are the same between the two editions, although substantially updated: "Models of Gene-Environment Interaction"; "The Development of the Brain"; and "Developmental Biology and Cognitive Development."

## Chapter 3: The Social Construction of Mind: Sociocultural Perspectives on Cognitive Development

The organization of this chapter has remained essentially the same between the two editions, although I added a short section titled "Sociohistorical Influences," reflecting a side of Vygotsky's theory that was not well represented in previous editions.

## Chapter 4: Infant Perception and Cognition

This chapter replaces most of the information that was in Chapter 6 (*Infant Perception*) in the 4th edition, but also covers research and theory related to infant cognition previously in Chapters 4 (*Piaget and the Neo-Piagetians*), 8 (*Spatial Cognition*) and 9 (*Representation*) of the 4th edition. The inclusion of both infant perception and cognition in a single chapter provides better integration of research and theory for students and better reflects how scientists investigating infant thought are thinking. In addition to covering most of the same topics that were spread among several chapters in the previous edition, I have added a new section titled "Core Knowledge," examining research and theory from the neonativist perspective.

## Chapter 5: Thinking in Symbols: The Development of Representation

This chapter replaces much of the information that was covered in Chapters 4 (*Piaget and the Neo-Piagetians*) and 9 (*Representation*) in the 4th edition. Piaget's theory is still discussed in some detail but given less coverage than in previous editions. I also examine some everyday expressions of the symbolic function in greater detail than in earlier editions, including symbolic play and distinguishing between fantasy and reality. Fuzzy-trace theory, which was covered in the *Information-Processing* chapter in the 4th edition, is examined here, emphasizing how the theory describes age-related changes in how children encode and process information (using verbatim versus fuzzy traces), in contrast to Piagetian theory.

## Chapter 6: The Development of Folk Knowledge

This is a new chapter, examining children's intuitive understanding of the major domains of their world, specifically folk psychology, folk biology, and folk physics. I start the chapter with a discussion of theory theories, which were covered in Chapter 4 (*Piaget and the Neo-Piagetians*) in the 4th edition. Much of the folk psychology section deals with the development of theory of mind, which was covered in Chapter 9 (*Representation*) of the 4th edition. I spend more space discussing the basic social-cognitive skills underlying theory of mind (e.g., seeing others as intentional agents, shared attention) than in previous editions. The section on folk biology is new to this edition, examining children's developing understanding of their biological world ("Is It Alive?"; "What Young Children Know and Don't Know about Biology"; and "Where do Babies Come From?"). The section on folk physics discusses the development of spatial cognition, previously examined in Chapter 8 (*Spatial Cognition*), object-oriented play and tool use, covered in Chapter 12 (*Problem Solving and Tool Use*) of the 4th edition, and children's understanding of time, a topic new to the 5th edition.

## Chapter 7: Learning to Think on Their Own: Executive Function, Strategies, and Problem Solving

The comparable chapter in the 4th edition was devoted to the development of cognitive strategies. This section is reduced in the current edition, but added to it are discussions of the basic assumptions of information-processing approaches and the development of basic-level processes (executive function), covered in Chapter 5 (*Information-Processing Approaches*) of the 4th edition, and problem solving and reasoning, previously covered in Chapter 12 (*Problem Solving and Reasoning*) of the 4th edition. Discussion of the basic assumptions of information-processing approaches has been streamlined compared to the 4th edition, whereas more space is devoted to the development of executive function than before.

## Chapter 8: Memory Development

Many of the same topics are examined in this chapter in the 5th edition as in the 4th (memory in infancy, the development of event memory, children as eyewitnesses, consistency and stability of memory). In the 5th edition I also discuss how knowledge is represented in the memory system, previously covered in Chapter 5 (*Information-Processing Approaches*) in the 4th edition, and have omitted coverage of "forgetting." I have added a section on "Remembering to Remember," which is devoted to the development of prospective memory and "mental time travel."

## Chapter 9: Language Development

Many of the same topics are examined in this chapter in the 5th edition as in the 4th (e.g., describing children's language development, nativist and social-interactionist perspectives of language development, gender differences, language and thought). I have omitted from the 5th edition the sections "Locke's Theory of Neurolinguistic Development" and "The Relation between Lexical and Syntactic Development: Is a Grammar Module Necessary," and added a section on bilingualism and second-language learning.

## Chapter 10: Social Cognition

Most of the same topics are examined in this chapter in the 5th edition as in the 4th (e.g., social learning, social cognitive theory, social information processing, the development of a concept of self, cognitive bases of gender identity). I have omitted discussion of Tomasello's cultural learning theory, integrating his ideas more thoroughly in the section on social learning. I have added a box on mirror neurons.

## Chapter 11: Schooling and Cognition

I cover the same topics in the 5th edition as I did in the 4th edition (the development of reading skills, children's number and arithmetic concepts, schooling and cognitive development). In addition, I've added a section on "Evolutionary Educational Psychology," describing mainly the ideas of David Geary.

## Chapter 12: Approaches to the Study of Intelligence

I cover most of the same topics in the 5th edition as I did in the 4th edition (the psychometric, information-processing approaches, Sternberg's, and Gardner's theories of intelligence). The major change in this chapter is the omission of the section "Piagetian Approaches to the Study of Intelligence."

## Chapter 13: Origins, Modification, and Stability of Intellectual Differences

I cover the same major topics in this chapter in the 5th edition as I did in the 4th edition (transactional approach to the study of intelligence, behavior genetics and heritability, experience and intelligence, the stability of intelligence).

## ACKNOWLEDGMENTS

Anyone who writes a book such as this does so with much help from many people. My greatest gratitude goes to my wife Barbara who provided constructive criticism on many chapters, while working on a textbook of her own—all in addition to being a supportive and understanding spouse. I would like to thank my editor, Jaime Perkins, and the many other specialty editors and support people at Cengage for making this book possible. I want to thank my students and colleagues for their comments on earlier versions of chapters, including Carlos Hernández Blasi, Kayla Causey, Amy Gardiner, Jason Grotuss, Marc Lindberg, and Virginia Periss. I especially want to thank Katherine Kipp who worked closely with me on the re-organization of the fifth edition. Finally, I would like to thank the conscientious professional reviewers for their consistently constructive comments.

One of the benefits of writing a textbook is how much you learn in the process. I hope that this book conveys the excitement I felt in discovering some of these new findings in the field of cognitive development. The book is not just about "what's new," however, but about the field as a whole, including classic studies from earlier decades. Although I have focused on the "new," I have attempted not to forget the "tried and true" research that still informs us about the nature of children's thinking today. And I have tried to make connections among different levels of analysis—macroprocesses and microprocesses, biology and environment, developmental function and individual differences—to provide a synthesis of the field of cognitive development. And I enjoyed (almost) every minute while doing it.

*David F. Bjorklund*
*Jupiter, Florida*

# An Introduction to Cognitive Development

**Basic Concepts in Cognitive Development**
Cognition
Development
Developmental Function and Individual
    Differences

**Five "Truths" of Cognitive Development**
Cognitive Development Proceeds as a
    Result of the Dynamic and Reciprocal
    Transaction of Internal and External
    Factors
Cognitive Development Is Constructed
    Within a Social Context
Cognitive Development Involves Both
    Stability and Plasticity over Time

**BOX 1-1:** The Adaptive Nature of Cognitive
    Immaturity
Cognitive Development Involves Changes
    in the Way Information Is Represented
Children Develop Increasing Intentional
    Control over Their Behavior and
    Cognition
Cognitive Development Involves Changes
    in Both Domain-General and
    Domain-Specific Abilities

**Goals of Cognitive Developmentalists**

SUMMARY
KEY TERMS AND CONCEPTS
SUGGESTED READINGS

No one can remember what 4-year-old Jason did to get his father so upset, but whatever it was, his father wanted no more of it.

"Jason, I want you to go over to that corner and just *think* about this for a while," his father yelled.

Instead of following his father's orders, Jason stood where he was, not defiantly, but with a confused look and quivering lips, as if he were trying to say something but was afraid to.

"What's the matter now?" his father asked, his irritation showing.

"But Daddy," Jason said, "I don't know *how* to think."

Jason did know how to think, of course. He just didn't know that he did. In fact, Jason had been "thinking" all his life, although in a very different way when he was an infant, and his current thinking would not be anything like the mental gymnastics he'd be capable of in just a few years.

Intelligence is our species' most important tool for survival. Evolution has provided other animals with greater speed, coats of fur, camouflage, or antlers to help them adapt to changing environments. Human evolution has been different. It has provided us with powers of discovery and invention by which we change the environment or develop techniques for coping with environments we cannot change. Although we are not the only thinkers in the animal kingdom, no other species has our powers of intellect. How we think and the technological and cultural innovations afforded by our intellect separate us from all other animals.

This remarkable intelligence does not arise fully formed in the infant, however. We require substantial experience to master the cognitive feats that typify adult thinking, and we spend the better part of two decades developing an adult nervous system. Little in the way of complex thought patterns is built into the human brain, ready to go at birth, although biology obviously predisposes us to develop the ability for complex thought. Our mental prowess develops gradually over childhood, changing in quality as it does.

In this first chapter, I introduce the topic of *cognitive development*—how thinking changes over time. In addition to describing developmental differences in cognition, scientists who study children's thinking are also concerned with the mechanisms that underlie cognition and its development. How do biological (genetic) factors interact with experiences in the physical and social world to yield a particular pattern of development? How do children of different ages represent their world? Does a 3-year-old understand the world in much the same way as a 10-year-old, or are these children qualitatively different thinkers? Once a pattern of intellectual competence is established, does it remain stable over time? Will the bright preschooler become the gifted teenager, or is making predictions about adult intelligence from our observations of children pointless? These and other issues are introduced in this chapter, but they are not answered until later in the book. Before delving too deeply into these issues, however, I need to define some basic terms. (See Table 1-1.) These definitions are followed by a look at some issues that define the field of cognitive development and have been the focus of controversy during the last century.

## BASIC CONCEPTS IN COGNITIVE DEVELOPMENT

### Cognition

**Cognition** refers to the processes or faculties by which knowledge is acquired and manipulated. Cognition is usually thought of as being mental. That is, cognition is a reflection of a mind. It is not directly observable. We cannot see the process whereby an 8-month-old discovers that the Mickey Mouse doll hidden under the blanket continues to exist even though it is out of her sight, nor can we directly assess the steps a 7-year-old takes to compute the answer to the problem $15 - 9 = ?$. Although we cannot see or directly measure what underlies children's performance on these and other tasks, we can infer what is going on in their heads by assessing certain aspects of their behavior. That is, cognition is never measured directly. It is inferred from the behaviors we can observe.

TABLE **1-1**
Some Basic Concepts in Cognitive Development.

*Cognition:* The processes or faculties by which knowledge is acquired and manipulated. Cognition is usually thought of as being mental. That is, cognition is a reflection of a mind. It is not directly observable but must be inferred.

*Development:* Changes in structure or function over time.

*Structure* refers to some substrate of the organism, such as nervous tissue, muscle, or limbs, or—in cognitive psychology—the mental knowledge that underlies intelligence.

*Function* denotes actions related to a structure and can include actions external to the structure being studied, such as neurochemical or hormonal secretions, and other exogenous factors that can best be described as "experience"—that is, external sources of stimulation. Development is characteristic of the species and has its basis in biology. Its general course, therefore, is relatively predictable. Development progresses as a result of a **bidirectional,** or reciprocal, relationship between structure and function and can be expressed as structure ↔ function.

*Developmental function:* The species-typical form that cognition takes over time.

*Individual differences:* Differences in patterns of intellectual aptitudes among people of a given age.

What psychologists can observe and quantify are things such as the number of words children remember from a list of 20, the number of seconds it takes to identify well-known pictures or words, or the amount of time 6-month-olds spend looking at a picture of a familiar face relative to that of an unfamiliar one. For the most part, cognitive developmental psychologists are not really interested in these overt, countable behaviors; what they *are* interested in are the processes or skills that underlie them. What mental operations does a 6-year-old engage in that are different from those performed by a 4-year-old or an 8-year-old? How does speed in identifying words reflect how information is stored in the minds of children of different ages? What kind of mental picture has the infant formed of the familiar face of his mother that allows him to tell her face apart from all other faces? How are such mental pictures created? How are they modified?

This is not to say that cognitive psychologists are unconcerned with socially important phenomena, such as reading, mathematics, or communicating effectively. Many are, and they have developed research programs aimed at improving in children these and other intellectual skills so critical for success in a high-tech society. But, for the most part, the behaviors themselves are seen as secondary. What is important and what needs to be understood are the mechanisms that underlie performance. By discovering the mental factors that govern intelligent behavior, we can better understand behavior and its development, which in turn can help us better understand children and foster their development.

Cognition includes not only our conscious and deliberate attempts at solving problems but also the unconscious and nondeliberate processes that are involved in routine daily tasks. We are not aware of the mental activity that occurs when we recognize a familiar tune on the radio or even when we read the back of a cereal box. Yet, much in the way of cognitive processing is happening. For most of us, reading has become nearly automatic. We can't drive by a billboard without reading it. It is something we just do without giving it any "thought." But the processes involved in reading are complex, even in the well-practiced adult.

Cognition involves mental activity of all types, including activity that is geared toward acquiring, understanding, and modifying information. Cognition includes such activities as developing a plan for solving a problem, executing that plan, and evaluating the success of the plan, making modifications as needed. These can be thought of as higher-order processes, or *macromechanisms* of cognition, which are often available to consciousness (that is, we are aware that we're doing them). Cognition also involves the initial encoding of a stimulus (that is, deciding how to define a physical stimulus so it can be thought about) and classifying what kind of thing it is ("Is this a letter, a word, a picture of something familiar?"). These can be thought of as basic processes, or *micromechanisms* of cognition, which occur outside of consciousness (we experience the product but are generally unaware of the process).

Cognition, then, reflects knowledge and what one does with it, and the main point of this book is that cognition develops.

## Development

### *Change over Time*

At its most basic, **development** (or **ontogeny**) refers to changes in structure or function over time. **Structure** refers to some substrate of the organism, such as nervous tissue, muscle, or limbs, or—in cognitive psychology—the mental knowledge that underlies intelligence. When speaking of cognitive development, we use *structure* to mean some hypothetical mental construct, faculty, or ability that changes with age. For example, children's knowledge of terms such as *dog, lion,* and *zebra* could be construed as existing in some sort of mental structure (think of it as a mental dictionary), with the meanings of these words changing over time. Or we could hypothesize some form of mental organization that permits children to place objects in serial arrays according to height, shortest to tallest.

In contrast to structure, **function** denotes actions related to a structure. These include actions external to the structure being studied, such as neurochemical or hormonal secretions, and other factors external to the individual that can best be described as "experience"—that is, external sources of stimulation. Function can also be internal to the structure itself—for example, the exercise of a muscle, the firing of a nerve cell, or the activation of a cognitive process, such as retrieving from memory the name of your first-grade teacher or computing the answer to the problem $26 + 17 = ?$. With respect to cognitive development, function refers to some action by the child, such as retrieving the definition of a word from memory, making comparisons between two stimuli, or adding two numbers to arrive at a third.

Development is characteristic of the species and has its basis in biology. Its general course, therefore, is relatively predictable. By viewing development as a biological concept that is generally predictable across all members of the species, I do not mean to imply that experience and culture do not also play a role in development. During the last several decades, developmental psychologists have become increasingly aware that a child's development cannot be described or understood outside of the context in which it occurs, and I will address this issue later in this and other chapters, especially Chapter 3.

### Structure, Function, and Development

Development is usually conceived as a bidirectional, or reciprocal, relationship between structure and function, in which the activity of the structure itself and stimulation from the environment can contribute to changes in the structure, which in turn contribute to changes in how that structure operates. Function does more than just maintain a structure (that is, prevent it from wasting away); function is necessary for proper development to occur. Function is limited, of course, to the actions that structures are capable of performing. This bidirectional relationship between structure and function can be expressed as structure ↔ function.

The **bidirectionality of structure and function** (or **structure ↔ function**) can perhaps be most easily illustrated with work in embryology. Chick embryos, for example, display spontaneous movement before muscle and skeletal development is complete. Such movement obviously stems from the maturation of the underlying structures—in this case, bones, muscle, and nervous tissue. When embryonic chicks are given a drug to temporarily paralyze them for as little as 1 to 2 days, deformations of the joints of the legs, toes, and neck develop, which in turn affect the subsequent movement of the limbs (Drachman & Coulombre, 1962). The spontaneous activity of moving the legs provides critical feedback to the genes, which in normal circumstances leads to a properly developed skeleton (Müller, 2003). In other words, the spontaneous activity (function) of the skeletal structures is necessary for the proper development and functioning of the joints. Development proceeds as a result of the interaction of genes with events and agents external to the genes, including functioning of the body itself, all in feedback loops that, when all goes right, produces a species-typical body.

Let me provide an example of the bidirectional relationship between structure and function at the behavioral level. Individual differences in activity level are found in newborns and are believed to be biologically based (Phillips, King, & DuBois, 1978). A highly active toddler will make it difficult for her parents to confine her to a playpen, resulting in a child who has a greater number of experiences outside of her playpen than a less active child has. These experiences will presumably affect the child's developing intellect (structure), which in turn will affect that child's actions (function). Thus, inherent characteristics of the child (biological structures) influence her behavior, the experiences she has, and the reactions of others to her—all of which influence the development of the child's underlying cognitive/behavioral structures, and so on.

The *functioning* of mental structures promotes changes in the structures themselves. This view is most clearly reflected in the work of the Swiss psychologist Jean Piaget. He believed that the activity of the child (or of the child's cognitive structures) is a necessary condition for development to occur. That is, for structures to change, they must be active. The structures making contact with the external world is responsible, to a large extent, for their development. Such a viewpoint makes children important contributors to their own development. Intellectual growth is the result of an active interaction between thinking children and their world, not simply the environment shaping children's intellect or genes dictating a particular level of cognitive ability. (More will be said of Piaget's theory throughout this book, especially in Chapter 5.)

I think it is fair to say that all developmental psychologists agree there is a reciprocal, bidirectional influence between "structures" (be they physical, such as neurons, or hypothetical, such as cognitive structures) and the activity of those structures (that is, the child's behavior). There is still much room for debate concerning *how* various subsystems of the child (neuronal, behavioral, social) interact to produce development, but developmental psychologists agree that development must be viewed as a two-way street. Development is *not* simply the result of the unfolding of genetic sequences unperturbed by variations in environment (structure → function), nor is it the product of "experience" on an infinitely pliable child (function → structure). The concept of the bidirectionality of structure and function is central to developmental psychology and will be a theme throughout this book. A more in-depth discussion of bidirectional models of development, along with more examples, is provided later in this chapter and in Chapter 2 during a discussion of the *developmental systems approach*.

## Developmental Function and Individual Differences

I will examine two aspects of cognitive development in this book: **developmental function**, or *cognitive development*, and **individual differences**. In the present context, developmental function refers to the form that cognition takes over time—to age-related differences in thinking. What are the mental abilities of infants? What is a 2-year-old's understanding of numbers, words, and family relations? What about that of a 4- or 6-year-old? How do school-age children and adolescents conceptualize cause and effect? How do they evaluate the relative worth of two products in the grocery store? People concerned with developmental function are usually interested in universals—what is generally true about the course and causes of development for all members of the species. Assessments of developmental function, then, are typically based on averages, with individual variations among children being seen as unimportant.

We all know that at some level, however, this variation *is* important. Our impressive intellectual skills are not uniform among members of the species. Some people at every age make decisions more quickly, perceive relations among events more keenly, or think more deeply than others. How can these differences best be described and conceptualized? What is the nature of these differences? Once differences have been established, to what extent can they be modified? Will differences observed in infancy and early childhood remain stable, or are some intellectual differences limited to a particular time during development?

Substantial variability in cognitive functioning also occurs *within* any given child. A particular 4-year-old will often show a wide range of behaviors on very similar tasks, depending on the context that child is in. Increasingly, developmental psychologists have come to realize the significance of individual differences and variability in cognitive performance among and within people of a given age and to see these variations as providing interesting and important information about developmental outcomes.

Although the people who study individual differences in thinking have traditionally not been the same people who study developmental function (Cronbach, 1957), the picture is changing, and I will attempt, where possible, to integrate the two concepts. Individual differences, like thought itself, have developmental histories, making the relationship between developmental function and individual differences a dynamic one. That is, individual differences do not simply constitute genetic or "innate" characteristics of a child. They emerge as children develop, often showing different manifestations at different times in development. Several chapters in this book are devoted exclusively to examining individual differences. In other chapters, individual differences in intellectual abilities are discussed in conjunction with the developmental function of those same abilities.

## FIVE "TRUTHS" OF COGNITIVE DEVELOPMENT

The field of cognitive development encompasses a broad range of topics. Moreover, cognitive developmentalists can be a contentious lot, disagreeing on the best way to conceptualize how thought changes from infancy to adulthood. Nonetheless, I believe there are some "truths" that typify the study of cognitive development—actually, generalizations that I think most cognitive developmentalists believe are true about cognitive development and around which controversy and differences of opinion swirl. In a recent overview of the field of cognitive development, I (Bjorklund, 2011) listed five such truths:

1. Cognitive development proceeds as a result of the dynamic and reciprocal transaction of internal and external factors;
2. Cognitive development is constructed within a social context;
3. Cognitive development involves both stability and plasticity over time;
4. Cognitive development involves changes in the way information is represented; and
5. Children develop increasing intentional control over their behavior and cognition.

In addition to these, I discuss briefly in this section two other issues that I think are central to the modern study of cognitive development: the importance of taking an evolutionary perspective and the distinction between domain-general and domain-specific mechanisms.

## Cognitive Development Proceeds as a Result of the Dynamic and Reciprocal Transaction of Internal and External Factors

This truth follows from the way we define development as the result of the bidirectional relationship between structure and function over time. In essence, this is modern developmental science's answer to the classic "nature/nurture" issue, which has been the granddaddy of controversies for developmental psychology over its history. How do we explain how biological factors, in particular genetics, interact with environmental factors, especially learning and the broader effects of culture, to produce human beings? At the extremes are two philosophical camps. Proponents of **nativism** hold, essentially, that human intellectual abilities are innate. The opposing philosophical position is **empiricism**, which holds that nature provides only species-general learning mechanisms, with cognition arising as a result of experience. As stated, each of these two extreme positions is clearly wrong. In fact, as far as developmental psychologists are concerned, there is no nature/nurture dichotomy. Biological factors are inseparable from experiential factors, with the two continuously interacting. This makes it impossible to identify any purely biological or experiential effects. It is often convenient, however, to speak of "biological" and "experiential" factors, and when psychologists do, there is always the implicit assumption of the bidirectional interaction of these factors, as discussed earlier in this chapter (that is, structure ↔ function).

At one level, it is trivial to state that biology and experience interact. There is really no other alternative. It's *how* they interact to yield a particular pattern of development that is significant. For example, one currently popular view holds that children's genetic constitutions influence how they experience the environment. A sickly and lethargic child seeks and receives less attention from others than a more active, healthy child does, resulting in slower or less advanced levels of cognitive development. A child who processes language easily might be more apt to take advantage of the reading material that surrounds him than will a child whose inherent talents lie in other areas, such as the ability to comprehend spatial relations. Environment is thus seen as very important from this perspective, but one's biology influences which environments are most likely to be experienced and, possibly, how those experiences will be interpreted. These issues will be discussed in greater detail in the chapters devoted to individual differences, particularly Chapter 13, in which the heritability of intelligence and the role of experience in individual differences in intelligence will be explored.

### What Does It Mean to Say Something Is "Innate"?

The term *innate* can be contentious, and many developmental psychologists would prefer not to see it used at all. The primary reason for many developmental psychologists' discomfort with the concept is that this term implies **genetic determinism**—the idea that one's genes *determine* one's behavior—which is the antithesis of a truly developmental (that is, bidirectional) perspective. If, in contrast, by innate we simply mean "based in genetics," then surely just about every human behavior can be deemed innate at some level, and the term is meaningless. If, however, we mean that a specific type of behavior or knowledge (of grammar, for example) is determined by genetics, with little or no input needed from the environment, then the term has a more specific meaning, but again, it is still not very useful. For, as we'll see more clearly in our discussions in Chapter 2, all genetic effects are mediated by "environment," broadly defined.

Some people equate the concept "innateness" with "instinct." The problem here is that instinct is not easily defined. This is made clear by Patrick Bateson (2002, p. 2212), who wrote:

> Apart from its colloquial uses, the term instinct has at least nine scientific meanings: present at birth (or at a particular stage of development), not learned, developed before it can be used, unchanged once developed, shared by all members of the species (or at least of the same sex and age), organized into a distinct behavioral system (such as foraging), served by a distinct neural module, adapted during evolution, and differences among individuals that are due to their possession of different genes. One does not necessarily imply another even though people often assume, without evidence, that it does.

Many developmental psychologists are just as uncomfortable (or more so) with the term *instinct* as they are with the term *innate*, and for the same reason—its association with genetic determinism. And, as Bateson's quote illustrates, it is not always clear which definition of instinct one is talking about.

The term *innate*, however, is not without its usefulness. Usually, when developmental psychologists use the term, they mean that there are some genetically based *constraints* on behavior or development. In cognitive development, by constraints we usually mean that the brain can only process a certain type of information in a certain way. Constraints here mean that the brain is not flexible enough to make sense of any information in any possible way. (I'll have more to say about such constraints in Chapter 2.) But even here there are different types of constraints. Jeffrey Elman and his colleagues (1996) have specified three general types of innate constraints—*representational, architectural,* and *chronotopic*—and I discuss each of them briefly.

**Representational constraints** (or **representational innateness**) refer to representations that are hardwired into the brain so that some types of "knowledge" are innate. For example, several theorists have proposed that infants come into the world (or develop very early in life) some basic ideas about the nature of objects (their solidity, for example), mathematics (simple concepts of addition and subtraction), or grammar (see Pinker, 1997; Spelke & Kinzler, 2007; and Chapters 4, 6, and 9 of this book). This type of innateness corresponds to what most people think of when they talk about innate concepts. This does *not* mean that there is no development. All abilities develop. But, according to this perspective, children (or animals) come into the world able to make sense of certain aspects of their environments given only minimal experience (basic notions of physics, or how to build webs if you're a spider, for example).

**Architectural constraints** (or **architectural innateness**) refer to ways in which the architecture of the brain is organized at birth. For example, some neurons are excitatory and others inhibitory, or neurons can differ in the amount of activation that is required for them to fire. At a somewhat higher level, neurons in a particular area of the brain might be more or less densely packed or have many or few connections with other local neurons. And at a higher level yet, different areas of the brain are connected with other areas of the brain, affecting the global organization of the organ. Architectural constraints limit the type of and manner in which information can be processed by the brain, not because the brain comes equipped with innate representations (for example, what a grammar is) but because certain neurons/areas of the brain can only process certain types of information and pass it along to certain other areas of the brain. Thus, architectural constraints imply limits on what is processed, as do representational constraints. Unlike representational constraints, however, architectural constraints permit (or require) a high degree of learning to occur.

For example, the architecture of a particular area of the brain might be best suited for processing a certain type of information—faces, for instance—but the architecture will change as a function of the information it receives. Structures in the brain are not preformed to "know" human faces, for example, but are biased toward processing information about faces and developing the skill of identifying and remembering faces as a result of interactions with the world. For instance, as early as 9 months of age, infants can more easily make decisions about upright human faces than about upside-down human faces. They treat upright human faces as "special," differentiating between them better than between upside-down faces, for example, which are processed much as other visual stimuli are. Things change, however, when monkey faces serve as stimuli. Now adults and 9-month-olds show no behavioral or neural differences when processing upright and upside-down faces. The "specialness" of upright faces is reserved for their own species. Not so for 6-month-old infants, however, who process upright faces differently (and more effectively) than upside-down faces for both humans and monkeys. This pattern suggests that the brain of young infants is biased to process right-side-up faces, perhaps the most important stimulus in the world of a young animal highly dependent on care from others. However, the fact that 6-month-olds do not give special privilege to human faces suggests that brain processing of faces becomes more specialized with age and experience (Johnson & de Haan, 2001; Lewkowicz & Ghazanfar, 2009; Pascalis, de Haan, & Nelson, 2002). According to Olivier Pascalis and his colleagues (2002, p. 1321), "the ability to perceive faces narrows with development, due in large measure to the cortical specialization that occurs with experience viewing faces. In this view, the sensitivity of the face recognition system to differences in identity among the faces of one's own species will increase with age and with experience in processing those faces." (The development of face processing over infancy will be discussed in greater detail in Chapter 4.) Such findings are consistent with the position that human infants are born with biases to process some information more effectively than others, but that such biases become modified with experience (Johnson, 2000; Nelson, 2001).

**Chronotopic constraints** (or **chronotopic innateness**) refer to limitations on the developmental timing of events. For example, certain areas of the brain might develop before others. This would mean that early developing areas would likely come to have different processing responsibilities than would later developing areas. Similarly, some areas of the brain might be most receptive to certain types of experiences (to "learning") at specified times, making it imperative that certain experiences (exposure to patterned light or language, for example) occur during this *sensitive period* of development (Thomas & Johnson, 2008). For example, children around the world acquire language in about the same way and at about the same time. If, however, for some reason children are not exposed to language until later in life, their level of language proficiency is greatly reduced. The human brain appears to be prepared to make sense of language, thus making it easy for children to acquire the language that they hear around them. But such neural readiness is constrained by time. Wait too long, and the ability to acquire a fully articulated language is lost. The issue of developmental timing (and sensitive periods) will be discussed in greater detail in Chapter 2 and with relation to language in Chapter 9.

### Nature/Nurture and Developmental Contextualism

During the past decades, I have noticed two shifts in emphasis in the cognitive development field that at first glance might seem contradictory. The first is a greater emphasis given to the role of context (including cultural context) in development. The second is a greater acknowledgment of the role of biological factors in development. In a field where nature and nurture have traditionally occupied opposite scientific, philosophical, and often political poles, seeing an increasing emphasis on both seems a contradiction, perhaps reflecting a field composed of mutual antagonists, each taking an extreme perspective to counterbalance the other (much like the U.S. Congress seems to function in recent years). This is not the case, however. The current perspective on the dynamic transaction of nature and nurture is one in which biological and environmental factors not only can peacefully coexist but also are intricately intertwined (Gottlieb, 2007; Lerner, 2006; Sameroff, 2009a).

Let me provide one brief illustration of how biology and environment are viewed as separate, interacting components of a larger system. Richard Lerner (1991, 2006) has been a proponent of the **developmental contextual model**. The basic contention of this model is that all parts of the organism (such as genes, cells, tissues, and organs), as well as the whole organism itself, interact dynamically with "the contexts within which the organism is embedded" (Lerner, 1991, p. 27). This means that one must always consider the organism-context as a unit and that there are multiple levels of the organism and multiple levels of the context. Figure 1-1 graphically presents the developmental contextual model, showing the many bidirectional influences between children, who are born with biological propensities and dispositions, and the contexts in which they find themselves. Perhaps more than anything else, this figure demonstrates the complexity of development. Of equal importance, however, it demonstrates the interactions that occur between the many levels of life, from genes and hormones to family and culture, and the fact that cultural effects cannot be meaningfully separated from their biological influences, and vice versa. The dynamic nature of development, which results from the interaction of a child at many different levels (genetic, hormonal, physical environment, social environment, self-produced activity, and so on), is a theme that runs through most contemporary theories of development.

### Dynamic Systems Approaches to Development

Related to developmental contextual models is the idea that development involves the continuous and bidirectional interaction between all levels of organization, from the molecular to the cultural, and that complex cognitive or behavioral characteristics *emerge* from the spontaneous interaction among simpler components (Lewis, 2000; Thelen & Smith, 2006). A **dynamic system** can be defined as a set of elements that undergoes change over time as a result of interactions among the elements. The system is dynamic because it is constantly changing. Changes in one part of the system—the length of a child's legs, the organization of a child's brain, or some aspect of the social environment, for example—disrupts the current child-environment relationship, causing the child to reorganize his or her behavior so the various parts fit together again, this time in a more sophisticated or effective manner. From this perspective, new patterns of behavior are not dictated simply by genes or the environment but emerge as a result of changes in the system or some aspect of the physical environment.

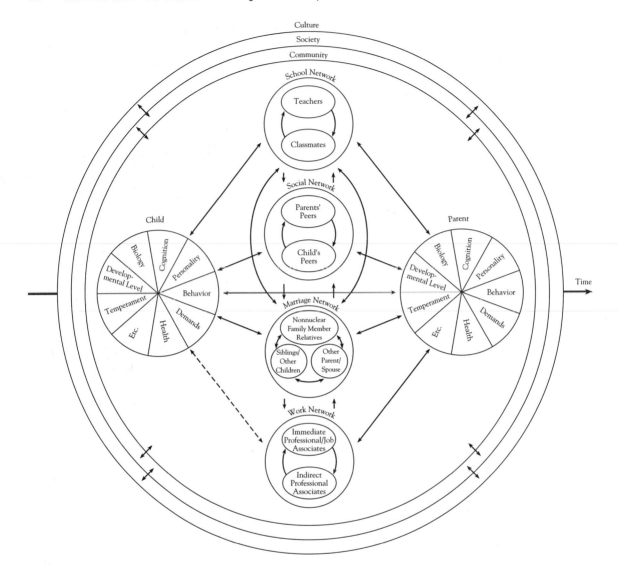

**FIGURE 1-1**

A developmental contextual model of person-context interaction.

Source: "Changing Organism-Context Relations as the Basic Process of Development: A Developmental Contextual Perspective," by R. M. Lerner, 1991, *Developmental Psychology*, 27, 27–32. Copyright © 1991 American Psychological Association. Reprinted with permission.

Perhaps the central idea behind dynamic systems theories is the concept of **self-organization**. Esther Thelen and Linda Smith (1998) defined self-organization as the process whereby "pattern and order emerge from interactions of the components of a complex system without explicit instructions either in the organism itself or from the environment" (p. 564). That is, order or structure in cognitive development (such as the linguistic ability to form the past tense, or being able to keep both the height and width of a container in mind when evaluating its volume) is not innately specified, waiting only for the right maturational conditions to be activated, nor is it simply the product of acquiring new knowledge (that is, learning). Rather, higher-level forms of cognition emerge from the self-initiated activity of the organism in interaction with all levels of its environment. According to Marc Lewis (2000), self-organization means that "structure does not have to be imported into a system from outside, as presumed by learning approaches, nor preordained from within, as presumed by nativist approaches. Structure is emergent" (p. 39).

Let me provide an example of emergence from meteorology, taken from Thelen and Smith (1994):

> In certain meteorological contexts, clouds form into thunderheads that have a particular shape, internal complexity, and behavior. There is clear directionality to the way thunderheads emerge over time ... But there is no design written anywhere in a cloud ... that determines the final community structure. There is no set of instructions that causes clouds ... to change form in a particular way. There are only a number of complex physical ... systems interacting over time, such that the precise nature of their interactions leads inevitably to a thunderhead ... We suggest that action and cognition are also emergent and not designed (p. xix).

Whether we're dealing with thunderheads or cognitive development, however, the types of changes brought about by self-organization are not straightforward. In fact, one characteristic of dynamic systems is that changes are *nonlinear* in nature. When a system changes linearly, the magnitude of the effect is proportional to the magnitude of the cause. So, for example, one might expect that giving children one extra word to keep in memory while performing a second task (for example, identifying tones that are played over headphones as high or low) would result in a corresponding decrease in performance on the second task. Keeping one word in mind may decrease performance by 10%, two words by 20%, three words by 30%, and so on. This would reflect a linear relationship between the two variables. At some point, however, change may become nonlinear, such that the magnitude of change in one variable is *not* proportional to the change in another. For instance, perhaps giving children in our hypothetical experiment four words to keep in mind reduces their performance on the second task to zero. The change from three words to four produced an abrupt and nonlinear change—the proverbial straw that broke the camel's back. Similarly, children may acquire individual "facts" about a concept, but they cannot reorganize their knowledge base, producing a more complex structure, until they have accumulated a sufficient number of such facts. Or relatedly, children may be able to remember a series of four or five words without using any particular strategy (they "just remember them"). But once the list nears 10 words, say, they must reorganize their approach to the problem, possibly by implementing a strategy of rehearsal or by mentally grouping words from the same category (for example, all the animal words). Thus, small changes in one factor can sometimes result in large changes in another factor.

Given the essential unpredictability of how individual elements will self-organize to produce new levels of functioning, the impression one can get is that dynamic systems are truly chaotic. Despite the impression of chaos, however, dynamic systems theories of human development are able to identify recurrent patterns or structures. For example, all children eventually understand that an object covered by a cloth doesn't disappear into oblivion but continues to exist in time and space. Such stable states will be attained by all, or most, children given a certain level of maturation and experience and, once acquired, are not easily modified, or perturbed. Immature cognitive states do change, of course (that's what development is all about), as elements interact and, through self-organization, the "system" (for example, a child's understanding of some physical phenomenon) moves toward another more stable state. This movement from one stable state to another is called a *phase transition.*

Phase transitions refer to changes in functioning that are relatively abrupt, or discontinuous. For instance, normal walking has associated with it a certain speed, gait, and coordination of the limbs. When one or more factors change, however, the system is "perturbed," such that the various components no long function smoothly together. For instance, if one walks faster or starts walking down a steep incline, maintaining a constant gait becomes difficult unless some changes in overall locomotive pattern are also made. At these points, there is instability and variability in performance, and subtle changes can move the system (in this case, the walker) into one of two forms (for example, walking or jogging). There comes a point when "the system" (here, the various integrated components involved in bipedal locomotion) makes the phase transition from walking to jogging because maintaining the coordination among elements within the system given the new parameters becomes difficult unless a new level of organization is implemented. (Think of Olympic speed walking as an example. The pace is faster than regular walking, but the gait and coordination are much more like walking than running, and it's very unnatural. People can do it, but without substantial deliberate control, the system—in this case, the walker—would make the transition into the more "natural" running.)

Phase transitions can be used to describe changes at a variety of levels, including major stage changes. For example, Hans van der Maas and Peter Molenaar (1992) proposed that transitions between major Piagetian stages (see Chapter 5) can be described as phase transitions. As children acquire more information about their surroundings, they must coordinate that information to form a coherent understanding of their worlds. But as they gather more information, contradictions arise (for example, taller people are not always older than shorter people), and this produces instability in the cognitive system (or "disequilibration in their structures," to use Piaget's terminology). During this period, children's performance is variable and, eventually, leads to a new, more stable structure. (Piaget referred to this process as *equilibration,* and it will be discussed in more detail in Chapter 5. The point here is that such transitions can be described using concepts from dynamic systems theory.)

As another example, consider children's problem solving on a visual analogy task (Siegler & Svetina, 2002). Children from 6 to 8 years of age were shown an incomplete matrix of pictures, similar to the example shown in Figure 1-2. In the top row on the left side is a picture of a large, light-gray mouse facing right and a picture of a large, light-gray bird facing right. Below them is a single picture of a small, light-gray mouse facing left. Children were to select from a group of six pictures on the right the one that best completed the analogy—in this case, a small, light-gray bird facing left. Although some children were able to solve these problems from the beginning, many were not. Of these, many began by making what the authors called "duplicate errors," selecting an object that was identical to the one in the problem (in this case, a small, light-gray mouse facing left). But several trials *before* they eventually learned how to solve the problems correctly, their pattern of errors changed. They generally stopped making duplicate errors and made other types of errors, apparently selecting randomly. But, just as suddenly, they made the transition to correct responding. This pattern of performance is shown in Figure 1-3. In the figure, trial block 0 corresponds

FIGURE **1-2**

Examples of a matrix problem. Children were to select the picture on the right that best completed the visual analogy. In this example, the correct answer is the small, light-gray bird facing left.

Source: From Siegler, R. S., & Svetina, M. (2002). A microgenetic/cross-sectional study of matrix completion: Comparing short-term and long-term change. *Child Development*, *73*, 793–809. Reprinted with permission of the Society for Research in Child Development.

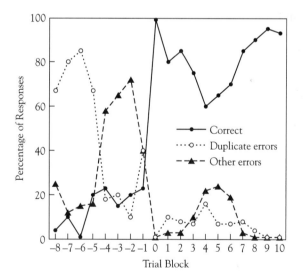

FIGURE **1-3**

Pattern of responses on the matrix problem as a function of when children first achieved perfect (100%) performance on a set of three trials (trial block 0). Negative trial blocks (–8 through –1) correspond to the sets of trials preceding the trial block on which perfect performance was first attained, and positive trial blocks (1 through 10) correspond to sets of trials following the trial block on which perfect performance was first attained.

Source: From Siegler, R. S., & Svetina, M. (2002). A microgenetic/cross-sectional study of matrix completion: Comparing short-term and long-term change. *Child Development*, *73*, 793–809. Reprinted with permission of the Society for Research in Child Development.

to the set of three trials on which children first performed at 100% accuracy. As can be seen, by definition, performance here was perfect and continued to be high (although not perfect) for all subsequent trial blocks (blocks 1 through 10). But on the trial blocks preceding block 0, performance was more variable. As can be seen, children made mostly duplicate errors on the earliest trials (blocks –8 to –5), but these declined abruptly, and "other errors" increased just as abruptly, on the four trials blocks immediately before block 0 (blocks –4 to –1). Stated in the language of dynamic systems theory, a period of instability and variable performance preceded a phase transition to a new level of organization, or to a new phase.

Much like Darwin's concept of natural selection (see Chapter 2), the concept of self-organization is not tied to a particular content but can be used to explain changes in any complex system. Thus, dynamic systems theories can serve as broad, metatheoretical accounts that can be adopted by researchers investigating a wide range of topics. The common ground on which developmental scientists with diverse interests can stand is the belief that development is a process of *emergence* rather than one of growth or learning. Although cognitive developmentalists who apply the often highly mathematical tools of dynamic systems theories to their areas of interest are still a minority, most believe in the dynamic nature of change and adopt, at some level, the metaphor of dynamic systems to explain development. This perspective will be implicitly (and sometimes explicitly) applied throughout the remainder of this book.

## Cognitive Development Is Constructed Within a Social Context

As I've presented the developmental contextual model, it should be clear that the social environment plays a central role in determining a child's development. A child's biology interacts with a child's social environment to influence a child's developmental trajectory. However, the social environment is not simply the place, so to speak, where development occurs. The culture in which children grow up also shapes, or constructs, their intellects.

We are a social species, and human development can only be properly understood when the influences of social relations and the broader social/cultural environment are considered. Development always occurs within a social context, culturally shaped and historically conditioned, although the specific details of a child's social environment can vary widely. From this perspective, one's culture not only tells children *what* to think but also *how* to think (Cole, 2006; Gauvain, 2009; Rogoff, 2003; Vygotsky, 1978).

### *Sociocultural Perspectives*

Several **sociocultural perspectives** on cognitive development have emerged over recent decades (Bronfenbrenner & Morris, 2006; Cole, 2006; Rogoff, 2003; see Chapter 3), stemming in large part from the rediscovery of the work of the Soviet psychologist Lev Vygotsky (1978). Writing in the 1920s and 1930s, Vygotsky proposed a sociocultural view, emphasizing that development was guided by adults interacting with children, with the cultural context determining largely how, where, and when these interactions would take place. There are many cultural universals, with children around the world being reared in socially structured, language-using groups. Thus, some aspects of development are also universal. But many aspects of culture, such as the available technology and how and when children are expected to learn the survival skills of their society (for example, formal schooling versus no formal schooling), vary greatly. Such differences can have considerable influence on how cognition develops. But how do different cultures construct different experiences for their children to learn, and what consequences does this have for *how* they learn?

Some researchers have noted that children living in traditional societies are more attentive to what adults do and, thus, develop a keener ability to learn through observation than children from schooled societies such as ours (Gaskins, 2000; Morelli, Rogoff, & Angelillo, 2003). These types of cultural experiences affect how children learn. For example, in one study, 6- to 10-year-olds observed a woman creating origami figures and were later asked to make figures of their own (Mejia-Arauz, Rogoff, & Paradise, 2005). Some of the children were of traditional Mexican heritage whose mothers had only basic schooling (on average, a seventh-grade education), and others were of Mexican or European background whose mothers had a high-school education or more. The children of the more educated mothers were more likely to request information from the "Origami Lady" than the children with the traditional Mexican heritage. These findings are consistent with the observations that these "traditional" children pay more attention to the actions of the adults and learn more through observation rather than seeking instructions from adults or learning through verbal instructions (see Cole, 2006).

### Integrating Approaches

There is an approach that takes an even longer view of historical influences on development that I think is important for understanding children, and that is *evolutionary theory,* which helps us better understand *why* children and adolescents behave as they do. I believe that a better understanding of the "whys" of development will help us to better understand the "hows" and the "whats" of development, as well as help us to apply knowledge of child development to everyday problems. Theodosius Dobzhansky (1964) famously said, "Nothing in biology makes sense except in the light of evolution" (p. 449). Many psychologists make the same argument for psychology, particularly for the understanding of infants, children, adolescents, and their development. The principles of evolutionary developmental psychology are reviewed in Chapter 2.

Developmental contextual, sociocultural, and evolutionary models of development also represent three levels of analysis (see Figure 1-4). Developmental contextual models examine the development of psychological processes over an individual's lifetime, beginning before birth. Sociocultural models also look at the immediate causes of behavior but, in addition, take into account the impact of humans' 10,000-year cultural history on development. Evolutionary theory takes a truly long view of human history, examining the role that natural selection has played in shaping human development, particularly since the emergence of humans about 2 million years ago. I do not view these three approaches as competing perspectives of development but as reflecting three different, but compatible, levels of analyses, each of which is important to properly understand development.

Because I believe that all of cognitive development (or at least most of it) can benefit from being examined through the lens of these three perspectives, you will find reference to them throughout the book. Also, some of the boxes presented will focus on issues related to one or more of these approaches. To get started, Box 1-1 presents an evolutionary-influence perspective on cognitive development—the adaptive nature of cognitive immaturity.

FIGURE **1-4**

Different levels of analysis of developmental phenomena.

Source: Bjorklund, D. F., & Hernández Blasi, C. (2012). *Child and adolescent development: An integrative approach.* Belmont, CA: Cengage.

## Cognitive Development Involves Both Stability and Plasticity over Time

Cognitive development is about change over time. Yet, once a level of cognitive competence is established, to what extent will it remain constant? Will a precocious infant become a bright 3-year-old and, later, a talented adult? Or is it just as likely that a below-average 5-year-old will become an above-average high-school student, or a sluggish infant a whiz-kid computer jock? Once patterns have been established, what does it take to change them? Can they be modified by later experience? How plastic, or pliable, is the human intellect?

The stability and plasticity of cognition are related. **Stability** refers to the degree to which children maintain their same relative rank order over time in comparison with their peers in some aspect of cognition. Does the high-IQ 3-year-old maintain her position in the intellectual pecking order at age 8 or 18? **Plasticity** concerns the extent to which children can be shaped by experience. More specifically with respect to cognition, once a pattern of cognitive ability is established, to what extent can it be altered? Is our cognitive system highly flexible, capable of being bent and re-bent, or, once a cognitive pattern has been forged, is it relatively resistant to change?

For the better part of the 20th century, psychologists believed that individual differences in intelligence, for example, were relatively stable over time and not likely to be strongly modified by subsequent environments. These views were held both by people who believed that such differences were mainly inherited and by those who believed such differences were mainly a function of environment, but for different reasons. People on the "nature" side assumed that intelligence was primarily an expression of one's genes and that this expression would be constant over one's lifetime. People on the other side of the fence emphasized the role of early

| BOX 1-1 | **The Adaptive Nature of Cognitive Immaturity** |

We usually think of development as something progressive—going from simple to more complex structures or behaviors, with children getting "better" or more "complete" over time. This is a wholly reasonable point of view, but such a perspective can cause us to interpret early or immature forms of cognition as merely less effective and incomplete versions of the adult model. And although this might generally be true, it is not always the case. Early or immature forms of development can serve some function of their own, adapting the infant or young child to his or her particular environment (Oppenheim, 1981). For example, young infants' relatively poor perceptual abilities might protect their nervous systems from sensory overload (Turkewitz & Kenny, 1982), preschool children's tendencies to overestimate their physical and cognitive skills might cause them to persist (and, thus, to improve) at difficult tasks (Shin, Bjorklund, & Beck, 2007), and infants' slow information processing might prevent them from establishing intellectual habits early in life that would be detrimental later on, when their life conditions are considerably different (Bjorklund & Green, 1992). The point I want to make here is that

infants' and young children's cognitive and perceptual abilities might, in fact, be well suited for their particular time in life rather than incomplete versions of the more sophisticated abilities they will one day posses (Bjorklund, 1997a, 2007a; Bjorklund, Periss, & Causey, 2009). In other words, what we consider to be immature and ineffective styles of thought might sometimes have an adaptive value for the young child at that particular point in development and should not be viewed solely as "deficiencies."

Consider the case of learning. Learning is good, of course, but is early learning always beneficial? Might providing an infant with too much stimulation or learning tasks too soon in development have a negative effect? There is little research on this issue. In one study, Harry Harlow (1959) began giving infant monkeys training on a discrimination-learning task at different ages, ranging from 60 to 366 days. For example, monkeys were to choose which of several stimuli that varied in several dimensions (size, shape, color, and so on) was associated with a reward. Beginning at 120 days of age, monkeys were given a more complicated learning task. In Figure 1-5, monkeys' performance on these more complicated

### FIGURE **1-5**

Discrimination learning set performance for monkeys as a function of age at which testing was begun.

Source: H. Harlow, (1959, December). The development of learning in the Rhesus monkey. *American Scientist*, 459–479. Reprinted with permission.

*(Continues)*

**BOX 1-1** **The Adaptive Nature of Cognitive Immaturity** (Continued)

problems is shown as a function of the age at which they began training. Chance performance for these problems was 50%. As can be seen, monkeys who began training early in life (at 60 and 90 days) seldom solved more than 60% of the problems and soon fell behind the monkeys who began training later (at 120 and 150 days of age). That is, despite having more experience with the problems, the early trained monkeys performed more poorly than the later trained monkeys. Harlow concluded, "There is a tendency to think of learning or training as intrinsically good and necessarily valuable to the organism. It is entirely possible, however, that training can be either helpful or harmful, depending upon the nature of the training and the organism's stage of development" (p. 472).

Might this relate to our species as well? In one of the few such experiments with humans, Hanus Papousek (1977) conditioned infants to turn their heads to a buzzer or a bell. Training began either at birth or at 31 or 44 days of age. Infants who began training at birth took many more trials (814) and days (128) before they learned the task than did infants who began later (278 and 224 trials and 71 and 72 days for the 31- and 44-day-old infants, respectively), causing Papousek to write that "beginning too early with difficult learning tasks, at a time when the organism is not able to master them, results in prolongation of the learning process."

Despite the lack of well-controlled studies investigating the effect of early and atypical learning experiences on infant development, the general belief is that "earlier is better," and many commercial products are available in the United States aimed at accelerating babies' cognitive development. For example, computer programs promoted as educational software for infants and toddlers as young as 6 months, called *lapware*, can be played while sitting on a parent's lap. For example, the *ToddlerToons*® website stated that "ToddlerToons allows babies and toddlers to build language skills and to learn concepts such as cause and effect, big and little, up and down, happy and sad, colors and shapes, body parts, and more." Who could ask for more?

The question is, of course, do these programs work? One recent study investigated vocabulary development in 12- to 24-month-old infants and found no evidence that watching baby DVDs enhanced infants' word learning (Richert et al., 2010). In another study, the amount of time children 8 to 16 months old watched "baby" DVDs/videos, such as Baby Einstein® and Brainy Baby®, was *negatively* related to the number of words they understood: Each hour children watched baby DVDs/videos was associated with six to eight *fewer* vocabulary words (Zimmerman, Christakis, & Meltzoff, 2007). Even having a TV playing in the background can adversely affect infants' and young children's behavior. For instance, 12-, 24-, and 36-month-old children were observed playing both with and without television broadcasting in the background (Schmidt et al., 2008; see also Courage et al., 2010). The quality of children's play and their focused attention was negatively affected by having the TV on in the background, even if they paid little attention to it. Although such findings are preliminary, they suggest these "educationally enriching" activities do not enhance young children's intellectual development, as many parents believe, and may actually be detrimental (see also Bjorklund, 2007a). A recent review of the literature concluded that television and other forms of infant-directed videos clearly attract and hold infants' attention, but it is not until 18 months of age that the *content* of the video, rather than the physical stimulus qualities of the display, will hold a child's attention (Courage & Setliff, 2010).

Infants need stimulation—interesting objects and, especially, responsive people to speak to and interact with. However, stimulation can be excessive, can distract infants and young children from other tasks, and may replace activities, such as social interaction, that are vital to their development. I am in no way advocating a "hands-off" policy on educating infants and young children. I am advocating a recognition that infants' limited cognitive abilities may afford them some benefits, such as allowing them to develop certain perceptual and cognitive skills without becoming overloaded with too much information.

Children's immature cognition can be seen as having an integrity and, possibly, a function of its own rather than being seen only as something that

*(Continues)*

| BOX 1-1 | The Adaptive Nature of Cognitive Immaturity *(Continued)* |
|---|---|

must be overcome. Such a perspective can have important consequences not only for how we view development but also for education and remediation. Expecting children who are developmentally delayed or have learning deficits to master "age-appropriate" skills might be counterproductive, even if possible. Young and delayed children's immature cognition might suit them for mastering certain skills. Attempting to "educate" them beyond their present cognitive abilities could result in advanced surface behavior; however, the general effectiveness of that behavior might be minimally, or even detrimentally, influenced despite considerable effort expended (Bjorklund & Schwartz, 1996; Goodman, 1992).

experience in shaping intelligence. Experience was the important component affecting levels of intelligence, with experiences during the early years of life being most critical.

Jerome Kagan (1976) referred to this latter view as the *tape recorder model* of development. Every experience was seen as being recorded for posterity, without the opportunity to rewrite or erase something once it has been recorded. Evidence for this view was found in studies of children reared in nonstimulating institutions (Spitz, 1945). Infants receiving little in the way of social or physical stimulation showed signs of intellectual impairment as early as 3 or 4 months of age. Not only did these deleterious effects became exacerbated the longer children remained institutionalized, they were maintained long after children left the institutions (Dennis, 1973). The finding of long-term consequences of early experience was consistent with Freudian theory, which held that experiences during the oral and anal stages of development (from birth to about 2 years) have important effects on adult personality. (This also seems to be the opinion shared by the media and general public.)

Evidence for the permanence of the effects of early experience was also found in the animal literature. For example, Harry Harlow and his colleagues (1965) demonstrated in a series of classic studies that isolating infant rhesus monkeys from their mothers (and other monkeys) adversely affected their later social and sexual behaviors. Without steady interaction with other monkeys during infancy, young monkeys grew up lacking many of the social skills that facilitate important adaptive exchanges, such as mating, cooperation with others, and play. Furthermore, their maladaptive behaviors apparently remained stable over the life of the animals.

Exceptions were found, however, and many began to believe that these exceptions were actually the rule. In one classic study, for instance, infants believed to be intellectually impaired were moved from their overcrowded and understaffed orphanage to an institution for the intellectually impaired (Skeels, 1966). There they received lavish attention by women inmates, and within the course of several years, these children demonstrated normal levels of intelligence. Figure 1-6 shows the average IQs of these children both before they were placed in the institution for the intellectually impaired and approximately 2.5 years later. Also shown are the IQ scores of "control" children, who remained in the same orphanage the experimental children were removed from and were tested about 4 years later. As you can see, the transferred children showed a substantial increase in IQ (27.5 points), whereas the control children showed a comparable degree of decline (26.2 points). (More recent research on the reversibility of intellectual impairment as a result of institutionalization will be presented in Chapter 13.) In other work, isolated monkeys were placed in therapy sessions with younger, immature monkeys on a daily

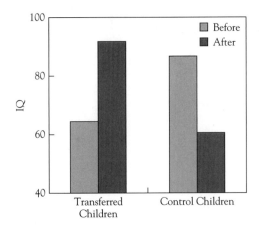

FIGURE **1-6**

Average IQ scores before placement and 2.5 years after completion of program for children in the experimental and control groups.

Source: Adapted from data presented in Skeels, H. M. (1966). Adult status of children with contrasting early life experiences. *Monographs of the Society for Research in Child Development, 31* (Serial No. 105).

basis over a 6-month period. By the end of therapy, these isolates were behaving in a reasonably normal fashion and became integrated into a laboratory monkey troop (Suomi & Harlow, 1972). Each of these studies demonstrates plasticity by a young organism and resilience concerning the negative effects of early environments.

Kagan (1976) proposed that one reason to expect resilience is that development does not proceed as a tape recorder. Rather, development is transformational, with relatively drastic changes occurring between adjacent stages, or phases. During these times, the "tapes" are changed. Alternatively, methods of representing and interpreting the world change so that the codes of the earlier tapes may be "lost" to the child. The tapes of our infancy might still reside in our heads, but we've lost the ability to play them or, maybe, the ability to understand the code in which they were written. In this view, plasticity should be the rule rather than the exception, especially for the experiences of infancy and early childhood.

One important thing to remember here is that, yes, stimulation and experience are important in the early years of life, but so is later experience. Although early intellectual stimulation is important to get children off to a good start, later experiences are necessary to maintain that positive beginning. And although most children who start life in nonstimulating circumstances remain there, enhancements in intellectual skills are apt to occur for such children if their environments change for the better. This does not mean that there is infinite plasticity in cognitive development, but merely that early experience is not necessarily destiny (just as biology is not) and that change is as much a characteristic of human cognition as is stability.

## Cognitive Development Involves Changes in the Way Information Is Represented

One key issue that all theories of cognitive development must address concerns age differences in how children represent experience. Most psychologists believe that there is more than one way to represent a thing, and children of different ages seem to use different ways to represent their worlds. Adults, as well, use a variety of techniques to represent knowledge. While providing directions to your house to someone over the phone, for instance, you must convey the route to your home verbally, through a language code. But how is it represented in your head? What is the nature of the **representation**—that is, the mental encoding of information? You might think of the route you take by generating visual images of the buildings and landmarks you pass and then convert those into words. Or perhaps you sketch a map and then transform it into words that can be understood by your listener. What the person on the other end of the phone must do is encode the information. At one level, your friend might attend only to the sounds of the words you speak, encoding the acoustic properties of your utterances. If she does, she will probably be late for dinner. More likely, she will attend to the semantic, or meaning, features of the words. Once a basic meaning has been derived, however, she might convert the message to a mental (or perhaps a physical) map, realizing that she will be better able to find your house if the relevant information is in the form of a visual image.

How children represent knowledge and how they encode events in their world change developmentally. Traditional theories have proposed that infants and toddlers much younger than 18 months are limited to knowing the world only through raw perception and through their actions on things, with little or no use of symbols. This position has been questioned recently, with research showing that even infants have access to some symbol systems (see Gelman & Williams, 1998; Spelke & Kinzler, 2007). Some researchers have even suggested that abstract, symbolic representation is innate, in that even newborns reveal behavior requiring seemingly symbolic representation, such as imitation of facial gestures (Meltzoff & Moore, 1985). Much of this research will be discussed in Chapter 4.

Let me provide a much-cited example concerning the question of whether infants are capable of simple arithmetic, a skill normally associated with much older children. Karen Wynn (1992) sat 5-month-old infants in front of a display. Infants were then shown a sequence of events that involved the addition or subtraction of elements. Two of these sequences are shown in Figure 1-7. One sequence (the "possible outcome") led to the conclusion that $1 + 1 = 2$; the other sequence (the "impossible outcome") led to the conclusion that $1 + 1 = 1$. Infants sat in front of a stage and watched as one object was placed on it (step 1 in Figure 1-7). A screen was then raised, hiding the object (step 2 in Figure 1-7). The infant then watched as a second object was placed behind the screen (steps 3 and 4 in Figure 1-7). The screen was then lowered, revealing either two objects (the "possible outcome") or one object (the "impossible outcome"). If infants have some primitive concept of addition, they should be surprised and, thus, spend more time looking at the "impossible" outcome. This was exactly what occurred, both for the addition problem shown in Figure 1-7 and for a simple subtraction problem ($2 - 1 = 1$). Although there is much debate about how to interpret this and similar findings (see Clearfield & Westfahl, 2006; Moore & Cocas, 2006), results such as these suggest that infants perhaps have more advanced representational skills than we once believed.

Most cognitive developmentalists agree that there are age differences in how children represent their world and that these differences are central to age differences in thinking. Researchers disagree, however, about the nature of these differences. Can children of all ages use all types of symbols, and do they simply use them with different frequencies? Or does representation develop in a stage-like manner, with the more advanced forms of

1. Object placed in case

2. Screen comes up

3. Second object added

4. Hand leaves empty

Then either: possible outcome

5. Screen drops ...

...revealing 2 objects

or: impossible outcome

5. Screen drops ...

...revealing 1 object

FIGURE **1-7**

Sequence of events for the 1 + 1 = 2 (possible) outcome and the 1 + 1 = 1 (impossible) outcome from the experiment by Wynn (1992).

Source: "Addition and Subtraction by Human Infants," by K. Wynn, 1992, *Nature, 358,* 749–750. Copyright © 1992 Macmillan Magazines Ltd. Reprinted with permission from *Nature.*

symbol use being unavailable to younger children? I believe most researchers today think that children, beginning in infancy, have multiple ways of representing information, although their ability to mentally represent people, objects, and events increases in sophistication over infancy and childhood. Research and theory pertinent to these and other issues related to changes in representation are central to the study of cognitive development, and they will be discussed in the pages ahead.

## Children Develop Increasing Intentional Control over Their Behavior and Cognition

Much cognitive developmental (and educational) research is concerned with how children solve problems. And much of what interests cognitive developmental psychologists is how children go about finding solutions to complex problems that might have multiple paths to a solution. For example, how do children solve a puzzle, how do they go about remembering a grocery list, or how do they study for a history exam? Problem solving begins in infancy, but the problems children face, and their solutions, become more complicated with age.

One central concern of cognitive developmentalists has been the degree to which children of different ages can intentionally guide their problem solving. Much research on this topic has addressed the use of strategies. **Strategies** are usually defined as deliberate, goal-directed mental operations that are aimed at solving a problem (Harnishfeger & Bjorklund, 1990a; Pressley & Hilden, 2006). We use strategies intentionally to help us achieve a specified goal. Strategies can be seen in the behavior of infants. Six-month-olds alter how hard they swing at mobiles over their cribs to yield slightly different movements from the inanimate objects. Eighteen-month-old toddlers will deliberately stack boxes one on top of another so that they can reach the kitchen shelf and the chocolate-chip cookies. These strategies are no less willful than the rhyming mnemonic the sixth-grader uses to remember how many days are in each month, or the plan the 15-year-old uses as he plays all his trump cards first in a game of bridge. Yet, strategies do change with development, and children seem increasingly able to carry out successful strategies as they grow older. So, one key research question in cognitive development concerns changes in the strategies children use and the situations in which they use them.

Although children around the world increasingly display goal-directed problem-solving behavior, this is especially evident for children from technologically advanced societies in which formal schooling is necessary to become a successful adult. Much of what children learn in school can be acquired only (or best) by deliberate study. This contrasts with how children in cultures without formal schooling often learn complicated tasks. In all cultures, much of what children learn about their world they acquire incidentally, without specific intention and, sometimes, even without specific awareness. This type of learning and development is important also, and recent research, particularly in the area of memory development, has recognized this (see Chapter 8).

Many factors are involved in the development of strategic cognition, one of them being how much knowledge children have of the information they are asked to process. For example, when children are asked to remember sets of categorically related words—such as different examples of fruits, clothing, and mammals—they are more likely to use a memory strategy (for instance, remembering all the items from the same category together in clusters) and to remember more of the words if they are *typical* of their category (Best, 1993; Schwenck, Bjorklund, & Schneider, 2009). Typical items for the category clothing, for example, would include words such as *shirt, dress,* and *coat,* whereas atypical clothing items would include *hat, socks,* and *belt.* The latter are all common words and would be well known to children, but they are less typical of what we think of as "clothes." How the role of knowledge base influences children's cognition has been a much-studied topic in cognitive development (Schneider & Bjorklund, 2003; Pressley & Hilden, 2006).

Becoming a strategic learner involves learning to regulate one's thought and behavior. This involves a set of basic-level cognitive abilities, referred to as executive function. **Executive function** refers to the processes involved in regulating attention and in determining what to do with information just gathered or retrieved from long-term memory. It plays a central role in planning and behaving flexibly, particularly when dealing with novel information. Among the basic cognitive abilities that comprise executive function is *working memory*—the structures and processes used for temporarily storing and manipulating information, selectively attending to relevant information, and inhibiting responding and resisting interference, among others. Thus, becoming a "self-directed thinker" (see Chapter 7) involves an understanding of the development of both lower-level cognitive processes (for example, executive function) and higher-level cognitive processes (for example, strategies).

## Cognitive Development Involves Changes in Both Domain-General and Domain-Specific Abilities

Theories that postulate **domain-general abilities** assume that at any point in time, a child's thinking is influenced by a single set of factors, with these factors affecting different aspects of cognition (that is, different domains of thought) equally. In contrast to domain-general accounts of cognitive development are theories that postulate **domain-specific abilities**. According to these theories, knowing a child's ability for one aspect of cognition might tell us nothing about his or her level of cognitive ability for other aspects of thinking because different cognitive domains are controlled by different mind/brain functions. At the extreme, domain-specific theories propose that different areas of the brain affect different aspects of cognition, with these areas being unaffected by what goes on in other areas of the brain.

The idea of the independence of different cognitive functions is best reflected in the work of philosopher Jerry Fodor (1983). Fodor proposed the concept of **modularity** in brain functions, meaning that certain areas of the brain are dedicated to performing specific cognitive tasks (such as processing language). These modules represent special-purpose systems that are "informationally encapsulated" (or "cognitively impenetrable"), meaning that other parts of the mind/brain can neither influence nor access the workings of the module. Many modules are proposed to be innate, part of the neural network an infant is born with and the result of millions of years of evolution; other modules can be developed as a result of experience and become encapsulated over time. Fodor proposed that the outputs of these modules become available to a central information processor (a domain-general mechanism), but that the activity of this central processor does not affect the domain-specific modules. Although Fodor's idea of domain-specificity in human cognition has been challenged (Elman et al., 1996; and see Fodor, 2000, for a revision of his earlier ideas), it remains a dominant perspective within cognitive psychology.

Robbie Case (1992) put the controversy between domain-general and domain-specific theorists succinctly: "Is the mind better thought of as a general, all-purpose computing device, whose particular forte is general problem solving? Or is it better thought of as a modular device, each of whose modules has evolved to serve a unique biological function that it performs in its own unique and specialized way?" (p. 3). As we'll see in Chapters 5 and 7, the predominant theories of cognitive development throughout the 20th century were domain-general ones. Domain-specific theories arose primarily because of the failure of the domain-general theories to account for the unevenness of cognitive function that is frequently observed in development.

Some compromises between these two approaches are possible and likely necessary. For example, many researchers have shown that children think differently as a function of how much background knowledge they have in a particular domain. For instance, Wolfgang Schneider and his colleagues (1989) evaluated German children in grades 3, 5, and 7 for their knowledge of soccer and classified children as either soccer experts or soccer novices. The children were also administered a series of intelligence tests, and these results, along with their school grades in math and German, were used to classify them as successful learners or unsuccessful learners. The children were then presented with a well-organized narrative text about soccer and were later asked to recall it. Amount remembered was computed by the number of idea units children recalled about the story. The patterns of results with respect to expertise and IQ were similar for the children at each of the three grade levels and are summarized in Figure 1-8 (averaged over grade). As would be expected, memory performance was better for the soccer experts than for the soccer novices. However, the researchers reported no difference in performance between the academically successful learners and the unsuccessful ones. That is, being a good learner (and having a high IQ) did not

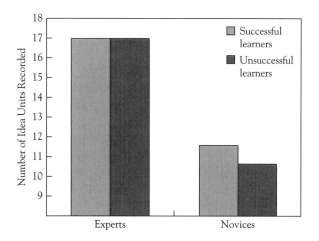

FIGURE **1-8**

Number of idea units remembered about a soccer story for high- and low-aptitude soccer experts and soccer novices. In this case, being an expert eliminated any effect of academic aptitude (IQ) on performance.

Source: Adapted from data presented in Schneider, W., Körkel, J., & Weinert, F. E. (1989). Domain-specific knowledge and memory performance: A comparison of high- and low-aptitude children. *Journal of Educational Psychology, 81,* 306–312.

result in better performance by either the expert children or the novice children. Having a detailed knowledge of the subject matter was enough to yield high levels of memory performance. Similarly, having an impoverished knowledge of the subject matter was enough to yield low levels of performance, regardless of a child's level of IQ (see also Recht & Leslie, 1988; Walker, 1987).

Yet, such differences in cognitive performance as a function of background knowledge (that is, such domain-specificity) can be explained by domain-general mechanisms. Children who are experts use fewer of their general information-processing resources in thinking about information from their domain of expertise than they do in thinking about information from other areas, accounting for their uneven performance without postulating innate, modular brain structures (Bjorklund, 1987a).

Modularity implies inflexibility, in that the individual is constrained by biology to process certain information in certain ways. This can be good, increasing the likelihood that complex information will be properly processed and understood. In discussing the benefits of constraints for infants, Annette Karmiloff-Smith (1992) states, "[T]hey enable the infant to accept as input only those data which it is initially able to compute in specific ways. The domain specificity of processing provides the infant with a limited yet organized (nonchaotic) system from the outset" (pp. 11–13). But the hallmark of human cognition is flexibility. Our species has come to dominate the globe, for better or worse, because we are able to solve problems that biology could not have imagined, and we have developed technological systems that expand our intellectual powers (such as writing, mathematics, and computers). Such cognition could not be achieved by a totally encapsulated mind/brain, and of course, no serious domain-specific theorist proposes this degree of modularity. What we must keep in mind is the certainty that both domain-general and domain-specific abilities exist, and we must be cautious of claims that postulate otherwise.

# GOALS OF COGNITIVE DEVELOPMENTALISTS

Although I believe the topics discussed in the previous sections reflect the major issues in the study of cognitive development, what underlies all of these issues, as I mentioned in the opening pages of this chapter, is a search for the mechanisms responsible for change. We can observe changes in how children represent their world and see evidence of enhanced intentional, goal-directed behavior with age, but as scientists, we very much want to know the causes of these changes. Thus, description of change is not enough, although it is a necessary start. Perhaps the principal goal of cognitive developmentalists is to discover the underlying mechanisms of change, and much of the research in the remainder of this book addresses this issue.

Another goal for many cognitive developmentalists is to produce research that can be applied to real-world contexts. For example, issues about the stability and plasticity of intelligence have direct applications to the remediation of intellectual impairment and to some learning disabilities. Understanding how children learn to use strategies of arithmetic, memory, and reading, for example, are directly pertinent to children's acquisition of modern culture's most important technological skills (see Chapter 11). Research on factors that influence children's recollection of experienced or witnessed events has immediate relevance to the courtroom, where children have increasingly been called to testify (see Chapter 8). Understanding the typical development of both basic (and unconscious) cognitive processes as well as forms of higher-order (and conscious) cognition provides insight into the causes of some learning disabilities, whether in math and reading (see Chapter 11) or, perhaps, as a result of attention deficit hyperactivity disorder (ADHD) (see Chapter 7). And although extensions to the schoolhouse or clinic may be the most obvious applications of cognitive development research and theory, I believe perhaps the greatest application is to an appreciation of children in general, particularly when they are your own.

# SUMMARY

The study of cognitive development involves the regular, age-related changes in children's cognition over time, referred to as *developmental function,* as well as *individual differences* in such cognition. *Cognition* refers to the acquisition and manipulation of knowledge. It includes conscious, effortful processes, such as those involved in making important decisions, and unconscious, automatic processes, such as those involved in recognizing a familiar face, word, or object. Cognition cannot be observed directly. It must be inferred from behavior.

*Development* refers to changes in *structure* or *function* over time, with such a relationship being conceived as *bidirectional* in nature (*structure ↔ function*). Development has its roots in biology, and its course is relatively predictable. Yet, within any given age or stage, there are individual differences in children's thinking, with the organism-environment interaction being critical for an understanding of the course of development. Although development is often viewed as being progressive, children's immature cognitions might provide them with some adaptive advantages.

With respect to the nature/nurture issues, extreme views of both *nativism* (a belief that all intellectual abilities are innate, and proposing a type of *genetic determinism*) and *empiricism* (a belief that all intellectual abilities are a result of experience) have been rejected and replaced by a belief in the bidirectional relation of biological and experiential factors, with children playing critical roles in their own development. Three different types of innate constraints have been proposed: *representational,* referring to innate representations; *architectural,* referring to innate characteristics of neurons and their connections with other groups of neurons; and *chronotopic,* referring to maturational (timing) constraints. Biological and environmental factors are seen as interacting in bidirectional relationships, as reflected by *developmental contextual models.*

*Dynamic systems* theories propose that new levels of organization emerge as a result of the *self-organization* among lower-level elements within a system. As such, development is viewed not as the product of learning or of innately specified information in the genes but, rather, as the process of emergence.

Contemporary theorists view the social environment as being particularly important for cognitive development, as reflected by *sociocultural perspectives.* Some further argue that developmental contextual and sociocultural models of development should be integrated with evolutionary theory to produce a coherent understanding of psychological development.

*Stability* refers to the degree to which children maintain their same rank order relative to their peers over time. *Plasticity* refers to the extent to which individuals can be shaped by the environment. For most of the 20th century, it was believed that intelligence is relatively stable over time and that experiences later in life cannot greatly affect patterns of intelligence established earlier. More recent research suggests that some characteristics are stable and that human intelligence can be substantially modified under certain circumstances.

Developmental differences in *representation* have been a central topic of concern for cognitive developmentalists. Most researchers today believe that children, beginning in infancy, have multiple ways of representing information, although their ability to mentally represent people, objects, and events increases in sophistication over infancy and childhood.

Children gain increasing control over their own problem-solving behavior, often by using deliberately implemented *strategies.* Strategic cognition is influenced by a host of factors, including how much knowledge a child has, and also by a child's levels of *executive function,* referring to processes involved in regulating attention and in determining what to do with information just gathered or retrieved from long-term memory.

Most traditional approaches to cognitive development have posited *domain-general abilities,* although recent research has shown that many aspects of cognition and its development are *domain-specific* in nature, with some forms of cognition being *modular.*

## KEY TERMS AND CONCEPTS

cognition

development (ontogeny)

structure

function

bidirectionality of structure and function

(structure ↔ function)

developmental function

individual differences

nativism

empiricism

genetic determinism

representational constraints (representational innateness)

architectural constraints (architectural innateness)

chronotopic constraints (chronotopic innateness)

developmental contextual model

dynamic system

self-organization

sociocultural perspectives

stability

plasticity (of cognition and behavior)

representation

strategies

executive function

domain-general abilities

domain-specific abilities

modularity

## SUGGESTED READINGS

### Scholarly Works

Bjorklund, D. F. (2011). Cognitive development: An overview. In P. D. Zelazo (Ed.), *Oxford handbook of developmental psychology*. Oxford, UK: Oxford University Press. This introductory article for an entire section devoted to cognitive development briefly reviews the major areas of research interest in the field.

Elman, J. L., Bates, E. A., Johnson, M. H., Karmiloff-Smith, A., Parisi, D., & Plunkett, K. (1996). *Rethinking innateness: A connectionist perspective on development*. Cambridge, MA: MIT Press. This book discusses the concept of innateness as it relates to developmental psychology. Although numerous aspects of development are discussed, most discussion is related to brain development and language development. The authors present a connectionist (computer modeling) perspective, but the book is valuable even for those who want to avoid such approaches.

Lerner, R. M. (2006). Developmental science, developmental systems, and contemporary theories of human development. In W. Damon & R. M. Lerner (Gen. Eds.), *Handbook of child psychology* (6th edition), R. M. Lerner (Vol. Ed.), Vol. 1, *Theoretical models of human development*, (pp. 1–17). New York: Wiley. This is a relatively lengthy and thorough examination of contemporary theorizing on developmental psychology, focusing on developmental contextual models.

Lewis, M. D. (2000). The promise of dynamic systems approaches for an integrated account of human development. *Child Development, 71,* 36–43. This short article presents the major concepts of dynamic systems as they are applied in developmental psychology. For a more in-depth discussion, the reader is directed to the chapter by Thelen and Smith in the 2006 *Handbook of Child Psychology.*

### Reading for Personal Interest

Bjorklund, D. F. (2007). *Why youth is* not *wasted on the young: Immaturity in human development*. Oxford, UK: Blackwell. This book, written for a general audience, takes an explicitly Darwinian view of childhood, including the potentially adaptive role of cognitive immaturity.

Rutter, M. (2006). *Genes and behavior: Nature-nurture interplay explained*. Malden, MA: Blackwell. This book provides a highly readable and up-to-date account of research in behavioral genetics, written by one of the leaders of the field who also knows a thing or two about development. I was tempted to include this in the category *Scholarly Works* because it is so thorough, but it is written so it can be understood by the educated layperson.

# Biological Bases of Cognitive Development

**Evolution and Cognitive Development**
Evolutionary Theory
Evolutionary Developmental Psychology

**Models of Gene-Environment Interaction**
The Developmental Systems Approach
The Genotype → Environment Theory

**The Development of the Brain**
   **BOX 2-1:** The Evolution of the Human Brain
Neuronal Development

How Do Young Brains Get Hooked Up?
The Development of the Neocortex
The Brain's Plasticity

**Developmental Biology and Cognitive Development**

SUMMARY
KEY TERMS AND CONCEPTS
SUGGESTED READINGS

Half of the first term had expired, and Tyler's first-grade teacher requested a conference with his parents. Tyler, the teacher said was a bright, creative, and likeable boy, but he was having some problems concentrating and staying on task. He would often blurt out answers to questions or say things that were not on topic, sometimes about one of his favorite TV shows. He was easily distracted and sometimes acted impulsively with the other children. After discussing some things his parents could do at home to help Tyler "stay on task" and proposing that he likely did not have attention deficit hyperactivity disorder, the teacher asked the parents in what month Tyler was born. Tyler's father's first thought was, "Uh oh, we've got a teacher who believes in astrology. What's next, Tarot cards?" But when they answered July, the teacher said, "I thought as much. He's a summer child, one of the youngest children in class, and a boy. His brain isn't as mature as most of the other children's. He'll catch-up. He's a bright boy."

This experienced first-grade teacher may not have known that it was the slow-developing frontal cortex of Tyler's brain that was primarily responsible for his control problems, or that psychologists refer to processing that involves staying on task, resisting interference, and planning as *executive function*. But this teacher had seen enough to know that "summer children," especially boys, were apt to get off to a slow start in first grade.

As I mentioned in Chapter 1, developmental psychology has become increasingly "biological" over the past decade or so. For some time now, I've begun including lectures on the biological basis of cognitive development in my undergraduate class, discussing brain development and the evolution of mental abilities. Invariably, one or two students will approach me after class and ask why we need to know anything about biology to understand children's thinking. These students didn't become psychology majors to study biology.

The question these students ask is not a trivial one. For much of the 20th century, social and behavioral scientists interested in cognition gave only lip service, at best, to biology. The mind might emanate from the brain, but understanding the brain was not seen as a prerequisite to understanding the mind. In fact, there existed in the social and behavioral sciences what can be called *biophobia* and an implicit belief that acknowledging biology was akin to rejecting the influence of environment or culture on behavior, something at odds with the central theme of the social sciences (see Tooby & Cosmides, 1992). The study of cognition was essentially isolated from the study of the brain.

Things have clearly changed. The new field of cognitive science takes as a given the close connection between mind and brain. As philosopher John Searle (1992) stated, "Mental phenomena are caused by neurophysiological processes in the brain and are themselves features of the brain.... Mental events and processes are as much part of our biological natural history as digestion, mitosis, or enzyme secretion" (p. 1). Moreover, cognitive scientists are concerned not only with immediate biological causes (for example, how the brain affects behavior) but also with factors that influenced the evolution of human cognition.

Looking at the biological basis of cognition and its development does not mean that one ignores the psychological level. Biology and psychology provide different levels of analysis. Much as psychology and anthropology present different pictures of human behavior (one at the level of the individual and the other at the level of the culture), so too do biology and psychology. Moreover, just as concepts in biology must be consistent with the known facts of chemistry, concepts in psychology must be consistent with the known facts of biology. Thus, proposing theories of mind that are inconsistent with what we know about physiology or evolution cannot lead to a productive theory of cognition (see Cosmides, Tooby, & Barkow, 1992).

Psychology, however, cannot be reduced to biology. Knowing how nerve cells function will not tell us all we need to know about how we think. Developing a theory of the brain is important, of course, but it is not enough. Having a theory of the brain does not obviate having a theory of the mind. Cognitive psychology is not just something to do until the biologists get better at their trade. Developmental psychologists should not blindly accept everything that biologists propose, but they should be mindful of the biological causes of cognitive development and formulate theories and design experiments accordingly (Bjorklund, 1997b).

In this chapter, I first look at ideas from evolutionary theory and how such Darwinian ideas can contribute to an understanding of the developing modern child. In the next section, I examine several developmental theories that take biology seriously, particularly the relation between genetic/biologic factors and environmental/experiential factors. I then provide a brief overview of brain development. In this chapter, as in later chapters, I will comment on the relation between brain and cognitive development. Although no one ever doubted that the brain was the seat of cognition, only recently, with the emergence of the field of **developmental cognitive neuroscience**, have brain-cognition relations in development been taken seriously (see Diamond & Amso, 2008; Johnson, 2007; Nelson, 2001). Developmental cognitive neuroscience takes data from a variety of sources—molecular biology, cell biology, artificial intelligence, evolutionary theory, as well as conventional cognitive development—to create a picture of how the mind/brain develops. As will be made clear soon, contemporary biologically based theories of development do not hold that "biology is destiny" but, rather, deal with the classic nature/nurture controversy by explaining how genes and environments interact to produce a particular pattern of development.

Because most research in cognitive development over the last century essentially ignored biological causation, most of what is covered in the rest of the book is at the psychological rather than the biological level. However, I firmly believe that we will develop an understanding of cognitive development only by taking biology seriously, and reference to biological factors will be made throughout the remainder of the book.

---

# EVOLUTION AND COGNITIVE DEVELOPMENT

What is the adaptive value of particular cognitive abilities? How might cognitive abilities have a different adaptive value at different times in development? In what contexts should certain cognitive abilities develop? How do some evolved human characteristics, such as bipedality or prolonged immaturity, affect the development of cognition? Developmentalists ask these questions relating to evolution.

## Evolutionary Theory

When biologists speak of **evolution,** they (usually) mean the process of change in gene frequencies within populations over many generations that, in time, produces new species. Modern evolutionary theory had its beginnings in the ideas of Charles Darwin, whose 1859 book *On The Origin of Species* represents one of the grandest ideas of science. The book made an immediate impact on the scientific community and is considered by many today to be one of the most important books ever written. The crux of the theory is that many more members of a species are born in each generation than will survive, and these members of the species all have different combinations of inherited traits (that is, there is substantial *variation* among members of a species). Conditions in the environment for that particular generation cause some members of that species to survive and reproduce whereas others do not, a process that Darwin referred to as **natural selection.** The inherited traits of the survivors will be passed on to the next generation of that species, whereas the traits of the nonsurvivors will not. Over the course of many generations, the predominant traits of a species will change by this mechanism. The major principle of Darwin's theory is *reproductive fitness,* which basically refers to the likelihood that an individual will become a parent and a grandparent.

Darwin's theory has gone through some substantial modifications during the last century or so, the most significant being the inclusion of modern genetic theory into formulations of evolution. Among scientists today, the *fact* of evolution is not questioned, although some lively debates center on the *mechanisms* of evolution (see Gould, 2002). Despite controversies, evolutionary theory is the backbone of modern biology, and because human cognition and behavior are rooted in biology, evolutionary theory should be the backbone of modern psychology.

One thing that evolutionary theory provides is a framework for interpreting all aspects of behavior and development. It does this, in part, by providing not only an explanation for *how* a particular mechanism came about (through natural selection) but also a possible explanation of *why* this mechanism evolved. In my early training, I was taught not to ask "why" questions. Scientists, I was taught, ask "how" questions—for example, "How do children come to appreciate that other people have perceptions and ideas other than their own?" rather than *why* do they develop this ability. Evolutionary theory provides answers to both the "how" and the "why" questions. The "how" is through natural selection over evolutionary time, in that children who could not learn to see the perspectives of another person did not grow up to have children of their own. Of course, this is not a sufficient answer to "how" this ability develops in individual children, but it does provide a mechanism for how it evolved in the species. The "why" suggests that this ability was likely important for survival, or that it was *adaptive*. Children who could understand the perspective of another were able to anticipate other people's actions and act accordingly. Such *adaptationist* reasoning must be used cautiously, of course. Not all aspects of present-day life were necessarily adaptive for our ancient ancestors. Some aspects might have been neutral, some associated with other adaptive characteristics, and others just not sufficiently maladaptive to result in extinction. But having a theory that provides a framework for asking why a particular behavior or pattern of development is present can help us to develop a better understanding of human nature and to ask better "how" questions.

Evolutionary theory is currently influencing cognitive development through the newly emerging field of **evolutionary developmental psychology** (Bjorklund & Hernández Blasi, 2005; Bjorklund & Pellegrini, 2002; Geary & Bjorklund, 2000). This field explains human development through evolutionary theory. It is important to understand that what might have been adaptive to our ancestors 100,000 or 1 million years ago might not be adaptive to us today. Our preference for sweets and fat is a good case in point. Although these foods would have been rare and much valued sources of energy for our ancient ancestors, they are easily available to people from postindustrial cultures today and are largely responsible for our high incidence of heart disease (Nesse & Williams, 1994). Many cognitive mechanisms can be seen in a similar light. Alternatively, many of the technological problems we must solve as modern humans are only centuries old at most, and no specific mechanisms have evolved to solve them.

## Evolutionary Developmental Psychology

Evolutionary psychologists have suggested that cognitive psychology is the missing link in the evolution of human behavior. Leda Cosmides and John Tooby (1987) proposed that information-processing mechanisms evolved and that "these mechanisms in interaction with environmental input generate manifest behavior. The causal link between evolution and behavior is made through psychological mechanisms" (p. 277). According to Cosmides and Tooby, adaptive behavior is predicated on adaptive thought. Natural selection operates on the cognitive level—information-processing programs evolved to solve real-world problems. How do I tell friend from foe? When do I fight, and when do I flee? From this viewpoint, it becomes fruitful to ask what kind of cognitive operations an organism must have "if it is to extract and process information about its environment in a way that will lead to adaptive behavior" (Cosmides & Tooby, 1987, p. 285). From an evolutionary perspective, we must ask what is the purpose of a behavior and the cognitive operations that underlie that behavior, and what problem was it designed to solve.

It is also important in the realm of cognitive development to remember that cognitive processes *develop* and that the problems infants and children face are different from the problems adults face. Researchers can fruitfully ask how children's cognitions are adapted to the cultural contexts in which they find themselves rather than to the contexts experienced by adults (Bjorklund, 2007a; Turkewitz & Kenny, 1982). For example, what type of information should helpless infants be attentive to? Might some information that is of vital importance to them be less important to older children and adults, and vice versa?

Most mainstream evolutionary psychologists assume that what evolved are domain-specific mechanisms designed by natural selection to deal with specific aspects of the physical or social environment, such as face recognition or the processing of certain types of social relationships. However, natural selection has also influenced the evolution of domain-general mechanisms (for example, executive function, ability to inhibit thoughts and actions), and a number of developmental psychologists believe that these should also be examined from an evolutionary perspective (Bjorklund & Kipp, 2002; Geary, 2005; Geary & Huffman, 2002).

Implicit in the idea that there are domain-specific mechanisms is that there are *constraints* (representational, architectural, and chronotopic; see Chapter 1) on learning (Gelman & Williams, 1998; Spelke & Kinzler, 2007). Constraints imply restrictions, and restrictions are usually thought of as being bad. Human cognition is exceptional for its flexibility, not for its restrictiveness. But constraints, from this perspective, *enable* learning rather than hamper it. Children enter a world of sights, sounds, objects, language, and other people. If all types of learning were truly equiprobable, children would be overwhelmed by the stimulation that bombards them from every direction. Instead, the argument goes, infants and young children are constrained to process certain information in "core domains" (such as the nature of objects, language) in certain ways, and this leads to faster and more efficient processing of information within specific domains. According to Gelman and Williams (1998), "From an evolutionary perspective, learning cannot be a process of arbitrary and completely flexible knowledge acquisition. In core domains, learning processes are the means to functionally defined ends: acquiring and storing the particular sorts of relevant information which are necessary for solving particular problems" (p. 600).

One way of thinking about how the mind is structured has been presented by David Geary (2005, 2009; Geary & Bjorklund, 2000), who proposes that what evolved is a set of domain-specific modules that develop as children engage their physical and social worlds. Geary's model is shown in Figure 2-1. As can be seen, there are two overarching domains—social (folk psychology) and ecological—with each consisting of more-specific domains (self, individual, and group for social and biological and physical for ecological), each of which in turn consists of more-specific domains.

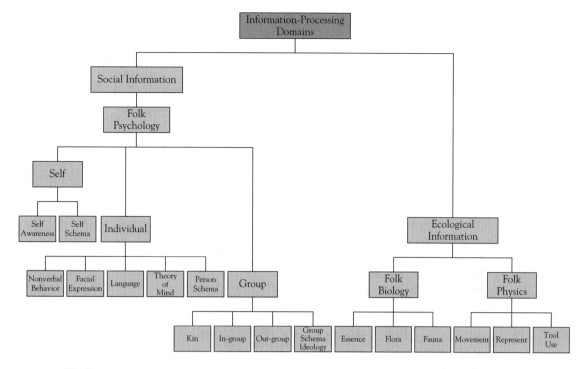

**FIGURE 2-1**

Geary proposed that the mind is hierarchically organized into domains. Within the social domain of folk psychology, domains are further organized into those dealing with self knowledge, dealing with individuals, and dealing with groups. Within the ecological domain, Geary proposes two subdomains, one dealing with the biological world and the other the physical world.

Source: Geary, D. C. (2005). *The origin of mind: Evolution of brain, cognition, and general intelligence.* Washington, DC: American Psychological Association.

Geary acknowledges that this list of domains is not complete (for example, there is no numerical domain listed here, which Geary believes exists), and one could argue about the organization of some of these domains (for example, should "language" be organized within the social domain, or is it best conceptualized as a separate domain?). Nonetheless, Geary's organization reflects one that is consistent with the dominant perspective of evolutionary psychologists (Buss, 2009; Tooby & Cosmides, 2005), and it captures much of the developmental data.

Despite the belief that many evolutionarily influenced cognitive abilities are domain-specific in nature, one should not lose track of the fact that human cognition is amazingly flexible. This implies that what evolved in *Homo sapiens* are not highly specific approaches to problems but genes and cognitive mechanisms that are sensitive to different environments and that yield different outcomes (phenotypes) in different contexts that are (or would have been, in ancient environments) adaptive to local conditions. Such mechanisms become more specific and finely tuned during development, primarily as a result of experience. And humans, more than any other mammal, have time to gather the experience that will be necessary to function optimally as an adult.

In fact, evolutionary developmental psychologists have emphasized the importance of our species' extended childhood for cognitive development (Bjorklund & Pellegrini, 2002; Flinn & Ward, 2005). Humans spend a greater proportion of their life spans as juveniles than any other primate species. There are great dangers associated with delaying reproduction, however, so there must be some substantial benefits to survival for this prolonged period of immaturity to have been selected. Although there is no single answer to the question of why humans have such an extended juvenile period, one reason proposed by many evolutionary developmental psychologists is that the long period of youth is necessary for children to master the complexities of human societies and technologies (Bjorklund, Periss, & Causey, 2009; Kaplan et al., 2000). This perspective argues that because of the variety of social and physical environments in which people live (both presently and in our evolutionary past), human cognition must be flexible, adapted not to a highly specific environment but to a broad range of potential environments, reflecting the diversity of social groups around the globe and throughout our species' history. To do this requires a long period of apprenticeship as well as a large brain capable of flexible learning and cognition.

Another insight relevant to cognitive development and to education derived from evolutionary psychology is the idea that much of what we teach children in school is "unnatural," in that it involves tasks never encountered by our ancestors. For example, although our species has apparently been using language for tens of thousands of years, reading is a skill that goes back only a few thousand years, and only during the past century have a majority of people on the planet have become literate. Geary (1995, 2007) has referred to cognitive abilities that were selected over the course of evolution, such as language, as **biologically primary abilities**, and to skills that build on these primary abilities but are principally cultural inventions, such as reading, as **biologically secondary abilities**. Biologically primary abilities are acquired universally, and children typically have high motivation to perform tasks involving them. Biologically secondary abilities, on the other hand, are culturally determined, and tedious repetition and external pressure are often necessary for their mastery. It is little wonder that reading, a supposed "language art," and higher mathematics give many children substantial difficulty. (See Table 2-1 for a summary of the characteristics of biological primary and secondary abilities.)

It is important to emphasize here that an evolutionary account of development is *not* one of biological determinism. That is, although evolution works through changing frequencies of genes within the population, natural selection requires a dynamic interaction between organisms and their environments. Organisms choose environments, the very act of which modifies those environments. Environments in turn affect the organism by "selecting" some behaviors that "match" those environments over others. Because of this dynamic interaction between organisms and environments, we must evaluate these interactions if we want to understand adaptation and cognitive development. Thus, this position rejects any simple notion of biological determinism (for example, "genes cause behavior") on cognitive development, intelligence, or the educability of children.

## MODELS OF GENE-ENVIRONMENT INTERACTION

All self-respecting developmentalists believe that development is the result of an interaction between genetic/biologic factors and environmental/experiential factors. There

TABLE **2-1**

Some distinctions between biologically primary and biologically secondary abilities. Language is a good example of a biologically primary ability, whereas reading is a good example of a biologically secondary ability.

| Biologically Primary Abilities |
| --- |
| • Have undergone selection pressure and evolved to deal with problems faced by our ancestors |
| • Are acquired universally |
| • Are acquired by children in all but the most deprived of environments |
| • Children are intrinsically motivated to exercise biologically primary abilities and do so spontaneously |
| • Most children attain "expert" level of proficiency |

| Biologically Secondary Abilities |
| --- |
| • Do not have an evolutionary history but are built upon biologically primary abilities |
| • Are culturally dependent, reflecting the cognitive skills that are important in a particular culture (such as reading in literate cultures) |
| • Children are not intrinsically motivated to exercise them and must often be pressured by adults to acquire these skills |
| • Tedious practice is sometimes necessary to master biologically secondary abilities |

Source: Adapted from Geary. D. C. (1995). Reflections of evolution and culture in children's cognition: Implications for mathematical development and instruction. *American Psychologist, 50,* 24–37.

is really no other alternative. Some theorists are more explicit about the nature of the interaction than others, however, and in this section, I examine two approaches that look at gene-environment interactions and their consequences for development. Each approach posits that the child is an active agent in his or her own development, that development proceeds through the bidirectional effect of structure and function, and that the context in which development occurs is as important as the genes the individual inherits. The two approaches are the *developmental systems approach* (or *developmental contextualism*), as advocated by Gilbert Gottlieb (2000, 2007; Gottlieb, Wahlsten, & Lickliter, 2006), Richard Lerner (2006), Susan Oyama (2000), and others (see Li, 2003; Lickliter, 1996, 2011), and a theory based on research in behavioral genetics, the *genotype → environment theory*, as presented by Sandra Scarr and Kathleen McCartney (1983; Scarr, 1992, 1993).

There are some important distinctions between the two approaches, centering mainly around the degree to which outside experience, influenced by one's genes, modifies the organism versus the degree to which a biological organism shapes its own development through epigenetic processes. Although debate between theorists in these two camps can be vigorous (see Moore, 2001; Scarr, 1993), the difference between the two approaches can be seen as a matter of degree. And the critical point for our purposes is that these two models take the transaction of biological and environmental factors seriously, making it clear that we need to give more than lip service to the interaction of the multiple factors that produce development. This is more easily said than done, but these approaches demonstrate how biology and environment can be included in serious scientific models that help us put development in proper perspective.

## The Developmental Systems Approach
### The Concept of Epigenesis

The **developmental systems approach,** so called because it views development as occurring within a system of interacting levels, is centered around the concept of **epigenesis.** Epigenetic phenomena have been defined as "any gene-regulating activity that doesn't involve changes to the DNA code and that can persist through one or more generations" (Pennisi, 2001, p. 1064). Epigenesis involves the action of genes, of course, but also the action of RNA, proteins, neurotransmitters, neurons, and so on, all in interaction with the "environment," broadly defined. Central to the concept of epigenesis is the activity of the organism itself in influencing its own development. According to Susan Oyama (2000), "Fate is constructed, amended, and reconstructed, partly by the emerging organism itself. It is known to no one, not even the genes" (p. 137). Along similar lines, Gottlieb (1991a) defined epigenesis as "the emergence of new structures and functions during the course of development" (p. 7) and states that epigenesis reflects a bidirectional relationship between all levels of biological and experiential variables, such that genetic activity both influences and is influenced by structural maturation, which is bidirectionally related to function and activity. This relationship can be expressed as follows:

$$\text{genetic activity (DNA} \leftrightarrow \text{RNA} \leftrightarrow \text{proteins)} \leftrightarrow$$
$$\text{structural maturation} \leftrightarrow \text{function, activity}$$

According to Gottlieb (1991a), "Individual development is characterized by an increase of complexity of organization (that is, the emergence of new structural and functional properties and competencies) at all levels of analysis (molecular, subcellular, cellular, organismic) as a consequence of horizontal and vertical coactions among the organism's parts, including organism-environment coactions" (p. 7). The point here is that functioning at any level influences functioning at adjacent levels. For example, genes clearly direct the production of proteins, which in turn determine the formation of structures, such as muscle or nerve cells. But activity of these and surrounding cells can turn on or off a particular gene, causing the cessation or commencement of genetic activity. Moreover, experience in the form of self-produced activity or stimulation from external sources can alter the development of sets of cells.

From this perspective, there are no simple genetic or experiential causes of behavior; all development is the product of epigenesis, with complex interactions occurring among multiple levels. This bidirectional approach to development is expressed in Figure 2-2. This figure suggests that we can never understand development merely by looking for genetic effects or for environmental effects; to understand development, we must look at the organism-context relationship (Lerner, 2006). Mark Johnson (1998), in his review of the neural basis of cognitive development, made this point especially clear: "Since it has become evident that genes interact with their environment at all levels, including the molecular, there is no aspect of development that can be said to be strictly 'genetic,' that is, exclusively a product of information contained in the genes" (p. 4).

This position should be reminiscent of the dynamic systems theories that were discussed in Chapter 1. The developmental systems approach *is* a dynamic systems

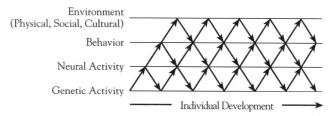

**Bidirectional Influences**

FIGURE **2-2**

A simplified schematic of the developmental systems approach, showing an hierarchy of four mutually interacting components.

Source: From *Individual development and evolution: The genesis of novel behavior* by G. Gottlieb. Copyright © 1991 by Oxford University Press, Inc. Used by permission of Oxford University Press, Inc.

theory, one that is specific to development. As such, new structures and functions emerge during development by means of self-organization through the bidirectional interactions of elements at various levels of organization (that is, genes, RNA, neurons, overt behavior, and so on). As Gottlieb (1991a) stated, "[T]he cause of development—what makes development happen—is the relationship between the … components, not the components themselves. Genes in themselves cannot cause development any more than stimulation in itself can cause development" (p. 7–8).

If the relations expressed in Figure 2-2 approximate reality, there should be substantial plasticity in development. Yet, it is undeniable that development is constrained by one's genes. Because our parents were humans, we develop in a way that a chimpanzee embryo can never develop, and vice versa. However, environments also constrain development. Genes will be expressed differently in different environments, yielding different patterns of development.

An example of how the effects of genes vary in different environments was provided in a study by Avshalom Caspi and his colleagues (2007), who examined the relationship between adult IQ, whether a person was breastfed or bottle-fed, and specific versions of a gene associated with processing fatty acid. Previous research had documented a relationship between breastfeeding and later IQ, with children, adolescents, and adults who were breastfed as babies having higher IQs than those who were bottle-fed (Mortensen et al., 2002). One explanation for this effect is that breast milk provides fatty acids (not found in cow's milk) that foster brain development early in life. Caspi and his colleagues (2007) identified a gene on chromosome 11 involved in processing fatty acids, as well as two variants of that gene. Recall from your basic biology class that we get one gene for a characteristic from our mother and one from our father, and that the genes, or alleles, can vary somewhat (like having one gene for brown eyes and one for blue eyes). Children who had two combinations of the alleles (called CC and CG) *and* who were breastfed as infants had significantly higher IQs (approximately 104) relative to children who had the same set of alleles but were not breastfed (approximately 97). In contrast, children with a third version of the genes (called GG) showed no effect on IQ from being either breastfed or bottle-fed (both groups had IQs of approximately 100; see Figure 2-3). Thus, the benefits of breastfeeding for subsequent IQ are influenced by a particular combination of alleles for a

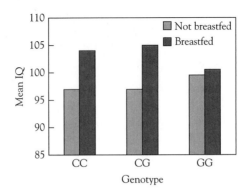

FIGURE **2-3**

The relation between breastfeeding and IQ for children with different versions of a gene for processing fatty acids.

Source: Caspi, A., Williams, B., Kim-Cohen, J., Craig, I. W., Milne, B. J., Poulton, R., Schalkwyk, L. C., Taylor, A., Werts, H., & Moffitt, T. E. (2007). Moderation of breastfeeding effects on the IQ by genetic variation in fatty acid metabolism. *Proceedings of the National Academy of Science, 104*, 18860–18865.

gene that influences how a person processes fatty acid. This study shows that even genes clearly associated with known specific biochemical and behavior outcomes (here, high IQ) are expressed differently in different environments (here, breastfed versus bottle-fed).

If there is so much plasticity in development, however, why do almost all members of a species (human or otherwise) develop in a species-typical pattern? The answer is that a child (or a puppy or a duckling) inherits not only species-typical genes but also a species-typical environment. This is expressed in Robert Lickliter's (1996) statement that "the organism-environment relationship is one that is structured on both sides. That is, it is a relation between a structured organism *and* a structured environment. The organism inherits not only its genetic complement, but also the structured organization of the environment into which it is born" (pp. 90–91). For example, ducks begin life in eggs, usually surrounded by other eggs, with their mother staying close by before they hatch. These ducks are able to hear and vocalize before hatching, and it turns out that these experiences contribute to an important aspect of posthatching behavior. Under normal conditions, when baby ducks, shortly after hatching, are put into a large container and hear the maternal call of two species of birds—their own and another—they invariably approach the call from their own species. They seem "instinctively" to know what their own species sounds like and to move toward that sound, something that makes good sense in the wild. However, when experimental procedures are performed so that the embryonic duck in the egg does not hear its mother or any of its siblings and its own vocal chords are temporarily prevented from functioning so that it can produce no sound itself, the duck fails after hatching to show the species-typical pattern of approaching the call of its own species (see Gottlieb, 1991b). In other words, prehatching experience, including hearing its own self-produced vocalizations, plays a major role in posthatching species-typical behavior. The reason that nearly all ducks approach the species-typical call after hatching is that nearly all ducks inherit not only the genetic disposition to make such a selection but also the species-typical environment that provides the necessary experiences for such a pattern to develop. Viewing development from this perspective provides a new meaning for the term *instinctive*. A behavior or function that is inborn in almost all members of the species might be instinctive, but if so, we must consider both the species-typical genes and the species-typical environment as factors contributing to that behavior.

Results such as these indicate that behaviors (here, related to infant-mother attachment) that are found in almost all typical members of a species are influenced by often-subtle characteristics of the environment. Psychological mechanisms at the human level can be viewed similarly. Strong species-universal biases may exist for certain behaviors, but how any particular behavior or mechanism is expressed will depend on the experiences of the individual at certain times in development.

This is fine for ducks, but how does this relate to human cognitive development? The idea is that human children develop in species-typical environments, both prenatal and postnatal, and that experiences in these environments may direct development in species-typical ways. Take, for example, a proposal by Gerald Turkewitz (1993) concerning the functioning of the two sections, called *hemispheres*, of the brain. These hemispheres are connected by a large bundle of nerves called the *corpus callosum*, and although similar, the two hemispheres are not identical. Each hemisphere controls the opposite side of the body, with one hemisphere typically predominating over the other, resulting in a left- or right-side preference. For example, there are far more right-handed people in the world than left-handed people, which reflects a hemispheric asymmetry, with the left hemisphere (which controls the right side of the body) being dominant relative to the right (which controls the left side of the body). Such an asymmetry is found even in neonates, with newborns turning their heads to the right more often than to the left. Also, newborns process speech sounds more effectively when the sounds are presented to the right ear (and, thus, the left hemisphere) than when they are presented to the left ear, further demonstrating hemispheric asymmetries. However, the right hemisphere seems to be more involved in recognizing faces, another important ability for human infants to have.

What is the origin of these asymmetries? Turkewitz (1993) proposed that they have to do with the timing of brain development and the nature of prenatal auditory experiences. Turkewitz presented evidence that the right hemisphere begins developing before the left hemisphere, but that later in prenatal development, the left hemisphere catches up and surpasses the right hemisphere in both size and complexity. Early in development, when the right hemisphere is developing most rapidly, the most salient auditory signals for a fetus, because of characteristics of the uterine environment and the relatively undeveloped state of the fetus's auditory system, are internally generated sounds, such as gastrointestinal gurglings and cardiovascular noises (that is, the heartbeat and the sound of pumping blood) produced by the mother. These are hardly important sounds for such a cognitively flexible and social species as *Homo sapiens*. As gestation proceeds and the fetus's auditory system improves, externally produced noises, particularly maternal speech, become more salient. This is when the left hemisphere is developing most rapidly. Turkewitz suggested that it is the interaction of the timing of development (faster development for the right hemisphere early and for the left hemisphere late) with auditory experiences (clearer signals from external speech sources later in development) that causes hemispheric asymmetries. Because the left hemisphere is developing most rapidly when maternal speech is most salient, it develops a specialty for processing speech. This leaves the right hemisphere "unspecialized," so to speak. Thus, after birth, when vision is possible, "the right hemisphere would be relatively unengaged and available for processing the facial information. In this way the right hemisphere could begin to develop a specialization for dealing with facial information" (Turkewitz, 1993, p. 136).

Turkewitz's proposal is intriguing. It suggests that asymmetries observed during infancy (and expressed later in visual and language processing in adults) have their origins in prenatal experiences, in interaction with genetically paced maturation. Turkewitz may be wrong, of course. But the argument is logically sound and consistent with what we know about development, and aspects of his hypothesis are testable.

As another example, take the perception of pain. Despite its obvious discomfort, perceiving painful stimuli "properly" is clearly adaptive. Might experiences early in life alter how the brain is organized for perceiving pain? This question was experimentally addressed in neonatal rats (Ruda et al., 2000). Neurons in the spinal cords of rats develop during the embryonic through early postnatal period, typically a time when rat pups are protected by their mothers from painful experiences. When newborn rats were exposed to painful stimulation, however, the nerve circuits that respond to pain were permanently rewired, changing the way they responded to sensory stimulation, making the animals as adults more sensitive to pain. These findings have obvious implications for humans. Only within the past 25 years have physicians bothered giving young human infants anesthesia for some medical procedures, believing that their perception of painful stimuli was minimal. But this study suggests that such unexpected stimulation, even if the infants seem not to perceive it as acutely painful, can alter the species-typical course of development in an adverse way.

### Developmental Timing

As any comedian will tell you, timing is everything. In the developmental systems approach, the timing of a particular event can influence substantially what effect that event will have on development.

Perhaps the concept most central to the issue of the timing of development is that of a **sensitive period**. The sensitive period (sometimes referred to as the *critical period*) for a specific skill or ability is the time in development (usually early in life) when it is most easily acquired. If a requisite experience occurs outside of this sensitive period (either too early or too late), the target skill will not be readily acquired—or possibly not acquired at all. Although the organism is most sensitive to a particular event at a particular time, similar or perhaps more intense experiences later in life can still have considerable influence on development. Figure 2-4 depicts the idea that a behavior is most easily acquired during a sensitive period.

Researchers have suggested that many aspects of human cognitive development can be described as sensitive periods (see Bornstein, 1989; Ceci, 1996), with language being perhaps the clearest example (Lenneberg, 1967; Newport, 1991). Both a first and a second language are acquired more easily when learned in early childhood. Although adolescents and adults can learn a second language, it is usually only with great difficulty, and they rarely attain the facility in that language observed when it is learned during childhood. (More will be said about a critical period for language acquisition in Chapter 9.)

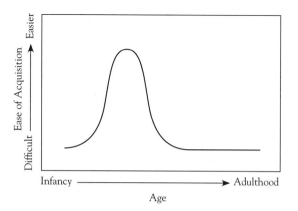

FIGURE **2-4**

Some cognitive abilities, such as language, might be most easily acquired during a sensitive period in (usually early) development.

Examples of the significance of timing of perceptual experience come from research by Lickliter (1990) involving auditory and visual stimulation of bobwhite quails. Like ducks, bobwhite quails approach the maternal call of their own species shortly after hatching. As demonstrated earlier by Gottlieb, this phenomenon has been attributed to auditory experiences the birds have before hatching. But, Lickliter reasoned, this is caused not just by the *presence* of auditory experiences before hatching but also by the *absence* of other sensory experiences, following an argument originally made by Turkewitz and Kenny (1982), who noted that the sensory systems in infants of many species function poorly at birth. Such inefficient functioning is actually adaptive, however, in that it protects the infant from sensory overload, permitting it to deal with small bits of simplified stimuli, which in turn makes it easier for the immature being to make sense of its world. Also, poor functioning in one sensory system (vision, for example) might permit an earlier developing sensory system (hearing, for example) to develop without undue competition for neural resources.

This is exactly the logic that Lickliter adopted for his study with bobwhite quails. In all vertebrates, hearing develops before vision (Gottlieb, 1971). Lickliter argued that the slower development of vision in bobwhite quails allows the auditory system to develop without competition from the visual system. If so, what would happen if quails were given extra visual experience before hatching? One possibility is that it might hinder important aspects of auditory development, such as showing a preference for the maternal call.

Lickliter (1990) developed a procedure whereby he removed part of the eggshell and provided visual experience to bobwhite quails 2 to 3 days before hatching. Control quails had the end of the egg opened but received no visual experience. This ensured that the behavior of the experimental birds would not be caused by removing part of the eggshell per se but by the additional visual experience the chicks received. Lickliter then examined those birds with an auditory preference test in which the birds were placed in an oval container having speakers at opposite ends. From one speaker came the maternal call of a bobwhite quail, and from the other speaker came the maternal call of a chicken. The researchers observed which speaker, if either, the chicks approached.

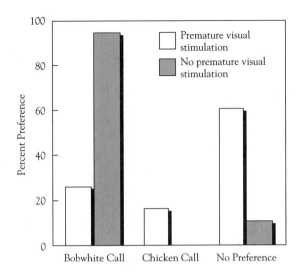

FIGURE **2-5**

Percentage of bobwhite quail chicks that approached the bobwhite maternal call, the chicken maternal call, or showed no preference as a function of whether they received premature visual stimulation or not.

Source: Adapted from R. Lickliter (1990), Premature visual stimulation accelerates intersensory functioning in bobwhite quail neonates. *Developmental Psychobiology, 23,* 15–27.

The results of this experiment are shown in Figure 2-5. The control birds demonstrated the species-typical pattern when tested, with nearly all the birds showing a preference for the maternal call of their own species (that is, approaching the speaker from which the bobwhite quail call came). This was not the case for the birds that had the extra visual experience, however. A majority of these birds showed no preference or approached the speaker producing the maternal call of a chicken! (I should note that these animals also displayed greater visual discrimination abilities. That is, the pre-hatching visual experience resulted in enhanced visual abilities, but at the expense of auditory abilities, which are important in their early development of attachment.)

This and other studies (see Bjorklund, 1997a) clearly demonstrate that the timing of perceptual experience is critically important and that earlier experience is not always better experience. This is worth remembering for human infants. Might their sensory limitations actually be adaptive, and might extra stimulation in one modality interfere with development in other modalities? Recall our discussion in Box 1-1, *The Adaptive Nature of Cognitive Immaturity,* and the demonstration that providing an infant with too much stimulation or "learning tasks" too soon in development might have a negative effect.

Although almost no research has been conducted with human infants on the topic of "sensory overstimulation," researchers have speculated that some of the deficits experienced by premature infants are caused by exposure to too much sensory information too soon. Neonatologist Heidelise Als (1995) suggests the early sensory stimulation that premature infants experience might adversely affect brain development by requiring these infants to process perceptual stimulation that they would not normally deal with for several more weeks (see also Lickliter, 2000). As in the research with quail chicks, "premature" stimulation might result in enhanced performance later in life in some domains, but at the expense of functioning in others, which often leads to forms of learning disabilities. And in fact, Als notes that these deficits are often accompanied by accelerated development or enhanced abilities in other areas, such as in mathematics. This idea is provocative, although still speculative. But it is consistent with the idea that the timing of developmentally sensitive periods in the brain is correlated with the species-typical timing of perceptual experiences. According to Bjorklund, Ellis, and Rosenberg (2007), "When animals receive stimulation from one modality earlier than 'expected' (i.e., when neural development and sensory experiences are uncoupled), it interferes with this choreographed dance between gene-influenced neural maturation and perceptual experience. This change in the gene-environment relation (in this case, a change in *timing* of different perceptual experiences) causes a species-atypical pattern of development" (p. 13).

More generally, the differential timing of maturation in various areas of the brain influences how the brain becomes organized. For example, Jeffrey Elman and his colleagues (1996) proposed that early developing brain regions effectively serve as filters for later developing areas. The type and manner in which these early developing areas can process information determines, in a very real sense, the type and way in which later developing areas can process information. These can be potent constraints on brain development, what I referred to in Chapter 1 as *chronotopic constraints*. From this perspective, it is the *timing of events*, rather than "knowledge" (representational constraints), that is inherited, and this timing is largely responsible for the species-typical patterns of brain and cognitive development that we see.

## The Genotype → Environment Theory

Related to the developmental systems approach are several theories that stem from the field of **behavioral genetics**, which studies genetic effects on behavior and complex psychological characteristics such as intelligence and personality (Plomin et al., 2008; Rutter, 2006). These theories have attracted much attention among mainstream developmentalists, in part because they use human behavioral outcomes such as personality or IQ scores as data rather than generalizing results from ducks, rats, or bobwhite quails to humans. This is also a reason for the substantial controversy the approach has produced.

Academic psychologists have long been reluctant to accept a strong influence of genetics on human behavior. The argument against a genetic influence on behavior goes something like this: If we are what our genes determine us to be, then there is little hope of modifying the human spirit or human behavior through environmental intervention. If genes affect not only blood type and eye color but also behavior, personality, and intelligence, then biology truly is destiny.

Yet, biology rarely dictates anything in an absolute way. As illustrated by Figure 2-2, all genetic effects are moderated by environmental ones. Even the genes for eye color must be expressed in a developing embryo, which is exposed to uncountable environmental factors as a result of its own development. The fact that genes influence behavior does not mean that environment plays only an inconsequential role. To deny the significant role of genetics in behavior is to place one's head in the sand, but to proclaim that genetics determines our personalities, intellects, and behavior is to seriously misinterpret reality.

### *Genotype → Environment Effects*

One of the most influential theories from behavioral genetics with respect to cognitive development is Sandra Scarr and Kathleen McCartney's (1983) **genotype → environment theory**. Basically, Scarr and McCartney propose that one's genotype (one's actual genetic constitution) influences which environments one encounters and the type of experiences one has. Their basic contention is that *genes drive experience*. One's genetic makeup determines how one organizes one's world. Thus, environment does play a significant role in shaping intellect, but a person's inherited characteristics largely determine what those experiences are and how they are perceived.

Figure 2-6 presents a schematic of Scarr and McCartney's model of behavioral development. A child's phenotype (his or her observed characteristics) is influenced both by the child's genotype and by his or her rearing environment. The child's genotype is determined by the genotype of his or her parents. The parents' genotype also influences the environment; the parents' genetic characteristics affect the types of environments they feel most comfortable in. But in this model, the child's genotype also has an impact on the environment, which affects the child's development. Thus, characteristics of the child, as well as the rearing environment and genetic contributions of the parents, influence the course of development.

Scarr and McCartney posit three types of genotype → environment effects that vary in influence over the course of development (see Table 2-2). They are *passive, evocative,* and *active*. Passive effects occur when genetically related parents provide the rearing environment of the child. When biological parents rear a child, the effects of genetics and environment cannot be separated because the people who provide the genetic constitution for a child also provide the environment. The influence of passive effects is proposed to decline with age.

Evocative effects occur when the child elicits responses from others that are influenced by his or her genotype. For example, an irritable child is responded to differently than a well-tempered child is, and the type of attention received by an infant who likes to cuddle is different from that received by an infant who does not want to be held. During early childhood, an attentive and cooperative child receives more

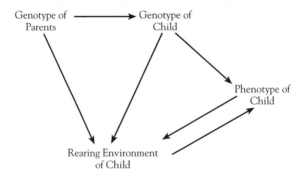

### FIGURE **2-6**

Scarr and McCartney's model of behavioral development.

Source: Adapted from "How People Make Their Own Environments: A Theory of Genotype-Environment Effects," by S. Scarr and K. McCartney, *Child Development, 54*, 424–435. Copyright © 1983 The Society for Research in Child Development, Inc. Adapted with permission.

TABLE **2-2**

Three types of genotype → environment effects in Scarr & McCartney's
Genotype → Environment Model.

| | |
|---|---|
| Passive: | Biological parents provide both genes and environment for child. Passive effects *decrease* with age. |
| Evocative: | Temperamental characteristics of child evokes responses from others. Evocative effects remain *constant* with age. |
| Active: | Children seek out environments consistent with their genotypes. Active effects *increase* with age. |

positive interactions from parents and teachers than an uncooperative, distractible child does. Evocative effects presumably remain constant throughout development.

Active effects occur when one's genotype influences the type of environments one chooses to experience. A person actively selects an environment in which he or she feels comfortable. For example, children interested in competitive sports would probably seek out other like-minded children to play with who would be very different from the type of people sport-phobic children would seek. Accordingly, people with different genotypes choose to interact in different environments and, thus, have different experiences that influence their development. Active effects increase with age as children become increasingly independent of their parents and able to select their own environments.

How does Scarr and McCartney's model relate to cognitive development? For one thing, this model suggests that parents' environmental influence on children should be greatest during the early childhood years and decrease with age as active genotype → environment effects increase. Evidence for this position comes from an adoption study by Scarr and Richard Weinberg (1978). They reported that the average correlations of the IQs of samples of adopted siblings (that is, genetically unrelated children living together) measured in early childhood ranged from .25 to .39. This indicates a moderate level of similarity between the IQs of biologically unrelated children growing up together, a reflection of an environmental influence on IQ. However, the correlation of the IQs for adopted siblings measured late in adolescence was 0! This means that knowing the IQ of one child would not help you predict, to any degree, the IQ of his or her adopted sibling. The predictive power is zero. These results reflect the fact that the longer these genetically unrelated siblings lived together, the less alike in IQ scores they became. Similar findings of reduced correlations of IQs with age have been reported for dizygotic (nonidentical) twins. Correlations of the IQs of dizygotic twins computed during the preschool years ranged from .60 to .75 but were reduced to .55 when measured later in childhood (Matheny et al., 1981). In fact, siblings in general become less alike in most respects the older they get (McCartney, Harris, & Bernieri, 1990; Sundet, Eriksen, & Tambs, 2008). Following Scarr and McCartney's model, passive genotype → environment effects, as reflected by the type of environments that parents provide for their children, decrease with age, and active genotype → environment effects increase. Why? Because as they get older, children are increasingly able to select environments that suit their particular needs, and such selection is determined primarily by one's genotype.

But then, do genes *cause* intelligence? Interestingly, Scarr and McCartney's theory ends up giving the environment a substantial role in directing development. Genotype causes a child to choose certain environments that are compatible with the child's genetic constitution, and the experiences in these environments shape the child's cognition (and other important psychological characteristics). From this perspective, one's genes serve to select "appropriate" environments, but experience is actually responsible for crafting the intellect. (The heritability of intelligence is discussed in greater detail in Chapter 13.)

Scarr and McCartney's model illustrates how genetic and environmental factors might interact to produce different patterns and levels of intelligence. What is particularly attractive about this model is its consideration of developmental effects. Genetic and environmental effects are viewed not as constants but as dynamic factors that have different effects on intelligence at different points in time. This theory in effect postulates a transaction between developmental function and individual differences. As children become more autonomous with age, the influence of genetic and environmental factors on individual differences changes.

### "Good Enough" Parents

Scarr expanded her initial position and proposed that "ordinary differences between families have little effect on children's development, unless the family is outside of a normal developmental range. Good enough, ordinary parents probably have the same effects on their children's development as culturally defined super-parents" (1992, p. 15). In other words, because of the strong influence of genotype → environment effects, individual differences in parenting should have little consequence for children's development. Although this is a logical extension of the original theory, it takes the theory to an extreme that many contemporary developmental psychologists don't like. In fact, several psychologists immediately criticized the theory harshly (see Baumrind, 1993; Jackson, 1993).

As we'll see in Chapter 13, differences in how children are reared are related to individual differences in their levels of intelligence and academic achievement. Scarr's point, reiterated and expanded in a response to her critics (Scarr, 1993), is that children around the world grow up to be productive (and reproductive) members of their societies despite considerable differences in child-rearing practices. A behaviorally flexible species that required high-quality parenting for survival would likely be extinct before too long. Thus, the species evolved so that children could tolerate great flexibility in child-rearing practices and still grow up to be "normal."

Scarr's critics are not concerned with this level of development, however. They point out that differences in parenting style and opportunities make a tremendous difference in the eventual outcome of a child (Baumrind, 1993), and that **"good enough" parents** are just not good enough for a sizable minority of children in our society. Scarr (1993) concurs. Children who lack opportunities and experiences associated with the dominant culture will show intellectual and social detriments relative to children in the majority culture. (Scarr notes that these effects can often be ameliorated by education.)

The difference between Scarr and her critics seems primarily to be one of focus: Scarr is taking an evolutionary perspective, looking at how individual children become functioning members of the species; her critics are focusing instead on individual differences among children within a culture. Each level is important, and each is legitimate. But it is easy for the two camps to argue right past one another, certain that the other camp is missing the point when in reality they are talking about different levels of human functioning.

In support of both Scarr and her critics is research on "resilient" children—children who develop social and intellectual competence despite growing up in impoverished and "high-risk" environments (Masten & Coatsworth, 1998). Why do some children from the worst environments "make it," whereas others flounder? Perhaps the single most important factor is competent parenting, starting early in life (Kim-Cohen et al., 2004). This fact is consistent with Scarr's critics, who point out that individual differences in how parents interact with their children is essential to their eventual success. However, Masten and Coatsworth point out that although many parents do fail to provide adequate warmth and support for their children, it does not take extraordinary efforts to raise a competent child, even in unfavorable environments. "Through the process of evolution, parenting has been shaped to protect development; nature has created in ordinary parents a powerful protective system for child development" (Masten & Coatsworth, 1998, p. 213).

## THE DEVELOPMENT OF THE BRAIN

The human brain is perhaps the most marvelous thing in the universe. Unlike the brains of any other species, ours provides us with self-awareness and a behavioral flexibility that has allowed humans to create culture and to adapt to a limitless diversity of environments. Other animal brains are quite impressive, but only the human brain has led to language, mathematics, physics, and art.

Differences in thinking between humans and other mammals are, of course, directly related to differences in their brains. But the human brain does not have any special structures that other mammals don't have. The major differences between human brains and those of other mammals are in the greater amount of area that is devoted to the cerebral cortex and the extended period of postnatal growth.

At birth, the human brain weighs about 350 grams—25% of its eventual adult weight of about 1400 grams. Compare this to overall body weight. At birth, an infant weighs only about 5% of what he or she will weigh as an adult. Stated another way, the brain accounts for about 10% of the overall body weight of a newborn, but for only about 2% of the overall body weight of an adult. By 6 months, the brain weighs 50% of what it will in adulthood; at 2 years, about 75%; at 5 years, 90%; and at 10 years, 95% (Lenroot & Giedd, 2007; Tanner, 1978). In contrast, total body weight is about 20% of eventual adult weight at 2 years and only 50% at 10 years. So the brain, which grows rapidly before birth, continues its rapid development postnatally. The rapid postnatal growth of the brain and head relative to the body in general is depicted in Figure 2-7. From this perspective, babies are brainy creatures indeed. But from another point of view, the brain of a newborn is grossly underdeveloped. Although the brain works effectively enough to direct basic physiological functions (for example, breathing, wake/sleep cycles), it cannot control coordinated movement, and it cannot perform the mental operations so characteristic of our species. Despite its size, the infant brain is far from the organ it will become.

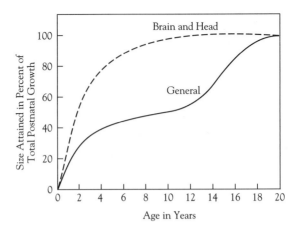

FIGURE **2-7**

Growth curves for the brain and head and the body in general.

Source: Adapted from "The Measurement of the Body in Childhood," by R. E. Scammon. In J. A. Harris, C. M. Jackson, D. G. Paterson, R. E. Scammon (Eds.), *The measurement of man,* University of Minnesota Press, 1930.

The human brain, directly or indirectly, is responsible for controlling all aspects of behavior, from respiration and digestion to our most advanced forms of cognition. Our concern here is with the portion of the brain most associated with thought—the neocortex, or cerebral cortex. The neocortex is the most recent structure to appear in evolutionary time, associated primarily with mammals and having its greatest manifestation in primates and, especially, humans (MacLean, 1990). Other areas of the brain—such as the limbic system, which is the seat of emotion—are also important and significantly influence human behavior, but the neocortex—particularly the *frontal lobes* (sometimes referred to as the prefrontal lobes) of the neocortex—provides the characteristics that we most associate with humanness. I will discuss briefly certain aspects of the neocortex and its development later in this section. Box 2-1 presents a brief overview of the evolution of the human brain.

Our knowledge of brain development and its relation to cognition has increased substantially during the past several decades, primarily because of new technologies that permit the imaging of brain activities (Amos & Casey, 2006; Johnson, 2007; Lenroot & Giedd, 2007). These **neuroimaging techniques** include, among others, *high-density event-related potentials,* which are a form of electroencephalography (EEG) that permits the detailed recording of brain activity when people solve cognitive tasks or are presented with specific stimuli; *positron emission tomography* (PET) and *single-photon emission computed tomography* (SPECT), in which radioactive materials are injected into participants and changes in radioactivity are used to reflect glucose consumption in specific areas of the brain; and *functional magnetic resonance imaging* (fMRI), which is a noninvasive technique that measures blood flow to the brain while people perform cognitive tasks. There are, of course, limits to such methods, but these and related new technologies promise that a new understanding of the relation between brain and cognitive development will be soon upon us. First, however, we must examine the basic building block of the brain—the neuron.

| BOX 2-1 | **The Evolution of the Human Brain** |

It seems without question that the brain is the seat of human intelligence. When we consider humans' superior cognitive ability relative to that of other species, it is good to realize that the brains of *Homo sapiens* didn't just "appear" on the scene 10,000 years ago but, rather, have a long evolutionary history. Humans are primates, closely related to chimpanzees (*Pan troglodytes*), bonobos (*Pan paniscus*), gorillas (*Gorilla gorilla*), and orangutans (*Pongo pygmaeus*). We are also descendants from a long line of *hominid*s (or *hominins*), animals that shared a common ancestor with modern chimpanzees 5 to 7 million years ago and of which we (that is, *Homo sapiens*) are the only surviving member.

The most notable characteristic of the human brain is its size. In comparison to other mammals, the human brain is much larger than expected for its body size. This is true for primates in general, but it is exaggerated in humans. Harry Jerison (1973, 2002) developed the **encephalization quotient** to evaluate the expected ratio between brain weight and body weight for animals. Animals with brains of the expected weight given their body weight have an encephalization quotient of 1.0. Animals with brains larger than expected for their body weight have an encephalization quotient of greater than 1.0, and animals with brains smaller than expected for their body weight have an encephalization quotient of less than 1.0. Using this measure, modern chimpanzees have an impressive encephalization quotient of about 2.3. This value is more than tripled in modern humans, however, who have an encephalization quotient of about 7.6 (Jerison, 1973, 2002; Rilling & Insel, 1999).

How long have humans had such big brains? As I mentioned, we last shared a common ancestor with chimpanzees between 5 and 7 million years ago. Did the shift to big brains occur early in the transition, or perhaps much later? Based on fossil evidence, hominid brains became progressively larger over the past 2 to 3 million years. Table 2-3 presents the average encephalization quotients for four species of hominids (*Australopithecus afarensis*, *Homo habilis*, *Homo erectus*, and *Homo sapiens*) over the past 3.5 million years based on fossil skulls as well as for modern chimpanzees. As you can see, the encephalization quotient for

*Australopithecus afarensis*, an early, small-brained hominid that lived 3 to 4 million years ago and, much like modern humans, walked on two legs, was only slightly greater than that of chimpanzees. From this point on, however, brain weight relative to body weight increased at a rapid rate.

TABLE **2-3**

## Estimated Encephalization Quotients (EQs) for Chimpanzees *(Pan Troglodytes)* and Four Hominid Species

Animals with brains that are the expected size given their body weight have an encephalization quotient of 1.0. Animals with "more brain" than expected for their body weight have an encephalization quotient of greater than 1.0. As you can see, hominids became increasingly "brainy" over the course of the last 4 or 5 million years.

| Species | EQ |
|---|---|
| *Pan troglodytes* (chimpanzees) | 2.3 |
| *Australopithecus afarensis* | 3.1 |
| *Homo habilis* | 4.0 |
| *Homo erectus* | 5.5 |
| *Homo sapiens* | 7.6 |

Not surprisingly, scientists have discovered genetic differences between modern humans and chimpanzees related to differences in brain size and function (Khaitovich et al., 2005; Pollard et al., 2006). Genes associated with other organs have also changed between humans and chimpanzees, of course, and many of those have changed even more than the genes associated with the brain. However, genes active in brain functioning have gone through more change in human evolution than in chimpanzee evolution (Khaitovich et al., 2005). For example, one version of a gene associated with increased brain size arose as early as 37,000 years ago (Evans et al., 2005) and another as recently as 5,800 years ago (Mekel-Bobrov et al.,

*(Continues)*

| BOX 2-1 | The Evolution of the Human Brain (*Continued*) |
|---------|-----------------------------------------------|

2005), suggesting that selection pressure for humans' increased brain size is an ongoing process.

Size isn't the only thing that has changed over the evolution of the human brain. For instance, humans have more cortical neurons than any other mammal (including the much larger whales) and nearly twice as many as chimpanzees (see Roth & Dicke, 2005). Moreover, some parts of the human brain have shown greater increases in size relative to other primates than other brain areas have. The human cortex, for example, has been estimated to be about 200% larger than expected for an ape of comparable body size (Barton & Harvey, 2000; Deacon, 1997). Although other areas of the human brain are also larger than expected for an ape of comparable body size, none is as large as the cortex, which plays a central role in complex human cognition. And other areas have actually displayed a decrease in size (for example, the olfactory cortex, some areas related to vision and motor control). Importantly, there have also been substantial evolutionary changes in the genes that affect the rate of brain *development* (Somel et al., 2009). Brain development is extended from the prenatal period into infancy in humans more so than in other primates, and genetic differences between humans and chimpanzees have been identified associated with this delayed brain development.

The reason that so much brain growth must occur after birth than is accomplished prenatally for other primates is because women's hips can only get so large and still permit upright walking. If the brain of a human neonate were as large, proportionally, as the brain of a chimpanzee at birth, it would never fit through the birth canal. Bipedality (upright walking) limited the size of newborns' brains. So if humans were going to have big brains and still walk on two feet and not four, then much of brain development would have to be done after birth. As a result, humans have an extended juvenile period, delaying sexual maturity well into the teen years. (See the discussion of the role of slow growth on brain and cognitive plasticity later in the chapter in the section *Slow Growth and Plasticity*.)

The human brain has taken a long time to evolve. Our ancestors used their large brains to deal with uncertain environments. These environments varied in climate, geography, availability of prey, presence of predators, and, perhaps especially important, other big-brained members of our own kind. Although our big-brained ancestors may not have been as strong or fast or keen-eyed as other animals in their ecological niche, they were able to survive and thrive because of their enhanced intelligence, and we are the inheritors of this evolutionarily unique set of abilities.

## Neuronal Development

The brain, and the nervous system in general, is a communication system. Electrical and chemical signals are transmitted from one **neuron**, or specialized nerve cell, to another. Estimates of the number of neurons in the mature human brain vary from 10 billion to more than 100 billion (Kolb, Gibb, & Robinson, 2003). Unlike most other cells in the human body, neurons are not compressed together but are separated.

Figure 2-8 presents a drawing of a neuron. The main part of the neuron is the cell body, which contains the nucleus. Extending from the cell body are many projections, one of which is called the **axon**, a long fiber that carries messages away from the cell body to other cells. The other, more numerous fibers are called **dendrites**, which receive messages from other cells and transfer them to the cell body.

Dendrites do not actually come in physical contact with other dendrites (or with dendrite-like branches on axons, called *axon terminals*) when receiving messages. Rather, there are small spaces between dendrites, called **synapses**, through which messages are passed. The result is many billions of connections (synapses) among neurons. Electrical messages flowing down the axon of one cell cause the release of certain

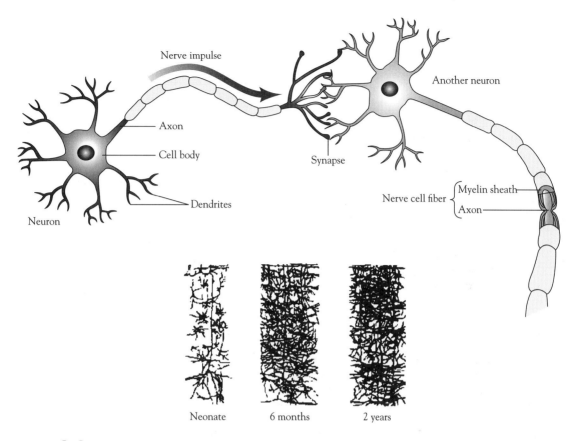

Nerve impulse

Another neuron

Axon

Cell body

Synapse

Dendrites

Nerve cell fiber
{ Myelin sheath
{ Axon

Neuron

Neonate        6 months        2 years

FIGURE **2-8**

Primary structures of the neuron.

chemicals, called **neurotransmitters**, into the synapse. Neurotransmitters, which include dopamine, acetylcholine, and serotonin, move across the space between the cells and are "read" at the dendrites of the adjacent cell, which convert the message back to an electrical signal and pass it on to its cell body. So two neurons do not actually touch one another, but pass their information chemically through the small gaps that separate them. Conditions at the synapse (amount and type of neurotransmitters available) affect the transmission of the messages among neurons.

Fully developed axons are covered by sheaths of **myelin**, a fatty substance produced by supportive brain cells called *glial cells*. Like the plastic cover of an electric wire, myelin protects and insulates axons, speeding the rate at which nervous impulses can be sent and reducing interference from other neurons. Compared with unmyelinated fibers, myelinated nerve fibers fire more rapidly, have lower thresholds of sensitivity to stimulation, and have greater functional specificity, meaning that there is less "leakage" of electrical impulse so that only the target set of neurons are likely to get activated.

*Myelination* increases throughout childhood and adolescence, not being complete until sometime during the third decade of life or beyond. Myelination proceeds at different rates for different areas of the brain. For example, myelination begins prenatally for the sensory system, with most sensory structures being completely myelinated within the first year. This corresponds to the well-developed sensory abilities of human infants and the adultlike sensory capacities they possess long before they can speak. Myelination of the motor areas follows closely, with most of these brain structures being completely myelinated before the second year. Again, this corresponds to the development of motor abilities in young children, most of whom are walking before their second birthdays. The frontal cortex, the so-called "thinking" part of the brain, is the last to become fully myelinated, not being complete until early adulthood (Giedd et al., 1999; Sowell et al., 1999).

When brains are stained with a chemical so that scientists can get a better look at their structure, myelinated areas appear white, whereas cell bodies and dendrites appear slightly pink or gray. This is a source of the terms *white matter*, reflecting mainly myelinated axons mostly beneath the surface of the brain, and *gray matter*, reflecting mostly cell bodies in both cortical and subcortical (that is, below the cortex) regions.

### Proliferation, Migration, and Differentiation

Neurons go through at least three stages of development (Lenroot & Giedd, 2007; Spreen, Risser, & Edgell, 1995). The first stage is referred to as **proliferation**, or **neurogenesis**, which is the process of cell division by mitosis. During its peak, several hundred thousand neurons are generated *each minute* (Nelson et al., 2006). Proliferation occurs early in development, during the prenatal period. It was once believed that the seventh month after conception essentially marked the end of neuron production. However, subsequent research in both laboratory animals (Gould et al., 1999) and humans (Eriksson et al. 1998) indicates that new neurons are produced in adults at least in some areas of the brain, specifically the hippocampus, a structure that has been implicated in the formation of new memories. New neurons are also produced throughout life in the olfactory bulbs, involved in the sense of smell, and there is some speculation that neurogenesis might occur after birth in several other brain areas (see Nelson et al., 2006). In general, unlike other cells of the body, new neurons are typically not produced after birth. So with a handful of exceptions, a person has all the neurons he or she will ever have at birth.

The second stage in neuronal development is **migration** (Aylward, 1997; Lenroot & Giedd, 2007). Once produced, the cells migrate, or move, to what will be their permanent position in the brain, where they collect with other cells to form the major parts of the brain. Not all cells migrate at the same time, but most cells have arrived at the final position in the brain by seven months after conception (Johnson, 2007; Nelson et al., 2006). Obviously, it is important that cells destined to be in a certain part of the brain be where they are supposed to be. Mistakes do occasionally happen, however, and faulty neural migration has been found to be associated with a variety of human disorders, including cerebral palsy, epilepsy, intellectual impairment, and learning disorders (Aylward, 1997).

The third stage in neuronal development is **differentiation** (or *cytodifferentiation*). Once at their final destination, neurons begin to grow in size, produce more and longer dendrites, and extend their axons farther and farther away from the cell body. Synapses are created during this stage. When an axon meets an appropriate dendrite from another neuron, a synapse is formed.

It is important to point out that differentiation does not stop at birth. In fact, most neuronal differentiation, particularly myelination (discussed earlier) and synaptogenesis (discussed below), takes place *after* birth, (see de Haan & Johnson, 2003; Lenroot & Giedd, 2007; Nelson et al., 2006).

### Synaptogenesis and Selective Cell Death

The process of synapse formation, or **synaptogenesis**, is rapid during the early years of life when the brain is first becoming organized. Synaptogenesis continues throughout life as the brain changes in response to new information, although the rate at which new synapses are formed is never as great as it is during those pre- and postnatal months when the brain is growing most rapidly. Synapse formation is perhaps more rapid in the months immediately following birth, but the peak of synapse formation varies for different parts of the brain. For example, a burst of synapse formation in the visual cortex begins at about 3 or 4 months of age and peaks between 4 and 12 months. At this time, the visual cortex has about 50% *more* synapses than there are in the adult brain. A similar pattern is found in the prefrontal cortex (the "thinking" part of the brain), but the peak number of synapses is not attained until about 24 months of age (Huttenlocher, 1994).

At this point, the infant brain has many more synapses and neurons than it needs, and a process of cell and synaptic pruning begins in earnest. (The pruning actually begins late during the prenatal period in a process known as **selective cell death**, or **apoptosis**.) Cell death and synaptic pruning occur at different rates for different parts of the brain. For example, the adult density of synapses for the visual cortex is attained between 2 and 4 years of age; in contrast, children continue to have more neurons and synapses in the prefrontal areas into their teen years than adults do (Giedd et al., 1999; Huttenlocher & Dabholkar, 1997; Spear, 2007; see Figure 2-9). Thus, by their middle to late teens, adolescents have fewer, but stronger and more effective, neuronal connections than they did as children. Interestingly, children with exceptionally high IQs tend to display an initial acceleration of growth in gray matter (mostly neurons) followed by a rapid (and equally early) loss of neurons by early adolescence. Adolescents with average IQs show the same pattern of development but at later ages (Shaw et al., 2006).

### Rises and Declines in Neural Development

The pattern just described for synaptogenesis is one of rapid development (that is, synapse creation) followed by a decline in the number of synapses (and neurons). Other aspects of brain development show a similar rise and decline over childhood. For example, evidence indicates that the basic metabolism of the brain (the rate at which it uses energy) increases sharply after the first year of life and peaks at about 150% of the adult rate between the ages of 4 and 5 (Chugani, Phelps, & Mazziotta, 1987). Evidence for this comes from studies using PET scans, which measure the amount of glucose uptake in the resting brain. After age 5 or so, the rate of glucose consumption slows down, reaching adult levels at about age 9. Thus, not only do infants and children have more neurons and synapses than adults, but their brains are also working harder (or at least using more calories) than those of adults.

In addition to changes in the actual structure of the neurons, developmental changes occur in the presence of various neurotransmitters—chemicals found in the

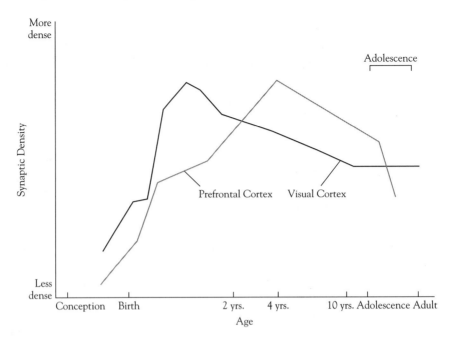

## FIGURE 2-9

Age differences in synapse production and pruning in the frontal and visual cortex. The number of synapses show sharp increases early in development but then experience "pruning," as the brain gets sculpted to its eventual adult form. Note the particularly sharp decline in synapses in the pre-frontal cortex during adolescence.

Source: Huttenlocher, P., & Dabholkar, A. S. (1997). Regional differences in synaptogenesis in human cerebral cortex. *Journal of Comparative Neurology, 387*, 167–178.

synapses that promote the electrical/chemical communication between cells. Several of these neurotransmitters show increases followed by decreases over infancy and child-hood, similar to the changes seen in synapses. These include glutamate, GABA, and serotonin (Johnson, 1998).

What function might there be in this rise and fall in several aspects of brain devel-opment? One proposal is that the hypermetabolism seen during the preschool years might be necessary for the rapid learning that occurs during this time (Elman et al., 1996). (Think of how children's language development proceeds from uttering only single words around 10 months to speaking in long paragraphs by age 3 or 4.) Pre-school children also have more neurons and synapses than older children and, I think it's fair to say, more to learn that is truly "new." These elevated levels of synapses and neurotransmitters also surely afford greater plasticity should brain damage occur. And although it may seem that slowing down the processes of synaptic pruning and cell death would afford children some advantages (more neurons and synapses can pre-sumably do more learning), the failure to display such losses has been linked to intel-lectual impairment, schizophrenia, and other developmental disorders (Feinberg, 1982/1983). A brief description of the major features of neuron development is presented in Table 2-4.

TABLE **2-4**
A Brief Description of Major Features in Neuronal Development.

| Developmental Event | Timeline | Brief Description |
|---|---|---|
| Proliferation (neurogenesis) | First 20 weeks after conception | Neurons are born from neural stem cells. This peaks in the third or fourth month of gestation. |
| Neural migration | 6–24 weeks after conception | Neurons move, or migrate, to their "adult" location in the brain. |
| Differentiation/ synaptogenesis | 3$^{rd}$ trimester through adolescence | Neurons extend their dendrites and axonal terminals, forming synapses with other neurons. |
| Postnatal neurogenesis | Birth-adulthood | New neurons develop in some parts of the brain, including the dentate gyrus of the hippocampus and the olfactory bulb. |
| Myelination | 3$^{rd}$ trimester to adulthood | Neurons become coated by a fatty tissue that results in faster transmission of nervous signals and a reduction of interference. |
| Selective cell death (apoptosis) | 3$^{rd}$ trimester to adulthood | Neurons die. |
| Synaptic pruning | infancy through adulthood | The number of synapses per neuron is greatest between 4 and 8 months of life and decreases with age. |

Why the slowdown in later childhood into adulthood? I have no good answer for this other than to suggest the tasks that must be solved by the older brain apparently require a different organization, needing less flexibility in number of neurons and perhaps synapses (much of what the brain will need to process "automatically" has already been established by 4 years of age) but greater differentiation in dendritic branching.

## How Do Young Brains Get Hooked Up?

I have described briefly the process of synaptogenesis and related development of neurons, such as myelination. But how do brains actually get wired? That is, what mechanisms are responsible for building a brain that eventually will be able to recognize faces, solve arithmetic problems, talk, and read? Perhaps the position accepted implicitly by most brain scientists throughout most of the 20th century was that the brain becomes specialized, and complex cognition thus arises, through intrinsic genetic and biochemical mechanisms. In other words, genes dictate the formation, migration, and differentiation of neurons, with experience serving only to "fine tune" the brain. Few developmental neuroscientists believe this today, however, arguing instead that brain development involves an extended process that is greatly influenced by postnatal experience (Fox, Levitt, & Nelson, 2010; Johnson, 2007; Nelson et al., 2006; Stiles, 2009).

It has become increasingly clear to those who study brain development that a reciprocal relationship exists between brain and behavioral development. To quote developmental neuroscientist Joan Stiles (2009): "Behavioral development is inextricably linked to brain development and vice versa. They are absolutely interdependent, exerting bidirectional influences that are essential for the normal development of the child" (p. 199). With respect to the survival of neurons and the process of synaptogenesis, William Greenough and his associates (Black et al. 1998; Greenough, Black, & Wallace, 1987) proposed that specific experiences produce neural activity that in turn determines which of the excess synapses will survive (see also Johnson, 2007; Nelson, 2001). The nervous system of animals (including humans) has been prepared by natural selection to expect certain types of stimulation, such as a three-dimensional world consisting of moving objects. Greenough and his colleagues referred to the processes whereby synapses are formed and maintained when an organism has species-typical experiences as **experience-expectant processes** (or **experience-expectant synaptogenesis**); as a result, functions will develop for all members of a species, given a species-typical environment. Early experience of merely viewing a normal world, for example, is sufficient for the visual nervous system to develop properly. Those neurons and connections that receive the species-expected experience live and become organized with other activated neurons, and those that do not receive such activation die. Thus, although the infant comes into the world prepared and "prewired" both for certain experiences and to develop certain abilities, these abilities are substantially influenced by experience. What is hardwired seems to be a susceptibility to certain environmental experiences rather than the circuitry for detailed behaviors themselves (a form of architectural constraints discussed in Chapter 1).

Examples of experience-expectant processes can be seen in research that restricts the species-typical perceptual experiences of an animal. For instance, cats or rats reared in total darkness or in the absence of patterned light later have difficulty making simple visual discriminations. That is, because they were not exposed to visual stimulation early in life, when later provided with visual experience they act as if they cannot see, or at least do not see normally (Crabtree & Riesen, 1979). In humans, cataract patients who suddenly gain sight via surgery have difficulty making simple visual discriminations. For example, for several weeks after surgery, they can tell the difference between a square and a triangle only by counting the corners (Senden, 1960). Visual abilities for both animals and humans improve with time, but the longer the period of deprivation, the less reversible are the effects (Crabtree & Riesen, 1979; Timney, Mitchell, & Cynader, 1980).

The behavioral effects of sensory deprivation are reflected in changes at the neuronal level. For example, when a kitten's eyes first open, about half of the neurons in the visual cortex respond selectively to direction of movement or orientation of a stimulus (that is, firing only when an object in their visual field moves in a certain direction or is in a particular orientation, such as diagonal lines or straight lines). Usually, after several weeks of normal visual experience, all the cells in the visual cortex become sensitive to the orientation of a stimulus or to direction of movement. Following the arguments of Greenough and his colleagues, this is what the cells are "expected" to do, given species-typical experiences. But when kittens are prevented from seeing any patterns (that is, when they experience only homogeneous light without any objects to see), the cells of the visual cortex make fewer connections with other cells and gradually lose their sensitivity to orientation. Experience (or lack of experience) changes the structure and organization of the young brain, even for something as basic as vision. As with behavior, recovery of normal neuronal structure and responsivity following exposure to pattern light occurs, although the amount or degree of recovery declines with longer periods of deprivation (Blakemore & Van Sluyters, 1975; Cynader, Berman, & Hein, 1976).

One cannot do these kinds of experiments with children, of course, but research by Daphne Maurer and her colleagues with infants born having cataracts over their eyes, including some infants who had their cataracts removed shortly after birth, is informative (Le Grand et al., 2001; Maurer, Mondloch, & Lewis, 2007; Maurer et al., 1999; see also Ostrovsky, Andalman, & Sinha, 2006). Maurer and her colleagues reported that infants who had their cataracts removed and new lenses placed in their eyes within several months of birth displayed a generally typical pattern of visual development. The longer the delay in removing the cataracts, however, the poorer vision was. Moreover, even for those infants who had their cataracts removed early and developed normal vision, some aspects of *face* processing were impaired (Le Grand et al., 2001). This finding suggests that there may be different sensitive periods for the brain areas associated with visual acuity and those associated with processing faces. It also points to the importance of identifying and correcting visual problems early to minimize their long-term effects.

Greenough and his colleagues (1987) proposed a second process of synapse development, which they called **experience-dependent processes** (or **experience-dependent synaptogenesis**). In this case, connections among neurons are made that reflect the unique experiences of an individual rather than the experiences that all members of a species can expect to have. In both cases, the overproduction of neurons enables an individual to make connections (and, thus, store information) that reflect his or her particular environment. When certain experiences are not had—when the world does not cause certain neurons to be activated and synapses to join—the neurons die.

Bennett Bertenthal and Joseph Campos (1987) relate the ideas of Greenough and his colleagues to the old nature/nurture issue and the question of whether infants come into the world fully prepared by biology or as blank slates. Bertenthal and Campos write, "What determines the survival of synaptic connections is the principle of use: Those synapses activated by sensory or motor experience survive; the remainder are lost through disuse. For Greenough et al., then, experience does not create tracings on a blank tablet; rather experience erases some of them" (p. 560).

Related to the ideas of Greenough and his colleagues are *selectionist models* of neural development that propose, essentially, that many more neurons are produced than can ever survive and that these neurons "compete" with one another for use (Changeux & Dehaene, 1989; Edelman, 1987). For example, Gerald Edelman proposed the concept of **neural Darwinism**, in which groups of neurons are in constant competition with one another, each attempting to recruit adjacent neurons to their group and, thus, perform a particular function. Groups that receive the most stimulation develop strong synapses, are able to recruit more neurons to their group, and survive. What determines which groups flourish (that is, receive the most stimulation) and which decline? One important factor is use. Neurons and groups of neurons are selected because they perform important tasks frequently, making them more likely to be used in the future. Because different groups are constantly competing for the same cells, changes in patterns of activation can result in changes in brain organization. Eventually, relatively stable patterns are achieved, but the process is an adaptive one, with the synaptic connections developing as a function of the types of information the young organism receives. Thus, through a process of activity-dependent competition, experience sculpts the brain into its final form.

In Chapter 1, I provided an example of how this process may work in the development of face perception. If you recall, infants as young as 6 months process right-side-up faces more efficiently than upside-down faces, regardless of whether the faces are those of other humans or of monkeys. This suggests an early developing bias for processing faces. By 9 months, however, infants, like adults, now process only human right-side-up faces more efficiently than upside-down faces (Pascalis, de Haan, & Nelson, 2002). Because of repeated experience with human faces (and lack of experience with monkey faces), their processing abilities (and brains) have become specialized for a type of stimulus that is of great importance to their survival.

The message here is that early brain development is not exclusively under genetic control, consistent with the developmental systems approach discussed earlier. Certainly, genes influence what the basic structure of the brain will be. But experiences play an important role in shaping the precise circuitry of the brain. From electrical and chemical activities of the growing nerve cells before birth to the information obtained through the senses after birth, the brain becomes organized by information it receives and by its own activation as much as or more so than by the instructions emanating from the genes.

## The Development of the Neocortex

When most people think of the brain, they think of what's on the surface, a convoluted series of lobes. This is the **neocortex**, or **cerebral cortex**, which is a multilayered sheet of neurons, only 3 to 4 millimeters thick, that surrounds the rest of the brain. Figure 2-10 provides a lateral view of the brain; except for the cerebellum and the spinal cord, all of the structures shown are part of the neocortex. Of course, there is much more to the brain than the neocortex, but because the neocortex is the part of the brain primarily associated with thinking, it is the only major part of the brain that I will discuss in this chapter.

The neocortex consists of two approximately equal halves, or hemispheres, connected by a thick mass of nerves called the **corpus callosum**. The neocortex can be further divided into regions. Some primary areas, such as the various sensory regions, receive information directly from the senses. Other primary areas, such as the motor regions, send instructions directly to muscles. Secondary areas consist of regions that integrate information and have many connections with other areas of the brain. These are the association (or thought) regions, which are responsible for our more complex mental functioning.

Let me provide a research example of the connection between development of the prefrontal lobes of the neocortex and cognitive development. Development of the prefrontal lobes in humans is rapid between birth and about 2 years of age. As I mentioned, the prefrontal lobes are proposed to be involved in many acts of "higher" cognition, but one important function of the prefrontal lobes appears to be in the inhibition of responses (Fuster, 1989). For example, for some tasks, children must *not* execute a previously acquired response (that is, they must inhibit that response) so that they can make a new response. One such task is Piaget's A-not-B object permanence task. (See Chapter 4 for a more in-depth discussion of object permanence.) On this task, infants watch as a toy is hidden in one of two wells. The infants are then distracted for

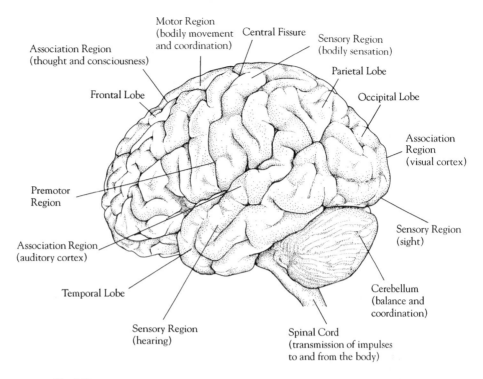

Motor Region
(bodily movement
and coordination)    Central Fissure

Association Region
(thought and consciousness)

Sensory Region
(bodily sensation)

Parietal Lobe

Frontal Lobe

Occipital Lobe

Association
Region
(visual cortex)

Premotor
Region

Sensory Region
(sight)

Association Region
(auditory cortex)

Temporal Lobe

Cerebellum
(balance and
coordination)

Sensory Region
(hearing)

Spinal Cord
(transmission of impulses
to and from the body)

FIGURE **2-10**

A lateral view of the left side of the human brain showing the major structures. All but the cerebellum and the spinal cord are part of the neocortex.

Source: D. F. Bjorklund and B. R. Bjorklund, 1992. *Looking at children: An introduction to child development.* Belmont, CA: Wadsworth, p. 129.

a delay period, after which they are allowed to retrieve the toy. Over trials, the hiding place is changed to well B following a series of correct retrievals from well A. Piaget reported that infants younger than 12 months have great difficulty performing this task and typically look for the hidden object at the A location, where they were successful previously.

Adele Diamond (1985) tested 25 infants in the A-not-B task, beginning at about 7 months of age and continuing until 12 months. She reported that the delay between hiding and searching that was necessary to produce the A-not-B error increased with age at a rate of about 2 seconds per month. That is, 7.5-month-old infants would search for the hidden object at the erroneous A position following only a 2-second delay. By 12 months of age, infants made the error only if approximately 10 seconds transpired between the hiding of the object and the beginning of the search.

Although such research suggests that memory might be a factor in infants' performance, Diamond believed that the more important factor is infants' ability to *inhibit* prepotent responses in solving the A-not-B task. Substantial research with adults (Luna et al., 2001), older children (Barkley, 1997), and infants (Bell, Wolfe, & Adkins, 2007) points to the frontal lobes as the locus of inhibitory control, and Diamond (1991) proposed that during the first year, infants' prefrontal lobes develop gradually, which results in their becoming increasingly able to inhibit their behavioral responses. Despite "knowing" that the object was hidden at location B, young infants cannot stop themselves from executing a response that has been correct in the immediate past. They have learned a response, and before they can learn a new one, they must inhibit the old one. This ability develops over the first year, with girls showing faster progress than boys, suggesting more rapid maturational development of the prefrontal cortex in girls through this age period (Diamond, 1985).

Support for Diamond's claim comes from a study showing significant relations between performance on the A-not-B task and scores on a task of inhibitory ability in 9-month-olds (Holmboe et al., 2008) and from neuroimaging studies that show connections between infants' performance on A-not-B tasks and frontal lobe activity (Baird et al., 2002; Bell & Fox 1992; Segalowitz & Hiscock, 2002). For example, Martha Bell and Nathan Fox (1992) recorded EEG activity from the frontal lobes of 7- to 12-month-old infants performing the A-not-B task. Consistent with Diamond's hypothesis, they reported systematic changes in EEG patterns as a function of age and length of delay. Age-related changes in the prefrontal cortex are also associated with developmental changes in executive function (Kuhn, 2006), and these will be examined in Chapter 7.

Age-related changes in brain structure and function associated with changes in cognition and behavior are not only observed in infancy and early childhood but also later in life. It will likely not surprise you to learn that major changes in brain organization occur in adolescence, a time of substantial change in behavior and thinking. Although some, such as Piaget (see Chapter 5), have noted the advent of adult-like cognitive abilities, a more common description of adolescent thought and behavior centers around a new self-centeredness, emotional instability, increases in risk-taking, and the seeking of novelty (see Spear, 2000). Not surprisingly, these behavioral changes are also associated with changes in the brain. Linda Spear (2000) reviewed some of these brain changes, and they include not only the formation of new neural connections but also the relatively rapid loss of others. Most prominently affected are the frontal lobes, which actually decrease in relative size during this time. The organization of the frontal lobes, as reflected by neural imaging studies (Luna et al., 2001), also changes substantially. In addition, changes occur in the distribution of various neurotransmitters, with some decreasing substantially in both the frontal cortex and the limbic system, an area of the brain associated with emotion.

These changes, which to varying degrees are also characteristic of other adolescent mammals, are likely adaptive, in that the emerging adult must seek independence from his or her parents, experiment with new environments, and establish a place in his or her social group. That there is a species-typical pattern of brain changes associated with such behavior should not be surprising. But what we have here is only correlation, and the correlation is far from perfect. Although many adolescents experience the storm and strife one might expect from a radical restructuring of the brain, others do not. There is a species-typical pattern of changes in cognition and behavior during adolescence, but there is also much variability. I am convinced that the brain mediates all such behavior; however, we must keep in mind that brain development is a dynamic process, influenced by both internal and external factors, rather than the simple consequence of the "unfolding" of a genetic blueprint.

## The Brain's Plasticity

**Plasticity**, discussed in Chapter 1, refers to the ability to change. To what extent can new synapses be formed and different parts of the brain take over a function intended for another part of the nervous system? Put another way, plasticity also refers to the potential outcomes that are possible for a single neuron, a bundle of neurons, or a larger brain structure. Given certain experiences at certain times during life, how might these cells become organized? Implicit in the theorizing of Johnson (2007), Nelson (2001; Nelson et al., 2006), and Greenough and his colleagues (1987) is the concept of plasticity.

### *Neuronal Plasticity*

There is apparently little or no plasticity in the production of new neurons, at least in the cerebral cortex. As I noted earlier, new neurons in the hippocampus are generated throughout life, but evidence of neurogenesis in the cortex of humans and other mammals is scarce. With few exceptions, a newborn comes into the world with more neurons than he or she will ever need. And from birth on, there is a loss of neurons (that is, cell degeneration)—a rapid loss during infancy and a gradual decline thereafter.

The picture is different for the formation of new synapses. Contemporary research indicates that new synaptic connections can be formed throughout life (see Greenough et al., 1987). What causes new synapses to form? The simple answer is experience. Perhaps the most convincing evidence of the effects of experience on brain structures comes from studies providing environmental stimulation for laboratory animals, mostly rats and mice. In studies dating back to 1949 (Hebb, 1949), researchers have raised groups of laboratory animals in environments constructed to be enriched or stimulating and then compared their brain development and learning ability with those raised in environments considered to be deprived (Hymovitch, 1952; Turner & Greenough, 1985). Enriched environments usually included animals raised together in large cages that were filled with a variety of objects with which they could interact. Various platforms, toys, and mazes filled some of the cages—not too dissimilar from the cages one might buy for the family gerbil.

These experiments have shown that rats and mice raised in enriched environments are superior at a wide range of complex tasks, such as maze learning. The differences in learning ability between enriched and nonenriched animals are of a general nature, with the most likely explanation for these effects being that "the groups differ in the amount of stored knowledge upon which they can draw in novel situations" (Greenough et al., 1987, p. 547). Concerning changes found in their brains, enriched animals have heavier and thicker neocortexes, larger neurons with more dendrites, and importantly, more synaptic connections. In one study, enriched rats had 20% to 25% more synapses per neuron in their visual cortexes than did rats raised in individual cages (Turner & Greenough, 1985). And these effects are not limited to infant animals; the behavioral and brain benefits of living in a stimulating environment are found even when experienced by older animals (Greenough et al., 1986).

Synaptic plasticity is greatest in infancy. With age and experience, neurons and synapses that were formed prenatally or in infancy die, and with their death, connections that could have formed are now impossible. Thus, experience serves not only to create new connections but also to make other ones impossible or less likely. But even though the plasticity to form new synapses decreases with age, it does not disappear;

we retain substantial neural plasticity throughout life. What does change is the degree to which experience can change the brain and the intensity of the experience needed to produce change.

Let me make it clear that losing plasticity should not be viewed completely negatively. As a result of genetic programming and experience, neurons become dedicated, or committed to certain functions, effectively eliminating plasticity. This commitment affords greater efficiency of processing, permitting sets of neurons to specialize. For a species such as humans, who have long life spans and must deal with a large diversity of social circumstances, retaining some plasticity into adulthood is necessary. However, much about human life does not change substantially over time and circumstances, and individuals are best served by a nervous system that early in life commits neurons to basic functions.

### Recovery of Function from Brain Damage

Perhaps the best-known evidence for the plasticity of the nervous system comes from case studies of people who have experienced brain damage and exhibit deficits in physical or mental functioning. These studies document the process of readjustment these people go through and the differences their ages make to their readjustment.[1]

The most studied type of brain damage of this sort concerns the areas of the brain controlling language. Since the 19th century, numerous reports have indicated that children who experience brain damage to the language areas of their left hemispheres before they are able to speak are eventually able to attain more advanced levels of language than are older children or adults who experience similar brain damage (Annett, 1973; Woods & Carey, 1979). Likewise, left-hemisphere brain injury for children who can already talk can produce an initial loss of language ability, but in many cases, language is recovered and the child talks again at normal or near-normal levels. Studies conducted on adults have not found the same degree of recovery (see Witelson, 1985). Even in young children, however, full recovery of language is rare, showing that the human brain is not completely plastic, even early in life (Witelson, 1987). Yet, the evidence clearly shows that "there is a remarkable functional plasticity for language functions following brain damage in childhood in that the eventual cognitive level reached is often far beyond that observed in cases of adult brain damage, even those having extensive remedial education. These results attest to the operation of marked neural plasticity at least in the immature brain" (Witelson, 1987, p. 676). This pattern is also seen for milder forms of brain injuries, such as concussions. Children tend to recover from the effects of concussion (for example, headaches, memory loss) faster than adolescents and adults do (see Yeats & Taylor, 2005).

This might lead one to believe that if one must have brain damage, have it early, for a young brain is more likely than an older brain to recover normal function. This is the so-called *Kennard effect*, and it is based on the observations of Margaret

---

[1] Before proceeding, I must mention some problems that are inevitable when using brain-damage research to understand brain function. These include the facts that (a) brain damage can rarely be narrowed to one area, (b) brain damage frequently involves complications beyond that of simple lesions, (c) disorders following brain damage might not reveal how the brain functions normally, and (d) lesions in one area of the brain can lead to changes in other areas of the brain (Fuster, 1989). Nevertheless, despite these and other reservations, much can be learned about brain functioning from studying brain damage, especially when viewed in combination with other sources of data.

Kennard, a pioneer in early studies on recovery of function from brain damage (Kolb, 1989). However, newer research has shown that the Kennard effect does not hold for all types of brain injuries. Rather, recovery depends on a wider series of variables than previously considered (de Haan & Johnson, 2003; Kolb, 1989). In fact, when the focus of damage is to an area of the brain that is involved with more general cognitive functioning rather than with a specific cognitive ability such as language, the reverse is often true (Stiles et al., 2005; Witelson, 1987). Evidence reviewed by Bryan Kolb and Ian Whishaw (1990) from both animal and human research demonstrates that younger children and animals show more permanent deficits than older children and animals after brain damage to the frontal lobes, which are associated with general processes such as those involved in IQ. For example, in one study, brain damage before the age of 1 year resulted in lower IQs for children than did similar brain damage that occurred after a child's first birthday (Riva & Cazzaniga, 1986); another study reported greater reductions in IQ for children who suffered brain damage before the age of 5 than for those who suffered similar injury after age 5 (Kornhuber et al., 1985). In research with rats, Kolb and Whishaw (1981) reported that brain lesions inflicted shortly after birth resulted in a smaller adult brain (approximately 25% smaller) than did lesions inflicted on adult animals (approximately 12% smaller).

What is the reason for this pattern? In some instances, early insults affect how large portions of a brain system will develop, making the consequences of early injury very severe. Likewise, the damage may interfere with learning, resulting in delayed development of cognitive skills. Again, such loss is especially apt to occur when the skill under question is a general one. Yet, in other cases, early brain insults can be compensated for by a pliable system that is not yet set in its ways and can adjust to unexpected changes. This is most apt to occur when the skill under question is highly specified, as in language. The relationship between age at injury and degree of plasticity for specific and general skills is shown in Figure 2-11. As can be seen, the degree of

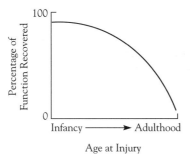

**A. Functional Plasticity for Specific Skills**

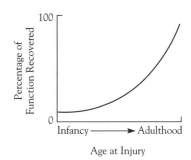

**B. Functional Plasticity for General Skills**

FIGURE **2-11**

Theoretical relationship between age of brain damage and recovery of function depending on whether the brain injury affects a specific skill (such as language) or a more general skill (such as intelligence or planning).

Source: Adapted from "Neurobiological Aspects of Language in Children," by S. F. Witelson, 1987, *Child Development, 58,* 653–688. Copyright © 1987 The Society for Research in Child Development, Inc. Adapted with permission.

plasticity observed is a function not only of age at injury but also of the nature of the brain injury.

### Slow Growth and Plasticity

As I mentioned in Chapter 1, through most of the 20th century, it was believed that if children suffered severe deprivation for much more than their first year after birth, they were destined to a life of intellectual impairment and psychopathology. Subsequent research with both human and animal participants has clearly shown that this is not true (Beckett et al., 2006; Suomi & Harlow, 1972). When the course of a young child's or young animal's life changes drastically, patterns of development can also be radically altered.

Let me provide one research example for the reversibility of the effects of negative early experience here. (I presented some research on plasticity in Chapter 1, and the topic is discussed in greater detail with respect to intelligence in Chapter 13.) With the political turmoil in Southeast Asia during the 1970s, many abandoned and sickly children from that part of the world were subsequently adopted by American families. Generally, follow-up interviews of adopted Asian children who were malnourished and socially deprived as infants revealed that their intellectual and social development was either at or above normal by early childhood (Clark & Hanisee, 1982; Winick, Meyer, & Harris, 1975). In the 1982 study by Audrey Clark and Jeanette Hanisee, for example, 25 adopted Asian children were given a test of verbal intelligence, the Peabody Picture Vocabulary Test (PPVT), and a test of social competence, the Vineland Social Maturity Scale (VSMS). The average age of the children at the time of testing was 44 months, and all the children had been in their adoptive homes for at least 23 months before testing. Before being adopted, most of the children had experienced physical and psychological deprivation. Sixteen of them were reported to have been malnourished sometime during infancy, with many displaying dehydration and muscle weakness. Despite their inauspicious beginnings, the children fared exceptionally well on the tests of verbal and social competencies. The national average on both the PPVT and the VSMS is 100. The adopted children's average scores were 120 on the PPVT and 137 on the VSMS. These children, impoverished and malnourished as infants, showed no residual signs of their early deprivation within 2 years of having been placed in upper-middle-class homes.

This plasticity of behavior and intelligence is attributed, in part, to the slow growth of the brain. As I noted earlier in this chapter, although the human brain is large relative to the rest of the body at birth, it continues to grow well into early adulthood. This prolonged immaturity provides humans the time necessary to master the complexities of social life. But it also provides the opportunity to change behavior and to acquire novel patterns later in life. Seen in this light, the extended immaturity of the human nervous system provides opportunities for behavioral flexibility and plasticity unsurpassed by any other species (see Bjorklund & Pellegrini, 2002).

An immature brain means a slow and inefficient brain. Partly because of the extent of myelination and partly because of a paucity of experience, young children process information more slowly than older children do (see Kail & Ferrer, 2008). This slower speed of processing translates directly into less-efficient processing (Case, 1985; Dempster, 1985) and means that more of the younger children's processing is effortful in nature, in that it uses substantial portions of their limited mental resources

(Hasher & Zacks, 1979; see Chapter 7). In contrast, more of older children's and adults' cognitive processing is automatic, in that it can be done quickly, without conscious awareness, and requires little or none of one's limited mental capacity. In other words, young children must work harder mentally to obtain the same results that older children can achieve more easily.

This inefficiency has its drawbacks, of course. You can't teach much of a complex nature to young children, you can't expect them to gain as much from experiences as older children do, and you can't rely on them to make many important decisions on their own. Despite the obvious disadvantages of a slow and inefficient brain, it also has its benefits. According to Bjorklund and Green (1992),

> [b]ecause little in the way of cognitive processing can be automatized early, presumably because of children's incomplete myelination, they are better prepared to adapt, cognitively, to later environments. If experiences early in life yielded automatization, the child would lose the flexibility necessary for adult life. Processes automatized in response to the demands of early childhood may be useless and likely detrimental for coping with the very different cognitive demands faced by adults. Cognitive flexibility in the species is maintained by an immature nervous system that gradually permits the automatization of more mental operations, increasing the likelihood that lessons learned as a young child will not interfere with the qualitatively different tasks required of the adult. (pp. 49–50)

This should not be seen as implying that the effects of early social or physical deprivation can always be reversed. As you'll see in later chapters, early experiences (or lack of them) can have relatively permanent, negative consequences. The experiences of infancy and toddlerhood establish patterns of behavior that can potentially influence the accomplishments of later years, particularly when those experiences are stable over childhood. But the inefficiency of the young brain does offer children some protection from the perils of an early damaging environment.

## DEVELOPMENTAL BIOLOGY AND COGNITIVE DEVELOPMENT

As the field of cognitive psychology evolved into cognitive science, people interested in mental functioning became increasingly aware of the need to coordinate the psychological level of explanation with the biological level. A similar realization is occurring now in the field of cognitive development. For example, a little more than a decade ago, James Byrnes and Nathan Fox (1998) reviewed some of the new neuroscience techniques and research findings from the developmental neurosciences and concluded that we are on the threshold of a new revolution, equivalent to the cognitive revolution. Since then, the discipline of *developmental cognitive neuroscience* has emerged, which focuses on the study of normal cognitive and neurological development (Johnson, 2007). Perhaps its greatest contribution is elucidating the neurological mechanisms that underlie behavioral observations made earlier by psychologists (Diamond & Amso, 2008). Admittedly, the presentation in this chapter is cursory, but I believe that it provides a foundation for the proper understanding of the ontogeny of human thought.

Many more topics could have been considered in this chapter. For example, hormones apparently play a major role in influencing cognition. Prenatal hormones are known to influence the brain and how later information is processed. More specifically, the class of male hormones called *androgens* are said to "masculinize" the brain, affecting certain sex differences in thinking (for example, spatial ability) as well as how sexual signals are processed (that is, sexual orientation) (see Money, 1988). The field of behavioral genetics has also blossomed in the past two decades, looking at the role of genetics in such diverse behaviors as alcoholism, religiosity, intelligence, learning disabilities, and amount of television viewing (see Plomin et al., 2008; Rutter, 2006). I will examine some of the data and claims of behavioral genetics in Chapter 13 when looking at individual differences in intelligence. I will also include contemporary neuroscience research in discussing a variety of other aspects of cognitive development, from social cognition to executive function and memory, and I hope that this chapter will have served as an adequate introduction for placing this new brain-based research into perspective.

By acknowledging the importance of biological factors to cognitive development, I do not mean to suggest that the future of the field lies in biology. But having an idea of both the neural and evolutionary causes of behavior and development will help the psychologist ask better research questions and achieve a better understanding of development. For example, knowledge of the developmental relationship between brain and behavior has important implications not only for theories of cognitive development but also for societal practices. How pliable is human intelligence? When, in development, can children most benefit from certain educational experiences? Is earlier always better, or are certain sensitive periods for particular experiences distributed throughout development?

The study of cognition, including its development, has gone through substantial changes since its beginnings in the 1950s. We cannot be certain what the future will hold, but it seems certain that part of the new paradigm will pay closer attention to the biological bases of cognition and cognitive development.

## SUMMARY

Developmental psychology has become increasingly concerned with the biological causes of cognition. Although psychology provides a different level of analysis than biology, concepts in psychology must be consistent with the known facts in biology. The new field of *developmental cognitive neuroscience* takes data from a variety of sources—molecular biology, cell biology, artificial intelligence, evolutionary theory, as well as conventional cognitive development—to create a picture of how the mind/brain develops.

Darwin's idea of variation and *natural selection* remains the cornerstone for theories of *evolution*. Proponents of *evolutionary psychology* believe that information-processing mechanisms have evolved in response to specific environmental pressures, equipping humans to solve specific problems; however, *evolutionary developmental psychologists* believe that domain-general mechanisms have also been modified over time as a result of natural selection. A distinction has been made between cognitive skills such as language that have been selected for in evolution (called *biologically primary abilities*) and those such as reading that are primarily determined by culture (called *biologically secondary abilities*).

The *developmental systems approach* centers around the concept of *epigenesis,* a bidirectional relationship between all levels of biological and experiential variables such that genetic activity both influences and is influenced by structural maturation, which is bidirectionally related to function and activity. Organisms inherit not only a species-typical genome but also a species-typical environment, and species-typical experiences early in life can greatly influence the course of development. Timing of experience can be crucial for development. Many early perceptual and cognitive abilities are governed by *sensitive periods,* those times in development when certain skills or abilities are most easily acquired.

Scarr and McCartney's *genotype → environment theory* proposes that genes drive experience. Based chiefly on research in *behavioral genetics,* this theory describes three kinds of genotype → environment effects: passive, which occur when biological parents rear the child; evocative, which occur when characteristics of the child elicit responses from others; and active, which occur when children select environments in which they choose to interact. Passive effects decrease in influence over time, whereas active effects increase. Data supporting this theory show that parents' environmental influence on their children's intelligence is greatest during the early years and wanes as the children approach adolescence. Because of the substantial influence of active genotype → environment effects, Scarr proposed that *"good-enough" parents* are sufficient to raise a child.

New *neuroimaging techniques,* such as high-density event-related potentials, PET, SPECT, and fMRI, are providing new knowledge about brain functioning and development.

The nervous system consists of *neurons,* which transport chemical and electrical signals. Neurons consist of a cell body; *axons,* long fibers that carry messages away from the cell body to other cells; and *dendrites,* more numerous fibers that receive messages from other cells and transfer them to the cell body. Electrical messages are transmitted through *synapses,* facilitated by various *neurotransmitters.* Neurons go through at least three stages of development: *proliferation (neurogenesis), migration,* and *differentiation.* The formation of synapses (*synaptogenesis*) occurs during this last stage. Synapse formation is rapid during prenatal development and during the early months of life. A complementary process of *selective cell death,* or *apoptosis,* also occurs, with many neurons dying. Nearly all the neurons an individual will ever have are produced before birth, although synaptogenesis occurs throughout life. *Myelin* is a fatty substance that surrounds axons, promoting faster transmission of electrical signals. Different areas of the brain begin and end the process of myelination at different times, and degree of myelination is related to certain sensory, motor, and intellectual levels of development.

Some neural connections are made by all members of a species given normal experiences (*experience-expectant processes*), whereas other connections are made because of the unique experiences of an individual (*experience-dependent processes*). Neurons live (and form synapses with other neurons) or die as a function of use, with groups of neurons apparently competing against one another to recruit other neurons, a process referred to as *neural Darwinism.* Evidence suggests that areas of infants' brains are only weakly specialized for processing certain information (for example, language) but become more domain-specific in nature as a result of experience.

The *neocortex* (or *cerebral cortex*) is divided into two *hemispheres* that are connected by the *corpus callosum*. Neuronal *plasticity* has been most clearly demonstrated in studies with animals, including those reared in deprived or enriched environments. With age, the plasticity needed to form new synapses declines, but it does not disappear. Examination of the recovery of function after brain damage shows that, at least for damage to areas of the brain that control specific abilities such as language, plasticity is greater the earlier the damage occurs. Humans' prolonged immaturity contributes to our behavioral plasticity and to children's abilities to overcome the effects of deleterious early environments.

## KEY TERMS AND CONCEPTS

developmental cognitive neuroscience

evolution

natural selection

evolutionary developmental psychology

biologically primary abilities

biologically secondary abilities

developmental systems approach

epigenesis

sensitive period

behavioral genetics

genotype → environment theory

"good enough" parents

encephalization quotient

neuroimaging techniques

neuron

axon

dendrites

synapses

myelin

neurotransmitters

proliferation (of neurons)

neurogenesis

migration (of neurons)

differentiation (of neurons)

synaptogenesis

selective cell death (or apoptosis)

experience-expectant processes (or

experience-expectant synaptogenesis)

experience-dependent processes (or experience-dependent synaptogenesis)

neural Darwinism

neocortex (or cerebral cortex)

corpus callosum

plasticity (of the brain)

## SUGGESTED READINGS

### Scholarly Works

Geary, D. C., & Bjorklund, D. F. (2000). Evolutionary developmental psychology. *Child Development, 71*, 57–65. This brief article introduces the basic tenets of evolutionary developmental psychology, particularly as it relates to cognitive development. For a more in-depth look at evolutionary developmental psychology, see Bjorklund, D. F., & Pellegrini, A. D. (2002). *The origins of human nature: Evolutionary developmental psychology.* Washington, DC: American Psychological Association.

Gottlieb, G. (2007). Probabilistic epigenesis. *Developmental Science, 10*, 1–11. This short article concisely presents the basic ideas of the developmental systems approach. Gottlieb was a major proponent of this perspective, and interested readers may want

to refer to his 1997 book, *Synthesizing nature-nurture: Prenatal roots of instinctive behavior* (Erlbaum).

Lenroot, R. K., & Giedd, J. N. (2007). The structural development of the human brain as measured longitudinally with magnetic resonance imaging. In D. Coch, K. W. Fischer, & G. Dawson (Eds.), *Human behavior, learning, and the developing brain: Typical development* (pp. 50–73). New York: Guilford. This chapter by leading researchers in the field of developmental neuroimaging provides an up-to-date review of structural changes in brain based on longitudinal data.

Scarr, S. (1993). Biological and cultural diversity: The legacy of Darwin for development. *Child Development, 64*, 1333–1353. Scarr presents a relatively detailed account of her genotype → environment theory, emphasizing the importance of an evolutionary theory to developmental psychologists. This paper is a response to critics of her theory (by Baumrind and by Jackson, same issue), and Scarr is careful to be precise about her theorizing.

## Reading for Personal Interest

Blumberg, M. (2007). *Basic instinct: The genesis of behavior*. New York: Basic Books. In this short book, developmental neuroscientist Mark Blumberg applies developmental systems theory to take on the notion of "instincts." In the process, he challenges theorizing in behavioral genetics and evolutionary psychology.

Healy, J. (2006). *Your child's growing mind: Brain development and learning from birth to adolescence*. Broadway: New York. Jane Healy, educational psychologist turned science writer, presents a well-written and authoritative book about brain development and learning that is accessible for the educated layperson.

# The Social Construction of Mind: Sociocultural Perspectives on Cognitive Development

**The Role of Culture in Cognitive Development**
Tools of Intellectual Adaptation
The Social Origins of Early Cognitive
　　Competencies
The Zone of Proximal Development
Apprenticeship in Thinking and Guided
　　Participation
Sociohistorical Influences
Assessing Cognitive Development from a
　　Sociocultural Perspective

**Implications for Education**

**Sociocultural Theory and Cognitive Development**

SUMMARY
KEY TERMS AND CONCEPTS
SUGGESTED READINGS

After impatiently helping her father complete an on-line purchase, complete with sighs and rolling eyes, 13-year-old Ashleigh's dad began the spiel that she had heard, in one form or another, many times: "When I was kid, we didn't have iPhones or MP3 players, and there was nothing like Facebook. I remember when Pong was the latest and greatest in video games! Most of the kids I went to school with didn't even have computers in their homes. It's no wonder why I can't keep up with you and your brother on all this Internet stuff. And your grandparents, for them computers were something that NASA had, not something that sits on your desk, or even in your pocket! I give them credit for trying, but I'm not surprised that they haven't made the jump to the high-tech world yet. So be patient with me, and especially your grandparents. We just can't think like you do!"

To some extent, Ashleigh and her dad grew up in different cultures. The tools Ashleigh is growing up with for communication, for problem solving, and even for recreation are very different from those her father knew as a child, and those of her grandparents were more different still. Ashleigh is a girl growing up in 21st-century America, and our culture has experienced a substantial technological change over the last two generations. In the distant past, cultures changed slowly, so the experiences of people in one generation were not so different than the experiences of people in previous (or future) generations. One question is central to this chapter: Can one's culture influence how one learns to think? And if so, how do the technologies, institutions, and values of a culture influence cognitive development? Will Ashleigh become a different type of "thinker" than her father and grandparents because of the technological differences in their "cultures"?

In the opening chapter, I stated that there were two obvious trends in cognitive development during the past several decades. The first trend was an increased emphasis on the biological basis of development. The second was an in creased emphasis on the social construction of cognition—the perspective that how children learn to think is governed largely by the culture in which they grow up. I hope, after reading Chapter 2, you agree that the "new view" of how biology influences psychological development gives experience a substantial role to play. But this is not the same as believing that the social environment plays a critical role in shaping development. For example, most researchers who examine the biological basis of development rarely investigate the social environment in detail and therefore rarely see how cognitive development is "constructed" by the social environment.

This is exactly the view that proponents of the **sociocultural perspective** of development take. Sociocultural psychologists believe that how we develop—and particularly how we learn to think—is primarily a function of the social and cultural environment in which we are reared. This viewpoint emphasizes what makes people different thinkers rather than what we all, as human beings, share in common. Traditional views of cognitive development, such as Jean Piaget's (discussed in detail in Chapter 5), emphasize *cognitive universals*—aspects of development that characterize all children in all parts of the world in essentially the same ways. For theorists like Piaget, and for other theorists such as Sandra Scarr, whose ideas of "good enough" parents were discussed in Chapter 2, individual differences in the environments children grow up in certainly affect their views of the world, but these differences do not affect the "big picture" of cognitive development much. Certainly, children growing up in an information-age society will have different things to think about than will children growing up in a hunter-gatherer society, but according to theorists such as Piaget, each will solve problems relevant to their daily lives using species-typical cognitive mechanisms that develop according to a species-typical schedule. Sociocultural theorists see cognitive development very differently.

The overriding theme of this chapter is that cognitive development is inseparable from its cultural context. The traditional dichotomy of the nature/nurture debate pitted culture *against* biology: "How much" of a child's development is governed by biology versus "how much" is shaped by culture? Contemporary theorists see the relation between biology and culture quite differently. Culture is considered to be as much a part of human nature as our big brains. *Homo sapiens* evolved a unique suite of physical and intellectual abilities, and these influenced how we fed ourselves, defended against predators, reared our children, and interacted with other members of our species, which in turn "created" culture. The effects of culture then influenced our behavior and served as pressures for natural selection and subsequent biological evolution (Cole, 2006; Rogoff, 2003). In the words of Henry Plotkin (2001), "Biology and culture relate to each other as a two-way street of causation" (p. 93). Or, as Michael Cole (2006) wrote, "Culture is, quite literally, a phylogenetic property of human beings" (p. 659).

Culture is transmitted to children by their parents and other members of society. Within the adult-child interchanges of daily life, children's intellectual processes are developed to handle the tasks and problems pertinent to their particular surroundings. Parents might not be conscious of their instructional techniques, but cultural practices of child-rearing are usually well suited for the type of life children can expect to face as adults. Sociocultural theory addresses how children come to understand and function in their social world. From the sociocultural perspective, how children understand their physical world "is embedded within knowledge of the sociocultural world … and it is the latter that enables and guides the former" (Nelson, 1996, p. 5). This should not be taken to mean that scientists with a sociocultural perspective give biology short shrift in influencing cognitive development. Most do not, but they realize that neurologically influenced, species-typical cognitive abilities emerge in species-typical social environments. This is captured in Mary Gauvain's (2001) statement that "cognitive development is an active constructive process that involves beings who are evolutionarily predisposed to live and learn in social context with other 'like-minded' beings. They are like-minded in terms of both the neurological system available and the social requirements that are in place" (p. 63).

The current interest in sociocultural perspectives in contemporary developmental psychology can be traced to the rediscovery of the ideas of the Russian psychologist Lev Vygotsky (1962, 1978; see Cole, 2006; Gauvain, 2001, 2009; Rogoff, 1990, 1998, 2003; Wertsch & Tulviste, 1992). Vygotsky, writing in the 1920s and 1930s, emphasized that development is guided by adults interacting with children, with the cultural context determining largely how, where, and when these interactions take place. Vygotsky proposed that cognitive development occurs in situations where a child's problem solving is guided by an adult. For Vygotsky and his contemporary followers, cognitive development progresses through the members of one generation collaborating with the members of another. In other words, children's development is embedded within a culture and proceeds as they are guided through life in collaboration with others. Elaborating on this perspective, Barbara Rogoff (1998) views development as a process of *transformation of participation*:

> Evaluation of development focuses on how individuals participate in and contribute to ongoing activity rather than on "outcome" and individuals' possessions of concepts and skills. Evaluation of development examines the ways people transform their participation, analyzing how they coordinate with others in shared endeavors, with attention to the purposes and dynamic nature of the activity itself and its meaning in the community. The investigation of people's actual involvement and changing goals in activities becomes the basis of understanding development rather than simply the surface to try to get past. (p. 18)

From this perspective, it is clear why Vygotsky and modern sociocultural theorists propose that it is impossible to evaluate the individual without also considering other significant people and institutions in the community.

# THE ROLE OF CULTURE IN COGNITIVE DEVELOPMENT

It is easy to think of cognitive development as something that "just happens" exactly the same way for children worldwide. After all, evolution has provided humans with a unique nervous system, and the center of our flexible intelligence is the brain. Yet, intelligence is also rooted in the environment, particularly in the culture. Understanding how cultural beliefs and technological tools influence cognitive development through child-rearing practices helps us better comprehend the process of development and our role as adults in fostering that process. Keep in mind, however, that sociocultural views are not intended as an alternative interpretation to those based on biology, which I discussed in the previous chapter. Rather, cognitive development must be seen as the result of interacting factors, with the social environment being a critical ingredient to this mix.

Vygotsky proposed that we should evaluate development from the perspective of four interrelated levels in interaction with children's environments—ontogenetic, microgenetic, phylogenetic, and sociohistorical. **Ontogenetic development** (or *ontogeny*), which refers to development of the individual over his or her lifetime, is the topic of this book and the level of analysis for nearly all developmental psychologists. **Microgenetic development** refers to changes that occur over relatively brief periods of time, such as the changes one may see in a child solving addition problems every week for 11 consecutive weeks (Siegler & Jenkins, 1989). This is obviously a finer-grained analysis than that afforded by the traditional ontogenetic level. **Phylogenetic development** (or *phylogeny*) refers to changes over evolutionary time (thousands and even millions of years). Here, Vygotsky anticipated the current evolutionary psychology perspective, believing that an understanding of the species' history can provide insight regarding child development. Finally, **sociohistorical development** refers to the changes that have occurred in one's culture and the values, norms, and technologies that such a history has generated. For example, children growing up in Western nations today have received a legacy of literacy, computers, and a legal and "human rights" tradition that influences their development in ways that children growing up in other cultures without literacy, computers, or Western values can't even imagine (and vice versa).

Vygotsky's claim that multiple aspects of a child's endowment (genetic, cultural) must be viewed in interaction makes his theory reminiscent of the developmental systems approach discussed in the previous chapter (see Gauvain, 2009; Tudge, Putnam, & Valsiner, 1996). Vygotsky stressed the need to understand how changing organisms develop in changing environments. Focusing only on the individual or only on the environment could not provide an adequate explanation of development (Hernández Blasi, 1996). However, what modern-day researchers have emphasized most about Vygotsky's ideas is his belief that development can only be meaningfully studied in the social and cultural context in which it occurs.

## Tools of Intellectual Adaptation

Vygotsky claimed that infants are born with a few *elementary mental functions*—attention, sensation, perception, and memory—that are eventually transformed by the culture into new and more sophisticated mental processes he called *higher mental functions*. Take memory, for example. Young children's early memorial capabilities are limited by biological constraints to the images and impressions they can produce.

However, each culture provides its children with **tools of intellectual adaptation,** which are methods of thinking and problem solving that children internalize from their interactions with more competent members of society and that permit children to use their basic mental functions more adaptively. Thus, children in information-age societies might learn to remember more efficiently by taking notes, whereas their age-mates in preliterate societies might have learned other memory strategies, such as representing each object they must remember by tying a knot in a string or reminding themselves to perform a chore by tying a string around their fingers. Such socially transmitted memory strategies and other cultural tools teach children how to use their minds—in short, the culture teaches children *how* to think. And because each culture also transmits specific beliefs and values, it teaches children *what* to think as well.

A subtle difference in cultural tools of intellectual adaptation that can make a noticeable difference on children's cognitive task performance can be found in how a language names its numbers. Today, most cultures in the world use a system with the concept of zero, negative numbers, and the possibility to enumerate quantities from one to infinity. Some cultures, however, have a more limited way of expressing quantities (for example, only having number words for "one," "two," and "many"), and this influences their ability to perform basic arithmetic operations. For instance, adult speakers of two Amazonia languages (Pirahã and Mundurukú) have no number words for quantities larger than five (Gordon, 2004; Pica et al., 2004). As a result, they perform arithmetic tasks involving small quantities easily, but they perform poorly on tasks involving larger quantities. Pirahã children who learn Portuguese, however, are able to perform arithmetic calculations with larger quantities, bolstering the interpretation that the language's ability to represent numbers is responsible for the pattern of numerical thinking in these cultures (Gordon, 2004).

Even more subtle differences in the *number names* that a language uses can affect children's mathematics. For example, in all languages, the first 10 digits must be learned by rote. After that, however, some languages take advantage of the base-10 number system and name numbers accordingly. English does this beginning at 20 ("twenty-one," "twenty-two," and so on). However, the teen numbers in English are not so easily represented. Rather, 11 and 12 also must be memorized. Not until 13 does a base-10 system begin ("three" + "ten" = "thirteen"), and even then, several of the number names do not correspond to the formula digit + 10. "Fourteen," "sixteen," "seventeen," "eighteen," and "nineteen" do, but the number names for "thirteen" and "fifteen" are not as straightforward (that is, they are not expressed as "threeteen" and "fiveteen"). Moreover, for the teen numbers, the digit unit is stated first ("fourteen," "sixteen"), whereas the decade unit is stated first for the numbers 20 through 99 ("twenty-one," "thirty-three"). Thus, the number system becomes very regular in English beginning with the 20s.

Other languages, such as Chinese, have a more systematic number-naming system. In Chinese, as in English, the first 10 digits must be memorized. From this point, however, the Chinese number-naming system follows a base-10 logic, with the name for 11 translating as "ten one," the name for 12 translating as "ten two," and so on. The Chinese and English languages are similar beginning at 20, and both use the base-10 logic once the "hundreds" are reached.

Kevin Miller and his colleagues (1995) reasoned that differences in the number-naming systems between English and Chinese might be associated with early

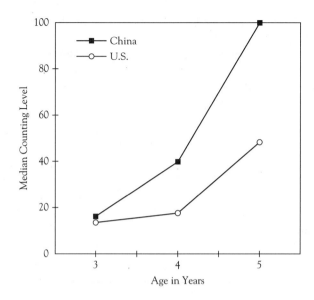

FIGURE **3-1**

Median level of counting (highest number reached) by age for Chinese and U.S. preschoolers. Because of the way numbers are named in Chinese versus English, Chinese-speaking children learn to count to 20 before English-speaking children.

Source: Miller, K. F., Smith, C. M., Zhu, J., & Zhang, H. (1995). Preschool origins of cross-national differences in mathematical competence. *Psychological Science, 6*, 56–60. Reprinted with permission.

mathematical competence, specifically counting. They tested 3- through 5-year-old children in Champaign-Urbana, Illinois, and in Beijing, China. They asked each child to count as high as possible. Differences between the Chinese and American sample are shown by age in Figure 3-1. As can be seen, no cultural differences were observed for the 3-year-olds, but the Chinese children began to show an advantage by age 4. This advantage was even larger at age 5. Further analyses indicated that cultural differences were limited to the teens decade. Although almost all children could count to 10 (94% of the American children and 92% of the Chinese children), only 48% of the American children could count to 20, compared with 74% of the Chinese children. Once children could count to 20, no cultural differences were noted for counting to 100. These findings indicate how differences in the naming-number system of a language can contribute to early differences in a cognitive skill. This early difference in a *tool of intellectual adaptation* might contribute to later differences in mathematical abilities found between Chinese and American children (see Chapter 11).

Other differences in how a language expresses its numbers can also influence children's development of basic arithmetic abilities. For example, expressing numbers between 21 and 99, English states the decade number first (47 is stated "forty-seven"), but some languages invert the ones and tens decade. For example, in German, 47 is said *siebenundvierzig*, literally "seven and forty," and so on. As a result of this inversion, German-speaking children have problems when learning how to convert spoken numbers (for instance, *fünfundzwanzig*, or "five and twenty") to numerals, with many children inverting the order of the numerals (for example, writing "52" instead of "25") (Zuber et al., 2009).

The relevance of tools of intellectual adaptation to cognitive functioning is not limited to subtle differences between languages or to comparisons between high-tech and stone-age cultures. It can be seen both within and between modern societies today. The 20th century saw the invention of many new tools of intellectual adaptation, but perhaps the one that will have the most profound impact is the personal computer. Like it or not, there is a global economy, and "information" is a valuable commodity. To a great extent, access to computers—and the ability to use them easily—differentiates those cultures that will experience economic boom versus economic bust in the 21st century and, within a culture, such as mainstream America, those who will reap the greatest benefits that an information-age society has to offer. Being computer literate affects not only what jobs we have and, thus, our income. It also influences how one learns, how (and what) one remembers, and how one solves problems—just as reading and writing did centuries before. In a sense, we are in the midst of natural experiment, one in which a new tool of intellectual adaptation has been introduced, and we should not be surprised if, in decades to come, we are a different-thinking people than we were before the computer revolution.

Most college students today, and certainly nearly all who will follow them, are *digital natives*, people who grew up with digital media and who take these media for granted. As illustrated by the story that opened this chapter, most members of Ashleigh's parents' and grandparents' generation have learned to use the new media, but it rarely comes easy to them. For people who did not grow up with it, using the new media is like using a second language, whereas for most people under 30 today, it is like using a first language. So it should not be surprising that such a near-universal change in how people gather information and communicate has had (and will continue to have) a significant impact on cognitive development. Moreover, access to digital media varies not only between generations and between developed and developing cultures but also within a culture. For example, in a 2001 survey of American homes, 77% of White and 76% of Asian households had computers in comparison to only 41% for both Black and Latino families (DeBell & Chapman, 2003; see also Calvert et al., 2003). However, a more recent survey of 12- to 17-year-old American teenagers reported that 97% played video games of some sort (Lenhart et al., 2008). This phenomenon is not limited to the United States. In a five-country survey (Brazil, Germany, Japan, the United Kingdom, and the United States) of the media habits of "Millennials" (people between the ages of 14 and 25), 75% stated that they view the computer as more of an entertainment device than their TV (Deloitte, 2009).

In sum, Vygotsky claimed that human cognition, even when carried out in isolation, is inherently *sociocultural* because it is affected by the beliefs, values, and tools of intellectual adaptation transmitted to individuals by their culture. And because these values and intellectual tools can vary substantially from culture to culture and even within a culture over time, Vygotsky believed that neither the course nor the content of intellectual growth was as "universal" as Piaget and others had assumed.

## The Social Origins of Early Cognitive Competencies

Vygotsky viewed young children as curious explorers who are actively involved in learning and discovering new principles. However, he placed little emphasis on *self-initiated* discovery, choosing instead to stress the importance of *social* contributions to cognitive growth. For example, Vygotsky believed that higher psychological processes (those involving self-awareness) have a social origin, developing first on the social plane and only later becoming internalized and developing on the psychological plane (Wertsch & Tulviste, 1992). Vygotsky referred to this dual nature of cognitive development as the **general genetic law of cultural development**. According to Vygotsky (1981), "[a]ny function in the child's cultural development appears twice, or on two planes. First it appears on the social plane, and then on the psychological plane. First it appears between people as an interpsychological category, and then within the child as an intrapsychological category. This is equally true with regard to voluntary attention, logical memory, the formation of concepts, and the development of volition" (p. 163). According to James Wertsch and Peeter Tulviste (1992), cognitive processes such as memory are not understood as characteristics of individuals but, rather, as functions that can be carried out either between people or internally. Such processes can be viewed as *socially constituted cognitive activity* (Gauvain, 2001), which is "individual thinking that has embedded within it the contributions of the social world" (p. 41). Children learn to use the symbols or the representational tools of the social community, regardless of whether they are sharing a memory with another person, for example, or contemplating a problem "in their head."

Following this logic, Vygotsky believed that to understand cognitive development, psychologists should not focus on individuals as they execute some context-independent process, as Western psychologists have traditionally done. Rather, psychologists should examine individuals as they participate in culturally valued activities.

It is not always practical, of course, to assess children's thinking in "naturalistic" settings, and even when it is, the loss of experimental control can limit greatly what one can say about the mechanisms underlying cognition. However, to the extent that children's thinking is applied to solve real-world problems (and what else is cognition for, and why else would we want to know about it?), an understanding of cognitive development requires that one appreciate the "larger social and cultural context that provides meaning and purpose" for children's cognitions (Gauvain, 2001, p. 28).

According to Vygotsky, many of the truly important "discoveries" that children make occur within the context of cooperative, or collaborative, *dialogues* between a skillful tutor, who might model the activity and transmit verbal instructions, and a novice pupil, who first seeks to understand the tutor's instruction and eventually internalizes this information, using it to regulate his or her own performance. The nature of that dialog may differ, however, as a function of culture. For example, as I mentioned in Chapter 1, children in traditional cultures are often more attentive to what adults *do* rather than to what they *say*. For instance, in one study, researchers observed 2- to 3-year-old children from each of four communities: Two of the communities were from the United States (the middle-class towns of West Newton, Massachusetts, and Sugarhouse, Utah), and two were from more traditional communities (the Efe, foragers from the Democratic Republic of the Congo, and an indigenous Mayan group from San Pedro, Guatemala) (Morelli et al., 2003). These communities vary in a number of ways, of course, but one was the extent to which children were exposed to the day-to-day lives of adults. In Western cultures such as ours, beginning in the preschool years, children are often segregated from adults and receive much culturally important information and instruction in school rather than

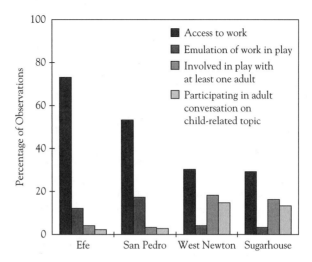

FIGURE **3-2**

Children in different cultures can have drastically different experiences that will affect what they learn and how they think. Children in more traditional cultures (Efe and San Pedro) observe adults at work and imitate work in their play more than children in middle-class communities, who engage more in child-focused activities.

Source: Adapted from Morelli, G. A., Rogoff, B., & Angelillo, C. (2003). Cultural variation in young children's access to work or involvement in specialized child-focused activities. *International Journal of Behavioral Development, 27,* 264–274.

"on the job." In contrast, in the Efe and San Pedro cultures, children are in close contact with adults during most of the day and observe and interact with adults while they perform important cultural activities.

One important finding of this study was the extent to which children in these communities observed adults at work. As can be seen from Figure 3-2, the Efe and San Pedro children frequently watched adults at work, whereas children from the middle-class American communities did so much less often. Also, the Efe and San Pedro children were more apt to emulate adult work in their play than the American children were. In contrast, the American children were more likely to be involved in specialized, child-focused activities, including lessons, play with at least one adult, scholastic play with an adult, and conversation with an adult on a child-related topic.

Let me provide an illustration from an everyday task in our own culture. Imagine Miguel, a 4-year-old, is trying to put together a jigsaw puzzle. His early attempts get him nowhere. His mother notices his difficulties, sits down beside him, and offers some assistance. She first suggests that Miguel look for the corner pieces, selecting one herself and then showing Miguel. Next, she suggests that Miguel look for other edge pieces, starting with those that match the patterns and colors of one of the corner pieces. Miguel selects several pieces, tries to put them together, and on his third attempt finds a piece that fits. Miguel continues to look for other pieces but soon becomes frustrated. His mother then selects two pieces, places them close together, and says, "See if these two fit." Miguel puts them together, smiles, and continues to look for other pieces. Miguel's mother gives him a few words of encouragement and continues to help when he runs into trouble. But Miguel is getting the hang of it, and his mother's assistance is needed less and less. This kind of social interaction, claimed Vygotsky, fosters cognitive growth.

## The Zone of Proximal Development

How does the kind of social interaction just illustrated by Miguel and his mother foster cognitive growth? First, Miguel and his mother are operating in what Vygotsky called the **zone of proximal development**—defined as the difference between a child's "actual developmental level as determined by independent problem solving" and his or her level of "potential development as determined through problem solving under adult guidance or in collaboration with more capable peers" (Vygotsky, 1978, p. 86). This is the zone in which sensitive instruction should be aimed and in which new cognitive growth can be expected to occur. Miguel obviously becomes a more competent puzzle-solver with his mother's help than without it. More important, he will internalize the problem-solving techniques that his mother uses in collaboration with him and will ultimately use them on his own, rising to a new level of independent mastery. In other words, children can best learn to solve problems at a level between their current ability and their ability when assisted by an adult, and within this zone adults can do the most effective teaching. One important thing to remember here is that the skills of the child continue to develop, requiring that adults modify their reactions to children. Thus, the sociocultural approach is by necessity dynamic—ever changing—with both adults and children progressing as a result of their repeated transactions.

Related to the concept of the zone of proximal development is the concept of **scaffolding** (Wood, Bruner, & Ross, 1976). Scaffolding occurs when experts are sensitive to the abilities of a novice and respond contingently to the novice's responses in a learning situation so that the novice gradually increases his or her understanding of a problem. Scaffolding will be most effective when done in the zone of proximal development, and it occurs not just in formal educational settings but any time a more expert person tailors his or her interactions to guide a child to a level near the limits of that child's performance. The behavior of Miguel's mother in the earlier example reflected scaffolding and working in the zone of proximal development.

Evidence of scaffolding can be seen in a study in which mothers were instructed to teach their 5-year-old children how to play a board game involving the use of dice to compute moves (Bjorklund, Hubertz, & Reubens, 2004). In this research, kindergarten children and their mothers played a board game of "Chutes and Ladders," with the spinner being replaced by a pair of dice. Children had to compute their moves by adding the numbers on the two dice. To what extent did mothers help their children add or attempt to teach their children arithmetic strategies in the process of playing the game? Mothers' behavior often varied with the competence of their children. For children who were using fact retrieval and mental arithmetic spontaneously (that is, children who did not have to count out loud or on their fingers to arrive at an answer), mothers usually provided little support or advice because little or none was needed. In contrast, mothers of less arithmetically competent children often prompted their 5-year-olds to count the dots on the dice, modeled or instructed the use of simple addition strategies (for example, counting all the dots on the dice), and often re-represented the problem by holding up their fingers to correspond to the dots on the dice. Some mothers used these overt procedures more during the early trials and gradually lessened their use of specific prompts and instructions as their children took more responsibility for solving the "problem" on their own. In other words, these mothers were "working in the zone of proximal development" to teach their children simple arithmetic strategies in the context of a social game.

There was variability in the degree of scaffolding shown by different mothers, of course. Let me provide one example from this research of a particularly effective mother. On her first move, 5-year-old Yolanda threw the dice, then just stared at them and said nothing, and then looked at her mother. Her mother asked, "How many is that?" Yolanda shrugged her shoulders, and her mother said, "Count them." Yolanda shrugged again, and her mother then pointed to the dots on the first die while saying, "One, two, three," then to the dots on the second die while saying "four, five. You have five. Now you count them." Yolanda complied, pointing to each dot as she counted out loud, and moved her piece on the board. The mother then threw the dice and asked Yolanda, "How many do I have?" Yolanda shrugged her shoulders, and her mother counted the dots on the dice out loud and then said, "You count them," which Yolanda did. The next five turns went very much the same, with Yolanda professing not to know what to do and her mother modeling counting and then directing Yolanda to count the dots on the dice. On the sixth move, Yolanda counted the dots on the dice immediately after her mother's request (no shrug and no modeling of counting by mother) and even did the same on her mother's turn. Her mother then hesitated on the next several turns before asking Yolanda how many dots she had. Eventually, Yolanda threw the dice and counted the dots herself spontaneously, without any prodding from her mother, and continued to do so on both her and her mother's turns throughout most of the game. The mother corrected Yolanda when she made mistakes counting, but she became less directive as Yolanda took more of the responsibility for the game herself.

Contrast the behavior of Yolanda's mother with that of Darrell's mother. Darrell would roll the dice and begin counting each dot on the dice, starting with the die closest to him ("one, two, three") and then continuing to count the dots on the second die ("four, five, six, seven, eight"). While he was counting, his mother would interrupt and instruct him to count from the larger number, a more sophisticated strategy. For example, when the child rolled a six and a five and started counting the dots, the mother would interrupt him by saying, "No, Darrell, start counting from the six here," pointing at the six and saying, "You know this is six." The child would start over counting each dot on the dice, asking his mother to stop telling him what to do. This continued throughout the game, with Darrell's mom rolling the dice during her turn and modeling retrieval of arithmetic facts (for example, "six plus four is ten"), which was apparently beyond this child's capability to execute on his own. Darrell usually ignored his mother's demonstrations and instructions and, as a result, showed no improvement in his use of arithmetic strategies over the course of the sessions.

All the responsibility for determining the extent of adult involvement is not on the adult. Adults and children jointly determine the degree to which children can function independently. For example, children who are less able to solve problems on their own will elicit more support from adults than more capable children will. More skilled children need less adult support, or scaffolding, to solve a problem (Plumert & Nichols-Whitehead, 1996).

I have been careful not to use the word "competence" in describing children's problem-solving abilities. In Vygotsky's sociocultural perspective, learning and development are the result of interacting in specific, culturally defined tasks that have specific rules. Unlike other theories of cognitive development (for example, Piaget's), "competence" is not an absolute level beyond which a child cannot exceed but, rather, is task specific (Fischer & Bidell, 1998; Laboratory of Comparative Human Cognition, 1983). A child can show a high level of ability on one highly practiced task but be much less adept on a very similar and perhaps even objectively less-demanding task. A child's level of intellectual functioning is always evaluated by performance on specific tasks or in specific, culturally determined situations.

## Apprenticeship in Thinking and Guided Participation

Adults' interactions with children vary depending on their culture. Although child-rearing in all cultures can take advantage of the zone of proximal development, what is taught will depend on what roles the child is eventually expected to play in society. Barbara Rogoff (1990, 2003; Rogoff et al., 1993) has viewed the transaction between children and adults as reflecting an *apprenticeship in thinking,* with novice children improving their "skills and understanding through participation with more skilled partners in culturally organized activities" (1990, p. 39). All the responsibility for the apprenticeship is not placed on the adults, however. Children might actively place themselves in positions to learn, prompting adults to increase the level of instruction as children become increasingly skilled.

Rogoff developed the concept of **guided participation** to extend Vygotsky's idea of the zone of proximal development. The zone of proximal development has typically been applied to situations where there is explicit instruction between an older, more skilled teacher and a younger, less knowledgeable learner. Rogoff uses the term *guided participation* to refer to adult-child interactions not only during explicit instruction but also during the more routine activities and communication of everyday life. Guided participation is "the process and system of involvement of individuals with others, as they communicate and engage in shared activities" (Rogoff et al., 1993, p. 6). Guided participation focuses on day-to-day activities in children's lives, such as doing chores, watching television, and eavesdropping on parents. Rogoff believes that children's cognitions are shaped during such mundane activities as much as or more so than in more formal educational settings.

The idea of an apprenticeship or guided participation might seem reasonable in cultures where children are integrated early into the daily activities of adult life, such as among the agrarian Mayans of Guatemala and Mexico or the !Kung of Africa, whose hunting and gathering lifestyles have remained virtually unchanged for thousands of years. But this idea is not as easily grasped for a culture such as our own. Many school-age children might not have seen their parents in action at their jobs— or even know what their parents do for a living. Moreover, children are generally excluded from adult activities, being segregated from adults for much of the day. Other children around the world, for example, sleep in the same room or even the same bed as their parents throughout childhood, and babies never leave home unless they are strapped to their mothers' backs.

### Shared Remembering

Many aspects of cognitive development in information-age cultures have been shifted from parents to professional educators, whose job is to teach important cultural knowledge and skills to children. Yet, much learning certainly transpires between parent and child in postindustrial societies, particularly during the preschool years; in many ways, these transactions are designed to prepare children for the schooling that will follow. For example, formal education in North America, Europe, and Japan involves children responding to adults' questions when the adults already know the answers. It also involves learning and discussing things that have no immediate relevance—knowledge for knowledge's sake. Such context-independent learning, foreign to many cultures, is fostered during infancy and early childhood in our own. For example, as will be discussed in Chapter 8, parents frequently prompt their young children to name objects or to recall recent events (Gauvain, 2001; Rogoff, 1990). Take, for instance, the following interchange between 19-month-old Brittany and her mother:

*Mother:* "Brittany, what's at the park?"

*Brittany:* "Babysing."

*Mother:* "That's right, the baby swing. And what else?"

*Brittany:* [Shrugs.]

*Mother:* "A slide?"

*Brittany:* [Smiling, nods yes.]

*Mother:* "And what else is at the park?"

*Brittany:* [Shrugs.]

*Mother:* "A see …"

*Brittany:* "See-saw!"

*Mother:* "That's right, a see-saw."

This type of interchange is not at all unusual for a mother and a child from mainstream America, and it is a good example of Vygotsky's zone of proximal development. Brittany, in this case, is learning to recall specific objects with her mother's help, but she is also learning the importance of remembering information out of context (mother and daughter are in their living room at the time, miles from the park). Brittany is learning that she can be called on to state facts to her mother that her mother already knows. And she is learning that she can depend on her mother to help provide answers when she is unable to generate them herself. Table 3-1, from

## TABLE **3-1**
### Some Functions of Shared Remembering in Children's Memory Development.

- Children learn about memory process, for example, strategies.
- Children learn ways of remembering and communicating memories with others, for example, narrative structure.
- Children learn about themselves, which contributes to the development of the self-concept.
- Children learn about their own social and cultural history.
- Children learn values important to the family and the community, that is, what is worth remembering.
- Social solidarity is promoted.

Source: Adapted from Gauvain, M. (2001). *The social context of cognitive development.* New York: Guilford, p. 111.

Gauvain (2001, p. 111) provides a list of some of the functions that such "shared remembering" between parent and child can have on memory development.

### Talking and Reading to Children

Another way parents in postindustrial cultures prepare their children for formal education is by talking to them. In the United States and most of the developed world, parents include their young children as conversational partners. Although the type of language environment children are exposed to does influence their language development (Hoff, 2009), children around the world acquire language at about the same time, even in cultures where children are "seen and not heard." But children who are not included as conversational partners by adults might not be prepared for the type of language interaction used in school. These children might become proficient users of language in their own community yet be perceived as language deficient in school (Rogoff, 1990).

Another school-related skill that might be associated with parent-child conversations is reading. We know that reading to children is an important predictor of children's later reading ability (see Chapter 11). There are substantial differences in how frequently preschool children are read to (see Adams, Treiman, & Pressley, 1998), and differences in how children are read to can have important implications for later language, and possibly reading, development. For example, Grover Whitehurst and his colleagues (1988) trained parents of 2- and 3-year-old children in a technique of *interactive story reading*. Instead of just reading to the children, parents were told to stop every so often and ask open-ended questions (such as "What is Eeyore doing?") and were encouraged to expand on their children's responses, suggest alternative possibilities, and make the questions progressively more challenging as children's understanding increased. A control group of parents was simply asked to read to their children. Analysis of tape recordings of the sessions indicated that the parents in the two groups did read to their children equally often and that parents in the experimental group followed the interactive story reading instructions. After 1 month of such reading, children in the experimental group were 8.5 months more advanced on a measure of verbal expression than were children in the control group, despite the fact that the two groups were equal at the beginning of the study. In later research, similar, though somewhat less substantial, gains were observed for a group of low-income 2-year-olds attending a public daycare facility in Mexico (Valdez-Menchaca & Whitehurst, 1992). The effect, it seems, is quite robust, and it demonstrates that the way in which parents or teachers read to young children—taking into consideration children's understanding of the task and encouraging their active participation—facilitates their subsequent language development and prepares them for life in a literate society. (For an example of interactive story reading, see the excerpt from Tudge, Putnam, & Valsiner [1996] in *Assessing Cognitive Development from a Sociocultural Perspective* later in this chapter.)

When most parents read picture-books with their young children, they are actually using a scaffolding strategy. Parents are more directive when children are younger and become less so as their children's language skills improve (DeLoache & DeMendoza, 1987). Parents establish a book-reading routine in which they may ask questions, point out and label pictures, provide feedback, and make categorical distinctions, such as saying "This is a dog and this is a bird; birds fly and make their nests in trees." They often elaborate about the stories' plots and the details depicted in the book (Simcock & DeLoache, 2006; Symons et al., 2005).

Is it just reading to children that prepares them for life in a literate society, or might talking to children also be related to later reading skills? Apparently, the latter is the case, but not all types of talking are equally effective at fostering later reading ability. Elaine Reese (1995) recorded conversations between mothers and their preschool children and related aspects of these conversations to children's understanding of print at 70 months of age. Most children were just beginning kindergarten, so few were actually reading. Children's understanding of print and prereading skills were assessed by their familiarity with letters and their ability to identify simple words (such as "cat" and "no"), a test of vocabulary, their knowledge about how books are read (front to back, with sentences running from left to right), and their ability both to comprehend and to produce coherent stories. Reese reported that mothers' conversations with their children about past events, especially when including elaborations of those events and associations with other events, was a good predictor of children's subsequent print skills (see the discussion of emergent literacy in Chapter 11). Reese proposed that mothers provide scaffolding by increasingly involving their children in collaborative conversations. According to Reese, "a tentative conclusion that can be drawn from this study is that children who participate to a greater degree in early adult-child conversations may be honing different abilities from those children who allow the adult to direct the interaction" (p. 402). In related research, Monique Sénéchal and Jo-Anne LeFevre (2002) assessed shared, or interactive, storybook reading at home and reported that it was positively related to the development of some receptive language skills, including listening comprehension and vocabulary, which in turn were related to children's reading level in the third grade.

### *Playing with More Skilled Partners*

Play is another area in which parents and older siblings guide children's development. One particularly important type of play for our purposes is *symbolic play*. Symbolic play is essentially pretending and can be solitary (for example, the child pretending that her chair is a car) or cooperative (for example, a child pretending that he's the driver of the car and his mother is a passenger). Symbolic play has been viewed by many as requiring mental representation and as an indication of children's general cognitive development (Piaget, 1962). According to Marc Bornstein and his colleagues (1996), "[i]n symbolic play, young children advance upon their cognitions about people, objects, and actions and in this way construct increasingly sophisticated representations of the world" (p. 2923).

But how do parents, or more expert siblings and peers, contribute to children's symbolic play development? It seems that young children are more likely to engage in symbolic play when they are playing with someone else rather than when they are playing alone, and that mothers in particular bring out high levels of symbolic play in their children (Bornstein et al., 1996; Youngblood & Dunn, 1995). Consistent with Vygotsky's idea of a zone of proximal development and Rogoff's idea of guided participation, young children who interact with a more skilled partner who structures the situation appropriately for them advance in their skills faster than when such support is not provided. Evidence for this comes from a study in which mothers and their 21-month-old children were videotaped during play sessions (Damast, Tamis-LeMonda, & Bornstein, 1996). Many mothers adjusted their level of play to that of their children or to slightly above the level their child was displaying. And mothers who knew more about play development were more likely to increase the level of play with their children than were less knowledgeable mothers and, thus, provided appropriately challenging play interactions. Other research with 2- and 3-year-old children indicated that children were much more apt to look at an adult immediately after performing a symbolic action in play rather than an instrumental action, reflecting, according to the authors, the essential social nature of symbolic play (Striano, Tomasello, & Rochat, 2001).

Why might it be important to facilitate symbolic play? Children learn about "people, objects, and actions" through symbolic play, and research indicates that such play might be related to other aspects of cognitive development. Researchers have found a relationship between the amount of cooperative social play in which preschoolers engage (often with a sibling or parent) and later understanding of other peoples' feelings and beliefs (Astington & Jenkins, 1995; Youngblood & Dunn, 1995). An understanding that other people have thoughts, feelings, and beliefs other than one's own reflects what has been called a *theory of mind* and will be discussed in Chapter 6. Developing an advanced theory of mind is necessary if children are to succeed in any society, and it appears that the guided participation afforded by parents, siblings, and other more expert partners during symbolic play contributes to this development.

### Cultural Influences on Guided Participation

Although the process of guided participation may be universal, how it is carried out varies as a function of how children are perceived and treated in a culture. Rogoff and her colleagues (1993) proposed that different parent-child interactions (that is, differences in the nature of guided participation) occur in different cultures. They made contrasts between two general types of cultures: (1) cultures such as ours, where beginning in the preschool years children are often segregated from adults and receive much culturally important information and instruction outside of the context of skilled activity (that is, in school); and (2) cultures where children are in close contact most of the day with adults and both observe and interact with adults while they perform culturally important activities. Rogoff and her associates observed 14 families with toddlers in each of four communities: two where culturally important information is transmitted mainly out of context, through formal schooling (Salt Lake City, Utah, and Keçiören, a middle-class community in Turkey), and two where culturally important information is transmitted mainly in context (the Mayan town of San Pedro, Guatemala, and Dhol-Ki-Patti, a tribal village in India). Rogoff and her colleagues observed toddlers and their caregivers while doing routine activities (for example, feeding, dressing), while playing social games (for example, peek-a-boo, finger games), and while playing with novel objects (for example, a clear glass jar with a small doll inside, an embroidery hoop, a jumping jack [a marionette that kicks its legs when its bottom string is pulled and the top string is held]). Following are examples of guided participation in each of the four communities.[1]

**Salt Lake City.** A 21-month-old boy and his mother, exploring a glass jar that contains a peewee doll:

> Sandy's mother held the jar up and chirped excitedly, "What is it? What's inside?" and then pointed to the peewee doll inside. "Is that a little person?" When Sandy pulled down on the jar, she suggested, "Can you take the lid off?"

---

[1] From "Guided participation in cultural activity by toddlers and caregivers," by B. Rogoff, J. Mistry, A. Göncü, C. Mosier, 1993, *Monographs of the Society for Research in Child Development*, 58 (Serial No. 236, No. 8). Copyright ©1993, The Society for Research in Child Development, Inc. Reprinted with permission.

Sandy inspected the round knob on top and said, "Da ball."

"Da ball, yeah," his mother confirmed. "Pull the lid," she encouraged, and demonstrated pulling on the knob. "Can you pull?" Sandy put his hand on hers, and they pulled the lid off together triumphantly. "What's inside?" asked his mother, and took the peewee out. "Who is that?"

Sandy reached for the lid, and his mother provided running commentary. "OK, you put the lid back on." And when Sandy exclaimed "Oh!" his mother repeated "Oh!" after him. When Sandy lost interest, his mother asked with mock disappointment, "Oh, you don't want to play anymore?" and suggested, "We could make him play peek-a-boo."

When Sandy took the peewee out, she [his mother] asked, "Where did she go?" and sang, "There, she's all gone," as she covered the peewee with her hands, "Aaall gone." (p. 81)

**Keçiören, Turkey.** A 14-month-old girl and her mother, playing with an embroidery hoop:

A mother introduced a game in which she and her 14-month-old daughter, Lamia, took turns putting the embroidery hoop on each other's head and then dropping it on the floor. The mother created a sense of pretend excitement by saying, "Ay ay ay … ," each time they dropped the hoop. This was followed by joint laughter. The game became explicitly pretend when the mother put the hoop on Lamia's head, making the girl look like a bug with the handles of the hoop sticking out like antennas. The older brother chipped in, saying, "Lamia is a bug, Lamia became a bug." "What kind of a bug?" asked the mother in a coquettish way. "A lady bug," the mother and brother said simultaneously. (p. 136)

**Dhol-Ki-Patti, India.** An 18-month-old girl and her mother, playing with a jumping jack [a wooden doll that does "jumping jacks" when a child pulls on a string]:

Roopa was not holding the top and bottom strings taut enough to cause the jumping jack to jump, so her mother took Roopa's hand in her own, grasped the bottom string with both hands, and pulled on the string twice, saying, "Pull here, pull here," as she demonstrated. She then released her hold of Roopa's hand to enable Roopa to do it on her own.

But the jumping jack fell to the ground because Roopa was not holding it tight. The mother, quick to help, lifted the jumping jack as Roopa reached for it. Twice again, she pulled on the bottom string with her left hand, repeating, "Pull it here." Then she released her hold, letting Roopa take the object. She held her hands close to (but not touching) Roopa's, ready to help if necessary. (p. 114)

**San Pedro, Guatemala.** A 19-month-old boy and his mother, playing with a jumping jack:

The mother used a firm manner of placing the child's hands on the strings to mark the importance of holding firmly onto them, positioning the jumping-jack toy in a position that indicated to the child to hold the bottom string lower, and tapping the child gently on the arm, indicating not to pull the string so hard. (p. 71)

Although toddlers and caregivers in all communities interacted in ways permitting all participants to develop an understanding of the task at hand and their own participation in that task, important differences were found between the middle-class and more traditional communities. Parents in Salt Lake City and Keçiören placed a greater emphasis on verbal than on nonverbal instruction, with the adults providing a good deal of structure to foster children's involvement in learning, including praise and other techniques to motivate the children. The middle-class parents also frequently instructed their children in specific tasks. In contrast, parents in the Mayan and Indian villages used more explicit nonverbal communication and rarely directly instructed their children in a particular task. In these communities, children are rarely segregated from adults; because children are around adults most of the day, they can observe competent adult behavior and interact with adults while they perform the important tasks of their society. Rogoff and her colleagues reported that observation skills are more important and better developed in the traditional communities than in the middle-class communities, with children in traditional communities being better at attending to relevant adult behavior. The acquisition of mature, culturally appropriate behaviors via observation has been termed **legitimate peripheral participation** (Lave & Wenger, 1991), and although adults seemingly play a less active role than in guided participation, it is nonetheless an important component of an apprenticeship in thinking.

The findings of Rogoff and her colleagues make it clear that there is no single path to becoming an effective member of society but that, depending on the demands of one's particular community, different forms of guided participation are apt to be used. One form is not necessarily better than another. It depends on how a competent adult in a society is supposed to behave.

## Sociohistorical Influences

Although Vygotsky's ideas about tools of intellectual adaptation and the zone of proximal development are well known, he also emphasized the importance of a culture's history in shaping cognitive development. For example, different cultures use different writing systems, and these systems can have consequences not only for how children learn to read and write but also for how they think. For example, one study examined the cognitive abilities in 8- to 14-year-old Greek and Chinese children (Demetriou et al., 2005). Although no differences were found in measures of general intelligence between the two groups, the Chinese children outperformed the Greek children on all measures involving visual/spatial processing. Why might Chinese children excel in this one area of cognitive ability? The researchers proposed that the Chinese children's extensive practice with their logographic writing system (pictorial symbols), in contrast to the phonetic system used by Greek children, was responsible for their greater spatial abilities. This is reminiscent of the counting advantage that Chinese-speaking children have relative to English-speaking children because of the way their language names the teen numbers (Miller et al., 1995).

Differences in thinking are even more substantial between literate cultures, which may also have books, newspapers, and computers, and illiterate cultures where reading and writing are not practiced. We would find similar differences in cognitive development between Western Europe today and 600 years ago, before the printing press, personal computers, cell phones, compulsory education, and laws limiting child labor. The differences in genes between people living in information-age societies and people living in hunter-gatherer cultures today are negligible, however, as are the genetic differences between Europeans of the early 21st century and those of the early 15th century. But because of differences in the tools of intellectual adaptation provided by different cultures at different historical times, and in the values and institutions of these cultures, children learn to think differently.

As I mentioned previously, sociocultural influences not only reflect differences between modern cultures and those hundreds of years ago, they represent dynamic forces at work today (Greenfield, 2009). For example, drastic changes in the economy such as the world financial crisis beginning in 2008, a natural disaster such as Hurricane Katrina in 2005, or an influx of immigrants to a community can affect people and, thus, children's development in significant ways, influencing how the local community is structured, what educational and economic opportunities are available, and how people interact with one another. In many parts of the developing world, children have their feet in two cultures, one traditional and the other modern, and their exposure to modern culture, including formal schooling, has been shown to affect important aspects of their cognitive development (Gauvain & Munroe, 2009).

Malcolm Gladwell (2008), in his best-selling book *Outliers,* shows not only how a culture's history can influence a child's development and, thus, adult accomplishments but also that such influences can extend back many generations and over different continents. Did one's ancestors make a living as independent farmers tending rice paddies, which required planning and persistent labor, or did they make a living as serfs growing potatoes, which required planting in the spring and harvesting in the fall, with little attention necessary in between? Are you a descendent of farmers, whose crops were relatively immune to theft, or of ranchers, whose livelihood could be rustled from under one's nose? Were people born in a time of economic plenty or hardship? Exceptional people (the "outliers" in the title of his book), Gladwell asserts, are not simply the product of hard work and native intelligence. They are the result of the practices of their culture at a particular time in history. Although Gladwell never mentions Vygotsky, his book illustrates the importance of sociohistorical influences that are central to sociocultural theory.

## Assessing Cognitive Development from a Sociocultural Perspective

From the perspective of the researcher, how can one effectively measure how a child and a more experienced partner interact in a particular context? One must look at the characteristics of the context (some contexts might constrain the possible interactions more than others), the child, and the more experienced partner, all in interaction with one another. It is not enough to assess what the child does and then, independently, what the experienced partner does. All factors must be evaluated together. Let me provide an example of such an interaction by examining what happens in a joint-reading activity between a 4-year-old child, whom we'll call Rose, and her mother (adapted from Tudge, Putnam, and Valsiner, 1996, pp. 215–216).

For her regular bedtime story, Rose chose *Mike Mulligan and the Steam Shovel* for her mother to read. (The text of the story is placed in quotation marks.)

*Mother:* "Mike Mulligan and the Steam Shovel." [She turns the page.]

*Rose:* "To Mike."

*Mother:* Good. "Mike Mulligan had a steam shovel. A beautiful red steam shovel. Her name was … ? [Mother pauses.] What was her name?

*Rose:* "Marianne."

*Mother:* Marianne. "Mike Mulligan was very proud of Marianne. It was Mike Mulligan and Marianne and some others who cut through the high mountains so that trains could go through. It was Mike Mulligan and Marianne and some others who lowered the hills and straightened the curves to make the long highways for the automobiles."

*Rose:* [Pointing to the picture.] And the holes for um er for the er um cars.

*Mother:*     Yep, there are some holes for the cars to go through. "It was Mike Mulligan and Marianne and some others who smoothed out the ground and filled the holes to make the landing fields for the airplanes." Rose, look at this airport. What do you think is strange about that airport? [Rose looks at the picture.]

*Mother:*     Have you ever been to an airport that looked like that? [Rose shakes her head, indicating No.]

*Mother:*     What's different about that airport? Why does it look different from the airports we've been to?

*Rose:*     Got houses.

*Mother:*     It's got houses, but that wasn't what I was thinking of. But that's true. I was thinking that the airports that we've been to, the airplane landing is a long rectangular-shaped road called a landing strip, a runway. Is that what this one looks like? [Rose shakes her head, No.]

*Mother:*     No. What's different about this one?

*Rose:*     Don't know.

*Mother:*     It's round! Have you ever seen … been to an airport where the airplane landed on a round road?

*Rose:*     No.

*Mother:*     [Laughs.] Pretty strange. Oooh, look at that. "Then along came new gasoline shovels, and the new electric shovels and the new diesel motor shovels and took all the jobs away from the steam shovels. Mike Mulligan and Marianne were …" [Pauses and looks down at Rose.]

*Rose:*     " … very sad."

*Mother:*     Why were they sad?

*Rose:*     Because they um, because, because um all the um gasoline shovels and all the [looks at mother] … shovels and all the mo … the motor shovels took all the jobs away from her.

*Mother:*     Aaaah [sad]. That's right. "All the other steam shovels were sold for …" [Pauses.]

*Rose:*     " … junk."

*Mother:*     " … or just left out in old gravel pits just to rust away."

What would one look at in this interaction to describe it in terms of a social constructivist perspective? First, the two are working toward the same goal (joint reading of the story) and seem to be jointly attending to the task. The two partners are also generally responsive to one another. This is obviously a familiar routine for mother and child, and each knows what to expect of the other. The two are not sharing the load equally, however. The mother takes the lead in most of the exchanges. Although we have a dyadic (two-way) interaction, the relations are not symmetrical. In this case, mother is doing most of the work, but that might change over time as Rose's reading improves. Note also that although the mother is contributing more to the interaction, Rose is not a passive participant. She selected the book, responded appropriately when her mother requested, and interjected her own comments at times. The mother seems to be providing adequate scaffolding for her daughter. When the context was clear, she requested that her daughter fill in parts of the text, but she read most of the text for Rose.

# IMPLICATIONS FOR EDUCATION

Vygotsky's theory has some rather obvious implications for education. He stressed active rather than passive learning and took great care to assess what the learner already knows, thereby estimating what he or she is now capable of learning. Teachers in a Vygotskian classroom would favor guided participation in which they structure the learning activity, provide helpful hints or instructions that are carefully tailored to the child's current abilities, and then monitor the learner's progress, gradually turning over more of the mental activity to their pupils. Teachers can also arrange **cooperative learning** (or **collaborative learning**) exercises in which students are encouraged to assist each other; the idea here is that the less competent members of the team are likely to benefit from the instruction they receive from their more skillful peers, who also benefit by playing the role of teacher (Palincsar, Brown, & Campione, 1993).

Is there any evidence that Vygotsky's guided-learning approach might be a particularly effective educational strategy? Consider a study by Lisa Freund (1990) in which 3- to 5-year-olds helped a puppet decide which furnishings (for example, sofas, beds, bathtubs, and stoves) should be placed in each of six rooms of a dollhouse that the puppet was moving into. Children were first tested to determine what they already knew about proper furniture placement. Next, each child worked at a similar task, either alone or with his or her mother (Vygotsky's guided learning). Then, to assess what they had learned, children performed a final, rather complex furniture-sorting task. The results were clear. Children who had sorted furniture with help from their mothers showed dramatic improvements in sorting ability, whereas those who had practiced on their own showed little improvement at all, even though they had received some corrective feedback from the experimenter (see also Diaz, Neal, & Vachio, 1991; Rogoff, 1998).

Similar advances in problem-solving skills have been reported when children collaborate with peers rather than working alone (Azmitia, 1992; Fleming & Alexander, 2001), and the youngsters who gain the most from these collaborations are those who were initially much less competent than their partners (Manion & Alexander, 1997; Tudge, 1992). Johnson and Johnson (1987) conducted a meta-analysis of 378 studies that compared achievement of people working alone versus cooperatively. They found that cooperative learning resulted in superior performance in more than half of the studies; in contrast, working alone resulted in improved performance in fewer than 10% of the studies.

There appear to be several reasons why cooperative learning is effective:

1. Motivation seems to be enhanced when children work on problems together (Johnson & Johnson, 1989).
2. Cooperative learning requires that children explain their ideas to one another, persuade, and resolve conflicts—each of which encourages children to examine their own ideas more closely and to be able to articulate them so that someone else can understand. Related to this are the results of a study in which fourth-grade children were given scientific reasoning problems to solve, either in pairs or alone, with some children asked to talk aloud while solving the problems and others given no special instructions about talking aloud (Teasley, 1995). Did working in pairs or talking aloud make any difference in children's performance? Children who worked in pairs and talked aloud were more apt to generate correct hypotheses than were children who did not talk aloud. This result suggests that collaborative learning leads to improved problem solving not simply because of the collaboration per se but because collaboration increases "the likelihood that children would engage in the kinds of talk that support learning" (Teasley, 1995, p. 218).

3. Children are more likely to use high-quality cognitive strategies and metacognitive approaches during cooperative learning (Johnson & Johnson, 1989), which results in generating ideas that no one in the group would likely have generated alone.

Peer collaboration, however, is not the cure-all that the results of some of these studies might seem to imply. Performance is not always enhanced by cooperative learning (Pine & Messer, 1998). In fact, when older peers as partners are compared with parents as partners in cooperative learning exercises, parents usually are the more effective collaborators (Ellis & Rogoff, 1986; Gauvain, 2001). For example, when peers work together on complex problems that involve planning and the use of strategies for their solutions, they tend not to talk as much as adults do about strategies and the task, to be concerned about coordinating their actions (for example, who's turn is next, who should decide what), and to have their interactions sometimes influenced by dominance relationships that can interfere with learning opportunities (see Gauvain, 2001; Radziszewska & Rogoff, 1988). Thus, although peer cooperative learning often has advantages over learning a similar task alone, it is not a panacea, and it typically does not result in as much learning as when an adult works with a child.

Performance on cooperative learning tasks also varies as a function of the competency of the "expert" in the pair. When the more competent peer lacks confidence or does not modify his or her behavior appropriately for the less-skilled peer (that is, does a poor job at scaffolding), achievement is usually no better than when working alone (Tudge, 1992).

As with other aspects of sociocultural theory, the effectiveness of cooperative learning will vary with culture as well. American children, accustomed to competitive and "do your own work" classrooms, seem to have particular difficulties adjusting to the shared decision making found in cooperative learning (see Rogoff, 1998), although they get better at cooperative decision making with practice (for example, Socha & Socha, 1994). As the structure of schools changes to support peer collaboration, with teachers becoming active participants in the children's learning experiences rather than simply directors of it, the benefits of cooperative learning correspondingly increase (see Rogoff, 1998).

One interesting finding about cooperative learning is that young children will sometimes remember the behaviors of others as their own, an error of *source monitoring*—the ability to determine the origins of one's knowledge, memory, or beliefs. For example, Mary Ann Foley and Hilary Ratner had children make a collage with an adult, with the child and adult taking turns putting pieces on the collage (Foley & Ratner, 1998; Foley, Ratner, & Passalacqua, 1993). After completing the collage, children were unexpectedly asked who had put each item on it, themselves or the adult. Foley and Ratner were interested in *attribution errors*—would children falsely attribute a piece to themselves that the adult had actually put on (an "I did it" error), or vice versa (a "You did it" error, when the child had actually placed the piece on the collage but said the adult had)? Four-year-olds made a disproportionate number of "I did it" errors, attributing actions to themselves that adults had actually performed. The children tended to re-code the actions of the adults as their own. Foley and Ratner suggested that this bias might lead to better learning of the actions of others, partly because misattributing others' actions to oneself could cause children to link the actions to a common source (themselves) and, thus, produce a more integrated and easily retrievable memory. In support of this, Ratner, Foley, and Gimpert (2002) reported that 5-year-old children who performed a collaborative task with adults (place furniture in a doll house, as in the study by Freund [1990] discussed earlier) made many "I did it" errors; however, these children later showed greater memory for the location of the furniture in each room than did children in a noncollaboration group. Thus, collaboration led to greater learning, but not in a way that might have been expected. Rather, young children's immature cognitive systems resulted in a high number of source-monitoring errors, which actually resulted in better learning (Bjorklund 1997a).

## SOCIOCULTURAL THEORY AND COGNITIVE DEVELOPMENT

The focus of sociocultural theory is unabashedly the social environment. But one need not reject any idea of looking at biological factors to adopt a sociocultural perspective. Contemporary sociocultural theorists clearly view development as occurring in a system of interacting levels (Gauvain, 2009; Rogoff, 2003), including the child and his or her behavior, people interacting with the child, other people in the immediate environment, and the school, the family, and the community. However, there is also the recognition that children's brains evolved to fit with children's environments, and those environments just happen to be essentially social in nature (Gauvain, 2001).

I think it is easy to espouse belief in the idea that development is the result of multiple levels of causation, each interacting in a bidirectional way. But it is more difficult to practice such a belief. I don't doubt that some researchers taking a sociocultural approach *do* view any mention of biological causation as unnecessary, and I believe some people who focus more on biological causation see the environment as nothing much more than a place for the genes to express themselves. These researchers, however, are in the minority. And at times, it is certainly convenient to talk about a pattern of development or a characteristic of a child as being primarily "environmental" or "biological" in origin, even though we know that *all* characteristics are the product of a complex interaction of bidirectional effects at multiple levels of organization. There are surely some spirited debates ahead for developmental scientists concerning *how* biological and sociocultural mechanisms interact to produce a developing child. But there should not be any debates concerning *if* they do. In my opinion, and in those of probably most leading developmental scientists, one cannot look at human development independently of culture. Humans' social, emotional, and cognitive abilities evolved for life in a human group. And such a perspective is not at odds with other, more biologically oriented models of development. Rather, models describing how the specific social environment in which a child lives influences development must be integrated with theories such as those presented in Chapter 2 on the biological bases of development. Only by studying children, with their genetic and congenital characteristics, in dynamic interaction with their environment, including the larger culture, can we attain a complete understanding of development.

## SUMMARY

*Sociocultural perspectives* of cognitive development hold that a child's cognition is constructed by the social environment. Contemporary sociocultural theories are based on the ideas of Soviet psychologist Lev Vygotsky, who proposed that development should be evaluated from the perspective of four interrelated levels in interaction with children's environments—*ontogenetic, microgenetic, phylogenetic,* and *sociohistorical.* Each culture transmits beliefs, values, and preferred methods of thinking or problem solving—its *tools of intellectual adaptation*—to each successive generation. Thus, culture teaches children what to think and how to think about it.

According to Vygotsky's *general genetic law of cultural development,* cognitive function occurs on two planes, first on the social (between individuals) and only later on the individual (internalized by the child). Children acquire cultural beliefs and problem-solving strategies in the context of collaborative dialogues with more skillful partners as they gradually internalize their tutor's instructions to master tasks within their *zone of proximal development.* Related to the concept of the zone of proximal development is *scaffolding,* which occurs when experts are sensitive to the abilities of a novice and respond contingently to the novice's responses in a learning situation, and *guided participation,* which refers to adult-child interactions not only during explicit instruction but also during the more routine activities and communication of everyday life. Children also acquire important cultural behaviors by working alongside and simply observing more skilled members of the community, a process termed *legitimate peripheral participation.*

Different cultures prepare their children for adult life differently. For example, in modern Western societies, parents talk to children extensively and prepare them for the types of tasks they will encounter in schools. In more traditional societies, adults are less likely to use language and more likely to demonstrate certain abilities to their children.

Sociocultural theory has been applied to educational settings, suggesting that *cooperative learning* (or *collaborative learning*) results in improved learning relative to when children solve problems on their own. Research has found that cooperative learning often produces better performance than individual learning does, but characteristics of the participants and the schools affect how beneficial cooperative learning is.

## KEY TERMS AND CONCEPTS

| | | | |
|---|---|---|---|
| sociocultural perspective | phylogenetic development | general genetic law of cultural development | guided participation |
| ontogenetic development | sociohistorical development | zone of proximal development | legitimate peripheral participation |
| microgenetic development | tools of intellectual adaptation | scaffolding | cooperative learning (or collaborative learning) |

## SUGGESTED READINGS

### Scholarly Works

Cole, M. (2006). Culture and cognitive development in phylogenetic, historical, and ontogenetic perspective. In W. Damon & R. M. Lerner (Gen. Eds.), *Handbook of child psychology* (6th edition), D. Kuhn & R. S. Siegler (Vol. Eds.), Vol. 2, *Cognition, perception, and language* (pp. 636–683). New York: Wiley. This excellent chapter takes into consideration both the evolutionary and sociohistorical contexts in explaining human development.

Gauvain, M. (2009). Social and cultural transactions in cognitive development: A cross-generational view. In A. Sameroff (Ed.), *The transactional model of development: How children and contexts shape each other* (pp. 163–182). Washington, DC: American Psychological Association. This article by Mary Gauvain, a leading proponent of sociocultural theory, presents a modern version of the sociocultural perspective and how it is integrated with evolutionary and developmental contextual viewpoints.

Miller, K. F., Smith, C. M., Zhu, J., & Zhang, H. (1995). Preschool origins of cross-national differences in mathematical competence. *Psychological Science*, 6, 56–60. This paper presents a good example of a study examining how cultural differences in "tools of intellectual adaptation" (in this case, how different languages represent numbers) can influence children's cognitive performance. It demonstrates how subtle differences between two cultures can have unexpected intellectual differences.

## Reading for Personal Interest

Gauvain, M. (2001). *The social context of cognitive development*. New York: Guilford. This book presents an authoritative yet highly readable account of research and theory from the sociocultural perspective. The first set of chapters discusses mainly theory, whereas the second set of chapters presents sociocultural research in areas of "higher mental functions," including the acquisition of knowledge, memory, problem solving, and planning.

Gladwell, M. (2008). *Outliers: The story of success*. New York: Little, Brown & Company. Popular writer Malcolm Gladwell explains how success is as much a function of a person's cultural heritage and time in history as it is of natural intelligence or hard work. Although never mentioning Vygotsky or the sociocultural approach to development, Gladwell's book provides many examples of how children's social surroundings and cultural traditions interact with other aspects of their personalities and intellects to produce successful people from Bill Gates to the Beatles to professional hockey players.

# Infant Perception and Cognition

**Basic Perceptual Abilities of Young Infants**

**Some Methodologies Used to Assess Infant Perception**
"This Sucks": Using Infant Sucking to Provide Insight into Infant Perception
Visual Preference Paradigm
Habituation/Dishabituation Paradigm

**The Development of Visual Perception**
Vision in the Newborn
The Development of Visual Preferences
The Development of Face Processing

**Auditory Development**
  BOX 4-1: The Development of Infants' "Specialization" for Processing Faces
Speech Perception
Music Perception

**Combining Senses**
Intermodal Integration
Intermodal Matching

The Intersensory Redundancy Hypothesis

**How Do We Know What Babies Know? The Violation-of-Expectation Method**

**Core Knowledge**
Object Representation
Early Number Concepts
Arguments Against Core Knowledge

**Category Representation**
How Is Categorization Measured?
The Structure of Infants' Categories

**What Is Infant Cognition Made Of?**

SUMMARY
KEY TERMS AND CONCEPTS
SUGGESTED READINGS

Audrey tells of an unusual preference in her healthy, 9-pound newborn daughter, Michelle. For the first several weeks of life, Michelle would nurse only from one breast, despite the fact that Audrey expressed milk equally well from both. Michelle's preference was the left breast, the one over her mother's beating heart, a sound Michelle had heard from the time her auditory system began to function several months after conception. Michelle would nurse from the left breast only and inevitably fall asleep, presumably being soothed not only by the milk she was consuming but also by the familiar sound she was hearing.

If you ask most people what newborn babies do, the answer you'll likely get is sleep, eat, cry, and occasionally, soil their diapers. This is true enough, but newborns are also making sense of their world. They are perceiving (hearing, seeing, smelling) and learning about events that surround them, and have been for some time prior to birth. Not all that many years ago, well-informed people believed that infants enter the world unable to perceive sights and sounds. When I was teaching my first child development class as a graduate student in the early 1970s, I stated that newborn infants can "see," meaning that they can tell the difference between two visual displays. A middle-age woman informed me that I was wrong, that newborns cannot see. She had had four children, and her obstetrician and pediatrician had both told her that babies were functionally blind at birth and "learned" to see during their first month of life. Newborns are far from mental giants, but they do enter the world able to perceive information with all their senses. Furthermore, babies have some perceptual biases. Some sights, sounds, and smells are inherently more pleasing to them than others, and they learn to prefer additional sensations during the first weeks of life.

But infants, even newborns, do more than "perceive" their world. As the example of Michelle suggests, they are also learning, something that most people call cognition. Even among experts, it's not always easy to know where perception ends and cognition begins (see, for example, Cohen & Cashon, 2006, for a review). Perception is usually defined as involving the organization of the sensations (for example, sights, sounds, smells), whereas cognition deals more with what we do with those perceived sensations (for example, classifying items or events into categories, solving problems, memorizing). In this chapter, I first examine the developing perceptual abilities in infants and then look at some basic cognitive abilities, focusing on aspects of what has been called *core knowledge*—specifically, infants' understanding of object representation and babies' abilities to make sense of quantitative information. I also look at research on infants' abilities to form categories. Other topics related to infant cognition will be examined in later chapters.

---

# BASIC PERCEPTUAL ABILITIES OF YOUNG INFANTS

The study of infant perception has been one of the most successful endeavors in the field of cognitive development over the past half-century. What infants perceive and know was once thought to be beyond the limits of science. However, the development of often simple techniques—using behaviors that infants, even newborns, can control themselves to peek into their minds—has permitted developmental psychologists to get a relatively clear picture of what infants perceive and how their perceptions change over time.

Most research on infant perceptual development has concerned audition (hearing) and vision. This is partly because of the importance of these two senses for human information processing and because vision in particular shows substantial development during the first year of life. The development of audition and vision will be discussed in separate sections later in this chapter.

Research on other senses has also been conducted, of course. For example, it was once believed that newborns were relatively insensitive to pain. More recent research, however, clearly demonstrates that they do, indeed, perceive pain (Delevati & Bergamasco, 1999), and some evidence indicates that, for extremely low birth weight (ELBW) infants (below 1000 grams, or about 2.2 pounds), their response to pain is affected by repeated painful episodes, which are often necessary for preterm infants (Grunau et al., 2001). When tested at 8 months of age, the number of invasive procedures ELBW infants had from birth was associated with reduced facial and heart-rate reactions to pain (blood collection). (Recall from Chapter 2 the research with rats that demonstrated painful experiences during the pre- and neonatal periods were associated with increased sensitivity to pain in adulthood [Ruda et al., 2000].) Newborns also respond to another skin sense, that of touch, or tactile stimulation. Actually, research with both animals and human preterm infants indicates that tactile stimulation is important in promoting normal growth and development. For instance, very small preterm infants who receive extra tactile stimulation gain more weight, spend more time awake, and display more advanced cognitive and motor skills than do normally treated preterm babies (see Schanberg & Field, 1987).

The chemical senses (olfaction and taste) tend to develop early and are quite well developed shortly after (and even before) birth. In fact, a pregnant woman's diet can influence taste preference in her newborn. This was illustrated by a study in which some women consumed anise-flavored food during pregnancy while others did not. At birth and 4 days later, infants born to anise-consuming mothers showed a preference for anise odor, whereas those born to non-anise-consuming mothers displayed aversion or neutral responses to anise (Schaal, Marlier, & Soussignan, 2000). Young infants can also tell the difference among a wide range of odors early in life (Steiner, 1979), and they develop preferences for certain odors within the first week. In a study by Aidan Macfarlane (1975), for example, 6-day-old nursing babies were able to discriminate the odor of their mothers from those of other women. In this study, mothers wore breast pads in their bras between nursings. Two breast pads—one from the baby's mother and the other from another woman—were placed on either side of an infant's head. Although no differences in infants' behaviors were seen in this situation at 2 days of age, by 6 days of age babies were turning to their own mother's pad more often than to the pad of another woman. That is, not only can babies discriminate odors, they quickly learn to make associations with odors and to modify their behavior accordingly. In subsequent work using a procedure similar to that of Macfarlane, researchers found that infants develop a preference for the odor of milk versus amniotic fluid (which they had been living in for 9 months) by 4 days of age (Marlier, Schaal, & Soussignan, 1998) and that bottle-fed, 2-week-old infants preferred the breast odor of a lactating female to that of a nonlactating female (Makin & Porter, 1989; Porter & Winberg, 1999).

# SOME METHODOLOGIES USED TO ASSESS INFANT PERCEPTION

How can a psychologist tell if an infant can see or hear something? That is, how can we determine if an infant can tell the difference between a bull's-eye pattern and a checkerboard pattern, for example, or between the mother's voice and that of another woman? This basic problem hampered serious investigation of infants' perceptual abilities for years, but the solution was really quite simple. What one must do is find some behavior that an infant can control and then use that behavior as an entry into what babies can perceive. For example, the Macfarlane (1975) study just presented took advantage of babies' abilities to turn their heads in one direction or another to determine if they could discriminate and develop a preference for certain odors.

## "This Sucks": Using Infant Sucking to Provide Insight into Infant Perception

Another behavior that very young infants can control is sucking. How might researchers use this behavior to tell if babies can discriminate between two different auditory signals? Anthony DeCasper and Melanie Spence (1986) used infants' ability to regulate their sucking to examine whether infants were learning something about the outside world while still in utero. DeCasper and Spence asked pregnant women to read aloud one of three passages twice a day during the last 6 weeks of their pregnancies. Shortly after birth, the neonates were tested for which passage, if any, would have more reinforcing value. Headphones were placed over the babies' ears, and various passages were played to the infants. Nonnutritive sucking (that is, sucking on a pacifier) was assessed as a function of which passage was being played. First, a baseline sucking rate was determined for each baby (that is, how rapidly the infant sucked on a nipple when no passage was being played). Changes in the babies' rate of sucking then determined whether they heard a familiar passage (the one their mothers had read during pregnancy) or a novel passage (one their mothers had not read). Some infants heard the familiar passage when they increased their sucking rate, whereas the contingency was reversed for other infants. The general finding was that the familiar passage was more reinforcing than the novel passage. That is, infants were more likely to alter their sucking rate to hear the familiar passage than to hear the novel passage. Furthermore, the reinforcing value of the passage was independent of who recited it, an infant's mother or another woman. These results present unambiguous evidence of prenatal conditioning to auditory patterns. The infants were able to discern the auditory characteristics (the rhythm and sound pattern) of these often-repeated passages, and the researchers were able to determine this by associating the various passages with changes in a behavior that infants could control themselves (sucking rate).

## Visual Preference Paradigm

The simplest (and first) technique to test infants' *visual* discrimination abilities was developed by Robert Fantz (1958, 1961). He placed alert babies in a looking chamber. Series of visual stimuli were placed in front of infants' eyes, and an observer peeking through a hole in the chamber above the infant recorded which stimuli the baby looked at the most. If groups of infants spent significantly more time gazing at one pattern than at another, it could be assumed that they can differentiate between the two patterns and prefer to look at one relative to the other. If they couldn't tell the difference between the paired stimuli, there would be no difference in their looking behavior. Using this **visual preference paradigm**, Fantz was able to show that babies younger than 1 week can tell the difference between stimuli such as a schematic face, a bull's-eye pattern, and an unpatterned disk (see Figure 4-1).

I use the term *preference* not to reflect a conscious liking for one thing over another—for alternative rock versus country music, for example—but only to indicate that an infant looks at one object more than another. *Preference*, as used here, is synonymous with *perceptual bias* and merely reveals that infants are not responding randomly.

If infants failed to show a preference (or perceptual bias) between two items, however, this would not necessarily mean that they could not tell them apart. Perhaps both are equally interesting. But if infants have no preference for one stimulus over

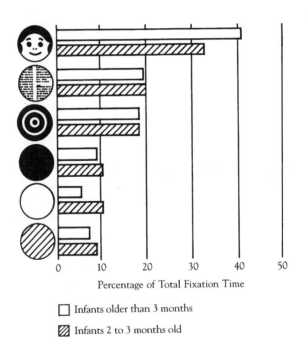

Percentage of Total Fixation Time

☐ Infants older than 3 months

▨ Infants 2 to 3 months old

## FIGURE **4-1**

Infants' visual attention to different patterns. Infants look longer at faces and patterns with more information.

another, how can you tell if they can discriminate them? One technique is the habituation/dishabituation paradigm, which I now describe.

## Habituation/Dishabituation Paradigm

A somewhat more complicated procedure is often used to evaluate infants' perception, memory, and concepts, and this is the *habituation/dishabituation paradigm*. **Habituation** refers to the decrease in response as a result of repeated presentation of a stimulus. The first day on the job in a noisy factory, for example, produces increased levels of physiological stress (heart rate, blood pressure). After a week in this environment, however, levels of stress decline, even though the noise remains. This is habituation. **Dishabituation** (sometimes referred to as *release from habituation*) occurs when, following habituation, a new stimulus is presented that increases the level of responding. If we switch from factory A to factory B, for instance, levels of physiological stress rise, even though the new factory is no louder than the old one was. The noises are different, however, which causes an increase in responding, or dishabituation.

How does this phenomenon relate to infant perception? The amount of time babies look at visual stimuli (or orient to auditory stimuli) is analogous to the worker's physiological reactions to loud noise. The longer infants are exposed to a visual stimulus, the less time they spend looking at it. Habituation is said to occur when an infant's looking time is significantly less than it was initially (often defined as when visual fixation to the stimulus is 50% of what it was on the early trials). At that point, a new stimulus is presented. If attention (that is, looking time) increases from the level of immediately before, dishabituation is said to occur. A typical habituation/dishabituation curve is shown in Figure 4-2.

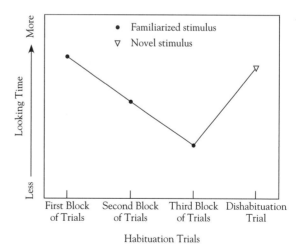

## FIGURE **4-2**

An example of results from a habituation/dishabituation experiment on infant visual attention. The amount of looking time decreases with repeated presentation of the same stimulus (habituation) but increases with the presentation of a new stimulus (dishabituation).

What does such a pattern mean? First, it demonstrates that infants can discriminate between the two stimuli. Babies might not prefer one to the other, but that they respond to the new stimulus with increased attention indicates they can tell the difference between the two. This paradigm is very useful in determining infants' discrimination abilities when researchers are using stimuli for which babies might not have a decided bias. Habituation and dishabituation also indicate memory. Infants are making a discrimination between one stimulus that is physically present and another that is present only in memory. They are not choosing between two stimuli that are before them, but between one stimulus that is in front of their eyes and another that is only in their minds.

Using this procedure, evidence of habituation/dishabituation (and, thus, of rudimentary memory) has been found in newborns for vision (Friedman, 1972) and haptic perception (identifying an object by active touch) (Strei, Lhote, & Dutilleul, 2000). Moreover, fetuses as young as 30 weeks habituate and later dishabituate (as demonstrated by their movement) to vibrations delivered via sound waves through the mother's abdomen (Dirix et al., 2009; Sandman et al., 1997). In one of the first studies to demonstrate habituation/dishabituation in newborns, Steven Friedman (1972) habituated 1- to 3-day-old infants to one visual pattern and then, immediately after habituation, showed the babies a novel pattern. These neonates displayed the classic increase in responding to the new stimulus, indicative of memory (be it ever so brief).

One word of caution about Friedman's results is in order, however. Of 90 newborns initially tested, 50 were excluded for reasons such as crying and falling asleep. Of the 40 remaining, only 29 displayed dishabituation. Thus, only 32% of the original sample demonstrated the habituation/dishabituation phenomenon. The high dropout rate challenges the generalizability of Friedman's (and others') findings. What Friedman's results do indicate, however, is that visual memory is within the capability of many human newborns, although the possibility exists that many infants do not possess such memory until several weeks after birth. (Dropout rates have been lower in some more recent studies. For example, of the 34 newborns tested by Alan Slater et al., 1991, only 10 [29%] were excluded for fussiness and related problems.)

These are not the only methods to assess infant perception. But these methodologies have been used for more than 40 years to evaluate what babies can perceive and what they know, and most of the research reviewed in this chapter involves variants of these well-developed techniques.

# THE DEVELOPMENT OF VISUAL PERCEPTION

When can infants begin to make sense of their visual world? When, for example, can they discriminate between two visual stimuli or form visual concepts? We, like our primate cousins, are a visual species. Survival during our prehistoric past would have been unlikely for a visually impaired child. Vision gives us information about both near and distant objects that touch and hearing cannot easily provide. Spatial cognition is an important "higher-order" skill (see Chapter 6), and such thinking is based on vision. Perhaps because of the importance of vision to the species, or perhaps because we're better at thinking about ways of testing vision, visual perception has been the most studied sense in psychology, both in children and in adults.

## Vision in the Newborn

Newborns can perceive light, as demonstrated by the pupillary reflex (constriction of the pupil to bright light and dilation to low levels of illumination). However, **accommodation,** or focusing, of the lens is relatively poor at birth, regardless of the distance an object is from an infant's eyes, and most of what newborns look at they see unclearly (Banks, 1980; Tondel & Candy, 2008). Development of the muscles of the lens is rapid, however, and under favorable stimulus conditions, accommodation is adultlike by as early as 3 months of age.

Newborns will visually track a moving object, but their eyes will not necessarily move in harmony. **Convergence** refers to both eyes looking at the same object, an ability apparently not possessed by newborns (Wickelgren, 1967). Convergence and **coordination** (both eyes following a moving stimulus in a coordinated fashion) improve during the first months of life and are adultlike by 6 months of age (Aslin & Jackson, 1979).

Studies attempting to determine the *acuity,* or the ability to see clearly, of infants have yielded varied results, depending on the technique used. Acuity improves substantially during the first year of life, but it is very poor at birth (Kellman & Banks, 1998). To assess visual acuity in infants, babies are shown high-contrast patterns of various sizes, such as the pattern of stripes shown in Figure 4-3. If they look at the striped pattern longer than at a plain gray one, we infer that they can "see" the lines. When they show no preference for any one pattern, we assume that they cannot tell the difference between them. With normal acuity for adults being 20/20 (that is, one can see at a distance of 20 feet what a person with "normal" vision can see at 20 feet), estimates of newborn acuity range from 20/400 to 20/600 (Slater, 1995), making the neonate legally blind in most states. Acuity improves substantially during

FIGURE **4-3**

If infants look at a striped pattern like this one longer than at a plain gray one, we know that they can "see" the lines. When they can no longer tell the difference between the gray pattern and the striped pattern, it reflects the narrowest width of stripes that an infant can discriminate, and this is used to determine their visual acuity.

the first year of life, although it does not reach adult levels until 6 years of age (Kellman & Arterberry, 2006; Skoczenski & Norcia, 2002).

An important reason for newborns' poor vision is the underdeveloped state of their foveas, the area of the retina where there is the highest concentration of cones (color perceiving cells that provide the clearest vision). Although the fovea of a newborn is larger than that of an adult, individual cells are arranged differently, cells vary in size and shape, and cones are more widely distributed in the foveas of newborns relative to adults. This makes the cones of newborns much less sensitive to light than those of an adult—by some estimates, by a difference of 350 to 1 (Kellman & Banks, 1998).

Do newborns see the world in color, the way adults do? Although newborns might not be color blind, they apparently do not perceive much in they way of color (Allen, Banks, & Schefrin, 1988). Research has shown newborns can likely discriminate between the colors red and white but cannot differentiate blue, green, and yellow from white (Adams, Courage, & Mercer, 1994). In general, newborns seem to process color information the same *way* adults do, but their color vision itself is extremely poor (Adams & Courage, 1998). However, by about 4 months of age, their color perception has improved greatly and is similar to that of adults (see Kellman & Arterberry, 2006).

The research just cited indicates that newborns can discriminate differences in intensity of light, can track a moving object, and likely can see differences between contrasting colors (see Photo 4-1). But what really interests most cognitive psychologists is the question of what infants can see: Can they tell the difference, for example, between a checkerboard pattern and a bull's-eye pattern? I described in the earlier section on methodology a simple procedure developed by Fantz (1958) in which infants are shown two pictures and the time they look at the various stimuli is noted. If the chosen stimuli are sufficiently different, even very young infants will show a bias for one over the other, demonstrating by their differential looking time that they can tell the difference between the two. Because of the relatively poor acuity of young infants' vision, however, stimuli must be reasonably discrepant before discriminations can be made, but newborns do make such discriminations (Slater, 1995).

## The Development of Visual Preferences

What a baby, or anyone else for that matter, chooses to look at depends on a variety of physical stimulus characteristics as well as psychological characteristics. Physical characteristics, such as movement, amount of contour or contrast, complexity, symmetry, and curvature of the stimulus, affect our looking behavior from a very early age. Familiarity and novelty, which determine the psychological significance of a stimulus for us, also affect the visual preferences of young infants, but these "psychological" factors increasingly influence infants' attention between 2 and 4 months of age. Until this time, babies' visual attention is affected chiefly (but not exclusively) by physical stimulus features.

### *Physical Stimulus Characteristics*

Movement is a potent stimulus characteristic influencing infants' visual attention. Everything else being equal, babies look more at a moving stimulus than at a comparable

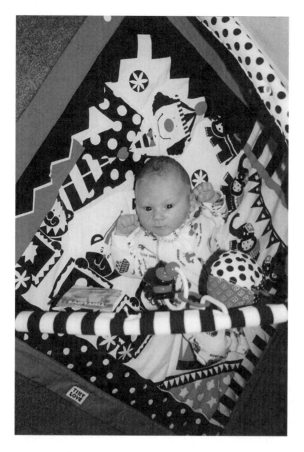

PHOTO **4-1**

Young infants' attention is attracted by high contrast. (Photo by Barbara Bjorklund.)

stimulus that is stationary. In an experiment by Marshall Haith (1966), newborns sucked on a nipple while watching a light display. On some trials, the light moved, tracing the outline of a triangle. Babies decreased their sucking on these trials relative to those when the light did not move, indicating increased attention to the moving light.

Infants are also attracted to areas of high contrast, as reflected by the outline, or contour, of an object. In a pioneering study, Philip Salapatek and William Kessen (1966) assessed the visual scanning of newborns. Infants less than 1 week of age were placed in a modified looking chamber with a white triangle painted on a black background situated before their eyes. The infants' eye movements were recorded and then contrasted with those that occurred when the triangle was not visible. Examples of the scanning patterns of the newborns when the triangle was present are shown in Figure 4-4. As can be seen, the infants' visual fixations were centered near the vertices of the triangles, the areas of most contrast. Subsequent research indicated substantial individual variability in newborn scanning, with many infants during the first 6 weeks of life showing no systematic visual attention to stimulus contours; much of this variation has been attributed to differences in infant neurological maturity at birth

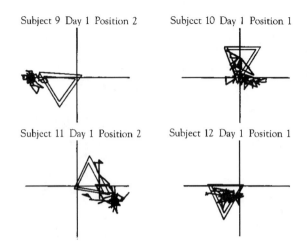

Subject 9 Day 1 Position 2    Subject 10 Day 1 Position 1

Subject 11 Day 1 Position 2    Subject 12 Day 1 Position 1

FIGURE **4-4**

Examples of scanning patterns of newborns.

Source: "Visual Scanning of Triangles by the Human Newborn," by P. Salapatek & W. Kessen, 1966, *Journal of Experimental Child Psychology, 3,* 155–167. Copyright © 1966 Academic Press. Reprinted with permission from Elsevier.

(Bronson, 1990). By about 2 months, however, infants in the Bronson (1990) study were able to consistently direct their attention toward stimulus contours. Work by Salapatek and his colleagues (Maurer & Salapatek, 1976; Salapatek, 1975) indicated that infants at 1 month of age direct their attention primarily to the outside of a figure and spend little time inspecting internal features. Salapatek referred to this tendency as the **externality effect.** By 2 months, however, most of infants' fixations are on internal stimulus features. An example of scanning patterns of 1- and 2-month-olds is shown in Figure 4-5.

Infants' preference for and processing of symmetrical forms have been shown for vertical stimuli. Although there seems to be no preference for *vertical symmetry* until the latter part of the first year, infants as young as 4 months process vertically symmetrical stimuli (stimuli that are the same on the left and right sides) more efficiently than they do vertically asymmetrical or horizontal stimuli (Bornstein, Ferdinandsen, & Gross, 1981). Efficiency of visual processing in these studies was measured by rates of visual habituation. Four-month-old infants acquired information about vertically symmetrical stimuli more effectively than they acquired information about asymmetrical or horizontal information, as reflected by their faster rates of habituation (that is, they looked at the symmetrical stimuli less on later trials than they looked at the asymmetrical or horizontal stimuli). According to Marc Bornstein and his colleagues (1981, p. 85), "The results ... support the view that verticality has a special status in early perceptual development.... Whether innate, early maturing, or based on experience, the special quality of verticality generally may derive from the importance of the vertically symmetrical body and face" (p. 85).

Another physical stimulus feature of importance is that of curvature, or *curvilinearity*. Some of Fantz's original work demonstrated infants' preferences for curved stimuli, such as a bull's-eye pattern, over linear (that is, straight-line) stimuli of

Scanning by a 1-month-old

Scanning by a 2-month-old

### FIGURE **4-5**

Examples of visual scanning of faces by 1- and 2-month-old infants. One-month-old infants explore the contour of faces, called the *externality effect*, whereas 2-month-olds spend more time looking at the internal features of faces.

Source: Adapted from Shaffer, D. R. (1993). *Social and personality development* (3rd edition). Pacific Grove, CA: Brooks/Cole.

|  | Curvilinear | | Straight | |
|---|---|---|---|---|
|  | Concentric | Nonconcentric | Concentric | Nonconcentric |
| 1 |  | IX |  | X |
| 2 | V | VI | VII | VIII |
| 3 | I | II | III | IV |

Number of Directions

### FIGURE **4-6**

Examples of stimuli used to assess infants' preferences for curvature. All other things being equal, infants prefer curvilinear and concentric stimuli.

Source: "Infant Visual Fixation: The Effect of Concentricity, Curvilinearity, and Number of Directions," by H. A. Ruff & H. G. Birch, 1974, *Journal of Experimental Child Psychology*, *17*, 460–473. Copyright © 1974 Academic Press. Reprinted with permission from Elsevier.

comparable contour (Fantz, 1958). Holly Ruff and Herbert Birch (1974) similarly observed a preference for curvilinear stimuli in 3- and 4-month-old infants, but they also found a preference for concentric stimuli (see Figure 4-6). This preference for curvature was reported even in a sample of newborns (Fantz & Miranda, 1975), although only when the stimuli differed in their outer perimeter (recall the externality effect).

### *Psychological Stimulus Characteristics*

Movement, contour, complexity, symmetry, and curvature continue to affect the attention of people throughout life. Beginning sometime around 2 to 4 months, however, the psychological characteristics of a stimulus—that is, the stimulus's familiarity or novelty—exert an increasing influence on whether and for how long it will be attended to. The fact that a stimulus's familiarity or novelty influences infants' attention implies some sort of memory for the stimulus event. For a stimulus to be regarded as familiar, it must be contrasted with some previous mental representation of that stimulus—that is, it must be contrasted with a stimulus that was previously known. Similarly, to be novel, a stimulus must be slightly different from something that the perceiver already knows (Rheingold, 1985).

Jerome Kagan (1971) proposed that beginning around 2 months, infants form **schemas**, or sensory representations, and that the similarity of a stimulus to previously formed schemas determines attention. A schema is not an exact copy of a stimulus. It is "a representation of an event that preserves the temporal and spatial arrangement of its distinctive elements without necessarily being isomorphic with the event" (Kagan, 1971, p. 6). Kagan proposed the **discrepancy principle** to explain infants' attention to novel stimuli. According to this principle, infants are most attentive to stimuli that are moderately discrepant from a schema. A stimulus that differs slightly from what a baby already knows (for example, a bearded face when the infant is familiar with nonbearded faces) is likely to maintain attention, whereas a highly familiar stimulus (a nonbearded face) or a highly discrepant one (a model of a face with its features scrambled) is likely to receive less of an infant's attention.

Robert McCall and his colleagues provided support for the discrepancy principle (McCall, Kennedy, & Appelbaum, 1977). In their experiments, infants between 2 and 4 months of age were familiarized with stimuli and later shown new stimuli that varied in their similarity to the originals. The researchers reported an inverted-U relationship between attention and similarity of the new stimulus to the standard (see Figure 4-7). Stimuli that were highly similar to the original or that were highly discrepant received less attention than stimuli that were moderately discrepant from the original. This preference for novelty implies that some representation of the original stimulus (a schema) was retained and used to guide subsequent visual processing.

Kagan's discrepancy principle, and much experimental data such as those presented by McCall and his colleagues, suggest that once infants have the ability to form long-lasting visual memories, they use those memories, or schemas, as a standard and direct their attention to stimuli that are somewhat novel to them. However, it has long been known that, under some circumstances, infants actually prefer to attend to familiar, not novel, stimuli (Bahrick & Pickens, 1995; Courage & Howe, 2001). In general, a preference for familiarity typifies the preference for younger infants, but also for older infants in the early phases of visual processing. For example, Susan Rose and her colleagues (1982; see Experiment 2 in that study) showed that groups of 3.5- and 6.5-month-old infants initially showed a preference for familiarity, followed by no preference, and eventually, a preference for novelty (see also Courage & Howe,

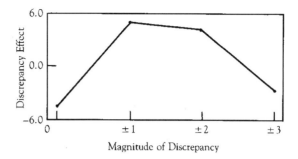

## FIGURE **4-7**

The relative amount of looking time (discrepancy effect) as a function of the magnitude of the discrepancy for 10-week-old infants.

Source: "Magnitude of Discrepancy and the Distribution of Attention in Infants," by R. B. McCall, C. B. Kennedy, & M. I. Appelbaum, 1977, *Child Development, 48,* 772–785. Copyright © 1977 The Society for Research in Child Development, Inc. Reprinted with permission.

1998, for similar results with 3-month-olds). In a similar vein, Richard Bogartz and his colleagues (Bogartz & Shinskey, 1998; Bogartz, Shinskey, & Speaker, 1997) proposed that infants prefer to look at familiar stimuli when processing is in its early stages. It takes time to create and store memory representations, so infants should prefer attending to familiar stimuli until memory representations are well developed. Once a stable memory representation has been formed, an infant's preference should switch to a novel stimulus (see also Bahrick & Pickens, 1995; Bahrick, Hernandez-Reif, & Pickens, 1997).

## The Development of Face Processing

Infants, like older children and adults, like faces. Infants' preferences for physical features, such as curvilinearity and vertical symmetry, may largely account for babies' more general bias to attend to faces. In Chapter 1, I discussed research that showed babies initially have a weak bias to attend to faces, which becomes stronger with age and experience. For example, whereas both adults and 6-month-old infants process upright and inverted faces differently, revealing what appears to be an appreciation of what the proper orientation of faces is "supposed" to be, adults show this bias only for human faces, and 6-month-olds show it for both human and monkey faces (de Haan, Oliver, & Johnson, 1998).

Although this and related research (Pascalis, de Haan, & Nelson, 2002) make it clear that the processing of faces develops during infancy, might a bias to attend to faces be present shortly after birth? Such a bias would not be surprising, for no single visual stimulus likely is of greater importance to a human infant than that of the face of another member of his or her own species. Human infants are highly dependent on their parents for support and protection for a far longer time than other mammals are, and human infants' survival is made more likely by the strong social attachment they establish with their parents. Given this, it makes sense from an evolutionary perspective for infants to be oriented to the most social of stimuli, the human face.

Research following Fantz's pioneering work pushed back the age at which infants show a preference for facelike stimuli to the newborn period. For example, Mark Johnson and his colleagues demonstrated that newborns can distinguish between facelike and non-facelike stimuli (Johnson et al., 1991; Morton & Johnson, 1991). These studies did not use a visual preference paradigm, however. Rather, they showed infants different head-shaped stimuli, moving each stimulus across the babies' line of visual regard. Investigators measured the extent to which the infants followed each moving stimulus (1) with their eyes and (2) by turning their heads. Using these measures, other researchers have reported significantly greater eye or head movement to facelike stimuli than to non-facelike stimuli for infants ranging in age from several minutes to 5 weeks. (Figure 4-8, from Johnson et al., 1991, presents the results of one such study.) Subsequent research using related methodologies has found special attention for facelike stimuli for newborns (Easterbrook et al., 1999; Mondloch et al., 1999).

Such evidence suggests that infants are born with some notion of "faceness" and will attend to such stimuli more than they will to others. Based on the results of their own studies plus those of others, Morton and Johnson (1991) concluded that "it can now be accepted with some degree of confidence that neonates find slowly moving faces with high-contrast definition particularly attractive stimuli" (p. 172). These researchers went on to caution, however, that this does not mean newborns understand the conceptual meaning of a face, merely that they are biased to visually track facelike rather than non-facelike patterns.

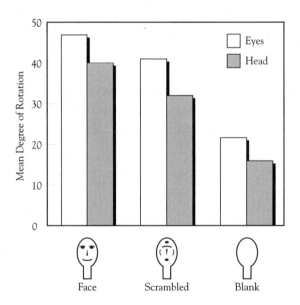

## FIGURE **4-8**

Newborn eye and head turns in following different stimuli.

Source: "Newborns' Preferential Tracking of Faces and Its Subsequent Decline," by M. H. Johnson, S. Dziurawiec, H. D. Ellis, & J. Morton, 1991, *Cognition, 40*, 1–19. Copyright © 1991 Elsevier Science Publishing Co., Inc. Reprinted with permission.

Morton and Johnson (1991) developed a two-process theory for infant face preference. An initial process is accessed primarily through subcortical pathways, and this controls newborns' tracking of faces. This system is responsible for human newborns' preference for the human face, but because of limited sensory capabilities, infants are not able to learn about the features of faces until about 8 weeks of age. Beginning around that time, this system loses its influence over infants' attention to faces, and the second process, which is under the control of cortical circuits, begins to take over. The functioning of this system depends on cortical maturation and experience with faces during the first 2 months of life, as infants begin to build a representation that enables them "to discriminate the human face from other stimuli and especially from faces of other species" (p. 178).

Some evidence suggests, however, that even newborns might be able to make discriminations among faces, looking longer at faces of their mothers than at those of other women, for example (Bushnell, Sai, & Mullin, 1989). In related research, Gail Walton and her colleagues (1992) reported that 12- to 36-hour-old infants would vary their rate of sucking to see a picture of their mother's face rather than that of another woman. This suggests not only that newborns can tell the difference between faces and nonfaces but also that they learn a preference for their mothers' faces shortly after birth. This bias toward faces and the early developing ability of preferring familiar faces may be evolutionarily quite old. Similar patterns have been reported for an infant gibbon (a lesser ape), which displayed a preference for looking at faces in general, and at familiar faces specifically, by 4 weeks of age (Myowa-Yamakoshi & Tomonaga, 2001).

One interesting discovery about infants' preference for faces is that babies find some faces more interesting than others—specifically faces that adults classify as being attractive. For example, Judith Langlois and her colleagues (1987) asked college men and women to judge the attractiveness of adult Caucasian women from photographs. From these ratings, photographs of eight attractive and eight less attractive faces were selected, although the distribution of attractiveness was relatively normal (that is, there were no extremely attractive or unattractive faces). The photographs were selected so that all women had neutral expressions, had medium to dark hair, and did not wear glasses. In one part of the study, 2- to 3-month-old and 6- to 8-month-old infants were shown pairs of faces from the selected photographs that varied in attractiveness (one attractive and one less attractive), and their looking time was measured. Both the younger and older infants spent significantly more time looking at the attractive faces than at the unattractive faces, with approximately two-thirds of the infants showing a preference for the more attractive faces. Furthermore, the preference for the more attractive faces was unrelated to how attractive an infant's mother was judged to be. Other research has shown that this bias toward attractive faces is found even in newborns (Slater et al., 1998), and that this preference extends across sex, race, and age of the modeled face: Six-month-olds consistently show a preference for attractive faces of both men and women, of both black and white adult females, and of 3-month-old infants, despite the fact that the infants had little or no experience with some of these classes of faces (Langlois et al., 1991).

One possible explanation for these findings is that attractive faces have more of the physical stimulus characteristics that draw infant attention than do unattractive faces. For example, attractive faces might be more curvilinear, concentric, and vertically symmetrical than unattractive faces (see earlier discussion). From this perspective, infants' preference for faces is simply a by-product of their preference for many of the physical features that happen to be characteristic of faces. Facial symmetry may be the most important factor here, for it is perhaps the single most potent determinate of attractiveness in adults (Gangestad & Thornhill, 1997). Evolutionary psychologists have indicated that symmetry is a sign of physical health (Gangestad & Thornhill, 1997) and of psychological health (Shackelford & Larsen, 1997), making it possible that a preference for facial symmetry when selecting mates may have been selected for in evolution. Although mate selection is not on the minds of infants, the preference may be a general one, which is weak early in life but becomes stronger with experience. However, evidence suggesting that the preference for attractive faces involves more than just symmetry comes from work with newborns, who displayed a preference for (that is, looked longer at) upright attractive faces versus less attractive faces but not for the same faces when presented upside down (Slater et al., 2000). Moreover, infants also show a preference for attractive faces versus less attractive faces of cats and tigers (as judged by an independent sample of adults), suggesting that this preference is not specific to human faces (Quinn et al., 2008).

The finding that newborns' preference for attractive faces is limited to upright stimuli suggests that they might be born with a schema, or abstract representation, of a human face and that attractive faces in the proper orientation (that is, upright) match that schema better than unattractive ones. But how could such a scheme be represented in the brain of a newborn baby? Some evidence indicates that attractive faces are those that reflect the "average" of a range of facial features (for example, average nose length, average distance between the eyes); that is, for both men and women, attractive faces are, in essence, average faces in terms of the features they possess (Langlois & Roggman, 1990). This would make sense from an evolutionary perspective. If attention to faces is important in forming social relations during early infancy and, thus, to survival, then the best bet would be to have an attentional bias toward "average" features (even if the combination of these "average" features results in an attractive and, thus, "above average" face). Other research has found a relationship between attractiveness and averageness not only for human faces but also for pictures of dogs, birds, and wristwatches (Halberstadt & Rhodes, 2000). This suggests the possibility that the preference for "average" faces is built, in part, on a mechanism for averageness in general rather than on a domain-specific mechanism exclusively for faces. Regardless of the reason, the data of Langlois and her colleagues indicate that what was once believed to be a learned preference (attractiveness) might have its basis in biology.

The face is a complicated stimulus with many defining features, but one that has attracted much attention (from both infants and researchers) is the eyes. For example, newborns prefer to look at faces with eyes opened (Batki et al., 2000), and mutual gaze (eye contact between two people) plays a critical role in social interaction. Research has shown that even newborns are sensitive to eye gaze and are more attentive to faces that are gazing at them than to faces with eyes are averted (Farroni et al., 2002). For instance, Teresa Farroni and her colleagues (2002) sat infants between 24 and 120 hours old in front of two photographs of the same female face. One face had a direct gaze, whereas the other face had its eyes averted to either the right

## FIGURE **4-9**

Newborns are attracted by eye movements, particularly by mutual gaze (like the face figure on the left).

Source: Drawings adapted from Farroni, T., Csibra, G., Simion, F., & Johnson, M. H. (2002). Eye contact detection in humans from birth. *Proceedings of the National Academy of Science, 99*, 9602–9605.

(for about half of the babies) or to the left (for the other half). Figure 4-9 shows an example of the type of faces babies saw. A flashing light attracted infants' attention, and then the two pictures were presented, side-by-side. Farroni and her colleagues reported that the newborns were more likely to orient toward the gazing face and spent significantly more time looking at the face with the direct gaze than at the picture with the averted eyes. A follow-up experiment with 4-month-olds demonstrated that infants showed enhanced neural processing, as indicated by patterns of brain activity (event-related potentials from EEGs) when they viewed faces looking directedly at them as opposed to looking at faces with averted gazes. Farroni and her colleagues concluded that infants' preference for direct gaze "is probably a result of a fast and approximate analysis of the visual input, dedicated to find socially relevant stimuli for further processing" (p. 9604).

Other research has shown that even newborns pay special attention to the eyes. For example, researchers showed newborns right-side-up and upside-down faces that were partially occluded, so that some faces showed the eyes whereas the eyes were hidden for others (Gava et al., 2008; see Figure 4-10). When babies could see the eyes, they looked longer at the right-side-up versus the upside-down faces, a pattern also shown by older infants and adults. They showed no preference, however, for either the right-side-up or upside-down face when the eyes were covered.

Research from a variety of perspectives using a variety of methodologies has illustrated that infants, from birth, are oriented toward faces, or facelike stimuli. This makes sense from an evolutionary perspective; it is also consistent with the speculation of Fantz, who wrote more than 50 years ago that infants' preferences for facelike patterns may "play an important role in the development of behavior by focusing attention to stimuli that will later have adaptive significance" (1961, p. 72). The development of infant face perception is examined in greater detail in Box 4-1.

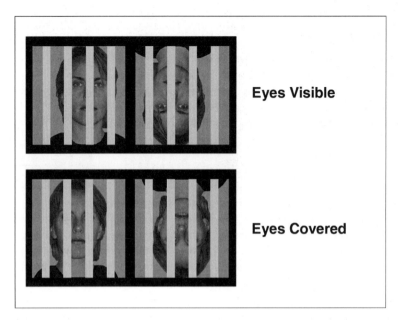

FIGURE **4-10**

Using a visual preference paradigm, Gava et al. found that newborns who could see the eyes of a person showed a stronger preference toward the right-side-up (versus the upside-down) face, as is typically found in research using faces without occlusions. In contrast, newborns showed *no* preference for either the upside-down or right-side-up faces in the condition in which the eyes were covered.

Source: Gava, L., Valenza, E., Turati, C., & de Schonen, S. (2008). Effect of partial occlusion on newborns' face preference and recognition. *Developmental Science, 11*, 563–574.

## AUDITORY DEVELOPMENT

Hearing is functioning before birth, so infants are born with some auditory experience, notably the voice of their mother, but also the sounds one would hear when living inside the body of another person (the heart beat, for instance). Despite this early experience, newborns' are often described as being a bit "hard of hearing" (Trehub & Schellenberg, 1995). Their audition improves substantially over the first year of life, but their hearing will not be adultlike until about 10 years of age (Johnson, Hannon, & Amso, 2005; Saffran, Werker, & Werner, 2006). To hear a sound clearly, newborns require that sound to be about 15 decibels louder than adults need. (A decibel is a measure of sound intensity. For example, a typical conversation is about 60 decibels, a train about 90 decibels, and conversation in a library about 30 decibels.) At birth, babies are relatively good at localizing the source of a sound, as reflected, for example, by turning their heads toward a sound, and this ability improves markedly by the end of the first year (Johnson, Hannon, & Amso, 2005; Morrongiello et al., 1994).

As with vision, infants enter the world with some auditory biases. For example, infants appear to be more sensitive to high-frequency than to low-frequency tones (Saffran & Griepentrog, 2001; Saffran, Werker, & Werner, 2006), and this might explain their preference for the voices of women (Jusczyk, 1997). As with smell, infants

| **BOX 4-1** | **The Development of Infants' "Specialization" for Processing Faces** |

Although babies seem to have some idea of what a face is shortly after birth and are sensitive to some features of faces, they are not really very good at discriminating among faces. This ability improves between about 3 and 9 months, as infants' skills at processing faces become increasingly specialized (Bhatt et al., 2005). At this time, babies begin to process right-side-up faces more efficiently than upside-down faces, suggesting that faces have "special" status compared to other visual stimuli (de Haan, Olivier, & Johnson, 1998). For instance, 4-month-olds look longer at internal facial features, especially the nose and mouth, when looking at right-side-up versus upside-down faces (Gallay et al., 2006).

As I noted elsewhere in the text, it takes time and experience for this special status for faces to develop. This can be seen in how infants process male versus female faces. For instance, 3- and 4-month-old infants can discriminate more easily between female than male faces, and they generally prefer to look at female faces, with the exception being when the father is an infant's primary caretaker (Quinn et al., 2002). Infants' increasing specialization at making distinctions between the faces of men and women and between different species (for example, monkeys versus humans; see de Haan, et al., 1998) clearly illustrates the importance of experience in processing this most important of social stimuli (Ramsey-Rennels & Langlois, 2006; Turati, 2004).

Infants not only become "specialized" in discriminating among faces of different species and between men and women, they also develop an increasing ability to discriminate between faces of their own race relative to those of other races. This is termed the **other-race effect**. For instance, infants are shown faces from a particular ethnic group until they habituate; later, they are shown photos of people from their own ethnic group and others (for example, Caucasian versus Asian). In studies by David Kelly and his colleagues (2007, 2009) with both British and Chinese infants, 3-month-olds showed no other-race effect. They were equally skilled at recognizing faces from all ethnicities tested (Caucasian, Chinese, and African, a well as Middle Eastern for the British infants). However, by 6 months of age, infants could only recognize faces from their own race plus one other (Chinese and Caucasian), and by 9 months, infants were only able to recognize faces in their own race (Chinese or Caucasian). This phenomenon is not an indication of implicit racism in infancy; rather, it reflects the role of familiarity in shaping infants' perceptual abilities.

Overall, infants' abilities to process faces is initially very general. Early on, they make no distinction among faces from different species, races, or genders, or as a function of the orientation of the face (upright versus upside down). This changes with experience. In the process, infants lose some plasticity—the ability to process all "face" information equally. This pattern of change is similar to that found for infants' abilities to process phonemes, the basic sounds of language. Infants are initially able to discriminate between the phonemes found in all language groups equally well, but they lose this ability as they become more proficient with their mother tongue (see Lewkowicz & Ghazanfar, 2009; Scott, Pascalis, & Nelson, 2007). In general, the consensus among researchers seems to be that there are dedicated and complex areas of the brain for processing faces, and these areas develop as a result of experience over infancy and childhood (Pascalis & Kelly, 2009).

less than 1 week old have been shown to recognize their mothers' voices (DeCasper & Fifer, 1980; Spence & Freeman, 1996). For example, Anthony DeCasper and William Fifer (1980) measured the rate at which 1- to 3-day-old infants sucked on a pacifier. They then conditioned the babies to alter their sucking rate (faster for half of the babies, and slower for the other half) to the tape-recorded voices of their mothers and of an unfamiliar woman. DeCasper and Fifer reported that these young infants varied their sucking rates to hear their mothers' voices, indicating not only that they could discriminate the voices of their mothers from those of other women but that they also acquired a distinct preference for the voices of their mothers in a matter of days.

I noted earlier that infants who heard stories being read to them by their mothers during the last 6 weeks of pregnancy were able to discriminate between that story and another and preferred the one their mother had read to them (DeCasper & Spence, 1986). The findings of DeCasper and his colleagues indicate not only that the auditory system in newborns is working well but also that babies are learning some things about the outside world while still in utero. Moreover, subsequent research following the same design as that of DeCasper and Spence has found changes in heart rate to familiar and novel passages among third-trimester fetuses, unambiguously indicating that learning occurs before birth (DeCasper et al., 1994).

## Speech Perception

One particularly interesting aspect of infant auditory perception is the extent to which it is attuned to language. For example, at birth, babies prefer to listen to language relative to comparably complex nonlanguage sounds. This suggests that infants begin life with a bias for listening to speech, thus giving them a leg up on acquiring language (Vouloumanos & Werker, 2007).

The basic units of speech are called **phonemes,** and evidence indicates that infants come into the world with the ability to perceive most, if not all, of the phonemes found in all human languages (see Aslin, Jusczyk, & Pisoni, 1998; Tsao, Liu, & Kuhl, 2004), suggesting substantial biological preparation for infants to learn language. This phenomenon caused Patricia Kuhl (2007) to describe young infants as "citizens of the world," in that they seem equally ready and able to acquire any of the world's 6000 or so languages.

Like colors, phonemes (such as "ba" and "pa") can be arranged on continua, with gradual changes between them. For example, there is a range of sounds that we hear as "pa" and another range that we hear as "ba." Despite this continuum, we categorize phonemes into distinct groups. For example, we tend to hear either a "pa" sound or a "ba" sound and not some hybrid of the two of them. And most of us agree on the point at which "ba" ends and "pa" begins, just like we agree on the division between orange and red. The gradual changes in phonemes (and in colors) are considered to be physical, and the dichotomies we perceive are considered to be perceptual.

In a classic study, Peter Eimas and his colleagues (1971) presented 1-month-old infants with one physical example of the "ba/pa" continuum until they had decreased the rate at which they sucked on a pacifier (habituation). The researchers then replaced the phoneme with another example along the "ba/pa" continuum. If the infants perceive the new sound as being from the same phonemic category as the previous sound (both "ba," for instance), then they should continue to habituate (that is, decrease their sucking). This is because even though the sound is physically different from the one they heard before, it is just another example of the sound they had just heard repeatedly (that is, just another "ba"). If, however, they recognize this new sound as being from a different phonemic category (a "pa" rather than a "ba," for example), they should increase their sucking rate (dishabituation). Using this technique, Eimas and his colleagues found that very young infants, like their parents and older siblings who already possess language, can categorize phonemes. They hear either "ba" or "pa," and the dividing line they make between the two is the same as older members of their species make.

Other studies have used reinforcement techniques to assess infants' abilities to discriminate among phonemes. For example, G. Cameron Marean, Lynne Werner, and Patricia Kuhl (1992) reinforced 2-, 3-, and 6-month-old infants by the activation of a mechanical toy for turning their heads when they heard a change from one vowel sound to another (either "A" to "I" or vice versa). This technique showed that even 2-month-olds were able to make the discrimination, despite changes in other auditory characteristics (that is, in the voice of the individual speaking).

If infants can discriminate basic phonemes shortly after birth, how is it they acquire the language sounds peculiar to their mother tongue? English-speaking adults have a difficult time discriminating phonetic contrasts that occur in Czech but not in English, for example. Yet, babies from English-speaking homes have little difficulty with these contrasts, suggesting that they were born with the ability (Trehub, 1976). Other studies have similarly shown that infants can make discriminations among speech sounds that are not found in their mother tongues and that their parents cannot make (Kuhl et al., 2006; Saffran et al., 2006). For example, Rebecca Eilers and her colleagues (1979) reported that 6- to 8-month-old infants from English-speaking homes were unable to discriminate some phonetic contrasts that are found in Spanish but not in English. Babies from homes where Spanish was spoken, however, had no trouble with such contrasts. What these and other data suggest is that babies can make some sound discriminations that adult speakers of their language communities cannot make; with time, babies lose the ability to make these contrasts because they rarely hear them.

At the same time that infants are losing their abilities to discriminate among "foreign" phonemes, they are becoming more sensitive to the speech regularities in the language they hear every day. For instance, they are able to make increasingly fine discriminations between the phonemes in their mother tongue (Kuhl et al., 2006). They also become increasingly able to recognize the stress patterns of their language (such as the first syllable of two-syllable words stressed in English, as in "table" and "carpet"), to identify some typical phoneme combinations and syllables that occur more often in their language, and to pay attention to the pauses between words (Aslin, Saffran, & Newport, 1998).

Other research has shown that young infants are able to differentiate sentences uttered in their native language versus those in a foreign language on the basis of vision alone, but as with sound discrimination, they lose this ability over time (Weikum et al., 2007). For instance, 4-, 6-, and 8-month-old infants watched silent video clips of a woman speaking sentences either in the infants' native language (English) or in a foreign language (French). After infants' looking time decreased to the videos (that is, after habituating), some were shown videos of a woman speaking the other language (for instance, French if infants had been habituated to English). The 4- and 6-month-old infants increased their looking time to the new video, indicating that they could tell the difference between sentences spoken in their native versus a nonnative language by vision alone—that is, just by watching the lips of the speaker. However, 8-month-old infants continued to habituate, indicating that they could not discriminate between the two languages on the basis of vision alone. These findings indicate that with experience, infants lose some of their ability to discriminate between languages on the basis of vision alone, much as they lose the ability to discriminate between sounds in nonnative languages. As children become more experienced with their native tongue, they lose some perceptual plasticity, becoming specialists in their own language.

Why should children lose this seemingly valuable ability? The flexibility to learn the sounds (or lip movements) of any possible human language would seemingly provide a great adaptive advantage, but keeping this flexibility beyond a certain age likely was not adaptive in practice. Once our ancestors learned one language, there was likely little need (or opportunity) to become proficient in another. Thus, it makes more sense for the brain to dedicate neurons to processing the sounds it hears early in life. The alternative would give individuals more flexibility, but likely less proficiency in perceiving or producing any one language. Infants exposed to more than one language are an interesting exception to this general rule. For instance, bilingual children are able to discriminate among a broader range of phonemes than monolingual children (see Bosch & Sebastián-Gallés, 2001; MacWhinney, 2005).

Speech perception is more than the ability to detect phonemes, of course. It involves the discrimination of individual words. And perhaps the word that young infants hear most frequently is their own name. Denise Mandel, Peter Jusczyk, and David Pisoni (1995) asked at what age can infants recognize the sound of their own name. They used a reinforcement technique (infants turned their heads to hear a name spoken, either their own or one of three other names) to test this. Infants at 4.5 months of age spent more time listening to their own names than to other names, regardless of whether the other names had the same stress pattern as their own (for example, "Johnny" versus "Abby") or a different stress pattern (for example, "Johnny" versus "Elaine"). These findings indicate that infants are able to recognize frequently heard sound patterns at least by 4.5 months of age.

## Music Perception

Although humans are especially prepared to process language, we also seem to be well prepared to process music. For example, some evidence indicates that young infants can imitate the pitch, loudness, melodic contour, and rhythm of their mothers' songs. Moreover, there are specific types of brain damage that affect musical abilities, suggesting that the ability to perceive and produce music is rooted in evolution and biology (see Gardner, 1983).

Many aspects of music perception appear to be adultlike very early in infancy (see Trehub, 2003, for a review). For example, babies seem to respond to changes in melody, rhythmic pattern, and redundancy much the same way that adults do and to be able to distinguish "good" from "bad" melodies (see Schellenberg & Trehub, 1999; Trehub, Trainor, & Unyk, 1993). Examples of telling the difference between "good" (regular or natural) musical patterns and "bad" (irregular or unnatural) musical patterns are particularly impressive given the diversity of human musical systems. Carol Krumhansl and Peter Jusczyk (1990) demonstrated this by having 4.5- and 6-month-old infants listen to segments of Mozart minuets. Some of the segments had pauses inserted at the end of each musical phrase (natural), whereas other segments had pauses inserted in the middle of phrases (unnatural). Infants learned to control which music they heard—natural or unnatural—by turning their heads in the direction of the speaker playing the music they preferred. Overall, infants spent more time listening to the natural than to the unnatural versions. Of the 6-month-olds, 22 of 24 showed this pattern; of the 4.5-month-olds, 20 of 24 showed this pattern. Other research has found that infants as young as 6 months prefer tones related by simple ratios (what most adults consider to be consonant, or pleasant sounding) over dissonant sounds (as found in atonal music) (Schellenberg & Trehub, 1996; Trainor & Heinmiller, 1998). Other research has shown that by 4 months of age, infants display a preference for the music of their own culture relative to that of another culture (Soley & Hannon, 2010). Given these infants' lack of musical experience, the results of these experiments suggest that music appreciation might not require a college class to attain and, in fact, might be a basic characteristic of the human nervous system.

Other research has shown that infants are prepared to hear more than just Western music; from an early age, they are able to distinguish regular from irregular patterns in culturally different music systems. For example, in one study, infants and adults heard a series of notes based on Western scales and Javanese pelog scales (Lynch et al., 1990). The formal description of these two musical systems is beyond the scope of this book (and my expertise); suffice it to say that the underlying scales differ considerably (to listen to some pelog music, Google "pelog music YouTube"). Adults and 6.5-month-old infants heard well-tuned or out-of-tune patterns of both types of music and were asked to distinguish between the two. The infants, of course, weren't asked to "tell" the difference; an operant-conditioning paradigm was used in which infants were rewarded for turning their heads toward out-of-tune series. The adults, who merely raised their hands for an out-of-tune series, were better able to distinguish between in-tune and out-of-tune patterns in the Western music than in the Javanese music, reflecting the influence of experience on their musical perception. (The adults were American, and all were familiar with the Western but not the Javanese system.) The infants, however, were equally good at distinguishing the out-of-tune series for both the Western and Javanese patterns, "suggesting that infants may be born with an equipotentiality for the perception of scales from a variety of cultures" (Lynch et al., 1990, p. 275). That is, just as children are capable of and biologically prepared for acquiring any human language, they seem also to be prepared for acquiring any system of music.

Numerous hypotheses have been advanced about the evolutionary origins of music, dating back at least to Darwin (1871). One hypothesis is that music played a social function, stemming from early humans' ability to synchronize body movements to an external beat. In support of this idea, Sebastian Kirschner and Michael Tomasello (2009) reported that 2.5-year-old children were better able to synchronize their body movements to a beat in a social situation (a person drumming to create the beat) versus a nonsocial situation (with the drumming done by a machine). Another proposal for the origins of music looks to early mother-infant interaction. The lullabies that mothers around the world sing to their babies are performed in an expressive and highly ritualized manner (see Masataka, 1999; Trainor, 1996) and serve to regulate infants' attention and emotion (see Trehub, 2003). In fact, although infants are highly attentive to infant-directed speech—the sing-songy and expressive style that mothers around the world use when talking to their babies (see Chapter 9)—they are even more attentive to their mothers' singing (Trehub & Nakata, 2001–2002).

# COMBINING SENSES

Although we often think of each sense as being distinct from all others, as adults we do a great deal of coordinating information between senses. We direct our vision to a loud noise, and we can identify our slippers by touch alone when we are awakened in the middle of the night by a barking dog outside our window. In fact, the environment for adults is "intrinsically multimodal" (Bahrick, Lickliter, & Flom, 2004). To what extent is such sensory integration available to infants, and how can we interpret such integration when we observe it?

## Intermodal Integration

**intermodal integration** (or **intersensory integration**) refers to the coordination of information from two or more sensory modalities. At one level, intermodal integration is present at birth. Newborns move their heads and eyes in the direction of a sound, as if they wish to see what all the noise is about. In a series of experiments examining the effects of sound on visual scanning in newborns, Morton Mendelson and Marshall Haith (1976) found that the presence of sound increased infants' visual attentiveness. The researchers suggested that this response to sound increases the likelihood that infants will discover something to look at.

Elizabeth Spelke (1976) provided an interesting demonstration of intermodal integration in young infants. Spelke showed 4-month-old infants two films on side-by-side screens. On one screen was a film of a woman playing peek-a-boo; on the other screen was a hand holding a stick and striking a block of wood. A single sound track was played, corresponding either to the peek-a-boo or the drumming. The babies somehow figured out which sound track went with which screen, devoting more looking time to the screen that matched the sound. That is, these 4-month-old infants realized that certain sound sequences go with certain visual displays, and they visually attended to those displays that provided such a match (see also Bahrick, 2002; Lewkowicz, 1992).

In somewhat related work, Lorraine Bahrick and John Watson (1985) investigated the ability of 5-month-olds to integrate proprioceptive (relating to perception of body movements) and visual information. The babies were seated in infant seats equipped with a type of tray that prevented them from seeing their legs. Two video screens were placed in front of the infants. One screen displayed the infant's own legs; that is, the picture was transmitted live. The other screen displayed a film of the legs of another infant (or in one experiment, the same infant's legs from a session recorded earlier). Thus, for one display (the contingent display), the movement of infants' legs was contemporaneous with their actual movement, whereas for the other display (the noncontingent display), the movement of legs was independent of the infants' current activity. Bahrick and Watson reasoned that if infants are able to integrate proprioception (as reflected by their own leg movements) and vision, they should be able to discriminate between the two films and spend more time looking at one than at the other. This was their finding. In three experiments, 5-month-olds spent, on average, 67% of their time looking at the noncontingent display. Presumably, the lack of contingency between their leg movements and those seen on the video produced some discrepancy, and this resulted in increased attention to the noncontingent display. In a another experiment, Bahrick and Watson tested 3-month-olds and found no overall preference for either the contingent or the noncontingent display. They concluded that proprioceptive-visual integration is well established by 5 months and that the ability to detect the congruency between one's movements and their visual representation plays a fundamental role in an infant's perception of self, possibly underlying the development of visual self-recognition (to be discussed in Chapter 10). Other researchers, using a similar design that varied the spatial orientation of the images that infants saw, report that even 3-month-olds can detect the congruence between their actual leg movements and a video image of those movements (Rochat & Morgan, 1995), suggesting that this might be an early developing ability.

Is intermodal integration present at birth? Although research clearly indicates that intermodal abilities improve with age (see Lewkowicz, 2000, for a review), even newborns are capable of recognizing the equivalence between stimuli in two different modalities (a bright light and loud sound, for instance; Lewkowicz & Turkewitz, 1980). Yet, this does not mean that such abilities are innate, at least not in the way that term is typically used. The developmental systems approach, introduced in Chapter 2, argues that all traits develop as a result of the bidirectional interaction between different levels of organization within the organism and that normal prenatal experiences are crucial in determining species-typical patterns of development. Such arguments have also been made for intermodal integration in infants (Lewkowicz, 2000; Lickliter & Bahrick, 2000). Perceptual experience begins before birth, and the specific experiences a fetus or an embryo receives can alter its development, including the ability to integrate information between senses. For example, I discussed in Chapter 2 research by Robert Lickliter (1990) in which exposure to patterned light before hatching augmented bobwhite quails' subsequent visual abilities but was detrimental to some important auditory skills (identifying their species' call). Although space limitations prevent me from discussing these ideas in any detail, what's important to keep in mind when seemingly advanced abilities are observed in very young infants is that these skills are not preformed and functioning without the benefit of prior experience. Rather, such skills are constructed from the interaction of genes and environment, broadly defined, which begin prenatally and continue throughout life.

## Intermodal Matching

A seemingly more complex intermodal feat concerns **intermodal matching** (or **cross-modal matching**). In intermodal matching, a child must be able to recognize an object initially inspected in one modality (touch, for example) through another modality (vision, for example). Susan Rose and her colleagues (1981) showed that 6-month-old babies can perform visual-tactual integration. The infants were presented an object (either through touch alone or vision alone) for 60 seconds (familiarization phase) and later presented a small set of objects through the alternative mode (transfer phase). The researchers reported that the infants spent more time during the transfer phase exploring the novel objects (by manipulating or gazing at them) than exploring the familiar ones. That is, the babies showed dishabituation by examining the novel stimuli more than the familiar stimuli, even though familiarization was done in a different sensory modality. Other studies using similar methods have demonstrated intermodal matching for 4- to 6-month-old infants (Streri & Spelke, 1989).

In related research, Andrew Meltzoff and Richard Borton (1979) reported visual-tactual integration in infants younger than 1 month. In their study, the infants were familiarized with one of two pacifiers (a sphere or a sphere with knobs, as shown in

FIGURE **4-11**

The shapes used in a cross-modal matching study by Meltzoff and Borton with 1-month-olds to assess tactual matching. One-month-old infants who held one of these two pacifiers in their mouths later looked longer at the pacifier they had sucked on than the one they had not.

Source: "Intermodal Matching by Human Neonates," by A. N. Meltzoff and R. W. Borton, 1979, *Nature, 282,* 403–404. Copyright © 1979 Macmillan Magazines Ltd.

Figure 4-11) and later shown three-dimensional models of the two pacifiers. In two experiments, the infants looked significantly longer at the visual display that corresponded to the pacifier they had orally (but not visually) inspected seconds earlier. The findings of Meltzoff and Borton have been confirmed by some researchers (Gibson & Walker, 1984) but not by others (Maurer, Stager, & Mondlach, 1999), and similar results have been found in 4- to 6-month-old babies (Rose, Gottfried, & Bridger, 1981; Streri & Spelke, 1989).

Substantial research has been done examining infants' developing ability to integrate sound patterns to the face patterns and movements that produce them. For instance, 4- to 5-month-old infants can associate lips movements congruent with the speech they are hearing (Spelke & Cortelyou, 1981) or with the utterance of specific phonemes, like "i" and "a" (Kuhl & Meltzoff, 1982). This early developing ability to associate auditory and visual information becomes more specific with experience. For instance, although 9-month-old infants can interconnect females' voices and faces, they can't reliably associate male voices and faces until about 18 months (Poulin-Dubois et al., 1994). This superiority of matching the voices and faces of females likely results from babies having more experience interacting with women than with men (Ramsey-Rennels & Langlois, 2006).

In Box 4-1, I described earlier that infants' abilities to discriminate between different phonemes in all the world's languages and to differentiate between faces from other races declines with age and experience. Something similar seems to be happening for intermodal perception. For instance, 2-month-old infants will look longer at a human face that corresponds to a sound (for instance, seeing a face saying "ee" and hearing the sound "ee") than at a face that that does not correspond to a sound (for instance, a face saying "ee" and the sound "ah"), and this ability improves with age

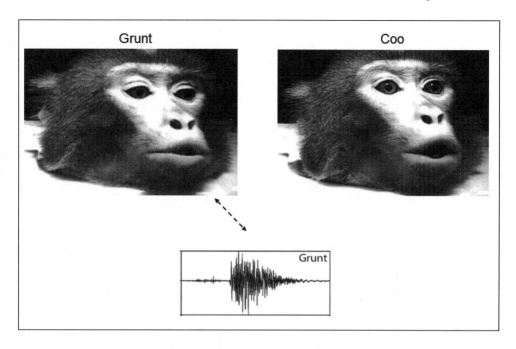

PHOTO **4-2**

The face of a monkey making a grunt sound (*A*) and making a coo (*B*). Both 4- and 6-month-old infants looked longer at the face making the sound, but older infants did not.

Source: Lewkowicz, D. J., & Ghazanfar, A. A. (2006). The decline of cross-species intersensory perception in human infants. *Proceedings of the National Academy of Sciences, 103,* 6771–6774.

(Kuhl & Meltzoff, 1982; Patterson & Werker, 2003). How general is this ability, and do children always get better at it with age? In one study, 4-, 6-, 8-, and 10-month-old infants watched the face of a monkey as it made one of two sounds, a coo or a grunt (see Photo 4-2, from Lewkowicz & Ghazanfar, 2006). Sometimes the infants heard a sound that corresponded with the face (for example, the coo face with the coo sound), and other times the sound and the face were mismatched (for example, the coo face with the grunt sound). The 4- and 6-month-old infants looked significantly longer at the faces that matched the sounds, but the 8- and 10-month-old infants did not. A later study found that even newborns looked significantly longer at the faces that matched the sounds (Lewkowicz, Leo, & Simion, 2010). Much like unimodal perception of language sounds, intermodal perception also shows a loss, or narrowing, of ability with age and experience. What begins as a general ability to match sounds and faces becomes specialized to the types of faces (humans) and sounds (native language) that one hears (for similar results see Pons et al., 2009; Weikum et al., 2007).

## The Intersensory Redundancy Hypothesis

Some stimuli provide redundant information from multiple senses. For example, looking at a face while the person is talking provides both visual (the moving mouth) and auditory (the sound coming out of the mouth) information about the same event. This is the case for many stimuli. Clapping hands and a bouncing ball, for instance, each provide both visual and corresponding auditory information. The information is redundant because the two sources occur simultaneously (for example, the ball hits the floor and simultaneously makes a noise). Some theorists have proposed that infants' exposure to repeated sources of intersensory redundant information (lots of talking faces or bouncing balls) causes them to explore *amodal* properties of those stimuli—that is, properties that are not specific to one modality (vision or audition) but cut across modalities, like, for example, rhythm, temporal synchrony, tempo, and changing intensity (Bahrick & Lickliter, 2002; Bahrick, Lickliter, & Flom, 2004). In contrast, exposure to information in a single modality (for instance, viewing a face or a bouncing ball without sound) causes infants to be attentive to modality-specific features (such as color, size, or shape). In support of this **intersensory redundancy hypothesis**, 3-month-old infants in one study were able to discriminate between various tempos (the speed, or pace) that a toy hammer struck a wooden platform when they received multimodal information (watching *and* listening to the toy hammer while moving) but not when they only received unimodal information (only watching or only hearing the toy hammer strike the platform) (see Bahrick et al., 2004).

Lorraine Bahrick and her colleagues (2004) proposed that infants are prone to amodal information processing because it provides a sense of unity to the items and events they perceive, particularly when compared with modality-specific information (that is, vision only or audition only). This would also help them to ignore the irrelevant information in their immediate environment. In this way, intersensory redundancy would be critical for infants' perceptual development and, furthermore, would guide infants' development of selective attention and cognition (see Chapter 7).

# HOW DO WE KNOW WHAT BABIES KNOW? THE VIOLATION-OF-EXPECTATION METHOD

Despite how much we have learned about infant perceptual development, we need to be cautious and not attribute too much "intelligence" to babies based on sucking rate or looking time (Haith, 1993; Hood, 2004). For instance, we should not view an infant's perceptual skills as fully developed the first time we see them. Like most aspects of development, perceptual development is context dependent, and an infant's response can vary substantially from one time or situation to the next. This becomes even more important when we go beyond perception and examine infant *cognitive* development.

As I mentioned earlier in this chapter, it is not always easy to tell when perception ends and cognition begins. Many of the feats I described in the previous sections on perception, such as discriminating between different faces, can be quite complex and perhaps better deserve the label "cognition" than "perception." In this section, I look at what many consider to be some lower-level cognitive abilities, including infants' understanding of objects, understanding of quantities, and abilities to form categories. Other "higher-level" forms of infant cognition, such as understanding social relations, memory, and problem solving, will be discussed in later chapters. Before examining specific aspects of infant cognition, however, I first look at the most frequently used method for assessing aspects of young infants' cognition—the **violation-of-expectation method**.

In the violation-of-expectation method, an infant's reaction to an unexpected event is used to infer what he or she knows. This method uses infants' looking behavior, much as in the preference-for-novelty and habituation/dishabituation procedures, to assess infants' reaction to unexpected events. The logic is simple: If infants see an event that deviates from what they expect—in other words, that violates their expectation—they should look longer at that event than at an "expected" event.

Let me provide an example from a study by Andréa Aguiar and Renée Baillargeon (1999) on the development of infants' understanding of objects. In this study, 2.5-month-old infants watched as a toy mouse disappeared behind one screen on the right side of a display and then reappeared seconds later from behind another screen on the left side of the display without appearing in the gap between the two screens (Aguiar & Baillargeon, 1999; see Figure 4-12). Infants looked longer at the magically appearing mouse than at the "expected" event (the mouse traveling through the gap between the two screens), suggesting that they were puzzled about how the mouse could have made the trip from one side of the display to the other without passing through the middle. As you can see, the violation-of-expectation method does more than simply inform researchers that infants "can tell the difference between two stimuli," and variants of this method have been frequently used to provide insights into the infant mind (see Aslin, 2007; Baillargeon, 2008; and discussion later in this chapter).

As I warned for measures of infant perception, we must be cautious and not attribute too much in the way of sophisticated cognition based on how long infants look at one event versus another. But when the looking behavior of groups of infants systematically varies between "expected" and "unexpected" events, a researcher can be confident that "something is going on" in the minds of babies to produce such reliable results. It's the job of the psychologist to determine what exactly that "something" is.

## CORE KNOWLEDGE

Infants are obviously not born as blank slates—beings with no biases and simply waiting for experience to mold their minds. As we saw in the previous sections, babies enter the world, or develop shortly thereafter, with things they are biased to look at and

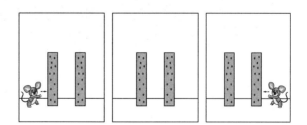

FIGURE **4-12**

An example of an "impossible" occlusion event. A toy mouse disappears behind a first screen and appears later behind a second screen, without appearing in the gap between them. Infants as young as 2.5 months of age seem to realize that objects cannot disappear at one point and then magically appear at another.

Source: Adapted from R. Baillargeon, 2004, Infants' physical world. *Current Directions in Psychological Science, 13* (3), 89–94; pg. 90.

TABLE **4-1**

According to the core-knowledge systems perspective, human infants are endowed with at least three core knowledge systems to represent and make inferences about relevant aspects of their surrounding environment. (Adapted from information in Spelke, E. S., & Kinzler, K. D. (2007). Core knowledge. *Developmental Science, 10,* 89–96.)

Core knowledge system 1: Inanimate objects and their mechanical interactions

1) *Cohesion* (objects have boundaries and their components are connected each other)
2) *Continuity* (objects move along unobstructed paths and cannot be in the same place)
3) *Contact* (one object must contact another to make it move)
4) *Number limitation* (infants cannot represent more than about 3 objects at a time)

Core knowledge system 2: Persons and their actions

1) *Goal-directness* (intentional human actions are directed to goals)
2) *Efficiency* (goals are achieved through the use of effective means)
3) *Contingency* (means are not applied rigidly but adjusted to the conditions found)
4) *Reciprocity* (such as: "turn taking" in conversation)
5) *Gaze direction* (the direction of a gaze is used to interpret social and non-social actions)

Core knowledge system 3: Number representation

1) *Abstractness* (number representations are abstract: they apply to different entities or things, from different sensory modalities: for example, sets of objects or set of sounds)
2) *Comparability and combinability* (number representations are comparable and can be combined by addition and subtraction operations)

listen to, and they are better at processing some types of information (faces, for instance) than others. Elizabeth Spelke and her colleagues (Spelke, 1991, 2000; Spelke & Kinzler, 2007), among others (for example, Baillargeon, 2008; Gelman & Williams, 1998), argue that babies possess **core knowledge** about several different domains from birth. They argue that infants are born with a small set of distinct systems of knowledge that have been shaped by natural selection over evolutionary time and upon which new and flexible skills and belief systems (such reading, arithmetic, navigating by maps, reasoning about other peoples' thoughts) are later built.

Spelke and her colleagues argue that strong evidence indicates the existence of at least three core-knowledge systems in infancy (see Table 4-1): (1) object representation, (2) knowledge of people and their actions, and (3) an ability to represent numbers, or quantities. David Geary (2005, 2007) has made a similar proposal, arguing that infants are born with a small set of *skeletal competencies* specialized to process information relating to the physical world (*folk physics*), the biological world (*folk biology*), and people (*folk psychology*). (Recall our discussion of Geary's theory in Chapter 2.) These skeletal abilities become fleshed out with time and experience, allowing children to deal effectively with a wide range of objects, events, and relationships as they develop. Infants thus enter the world prepared to learn and understand some things better than others, but such biases are modified, in a species-typical way, as a result of experience.

Core-knowledge systems are inferred not only by evidence from experiments with infants but also from research with nonhuman animals and with people from traditional cultures. For example, in some cases, evidence suggests that humans share some of these abilities, such as aspects of object representation (see Dore & Dumas, 1987), basic arithmetic abilities (see discussion later in this chapter), and understanding of so-cial partners (see Chapters 6 and 10), with other animals, although some abilities, such as shared attention (for example, mother and infant sharing information and attention about a third object) may be unique to *Homo sapiens* (Tomasello, 2000; see Chapter 6). Finding commonalities of early developing abilities with other species, especially those closely related to humans, is central to a core-knowledge perspective, based on the idea that each system has a phylogenetic history, with at least hints of these abilities being found in our genetic relatives and, presumably, our common ancestors.

In this chapter, I examine some research motivated by the core-knowledge approach with respect to object representation and understanding of numbers. Research looking at infant and children's folk psychology will be explored in Chapters 6 and 10.

## Object Representation

A basic question in infant spatial cognition concerns what they know about the nature of objects—for example, the extent to which they understand that physical objects follow the basic Newtonian laws of physics. (Must everything that goes up eventually come down?) Infants have to recognize at least three features related to objects: (1) *object constancy*, (2) *object continuity and cohesion*, and (3) *object permanence*. Object constancy refers to the fact that an object does not change size or shape depending on how one views it. It may *look* different from a different angle, but it's still the same size and shape. Object continuity and cohesion refers to the fact that individual objects are seen as cohesive wholes with distinct boundaries. Object permanence refers to the fact that objects are permanent in time and space, whether we are perceiving them or not (that is, objects continue to exist even if they are out of our sight). In the following sections, I discuss the development of each of these aspects of object representation.

### Object Constancy

Perhaps the most basic form of spatial cognition concerns infants' understanding of the constancy of physical objects in time and space. **Object constancy** refers to the knowledge that an object remains the same despite changes in how it is viewed. Consider a table, for instance. When we see the table at a certain distance, it makes a specific impression on the retinas of our eyes. As we move away from the table, that image on the back of our eyes gets smaller, but we continue to perceive the table as maintaining a constant size and shape. We don't act as if the table is chang-ing before our eyes; although the literal sensation changes, we maintain a type of perceptual constancy in our minds.

This would seem to be a very basic form of spatial cognition, and in fact, it is possessed, to varying degrees, even by newborns. Imagine, for example, that new-borns are habituated to an object of a particular size and then shown one of two new objects: the same object, but as seen from a different distance, and a new object of a different size, but presented so that the retinal image it projects is the same as the retinal image projected by the original habituated object (see Figure 4-13). If in-fants possess size constancy, they should continue to habituate to the same object/different distance, even though the actual retinal image is different. If they do *not* possess size constancy, however, they should dishabituate to the same object at a dif-ferent distance and habituate to the new object that produces the same retinal image. In one such study (Slater, Mattock, & Brown, 1990), newborns show the former pattern, displaying a degree of size and shape constancy that, although not quite

### FIGURE **4-13**

Size constancy experiment. After becoming accustomed to looking at a small cube at different distances (habituation to changes in retinal image), infants are presented a second, larger but more distant cube (same retinal image for both cubes). If infants pay more attention to the larger than to the smaller cube, researchers conclude that they are distinguishing the cubes on the basis of their actual, not their retinal, size. That is, infants are demonstrating size constancy.

Source: Adapted from Slater, A. M., Mattock, A., Brown, E., & Bremner, G. J. (1991). Form perception at birth: Cohen and Younger (1984) revisited. *Journal of Experimental Child Psychology, 51*, 395–406.

adultlike, indicates that human infants are well-prepared at birth for making sense of physical objects.

Despite this precocious ability, older children sometimes reveal what appears to be a surprising ignorance of size and shape constancy. For example, I recall sitting with 4-year-old Brendan, looking at planes flying overhead. "How do they get so small?" he asked. "Huh?" was probably my response, and he went on to wonder how big planes like he sees at the airport can get so tiny when they go up in the air. He seemed not to have realized that the plane stays the same size despite the vastly changing retinal image it projects as it soars away. Brendan is not unique in his confusion, for I have heard other people describe their children's mystification of the "amazing shrinking abilities" of airplanes. ("When do we get small?" asked one preschool child of her mother on her first airplane trip. This child figured out that if the plane gets smaller, then so, too, must the people inside it.) What we seem to have here is a discrepancy between the implicit knowledge of the infant, assessed by looking-time or operant-conditioning procedures, and the explicit, verbalizable knowledge of the older child. Granted, in most of children's everyday experiences, they behave as if objects maintain their size and shape despite changes in retinal image. Yet, for extraordinary events—extraordinary in that they were unlikely to be experienced by our ancestors hundreds of thousands or even millions of years ago, such as large, rapidly moving, flying objects—the appearance of a change in size seemingly overpowers children's intuitive knowledge of object constancy, reflecting a disconnect between what they know implicitly (without conscious awareness) and what they know explicitly (with conscious awareness).

### *Object Continuity and Cohesion*

Another form of basic spatial cognition in infancy concerns the Gestalt concept of continuation. As mentioned earlier, **object continuity and cohesion** refers to the fact that individual objects are seen as cohesive wholes with distinct boundaries. For example, Figure 4-14 shows a solid rectangle with two bars extending from its top and bottom. Adults infer that the rectangle is occluding a solid bar, although no solid bar is actually seen. Will infants make the same inference? How can one tell? One way is by repeatedly showing infants the stimulus until their attention to it decreases (habituation) and then showing them a picture of a solid bar in the same orientation as the partial bars in the original stimulus. If the infants increase their attention to this stimulus, they would be treating it as if it were novel, indicating that they had *not* inferred the two partial bars in the original stimulus were connected. If, however, when shown the solid bar they show little interest in it (that is, they continue to habituate), they would be treating it like an "old" stimulus, one they've gotten tired of looking at. But it is not literally the "same old thing." It is a different physical stimulus. If they treat it like an "old" stimulus, it would be because they have inferred that the rectangle in the original stimulus was occluding a solid bar.

When doing experiments like this, how do babies respond? Infants at 4 months of age treat the solid bar as if it were an old stimulus (that is, they continue to habituate), but only for moving stimuli (as shown in by the arrows in Figure 4-14), not for stationary stimuli (Johnson & Aslin, 1996; Kellman & Spelke, 1983). Elizabeth Spelke (1985) speculated that this is an indication that infants are born with the notion of the persistence, coherence, and unity of objects. They "know," at some level, that objects are continuous in space. However, more recent research indicates that 2-month-old (Johnson & Aslin, 1995) and 4-month-old (Eizenman & Bertenthal, 1998) infants will show evidence of inferring object unity in some, but not in other,

### FIGURE **4-14**

Example of the Gestalt concept of continuation. An important acquisition in visual perception is identifying objects that appear connected, or together, visually as independent objects. A widely used stimulus has been this rectangle with two broken rods. Typically, adults infer that the rectangle covers a solid bar behind it. Four-month-old infants (and even 2-month-old infants, in some cases) infer the same, but only if both rods exhibit a continuous same speed movement.

situations and that newborns *increase* their attention to the solid bar (Slater et al., 1990), suggesting that babies are likely *not* born with this knowledge.

Spelke and her colleagues have conducted other studies consistent with the interpretation that infants as young as 2.5 months of age have a knowledge of the solidity and continuity of objects (the fact that a moving object continues on its path) (see Spelke & Kinzler, 2007). More recently, Renée Baillargeon and her colleagues have investigated young infants' understanding of support (an object must be supported or it falls) (Baillargeon, Kotovsky, & Needham, 1995) collisions (an object that is hit by another object moves) (Baillargeon et al., 1995), and containment (a larger object cannot fit into a smaller object) (Aguiar & Baillargeon, 1998).

I discussed infants' understanding that objects must travel through space to get from point A to point B earlier in this chapter when describing the violation-of-expectation method. As you may recall, infants as young as 2.5 months of age looked longer at an event in which an object somehow moved behind one barrier and appeared seconds later from another without traversing the area in-between (Aguiar & Baillargeon, 1999). The concept of "collision" seems to develop at about the same time. For example, 2.5-month-old infants increased their looking time when a toy bug on wheels remained stationary after being hit by a cylinder rolling down a ramp or, conversely, when the bug moved in the absence of contact (Kotovsky & Baillargeon, 1994, 2000; Wang, Kaufman, & Baillargeon, 2003). Based on looking time, young infants behave as if they understand that objects are solid and move only when contacted by some outside force.

Another interesting expectation of infants' is that objects require support—that an object cannot remain suspended in midair or it will fall—and this, too, develops gradually over infancy. Baillargeon and her colleagues (1995) showed infants possible and impossible events reflecting the notion of support (see Figure 4-15). A gloved hand would push a box that sat atop a platform from left to right. In the possible event, the box stopped while firmly situated on the platform. In the impossible event, the box was pushed until only 15% of it rested on the platform. How did babies react to the impossible event? If they understand that objects need to be supported lest they fall, they should show "surprise" and increased looking time when observing the impossible event. The youngest infants (3-month-olds) weren't surprised. As long as the box maintained some contact with the platform, they acted as if they expected it to remain on the platform and not fall. Beginning about 4.5 months of age, the amount of contact between the box and the platform became important, and by 6.5 months, infants expected that the box will fall unless a significant portion of it was in contact with the platform.

Other studies indicate that infants' understanding of object cohesion and continuity continues to develop over the first year. For example, Figure 4-16 (p. 136) presents three ways in which Baillargeon and her colleagues have tested infants' understanding of the role of height in object continuity. The first is in an occlusion experiment. A tall object is placed behind and, thus is occluded by a shorter object, as shown in the top row of Figure 4-16. This is impossible, of course, and 4.5-month-old infants act surprised when this happens (Baillargeon & DeVos, 1991). Now consider nearly the same situation, but instead of the taller object being placed *behind* the shorter object, it is placed *within* it, a containment event, as shown in the second row of Figure 4-16. Now infants do not show surprise until about 7.5 months (Hespos & Baillargeon,

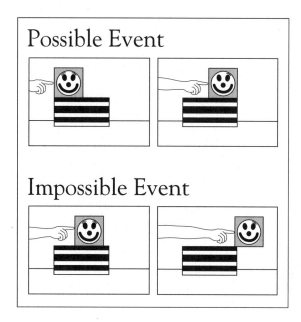

**FIGURE 4-15**

Example of possible and impossible events for object support. Although 3-month-old infants were not surprised by the impossible event, by 4.5 months of age infants begin to understand that the *amount* of contact between the box and the platform is important.

Source: Baillargeon, R. (1994). How do infants learn about the physical world? *Current Directions in Psychological Science, 3*, 133–140. Reprinted with permission.

2001), and it is not until 12 months that they show surprise when a shorter object covers a taller object (Wang et al., 2005), as seen in the bottom row of Figure 4-16. This pattern reflects what Piaget referred to as *horizontal décalage* (see Chapter 5), in which an ability—in this case understanding the physical relationship between short and tall objects—develops at different rates in different contexts.

As we have seen, young infants' knowledge of objects seems to be dominated by an expectation that inanimate objects behave in continuous (in the sense of being permanent and solid entities) and cohesive (as a bounded whole) ways, that contact is necessary for an inanimate object to move, and that objects must be supported or they will fall. Some of these expectations seem to develop earlier than others, and the range of contexts in which infants will show this knowledge increases with age and experience. Baillargeon (2008) proposed that infants possess an innate idea she called the **principle of persistence,** defined as "objects not only exist continuously and remain cohesive, they also retain their individual properties. According to this principle, no object can undergo a spontaneous or uncaused change in the course of an event" (p. 3). The principles of continuity and cohesion would be derivations of this more general principle. This does not mean that experience is unnecessary, however. According to Baillargeon and her colleagues, when infants watch a physical event for the first time, their representation of it is initially impoverished, so that they may be attentive to only some violations of persistence (for example, an object cannot

**FIGURE 4-16**

Three different ways of assessing infants' understanding of the role of height in object continuity.

Source: Baillargeon, R. (2008). Innate ideas revisited: For a principle of persistence in infants' physical reasoning. *Perspectives on Psychological Science, 3,* 2–13.

disappear at one location and appear at another without traversing the area in between) but not to others (for example, the height or color of the objects). With increasing experience, their representations become enriched, and infants will demonstrate sensitivity to a broader range of violations of persistence (for example, they will notice when the color or height of an object has unexpectedly changed). However, infants can develop a sensitivity to these "secondary" characteristics of objects (for example, their color, height, shape) earlier under certain task conditions, such as when their attention is deliberately drawn to these features (Wilcox & Chapa, 2004).

There is an interesting aside to the work demonstrating infant's often-substantial knowledge of support and solidity. Recall my comments about the discrepancy between infants' (even newborns') appreciation of object constancy and that of the preschooler ("How does the plane get so small?"). This discrepancy is also found for an understanding of support and solidity. For example, in search tasks, in which children must find an object hidden in one of several locations, 2-year-olds generally fail to display knowledge of these concepts, unlike their younger, 6-month-old counterparts (Berthier et al., 2000; Hood, Carey, & Prasada, 2000). For example, Bruce Hood and his colleagues (2000) showed groups of 2- and 2.5-year-old children a ball being dropped onto a stage behind a screen. The screen was removed to reveal the ball resting on the floor of the stage (Experiment 1). After the children witnessed this event three times, the experimenter placed a cup on the floor of the stage, a shelf over the

Familiarize x 3                    Introduce Shelf + Cups, Then Search

## FIGURE **4-17**

The apparatus used in study by Hood et al. with 2- and 2.5-year-old children. Children watched as a ball was dropped behind the screen and saw that it rested on the floor. A shelf and two cups were then added to the stage, and the ball was dropped again behind the screen. Children were then asked to retrieve the ball.

Source: Hood, B., Carey, S., & Prasada, S. (2000). Predicting the outcomes of physical events: Two-year-olds fail to reveal knowledge of solidity and support. *Child Development, 71*, 1540–1554. Adapted with permission of the Society for Research in Child Development.

cup, and then a second cup on that shelf. This is illustrated in Figure 4-17. The screen was then replaced, and the ball was dropped behind the screen again. The children then saw the two cups, one on the shelf and one on the stage floor, and were asked to retrieve the ball. If they possessed a sense of solidity, as 6-month-old infants presumably do on the basis of looking-time procedures, they should search in the upper cup. However, if their sense of solidity is not fully developed, they should be just as likely to search in the cup on the floor of the stage, particularly since that is where they had successfully retrieved the ball three times before. Hood and his colleagues (2000) reported that only 40% of the 2-year-olds searched in the upper cup, whereas this percentage rose to 93% for the 2.5-year-olds.

This perplexing result, suggestive that infants have a more sophisticated understanding of spatial relations than 2-year-olds, likely is caused by the very different nature of the tasks (Keen, 2003). Older children must demonstrate an explicit (that is, conscious) understanding of solidity and support in the search tasks, whereas the looking-time tasks used with infants require only implicit (that is, out of conscious awareness) knowledge. As such, postulating that infants who look longer at an "impossible" than at a "possible" event have the same type of knowledge as older children have for the phenomenon under question (here, support) is likely unwarranted. What young infants appear to posses, or to develop early, is implicit knowledge, which likely cannot be used as flexibly as explicit knowledge can.

### *Object Permanence*

If a tree falls in the middle of the forest and no one is there to hear it, is there any noise? Young infants (presuming, of course, that they could communicate their response to us) would answer this perennial philosophical question very easily. Their answer would be no, for there can be no noise unless someone is there to perceive it. But the young infant would go on to say that there is also no tree and no forest. Nothing exists unless it is directly perceived or, more precisely, unless it is personally perceived by them.

This hypothetical philosophical discussion illustrates the concept of **object permanence** or, more appropriately, the lack of object permanence. For infants who lack object permanence, out of sight is literally out of mind. Object permanence is obviously a cognitive skill necessary for normal intellectual functioning in all human cultures. The concept of object permanence was introduced by Jean Piaget (1954), and in this section, I first describe Piaget's account of object permanence. I then examine newer research, some of which challenges the interpretation, if not the findings, of Piaget.

**Piaget's account of object permanence.** Piaget believed that between birth and 4 months, infants understood objects only as extensions of their own actions. Objects have no reality for babies independent of their perceptions or actions upon them. For example, a 2- or 3-month-old follows his mother with his eyes, but when she leaves his visual field, he continues to gaze at the point where he lost sight of her, not anticipating her reappearance at another location. Piaget saw the first semblance of object permanence at about 4 months. At this age, infants now attempt to retrieve an object that "disappears," but only if the object is still partially visible. For example, babies at this stage fetch a toy that has been partially covered by a cloth, apparently realizing that the entire toy exists under the cloth even though they can see only a portion of it. They do not search, however, for a toy that is completely hidden, even if the hiding occurred right before their eyes. (An exception to this behavior seems to be that late in this substage, infants search for a completely hidden object if they are moving in that direction when the object is hidden. So, for example, a 6-month-old infant playing with a favorite toy does not attempt to retrieve that toy when her father places it under a blanket while she is watching. She does retrieve it, however, if she is reaching for the toy in front of her as Dad places the blanket over it.) Beginning at about 8 months, infants can retrieve a completely hidden object. However, object permanence is not yet complete, for if an object is hidden in one location and then later moved to a second, all while the child is watching, the infant searches at the first location and often acts quite surprised not to find the desired object. This is the **A-not-B object-permanence task**, which I discussed briefly in Chapter 2.

Let me provide a real-life example of the A-not-B object-permanence task. At approximately 10 months, my daughter Heidi was seated in her high chair, having just completed lunch. She was banging her spoon on the tray of the chair when it fell to the floor to her right. She leaned to the right, saw the spoon on the floor, and vocalized to me; I retrieved it for her. She began playing with the spoon again, and it fell to the right a second time. She again leaned to the right, saw the spoon on the floor, and vocalized until I returned it to her. Again, she played with the spoon, and again, it fell to the floor, but this time to her left. After hearing the clang of the spoon hitting the floor, Heidi leaned to the right to search for the spoon, and she continued her search for several seconds before looking at me with a puzzled expression. Heidi had been watching the spoon at the time it fell. Thus, when it fell the third time, she had both visual and auditory cues to tell her where it must be. But she searched where she had found the vanished object before. She trusted her past experience with the fallen spoon more than her perceptions. At this age, children still understand objects by their actions on them, in these cases, by their prior actions.

Beginning around 12 months, infants can solve problems like the one just described. What they cannot yet do, however, is solve what Piaget called *invisible displacements*. In invisible displacements, an object is hidden in one container and then hidden under another container out of the vision of the observer. An example from Piaget (1954) will help clarify this task:

> Jacqueline is sitting on a green rug playing with a potato which interests her very much (it is a new object for her). She says "po-terre" [pomme de terre] and amuses herself by putting it into an empty box and taking it out again.... I then take the potato and put it in the box while Jacqueline watches. Then I place the box under the rug and turn it upside down, thus leaving the object hidden by the rug without letting the child see my maneuver, and I bring out the empty box. I say to Jacqueline, who has not stopped looking at the rug and who has realized that I was doing something under it: "Give papa the potato." She searches for the object in the box, looks at me, again looks at the box minutely, looks at the rug, etc., but it does not occur to her to raise the rug in order to find the potato underneath. During the five subsequent attempts the reaction is uniformly negative.... Each time Jacqueline looks in the box, then looks at everything around her including the rug, but does not search under it. (p. 68)

To solve invisible displacement problems, according to Piaget, children must be able to mentally represent objects, something that is not found, according to Piaget, until about 18 months.

Piaget's basic observations of the development of object permanence have been replicated in both large- and small-scales studies, using variants of the procedures he described (Kopp, Sigman, & Parmelee, 1974; Marcovitch & Zelazo, 1999; Uzgiris & Hunt, 1975). However, researchers using some of the new techniques developed to study infant cognition believe that babies possess knowledge of the permanency of objects at earlier ages than Piaget proposed.

**A new look at object permanence.** Evidence of object permanence in very young infants is probably best exemplified by Baillargeon's work (Baillargeon, 1987; Baillargeon & De Vos, 1991) using the violation-of-expectation method, much as was done in her work on understanding support. In Baillargeon's experiment (1987), infants 3.5 and 4.5 months of age were habituated to a moving screen (see Figure 4-18). The screen was rotated 180 degrees, starting from being flat in a box with its leading edge facing the infant and rising continuously through an arc until it rested in the box with its leading edge farthest away from the infant. Once habituated to this event, infants in the experimental group were shown a colorful wooden block with a clown face painted on it, placed to the rear of the flat screen. In the "impossible event" condition, the screen was rotated upward (exactly as in the habituation trials), which in the process obscured the wooden block from the infant's sight. When the screen reached 90 degrees, the wooden block was removed, out of the view of the infant. The screen then continued its downward rotation until it lay flat. After this, the screen was rotated upward again, and the wooden block was replaced, again unbeknownst to the infant, so that it reappeared once more when the screen was being rotated toward the infant. From the infant's perspective, such a series of events (the continuous movement of the screen, despite the presence of an obstacle) should be impossible and violate the infant's expectation of what should happen. If the wooden object were real in space and time, the screen should have stopped when it reached it. This, in fact, is what infants did see on some trials (the "possible event"), with the screen stopping at the point where it should have, given that there was an object on the other side. If the infants believed that the wooden block continued to exist, they should have shown surprise or increased looking

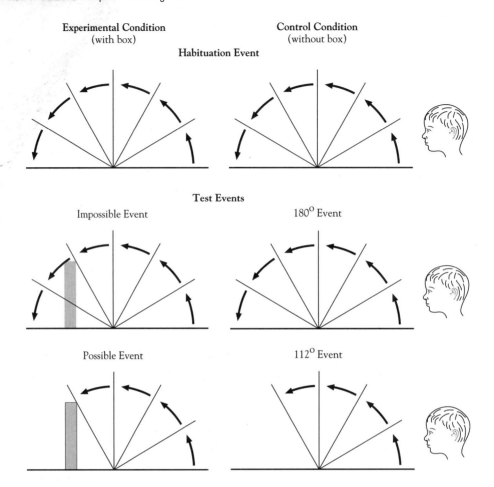

## FIGURE **4-18**

The habituation and test (dishabituation) events shown to infants in the experimental and control conditions in the object-permanence experiment by Baillargeon.

Source: From "Object Permanence in 3½- and 4½-month-old infants," by R. Baillargeon, 1987, *Developmental Psychology*, *23*, 655–664. Copyright © 1987 American Psychological Association. Reprinted with permission.

time at the "impossible event" relative to the "possible event." Infants in the control condition saw the same sequence of screen movements but were never shown the wooden block. Thus, these infants had no reason to express surprise. Infants in all conditions received four test trials.

The results of this experiment for the 4.5-month-old infants are graphed in Figure 4-19. As you can see, the infants in the experimental condition looked significantly longer at the "impossible event" than at the "possible event." For the experimental infants, there was apparently nothing surprising about the "possible event," but they knew that something was amiss when the screen failed to stop. No differences in looking time were found for the infants in the control condition. Similar findings were reported for 3.5-month-old infants (see Experiments 2 and 3 in Baillargeon, 1987; Baillargeon & De Vos, 1991). Other studies using this (Baillargeon & De Vos, 1991)

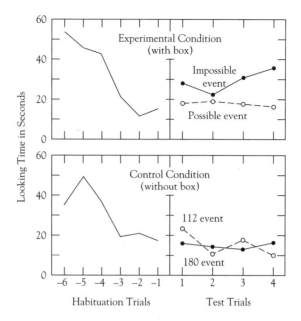

FIGURE **4-19**

Looking times of infants in the experimental and control conditions during habituation and test trials in Baillargeon's experiment. Note the increased looking time for the infants in the experimental condition during the test trials for the impossible event.

Source: "Object Permanence in 3½- and 4½-month-old infants," by R. Baillargeon, 1987, *Developmental Psychology*, *23*, 655–664. Copyright © 1987 American Psychological Association. Reprinted with permission.

and similar (Baillargeon, 2004) methods have produced similar results. This does not necessarily mean that Piaget was wrong, but that infants' understanding of the permanence of objects varies with the type of task used to assess it.

The most straightforward interpretation of these results is that the infants believed the block continued to exist even though it was out of their sight and were surprised when the screen failed to stop. Their performance in the "impossible event" condition reflects not only a knowledge of the permanence of objects but also a knowledge that one solid object cannot pass through another (see the earlier discussion of solidity).

Other research using looking-time measures has shown that 5-month-olds code the spatial location of hidden objects. In a study by Nora Newcombe and her colleagues (1999), for instance, babies watched as an object was buried in a sandbox. After a 10-second delay, the object was dug out. This was repeated four times. On the fifth occasion, instead of digging up the object at the location where it had been hidden, the experimenter dug out the object from a different location (as near as 6 inches from where the first had been hidden). Babies looked significantly longer at these "trick" trials than at the previous trials, suggesting that they had coded the specific location of the objects. During a final experiment in this same study, infants were not surprised (that is, did not look longer) when a *different object* was retrieved from the sand. This finding suggests that spatiotemporal characteristics may play a central role in defining objects to young infants, with shape and color being unimportant.

One very interesting aspect of the findings of this study by Newcombe and her colleagues is that toddlers usually fail an analogous hiding task. In this task, toddlers watch as an object is hidden in a sandbox, then move to the opposite end of the box and are asked to retrieve the object. Not until 21 months of age can children solve this problem reliably (Newcombe et al., 1998), calling into question what, exactly, are the skills involved in solving these simple spatial tasks (Newcombe, 2002). Maybe the act of moving around the sandbox makes the task too demanding of children's limited mental resources or disrupts their memory, accounting for the discrepancy. It is also possible that the difference between the implicit and explicit natures of the two tasks is responsible for the different findings. Children may possess an understanding of spatial relations at first only implicitly (Bremner & Mareschal, 2004; Karmiloff-Smith, 1992; Newcombe, 2002), with explicit understanding, as reflected by an overt search task, being displayed only later in development. Recall that a similar interpretation was made for differences between infants and 2-year-olds' understanding of support (Hood, et al., 2000). That is, the violation-of-expectation method assesses perceptual knowledge, whereas the reaching task assesses self-aware thought, the ability to combine an old habit (finding the object) with a new cognitive update (looking under something). This is not to say that one method is better than the other, but that the meaning of "infants possess object permanence" may differ depending on how object permanence is measured.

Other research has questioned Piaget's results for the A-not-B task. As you may recall from Chapter 2, infants as young as 7.5 months of age will sometimes reach correctly on the B trials if the delay between hiding the object and searching for it is very brief (Diamond, 1985). As the delay increases, infants are more likely to look where the toy was previously hidden (that is, at the A location). This has caused some people to propose that memory or inhibition is involved in solving this task. It is not so much that infants fail to understand that objects have permanence in time and space, but that they forget the object's location or do not have the neurological maturation to inhibit a previously practiced behavior (reaching to the correct A location) (Diamond, 1991).

Even when using Piaget's reaching paradigm, differences in infants' tendencies to successfully retrieve a hidden object are affected by some simple task variables, such as the number of times infants retrieve the object at the A location before it is switched to the B location in the A-not-B task (Marcovitch, Zelazo, & Schmuckler, 2002), or the familiarity of the objects being hidden. For example, in one study, 7.5-month-old infants were tested in the classic Piagetian object permanence tasks (retrieve an object hidden under a cloth) either for familiarized items (clay objects they had seen and reached for many times) or novel objects (Shinskey & Munakata, 2005). Infants were tested both for their preference (reaching for the items when *uncovered*) and their understanding of object permanence (reaching for the items when *covered*) for the novel versus familiar items. The results are shown in Figure 4-20. When the familiar and novel objects were visible, the infants almost always reached for the novel items, showing a classic novelty bias. However, when the object was hidden, they were more likely to reach for the familiar item. Infants had a stronger mental representation for the familiar objects, and, as a result, showed greater sensitivity for the continued existence of the familiar object when hidden. In other words, they displayed evidence of object permanence for the familiar objects but not for the novel objects. That is, infants' understanding of the

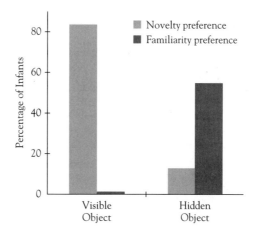

FIGURE **4-20**

Infants at 7.5 months of age reach more for novel versus familiar objects when the objects are in plain sight. When objects are covered as infants watch, however, they are more apt to reach for the familiar object. This indicates that infants' familiarity with objects affects their understanding for the permanence of the objects.

Source: Shinskey, J. L., & Munakata, Y. (2005). Familiarity breeds searching: Infants reverse their novelty preferences when reaching for hidden objects. *Psychological Science, 16*, 596–600.

permanence of objects, counter to Piaget, gradually develops as infants acquire stronger mental representations of objects through experience.

## Early Number Concepts

A second proposed core-knowledge system is an understanding of quantities and numbers. David Geary (1995, 2005) proposed that infants and young children possess skeletal competencies in four abilities related to mathematics: (1) numerosity, (2) ordinality, (3) counting, and (4) simple arithmetic (see Table 4-2). With the exception of counting, which I'll discuss in Chapter 11, evidence of each ability has been observed in infancy.

### Numerosity and Ordinality

**Numerosity** refers to the ability to determine quickly the number of items in a set without counting, whereas **ordinality** refers to a basic understanding of *more than* and *less than*—for instance, that the number of items in one array is more (or less) than the number of items in another array. To do this, one does not necessarily have to understand the concept of "two" or "three." Rather, infants display numerosity and ordinality by consistently being able to differentiate between two arrays with different numbers of items in them. For example, very young infants can tell the difference between two arrays that differ in the number of objects they contain (Antell & Keating, 1983; van Loosbroek & Smitsman, 1990). In research with slightly older infants, 10- and 12-month-olds watched as different numbers of crackers were placed inside two boxes (Feigenson, Carey, & Hauser, 2002). The boxes were then separated, and infants could crawl to retrieve the crackers in whichever box they pleased. Infants consistently

TABLE **4-2**

Potential Skeletal Mathematical Abilities.

*Numerosity*

The ability to accurately determine the quantity of small sets of items or events without counting. In humans, accurate numerosity judgments are typically limited to sets of four or fewer items.

*Ordinality*

A basic understanding of *more than* and *less than* and, later, an understanding of specific ordinal relationships.

For example, understanding that 4 > 3, 3 > 2, and 2 > 1.

For humans, the limits of this system are not clear, but it is probably limited to quantities < 5.

*Counting*

Early in development there appears to be a preverbal counting system that can be used for the enumeration of sets up to three, perhaps four, items. With the advent of language and the learning of number words, there appears to be a pan-cultural understanding that serial-ordered number words can be used for counting, measurement, and simple arithmetic.

*Simple Arithmetic*

Early in development there appears to be sensitivity to increases (addition) and decreases (subtraction) in the quantity of small sets. This system appears to be limited to the addition or subtraction of items within sets of three, perhaps four, items.

Source: From D. C. Geary. (1995). Reflections of evolution and culture in children's cognition: Implications for mathematical development and instruction. *American Psychologist, 50*, p. 36.

crawled to the box that contained the larger number of crackers when the boxes contained one versus two and two versus three crackers, but they responded indiscriminately when the larger quantity was four or greater (for example, three versus four, two versus four, and three versus six).

This pattern of results with 10- to 12-month-old infants is similar to one reported for a group of rhesus monkeys (Hauser, Carey, & Hauser, 2000). In that study, researchers placed pieces of apples, one at a time, into one of two containers as the monkeys watched. The researchers then stepped back and watched to see which container the monkeys, living wild on an uninhabited island but accustomed to the human researchers, would approach first. Much like the human babies, the monkeys approached the box with the larger number of apple pieces in it for contrasts of zero versus one, one versus two, two versus three, and three versus four (the latter contrast being one the babies failed). When the number of apple pieces in a box exceeded four, the animals responded randomly. These findings suggest that both human infants within their first year of life and adult rhesus monkeys develop a "natural" understanding of *more than* and *less than*, at least for small quantities, making this ability evolutionarily old and not unique to humans.

Other research indicates that 6-month-old infants can tell the difference between quantities larger than four, but that the *ratio* of the larger and smaller quantities must be large. For example, using preferential-looking methods, 6-month-olds can tell the differences between large arrays of dots on a computer screen when the larger quantity is twice as numerous as the smaller quantity, such as 8 versus 16 or 16 versus 32. However, 6-month-olds fail to discriminate between arrays with smaller ratios, such as 8 versus 12 or 16 versus 24 (Cordes & Brannon, 2009; Xu & Spelke, 2000; Xu, Spelke, & Goddard, 2005). A variety of factors influence infants' abilities to discriminate different quantities of objects in arrays, including the density of the items in arrays (spaced out or packed together) and the size of the items (large items versus small items), making any definitive statements about what underlies these early abilities difficult. However, these abilities seem to represent more than simple differences in visual perception, as infants' quantity judgments are not limited to visual arrays. For example, 6-month-old infants can also distinguish the difference between two sequences of 8 and 16 sounds (Lipton & Spelke, 2000) as well as between sequences of events (for example, a puppet jumping up and down four versus eight times) (Wood & Spelke, 2005).

### Simple Arithmetic

No one claims that infants really "know" arithmetic the way that a first-grade child knows how to add and subtract small quantities. But some provocative evidence indicates that 5-month-old babies can keep track of small changes in quantities, equivalent to understanding how to add and subtract.

This is best illustrated in the study by Karen Wynn (1992) that I discussed in Chapter 1. As you may recall, Wynn used the violation-of-expectation method to determine if 5-month-old infants could "add" and "subtract" small quantities. For example infants watched as a screen moved in front of a single doll. They then watched as a hand placed a doll behind the screen. When the screen dropped, some infants saw two dolls, as one would expect if they had a basic understanding of arithmetic ($1 + 1 = 2$). Others, however, saw only one doll, and these babies looked longer at this impossible outcome ($1 + 1 = 1$) than at the possible outcome ($1 + 1 = 2$).

How can these results best be interpreted? On the surface, at least, infants seem not to be making only a perceptual discrimination between two arrays (that is, telling the difference between an array with one item in it and another with two). Rather, when they watch as one item is added to another behind a screen, they expect to see two items when the screen is dropped. This seems to require some rudimentary ideas about addition. They must infer that the second object was added to the first, without actually seeing that this was done (recall that the screen occluded their vision).

Others have replicated these results (Simon, Hespos, & Rochat, 1995), and recent research using methods much like those used with human babies has shown that 3- and 4-day-old chickens show similar quantitative abilities (Rugani et al., 2009), suggesting that such basic computation is not unique to humans. However, the interpretation of these findings is not without debate (Clearfield & Westfahl, 2006; Moore & Cocas, 2006). For example, some researchers suggest that babies are not responding to *number* but to the total amount of *substance* present (Mix, Huttenlocher, & Levine, 2002). In other words, infants are not doing primitive (and unconscious) addition and subtraction. They are responding to changes in the amount of "stuff" that is present in the various arrays. For example, rather than reflecting infants' abstract understanding of integers (that is, there should be "1" or "2" objects behind the screen), performance on such tasks may be based on representations of the actual objects (for example, ♥ versus

♥ ♥ suggesting that decisions are based more on perceptual than on conceptual relations (Uller et al., 1999; see Mandler, 2000).

This line of work is provocative and, regardless of interpretation, suggests substantially greater quantitative knowledge in young infants than was previously believed. However, it does not mean that infants and toddlers should be able to learn complicated mathematics given the proper instructions. The nature of their numerical competencies might not be fully known, but it seems relatively certain that it is not equivalent of the abilities found in children only a few years older.

## Arguments Against Core Knowledge

I think it's fair to say that research over the past 25 years or so using the "new" infant technologies has demonstrated that babies have far more cognitive abilities than we once thought. However, not everyone believes that systematic changes in looking time reflect complex underlying cognitive abilities. For example, Richard Bogartz and his colleagues (Bogartz & Shinskey, 1998; Bogartz, Shinskey, & Speaker, 1997; see also Spencer et al., 2009) have argued that it is not necessary to attribute innate knowledge of physical objects to account for the findings of studies that use infants' looking behavior as an indication of what they know. Bogartz and his colleagues (1997) "assume that young infants cannot reason, draw inferences, or have beliefs" (p. 411) and "that the infant does not enter the world with [knowledge of objects] nor does it acquire such knowledge of physical laws in the first 6 months of life" (p. 412).

How, then, can one explain the data if there are no innate conceptual constraints? Bogartz and his colleagues suggest that young infants come into the world with a set of mechanisms for processing perceptual information and that infants acquire knowledge of objects through perceptual experience. The nature of perceptual processing produces looking patterns that Baillargeon, Spelke, and others interpret as "innate knowledge." According to Bogartz and his colleagues (1997), however, infants' perceptual processing "consists of analysis of the immediate representations of events, the construction in associative memory of the transformations of these immediate representations, abstraction of their forms, and the comparison of immediate perceptual representations to the representations stored in memory" (p. 411). All this processing takes time. In habituation/dishabituation tasks, infants look at familiar stimuli because it takes time to store memory representations. Novel events (that is, impossible events in the studies described earlier) take even more time because initial encoding of the stimuli needs to be done. Infants show a preference for looking at the novel (impossible) event over the familiar (habituated and possible) event simply because more processing is required to make sense of the former than the latter. There is no need to postulate innate knowledge of physical laws, only laws about how infant perception and memory work.

There has been much debate about the nature of infant cognition. Some researchers propose that infants are born with "core knowledge" for important aspects of their world that develop rapidly with experience (for example, Spelke & Kinzler, 2007), and still others propose that infants' and toddlers' cognitive skills are influenced by more domain-general mechanisms (for example, Newcombe, 2002; Spencer et al., 2009). Although I believe that humans, and others species, have been prepared by evolution for processing spatial information (a form of architectural constraints), such constraints require substantial input from the environment to develop properly during early childhood.

# CATEGORY REPRESENTATION

As we've seen, babies have distinct preferences for what they look at, and they display a rudimentary form of visual memory, as reflected by the effects that novelty and familiarity have on their preferences. As important as these basic processes are, however, our ability to deal effectively with new information would be hopelessly impaired if we did not form *categories*. By the process of categorization, one can treat objects that are perceptually different as being the same kind of thing. Uncle Joe, Aunt Mary, Mommy, Daddy, and the stranger on the street are all unique individuals, but at one level, they're all the same: They're all people. Our ability to categorize allows us to reduce an enormous diversity of information into manageable units. A 6-month-old given a new stuffed animal, rattle, or bottle can identify each object and act toward it accordingly, even though he or she has never seen the object before. Each object is similar to something the child already knows, and the objects can be categorized and dealt with easily. The process of categorization is ubiquitous, permeating every aspect of our intellectual life, and the origins of categorization can be found in early infancy.

## How Is Categorization Measured?

One technique that has been used to assess infants' perceptual categories is the habituation/dishabituation paradigm, discussed earlier in this chapter. How can this paradigm be used to assess infants' categories, or concepts? One way is by varying the stimuli that are presented during habituation trials. Rather than habituating infants to a picture of the face of a single individual (Sally), for example, pictures of different individuals can be presented (Sally, Maria, Barbara, and Teresa). In both the single- and multiple-face cases, looking time declines with repeated exposure (that is, habituation). In the former case, infants are habituated to a specific stimulus (Sally), and in the latter case, infants are habituated to a category of stimuli (women's faces). After habituation has occurred, a new female face can be presented (Elizabeth). Infants who were habituated to a single face should recognize this new face as a novel stimulus and increase their attention to it (that is, show dishabituation). In contrast, infants who were habituated to women's faces in general should recognize it as just another example of a woman's face and continue to habituate. That is, even though they have never seen this face before, they should categorize it as familiar and direct relatively little of their attention to it.

The procedure and results just described are similar to those reported by Leslie Cohen and Mark Strauss (1979) for a group of 30-week-old infants. Cohen and Strauss interpreted their findings as evidence that such infants can abstract "appropriate conceptual categories regarding the human face" (p. 422). By continuing to habituate to the new stimulus, infants are, in effect, telling us that although the face is perceptually different from anything they have seen before, it is similar in general form to what they already know. They are telling us that they have acquired a category for female faces.

Research during the past 30 years has shown that infants as young as 3 months can organize objects into perceptual categories during relatively brief experimental sessions (Eimas & Quinn, 1994; Younger & Gottlieb, 1988). For example, in a series of experiments by Peter Eimas and Paul Quinn (1994), 3- and 4-month-old infants were habituated to a series of pictures of either horses or cats. Following habituation, the infants were shown a pair of new pictures, one from the habituated category (a "new" picture of a horse, for instance) and one from a different, but related, category (a zebra or giraffe, for instance). Note that both pictures on these test trials were "new" to the infants, in that they had never been shown the specific picture of this horse before, nor a picture of any giraffe or zebra. However, if the infants had formed a concept of "horse," they would recognize the new picture of a horse as "just another horse" and, thus, look longer at the giraffe (or zebra) than at the horse. This, in fact, is what Eimas and Quinn found. Infants formed categories of horses that were distinct from zebras, giraffes, and cats, and they formed categories of cats that were distinct from horses and tigers. However, these babies were not able to distinguish between cats and female lions, indicating that the perceptual similarity between cats and female lions is too great for infants of this age to form separate categories of them, at least with this little experience. But when 3- and 4-month-old infants were given more experience with cats before being tested for category formation, they were able to make the "cat versus female lion" categorical distinction (Quinn & Eimas, 1996), indicating that perceptual category formation for "natural" categories is quite well developed early in life.

It's worth asking what these categorization experiments are really assessing. If 3-month-old infants habituate to a category of vehicles, for example, and then dishabituate to pictures of animals (Arterberry & Bornstein, 2001), does this mean that they came into the laboratory with these categories already "in mind," and that the experimenter is discovering how they classify their world? Or do these results indicate that infants are able to distinguish physical features of items that correlate with one another (for example, four legs of mammals, certain characteristics of faces) and discover for themselves the categories in the minds (and the stimuli) of the experimenters (Oakes & Madole, 2000)? In most experiments, a little of both is likely going on. At one level, these experiments reveal something of the processes underlying infants' categorization. What types of features do they use to form categories? How much overlap, or correlation, among features is necessary for them to treat two different members of a concept as the same? From this perspective, it would be foolhardy to assume that 3-month-olds have a concept of "vehicles." It would be more sensible to assume that they are able to identify the perceptual similarity among the different pictures of vehicles to form a category, one they formed in the course of the experiment. Then again, even 3-months-olds have substantial perceptual experiences. Although they may never have seen a giraffe, their parents may have shown them pictures of such bizarre animals in books, and to assume that their behavior in the laboratory is independent of their past experience is equally foolhardy (Quinn, 2002). In general, results from infant categorization studies reveal something about both the content of children's categories and the processes by which such content is acquired. It takes careful experimentation, however, to know which is which.

## The Structure of Infants' Categories

When infants form categories, how do they do it? One popular way of describing adult concepts is through *category prototypes*. A **category prototype** is an abstract representation of a category. It reflects the central tendency, or "best example," of a category. Items that share many features in common with the prototype are said to be typical category exemplars (for instance, *robin* for the category *birds*), whereas items that share fewer features with the prototype are said to be atypical category exemplars (for instance, *ostrich* for the category *birds*) (see Rosch, 1975).

a

b

c

d

e

f

PHOTO **4-3**

Infants seem to form categories based on typicality. For instance, if habituated to examples of category-typical birds (blue jay, robin, and sparrow ), they will later dishabituate (increase looking time) to a picture of a nonbird, demonstrating that they formed a "bird" category. However, they will not dishabituate to a picture of a nonbird if they were initially habituated to photos of category-a typical birds (ostrich, turkey and penguin).

Several researchers have demonstrated that infants form category prototypes much as adults do. Kenneth Roberts and Frances Horowitz (1986; see also Roberts, 1988) showed that 9-month-old infants formed a category for the concept "birds" when habituated to highly typical exemplars of the category (for example, *sparrow, robin,* and *blue jay*). They found no evidence of concept formation, however, when atypical exemplars served as the habituation stimuli (for example, *turkey, ostrich,* and *chicken*) (see Photo 4-3). Like young children, infants are more apt to identify or form a category when provided with typical, rather than atypical, category exemplars (Anglin, 1977). Similarly, infants seem to develop a prototype for female faces before male faces (Ramsey et al., 2005; Rubenstein, Kalakanis, & Langlois, 1999) as a result of their greater experience with women's faces. As you may recall, babies generally prefer to look at female faces than at male faces, and they are better able to distinguish among female faces than among male faces (Quinn et al., 2002). The findings of these experiments are enlightening, suggesting that the categorization process of infants is qualitatively similar to that of older children and adults.

## WHAT IS INFANT COGNITION MADE OF?

There is little debate that cognition and behavior change drastically over infancy. Brain growth is more rapid during the first 2 years than at any other time in postnatal life. Cognitive differences between the 10-month-old and the 2-year-old are dramatic, obvious to anyone who takes the time to look. Yet, increasing evidence indicates that the huge changes in overt behavior that are apparent to all might be masking much smaller changes in underlying competencies. Infants seem to know a lot about their physical world from birth or shortly thereafter, and they may even be able to do simple computations.

Some of these skills may be domain specific in nature. For example, we saw that very young infants can recognize faces and perhaps are even born with a prototype for the human face (as reflected by their preference for "attractive" faces; see Langlois et al., 1987). Such skills are likely limited to face identification and recognition and do not generalize to other aspects of cognition. Similarly, knowledge of addition and subtraction might be domain specific, with the symbolic skills underlying simple computation being unavailable to other conceptual systems.

Other aspects of young infants' cognition might be more domain general in nature. For example, Catherine Sophian (1997) suggested innate structures are more like tools that might be best suited for some contents (understanding objects, for example) but can also be used flexibly for other purposes (see also Gelman & Williams, 1998).

Some, such as Andrew Meltzoff (1990), argue that infants' minds have more in common with those of older children than we once thought. In reviewing his own and other people's research on cognitive development over infancy, Meltzoff concluded that "*in a very real sense, there may be no such thing as an exclusively 'sensorimotor period' in the normal human infant*" (p. 20, italics in the original). Jean Mandler (1992, 2000) takes a similar, though somewhat less drastic, position. Mandler interprets the wealth of new information about infant cognition as requiring new theories. According to Mandler (1992), infants from the first few months of life are able to abstract certain types of perceptual information and redescribe their perceptions (presumably including both the sensory and motor representations) into conceptual form (see also Karmiloff-Smith, 1992). This conceptual knowledge can coexist with purely sensory and motor knowledge, and such redescription, rather than having a late onset, develops alongside sensorimotor functioning. It is not necessary to posit substantial amounts of innate knowledge, Mandler suggests.

Not everyone believes that the new research findings truly reflect advanced symbolic functioning or innate knowledge, of any type. For example, Kurt Fischer and Thomas Bidell (1991) argue that any particular infant skill should not be viewed in isolation but in the context of overall development. Rather than asking, for instance, when infants "really" have object permanence, Fischer and Bidell suggest that developmental researchers ask more fruitful questions, including these: "What is the developmental sequence of object knowledge from earliest infancy through early childhood? How is the development of this sequence related to developments in other domains? How is it constrained by the nature of perceptual and sensorimotor processes, which are partly regulated by the genome, and by environmental inputs? How are such constraints evident at various points in developmental sequences?" (pp. 223–224). These are similar to the arguments Marshall Haith (1993) made regarding infant perceptual abilities.

Who's right? We can't yet answer that question, and perhaps one group doesn't have to be wrong for the other group to be right. Cognitive development does not follow a single course for all aspects of intelligence. It is possible—and I believe likely—that infants' cognition is multiply determined. Infants might possess some innate knowledge (representational constraints) and some innate processing mechanisms (architectural constraints), but at other times, their behavior might be better explained by referring to more domain-general perceptual and memory mechanisms rather than to highly constrained, domain-specific processes. And most likely, infants' brains are structured so that domain-specific constraints (both representational and architectural) and domain-general mechanisms interact (see Bjorklund & Pellegrini, 2002; Geary & Huffman, 2002).

There is much excitement in infant research these days. Regardless of which interpretation one prefers, I think most researchers would agree that infants have far greater conceptual abilities than was previously believed, and every year we learn something else that infants know or can do. We should not lose sight, however, of what infants cannot do. There is no evidence, for example, that infants can be taught arithmetic, reading, or chemistry. Infancy is still a special time, and the infant mind remains far different from the mind that resides in the 3-year-old child. Remembering the limits of infant cognition is sometimes difficult when we look at all the things infants can do, but it is a thought we shouldn't lose.

## SUMMARY

From birth, infants actively use their perceptual systems to acquire information from their surroundings. By 1 week of age, babies can discriminate their mothers from other women by smell and by the sound of their voices. A number of techniques have been used to assess infants' perceptual abilities, including changes in their sucking rate to different stimuli, the *visual preference paradigm* (in which differences in the amount of time infants spend looking at two stimuli is used to infer that they can discriminate between the stimuli and prefer to look at one versus the other), and the habituation/ dishabituation paradigm. *Habituation* occurs when infants' looking time diminishes as a result of repeated presentation of a stimulus. *Dishabituation*, or release from habituation, occurs when looking time increases with the presentation of a new stimulus. Habituation and dishabituation to visual stimuli are found for some newborns and reflect both discrimination and memory.

Vision is not well developed at birth, although the abilities of *convergence, coordination,* and *accommodation* of the lens improve rapidly during the first 6 months. From birth, infants look longer at some stimuli than at others, indicating they can discriminate between the stimuli and have preferences, or perceptual biases. During the first month of life, infants tend to direct their attention to the outside of a figure, which is referred to as the *externality effect*. Among the physical characteristics of a stimulus that attracts infants' visual attention are movement, contour and contrast, certain levels of complexity, vertical symmetry, and curvature.

Beginning around 2 months of age, infants' attention is increasingly influenced by psychological factors, such as the familiarity or novelty of a stimulus. Infants form long-term sensory representations, or *schemas*. Kagan proposed the *discrepancy principle* to explain infants' preferences for novel stimuli, stating that stimuli that are moderately discrepant from a previously acquired schema are most likely to be attended to.

Very young infants also seem to have a bias toward attending to the human face and look longer at attractive compared to less attractive faces. The eyes in particular are important in processing faces. Over the first year, face processing becomes increasingly specialized, and infants develop an increasing ability to discriminate between faces of their own race and experience a decreasing ability to discriminate between faces of other races, termed the *other-race effect.*

Newborns show a preference for high-pitched voices, and this preference might have its origins in the womb. Young infants can discriminate among *phonemes* and categorize language sounds much as adults do, and they appear to be biologically prepared to perceive music.

*Intermodal* (or *intersensory*) *integration* refers to the coordination of information from two or more sensory modalities. *Intermodal* (or *cross-modal*) *matching* refers to the ability to recognize a stimulus initially inspected in one modality (vision, for example) through another modality (touch, for example). These abilities may be present at birth or shortly thereafter. The *intersensory redundancy hypothesis* proposes that when infants repeatedly receive redundant information from two senses (for example, watching lips move and hearing sound), they become more attuned to amodal properties of the events (for example, tempo) than when they attend to unimodal stimuli.

In the *violation-of-expectation method*, infants' attention to an unexpected, often impossible event increases relative to baseline or to expected events.

*Core knowledge* refers to the idea that infants possess a small set of domain-specific systems of knowledge that have been shaped by natural selection and upon which new and flexible skills are built. There are at least three core-knowledge systems in infancy: object representation, knowledge of people and their actions, and an ability to represent numbers, or quantities. From birth, infants seem to have a rudimentary understanding of *object constancy,* the knowledge that an object remains the same despite changes in how it is viewed. Infants' understanding of *object cohesion and continuity* (understanding that objects have boundaries) develops over the first year, as reflected by experiments using the violation-of-expectation method. Baillargeon proposed that infants possess at birth the *principle of persistence* (knowledge that objects remain cohesive and cannot undergo a spontaneous or uncaused change in the course of an event). *Object permanence* refers to the belief that objects exist independent of one's perceptions or actions. Piaget was the first to describe the development of object permanence and proposed that infants cannot retrieve a hidden object until about 8 months, cannot solve the *A-not-B task* until about 12 months, and cannot understand invisible displacements until about 18 months. By using variations of the violation-of-expectation method, researchers have demonstrated evidence of object permanence earlier than Piaget had proposed.

Using variations of the violation-of-expectation method, researchers have also demonstrated evidence for simple quantitative abilities in infants. Among these are *numerosity* (the ability to determine quickly the number of items in a set without counting), *ordinality* (a basic understanding of "more than" and "less than" relationships), and simple arithmetic, although there is some debate about the interpretation of these findings.

Using the habituation/dishabituation paradigm, researchers have been able to demonstrate that infants can form categories and that they do so much the same way that older children and adults do. Infant categories are formed around a category prototype which is an abstract representation reflecting the central tendency, or "best example," of a category.

## KEY TERMS AND CONCEPTS

visual preference paradigm

habituation

dishabituation

accommodation (of the lens)

convergence (of the eyes)

coordination (of the eyes)

externality effect

schemas

discrepancy principle

other-race effect

phonemes

intermodal integration (or intersensory integration)

intermodal matching (or cross-modal matching)

intersensory redundancy hypothesis

violation-of-expectation method

core knowledge

object constancy

object cohesion and continuity

principle of persistence

object permanence

A-not-B object permanence task

numerosity

ordinality

category prototype

## SUGGESTED READINGS

### Scholarly Works

Baillargeon, R. (2008). Innate ideas revisited: For a principle of persistence in infants' physical reasoning. *Perspectives on Psychological Science*, *3*, 2–13. This article reviews research by Reneé Baillargeon and her colleagues on object representation in infants using the violation-of-expectation method. She proposes the principle of persistence, in which babies seem to know coming into the world something about the continuity of objects.

Kellman, P. J., & Arterberry, M. E. (2006). Perceptual development. In W. Damon, D. Kuhn, & R. Siegler (Eds.), *The handbook of child psychology: Cognition, perception, and language*, 6th edition (pp. 109–160). New York: John Wiley. This chapter provides an extensive review of perceptual development in infancy and childhood.

Kelly, D. J., Quinn, P. C., Slater, A. M., Lee, K., Ge, L., & Pascalis, O. (2007). The other-race effect develops during infancy. *Psychological Science*, *18*, 1084–1089. These leading researchers in the field of face processing in infants present findings demonstrating the "other-race effect" in infancy. The article also provides a good example of how

researchers test hypotheses regarding how infants process complicated information.

Spelke, E. S., & Kinzler, K. D. (2007). Core knowledge. *Developmental Science*, *10*, 89–96. Elizabeth Spelke and Katherine Kinzler present evidence for the core-knowledge perspective of infant cognition, listing five areas in which core knowledge is proposed to exist.

### Reading for Personal Interest

Dobbs, D. (2005). Big answers from little people. *Scientific American Mind*, Vol. 16, Issue 3, 38–43. This article, written for the layperson, examines the latest research into infants' cognitive abilities, focusing on the work of Elizabeth Spelke, Harvard developmental psychologist and advocate of the core-knowledge approach.

Rochat, P. (2004). *The infant's world*. Cambridge, MA: Harvard University Press. Philippe Rochat examines the development of infant social cognition, taking an ecological perspective somewhat different from the core-knowledge perspective as advocated by Elizabeth Spelke and her colleagues.

# CHAPTER 5

# Thinking in Symbols: The Development of Representation

**Learning to Use Symbols**
Young Children's Interpretation of Pictures
   and Models
The Appearance/Reality Distinction

**Piaget's Theory**
Some Assumptions of Piaget's Theory
Stages of Development
   **BOX 5-1:** Culture and Symbolic Development
The State of Piaget's Theory Today

**Everyday Expressions of the Symbolic
Function**

Symbolic Play
Distinguishing Between Fantasy and
   Reality

**Fuzzy-Trace Theory**
Assumptions of Fuzzy-Trace Theory
Developmental Differences

**The Symbolic Species**

SUMMARY
KEY TERMS AND CONCEPTS
SUGGESTED READINGS

Three-year-old Nicholas sometimes spent the night with his grandparents, who would take him to preschool the following morning. Nicholas especially liked to ride with his grandfather because he drove a somewhat battered, stick-shift Chevy, which Nicholas called "Papa's car." Nicholas's grandmother, however, only drove cars with automatic transmissions. Thus, she was unable to take Nicholas to school in Papa's car. One morning when Grandma was about to drive Nicholas to school, he said, "Grandma, dress up like a man this morning. Put on Papa's shirt and wear his hat." When asked why he wanted her to do that, he responded, "Then you can take me to school in Papa's car." Nicholas had a problem and attempted to solve it by changing his grandmother's appearance, which he believed would temporarily transform her into a man and give her the ability to drive a stick-shift car.

What's going on here? Does little Nicholas really think that clothes, quite literally, make the man? His thinking may reflect many things, but one is his ability to represent reality. I noted in Chapter 1 that one of the major issues in cognitive development concerns changes in the way children represent information. **Representation** refers to the mental coding of information, and as I also noted in previous chapters, children can represent information in a variety of forms. (I discussed some aspects of representation in infancy in Chapter 4.) Most (but not all) of the focus in this chapter will be on slightly older children, as I examine different aspects of children's developing abilities to symbolically represent their worlds.

I start by examining what it means to use symbols—specifically to use one object to represent another. I then look at the theory of the Swiss psychologist Jean Piaget, who brought to light many of the phenomena of symbolic functioning that psychologists are researching today and who made the study of the development of representation a central issue of our field. I next examine two expressions of symbolic functioning in children and how they change with age: symbolic play and distinguishing between fantasy and reality. I conclude by looking at a very different type of approach to the development of representational abilities and their relationship to thinking: Charles Brainerd and Valerie Reyna's fuzzy-trace theory.

---

## LEARNING TO USE SYMBOLS

In everyday parlance, the term *symbol* usually refers to external referents for objects and events. For example, a picture or a photograph of an object is a stand-in for the real thing—it is a concrete yet symbolic representation of an object that is not physically present. Likewise, scale models, such as a miniature room complete with doll-sized furniture, can serve as a symbolic representation of a larger, real room. Similarly, some things are not exactly what they seem. The ubiquitous refrigerator magnet attests to this. Cookies, candy bars, and many other "real" things are, in actuality, only magnets that look like something else. At a more abstract level, the letters and numbers so central to our technological culture are not what they seem to be but, rather, are symbols necessary for reading and computation. Judy DeLoache (1987; DeLoache & Marzolf, 1992) has referred to the knowledge that an entity can stand for something other than itself as **representational insight**. When can children understand and effectively use external forms of representation, such as pictures and models, and what does this tell us about their representational development?

In this section, I examine two areas of research related to young children's use of external symbols. The first is the research of DeLoache and her colleagues regarding children's abilities to use pictures and scale models as representations for the real things. The second is research examining children's abilities to distinguish the differences between the appearance and the reality of objects.

## Young Children's Interpretation of Pictures and Models

How do children come to understand that pictures and models are symbols for other things? Judy DeLoache and her colleagues have investigated this question, and their studies have produced some interesting and, at first look, counterintuitive findings (DeLoache, 2000; DeLoache & Marzolf, 1992; see also Kuhlmeier, 2005). In DeLoache's studies, 2- and 3-year-old children are asked to find a toy hidden in a room. Before searching for the object, they are shown a picture or scale model of the room, with the location of the hidden object made obvious in the picture or model. For example, children are shown a scale model of a room, and they watch as the experimenter hides a miniature toy behind a miniature chair in the model. The miniature toy and the model chair correspond to a large toy and a real chair in the adjoining real room. Children are then asked to find the toy in the room (Retrieval 1). After searching for the toy in the room, they return to the model and are asked to find where the miniature toy was hidden (Retrieval 2). If children cannot find the large toy in the room (Retrieval 1) but can find the miniature toy in the scale model (Retrieval 2), then their failure to find the large toy cannot be because they forgot where the miniature toy was hidden. A better interpretation would be that the children cannot use the model in a symbolic fashion.

The results of one such experiment with 2.5- and 3-year-old children are graphed in Figure 5-1 (DeLoache, 1987). As can be seen, 3-year-olds performed comparably in both retrieval tasks, indicating that they remembered where the miniature toy was hidden and used the information from the scale model to find the large toy in the real room. The younger children showed good memory for where the miniature toy was hidden (Retrieval 2 in the figure) but performed very poorly when trying to find the large toy in the real room (Retrieval 1 in the figure). This pattern of results suggests that 2.5-year-old children failed to recognize that the scale model was a symbolic representation of the large room. Recalling DeLoache's definition of representational insight as realizing that one entity can stand for another, it appears that, on the scale-model task, 3-year-olds possess representational insight whereas 2.5-year-old children do not.

A similar pattern of results was found when *pictures* of a room were used, with an experimenter pointing to the location in a picture where the toy was hidden

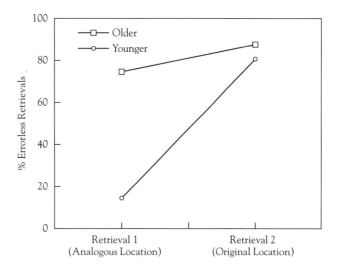

FIGURE **5-1**

The number of errorless retrievals (correctly locating the hidden toy) for 2.5-year-olds (younger) and 3-year-olds (older) on a model task. Retrieval 1 involved locating the real toy in the real room; retrieval 2 involved locating the miniature toy in the model.

Source: "Rapid Change in the Symbolic Functioning of Very Young Children," by J. S. DeLoache, 1987, *Science, 238*, 1556–1557. Copyright © 1987 American Association for the Advancement of Science. Reprinted with permission.

(DeLoache, 1987, 1991; Suddendorf, 2003). The primary difference between the picture and scale-model experiments was that the picture task was solved by 2.5-year-old children but not by 2-year-olds. Thus, when pictures are used as symbols, 2.5-year-olds demonstrate representational insight. Such competence is not achieved until 3 years of age, however, when a scale model is used.

Why should children perform more poorly using the scale model than when using the pictures? If I had been asked to make a prediction of which task would be the easier, my guess would have been exactly the reverse. The model, being a more concrete stimulus, is more like the real room, and it would seem that less symbolic sophistication would be required to use it to guide behavior. In fact, when young children are given toy objects versus pictures of objects to use in memory and simple problem-solving tasks, they usually perform better with the objects, not the pictures (Daehler, Lonardo, & Bukatko, 1979). Such was not the case with DeLoache's study, of course, and she proposed that one reason for the pattern of results was related to children's difficulty in thinking about an entity in two different ways at the same time, or what she refers to as **dual representation** (or **dual orientation**). A model, she argues, is an object worthy of attention all by itself. A picture, by contrast, is itself uninteresting, with its primary purpose being to represent something else. When models are made less interesting and less concrete, or when pictures are made more salient, performance should change.

This is exactly what DeLoache (1991) found. When models were viewed through a window, 2.5-year-olds' performance increased substantially relative to the standard model task. Likewise, when 3-year-olds were allowed to play with the model before the hiding task, their performance significantly *decreased*. Making the model *less* salient for the 2.5-year-olds (by requiring that they view it through a window) enabled them to more easily represent the model as both an object and a model. Making the model *more* salient for the 3-year-olds (by encouraging them to play with it) made it more difficult for them to treat it as a representation for something else, and their performance deteriorated. A similar result was found when pictures were made more salient (DeLoache, 1991), while other studies have shown that under favorable conditions, even 2-year-olds can appreciate that a picture can relate both to something else and be an object itself (Preissler & Bloom, 2007; Suddendorf, 2003; Troseth, 2003).

If dual representation is the key here, as DeLoache proposes, what would happen if young children had to use a model to find a hidden toy *without* dual representation? How can this be done? DeLoache, Kevin Miller, and Karl Rosengren (1997) convinced children that a "shrinking machine" (an oscilloscope with flashing lights and computer-generated sounds) could actually shrink a room, something that the 2.5-year-old children easily believed. The children were then given the "hiding" test as in previous research. First, a toy was hidden in the large room. Then, the room was "shrunk," and the children searched for the toy in the miniaturized model. Their performance this time was exceptional. Whereas children who were given the standard (no shrinking room) instructions successfully found the toy on only 19% of all trials (about what one would expect by chance), children who searched in the shrunken (model) room were correct nearly 80% of the time. Why the difference? DeLoache and her colleagues reasoned that the children believed *the miniaturized room was the same room as the larger room*; it was not a model and, thus, not a symbol. In this case, as far as the children were concerned, dual representation was not necessary.

The ability to use one object to represent another is the essence of what we mean when we refer to symbol use. At a very basic level, we see this ability in very young children, most easily perhaps in symbolic play. For example, an 18-month-old might hold a shoe to her ear and pretend that it's a phone, or a 20-month-old might place a napkin on his head and parade around the living room drawing attention to his "hat." In these cases, one object is being used as a symbol for another. But this is not quite what DeLoache means when she refers to representational insight. It is not enough to use an object as a symbol; one must know that the object can be both a symbol (for example, a representation of a room) and an object (for example, a model) at the same time. DeLoache and Donald Marzolf (1992) make this point nicely, stating, "Young children are capable of responding to a single entity either concretely, as an object itself, or abstractly, as a representation of something else. It is very difficult for them to do both at once, that is, to achieve dual representation" (p. 328).

Subsequent research has documented the development of dual representation for children's understanding of one common symbolic entity—pictures. DeLoache and her colleagues (1998) presented pictures of objects to children between the ages of 9 and 19 months in the United States and the Ivory Coast. The youngest children in both countries initially touched the pictures as if they were real objects, sometimes even trying to pick them off the page. By 19 months of age, however, children in both countries realized that the pictures represented something else: They now pointed at the depicted objects rather than try to manipulate them. DeLoache and her colleagues propose that infants' initial uncertainty about pictures causes them to explore the pictures, which gradually results in their acquisition of the concept of "picture" and the understanding that they represent something else. Later research has indicated that, under some contexts, infants as young as 15-months old understand that pictures are representations of objects (Ganea et al., 2009).

## The Appearance/Reality Distinction

Adults know very well that things are not always what they seem to be. We realize that the appearance of an object does not necessarily correspond to its reality. This is not knowledge we are born with but knowledge that has a developmental history. The **appearance/reality distinction** refers to the knowledge that the appearance of an object does not necessarily correspond to its reality. This is illustrated in a pioneering study by Rheta De Vries (1969). In this study, De Vries first familiarized 3- to 6-year-old children with a trained cat named Maynard. In one condition, after the children petted Maynard, the cat was fitted with a realistic dog mask. (I did mention that he was a trained cat.) Although the children did not actually see the mask being placed on Maynard, the cat's body and tail remained in full view of the children during the transformation. They were then asked questions about the identity of the animal. What kind of animal is it now? Would this animal eat dog food or cat food? Does it bark or meow? In general, 3-year-olds frequently believed that the mask had actually changed the identity of the animal, whereas most 5- and 6-year-olds believed that changes in the appearance of the animal had not altered its identity. De Vries referred to this type of qualitative constancy as *generic identity*.

In addition to her research on changing the appearance of animals, De Vries also interviewed children regarding their beliefs about people wearing masks and about the constancy of gender as a result of certain irrelevant changes (for example, boys wearing dresses). Again, she reported that 3-year-olds tended to believe that changes in appearance result in changes in identity. This can account for young children's sometimes puzzling responses to costumes worn both by others and by themselves. For example, it is not uncommon at Halloween for 2- and 3-year-old children to be excited about wearing a costume, only to become distressed when the masks are placed over their faces or when they look at themselves in the mirror. Wearing a SpongeBob SquarePants outfit is one thing, but wearing the mask is another story. Not all transformations of personal identity are upsetting, however, as evidenced by the number of scraped elbows and knees on children who wear their Superman underwear, tie capes around their necks, and jump from tables and fences, convinced that they can fly. These children's behaviors are consistent with the belief that a significant change in appearance results in a change in identity. (The story that opened this chapter reflects a young boy's wish to change his grandmother into a man, temporarily, so she can drive him to school in "Papa's car.")

In related research, John Flavell and his colleagues extensively investigated young children's knowledge about the distinction between appearance and reality (Flavell, Green, & Flavell, 1986; Taylor & Flavell, 1984). In some experiments, children were presented with a realistic-looking fake rock made of sponge, or they watched as white milk was poured into a red glass. The children were then asked two questions. The first concerned what the objects looked like, "how they look to your eyes right now." The second concerned the actual identity of the objects, "how they really and truly are." Somewhat surprisingly, Flavell and his colleagues reported that most 3-year-olds could not solve these seemingly simple problems. Children stated, for example, that the milk looked red and "really and truly" was red, or they would say that the fake rock was, indeed, a sponge and looked like a sponge. In general, when children erred, they did so by giving the same answer to both questions. Subsequent research that simplified the task or provided training to young children generally failed to find any enhancement in performance for 3-year-olds (Deák, Ray, & Brenneman, 2003; Flavell, Green, & Flavell, 1986), causing Flavell and his colleagues (1986) to conclude that 3-year-olds "truly did not understand [the appearance/reality distinction], even minimally" (p. 23).

Flavell and his colleagues (1986) speculated about the factors that can mediate children's development of the appearance/reality distinction. One likely candidate is *dual encoding*. Three-year-olds' inability to differentiate between the appearance of an object and its actual identity might stem, in part, from their difficulty with representing an object in more than one form at a time. That is, young children might focus on one aspect of a stimulus (its appearance or its actual identity) and give the same answer, based on either appearance or reality, regardless of the question asked. Thus, on the one hand, if the change in color is more salient to a child, the object *looks* red and *is* red. If, on the other hand, the identity of the object is more salient, it *is* a sponge and *looks like* a sponge. Young children cannot act on multiple representations of an object simultaneously. With increasing age, they become more adept at dual encoding, but not until later childhood or early adolescence can they "think about notions of 'looks like,' 'really and truly,' 'looks different from the way it really and truly is,' and so on in the abstract, metaconceptual way that older subjects can" (Flavell, 1986, p. 59).

The findings and interpretation of Flavell and his colleagues are similar to those DeLoache (1987; DeLoache & Marzolf, 1992) reported with respect to dual representation for pictures and models. Together, the findings of Flavell and DeLoache suggest that there is not a single dual-representational ability that emerges at a single time and affects thinking across all tasks. Rather, this ability appears to develop gradually from ages 2 to 5, being found early (2.5 years) in some circumstances (using pictures as symbols), a bit later (3 years) in others (using models as symbols), and later yet (4 to 5 years) in still other situations (making the appearance/reality distinction).

## PIAGET'S THEORY

Jean Piaget (1896–1980) has had a greater impact on the field of cognitive development than any other person in the brief history of our science. The self-proclaimed experimental philosopher formulated a grand theory of intelligence that made children themselves, rather than their environment or their genetic constitution, the primary force in the development of thought. Piaget changed the way we look at children. Following Piaget, we no longer view the child as an incomplete adult. Piaget taught us that children's thinking, at any age, reflects a unique way of interpreting the world (for example, changes in appearance can produce changes in reality). Development is more than the simple acquisition of skills and knowledge. The 4-year-old is not just a smaller model of the 12-year-old who merely lacks the experience and knowledge of his older peer. Rather, in addition to quantitative differences in what these two children know (that is, differences in amount, degree, or speed), there are qualitative differences in how they know it (that is, differences in form, or type). Because of Piaget's work, it is difficult today for us to conceive of the child as a passive organism, shaped and molded by environmental pressures. At any given developmental level, children are seekers of stimulation who act on their environment as much as their environment acts on them.

Many cognitive developmentalists hold great reverence for Piaget's theory because of the impact it has had on the field of developmental psychology (see Brainerd, 1996). Although the number of active researchers today who are strict adherents of Piaget's theory is relatively small (many would describe themselves as neo-Piagetians), familiarity with Piaget's theory is essential for understanding cognitive development as it is studied today.

## Some Assumptions of Piaget's Theory

Piaget was a stage theorist. He believed that cognition develops in a series of discrete stages, with children's thinking at any particular stage being qualitatively different from that which preceded it and that which will follow it. In other words, Piaget did not view cognitive development as the gradual accretion of knowledge or skills. Rather, he viewed cognitive development as a series of transformations, with children's thinking going through abrupt changes over relatively brief periods. Despite his belief in the discontinuous nature of changes in children's thinking, Piaget did believe that the *functions* underlying cognitive development are continuous. New abilities do not just pop up but emerge from earlier abilities. Given this underlying continuity, Piaget hypothesized transition, or preparatory, phases between stages—brief times when a child can have one foot in each of two qualitatively different cognitive worlds.

Piaget also believed that the mechanisms of cognitive development are domain general. Children come into the world with a general, species-typical nervous system—a nervous system that is not specially prepared to acquire any one type of information more than another. Thus, all intellectual accomplishments of infancy, for example, are governed by a general developmental function. Infants' mastery of early language, knowledge of objects, imitation abilities, and problem-solving skills are all interrelated and are the products of changes in a single cognitive system.

Piaget viewed children as being *intrinsically active*. They are not passive creatures, waiting to be stimulated by their surroundings before they behave. Rather, they are active initiators and seekers of stimulation. Intrinsic activity in children can be viewed as curiosity. Children are not content with what they already know, and they seek to know more. Although a child can be enticed to acquire certain information through external rewards, such exogenous reinforcements are not necessary to motivate learning and development. The motivation for development is within the child, who Piaget made not only the focus of development but also its major perpetrator. Children are the movers and shakers of their own experiences and, thus, are primarily responsible for their own development. Environmental and genetic sources play a role in influencing development as well, of course, and Piaget most explicitly believed that development is the result of an interaction between a biologically prepared child and his or her environment. Nevertheless, unlike most of his contemporaries, Piaget placed his emphasis squarely on the child.

Related to the concept of intrinsic activity is Piaget's belief that cognition is a *constructive* process. According to Piaget, our current state of knowledge guides our processing, substantially influencing how (and what) new information is acquired. In other words, the world is not out there for everyone to perceive in exactly the same manner. Knowing is an active, constructive process—an interaction between the environment and the active individual.

If reality is a construction, however, then children at different developmental levels must surely construct different realities. The same event experienced by a 2-, a 7-, and a 14-year-old will be interpreted very differently by each. This is true not only because of differences in the amount of knowledge possessed by these children (that is, quantitative differences) but also because of differences in how each child can process information (that is, qualitative differences). For a 6-month-old whose rattle is hidden by a blanket, reality is that the rattle no longer exists; a 3-year-old boy believes that wearing girls' clothes or playing girls' games transforms him temporarily into a girl; and a 6-year-old is convinced that a baloney-and-cheese sandwich cut into quarters provides more to eat than when it is cut into halves. An older child or adult believes none of this, but for Piaget, reality is not an absolute. It is a construction based on our past experiences and our current cognitive structures.

But how do children "construct" the world in their minds? Piaget proposed that infants initially come to "know" objects by physically acting on them. He referred to organized and sequential series of actions as *action schemes*, as, for example, when an infant voluntarily grasps things with her hands (grasping scheme) or sucks everything that comes in contact with her mouth (sucking scheme). A **scheme** (sometimes referred to as *schema*)is the basic unit of knowledge for Piaget. Later in development, children internalize these actions so they can "think without hands"—that is, mentally manipulate the things they perceive (like we do, for example, when thinking of the different possible arrangements for furniture in a living room). Piaget called these internalized actions *operations,* or *operational schemes.* Operations are organized and follow a system of logical rules. According to Piaget, the nature of schemes varies over development. Roughly speaking, they correspond to the four stages in the development of thought described later in this chapter.

### Functional Invariants

Piaget used the term **functional invariants** to describe two processes that characterize all biological systems (including intelligence) and operate throughout the life span: *organization* and *adaptation.*

**Organization.** Organization refers to the fact that intellectual operations are integrated with one another in a hierarchical nature. Through the process of organization, every intellectual operation is related to all other acts of intelligence. Thus, one scheme does not exist independently of other schemes but is coordinated with them. Similarly, organization is the tendency to integrate schemes into higher-order systems. For example, a week-old infant has one scheme for sucking and another for hand and arm movements. It doesn't take long, however, for these two schemes to become coordinated, resulting in a thumb-sucking scheme. Thumb sucking is not innate but represents the organization of two initially independent schemes into an integrated, higher-order scheme (even if these schemes become coordinated before birth).

**Adaptation.** Adaptation is the organism's tendency to adjust its schemes to environmental demands. Piaget defined two aspects of adaptation: **assimilation** and **accommodation.** Basically, assimilation is the incorporation of new information into already-existing schemes. Assimilation is not a passive process; it often requires that children modify or distort environmental input (hence, one source of cognitive errors) so that they can incorporate it into their current schemes.

Complementary to assimilation is the process of accommodation, in which a current scheme is changed to incorporate new information. Accommodation occurs when children are confronted with information that cannot be interpreted by current cognitive schemes. Accommodation is obviously an active process, resulting in the modification of existing schemes as a result of the interaction of those schemes with the environment.

As a simple example of assimilation and accommodation, consider the grasp of an infant. Babies will reflexively grasp objects placed in the palms of their hands. This grasping scheme can be applied to a variety of objects that fit easily into the infant's hand. So grasping the handle of a rattle, Daddy's finger, or the railing of a crib all involve (primarily) assimilation. The infant is incorporating information into an existing scheme. If the same infant is presented with a small ball, some small modifications in hand movements are required if the infant is to "know" this new object and successfully apply the grasping scheme to it. These modifications constitute (primarily) accommodation, permitting the infant to incorporate new data by slightly changing current schemes.

Piaget stressed that every act of intelligence involves both assimilation and accommodation. However, some actions involve a predominance of one over the other. For example, Piaget proposed that play is the purest form of assimilation, with children modifying the information in the environment to fit their make-believe actions. Conversely, Piaget proposed that there is a relative predominance of accommodation in imitation, with children adjusting their schemes to match those of a model.

For Piaget, children enter the world possessing the functional invariants of organization and adaptation, with little else, if anything, pre-specified. Thus, counter to neo-nativists or core-knowledge theorists (see Chapter 4), children are not specifically "prepared" to process some information more readily than others; rather, they actively construct knowledge, chiefly through the mechanisms of assimilation and accommodation.

### Equilibration

Piaget stated that at least four major factors contribute to development: (1) maturation, or the gradual unfolding of genetic plans; (2) the physical environment, or the child's actions on objects in his or her world; (3) social transmission, or the knowledge abstracted from people in the environment; and (4) equilibration, a concept unique to Piagetian theory.

**Equilibration** refers to the organism's attempt to keep its cognitive schemes in balance. This concept explains the motivation for development; it is meant to answer the questions "Why should we develop at all?" and "Why do cognitive schemes change?" When a child encounters some information that does not match his or her current schemes, an imbalance, or disequilibrium, results. The child experiences cognitive incongruity, with the new information not quite fitting his or her current state of knowledge. States of disequilibrium are intrinsically dissatisfying, and the child attempts to reinstate equilibrium.

How is this equilibration achieved? According to Piaget, equilibration is achieved by altering one's cognitive schemes. That is, given the disconfirming information, accommodation can occur, with the child slightly modifying current schemes to match the environmental data. As a result, a new and more stable scheme develops. This new scheme is more stable because fewer intrusions will set it into a state of disequilibrium than the immediately previous scheme was vulnerable to.

Discrepant information, however, is not always dealt with in such a way as to produce cognitive change (that is, by accommodation). If new information is too discrepant from a child's current schemes, for example, accommodation becomes impossible, and assimilation becomes unlikely. The alternative is to ignore (that is, not act on) the information, thus returning the schemes to their original state. For instance, a first-grader given algebra problems to solve will likely remain in a state of disequilibrium only briefly, realizing very soon that he or she hasn't the foggiest idea what these symbols mean, and will go on to something else.

Another alternative is to distort the new information by assimilation, making it compatible with the old schemes. In this case, no qualitative change in the schemes occurs, only a possible broadening of the original schemes. Nevertheless, the environmental intrusion is dealt with effectively, although it might not appear that way to an outsider. For example, the same algebra problem given to a 9-year-old will likely be recognized as a math problem, and the child might apply his or her basic arithmetic schemes to derive an "answer." Such an answer will probably be wrong, but by distorting an algebra problem to an arithmetic one can re-establish a temporary equilibrium. The equilibration process is schematically represented in Figure 5-2.

Let me provide one more example of how the equilibration process might work. A 3-year-old in the bathtub is confronted for the first time by a bar of soap that floats. The child has no scheme for floating soap. Toy boats float, but soap sinks. This new information produces cognitive incongruity, or a state of disequilibrium. At this point, the child can distort somewhat the characteristics of the soap in her mind and assimilate it into her "toy boat" scheme. She also has the option of hiding it under the washcloth and pretending it was never there. Her third option is to modify her current "soap" scheme by accommodating this new information and changing slightly her knowledge of soaps.

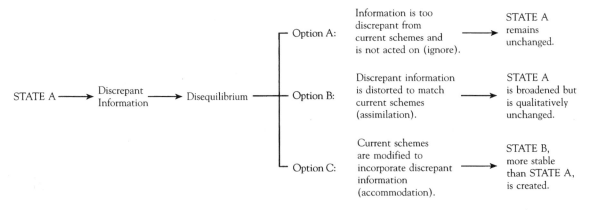

## FIGURE **5-2**

A schematic representation of the equilibration model. Although Piaget specified that equilibration involves accommodation (Option C), Options A and B reflect ways in which children may achieve temporary states of stability.

Accommodation—and, thus, the attainment of more stable schemes—is most apt to occur when the new information is only slightly discrepant from current schemes. Information that exactly matches current schemes can be assimilated into those schemes, and information that is too different from what a child already knows is likely to be either distorted or ignored. Regardless, children remain active operators on their environments both throughout and following the re-establishment of equilibrium.

## Stages of Development

Piaget divided cognitive development into four major stages, or periods: (1) sensorimotor, (2) preoperations, (3) concrete operations, and (4) formal operations. A brief description of the major characteristics of children's thinking during each of these stages is provided in Table 5-1. Piaget insisted that the order in which children progress through these stages is invariant and culturally universal; stages cannot be skipped. This assumption of the invariant order of stages is a direct consequence of Piaget's belief that development is *epigenetic* in nature—that it proceeds gradually, with later developments being based on earlier developments (see discussion of epigenesis in Chapter 2). So, from a Piagetian perspective, a precocious 8-year-old who has mastered analytic geometry acquired these skills by going through the same sequence of stage as his adolescent peers, but he went through those stages at a faster rate.

### The Sensorimotor Stage

The first major stage in Piaget's theory is the **sensorimotor stage**, or sensorimotor period, which lasts from birth to approximately 2 years of age (Piaget, 1952, 1954, 1962). In this period, children's intelligence is limited to their own actions. During

TABLE **5-1**
Characteristics of Major Periods in Piaget's Theory.

| Period and Approximate Age Range | Major Characteristics |
|---|---|
| Sensorimotor: birth to 2 years | Intelligence is limited to the infant's own actions on the environment. Cognition progresses from the exercise of reflexes (for example, sucking, visual orienting) to the beginning of symbolic functioning. |
| Preoperations: 2 to 7 years | Intelligence is symbolic, expressed via language, imagery, and other modes, permitting children to mentally represent and compare objects out of immediate perception Thought is intuitive rather than logical and is egocentric, in that children have a difficult time taking the perspective of another. |
| Concrete operations: 7 to 11 years | Intelligence is symbolic and logical. (For example, if A is greater than B and B is greater than C, then A must be greater than C.) Thought is less egocentric. Children's thinking is limited to concrete phenomena and their own past experiences, that is, thinking is not abstract. |
| Formal operations: 11 to 16 years | Children are able to make and test hypotheses: possibility dominates reality. Children are able to introspect about their own thought processes and, generally, can think abstractly. |

their first 18 months or so, children develop some complex problem-solving skills, but they do this without the benefit of mental representation. They know the world only by their direct actions (both sensory and motoric) on it.

Movement through the sensorimotor period can be described in terms of a cognitive developmental "trip" in two basic dimensions. The first dimension is in terms of representation. Infants progress from an action-based to a symbol-based intelligence—in other words, from sensorimotor to representational thought. The second dimension is in terms of personal perspective. Piaget described infants at birth as being unable to differentiate themselves from the external world; all the world is one, with themselves at the center. By the time children are 2 years old, they realize they are independent from the objects they act on and that objects exist in time and space even when they are not interacting with them (object permanence, discussed in Chapter 4). In general, over the course of the first 2 years of life, infants move from cognition centered on their own bodies and actions to cognition that displaces them in time and space from the things they think about.

Piaget's basic description of development through the sensorimotor period has been replicated using variants of the procedures he described and almost always with greater experimental control than in the original studies (Kopp, Sigman, & Parmelee, 1974; Uzgiris & Hunt, 1975). However, as we saw in Chapter 4, subsequent research has demonstrated that young infants may have substantially greater cognitive abilities than Piaget proposed.

Piaget divided the sensorimotor stage into six substages. As with Piaget's theory in general, infants progress through these increasingly complex substages in an invariant sequence, with the successful accomplishments of earlier substages forming the basis for the accomplishments of later substages. Central to each substage is children's problem-solving skills, particularly the extent to which they display intentionality, or **goal-directed behavior**, and this will be the focus of my description of Piaget's sensorimotor substages. A brief description of the major characteristics of children's intelligence at each sensorimotor substage is presented in Table 5-2.

**Substage 1: Basic reflexes (birth to 1 month).** In the first substage of *basic reflexes*, infants apply the set of action patterns, or reflexes, they were born with to interpret their experiences. Piaget used the term *reflex* broadly, so that infant reflexes include not only obvious behaviors, such as sucking and grasping, but also more subtle behaviors, such as eye movements, orientation to sound, and vocalization. If an object "fits" an infant's reflex, he or she applies that reflex to the object and assimilates it to existing schemes. However, accommodation also occurs during the first weeks of life. For example, Piaget (1952) made careful observations of his son, Laurent, who was adjusting to nursing. Piaget noted how Laurent would suck his hand or a quilt even when not hungry, the reflex being released by almost anything that touched his lips. Piaget also observed that Laurent's ability to locate the nipple and nurse successfully improved gradually over the first 3 weeks of life, as he learned to apply his sucking reflex selectively to the nipple (rather than to the skin surrounding the nipple) when hungry.

**Substage 2: Primary circular reactions.** Piaget called the second substage *primary circular reactions* (1 to 4 months). According to Piaget, primary circular reactions are the first class of repetitive actions, and they are based on hereditary reflexes. Piaget discussed these first circular reactions primarily with regard to sucking, vision,

TABLE **5-2**

Characteristics of the Sensorimotor Substages in Piaget's Theory.

| Substage and Approximate Age Range | Major Characteristics |
|---|---|
| Substage 1 (basic reflexes): birth to 1 month | Cognition is limited to inherited reflex patterns. |
| Substage 2 (primary circular reactions): 1 to 4 months | Infant acquires first adaptations, extends basic reflexes: reflex is activated by chance (for example, thumb comes in contact with lips, activating sucking reflex): infant attempts to reproduce reflex, resulting in acquisition of new, noninherited behavior (thumb sucking) that can be activated at the infant's discretion: initial occurrence of behavior is by chance, so need follows action. |
| Substage 3 (secondary circular reactions): 4 to 8 months | By chance, infant causes interesting event in environment to occur (for example, infant kicks mattress, causing mobile over crib to move) and tries to re-create event: beginning of control of objects and events external to infant; as in previous stage, initial occurrence of interesting event is by chance so need follows action. |
| Substage 4 (coordination of secondary circular reactions): 8 to 12 months | Infant uses two previously acquired schemes in coordination with each other to achieve a goal; First sign of need preceding action, or goal-directed behavior, is exhibited. |
| Substage 5 (tertiary circular reactions): 12 to 18 months | Infant discovers new means through active experimentation and develops new techniques to solve problems; goal-directed behavior is exhibited, but entire problem-solving process is conducted by overt trial and error: intelligence is still limited to child's actions on objects. |
| Substage 6 (mental combinations): 18 to 24 months | Infant shows first signs of symbolic functioning; infant is able to represent events in environment in terms of symbols (for example, language, imagery); problem solving can now be covert. |

hearing, vocalizations, and grasping. For example, Piaget detailed how Laurent, between 1 month 1 day and 1 month 21 days, acquired the ability to suck his thumb. The initial contact between Laurent's hand and his mouth was by chance. That is, babies don't start out thinking, "Gee, I'd like to suck my thumb. I wonder how I should go about doing it?" Rather, in the process of random activity or activity directed toward a biological outcome (for example, nursing), reflexes are fortuitously activated. Once Laurent's thumb or fingers were in his mouth, sucking occurred. And Laurent repeatedly attempted to re-create the experience, gradually coordinating his arm, hand, and finger movements with his mouth until he had established the ability to suck his thumb whenever (presumably) he pleased.

**Substage 3: Secondary circular reactions.** This is followed by the stage of *secondary circular reactions* (4 to 8 months) and the first acquired adaptations of new (that is, not reflexive) behaviors. With no intention beforehand, babies cause something interesting to happen and then attempt to re-create the interesting event. A major difference between primary and secondary circular reactions is that for the former, the interesting events are based on reflexes and, thus, are necessarily centered on the infant's body. In contrast, for secondary circular reactions, interesting events are found in the external world. This is especially true of visual events, although Piaget also discussed secondary circular reactions for other schemes, particularly grasping and hearing.

Let me provide an observation of my own. My daughter, Heidi, at 4 months of age, was lying in her playpen. She did not seem particularly interested in any of the toys that surrounded her, although she was awake, alert, and active. Strung over her head was a "crib gym," a complex mobile with parts that spin when they are hit. I had spun the objects for her on several occasions, and when I did, Heidi seemed to like it. But today was to be different. While flailing her arms and legs, she hit the mobile, causing it to spin. She happened to be looking at the mobile, and its movement caught her attention. She suddenly stopped and stared intently at the moving object over her head. It ceased moving, and she began to shake her arms and legs, to squirm, and finally, to cry. Again she hit the mobile, and again, she froze and quieted, staring straight ahead at the wonderful event she had caused.

**Substage 4: Coordination of secondary circular reactions.** Beginning around 8 months of age, infants enter substage 4, the *coordination of secondary circular reactions* (8 to 12 months). A major change in intentionality is found in substage 4, in that the need now precedes the act. That is, we have for the first time, *goal-directed behavior* and the beginning of the differentiation between means and ends (that is, cause and effect). This means/ends separation is first accomplished by the coordination of two previously acquired secondary schemes to obtain a specific goal. Piaget suggested that one of the simplest coordinations is that of removing an obstacle to retrieve a visible object. Piaget (1952) provided a lengthy description of experiments in which he placed obstacles, such as his hand, between his son, Laurent, and some desired object. Laurent acquired the ability to brush aside his father's hand to obtain the desired goal. That is, Laurent was able to use one well-established scheme (striking) so that another scheme (reaching, grasping, and retrieving an object) could be activated.

**Substage 5: Tertiary circular reactions.** Between 12 and 18 months of age, infants enter substage 5 and develop *tertiary circular reactions*. Infants in this substage are not restricted to applying previously acquired and consolidated schemes to achieve a goal. Rather, when faced with a problem, children can now make subtle alterations in their existing schemes that are directly related to obtaining a solution to their conundrum. This, Piaget stated, reflects a process of active experimentation.

Along with their new intellectual tools come increasing locomotive abilities. By 12 months of age, most babies can get around well, be it on two limbs or four, and this combination of increased locomotor and cognitive skills results in a child who is apt to be into everything. Children of this age often show a peak in curiosity. They want to know what makes things tick, and more importantly, how *they* can make them tick. They are explorers and adventurers. Is it possible to unravel the toilet paper, getting it all into the toilet without breaking the paper? How does one get into the bathroom sink? Isn't it interesting how by turning one knob the music becomes so much louder? Adults are often perplexed about why 15-month-olds find dog food and kitty litter so fascinating, why they are so interested in electric sockets and wastebaskets, and why they insist on climbing out of their high chairs and manipulating and mouthing everything on the kitchen table.

Although children during this substage are wonderful problem solvers, their intelligence, according to Piaget, is still basically limited to physical actions on objects. They know objects by acting on them and cannot yet make mental comparisons or represent objects and events symbolically. These children solve problems by a trial-and-error process, with all their trials available for public examination. So, for example, if a 15-month-old wants to see if her brother's tricycle fits beneath the coffee table, she will have to do it by physically attempting to place it there. It makes no difference that the tricycle rises a foot above the table. She cannot simply examine the two objects and discern that one is too big to fit under the other. She can learn this, however, by attempting it, although it may take several such tries before she concludes what, to an adult, is obvious.

**Substage 6: Invention of new means through mental combinations.** In the final substage of the sensorimotor period, *invention of new means through mental combinations* (18 to 24 months), children show the first glimmer of mental (symbolic) representation—of being able to think about objects without having to directly act on them. With the advent of mental representation, the process of children's problem solving is no longer totally in the open. Trial-and-error procedures can occur covertly in the head, producing what appears to be sudden comprehension or insight. New means can be invented through mental combinations.

What develops at this time, according to Piaget, is the *symbolic function,* which is expressed by language, deferred imitation (imitating a model after a significant delay), gestures, symbolic play, and mental imagery. These varied mental abilities arise alongside the more action-based forms of intelligence during the latter part of the second year. During this substage, the cognitions of the sensorimotor stage begin to be internalized as representational thought, setting the stage for a revolutionary change in the nature of human intelligence.

### The Development of Operations

With the advent of symbols, children's thinking becomes uniquely human. We might not be the only thinking species, and other species may occasionally use symbols (Savage-Rumbaugh et al., 1993), but the intellectual prowess that language, imagery, and deferred imitation provide us makes humans different from any other creature on the planet. In comparing the intellectual abilities of a 12-month-old infant, a 3-year-old child, and a 21-year-old adult, most would agree that, despite their vast age difference, the 3-year-old and the 21-year-old are more alike, cognitively speaking, than the 12-month-old and the 3-year-old. But no one would mistake a 3-year-old and 21-year-old as intellectual equals. Both the young child and the adult possess and use symbols, but there are many differences in their cognitions.

The three stages that follow the sensorimotor period are all similar in that children have symbolic (that is, mental representational) abilities, but they differ in how children are able to use these symbols for thought (Piaget & Inhelder, 1969). Piaget labeled these three stages **preoperations,** describing children's thinking between the ages of 2 and 7 years, **concrete operations,** occurring between the ages of 7 and 11 years, and **formal operations,** characterizing the advent of adult thinking and beginning about 11 years of age (see Table 5-1). As the names denote, each stage is characterized by operations (or in the case of preoperations, the lack of them). Most of Piaget's work beyond the period of infancy dealt, in one way or another, with the development of operations.

As I mentioned previously, **operations** are particular types of cognitive schemes, and they describe general ways that children act on their world. Piaget specified four characteristics of operations. First, they are mental; thus, they require the use of symbols. Second, operations derive from action, so operations can be thought of as internalized actions. For example, children will first count on their fingers or physically line up red checkers with an equal number of black checkers, discovering through action that the one-to-one correspondence between red and black checkers remains the same no matter where they start counting or how they arrange the pieces. Third, operations exist in an organized system. Piaget believed that all cognitive operations are integrated with all other operations, so a child's cognition at any particular time should be relatively even, or homogeneous. And fourth, operations follow a system of rules, the most critical of which is that of **reversibility**, the knowledge that an operation can be reversed or that, for any operation, another operation can compensate for the effects of the first. For example, in arithmetic, subtraction is the inverse of addition. If 5 plus 2 equals 7, then 7 minus 2 must equal 5. Such a rule would seem to be obviously critical in children's learning basic arithmetic. (This brings to mind the 5-year-old who proudly announced to his mother that he had learned at school that 3 plus 2 equals 5. After praising him for his new knowledge, his mother asked him how much 2 plus 3 equaled, and the child answered that he didn't know; he hadn't learned that one yet.) Reversibility is also reflected in the knowledge that a change in one dimension can be compensated by a change in another dimension. For example, if water is poured from a short, fat glass into a tall, thin glass, the increased height of the water level in the second glass is compensated by a decrease in the breadth of the water.

The following subsections give a general account of Piaget's description of the thought of preoperational, concrete operational, and formal operational children. Many other topics relating to the development of operations in Piaget's theory will be discussed in later chapters.

**Transition from preoperational to concrete operational thought.** Piaget described preoperational thought, although based on symbols, as lacking the logical characteristics of concrete operations. By this, Piaget meant that operations do not generate contradictions. In contrast to concrete operational children, preoperational children are greatly influenced by the appearance of things, and their thought is said to be *intuitive*. Thus, young children are less affected by what, according to logic, must be and are more affected by what, according to appearance, seems to be.

Perhaps giving an example is the easiest way to explain the distinction between preoperational and concrete operational thought. **Conservation**, the realization that an entity remains the same despite changes in its form, is the sine qua non of concrete operations. For Piaget, conservation is not just a convenient task to illustrate cognitive differences among children; it represents the basis for all rational thinking (Piaget, 1965/1932). The concept of conservation can apply to any substance that can be quantified, and conservation has been studied with respect to length, number, mass, weight, area, and volume. In general, Piaget's conservation tasks take the following form:

$$A = B$$
$$B \rightarrow B'$$
$$A \; ? \; B'$$

In words, the equivalence between A and B is first established (for example, two balls of clay). Object B is then transformed while children watch (for example, rolling one ball of clay into a sausage). The children are then asked to judge the equivalence of the transformed object with the initial, unchanged object and to provide a justification for their decision. Basically, children must realize that the quantitative relation between the two objects remains the same despite changes in the appearance of one. You may recognize this as a form of the appearance/reality distinction discussed earlier. The question here is whether children realize that, despite changes in appearance, the actual amount of substance remains the same.

Piaget's conservation-of-liquid task is illustrated in Figure 5-3. A child is presented with two identical glasses containing equal amounts of water. A third glass is introduced that is taller and thinner than the original two containers. The water in one of the original glasses is then poured into the third, taller glass while the child watches. The water level in the new glass is, of course, higher than the water level in the original glass because of its narrower width. The child is then asked if the two glasses have the same amount of water in them and to justify his or her answer.

Most 5-year-old children answer by saying no, the amounts of liquid are not the same anymore—there is more water in the new, taller glass. Ask them why this is so, and they will point out the difference in the height of the water. They will ignore the fact that the shorter glass is wider, and if this is pointed out to them, they will either dismiss it as insignificant or, in some cases, actually change their minds and tell you that there is more water in the shorter glass because it is so fat. They will admit that the water in the two glasses was the same to begin with, and they do not think that anyone is playing a trick on them. The difference in appearance between the water levels in the two glasses is too great for them to believe that the same amount of water is contained in both.

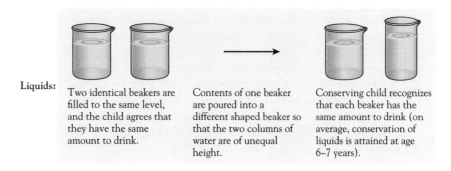

Liquids: Two identical beakers are filled to the same level, and the child agrees that they have the same amount to drink.

Contents of one beaker are poured into a different shaped beaker so that the two columns of water are of unequal height.

Conserving child recognizes that each beaker has the same amount to drink (on average, conservation of liquids is attained at age 6–7 years).

FIGURE **5-3**

Piaget's conservation-of-liquid problem.

In contrast, most 8-year-olds given the same problem tell you that the two glasses still contain the same amount of water. When pressed to explain why, they say that all you did was pour the water from one glass to the other, and that you could just as easily pour it back to confirm equivalence (reversibility). If you ask them "Why do they look so different then?" they will likely comment that although the water level is much higher in the tall, skinny glass, it is much wider in the short, fat glass, and that the difference in height is made up by the difference in width. Children's responses to such questions are important, for in conservation problems, it is not sufficient just to provide the correct answer to demonstrate concrete operations; a justification that involves the concept of reversibility is also necessary.

This example demonstrates the intuitive thinking of the preoperational child. There really seems to be more water in the tall, skinny glass. In fact, most objective adults would probably concur, although we know that this cannot be so. The young child's intuitive approach to the problem leads to some contradictions, however. What happens when the water in the tall glass is returned to its original container? Most preoperational children will tell you that the water in the two glasses is now the same as it was to begin with. The contradiction, however, is one of objective fact; there is no apparent contradiction to the child. Some cognitive discrepancy (disequilibrium) may be experienced by slightly older and cognitively more advanced children, who realize that something is not quite right but can't figure out exactly what it is. For Piaget, these children are in a transition phase between preoperations and concrete operations. Their cognitive structures are thrown into states of disequilibrium, and within a short time, they will make the accommodations necessary to achieve conservation. No such disequilibrium is experienced by younger children; they assimilate the information to their preoperative schemes.

With a few mainly laboratory-based exceptions, conservation is not something that children are taught. The notion of conservation develops gradually, and once it is acquired, most children assume they always thought that way. Ask most 8-year-old conservers if they ever in their lives thought the glass with the higher water level had more water, and they will answer "No"—and often give you a funny look as well. After all, why would an adult even ask such a question?

An operational knowledge of conservation does not develop simultaneously for all properties of material; conservation develops for some properties before others. Piaget referred to this phenomenon as *horizontal décalage*. When children acquire the concept of conservation for one property, they do not realize that the same general principle applies to other properties. Piaget claimed that the order in which conservation is acquired for different properties is constant across children. Thus, conservation of number is acquired before conservation of mass, and both of these are acquired before conservation of weight, which precedes the conservation of volume. Other researchers have generally confirmed this pattern of development (for example, Brainerd & Brainerd, 1972; Uzgiris, 1964).

Conservation is only one of the many phenomena described by Piaget that concrete operational children "pass" and preoperational children "fail." Table 5-3 summarizes several other phenomena Piaget investigated that differentiate preoperational from concrete operational children.

Piaget's description of children's performance on conservation tasks illustrates the importance of the concept of reversibility, discussed earlier. Preoperational children,

TABLE **5-3**

Several Piagetian tasks that preoperational children "fail" and concrete operational children "pass." Note, however, that subsequent research found that, under certain stimulus or training conditions, preoperational children could "solve" many of these tasks.

*Conservation:* The ability to realize than changes in the physical appearance of things have no influence on changes in their substantial, real properties, like number, length, area, mass, liquid weight, or volume. Children are first able to conserve number, followed by conservation of mass, and these are acquired before conservation of weight, which precedes the conservation of volume.

*Multiple classification*: The ability to classify objects simultaneously on two dimensions (size and shape, for instance). Preoperational children can classify' objects on a single dimension (size or shape), but not both simultaneously. Concrete operational children realize that a woman can be both a mother and a daughter at the same time, something that preoperational children have a difficult time doing.

*Class inclusion:* The knowledge that a class must always be smaller than any more inclusive class in which it is contained. In a typical class-inclusion problem, children are given several examples from two subordinate categories of a single superordinate category (for example, seven pictures of dogs and three pictures of cats). They are then asked whether there are more dogs or more animals. Although preschool children can easily make correct numerical judgments when comparing two subordinate sets (for example, dogs versus cats), correct responses on class-inclusion problems are not found reliably until late childhood or early adolescence (see Winer, 1980).

*Seriation:* The ability to order objects according to the quantitative dimension of a certain trait, such as size. For example, concrete operational children can order a pair of scissors, a pen, and a paper clip by length.

*Transitive inference:* Ability to infer quantitative relationship between three or more elements. For example, if a concrete operational child is told that a pair of scissors is longer than a pen, and a pen is longer than a paper clip, he or she can infer that the pair of scissors is longer than the paper clip (that is, if $A > B$ and $B > C$, therefore $A > C$). There is no need to actually check the difference in length between A and C.

stated Piaget, are unable to apply the rules of reversibility to arrive at correct solutions to conservation problems. Preoperational and concrete operational children differ in ways other than reversibility, however. Generally, Piaget described preoperational children as being more influenced by their immediate perceptions and more egocentric, all relative to concrete operational children. These factors are discussed briefly in the following subsections.

**Perceptual centration versus decentration.** Preoperational children's perception is said to be *centered* in that they attend to and make judgments based on the most salient aspect of their perceptual fields, which Piaget referred to as perceptual **centration**, They are highly attentive to particular portions of a perceptual array and often are unable to integrate various parts into a whole. In the conservation-of-liquid problem discussed earlier, their attention is directed only to the difference in heights of the water levels, and they are unable (according to Piaget) to coordinate the two dimensions of height and width simultaneously. In contrast, concrete operational children's perception is said to be *decentered* in that they can divorce themselves from specific aspects of a perceptual array and attend to and make decisions based on the entire perceptual field, which Piaget referred to as perceptual **decentration**. Unlike their younger peers, they can consider two dimensions at once, partly because they are not so highly focused on one dimension that differences in the other escape their awareness.

Perceptual centration is not limited to young children's performance on laboratory tasks but is reflected in their everyday thinking. For example, Piaget (1929) noted that preoperational children often use height as a means of estimating age. Take, for example, the 5-year-old who told her 35-year-old, 4-foot-11-inch mother that she was the "youngest mommy in the whole neighborhood." In actuality, she was the shortest mommy in the whole neighborhood and, if truth be known, one of the oldest among her daughter's friends.

Consider another example of young children interpreting age on the basis of height. As a young graduate student, I was finishing a day of testing at a kindergarten when I ran into the mother of one of the children. We talked for a while about the project, and then she said she was surprised to see that I was so young. She had questioned her son about me, and he had told her that I was older than his mother and much older than his teacher. In reality, I was 22 years old at the time, the child's mother looked to be in her early 30s, and his teacher was a woman nearing retirement. How could a 5-year-old child be so far off? The answer is that I am about 6 feet tall, the boy's mother was about 5-feet-3-inches, and his teacher was a petite woman, likely no more than 5-feet tall. To this child's mind (and eyes), I was a good "foot older" than his teacher.

**Egocentricity.**  In general, Piaget described preoperational children as being more egocentric than older, concrete operational children. Piaget used the term **egocentricity** to describe young children's intellectual perspective. Young children interpret the world through preoperative eyes and generally assume that others see the world as they do. Their cognition is centered around themselves, and they have a difficult time putting themselves in someone else's shoes. Preoperational children are, of course, less egocentric than sensorimotor children, who know objects and events only by direct action on them. Yet, young, preoperational children are more self-centered in cognitive perspective than concrete operational children.

According to Piaget, this egocentric perspective permeates young children's entire cognitive life, influencing their perceptions, their language, and their social interactions. For example, 6-year-old Jamal assumes that all children in the first grade have older siblings and can never be the eldest child in their family. Jamal himself is in first grade and has an older brother; therefore, all first-graders, if they have siblings at all, must have older siblings. Or consider, for example, my encounter with a neighbor child, Maurice, when I, and he, were about 6. Maurice asked about the ages of my parents. I told him I wasn't sure about their ages, but I knew that my mother was older than my father. Maurice quite emphatically told me that that was impossible. "Daddies are *always* older than mommies. It's the law." That evening, I talked to my parents and was told that my mother was, indeed, a few months older than my father, and that this was perfectly legal in the state of Massachusetts. Maurice's assertions were related to the structure of his own family. His father was about 15 years older than his mother, so Maurice assumed that *all* fathers must be older than *all* mothers. There is also the fact that my father was nearly a foot taller than my mother, so Maurice's egocentrically based belief in age differences between mothers and fathers may have been further influenced by his centering on the difference in height between my parents.

Like most other aspects of preoperational thought, the young child's egocentricity is viewed as ineffective—and in most situations, it is. However, there might be some adaptive advantage to a young child's egocentricity (Bjorklund, 1997a; Bjorklund & Green, 1992). From a global perspective, young children should be self-centered and less concerned with the thoughts, feelings, and behaviors of others. They are universal novices and need to learn the complicated ways of their culture, making a self-centered perspective for young children likely to be beneficial from a Darwinian point of view. For instance, research with both adults and children has shown that when information is related to oneself (for example, when one is asked to determine how words on a list or events in a story relate to you), it is remembered better than when no self-referencing is done (Kail & Levine, 1976; Mood, 1979). Young children's tendencies to relate new information to themselves might thus give them a learning advantage, making egocentricity beneficial and not detrimental for the young child (Bjorklund & Green, 1992; Mood, 1979).

**Transition from concrete to formal operational thought.** Children in the concrete operational stage are impressive thinkers. Compared to preoperational children, they can reverse thought (as reflected by their answers to conservation problems), can decenter their perception, and are less egocentric. Given a set of data, they can arrive at an answer (generally) free of contradictions. They can solve reasonably complex problems as long as the general form of the problem and of the solution are previously known to them. Their thought is directed to the objects and events in their immediate experience, and "thinking about things" suffices to get most people, of any age, through most of the routine tasks of everyday life.

Most of us also recognize, however, that a change takes place in early adolescence. Children are no longer tied to thinking about concrete objects. Their thought can roam to discover or invent objects, events, and relations independent of their previous experiences. Their thinking is no longer restricted to things but can be applied to itself. As one Piagetian scholar put it: "Concrete operations consist of thought thinking about the environment, but formal operations consist of thought thinking about itself" (Brainerd, 1978, p. 215).

The benchmark of formal operations is what Piaget referred to as **hypothetico-deductive reasoning** (Inhelder & Piaget, 1958). Deductive reasoning, which entails going from the general to the specific, is not in itself a formal operational process. Concrete operational children can arrive at a correct conclusion if they are provided with the proper evidence. However, their reasoning is confined to events and objects with which they are already familiar. "Concrete" operations are so named because children's thinking is limited to tangible facts and objects; it does not include hypotheses. Formal operational children, on the other hand, are not restricted to thinking about previously acquired facts but can generate hypotheses—for these children, what is possible is more important than what is real.

Thinking during the formal operational period can be done solely on the basis of symbols, with no need for referents in real life. Although this might bring to mind a person whose head is perpetually in the clouds and who cannot carry on a conversation without getting into metaphysics, this was not Piaget's intention. Rather, we have a person who is not tied to facts in his or her thinking but can postulate what might be as well as what is. The formal operational thinker can generate ideas of things not yet experienced, accounting for the novel (to the child) and often-grand ideas adolescents generate concerning morality, ethics, justice, government, and religion. Adolescents are entering, cognitively, the adult arena and ponder many of the weighty issues of the day without having had to experience directly the things they think about. The theories of most adolescents are naive because of their limited knowledge, but Piaget believed these children are flexing their mental muscles, using their newly acquired symbolic skills to deal with ideas rather than with things.

Hypothetical thinking is also critical for most forms of mathematics beyond arithmetic. If $2x + 5 = 15$, what does $x$ equal? The problem does not deal with concrete entities, such as apples or oranges, but with numbers and letters. Mathematics in general is based on hypotheses and not necessarily in reality. Let $y$ be 22, or let it be 7, or $-12$, or 45 degrees, or the cosine of angle AB. Once provided with a premise, formal operational thinkers can go on to solve the problem. They don't ask, "Is $y$ *really* 22?" It is an arbitrary, hypothetical problem—and one that can be answered only if it is approached abstractly, using a symbol system that does not require concrete referents.

In addition to developing deductive reasoning abilities, Piaget theorized that formal operational children are able to think inductively, going from specific observations to broad generalizations. **Inductive reasoning** is the type of thinking that characterizes scientists, in which hypotheses are generated and then systematically tested in experiments. By controlling for extraneous or potentially confounding factors, experiments lead to conclusions about nature. Inhelder and Piaget (1958) used a series of tasks to assess scientific reasoning, one of which, the *pendulum problem*, I will discuss briefly.

In the pendulum problem, children are given a rod from which strings of different lengths can be suspended. Objects of varying weight can be attached to the strings. The children are shown how the pendulum operates (one places a weighted string on the rod and swings it) and are asked to determine the factors responsible for the speed with which the pendulum swings (the rate of oscillation) (see Figure 5-4). The children are told that in addition to varying the length of the string and the weight of the object attached to it, they can drop the object from varying heights (for example, high versus low) and alter the force of the push they give the object when initially propelling it. Thus, in attempting to solve the problem of the oscillating pendulum, the children can consider four possible factors (string length, weight of object, height of release, and force of push), with several levels within each factor (for example, three lengths of string, four weights of objects). The children are given the opportunity to experiment

## FIGURE **5-4**

The pendulum problem. Children are to determine what factors or combination of factors are responsible for the rate at which the pendulum oscillates.

with the apparatus before providing an answer to the question of which factors are responsible for the pendulum's rate of oscillations. (The correct answer is the length of the string—short strings swing faster than long strings, regardless of all other factors.)

How might a scientist go about solving this problem? The first step is to generate a hypothesis. It doesn't matter if the hypothesis is correct or not, merely that it be testable and yield noncontradictory conclusions. This initial step is within the ability of concrete operational children. The next step is what separates the concrete from the formal operational thinkers—the testing of one's hypothesis. The trick is to vary a single factor while holding the others constant. For example, a child might examine the rate of oscillation for the 100-gram weight in combination with all the other factors (that is, short string, high release, easy push; short string, high release, hard push; short string, low release, short push; and so on). This can then be done for other weights, until the child has tested all of the various combinations.

Concrete operational children often get off to a good start on this problem, but they rarely arrive at the correct answer. Their observations are generally accurate (which is not the case for preoperational children), but they usually fail to isolate relevant variables and will arrive at a conclusion before exhaustively testing their hypotheses. For example, children might observe that the pendulum swings fast with a short string and a heavy weight and then conclude that both string length and weight are jointly responsible for the rate of oscillation. According to Inhelder and Piaget (1958), it is not until the formal operational stage that children can test their hypotheses correctly and arrive at the only possible, logical conclusion. (More will be said about scientific reasoning in Chapter 7.)

A further formal operational characteristic involves the ability to examine the contents of one's thought, or to *think about thinking*. Concrete operational thinkers have available to them some powerful problem-solving skills. But according to Piaget, they are not able to reflect on the content of their thinking to arrive at new insights. Concrete operational children gain knowledge from the outside world but cannot learn anything new by contemplating what they already know. In contrast, formal operational children can acquire new information as a result of internal reflection. Piaget (1971) used the term **reflective abstraction** to refer to "a rearrangement, by means of thought, of some matter previously presented to the subject in a rough or immediate form" (p. 320). In other words, formal operational children can reflect on knowledge they already possess and, without needing additional information from the external environment, arrive at a previously unknown truth. Reflective abstraction is thinking about thinking, and it might allow a child to apply more readily information that he or she knows to new situations or to discover alternative cognitive routes to solving old problems.

**Egocentricity in adolescence.** One interesting observation Piaget made about adolescents that ties their cognition to that of much younger children concerns egocentricity, which is usually associated with preoperational thought. Piaget, however, defined egocentrism broadly, as an inability to decenter, and proposed that adolescents demonstrate their own form of centration.

Piaget stated that adolescents are concerned about their future in society, and often with how they might transform society, but many of the grand social and political ideas of adolescents conflict with the beliefs or attitudes of others (particularly people in authority). Adolescents also might believe that these abstract ideas are unique to them, making them impatient with the "stodgy and simple-minded" ideas of their elders. This view changes as the adolescent approaches adulthood, and many of us can identify with Mark Twain, who (supposedly) professed to be impressed by how much his father had learned between Twain's 14th and 21st birthdays.

Adolescence is a time when young people are trying to leave childhood behind and adopt adult roles, an attempt that often results in extreme self-consciousness. Adolescents' self-centered perspectives result in the mistaken belief that other people are as concerned with their feelings and behavior as they are, which only enhances their self-consciousness. David Elkind (1967; Elkind & Bowen, 1979) hypothesized that adolescents feel they are constantly "on stage" or playing to an **imaginary audience**. This hypothesis has been confirmed in several studies, where adolescents' responses to potentially embarrassing situations and their tendencies to reveal aspects of themselves to others were related to age and formal operational abilities (Elkind & Bowen, 1979; Gray & Hudson, 1984). Although there are some discrepancies in the findings, the effect of the imaginary audience seems to peak during early adolescence and to decline as formal operational skills increase.

Elkind also proposed that the egocentrism of adolescence leads to what he called the **personal fable**, a belief in one's uniqueness and invulnerability. This is reflected in the often-reckless behavior of adolescents and the belief that bad things happen only to other people (for example, "I won't get pregnant," or "I can get off the tracks before the train gets here") (Arnett, 1992).

The risk-taking behavior that springs from adolescents' personal fables clearly has its drawbacks, but it might also have some adaptive value, just as preschool children's egocentricity might. For example, teenage egocentricity ensures that adolescents will experiment with new ideas and generally behave more independently (Bjorklund & Green, 1992). Many of these experiences will be beneficial to adult functioning and might hasten entry into adult life. Many parents do not welcome such independence, of course, for the negative consequences of much adolescent risk-taking are real, but for most adolescents, their egocentricity might be adaptive in the long run.

Piaget saw adolescence as a time of great intellectual awakening rather than a time of emotional storm and strife. But few scientists today believe that Piaget's picture of adolescent (and adult) intelligence as reasonable, systematic, and logical is correct. Adults in general are not nearly as logical in their thinking as Piaget would have us be. We take mental shortcuts, make estimations, and arrive at conclusions before exhausting all possibilities. In fact, formal operational thinking does not seem to be typically used by adults in daily life (Capon & Kuhn, 1979), and it is rare in cultures where formal schooling is not the norm (Cole, 1990; Dasen, 1977). (See Box 5-1 for a discussion of the role of culture in the expression of symbolic thinking.) Moreover, among educated people from developed cultures, formal operational abilities may be used in some contexts but not others. For instance, when college students were given a series of formal operational problems to solve, they tended to perform best when the problems were in their area of expertise—physics majors on physics problems (the pendulum problem), political science majors on political problems, and English majors on literary problems (De Lisi & Staudt, 1980; see Figure 5-5). Piaget's description of formal operations may reflect the best adults

| **B O X 5-1** | **Culture and Symbolic Development** |

The description Piaget and others have provided of cognitive development is intended to be universal: Children across the globe develop the use of symbolic representation at about the same time and in the same manner. Culture, however, does matter. As we noted in Chapter 3 when discussing sociocultural perspectives of development, the culture that a child grows up in not only limits *what* that child thinks about but also *how* that child thinks. How might culture influence thinking as studied by Piaget?

Although Piaget argued that the developmental sequence for attaining the various accomplishments of concrete operations is universal, there are individual differences in the rate at which conservation and other concrete operational abilities are achieved. Cultural differences in the rate of attaining conservation have been repeatedly observed, with most studies finding a slower rate of development for nonschooled children relative to schooled children (Dasen, 1977). Yet, these cultural differences in the rate of development might be attributed less to differences in the actual competence of these children than to cultural differences in the nature of the tasks and how they are administered. For example, in many studies, children from traditional cultures were tested either through interpreters or in their second or third language (see Nyiti, 1982). This contrasts sharply with the way that American or European children are tested and makes it difficult to interpret differences in performance found between these groups.

For example, in a study of conservation, Raphael Nyiti (1982) compared two cultural groups of Canadian children: Europeans (white and English speaking) and Micmacs (a First Nations people of eastern Canada). The Micmac children attended school, where they learned English, but they spoke their native language (Micmac) at home. Both the European and Micmac children were given a series of conservation tasks, following standard Piagetian procedures. The European children were all tested in English. The Micmac children were divided into two groups, with half being tested in English by a European and the other half being tested in Micmac by a Micmac. No difference was found in how the European and Micmac children performed the tasks when tested

in their "home" language—European children in English and Micmac children in Micmac. When the Micmac children were tested in English by a European examiner, however, they gave much shorter and less complete answers, and they were significantly less likely to be classified as conservers than their European counterparts. These results bolster Piaget's contention that certain aspects of cognitive development are universal and that concepts such as conservation develop on a predictable schedule in all cultures. This truism can be overlooked, however, if one is not mindful of the cultural context in which performance is assessed.

Cultural differences have also been found in the attainment of formal operations, with adults from nonschooled cultures often failing to display formal operational thinking, at least as measured by Piaget. People who lack formal schooling might not have had sufficient exposure to the kinds of thinking that stress logic, mathematics, and science—experiences that Piaget believed help children to reason at the formal level (Cole, 1990; Dasen, 1977). Indeed, Steven Tulkin and Melvin Konner (1973) found that preliterate Bushman hunters who fail Piaget's problems often do reason at the formal level on at least one task—tracking prey. Clearly, this is an activity of great importance to them that requires the systematic testing of inferences and hypotheses.

Consider children's classification abilities. In the 1930s, the Russian neuropsychologist Alexander Luria (1976) evaluated the cognitive styles of inhabitants from a remote area in the former Soviet Union (Uzbekistan) and reported that, unlike Westerners, most of the adults he studied did not develop a conceptual, or taxonomic, way of classifying objects. Rather, they used a more functional approach, one perhaps better suited for their ecology. Consider the following example from Rakmat, a 38-year-old illiterate peasant (from Luria, 1976, pp. 55–57):

He is shown drawings of the following: *hammer-saw-log-hatchet.*

"They're all alike. I think all of them have to be here. See, if you're going to saw, you need a saw, and if you have to split something you need a hatchet. So they're all needed here."

*(Continues)*

| BOX 5-1 | **Culture and Symbolic Development** (*Continued*) |
|---|---|

We tried to explain the task by another, simpler example: "Look, here you have three adults and one child. Now clearly the child doesn't belong in this group."

"Oh, but the boy must stay with the others! All three of them are working, you see, and if they have to keep running out to fetch things, they'll never get the job done, but the boy can do the running for them.... The boy will learn; that'll be better, then they'll be able to work well together" (p. 55).

Subject is then shown drawing of: *bird-rifle-dagger-bullet*.

"The swallow doesn't fit here.... No ... this is a rifle. It's loaded with a bullet and kills the swallow. Then you have to cut the bird up with the dagger, since there's no other way to do it.... What I said about the swallow before is wrong! All these things go together." (pp. 56–57)

When we look at the way illiterate Uzbekistani peasants classify objects, we might feel tempted to evaluate them as being "less cognitively advanced" than the classifications used by Western people. (In fact, a functional type of classification is typical of many 5-year-old children in Western societies.) However, this would be a mistake, for these differences in classification style are, in fact, well suited to the local environment

Culture certainly counts in shaping children's thinking. However, children across the globe possess the same set of symbolic abilities, and these abilities develop in much the same fashion. What seems to differ is how children in different cultures express their symbolic abilities, not the abilities themselves.

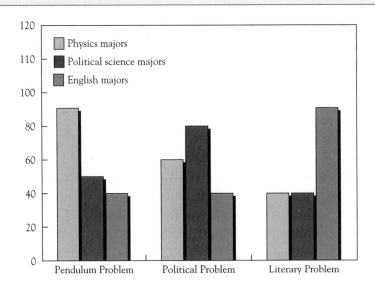

## FIGURE **5-5**

Percentage of college students displaying formal thought. College students performed best on formal-operational problems in their area of expertise – physics major on physic problems, political science majors on political science problems, and English majors on English problems.

Source: De Lisi, R., & Staudt, J. (1980). Individual differences in college students' performance on formal operations tasks. *Journal of Applied Developmental Psychology, 1*, 163–174.

can do, but it fails to capture how grown-ups deal with real-world problems on a daily basis. To quote Peter Wason and Philip Johnson-Laird (1972): "At best, we can all think like logicians: At worst, logicians all think like us" (p. 245). Even with its shortcomings, however, Piaget's account of adolescent thought captures some of the uniqueness of adolescence and has provided insight to psychologists, educators, and parents about the teenage mind.

## The State of Piaget's Theory Today

Piaget is a giant in the field of human development. As one scholar quoted by Harry Beilin (1992) put it, "[A]ssessing the impact of Piaget on developmental psychology is like assessing the impact of Shakespeare on English literature or Aristotle on philosophy—impossible" (p. 191). But what does Piaget's theory, initially formulated more than three-quarters of a century ago, tell us about development today? Table 5-4 lists some of the major contributions that Piaget made to the field of cognitive development. The list is based, in part, on an assessment of Piaget's contributions made by

TABLE **5-4**
Contributions of Piaget to the Study of Cognitive Development.

1. Piaget founded the field of cognitive development as we know it. The study of children's thinking has focused on high-level cognitive tasks, very different from the emphasis on basic-level and mainly unconscious cognition that has characterized the study of adult cognition. Because of Piaget, cognitive development is a unique field to itself and not simply the application of ideas and methods developed in the study of adult cognition to children.

2. The child is an active, self-motivated agent, playing an important role in his or her own development. This might seem obvious to anyone today who has seriously considered the nature of cognitive development, but it was an innovation of Piaget and counter to the dominant perspective of his time.

3. Piaget's equilibration model was one of the first attempts to explain, rather than just describe, the process of development. Despite the many years since Piaget originally formulated this model, only recently have psychologists taken seriously the challenge to explain, rather than just describe, developmental transitions (Case, 1992; Fischer, 1980; Siegler, 1996).

4. Piaget introduced many interesting and useful concepts to cognitive development, including *scheme, object permanence, egocentrism, centration, decentration,* and *conservation,* among many others. Accompanying these concepts were many experimental tasks used to assess them, many of which are still used by psychologists today.

5. Piaget provided a highly memorable description of cognitive development that gave a relatively accurate picture of how children of different ages think. Piaget's description of development still captures much of the richness and uniqueness of children's thinking. Children can, under certain circumstances, be trained or biased to think in a more advanced way, But such training is usually limited and rarely transforms the child into a totally different type of thinker. In other words, Piaget's description of intellectual development has ecological validity in that it depicts well the day-to-day functioning of most children.

6. Piaget's influence extended beyond the field of cognitive development to other areas of development (social, emotional), and, importantly, to education.

7. Piaget made more important empirical discoveries, on a wider range of topics, than any other developmental psychologist, and he is not likely to be displaced from this lofty seat of honor soon.

8. Finally, Piaget asked important questions and drew literally thousands of researchers to the study of cognitive development. And as often happens when heuristic theories such as Piaget's are repeatedly scrutinized, some of his research led to new insights.

Source: This list is based, in part, on an assessment of Piaget's contributions made by several prominent researcher, written in honor of the centennial of Piaget's birth (see Brainerd, C. F. (1996). Piaget: A centennial celebration. *Psychological Science, 7,* 191–195.)

several prominent researchers, written in honor of the centennial of Piaget's birth (Brainerd, 1996; Elkind, 1996; Fischer & Hencke, 1996; Flavell, 1996; Gopnik, 1996; Kessen, 1996; Siegler & Ellis, 1996).

Piaget's theory has undergone more scrutiny than any other theory in cognitive development, and nearly 40 years of intense investigation (some would say 40 years of Piaget bashing) has shown that Piaget's theory is not the final word. For example, children often display greater abilities than Piaget proposed. For instance, we saw in Chapter 4 that infants display what appear to be glimmers of representational thought much earlier than Piaget proposed (Spelke & Kinzler, 2007). And we'll see in later chapters at least rudimentary evidence that infants, in their first year of life, show deferred imitation, a landmark measure of the symbolic function for Piaget (Bauer, 2007), and represent other people as intentional agents (Tomasello & Carpenter, 2007).

Perhaps most research has focused on Piaget's underestimation of the representational abilities of preschool children. This is illustrated by studies examining preoperational children's egocentricity. For instance, preschool children can identify and empathize with the emotions of others (Hoffman, 1975), can take the visual perspective of another person (Borke, 1975), and can realize that they possess knowledge that others do not share (see discussion of the development of theory of mind in Chapter 6). In fact, research during the last three decades has indicated that Piaget underestimated the perspective-taking abilities of young children and that egocentricity is far from an all-or-none matter.

Other researchers have shown that children who do not spontaneously solve problems in a concrete operational way can be trained to do so. For example, although scientists have replicated the stages involved in the acquisition of conservation proposed by Piaget (Brainerd & Brainerd, 1972), many have demonstrated that children as young as 4 years of age can be trained to conserve by way of a variety of techniques, at least in the laboratory (Brainerd & Allen, 1971; Gelman, 1969). Other researchers have successfully trained concrete operational children to perform formal operational tasks (Adey & Shayer, 1992; Stone & Day, 1978).

In still other situations, research has shown that Piaget's account of formal operations greatly overestimates how adults actually think (Capon & Kuhn, 1979; De Lisi & Staudt, 1980). For example, Noel Capon and Deanna Kuhn (1979) investigated whether adults tend to use formal operational abilities in a practical task. These researchers interviewed 50 women in a supermarket and asked them to judge which of two sizes of the same product was the better buy. For example, one task involved two bottles of garlic powder: a smaller bottle containing 1.25 ounces (35 grams) and selling for 41 cents, and a larger bottle containing 2.37 ounces (67 grams) and selling for 77 cents. The women were provided with pencil and paper to use if they wished and were asked to justify their explanations. The most direct way to arrive at the correct answer is to compute the price per unit of weight for each product and then compare the two. This involves reasoning about proportions, which Inhelder and Piaget (1958) said was a scheme characteristic of formal operations. Fewer than 30% of the women used a proportional reasoning strategy, however, and at least 50% of the women used a strategy that yielded inconclusive evidence at best and was just as likely to be wrong as to be right. For instance, some women used a subtraction strategy, saying, for example, "With the bigger one you get 32 more grams for 36 more cents," concluding that the bigger one was thus the better buy. Others merely relied on their past experiences, making statements such as "The big one must be cheaper" without providing any justification for the statement. In general, formal operational reasoning was not observed for a majority of these women. This does not mean that these adults would not have displayed formal reasoning under some other conditions, but it does suggest that formal operations are not typical of adult thought in general.

Researchers have also questioned Piaget's stage account of development. Children are not as even, or homogeneous, in their cognitive abilities as Piaget's stage theory suggests. For example, a particular child may display a highly egocentric attitude in one situation but show impressive perspective-taking skills in another. The success of training studies mentioned above, for example, indicates that, in some contexts, children can acquire a skill that would otherwise have to wait for several years, or can show advanced cognitive abilities in one context (knowledge of the win-loss percentage of favorite NASCAR drivers, for example) but not in a related context (long division problems in school). As an aside, I know of no studies that have taught children to conserve on a laboratory task and then examined the transfer of this ability to everyday life. Will a 4-year-old child who has been taught to conserve liquid or mass be fooled when her sandwich is cut into four pieces instead of two at lunch? Cognitive development is more heterogeneous, or variable, both across and within stages than Piaget proposed, and his whole notion of underlying cognitive structures as the basis for cognitive development has been seriously questioned.

Such findings challenge Piaget's notion of stages of development that represent qualitatively unique forms of thinking, with transitions between stages reflecting discontinuities in development (see Brainerd, 1978; Courage & Howe, 2002). As John Flavell (1978) wrote, "However much we may wish it otherwise, human cognitive growth may simply be too contingent, multiform, and heterogeneous—too variegated in developmental mechanisms, routes, and rates—to be accurately characterized by any single stage theory of the Piagetian kind" (p. 187).

Yet, homogeneity of cognitive function is a relative thing. Although most researchers concur that cognitive development is not as even as Piaget proposed, most children's thinking most of the time can be described as being well integrated and relatively homogenous. For example, Robbie Case (1992) acknowledged that children's thinking is more heterogeneous, or uneven, than proposed by Piaget and is likely governed by many domain-specific mechanisms; nonetheless, he argued that some important aspects of cognition are likely under the influence of a domain-general mechanism, much as proposed by Piaget, and are relatively even. In sum, Piaget's account of development does not fully capture what actually occurs, but it does provide a reasonable picture of the behavior of most children most of the time and a good jumping-off point for further investigation.

# EVERYDAY EXPRESSIONS OF THE SYMBOLIC FUNCTION

In this section, I provide a more detailed look at two aspects of the "symbolic function" that reflect not just what children say and do when being interviewed by psychologists but also how their developing symbolic abilities are expressed in their daily activities: symbolic play and distinguishing between fantasy and reality.

## Symbolic Play

Play is usually seen as a "purposeless" activity, in that it is done voluntarily and without any obvious immediate function (Rubin, Fein, & Vandenberg, 1983). Children play for the sake of playing. Yet, most people who have given the topic serious thought believe that play does, in fact, serve a number of functions (see Pellegrini, 2011).

**Symbolic play** (or **fantasy play**), which is also called *pretend* or *make-believe play*, includes an "as if" orientation to objects, actions, and peers (Lillard, 2001; Pellegrini & Bjorklund, 2004). At its simplest, symbolic play involves substituting one thing for another in a playful setting. The simplest forms of symbolic play are first seen late in the second year of life, usually between 15 to 18 months of age, consistent with Piaget's (1962) observations. At this time, children substitute perceptually similar objects for the "real thing." For instance, a banana may be used as a telephone, or children may take an empty teacup, put it to their lips, and make drinking noises. For older children, the physical similarity between the objects they use in play and the "real things" diminishes. For instance, a 3-year-old child may take a baby bottle and comb her doll's hair with it (Ungerer et al., 1981).

Although symbolic play can be solitary (for example, a child pretending he is driving a car or making a phone call), most such play, especially for children beyond 3-years of age, is social (for example, playing "doctor," "school," or "store" with other children) (Rubin, Fein, & Vandenberg, 1983). As I noted in Chapter 3, mothers in particular promote symbolic play in their preschool children (Bornstein et al., 1996; Youngblade & Dunn, 1995). One social form of symbolic play that is not seen until about 3-years of age is called **sociodramatic play**, in which children take on different roles and follow a story line as if they were in a theatrical performance. For example, children may play "school," taking turns as the teacher and the student and follow a script that involves what children think goes on at school. Sociodramatic play requires more than using one object as a substitute for another; children must also be able to represent the actions and thoughts of other people (If I'm a pretend teacher, you're a pretend student).

Symbolic play is virtually nonexistent until about 15 months of age, peaks between 5 and 7 years, and decreases thereafter (Rubin et al., 1983; Smith, 2005). When measured during preschool or in children's homes, symbolic play accounts for between 10% and 33% of children's waking time, making it one of the most frequent behaviors in which children of this age engage (Fein, 1981; Haight & Miller, 1993). Part of the decline in symbolic play during the school years may involve parents and, especially, teachers discouraging such play, as well as the increase in other types of playful activities, such as games. Yet, older children continue to engage in symbolic play from time to time, such as building LEGO® "monsters" and other characters and inventing make-believe scenarios in which they interact.

There are sex differences in the content or themes of symbolic play. For instance, girls are more apt to engage in various types of play parenting and in play involving relationships and families than are boys. In contrast, the themes of boys' symbolic play are more likely to involve aggression, power, and dominance, frequently finding their expression in rough-and-tumble play (often involving superheroes). Such play may serve to prepare both girls and boys for roles they would have played in traditional environments. Girls' symbolic play also tends to be more complicated, as reflected by the use of language, and to last longer than that of boys (Pellegrini & Bjorklund, 2004).

Symbolic and sociodramatic play are strongly influenced by culture (Smith, 2005). In all cultures, children's symbolic play is based on the materials they have available (various toys, or cardboard boxes that can be used as spaceships for children in contemporary society, for instance) and on the activities and roles of adults in their culture that they can emulate during play. For example, children from traditional cultures are more likely to include real or toy tools and imitation of real adult work in their symbolic play than children from developed countries. This is because children from hunter-gatherer or horticultural societies are more likely to observe adults at work on a daily basis than are children in schooled cultures (see Chapter 3). In some traditional societies, children are given toy tools, often made by their parents, to use in play. For instance, among the Parakanãs of the Amazon rainforest, mothers give their daughters small baskets, and fathers give their sons toy bows and arrows, both tools that adults use and that children then use in their play. Four- to 6-year-old Parakanã girls make small baskets with palm leaves, imitating their mothers' activities, although the baskets are not strong enough to be useful. By 8 years of age, however, most girls are making functional baskets (Gosso et al., 2005).

## Distinguishing Between Fantasy and Reality

Related to fantasy play is children's ability to distinguish what they imagine from what they experience. In other words, do children realize that thinking or imagining something is distinct from actually doing or experiencing something? Does pretending make it real? At one level, even young children clearly know the difference between imagining and doing. For example, although dreams can seem quite real to people of any age, apparently even 3- and 4-year-olds know the difference between dreams and reality, although many 3-year-olds seem to believe that the same dream is experienced by different people (Woolley & Wellman, 1992) and that dreams are highly controllable (Woolley & Boerger, 2002). Also, several researchers have shown that 4- and 6-year-olds can easily distinguish between real and pretend items (Golomb & Galasso, 1995; Harris et al., 1991). For example, when a pencil is placed on a table in front of a child, 4-year-olds can state that both they and a person sitting opposite them can see the pencil. When asked to close their eyes and imagine a pencil, however, they can state quite correctly that the person sitting across from them cannot see the imagined object.

Yet, the ability to make the distinction between imagined and experienced events is far from complete by age 4. For example, in research evaluating developmental differences in **source monitoring**—the awareness of the origins of one's memories, knowledge, or beliefs—children and adults are asked to perform certain actions (for instance, "touch your nose") or to imagine performing certain actions (for instance, "imagine touching your nose") (Foley & Ratner, 1998). The ability to distinguish imagined from real actions improves during the preschool years (Sussman, 2001; Welch-Ross, 1995), but even 6- and 7-year-olds have greater difficulty making such distinctions than older children or adults do (Foley & Ratner, 1998; Parker, 1995). When children make errors in studies such as these, they usually claim that they had performed an action they had actually only imagined.

Related to distinguishing real from imagined events is the distinction between real and imaginary characters. Young children are more apt to believe in fantasy figures such as superheroes, monsters, Santa Claus, and the Tooth Fairy (the latter two of which adults heartily promote) than are older children (Principe & Smith, 2008).

Young children's tenuous grasp of the distinction between fantasy and reality is seen in experiments by Paul Harris and his colleagues (1991). These researchers demonstrated that 4- and 6-year-olds could easily distinguish between real and imagined objects. For example, when asked to imagine that there was either a bunny or a monster in a box on a table in front of them, few children had any difficulty with the task. Most stated quite clearly that the bunny or the monster was pretend and not real, but this knowledge was tenuous for many of the children. For example, after asking children to imagine a bunny or a monster in the box, the experimenter said she had to leave the room for a few minutes. Of the twelve 4-year-olds who had imagined a monster in the box, four became frightened and wouldn't let the experimenter leave. (No child who was asked to imagine a bunny became frightened.) When the experimenter returned and questioned the children, nearly half of both the 4- and 6-years-olds admitted to wondering whether there was, indeed, a monster or a bunny in the box. That is, although nearly all of the children admitted that the bunny or the monster was make-believe at the beginning of the experiment, many had second thoughts at the end. Perhaps imagining really did make it so.

Harris and his colleagues view this contradiction between children's beginning and final beliefs as a reflection of the uncertain state of young children's knowledge of fantasy versus reality. "Our general explanation is that when children imagine a creature such as a monster or rabbit in a box they start to wonder whether there is such a creature in the box, and they cannot completely discount that possibility. Thus, children's imagination increases the subjective likelihood that certain fantasy creatures might become encountered" (1991, p. 121). These results help explain why young children are often frightened by imagining bogeymen in the closet or monsters under the bed. Although at one level they know the difference between imagined and real, at another level they possess a belief in magic, making the fantasy/reality distinction a fragile one.

Let me provide an anecdote to illustrate young children's uncertainty about what is real and what is fantasy. Five-year-old Jeffrey was very impressed with the Disney movie *The Lion King*. He knew the cartoon was fiction, of course, and was quite aware that lions and hyenas can't actually talk. He was especially impressed with the character of Simba, the young lion cub and star of the movie. "Simba was so sad when his father died," he said. "Boy, what a good actor he is. He *really* looked sad." Jeffrey knew that this was fiction and that the characters were not real. But he still got confused.

It's not just cartoon characters and possible monsters or bunnies in boxes that young children attribute life qualities to but also "people" in their daily lives. At about the same time that children begin to engage in sociodramatic play, many create **imaginary friends**. By 3 or 4 years of age, children endow these invisible agents (usually make-believe children but sometimes talking animals or beings from another planet) with personalities, feelings, ideas, and motivations of their own (Taylor, 1999). Having imaginary friends is quite common. In one study, 65% of children up to age 7 had had an imaginary friend sometime in their lives (Taylor, Batty, & Itier, 2004). There may even be some cognitive advantage to having imaginary friends. One recent study found that 5-year-old children with imaginary friends tell more detailed stories than children without such friends (Trionfi & Reese, 2009).

Believing in fantasy beings requires a relatively sophisticated cognitive system. For example, Jacqueline Woolley and her colleagues introduced 3- to 5-year-old children to a new fantasy character, the Candy Witch (Woolley, Boerger, & Markman, 2004). The Candy Witch comes on Halloween night into children's homes and replaces candy she finds under children's pillows with a toy. Children were shown a doll representing the Candy Witch but were not told anything about whether she was real.

The parents of some of the children exchanged a toy for candy after their children were asleep. When later interviewed, for children who had actually been visited by the Candy Witch (much as they are visited by the Tooth Fairy), older preschoolers (average age = 5.3 years) were more likely to express belief in the Candy Witch than younger preschoolers (average age = 3.7 years). In other words, it was the older and, presumably, more cognitively advanced children, not the younger children, who were more likely to believe in the Candy Witch.

In another study by Jesse Bering and Becky Parker (2006), three groups of children (ages 3 to 4 years, 5 to 6 years, and 7 to 9 years) were asked to perform a task in which they had to guess in which of two boxes a prize was hidden. Children could place a hand on either box, and whichever box their hand was on at the end of each trial, they would get whatever was in the box (the prize or nothing). Some children were shown a picture of Princess Alice—an invisible princess who was in the room and wanted to help them win the prize. They were told that "Princess Alice will tell you when you pick the *wrong* box." Other children were told nothing about Princess Alice. During two of the trials, "unexpected" events happened: a picture of Princess Alice fell from the wall or a table lamp flashed on and off in rapid succession. Bering and Parker were interested in whether children would view these unexpected events as messages from Princess Alice and move their hand from one box to the next.

Figure 5-6 presents the percentage of trials on which children moved their hands in response to the unexpected even (percentage of "receptive trials"). As you can see, the two younger groups of children in the experimental ("Princess Alice") condition were no more likely to move their hand on the critical trials than were children in the control group, who knew nothing of Princess Alice. Only the 7- to 9-year-old children in the Princess Alice condition moved their hands significantly more on these

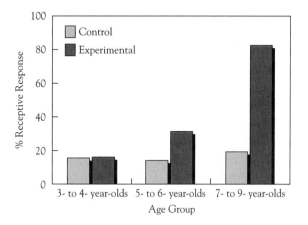

FIGURE **5-6**

Only older children in the Experimental condition who were told that "Princess Alice wants to help you win the prize" were more likely to move their hand from one box to the other (that is, make a "receptive response") than children in the Control condition who did not hear the story about Princess Alice.

Source: Bering, J. M., & Parker, B. D. (2006). Children's attributions of intentions to an invisible agent. *Developmental Psychology, 42,* 253–262.

"receptive trials" than did children in the control group. Children were later asked what they thought the unexpected events "meant." The youngest children usually stated some physical cause for the event (for instance, "The picture fell because it wasn't sticking very well"). The 5- and 6-year-olds most often attributed the unexpected events to Princess Alice but said it had nothing to do with helping them win the prize (for example, "Princess Alice did it because she wanted to"). Only the older children attributed the unexpected events to Princess Alice doing something to communicate to the child (for instance, "Princess Alice did it because I chose the wrong box"). Thus, similar to the findings in the study about children's belief in the Candy Witch, only the older children attributed intention to Princess Alice, suggesting that mature, not immature, cognition is associated with how imaginary (and supernatural) agents behave.

Preschool children are also especially prone to interpret events they don't understand as magic. Karl Rosengren and Anne Hickling (1994) asked 4- and 5-year-old children how certain objects could be changed (for example, "How can you make this piece of string look different?"), and most provided answers based on physical mechanisms (for instance, "Cut it in two"). Children were then shown some magic tricks (for example, putting two pieces of string together to make one piece) and asked for their explanations of the transformations. Whereas most 5-year-olds explained the changes as tricks that anyone could learn, many 4-year-olds explained them as magic that could only be performed by a magician.

How different are children from adults regarding magical thinking? Woolley (1997) thinks not too much. Children are more likely to attribute unfamiliar events to magic and to believe that "just wishing" can make something come true. But such thinking does not disappear at adolescence or adulthood. The belief systems of most cultures include supernatural beings who intervene in the physical world on a regular basis and who can be asked to intervene on people's behalf, and many adults are highly superstitious. They believe that blowing on dice before a roll will produce a good outcome, knocking on wood will prevent a bad one, and breaking a mirror will result in bad luck. Belief in the paranormal approaches 50% among American adults, including faith healing, demonic possession, and astrology. Thus, the tendency to provide a magical explanation for phenomena about which we have no known physical explanation is not unique to children. One likely reason for children's greater tendency to believe in fantasy, however, is knowledge. Older children and adults know more about how the physical world works, and they also know the domains in their culture where belief in supernatural explanations is accepted (for example, religion) and where it is not (for example, Criss Angel's illusions).

## FUZZY-TRACE THEORY

Theories like Piaget's emphasize that the quality of children's mental representation changes with age. But as important as Piaget's theory has been to understanding children's thinking, as we saw earlier in this chapter, cognitive development just doesn't work this way, at least not exclusively. New forms of thinking do not necessarily replace (or emerge from) earlier forms. Older children and adults sometimes still solve problems using the same type of illogical, intuitive thinking that characterizes preschoolers. They do it, however, with more "processing power" than preschoolers do (such as enhanced working memory and faster speed of processing) and with greater logical abilities. Collectively, theories that propose there are multiple (usually two general) "ways of knowing" that people use to solve problems are referred to as *dual-processing theories* (Brainerd & Reyna, 2002; Klaczynski, 2009).

One influential dual-processing theory of cognitive development is **fuzzy-trace theory** of Charles Brainerd and Valerie Reyna (1993, 2002, 2005), who proposed the metaphor of *intuitionism*, in which people prefer to think, reason, and remember by processing inexact, "fuzzy" memory representations rather than by working logically from exact, verbatim representations. In a nutshell, according to Brainerd and Reyna (1993), most cognition is intuitive, in that it is based on "fuzzy representations (senses, patterns, gists) in combination with construction rules that operate on those representations" (p. 50).

Fuzzy-trace theory makes several basic assumptions about aspects of cognitive processing as well as about how these aspects of processing vary with development. I will first mention each of the assumptions, outlined in Table 5-5, and then discuss how they relate to cognitive development.

## Assumptions of Fuzzy-Trace Theory

At the core of fuzzy-trace theory is the idea that memory representations (or memory traces) exist on a continuum from literal, verbatim representations to fuzzy, imprecise,

TABLE **5-5**
## Some Assumptions of Fuzzy-Trace Theory and Their Relation to Cognitive Development.*

1. *Gist extraction and the fuzzy-to-verbatim continua*

**Basic Assumption:** People extract fuzzy, gistlike information from the stimuli and events they experience, following the reduction to essence rule. Traces for an event exist on a fuzzy-to-verbatim continuum. At one extreme are fuzzy traces that are vague, degenerated representations that maintain only the sense or pattern of recently encoded information. At the other extreme are verbatim traces, which are elaborated, exact representations of the recently encoded information.

**Age Differences:** Young children's memory is specialized for encoding and processing verbatim information; with age, their ability to extract gist improves.

2. *Fuzzy-processing preference (intuition)*

**Basic Assumption:** People prefer to reason, think, and remember intuitively, processing fuzzy rather than verbatim traces.

**Age Differences:** There is a shift in the reliance on verbatim and gist traces, sometime during the elementary school years, with children becoming increasing facile processing gist traces. Processing of verbatim traces declines in efficiency during adolescence.

3. *Output interference*

**Basic Assumption:** As people make responses, output interference occurs and interferes with subsequent processing.

**Age Differences:** Young children are more sensitive to the effects of output interference than are older children or adults.

*A fourth assumption of fuzzy-trace theory is that short-term memory is reconstructive. However, because the theory predicts few developmental differences in reconstructive processes, this aspect of the theory is not discussed here.

gistlike traces. Take, for example, a transitive-inference problem in which children are shown a series of sticks that vary in length. Stick A is 20 centimeters long, stick B is 20.5 centimeters long, and stick C is 21 centimeters long. Children are shown each of two adjacent pairs of sticks (A and B; B and C) and asked to judge which item of each pair is longer. They then are asked to decide whether stick A or stick C is longer, without having seen these two particular sticks together and without being allowed to make a visual comparison of their lengths. Verbatim traces would correspond to the actual lengths of the sticks (expressed, perhaps, in the form of visual images). Fuzzy or gistlike traces would be of a less exact form, such as "C is long, B is not long and not short, A is short," or "The sticks get taller to my right." Either of these forms of representation can be used to solve the problem. Fuzzy-trace theory poses such questions as these: Which representation is cognitively easier? Which representations do people actually use? And, important for us, what develops?

An important assumption in fuzzy-trace theory is the idea that gist can exist at several different levels for the same information (for example, "A is short, C is long" and "The sticks get taller to my right") and that a single event will be represented in memory by a number of different traces, from exact **verbatim traces** to a variety of inexact **fuzzy traces**. Moreover, these various traces are independent of one another. That is, gist traces are not simply the result of the deterioration of verbatim traces.

A central assumption of fuzzy-trace theory is that people of all ages prefer to use fuzzy traces when solving problems, although this preference does vary with age (see *Developmental Differences*). Brainerd and Reyna refer to this as the *reduction to essence rule*. Fuzzy traces cannot always be used to solve a problem, but according to Brainerd and Reyna (1990), "it is a natural habit of mind to process traces that are as near to the fuzzy ends of fuzzy-to-verbatim continua as possible" (p. 9). In other words, there is a bias in human cognition toward thinking and solving problems intuitively rather than logically.

Fuzzy traces and verbatim traces differ in important ways. First, relative to verbatim traces, fuzzy traces are more easily accessed and generally require less effort to use. Also, verbatim traces are more susceptible to interference and forgetting than are fuzzy traces. For example, when a shopper is comparing the prices of sweaters at two stores, he or she will quickly forget the exact prices of the sweaters. More resistant to forgetting, however, will be the less-precise information that the sweater at Sears was cheaper than the comparable sweater at JCPenney. If your problem is to decide which sweater is the better buy, you can rely on the degraded, fuzzy knowledge of the relative prices of the two sweaters. If, however, you are required to write a check for one of the sweaters, you will need the verbatim information, and in that case, it would be helpful if you wrote the exact price down, for it is unlikely that you will have remembered it.

A final assumption of fuzzy-trace theory has to do with the role of *output interference* and how it varies with development. Brainerd and Reyna hold that the act of making responses produces output interference that hinders subsequent performance. According to Brainerd and Reyna, output interference occurs in two forms: *scheduling effects* and *feedback effects*. Scheduling effects are caused by the serial nature of response systems. Although people can perform several different cognitive operations simultaneously (that is, in parallel), responses are made serially (that is, one at a time). This leads to a parallel-to-serial bottleneck at output, or response competition, with the various possible responses competing for priority of execution. Once a response is made, Brainerd and Reyna (1990) propose, irrelevant feedback is generated "that reverberates through the systems, degrading performance as it goes ... [and] introducing noise into working memory" (p. 29).

## Developmental Differences

How does processing of fuzzy traces and verbatim traces vary with development? Fuzzy-trace theory makes specific predictions, some of which have been confirmed by research. First, there are age differences in gist extraction. Early in life, children are biased toward storing and retrieving verbatim traces. They do extract gist, of course, but relative to older children and adults, young children are biased toward the verbatim end of the continuum. A verbatim → gist shift occurs sometime during the early elementary school years, with children now showing a gist bias. Thus, the memory system for processing verbatim information should develop earlier than the system for processing fuzzy, gistlike information. Moreover, the memory system used for processing verbatim information should decline relatively early in development, likely during adolescence or young adulthood.

Evidence from a variety of sources supports the idea that preschool and early school-age children are more biased toward encoding and remembering verbatim traces, whereas older children, like adults, are more prone toward encoding and remembering gist traces (Brainerd & Gordon, 1994; Odegard et al., 2009). For example, in research by Brainerd and L. L. Gordon (1994), preschool and second-grade children were given simple numerical problems. In one problem, children were given the following background information: "Farmer Brown owns many animals. He owns 3 dogs, 5 sheep, 7 chickens, 9 horses, and 11 cows." They were then asked a series of questions, some requiring verbatim knowledge for their correct answer, such as "How many cows does Farmer Brown own, 11 or 9?" and others requiring only gist information, such as "Which of Farmer Brown's animals are the most, cows or horses?" (called global) and "Does Farmer Brown have more cows or more horses?" (called pairwise). The results of this experiment are shown in Figure 5-7. Brainerd and Gordon found that preschool children were better at remembering the verbatim numbers than the numerical gist, whereas the reverse was true for second-graders.

Note that the theory does *not* say that young children are better at processing or remembering verbatim traces than older children are; the ability to deal with *both* verbatim and fuzzy traces improves with age. Young children merely start with a bias toward processing verbatim relative to gist traces, and this tendency shifts with age. Children become increasingly biased toward processing at the fuzzy end of the continuum, but the overall processing effectiveness for both types of traces improves.

Age differences have been also found in sensitivity to output interference, with younger children being more adversely affected than older children. Support for this contention has come from studies of selective attention (for example, Ridderinkhof, van der Molen, & Band, 1997), including research that has used developmental differences in evoked brain potentials on tasks involving interference (Ridderinkhof & van der Molen, 1995). One reason for young children's greater interference sensitivity is their reliance on verbatim traces, which are more susceptible to interference than fuzzy traces are.

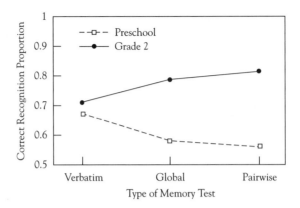

FIGURE **5-7**

Proportion of correct recognition responses for verbatim, global, and pairwise problems for preschool and second-grade children. As you can see, preschool children were better at remembering the verbatim numbers than the numerical gist, whereas the reverse was true for second-graders.

Source: Brainerd, C. J., & Gordon, L. L. (1994). Development of verbatim and gist memory for numbers. *Developmental Psychology, 30*, 163–177. Copyright © 1994 by the American Psychological Association. Reprinted with permission.

## THE SYMBOLIC SPECIES

Humans are a symbolic species—perhaps *the* symbolic species. How people come to mentally represent their experiences has been of great concern to psychologists, as has how such representational abilities develop. Piaget contended that children lack symbolic ability until late in their second year of life, and that their mental world changes in a stagelike fashion over early childhood (preoperational thought), the elementary school years (concrete operational thought), and into adolescence and adulthood (formal operational thought). As we saw in Chapter 4 on infant perception and cognition, many scientists now believe that infants, perhaps even newborns, are not totally devoid of symbolic abilities. However, as much of the research reviewed in this chapter indicates, children seem to have available to them at any one time multiple ways of representing experiences. There does not seem to be a time when children "have" versus "don't have" a particular symbolic skill. Rather, such ways of knowing develop over infancy and childhood, and their expression is influenced not only by their inherited mental architecture but also by aspects of the task and context in which they are "thinking." Young children are able to treat pictures as symbols before models, but depending on context, this too can change. College students can solve formal operation tasks best in their area(s) of expertise (for example, English majors for literary problems). In many ways, human symbolic functioning and its development, perhaps more than any other single factor, make us the species that we are. We should not be surprised that figuring out how such ability develops is complicated.

## SUMMARY

*Representation* refers to the mental coding of information. The knowledge that an entity can stand for something other than itself has been referred to as *representational insight*. Whereas children as young as 2.5 years show representational insight when pictures are used, they do not show representational insight with models until age 3. *Dual representation* (or *dual orientation*), the ability to think about an entity in two different ways at the same time, is required before children can show representational insight. Young children also have a difficult time distinguishing between an object's appearance and its actual identity (*appearance/reality distinction*).

Jean Piaget's theory of intellectual development has had a profound impact on how we view children, their thinking, and their development. Piaget believed that *schemes* are systematic patterns of actions or mental operations that underlie intelligence, and he viewed children as being *intrinsically active* and, thus, largely responsible for their own development. Piaget also believed that cognition is a constructive process and that our current state of knowledge influences how we perceive and process new information.

Piaget described the *functional invariants* of *organization* and *adaptation* as processes that are characteristic of all biological systems (including intelligence) and that operate throughout the life span. Organization is an organism's tendency to integrate structures into higher-order systems or structures. Adaptation is the process of adjustment the organism goes through in response to the environment; this process has two complementary components: *Assimilation* is the structuring of environmental input to fit a child's current schemes, and *accommodation* is the structuring of the child's schemes to match environmental data. Piaget proposed *equilibration* as a mechanism for development. When confronted with information that cannot be assimilated into existing structures, one enters a state of cognitive incongruity, or disequilibrium. When disequilibrium is resolved by accommodation, a new, more stable scheme results.

Piaget postulated four major stages, or periods, of cognitive development. During the *sensorimotor period* (from birth to about 2 years), children's thinking is limited to their own actions on objects. Piaget also described six substages during the sensorimotor period. During the earliest substages, cognition is limited to inherited reflexes and simple extensions of these reflexes. *Goal-directed behavior* is seen first in substage 4. Infants become capable of mentally representing environmental events in the final substage of the sensorimotor period.

Sometime between 18 and 24 months, children begin to use symbols, exemplified by language, imagery, symbolic play, and deferred imitation. From this point on, development consists of the acquisition of operations. Piaget described three major periods between the ages of approximately 2 and 16 years: *preoperations* (between 2 and 7 years), *concrete operations* (between 7 and 11 years), and *formal operations* (between 11 and 16 years). Piaget proposed four characteristics of *operations:* (1) They are mental, (2) they are derived from action, (3) they integrated with one another, and (4) they can be reversed.

Piaget considered the thought of preoperational children to be intuitive, in contrast with the logical thought of concrete operational children. Differences between preoperational and concrete operational children are displayed on many tasks, the most critical of which is *conservation*. Conservation represents the cognitive constancy of quantitative relations and refers to the knowledge that the quantity of a substance remains the same despite a perceptual transformation of that substance.

Piaget proposed that preoperational and concrete operational children differ on several factors. Most critically, the thought of preoperational children lacks *reversibility,* the knowledge that an operation can be reversed or that, for any operation, another operation can compensate for the effects of the first. Piaget described the perception of preoperational children as being *centered* on the most salient aspects of a perceptual array, in contrast with the *decentered* perception of concrete operational children. Preoperational children are said to be *egocentric,* in that they have a difficult time seeing the perspective (visual, communicative, or social) of another.

The major factor in the transition from concrete to formal operations is the advent of *hypothetico-deductive reasoning,* in which thinking can be done solely in terms of symbols, without need for referents in real life. The child can think about what is possible as well as what is real. Piaget described the formal operational child as being able to think like a scientist, or to use *inductive reasoning.* Formal operational children are able to think about thinking, or to reflect on the outcome of their own thought (*reflective abstraction*). Adolescents display a form of egocentrism reflected in their feeling as if they are constantly "on stage" or playing to an *imaginary audience* as well as a belief in their uniqueness and invulnerability, which Elkind referred to as the *personal fable.*

Although Piaget's account of the development of operations has generated tremendous interest for more than eight decades, research investigating his account has frequently been critical. Piaget often underestimated the cognitive competencies of children, and numerous studies have demonstrated that children can be easily trained to display both concrete and formal operational abilities. Young children can display sophisticated cognitive processing in certain situations and, in general, are less homogeneous in cognitive functioning than Piaget proposed.

Children use their symbolic abilities in everyday interactions with family members and peers. *Symbolic play,* or *fantasy play,* involves an "as if" orientation to objects, actions, and peers. *Sociodramatic play* is first seen at about 3 years of age and involves children playing roles, usually with parents or peers. Symbolic play is based on the materials children have available and on the activities and roles of adults in their culture. In cultures that lack industry, play tends to develop into work as children grow into adults.

Although 3- and 4-year-old children can distinguish between imagined and experienced events, this distinction is tenuous, with preschoolers often thinking that make-believe objects can become real by imagining them as real. Young children also often show *source-monitoring* errors, confusing whether they had imagined or experienced an event. Most children have *imaginary friends* sometime during childhood and believe in fantasy characters, such as Santa Claus or the Easter Bunny. Although belief in such fantasy characters decreases with age, a certain level of cognitive development is required for such a belief in the first place.

Brainerd and Reyna's *fuzzy-trace theory* suggests intuitionism as a metaphor for cognition. Fuzzy-trace theory assumes that memory representations exist on a continuum from *verbatim traces* to *fuzzy traces* (or gistlike traces). People generally prefer to think with fuzzy traces rather than verbatim traces, following the reduction to essence rule, but this preferences develops over time, with young children showing more of a verbatim bias than older children. Processing of verbatim traces is relatively good in young children but declines in efficiency during adolescence. Fuzzy-trace theory assumes that output interference, resulting from scheduling effects and feedback effects, causes deterioration of performance and that younger children are more susceptible to the effects of output interference than older children or adults are.

# KEY TERMS AND CONCEPTS

representation

representational
insight

dual representation
(or dual orientation)

appearance/reality
distinction

scheme

functional invariants

organization

adaptation

assimilation

accommodation

equilibration

sensorimotor stage

goal-directed behavior

preoperations

concrete operations

formal operations

operations

reversibility

conservation

centration

decentration

egocentricity

hypothetico-deductive
reasoning

inductive reasoning

reflective abstraction

imaginary audience

personal fable

symbolic play
(or fantasy play)

sociodramatic play

source monitoring

imaginary friends

fuzzy-trace theory

verbatim traces

fuzzy traces

# SUGGESTED READINGS

## Scholarly Work

Bering, J. M., & Parker, B. D. (2006). Children's attributions of intentions to an invisible agent. *Developmental Psychology*, 42, 253–262. This clever experiment shows how to assess age differences in children's beliefs and reactions to invisible agents (here, the kindly Princess Alice).

Brainerd, C. F. (1996). Piaget: A centennial celebration. *Psychological Science*, 7, 191–195. This is the introductory article to a special issue of *Psychological Science* devoted to commemorating the centennial of Piaget's birth. Piaget's many contributions are summarized in the articles written by prominent cognitive developmental psychologists, documenting that Piaget's influence and legacy lives on.

DeLoache, J. S. (1995). Early understanding and use of symbols: The model model. *Current Directions in Psychological Science*, 4, 109–113. Judy DeLoache provides a brief and easily comprehensible account of her research and theory about preschool children's developing understanding of symbols.

Piaget, J. (1952). *The origins of intelligence in children*. New York: Norton. This is Piaget's first book in his series of three on infant cognition, and it presents many of the central concepts of his theory of sensorimotor intelligence. It was the first book by Piaget I ever read, perhaps accounting for my fondness toward it.

## Reading for Personal Interest

Gopnik, A. (2009). *The philosophical baby: What children's minds tell us about truth, love, and the meaning of life*. New York: Farber, Straus, and Giroux. In this delightfully written book, developmental psychologist Alison Gopnik examines how babies and young children form and test theories, how they use their imagination, and what it's like to be a baby.

Paley, V. G. (2004). *A child's work: The importance of fantasy play*. Chicago: University of Chicago Press. In this book, well-known preschool educator and researcher Vivian Gussin Paley tells us about the importance of storytelling and fantasy play in children's development in contemporary societies, describing their positive effects on children's academic and social development.

# CHAPTER 6

# The Development of Folk Knowledge

**Theory Theories of Cognitive Development**

**Folk Psychology: Developing a Theory of Mind**

Basic Social-Cognitive Skills Underlying Theory of Mind

The Development of Mind Reading

BOX 6-1: Do False-Belief Tasks Overestimate Children's Theory of Mind? Solving True-Belief Tasks

Theory of Mind, Evolved Modules, and Autism

Extending Theory of Mind

Some Final Reflections on Theory of Mind

BOX 6-2: Do Chimpanzees Have a Theory of Mind?

**Folk Biology: Understanding the Biological World**

Is It Alive?

What Young Children Know and Don't Know about Biology

Where Do Babies Come From?

**Folk Physics: Understanding the Physical World**

The Development of Spatial Cognition

Object-Oriented Play and Tool Use

Children's Understanding of Time

Some Final Reflections on Children's Understanding of the Physical World

SUMMARY

KEY TERMS AND CONCEPTS

SUGGESTED READINGS

Eight-year-old Mitchell sat beside the tree stump in his back yard, watching the ants and other insects crawling in and out of the rotten log. From time to time, he would poke a stick into the log or flake off some loose pieces of wood to see where the crawly bugs were going and what else resided inside the dead tree. Eventually, he went to his house, returned with a jar, and placed some wood, ants, and what he assumed were ant eggs into it, then punched holes in the top. He put the jar on top of his dresser, where for more than a week he examined it every morning when he awoke and every night before he went to bed. For his birthday, he asked his parents for an ant farm.

Kids have a fascination with animals and the natural world. Although this is most easily seen in children's love of pets like cats and dogs and in their fascination with petting zoos, for some youngsters it extends to other creatures, such as ants living in dead trees. Recently, psychologists have recognized that children may possess an early and intuitive understanding of the biological world and acquire biological facts relatively easily. However, it not just biology that children seem to have a propensity to learn about, but also physics and psychology. This may make it appear that children are like young scientists, and this is exactly how one group of not-so-young scientists views them. Others see children less as scientists and more as young animals who have inherited evolved mechanisms that are sensitive to psychological (that is, other people), biological, and physical features of their environment. In other words, children possess or acquire very easily naïve or intuitive notions about how the psychological, biological, or physical world works. These intuitive theories are often referred to as the domains of **folk psychology**, **folk biology**, and **folk physics**—or collectively, **folk knowledge** (Geary, 2005). Folk knowledge reflects how people "naturally" come to understand aspects of their world and is differentiated from scientific knowledge. For example, children perceive the Earth as a flat surface, with people standing on top of it, and not as a globe with people on both the northern and southern hemispheres being held to the ground by gravity that science informs us it is.

We encountered the concept of folk knowledge earlier in this book, initially in Chapter 2, when discussing David Geary's (2005) model for the "structure of the mind," and in Chapter 4, when discussing core-knowledge theories (Spelke & Kinzler, 2007). As you may recall, Geary argued that the mind consists of hierarchically organized modules within the social (psychological), physical, and biological domains. Children are born with *skeletal competencies* within these domains, which become fleshed out with experience. In other words, natural selection has biased children to process information within these broad domains of knowledge, with experience shaping the eventual form of a child's mind. Similarly, core-knowledge theorists argue that infants possess knowledge about aspects of their physical and social environments from birth or shortly thereafter and upon which new and flexible skills and belief systems are built.

As both Geary and core-knowledge theorists recognize, however, folk knowledge is not complete in infancy but develops over childhood. In this chapter, I look at the development of children's intuitive psychology, biology, and physics (that is, their folk knowledge) past infancy. Much of this research has been done following a particular theoretical perspective called **theory theory**, and I start the chapter with an overview of this approach. I then examine three aspects of the development of folk knowledge, beginning with folk psychology (children's understanding of other people, including their mental lives). Next, I examine the development of folk biology (children's understanding of plants, animals, and biological processes). In a final section, I look at the development of folk physics (children's knowledge of the physical world, such as physical objects and their movement). Much of Piaget's research on conservation, for example, can be seen as reflecting children's developing, naïve theories of physics (how does the physical world "behave?"). This is an extension of infants' understanding of objects, discussed in some detail in Chapter 4.

------------

## THEORY THEORIES OF COGNITIVE DEVELOPMENT

A growing group of developmental psychologists view infants and children as having sets of intuitive theories that they modify over the course of childhood until their understanding of the world is like that of adults in their culture. In many respects, these theories are very different from Piaget's, particularly in their proposals that children are born with, or develop very early, substantial knowledge or processes and that there is no domain-general set of logical schemes, as Piaget believed. But in another way, many *theory theorists* see themselves as the inheritors of Piaget's tradition. They see cognitive development as being a constructive process, much as Piaget did, with mechanisms of change that are not so dissimilar from those hypothesized by Piaget.

Advocates of theory theories propose that the process of cognitive development is similar, or perhaps even identical, to the process of scientific discovery. An initial theory is tested (experimentation), and when the old theory can't explain the new data, the theory is revised. Children use these theories to predict, interpret, and explain the world, just as scientists do. In fact, Alison Gopnik and Andrew Meltzoff (1997) suggest that scientific reasoning is not a *late* invention (either in evolutionary time or over the course of childhood) but has long characterized not only our species as a whole but also infants and children. The nature of theories and how they're tested might change in adulthood, but the basic processes of theory generation, theory testing, and theory change (what is refer to as *conceptual change*) are characteristics not just of people in white lab coats but of children from birth.

Theory theories have much in common with the core-knowledge theories discussed in Chapter 4 (Spelke & Kinzler, 2007), in that each assumes children possess rudimentary ideas about how a specific segment of their world works, yet each also assumes that these naïve theories are modified by experience (Gopnik & Meltzoff, 1997; Siegal, 2008). They tend to differ in terms of the degree to which knowledge is viewed as being "innate" or constructed (á la Piaget) by experience (see Siegal, 2008). At the extreme, core-knowledge (or neonativist) theorists propose that cognitive processes that Piaget claimed undergo gradual, constructivist development are actually innate and await only the requisite motor or sensory skills for their demonstration. Theory theorists rarely take this strong perspective, proposing instead that children are born with sets of rules for operating on particular representations that are altered by experience (Gopnik & Meltzoff, 1997). However, as these research disciplines mature, the distinction between the various theories on this point seems to be diminishing (see Spelke & Kinzler, 2007). Both approaches adopt an evolutionary perspective, arguing that infants and children have been prepared by natural selection to make sense of their world, with infants and children's initial, naïve theories changing with experience (Gelman & Williams, 1998; Gopnik & Meltzoff, 1997; Spelke & Kinzler, 2007). Infants and children's cognition is *constrained*, in that they are not able to process all information equally well, but they are especially able to make sense of some information, particularly information in *core domains* (for example, psychological, biological, and physical information).

Essentially, theory theorists see children as little scientists, much as Piaget did. Children test theories about how different aspects of the world work, and when their experiences contradict their existing theories, they eventually change those theories (that is, they make a conceptual change) and, as a result, develop a more reliable mental map to navigate in the real world. In fact, Alison Gopnik and Andrew Meltzoff (1997) turn this idea on its head, stating, "It is not that children are little scientists but that scientists are big children. Scientific progress is possible because scientists employ cognitive processes that are first seen in very young children" (p. 32).

## FOLK PSYCHOLOGY: DEVELOPING A THEORY OF MIND

During the last three decades, the topic of children's **theory of mind** has become immensely popular. In general, the phrase "theory of mind" is used to refer to children's developing concepts of mental activity. A theory of mind is more than just a collection of concepts, however. "Theory" implies some coherent framework for organizing facts and making predictions. Having a theory of mind implies recognizing different categories of mind, such as dreams, memories, imagination, beliefs, and so on, and having some causal-explanatory framework to account for the actions of other people (that is, to explain why someone behaves as he or she does). For example, Henry Wellman (1990) believes that adults' theory of mind is based on **belief-desire reasoning**. Basically, we explain and predict what people do based on what we understand their desires and beliefs to be—that is, by referring to their wants, wishes, hopes, and goals (their desires) and to their ideas, opinions, suppositions, and knowledge (their beliefs).

Such belief-desire reasoning is depicted in Figure 6-1. Basically, this is what researchers mean when they talk about children developing a theory of mind: To what extent do children have a coherent explanatory "theory" to understand, predict, and explain behavior?

Developmental differences in theory of mind are reflections of developmental differences in how children represent the world—in this case, the mental world. In fact, some of the research reviewed in Chapter 5 examining children's ability to distinguish between appearance and reality (Flavell, Green, & Flavell 1986) or between imagining and experiencing (Harris et al., 1991) could properly be classified as theory-of-mind research (see Flavell & Miller, 1998).

The aspect of theory of mind that has spawned the most research, however, concerns children's abilities to "read the minds" of others (Perner, 1991; Wellman, Cross, & Watson, 2001). To what extent do young children understand that the perceptions, knowledge, and thoughts of others are different from their own? Children's representation of others and of themselves as thinkers is vitally important to our species' way of life. Cooperation, competition, and social interaction in general would be radically different if we did not develop a theory of mind and the ability to "read" others' minds. I believe that one reason for the popularity of this topic is its significance for understanding the human condition. "Mind reading," however, is a relatively advanced aspect of theory of mind and is based on more basic social-cognitive abilities, which I examine in the following section.

## Basic Social-Cognitive Skills Underlying Theory of Mind

What are the most elementary social-cognitive abilities required for a theory of mind? The best candidates I believe are (1) viewing oneself and other individuals as **intentional agents**—that is, as individuals who *cause* things to happen and whose behavior is designed to achieve some goal (they do things "on purpose") (see Bandura, 2006; Harris, 2006; Tomasello & Carpenter, 2007; Tomasello & Moll, 2010; Woodward, 2009)—and (2) the ability to take the perspective of another, which is to understand what the intentions of other people are.

Infants are not born with this knowledge; it develops over the first several years of life, beginning in infancy with **shared attention** (sometimes called *joint attention*) (Carpenter, Nagell, & Tomasello, 1998; Tomasello & Carpenter, 2007). Shared attention refers to the *triadic interaction* between two social partners (for example, an infant and her mother) and a third object (which can sometimes be another person). For instance, a mother may point or gaze at the family dog while catching her infant's attention, drawing the baby into a social relationship that extends beyond the mother-infant dyad. Although mothers (and fathers) may engage in this type of behavior from the earliest days of a baby's life, it takes infants a while to catch on, although they do seem to be oriented to social interactions from birth. For instance, neonates orient to the human face and quickly learn to seek their mothers' faces (Feldman & Eidelman, 2004).

Shared attention, however, is typically not seen in babies until about 9 months of age, when they will gaze in the direction adults are looking or pointing, engage in repetitive interaction with an adult and an object, imitate an adult's actions, and point or hold up objects to another person (see Carpenter, Nagell, & Tomasello, 1998; Tomasello, 1999). Pointing out distant objects is a form of *referential communication* and indicates the "pointer" understands that he or she sees something the observer does not. These abilities increase over the next year. For example, 12-month-olds will point to alert

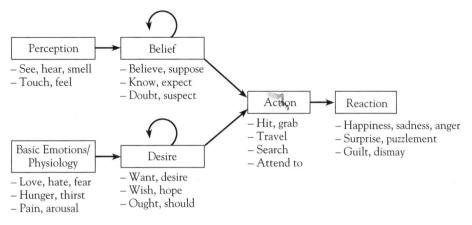

### FIGURE **6-1**

Children's perception of the world affects their knowledge, or beliefs, and their emotions influence their wants and desires. Beliefs and desires, in turn, motivate one's actions. Children learn that such belief-desire reasoning not only describes their own behavior but also that of other people.

Source: *The Child's Theory of Mind*, by H. M. Wellman. Copyright © 1990 Massachusetts Institute of Technology Press. Reprinted with permission.

" I KNOW WHAT I THINK , BUT WHAT'S IMPORTANT IS WHAT MY MOM THINKS I THINK ! "

Knowing that someone else has thoughts and being able to infer those thoughts have important social and intellectual implications.

Source: DENNIS THE MENACE® used by permission of Hank Ketcham and © 1990 by North America Syndicate.

others about events they are not aware of (Liszkowski, Carpenter, & Tomasello, 2007), and between 12 and 18 months of age, infants use the eye gaze of others to achieve shared attention (Brooks & Meltzoff, 2002) and point to objects to direct an adult's attention to something that adult is searching for (Liszkowski et al., 2007). Between 18 and 24 months of age, toddlers use eye gaze along with other directional cues, such as pointing and head orientation, for word learning and social referencing (Poulin-Dubois & Forbes, 2002). These findings indicate that beginning about 9 months of age, infants view other people as intentional agents, with this knowledge increasing over then next year or so (see Tomasello, 1999; Tomasello, Carpenter, & Liszkowski, 2007).

Is there other evidence, independent of shared attention, that indicates more directly that infants and toddlers view others as intentional agents? Research on imitation indicates that babies are more likely to copy the behavior of a model when the model engages in the action "on purpose" as opposed to accidentally. (More will be said about the development of imitation in Chapter 10.) For example, in research by Malinda Carpenter and her colleagues (Carpenter, Akhtar, & Tomasello, 1998), 14- to 18-month-old infants watched adults perform complex behavior sequences, some of which appeared to be intentional, as reflected by the model's vocal behavior, and others of which, based on what the models said, were accidental. When the infants were later given the chance to imitate the model, they reproduced twice as many "intentional" as "accidental" behaviors. One study even suggests that infants understand and selectively imitate a model's goal as young as 7 months (Hamlin, Hallinan, & Woodward, 2008). In other research, Andrew Meltzoff (1995) had 18-month-old infants watch as an adult performed actions on objects both "successfully" and "unsuccessfully." For one task, a model picked up a dumbbell-shaped object and made deliberate movements to remove the wooden cube at the ends of the dumbbell (successful condition). In the unsuccessful condition, toddlers watched as the model pulled on the ends of the dumbbell, but her hand slipped off the cubes, which stayed on the dumbbell. When the infants were later given the dumbbell, those who had watched both the successful and the unsuccessful demonstrations removed the ends of the dumbbell significantly more often than those infants in control conditions (who did not see a demonstration of the dumbbell). They seemed to understand what the model in the unsuccessful condition *intended* to do, and they imitated her behavior to achieve an inferred (but not witnessed) goal.

Eighteen-month-old infants also discriminate between intentional and unintentional actions of another person when deciding whether to render help. In a study by Felix Warneken and Michael Tomasello (2006), 18-month-old infants sat across a table from an adult who performed a series of tasks. The adult had difficulty performing the tasks, but in some cases it was obvious that the adult was trying to achieve a specific outcome (the "intentional" condition). For instance, in one task, the adult accidentally dropped a marker on the floor and reached unsuccessfully to retrieve it. In a control condition, the adult deliberately threw the marker on the floor. In another task, the adult attempted to place a book on a stack of other books, but it slipped and fell beside the stack. This was contrasted with a control condition, in which the person simply placed the book beside the stack. In 6 of 10 tasks, children helped the adult (for example, retrieved the marker, placed the book on top of the stack) more in the experimental than in the control condition, reflecting not only an understanding of another person's intention but a willingness to help (a form of altruistic behavior).

You may find it difficult to get too excited about infants and young children's abilities to share attention and attribute intention to others. These hardly appear to be high-level cognitive accomplishments. Yet, nearly all forms of complex human social interaction rest on the premise that the people we are dealing with are intentional agents—that they do things "on purpose" and that they see us the same way. Treating others as intentional agents is a necessary, but not sufficient, condition for "mind reading."

## The Development of Mind Reading

When and how do children come to appreciate that other people have beliefs and desires, often different from their own, that motivate their behavior? To assess this question, researchers have developed tasks in which children must predict what another person will do or state, or what another person thinks, in an effort to determine what young children know about the minds of others.

### *False Belief*

The most frequently used tool to assess children's theory of mind is the **false-belief task**, first developed for use with chimpanzees (Premack & Woodruff, 1978). In a standard false-belief task (first used with children by Wimmer & Perner, 1983), children watch as candy (or some other treat) is hidden in a special location (in a cupboard, for example). Another person—for example, Maxi—is present when the treat is hidden but then leaves the room. While Maxi is out of the room, the treat is moved from the cupboard to another container. When Maxi returns, will he know where the treat is hidden? The results of studies using variants of this standard task are relatively straightforward. Most 4-year-old children can solve the problem, stating that Maxi will look where the candy was originally hidden. Three-year-olds, in contrast, generally cannot solve the problem, stating that Maxi will look for the candy in the new hiding place, apparently not realizing that Maxi is not privy to the new information (Wellman et al., 2001). This pattern has been reported across the globe (Sabbagh et al., 2006; Tardif & Wellman, 2000), even among the children of Baka Pygmies living in the rain forests of Cameroon (Avis & Harris, 1991), although the timetable for passing false-belief tasks has been found to vary for children in different cultures (see Lillard, 1998; Liu et al., 2008; Wellman et al., 2006, for a discussion of cultural variations in theory of mind).

Why do 3-year-olds fail false-belief tasks? For one thing, they seem not to remember what they originally believed before any switch was made (Gopnik & Slaughter, 1991; Zelazo & Boseovski, 2001). For example, in a modification of the false-belief task, called the "Smarties" task, developed by G.-Juergen Hogrefe, Heinz Wimmer, and Josef Perner (1986), children are shown a box of Smarties® (a type of candy in a distinctive box, with which British children are highly familiar) and asked what they think is in the box. Naturally, they say, "Smarties." The box is then opened, revealing not candy but pencils. Children are then asked what they originally thought (that is, what they believed was in the box before being shown the contents) and to predict what another child (who is not privy to the trick) will think is in the box. The first question assesses children's memory for their initial belief, whereas the second question assesses their ability to understand false belief. The correct answer to both of these questions, of course, is "Smarties," but most 3-year-olds say "pencils" to both questions—that is, they seem to forget their initial belief. Alison Gopnik and Virginia

Slaughter (1991) found that this memory deficit is not a general one but is specific to beliefs (referred to as *representational change*). Three-year-olds have little difficulty remembering their past images, perceptions, or pretenses, but they have particular difficulty remembering their past beliefs.

If young children's problem with false-belief tasks is not one of general memory, what can account for their poor performance? Josef Perner (1991), among others, has proposed that 3-year-old children lack the conceptual structures necessary to solve problems dealing with beliefs. In other words, they have a *representational deficit* and do not possess a true theory of mind. One possibility along these lines, originally proposed by Heinz Wimmer and Perner (1983), is that young children have difficulty with contradictory evidence. They cannot deal with two representations of a single object simultaneously (the candy in location 1 and in location 2). This is similar to the *dual-encoding hypothesis* (or *dual-representation hypothesis*) John Flavell and Judy DeLoache proposed to explain representational differences between younger and older preschoolers discussed in Chapter 5. Basically, this position argues that young children will fail in situations where they must consider two different beliefs or representations for one target.

Support for this position comes from a study by Alison Gopnik and Janet Astington (1988), in which they assessed 3-, 4-, and 5-year-old children's performance on a series of tasks, each requiring the children to deal with contradictory evidence: false belief, appearance/reality distinction (Flavell et al., 1986), and representational change (remembering their past beliefs). The results of this study are graphed in Figure 6-2.

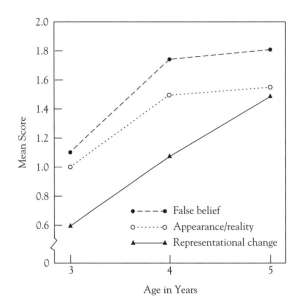

## FIGURE **6-2**

Scores on false-belief, appearance-reality, and representational change questions for 3-, 4-, and 5-year-olds. Note the similar pattern of developmental change for each task.

As you can see, performance on each of the three tasks varied with age, consistent with the idea that a single, domain-general mechanism underlies preschool children's representational abilities.

Related to this interpretation is the idea that young children have a general lack of *executive function* (Carlson & Moses, 2001; Perner & Lange, 2000; Rakoczy, 2010). Executive function refers to the basic cognitive abilities involved in planning, executing, and inhibiting actions, which I will discuss in greater detail in Chapter 7. From this perspective, rather than seeing young children's failure to solve false-belief tasks as a representational deficit, their failure results from an inability to regulate their own behavior. In other words, before children can display advanced levels of theory of mind, they must first develop some requisite, lower-level information-processing skills. Emma Flynn and her colleagues (2004) provided support for this hypothesis in a study in which 3-year-old children were tested on a battery of false-belief and executive-function tasks once every 4 weeks for six phases (24 weeks in all). They reported that most children performed well on the executive-function tasks *before* they performed well on the false-belief tasks. That is, having good executive control preceded and was necessary for successful performance on false-belief tasks (see also Hughes & Ensor, 2007).

Of the various components of executive function related to theory of mind, inhibition mechanisms have received the most attention (Bjorklund & Kipp, 2002; Perner & Lange, 2000). Cognitive inhibition refers to the ability to inhibit certain thoughts and behaviors at specified times. With respect to theory of mind, many tasks require children to inhibit a dominant response to "pass" the task. For example, Joan Peskin (1992) showed preschool children a series of stickers, some more attractive than others. She then introduced "Mean Monkey," a hand puppet controlled by the experimenter, who played a game with the children. Mean Monkey would ask the children which of the stickers they really wanted and which of the stickers they did not want; he then selected the children's favorite sticker, leaving them with the least desirable ones. By 4 years of age, children understood the dynamics of the interchange and quickly learned to tell Mean Monkey the opposite of their true desires. Younger children rarely caught on, however, and played most of the game telling Mean Monkey the truth and not getting the stickers they wanted. Similarly, in research by James Russell and his colleagues (1991), 3-year-old children were shown a series of windows, some of which had treats in them. To get the treat, the children had to select the nontreat window. Children had a difficult time doing this, and they repeatedly failed to get a treat, seemingly being unable to inhibit their "pick-the-treat" response.

Do other factors contribute to individual differences in children's attainment of theory of mind? Research has found a host of factors that predict children's performance on these tasks, among them quality of attachment, parenting styles, and parent-child communication (Carpendale & Lewis, 2004); language skills (Lockl & Schneider, 2007; Milligan, Astington, & Dack, 2007); and maternal warmth and the extent to which mothers use mental-state talk (that is, talking about what they and their children are thinking) (Ruffman et al., 2006; Taumoepeau & Ruffman, 2006, 2008).

One interesting finding is that 3- and 4-year-old children's performance on false-belief tasks is related to family size (Jenkins & Astington, 1996; Perner, Ruffman, & Leekam, 1994). Children from larger families perform false-belief tasks better than do children from smaller families. Why should there be a relation between family size and theory-of-mind reasoning? One explanation has to do with the role of siblings.

The type of interaction provided by siblings facilitates developing a sophisticated theory of mind. Jennifer Jenkins and Janet Astington (1996) showed that family size is particularly important for children with low linguistic skills. Apparently, having siblings can compensate for delayed language development in influencing performance on false-belief tasks. Subsequent research indicates that it is only having *older*, not younger, siblings that has a facilitative effect on theory-of-mind reasoning (Ruffman et al., 1998). Ted Ruffman and colleagues (1998) believe that having older siblings stimulates pretend play, which helps younger children represent "counterfactual states of affairs," a necessary skill for solving false-belief tasks.

Although siblings may be important, they are not necessarily more effective tutors than adults. Charlie Lewis and his colleagues (1996) administered a series of theory-of-mind tests to 3- and 4-year-old children and found that the number of adults children interact with daily is the best single predictor of a child's performance on theory-of-mind tasks.

Denise Cummins (1998) suggested an alternative explanation based on dominance theory. Siblings are always competing for resources, with older siblings typically having the advantage because of their greater size and mental abilities. Younger children would be motivated to develop whatever latent talents they have to aid them in their social competition with their older siblings, and developing an understanding of the mind of one's chief competitor sooner rather than later would certainly be to the younger child's advantage. A similar argument can be made for interacting with older peers.

Despite the impressive demonstrations that most 3-year-old children cannot solve false-belief tasks, evidence that 3-year-olds do solve other tasks that seemingly require an understanding of other minds challenges the strong version of the representational-deficit hypothesis (see Caron, 2009). In one particularly interesting study, Wendy Clements and Josef Perner (1994) evaluated children's *implicit* understanding of false belief. In this study, children ranging in age from 2 years 5 months to 4 years 6 months were told a story about a mouse named Sam, who had placed a piece of cheese in a specific location (Location A) so that he could get it later when he was hungry. While Sam was sleeping, a mouse named Katie found the cheese and moved it to another place (Location B). When Sam woke up, he said, "I feel very hungry now. I'll go get the cheese." Children were then asked, "I wonder where he's going to look?" The answer most older children should give is Location A, where he originally hid it, whereas most younger children should say Location B, reflecting their lack of understanding of false belief. This is the standard, or *explicit*, false-belief task, and this was the pattern of results that Clements and Perner found. However, Clements and Perner also recorded where children *looked*, at Location A or Location B. This is an *implicit task*, requiring no verbal response and, presumably, no conscious awareness. Now all but the youngest children showed high levels of correct responding (that is, they looked at Location A). Figure 6-3 shows the average explicit and implicit understanding scores, based on children's performance on the tasks in this experiment. This finding has been replicated (Clements, Rustin, & McCallum, 2000; Garnham & Ruffman, 2001), and other studies, using looking time and the violation-of-expectation paradigm, have suggested that infants as young as 15 months may have an implicit understanding of false belief (Onishi & Baillargeon, 2005; Song & Baillargeon, 2008). What these findings suggest is that by about 3 years of age, and

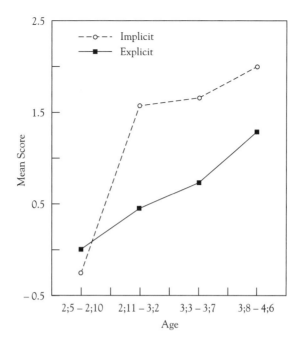

FIGURE **6-3**

Average implicit and explicit understanding scores on false-belief tasks by age. Although most children much under 4 years of age could not correctly say where Sam the mouse would look to find the piece of cheese he had hidden earlier (explicit false-belief task), 3-year-old children *looked* in the proper location (implicit false-belief task), suggesting that they may have greater knowledge of false beliefs than they can verbalize.

Source: Clements, W. A., & Perner, J. (1994). Implicit understanding of belief. *Cognitive Development, 9,* 377–395.

perhaps younger, children have a well-developed *implicit* understanding of false belief that exceeds their explicit (verbalizable) knowledge.

In other research, the first inkling of a theory of mind has been found in 18-month-old toddlers (Repacholi & Gopnik, 1997). In this study, 14- and 18-month-old infants were first tested for their preference regarding two types of food (Pepperidge Farm Goldfish® crackers and raw vegetables). They then watched as a woman tasted the two types of food. She expressed disgust for one type and happiness for the other. The woman then placed her hand, palm up, between the two bowls of food and said, "Can you give me some?" What did the infants do? The 14-month-olds gave the woman the type of food *they* liked, regardless of what food the woman liked. In contrast, the 18-month-olds were more likely to give the woman the food she had expressed a preference for, independent of whether it was what they liked best. That is, whereas the 14-month-olds responded egocentrically, the 18-month-olds did not. Instead, they recognized that their likes were different from those of another person.

Although the research findings concerning children's performance on false-belief tasks is quite robust, some researchers have suggested that they may actually be overestimating children's ability to understand false belief. This is examined in Box 6-1.

| BOX 6-1 | **Do False-Belief Tasks Overestimate Children's Theory of Mind? Solving True-Belief Tasks** |
| --- | --- |

Would a 5-year-old child who passes the false-belief Smarties task ever look at a real M&M'S® bag that she knows really contains M&M'S and say that someone else will think it contains a pencil? If children pass false-belief tasks and simultaneously fail true-belief tasks, what would that tell us about their reasoning about the mind?

Although age-related changes in children's performance on false-belief tasks are quite consistent, some evidence indicates that standard false-belief tasks actually overestimate children's theory of mind ability and that children cannot actually reason about false belief until age 6 or so. William Fabricius and his colleagues (Fabricius & Imbens-Bailey, 2000; Fabricius & Khalil, 2003; Fabricius et al., 2010) have argued that children who pass false-belief tasks may not truly understand that someone else has a false belief, but only that the person lacks information. For example, in the task in which a treat is moved from one location to another when Maxi leaves the room, children may not actually understand that Maxi has a false belief (that he believes the treat is still in the cupboard where it was originally hidden), only that he now doesn't know where it is. In the absence of knowledge, children may simply assume that Maxi will look in the wrong location. But in traditional false-belief tasks, there is only one wrong (that is, empty) location, and that location happens to be the correct answer! Similarly, in the Smarties task, children only know that an unsuspecting person can't see what is in the box (for example, a pencil). In the absence of this knowledge, they may simply assume that the person will be wrong and that she will say there are Smarties in the Smarties box—again, arriving at the correct answer without reasoning about false beliefs. The researchers called this *perceptual access reasoning*.

To test this hypothesis, Fabricius and his colleagues used *true-belief tasks*. For example, in a true-belief version of the Smarties task, 3.5- to 6.5-year-old children were shown a bag of M&M's and learned, to their surprise, that there was a pencil in it. The pencil was removed, and the experimenter placed M&M's into the bag while the children watched. Children were then asked what was in the bag, and they stated, correctly, "M&M's." They were then asked what another person, waiting outside the room, would think is in the bag, M&M's or a pencil. This is different from a false-belief task, in which the content of the bag would be something different from what everyday experience tells us (of course, there are M&M's in the bag). A similar true-belief task was generated for the Maxi problem.

Figure 6-4 presents the proportion of children who correctly answered the true-belief M&M's task (called the content task in the figure) and the true-belief Maxi task (called the location task in the figure) by age. As you can see, most of the youngest (3.5 years) and oldest (6.5 years) children passed the true-belief questions whereas only about half of the 4.5- and 5.5-year-old children did so, although the patterns differed somewhat for the 5.5-year-olds for the two tasks. How can these data be explained? Fabricius and his colleagues proposed that the 3.5-year-old children based their judgment on what they termed *reality reasoning*. They assume people's answers to questions will reflect reality. There really are M&M's in the bag, and so an unknowing child will think there are M&M's in the bag. This is also how they approach false-belief tasks. There really are crayons in the Smarties box, so they say an unknowing child will think there are crayons in the box. As a result, they get the true-belief questions right and the false-belief questions wrong. In contrast, the oldest children really understand that the picture on the bag will cause the person to believe (truly or falsely) that M&M's are inside and so use *belief reasoning*. Children 4.5 to 5.5 years of age, however, engage in perceptual access reasoning. Children at this age assume that ignorance (that is, not having perceptual access to something) leads to errors. In other words, if someone does not know something (such as what is in an M&M's bag), then when asked, they will be mistaken. They couldn't have known that the bag has M&M's in it. They weren't there when the switch was made! They never saw it! As a result, they get the true-belief questions wrong. This same

*(Continued)*

| **BOX 6-1** | **Do False-Belief Tasks Overestimate Children's Theory of Mind? Solving True-Belief Tasks** (*Continued*) |
|---|---|

perceptual access reasoning allows them to get false-belief questions right. Developmental differences on these true-belief tasks are admittedly a bit surprising, and it took me a while to get my head around such findings. But they are replicable and suggest that many children may pass false-belief tasks without truly understanding false beliefs.

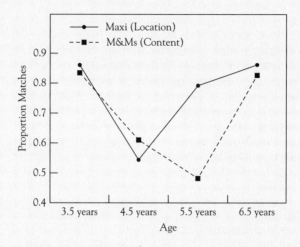

### FIGURE **6-4**

When children are given true-belief tasks, both the youngest (3.5 years) and the oldest (6.5 years) children get them right, but for different reasons. Whereas the oldest children understand both true and false belief, the 3.5-year olds base their decisions on *reality reasoning*–people's answers reflect the true state of affairs. Children 4.5 to 5.5 years of age, however, base their decisions on *perceptual access reasoning*, and as a result get true-belief questions wrong and false-belief questions right.

Source: Fabricius, W. V., Boyer, T., Weimer, A. A., & Carroll, K. (2010). True or false: Do five-year-olds understand belief? *Developmental Psychology.*

### *Deception*

One research area that has produced compelling evidence that young children have knowledge of the beliefs of other people concerns *deception*. Perhaps the consummate political skill, deceptions is useful in love, war, and poker games. In fact, some theorists have speculated that early hominids' abilities to deceive may have contributed significantly to the evolution of intelligence in our species (Bjorklund & Harnishfeger, 1995; Humphrey, 1976). But deception also reflects knowledge of other minds. However, if children are so self-centered in perspective that they assume that if they know something (for example, where an apple is hidden) then other people must know it too, they will see trying to deceive as fruitless. Deception is only reasonable when a person (the deceiver) knows something that another person (the deceived) doesn't know; only then can attempts be made to mislead or conceal information.

Despite young children's inability to solve false-belief tasks, when preschoolers play tricks on others, they sometimes seem to be aware of what the other person does and doesn't know. Observations by many parents would suggest that 2- and

3-year-old children frequently practice (sometimes successfully, sometimes not) deception. For example, 3-year-old Tamara had gotten into her mother's makeup and spilled powder over the top of the bureau. She found a handkerchief and covered up the offending mess, acting as if nothing had happened. In this case, the ruse did not work. Kate Sullivan and Ellen Winner (1991) relate an example of more successful deception by a 2-year-old. The child pretended to cry when his aunt said that she could not come over to play with him. When she relented, the child turned to his mother and said, "I tricked her. I made her think I was sad so she would come" (p. 160).

These observations have been supported by empirical science. For example, Michael Chandler, Anna Fritz, and Suzanne Hala (1989; see also Hala, Chandler, & Fritz, 1991) assessed deception in hide-and-seek tasks in children ranging in age from 2.5 to 4 years. In these studies, children were introduced to a hiding task involving several containers placed on a white surface made of a washable oilcloth material (see Figure 6-5). A puppet hid various pieces of "treasure," making footprints on the cloth from the start box to the container in which the treasure was hidden. A sponge was available that could be used to wipe up the puppet's footprints. After ensuring that the children understood the basics of the game, one of two experimenters (E1) left the room, and the remaining experimenter explained to the child that he or she should help the puppet hide the treasure so that E1 wouldn't be able to find it. The hide-and-seek game went on for several trials, with the sponge being taken away on later trials so that the puppet's footprints could not be wiped off. If children didn't think of it themselves on these later trials, they were shown how false tracks could be made (that is, tracks leading to the wrong container). The question of interest was the extent to which children would use a variety of deception strategies to make it difficult for E1 to find the treasure.

## FIGURE **6-5**

Illustration of the hide-and-seek game used in research by Chandler and colleagues (1989). The puppet would hide a "treasure" in one of the four containers, leaving footprints tracing her path.

Source: "Small-Scale Deceit: Deception as a Marker of Two-, Three-, and Four-Year-Olds' Early Theories of Mind," by M. Chandler, A. S. Fritz, & S. Hala, 1989, *Child Development*, *60*, 1263–1277. Copyright © 1989 The Society for Research in Child Development. Reprinted with permission.

Several different types of deception were scored. The simplest involved withholding information—for example, by making sure that E1 was out of earshot before commenting on the hiding strategy they would use. Another involved destroying evidence by wiping away the tracks, leaving no sign of the path that the puppet took in hiding the treasure. A third involved openly lying—for example, telling E1 to look in an incorrect container. A fourth involved leaving a false trail of footprints leading to an incorrect container. The most sophisticated deceptive strategy involved a combination of both destroying the correct trail and laying a false one.

Table 6-1 shows the percentage of 2-, 3-, and 4-year-olds who used the various deceptive strategies. As can be seen, children of all ages used deception, with no age differences between the three groups. Chandler and his colleagues (1989) concluded that these findings "leave little room for doubt that even children as young as 2.5 are already capable of engaging in a variety of well-crafted deceptive practices, best interpreted as strategies aimed at instilling false beliefs in others" (p. 1274).

In a related study (Hala & Chandler, 1996), 3-year-olds were asked to play a trick on a person (Lisa) by moving some biscuits from their distinctive jar to a hiding place so that Lisa would be fooled. When later asked where Lisa will look for the biscuits and where she will think the biscuits are, children who helped plan the deception performed quite well. In contrast, children who merely observed the experimenter planning the deception or other children who planned a nondeception themselves (for example, moving the biscuits to a new location but not trying to deceive Lisa), did not perform so well. Rather, they were more likely to perform this false-belief task erroneously, stating that Lisa would look for the biscuits in the new hiding place. In other words, when they planned to deceive someone, they were later able to take the perspective of that person; when they were not actively involved in the deceit, however, they performed egocentrically, stating that the unsuspecting person would look for the biscuits where the children knew them to be.

In other research, Sullivan and Winner (1993) reported that 3-year-old children can solve the Smarties false-belief task (discussed earlier), but only when they are asked to actively trick another person. When the same task is used without the "trick" instructions, 3-year-olds perform poorly. Sullivan and Winner interpreted

TABLE **6-1**

Percentage of 2-, 3-, and 4-Year-Olds Using Various Deceptive Strategies.

| Deceptive Strategy | Age Years | | |
| --- | --- | --- | --- |
| | 2-Year-olds | 3-Year-olds | 4-Year-olds |
| Withholding evidence | 80 | 90 | 100 |
| Destroying evidence | 50 | 60 | 80 |
| Lying | 30 | 60 | 55 |
| Producing false trails without destroying evidence | 20 | 35 | 20 |
| Destroying evidence and producing false trails | 50 | 25 | 50 |

Source: Chandler, M., Fritz, A. S., & Haul, S. (1989). Small-scale deceit: Deception as a marker of two-, three-, and four-year-olds' early theories of mind. *Child Development, 60,* 1263–1277.

these findings as indicating that 3-year-olds can understand false belief when it is embedded within a deceptive context. Subsequent research has similarly shown that 3-year-olds are able to use deception successfully under some situations (Carlson, Moses, & Hix, 1998).

Unfortunately, the picture is not as simple as the research by Chandler and his colleagues and by Sullivan and Winner suggests, with more than a little room for doubt, at least according to some researchers. Most other studies report little evidence that children much under 4 years of age use deception in a way that reflects "mind reading" (Peskin, 1992; Sodian et al., 1991). For example, Beate Sodian and her colleagues (1991) reported that 3-year-olds were just as likely to use a deceptive strategy whether they were asked to mislead a competitor or to help a collaborator (although Hala et al., 1991, reported evidence that 3-year-olds can use a deceptive strategy selectively). Subtle differences in the way the deception tasks are performed seem to make a big difference in whether children younger than 4 years use deception selectively or not.

Related to deception is lying. Perhaps not surprisingly, children's tendencies to tell lies (and the effectiveness of those lies) increases over the preschool years and is related to their improved executive function and theory-of-mind skills (Talwar & Lee, 2008).

### Do Three-Year-Olds Have a Theory of Mind?

What can we make of the often-contradictory evidence concerning young children's theory of mind? There is actually much that the various researchers agree on. Three-year-olds seem to have a limited knowledge of other minds. In some circumstances, particularly involving deception or when implicit tasks are used, even 2.5-year-old children seem to be aware that they have knowledge not possessed by others. But young children's theory of mind, or belief-desire reasoning, is tenuous at best.

In general, there have been two camps of theory-of-mind researchers (Wellman et al., 2001). Members of the first camp argue for early competence, proposing that 3-year-olds (and perhaps even younger children) posses the same basic competence as older children, but that overly demanding tasks, confusing questions, or limits on information processing prevent them from displaying this competence in most situations. Members of the second camp propose that there is real conceptual change during the preschool years, that is, age-related differences in performance on false-belief tasks are the result of "genuine changes in children's conceptions of persons" (Wellman et al., 2001, p. 671). To differentiate between these two positions, Henry Wellman, David Cross, and Julanne Watson (2001) conducted a meta-analysis including 178 separate false-belief studies. They reported a substantial age effect in every analysis performed, and they found patterns of change generally consistent with the conceptual-change position. Although different task and instruction variables did influence young children's performance, there was little evidence that 3-year-old children possess the conceptual understanding to perform false-belief tasks. According to the authors, "early competence accounts that claim apparent development during the ages of 3 to 5 years are solely the products of overly difficult tasks masking young children's essentially correct understanding of belief are not substantiated in several key regards" (p. 678).

## Theory of Mind, Evolved Modules, and Autism

Some theorists have proposed that theory of mind evolved during the course of human evolution and is the basis of our social intelligence (Baron-Cohen, 1995; Leslie, 1994). The social complexity of human groups demands attention to the actions of fellow members, and having an idea of the beliefs and desires of others would provide a tremendous political advantage for anyone trying to predict the actions of other members of a group or of rival groups. Consistent with the premises of evolutionary psychology (see Chapter 2), many of the cognitive and brain mechanisms underlying theory of mind have been proposed to be domain specific and modular in nature rather than resulting from some domain-general ability. Thus, the theory goes, our ancestors developed specific skills relating to mind reading, and these skills are relatively independent of more general cognitive abilities. One modular-type account of theory of mind was presented by Simon Baron-Cohen (1995, 2005), who proposed two complementary systems of interacting modules involved in mind reading that develop during infancy and early childhood: (1) the *Mindreading System* and (2) the *Empathizing System* (see Table 6-2).

### The Mindreading System

The earliest developing module in the Mindreading System is the *Intentionality Detector (ID)*, which interprets moving objects as having some volition or intention. For example, an object that is moving toward an individual might be perceived as an

TABLE **6-2**

A Description of Baron-Cohen's Mindreading and Empathizing Systems of Theory of Mind.

| The Mindreading System | |
|---|---|
| Intentionality Detector (ID) | Interprets moving objects as having some volition or intention. Develops by 9 months. |
| Eye-Direction Detector (EDD) | Detects the presence of eyes or eye-like stimuli, determines whether the eyes are looking toward it or toward something else, and infers that if an organism's eyes are looking at something, then that organism sees that thing. Develops by 9 months. |
| Shared-Attention Mechanism (SAM) | Involves triadic (three-way) interactions or representations, such as those that babies and their parents engage in during joint-attention episodes. Develops between 9 and 18 months. |
| Theory of Mind Module (ToMM) | Roughly equivalent to the belief-desire reasoning and is reflected by passing false-belief tasks. Develops between 24 and 48 months. |
| The Empathizing System | |
| The Emotion Detector (TED) | Represents affective, or emotional, states between two people. Develops by 9 months. |
| The Empathizing SyStem (TESS) | Permits an empathic reaction of another person's emotions and assumes that there is an associated drive to help other people. Develops by 14 months. |

Source: Adapted from Baron-Cohen, S. (2005). The Empathizing System: A revision of the 1994 model of the Mindreading System. In B. J. Ellis & D. F. Bjorklund (Eds.), *Origins of the social mind: Evolutionary psychology and child development* (pp. 468–492). New York: Guilford.

agent with some intention toward that individual (for instance, it wants to harm me, to be near me). All animals that have nervous systems likely possess this very primitive skill, as do human infants by 9 months of age, if not younger. For example, in one study, 12-month-old infants watched a computer screen that depicted a ball repeatedly "jumping" over a barrier to land beside a ball on the other side (Csibra et al., 2003; Gergely et al., 1995). When adults see something like this, they attribute it to the ball "wanting" to jump the barrier to join the other ball. Infants apparently see this similarly. When the barrier was removed, the babies increased their looking time when the ball continued to jump, apparently surprised that it didn't just move straight across the screen to achieve its "intention" of getting to the other side.

The second module is the *Eye-Direction Detector (EDD)*, which has three related functions: (1) It detects the presence of eyes or eye-like stimuli, (2) it determines whether the eyes are looking toward it or toward something else, and (3) it infers that if an organism's eyes are looking at something, then that organism sees that thing. In other words, this module is responsible for our belief that knowledge is gained through the eyes (both ours and the eyes of others). According to Baron-Cohen (1995), this module also develops between birth and 9 months of age.

The third module in Baron-Cohen's Mindreading System is the *Shared-Attention Mechanism (SAM)*. Whereas the ID and EDD involve only two objects/individuals (that is, dyadic interactions/representations), the SAM involves triadic (three-way) interactions/representations. These are the interactions that babies and their parents engage in during shared-attention episodes, and as noted previously, these abilities develop between about 9 and 18 months of age (Tomasello, 1999).

The final module, the *Theory-of-Mind Module (ToMM)*, is roughly equivalent to the belief-desire reasoning described earlier and is reflected by passing false-belief tasks. As we've seen in the research discussed in this section, this develops between the ages of about 24 to 48 months.

### The Empathizing System

More recently, Baron-Cohen (2005) updated his model, proposing that the Mindreading System is accompanied in development by the *Empathizing System*. In addition to the ID and EDD, Baron-Cohen proposed a new, early developing mechanism, *The Emotion Detector (TED)*. According to Baron-Cohen, infants from an early age are sensitive to the emotions of others. The emotion detector can represent affective, or emotional, states between two people. For instance, an infant can represent the idea that "Mother is happy" or "Father is angry at me." Within their first 6 months of life, infants can detect another's emotional state through facial expressions or vocalizations, with infant-directed speech (see Chapter 9) being a particularly effective means by which infants pick up on the emotions of their mothers (or others). TED permits infants to detect the basic, or primary, emotions—for example, joy, anger, and sadness.

Beginning around 9 months, emotional information derived from TED can be converted into a triadic representation by the SAM (just as information derived from the EDD can be converted into a triadic representation). So, for example, infants who months before could represent the idea that "Mother is sad" can now represent the idea that "I'm sad that Mother is sad," or "Mother is sad that I am sad."

Beginning around 14 months of age, more than 2 years before the development of the ToMM, *The Empathizing SyStem* (*TESS*) comes on-line. TESS permits an empathic reaction to another person's emotions and assumes that there is an associated drive to help other people. Baron-Cohen (2005, p. 473) illustrates the distinction between the TESS and the ToMM by using the following example: "I see you are in pain" requires ToMM. A child must use facial cues (perhaps) to infer the state of mind (in this case, pain) of another individual. In contrast, "I am devastated that you are in pain" requires TESS. The reactions of another individual trigger an empathic response and may cause children to act appropriately (for example, consoling the hurt person). This type of empathy is a secondary, or self-conscious, emotion, typically emerging late in the second year of life (Lewis, 1993). Baron-Cohen places the initial emergence of empathy as reflected by TESS a bit earlier, but all agree that the expression of empathy develops much earlier than theory of mind, as reflected by false-belief reasoning.

Baron-Cohen's proposal is that his various modules are specific to theory of mind and that they evolved to deal with the types of problems that are posed by having to cooperate and compete with other people. In other words, theory of mind is not a reflection of "general" intelligence. It is a set of mechanisms shaped by natural selection to handle the problems of living in a complex social world.

### Mindblindness

Baron-Cohen's primary source of evidence for his model is that the more advanced forms of mind reading (SAM and ToMM) and empathizing (TESS) are typically absent or significantly delayed in one particular class of childhood psychiatric disorder, *autism*, which is characterized by severe social and communication disabilities. Baron-Cohen claims that the primary deficit of these children is an inability to read minds, or what he calls **mindblindness**. Evidence for this comes from studies in which children with autism are presented with false-belief and other theory-of-mind tasks and consistently fail them, despite performing well on other, nonsocial tasks. This is in contrast to children with intellectual impairment, such as Down syndrome, who perform the theory-of-mind tasks easily, despite often doing poorly on other tasks that assess more general intelligence (Baron-Cohen, Leslie, & Frith, 1985; Peterson, Wellman, & Liu, 2005). Most children with autism are able to perform well on the simpler tasks requiring the ID, EDD, or TED modules, but they fail tasks involving SAM and, especially, ToMM and TESS.

However, it is not just the more advanced forms of theory-of-mind abilities that children with autism lack. For example, 3- and 4-year-old children with autism perform significantly worse than typically developing children in social orientation, shared attention, attending to the distress of another, and attending to faces (Dawson et al., 2004; Hobson et al., 2006; Kikuchi et al., 2009). According to Baron-Cohen (2005), autistic children are unable to understand other people's different feelings and beliefs, and as a result, the world consisting of humans must be a confusing and frightening one, even for those children who are functioning at a relatively high intellectual level.

## Extending Theory of Mind

As we've seen from our discussion so far, theory of mind seems to be based on two underlying abilities. The first is the tendency to view the actions of others as intentional, executed "on purpose" to achieve specific goals (that is, to view other individuals as *intentional agents*). The second is *perspective taking*, specifically being able to "read the minds" of other people. Might these aspects of theory of mind be extended to nonsocial phenomena?

### Finalism, Promiscuous Teleology, and Artificialism

Some researchers have suggested that such intentional reasoning causes children to interpret natural phenomena as being caused or created by someone with a purpose in mind (Bering, 2006; Evans, 2001; Kelemen, 2004). For example, 4- and 5-year-old children will say that mountains are "for climbing," clouds are "for raining," and pointy rocks are "so animals could scratch on them when they get itchy," and school-age children will say things such as "the sand was grainy so that animals could easily bury their eggs in it" (Kelemen, 1999a, 1999b). Piaget termed such thinking **finalism**. Deborah Kelemen (2004) goes a step further, referring to such thinking a **promiscuous teleology**. Teleology refers to the tendency to reason about events and objects in terms of purpose—what they are "for." Young children, claims Kelemen, see purpose everywhere, and this is a product of their sophisticated social cognition, interpreting people's actions in terms of intentions.

Closely related to finalism is **artificialism**, the belief that everything that exists was constructed by people (or God) for specific purposes, much as artifacts (for example, tools, tables, automobiles) are constructed. According to Piaget (1929), artificialism "consists in regarding things as the product of human creation, rather than in attributing creative activity to the things themselves" (p. 253). An example of this would be a preschool-age child, upon being asked where the rain comes from, answering that the rainmaker in the sky pushes the button to make the rain fall down. Piaget believed that young children were incapable of understanding physical causation, accounting for their mental errors. We now know, however, that young children, and even infants, have some understanding about physical causality and that they understand people make artifacts but not natural objects (Gelman & Kremer, 1991). Despite this knowledge, children still seem to view objects and events as existing for a purpose and to believe that natural phenomena are created intentionally, although not necessarily by humans; supernatural agents may be involved (Evans, 2001; Gelman & Kremer, 1991; Kelemen, 2004). Such a perspective may help explain how children understand the natural world and their belief in supernatural beings.

### Children as Intuitive Theists

All cultures have religion and a belief in some supernatural beings or powers. There have been a number of explanations for the universality of religion, including the idea that God is innate (although one's conception of a deity varies radically among cultures), that religion serves to combat our fear of death, and that religion serves a social function, bringing people together and providing rules to live by. An alternative view now developing among a set of scientists is that religion (or at least belief in supernatural agents) is a by-product of our developing social-cognitive system (Atran, 2002; Bering, 2006; Bloom, 2004; Boyer, 2001).

What aspects of children's developing social cognition may be extended to the belief in the supernatural? Kelemen (2004) proposes that children's beliefs that things occur "for a reason" and their endowment of fantasy creatures with opinions, desires, and knowledge (see the discussion of children's belief in fantasy beings in Chapter 5) makes them susceptible to cultural beliefs of the supernatural, particularly to the idea of God or gods. Kelemen refers to children as *intuitive theists*. They believe in the existence of supernatural beings, attribute belief-desire reasoning to such characters, and assume that everything happens for a reason. Children do not come into the world with a concept of God, but their social-cognitive system develops over the preschool years to make it likely that they will acquire the supernatural beliefs of their culture. Kelemen (2004) argues that "children make sense of the world in a manner superficially approximating adult theism, by forming a working hypothesis that natural phenomena derive from a nonhuman 'somebody' who designed them for a purpose—an intuition that may be elaborated by a particular religious culture but derives primarily from cognitive predispositions and artifact knowledge" (p. 297). From this perspective, children generalize what they know about how people make decisions (that is, based on belief-desire reasoning) to explain natural objects and events (the weather, good fortune, the Rocky Mountains).

Paul Bloom (2004) has made similar arguments, proposing that children (and adults, for that matter) are intuitive Cartesians, easily making a distinction between body and soul, following the 18th-century French philosopher René Descartes. Descartes proposed that nonhuman animals were "beast-machines," or automata without minds or souls. Humans, by contrast, have both bodies and minds/souls. Despite modern science's demonstration that the mind is the product of the physical brain, Bloom claims that the mind-body distinction feels "right" to all of us. Bloom proposes that this separation originates in children's distinction between social beings who intentionally make things happen and physical objects that do not do things themselves but obey the laws of nature (for example, unsupported objects will fall). With the development of theory of mind, children come to understand that what people do is based on what they think—their unseen (and unseeable) desires and knowledge—and this serves to solidify the distinction between body and soul. With this distinction, children can easily grasp the death of the body—pets die, people die, and their bodies cease to function. However, children (or adults, for that matter) have no experience, other than perhaps sleep, with the cessation of the mind. How do we conceive of the mind "not working"? Children's (and, later, adults') "natural" mind-body dualism makes the belief in the continuation of the mind/soul after death a reasonable thing.

Nearly all religions have some belief in life after death. How do such beliefs develop, and are they based on children's folk psychology and their level of cognitive development? Jesse Bering and his colleagues (Bering & Bjorklund, 2004; Bering, Hernández Blasi, & Bjorklund, 2005) set out to examine this question. In one study (see Experiment 3 in Bering & Bjorklund, 2004), kindergarten children, fifth- and sixth-grade children (late elementary), and college students saw a puppet show about an anthropomorphized mouse who had a series of experiences (he was lost, smelled some flowers, ate some grass) and who expressed some thoughts and emotions (he loved his mother, thought he was better at math than his brother, wanted to go home). At the end of the show, the mouse was eaten by an alligator, and the participants were told that "Brown Mouse is not alive any more." They were then asked a series of questions about various aspects of the physical and psychological functioning of the now-dead mouse. Six types of functioning were identified:

1. *Biological*: "Now that Brown Mouse is not alive any more, will he ever need to eat food again?"
2. *Psychobiological*: "… is he still hungry?"

3. *Perceptual*: "... can he still smell the flowers?"
4. *Emotional*: "... does he still love his mother?"
5. *Desire*: "... does he still want to go home?"
6. *Epistemic*: "... does he still think he's better at math than his brother?"

Figure 6-6 presents the percentage of participants who said that the various types of biological or psychological functioning continued after death for each age (that is, who said, for example, "Yes, he still loves his mother."). As you can see, kindergarten children were more likely to say that all forms of functioning would continue after death than the older children or adults. However, even most of these children stated that biological functioning stops with death (Brown Mouse will not need to eat again; his brain doesn't work any more; he'll never grow up to be an old mouse). Yet, most of these same children said that psychobiological functioning would continue after death (Brown Mouse will still get thirsty, hungry, and sleepy). Although most of the children in late elementary school and the adults said that biological, psychobiological, and perceptual functioning ceased with death, about 50% of these older participants said that emotions, desires, and epistemic ("thinking") functions continued after death. Given that greater than 95% of American adults believe in an afterlife (Lester et al., 2002), one might expect that children would be *more* apt to say that feelings and thoughts continue after death. In fact, in a study that presented college students with death scenarios involving people rather than mice, adults who professed

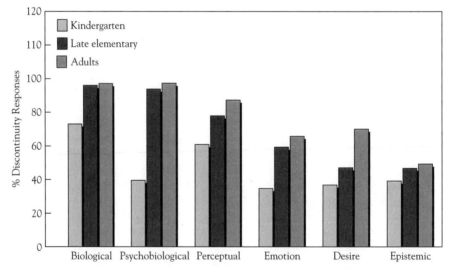

## FIGURE **6-6**

**Percentage of participants stating that different types of psychological functioning ceases after death (discontinuity responses).**

At all ages, participants were more likely to say that emotional, desire, and epistemic ("thinking") functions would continue more than biological, psychobiological, or perceptual functions. The youngest children were least likely to say that functioning of all types would cease after death.

Source: Adapted from Bering, J. M., & Bjorklund, D. F. (2004). The natural emergence of afterlife reasoning as a developmental regularity. *Developmental Psychology, 40*, 217–233.

traditional Judeo-Christian beliefs in the afterlife almost unanimously said that these psychological functions continue after death (Bering, 2002). Instead, as children become more biologically literate, they realize that biological and psychological functioning stops with death. This knowledge may be in conflict with religious beliefs about the afterlife, so many older children and adults profess that the some psychological functioning continues after death. Younger children, however, are steeped neither in biological nor in religious training. Bering and Bjorklund (2004) argued that young children's belief that psychological functioning continues after death is less a matter of learning the religious traditions of their community "but is more likely a natural disposition that interacts with various learning channels" (p. 218).

## Some Final Reflections on Theory of Mind

The centrality of theory of mind to human social functioning seems incontrovertible. Although the beginnings of theory of mind are seen in the first year of life, the ability to "read minds" develops over the preschool years and into childhood. The ability to track and anticipate the thoughts and behaviors of others continues to improve with age, of course, as older children and adolescents perform what are known as third- and fourth-order theory-of-mind tasks (for example, "Shelia knows that Daphne knows that I was lying when I told Karl that Makayla likes him") (see Miller, 2009).

Is theory of mind unique to humans? We tend to attribute intentions to our pets and other animals in general. Do they see us (and other members of their own species) the same? Of particular interest, to what extent do our close genetic relatives, chimpanzees, possess theory of mind? How much "like us" are they, and what type of social cognition might our common ancestor with these animals have had? These controversial issues are examined briefly in Box 6-2.

---

| **BOX 6-2** | **Do Chimpanzees Have a Theory of Mind?** |

Are humans the only animal with theory of mind? How much "like us," cognitively speaking, are our closest living genetic relatives? Chimpanzees (*Pan troglodytes*) and the closely related bonobos (*Pan paniscus*) are like humans in many ways. Compared to other mammals, they live in socially complex communities, have relatively large brains for their body size (see Chapter 2), and have an extended juvenile period. They even possess "culture," in that they transmit nongenetic information across generations, such as forms of greeting, grooming, and tool use (Whiten et al., 1999). We would expect this from species we last shared a common ancestor with just 5 to 7 million years ago. Following Darwin, we would also expect

to share some cognitive abilities with them. The question is, of course, how much? Are the cognitive differences between modern humans and chimpanzees best described in terms of quantitative differences—that is, we're the same type of thinkers, we just have more computing power than they do, accounting for our intellectual edge—or in terms of qualitatively differences types—that is, we possess theory of mind whereas chimpanzees and bonobos do not?

Let's start with the basics of theory of mind: seeing others as intentional agents, as reflected by shared attention. Like human infants and toddlers, chimpanzees (and even some monkeys) will follow the gaze of another individual in some

*(Continued)*

| BOX 6-2 | Do Chimpanzees Have a Theory of Mind? (*Continued*) |
|---|---|

contexts (Bräuer, Call, & Tomasello, 2005; Pitman & Shumaker, 2009); however, most researchers believe there is no evidence of shared attention in chimpanzees (Herrmann et al., 2007; Tomasello & Carpenter, 2005). Mother chimpanzees and their infants do not engage in triadic interactions—pointing out objects for the other to attend to—as human mothers and infants do.

When describing theory of mind in children, I mentioned the ability to deceive, at least in some cases, as involving the ability to take the perspective of another, an important component in theory of mind. There is some evidence that chimpanzees engage in deception (see Byrne & Whiten, 1988), although whether such actions require mind reading or not is a matter of debate. For example, the captive chimpanzee Belle was shown the hiding place of some food and, when released to the open area, quickly retrieved it (Menzel, 1974). However, when the dominant chimp Rock was around, he would follow Belle and take the food for himself. Belle quickly learned to wait until Rock was out of sight before getting the food, and even led Rock to a wrong location, doubling back to get the food while Rock was busy. These are sophisticated social behaviors, but do they require a theory of mind? Belle may not be reading Rock's mind but may simply have learned that "When Rock's around and I go for the food, he gets it. When I wait, or move to another location, I can get the food." This may reflect a "theory of behavior," but not necessarily a "theory of mind."

In a more recent experiment involving food competition between chimpanzees and humans, chimpanzees were able to deceive the human by selectively reaching through tunnels to retrieve food so that the human competitor either could not see the chimpanzee's hand or could not hear anything when the tunnel was opened, behaviors indicative of deception as well as the idea that eyes (and ears) possess "knowledge" (Melis, Call, & Tomasello, 2006). Again, these are sophisticated social behaviors, and they require substantial control of one's actions and the inhibition of prepotent responses. Like Belle's behavior when interacting with Rock, however, they do not, in and

of themselves require an understanding of what another being "knows."

Food competition may well be a good place to assess theory-of-mind abilities in chimpanzees, for in the wild, these animals are more apt to compete over food than to share it. In an interesting series of studies, Brian Hare and his colleagues (Hare et al., 2000; Hare, Call, & Tomasello, 2001) reported that lower-ranking chimpanzees would retrieve food placed in a room only if it were placed out of sight of a higher-ranking animal, suggesting that these animals understand that if another individual is looking at something, they "see" it, and that these animals use this information adaptively. However, in other research in which chimpanzees must make a begging gesture to get food from one of two human caretakers, the animals were as likely to beg to a person wearing a blindfold or having a bucket over her head as to a sighted person (Povinelli & Eddy, 1996). Together, these findings indicate that an awareness that "the eyes have knowledge" is not well developed in chimpanzees and that they do not use such information across social settings, as human children do.

The definitive test for theory of mind, however, is passing false-belief tasks. How do chimpanzees do on these? First, one has to develop a nonverbal false-belief task. Several researchers have done just that, and they report that human children solve these more difficult tasks around 5 years of age (Krachun et al., 2009). When chimpanzees or bonobos are given such tasks, however, they consistently fail them (Herrmann et al., 2007; Krachun et al., 2009).

It seems clear that chimpanzees do not possess theory-of-mind abilities comparable to those of 4-year-old human children. Yet, chimpanzees obviously have some understanding about the psychological states of others. The task of researchers is to determine which states the chimpanzees understand and the extent of their understanding (Tomasello, Call, & Hare, 2005). These findings also suggest that our common ancestor with chimpanzees likely possessed the social-cognitive abilities that would one day lead to human theory of mind.

# FOLK BIOLOGY: UNDERSTANDING THE BIOLOGICAL WORLD

The story that opened this chapter—of a boy's fascination with creepy-crawly things living in a rotting log—illustrates some children's interests in the biological world. In fact, most children across the globe are interested in the "natural world" and, like social relations, seem especially prepared to make sense of it (see Inagaki & Hatano, 2002, 2006). Given the central role that animals would have played in the lives of our ancestors—both as predators and prey—it is perhaps not surprising a number of theorists have proposed that natural selection produced mechanisms that made it easy for children to acquire knowledge about those animals (Barrett, 2005; Geary, 2005).

## Is It Alive?

A good place to begin our discussion of children's understanding of the biological world is their ability to distinguish (1) animate from inanimate objects and (2) agents (things that act intentionally, like people and nonhuman animals) from nonagents (things that do not act intentionally, like rocks and trees). Within the first year of life, infants are able to distinguish between animate and inanimate objects based on self-propelled movement (Schlottmann & Ray, 2010). For instance, babies can recognize biological motion as young as 3 months of age. To assess this, infants watch a human figure walking with 10 to 12 light patches at the joints, as well as other displays with randomly moving patterns of light (see Figure 6-7). Infants from 3 to 5 month of age usually look longer at light patterns generated by a walking person than at randomly generated patterns, although they do not seem to recognize the same walking figure if it is presented upside down (middle panel in Figure 6-7; Bertenthal, Proffitt, & Cutting, 1984). However, although they spend more time looking at displays showing biological motion, they do not seem to treat it as a person until about 9 months (Bertenthal, 1996; Bertenthal, Proffitt, & Kramer, 1987; see also Yoon & Johnson, 2009). And it will be several more years before they understand that animate beings "cause" things to happen, whereas inanimate objects do not. Relatedly, the lack of spontaneous movement seems to be the major reason children have a difficult time identifying plants as living things. It is not until about 7 to 9 years of age before children agree that plants are alive (Hatano et al., 1993; Opfer & Gelman, 2001).

Once children get it into their minds, however, that living things can have thoughts, feelings, and can act intentionally, they tend to generalize such beliefs to inanimate objects. Piaget (1929) was one of the first people to describe this form of "magical thinking" in children and referred to it as **animism**. Children attribute human properties, like hopes, feelings, and thoughts, to inanimate things ("The wind came and blew on me because I was hot"). I recall as a not-too-young elementary school student having mixed feelings about getting a new baseball glove, not wanting to "hurt the feelings" of my old, trusty glove, or being careful to use all the ink in a favorite pen so not to "disappoint" the unused ink. I knew very well that baseball gloves and ink were inanimate and had no thoughts or emotions, and I remember, even then, believing how silly such thinking was. But I could not avoid my intuitions of attributing intentions and emotions to some of the inanimate objects that I was particularly fond of (from Bjorklund, 2007a, p. 108).

Animistic thinking doesn't totally disappear with the advent of concrete operations, either. William Looft and Wayne Bartz (1969) summarized research examining animistic thinking in adults and reported that between 50% and 75% of adults

### FIGURE **6-7**

Biological motion.

Three- to five-month-old babies look longer at the first panel of moving lights, that is, the one depicting biological (here, specifically human) motion than to the other patterns of moving lights.

Source: Bertenthal, B. I., Proffitt, D. R., & Cutting, J. E. (1984). Infant sensitivity to figural coherence in biomechanical motions. *Journal of Experimental Child Psychology, 37,* 213–230.

tested displayed some animistic thinking. For example, some college students stated that the sun is alive "because it gives off heat," or that a lighted match was alive because "it has a flame which indicates life." Looft and Bartz believed that the animism shown by adults was qualitatively different from that shown by children; nonetheless, the high frequency of adults, even those with college educations, who attribute life characteristics to inanimate objects indicates that this tendency extends beyond early childhood. This, along with newer research (for example, Goldberg & Thompson-Schill, 2009, who show that even biologists display some remnant of animistic thinking), suggests that adults retain some of the same biases about living things as children do, but that they overcome these biases, for the most part, as they learn the scientific way to classify living and nonliving things. So, despite lingering beliefs in animism, children's knowledge of the biological world becomes more adult-like with time.

## What Young Children Know and Don't Know about Biology

Susan Carey and her colleagues (Carey, 1985, 1999; Slaughter, Jaakkola, & Carey, 1999) were pioneers in investigating children's understanding of the biological world and how it develops. Carey (1985, 1999) argued that children much before the age of

7 do not have an organized understanding of the natural world but, instead, possess a series of isolated pieces of knowledge. According to Carey, preschool children fail to differentiate between folk biology and folk psychology, generalizing what they know about people to animals in general. For instance, 4- and 5-year-old children attribute human properties, such as having a heart, having bones, thinking, and sleeping, to different species depending on their similarities to humans (Carey, 1985). A major conceptual change occurs sometime between 7 and 10 years, as children gain more knowledge about biology. Similarly, Kayoko Inagaki and Gyoo Hatano (1991) have described young children's animistic beliefs as reflecting an egocentric tendency to explain things in terms of what is familiar to them, such as human behavior. However, when preschool children have more knowledge about living things, they are less apt to characterize other animals in terms of what they know about people. For example, urban children who have had experience caring for goldfish at home do not attribute human characteristics to goldfish, unlike other urban children without this experience (Inagaki, 1990; Hatano Inagaki, 1992).

By 3 years of age, children easily attribute intention and agency to animals. For example, a majority of 3-year-old Shuar children from the rainforests of Ecuador made "appropriate" attributions to both predator ("The lion wants to eat the zebra") and prey ("The zebra wants to escape from the lion") animals (Barrett, 2004). This rose to over 80% for 4- and 5-year-old children. Similar findings were found for German children, whose only exposure to wild animals was from television, books, and zoos. In fact, in many ways the biological knowledge of preschoolers is quite impressive. For example, Inagaki and Hatano (1993, 2002) reported that 4- and 5-year-old children understand that eye color, one's heartbeat, and breathing are not under voluntary control, and that children who are poorly nourished are susceptible to illness. Other research has shown that 4- and 5-year-old children understand that dead animals cannot exhibit living functions, such as moving, but that, in contrast, sleeping animals can act once they awaken (Barrett & Behne, 2005). Preschool children show an understanding of the distinction between living and nonliving things by asking different questions when trying to discover the identity of animals (category membership, "Is it a bear?") and location ("Where does it live?") than of artifacts (functions, "What does it do?") (Greif et al., 2006). They can also understand some complex biological phenomena, such as contamination (for example, if a cockroach is in a glass of orange juice, the juice should not be drunk, even if the cockroach is removed; see Siegal & Share, 1990) and reproduction (that babies grow inside their mothers, and that seeds of a certain species of plant produce a new plant of the same species; see Springer, 1999; Hickling & Gelman, 1994). I'll have more to say about children's understanding about where babies come from in the next section.

Young children's understanding of biological life is far from that of adults, however (see Inagaki & Hatano, 2006; Siegal, 2008). For instance, it is not until children are about 7 years old that they understand that some traits are linked to one's biological family whereas others are not (for example, beliefs). Four-year-old children in both Western and non-Western cultures initially believe, for example, that the inheritance of some physical traits, such as eye color, depends on environmental factors, such as the family children are living with, regardless of whether children live with their biological or adoptive parents (Astuti, 2001; Astuti, Solomon, & Carey, 2004). In other research, children in preschool through second grade believe that you are more apt to catch a cold from a stranger than from a relative or friend (Raman & Gelman, 2008). Other studies have demonstrated that young children often think that dead people retain some biological properties of life, like eating and breathing (Bering & Bjorklund, 2004; Slaughter et al., 1999; see discussion of children's afterlife beliefs earlier in this chapter). Although young children show quite a sophisticated understanding for some aspects of biological life, others take a while to develop.

## Where Do Babies Come From?

Most parents have stories they tell about awkward moments when their children ask, "Where do babies come from?" Although anecdotes abound about children's understanding—and misunderstanding—of reproduction, there is relatively little research on the topic. Exceptions to this are studies by Anne Bernstein and Philip Cowan (1975) and by Ronald and Juliette Goldman (1982), who examined children's understanding of "where babies come from" from an explicitly Piagetian perspective. Both investigations reported several well-defined levels of understanding that followed

TABLE **6-3**
Development of Children's Thinking about Reproduction.

| Level | Piagetian Stage | Ages | Name | Description | Example |
|---|---|---|---|---|---|
| 1 | Preoperational | 3–7 | Geographer | Babies have always existed in completed form; need to be acquired (bought, found, ordered, delivered). | Mommy got me at the hospital. |
| 2 | Preoperational | 4–8 | Manufacturer | Babies haven't always existed in completed form; need to be assembled. | Mommy made me out of blood and bones she had left over from my brother. |
| 3 | Transitional | 5–10 | In-betweens | Babies need two parents in special relationship, sexual intercourse, sperm and egg; process is unclear. | Doctor put a seed in Mommy; and Daddy put some stuff in to make the seed grow. |
| 4 | Concrete operations | 7–12 | Reporters | Know the basic facts but don't speculate on why; only accuracy counts. | Daddy puts sperm in Mommy, and the baby starts growing. (Why?) I guess it loosens up the egg or something. |
| 5 | Transitional | 10–13 | Theoreticians | Know basic facts and basic why's; don't understand that eggs and sperm can join to produce a third entity. | Baby is in the egg, and the sperm makes it start growing. |
| 6 | Formal operations | 14–adult | Putting it all together | Know that two distinct entities, sperm and ovum, can become one qualitatively different entity, the embryo. | The male injects sperm into the female's womb and fertilizes the egg and it grows into a fetus, and nine months later a baby is born. |

Source: Adapted from Bernstein, A. C. (1978). *Flight of the stork*. New York: Delacorte Press.

Piaget's stages of cognitive development. Table 6-3 presents Bernstein and Cowan's description of the stages children pass through while learning the origin of babies.

At Level 1, many children think that babies have always existed and were somehow given to their mothers. Parents in generations past have supported this type of thinking by telling children, for example, that the stork brings babies. At Level 2, children think that babies are somehow "made," but they do not understand the process. Consider 4-year-old Carlos, who had been pondering the process whereby his new baby sister came into the world. Out of the blue one afternoon, he stated that his mother had gone to the paint store, drew a picture of a baby, and then she "popped" out of his mother's tummy. Children in Level 3 realize the importance of mothers and fathers to produce a baby, but they are unclear about the process. For example, 8-year-old Christopher was confused how his divorced mother could be pregnant. Didn't she have to be married to get pregnant? The presence of her live-in boyfriend did not seem to make a difference. Children at this stage understand that a special relationship between a man and a woman is needed for reproduction, but they do not understand the nature of that relationship. Children seem to understand the basic facts of reproduction between 7 and 11 years of age (Level 4), but it takes them some time to fully understand the biology of the process. For example, many preadolescents in Level 5 often believe that babies exist in the egg fully formed, waiting for the sperm to initiate growth. (This is also how most educated people several centuries ago, before the advent of modern biological science, thought about reproduction.)

Bernstein and Cowan concluded that children do not wait to be told about reproduction but construct their own notions about where babies come from. Consistent with Piagetian theory (see Chapter 5), these self-constructed ideas reflect the children's present cognitive structures. The more extensive research by Goldman and Goldman (1982) basically replicated the findings of Bernstein and Cowan, but it also found national differences in the attainment of knowledge of reproduction. For example, Swedish children had the most advanced understanding of where babies come from, well ahead of Australian and English children, with North American children being the slowest. Subsequent research has confirmed that preschool children know little about procreation and also have little knowledge of adult sexual behavior (Volbert, 2000).

## FOLK PHYSICS: UNDERSTANDING THE PHYSICAL WORLD

According to theory theorists and others (Geary, 2005), children are not only specially prepared to make sense of their social and biological world but also their physical world. For example, we saw in Chapter 4 that infants develop early an understanding of objects, culminating in the attainment of object permanence. Core-knowledge theorists, however, argue that children's understanding of objects in space continues to develop, and this is often studied under the term *spatial cognition*. Children are not only biased to *perceive* the physical world but also to *act* upon it. For example, David Geary (2005), among others (see Bjorklund & Gardiner, 2010; Smith, 2005), proposed that children are biased to interact with objects, often through what is called object-oriented play, to learn properties of those objects that can later be used as tools. Children also develop an understanding of how events unfold over time, an important component in how people interact with their social and physical environments. In this section, I examine three aspects of children's developing folk physics: (1) spatial cognition, (2) object play and tool use, and (3) understanding time.

## The Development of Spatial Cognition

**Spatial cognition** refers to processing information with respect to spatial relations. Most animals, including humans, need to navigate their environment (find their way home after roaming in the backyard), judge the distances between different objects (and oneself), and regulate one's action in time and space (knowing when to execute a jump over a log, lest you end up tripping on it). This is why most experts in psychology think that the ability to deal with spatial information must have deep evolutionary roots (see Newcombe & Huttenlocher, 2006). Basically, spatial cognition involves coding information about the environment (where something is in relation to you, or how something might look from a different orientation). Table 6-4 lists 10 spatial skills that develop through childhood and adolescence that children seem prepared to acquire.

Spatial cognition shows substantial improvements during the preschool years and into the school years (Newcombe & Huttenlocher, 2006). Spatial cognition is sometimes divided into three broad categories: (1) *spatial orientation*, (2) *spatial visualization*, and (3) *object and location memory*. **Spatial orientation** refers to how people understand the placement of objects in space with themselves as the reference point. Spatial-orientation tasks include those in which participants are asked to distinguish geographic directions in an unfamiliar locale or to draw their way from point A to point B on a map. In contrast, **spatial visualization** is tested using tasks that involve visual operations, such as mentally rotating a figure or adjusting a tilted object to bring it to an upright position. **Object and location memory** is tested by having participants remember objects and their location from a spatial array. Both developmental and sex differences have been reported in each of these areas.

### Spatial Orientation

Aspects of children's spatial-orientation abilities are relatively well developed during the preschool years. For instance, in one study, toddlers watched as an object was

---

TABLE **6-4**

Ten spatial skills that young children exhibit and develop. This listing does not pretend to be exhaustive (based partially on Newcombe & Huttenlocher, 2006).

- Geometric sensitivity (mostly to angles, distances and handedness/sense)
- Dead reckoning or inertial navigation (that is, coming back to a starting point)
- Voluntary or conscious navigation (that is, orient/reorient in a physical space)
- Use of beacons/landmarks to represent spatial information
- Perspective taking (that is, to "read" others' spatial perspective)
- Mental rotation (that is, exploring objects by mentally moving them)
- Building "cognitive maps" about physical environments
- Making spatial inferences (that is, applying logical thinking to space)
- Communicating linguistically spatial information to others
- Using real maps, models, and understanding graphs and diagrams

Source: Information from Newcombe, N. S., & Huttenlocher, J. (2006). Development of spatial cognition. In W. Damon & R. Lerner (Series Eds.) & D. Kuhn & R. S. Siegler (Vol. Eds.), *Handbook of child psychology: Vol 2: Cognition, perception, and language* (6th edition) (pp. 734–776). New York: Wiley.

hidden in a room, were disoriented, and then were asked to find the hidden object. Most were able to find the object if it was hidden in a distinctive location, such as a corner in both rectangular- and triangular-shaped rooms (Huttenlocher & Vasileya, 2003). Even 5-month-old infants code distances about a hidden object in a 3-foot-long sandbox (Newcombe, Huttenlocher, & Learmonth, 1999). In other research, 1- to 2-year-old children were able to successfully trace their paths back to the appropriate place in a sandbox where a toy was previously hidden after they had been distracted and brought to a different place by a route where no landmarks were available (Newcombe et al., 1998). This is called *dead reckoning*, or inertial navigation, the ability to come back to an initial starting point.

Spatial orientation increases with age as the tasks become more demanding. This is reflected by children's ability to form *cognitive maps* of large areas. In one study, 5-, 7-, and 10-year-old children walked repeatedly through a large model town consisting of buildings, streets, railroad tracks, and trees. After the walks, the children were asked to re-create the layout from memory. Performance increased with age (Herman & Siegel, 1978). Similar age changes in cognitive maps have been reported between 3- and 5.5-year-old children, although the spatial representations were not that sophisticated for either group (Herman, Shiraki, & Miller, 1985).

The use of "real" maps also develops over the school years (Liben, 2009). Preschoolers have a difficult time using maps, even if they are very simple and depict a familiar environment (Liben & Yekel, 1996). The ability to deal with maps improves by the age of 6 (Sandberg & Huttenlocher, 2001), but it is not adultlike until about the age of 10 (Uttal, Fisher, & Taylor, 2006). However, even younger children can use maps effectively under certain conditions. A good example of this is an experiment reported by David Uttal and colleagues (2001), in which a group of 3-, 4-, and 5-year-old children were shown a 10- × 10-foot yellow carpet with 27 cups spread on it (see top of Figure 6-8). Children were told that there were stickers under some cups that they should find, and they were given a simple map to show them where the stickers were hidden. For half of the children, the maps included lines that were drawn connecting the dots that represented the cups, producing an image of a dog (see bottom left of Figure 6-8); for the remaining children, no lines were drawn on the map (see bottom right of Figure 6-8). One sticker was hidden on each of 10 trials, and children had up to three attempts on each trial to find the sticker. Older children did better on this task than younger children, but connecting the lines improved performance only for the 5-year-olds, not for the younger children. In fact, the 3-year-olds actually performed slightly better using the map *without* lines.

In any case, remember that maps (like models, diagrams, or graphs) are not just devices to assess spatial skills in children but also a way to promote them. In this sense, maps can be seen as a *tool of intellectual adaptation* that a culture provides its members to think about important aspects of their environments (Vygotsky, 1978, see Chapter 2). The relation between maps and spatial development is thus reciprocal: Children's developing spatial skills influences their ability to use maps, but the very process of using maps influences spatial cognition (Uttal, 2000). According to Uttal (2000), "Maps provide a cognitive tool that helps children extend their reasoning about space in a new way. Over time, children can internalize the tool and think about space in maplike ways, even if they are not looking at a map at the time" (p. 249). Tentative evidence for Uttal's position was found in an experiment in which

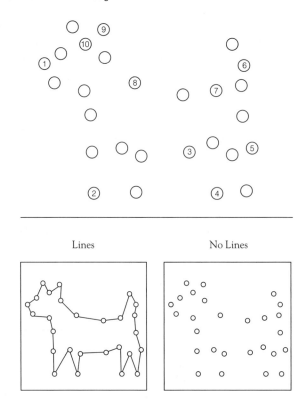

FIGURE **6-8**

The pattern of cups on the 10- × 10-foot carpet and the hiding location of each sticker (top), and the maps children saw in the Lines and No Lines conditions (Experiment 1). Note that the configuration of dots produces an image of a dog. Five-year-old, but not 3-year-old, children were better able to find the stickers when using the maps with lines.

Source: Uttal, D. H., Gregg, V. H., Tan, L. S., Chamberlin, M. H., & Sines, A. (2001). Connecting the dots: Children's use of a systematic figure to facilitate mapping and search. *Developmental Psychology, 37,* 338–350. Copyright © 2001 by the American Psychological Association. Reprinted with permission.

4- to 7-year-old children were asked to learn which of six animals went with each of six rooms in a life-sized playhouse (Uttal & Wellman, 1989). One group of children was given a simple map, with each room represented by a box that contained a picture of the animal. A control group of children was shown a series of flash cards, with the picture of one animal on each of six cards. Children in both groups learned perfectly the six animals that went with the playhouse. They then were walked through the playhouse and asked to anticipate which animal would be found in each room. Although both groups of children had, as mentioned, learned the list of animals perfectly, the children in the map group performed significantly better than the children in the control group. Why did the children in the map group do so well? Uttal and Wellman argued that the experience with the map changed the way those children represented space, allowing them to more easily see spatial relationships among elements. Thus, the development of spatial cognition is influenced not only by endogenous (internal, or maturational) factors but also by children's experience in the real world. In this case, a cultural invention (maps) not only permits children (and adults) to apply their spatial skills to solve problems but also influences how those skills develop.

### Spatial Visualization

In contrast to spatial-orientation tasks, *spatial-visualization tasks* involve visual/mental operations, such as mentally rotating a figure or adjusting a tilted object to bring it to an upright position. One type of spatial-visualization task that shows substantial improvement over development is **mental rotation** (see Figure 6-9), in which a person must mentally rotate a visual stimulus to determine if it matches another stimulus (see Halpern, 1992). Both 4- and 5-year-old children are able to mentally rotate simple stimuli (see Newcombe & Huttenlocher, 2006), but even adults have difficulty mentally rotating more complex stimuli, such as the ones shown in Figure 6-9.

A relatively simple test of spatial visualization is Piaget and Inhelder's (1967) water-level problem (see Figure 6-10). Children are shown a tipped bottle, then asked to imagine the bottle half-full and to draw a line depicting the water level. The correct solution to this is to draw a line parallel to the ground, horizontal across the bottle. However, most preschool children draw a line parallel to the bottom of the bottle. This is a seemingly simple task that Piaget and Inhelder found was mastered by most

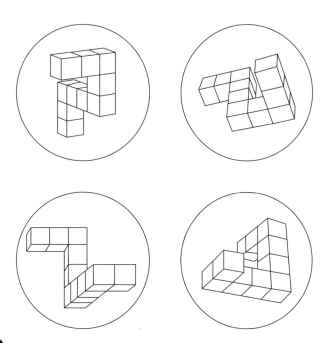

FIGURE **6-9**

A mental rotation task. Are the two figures in each pair alike or different? The task assesses the ability to mentally rotate visual information and is a task on which average differences between males and females are large. Males typically outperform females on this task.

FIGURE **6-10**

Piaget and Inhelder's (1967) water-level task. Children are to draw the water line in each bottle to represent how it would look if it were half-filled with water. Although Inhelder and Piaget reported that most children draw the line correctly by age 7 or so, other researchers report that even adolescents and adults have difficulty with this problem.

children by the time they reached concrete operations, around 7 years of age. Other researchers, however, have reported that many adolescents and young adults continue to have difficulty with the concept (see Kalichman, 1988; Vasta & Liben, 1996), with females making more errors than males.

### Object and Location Memory

Another early developing spatial ability is object and location memory (Plumert & Hund, 2001; Schumann-Hengsteler, 1992). Consider the board game *Concentration* (or *Memory*), in which players must find matches to cards placed facedown on a table by turning over two cards on each turn. During the early stages of such games, when strategies are less important (older children and adults use strategies more effectively than younger children; see Chapter 7), 5-year-olds perform as well as, and sometimes better than, adults (Baker-Ward & Ornstein, 1988). Five-year-old children's object and location memory performance is especially impressive, given their generally limited memory abilities (Schneider & Bjorklund, 1998; see Chapter 8).

### Sex Differences in Spatial Cognition and Evolutionary Hypotheses

Although the job of developmentalists is to describe and explain age-related changes in functioning, sometimes reliable individual differences are also found that pique researchers' attention as much as, or even more than, developmental difference. This has been the case for spatial cognition. In fact, some of our culture's most familiar gender stereotypes relate to spatial cognition. Women, for example, are alleged to have difficulty using maps, especially when one must turn the map (that is, mentally rotate it) to find where one is and where one wants to go. (This disability afflicts some men—your author included. I do just fine as long as both the map and I are facing north, but rotation of either the map or myself leaves me confusing my left from my right. This less-than-exceptional mental-rotation ability had me heading west to the outskirts of the Everglades at midnight one evening, when my destination was east, near the Atlantic Ocean.) And men are supposed victims of the "Where's the mayonnaise, Honey?" syndrome, in which they stare into a crowded refrigerator searching futilely for the mayonnaise, which their wives find with little difficulty. (I plead guilty to this fault as well.) Do these stereotypes have any basis in reality? Like all stereotypes, they do not describe the abilities of all men or all women (or perhaps even most of them), but does the research literature suggest at least a general trend in these directions?

In general, the answer is yes, with many of the gender differences being found early and persisting into adulthood (see Halpern, 2000, 2004). In fact, several theorists have proposed that some sex differences in spatial cognition may have been selected for over the course of human evolution. For example, David Geary (2007, 2009) proposed that there has been selection pressure on human males to develop spatial abilities, primarily for the purpose of navigation, which is important in hunting and for eye-hand coordination, which is important in tool and weapon use. Sex differences favoring males in map reading and mentally rotating figures (see Figure 6-8) have been found in the preschool years (Anooshian & Young, 1981; Levine et al., 1999), with sex differences in mental rotation favoring males being observed even in infancy (Moore & Johnson, 2009; Quinn & Liben, 2009).

Although gender differences in spatial cognition have been consistently found, the absolute magnitude of those differences is small. One way of evaluating the size of such differences is to conduct a *meta-analysis*—a statistical technique that allows an investigator to evaluate the magnitude of a significant effect across a large number of studies. Janet Hyde (1981) performed such an analysis, re-analyzing the findings of spatial cognition studies initially reviewed by Eleanor Maccoby and Carol Jacklin in 1974. Hyde reported that differences in spatial ability attributed to the gender of the child accounted for less than 5% of the difference in performance. Other meta-analyses have reported similar findings. For example, Marcia Linn and Anne Petersen (1985) reported that only between 1% and 5% of differences in spatial abilities can be attributed to gender, depending on the particular task. One exception Linn and Petersen noted was mental rotation, in which males of all ages performed better than females did. Robert Rosenthal and Donald Rubin (1982) similarly reported small differences between the sexes in their meta-analysis, and that the size of the effect diminished across the years, with females showing a substantial gain in cognitive performance (relative to males) in recent years. One exception to this trend is, again, mental rotation, which has shown no diminution in the gender difference over time (Masters & Soares, 1993).

Not all sex differences in spatial cognition favor males, however. Females typically show greater performance in object and location memory than males do, and these abilities may have been selected to promote the survival of ancestral women. As Geary (2009) has argued, ancestral males were likely responsible for hunting large game, which required accurate throwing, eye-hand coordination, and long-distance travel—and, thus, the development of good spatial-orientation skills. Ancestral women, in contrast, likely stayed near camp, where they tended to children and gathered food, the latter requiring fine-motor capabilities and the recognition of small perceptual differences (to tell the difference between poisonous and edible berries, for instance). Different evolutionary pressures should have led to different patterns of spatial abilities in males and females.

Females' superior performance on object and location memory tasks is illustrated in studies in which people are shown an array containing many objects (see Figure 6-11A) and, after studying it for a short while, are shown a larger array (see Figure 6-11B). Their task is to identify only objects that were in the initial array. Females of all ages tested perform better than males on this task (Silverman & Eals, 1992).

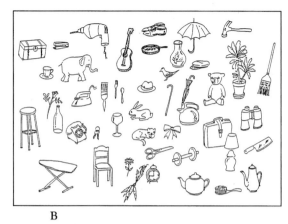

A          B

# FIGURE **6-11**

(*A*) The initial stimulus array shown to participants in a test of object and location memory. (*B*) The stimulus array with objects added. Participants were to cross out all items not found in the original array. One hypothesis for this sex difference is that females evolved spatial skills for detecting small perceptual differences, important in food gathering.

Source: "Sex Differences in Spatial Abilities: Evolutionary Theory and Data," by I. Silverman & M. Eals. In J. H. Barkow, L. Cosmides, & J. Tooby (Eds.), *The Adapted Mind: Evolutionary Psychology and the Generation of Culture*, pp. 537 (*A*) and 538 (*B*). Copyright © 1992 by Oxford University Press. Used by permission of Oxford University Press, Inc.

How can these gender differences in spatial ability be explained? Myriad factors have been proposed to explain these differences, including differential experience for males and females, genetics, prenatal hormones, and evolutionary accounts (see articles in Halpern, 1995). For example, boys typically engage in more spatial activities, including object-oriented play (see discussion to follow), and these differences may be related to sex differences in spatial cognition (Connor & Serbin, 1977). Research examining the "differential-experience" hypothesis has shown that spatial abilities in women are related to personality measures of masculinity (Newcombe & Dubas, 1992; Signorella, Jamison, & Krupa, 1989). One reason for the relationship between masculine personality characteristics and spatial abilities might have to do with the types of activities in which girls engage (Baenninger & Newcombe, 1995). For example, Nora Newcombe and her colleagues (1983) found that differences in spatial experience accounted for observed differences in spatial performance. They created a list of everyday activities that might occur in a population of high school and college students. In the first part of the study, college students were asked to classify the activities as masculine, feminine, or neutral. The raters typically selected those tasks judged to have high spatial content as masculine and as having more male participants (see Table 6-5). Subsequently, the researchers found small but significant gender differences among college students on a psychometric test with strong spatial components. Newcombe and her colleagues also reported a significant correlation between spatial activities and aptitude scores, particularly for females; that is, the more spatial activities one engages in, the greater one's spatial ability is likely to be (see also Newcombe & Dubas, 1992; Signorella, Jamison, & Krupa, 1989).

TABLE **6-5**

Examples of Masculine, Neutral, and Feminine Activities.

| Masculine | Neutral | Feminine |
|---|---|---|
| Touch football | Bowling | Figure skating |
| Baseball | Softball | Field hockey |
| Basketball | Advanced tennis | Gymnastics |
| Darts | Table tennis | Ballet |
| Hunting | Diving | Disco dancing |
| Skateboarding | Drawing | Embroidery |
| Shooting pool | Sculpting | Knitting |
| Car repair | Photography | Baton twirling |
| Electrical circuitry | Navigating in a car | Tailoring |
| Sketching house plans | Marching in a band | Touch typing |

Source: Adapted from Newcombe, N., Bandura, M. M., & Taylor D. C. (1983). Sex differences in spatial ability and spatial activities. *Sex Roles*, 9, 377–386.

Not surprisingly, the most sophisticated explanations of sex differences in spatial abilities consider interactions of biological and experiential factors during development. For example, Diane Halpern (2000, 2004) developed a model designed to explain sex differences in cognitive abilities; this model is illustrated in Figure 6-12. Halpern argues that to understand sex differences on academic and cognitive tasks, one must examine how information is acquired, stored, selected, retrieved, and used,

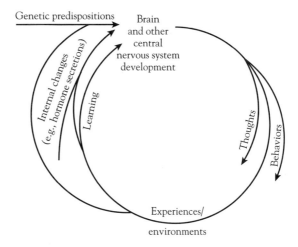

FIGURE **6-12**

A psychobiosocial model that can be used as a framework for understanding cognitive sex differences. It replaces the older idea that nature and nurture are separate influences and instead indicates that biological and psychosocial variables exert mutual influences on each other (graphically represented as a circle).

Source: From *Sex Differences in Cognitive Abilities*, 3rd ed. (p. 18), by D. F. Halpern, 2000, Mahwah, NJ: Erlbaum. Copyright 2000 by Lawrence Erlbaum Associates. Reprinted with permission.

each of which can vary depending on a variety of personal and contextual factors. Halpern argues that we cannot specify "how much" of average differences between males and females on any task is the result of "nature" or "nurture." Rather, the relation between nature and nurture is dynamic, interacting and varying over time. What children learn alters their brains. This in turn affects their ability to acquire and perform specific skills, which leads children to select new experiences, which will change the structure of their brains. According to Halpern (2004), "Differences in the interests of females and males both derive from differences in the areas in which they have achieved success and lead to further differential success in these areas because of differential knowledge and experience. Learning is both a biological and an environmental variable, and biology and environment are as inseparable as conjoined twins who share a common heart" (p. 138).

Even infants are able to process objects in space as they relate to them. These abilities, however, should not be thought of as inborn; they develop with experience. Over the preschool and early school years, children learn to form and use cognitive maps of their surroundings and to use real maps to help them navigate. During this same time, children become increasingly skilled at spatial visualization, such as mentally rotating an object, and at object and location memory, the latter of which seems to be particularly well developed even in 5-year-olds. Reliable sex differences are also found for various forms of spatial cognition, with males generally showing higher levels of performance on spatial-orientation and spatial-visualization tasks and females performing better on object and location as well as memory tasks. Like many other aspects of development, children seem prepared to make sense of spatial information. However, the way they engage their environment (for example, differences in play styles between boys and girls) interacts with their intuitive notions of space, producing ever-increasing spatial-cognitive abilities.

## Object-Oriented Play and Tool Use

Just as infants and young children seem oriented to attend to people, they also seem biased to explore and "play" with objects and to use objects as tools (Bjorklund & Gardiner, 2010; Geary, 2005). In this section, I first explore briefly the development of *object-oriented play*, followed by a more in-depth look at the development of *tool use*, and then conclude by examining the relation between the two.

### The Development of Object-Oriented Play

In Chapter 5, I defined "play" as a "purposeless" activity, in that it is done voluntarily and without any obvious immediate function (Rubin, Fein, & Vandenberg, 1983). Yet, as I mentioned then, most researchers see different types of play as having some functions important for children's development (see Pellegrini, 2011). Although **object-oriented play (or object play)** has been viewed differently by different authors, it is usually defined as the active manipulation of objects, such as banging them and throwing them, but also as the use of objects to build something (Bjorklund & Gardiner, 2010).

Object play is differentiated from *exploration*, which involves gaining information about an object by manipulating it, possibly with visual inspection (Belsky & Most, 1981; Hutt, 1966). Particularly in infancy, however, it can be difficult to know when exploration ends and object play begins. It seems safe to say that nearly all interaction with objects in infants before 9 months of age can be considered exploration, but that most of an infant's interaction with objects from 12 months onward can be better described as play (Belsky & Most, 1981), with boys engaging in both object exploration and object play more than girls (Bornstein et al., 1996).

Much object play in infants and toddlers involves making noise—for instance, by banging or shaking objects (Goldberg & Lewis, 1969; Morgante & Keen, 2008). Such "perceptually contingent" play gives way to more sophisticated forms of object play, such as building things, or constructive play, with boys usually engaging in such play more than girls (Caldera et al., 1999; Gredlein & Bjorklund, 2005). Other research has shown that girls exposed to high levels of androgen prenatally (congenital adrenal hyperplasia) engage in more object-oriented play than unaffected girls (Berenbaum & Hines, 1992; Collaer & Hines, 1995), suggesting a biological origin, at least in part, for this sex difference. Because object play is sometimes confused with exploration, and because some researchers exclude constructive play (for example, children building a fort with boxes or a house with LEGOS®) from their definition of object play, it is difficult to get an accurate measure of how frequently children engage in it. However, a fair estimate would seem to be that preschool children devote about 10% to 15% of all behaviors to object play (Smith & Connolly, 1980). As with other forms of play, object play is typically low in frequency during the early preschool years, peaks in childhood, and declines in early adolescence (see Pellegrini, 2011). Similar frequencies and patterns of developmental change have been observed for children from hunter-gatherer and other traditional cultures (Bakeman et al., 1990; Bock, 2005; Sigman et al., 1988).

What function might object play serve for children? One prominent hypothesis is that through object play, children discover *affordances* of objects (functional relationships between objects and the environment) and how objects can be used as *tools* (Bjorklund & Gardiner, 2010; Geary, 2005; Smith, 2005). Humans are one of only a handful of species that uses tools to any significant degree. In fact, it was not long ago that anthropologists considered tool use to be a defining feature of *Homo sapiens*. We now know that many other species use tools to solve problems and that chimpanzees, like humans, actually make tools (for example, the sticks used in termite fishing) (Whiten et al., 1999). However, no other species constructs and uses tools to the extent that humans do, and tool use begins early in life.

### *Learning to Use Tools*

By the time children are 3 or 4 years old, they are using, on a regular basis, many of the tools a culture offers, such as forks, spoons, chopsticks, pencils, hammers, or scissors. As such, the origins of tool use must be sought in infancy and the preschool years. How is it that children come to use objects (that is, tools) to solve problems? What factors are involved in early tool use, and how might they relate to cognitive functioning both in infancy and in later childhood?

Jeffrey Lockman (2000) has argued that children's eventual use of tools to solve problems may have its origins in infants' manipulation of their physical world. According to Lockman, "the origins of tool use in humans can be found during much of the first year of life, in the perception-action routines that infants repeatedly display as they explore their environments" (p. 137). From this perspective, tool use develops continuously over infancy and early childhood, and it should be thought of as a gradual process of discovery (often through play and exploration) rather than as resulting from the emergence of new representational skills. It develops from infants and young children's interactions with objects in the real world (for example, seeing what objects "do," hitting two objects together), often to obtain some perceptual outcome, such as noise. In the process, children learn how objects relate together, and they learn, often through trial and error, how best to manipulate one object (a spoon, for example) in relation to other objects (various types of food, for instance) to achieve specific goals (getting food to one's mouth) (see Bjorklund & Gardiner, 2010).

**The Development of Tool Use in Young Children.** According to Piaget (1954), the first signs of tool use in infants are seen around their first birthdays. However, subsequent research has indicated that infants are able to use tools earlier than Piaget proposed. Most tool-use research with infants and young children has used a variant of the *lure-retrieval task*, first developed by Köhler (1925) for use with chimpanzees, in which a desired object is placed out of the child's reach and a number of potential tools are available to use to retrieve the object. Infants as young a 9 and 10 months of age are able to use tools to solve lure-retrieval problems, although performance is influenced by features such as physical proximity (performance is greater when the tool is close to the target item) and perceptual similarity (performance is greater when the tool and lure are of contrasting colors and textures) (Bates, Carlson-Luden, & Bretherton, 1980).

In a study with slightly older children by Zhe Chen and Robert Siegler (2000), 1.5- and 2.5-year-old children were shown an out-of-reach toy and a group of toy tools, only one of which could be used to get the toy. The setup for their experiments is shown in Figure 6-13. As can be seen from the figure, only one tool, the rake, was both long enough and had the appropriate shape to retrieve the toy. Children sat with

FIGURE **6-13**

Example of the lure-retrieval task used by Chen and Siegler (2000). The child needed to choose the appropriate tool (here, the rake) to retrieve that toy (here, the turtle).

Source: Chen, Z., & Siegler, R. S. (2000). Across the great divide: Bridging the gap between understanding of toddlers' and older children's thinking. *Monographs of the Society for Research in Child Development* 65 (Issue no. 2, Serial no. 261). Reprinted with permission of the Society for Research in Child Development.

their parents, and for three consecutive trials, an experimenter urged them to get the toy. If they did not retrieve the toy after these trials, some children were given hints about using the tool (hint condition), whereas others saw the experimenter retrieve the toy with the appropriate tool (model condition). Children were then given a second (and third) set of trials using different tools and toys. Chen and Siegler found that older children (about 30 months) were more likely to use the tools to retrieve the toy before any instruction (hint or model) than younger children (about 21 months), but even these children retrieved the toy successfully only 15% of the time. Following the hint or modeling, however, even the youngest group of children used the tool to retrieve the toys (see also Gredlein & Bjorklund, 2005).

Chen and Siegler also examined the types of strategies children used to get the toy. The *forward strategy* involved the children leaning forward to reach the toy with their hands; the *indirect strategy* involved turning to their parent for help; and the *tool strategy* involved using one of the tools. Figure 6-14 shows changes in strategy use over the three trials (1, 2, and 3 in the figure) on each of the three problems (A, B, and C in the figure). As can be seen, the incidence of tool use increased over the problems, although children continued to use the forward strategy on the same trials they used the tool strategy. Thus, these young children, although not spontaneously using tools to retrieve the out-of-reach toy initially, could do so easily after receiving a simple hint or demonstration, and they generalized their new-found skill to a similar, but new, task.

FIGURE **6-14**

Percentage of children who used each strategy on the pretraining trials of the Chen and Siegler (2000) study.

Source: Chen, Z., & Siegler, R. S. (2000). Across the great divide: Bridging the gap between understanding of toddlers' and older children's thinking. *Monographs of the Society for Research in Child Development 65* (Issue no. 2, Serial no. 261). Reprinted with permission of the Society for Research in Child Development.

One interesting finding in the Chen and Siegler study was that boys were more likely than girls to choose a tool-use strategy. This difference was particularly large initially, but it was greatly reduced (though not eliminated) when hints were given. Although not all studies find sex differences in tool use, when such differences are found, they usually favor boys (Barrett, Davis, & Needham, 2007; Bates et al., 1980; Bjorklund & Gredlein, 2005).

### The Design Stance

When a person sees someone use a tool to achieve a goal, he or she assumes that that tool was designed for that intended purpose. This is referred to as the **design stance** (Dennett, 1990). Thus, pencils were made for writing, hammers were made for hammering, and objects that resemble pencils and hammers were likely made for writing and hammering, respectively. As a result, selecting tools becomes very efficient, although it sometimes results in "functional fixedness," the tendency not to identify alternative uses for familiar objects (German & Johnson, 2002). Children as young as 3 years tend to believe that an object designed for one purpose (catching bugs, for instance) is, indeed, only a "bug catcher," even though it can be successfully used for another function (collecting raindrops, for example) (Bloom & Markson, 1998; German & Johnson, 2002).

Research has shown that even 12-month-olds have learned that some tools are special-purpose objects. For example, by 1 year of age, children already have extensive experience with spoons. In one study (Barrett, Davis, & Needham, 2007), 12- and 18-month-old infants saw a box with a light display and a small hole on its side (see Figure 6-15). The experimenter then grasped the round end of either a spoon or a novel spoon-like object and inserted the object's straight end into the box, turning on the light. Infants were then given the opportunity to turn the light on themselves ("Now it's your turn"). When the familiar spoon was used, infants grasped the round end less than 25% of the time, failing to insert the tool into the box and turn on the light. In contrast, when they used the novel tool, they succeeded about 60% of the time, with most grasping the tool by the round end and inserting the straight end into the box. That is, even 12-month-old infants had formed a category of "spoon" and knew how

### FIGURE **6-15**

The light box and the spoon and novel tool used in the study by Barrett and colleagues (2007). Twelve and 18-month-old children used the novel tool to turn on the light but displayed "functional fixedness" with the spoon, failing to use it in a novel way.

Source: Barrett, T. M., Davis, E. F., & Needham, A. (2007). Learning about tools in infancy. *Developmental Psychology, 43*, 352–368.

they should interact with it (hold it by the straight end). In this case, it resulted in less flexible problem solving on a novel task, but like their older peers, they had learned how an important cultural tool was usually used and behaved accordingly.

Young children will apparently treat a novel tool as having a "special function" after only limited exposure. For example, in one study, 2- and 3-year-old children were shown a box with a slot in it and two similar objects (see Figure 6-16), both of which could fit into the slot (see Experiment 2 in Casler & Kelemen, 2005). An adult then took one of the objects (tool i in Figure 6-16B) and placed it in the slot of the box, which turned on a light. The children were told that they could do the task themselves if they wanted, and the experimenter handed them both of the tools. The adult even inserted the alternative object (tool ii) into a case similar to the slot on the box (although the light did not turn on). The adult also commented about the similarity of the bottoms of the two objects ("Hey, I noticed something. These look really different, but at the bottom, they're exactly the same size. Wow! See that?"). Children were later

## FIGURE **6-16**

The box and two tools in the study by Casler and Kelemen (2005). Two- and 3-year-old children who watched an experimenter insert tool i (below) to turn on a light were reluctant to use it for another purpose (crushing a cracker).

Source: Casler, K., & Kelemen, D. (2005). Young children's rapid learning about artifacts, *Developmental Science, 8,* 472–480.

given both tools (sometimes of different colors) and asked to select one to (1) turn the light on the box (the original task) or (2) crush a cracker. To turn on the light, the children consistently chose the same tool that the adult had demonstrated, even when it was a different color. In contrast, they consistently used the alternate tool to crush the cracker, even though the original tool would have worked equally well.

What these results reflect is that young children do not select a tool based solely on its properties to solve a problem but on their past history with a tool. From a single demonstration by an adult, children acquired a "tool category" for an object and acted as if the tool was invented "for that purpose." This reflects a primitive form of the design stance that older children and adults have toward tools, and it seems to be based on young children's belief that other people's behavior is based on intention (that is, they perform actions "for a reason") (Tomasello, 1999; see the discussion of treating people as intentional agents earlier in this chapter). As a result, they quickly learn that a tool has a specific function. According Krista Casler and Deborah Kelemen (2005), "young children exhibit rapid learning for artifact function, already possessing an early foundation to some of our most remarkable capacities as tool manufacturers and users" (p. 479). These findings are consistent with David Geary's (2005) proposal that tool use is part of children's intuitive notions of physics. An ability to understand how objects can be used to affect other objects and change the environment underlies tool use in humans and develops as children interact with their world (see also Smitsman & Bongers, 2002).

Nonhuman primates seem not to see tools in this way. Tool-using chimpanzees, bonobos, gorillas (Buttelmann et al., 2008), and monkeys (Cummins-Sebree & Fragaszy, 2005), for example, don't seem to be influenced by having used a tool to solve a problem when other, equally useful but novel tools are available. They seem to make their selection based on what will likely work, regardless of whether they have had prior experience with a tool.

## The Relationship between Tool Use and Object-Oriented Play

Many factors influence children's tool use, and one is children's tendencies to interact or "play with" objects. Some researchers have proposed that object-oriented play should enhance problem solving by creating a flexible cognitive set whereby children learn that materials can be used in a variety of ways, which will help them develop generalized approaches for solving problems (Bruner, 1972; Cheyne & Rubin, 1983). Based on research with preschool children, Peter Smith (1982, 2005) speculated that object-oriented play, often done as part of sociodramatic play (see Chapter 5), encourages children to understand that objects can be used in a variety of ways to solve problems. According to Smith (1982), object exploration and play may help prepare children to use tools "over and above what could be learnt through observation, imitation, and goal-directed practice" (p. 151).

For example, in some studies, children must select a properly shaped tool in order to retrieve a toy (for instance, a rake-like object long enough to reach a toy placed out of a child's reach, as described earlier). Children who are given the opportunity to play with the objects beforehand are more likely to later use the objects as tools to retrieve the toy than children who did not play with them and are just as good or better at the task as children who are given specific instructions (Cheyne & Rubin, 1983; Smith & Dutton, 1979). In related research, the amount of object-oriented play

3-year-old children engaged in on a separate task with different objects predicted their later performance on a toy-retrieval task (Gredlein & Bjorklund, 2005). Boys were more apt to engage in object-oriented play than girls, and boys were more likely to use a tool to solve a lure-retrieval task than girls. Similar to the findings of Chen and Siegler (2000) discussed earlier, the sex difference in using tools to solve the problem was greatly reduced when girls were given hints, indicating that girls were as capable of solving the problems as boys: They were just less likely to spontaneously use a tool than the boys were. When examining the relation between object-oriented play and tool-use scores, there were no significant effects for girls. In contrast, the amount of object-oriented play was significantly correlated with tool use scores for boys ($r = .59$). These findings are consistent with arguments made by Geary (2005, 2009) and others (Bjorklund & Pellegrini, 2002; Pellegrini & Bjorklund, 2004) that sex differences in early behavior interact with inherent, but still developing, folk-physics systems, yielding differential behavioral competencies in males and females. According to Geary (2009), the relation between object play and tool use is consistent with the idea that "the early skeletal structure of folk domains is enhanced during children's self-initiated social and play activities" (p. 316). Moreover, also consistent with evolutionary theory, there are sex differences in some aspects of children's folk physics. Geary continues: "In this case, sex differences in some folk physical abilities ... may be accompanied by early sex differences in sensitivity to corresponding forms of information (e.g., attending to objects and implicitly framing them as potential tools)" (p. 316).

Children seem to use tools to solve problems soon after the first glimmers to goal-directed behavior. Children's effective use of tools increases with age and is influenced by a host of factors, possibly even their tendencies to engage in object-oriented play (Gredlein & Bjorklund, 2005). Once children learn about tools, however, they seem to become part of their basic toolkit of problem-solving skills—and an essential component of human cognition.

## Children's Understanding of Time

A topic that can fall through the cracks when examining children's folk physics is their understanding of *time*. Typically, when we speak of "understanding the physical world," we think of perceiving or acting on solid "stuff," something that time is not. However, if it was good enough for Einstein, it should be good enough for us. In fact, it was Albert Einstein's question in 1928 about the origins and relations of the speed, time, and movement concepts in children that prompted Piaget (1946) to first investigate the topic. In this section, I examine briefly some of the research literature on children's developing understanding of time.

Perceiving and understanding time is both a very basic and a very complex thing. At its most basic, the understanding that events follow one another in time is almost self-evident and, as we will see, within the grasp of young infants. On the other hand, understanding concepts such as "past" and "future," and knowing when future events, such as one's birthday, will occur relative to other future events, such as Halloween, for example, take many years to master (see Friedman, 2003, 2008, for reviews).

### Understanding Temporal Order and "Causality"

Lets start with the "easy" concepts. Consider a sequence of different objects (a circle, A; a triangle, B; a square, C; and a diamond, D) falling from the top to the bottom of

## FIGURE **6-17**

After 4- and 8-month-old infants were habituated to one sequence of "falling objects" (circle, triangle, square, diamond) they were shown a different sequence of falling objects in the test phase (circle, diamond, triangle, square). Infants' attention increased during the test phase, indicating that they recognized that the temporal order of the falling objects had changed.

Source: Lewkowicz, D. J. (2004). Perception of serial order in infant. *Developmental Science, 7,* 175–184.

a computer screen in a particular order, ABCD, each making a distinctive sound when it hits bottom (see Figure 6-17). When 4- and 8-month-old infants watch such a display for a while, their attention wanes (that is, they habituate). When they are then shown the same objects falling in a different temporal sequence (circle, diamond, triangle, and square, or ADBC), their attention increases, demonstrating that they recognize something has changed (Lewkowicz, 2004). What has changed is not the objects or what they do but the temporal order in which they fall. Two-month-old babies are also sensitive to the order in which words in a sentence are spoken (for example, "cats would jump benches" to "cats jump wood benches") (Mandel, Kemler Nelson, & Jusczyk, 1996), indicating that babies from their first months of life have some rudimentary notion of "time" (see Lewkowicz, 2000).

Infants' understanding of temporal sequencing, as in "event A comes before event B," is further illustrated by research in **causal perception**. For example, when adults watch a computer screen and see a moving shape collide with a stationary shape, they expect the stationary shape to move. The first shape is seen as an *intentional agent*, hitting and "launching" the other (Michotte, 1963). Infants behave similarly, interpreting events of moving and colliding shapes much as adults do, making movement an important clue to agency (Leslie & Keeble, 1987; Oakes, 1994). For example, 2.5-month-old infants act surprised when a toy bug on wheels remains stationary after being hit by a cylinder rolling down a ramp or, alternatively, if the bug moves in the absence of the cylinder contacting it (Kotovsky & Baillargeon, 1994, 2000; Wang, Kaufman, & Baillargeon, 2003).

### *Yesterday, Today, and Tomorrow*

Children still have a lot to learn about time, particularly as we use it to organize our everyday lives. Some things happen at about the same time and in the same order every day: We wake up in the morning, have breakfast, go to school or work, have lunch, have dinner, and go to bed. We understand concepts such as "yesterday," "today," and "tomorrow," and we understand that Tuesday comes after Monday, June comes before October, and Halloween comes before Thanksgiving. These are all recurring events—things that happen every day, week, month, or year—and we are able to place ourselves in time along these various continua. When can children understand sequences of events like these?

Even 2- and 3-year-old children use temporal terms such as *yesterday, last night,* and *tomorrow,* but they frequently use such terms incorrectly (see Friedman, 2008). By 4 years of age, children have a relatively firm grasp on concepts such as "before" and "after," being able to state, for example, that an event that happened 1 week ago did, indeed, occur more recently than one that happened 7 weeks ago (Friedman, 1991). However, preschool children still have a difficult time judging the recency of important future (and past) events, such as determining which will occur sooner, their birthday or Valentine's Day (Friedman, Gardner, & Zubin, 1995).

How can one tell what children know about the timing of future events? In one study, William Friedman (2000) showed 4-, 7-, and 10-year-old children a road map with various features marked on it. Some were marked very close to where the child sat, representing events that would happen soon in the future, and some were marked farther away, representing events that would happen in the more distant future (see Figure 6-18). Children were then given a series of future events and asked to show on the road map where each belonged. Testing was done in October, a few weeks before Halloween. Children were asked about the timing of the following events: dinnertime, Saturday (when they watch cartoons in the morning), Halloween, Christmas, Valentine's Day, and summer. The 4-year-olds' responses were generally random, although about half of the youngest children in the study responded properly that Halloween was coming soon. Seven-year-olds did a better job, distinguishing mainly between "near" and "distant" events, whereas the 10-year-old children used the entire road map and produced generally accurate judgments.

Four- and 5-year-olds are not totally incompetent when judging the timing of events, however, especially when dealing with recurrent events that happen daily. For example, 4- and 5-year-olds can distinguish between events that happen during the course of a day (waking up, eating breakfast, eating lunch, etc.), but events occurring at longer intervals (for example, days of the week or seasons of the year) still give them trouble (see Friedman, 2008). For instance, although most 6- and 7-year-old children can recite in correct order the days of the week, and many can do the same for the months of the year, they have difficulty thinking about days of the week in relation to one another (for example, "If this is Saturday and you go backward in time, which will you come to first, Thursday or Tuesday?"). It's not until midadolescence that children can solve problems such as these (Friedman, 1986).

It is interesting that the language a culture uses may affect how easily children learn calendar systems (for instance, days of the week, months of the year). For example, in Mandarin Chinese, the names of the days of the week (except Sunday) include numbers. Monday, for example, is *xing qi yi* (day one), Tuesday is *xing qi er* (day two), Wednesday is *xing qi san* (day three), and so forth. In one study, Chinese and American 8- and 10-year-olds were given the name of a day and asked to tell what day came some specified time before it, much like the example in the last paragraph

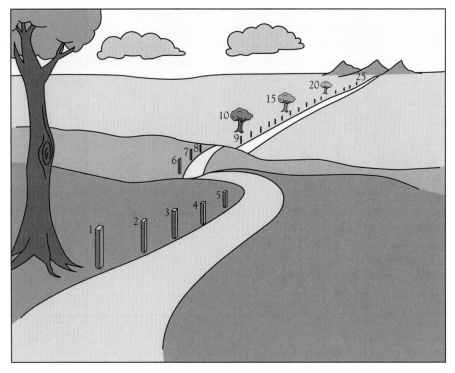

FIGURE **6-18**

Children pointed to various points on the road map to designate when an event would happen—points near them (to the left of the picture) for events that would happen soon, such as dinner time, and points farther way from them (to the right side of the picture) for events that would happen later in time, such as Valentines Day. Four-year-olds generally did not differentiate the timing of events, whereas 10-years olds performed much as adults would.

Source: Friedman, W. J. (2000). The development of children's knowledge of the times of future events. *Child Development, 71*, 913–932.

("If this is Saturday and you go back two days …"). Unlike American children, most Chinese children solved these problems by arithmetic calculation. For example, to find the day that was 2 days before Saturday (*xing qi liu*, or day six), they would subtract two and arrive at the answer *xing qi si*, or "day four" (Thursday) (Kelly et al., 1999). As a result, the Chinese children performed substantially better than the American children, with 8-year-old Chinese children solving problems as quickly as English-speaking adults. This is another example of how something as basic as the language one speaks can serve as a *tool of intellectual adaptation* (Vygotsky, 1978; see Chapter 3), influencing cognitive development in subtle ways.

Time, of course, is a complicated concept, but one that most of us have a reasonable grasp of by adulthood (although understanding the time-space continuum of modern physics remains beyond most of us). Even infants have an understanding of some aspects of time—for example, simple causality (events that happen first cause events that happen second). However, it takes children years to fully grasp time as adults do, with even something as fundamental as the language one speaks influencing its rate of development.

## Some Final Reflections on Children's Understanding of the Physical World

A true understanding of the physical world requires an understanding of both the main facts involved about a topic and the causal links among them. This is how scientists usually operate. Some of these facts and causes are easier to understand than others, and infants and young children seem to have a better grasp of many of these concepts than scientists once believed (as some core-knowledge and theory-theory theorists have pointed out). Others require more time, cognitive effort, and cultural instruction to be acquired (for example, understanding time). It's worth noting that children's and adults' thinking about many aspects of reality are often not so different from one another. Modern science is only about 500 years old, and knowledge provided by telescopes, moon trips, microscopes, and other technologies were not available when our psychological structures were shaped by natural selection. When, as a parents or teachers, we feel pleased seeing our children overcome their temporary erroneous explanations about why the sun is not out, how mountains and lakes are formed, or where babies come from, we should not forget that scientific explanations about those phenomena are historically quite recent. Forms of "magical thinking" about reality have pervaded throughout human history, and they still seem to operate today when facing the unknown.

## SUMMARY

Children possess naïve, or intuitive, notions about how the psychological (*folk psychology*), biological (*folk biology*), and physical (*folk physics*) world works, collectively known as *folk knowledge. Theory theories* extend Piaget's ideas, assuming that children possess some rudimentary naïve theories to represent and reason about the principal domains of knowledge.

*Theory of mind* refers to children's developing concepts of mental activity, including the understanding that peoples' behavior is motivated by what they know, or believe, and by what they want, or desire (*belief-desire reasoning*). The beginnings of theory of mind are seen in infants viewing other people as *intentional agents* (beings who are goal-directed). *Shared attention*, which is reflected in gaze following, pointing, and other forms of triadic interaction, is seen as early as 9 months and continues to improve over the next year, reflecting infants' increasing abilities to take the perspective of others.

Concerning children as "mind readers," 3-year-olds usually fail *false-belief tasks*. One explanation for young children's poor performance on false-belief tasks is that they have a representational deficit. Other explanations look at children's executive function or their reasoning about true-belief tasks. Children with autism are particularly deficient in "mind reading" skills and have been described as having *mindblindness*. Chimpanzees and other great apes show only limited evidence that they possess components of theory of mind.

Preoperational children have a tendency toward *finalism*, believing that natural objects and events must have a specifiable cause, with some people describing such thinking as *promiscuous teleology*. Preoperational children also display *artificialism*, the belief that everything that exists was constructed by people (or God) for specific purposes.

Children in all cultures are interested in animals and biological life. Movement is a key component in whether children think something is alive or not. With increasing age, children make clearer distinctions between animate and inanimate objects, although some aspects of *animism* persist in adults. Children's understanding of folk biology becomes more adultlike with age and is affected by culture and children's experience with animals. Children's knowledge about reproduction follows a developmental course similar to that suggested by Piaget.

*Spatial cognition* develops over childhood, with age differences being found on tasks of *spatial orientation*, which measure how people understand the placement of objects in space with themselves as the reference point, and on tasks of *spatial visualization*, which deal with the mental manipulation of visual stimuli, such as performing tasks involving *mental rotation*. Sex differences favoring males are found on tasks of spatial orientation and spatial visualization, whereas females usually perform better on tasks assessing *object and location memory*.

Infants and young children explore objects and engage in *object-oriented play* (or *object play*), with boys usually engaging in such play more than girls. Even young children adopt the *design stance*, assuming tools are designed for an intended function. Higher levels of tool use are sometimes found for boys than for girls.

Even infants have a rudimentary understanding of time, as reflected, for example, by research on *causal perception*, in which one object is seen as "launching" another when it hits the second object. However, children's understanding of the relation between past, present, and future events continues to develop into adolescence.

## KEY TERMS AND CONCEPTS

| | | | |
|---|---|---|---|
| folk psychology | intentional agents | animism | object-oriented play (or object play) |
| folk biology | shared attention | spatial cognition | |
| folk physics | false-belief task | spatial orientation | design stance |
| folk knowledge | mindblindness | spatial visualization | causal perception |
| theory theory | finalism | object and location memory | |
| theory of mind | promiscuous teleology | | |
| belief-desire reasoning | artificialism | mental rotation | |

## SUGGESTED READINGS

### Scholarly Work

Geary, D. C. (2005). *The origin of mind: Evolution of brain, cognition, and general intelligence.* Washington, DC: American Psychological Association. This is Geary's magnum opus (at least to date) concerning his theory about the evolution and development of human cognition. It covers, among other topics, evolutionary theory and his views about the development of folk psychology, folk biology, and folk physics.

Gopnik, A., & Meltzoff, A. N. (1997). *Words, thoughts, and theories.* Cambridge, MA: MIT Press. Gopnik and Meltzoff present their version of a theory theory of cognitive development, focusing primarily on development in infants and young children. This is a clear presentation of the basic ideas behind theory theories of cognitive development.

Kelemen, D. (2004). Are children "intuitive theists"? Reasoning about purpose and design in nature.

*Psychological Science, 15,* 295–301. This paper presents the argument that young children's tendencies to see "purpose" in all things makes them susceptible to cultural beliefs of the supernatural, particularly to the idea of God or gods.

Newcombe, N. S., & Huttenlocher, J. (2006). Development of spatial cognition. In W. Damon & R. Lerner (Series Eds.) & D. Kuhn & R. S. Siegler (Vol. Eds.), *Handbook of child psychology: Vol 2: Cognition, perception, and language* (6th edition) (pp. 734–776). New York: Wiley. This chapter presents a state-of-the-art review of research on the development of spatial cognition by two prominent researchers in the field.

## Reading for Personal Interest

Siegal, M. (2008). *Marvelous minds: The discovery of what children know.* Oxford, UK: Oxford University Press. Developmental psychologist Michael Siegal presents a clear and comprehensive review of research over the last several decades of children's developing understanding of people, biology, and the physical world.

# Learning to Think on Their Own: Executive Function, Strategies, and Problem Solving

**Assumptions of Information-Processing Approaches**

**The Development of Basic-Level Processes: Executive Function**
Speed of Processing
Memory Span and Working Memory
Attention
Learning How Not to Respond: Inhibition and Resistance to Interference
Cognitive Flexibility
Some Final Thoughts on Executive Function

**The Development of Strategies**
Increases in Strategy Use, Improvements in Performance
  BOX 7-1: Executive Functioning and Brain Development

Utilization Deficiencies
How Do Children's Strategies Develop?
  Siegler's Adaptive Strategy Choice Model
The Development of Memory Strategies
Factors that Influence Children's Strategy Use and Effectiveness
Culture and Strategies
Strategies in the Classroom

**Learning to Solve Problems**
The Development of Problem Solving Reasoning

SUMMARY
KEY TERMS AND CONCEPTS
SUGGESTED READINGS

Four-year-old Benjamin was a talkative child, and unlike many other preschoolers, he almost always had plenty to say when his parents asked him, "So what did you do in preschool today?" On this occasion, Benjamin was excitedly telling his parents about the pet iguana that one of his classmates had brought in for show-and-tell when, without warning, he started talking about a character on one of his favorite TV shows. Within a few seconds, Benjamin paused and then said, "Oops, I just interrupted myself." He couldn't keep the distracting thought about the TV show from intruding on his story about his day at school.

Benjamin may be more talkative than most 4-year-olds, but he is very much like his peers when it comes to being distracted and getting off task. He is not easily able to keep intruding thoughts from his mind (and mouth), and this shortcoming makes it difficult for him to successfully control his thought and behavior to solve problems effectively. As I mentioned in Chapter 1, one of the major issues in cognitive development is how children gain control over their own cognition—how they intentionally regulate their actions and thoughts.

In this chapter, I examine how children come to "learn to think on their own." Most of the research and theorizing on this topic can trace its roots to *information-processing theories* of cognitive development. Information-processing theories use the computer as a model for how the mind works and changes with age. From this perspective, cognitive development can be seen as reflecting changes in *hardware* (such as the capacity of memory systems and the speed with which information is processed through the systems), *software* (such as children's access to and ability to use strategies), or both. After reviewing briefly some assumptions of information-processing approaches to cognitive development, I examine the development of *executive function*—a set of lower-level cognitive processes that are associated with planning and self-regulation. I then look at the development of strategies and, finally, the development of problem solving, including both analogical and scientific reasoning.

## ASSUMPTIONS OF INFORMATION-PROCESSING APPROACHES

There is no single information-processing theory of cognition or cognitive development. Rather, information-processing theories are built on a set of assumptions concerning how humans acquire, store, and retrieve information. A core assumption of information-processing approaches is that information moves through a system of

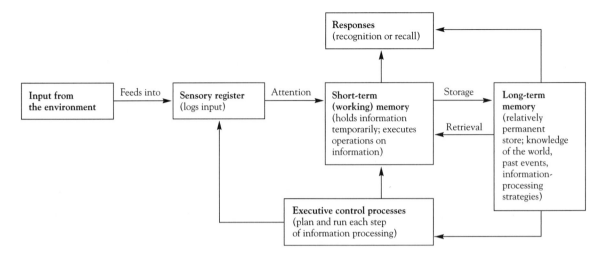

**FIGURE 7-1**

The flow of information through the memory system.

Source: Based on Shaffer, D. R. (1996). *Developmental psychology: Childhood and adolescence* (4th ed.) Pacific Grove, CA: Brooks/Cole, as adapted from "Human Memory: A Proposed System and Its Control Processes," by R. C. Atkinson & R. M. Shiffrin, 1968, in K. Spence and J. T. Spence (Eds.), *The psychology of learning and motivation: Advances in research and theory* (Vol. 2), Copyright © 1968 by Academic Press, Inc.

stores, as reflected in Figure 7-1. Typically, processing is viewed as occurring serially, with the product of one stage of processing serving as the input for the next stage, and so on, until some final response or decision is made. The initial multistore models of the sort shown in the figure were first suggested as theories of memory (Atkinson & Shiffrin, 1968). At the risk of oversimplification, these theories assume that information from the external world is initially represented, perceptually intact, in *sensory registers*. There is a separate sensory register, or *sensory store,* for each sense modality (for example, vision, audition), and these registers can presumably hold large quantities of information—but only for a matter of milliseconds. From this initial registration, information is passed through to the **short-term store**, where capacity is smaller but the representations are more durable, lasting for seconds. The short-term store has also been referred to as *primary memory, working memory,* or the *contents of consciousness.* Our short-term store makes contact with the world, holding information long enough for us to evaluate it. We apply strategies for remembering or solving problems in the short-term store. The short-term store is where we live, mentally speaking. Its capacity is limited, however, and if something is not done to information once it is in the short-term store, that information will be lost. But if we apply some cognitive operation to the information in the short-term store, that information is transferred to the **long-term store**, where it presumably is retained indefinitely.

Central to information-processing approaches is the idea of **limited capacity**. We can deal with only so much information at any single time. Theorists have used a variety of metaphors for capacity, including a space metaphor (one has only so much mental space in which to store or operate on information), a time metaphor (one can only perform operations so fast), and an energy metaphor (one has only so much energy to allocate to the storage or execution of cognitive operations). Some researchers have taken the energy metaphor seriously and shown, for instance, that glucose consumption in areas of the brain associated with cognitive processing is elevated for difficult (that is, for resource-consuming) tasks relative to easier (that is, for less-resource-consuming) tasks (Haier et al., 1988). For example, most of us have enough mental space or energy to walk and chew gum at the same time. Add to these operations a nontrivial arithmetic problem, however, and a change in our rate of gum chewing or walking will be discerned. We have added something else to do, and doing it will interfere with the execution of other operations.

Cognitive theorists also assume that mental processes can be placed on a continuum relative to how much of one's limited capacity each process requires for its execution (Hasher & Zacks, 1979). At one extreme are **automatic processes**, which require none of the short-term store's limited capacity; at the other extreme are **effortful processes**, which require the use of mental resources for their successful completion. In addition to not requiring any mental effort, truly automatic processes are hypothesized (1) to occur without intention and without conscious awareness, (2) not to interfere with the execution of other processes, (3) not to improve with practice, and (4) not to be influenced by individual differences in intelligence, motivation, and education (Hasher & Zacks, 1979). In contrast, effortful processes, which have also been called strategies or control processes, are hypothesized (1) to be available to consciousness, (2) to interfere with the execution of other effortful processes, (3) to improve with practice, and (4) to be influenced by individual differences in intelligence, motivation, and education.

Within this general framework, researchers have investigated age differences in both lower-level, or basic, processes, such as speed of processing and working memory, and higher-level processes, such as the use of strategies and problem solving. I examine the development of both basic and higher-level processes in this chapter, starting with the processes involved in executive function and moving to an examination of the development of cognitive strategies and, finally, to problem solving, with a special look at the development of analogical and scientific reasoning. Other topics that have been examined mainly from an information-processing perspective will be the topics of later chapters, such as memory in Chapter 8. The major emphasis in this chapter is not an evaluation of information-processing theories of cognitive development, however, but how children come to control their own thinking and problem solving—how they become *self-directed thinkers*.

## THE DEVELOPMENT OF BASIC-LEVEL PROCESSES: EXECUTIVE FUNCTION

How do children learn to exert control over their problem solving and "thinking"? Stated another way, how do children acquire the ability to control or regulate their own thought and behavior? Researchers have argued that attaining cognitive self-control requires the development of a set of basic-level abilities that, collectively, are referred to as **executive function** (or **executive control**) (Jones, Rothbart, & Posner, 2003; Wiebe, Espy, & Charak, 2008).

Executive function refers to the processes involved in regulating attention and in determining what to do with information just gathered or retrieved from long-term memory. It plays a central role in planning and behaving flexibly, particularly when dealing with new information. It involves a related set of basic information-processing abilities, including (1) working memory, or how much information one can hold in the short-term store and "think about" at a time; (2) how well one can inhibit responding and resist interference; (3) selectively attending to relevant information; and (4) cognitive flexibility, as reflected by how easily individuals can switch between different sets of rules or different tasks (see Garon, Bryson, & Smith, 2008; Zelazo, Carlson, & Kesek, 2008). In addition, each of these abilities is related to how quickly one can process information. Each of these abilities develops over time, and age differences in these functions determine how well children are able to regulate their behavior and thinking.

Individual differences in various measures of executive function are related to a host of higher-level cognitive abilities, including reading, mathematics, theory of mind, and IQ, among others (each of which will be discussed in later chapters). Children's executive-function abilities have been shown to have high genetic heritability (Friedman et al., 2008) but are also significantly associated with "environmental" factors, such as exercise (Hillman et al., 2009), patterns of mother-child interactions (Hughes & Ensor, 2009), and culture (Lewis et al., 2009).

I examine the development of five cognitive abilities associated with executive function in this section, beginning with speed of processing and followed by memory span and working memory, various aspects of attention, inhibition and children's abilities *not* to respond, and finally, cognitive flexibility.

## Speed of Processing

With respect to overall speed of processing, young children require more time (and, thus, presumably use more of their limited capacity) to execute most cognitive processes than do older children (Dempster, 1981). In a series of studies, Robert Kail (1991, 1997; Kail & Ferrer, 2008) reported that the general developmental changes in processing speed are similar across different tasks. In Kail's studies, participants ranging in age from 6 to about 21 years were given a series of reaction-time tasks. For example, in some experiments, participants were presented with a pair of letters in different orientations and were to determine as quickly as possible whether the two letters were identical or mirror images of each other. To do this, participants had to mentally rotate one letter into the same orientation as the other. In a name-retrieval task, the participants were shown pairs of pictures and asked to determine whether they were physically identical or had the same name (for instance, different examples of a banana, one peeled and one unpeeled). Patterns of responses over these two and several other tasks were highly similar, with reaction times becoming faster with age (see also Hale, Fry, & Jessie, 1993; Miller & Vernon, 1997).

Figure 7-2 presents the pattern of reaction times across age for a variety of tasks used in Kail's experiments. Note that despite substantial differences in the task requirements and the length of time it takes to perform the tasks (processing time is measured in milliseconds for some tasks and in seconds for others), all show essentially the same pattern of changes in reaction time across age. Subsequent research even showed a similar (though not identical) age trend in reaction time over the first year of life (Canfield et al., 1997; Rose et al., 2002), and between 22 and 32 months of age (Zelazo, Kearsley, & Stack, 1995).

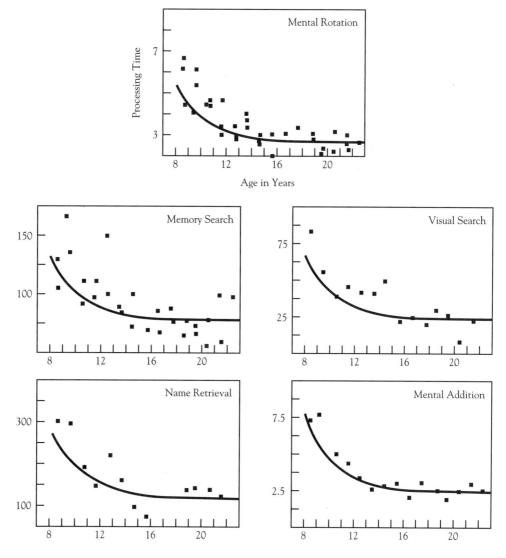

FIGURE **7-2**

Developmental patterns of speed of processing for five cognitive tasks. For both simple and complex tasks, children become faster with age.

Source: "Development of Processing Speed in Childhood and Adolescence," by R. Kail. In H. W. Reese (Ed.), *Advances in Child Development and Behavior, 23*, 151–187. Copyright © 1991. Reprinted with permission from Elsevier.

Kail interpreted these findings as reflecting age-related increases in the amount of processing resources available for the execution of cognitive operations. Kail acknowledged that knowledge influences speed of processing and, thus, levels of performance on cognitive tasks, but he argued that maturationally based factors are primarily responsible for age-related differences in speed and, therefore, efficiency of processing (see Kail & Salthouse, 1994). One maturationally based change likely involves the myelination of nerves in the associative ("thinking") area of the brain. As noted in

Chapter 2, myelin is a fatty substance that surrounds nerves and facilitates transmission of nerve impulses. Whereas myelination of most sensory and motor areas of the brain is adultlike within the first several years of life, myelination of the associative area is not complete until the teen years and beyond (see Lenroot & Giedd, 2007).

## Memory Span and Working Memory

Central to information-processing models of cognition is the idea that people can hold only so much information in the short-term store before it deteriorates. While information is in the short-term store people can process that information, that is, think about it. Two useful concepts that relate to how much information people can hold and process in the short-term store are *memory span* and *working memory*, and I discuss the development of each here.

### Age Differences in Memory Span

Traditionally, the capacity of the short-term store has been assessed by tests of **memory span** that measure the number of (usually) unrelated items that can be recalled in exact order. Presentation of items is done rapidly (usually one per second), so there is minimal time for the application of strategies to aid recall. A child's memory span is considered to be a reflection of the size of the short-term store, or the capacity of working memory. Basically, when children are presented with randomly ordered items, the number of items they can recall in exact order increases with age (Dempster, 1981; Schneider, Knopf, & Sodian, 2009). The average memory span of 2-year-olds is about two items; of 5-year-olds, about four items; of 7-year-olds, about five items; and of 9-year-olds, about six items. The average memory span of adults is about seven items. Figure 7-3 shows the highly predictable growth of the memory span for digits (digit span) from age 2 years through adulthood.

Evidence for developmental differences in the capacity of the short-term store comes from a study by Nelson Cowan and his colleagues (1999) assessing **span of apprehension,** which refers to the number of items that people can keep in mind at any one time or the amount of information that people can attend to at a single time. The span of apprehension for adults is about four items. This is lower than the average adult memory span of seven items because factors such as focused attention, knowledge of the to-be-remembered information, and encoding strategies can affect memory span when items are presented more slowly.

Does the span of apprehension represent an absolute capacity of the short-term store, and does it increase with age? In the critical condition in the study by Cowan and colleagues (1999), first-grade and fourth-grade children and adults played a computer game. Over earphones, they also heard series of digits that they were to ignore. Occasionally and unexpectedly, however, they were signaled to recall, in exact order, the most recently presented set of digits they had heard. Participants were not explicitly attending to the digits, making it unlikely that they were using any encoding strategies to remember them. Thus, performance on this task seems to be a fair test of span of apprehension. Average span of apprehension was about 3.5 digits for adults, about 3 digits for fourth-graders, and about 2.5 digits for first-grade children. Cowan and his colleagues interpreted these significant age differences as reflecting a true developmental difference in the capacity of the short-term store. There seems to be an underlying difference in capacity, as reflected by differences in the span of apprehension, that serves as the foundation for age differences on memory span tasks.

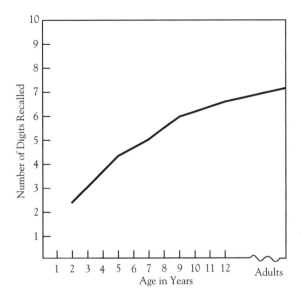

FIGURE **7-3**

Children's memory span for digits (digit span) shows regular increases with age. With increasing age, children are able to hold more things in mind (here digits) at once, and this affects their ability to perform more complicated tasks.

Source: "Memory Span: Sources of Individual and Developmental Differences," by F. N. Dempster, 1981, *Psychological Bulletin, 89*, 63–100. Copyright © 1981 American Psychological Association. Reprinted with permission of the author.

Despite these impressive and robust findings, researchers have seriously questioned the idea that the capacity of the short-term store is the only (or even the most important) source of age differences on memory span tasks. For example, in one often-cited study, a group of graduate students at the University of Pittsburgh were given two simple memory tests (Chi, 1978). On one, they were read a series of numbers quickly (about one per second) and were asked to recall them immediately in exact order. On a second test, they were briefly shown chess pieces on a chessboard in game-possible positions (again, about one chess piece per second) and then given the pieces and asked to place them at their previous positions on the board. Their performance on these tasks was compared with that of a group of 10-year-olds. In all fairness, these were not typical 10-year-olds—they were all chess experts, either winners of local tournaments or members of chess clubs. When memory for the chess positions was tested, the children outperformed the adults. This finding is probably not surprising, given the expert status of the children. But the critical question is how they did when remembering the numbers. Does being a chess expert cause one's memory capabilities to improve overall, or was the children's remarkable performance limited to what they knew best? The results supported the latter interpretation. The adults, despite being outdone by the children when memory for chess positions was tested, were superior to the children when the test stimuli were numbers. The results of this experiment can be seen in Figure 7-4 (see also Schneider et al., 1993).

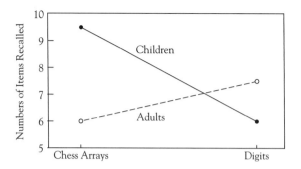

FIGURE **7-4**

The average memory span for digits and chess arrays by chess-expert children and college-educated adults.

Source: Adapted from "Knowledge Structures and Memory Development," by M. T. H. Chi. In R. Siegler, (Ed.), *Children's Thinking: What Develops?* Copyright © 1978 Lawrence Erlbaum Associates, Inc. Reprinted with permission.

## The Development of Working Memory

A distinction is made between short-term memory and **working memory**. The former involves only the storage of information held in the short-term system, whereas the latter involves storage capacity plus the ability to transform information held in the short-term system (Schneider & Pressley, 1997). Digit-span tasks described earlier assess the capacity of short-term memory. An example of a working memory task can be found in the research of Linda Siegel and Ellen Ryan (1989), who gave children sets of incomplete sentences, requiring them to supply the final word (for example, "In the summer, it is very _____"). After being presented with several such sentences, children were asked to recall the final word in each sentence, in order. Such a test requires not only the short-term storage of information but also some mental work dealing with the to-be-remembered information. Similar to the findings reported for digit span, reliable age differences in working memory are found, although working memory span is usually about two items less than a child's memory span (see Alloway, Gathercole, & Pickering, 2006; Case, 1985; Cowan & Alloway, 2009).

Alan Baddeley and Graham Hitch (1974) presented one popular account of working memory and its development (see also Baddeley, 1986). According to the Baddeley and Hitch model, working memory consists of a central executive that stores information and two temporary systems, one for coding verbal information, called the **articulatory loop,** and another for coding visual information, which is referred to as the *visuo-spatial scratch pad*. Because relatively little developmental research has been conducted on the visuo-spatial scratchpad, my discussion here will focus on the articulatory loop. Figure 7-5 presents a simplified model of the working memory system as Baddeley and Hitch think of it. According to the theory, age differences in verbal memory span (for example, recall of digits or words) are primarily caused by developmental differences in the articulatory loop. On verbal-span tasks, phonological information is stored in the articulatory loop. These verbal representations (or memory traces) decay rapidly but can be maintained in working memory by verbal rehearsal. Although age differences in the rate that information decays in working memory have been reported (see Cowan & Alloway, 2009), most researchers believe that age

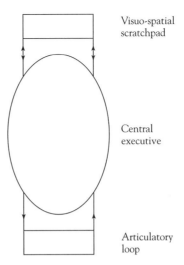

Visuo-spatial
scratchpad

Central
executive

Articulatory
loop

FIGURE **7-5**

A simplified version of Baddeley and Hitch's working memory model.

Source: Baddeley, A. D. (1983). Working memory. *Philosophical Transactions of the Royal Society, B302,* 311–324. Reprinted with permission of the Royal Society.

differences in rehearsal rate are the primary reason for developmental differences in memory span. The faster one rehearses, the more memory traces one can rehearse, the more information that can be kept active in working memory, and the more one can remember.

Baddeley and Hitch assume that the articulatory loop involves a literal subvocalization process, with people saying the items to themselves. One factor that influences rehearsal rate is word length. Longer words require more time to say, thus leaving less time to rehearse other words before they decay and are lost from working memory. There is good evidence from the adult literature that such a process (or one very like it) actually occurs (see Baddeley, 1986, for an extensive review). In the developmental literature, research has shown a relationship between the speed with which children can say words and memory span. With age, children are able to read or say words at a faster rate, and memory span increases accordingly (Chuah & Maybery, 1999; Hulme et al., 1984). Figure 7-6 presents data from a study by Charles Hulme and his colleagues (1984) showing a very regular, age-related relationship between speech rate (that is, how fast people can say the words) and the number of words recalled on a word-span task. Older children and adults have a faster rate of speech than younger children do, and their memory spans vary accordingly.

It is interesting to note that differences in digit span have been found as a function of the language a person speaks. For example, Chinese speakers have considerably longer digit spans than English speakers do; this difference is apparent as early as age 4 and extends into adulthood (Chen & Stevenson, 1988; Geary et al., 1993). This cultural effect seems to be caused by differences in the rate with which number words (*one, two,* and so on) in the two languages are spoken. Languages such as Chinese, with relatively short number words that can be articulated quickly, enable longer digit

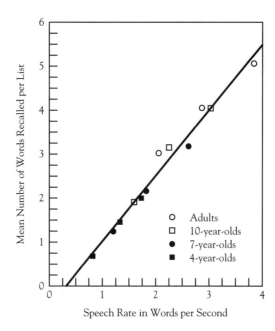

FIGURE **7-6**

The relationship between word length, speech rate, and memory span as a function of age. As speech rate increases, more words are recalled, with both speech rate and words recalled increasing with age.

Source: "Speech Rate and the Development of Spoken Words: The Role of Rehearsal and Item Identification Processes," by C. Hulme, N. Thomson, C. Muir, & A. Lawrence, 1984, *Journal of Experimental Child Psychology, 38,* 241–253. Copyright © 1984 Academic Press. Reprinted with permission.

spans than do languages such as English, with relatively long number words that are articulated more slowly (Chen & Stevenson, 1988). In fact, in one study with bilingual children, the children had longer digit spans in their *second* language (English) than in their first language (Welsh). This counterintuitive finding was because number words can be articulated more rapidly in English than in Welsh (Ellis & Hennelley, 1980). Thus, the greater digit spans of Chinese children relative to American children, for example, seem not to be the result of some inherent cognitive or educational superiority for the Chinese children but, rather, the result of the language they speak. From a Vygotskian perspective (see Chapter 3), the number words in a language are a "tool of intellectual adaptation," provided by the culture, that influences cognition.

## Attention

Resources are sometimes conceptualized in terms of *attention*. We all know what is meant by attention. In everyday parlance, we use the term interchangeably with *concentration*. When we tell a child to "pay attention," we usually want that child to concentrate on the task at hand and not let his or her mind wander to other things. One assumption about attention is that it consumes limited mental resources. Thus, age differences in the ability to attend to or focus one's attention on a particular stimulus or task have been presumed to reflect differences in the availability of and ability to allocate limited mental resources.

One aspect of attention involves sustaining one's focus on a particular task—that is, to sustain, or pay, attention. To some extent, we can measure this even during infancy, with some babies staying "on task" better than others do. Some interesting evidence indicates that variations in attention in infants and toddlers (1- and 2-year olds) predict attention in early childhood (3.5 years) (Ruff et al., 1990). Such a finding suggests that some common factor may underlie individual differences in attentiveness, both in infancy and childhood, and may make possible the prediction of attention disorders from measurements taken during infancy.

The ability to sustain attention becomes increasingly important for children beyond infancy, and ample evidence indicates that children's *attention spans*, the length of time for which they can sustain focused attention, increases with age. For example, Holly Ruff and Katherine Lawson (1990) observed children between the ages of 1 and 4.5 years during free play. They noted a regular increase in focused attention during play over this time, and they attributed such increases, in part, to improved abilities to inhibit extraneous information. In other research, children between the ages of 30 and 54 months were given a series of tests of sustained visual attention—for example, attention during play, while watching television, and during a reaction-time task (Ruff, Capozzoli, & Weisberg, 1998). For each measure, attention increased with age, although it differed among the tasks, with attention during play and for television viewing developing earlier than attention during the reaction-time task. Also, only low to moderate correlations were found among the tasks, indicating that individual differences in attention were relatively domain specific in nature, tied to particular contexts.

Another important aspect of attention is the ability to focus only on chosen stimuli and not be distracted by other "noise" in the environment, which is referred to as **selective attention**. Young children are notorious for their relatively poor selective attention abilities, focusing their attention disproportionately on aspects of a situation that are irrelevant to the task at hand. They are easily distracted and spend much time "off task." These abilities improve with age, as children are increasingly able to stay on task and select appropriate information to attend to (Lane & Pearson, 1982).

Research has documented cultural differences in aspects of selective attention. For example, some have proposed that Westerners are socialized to focus their attention on key features of objects, whereas East Asians are socialized to divide their attention between objects and events in their environments (Duffy & Kitayama, 2007). This is related to hypothesized differences in holistic (Asian) versus analytic (North American) styles of reasoning that have been proposed to characterize the two cultures (Nisbett et al., 2001; Varnum et al., 2010). For instance, it is hypothesized that Asians see the world in a more holistic way, being especially sensitive to relationships among objects within the current context, whereas Westerners are more apt to take an analytic perspective, focusing on individual "target" items. This is illustrated in a study in which Japanese and American adults were shown stimuli similar to those presented in Figure 7-7 (Kitayama et al., 2003). In this study, participants were shown a box with a line drawn in it and, in a smaller box, had to reproduce either the absolute length of the line (bottom left in Figure 7-7) or the relative length of the line (bottom right in Figure 7-7). Consistent with the divided-versus-focused-attention hypothesis, the American adults were more accurate performing the absolute task, whereas the Japanese adults were more accurate performing the relative task.

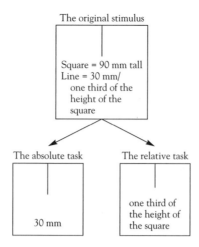

FIGURE **7-7**

The frame-line test. Children are asked to draw the line in the boxes at the bottom that is either the same absolute length as the line in the top box (absolute task) or the same relative length (relative task). Beginning at age 6, Americans perform better on the absolute task and Japanese perform better on the relative task. However, 4- and 5-year-old children in both America and Japan make more errors on the absolute task.

Source: Kitayama, S., Duffy, S., Kawamura, T., & Larsen, J. T. (2003). Perceiving an Object and its Context in Different Cultures: A Cultural Look at New Look. *Psychological Science, 14*, 201–206.

When does this cultural pattern develop? By 6 years of age, both Japanese and American children display the same pattern as adults in their culture do (Duffy et al., 2009; Vasilyeva, Duffy, & Huttenlocher, 2007). However, 4- and 5-year-old children in both America and Japan make more errors on the absolute tasks (Duffy et al., 2009). This and other research (Duffy, Huttenlocher, & Levine, 2005) suggest that both American and Japanese young children initially have an easier time dealing with relative information. However, depending on cultural practices, sometime around 6 years of age some children (in this case, Americans) become socialized to *focus* their attention, whereas others (in this case, Japanese) become socialized to *divide* their attention. A similar interpretation has been proposed for the development of analogical reasoning, with Asian preschool children performing better on complex problems dealing with relations among objects than Western (American) children (Richland et al., 2010).

## Learning How Not to Respond: Inhibition and Resistance to Interference

To this point, the cognitive processes I have discussed all involve some process of activation. Children must *encode* information, *hold* it in short-term store, *rehearse* it in the articulatory loop, and do it all as fast as possible if performance is to be optimal. There should be no surprise here, for thinking is nothing if not an active process, and one important point of cognitive development would seem to be that children can do "more" thinking "more effectively" with age. Well enough. But sometimes what one *doesn't* do is as important to effective thinking as what one does do. Sometimes people must inhibit thoughts and action if they expect to get a job done. Of course, "not doing" something is actually a very active process itself, so I have perhaps mislead the reader a bit to make a point—that sometimes inhibiting processes are just as important as activating them, and that these abilities change during development.

**Inhibition** refers "to an active suppression process, such as the removal of task-irrelevant information from working memory" (Harnishfeger, 1995, p. 188). Many of children's cognitive errors and everyday "problem" behaviors come from things they do despite instructions otherwise (for example, "I didn't mean to trip Josh when he walked up the aisle, it just happened"). The basic idea at its simplest is that, with age, children are increasingly able to inhibit prepotent (primary) and often inappropriate mental or behavioral responses from both internal and external sources and that these improved skills permit the more efficient execution of other cognitive operations.

Related to the concept of inhibition is **resistance to interference**, which refers to "susceptibility to performance decrements under conditions of multiple distracting stimuli" (Harnishfeger, 1995, p. 188–189). Resistance to interference, for example, is shown on dual tasks, when performing one task (chewing gum or watching television) interferes with performance on a second task (walking or doing one's homework). Inhibition and resistance to interference have often been treated as reflecting the same underlying mechanisms, which is likely true, but the two concepts, although highly related, are not synonymous. Nevertheless, they do seem to have a similar neurological locus and to follow the same developmental function. As such, I will discuss them in this section as reflecting a single set of processes.

### *Developmental Differences*

Inhibition abilities develop over infancy, early childhood, and into adolescence and are assessed by a variety of simple tests (see Kochanska et al., 1996; Sabbagh et al., 2006). For example, in the *day-night task*, children must say "day" each time they see a picture of the moon and "night" each time they see a picture of the sun, which is very difficult for preschoolers, presumably because they cannot inhibit the response to say the highly associated word with its corresponding picture (for example, "day" with the sun). Young children's difficulties are eliminated when they are requested to pair unrelated words (for example, "dog" and "pig") with the pictures (Diamond, Kirkham, & Amso, 2002). Preschoolers also have difficulty in the *tapping task*, in which they must tap once each time the examiner taps twice, and tap twice each time the examiner taps once, in the *opposites task*, where they point to one of two pictures an interviewer did *not* point to (Baker, Friedman, & Leslie, 2010), and in playing *Simon Says*, where they must perform an action only when Simon says so (for example, "Simon says, touch your nose"). Simplifying the Simon Says game helps, but young children still make many more inhibitory errors than older children do (Diamond & Taylor, 1996; Sabbagh et al., 2006).

Children also have a difficult time inhibiting their speech. For example, when children were to name out loud only certain pictures on a page (for example, animals) but not say the names of distractor items (for example, people), kindergarten children showed no evidence of inhibiting their responses. They mentioned the distractor items as frequently on trials when they were told not to mention them as on trials when they were told to mention them (Kipp & Pope, 1997).

Changes in inhibitory processes over childhood have been related to a number of cognitive tasks. For example, children's ability to selectively forget information is affected by their ability to keep the to-be-forgotten information out of mind. Older

Young children often have a difficult time not saying whatever is on their minds.

Source: © Baby Blue Partnership. Reprinted with special permission of King Features Syndicate.

children are better able to execute these inhibitory processes than are younger children (Harnishfeger & Pope, 1996; Lehman et al., 1997; see Wilson & Kipp, 1998). Age differences in selective attention can be explained by young children's difficulty ignoring task-irrelevant stimuli. Although task instructions make it clear that they are to attend only to the central stimuli and ignore peripheral stimuli, they have a difficult time doing so (see Ridderinkhof, van der Molen, & Band, 1997). And young children's difficulty in inhibiting some behaviors (such as pointing to where an object is hidden) has been linked to the ability to deceive others and in the development of theory of mind (Carlson, Moses, & Hix, 1998; see Chapter 6).

### Inhibition and Attention Deficit Hyperactivity Disorder

In recent decades, the phenomenon of **attention deficit hyperactivity disorder (ADHD)** has gained substantial attention, with children (and adults) who have this disorder displaying hyperactivity, impulsiveness, and great difficulty sustaining attention. The incidence of ADHD in the United States is approximately 3% to 7% of the childhood population; it is more common in boys than in girls, with between about a third to half of all childhood cases of ADHD persisting into adulthood (see Barkley, 1998). Children with ADHD are more likely to experience school problems, including poor academic performance, grade retention, suspensions, and expulsions, than are children without ADHD, and they are also at greater risk for delinquency, substance abuse, and troubled social relationships in adulthood (see Barkley, 1997; Loe et al., 2008).

Russell Barkley (1997) proposed that the principal cause of ADHD is deficits in behavioral inhibition. Behavioral inhibition, claims Barkley, influences working memory, self-regulation of emotion, internalization of speech (critical in directing problem solving and reflecting upon one's behavior), and what Barkley calls *reconstitution*, which involves the "creation of novel, complex goal-directed behaviors" (p. 72). Given the importance of these abilities for cognition and successful day-to-day functioning, children with deficits in behavioral inhibition would be especially disadvantaged.

There is ample support for Barkley's contention that children with ADHD show deficits in these areas (see Barkley, 1997, for a review). For example, relative to non-ADHD controls, children with ADHD:

1. Do more poorly on working memory tasks (Mariani & Barkley, 1997).
2. Are less proficient at imitating lengthy sequences of actions (Mariani & Barkley, 1997).
3. Have a poorer sense of time (Barkley et al., 1997).
4. Are more adversely affected by delay (Songua-Barke et al., 1992).
5. Are more likely to be described as irritable, hostile, and excitable (see Barkley, 1990).
6. Perform more poorly on comprehension tasks (Bailey et al., 2009).
7. Are less likely to use strategies on memory tasks (August, 1987).

Some have speculated that many youngsters diagnosed with ADHD may merely be highly active children within the "normal range" of functioning but who have a difficult time adjusting to the "sit still and listen" regime of school (Panksepp, 1998). Others have suggested that high activity levels and frequent switching of attention may actually be beneficial in some environments and was adaptive to our hunter-gatherer ancestors (Jensen et al., 1997). For example, the benefits of having individuals in a group who constantly scanned the horizon for signs of predators or prey would seem to be obvious. One must be cautious, however, in taking these arguments too far. As Sam Goldstein and Barkley (1998) comment, it is unlikely that any person with a true case of ADHD would be at an advantage in any environment, modern or ancient. But one must keep in mind that schools are a recent invention for our species. Although sometimes interfering with ideal educational practices, "normal" levels of activity and playful behavior (especially as displayed by preadolescent boys) may not, in and of themselves, be signs of pathology.

## Cognitive Flexibility

**Cognitive flexibility** refers to the ability to shift between sets of rules or tasks (Garon et al., 2008; Zelazo et al., 2003). Philip Zelazo and his colleagues (2003, 2008) have argued that the development of executive function involves the increasing ability to formulate and maintain rules, as illustrated on simplified "shifting tasks" in which children must change from following one criterion to another (see Hanania & Smith, 2009 for a review). Such "shifting" is seen in the *Dimensional Card Sorting Task*, developed by Zelazo and his colleagues (Zelazo, Frye, & Rapus, 1996). In this task, children are shown sets of cards that vary on two dimensions. Figure 7-8 provides an example of the cards used in these experiments. Children are shown two target cards, a yellow car and a green flower, for instance. When playing the *color game*, they are told that all the yellow cards go in one pile (with the yellow car) and all the green cards go in the other pile (with the green flower). Children then are given a series of test cards (for instance, yellow flowers and green cars), and are asked to sort them by color. Most 3-year-olds do this easily. Then, children are told they are going to play a new game, the *shape game*. (For half the children, the shape game is played first, and

Target Cards

Test Cards

## FIGURE **7-8**

Dimensional Card Sorting Task. Children are to sort cards initially by one dimension (color) and later by a second dimension (shape). Children much younger than 4 years of age have difficulty on the "switch" trials, and usually continue to sort by the original dimension.

Source: Zelazo, P. D., Frye, D., & Rapus, T. (1996). An age-related dissociation between knowing rules and using them. *Cognitive Development, 11*, 37–63. Copyright © 1996, reprinted with permission from Elsevier.

for the other half, the color game is played first.) In the shape game, children are to place cars in one box (with the yellow car) and flowers in the other box (with the green flower). These are called *switch trials*, because the rules have been switched (from sorting on the basis of color to shape, or vice versa). Now, most 3-year-old children fail, continuing to sort the cards according to the original dimension. Yet, when asked what the new rule is, most can easily and correctly tell the experimenter. That is, 3-year-olds can verbalize the rule but cannot execute the problem. By 4 years of age, however, most children do fine on both tasks.

Why do children have difficulties on these tasks, and what develops so that, by 4 and 5 years of age, most children can follow simple rule systems relatively easily? According to Zelazo and his colleagues, children gain increasing conscious control over their problem solving, and this is captured by *cognitive complexity and control (CCC)* theory (Zelazo, 2000; Zelazo & Frye, 1997). Zelazo and Douglas Frye (1997) propose that there are age-related changes in the complexity of rule systems that children can represent. According to Zelazo and his colleagues (1997), developmental differences in *reflection* give children increased control over their behavior and cognition. "Reflection is defined as a recursive process whereby the contents of consciousness become an object of consciousness so that they can be operated on and modified … [H]igher order rules mediate reflective awareness of lower order rules and make possible the deliberate selection of lower order rules for use. In the absence of a higher order rule, children will perseverate on whichever lower order rules are most compelling" (p. 218). In other words, children acquire rules early on and can follow them in certain situations. But coordinating rules requires greater conscious reflection, and this develops over the preschool years.

## Some Final Thoughts on Executive Function

Developmental changes in speed of processing, working memory, inhibition, and cognitive flexibility are all related to one another and to changes in neurological development, particularly the frontal cortex (see Box 7-1). Developing control over one's thoughts, emotions, and behavior is essential to the performance of most, if not all, higher-level cognitive tasks. David Geary (2005) has speculated that the evolution of executive function was an important component in the emergence of the modern human mind. Inhibiting inappropriate behavior, resisting distraction, and controlling one's actions in general are critical to effective functioning in any social group, as well as for activities such as constructing tools, hunting, and preparing meals, among many others. These abilities are better developed in humans than in other primates, and in older children than in younger children, and may be a key to understanding both human cognitive development and human evolution.

# THE DEVELOPMENT OF STRATEGIES

Strategies are relevant to most aspects of cognitive development. For example, in memory development, commonly used strategies include rehearsing information and grouping to-be-remembered items by conceptual categories (for example, remembering all the outfielders on a baseball team in one group and all the pitchers in another). In mathematics, simple strategies of addition include counting on one's fingers and mental counting (for instance, for the problem $3 + 2 = ?$, mentally starting with 3 and counting up two to arrive at 5). Strategies can be much more complicated and involve an evaluation component, a form of *metacognition*—knowledge about one's own cognition and factors that influence thinking. For example, in reading, one must occasionally determine how well the recently read information has been understood. In all cases, strategies are used to achieve some cognitive goal (remembering, adding, comprehending).

**Strategies** are usually defined as deliberate, goal-directed mental operations that are aimed at solving a problem. Strategies are usually viewed as being deliberately implemented, nonobligatory (one does not have to use them to perform a task), mentally effortful, and potentially available to consciousness (Harnishfeger & Bjorklund, 1990a; Pressley & Hilden, 2006). To some extent, strategies lie at the heart of what it means to be a "self-directed learner" or to "think on one's own." Children use strategies to achieve goals that they cannot achieve "without thinking." A 2-year-old stares at the place where a favorite toy is hidden so that she can find it again after a time-out; a 6-year-old counts on his fingers, holding up one finger for each item counted, to determine how many cookies he has; and a 10-year-old memorizes a simple rhyme so that she can remember the number of days in each month ("Thirty days has September, April, June, and November..."). These are all deliberate strategies, effortful cognitive operations that are used to solve some problem. Children discover many strategies themselves while trying to come up with answers to everyday problems, and parents or teachers explicitly teach other strategies to them. The frequency and effectiveness of strategy use changes with age, as children become increasingly able to direct their own learning and problem solving.

## Increases in Strategy Use, Improvements in Performance

For most cognitively effortful tasks, older children are more likely to use strategies, select more effective and efficient strategies, and perform better on tasks than younger children. Younger children can often be taught strategies that they do not use

## BOX 7-1    Executive Functioning and Brain Development

Executive function consists of different components that are related to one another and are associated with age-related changes in different areas of the *prefrontal cortex* (Bunge & Zelazo, 2006; Moriguchi & Hiraki, 2009). The frontal lobes of the neocortex have many projections to other areas of the brain, including the limbic system (the "emotional" part of the brain). The prefrontal cortex is one of the last areas of the brain to reach full maturity. Development of the frontal lobes in humans is rapid between birth and about 2 years of age. Another, less pronounced growth spurt occurs between about 4 and 7 years, with additional changes occurring over adolescence into adulthood (see Zelazo et al., 2008).

Much evidence for the role of the frontal lobes in executive function in humans comes from cases of brain damage. Humans with frontal lobe damage have difficulty with planning and concentration. Frontal lobe dysfunction has been implicated in some psychiatric syndromes, such as obsessive-compulsive disorder (Malloy, 1987). One test that demonstrates the difficulty frontal-lobe patients have with executive function is the Wisconsin Card Sorting Test (WCST). The WCST consists of cards on which are depicted different objects (such as squares, stars, and circles) that vary in color and number (see Figure 7-9). The

participant's task is to sort the cards into specified categories (that is, according to color, number, or shape), which is reinforced by the examiner. Without specifically informing the participant, the examiner then switches reinforcement to another category. (This is similar in form to the Dimensional Card Sorting Task described earlier in the main chapter text.) For example, the initial category may be number, in which case participants would be reinforced for sorting all the target cards with four items on them under the cue card consisting of four circles, all the cards with three items on them under the cue card with the three crosses, and so on, regardless of the color or shape of the items on the cards. The examiner may then switch from number to shape, so that all target cards are now to be placed with the cue card consisting of the same shape (stars with stars, triangles with triangles, and so on), with color and number being irrelevant. Participants are corrected after a mistake, so they should presumably be able to learn a new classification scheme after only a few trials. People without brain damage do exactly this. However, patients with lesions in the frontal lobes do poorly on this task, often finding it difficult to make a new response (Milner, 1964). This reflects an inability to inhibit a previously acquired response and a lack of cognitive flexibility. Based on these and related findings, it has become clear that the

### FIGURE **7-9**

The Wisconsin Card Sorting Test.

Source: "Some Effects of Frontal Lobotomy in Man," by B. Milner. In J. M. Warren & K. Akert (Eds.), *The frontal granular cortex and behavior*. New York: McGraw-Hill, 1964.

| **BOX 7-1** | **Executive Functioning and Brain Development** (*Continued*) |

frontal lobes play a central role in the selection and regulation of behavior by inhibiting previous responses and fostering resistance to interference from extraneous stimuli (see Dempster, 1993; Luria, 1973).

Both executive function and the prefrontal lobe take time to develop. We saw in Chapter 2 that infants' performance on A-not-B object-permanence tasks was related to the ability to inhibit responses and development of the prefrontal lobes (Bell, Wolfe, & Adkins, 2007; Holmboe et al., 2008). During childhood, age differences are found in performance on the WCST, with young children performing much the way that adults with frontal lesions do (Chelune & Baer, 1986).

More recently, Deanna Kuhn (2006) has argued that adolescents display improvements in various aspects of executive functioning and that these cognitive and behavioral improvements are associated with neurological changes occurring at this same time. In support of this, Beatriz Luna and her colleagues (2001) gave participants between the ages of 8 and 30 years tasks that assessed inhibition abilities. They reported that adultlike abilities to inhibit inappropriate responses developed gradually and were correlated with patterns of brain activity. Using fMRI techniques, Luna and her colleagues found that the prefrontal cortex was more active on these inhibition tasks in adolescents than in either children or adults. Thus, age-related changes in task performance were not related to underlying

brain activation in a straightforward, linear way. Task performance increased gradually with age, while brain activation in the frontal cortex on this task increased sharply between childhood and adolescence, only to decrease again in adulthood. This sensitive period of cortical development in adolescence has prompted some brain scientists to suggest that drinking alcohol to excess can have the most deleterious effects during late adolescence and early adulthood (Volkow, 2007).

Developmental lags in the frontal cortex are associated with the incidence of ADHD. For example, in one study, development of the frontal cortex of 7- to 13-year-old children with ADHD lagged about 3 years behind those of children without ADHD, whereas development of their motor areas developed slightly earlier (Shaw et al., 2007). This uneven pattern of brain development may account for the increased fidgeting and restlessness seen in children with ADHD.

It should not be surprising that brain and cognitive development are closely related. The brain, quite obviously, is the source of our thought. The relation between prefrontal cortex development and various components of executive function has been especially well documented, both in adults and over the course of development. These discoveries not only tell us about the brain but also provide insights into the types of cognitive mechanisms that underlie both basic and more sophisticated cognitive operations and their development.

spontaneously and, as a result, improve their performance (Schwenck, Bjorklund, & Schneider, 2007; see Bjorklund, Dukes, & Brown, 2009; Ornstein & Light, 2010). For example, simply telling young children to repeat, or rehearse, words that they are asked to remember results in children remembering more words (Ornstein, Naus, & Stone, 1977). This phenomenon has been termed a **production deficiency** (Flavell, 1970). That is, although children do not *produce* strategies spontaneously, they can be trained to use them and enhance their performance as a result. However, the performance of trained younger children rarely reaches the levels of the performance of older children who use strategies spontaneously, and young children frequently fail to generalize a trained strategy to new tasks, often resorting to their nonstrategic ways (see Bjorklund, Dukes, & Brown, 2009, for examples with respect to memory strategies).

If young children are not using strategies (unless we train them), then what are they doing? The answer is, basically, that they are still being "strategic." Preschool children, who do not spontaneously conserve liquid (see Chapter 5) or organize sets of pictures according to familiar categories (such as animals, tools, and vegetables), nevertheless do things to help them perform tasks (see Ornstein & Light, 2010, and Wellman, 1988, for reviews). These strategies often result in incorrect answers, but they are strategies nonetheless.

For instance, Judy DeLoache, Ann Brown, and their colleagues engaged children as young as 18-months-old in a hide-and-seek game, in which a toy (a stuffed animal, for example) was hidden in one of several locations in a child's home. Following delays of several minutes, the child was asked to retrieve the toy. DeLoache and Brown reported that children as young as 18 months engaged in strategic behavior during the delay periods, including looking or pointing at the hiding location and repeating the name of the toy (DeLoache & Brown, 1983; DeLoache, Cassidy, & Brown, 1985). These results, and others like them (Cohen, 1996), make it clear that production deficiencies are relative. Even very young children use strategies, although the strategies that they use tend to be simple and to increase in efficiency with age.

Following these findings, it seems clear that preschool children engage in some planning that warrants being called strategic. Still, their strategies lack the effectiveness of the procedures used by older children and often may not aid task performance at all. However, Henry Wellman (1988) asserted that preschoolers' strategies are every bit as goal-directed and performance-influencing as the strategies of older children and that they are used in a wide range of situations. Subsequent findings support Wellman's interpretation (see Bjorklund, Dukes, & Brown, 2009). However, we must be careful not to attribute too much in the way of strategic competence to the preschool child, for cognitive skills are clearly more effective and more easily observed in older children.

## Utilization Deficiencies

Sometimes children will use a strategy, either spontaneously or as a result of training, but their performance will not improve. For example, in one set of studies, 3- and 4-year-old children were shown a miniature room containing toy animals and furniture (Blumberg & Torenberg, 2005; Blumberg, Torenberg, & Randall, 2005). Children were told that one set of items was special (for example, "It's very important that the animals get fed regularly"), and the children's job was to help the experimenter take care of these special things. They were then told to remove all of the objects from the room, and later, they were asked to put them back in the room where they had been placed before. A simple strategy for achieving this goal would be to remove the items according to category membership (that is, take out the "special" objects one after the other), something that 70% of the preschoolers did. However, using this strategy did not help them put the items back in their proper place. In other words, although children used a strategy, it did not help them achieve their goal.

Using a strategy that does not improve performance is called a **utilization deficiency** (Miller, 1990; Miller & Seier, 1994) and is something that is frequently observed in children's strategy use. Utilization deficiencies are not limited to preschool children; they are also seen in the behavior of older children as well (see Bjorklund, Dukes, & Brown, 2009; Miller, 1990). For example, Patricia Miller and Wendy Seier (1994) reported strong or partial evidence of utilization deficiencies in more than 90% of all experiments examining children's spontaneous use of memory strategies.

Similarly, utilization deficiencies were found in more than 50% of memory training studies conducted during a 30-year period (Bjorklund et al., 1997).

Let me provide an example of a utilization deficiency in research by Patricia Miller and her colleagues, which involved children's use of a selective-attention strategy (DeMarie-Dreblow & Miller, 1988; Miller et al., 1986). In this research, children (usually between 3 and 8 years of age) are shown a series of boxes with doors on top arranged into two rows of six columns (see Photo 7-1). On half of the doors are pictures of cages, meaning that those boxes contain pictures of animals. On the remaining doors are pictures of houses, meaning that those boxes contain pictures of household objects. Children are told to remember the location of one group of objects, either the animals or the household objects. They are also told that they can open any doors they wish during a study period. Children's strategies can be examined by looking at the doors they choose to open during this study period.

The most efficient strategy, of course, is to open only those doors that have a drawing of the relevant category. In a series of experiments, Miller and her colleagues found a developmental sequence in strategy use. In the first phase, preschoolers show no selective strategy, usually opening all the doors on the top first and then all the doors on the bottom, regardless of what picture is on the door. In the second phase, children use the selective strategy, but only partially: They still open many irrelevant doors. In the third phase, children use the most efficient strategy (that is, open mainly the relevant doors), but the strategy does not help them remember the locations of the items. This third phase constitutes a utilization deficiency. Not until the fourth phase, usually late in the preschool years, are children able to use the strategy and to benefit from its use.

If strategies are so important to children's cognitive performance, why should they sometimes *not* benefit from them? And when strategies don't do the children any good, why do they bother using them? There is surely no single reason for utilization

PHOTO **7-1**

Apparatus used in studies of children's attentional strategies by Patricia Miller and her colleagues.

Source: Courtesy of Patricia Miller.

deficiencies. But perhaps the factor that is most responsible for utilization deficiencies, especially in young children, is lack of mental resources. By definition, strategies are effortful to use, and children who use a strategy may not have enough mental resources left over to devote to solving the problem at hand (Bjorklund & Harnishfeger, 1987; Miller et al., 1991). Other factors that are likely involved include children's lack of awareness that the strategy is not helping them. That is, children may possess poor metacognition and fail to realize that all the extra effort they are putting in isn't resulting in any benefit (Ringel & Springer, 1980). In fact, young children frequently overestimate their physical and cognitive abilities, thinking they are performing better than they actually are. This may not always be such a bad thing, however. Children who practice strategies eventually get good at them, and their task performance does, indeed, improve (Shin, Bjorklund, & Beck, 2007). That is, utilization deficiencies are often short lived (Bjorklund, Coyle, & Gaultney, 1992). If young children realized how poorly they were doing, they might stop using the strategy and, although saving themselves some effort in the short term, hinder their overall effectiveness in the long term. Finally, children may use a new strategy just for the sake of novelty (Siegler, 1996). Although from an adult perspective the number-one reason to use a strategy is to improve task performance (that's what strategies are "for," after all), this may not reflect the child's point of view. Trying something new may be a goal unto itself, and the fact that it does not improve performance may be relatively unimportant to children.

## How Do Children's Strategies Develop? Siegler's Adaptive Strategy Choice Model

For any given task, children have a variety of strategic options available to them. Although psychologists may study a single strategy at a time, in actuality children use multiple strategies to solve a single problem—and sometimes even several strategies at a single time. Evidence for multiple and variable strategy use has been found everywhere it has been looked for, including arithmetic (Alibali, 1999), scientific reasoning (Schauble, 1990), memory (Schwenck et al., 2007), spelling (Rittle-Johnson & Siegler, 1999), and conservation (Church & Goldin-Meadow, 1986), among others (see Siegler, 2006).

Robert Siegler's (1996, 2006) **adaptive strategy choice model** best exemplifies this perspective of multiple and variable strategy use. Basically, Siegler proposes that, in cognitive development, children generate a wide variety of strategies to solve problems. Depending on the nature of the task and the goals of the child, certain strategies are "selected" and used frequently, whereas others that are less effective are used less often and eventually decrease in frequency.

The technique Siegler and his colleagues used to assess children's multiple strategy use has been referred to as the *microgenetic method*, which involves looking at developmental change within individuals over short time intervals—usually days or weeks (see Miller & Coyle, 1999; Siegler, 2000). Not all aspects of development (cognitive or otherwise) fit this bill, so one must be careful in selecting phenomena to study and to assess children who are most susceptible to changing how they think over relatively short intervals. But cognitive strategies are good candidates for examination from a microgenetic perspective, and research following Siegler's general approach has produced some interesting results.

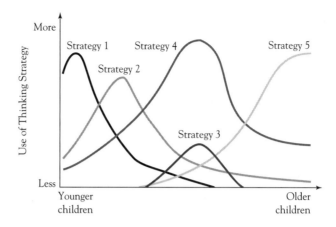

FIGURE **7-10**

Siegler's strategy choice model of development. Change in strategy use is seen as a series of overlapping waves, with different strategies being used more frequently at different ages.

Source: Adapted from Siegler, R. S. (1996). *Emerging minds: The process of change in children's thinking.* New York: Oxford University Press. Thanks to Robert Siegler.

Basically, Siegler sees multiple strategies existing within a child's cognitive reportoire at any one time, with these strategies competing against one another. Early in development, or when a child is first learning a new task, relatively simple strategies will "win" most of the time. With practice and maturation, the child will use other, more effortful but more efficient strategies more frequently. Thus, Siegler believes that development does not occur in a steplike fashion but, rather, as a series of overlapping waves, with the pattern of those waves changing over time. Figure 7-10 presents Siegler's wave approach to cognitive development. Multiple strategies are available to children at every age, but which strategies are used most frequently changes with age.

Perhaps the single most investigated topic using the microgenetic method and following Siegler's adaptive strategy choice model is simple arithmetic. For example, in learning to add, children frequently use a strategy that involves counting out loud both addends, called the *sum strategy* (for example, for 5 + 3 = ?, saying "1, 2, 3, 4, 5 [pause], 6, 7, 8"). A more sophisticated strategy, called the *min strategy,* begins with a child identifying the larger addend (in this case, 5) and counting up from there (for example, saying "5 [pause], 6, 7, 8"). A still more sophisticated strategy, known as *fact retrieval,* is "just knowing" the answer—retrieving it directly from long-term memory without having to count at all (for example, simply saying "8" to the question "How much is 5 + 3?"). When looking at group data, one gets the impression that children progress from using the sum strategy to using the min strategy to using fact retrieval. Yet, closer examination reveals that individual children use a variety of these strategies at any one time, and the frequencies with which these strategies are used vary with age. (More will be said of children's arithmetic strategies in Chapter 11.)

Children's multiple strategy use can be seen in more naturalistic settings as well. For example, in one study, kindergarten children computed moves on a board game (Chutes and Ladders®) by throwing a pair of dice (Bjorklund & Rosenblum, 2002). Children used a variety of strategies to compute their moves. Moreover, these strategies were not random but varied with the numbers on the dice. For example, children used fact retrieval for most doubles (for example, 6 + 6, 5 + 5), the min strategy when the difference between the two addends was large and the smaller number was (usually) a 1 or 2 (for example, 5 + 1, 6 + 2), and the sum strategy for all others (for example, 4 + 2, 5 + 3). Thus, not only do children use multiple and variable strategies on a task, they are highly sensitive to factors within the testing context (here, the particular combination of numbers they were asked to add) when choosing which strategy to use.

Other examples of children's multiple strategy use come from experiments assessing memory development. For example, Kate McGilly and Siegler (1990) gave children in kindergarten, second grade, and fourth grade a serial-recall task (remember a list of digits in exact order). McGilly and Siegler observed the strategies the children used and later questioned the children about their strategy use. They reported that the children used a variety of strategies on these tasks (single word rehearsal, repeated rehearsal), with any given child using a combination of strategies over repeated trials. That is, multiple strategy use was the rule rather than the exception (see also Coyle & Bjorklund, 1997; Schwenck, Bjorklund, & Schneider, 2009).

Siegler believes that age differences in how strategies are selected and used reflect an important way of viewing cognitive development that differs from conventional Piagetian and information-processing models. Perhaps the most important message from Siegler's work is that children use strategies *selectively* and *adaptively* and that, at any point in time and for any given task, children have a variety of strategies available to them. The issue facing cognitive developmental psychologists is not whether children are being strategic. Rather, we are seeking to discover what strategies and combination of strategies children of different ages use and how the simpler strategies used by young children develop into the more sophisticated and effective strategies used by older children and adults.

## The Development of Memory Strategies

Children's strategies have been investigated for a wide range of topics. To provide an example of strategy development for a particular content, in this section I describe the development of **memory strategies** (or **mnemonics**). Developmental researchers have studied a variety of memory strategies, and here I will review briefly the two most investigated: **rehearsal**, in which a child repeats the target information, and **organization**, in which the child combines different items into categories, themes, or other units.

### *Rehearsal*

In a pioneering study by John Flavell and his colleagues (Flavell, Beach, & Chinsky, 1966), children in kindergarten and the second and fifth grades were shown a set of pictures that they were asked to remember. Following the presentation, a 15-second delay allowed the children to prepare for the recall test. An experimenter, who was trained to identify lip movements corresponding to the words the children were trying to remember, watched the children's mouths. Flavell and his associates reported age-related increases in recall with corresponding increases in the amount of rehearsal. Eighty-five percent of the fifth-graders displayed evidence of some spontaneous rehearsal, whereas only 10% of the kindergarten children did so. Furthermore, within a grade level, children who rehearsed more recalled more, on average, than did children who rehearsed less. These findings led the researchers to conclude that rehearsal is a powerful mnemonic that increases with age, with the frequency of rehearsal (the absolute number of times one rehearses) determining memory performance.

Later research by Peter Ornstein, Mary Naus, and Charles Liberty (1975) questioned Flavell's frequency interpretation. These researchers used an *overt rehearsal procedure* with children in the third, sixth, and eighth grades. In this procedure, children are presented with a series of words to recall, with several seconds between each successive word. During this interval, the children are told they must repeat the most recently presented word at least once and, if they wish, that they may practice any other words they like. Thus, rehearsal is made obligatory (they must "rehearse" at least one word once during each interval), and the experimenters can determine exactly what the children are doing. Using this procedure, the researchers found no differences in the frequency of rehearsal across the three grade levels. Despite this equivalence in quantity of rehearsal, age differences in recall persisted—a perplexing finding given the interpretation of the earlier study by Flavell and his colleagues. However, Ornstein and his associates did report differences in the quality, or *style,* of rehearsal.

Typical rehearsal protocols for a third- and an eighth-grade child are shown in Table 7-1. The number of words actually rehearsed is similar for the two children, but the style of rehearsing is very different. The younger child includes only one or, at best, two unique words per rehearsal set. (A rehearsal set refers to the words repeated during the interstimulus interval.) The researchers referred to this method as a **passive rehearsal** style. In contrast, the older child includes several different words per rehearsal set, a style labeled **active rehearsal** (or **cumulative rehearsal**). The child repeats the most recently presented word and then rehearses it with as many other different words as possible. From these and other data, Ornstein and his colleagues asserted that the important developmental changes are in style rather than frequency of rehearsal (see also Guttentag, Ornstein, & Siemens, 1987).

A causal relationship between differences in the frequency and style of rehearsal and age differences in memory performance has been demonstrated in training studies. Preteen-age children trained to use a cumulative rehearsal strategy display elevated

## TABLE **7-1**

Typical rehearsal protocols for an eighth-grade child and a third-grade child. Note the use of cumulative rehearsal by eighth graders and the more passive rehearsal style by third graders.

| Word Presented | Rehearsal Sets | |
|---|---|---|
| | Eighth-grade Child | Third-grade Child |
| l. Yard | Yard, yard, yard | Yard, yard, yard, yard, yard, |
| 2. Cat | Cat, yard, yard, cat | Cat, cat, cat, cat, yard |
| 3. Man | Man, cat, yard, man, yard, cat | Man, man, man, man, man |
| 4. Desk | Desk, man, yard, cat, man, desk, cat, yard | Desk, desk, desk, desk |

Source: Ornstein, P. A., Naus, M. J., & Liberty, C. (1975). Rehearsal and organizational processes in children's memory. *Child Development,* 46, 818–830. Copyright © The Society for Research in Child Development, Inc. Reprinted with permission.

levels of recall (Cox et al., 1989; Ornstein, Naus, & Stone, 1977). Thus, young children can be trained to use a rehearsal strategy, resulting in increases in memory performance (although age differences are rarely eliminated). What differs in development is children's inclination to implement a strategy rather than their ability to use it (that is, a *production deficiency*). This general pattern is not unique to rehearsal but, as you will see, typifies other strategies as well.

## Organization

One reason that active rehearsal benefits memory might be that conceptual relations are noticed among items that are rehearsed together (Ornstein & Naus, 1978). *Organization* in memory refers to the structure discovered or imposed on a set of items that is used to guide subsequent performance. In attempting to remember what groceries one must buy at the store, for example, we benefit by organizing the information by categories (dairy products, meats, vegetables) or meals (food necessary for pot roast, food necessary for Saturday's barbecue).

In a typical study of organization and recall, children are given a randomized list of items that can be divided into categories (several instances of furniture, tools, and occupations, for example). Children are sometimes given the opportunity to sort items into groups before recall (a *sort-recall* task). Will children sort categorically similar items together? And when they recall the items, will they remember different ones from the same category together, even though they were not originally presented together? Recalling items from the same category together has been referred to as *clustering*, and adults who display high levels of clustering in their recall typically remember more than adults who display lower levels of clustering. Developmentally, levels of sorting, clustering, and recall usually increase with age (see Bjorklund, Dukes, & Brown, 2009; Schneider, 2010). In fact, preschool children's clustering is often at chance levels (see Salatas & Flavell, 1976; Schwenck et al., 2009). Older children are more likely to group items by meaning and, as a result, realize higher levels of recall (Best & Ornstein, 1986; Hasselhorn, 1992). Yet, when the instructions are modified, stressing to children that they should make their groups on the basis of meaning, even preschoolers comply and demonstrate enhanced levels of memory performance (Lange & Jackson, 1974; Sodian, Schneider, & Perlmutter, 1986).

Other experiments that more explicitly training children to use an organizational strategy have also yielded positive results. Young children, under certain instructional conditions, use an organizational strategy and display elevated levels of memory performance (Lange & Pierce, 1992; Schwenck et al., 2007). In other words, young children are capable of organizing information for recall, but they generally fail to do so spontaneously. As with rehearsal, training children to use an organizational strategy rarely eliminates age differences, and under most conditions, young children fail to generalize the strategy to new situations or new sets of materials (Cox & Waters, 1986).

## Longitudinal Assessment of Memory Strategy Development

The impression one gets when looking at the memory strategy literature is that children show regular and gradual changes in strategy use (rehearsal or organization) with time. Most data looking at age-related changes in strategy use, however, are cross-sectional in nature, with different children of different ages being tested to assess developmental changes. Although cross-sectional studies have many benefits (their economy in time, effort, and expense being the foremost values), they cannot adequately test developmental hypotheses. Only longitudinal studies can do this, and unfortunately, there have been very few longitudinal studies of basic strategic processes.

An exception is the Munich Longitudinal Study on the Genesis of Individual Competencies (LOGIC) (Schneider & Bullock, 2009; Sodian & Schneider, 1999; Weinert & Schneider, 1992), which followed participants between the ages of 4 and 18 years and evaluated performance on sort-recall tasks as part of their assessments. Beate Sodian and Wolfgang Schneider (1999) observed changes in strategy use over time by individual children and noted that only about 8% of the children showed a gradual improvement in the use of organizational memory strategies (sorting items into categories and clustering), with 81% "jumping" from chance sorting or clustering scores at one test interval to near-perfect scores at the following measurement point. Although cross-sectional data can give the impression of a gradual change in strategic functioning over childhood, longitudinal data indicate that, for most children, the transition from astrategic to strategic, at least for organizational memory strategies, occurs relatively quickly and at different ages for different children.

One shortcoming of the Munich Longitudinal Study is that memory strategies were assessed only every other year. Children may have experienced relatively gradual change over the 2-year period, but because of the lengthy time between assessments, the change appeared more abrupt than it actually was (Ornstein, 1999). This problem was addressed in the Würzburg Longitudinal Memory Study (Schneider et al., 2004; Schneider, Kron-Sperl, & Hünnerkopf, 2009), which followed children between the ages of 6 and 9 years at intervals as short as 6 months. Again, Schneider and his colleagues reported that relatively few children displayed gradual change in memory strategy development as reflected by the cross-sectional data. Figure 7-11 presents the patterns of strategy change in the LOGIC and the Würzburg longitudinal studies (from Schneider, Knopf, & Sodian 2009). A few children in each study were strategic from the beginning, and a few others never developed strategic proficiency. However, most children in both studies showed significant improvement in strategy use over time, with more children in both studies (but especially with older children the LOGIC study) demonstrating "jumps" rather than gradual increases. These findings indicate that, despite the impression of gradual change in strategic functioning obtained from cross-sectional studies, most children actually display a relatively abrupt change from astrategic to strategic memory functioning, with the change happening at different ages for different children.

Even the 2-month interval used in the Würzburg Longitudinal Memory Study, however, may cause a researcher to interpret a relatively gradual change as a true discontinuity. This was addressed in a microgenetic study, in which 8- to 12-year-old children performed a series of sort-recall tasks over 11 consecutive weeks (Schlagmüller & Schneider, 2002). Changes in organizational strategies were assessed weekly. The researchers reported that children made the transition from astrategic to strategic functioning quickly, not gradually, and that once children started to use an organizational strategy, they continued to do so and also showed corresponding improvements in their recall.

## Factors that Influence Children's Strategy Use and Effectiveness

A number of factors contribute to both developmental and individual differences in children's tendencies to use and benefit from strategies. Three important ones that I discussed here are (1) *mental capacity,* (2) *knowledge base,* and (3) *metacognition.*

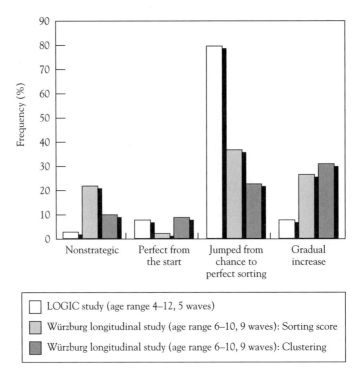

FIGURE **7-11**

Patterns of strategy change in the LOGIC and the Würzburg longitudinal studies. As can be seen, most children showed abrupt jumps from being nonstrategic to being strategic.

Source: Schneider, W., Kron-Sperl, V., & Hünnerkopf, M. (2009). The development of young children's memory strategies: Evidence from the Würzburg Longitudinal Memory Study. *European Journal of Developmental Psychology, 6*, 70–99.

### *Mental Capacity*

By definition, strategies are effortful cognitive operations, and one factor that affects whether children will use strategies and their effectiveness if used is limited mental capacity. That is, strategy use has a cost in mental effort, and young children exert so much of their limited resources executing the strategy that they do not retain sufficient mental capacity to perform other aspects of the task efficiently (Case, 1985; Cowan et al., 2005).

This is seen in research showing a relation between strategy use and working memory (Lehmann & Hasselhorn, 2007; Woody-Dorning & Miller, 2001) as well as in *dual-task experiments* that are based on the simple idea that it is difficult to do two things at once (Guttentag, 1984; Miller et al., 1991). Katherine Kipp Harnishfeger and I demonstrated this possibility in a dual-task memory experiment (Bjorklund & Harnishfeger, 1987). Third- and seventh-grade children were instructed in the use of an organizational memory strategy (remembering all the words from a category together). In addition, the children were required to tap an index finger on the space bar of a computer as fast as they could. Their tapping rates during the memory training were compared with their rates during a baseline period when no memory task was given and during a free-recall memory task for which no training instructions had been provided. Decreases in tapping rate during the memory tasks were used as an indication of how much mental effort the children were expending on the tasks. The more slowly the children tapped (relative to when they were performing no memory task), the greater the mental effort required to perform the memory task was presumed to be. That is, the more mental effort required for the memory task, the more interference (as measured by the decreased tapping rate) there should be on the secondary task (tapping).

Both the third- and seventh-graders showed increased interference relative to the free-recall task as a result of the training (see Table 7-2). Furthermore, both groups later used the strategy that they had been shown during training. This use was indicated by increased clustering scores in recall, with children remembering words from the same category together. Only the seventh-grade children, however, showed a corresponding improvement in the number of words they remembered relative to the free-recall task. The third-graders remembered no more words during training than they did when no memory instructions had been given, despite the fact that they used the strategy and expended greater amounts of mental effort. We interpreted these results as indicating that the third-graders used too much of their limited mental capacity in executing the strategy to have enough left over for other aspects of the memory task, such as retrieving specific words. Strategies are supposed to provide greater efficiency in processing, and had the third-grade children mastered the strategy to a greater degree, their memory performance would probably have improved. Nevertheless, under the conditions of this experiment, their memory performance did not improve. Similar findings and interpretations have been reported for other strategies, including rehearsal (Guttentag, 1984), simpler attentional strategies (Miller et al.,

TABLE **7-2**

Mean recall, clustering, and percentage interference scores for free recall (baseline) and trained recall for third and seventh grade children. Both the third- and seventh-grade children transferred the trained strategy, as reflected by significant increases in clustering, and experienced significant increases in interference. However, only the seventh graders showed an increase in recall as a result of training.

|  | Free Recall | Trained Recall |
| --- | --- | --- |
| **Third Grade** | | |
| Percent interference | 17.31 | 21.29* |
| Clustering (ARC) | .14 | .53* |
| Recall | 4.60 | 5.07 |
| **Seventh Grade** | | |
| Percent interference | 18.07 | 23.53* |
| Clustering (ARC) | .09 | .80* |
| Recall | 5.89 | 7.73* |

*Significant difference between trained-recall and free-recall trial.

Source: Bjorklund, D. F., & Harnishfeger, K K. (1987). Developmental differences in the mental effort requirements for the use of an organizational strategy in free recall. *Journal of Experimental Child Psychology, 44,* 109-125; Experiment 2.

1991), and a more complex elaboration memory strategy (Rohwer & Litrownik, 1983; see also Bjorklund, Dukes, & Brown, 2009).

Strategies are effortful. Young children process information less efficiently than older children do, making them less likely to use a strategy spontaneously and less likely to benefit from the imposition of a strategy. Cognitive processing becomes more efficient with age, allowing children to execute more strategies and to use them with greater effectiveness.

### Knowledge Base

I discussed earlier the role that children's **knowledge base** could have on their memory performance. For example, the research with chess-expert children by Chi (1978) demonstrated that when someone knows a lot about a specific topic, memory span for information *in one's area of expertise,* but not beyond it, is significantly enhanced. Perhaps the relationship between knowledge and processing is most easily seen with respect to strategies. According to Daniel Kee (1994), "most researchers acknowledge that strategic processing is dependent on the availability and accessibility of relevant knowledge" (p. 9; see also Bjorklund, Muir-Broaddus, & Schneider, 1990; Rabinowitz & Kee, 1994). The primary reason hypothesized for this relationship is that having a detailed, or elaborated, knowledge base results in faster processing for domain-specific information, which in turn results in more efficient processing and greater availability of mental resources. The relationship between knowledge and strategy use has been demonstrated for a variety of domains, including mathematics (Ashcraft, 1990), reading (Daneman & Green, 1986), text comprehension (Schneider, Körkel, & Weinert, 1989), problem solving (Chi, Feltovich, & Glaser, 1981), communication (Furman & Walden, 1990), memory (Ornstein, Baker-Ward, & Naus, 1988), and forming inferences (Barnes, Dennis, & Haefele-Kalvaitis, 1996), among others.

The role of knowledge base on children's memory strategies is perhaps most easily illustrated on sort-recall tasks, in which children are given lists of words or pictures from different categories to remember. Children's knowledge of relations among the to-be-remembered items can then be manipulated, so that some items are typical of their categories (for example, *pants, dress, sweater* for clothing) whereas others are equally familiar but atypical of their category (for example, *belt, shoes, necklace* for clothing). Children are more likely to use one or more strategies and to remember more items when recalling the more typical and categorically integrated sets of items than the atypical items (Best, 1993; Schwenck et al., 2007, 2009). In general, as children's world knowledge increases with age, so does their strategic performance.

But *how* does knowing a lot (or a little) about the task materials influence performance? This will vary with the nature of the task, but knowledge should influence task performance in some general ways. One theory (Bjorklund, 1987b) proposed three ways, some of which are directly related to strategies, in which knowledge may enhance children's performance: (1) by increasing the accessibility of specific items (item-specific effects), (2) by the relatively effortless activation of relations among sets of items (nonstrategic organization), and (3) by facilitating the use of deliberate strategies. *Item-specific effects* are most easily observed when children are asked to recall sets of unrelated items (for example, *apple, army, clock, day, dress, flower, hammer, snow*). Recall typically improves with age, but there are no corresponding improvements in measures of organization (Ornstein, Hale, & Morgan, 1977). One interpretation of these findings is that individual items are more richly represented in the long-term memories of older children than in those of younger children, resulting in greater ease of retrieval (Chechile & Richman, 1982; Ghatala, 1984).

Nonstrategic organization occurs when children have highly developed knowledge of relations among sets of to-be-remembered items and the retrieval of one item acts to automatically activate the retrieval of related items without the need of implementing a deliberate (that is, effortful) strategy. For instance, highly associated words (for example, *dog* and *cat, hand* and *glove, mouse* and *cheese*) are processed faster and are more likely to be remembered together by young children than are nonassociated words that are categorically related (for example, *dog* and *lion, cheese* and *milk, hand* and *head*) (Bjorklund & Jacobs, 1985; Schneider, 1986). In other studies, age differences in recall have been eliminated or greatly reduced when children have detailed knowledge about the information they are asked to remember (Bjorklund & Zeman, 1982; Lindberg, 1980). For example, Barbara Zeman and I (Bjorklund & Zeman, 1982) asked children in the first, third, and fifth grades to recall the names of their current classmates. Age differences in class recall were small and were significantly less than age differences found for lists of categorically related words (see Figure 7-12). Furthermore, children's recall of their classmates' names was not random but was highly organized (by seating arrangement, reading groups, sex, and so on). Yet, when queried about their use of strategies, most of the children in all grades

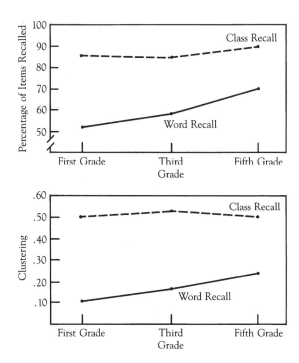

FIGURE **7-12**

The average recall and clustering on class- and word-recall tasks by children in first, third, and fifth grades.

Source: Bjorklund, D. F., & Zeman, B. R. (1982). Children's organization and metamemory awareness in their recall of familiar information. *Child Development, 53*, 799–810. The Society for Research in Child Development, Inc.

were unaware of using any special technique to remember the names. We proposed that the classmates' names represented a well-established knowledge base, with relations among names being activated with relatively little effort. Thus, a strategy was not necessary for successful retrieval. In other words, although the outcome of the children's recall appeared to be strategic (highly organized retrieval), the processes underlying their performance were not. Rather, they represented the relatively automatic activation and retrieval of relations among items in memory.

Another interpretation for our findings is that the elaborated knowledge base the children had for their classmates' names allowed them to use memory strategies efficiently. In fact, we proposed this possibility for the oldest children, who might have identified categorical relations in their recall while retrieving names on the basis of the relatively automatic activation of long-term memory relations and then continued to use this fortuitously discovered strategy for the remainder of their recall ("Hey, all those kids sit in the same row. I think I'll remember the rest of the kids by where they sit"). Peter Ornstein and his colleagues have championed this position—namely, that an elaborated knowledge base for sets of items allows the effective use of mnemonics (Folds et al., 1990; Ornstein et al., 1988). Ornstein and his colleagues propose that the use of memory strategies is facilitated by the automatic execution of certain parts of a task, even in very young children. Later in development, when children have a more sophisticated knowledge base and more experience, entire problem-solving routines can become automated.

Although knowledge typically is positively correlated with memory performance (that is, the more one knows about a topic, the better one remembers), there is at least one interesting exception. In what is known as the Reese/Roediger-McDermott (DRM) paradigm (named after the researchers who developed it), participants are given a list of words all related to a single concept. For example, the words on the list might include *butter, food, eat, sandwich, jam, milk, flour, jelly, dough, crust, slice, wine, loaf,* and *toast.* You've probably figured out that what's missing here is the word *bread,* associated with each of the words on the list. When adults are given such a list and later asked to recall the items, they frequently remember *bread* or, when given a recognition list, erroneously select *bread* as being on the list (see Brainerd, Reyna, & Ceci, 2008). What's interesting is that children are generally *less* apt to make such mistakes, thus making fewer false responses than adults (see Brainerd et al., 2008; Brainerd, Reyna, & Zember, 2011; Dewhurst, Pursglove, & Lewis, 2007; Howe, Courage, & Rooksby, 2009).

What can account for this developmental reversal in accurate memory performance? One explanation involves the ease with which children can identify and activate semantic relations among category members. The better-elaborated knowledge base of older children and adults causes them to spontaneously activate the word *bread* when they hear or read *butter, sandwich,* and *jam.* Younger children, because of their less-elaborated knowledge base, are less apt to automatically activate such relations (Wimmer & Howe, 2010) or to identify category relations among items (Bjorklund, 1980) and, thus, are less likely to falsely remember *bread* when presented with a long list of its associates. So, although increasing knowledge base usually is positively associated with their strategic and nonstrategic memory performance, it can sometimes be a double-edge sword, resulting in increased false memories.

The relationship between knowledge, strategies, and task performance is a complicated one and centrally important to cognitive development. What is important to remember is that what and how much one knows influences both how and how well one thinks. With age, children acquire more knowledge and, simply as a result of these quantitative increases, process information differently. Because knowledge affects processing, children (and adults) think differently about topics on which they have detailed knowledge versus those on which they have less knowledge.

### Metacognition

Earlier, I defined **metacognition** as the knowledge of one's cognitive abilities. Every type of cognition has a corresponding type of metacognition—that is, metamemory, meta-attention, meta-comprehension, and so on. Someone with high metacognitive awareness should be aware of the cognitive operation he or she is engaged in and perhaps how successful his or her attempts at solving a particular problem are. Strategies as I defined them earlier in the chapter almost require a degree of metacognitive awareness. If strategies are available to consciousness, it implies that children "know" (that is, are self-aware) of using them. At one level, this is true, but much room for variability remains. Children differ greatly in the degree to which they know what strategies they have available in their cognitive arsenal, their relative effectiveness, when they are needed and when they are not, and in monitoring task performance. These various factors can influence strategy use and effectiveness and, not surprisingly, they each develop.

Children with higher levels of metacognition usually (but not always) display higher levels of cognition, and young children are generally more out of touch with their cognitive abilities than older children are. This is especially true when it comes to using strategies, as has been found for a host of cognitive domains, including scientific reasoning (Kuhn, Amsel, & O'Loughlin, 1988), arithmetic (Carr & Jessup, 1995), attention (Miller & Weiss, 1982), and memory (DeMarie et al., 2004), among others.

Metacognition can be divided into two types: *declarative* and *procedural* (Schneider & Lockl, 2002). **Declarative metacognition** refers to the explicit, conscious, and factual knowledge a person has about the characteristics of the task he or she is performing, one's own weak and strong points with respect to performing the task, and the possible strategies that could be used on the task. For example, for simple addition problems, are children aware of their own abilities to add and subtract numbers? Do they realize that computing sums may be easier if they use some external aids, such as their fingers or pips on a pair of dice, rather than doing the computation in their heads? Do they know that they can derive an answer to the problem by counting all the numbers (for example, for the problem $3 + 2 = ?$, saying, "1, 2, 3, ... 4, 5"), by counting from the larger number (for example, saying "3 ... 4, 5"), or in some cases, "just knowing" the answer ("5!")? In contrast to declarative metacognition is **procedural metacognition**, which refers to the knowledge about when strategies are necessary ("Do I need to do something special to remember this telephone number?") as well as to monitoring how well one is performing on a task (see Schneider & Pressley, 1997). In the following subsections, I describe research into two types of metacognition—meta-attention and meta-memory—and their relation to strategy use and development.

**Meta-attention.**   **Meta-attention** refers to children's knowledge of their attentional abilities. As noted earlier in this chapter, young children often attend as much (or more) to task-irrelevant stimuli as to task relevant ones. Might such performance be attributed (or at least related) to deficits in meta-attention? Well, yes and no. Even though

4-year-olds generally cannot overcome distractions when performing selective-attention tasks, they are apparently aware that distractions are a problem, for they realize that two stories will be harder to understand if the storytellers speak simultaneously rather than taking turns (Pillow, 1988). In contrast, 3-year-olds would just as soon listen to stories told simultaneously as to have the storytellers take turns. In other research, Patricia Miller and Michael Weiss (1982) asked 5-, 7-, and 9-year-olds to answer a series of questions about factors known to affect performance on an incidental-learning task, in which they must attend to relevant stimuli and ignore irrelevant stimuli. Although knowledge about attentional processes generally increased with age, even the 5-year-olds realized that one should at least *look first* at task-relevant stimuli and then *label* these objects as an aid to remembering them. The 7- and 10-year-olds further understood that one must *attend selectively* to task-relevant stimuli and *ignore* irrelevant information to do well on these problems.

At other times, however, young children seem unaware that paying attention is something special. In one study, John Flavell and his colleagues (Flavell, Green, & Flavell, 1995) asked 4-, 6-, and 8-year-old children a series of questions about attention. For example, if a woman were examining a set of decorative pins so that she can select one as a gift, what would be on her mind? Would she be focusing just on the pins, or might she have other things on her mind as well? Whereas almost all 8-year-olds and most 6-year-olds were aware that the woman would be thinking primarily about the pins and not likely thinking about other things, few 4-year-olds had this insight. It's as if they did not realize what is involved in selective attention. By 8 years of age, however, children's understanding of attentional focus was about as good as that of adults.

**Metamemory.** As another example, consider **metamemory** (see Schneider, 2009; Waters & Kunnman, 2009, for reviews). In a pioneering study of children's metamemory abilities, Mary Anne Kreutzer, Catherine Leonard, and John Flavell (1975) asked children in kindergarten and the first, third, and fifth grades a series of questions about memory. For example, the children were asked if they ever forget things, if it would be easier to remember a phone number immediately after being told the number or after getting a drink of water, and if learning pairs of opposites (for example, boy/girl) would be easier or harder than learning pairs of unrelated words (for example, Mary/walk)—all of which are forms of declarative metacognition. Some kindergarten children asserted that they never forget things, and fewer than 50% believed that phoning the friend immediately would yield more accurate recall. About half of the kindergarten and first-grade children believed that the arbitrary pairs would be just as easy (or even easier) to learn as the opposites.

Let me relate an anecdote about how young children can be out of touch with their memory performance. I was conducting a memory test with a 5-year-old boy. I showed him 16 pictures of familiar objects from four categories (fruit, tools, body parts, and animals), which he had 2 minutes to study. After the 2 minutes, I asked him a few questions as a simple distraction task ("How old are you? When's your birthday?"), and then I asked him to remember as many of those pictures as he could, out loud, in any order that he wanted. The child did not hesitate and quickly said, "Cow, hammer, screwdriver, apple," then just as quickly stopped and sat quietly, waiting for me to say something. After sitting silently for about 10 seconds, I asked, "Can you remember any more of the pictures?" He looked incredulously at me and said, "You mean there were *more* pictures?" This child had told me all he could remember of the list, and as far as he was concerned, his recall was perfect. His ability to monitor his performance (procedural metamemory) would (one hopes) improve considerably in the years to come.

More specifically with respect to strategies, are children aware that strategies are necessary to perform a task well and of the relation between using strategies and task performance (procedural metacognition)? Not surprisingly, young children are often unaware of simple strategies they can use to solve problems, or at least they are not conscious that such techniques can be useful when they are given a specific task. For example, children who are aware of the connection between strategies such as rehearsal and organization and memory performance often remember more information than do children who do not posses such awareness (Justice et al., 1997). Furthermore, young children who have been taught a strategy are often unaware that using it facilitated their memory performance. This is illustrated in an experiment by Barbara Ringel and Carla Springer (1980). They trained first-, third-, and fifth-grade children to use an organizational memory strategy. The children were given pictures and instructed to sort them into groups by meaning and to use the groupings to help them remember the pictures. Each group of children showed improved memory performance after training (relative to an earlier baseline phase). The children were then given a third memory task to assess transfer of training. After completing the training but before beginning the transfer list, some of the children were provided with explicit feedback concerning their improved performance on the task, whereas others were not. The fifth-grade children transferred the organizational strategy to the new task under all conditions, whereas Ringel and Springer found no evidence of significant transfer for any group of first-graders. For the third-grade children, however, feedback made a difference. Those third-graders who had received feedback concerning their memory performance transferred the organizational strategy to a new set of pictures. Third-graders receiving no feedback did not; for the most part, they reverted to a nonstrategic style characteristic of their pretraining behavior. In other words, knowing how well they were doing influenced the third-graders' generalization of a strategy. The older children, apparently being better able to assess their own progress, did not require such explicit feedback to transfer the strategy, and the younger children either were unable to transfer the strategy or, at best, needed more intensive instructions before generalization would take place. Other researchers have emphasized the role of metamemory in the effectiveness of strategy use and transfer, demonstrating that training in memory monitoring or other aspects of metamemory is responsible for the effectiveness and maintenance of strategy training (Ghatala et al., 1986; Melot, 1998).

I will have more to say about metacognition with respect to specific types of cognition in other chapters in the book. For now, it's important to keep in mind that possessing and using strategies are not enough to ensure competent performance. Being aware of when to use strategies, of which ones to use, and of how effective the strategies you're using really are will all influence task performance.

### *Transactions among Capacity, Knowledge, and Metacognition*

Metacognition is obviously an important component in children's cognitive development. However, research findings suggest that metacognitive competence is as much a consequence as it is a cause of competent cognitive behavior, with the two being intimately entwined, and that this relationship varies as a function of age and task

FIGURE **7-13**

A model of children's memory development. Mental capacity and metamemory interact over age to produce patterns of strategic memory performance.

Source: DeMarie, D., Miller, P. H., Ferron, J., & Cunningham, W. R. (2004). Path analysis tests of theoretical models of children's memory performance. *Journal of Cognition and Development, 5,* 461–492.

variables (Schneider & Bjorklund, 1998). For example, children who are experts in a domain will perform better in that domain than will less-expert children (Schneider, Bjorklund, & Maier-Brücker, 1996). However, expert children's cognitive performance will be greatest when they also have substantial metacognitive knowledge (Schneider, Schlagmüller, & Visé, 1998).

Darlene DeMarie and her colleagues have investigated how mental capacity, knowledge base, and metamemory transact to produce changes in children's memory performance (DeMarie & Ferron, 2003; DeMarie et al., 2004). Children 5 to 11 years of age were administered a series of strategic memory tasks, measures of memory capacity (for example, working memory), and metamemory assessments. DeMarie et al. (2004) then performed a series of analyses, evaluating different theoretical models of memory development. The model that best fit the developmental data is shown in Figure 7-13. DeMarie and colleagues concluded that capacity and metamemory interact over age to produce patterns of strategic memory performance, and that (1) both strategy production (that is, whether children produce a strategy or not) and strategy efficiency (that is, how much a strategy helps in enhancing recall) are important factors in memory development; (2) multiple strategy use must be considered; and (3) metamemory plays a significant role in predicting multiple strategy use and strategy effectiveness. They further speculated that different factors have greater impact at different times in development. For example, individual differences in capacity may be more important in influencing memory strategies for young children (Woody-Dorning & Miller, 1988), whereas individual differences in metamemory may be more important for older children.

## Culture and Strategies

Cultures clearly differ in the extent to which they support and encourage particular strategic activities (Kurtz, 1990; Mistry, 1997). For example, the memory strategies of rehearsal and organization are especially helpful to children from Western industrialized societies, where school activities involve a great deal of rote memorization and list learning. Yet, these same strategies might not be so useful to unschooled children from nonindustrialized societies, where the most important memory tasks might involve recalling the location of objects (water, game animals) in a natural setting or remembering instructions passed along in the context of proverbs or stories.

For example, in list-learning experiments, Western children rely heavily on strategies acquired at school and clearly outperform their unschooled peers from nonindustrialized societies (Cole & Scribner, 1977; Rogoff & Waddell, 1982). The picture is much different, however, when the memory task is embedded in a meaningful and structured context. When tests are structured so that people must recall organized prose (as in a story) or items from spatially organized arrays (as in familiar scenes), few cultural differences in memory performance are found (see Rogoff, 1990).

There are also differences in strategy use between children in different schooled cultures. For example, in studies comparing German and American second- and third-grade children, German children were found to use more memory strategies than American children (Carr et al., 1989; Kurtz et al., 1990). The reason for these cultural differences can be traced to the behaviors and attitudes of children's parents and teachers. German parents buy their children more games that require strategic thinking, give them more direct strategy training, and check their homework more than American parents do. Similarly, German teachers provide more direct strategy instruction than American teachers (Carr et al., 1989; Kurtz et al., 1990).

## Strategies in the Classroom

I'd like to think that all (or nearly all) aspects of cognitive development have some practical utility, but this seems to be especially the case for strategies. Many aspects of cognition develop because of children's normal, day-to-day interaction with their environment. Change happens when no one (including the child) is watching. Many strategies are different. Although children often discover strategies on their own in the process of performing a task (Siegler & Jenkins, 1989), many important cognitive strategies are explicitly taught in school (Moely et al., 1992; Pressley & Woloshyn, 1995), or sometimes by parents (Güler et al., 2010; Larkina et al., 2008). As such, knowledge of how strategies develop and factors that influence their use can be of great practical value for the educator or parent of a school-age child.

But how much explicit strategy instruction do children get in school? This, of course, will vary from school to school and from teacher to teacher, but it may surprise you to learn that strategy instruction is rarely on the top of most teachers' "to do" list. In a classroom observational study, Barbara Moely and her colleagues (1992) reported that teachers in kindergarten through sixth grade taught a wide range of strategies that varied with the age of the child and the nature of the task. These included rote learning for simple and repetitive tasks, imagery, and self-checking, among others. Despite the diversity of strategies taught, Moely and colleagues reported that the absolute frequency of strategy instruction was low. For example, specific strategy instruction was observed on an average of fewer than 3% of the teacher observations, with teachers providing some general instruction about how to deal with a task strategically in 9.5% of the observations. In fact, 10% of the teachers observed in this study provided no strategy instruction at all. Thus, strategy instruction in school varies with the teacher, the task, and the age of the children, with teachers generally providing children with instruction that is age-appropriate (that is, neither too simple nor too complicated for them to understand).

In other research, first-grade teachers who used a "mnemonic orientation" in their classroom and related it to children's strategic memory behavior (for example, "How did you study those words?"; "If you make a picture in your mind, it will help you to remember") had children who displayed higher levels of strategic memory performance compared to children with less "mnemonically oriented" teachers (Coffman et al., 2008). This benefit extended to the second grade when children were taught by other teachers (Ornstein, Grammar, & Coffman, 2009; see Ornstein et al., 2010).

Strategy instruction is more likely to occur for some subjects than for others and, especially, for children just beginning to tackle a new challenge. For example, teachers (and parents) often give children specific instruction in simple arithmetic strategies— teaching them, for instance, how to use the min strategy ("Start with the bigger number, 6, and then count from there, 7, 8, 9")—and provide quite explicit directions about how to decode letters and printed words into spoken sounds and language (Moely, Santulli, & Obach, 1995; Pressley & Woloshyn, 1995). In a study of preschoolers and their teachers, the amount of "math talk" that teachers did (much of which could be considered pointing out simple strategies) was related to children's growth of mathematical knowledge over the school year (Klibanoff et al., 2006). Strategy instruction occurs less frequently for higher-level cognitive tasks, such as reading comprehension, yet researchers have investigated such strategies with known positive effects of instruction on children's performance (Gaultney, 1995; Mastropieri & Scruggs, 1991).

The goal of strategy instruction is to make children into effective learners. Michael Pressley and his colleagues (Pressley, Borkowski, & Schneider, 1989; Schneider & Pressley, 1997) proposed three stages in which knowledge is acquired via instruction:

1. Children are taught by teachers or parents to use a strategy, and with practice, they come to learn the attributes and advantages of the strategy (*specific strategy knowledge*).
2. Teachers demonstrate similarities and differences of various strategies within a domain (for example, rehearsal versus organization for memory), allowing children to make comparisons among strategies (*relational knowledge*).
3. Children come to recognize the general usefulness of being strategic, leading to *general strategy knowledge*.

Although methods of instruction will vary depending on the age of the child and the specific strategy that is being taught, Michael Pressley and Vera Woloshyn (1995) provide a general model for how to teach strategies (see Table 7-3). As a result, children learn to attribute their academic successes to the effort they spend using a strategy, and they also gain higher-order skills, such as selecting and monitoring strategies appropriate for the task (*metacognitive acquisition procedures*).

## LEARNING TO SOLVE PROBLEMS

Life is full of problems that we seek to solve. Problems and their attempted solutions start early. Infants will strive to retrieve a fallen toy, overcoming obstacles along the way. The problems we face (and their solutions) become more complicated as we get older, but they all have certain things in common. We say that someone is solving a problem when there is a specific goal in mind that cannot be attained immediately because of the presence of one or more obstacles. We solve problems by learning rules or by using (and sometimes discovering) one or more strategies. Sometimes a problem takes several attempts before it is solved, and we must be able to evaluate our progress toward the goal, if for no other reason than to know when the problem has been

TABLE **7-3**
General Model of How to Teach Strategies.

Teach a few strategies at a time, intensively and extensively, as part of the ongoing curriculum; in the beginning, teach only one at a time, until students are familiar with the "idea" of strategy use.

Model and explain each new strategy.

Model again and re-explain strategies in ways that are sensitive to aspects of strategy use that are not well understood. (The students are constructing their understanding of the strategy, refining the understanding a little bit at a time.)

Explain to students where and when to use strategies, although students will also discover some such metacognitive information as they use strategies.

Provide plenty of practice, using strategies for as many appropriate tasks as possible. Such practice increases proficient execution of the strategy, knowledge of how to adapt it, and knowledge of when to use it.

Encourage students to monitor how they are doing when they are using strategies.

Encourage continued use of and generalization of strategies, for example, by reminding students throughout the school day about when they could apply strategies they are learning about.

Increase students' motivation to use strategies by heightening student awareness that they are acquiring valuable skills that are at the heart of competent functioning with learning tasks.

Emphasize reflective processing rather than speedy processing; do all possible to eliminate high anxiety in students; encourage students to shield themselves from distraction so they can attend to the academic task.

Source: Pressley, M., & Woloshyn, V. (1995). *Cognitive strategy instruction that really improves children's academic performance* (2nd edition). Cambridge, MA: Brookline Books. Reprinted with permission.

solved. Thus, the four basic requirements of problem solving are (1) goals, (2) obstacles, (3) strategies for overcoming the obstacles, and (4) an evaluation of the results (DeLoache, Miller, & Pierroutsakos, 1998).

Much of what we have covered in this book to this point can be considered as being in the realm of problem solving. The classic Piagetian tasks of retrieving covered objects and conservation, for example, are problem-solving tasks. Arithmetic problems, which will be discussed in Chapter 11, are clearly problem-solving tasks. In this section, I describe children's general problem-solving abilities beginning in infancy, and I conclude by looking at a special type of problem solving: reasoning.

## The Development of Problem Solving

When do children first solve problems? Based on the definition of what constitutes **problem solving** (having a goal, obstacles to that goal, strategies, and evaluation of results), infants cannot be said to solve problems until they demonstrate some sense of **goal-directed behavior**. Recall from our discussion of Piaget's theory of sensorimotor development (see Chapter 5), goal-directed behavior requires that "need precedes action." That is, infants do not discover an interesting outcome fortuitously (for example, hitting a mobile with their arm) but, rather, first seek to achieve a specific goal (move a mobile) and then act accordingly. This is also the beginning of cause and effect (means-end) thinking. Infants must realize that they must do something quite specific (make physical contact with the mobile) before the mobile will move.

Piaget proposed that infants are not able to accomplish this until about 8 months of age. At this time, they can use one behavior *strategically* in the service of another (for example, push aside a cloth to retrieve a toy hidden underneath). Thus, following from Piaget's classic work, we can say that problem solving begins at least during the latter part of the first year of life.

Peter Willatts (1990) performed some interesting experiments demonstrating means-end problem solving in infants. In one study, 6-, 7-, and 8-month-old infants were placed on a table. In front of the infants was a long cloth with a toy placed on it, out of the infants' reach. Here's a goal (get the toy) and an obstacle (the toy is out of reach). The solution is to strategically use one behavior (pull the cloth toward them) to achieve the goal (get the toy). How did the infants do? The 6-month-olds often retrieved the toy, but their behavior was not always intentional. Instead of pulling the cloth toward them and fixing their attention on the toy, these youngest infants often simply played with the cloth, looked away from the toy, and after a while, the toy finally was in their reach. By 8 months of age, infants were much less apt to play with the cloth. They grabbed the cloth and immediately began pulling it to bring the toy closer to them. They kept their fixation on the toy and quickly and efficiently brought the toy within their grasp, often holding out a hand in anticipation of the toy's arrival. The 7-month-olds fell between the 6- and 8-month-olds.

In other research, Zhe Chen, Rebecca Sanchez, and Tammy Campbell (1997) assessed means-end problem solving in 1-year-old infants. The basic task involved placing a desirable toy out of reach of the infant, with a barrier between the baby and the toy. Two strings, one attached to the toy and one not, were also out of the infant's reach, but each string was on a cloth that *was* within reach. To get the toy, the infants had to pull the cloth toward them and then pull the string attached to the toy. There were three similar tasks, although the toy, the barrier, and the color of the cloth varied among the three tasks. These are illustrated in Figure 7-14. If infants did not solve

## FIGURE **7-14**

The configuration of the three problems 1-year-old infants solved.

Source: Chen, Z., Sanchez, R. P., & Campbell, T. (1997). From beyond to within their grasp: The rudiments of an-alogical problem solving in 10- and 13-month-olds. *Developmental Psychology, 33,* 790–801. Copyright © 1997 by the American Psychological Association. Reprinted with permission.

the problem after 100 seconds, their parents modeled the correct solution for them. The primary research question concerned whether, after solving an initial problem with or without parental modeling, the infants would see the similarity with the later problems and be more apt to solve them.

Few children solved the first problem spontaneously (most required help from a parent). However, the percentage of infants solving the problems increased from 29% for the first problem to 43% for the second and to 67% for the third. Infants' problem solving was also rated for "efficiency," with higher scores reflecting a greater goal-directed approach, as opposed to a trial-and-error approach to the problem. As can be seen in Figure 7-15, efficiency increased steadily over the three problems.

Although means-end problem solving might be within the capacity of infants as young as 7 and 8 months of age, it does not mean that children will display such behavior on more complicated tasks. This is illustrated in an interesting study by Merry Bullock and Paul Lütkenhaus (1988), who asked children between the ages of 15 and 35 months to perform one of several tasks—for example, stacking blocks to copy a house built by an adult. The youngest children (average age, 17 months) showed little specific goal-directed behavior. They did play with the blocks and built "something," but there was little evidence that they kept the goal of building a house in mind during their activities. In contrast, most 2-year-olds were able to keep the goal in mind and build the house. These children also did a good job at monitoring their performance (evaluating the results of their behavior). Almost all these children made at least one correction, and 85% of the 2-year-olds stacked all the blocks correctly on at least one trial. The reactions of the children to their problem-solving attempts also revealed their evaluations of their behavior toward achieving their goal. Only about a third (36%) of the 17-month-olds showed some clear sign of emotion with their performance (smiling or frowning), whereas 90% of the older children (32-month-olds) did so.

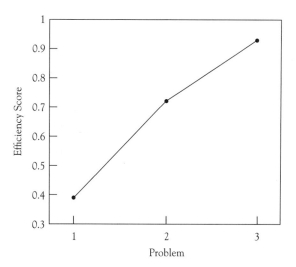

FIGURE **7-15**

Infants' problem-solving efficiency scores.

Source: Chen, Z., Sanchez, R. P., & Campbell, T. (1997). From beyond to within their grasp: The rudiments of analogical problem solving in 10- and 13-month-olds. *Developmental Psychology, 33,* 790–801. Copyright © 1997 by the American Psychological Association. Adapted with permission.

The tasks children need to solve get more complicated as they grow older, so their problem-solving abilities must also improve. One factor that has been found to have a significant impact on problem solving is knowledge. The more one knows about a particular topic or the more familiar one is with the context, the more sophisticated problem solving will be. Let me provide an example for learning the rules behind a computer game. Stephen Ceci (1996) proposed that context influences how people approach and solve problems. Ceci defined context as the way in which a problem is represented in long-term memory; that is, it consists of what a person knows about a task, including the reason for performing it. Ceci reported an experiment in which 10-year-old children were asked to predict where on a computer screen an object would land by using a joystick to mark on the screen the next position of the object. The object varied in size (big or small), color (dark or light), and shape (square, circle, or triangle), producing 12 combinations of features (two sizes × two colors × three shapes). A simple algorithm was written so that (1) squares would move upward, circles downward, and triangles would stay on the horizontal; (2) dark figures would move to the right and light figures to the left; and (3) large objects would move diagonally from lower left to upper right, whereas small objects would move in the opposite direction. For example, a large, light square would move upward, leftward, and from the lower left to the upper right.

Figuring out how the object would move (that is, where it would be on the next trial) seems like it would be a difficult task for children (as well as for adults), and it was. The children were given 15 sessions with the task, with 50 trials per session. Some children were simply asked to predict where the object would move on each trial. Other children were told that this was a video game, the purpose of which was to capture flying animals; for these children, the three shapes were changed to a butterfly, a bee, and a bird. These children were told to use the joystick to place the "butterfly net" so that they could "capture the prey" on each trial. The rule by which the target moved on each trial was identical in both conditions.

The results of this study are graphed in Figure 7-16. As can be seen, the two groups started out similarly, performing poorly over the first five sessions. However, the children in the video-game context then took off, performing at levels approaching 90% by the ninth session. In comparison, the children given the laboratory context continued to perform poorly, never really improving on the task over the 15 sessions. Discovering the algorithm depended on the mental context in which the problem was presented. The rules were the same for all children, but the context, a form of knowledge, influenced greatly children's problem-solving performance.

## Reasoning

**Reasoning** is a special type of problem solving. Reasoning usually requires that one make an inference—that is, to reason, one must go beyond the information given. It is not enough to figure out the rules of some game. That's problem solving, but not necessarily reasoning. In reasoning, one must take the evidence presented and arrive at a new conclusion based on that evidence. The result is often new knowledge (DeLoache, Miller, & Pierroutsakos, 1998).

We use some forms of reasoning in our everyday lives, and we are so accustomed to thinking this way that we are often unaware of it. Other types of reasoning are more formalized. Most of us do not engage in these forms regularly, so when we do, we are certainly conscious of it. In the following sections, I discuss the development of two types of reasoning: analogical reasoning and scientific reasoning.

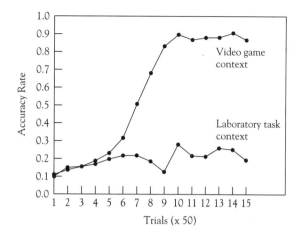

FIGURE **7-16**

Children's mean proportion of accurate predictions of the position of a moving object in a video game versus laboratory context.

Source: From Stephen J. Ceci, *On intelligence ... more or less: A bioecological treatise on intellectual development,* © 1990, p. 39. Reprinted by permission of Prentice Hall, Englewood Cliffs, New Jersey.

### Analogical Reasoning

**Analogical reasoning** involves using something you already know to help you understand something you don't know yet. Analogical reasoning involves **relational mapping**—the application of what one knows about one set of elements (the relation of A to B) to relations about different elements (the relation of C to D). Classic analogical reasoning problems are stated A:B :: C:?. For example, *dog* is to *puppy* as *cat* is to ?. The answer here, of course, is *kitten*. By knowing the relation between the first two elements in the problem (a *puppy* is a baby *dog*), one can use that knowledge to complete the analogy for a new item (*cat*). Analogies are thus based on *similarity relations.* One must understand the similarity between dogs and cats and puppies and kittens if one is to solve the above analogy.

How basic is analogical reasoning to cognitive development? How well adults are able to solve analogies is related to general intelligence as measured by IQ tests (Sternberg, 1985), and one advantage gifted children have over nongifted children is in their ability to solve analogies (Muir-Broaddus, 1995). This suggests that it is a complex skill that is influenced by a variety of other cognitive abilities and does not peak early in life. According to Piagetian theory (Inhelder & Piaget, 1958), analogical reasoning is a sophisticated ability that is not seen until adolescence, although others have proposed that analogical thinking serves as the basis for other reasoning and problem-solving tasks (Halford, 1993) and might be present at birth (Goswami, 1996).

The first study to demonstrate analogical reasoning in young children using a traditional A:B :: C:? task was performed by Keith Holyoak, Ellen Junn, and Dorrit Billman (1984). In their study, preschool and kindergarten children had to move some gumballs in one bowl on a table to another, out-of-reach bowl, without leaving their chair. The children had various objects available to them that they could use to solve the problem, including scissors, an aluminum cane, tape, string, and a sheet of paper. Before solving the problem, children heard a story about a genie who had a similar problem. The genie's problem was to move some jewels from one bottle within his reach to another bottle, out of his reach. One way in which he solved this problem was to roll his magic carpet into a tube and pass the jewels down the tube into the second bottle. Another solution that other children heard was to use his magic staff to pull the second bottle closer to him. After hearing the stories, children were told to think of as many ways as they could to solve *their* problem—to get the gumballs from one bowl to another. About half of the preschool and kindergarten children solved the "magic staff" problem, and the remainder did so after a hint. That is, these 4.5- to 6-year-old children were able to reason by analogy. However, they were less successful with the "magic carpet" analogy, suggesting that young children's performance on analogical-reasoning tasks is highly dependent on the similarity between objects. Holyoak and his colleagues argued that the "magic staff" and the aluminum cane were more perceptually similar to one another than were the "magic carpet" and the sheet of paper, making the former analogy easier to use for these young children than the latter. But the basic finding that preschool children could use the similarity in one story to solve an analogous problem suggests that such reasoning is well within the capability of these children, counter to the traditional Piagetian position.

Not all similarity is perceptual, however. Sometimes the similarity between objects is *relational*. This is illustrated in a study by Usha Goswami and Ann Brown (1990), who showed 4-, 5-, and 9-year-old children sets of pictures of the A:B :: C:? type. Children were given four alternatives and had to choose which of the four best completed the analogy. An example of a problem used in this study is shown in Figure 7-17. In this problem, children must discover the relation between bird and nest (a bird lives in a nest) and find the proper match for dog (here, dog house). Chance performance on this task was 25%, and children of all ages performed greater than expected by chance (59%, 66%, and 94% correct for the 4-, 5-, and 9-year-olds, respectively). Note that children were not

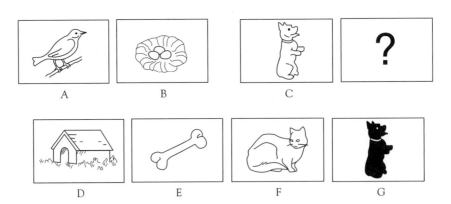

## FIGURE **7-17**

Example of problems used by Goswami and Brown (1990). Children must select from the set of pictures in bottom row (pictures D through G) the one that best completes the visual analogy on the top row. (The correct answer is D.)

Source: Goswami, U., & Brown, A. L. (1990). Higher-order structure and relational reasoning: Contrasting analogical and thematic relations. *Cognition, 36,* 207–226. Reprinted with permission of Elsevier Science.

solving the problem based on *perceptual similarity*. The bird and dog look nothing alike, nor do the nest and the dog house. To solve this problem, they must do so on the basis of *relational similarity*—the relation between the A and B terms (bird and nest) is used to find the best match for the C term (dog).

Children might not have been using analogical reasoning to solve this problem, however. Maybe they were simply selecting the item the "went best with" the dog. This apparently was not the case. Children in a control group were given exactly this directive—pick the one that "goes best" with the C term (in this case, dog). When asked to do this, children were no more likely to select the analogical choice (dog house) as they were a highly associated choice (bone). Thus, children's performance on the analogical-reasoning task cannot be attributed to responding on the basis of strictly associative or thematic relations; rather, it reflects the use of true analogical reasoning.

That at least some young children were solving these problems using true analogical reasoning was reflected by the type of errors they made. For example, Goswami (1996) reported a 4-year-old child, Lucas, who, after seeing the *bird*:*nest* :: *dog*:? problem, figured out what the answer should be without seeing the alternatives. However, what he figured was wrong. "Lucas first told us that the correct solution was *puppy*. He argued, quite logically, 'Bird lays eggs in her nest … dog—dogs lay babies, and the babies are—umm—and the name of the babies is puppy'" (p. 102). Lucas quickly changed his mind when he saw that a puppy was not among the alternatives, re-thought the problem, and identified the "lives in" relation. However, his first idea was also relational. He had simply identified a type of relation (*type of offspring*) different than that identified by the experimenters. Successful analogical reasoning requires identifying the "right" relation. However, there can be many different relations existing between sets of items, and outside of the laboratory or classroom, there might not be clear-cut "right" and "wrong" answers.

### Factors Affecting Children's Analogical Reasoning

Many factors influence children's success on any given task. For example, Graeme Halford (1993) proposed that analogical reasoning develops in a stagelike fashion reminiscent of Piaget, based on the availability of mental resources, and others have assumed that age-related differences in various aspects of executive function greatly influence children's ability to solve analogical reasoning problems (Richland Morrison, & Holyoke, 2006; Thibaut, French, & Vezneva, 2010). A child's ability to symbolically represent concepts and relations will also affect whether and how a child will use analogical reasoning (see DeLoache, Miller, & Pierroutsakos, 1998).

**Analogical reasoning and relational shift.** Related to how children represent a problem are the types of relations they identify and base their reasoning on. For example, although the research of Goswami and Brown (1990) indicates that young children *can* use analogies based on relational similarity, this does not mean that they do so easily, especially when they can form analogies based on perceptual similarity. Dedre Gentner (1989) argued that a **relational shift** occurs in the development of analogical reasoning, in which young children are more likely to focus on perceptual similarity whereas older children and adults focus more on relational similarity in solving problems. For example, infants and young children are more influenced by the surface similarity of objects, such as an object's shape. Older children, on the other hand, are more tuned to the underlying relation between sets of objects. For example, the better performance of the preschool children for the "magic staff" than the "magic carpet" analogy in the study by the Holyoak and his colleagues (1984) was attributed to the greater perceptual similarity between the magic staff and the aluminum cane available to solve the "gumball" problem, than between the magic carpet and the sheet of paper (for other examples, see Daehler & Chen, 1993; Pierce & Gholson, 1994). When there is a conflict between perceptual similarity and relational similarity, young children's ability to use relational similarity is hindered (see Goswami, 1996).

**Knowledge.** One factor that affects whether children will use relational similarity to solve an analogical-reasoning problem is knowledge, or familiarity. How familiar are children with the underlying relations used to make the analogy? Remember, the function of analogical reasoning is to use something you know to help you understand something you don't know. From this perspective, analogical reasoning can only make sense if a child is familiar with the base relation. You might get a better understanding of the human nervous system, for example, if you see it as analogous to electrical circuits. But if you know nothing about electrical circuits, this won't help you understand the nervous system at all, no matter how well developed your analogical reasoning abilities are. It is fair to say that all major theorists acknowledge the importance of knowledge and familiarity on the development of analogical reasoning, although they might disagree on the exact role that knowledge plays in such development (see DeLoache, Miller, & Pierroutsakos, 1998; Goswami, 1996).

The role of familiarity is illustrated in a study by Goswami (1995) that used a familiar children's story as the basis for analogical reasoning. Goswami used the familiar story of *Goldilocks and the Three Bears* ("The Daddy Bear has all the big things, the Mummy Bear has all the medium-sized things, and the Baby Bear has all the tiny things") to help children make *transitive mappings*. A transitive relation involves at least three objects varying in some dimension, such as length. If object A is longer than object B, and object B is longer than object C, then object A must be longer than object C (that is, A > B > C). Can young children use the transitive relation on one dimension as a basis for mapping transitive relations on another dimension? Or, stated somewhat differently, can children map the transitive relation from one dimension (the Daddy, Mummy, and Baby bears) to another (size, for instance)?

In Goswami's study, 3- and 4-year-old children were asked to use the relations in the Goldilocks story (Daddy Bear > Mummy Bear > Baby Bear) to classify objects that differed in quantity (a lot versus a medium amount versus a little of pizza, candy, or lemonade) or to rank order (three levels) certain phenomena on the basis of loudness (of footsteps), pitch (of voices), temperature (of porridge), saltiness (of porridge), width (of beds), or height (of mirrors). Four-year-olds generally performed well on all these tasks, using the Three Bears analogy to map onto other dimensions. Three-year-olds did less well, although they performed above chance levels on most tasks, indicating that they, too, could use the familiar (perhaps less familiar to them than to the 4-year-olds) story as a basis for making analogical relations.

**Metacognition.** To what extent is explicit awareness of the relations between entities on analogical-reasoning tasks important in solving problems? That analogical relations can be explicit to young children was illustrated by the previously discussed example of 4-year-old Lucas, who generated an analogical relation (albeit an incorrect one) for the *bird:nest* :: *dog*:? problem before seeing the alternatives. Successful training of analogical reasoning is often best accomplished when children receive explicit instruction about the rationale behind the training (Brown & Kane, 1988; Daehler & Chen, 1993), similar to what has been found in the training of memory strategies, as discussed earlier in this chapter. This suggests, not at all surprisingly, that knowing what one is doing (that is, having metacognitive knowledge) facilitates analogical reasoning.

One set of studies relevant to metacognitive knowledge was done by Ann Brown, Mary Kane, and their colleagues (Brown & Kane, 1988; Brown, Kane, & Long, 1989), who assessed children's *learning to learn* on a series of analogical-reasoning tasks. Learning to learn refers to improvements in performance on new tasks as a result of performance on earlier tasks, during which time children learn a general rule or approach to problems. That is, participants learn a general set of rules that they can apply to new tasks so that performance on later tasks is enhanced relative to performance on earlier tasks.

In Brown and Kane's studies, preschool children were given a series of problems similar to the "magic carpet" story used by Holyoak and his colleagues (1984). For example, some children were first given the genie problem. If they did not solve it, they were told about how rolling the "carpet" could be used to transport the jewels. They were then given a second similar problem (the Easter Bunny needing to transport eggs by using a rolled-up blanket) and then a third (a farmer transporting cherries using a rolled-up rug). Children who received this series of problems and were given the solution to a problem when they failed showed a large learning-to-learn effect. For the "rolling" solution, 46% of the children used analogical reasoning to solve the second problem, and 98% of the children did so for the third task. The control group, who received the three sets of "rolling" problems but did not receive the hints, showed only 20% transfer on the second problem and 39% on the third.

Does a learning-to-learn effect have to involve metacognition? Not necessarily. But some of the children's comments suggested that their improved performance on the later problems was the result of their awareness of analogical reasoning strategies. For example, one 4-year-old child in the Brown and Kane (1988) study, after solving two "rolling" problems, said at the beginning of the third problem: "And all you need to do is get this thing rolled up? I betcha!" (p. 517). Brown and Kane (1988) commented that children had developed a mind-set to look for analogies, expecting to extract some general rule to solve problems and to be able to use knowledge they acquired in one context elsewhere.

### Scientific Reasoning

**Scientific reasoning** involves generating hypotheses about how something in the world works and then systematically testing those hypotheses. Basically, one uses scientific reasoning by identifying the factors that can affect a particular phenomenon (for instance, the rate at which a pendulum oscillates, as in the example provided in Chapter 5) and then exhaustively varying one factor at a time while holding the other factors constant. As you will recall, Piaget proposed that scientific reasoning is not found until adolescence (Inhelder & Piaget, 1958). Subsequent research has not always supported Piaget's theories, but it is generally agreed that scientific reasoning is a late-developing ability that is not easily demonstrated by many adults (Bullock, Sodian, & Koerber, 2009; Kuhn, Amsel, & O'Loughlin, 1988).

Let me provide an example from research by Deanna Kuhn and her colleagues (1988), who presented hypothetical information about the relation between certain foods and the likelihood of catching colds to sixth- and ninth-grade students and to adults of varying educational backgrounds. Participants were first interviewed to determine which foods they thought might be associated with colds. Then, over several trials, they were given a series of foods (for example, oranges, baked potatoes, cereal, Coca-Cola), each associated with an outcome (cold or no cold). Some foods were always associated with getting a cold (baked potatoes, for instance), some were always associated with not getting colds (cereal, for instance), and others were independent of getting colds (that is, sometimes they were associated with getting colds and sometimes not). At least one outcome was consistent with a participant's initial opinion about the "healthiness" of a food, and at least one outcome was inconsistent with it.

Scientific reasoning involves hypotheses, but what is most crucial about the scientific method is that it involves *evidence*. Maybe you have grown up believing that eating chicken soup will make you healthy, but science requires that evidence, when available, be used to provide an answer. Initial responses on these questions were usually based on prior beliefs, but as more evidence accumulated, most adults increased their decisions based on that evidence. The adolescents, however, were much less apt to consider evidence in their decisions and, instead, relied more frequently on extra-experimental beliefs (for example, "The juice makes a difference because my mother says orange juice is better for you"). In fact, 30% of the sixth-graders never made a single spontaneous evidenced-based response. Yet, when asked how they knew one food did, or did not, have an effect, most participants of all ages were able to provide an evidenced-based answer, although children were still less likely to do so than adults. This indicates that reasoning from evidence is something that sixth-graders can do, but that they tend not to do it spontaneously. It's also worth noting that the adults did not perform perfectly on these problems, either. Only the most highly educated adults (philosophy graduate students) consistently solved these problems using the evidence that was presented.

Scientific reasoning can improve with practice. Several researchers have given participants of varying ages sets of scientific problems to solve over repeated testing sessions (Kuhn, Pease, & Wirkala, 2009; Schauble, 1996). In these studies, participants' performance improved over sessions and generalized to different scientific problems (for example, from determining what factors affect the speed of a car to determining what factors influence school achievement). Although participants of all ages showed improvements over sessions, preadolescent children showed fewer gains than adults.

There is evidence that elementary school children can be trained to use scientific reasoning with explicit instruction and then transfer such strategies to new tasks. Zhe Chen and David Klahr (1999) trained second-, third- and fourth-grade children to use the control of variables strategy (CVS), which essentially involves setting up experiments so that contrasts are made between experimental conditions one at a time. This is essential in being able to assess properly a scientific hypothesis. Children received explicit instruction in how to use the CVS as well as implicit training via the use of probes, in which children were asked systematic questions about factors in the experiments as they were conducting them. Children performed hands-on experiments—for example, testing factors that influence how far a ball will travel down an inclined plane (such as degree of the slope, surface of the ramp, length of the ramp, and type of ball). To assess transfer of training, children were given new problems 1 and 2 days after training.

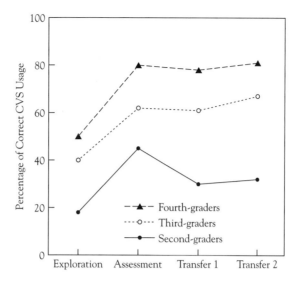

FIGURE **7-18**

Percentage of correct control of variables strategy (CVS) usage by phase and grade for children receiving both explicit training and probes.

Source: Chen, Z., & Klahr, D. (1999). All other things being equal: Acquisition and transfer of the control of variables strategy. *Child Development, 70*, 1098–1120. Reprinted with permission of the Society for Research in Child Development.

Figure 7-18 presents the percentages of correct CVS usage for the condition in which children received both direct training and probes for second-, third-, and fourth-grade children. The exploration phase in the figure can be considered a baseline, whereas the assessment phase reflects children's performance on the training trials. As can be seen, all groups of children improved as a result of training, although the improvement for the second-graders was only marginally significant. Perhaps more critically, both the third- and fourth-grade children continued their high level of CVS use on the 1- and 2-day transfer tests. These results indicate that elementary school children can, indeed, learn to use scientific reasoning to solve problems and then generalize them to new tasks. However, when some of the third- and fourth-grade children were tested 7 months later, only the fourth-graders showed any long-term benefits of training, indicating that the instruction given to the younger children was not sufficient to have lasting effects.

Why do children, adolescents, and many adults perform so poorly on scientific reasoning problems? Kuhn and her colleagues (1988) argued that scientific reasoning involves thinking *about* theories rather than just working with them. In other words, scientific reasoning requires a high level of metacognition. It requires integrating theories (or hypotheses) with data (or evidence). When the two agree, there is little problem. When hypotheses and evidence are in conflict, however, problems occur. Kuhn (1989) has speculated that children (and many adults) take one of two extreme approaches to theory-data conflicts: *Theory-bound children* distort the data to fit the theory, whereas *data-bound children* focus not on the global theory to explain their results but on isolated patterns of results (to avoid conflict with the theory).

Although poor metacognition might be the overarching reason for peoples' difficulties with scientific reasoning, it is not the only one. Children and adolescents often do not conduct effective experiments. They frequently fail to vary one factor systematically, or they come to a decision before all possible factors have been tested. Children (and, to a lesser extent, adults) have a positive-results bias. They put more weight on results that produce good outcomes (for example, good academic performance, good health) than on results that yield negative outcomes (see DeLoache, Miller, & Pierroutsakos, 1998). Adolescents' pre-existing beliefs also strongly influence their scientific reasoning. Outcomes that are consistent with their prior beliefs are quickly and uncritically accepted, whereas evidence counter to their beliefs is regarded more critically (Klaczynski, 1997; Klaczynski & Narasimham, 1998).

In general, the "big" picture of scientific reasoning painted by Inhelder and Piaget (1958) more than 50 years ago has not changed drastically. Scientific reasoning is rarely found in children. What the new research indicates, however, is that scientific reasoning is only occasionally found in adolescents and adults without specific training. Given these findings, it makes good sense for university-level psychology students to have a course in research methods, in which the logic of experimental design is made explicit. College students are clearly capable of such thinking, but we should not be surprised that it does not come spontaneously or easily to them.

# SUMMARY

Information-processing approaches to the study of cognition emphasize the flow of information through a *limited capacity* processing system—specifically, the sensory registers, the *short-term store*, and the *long-term store*. Cognitive operations are conceptualized as existing on a continuum, with *automatic*, or effortless, *processes* at one extreme and strategic, or *effortful processes* at the other.

*Executive function (executive control)* refers to the processes involved in regulating attention and in determining what to do with information just gathered or retrieved from long-term memory. It involves a related set of basic information-processing abilities, including speed of processing, *memory span* and *working memory*, *selective attention*, *inhibition* and *resistance to interference*, and *cognitive flexibility*, each of which develops with age. *Span of apprehension* refers to the amount of information people can attend to at a single time and is several items less than memory span. According to one popular model, working memory consists of a central executive, which stores information, and two temporary systems, one for coding verbal information, called the *articulatory loop*, and another for coding visual information, referred to as the visuo-spatial scratch pad. *Attention deficit hyperactivity disorder (ADHD)* is a common childhood disorder associated with deficient executive control.

*Strategies* are deliberately implemented, nonobligatory operations that are potentially available to consciousness and are used to improve task performance. Children who fail to use a strategy spontaneously can often be trained to use one and, thus, improve task performance, a phenomenon called a *production deficiency*. Although both strategy use and task performance typically increase with age, children frequently display a *utilization deficiency*, using a strategy without experiencing any benefit from its use. Siegler's *adaptive strategy choice model* proposes that children have a variety of strategies available to them at any one time and that these strategies "compete" for use, with strategies changing in frequency over time.

Two frequently studied *memory strategies*, or *mnemonics*, are *rehearsal* and *organization*. Younger children frequently engage in *passive rehearsal*, repeating only one unique word at a time, whereas older children are more apt to engage in *active*, or *cumulative rehearsal*, repeating many different words in the same rehearsal set. Organization in recall is reflected by children sorting or remembering related items together.

Many factors influence children's strategy use, including *mental capacity*; *knowledge base*, or how much children know about the problems they are trying to solve; and *metacognition*, or an awareness of one's cognitive abilities. *Declarative metacognition* refers to explicit, conscious, factual knowledge about person or task variables. *Procedural metacognition* refers to knowledge about when strategies are necessary as well as to monitoring one's progress on a task. Metacognitive knowledge increases with age, as reflected by studies of *meta-attention* and *metamemory*.

Strategies are particularly important to children in schooled societies, and classroom teachers instruct children in the use of a variety of different strategies. The absolute level of strategy instruction in school is often low and varies with subject, and children who receive more strategy instruction tend to show more strategic behavior.

*Problem solving* involves a goal, obstacles to that goal, strategies for overcoming the obstacles, and an evaluation of the results. Infants show signs of *goal-directed behavior* and problem solving in the latter part of the first year. Problem solving improves over the preschool years and is influenced by how much knowledge the problem solver has about the task to be solved or the context in which the task is embedded.

*Reasoning* is a special type of problem solving that requires one make an inference. *Analogical reasoning* involves *relational mapping*—the application of what one knows about one set of elements to relations about different elements. There appears to be a *relational shift* in the development of analogical reasoning, in which young children are more likely to focus on perceptual similarity whereas older children and adults focus more on relational similarity in solving problems. Other factors that influence children's success at analogical reasoning are knowledge for the relations on which the analogy is based and metacognition.

*Scientific reasoning* involves generating hypotheses about how something in the world works and then systematically testing those hypotheses. Scientific reasoning is a late-developing ability, in part because of the metacognitive difficulty involved in reasoning about theories.

## KEY TERMS AND CONCEPTS

| | | | |
|---|---|---|---|
| short-term store | memory span | resistance to interference | production deficiency |
| long-term store | span of apprehension | | utilization deficiency |
| limited capacity | working memory | attention deficit hyperactivity disorder (ADHD) | adaptive strategy choice model |
| automatic processes | articulatory loop | | |
| effortful processes | selective attention | cognitive flexibility | memory strategies (or mnemonics) |
| executive function (or executive control) | inhibition | strategies | rehearsal |

organization

passive rehearsal

active rehearsal
(or cumulative
rehearsal)

knowledge base

metacognition

declarative
metacognition

procedural metacogni-
tion

meta-attention

metamemory

problem solving

goal-directed behavior

reasoning

analogical reasoning

relational mapping

relational shift

scientific reasoning

## SUGGESTED READINGS

### Scholarly Work

Bjorklund, D. F., Dukes, C., & Brown, R. D. (2009). The development of memory strategies. In M. L. Courage & N. Cowan (Eds.), *The development of memory in infancy and childhood* (pp. 145–175). New York: Psychology Press. This chapter presents an up-to-date review of research in memory strategy development.

Siegler, R. S. (2000). The rebirth of learning. *Child Development, 71*, 26–35. This short paper presents some of the basic ideas of Siegler's adaptive strategy choice model, including how to use the microgenetic method to study children's learning.

Zelazo, P. D., Carlson, S. M., & Kesek, A. (2008). The development of executive function in childhood. In C. A. Nelson & M. Luciana (Eds.), *Handbook of cognitive developmental neuroscience* (2nd edition) (pp. 553–574). Cambridge, MA: MIT Press. This article presents a state-of-the-art review of thinking about the development of executive function in childhood, including a discussion of correlated changes in brain development.

### Reading for Personal Interest

Thornton, S. (1998). *Children solving problems*. Cambridge, MA: Harvard University Press. This relatively old book from the *Developing Child* series still offers an accessible and interesting summary of some post-Piagetian research findings on cognitive development as well as a readable account of why problem solving should be at the foundation of cognitive development research.

# Memory Development

**Representation of Knowledge**

**Memory Development in Infancy**
Preference for Novelty as an Indication of
Memory
Kicking Up Their Heels
Deferred Imitation as a Measure of
Memory
Neurological Basis of Infant Memory

**Infantile Amnesia**
Why Can't We Remember Events from
Infancy and Early Childhood?
Infantile Amnesia and Hypnotic Age
Regression

**Implicit Memory**

**The Development of Event Memory**
Script-Based Memory
The Role of Parents in "Teaching"
Children to Remember

**Children as Eyewitnesses**
Age Differences in Children's Eyewitness
Memories
Age Differences in Suggestibility
Some Final Thoughts on Children as
Eyewitnesses
   BOX 8-1: Assessing Children's Memories in
   Real-Life Settings

**Remembering to Remember**

**Consistency and Stability of Memory**
Is "Memory" a Domain-General Faculty
or a Set of Domain-Specific Abilities?
How Stable Is Memory Performance over
Time?

SUMMARY
KEY TERMS AND CONCEPTS
SUGGESTED READINGS

Although rare, some people have one or more vivid memories from infancy or early childhood. I have one, for example, stemming from my first year of life. My memory is of me as a sick baby. I had the croup (something like bronchitis). When I recall this memory, I can feel the congestion in my chest, hear the vaporizer whir, smell the Vicks® VapoRub®, and see the living room of my grandparents' house while looking through the bars of my crib. The memory is like a multisensory snapshot. I have no story to tell, only the recall of an instant of my life as a sickly baby. My mistake was relating this vibrant and personally poignant memory to my mother. She listened carefully and then told me that I had never had the croup; my younger brother Dick had the croup as a toddler. I was about 4 years old at the time. My "memory" was a reconstruction—and of an event I had only *observed,* not one I had actually *experienced.* Most memories of infancy, it seems, are like mine—reconstructions of events that never happened or, perhaps, that happened to someone else, but what one is remembering is the re-telling of that event by other people.

It's hard to overestimate the significance of memory for our lives. Our memories define for us what we've done, who and what we know, and even who we are. Nearly all acts of cognition involve memory. A 4-month-old looks longer at a new picture than at one he has seen repeatedly; a 3-year-old recounts her class field trip to a bakery; a 7-year-old lists for her mother the names of all her classmates in preparing to send Valentine's Day cards; and a high school sophomore attempts to remember everything his father asked him to get at the corner store. Each of these diverse activities involves memory. The 4-month-old can recognize a new stimulus only if he has some notion that it is different from a previously experienced but currently unseen one. The memory requirements for the three older children are more demanding, but all involve retrieving from memory some previously stored information.

Memory is not a unitary phenomenon. Information must be encoded and possibly related with other information known to the individual. What knowledge already resides in memory influences the ease with which new information is stored and later retrieved.

Memory development is one of the oldest, continuously researched topics in the field of cognitive development. But how it is researched, and the theoretical focus of the researchers, is much different today than it was 30 years ago. In the previous chapter, we discussed that how much children remember is influenced by developmental differences in basic information-processing abilities of encoding, storage, and retrieval and by the strategies they use to intentionally learn information. Today, however, there is an increasing awareness that memory is used *for* specific purposes and *in* specific social contexts (Kuhn, 2000; Ornstein & Haden, 2001; Ornstein & Light, 2010). It is not enough merely to assess children's memory behavior in one context, particularly a context devoid of social meaning. How and what children remember depends on a host of dynamically interacting factors that vary over time. Despite the wealth of information we have about children's memory today, we are just beginning to develop an appreciation for the factors and contexts that influence children's memory performance and the development of those abilities.

In this chapter, I examine research and theory dealing with the development of memory in children. I open the chapter with a brief examination of the different ways knowledge can be represented in memory. I then examine memory development in infancy, followed by a look at children's implicit memory. Children's memories for events—specifically, autobiographical memories—are then examined. Research on children as eyewitnesses, and the factors that influence their suggestibility, is reviewed in some detail. This is followed by a brief look at the development of "remembering to remember," or prospective memory, and finally, the topics of the consistency and stability of memory.

---

## REPRESENTATION OF KNOWLEDGE

As we saw in Chapters 5 and 6, how people represent information changes with age, and this is a central issue in cognitive psychology. We take it for granted that knowledge is represented somehow in our brains and that we can access it whenever we want. But knowledge is not quite so simple. Is everything we know represented in such a way that we can easily (and consciously) retrieve it "on demand"? Might there be some things we "know" that affect our thoughts and behavior that are difficult or impossible to bring to consciousness? And if so, how do these things develop?

Endel Tulving (1985, 2005) proposed that information in the long-term store can be represented in one of two general ways: declarative memory and nondeclarative memory. **Declarative memory** refers to facts and events and comes in two types: episodic memory and semantic memory. **Episodic memory**—literally, memory for episodes, such as what you had for breakfast this morning, the gist of a conversation you had with your mother last night, and the Christmas visit to your grandparents when you were 5 years old—can be consciously retrieved. Such memory is sometimes called **explicit memory**, which refers to the fact that it is available to conscious awareness and can be directly (explicitly) assessed by tests of recall or recognition memory.

**Semantic memory** refers to our knowledge of language, rules, and concepts. So, for instance, the meaning of the term *democracy* or the rules for multiplication are examples of semantic memory. For instance, the definition for the word "avuncular" is part of my semantic memory, but my recollections of the events surrounding my learning the word (preparing for the Graduate Record Exam) are part of my episodic memory.[1]

The second general type of memory has been termed **nondeclarative memory** (or **procedural memory**). Nondeclarative memory refers to knowledge of procedures that are unconscious. For example, some have argued that the learning and memory observed in classical and operant conditioning are unconscious, as are many familiar routines once they have become well practiced (tying one's shoe, for example). Such memory is sometimes called *implicit memory*, which refers to the fact it is unavailable to conscious awareness ("memory without awareness") and can be assessed only indirectly (that is, you just can't ask someone to remember something he or she knows only implicitly).

Consider the classic case of amnesia, where a person walks into a police station and announces to the desk sergeant that he has no idea who he is or how he got there—the perfect beginning of a mystery novel. Now consider a person who knows very well who she is and can carry on a conversation just fine, but 5 minutes after meeting you, she has forgotten who you are and anything you talked about. Yet, were you to meet with her every day and teach her how to tie a complicated knot, after a week of practice she would be able to tie the knot expertly without having any awareness of doing it before. These are both forms of amnesia (*retrograde amnesia* in the first case and *anterograde amnesia* in the second), but different memory systems are involved. In the first case, the person has lost his personal history. He remembers nothing about "the self." In the second case, the person's sense of self and personal history are intact. However, she can learn no new information other than some procedures (tying knots), and she will have no recollection of having ever learned them. In both cases, people keep their knowledge of their language, multiplication tables, and basic facts of the world. For example, if they were American citizens, they would likely know the current President and who the first U.S. President was. The person with retrograde amnesia who forgot who he was displays a deficit in a form of *explicit/declarative memory*—specifically, *episodic memory*. The person with anterograde amnesia has access to past episodic memories but cannot form new ones (usually because of damage to the hippocampus), although she can form new procedural memories. Figure 8-1 shows the various components of the explicit and implicit memory systems.

In addition to tapping different "types" of memories, evidence also indicates that different areas of the brain are involved in declarative and nondeclarative memories (Schacter, 1992). This supports the argument that memory is not a single phenomenon (that is, domain-general) but, rather, is a set of domain-specific mental operations that may show different patterns of developmental function.

---

[1] *avuncular:* Of, pertaining to, or resembling an uncle *(The American Heritage Dictionary of the English Language).*

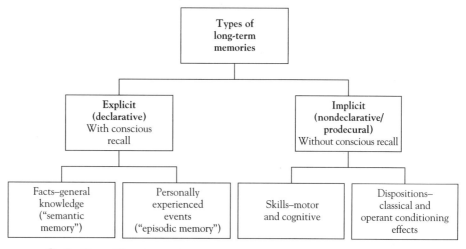

FIGURE **8-1** Classification of different types of memory.
The human memory system can be divided into twogeneral types of memory: explicit, or declarative, which is available to consciousness, and implicit, or nondeclarative, which is not available to consciousness, which themselves can be divided further. Age differences are greater in explicit than implicit memory.

## MEMORY DEVELOPMENT IN INFANCY

Babies obviously remember things. The questions of interest are when and under what conditions infants demonstrate memory and how long these memories last. For example, research examining infants' search behavior, as reflected by object permanence tasks (see Chapter 4), indicates changes in memory with age during the first year (Diamond, 1985). Recall Adele Diamond's findings that the amount of delay necessary to yield the A-not-B error increased with each successive month between 7 and 12 months of age. Although Diamond proposed that developmental differences in the ability to inhibit a prepotent response were partly responsible for this effect, she also acknowledged that such results reflect age changes in memory during this 6-month period (Diamond, Cruttenden, & Neiderman, 1994).

### Preference for Novelty as an Indication of Memory

The bulk of research assessing infant memory, particularly in the early days of such research, used variants of the habituation/dishabituation paradigm discussed in previous chapters. To review, infants' attention declines as a result of repeated presentation of a stimulus (habituation) but returns to its previously high levels when a new stimulus is presented (dishabituation). Such a finding not only indicates that infants can discriminate between the two stimuli but also implicates memory, in that the discrimination is being made between one stimulus that is physically present and another that is present only memorially. In a related procedure, infants are familiarized with a stimulus and later shown two stimuli: the original, familiarized stimulus and a novel one. As in the habituation/dishabituation paradigm, preference for the novel stimulus is (usually) taken as evidence of memory for the original. Using these **preference-for-novelty**

**paradigms,** memory for visual stimuli has been found for some newborns. Research by Steven Friedman (1972) illustrated that some newborns demonstrate dishabituation (discussed in Chapter 4), although other research suggests that this ability likely characterizes only the more maturationally advanced neonates. Nonetheless, basic visual memory is an early developing ability—certainly within the capacity of most infants during their first months of life.

Perhaps the most influential work demonstrating memory in infants using the preference-for-novelty paradigm is that of Joseph Fagan (1973, 1974). One study showed that 5- and 6-month-old babies formed visual memories following brief exposures (5 to 10 seconds) and that these memories lasted as long as 2 weeks (Fagan, 1974). Fagan's procedures have been widely used by researchers, and later work suggested a relationship between individual differences in preference for novelty during infancy and childhood memory and intelligence. This research will be examined in Chapter 13.

Subsequent research has shown that even 1-month-old infants demonstrate relatively long-lived memories. For example, in one study, the mothers of 1- and 2-month-old infants read their babies one of two nursery rhymes over the course of 2 weeks. Infants were then brought into the laboratory, and their preferences for the familiar versus a novel nursery rhyme were tested. This was done by permitting infants to choose hearing either the familiar or a novel nursery rhyme by modifying their sucking on a pacifier (for example, increase sucking rate to hear one rhyme, decrease sucking rate to hear the other). After a 3-day delay between the time infants last heard their mothers read the familiar nursery rhyme and being tested in the lab, even 1-month-old babies showed a preference for the familiar rhyme, indicating memory for the auditory event (Spence, 1996).

It's worth noting here that infants' preference in Melanie Spence's (1996) study was for the familiar stimulus, not for the novel one. To demonstrate memory, all that is required is that infants show a decided preference for one stimulus over the other. As I noted in earlier chapters, infants' preferences for novel versus familiar objects/ events varies as a function of their age and stage of learning in a task, among other factors (Bogartz & Shinskey, 1998). For example, Mary Courage and Mark Howe (2001) showed 3.5-month-old infants a stimulus for 30 seconds and then tested their preference for the old (familiar) versus a new (novel) stimulus after delays of 1 minute, 1 day, and 1 month. The researchers reported a preference for novelty after the 1-minute delay, no preference after the 1-day delay, and a preference for familiarity after the 1-month delay (see Figure 8-2). Following the theorizing of Lorraine Bahrick and Jeffrey Pickens (1995), Howe and Courage (2001) interpreted these findings as indicating that infants' attention to novel versus familiar stimuli varies as a function of the strength of the familiar information in long-term memory at the time of testing. Infants will attend more to novel stimuli when memory traces are strong (after the 1-day delay) and attend more to familiar stimuli when the memory traces are weak (after the 1-month delay). Null effects (that is, neither a preference for the novel nor a preference for the familiar stimuli) reflect a transition phase in which both stimuli compete equally for attention.

## Kicking Up Their Heels

Other research by Carolyn Rovee-Collier and her colleagues has used conditioning techniques, demonstrating retention over relatively long periods for very young infants (see Rovee-Collier, 1999, and Rovee-Collier & Cuevas, 2009, for reviews). In their

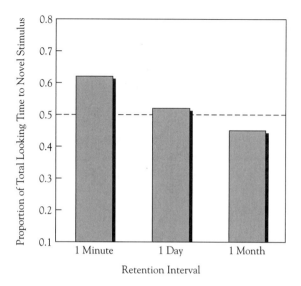

FIGURE **8-2**

Mean proportion of total looking time infants directed to the novel stimulus during the 1-minute, 1-day, and 1-month delays. Chance is .5. Mean looking time significantly greater than chance reflects a preference for novelty. Mean looking time significantly less than expected by chance reflects a preference for familiarity.

Source: Courage, M. L., & Howe, M. L. (2001). Long-term retention in 3.5-month-olds: Familiarization time and individual differences in attentional style. *Journal of Experimental Child Psychology, 79,* 271–293. © 2001 Elsevier. Reprinted with permission.

**conjugate-reinforcement procedure,** a ribbon is tied to an infant's ankle and connected to a mobile that is suspended over the crib (see Photo 8-1). Infants quickly learn that the mobile moves when they kick their feet, and they soon make repeated kicks, controlling the movement of the mobile overhead. In a typical experiment, for the first 3 minutes the ribbon is not connected to the mobile, so kicks do not cause it to move (baseline nonreinforcement period). This is followed by a 9-minute reinforcement period in which the ribbon and mobile are connected, and infants quickly learn to kick to make the mobile move. What will happen when the infants are hooked up to the apparatus hours or days later? Will they resume kicking (even when the ribbon is not connected to the mobile), or will their level of kicks be comparable to that observed during the 3-minute baseline? If the kicking rate is high on these delayed trials, it reflects memory; if it is low, it reflects forgetting.

Rovee-Collier and her colleagues have used this procedure successfully with infants as young as 2 months of age. For example, Margaret Sullivan, Carolyn Rovee-Collier, and Derek Tynes (1979) varied the delayed memory test between 48 and 336 hours (2 weeks) with 3-month-old infants. The researchers reported no forgetting by these young infants for as much as 8 days, and some babies displayed memory for the full 2-week interval. In related work, retention of conditioned responses during a 2-week period was obtained for infants as young as 8 weeks, although evidence of memory was obtained only under optimal conditions (distributing training over several sessions) (Vander Linde, Morrongiello, & Rovee-Collier, 1985). These results

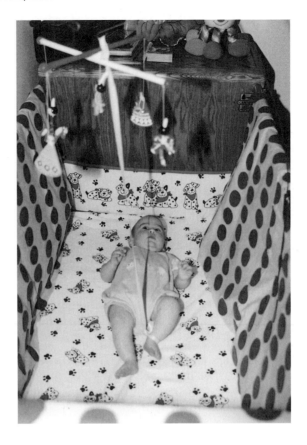

PHOTO **8-1**

An infant connected to a mobile in an experiment to assess memory used by Carolyn Rovee-Collier and her colleagues. (Thanks to Carolyn Rovee-Collier.)

indicate that young infants can remember events over long intervals, although these skills do improve over the first several months of life.

Subsequent research by Rovee-Collier and her colleagues focused on the role of context in infants' memories. How similar must the learning environment and testing environment be for babies to show retention? This was assessed by a study in which different aspects of the learning environment (in this case, the playpens in which the infants were tested) were changed between the time of learning and the time of testing (Rovee-Collier et al., 1992). Six-month-old infants were tested using the conjugate-reinforcement procedure described earlier, but the testing situation was made very distinctive. Infants sat in an infant seat that was placed in a playpen. The sides of the playpen were draped with a distinctive cloth (for example, yellow liner with green felt squares). Some infants were tested 24 hours later with the same cloth, whereas others were placed in the playpen that was draped with a blue liner and vertical red felt strips. The results of this experiment are presented in Figure 8-3 (expressed as kicking rate during testing relative to kicking rate during baseline). As you can see, infants in the "No Change" condition demonstrated significantly better retention of the learned

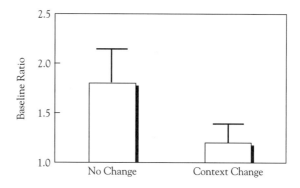

FIGURE **8-3**

Mean baseline ratios for 6-month-old infants in a No Change (control) condition and a Context Change condition. The higher ratio for infants in the No Change condition reflects greater retention of the behaviors that were learned 24 hours earlier.

Source: Adapted from Rovee-Collier, C., Schechter, A., Shyi, C.W. G., & Shields, P. (1992). Perceptual identification of contextual attributes and infant memory retrieval. *Developmental Psychology, 28,* 307–318.

behavior than infants in the "Context Change" condition, indicating the important role that context plays in reinstating infants' memories.

Rovee-Collier et al. (1992) performed six other experiments, varying different aspects of the context. They concluded that infants do not respond to the context "as a whole" but, rather, seem to process individual components of a context. For instance, changes in visual patterns (for example, strips versus squares) or reversal of the foreground and background (for example, yellow liner with green squares versus green liner with yellow squares) disrupted memory, but changes in color did not (for other examples, see Bhatt, Rovee-Collier, & Shyi, 1994; Fagen et al., 1997). Rovee-Collier and Gary Shyi (1992) speculated that infants' reliance on specific aspects of a context prevents them from retrieving memories in "inappropriate" situations. This may be especially important for infants with poor inhibitory abilities, who would be apt to retrieve previously acquired memories (actions) in a wide range of often-inappropriate situations unless there were some potent constraints (such as context specificity) on the memory system. The role of inhibitory factors in infant cognition has been addressed by several researchers, most notably Diamond, and some of this work was discussed in Chapter 2.

Rovee-Collier and her colleagues have also used conjugate-reinforcement procedures to assess age-related changes in long-term memory in infants. For example, in addition to the mobile task, they developed the *train task,* which uses the same logic as the mobile task but is appropriate to use with older babies. In the train task, infants sit in front of a display that includes a miniature train set. They can learn to move the train around the set by pressing a lever in front of them, and retention is tested as it is in the mobile task, with infants sitting in front of the display after a delay and the rate with which they press the lever (when it is now not connected to the train) being measured. With these two comparable tasks, it is now possible to ask how long memories last for infants of different ages. Figure 8-4 presents the maximum number of weeks that infants between 2 and 18 months of age demonstrated retention on the mobile

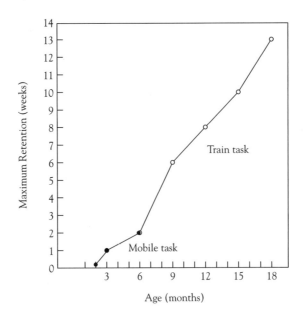

FIGURE **8-4**

Maximum duration of retention from 2 to 18 months of age. Filled circles show retention on the mobile task, and open circles show retention on the train task. Six-month-olds were trained and tested on both tasks.

Source: Rovee-Collier, C. (1999). The development of infant memory. *Current Directions in Psychological Science, 8,* 80–85. © 1999 Blackwell Publishers. Reprinted with permission.

and train tasks. As can be seen, the duration of infants' memories showed gradual but steady increases with age, reflecting a continuously developing memory system.

## Deferred Imitation as a Measure of Memory

Another task that has been used to assess infants' long-term memory is **deferred imitation**, which refers to imitating a model after a significant delay. In most deferred-imitation experiments, infants watch as an experimenter demonstrates some novel behavior with an unfamiliar object. At some later time, they are given the object. If they display the novel behavior more than a control group of infants who had not previously been shown the object, it implies that the study group formed a long-term memory for the action. The results of this research are quite striking, showing that infants form long-term memories for these novel actions that can last as long as 1 year (see Bauer, 2002, 2007). These results suggest that preverbal infants and toddlers do represent events in their long-term memories and, under the right conditions, can access those memories months later.

At what age do infants display deferred imitation? Although results vary with the specific task used, infants as young as 9 months old will imitate simple actions up to 5 weeks later (Carver & Bauer, 1999), and 6-month-olds have been shown to imitate simple behaviors after a 24-hour delay (Carver & Bauer, 1999).

Once infants observe an action, how long do those memories last? The answer depends primarily on the age of the infant, with older infants being able to remember more complicated sets of behaviors over longer periods of time. For example, Patricia Bauer and her colleagues (Bauer, 2002, 2007; Bauer et al., 2000; 2001) showed infants a series of three-step sequences. (For example, the researcher placed a bar across two posts, hung a plate from the bar, and then struck the plate with a mallet; see Photo 8-2.) After delays ranging from 1 to 12 months, the babies were given the objects, and the incidence of deferred imitation was noted. About half of the 9-month olds tested displayed imitation of simpler two-sequence actions after a 1-month delay, and these infants required at least three exposures to the events to achieve this level of performance. Rate of deferred imitation increased substantially for 13-, 16-, and 20-month-old infants, with older infants demonstrating higher levels of deferred imitation during each delay interval than younger infants did (Bauer et al., 2000). Figure 8-5 shows results of long-term retention as a function of age of infant and length of delay from this study. These findings are similar in form to those Rovee-Collier and colleagues reported using the conjugate-reinforcement procedures, and they illustrate that infants are able to form long-term memories early in life and that the ability to retain these memories increases gradually during the first 2 years.

Is deferred imitation a type of explicit, or declarative, memory? Recall from earlier in this chapter that *explicit* memory is contrasted with *implicit* memory. The former

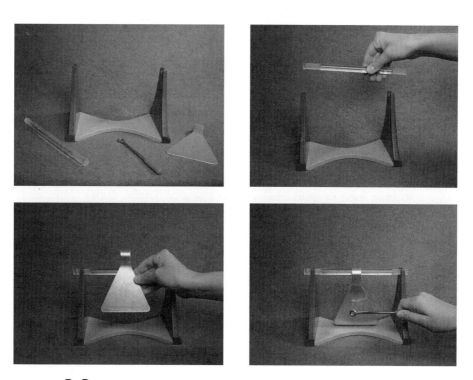

PHOTO **8-2**

Bauer's three-step sequence as shown by the "gong" task. Infants watched as a model performed a three-step sequence: placing the bar across two posts, hanging a plate on the bar, and striking the plate with a mallet. Infants were later given the opportunity to reproduce the sequence, demonstrating evidence of deferred imitation, and thus memory. (Thanks to Patricia Bauer)

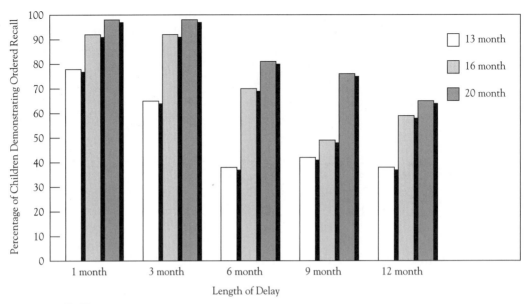

## FIGURE **8-5**

Percentage of 13-, 16-, and 20-month-old infants displaying deferred imitation of three-step sequences as a function of length of delay.

Source: Data from Bauer, P. J., Wenner, J. A., Dropik, P. L., & Wewerka, S. S. (2000). Parameters of remembering and forgetting in the transition from infancy to early childhood. *Monographs of the Society for Research in Child Development, 65* (Issue No. 4, Serial No. 263). Figure from Bauer, P. J. (2002). Long-term recall memory: Behavioral and neuro-developmental changes in the first 2 years of life. *Current Directions in Psychological Science, 11*, 137–141. © 2002 Blackwell Publishers. Reprinted with permission.

represents a deliberate attempt to remember and is potentially available to conscious awareness, whereas the latter is often referred to as "memory without awareness." Most researchers who have investigated deferred imitation in older infants believe it to be a form of nonverbal explicit memory (Bauer, 2007; Collie & Hayne, 1999). If so, it would be using the same type of representational system as that used by older children on verbal memory tasks.

How can one tell the difference between explicit and implicit memory in preverbal children? Perhaps one can't definitively, but support for this distinction comes from a study of adults with *anterograde amnesia,* like the woman I described earlier who learned to tie complicated knots but had no recollection of doing so. People with anterograde amnesia are unable to acquire new declarative memories (memory with awareness) but perform well on implicit memory tasks (memory without awareness). How do they perform on deferred imitation tasks? Just like they do on declarative memory tasks—they fail them (McDonough et al., 1995). These findings suggest that deferred imitation tasks tap the same memory system as do declarative tasks used with older children (for example, "Tell me what you had for breakfast this morning") and "that the neurological systems underlying long-term recall are present, in at least rudimentary form, by the beginning of the second year of life" (Schneider & Bjorklund, 1998, p. 474).

## Neurological Basis of Infant Memory

The pattern of deferred imitation shown by infants between 9 months and approximately 2 years is consistent with what is known about brain development during this time (see Bauer, 2007, 2009; Nelson, 1997). Long-term memory requires the integration of brain activity from multiple sites, including the hippocampus and the prefrontal cortex and structures within the temporal lobe. Most parts of the hippocampus develop early and are adultlike before birth, although the **dentate gyrus**, which plays an important role in memory, continues to develop after birth (Richmond & Nelson, 2007). In fact, one layer of the dentate gyrus includes at birth only about 70% of the number of cells that it will have in adulthood (Seress, 2001), meaning that about 30% of the neurons in this layer will be generated after birth. As we saw in Chapter 2, it was once believed that no new neurons were generated after birth. However, we now know that neurogenesis continues throughout life in the hippocampus, particularly the dentate gyrus. Once neurons are generated, synapses between neurons need to be formed, and this reaches its peak in the dentate gyrus during the fourth or fifth month after birth. Synapses are then pruned to adult levels by about 10 months. The early developing hippocampus presumably underlies the deferred imitation of simple actions by 6-month-olds (Collie & Hayne, 1999), but other brain areas must mature before infants can retain more complicated information for longer periods.

The frontal cortex is important in the formation and retrieval of declarative memories, and this develops more slowly than the hippocampus (Monk, Webb, & Nelson, 2001). For instance, synaptic density reaches its peak in the frontal cortex between 15 and 24 months after birth, and significant pruning takes place during childhood (Huttenlocher, 1979). Not until the second year of life do these and other systems (hippocampus, prefrontal lobe, temporal lobe) begin to coalesce, with development continuing well into the third year. The relatively gradual development of these brain structures correlates with the relatively gradual improvement in long-term retention of infants during this same period (Liston & Kagan, 2002; Bauer et al., 2000).

Additional evidence of the relation between brain and memory development in infancy comes from studies of premature infants. For example, Michelle de Haan and her colleagues (2000) administered deferred imitation tasks to three groups of 19-month-old children. One group of babies was born full term. Another group of infants had been born premature, after 35 to 37 weeks of gestation, but were physiologically healthy. A third group had been born premature after 27 to 34 weeks and were physiologically immature. The three groups of infants showed comparable levels of immediate imitation; however, they differed on deferred-imitation tasks, with the preterm infants, especially those who were physiologically immature, having significantly lower levels of memory. These results suggest that the declarative memory system of these preterm infants was adversely affected by depriving them of the last several weeks of their prenatal environment.

Other research indicates that the memory abilities (and, presumably, the underlying brain structures) of infants are impaired as a result of living in deprived environments. For example, the deferred imitation abilities of 20-month-old infants, some of whom had been adopted about 8 months earlier from a Romanian orphanage, where they had experienced extreme deprivation, were impaired relative to typically developing children (Kroupina et al., 2010). Toddlers who had spent their first year or so in conditions of extreme deprivation showed immediate imitation similar to that of home-reared children but displayed significantly poorer levels of deferred imitation. As I noted in

Chapter 2, postnatal experience plays a critical role in getting the brain "hooked up" properly, and when infants receive less-than-optimal experiences during their first year of life, their brains and memories suffer.

# INFANTILE AMNESIA

The results of Rovee-Collier, Bauer, and their colleagues indicate that infants do, indeed, form long-term memories. This is a relatively new finding, and one that, on the surface, contradicts the phenomenon of **infantile amnesia**—the seeming inability to recall information from early childhood. Such amnesia is bothersome not only to researchers but also to some parents. For example, my wife and I used to write a column for a parenting magazine and would occasionally get letters from concerned parents. One letter came from a woman who was worried because her 10-year-old son could remember very little from his preschool days. She said that she and her husband had always tried to be good parents but thought her son's inability to remember things from early childhood was an indication that either they hadn't done a very good job after all or, worse yet, they had done a truly terrible job and her son was repressing this painful period of his life. We wrote back to the woman, assuring her that her son's inability to remember events much before his fourth birthday is quite normal and that just because her child can't remember his experiences from this age doesn't mean that they didn't have an impact on him.

It is not just memories from infancy that escape us. For the most part, we are unable to remember much of anything before the age of 3.5 or 4 years (Rubin, 2000; West & Bauer, 1999). Most of us have a few memories for events that happened between the ages of about 3 and 6 years, but these memories are very few in comparison with what we can remember from after this time (Pillemer & White, 1989). What we lack specifically are **autobiographical memories**, which refer to personal and long-lasting memories and are the basis for one's personal life history (Nelson, 1996).

**CALVIN & HOBBES**

Most people cannot remember anything from the first few years of their lives, but this does not mean that this information is being repressed.

JoNell Usher and Ulric Neisser (1993) studied this lack of memory for the early years by questioning college students about experiences they had had early in life—experiences such as the birth of a younger sibling, a stay in the hospital, a family move, or the death of a family member. To assess recall, a series of questions was asked about each event the person had experienced (Who told you your mother was going to the hospital to give birth? What were you doing when she left? Where were you when you first saw the new baby?) The percentage of questions college students could answer increased substantially the older the person was when he or she had experienced the event. Usher and Neisser concluded that the earliest age of *any* meaningful recall was about 2 years for the birth of a sibling or a hospitalization and age 3 years for the death of a family member or a family move.

Of course, many people do claim to have memories from infancy or even from birth (or before). But are these memories to be trusted? The story that opened this chapter (a sick baby looking out the bars of his crib) is an example of how a vivid memory from infancy can be a reconstruction of an event and not the recollection of an event that actually happened to the "rememberer." Are all early memories like this? And, perhaps more to the point, does the inability to retrieve memories from infancy contradict the new research findings of long-term retention in early infancy?

## Why Can't We Remember Events from Infancy and Early Childhood?

Sigmund Freud (1963) was the first to speculate on the reason for infantile amnesia, proposing that the events of infancy and early childhood are rife with sexual overtones toward one's mother and are just generally so traumatic that they are actively repressed. We protect our adult egos, claimed Freud, by preventing these disturbing memories from rising to consciousness.

Few scientists today agree with Freud's interpretation. Other, more cognitively based interpretations propose the possibility that (1) information is not stored for long-term retention before about 2 years of age and (2) information is encoded differently by infants and toddlers than by older children and adults (see Bauer, 2007; Howe, Courage, & Rooksby, 2009). The first possibility seems unlikely. As we've seen, research using the deferred-imitation procedure (Bauer, 2007; Meltzoff, 1995), discussed earlier in this chapter, has shown that infants between 6 and 16 months of age can encode and retain a simple experience for as long as 1 year.

The second alternative, that information is encoded differently during the early and later years of life, is consistent with observations made by Jean Piaget and others that the nature of representation changes from infancy to early childhood and then again (although less drastically) somewhere between the ages of 5 and 7 years. The minds that resided in our heads when we were infants are no longer there, replaced by minds that process symbols, especially verbal ones. We reconstruct memories through adult schemes and representations, which are not suitable for events encoded in infancy and early childhood. For example, the memories tested in infancy all involve recall of action patterns, whereas the recall assessed in childhood and adulthood involve verbal recall, using language. Perhaps the inability to convert motor memories into verbal ones prevents children from recalling events from infancy.

Evidence for this latter interpretation has been accumulating over the past decade or so (Bauer, Wenner, & Kroupina, 2002; Hayne & Simcock, 2009; Richardson & Hayne, 2007; Simcock & Hayne, 2002). For example, Gabrielle Simcock and Harlene

Hayne (2002) showed children ranging in age from 27 to 39 months sequences of actions and then interviewed them 6 and 12 months later for their verbal and nonverbal memory of the events. Despite having the verbal ability to describe their previous experience, none of the children did so spontaneously. To the extent that children did talk about these prior events, they did so only if they had the vocabulary to describe the event *at the time of the experience*. That is, children who were more verbally sophisticated at the time of initial testing tended to verbally recall some aspects of the event, but children were seemingly not able to translate earlier preverbal experiences into language. According to Simcock and Hayne, "[C]hildren's verbal reports were frozen in time, reflecting their verbal skill at the time of encoding, rather than at the time of test" (p. 229).

Such an interpretation can account for our inability to retrieve memories from infancy, but 3- and 4-year-old children are clearly verbal and would presumably represent information in a symbolic form similar to the way adults do. The fact that 3- and 4-year-old children can recount verbally events that happened many months or even years ago suggests that this interpretation cannot be the entire answer (Fivush & Hamond, 1990).

A number of alternative explanations for infantile amnesia have been proposed. For example, several authors have suggested that for autobiographical memories to be laid down and later retrieved, there needs to be a sense of self (the "auto" in autobiographical) (Fivush, 1988; Howe, Courage, & Rooksby, 2009). Research has shown that the sense of self develops gradually during the preschool years (see discussion of the development of self-concept in Chapter 10) and that, although young children have "memories," the experiences of early childhood occurred when the sense of self was poorly developed, thus providing no anchor for such events. Unless events can be related to the self, they cannot be retrieved later.

Another alternative is that infantile amnesia is merely a consequence of the child's developing information-processing system (Leichtman & Ceci, 1993). Following the tenets of fuzzy-trace theory (Brainerd & Reyna, 2002; see discussion in Chapter 5), Michelle Leichtman and Stephen Ceci (1993) proposed a developmental shift in how events are represented, with young children encoding events primarily in terms of verbatim (precise) memory traces and older children relying more on gist (less precise) traces. Verbatim traces are more susceptible to forgetting than gist traces are. Thus, the heavy reliance on the highly forgettable verbatim traces makes memories from infancy and early childhood unavailable. Gist traces become increasingly available by the early school years, about the time when more memories can be retrieved.

Other theorists have proposed changes in language and how language is used as an explanation for the phenomenon of infantile amnesia (Fivush & Hamond, 1990; Nelson, 1993, 1996). This was illustrated in Simcock and Hayne's (2002) research, which showed that 2- and 3-year-old children were not able to translate a preverbal memory into language 6 months later. But language is not fully developed by 3 years of age, and other language-related changes may further influence children's ability to remember events from their past. Young children, in trying to understand and predict their world, are attentive to routines and embed novel events in terms of these routines (for example, what happens at breakfast, what happens on a trip to the grocery store). Such memories, ensconced as they are in routines, are not very distinctive and, thus, are not easily retrieved later on. Even when events *are* distinctive, however, young children do not necessarily know how to organize them in a memorable form. As I'll discuss in more detail later in this chapter, children "learn" to remember through interactions with adults. Adults provide the cues and structure for children to form narratives—stories for embedding events and, later, for remembering them. Only after being guided by adults can children learn to code memories and realize that language can be used to share memories with others.

Katherine Nelson (1993) makes this point especially clear:

> The claim here is that the initial functional significance of autobiographical memory is that of sharing memory with other people, a function that language makes possible. Memories become valued in their own right—not because they predict the future and guide present action, but because they are shareable with others and thus serve a social solidarity function. I suggest that this is a universal human function, although one with variable, culturally specific rules. In this respect, it is analogous to human language itself, uniquely and universally human but culturally—and individually—variable. (p. 12)

Research examining the earliest memories of people from different cultures lends some support for Nelson's ideas. For instance, in a series of studies, White North Americans reported earlier memories than Asians, in most cases by about half a year (Peterson, Wang, & Hou, 2009; Wang, 2006). In addition, American adults' earliest memories were more likely to include emotions and less likely to involve family activities than were the childhood memories of Chinese adults (Wang, 2001). These patterns are correlated with cultural differences in parent-child interaction. For example, compared to Korean mothers, American mothers talk about past events more with their 3-year-old children (Mullen & Yi, 1995) and also have earlier memories than Korean adults (Mullen, 1994).

Nelson's (1993) claim suggests that infantile amnesia might not be so significant in its own right, as Freud believed, but, instead, reflects an important transition in human cognition. This transition is based on everyday adult-child interaction and the developing language system, and it transforms the child into an individual who has a personal past that can be shared with others. This does not preclude the possibility that changes in the self-system (Howe, Courage, & Rooksby, 2009) or in the information-processing system (Leichtman & Ceci, 1993) also play an important role. My guess is that they do. The most recent research suggests that infantile amnesia reflects important changes occurring during early childhood—changes that permit autobiographical memory and that truly separate our species from all others.

## Infantile Amnesia and Hypnotic Age Regression

Are memories from infancy and early childhood really gone, or are they just not retrievable by our conscious minds? What about hypnosis? Don't psychologists often use hypnosis to help people remember "forgotten" or "repressed" memories, and doesn't that sometimes include remembering events from one's early childhood? Yes, indeed, between 20% and 34% of psychotherapists report using hypnosis to help their patients "recall the unrecallable" (Lynn et al., 1997), and this sometimes includes memories from early childhood. But are memories recalled using hypnosis reliable, and are these memories even real? In general, people under hypnosis often do recall more details about an event than people not under hypnosis do, but many of these details turn out to be false (Erdelyi, 1994).

In hypnotic age regression, adults are hypnotized and "brought back" to an earlier age. In doing so, will the adults now truly think like they did as children, and will they remember events from their childhood better than nonhypnotized people? Michael Nash (1987) reviewed more than 60 years of this literature, and his answer is a definitive "no." For example, in research during which adults are regressed to the preschool years and then given Piagetian tasks such as conservation (see Chapter 5), they act more like adults who are asked to *pretend* to solve the problem like a 4-year-old would than like an actual 4-year-old child. In one study, adults were regressed to 3 years of age and asked to identify objects such as dolls, blankets, or teddy bears that were of particular importance and comfort to them at that time (Nash et al., 1986). The parents of both hypnotized and control participants were contacted to confirm the subjects' recollections. The hypnotized people were substantially *less* accurate in identifying favorite objects from their early childhoods than were the controls. The reports of the hypnotized participants matched those of their parents just 21% of the time, whereas the hit rate for the controls was 70%.

People who experience age regression might have the feeling of recalling a "real" memory. However, how confident one is in the veracity of a memory, unfortunately, does not always predict the truth of the memory. There is no evidence that hypnotic age regression can succeed in retrieving "repressed," or simply forgotten, memories from childhood, despite many people's claims to the contrary.

## IMPLICIT MEMORY

The memory infants show in the preference-for-novelty task or in Rovee-Collier's conditioning experiments do not seem to require conscious awareness. Typically, conscious awareness has been a prerequisite for explicit, or declarative, memory, with the "unconscious" memories of infants typically being classified as a form of **implicit memory**. (See, however, Howe, 2000, and Rovee-Collier, 1999, for arguments against this distinction.) Implicit memory is "memory without awareness" (see Schacter, 1992), and it is not limited to preverbal infants and toddlers but occurs also in older children and adults.

The distinction between implicit and explicit memory has more than heuristic value, for the two types of memories seem to be governed by different brain systems, as revealed by research on people with brain damage (Schacter, 1992; Schacter, Norman, & Koustall, 2000). For instance, as I mentioned previously, the hippocampus is involved in transferring new explicit information from the short-term store (the "location" of immediate awareness) to the long-term store. People with damage to the hippocampus can acquire a new skill as a result of repeated practice, but they will have no awareness of ever learning such skills. For example, Brenda Milner (1964) reported the case of H.M., a patient with hippocampal brain damage. H.M. was given a mirror-drawing task over several days, in which he had to trace figures while watching his hand in a mirror. H.M.'s performance was quite poor initially but improved after several days of practice, despite the fact that he had no recollection of ever performing the task before. The enhancement of performance as a result of practice is a reflection of intact implicit (procedural) memory, whereas H.M.'s failure to recall previously performing the task is a reflection of a lack of explicit memory.

There has been less developmental research on implicit memory compared to explicit memory, but what research has been done presents a consistent picture. Although substantial age differences are found on tests of declarative memorization, few age differences are found when implicit memory is tested (Billingsley, Smith, & McAndrews, 2002; Lum et al., 2010; Newcombe et al., 1998; see Lloyd & Newcombe, 2009, and Schneider, 2010, for reviews). Performance on implicit memory tasks is associated with the basal ganglia and cerebellum (Gareil, 1988), which develop earlier than areas of the brain associated with declarative memory (Giedd et al., 1999; Lenroot & Giedd, 2007).

One procedure used to assess implicit memory in children involves the use of fragmented pictures. Here, a fragmented picture is presented, and children are asked to identify it. This is very difficult to do initially, but as more of the picture is completed, it becomes increasingly easier to identify the object. In experiments using this task, children are shown a series of fragmented pictures and, later, are given another task involving those pictures. Do children perform this second task better (faster or more accurately) for pictures they had previously seen, despite the fact that they might not remember seeing those pictures before? The answer is generally "yes," and more important, few age differences are found in the magnitude of the effects (Drummey & Newcombe, 1995; Hayes & Hennessy, 1996).

Let me provide an example of a study using this procedure. Brett Hayes and Ruth Hennessy (1996) showed 4-, 5-, and 10-year-old children a series of pictures and asked the children to identify them or to answer some questions about each item (for example, "What would you use an X for?"). Two days later, the children were shown some of the previous pictures and some new ones to identify in a fragmented-picture task. Children were also asked if they had remembered seeing each picture 2 days earlier. Although older children correctly identified more pictures than the younger children did, the *priming effect* (that is, the degree to which children identified "old" pictures sooner than "new" pictures) was equal for children of all ages. Also, no relation was found between how many pictures children of any age recognized (their explicit memory) and priming effects (their implicit memory). In other words, although children exhibited substantial age differences in explicit memory, no developmental differences were found in implicit memory.

One interesting study of implicit memory involved showing 9- and 10-year-olds pictures of preschool children, including some who had been their classmates 4 and 5 years earlier (Newcombe & Fox, 1994). Children were asked to determine whether each picture they were shown was that of a former classmate (an explicit recognition memory task); changes in the electrical conductance of their skin were also recorded. Greater changes in skin conductance for former classmates' pictures relative to pictures of unfamiliar children was used as a reflection of implicit recognition memory (that is, requiring no conscious awareness). Not surprisingly, children's performance was relatively poor on both the explicit and implicit tasks (although greater than expected by chance, indicating some memory of both the explicit and implicit types). However, no difference in skin conductance was found between children who performed well on the explicit task and those who performed poorly. This suggests that even the children whose performance on the explicit memory task was no greater than chance still "recognized," implicitly, as many of their former classmates as those children who had performed better. This pattern of data indicates that some children "remembered" (implicitly) more than they "knew" (explicitly). Eunhui Lie and Nora Newcombe (1999), using a different method of implicit memory, reported similar results of greater implicit than explicit recognition of former classmates.

These findings suggest that implicit memory is an early developing ability, perhaps more related to the development of semantic memory than to episodic memory (Tulving, 1987). Some theorists have speculated that implicit memory is under the control of automatic rather than effortful processes (Jacoby, 1991) and, following the theorizing of Lynn Hasher and Rose Zacks (1979), that these processes show little development across childhood (Newcombe et al., 2000). Actually, the procedures used to assess memory in infants (habituation/dishabituation and conditioning techniques) likely are more similar in nature to the tests used to assess implicit memory in older children than they are to the tests used to assess explicit memory. Marshall Haith (1993) argued that researchers need to bridge the gap between cognition in infancy and cognition in childhood by developing new research techniques and theories, and research using implicit memory techniques might be that bridge. In this spirit, Jayne Ausley and Robert Guttentag (1993) suggested that "research using indirect [implicit] methods of memory assessment with children probably does provide a real avenue of continuity with infancy research, because these tests do not require an awareness of the previous occurrence of events for successful performance" (p. 254).

# THE DEVELOPMENT OF EVENT MEMORY

Much of what we remember is for *events*, things that happen to us during the course of everyday life. Unlike implicit memory, **event memory** is explicit. We are aware that we are remembering. For most aspects of event memory, however, we did not specifically *try* to remember the event when we experienced it. In other words, for most event memories, the encoding of the event was unintentional. Because we did not intend to learn new information, our unintentional memory is not influenced by the use of deliberate encoding strategies, which accounts for much of the age differences observed on intentional memory tasks. (See discussion of strategic memory in Chapter 7.) Rather, memory representations can be laid down involuntarily as part of ongoing activity, and several researchers have speculated that, in some cases, such "naturalistic learning" could actually produce higher levels of memory performance than would more deliberate memorization attempts, especially for young children (Istomina, 1975; Piaget & Inhelder, 1973).

The issue at hand is when and how children remember the experiences of their everyday lives. How are these memories organized? How long do they last? And how is it that children acquire them?

A young child must master many aspects of memory if he or she is to remember important events. First, an event must be attended to and perceived. Then, the child must make some sense of that event so that it can be represented in his or her mind and recalled later on. If a child doesn't attend to the important aspects of an event or cannot make sense of what he or she experienced, there is really nothing to remember. One important thing to realize is that young children pay attention to different aspects of events than adults do, and they do not necessarily know which aspects of an event are important and which are trivial. For example, as adults, we know that the purpose of a baseball game is to watch the players on the field play ball. We automatically pay less attention to the field maintenance staff, the players on the bench, and most of the other spectators. However, young children don't always select the "right" things to pay attention to. At a baseball game, they might spend more time watching the hot dog vendors, the batboys, and the second-base umpire. What they remember of the game will thus be very different than what an older child or adult remembers.

It is also worth noting that event memory is *constructive* in nature. Event memory does not involve the verbatim recall of a list of facts or the memorization of lines, like an actor in a play (although children, and adults, do retain some specific, or verbatim, aspects of events; see Brainerd & Reyna, 2005). Rather, we recall the gist of the message, and in the process, we transform what was actually said or done. That is, we interpret our experiences as a function of what we already know about the world, and our memory for events is colored by previous knowledge (Bartlett, 1932). Memory, in general, is not like a tape recorder. True, we sometimes do retain verbatim information and use that information to construct stories. But the tales we tell about our lives are best thought of as constructions, based on our actual experiences, our background knowledge of the things we are trying to remember, our information-processing abilities, and the social context in which the remembering is being done.

## Script-Based Memory

What is it that young children remember? One thing they tend to remember well is recurring events—what typically happens on a day-to-day basis (Hudson & Mayhew, 2009). Katherine Nelson and her colleagues have demonstrated that preschool children tend to organize events in terms of **scripts**, which are a form of schematic organization with real-world events organized in terms of their causal and temporal characteristics (Nelson, 1993, 1996; see also Fivush, 2008). For example, a "fast-food restaurant" script might involve driving to the restaurant, entering the restaurant, standing in line, ordering, paying the cashier, taking the food to the table, eating, and then throwing away the trash before leaving. Children learn what "usually happens" in a situation, such as what happens during snack time at school, a birthday party, or breakfast, and they remember novel information in the context of these familiar events.

Substantial research demonstrates that even very young children organize information temporally in a scriptlike fashion (see Bauer, 2007; Fivush, Kuebli, & Clubb, 1992) and that such schematic organization for events doesn't change appreciably into adulthood (for reviews of this literature, see Fivush & Hudson, 1990; Nelson, 1996). Perhaps even more impressive is evidence that even preverbal infants use temporal order to remember events. For example, Patricia Bauer and Jean Mandler (1989, 1992) tested infants ranging in age from 11.5 to 20 months on imitation tasks. The toddlers were shown a sequence of events (for example, putting a ball in a cup, inverting a smaller cup on top of the larger one, and shaking the cups) and, later, given the opportunity to interact with the materials again. Bauer and Mandler reported that the children re-enacted the sequence of events in the same temporal order they had been shown. This finding argues for the existence of a script-style memory organization long before children are able to talk.

Young children's tendencies to organize information following familiar scripts seem to result in their tendency *not* to remember much in the way of specific (that is, nonscript) information. For example, Robyn Fivush and Nina Hamond (1990) asked 2.5-year-old children specific questions about recent special events, such as a trip to the beach, a camping trip, or a ride on an airplane. Rather than recalling the novel aspects of these special events, the children were more apt to focus on what adults would consider routine information. Take, for instance, the following conversation reported by Fivush and Hamond between an adult and a child about a camping trip. The child first recalled sleeping outside, which is unusual, but then remembered very routine things:

*Interviewer:* You slept outside in a tent? Wow, that sounds like a lot of fun.

*Child:* And then we waked up and eat dinner. First we eat dinner, then go to bed, and then wake up and eat breakfast.

*Interviewer:* What else did you do when you went camping? What did you do when you got up, after breakfast?

*Child:* Umm, in the night, and went to sleep. (p. 231)

It seems strange that a child would talk about such routine tasks as waking up, eating, and going to bed when so many new and exciting things must have happened on the camping trip. But the younger the child, the more he or she might need to embed novel events into familiar routines. According to Fivush and Hamond, everything is new to 2-year-olds, and they are in the process of learning about their surroundings.

Why should young children's memory be so tied to recurring events? One way to answer this question is to ask what the function of memory is for young children. Katherine Nelson (1996, 2005) has taken such a functional view, arguing that memory has an adaptive value of permitting children to predict the likelihood of events in the future. Basically, by remembering the likelihood of an event's occurrence in the past, one can predict its likelihood of occurring in the future. From this perspective, some events (recurring ones) are more likely to be remembered than are others (single events). According to Nelson (1996):

> Memory for a single, one-time occurrence of some event, if the event were not traumatic or life-threatening, would not be especially useful, given its low probability. Thus, a memory system might be optimally designed to retain information about frequent and recurrent events—and to discard information about unrepeated events—and to integrate new information about variations in recurrent events into a general knowledge system. (p. 174)

Nelson makes the point that memory for routine events allows infants to anticipate events and to take a part in (and, possibly, control of) these events. There is no such pay-off for a novel event; thus, it makes sense to forget it.

Children do, however, eventually remember specific events, not just some generalized event memory. In fact, although 2- and 3-year-old children may rely heavily on scripts, they have been shown to remember specific information for extended periods (Hamond & Fivush, 1991; Howe, 2000). Hamond and Fivush (1991) presented research that demonstrates how long memories for specific events can last for young children. They interviewed 3- and 4-year-old children 6 or 18 months after they had gone to Disney World. All children recalled a great deal of information about their trip, even after 18 months. The older children recalled more details and required fewer prompts (cues) to generate recall than did the younger children, and children who talked more about the trip with their parents recalled more information about the trip. Nevertheless, recall for this single, special event was quite good, even though it did not fall nicely into a familiar routine.

## The Role of Parents in "Teaching" Children to Remember

Hamond and Fivush's research is an early example of an investigation into the role that parents play in "teaching" children how to remember (see Haden & Ornstein, 2009). As it turns out, parents, especially mothers (but also sometimes fathers; see Fivush et al., 2009), and their children spend a good deal of time reminiscing about the past, and individual differences in how this is done are related to how well children remember past events. This suggests that parents can play an important role in children's early remembering, a point that has been made by several theorists (Fivush, 2009; Haden & Ornstein, 2009; Ornstein & Haden, 2001) and that is consistent with the theorizing of Lev Vygotsky (1978) and the sociocultural perspective discussed in Chapter 3 (see the discussion of shared remembering; Gauvain, 2001). For example, Judith Hudson (1990) argued that children learn how to remember by interacting with their parents, that "remembering can be viewed as an activity that is at first jointly carried out by parent and child and then later performed by the child alone" (p. 172). In most families, Hudson proposed, parents begin talking with young children about things that happened in the past. They ask questions such as "Where did we go this morning?," "What did we see at the zoo?," "Who went with us?," and "What else did we see?" From these interchanges, children learn that the important facts to remember about events are the whos, whats, whens, and wheres of their experiences. Through these conversations with their parents, they are learning to notice the important details of their experiences and to store their memories in an organized way so that they can be easily retrieved when needed. Parents also often discuss future events with children (for example, an upcoming trip to Disney World), and when they do, particularly when they include photographs of what they may see, children later remember more about the event (Salmon et al., 2008).

In studying these interchanges between parents and preschoolers, Hudson found that parents do more than just ask the right questions. They also give the right answers when the child can't remember, showing children how the conversation should go. Young children generally show low levels of free recall when remembering an event, but they can remember much more when specific cues are presented. In fact, Fivush and Hamond (1990) stated that "young children recall as much information as older children do, but they need more memory questions in order to do so" (p. 244). By asking repeated questions to children, adults are structuring the conversation, showing children how "remembering" is done. Moreover, by providing the missing information, children also learn that their parents will help them out when they can't seem to retrieve the information called for.

A good example of this was a conversation I overheard while riding on the Metro in Washington, D.C. A young mother and her 19-month-old daughter, Tanya, were returning home after a trip to the zoo.

*Mother:*  Tanya, what did we see at the zoo?

*Tanya:*  Elphunts.

*Mother:*  That's right! We saw elephants. What else?

*Tanya:*  [shrugs and looks at her mother]

*Mother:*  Panda bear? Did we see a panda bear?

*Tanya:*  [smiles and nods her head]

| | |
|---|---|
| *Mother:* | Can you say "panda bear?" |
| *Tanya:* | Panda bear. |
| *Mother:* | Good! Elephants and panda bears. What else? |
| *Tanya:* | Elphunts. |
| *Mother:* | That's right, elephants. And also a gorilla. |
| *Tanya:* | Go-rilla! |

Hilary Ratner (1984) illustrated the importance of these parent-child conversations. She observed 2- and 3-year-old children interacting with their parents at home and recorded the number of times the mother asked the child about past events. She then tested the children's memory abilities. The children who showed better memory abilities at that time, and also a year later, were those whose mothers had asked them many questions about past events. Other research has shown that mothers who provide their preschool children with more evaluations of their memory performance, and who use more elaborative language when talking about memory with their children, have children who remember past events better than do children with less elaborative mothers (Cleveland & Reese, 2005; Fivush, Haden, & Reese, 2006; Wenner et al., 2008). That is, after making a statement about some previous event (for example, "Then we ate the cake"), *elaborative* mothers are more likely to provide comments that confirm or negate a child's statement (such as "That's right," "Yes," or "No") than less elaborative mothers are. Recent research has even shown that preschool children whose mothers used more elaborative language in talking with them about past events had earlier memories as adolescents than did children with less elaborative mothers (Jack et al., 2009).

In other research, mothers and their young children engaged in three novel events, one when children were 30 months, a second at 36 months, and a third at 42 months (Haden et al., 2001; Hedrick et al., 2009). For example, in one study (Haden et al., 2001), children were tested for their memory of each event at 1 day and at 3 weeks following each episode. The events were carried out in children's homes and involved the investigator setting up props and asking the mother and child to carry out an elaborate make-believe activity. For example, for the "camping event," the mother and child first loaded supplies in a backpack, hiked to a fishing pond, caught a fish with a fishing rod and net, and then moved to their campsite, where they found sleeping bags, pots, pans, and utensils, which they used to cook and eat their food. The frequency with which mothers and children jointly carried out these activities, and the degree to which language was involved during the execution of the task, were observed and related to children's subsequent memory performance. First, and not surprisingly, children's overall memory performance increased with age and was greater for the 1-day delay than the 3-week delay. Most pertinent for our discussion here was the relation between mother-child activities during the event and children's later recollections. Features of the events (for example, putting food in the backpack) that were jointly handled and talked about by the mother and child were better remembered than were features that were handled and talked about only by the mother, or that were jointly handled by the mother and child but not discussed. This result clearly points out the important role of joint activity guided by the mother, including the use of language, in fostering young children's event memory.

The results of recent research point to the interactive role of parents and children in the process of "learning" how to remember. Thus, remembering becomes a cultural phenomenon, consistent with the ideas of Vygotsky and others who propose a socio-cultural perspective of development (see Chapter 3). Parents teach children how to construct narratives (that is, create stories) in which to embed the important things that happen to them. This in turn allows children to share their experiences with others. This is a practice that may vary somewhat, however, between cultures. For example, Mary Mullen and Soonhyung Yi (1995) examined how frequently Korean and American mothers talked to their 3-year-old children about past events and reported that the American mothers talked about the past with their young children nearly three times as often as the Korean mothers did. This is consistent with reports that American children talk about past events more than Korean children do (Han, Leichtman, & Wang, 1998) and that American adults report earlier childhood memories than Korean adults (Mullen, 1994). This suggests that early language experience contributes to the onset of autobiographical memory, consistent with the argument made by Katherine Nelson (1996, 2005).

It is also worth noting that there are differences in the event memories reported by girls and boys. When asked to remember information about earlier experienced events, girls tend to remember more information than boys do (Reese, Haden, & Fivush, 1996), but not always (see Lewis, 1999; Weber & Strube, 1999). For example, in a study by Elaine Reese, Catherine Haden and Robin Fivush (1996), children between the ages of 40 and 70 months participated in several sessions during which their mothers, fathers, or an experimenter asked them to recollect about salient events that had occurred in the recent past. Regardless of who interviewed the children (that is, their mothers, fathers, or the experimenter), girls remembered more details about past events than boys did. These gender differences were related to ways in which parents conversed with their sons and daughters about the past. Girls generally received more evaluations of their memory responses than boys. These findings suggest that the roots of females' greater event memory lie early in development and might result, in part, because of the way parents talk to boys and girls during attempts at remembering, with daughters being encouraged to embellish their memories more than sons are. Other research indicates that mothers talk to their male and female preschool children about different topics. For example, Dorothy Flannagan, Lynne Baker-Ward, and Loranel Graham (1995) reported that in their conversations about school, mothers talked to their sons more about learning and instruction, whereas they tended to talk to their daughters more about social interactions. Thus, there are differences both in how parents talk to boys and girls about remembering events and in what they are asked to remember, both of which seemingly affect what and how well children remember.

It's hard to minimize the significance of autobiographical memory and to think that there may have been a time in our lives when it didn't exist. Our recollections about what we've experienced in the past define for us who we are and how we interact with others. But autobiographical memory develops over the course of infancy and early childhood. In fact, Alison Gopnik (2009) proposed that although 2- and 3-year-old children can remember specific events, a reflection of episodic memory, they lack true autobiographical memory. According to Gopnik, "[T]hey do not experience their lives as a single time line stretching back into the past and forward into the future. They don't send themselves backward and forward along this time line as adults do ... Instead, the memories images, and thoughts pop in and out of consciousness as they are cued by present events, or by other memories, images, and thoughts" (pp. 153–154, see also Bogdan, 2010).

# CHILDREN AS EYEWITNESSES

One topic in event memory that has attracted substantial research attention concerns the reliability of children as eyewitnesses. How reliable is children's testimony? How much do they remember, and for how long? How suggestible are children? Can a persuasive interviewer make children report things that didn't really happen, and can faulty interviewing techniques actually result in children believing they were victims of (or witnesses to) a crime when they were not? These are questions not only for the justice system but also for psychologists because they deal with the nature of children's developing memory systems and the construction of a particular kind of event memory.

In the following sections, I review research and theory into children as eyewitnesses and the degree to which their testimonies and their memories are subject to change. In the first section, I review age differences in children's eyewitness reports when no one is trying to change their minds. That is, what do children remember, and what factors influence their memory, when they are asked to report what they witnessed or experienced? In the second section, I examine the large literature on age differences in suggestibility. How susceptible are children to suggestion, and to what extent will they change their answers or their memory representations as a result of suggestive questioning?

First, however, let me provide a general framework for making sense of this research literature. Children's eyewitness testimony and suggestibility, like event memory in general, are influenced by a host of interacting factors. Which factors are most important? Can we specify how the various factors will interact to predict performance? And can we be confident enough in our conclusions to inform the legal system? Marc Lindberg (1991; Lindberg, Keiffer, & Thomas, 2000) has suggested three major categories of factors that we should consider in evaluating studies of children's eyewitness memory and suggestibility (see Figure 8-6). The first category in Lindberg's scheme is *memory processes,* and these concern the different memory operations of encoding, storage, and retrieval. *Encoding* refers to children's representation of an event and how children respond to information they receive before the event. For example, how are children influenced by being told that someone they are about to meet is a "bad boy" or prone to breaking things? *Storage* refers to information provided to participants after witnessing an event. This may be in the form of suggestive questions (for example, "He spilled chocolate milk over the book, didn't he?"), or postevent information, which includes any experiences that intervene between witnessing an event and recollecting it. *Retrieval* refers to manipulations at the time of testing. For instance, how is memory tested? With open-ended, free-recall questions (for example, "Tell me everything you can remember about what happened at the park last week"), cued-recall questions (such as "Tell me what color was the boy's t-shirt"), or recognition (for instance, "Look at these pictures. Was one of these the boy who took the bike?")? How are these questions posed?

Lindberg refers to the second category of his taxonomy as *focus of the study,* by which he means the type of information that is being assessed. For example, is the

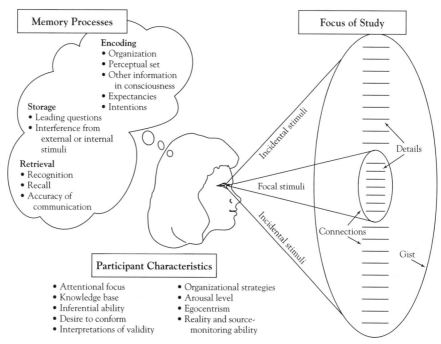

FIGURE **8-6**

Three major interacting classes of variables in interpreting children's eyewitness memory and suggestibility.

Source: Lindberg, M. A. (1991). An interactive approach to assessing the suggestibility and testimony of eyewitnesses. In J. Doris (Ed.), *The suggestibility of children's recollections: Implications for eyewitness testimony* (pp. 47–55). Copyright © 1991 by the American Psychological Association. Reprinted with permission.

interviewer concerned with psychologically and legally central (or focal) information (who did what to whom, which is critical in determining innocence or guilt in court), or is peripheral (incidental) information (for example, "What color pants was the man wearing?" or "How tall was the girl?) also important? Similarly, is the memory for gist information or for details, or verbatim information (as in fuzzy-trace theory's description of memory traces; see Brainerd & Reyna, 2005)?

And, finally, one must consider *participant factors*. Here, developmental level and the associated social, emotional, and cognitive skills of children are important. Also of potential importance are personality characteristics of the participants, their level of stress at the time of the event (or at the time of retrieval), their past experiences with a situation, and their more general knowledge of the things they witness. No single study will include all relevant factors from this taxonomy, but it is worthwhile to keep these categories in mind if for no other reason than to remember that understanding children's eyewitness memory is not child's play.

## Age Differences in Children's Eyewitness Memories

Although there is much variability in methods from study to study, most investigations of children's eyewitness memory begin by showing children a video of some event, having them observe some activity in their school, or involving them personally in an activity. Usually, children are not told that they will be asked to remember what they view. Later, often minutes after the event but in some cases days or weeks later, children are asked what they remembered (for example, "Tell me what happened in the video you saw" or "Tell me what happened in your classroom yesterday morning"). This is essentially a request for free recall. Typically, children will then be asked some more specific recall questions (for example, "What was the girl in the video wearing?" or "What did the man who came into your class yesterday morning do?"), which constitute cued recall. Often, children will be asked some recognition memory questions (for example, "Was the girl wearing a white t-shirt?" or "Did the man play with the teddy bear?"). In some studies, the same or similar questions may be repeated, and in others, questions are often intentionally suggestive, sometimes directing children to a "correct" answer (such as "Did the man play nicely with the teddy bear?") and sometimes leading to an "incorrect" answer (such as "Did the man rip the book?"). There are, of course, many variations, depending on the purpose of the study, but in most cases, children's memories for specific events are probed, often with the purpose of seeing how likely children are to change their answers or to be swayed by leading questions posed by an interviewer (see Brainerd & Reyna, 2005; Bruck, Ceci, & Principe, 2006).

### How Much Do Children Remember, and How Accurate Are They?

First, how much do children of different ages remember shortly after witnessing an event? When examining immediate (that is, within the same experimental session) free recall, substantial age differences are found (Ornstein, Gordon, & Larus, 1992; Poole & White, 1995). How much is remembered differs from study to study, but preschool children typically recall only a small proportion of information from an event in answer to free-recall questions. Although young children remember very little information, what they do recall is highly accurate and central to the event—if there are no suggestions or coaching (Goodman, Aman, & Hirschman, 1987; Poole & White, 1995). For example, in a video involving a boy and a girl in a park, with the boy stealing a bike, young children typically recall the bike theft but are much less apt than older children or adults to mention in their free recall descriptions of the participants, characteristics of the bicycle, or things about the setting (Cassel & Bjorklund, 1995; Cassel, Roebers, & Bjorklund, 1996). Thus, young children's free recall is typically low, accurate, and about central aspects of an event.

When children are provided general cues (for example, "Tell me what the girl looked like"), they recall more information, as you would expect. However, in addition to remembering more *correct* facts, they also tend to remember some *incorrect* "facts" as well, reducing the overall accuracy of their recall (Bjorklund et al., 1998; Lindberg et al., 2000).

When children do falsely remember information to cues, does this actually change their memory representations? Will these children, when interviewed later, remember this misinformation again? The answer seems to depend on several factors, including the amount of time between the initial and later interviews. With delays of only several weeks or less, children seem *not* to recall their earlier false memories (Cassel & Bjorklund, 1995). But, when delays are longer (Poole, 1995) or when children are merely asked to recognize rather than to recall information

(Brainerd & Reyna, 1996; Brainerd, Reyna, & Brandse, 1995), these false memories not only tend to persist, they might even be *more* resistant to forgetting than true memories (Brainerd & Mojardin, 1999).

These counterintuitive findings have been interpreted in terms of fuzzy-trace theory (Brainerd & Poole, 1997; Brainerd & Reyna, 2002, 2005; Brainerd et al., 2008; see also Chapter 5). According to fuzzy-trace theory, correct recognition is based on literal, or verbatim, memory traces, which are more susceptible to forgetting than are less-exact fuzzy, or gist, traces. In contrast, false recognition must be based on gist traces because there are no verbatim traces for false memories. Gist traces are more resistant to forgetting than verbatim traces are, so the gist-based false memories become more likely to be remembered over long delays than the more easily forgettable, verbatim-based true memories.

### How Long Do Memories Last?

Although most studies have not assessed the long-term recollections of children, several have investigated children's memories of specific events for periods ranging from several weeks to 2 years (Flin et al., 1992; Salmon & Pipe, 1997). This is important for the legal system, given that children are sometimes asked in forensic interviews to remember events they witnessed weeks, months, or even years earlier (Paz-Alonso et al., 2009; Pipe & Salmon, 2009). Although the results of these studies are not always consistent, a picture emerges of greater age differences in the accuracy of recall with increasing delays. *Accuracy*, as used here, does not refer to "how much" was remembered but, rather, to the ratio of incorrect-to-correct information remembered. Children who recall very little, for example, but correctly recall what they do remember, have perfect accuracy. In contrast, a child who recalls a substantial amount of both correct (accurate) and incorrect (inaccurate) information might demonstrate more recall but less accuracy.

First, with delays of about 1 month or less, children of all ages and adults remember about the same proportion of accurate and inaccurate information as they did originally (Baker-Ward et al., 1993; Cassel & Bjorklund, 1995). Age differences in recall accuracy are found with longer delays, however. For example, Rhona Flin and her colleagues (1992) reported that both 6-year-olds and adults recalled as much correct information after a 5-month delay as they had originally, but that recall by the 6-year-olds was less accurate than recall by the adults. Thus, the ratio of incorrect-to-correct recall became higher for the children than for the adults during the 5-month period (see also Poole & White, 1993). The conclusion from these studies is that age differences in accuracy are found, but only when memory is assessed after extended delays. Fuzzy-trace theory (Brainerd & Reyna, 2005; Brainerd et al., 2008; see also Chapter 5) explains these findings by the greater rate of trace decay of verbatim (exact) traces relative to gist traces. Verbatim traces, favored by younger children, deteriorate more rapidly than the gist, or fuzzy, traces favored by older children, resulting in greater loss of information over delays and corresponding increases in erroneous recall. These are the same arguments that have been used to explain the phenomenon of infantile amnesia (see earlier discussion). The verbatim traces favored by infants and young children are especially susceptible to deterioration, making it highly unlikely that these memories would be available years after their original encoding (Leichtman & Ceci, 1993).

### Factors Influencing Children's Eyewitness Memory

A host of factors other than age and length of delay have been found to influence the amount and accuracy of children's eyewitness memories. For instance, children with high IQs show higher levels of eyewitness recall than do their peers with lower IQs (Roebers & Schneider, 2001); children given incentives to be accurate in their recall are, indeed, more accurate than children not given incentives (Roebers, Moga, & Schneider, 2001); intermediate levels of stress (when experiencing the event) seem to facilitate recall of an event relative to overly high or low levels of stress (Bahrick et al., 1998); and children having emotionally supportive mothers who discuss upcoming medical procedures with them recall less inaccurate information about the procedure than children having less sympathetic or talkative mothers (Goodman et al., 1994; 1997). Two sets of factors that have substantial influences on children's eyewitness reports are children's background knowledge for the event (Ornstein et al., 2006) and the characteristics of the interview (Ceci, Bruck, & Battin, 2000), each of which I will discuss in greater detail below.

**The role of knowledge.**  We saw in Chapter 7 that knowledge has a potent role in children's working memory and strategic memory, so we should not be surprised that it also plays an important role in eyewitness memory (Elischberger, 2005; Ornstein & Greenhoot, 2000). For example, children's recollections of stressful and invasive medical procedures are related to their knowledge of the procedures; children who know more about the procedure remember more accurate information (Clubb et al., 1993; Ornstein et al., 2006) and recall less inaccurate information (Goodman et al., 1994). Yet, although knowing a lot about an event (that is, how actions in an event are "supposed to go") is usually associated with increased memory accuracy, knowledge can be a double-edged sword. For example, in a study of 4- and 6-year-old children's recall of a mock physical examination, Peter Ornstein and his colleagues (1998) included some typical, expected features in the exam (for example, the doctor listened to the children's hearts with a stethoscope and looked into their ears), but they also included some atypical, unexpected features (for example, the doctor measured children's head circumference and used alcohol to wipe their belly buttons). In addition, some expected features were omitted from the exams (for example, measuring blood pressure and looking in children's mouths). Children were interviewed about the exam both immediately and after a 12-week delay. They were first asked open-ended questions (for example, "Tell me what happened during your checkup" and "Tell me what the doctor did to check you"), followed by increasingly specific questions (for instance, "Did the doctor check any parts of your face?" and "Did the doctor check your eyes?"). In addition to being asked questions about what really did happen during the exam, children were also asked specific questions about things that did not happen. For example, children for whom the doctor did not check their ears would be asked, "Did the doctor look into your ears?" Some of the questions referred to events that are likely to occur in an exam, such as looking into children's ears, whereas others were for events that were unlikely to occur (for example, "Did the doctor give you some stitches?").

How did the children do? The results for the 12-week assessment of this study are shown in Figures 8-7 and 8-8. The first figure reports the percentage of correct responses for the 4- and 6-year-old children for the present-typical and present-atypical features (that is, aspects of the exam that children actually experienced) for the open-ended question and for the specific questions. As can be seen, children of both ages recalled more typical features correctly than atypical features, for both types of questions. This reflects the positive effects of knowledge base. This was not the first medical exam for any of the children, and they presumably had a script for what usually happens in such an exam. As a result, features that are typically found in medical exams, based on children's past experiences, were more likely to be remembered than atypical features. But there was a negative side to knowledge, and this is reflected in the results displayed in Figure 8-8. Correct denials (the dark portion of the bars in Figure 8-8) refer to children correctly stating that an event did not happen. (Did the doctor give you stitches? *No.*) As can be seen, children were more likely to correctly reject these nonevents for the atypical features. False alarms (the light portion of the bars in Figure 8-8) refer to children *incorrectly* agreeing that an event happened when it did not. (Did the doctor look into your ears? *Yes.*) Here, both the 4- and 6-year-old children were more likely to erroneously say that these events did, indeed, happen when they were typical rather than atypical features of a physical exam. Knowing what usually happens caused children to falsely remember what did happen, at least when their memory was tested 12 weeks after the event.

**Characteristics of the interview.** Not surprisingly, how children are interviewed can greatly affect what they remember and the accuracy of their recollections (Bruck et al., 2006; Ceci et al., 2000). The type of questions asked, for example, influences what children remember. As I noted earlier, young children tend to recall relatively little to open-ended, free-recall questions ("Tell me everything that happened when the man came into your classroom"), but what they do recall tends to be highly accurate.

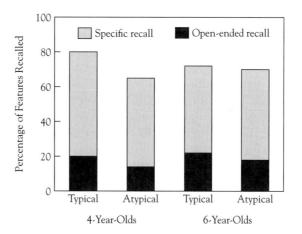

FIGURE **8-7**

Percentage of present-typical and present-atypical features recalled correctly in response to open-ended and specific questions for 4- and 6-year-old children, 12-week assessment.

Source: Ornstein, P. A., & A. F. Greenhoot, "Remembering the distant past: Implications of research on children's memory for the recovered memory debate." In D. F. Bjorklund (Ed.), *False-memory creation in children and adults: Theory, research, and implications.* © 2000 Lawrence Erlbaum Associates, Inc. Reprinted with permission. Based on data in Ornstein, P. A., K. A. Merritt, L. Baker-Ward, E. Furtado, B. N. Gordon, & G. F. Principe (1998). Children's knowledge, expectation, and long-term retention. *Applied Cognitive Psychology, 12,* 387–405.

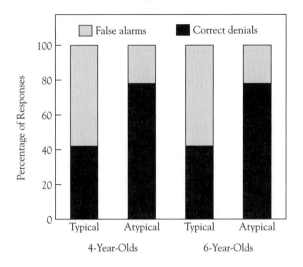

FIGURE **8-8**

Percentage of absent-typical and absent-atypical features to which children responded with correct denials and false alarms for 4- and 6-year-old children, 12-week assessment.

Source: Ornstein, P. A., & A. F. Greenhoot, "Remembering the distant past: Implications of research on children's memory for the recovered memory debate." In D. F. Bjorklund (Ed.), *False-memory creation in children and adults: Theory, research, and implications.* © 2000 Lawrence Erlbaum Associates, Inc. Reprinted with permission. Based on data in Ornstein, P. A., K. A. Merritt, L. Baker-Ward, E. Furtado, B. N. Gordon, & G. F. Principe (1998). Children's knowledge, expectation, and long-term retention. *Applied Cognitive Psychology, 12,* 387–405.

Children recall more when given neutral cues, but the accuracy of their recall declines (that is, they also recall more false information).

Interviewer characteristics, such as whether the interviewer is warm and supportive or high status (for example, a police officer), influences the accuracy of children's memory, as does the use of any special recall-facilitating technique or props. For example, many forensic interviews make use of anatomically correct dolls when questioning children who are suspected of being victims of sexual abuse. Does the use of such dolls increase the accuracy of children's reports? Maggie Bruck and her colleagues (1995) interviewed 3-year-old children following a routine medical exam (that is, these children were *not* suspected child-abuse victims). Half of the children received a genital exam by the doctor, and half did not. Immediately after the examination, children were shown an anatomically correct doll and were asked, with the interviewer pointing to the genital area of the doll, "Did the doctor touch you here?" Only about half of the children who did receive the genital exam answered correctly, whereas about half of those who did not receive a genital exam also said "yes." When simply asked to "show on the doll" how the doctor had touched their genitals or buttocks, only 25% of the children who had received the genital exam responded correctly, and 50% of the children who were not given such an exam falsely showed anal or genital touching. Similar results have been reported by other researchers (Gordon et al., 1993). Other research indicates that interviewers who use dolls and other objects to aid recall ask fewer open-ended questions and are less likely to stay on topic than interviewers who do not use such objects (Melinder et al., 2009). Findings such as these call into question the use of anatomically correct dolls, at least with young children, indicating that the dolls themselves may cause children to "make accusations" of abuse when no abuse occurred.

How warm or supportive an interview is can also influence the accuracy of children's recollections. For instance, children remember more correct information, and less incorrect information, when they are questioned by a warm and supportive interviewer (Quas et al., 2007). In one study, 4- to 6-year-old children who had high levels of stress showed increased levels of recall accuracy when they were questioned by an emotionally supportive interviewer but reduced levels of accuracy when questioned by a nonsupportive interviewer (Quas, Bauer, & Boyce, 2004).

## Age Differences in Suggestibility

Perhaps the single most investigated area of eyewitness testimony in both the adult and child literatures concerns suggestibility (for reviews, see Brainerd & Reyna, 2005; Bruck et al., 2006; Ceci & Bruck, 1998). To what extent are children susceptible to suggestion? Research has shown that people of all ages report more inaccurate information when misleading questions are posed (that is, questions suggesting incorrect "facts"). The questions for developmentalists, and for the legal profession, include are children more suggestible than adults, what factors influence their suggestibility, and how to maximize memory accuracy and minimize suggestibility.

The general consensus regarding the question of whether children are more suggestible than adults seems to be "yes." In an extensive review of the early literature, Stephen Ceci and Maggie Bruck (1993) concluded, "There do appear to be significant age differences in suggestibility, with preschool children being disproportionately more vulnerable to suggestion than either school-age children or adults" (p. 431). Most investigators looking for age differences in suggestibility have found it, although in varying degrees and sometimes only under certain circumstances (Ackil & Zaragoza, 1995; Bruck et al., 1995; see also Brainerd et al., 2008).

### How Do Children Respond to Misleading Questions?

Let me provide an example from research that asked children different types of suggestive (leading) questions. William Cassel and I (1995) showed groups of 6- and 8-year-old children and college adults a brief video of a boy and a girl in a park, with the boy eventually taking the girl's bike without permission. Participants were interviewed 15 minutes after viewing the video and then again 1 week and 1 month later. During these later interviews, participants were given either sets of misleading questions, suggesting things that did not happen (for example, "The girl said it was okay for the boy to take her bike, didn't she?"), or positive-leading questions, suggesting things that did, indeed, happen (for example, "The girl told the boy not to take the bike, didn't she?"). Figures 8-9 and 8-10 present some of the results for the 1-week interview. As can be seen, the 6- and 8-year-olds tended to follow the lead of the interviewer, agreeing both with the misleading questions (see Figure 8-9), thus getting more wrong than the adults did, and with the positive-leading questions (see Figure 8-10), thus getting more right than the adults did. In fact, as can be seen in Figure 8-9, both the 6- and 8-year-olds had more incorrect than correct responses to the misleading questions, whereas the reverse was true for the adults.

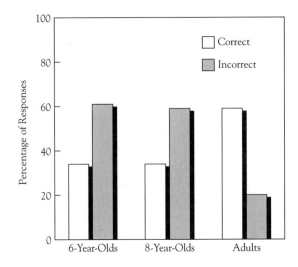

FIGURE **8-9**

Percentage of correct and incorrect responses by age to misleading questions.

Source: Based on data from Cassel, W. S., & Bjorklund, D. F. (1995). Developmental patterns of eyewitness memory and suggestibility: An ecologically based short-term longitudinal study. *Law & Human Behavior, 19*, 507–532.

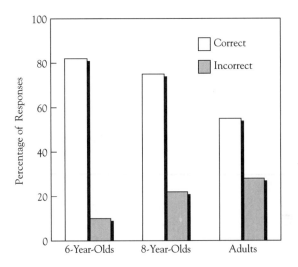

FIGURE **8-10**

Percentage of correct and incorrect responses by age to positive-leading questions.

Source: Based on data from Cassel, W. S., & Bjorklund, D. F. (1995). Developmental patterns of eyewitness memory and suggestibility: An ecologically based short-term longitudinal study. *Law & Human Behavior, 19*, 507–532.

In the 1-month interview, participants were first asked sets of leading questions by one examiner suggesting one interpretation (either misleading or positive-leading) and then immediately thereafter were asked a second set of questions by a second examiner, asking for the *opposite* interpretation (misleading if positive-leading had been asked first, and vice versa). How would children respond to the same question they had just been asked, but with an opposite "spin"? The answer is that children often changed their answers. For example, when asked about the color of the bike, 71% of the 6-year-olds who had agreed with the suggestion of the first interviewer later changed their answers to comply with the suggestion of the second interviewer. The corresponding percentages for the 8-year-old children and adults were 53% and 35%, respectively. For the more critical central question—that is, whether the girl had given the boy permission to take her bike—42% of the 6-year-old children changed their answers in response to the second interviewer, whereas only 7% of 8-year-olds and 12% of adults did so. These results make it clear that younger children are highly susceptible to the suggestion of an adult interviewer, modifying their answers, it seems, to suit the desires of whomever is interviewing them.

Yet, despite the ease with which young children can be led to give answers consistent with the suggestion of any adult, are their memories actually changed as well? Research that has asked children misleading questions over repeated interviews indicates that such repetition will, indeed, cause some children to report the incorrect information in later tests of free recall and recognition, particularly information that is peripheral, or incidental, to the event. Such findings indicate that suggestive questioning changes not only children's answers but also their memories. However, in many other cases, children who follow the lead of an interviewer fail to incorporate that misinformation, especially information that is central to the event, in their subsequent free recall of the event, suggesting that it is far easier to change children's answers with such questions than it is to change their minds (see Bjorklund, Brown, & Bjorklund, 2002).

In an early investigation, Gail Goodman and Allison Clarke-Stewart (1991) illustrated the extent to which young children's reports of a witnessed event can be swayed and the extent to which they will stick to their interpretation. Preschool children watched a man, posing as a janitor, who either cleaned and arranged some toys, including a doll, or played with the toys in a somewhat rough and inappropriately suggestive manner. About an hour later, the janitor's "boss" interviewed the children about what they had seen. Of primary concern here is the situation in which children watched the janitor merely cleaning the toys, although it was suggested to them that he had actually been playing with the toys improperly instead of doing his job. If a child in this situation initially did not agree with the interviewer's suggestion, subsequent leading questions were asked, with each question becoming increasingly stronger in its suggestion (that is, more explicitly suggesting misbehavior). Two-thirds of these children eventually followed the interviewers' suggestions, even though the suggestions did not correspond to what they had seen. Moreover, when the children were questioned by their parents at the end of the session, all stuck with the story that they had given the interviewer. In sum, when suggestions and accusations were strong and persistent, young children were easily led and did not alter their newfound interpretations when later questioned by their parents.

In other research, Leichtman and Ceci (1995) assessed the effects of negative stereotyping and suggestion on preschool children's recollections of an event that happened at their school. An unfamiliar person, Sam Stone, came into children's classrooms, talked to the teacher, sat with the children during the reading of a story and made a comment about the story ("I know that story; it's one of my favorites!"), walked around the classroom, and finally, left the room, waving good-bye to the children. Children in the *stereotype* condition were given information about Sam Stone before his visit that depicted him as accident prone and irresponsible ("That Sam Stone is always getting into accidents and breaking things!"). Children in the *suggestion* condition were interviewed several times after Sam Stone's visit and given misinformation about the visit (Sam ripped a book and soiled a teddy bear when he visited). Children in the *stereotype-plus-suggestion* condition received both the negative stereotype before Sam Stone's visit and the misinformation afterward, and children in the *control* condition received neither the stereotyped information nor the misinformation about Sam.

Ten weeks after the visit, the children were given an open-ended interview about what happened the day Sam Stone visited the classroom. Leichtman and Ceci (1995) reported that, relative to children in the control condition, children who had been given the stereotypes made a modest number of false statements about Sam in the interview and that children in the suggestion condition made a substantial number of false reports. The highest levels of false reports about Sam's visit, however, came from children who had received both the stereotyped information before and the misinformation after the visit: 46% of 3- and 4-year-old children and 30% of 5- and 6-year-old children said that Sam had either ripped a book, soiled a teddy bear, or both. The percentage of erroneous responses increased to 72% and 44% for the younger and older preschoolers, respectively, when children were asked specific follow-up questions concerning whether Sam had ripped a book or soiled a teddy bear.

Why are younger children often more susceptible to the effects of misinformation and suggestion than older children are? One explanation comes from fuzzy-trace theory, as discussed earlier (Brainerd & Poole, 1997; Brainerd & Reyna, 2002, 2005). Because verbatim traces deteriorate rapidly, they may not be available when postevent information is provided or when suggestive questions are asked. Thus, the erroneous information has an excellent chance of being incorporated with "real" memories and becoming indistinguishable from them. Similarly, it would seem that young children's elevated rates of erroneous information to unbiased cues (that is, questions that ask for more information but do not attempt to bias a child's answer one way or the other) might be the result of their greater reliance on verbatim traces.

Many factors influence suggestibility in children. For example, social factors, such as a desire to comply with adult requests, surely play a role in children's greater suggestibility (Bjorklund et al., 1998). Children are more likely to comply with the suggestion of a high-status versus a low-status person (Ceci, Ross, & Toglia, 1987). Children's background knowledge for the witnessed event also influences their performance (Ornstein et al., 2006), as does the number of times an event is experienced (Powell et al., 1999). Much research has investigated how other aspects of children's cognitive development influence suggestibility. For example, developmental and individual differences in working memory and inhibitory control are related to suggestibility in children (Ruffman et al., 2001). Preschool children who perform better on theory-of-mind tasks tend to be less suggestible than are children with poorer theory-of-mind abilities (Welch, 1999), and children and adults with better metacognitive skills are more accurate in suggestive interviews than are their less-metacognitively sophisticated peers (Roebers, 2002).

One topic that has received considerable attention is that of **source monitoring**, which refers to being aware of the source of information one knows or remembers. For example, did a particular experience happen to them, to a friend, or did they see it on TV? This can be particularly important in cases of eyewitness testimony. "Was the information that the boy stole the bike something I saw, or something someone told me?" Research has shown that preschool and early school-age children often have difficulty monitoring the source of their memories (see discussion in Chapter 5). For example, children sometimes have difficulty determining whether they actually performed an act or just imagined it (Foley, Santini, & Sopasakis, 1989), and they often incorrectly remember that an action carried out by another person during a joint activity was actually performed by them (Ackil & Zaragoza, 1995; Foley, Ratner, & Gentes, 2010; Foley, Ratner, & Passalacqua, 1993). When young children make errors in such situations, they are much more likely to attribute an action to themselves that someone else actually did than vice versa. Findings such as these have caused some researchers to propose that young children's increased susceptibility to suggestion might be caused largely by their difficulty in monitoring the source of what they know (Ceci & Bruck, 1995). Some research supports these speculations, showing that 6-year-olds who are poor at source monitoring are more prone to the effects of suggestion (Mazzoni, 1998). Moreover, children who are given some source-monitoring training (for example, training in distinguishing between events they experienced directly versus events they heard about in a previous interview) make fewer false statements to misleading questions (Thierry & Spence, 2002), although some researchers have found this effect only for older (7- and 8-year-old) children and not for preschoolers (Poole & Lindsay, 2002).

Another reason contributing to young children's suggestibility might be their beliefs that their memory is invulnerable to suggestion. For example, Julia O'Sullivan, Mark Howe, and Tammy Marche (1996) interviewed preschool, first-grade, and third-grade children about factors that might influence their memories. Although children of all ages believed that central aspects of a story would be more likely to be remembered than peripheral details, only the third-grade children believed that their memories would be susceptible to suggestion. The preschool and first-grade children were confident that suggestion from a parent or sibling would not affect their recollection of an event.

### False-Memory Creation

How easy is it to create a false memory in a person? Asking children misleading questions about an event they have seen can cause children to confuse the source of the information, thinking that the misinformation was actually something they experienced and not just something they heard someone else say (Ackil & Zaragoza, 1995). But how easy is it to actually get children, or adults, to believe an event happened to them that never really did?

Elizabeth Loftus and her colleagues first investigated this with adults (Loftus & Pickrell, 1995). College students were interviewed about four events that had supposedly happened to them in childhood (based on reports of parents and older siblings). One event, being lost in a mall at age 5, never actually occurred. The students were asked to write as much about each event as they could remember. They remembered, on average, 68% of the true events; they also "remembered" 25% of the false events, sometimes vividly (see also Oakes & Hyman, 2000).

It seems that preschool children are even more susceptible to creating false memories than are adults. Ceci and his colleagues (1994) used a similar technique to that used by Loftus and Pickrell (1995) and interviewed children throughout an 11-week period about events that might have happened to them. For example, children were asked if they remember ever getting their finger caught in a mousetrap. The percentage of false reports (that is, recalling something about the event) for the 3- and 4-year-old children and for the 5- and 6-year-old children in this study over the 11-week period is shown in Figure 8-11. Although few children admitted to experiencing these false events in the initial interviews, by the conclusion of the study more than 50% of the preschool children and about 40% of 5- to 6-year-olds assented that these events did, indeed, happen—and often provided substantial detail about the events. Moreover, many children continued to believe that these events actually happened even after being told by the interviewers and their parents that the events were just made up. It seems that false memories of plausible but extraordinary events are relatively easy to put into young children's minds.

*Plausibility* is an important factor here. Even though getting one's finger caught in a mousetrap might be an event that few children have ever actually experienced, it is one that "could" happen in many households. Kathy Pezdek and Danelle Hodge (1999) demonstrated that about one-third of 5- to 7-year-old children "remembered" being lost in a mall (which they had not been), whereas only 1 of 19 children (about 5%) "remembered" being given an enema. Although most of these children knew

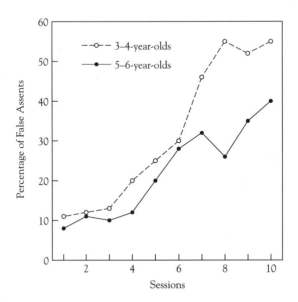

FIGURE **8-11**

Percentage of false reports over sessions for 3–4-year-olds and 5–6-year-olds.

Source: Ceci, S. J., Loftus, E. F., Leichtman, M., & Bruck, M. (1994). The role of source misattributions in the creation of false beliefs among preschoolers. *International Journal of Clinical and Experimental Hypnosis, 62,* 304–320. © 1994 by Sage Publications, Inc. Reprinted by permission.

what an enema was, the event was implausible. If such an embarrassing and invasive event had happened to them, they certainly would have remembered.

Other research has examined how *rumors* may influence children's memory of events. For example, in research by Gabrielle Principe and her colleagues (Principe et al., 2006, 2010), preschool children witnessed a magic show by Magic Mumfrey, during which, toward the end of the show, Mumfrey tried to pull a rabbit out of his hat but failed. After the show, some children heard an unfamiliar adult tell their teacher that she knew why the trick failed: The rabbit had escaped and was in the classroom eating carrots. Other children didn't hear the rumor from an adult but were classmates of the children who did, and they heard the rumor as they interacted with children in their classroom. Finally, some children saw the show but were not exposed to any rumor. One week later, children were interviewed about the show. A majority of children in both rumor conditions reported that the rabbit had gotten loose in the classroom, and many of these children actually professed seeing the runaway bunny. Five- and six-year-old children who were warned that there was a false rumor going around about what had happened in the school made fewer such claims when they heard the rumor from their classmates, although such a warning did not affect 3- to 4-year-old children's reports. Moreover, children who said they saw the rabbit in the classroom provided more vivid descriptions of the (non)event than children who did not, suggesting that the implanted rumor produced a true false memory, complete with perceptual details, and was not simply the result of children wanting to conform with what other children had witnessed (Principe et al., 2010).

The investigations described in this section are laboratory studies. Researchers know what children witnessed or experienced, and they often manipulated some aspect of the experience or characteristics of the interview to see what would happen. However, because children's testimony may have significant legal consequences, it is important to do research in "the real world," developing paradigms where researchers have some control over the situation but where children remember "real" events that may have legal implications. Some of this research is reviewed in Box 8-1.

## Some Final Thoughts on Children as Eyewitnesses

Children do not have perfect memories, making them less than ideal witnesses. Of course, adults' memories are also fallible, so how different are children from adults when it comes to providing reliable testimony? As we've seen, young children's spontaneous recall is typically sparse, but it also tends to be accurate and about psychologically and legally central aspects of an event. They are also more prone to suggestion than adults, at least in most contexts (but see Brainerd et al., 2008; 2010 for important exceptions). Since the 1980s, when issues about the accuracy of children's testimony became of increasing interest to the legal community (Ceci & Bruck, 1995), developmental psychologists have investigated children's event memories for forensically relevant information and have discovered important things about the emotional, social, and cognitive factors that influence children's reports and memories. This research has made significant contributions to the legal system, affecting how children are interviewed by police officers, social workers, and lawyers (Bruck et al., 2006). We may never know with 100% certainty the veracity of a child's recollections (or that of an adult, for that matter), but developmental science has made great leaps in understanding children's memory and factors that affect its accuracy.

## BOX 8-1  Assessing Children's Memories in Real-Life Settings

As you likely learned early in your academic studies, psychologists are rightly concerned about experimental control, and this is no less true for the topic of children's memory development than it is for any other topic. However, because issues related to children as eyewitnesses have substantial consequences for the legal and medical professions, it is important to get out of the laboratory and into the field, assessing children's memories and factors that affect them in real-life settings.

Some researchers have assessed children's recollections of events surrounding natural disasters (Ackil, Van Abbema, & Bauer, 2003; Bahrick et al., 1998). For example, Hurricane Andrew struck South Florida in August 1992 with devastating winds, destroying many homes. Lorraine Bahrick and her colleagues (1998) interviewed 3- and 4-year-old children between 2 and 6 months after the storm, and their memories were related to the amount of destruction that occurred to each child's home (low, moderate, or high). Older children recalled more than younger children, and the amount that children remembered varied with the severity of damage. Children whose homes were moderately damaged remembered more than children whose homes suffered low or high levels of damage. Children's memory for the storm remained high 6 years later, although a significant relation between recall and severity of stress was no longer found. However, children whose homes suffered the most damage required more prompts to recall information than did children in the low- and moderate-stress groups (Fivush et al., 2004).

Other "real-life" research paradigms involve assessing children's recollections of invasive medical procedures—some traumatic (such as trips to the emergency room) and others not (such as well-child pediatric exams). In general, older children remember more than younger children, and prior knowledge of the exam procedure is positively related to amount of initial (but not delayed) recall of the events (Ornstein et al., 1997, 2006). Examinations that involve bodily contact and discomfort can be analogous to instances of child abuse (Ornstein et al., 1997, 2006). One particularly invasive procedure is the voiding cystourethrogram. Children are frequently restrained while a urinary

catheter is inserted, and they are required to urinate during the procedure. Children as young as 5 years of age report relatively accurate accounts of such procedures over delays of longer than 1 month (Merritt, Ornstein, & Spicker, 1994; Pipe et al., 1997).

Other studies attempt to construct forensic interviews similar to those that abused children would experience (Lamb & Thierry, 2005; Orbach & Lamb, 2007; Pipe & Salmon, 2009). Such studies afford control of variables that are difficult, if not impossible, to control in real life. However, there is always the question of the ecological validity of the studies. How do we know that children who experience child abuse behave in the same way? This is where field studies, interviewing children who are suspected victims of child abuse, become important (Lamb & Thierry, 2005). Of course, field studies lack control of important factors, and one does not know for certain what children actually experienced. But the combination of laboratory and field studies can provide greater insight into the reliability and accuracy of children as witnesses.

Do the factors that influence children's testimonies in laboratory studies similarly affect children's testimonies in field studies? For the most part, the answer is "yes." In general, in studies with children who are suspected victims of abuse, younger children remember less information than older children, memory performance declines over delays, open-ended questions apparently produce more accurate information than more specific cued questions, and suggestive questions increase levels of inaccurate information (see Lamb & Thierry, 2005). However, field studies have also shown that young children can often recall more information about abuse than many laboratory studies would suggest when nonsuggestive, open-ended prompts are used (Sternberg et al., 2001).

The abundance of research on children as eyewitnesses over the past two decades has led to changes in how children are interviewed by legal professionals. Many of the techniques previously used by people when interviewing suspected victims of child abuse turned out to be highly suggestive—and the statements of the children highly questionable (Ceci & Bruck, 1995; Poole & Lamb, 1998). Subsequently, a number of protocols were designed to help those in the legal profession

**Assessing Children's Memories in Real-Life Settings** (*Continued*)

get the most accurate information possible when interviewing children (see Poole & Lamb, 1998; Larsson & Lamb, 2009, for reviews). For example, the National Institute of Child Health and Human Development (NICHD) protocol incorporates research findings from both laboratory and field settings (Lamb, Sternberg, & Esplin, 1998). It provides children with practice in recalling detailed accounts of events, and it admonishes children to tell the truth and to say "I don't know" when they are uncertain. Table 8-1 presents the sequence of phases recommended by the NICHD guidelines.

Note that the NICHD guidelines call for the use of open-ended (free recall), cued, and even leading questions, where necessary. However, the child is always first encouraged to provide a narrative (open-ended) account of each incident that he or she experienced before resorting to cued and, if necessary, leading questions.

TABLE **8-1**

For Box 8-1: Sequence of Phases Recommended by the NICHD Guidelines.

1. Introduction of parties and their roles
2. The "truth and lie ceremony" (warning the child of the necessity to tell the truth)
3. Rapport building
4. Description of a recent salient event
5. First narrative account of the allegation
6. Narrative accounts of the last incident (if the child reports multiple incidents)
7. Cue question (for example, "You said something about a barn. Tell me about that.")
8. Paired direct-open questions about the last incident
9. Narrative account of first incident
10. Cue questions
11. Paired direct-open questions about the first incident
12. Narrative accounts of another incident that the child remembers
13. Cue questions
14. Paired direct-open questions about this incident
15. If necessary, leading questions about forensically important details not mentioned by the child
16. Invitation for any other information the child wants to mention

Source: Adapted from Poole, D. A., & Lamb, M. E. (1998). *Investigative interviews of children: A guide of helping professionals.* Washington, D.C.: American Psychological Association, pp. 98 & 99.

# REMEMBERING TO REMEMBER

To this point, our discussion of memory has focused on what is called *retrospective memory*, or remembering something that happened in the past. But another type of memory, one that we engage in every day, is **prospective memory**, or remembering to do something in the future (Einstein & McDaniel, 2005). For example, if you need to pick up a bottle of wine tonight on your way home from school or work for that "special dinner" and remember to do so, you are demonstrating good prospective memory. If you neglect to do so, you are displaying a failure of prospective memory (and, perhaps, a less successful evening than you had hoped for). Prospective memory involves what some people refer to as *mental time travel,* or anticipating the future and planning for it (Suddendorf & Corballis, 2007; Tulving, 2005). This requires a sophisticated cognition/memory system.

Researchers have paid less attention to the development of prospective memory relative to retrospective memory, but this is gradually changing (see Kvavilashvili, Kyle, & Messer, 2008, for a review). One of the first studies to examine prospective memory in young children was performed by Susan Somerville and her colleagues (1983), who asked the parents of 2-, 3-, and 4-year-old children to remind them to perform some task in the future, some of which were of low interest to the children (for example, "Remind me to buy milk when we go to the store tomorrow") and others of which were of high interest (for instance, buying candy at the store). Figure 8-12 shows the performance of the children for the high- and low-interest tasks for short (5 minutes or less) and longer (for example, from morning to afternoon) delays. As you can see, even the 2-year-olds were very good at reminding their parents when the task was one of high interest and over short delays. Performance for all children dropped sharply, however, for the low-interest and long-delay tasks. In fact, none of the 2-year-olds spontaneously remembered to remind their parents about a low-interest task over a long delay. Children improved when given a clue ("Was there something you were supposed to remind me to do?"), increasing their performance by about a third, on average. These results suggest that motivation plays an important role in when children display prospective memory, as does the length of time they have to wait.

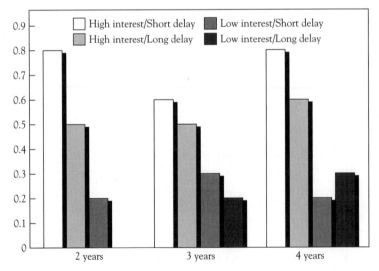

### FIGURE **8-12**

Proportion of children who reminded their parents to perform some task for 2-, 3-, and 4-year-old children for high- and low-interest tasks over short and long delays

Source: Adapted from Somerville, S. C., Wellman, H. M., & Cultice, J. C. (1983). Young children's deliberate reminding. *Journal of Genetic Psychology, 143,* 87–96.

More recent research using controlled laboratory experiments has shown that 2-year-olds rarely perform as well as Somerville's youngsters did (Kliegel & Jager, 2007) and that prospective memory continues to improve over the preschool (Quon & Atance, 2010) and school years (Atance, 2008; Smith, Bayen, & Martin, 2010). For instance, in one study, 7- to 12-year-old children played a computer game called CyberCruiser in which they used a joystick to maneuver around obstacles. They also had to occasionally check the fuel gauge to make sure they did not run out of gas and to fill up when they had less than a quarter of a tank. Perhaps not surprisingly, younger children ran out of gas more often than older children (Kerns, 2000).

Like performance on some retrospective memory tasks (Lehmann & Hasselhorn, 2007), children's performance on prospective memory tasks is influenced by individual differences in executive function (Causey & Bjorklund, 2009; MacKinlay, Kliegel, & Mäntylä, 2009). For example, in the study by Kimberly Kerns (2000) described in the previous paragraph, the author reported a moderate but significant negative correlation ($r = -.29$) between executive-function measures and the number of times children ran out of gas. Subsequent research reported significant relations between a measure of strategic prospective memory (checking a clock to indicate the passage of every 5 minutes while watching a film) and measures of executive function (Mäntylä, Carelli, & Forman, 2007). Other research has shown that executive function predicts 3-year-olds' performance on a low-interest prospective memory task ("Remind me to remove the sign on the door when we leave") but not for high-interest tasks ("Remind me to get you a prize when we finish") (Causey & Bjorklund, 2009). These patterns of findings suggest that the relation between executive function and prospective memory is complex and highly task dependent.

Propsective memory involves a host of cognitive skills, among them a symbolic system that can represent the self in the future, which is the essence of episodic memory, and executive function (Causey & Bjorklund, 2009; MacKinlay et al., 2009). In fact, some peoples have referred to this type of memory as *episodic future thought* (Quan & Atance, 2010; Szpunar, 2010). Apparently, under some limited conditions with delays of five minutes or less, this is something that 2-year-old children can do. However, the tendency to travel through time and to remember to do something in the future develops with age, as children's representational abilities, memories, and executive functions improve (see Atance, 2008; Kerns, 2000).

# CONSISTENCY AND STABILITY OF MEMORY

With a chapter titled "Memory Development," your expectation may be that we are talking about a single cognitive skill. Memory can be tapped in different ways (recognition, recall), can occur in different situations (event memory, school- or laboratory-type tasks), and can involve deliberate strategies or be indirect and unintentional, but the implication remains that there is a single, underlying "memory" ability. This, of course, is an empirical question, and there is every reason to believe that the phenomenon we call "memory" is not a domain-general skill but, rather, comprises different domain-specific abilities.

## Is "Memory" a Domain-General Faculty or a Set of Domain-Specific Abilities?

The way to assess this question is to administer different memory tasks to children and note the intertask correlations. That is, do children who perform well on one memory task perform well on others, and do children who perform poorly on one task perform poorly on others? Early developmental studies using this technique reported relatively high correlations among tasks, with the correlations increasing with age (Cavanaugh & Borkowski, 1980). These studies used strategic, laboratory tasks (discussed in Chapter 7), and the results suggest not only a general memory ability but also a general strategy ability, at least for children 8 years and older. (Recall that young children show little spontaneous strategic behavior, at least on the tasks used in these investigations.)

Later research used a wider variety of tasks, including laboratory tasks, such as digit span and sort-recall (see Chapter 7), and "everyday" memory tasks, such as story recall (Kurtz-Costes, Schneider, & Rupp, 1995; Schneider & Weinert, 1995). These studies reported lower intertask correlations, suggesting that deliberate memory could better be thought of as a set of specific abilities rather than as a domain-general faculty. For example, Beth Kurtz-Costes and colleagues (1995) administered a set of 12 memory tasks to 5-, 7-, and 9-year-old children, including several tasks reflecting everyday activities (for example, remember to remind the interviewer of something at the end of the session or "shopping" for items at a store), school-related tasks (for example, remembering a geography "lesson" or recalling a story), and laboratory tasks (sort-recall and paired associates). The researchers reported little intertask consistency among the 12 tasks at any age, with only slightly more correlations reaching statistical significance than would be expected by chance. The average correlations among tasks did increase slightly with age (average correlations = .07, .08, and .13 for 5-, 7-, and 9-year-olds, respectively); overall, few developmental differences were observed.

In related research, as part of a longitudinal study, Wolfgang Schneider and his colleagues (Schneider, Knopf, & Sodian, 2009; Schneider & Weinert, 1995) assessed the intertask correlations in the same group of individuals from 4 to 23 years of age for a variety of memory tasks, including memory-span tasks (word span, sentence span), sort-recall tasks, and two story-recall tasks. The researchers reported relatively high intertask correlations among the two span tasks and the two story-recall tasks. That is, consistency was high only when the parallel measures of story recall and word span were used. Like the results of Kurtz-Costes and her colleagues, these findings are consistent with the position that there is no unitary "memory" construct and little change in the relationship among memory tasks with development.

## How Stable Is Memory Performance over Time?

One issue that interests developmental psychologists is *stability*. In this case, stability refers to maintaining the same rank order with respect to ability over time. That is, will children who remember well at one age also remember well on a similar task several years later? Research investigating stability requires longitudinal assessment, and such expensive and laborious work has rarely focused on basic cognitive processes, such as memory. One notable exception is the Munich Longitudinal Study on the Genesis of Individual Competencies (LOGIC), which has followed children from age 4 through 23 years of age and was discussed briefly in Chapter 7 and in the preceding paragraph (Schneider, Knopf, & Sodian, 2009; Schneider & Weinert, 1995).

When looking at the stability of children's performance on a sort-recall task, Schneider and his colleagues (Schneider, Knopf, & Sodian, 2009) reported relatively low long-term stability, with correlations of recall, sorting (the degree to which participants sort items into categories), and clustering never exceeding .36 over a 4-year period and .39 over a 2-year period. Table 8-2 presents the pattern of correlations for different intervals and at different ages from the LOGIC sample. These relatively low correlations (22 out of 30 being .20 or lower) are not caused by the unreliability of the tasks themselves. The column in Table 8-2 labeled "Short Term" presents correlations between tasks given to the same children within a 6-week period. As you can see, these correlations were quite high (.68 for recall, .85 for sorting, and .64 for clustering), indicating that children's performance is stable when tests are given over very brief intervals, which suggests that the tests themselves are reliable. What is not reliable is performance over longer periods.

Schneider and his colleagues noted that long-term stability is higher for other memory tasks, however. For example, the correlations over a 2-year period for sentence span, word span, and several measures of story recall were usually quite high (most in the .40 to .70 range) (Schneider & Weinert, 1995). Similarly, there was relatively high cross-age stability in text recall, with young children who remember more of a story than their peers becoming adults who also show high levels of text recall (Schneider, Knopf, & Sodian, 2009). This suggests that the ability to acquire, store, and retrieve text information develops early in childhood and remains relatively stable into adulthood. In contrast, the lower stabilities for sort recall are related to the

## TABLE **8-2**

Short-term[a] and Long-term Individual Stabilities for the Recall, Sorting, and Clustering Measures from the Munich Longitudinal Study (LOGIC). In General, Cross-age Correlations were Low, Especially for Periods over Four Years, Reflecting Low Levels of Stability.

| A. Short-Term Stabilities | | | | | |
|---|---|---|---|---|---|
| | Age | | | | |
| | 4–6 | 6–8 | 8–10 | 10–12 | 12–18 | Short Term |
| Recall | .36 | .29 | .39 | .38 | .36 | .68 |
| Sorting | .17 | .12 | .07 | .16 | .06 | .85 |
| Clustering | .12 | .16 | .12 | .29 | .17 | .64 |

| B. Long-Term Stabilities | | | | |
|---|---|---|---|---|
| | Age | | | |
| | 4–8 | 8–12 | 6–12 | 4–12 | 4–18 |
| Recall | .30 | .36 | .30 | .16 | .14 |
| Sorting | .08 | .16 | −.09 | .06 | .07 |
| Clustering | .08 | .17 | .004 | .22 | .10 |

[a]"Short-term" stabilities assess performance on tasks given to the same children within a six-week period.

Source: Schneider, W., Knopf, M., & Sodian, B. (2009). Verbal memory development from early childhood to early adulthood. In W. Schneider & M. Bullock (Eds.), *Human development from early childhood to early adulthood: Findings from a 20-year longitudinal study* (pp. 63–90). New York, NY: Psychology Press.

substantially greater strategic component required for these tasks (Schneider & Weinert, 1995). That is, stability is relatively high for tasks involving relatively little in the way of deliberate strategic functioning (memory span and story recall) but lower when strategies play a crucial part in task performance.

## SUMMARY

Memory is multifaceted, involves a host of other cognitive operations, and is involved in all complex forms of thinking. Memories can be represented in different forms. *Declarative (explicit) memory,* which includes *episodic* and *semantic memory,* is proposed to be available to consciousness and is often contrasted with *nondeclarative (procedural* or *implicit), memory,* which is unavailable to consciousness.

Infants display memory in habituation/dishabituation and *preference-for-novelty paradigms* shortly after birth. Conditioning techniques, particularly *conjugate reinforcement procedures,* have been used to demonstrate memory in infants as young as 3 months for periods as long as 2 weeks, with infants' memories in these situations being greatly influenced by context effects. *Deferred imitation* tasks have shown that older infants can retain information over relatively long periods, with infants' long-term memory for actions increasing gradually over the first 2 years of life. Maturation of an area of the hippocampus, the *dentate gyrus,* as well as of the frontal cortex is associated with infants' ability to display deferred imitation.

*Infantile amnesia* refers to the inability to recall information from infancy and early childhood. Current theories about the reason for infantile amnesia focus on the development of self-concept, developmental differences in how information is encoded, and changes in children's use of language to communicate their memories to others. The use of hypnotic age regression is not successful in retrieving memories from infancy.

In contrast to explicit memory, few age differences are observed for *implicit memory,* when there is no conscious intention to remember something.

Young children's *event memory* is based on *scripts,* a form of schematic organization with real-world events organized by their causal and temporal characteristics. Children's early memories are for general routines and not for specific *autobiographical* experiences. Parents "teach" children how to remember by interacting with them and providing the structure for putting their experiences into narratives.

Recent research in event memory has focused on children as eyewitnesses. Age differences are found in the amount of information children remember, but what young children do recall tends to be accurate and for central components of an event. The accuracy of children's event memory is influenced by a host of factors, including their knowledge for the event they experienced and the characteristics of the interview, such as the use of an anatomically correct doll. Recent research has documented that young children are generally more susceptible to misleading questions (suggestions) and misinformation than are older children and can easily be caused to form false memories. Many factors influence children's suggestibility, including deficits in *source monitoring,* with children confusing the source of information they know or remember.

Developmental differences are also found in *prospective memory,* which refers to remembering to do something in the future.

Research has shown that memory is best conceptualized as a set of different, domain-specific skills rather than as a single mental faculty. There is relatively little stability of strategic memory but greater short-term stability (2 years) for less obviously strategic tasks, such as memory span and story recall.

## KEY TERMS AND CONCEPTS

declarative memory

episodic memory

explicit memory

semantic memory

nondeclarative memory

procedural memory

preference-for-novelty paradigms

conjugate-reinforcement procedure

deferred imitation

dentate gyrus

infantile amnesia

autobiographical memories

implicit memory

event memory

scripts

source monitoring

prospective memory

## SUGGESTED READINGS

### Scholarly Work

Bauer, P. J. (2007). *Remembering the times of our lives: Memory in infancy and beyond.* Mahwah, NJ: Erlbaum. This book, by one of the leading researchers in infant memory, provides an up-to-date review of research and theory on memory development in infancy and early childhood and includes several chapters on the neurological basis of memory development. A concise summary of this work can be found in Bauer, P. J. (2002). Long-term recall memory: Behavioral and neuro-developmental changes in the first 2 years of life. *Current Directions in Psychological Science, 11,* 137–141.

Brainerd, C. J., & Reyna, V. F. (2005). *The science of false memory.* Oxford, UK: Oxford University Press. This book, by the originators of the fuzzy-trace theory, provides a detailed look at the research and theory pertinent to false-memory creation in general, including research on children as eyewitnesses and the extent to which they remember falsely or can be mislead. The book also provides an excellent account of fuzzy-trace theory. A concise summary of this work can be found in Brainerd, C. J., & Reyna, V. F. (2002). Fuzzy-trace theory and false memory. *Current Directions in Psychological Science, 11,* 164–169.

Bruck, M., Ceci, S. J., & Principe, G. F. (2006). The child and the law. In W. Damon & R. M. Lerner (Gen. Eds.), *Handbook of Child Psychology (6th edition)*, K. A. Renninger & I. E. Sigel (Vol. Eds.), Vol. 4, *Child psychology in practice* (pp. 776–816). New York: Wiley. This chapter presents the latest research on children's eyewitness memory and suggestibility, including summaries of important legal cases in which children's testimony played a central role.

Courage, M. L., & N. Cowan, N. (Eds.) (2009). *The development of memory in infancy and childhood* (pp. 242–282). New York: Psychology Press. This edited volume includes up-to-date reviews written by leading researchers in the field, reviewing specific topics in children's memory development.

### Reading for Personal Interest

Lamb, M. E., Hershkowitz, I., Orbach, Y., & Esplin, P. W. (2008). *Tell me what happened: Structured investigative interviews of children victims and witnesses.* West Sussex, UK: Wiley. Child forensic science is one of the fields in which cognitive development research has had a great practical impact. This book, written by leading researchers in the field, provides a recent summary of how professionals (for example, psychologists, police officers, social workers) should approach children suspected of abuse and child witnesses to obtain reliable accounts of what happened.

CHAPTER **9**

# Language Development

**BOX 9-1:** Is Language Unique to Humans?
Can Apes "Talk"?

## What Is Language?

## Describing Children's Language Development

Phonological Development
Morphological Development
Syntactic Development
Semantic Development
Pragmatics
Speech Registers: The Case of Black
  English

## Some Theoretical Perspectives of Language Development

Nativist Perspectives on Language
  Development

**BOX 9-2:** The "Less Is More" Hypothesis
Social-Interactionist Perspectives of
  Language Development

## Bilingualism and Second-Language Learning

## Gender Differences in Language Acquisition

## Language and Thought

SUMMARY
KEY TERMS AND CONCEPTS
SUGGESTED READINGS

"Up, Daddy," 2-year-old Darius called to his father, who turned around and put out his arms to pick up his son. But Darius immediately protested, pointing to the candy dish his mother recently placed on a high shelf out of his reach and saying, "No, Daddy! Up!". Seeing this, his father said, "No, Darius, no candy right now." Darius whined, "Please, Daddy," and then again pointed to the out-of-reach dish and said, "Up!"

Darius can barely string more than two words together at a time and has few verbs in his limited vocabulary. Yet, by speaking just one or two words at a time, along with pertinent gestures and a social context shared with a familiar person, Darius is able to get his message across, even if he doesn't always get what he wants. Darius is at the early stages of learning language, something that he will master in a very short time and that, perhaps more than any other single ability, will distinguish him from all other animals.

Children around the globe acquire language without formal instruction. Language belongs to the class of abilities that are too important to be relegated to our conscious awareness and "free will" (Spelke & Newport, 1998). Some scientists believe that the evolution of language made human thought possible (Bickerton, 1990; Nelson, 1996). Although a few nonhuman primates have shown simple language abilities (see Savage-Rumbaugh et al., 1993, and Box 9-1), none has approached the level found in all typical humans. And despite the universality of language (that is, all groups of people possess it and develop it at about the same age), the language people learn depends on what is spoken around them. Language is thus strongly influenced both by humans' general biological inheritance and by the uniqueness of the environments in which they grow up.

In this chapter, I examine some of the fascinating and often controversial research and theory related to language development. I first consider what characteristics a communication system has to have to be considered "language." I then provide a brief sketch of children's developing language abilities, from cooing and babbling to communicative competence. Next, I investigate some of the major theoretical perspectives of language development, particularly the contrast between *nativist theories*, which hold that the mechanisms and structures underlying language acquisition (specifically, the acquisition of syntax, or grammar) are largely innate, and *social-interactionist theories*, which hold that the social environment plays a substantial role in language development. I then examine the development of bilingualism, followed by a brief look at gender differences in language development and, finally, a look at the developmental relationship between language and thought.

––––––––––––

| **BOX 9-1** | **Is Language Unique to Humans? Can Apes "Talk"?** |

Scientists have long looked for abilities that separate humans from all other animals, and language seems to be the last candidate standing. Or is it? First, other species have complicated communication systems, but they don't qualify as language, at least not as defined by human linguists. Vervet monkeys, for example, have specific calls that correspond to certain dangers in their environment: one for snakes, one for eagles, and another for leopards (Cheney & Seyfarth, 1990). These calls are learned, so they are not innate. But they are also not arbitrary. In other words, unlike human languages, they are specific calls associated with specific objects or events, not arbitrary symbols that can be put together in creative ways.

From an evolutionary perspective, however, language had to come from somewhere. New adaptations do not arise fully formed from nothing but can trace their history to earlier generations. One reason why chimpanzees don't use language, of course, is because they don't talk—or rather the structure of their mouth and vocal tract prohibits them from making the sounds found in human language. Early attempts to teach chimpanzees spoken language failed essentially because of the physical limitations of these apes' abilities to make language-like sounds (Hayes, 1951; Kellogg & Kellogg, 1933).

Even so, apes can form signs with their hands, and in the 1960s scientists began teaching a form of sign language to chimpanzees, getting around the physical limitations of their vocal apparatus. Perhaps the most successful and best-known work in this area was by Howard and Beatrix Gardner (1969; see also Fouts, 1997), who taught a version of American Sign Language to the chimpanzee Washoe. The Gardners raised Washoe in their home and treated her much as a child. Washoe was able to understand simple sentences, knew more than 130 words, and was able, some claim, to use language creatively. For instance, when seeing a duck for the first time, Washoe made the signs for "bird" and "water." In her later years, she was observed teaching a younger chimpanzee, Loulis, some signs. For example, Washoe brought a chair over to Loulis and signed "chair" repeatedly. Another time,

Washoe saw Loulis begging for a candy bar from one of the trainers. She took Loulis' hands and molded his fingers into the sign for "food" (Fouts & Fouts, 1989). Other researchers have used sign language with orangutans (Miles, 1990) and gorillas (Patterson, 1978), but with limited success.

Because language is symbolic, it can be represented with arbitrary symbols beyond words and hand signs (consider the marks on the page you are reading now). Scientists at the Yerkes Regional Primate Research Center at Georgia State University developed a communication system in which chimpanzees used symbols, or lexigrams, on a computer keyboard to communicate with their human caretakers and fellow chimps (Rumbaugh, 1977; Savage-Rumbaugh, 1986). A number of chimpanzees (*Pan troglodytes*) and bonobos (*Pan paniscus*) have learned this language, called "Yerkish." For example, two male chimpanzees, Sherman and Austin, were raised together and were tested on a variety of tasks that required cooperation. On one occasion, Sherman had a jar of peanut butter but needed a can opener to remove the lid. Out of sight in another room, Austin had access to various tools. Sherman had to use the computer keyboard to communicate to Austin that he needed a can opener. When the task was completed, Sherman and Austin had been taught to share the prize.

The champion of the "talking" apes is the bonobo Kanzi (Savage-Rumbaugh et al., 1993; see Rumbaugh, Beran, & Savage-Rumbaugh 2003). Kanzi was not originally the researchers' subject in their language-learning study but, as an infant, spontaneously learned many of the lexigrams that the researchers were trying to teach to his mother. His mother never caught on, but young Kanzi did and soon became the focus of the study. Like Washoe, Kanzi was raised much as a human child would be raised, with language training being embedded within the social interaction with his human caretakers. Kanzi has acquired a vocabulary of about 150 words and can generate and understand short sentences. For instance, Sue Savage-Rumbaugh and her colleagues (1993) presented Kanzi and a 2.5-year-old human child, Alia, with 660 simple sentences. For example, both Kanzi and Alia were asked to take an object

*(Continues)*

| **BOX 9-1** | **Is Language Unique to Humans? Can Apes "Talk"?** (*Continued*) |

to a specific person ("Give Karen the apple") or place ("Take the shoe to the bedroom") or to do something with an object ("Put the pine needles in the refrigerator"). The ape and the child performed comparably, with Kanzi actually slightly outperforming Ali on comprehending sentences (72% versus 66%). This research clearly indicates that an ape is able to learn an arbitrary system of symbols to communicate. This ability emerges as a result of exposure to language in the context of daily and routine social interaction, much the same way that human children learn language (Rumbaugh et al., 2003).

These results are definitely impressive and tell us something about ape thinking, but what do they tell us about language? Not everyone believes that the performance of these accomplished apes actually reflects evidence of language but, rather, shows an ability to learn complex chains of behaviors (Terrance et al., 1979). The "language" of these apes lacks all but the simplest grammar—a rule system that allows the speaker to produce

and understand novel statements. Even Kanzi's impressive performance is limited, and if he possesses grammar, it does not exceed the level of a typical 2.5-year-old child (Gómez, 2005).

Is it only the lack of complex grammar that prevents apes from using (and, perhaps, "inventing") language? Some argue that apes also lack the necessary social-cognitive abilities that make language-learning so easy (or at least nearly inevitable) in children (Tomasello, Kruger, & Ratner, 1993; see discussion of the social-interactive perspective of language development later in this chapter). What apes lack is a well-developed theory of mind (see Box 6-2 in Chapter 6), which makes the acquisition of a complicated communication system possible. If chimpanzees had greater social-cognitive skills, perhaps language would come more easily to them. This suggests that human language may have coevolved with social intelligence, with language providing a decided advantage in terms of social communication and social cohesion.

# WHAT IS LANGUAGE?

Perhaps the first thing to realize is that language is a special form of communication, qualitatively different from the ways in which other animals send messages back and forth to one another. Language is also multilayered, involving actual speech sounds, rules for combining words into sentences, the meanings those words and sentences convey, and use in social interaction. And each of these different layers of language develops.

At its most basic level, language refers to the systematic and conventional use of sounds, signs, or written symbols for the intention of communication or self-expression (Hoff, 2009). Although other animals have communication systems, they differ from humans in at least three important ways (Tomasello, 2006): Human language is *symbolic*, *grammatical*, and although all biologically typical people acquire language, *the particular language children learn to speak varies with culture.*

By symbolic, psychologists mean that the sounds of spoken language, or the hand movements of sign language, *represent* something independent of the actual sounds or movements. Moreover, the meaning of any pattern of sound is arbitrary. A word is not necessarily related to the concept it represents. In English, for example, we refer to man's best friend as a "dog" and to the purring and usually more independent domesticated pet as a "cat." The words themselves are arbitrary. If we wished, we could agree to reverse the names. For instance, the word "bad," when used in the right context with the proper pronunciation, has come to have a positive, not a negative, connotation. Moreover, because it is symbolic, language can displace the speaker in time and place, referring to events that happened in the past, that will happen in the future, and that happen in locations that may be miles away from the speaker (that is, language allows mental time travel; see Chapter 8).

By grammatical, psychologists mean that language has a system of rules that permits a speaker to produce and understand sentences that have never been uttered before. A language does not have a set number of sentences that all speakers memorize. Rather, speakers can generate an infinite number of sentences—and, thus, meanings—using a finite number of words. There are two aspects of grammar that concern us here: morphology and syntax. *Morphology* refers to the structure of words and to a system of rules for combining units of meaning into words (for instance, adding *ed* to verbs to make them past tense). *Syntax* refers to a system of rules for creating phrases and sentences out of words.

Finally, there are many different languages with different vocabularies and rules. Currently, the world is estimated to have about 6000 languages, many with only a handful of speakers, whereas some languages, such as English, Spanish, and Mandarin Chinese, are spoken by many hundreds of millions of people. This means that although language may be rooted in human biology, experience with a specific language is required. That language is rooted in biology is evidenced by the fact that all biologically normal members of the species acquire language in much the same way, regardless of the specific language they speak. Language fits the description of a biologically primary ability (Geary, 1995; see Chapter 2) that develops in all normal members of the species without the need of special instruction or motivation.

As a communication system, language serves many functions. Linguist Michael Halliday (1973) identified seven functions of language that motivate children to use language to attain a variety of goals. Those functions and some examples are presented in Table 9-1.

# DESCRIBING CHILDREN'S LANGUAGE DEVELOPMENT

There are at least five different aspects of language: (1) *phonology,* (2) *morphology,* (3) *syntax, (4) semantics*, and (5) *pragmatics*, and they all develop over time. Figure 9-1 (from Hoff, 2009) presents a schematic overview of some of the major developmental milestones for each of these aspects of language over the preschool years. In this section,

TABLE **9-1**

Seven Functions of Language According to M. A. K Halliday.

**Instrumental**: Using language to express needs (for example. "More milk")

**Regulatory**: Using language to tell others what to do (for example, "Get me juice")

**Interactional**: Using language to make contact with others and form relationships (for example." I love you, mommy")

**Personal**: Using language to express feelings, opinions, and individual identity (for example. "I'm a good boy")

**Heuristic**: Using language to gain knowledge about the environment (for example, "What's that?")

**Imaginative**: Using language to tell stories and jokes and to create an imaginary environment.

**Representational**: Using language to convey facts and information.

Source: Halliday, M. A. K. (1973), *Explorations in the functions of language.* London, Edward Arnold.

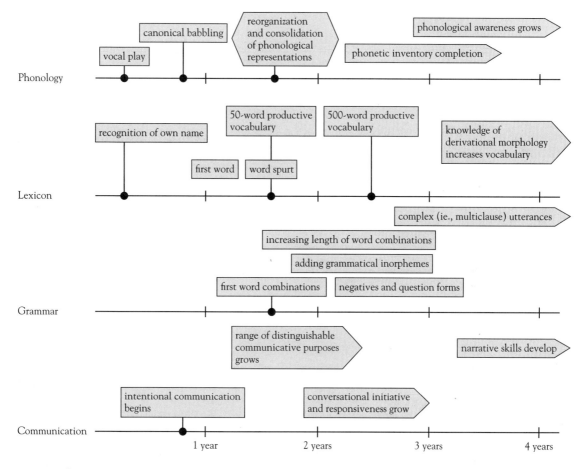

FIGURE **9-1**

Major milestones in early language development. "Lexicon" refers to the words that a child knows (semantics), and "communication" refers to a child's ability to use language in social situations (pragmatics).

Source: Hoff, E. (2009). *Language development (4th edition)*. Belmont, CA: Wadsworth.

I look at the five aspects of language just mentioned and provide a brief description of children's development for each aspect.

## Phonological Development

**Phonology** refers to the sounds of a language. Our unique anatomy permits us to make a wide range of sounds that can be combined into sequences of words. Age-related changes occur in the tongue, mouth, and position of the larynx in the throat, and these physical differences mean that the sounds infants and children are able to produce change over time (Stoel-Gammon & Menn, 1997).

Infants begin cooing and laughing between 2 and 4 months, and these vocalizations increase until 9 to 12 months, when they decline and one-word utterances begin (see Table 9-2). Sounds made during babbling vary widely, including both sounds heard in the baby's native language and sounds that are not. Over the course of the first year,

TABLE **9-2**
Developmental Stages of Infants' Babbling.

*Stage 1: Reflexive crying and vegetative sounds (0 to 8 weeks)*

Infants in stage 1 cry as a reaction to a distressed state and make various vegetative sounds associated with feeding and breathing, such as burps, coughs, and sneezes. The vocal tract of these young infants closely resembles that of nonhuman primates; their tongue fills their oral cavity and their larynx is high in their neck (which permits them to breathe and swallow simultaneously). This leaves little room for making different sounds. As the infant's head and neck grow, a greater variety of sounds become possible.

*Stage 2: Cooing and laughter (8 to 20 weeks)*

Infants at this age begin to make pleasant noises, especially during social interactions. These are mostly vowel sounds such as "oooh" and are termed cooing because they resemble the sounds made by pigeons. A few of the sounds will also contain some consonants such as *g* and *k*. Crying decreases and takes distinct forms that convey meaning to caregivers—discomfort, call, and request. Sustained laughter appears.

*Stage 3: Vocal play (16 to 30 weeks)*

This is a transition between cooing and true babbling. Infants begin to utter single syllables with prolonged vowel or consonant sounds.

*Stage 4: Reduplicated babbling (25 to 50 weeks)*

True babbling sounds appear, such as "bababa" and "nanana." Consonant-vowel patterns are repeated, and playful variations of pitch disappear. This type of vocalization is not just a response to caregiver's social interaction, but often occurs when no one is present. Deaf infants, although going through the first three stages, do not engage in true babbling at this time (Oller & Eilers, 1988).

*Stage 5: Jargon (9 to 18 months)*

Babbling consists of many nonrepeated consonant-vowel patterns. Jargon babbling is strings of sound filled with a variety of intonations and rhythms to sound like meaningful speech. Infants at this stage often sound as if they are carrying on their end of a conversation, with their intonations sometimes sounding as if they reflect questions or explanations, but their "words" are only babble sounds.

Source: Stark, R. (1978). Features of infant sounds: The emergence of cooing. *Journal of Child Language*, 5, 1–12; and Stoel-Gammon, C., & Menn, L. (1997). Phonological development: Learning sounds and sound patterns. In J. Berko Gleason (Ed.), *The development of language* (4th ed.). Boston: Allyn & Bacon.

babies' babbles come to resemble the sounds they hear around them (for instance, Chinese babies babble in "Chinese" and Spanish babies in "Spanish"), indicating that babbling development is based, at least partially, on children reproducing sounds that they hear. Some evidence consistent with this is that deaf children do not engage in true babbling, although they pass successfully through the earlier stages of speech production (Oller & Eilers, 1988; Petitto, 2000). This evidence is important because it points out that speech production before 6 months of age (that is, before true babbling begins) is driven primarily by endogenous (internal) forces rather than by the language environment. However, even deaf babies in the latter part of the first year "babble," but they do so with their hands. For instance, deaf infants exposed to American Sign Language from early in life begin "babbling" with their hands around 8 months, following patterns identical to those of hearing infants (Petitto, 2000; Petitto & Marentette, 1991).

It has been suggested that babbling plays a more important role in language development than just a poor attempt at spoken words (Sachs, 1977). Babbling might serve as a way to relate socially with family members long before the cognitive system is able to appreciate the intricacies of language. In addition, evidence suggests that although the *sounds* of babbling don't gradually approximate speech, the *intonation* of babbling does. Infants begin to "converse" in many ways that do not involve words but that do involve the conventions of speech. Infants develop the ability to take turns (Snow & Ferguson, 1977), match the speaker's tone of voice, pause between strings of syllables, end phrases with upward or downward inflections (Tonkova-Yompol'skaya, 1969), and match the pitch of adults speaking to them—higher for mother, lower for father (Lieberman, 1967).

But is babbling truly a component of language, using the same neurological structures that, later, "real" language does? Or is it simply the infant exercising his or her vocal apparatus? Siobhan Holowka and Laura Ann Petitto (2002) investigated this question. In most adults, language is principally localized in the left hemisphere of the brain, which controls the right side of the body. When adults are engaged in linguistic tasks, mouth openings are generally greater on the right-hand side (and, thus, controlled by the language-dominant left hemisphere) compared with when adults are engaged in nonlinguistic tasks, such as smiling, when mouth openings are greater on the left-hand side (and, thus, controlled by the right hemisphere). According to Holowka and Petitto (2002), "If babbling is fundamentally linguistic in nature, then left hemispheric specialization should be reflected in right mouth asymmetry while babbling. If babbling is fundamentally motoric in nature, then equal hemispheric participation should be reflected in equal mouth opening while babbling" (p. 1515). To test this, they videotaped 10 babies (five from English-speaking parents and five from French-speaking parents) between the ages of 5 and 12 months while making three types of expressions: babbles, nonbabbles, and smiles. Holowka and Petitto reported that all babies opened their mouths to the right side when babbling, opened their mouths to the left side when smiling, and showed no significant left-right difference when they made nonbabbling sounds. These findings suggest that brain lateralization for language is present before children's first words and that babbling is more than motor exercise, reflecting infants' "sensitivity to and production of patterns in the linguistic input" (p. 1515). (These findings also suggest that, like adults, infants' *emotional* expressions, reflected here by smiling, may be controlled principally by the right hemisphere.)

The variety of sounds children can make increases from about 18 months to 8 or 9 years of age. For instance, 2-year-olds can produce between 10 and 20 consonants. Preschool and early school-age children often drop the unstressed syllables of words ("spaghetti" is pronounced as *getti*), repeat consonants ("Daddy" is pronounced as *dada*), and oversimplify complex consonants ("blanket" is pronounced as *bankee*). Children can pronounce most vowels and consonants in their language by 4 to 6 years, but they often have trouble with *fricatives* such as z and s (as in zone, song, this), the l (as in lamb), and the r (as in rope). By 6 to 9 years of age, children can pronounce all the sounds of their language correctly about 75% of the time (Kent, 2005).

Speech perception (as opposed to production) was discussed in Chapter 4. To reiterate briefly, very young infants can perceive *phonemes,* the basic sound units of language, and they categorize them much as adults do (Eimas et al., 1971). Young infants can also discriminate between the sounds of many different languages, something that their parents cannot do (see Saffran, Werker, & Werner, 2006; Tsao, Lui, & Kuhl, 2004). Over time, however, infants lose the ability to tell the difference between sounds that are not found in their mother tongue. Thus, infants' auditory systems seem prepared to make sense of human speech, although their audition is modified over childhood as a function of what language sounds they hear.

Speech perception skills are not complete by the end of infancy, however. An important aspect of speech perception that is related to reading is **phonemic awareness,** which refers to the knowledge that words consist of separable sounds. Preschool children first become aware of syllables, followed by the sounds at the beginning of words (for example, "dog" begins with a *d* sound and "cat" with a *k* sound), rhymes, and eventually, the identification of individual phonemes (Carroll et al., 2003; Hoff, 2009). Phonemic awareness is important in proficient reading (see Chapter 11), and some believe improvement in phonemic awareness is influenced by learning to read.

## Morphological Development

**Morphology** refers to the structure of something—in the case of language, the structure of words. Counter to what you might think, the word is *not* the smallest unit of meaning in a language. In English, for example, we add sounds to words to make them past tense (add *ed*), to express the present progressive (add *ing*), or to make a word plural (add *s*), and these word endings are also units of meaning. The smallest unit of meaning in a language is called a **morpheme,** and these occur as two types. **Free morphemes** can stand alone as words, such as "fire," "run," or "sad." In contrast, **bound morphemes** cannot stand alone but, rather, are attached to free morphemes. They convey meaning by changing the free morpheme they are attached to. These include the rules for making nouns plural (add an *s*), for making a verb past tense (add an *ed*), as well as prefixes (*un*likable) and suffixes (like*ness*). The average number of morphemes a child uses in a sentence, or the **mean length of utterance (MLU),** is one indication of young children's linguistic development. MLU is measured by recording a child's speech during a period and then computing the average number of morphemes (both free and bound).

Roger Brown (1973) identified many of the morphemes used in children's early language and analyzed the speech of three unacquainted children (Adam, Eve, and Sarah) to determine the order in which these morphemes appear in development. He found 14 morphemes that occurred in almost the same order for the three children in his sample (see Table 9-3). Later research by Jill and Peter de Villiers (1973) extended these findings to 21 other preschoolers and found a high correlation between their sample and Brown's.

As can be seen from Table 9-3, many of the morphemes children learn are word endings. Once children learn these rules, they tend to apply them, even when it is not correct. For example, 2- and 3-year-olds learn that adding *ed* to a verb makes it past tense and *s* to a noun makes it plural. Although this may be generally true, there are many irregular verbs and nouns (especially in English), and although words such as "goed" (or "wented"), "drinked," "runned," "feets" (or "footes"), and mices follow the rules, they are incorrect. Children make these kinds of mistakes even when they

TABLE **9-3**

Mean Order of Acquisition of 14 Morphemes for Three Children.

Children start using the present progressive (verb + *ing*) when their *mean length of utterance* is about 2.5 morphemes. They do not start using contractions of the verb "to be" ("the dog's big"; "I'm going") until their mean length of utterance is about 4.0 morphemes [Adapted from Brown. R. (1973). *A first language: The early stages.* Cambridge, MA: Harvard University Press.]

| Morpheme | Example |
|---|---|
| 1. Present progressive (verb + *ing*) | I *singing*, He *walking* |
| 2. Preposition "in" | *in* chair, *in* car |
| 3. Preposition "on" | *on* table; *on* head |
| 4. Plural (noun + *s*) | apples; shoes |
| 5. Past tense, irregular verbs | *went; saw, ran* |
| 6. Possessives (noun + *'s*) | Eve's; hers |
| 7. Use of "to be" (uncontracted) | The dog *is* big; I *am* tired |
| 8. Articles "a" and "the" | *the* man; *a* toy |
| 9. Past tense, regular verbs (verb + *ed*) | talk*ed*, throw*ed* |
| 10. Third person regular verbs (adding *s* to verb) | he runs: she swims |
| 11. Third person irregular verbs | he *does*; she *has* |
| 12. Auxiliary verb, not contracted | I *am* going; He *is* drinking. |
| 13. The verb "to be" contracted | the dog's big; I'*m* scared; they'*re* here |
| 14. The verb "to be" contracted and used as an auxiliary | I'*m* going; she'*s* running |

have previously used the proper irregular word forms (for example, "went," "drank," "ran," "feet," and "mice"). This phenomenon is referred to as **overregularization** and usually begins around 20 months of age. Children continue to overregularize words throughout the preschool years, although beginning around age 3, they are increasingly likely to use the irregular forms of verbs and nouns properly (Marcus, 1995; Marcus et al., 1992). With overregularization, children have learned a rule for regular words and generalize it to irregular words. Apparently, having a history of being understood is not as potent a motivator for using a certain form of language as is the acquisition of a rule and its generalization to all situations where it might apply. This phenomenon is not limited to children learning English; it has been found in a wide variety of languages, suggesting that children around the world approach the problem of language acquisition in a similar way (Slobin, 1970).

How can you know whether children understand the morphological rules of their language? One technique that has been quite successful is the "wug test" (Berko, 1958; see Figure 9-2). Children are shown a series of unfamiliar objects (for example, "This is a *wug*") or pictures of people performing unfamiliar actions (for example, "This man knows how to rick"). For the "wug" example, children are then shown two of these creatures and told, "Now there are two of them. There are two _____." If children

This is a wug.

Now there is another one.
There are two of them.
There are two _____.

This is a man who knows how to rick.
He is ricking. He did the same thing
yesterday. What did he do yesterday?
Yesterday he _____.

FIGURE **9-2**

Two examples from the "wug" test.

Source: Berko, J. (1958). The child's learning of English morphology. *Word, 14,* 150–177. Reprinted with permission.

know the regular rules for making plurals, they will say "wugs." When shown a picture of a man who knows how "to rick," when asked what he did yesterday, children who know the rule for making a verb past tense will say that "he ricked," and if they know the rules for the present progressive, they will say that currently "he is ricking" (Marcus et al., 1992).

## Syntactic Development

*Syntax* is the knowledge of sentence structure, or grammatical rules—rules for how words are combined into sentences and how sentences are transformed into other sentences. Competent speakers of a language can use the same set of words to create very different meanings by applying basic grammatical rules. For example, the sentence "The man drove the car" can be made negative ("The man didn't drive the car"), transformed to pose a question ("Did the man drive the car?"), or expressed in the passive voice ("The car was driven by the man"). If you followed these simple transformations of these English sentences, it means that you know the underlying structure, or syntax, of English. You might not be able to pass a freshman test of English grammar, and these rules might not be part of your explicit (declarative) knowledge, but you implicitly know the rules. Few of us can actually state the rules used for transforming an active declarative sentence into a question or to the passive voice, but nonetheless, we are all linguistic experts when it comes to actual performance. Our syntactic expertise is so good that we can even recognize grammatical sentences that contain nonsense words. For example, the sentence "The golup was pudaded under his limnex" is meaningless because "golup," "pudaded," and "limnex" are all meaningless. But because you are an expert at English syntax, you know that the subject of the sentence is "golup" (and that it is animate and masculine), that "pudaded" is a verb (specifically, an action that was done to the "golup"), and that a "limnex" is something (a noun) possessed by the "golup" (possibly a body part). Not bad for nonsense.

Although technically you can't have syntax until you have two-word sentences, which usually happens around 18 months, toddlers begin speaking one word at a time and can often convey complicated meaning from such utterances. "MOMMY!" can be a clear cry of distress, whereas "Mommy?" can be the initiation of a light conversation. Add a little hand waving and an empty cup, and "Mommy" becomes a request for a drink refill. And coming from behind a chairback, "Mommy" can be the beginning of a round of peek-a-boo. Take, for example, the toddler who gets his mother's attention by climbing up next to her on the sofa, putting one hand on each of her cheeks, and turning her face toward his as he finally says "Cookie?" These have been termed **holophrases** (one-word sentences, sometimes referred to as **holophrastic speech**), and children from language groups all over the world use them to achieve different functions or purposes (Tomasello, 2006).

When children get beyond the two-word phase, they do so mostly by including only those words that convey the most meaning and omitting the "little" words that make language easy to understand but that are not absolutely necessary for comprehension. For example, a child might say "Daddy give milk me" or "Amy me go Grandma's?" rather than "Give me the milk, Daddy" or "May Amy and I go to Grandma's?" When heard in context, the meanings of these abbreviated sentences are straightforward. Children are economical in their word choice, using only the concrete and high-information words that are most important in conveying meaning. Such speech has been described as **telegraphic speech**, in that it is accomplished much as telegrams were once written and text messages are written today—including only the high-content words and leaving out all the ifs, ands, and buts.

By about 3 years of age, most children begin to use longer and more complex sentences and to understand that word order is important (see Tomasello, 2006). For instance, between 2 and 3.5 years, children can recognize an improperly worded sentence; within another year, they can recognize incorrect word order even when unfamiliar verbs are used. For example, Nameera Akhtar (1999) presented English-speaking children with sentences including made-up verbs, sometimes in a familiar Subject-Verb-Object order (for instance, "Ernie meeking the car") and sometimes in a less-familiar Subject-Object-Verb order (for example, "Ernie the cow taming") or Verb-Subject-Object order (for example, "Gopping Ernie the cow"). As can be seen in Figure 9-3, even 2-year-olds were able to understand the familiar Subject-Verb-Object sentences, but about half of these young children "corrected" the Subject-Object-Verb or Verb-Subject-Object sentences to make them fit "standard" Subject-Verb-Object order (for example, "Ernie gopping the cow"). By 4 years of age, about 90% of children corrected the unusual adult speech, demonstrating children's increasing sensitivity to the familiar word order as well as, perhaps, their comfort in correcting an adult.

In general, children begin to produce more complicated sentences around the age of 2, when they are able to put four words together in their utterances (Bowerman, 1979), with most children using complex sentences by 4 years of age (Bloom, 1993; Bowerman, 1979). The earliest types of complex sentences involve object complementation (that is, sentences

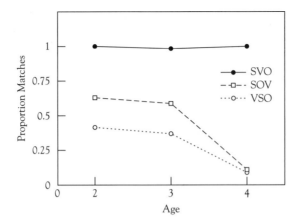

FIGURE **9-3**

Proportion of matches by children to sentences of different word order. SVO = Subject-Verb-Object, SOV = Subject-Object-Verb, VSO = Verb-Subject-Object.

Source: Akhtar, N. (1999). Acquiring basic word order: Evidence for data-driven learning of syntactic structure. *Journal of Child Language, 26*, 339–356.

with direct objects: "Look at me hit the ball") and "wh"-embedded clauses (that is, sentences with "wh" words embedded in them: "Do you want to play when we get home?"). The coordination of sentences (using "and" to connect two simple sentences: "I tripped Justin, and he fell") appears later, around the age of 3. More complex sentences linking a subordinate clause with a main clause using words such as "if," "because," "although," "until," "while," and "since" ("I'll go to the park if Jesse goes"), are usually mastered by age 4.

One way of assessing syntactic development is to look at common grammatical forms and see how children of different ages use them. Here, I examine briefly young children's development of negatives, questions, and passive sentences.

### Negatives

Early in the preschool years, children learn the power of negatives. Actually, many problems during the so-called "terrible twos" spring from children's new knowledge that they can have thoughts and wishes that don't necessarily reflect those of their parents and that they can express these by using negatives. Early use of negatives involves tacking "n" words onto positive sentences, as in "No drink milk" or "Not bath, Mommy." Children sometimes add the negative to the end of a sentence, as in "Drink milk no."

Following this stage, the negative term is moved inside the sentence next to the main verb—for example, "I no do it" or "She no go." Eventually, children learn to use auxiliaries much as adults do and as reflected in sentences such as, "I don't want to do it" and "She can't have it." These later, more sophisticated negatives are also associated with longer sentences (Bloom, 1993).

### Questions

Questions develop from adding a raised intonation at the end of declarative sentences ("Aaron go outside, Mommy?") to more adultlike forms ("Can I go outside,

Mommy?"). Sometime during the third year, the "wh" questions begin: "Where Daddy?" and "What's this?" and the all-too-common "Why?" (Van Valin, 2002).

More significant to developmentalists is the child's growing ability to *answer* "wh" questions. Different "wh" words refer to different parts of speech—"who," "what," and "where" refer to people, objects, and locations and are easily answered by young toddlers. For example, "Where's Mommy?" requires a simple response of "Outside" or "In the kitchen." In contrast, "when," "which," "how," and "why," require more difficult concepts and greater language ability. For example, asking a toddler "When did Daddy go to work?" or "Why did you leave the door open?" could result in great frustration for both the adult asking the question and the child trying to answer it (de Villiers & de Villiers, 1978).

### Passive Sentences

Late in the preschool years, around age 5 or 6, children learn about passive sentences. With active sentences, the word order tells the story ("John hit the ball"). Passive sentences take away that cue ("The ball was hit by John"), and young preschoolers get confused (Goodz, 1982). Interestingly, children first learn to interpret passive sentences when the verb refers to some observable event, such as "The horse was kicked by the cow." Later, they learn passive sentences with less observable verbs, such as "Tommy was remembered by the teacher."

Passive sentences are used relatively infrequently in English (Hoff, 2009), and they are not typically produced by English-speaking children until 4 or 5 years of age (Budgwig, 1990). However, with languages that make greater use of passive sentences (Inuktitut, K'ich'e Mayan, Sesotho, and Zulu), children 2 to 3 years of age produce them (see Tomasello, 2006).

Syntactic development does not stop at age 5, of course, but the differences between the grammar used by 6- and 7-year-olds and adults are subtle and minor. For instance, school-age children still must master subject-verb agreement (for example, "They were going" instead of "They was going") and the use of personal pronouns (for example, "He and she went" instead of "Him and her went"). But in general, the basic grammatical structure of school-age children's sentences varies little from that of adults.

## Semantic Development

**Semantics** refers to meaning—specifically, the meaning of language terms. Here, however, "meaning" refers to more than just a simple definition. For example, children must learn not only that "dog" refers to a four-legged family pet called Spot but also to other perceptually similar creatures, who themselves are members of the larger group of "mammals" and "animals." In this section, I look at the development of children's store of word meanings (basically, vocabulary development) and how it is that children acquire the meaning of language utterances so readily.

### Vocabulary Development

Perhaps the simplest indication of children's semantic development is the number of words they know. Children typically say their first words late in the first year of life or shortly thereafter. Early words are sometimes only recognized by family members and usually refer to people in the family ("Mama," "Dada") or important objects.

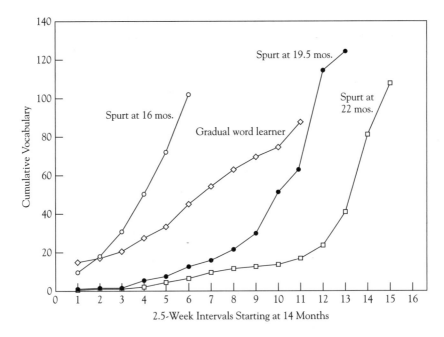

FIGURE **9-4**

Different children show different times of onset of their growth spurt, although most (but not all) children show an abrupt and rapid increase in vocabulary.

Source: Goldfield, B. A., & Reznick, J. S. (1990). Early lexical acquisition: Rate, content, and the vocabulary spurt. *Journal of Child Language, 17*, 171–184.

By 6 years of age, most children have a vocabulary of over 10,000 words, which will double by third grade and steadily increase to about 60,000 words by 18 years and 100,000 words by adulthood (Aitchinson, 1994; Carey, 1978).

Children speak their first words at about 10 to 12 months of age and learn new words at a rate of about 8 to 11 per month. However, at about 18 months of age, or when children have about 50 words in their active vocabulary, the rate at which they learn new words increases substantially, to between 22 and 37 words per month (Benedict, 1979; Bloom, 1998). This has been termed the **word spurt**. Most of the words children learn during this time are nouns, often labels for objects. Some children begin their word spurt shortly after their first birthdays, whereas others don't start until age 2 or later (Mervis & Bertrand, 1994; see Figure 9-4). There has been some debate about whether all children have this word spurt (Bloom, 2000; Goldfield & Reznick, 1990), with some research using different methodological procedures suggesting that it might actually be typical for only about 20% of children, with the rest following a more linear, gradual progression of vocabulary development (Ganger & Brent, 2004).

Some research indicates that infants in their second year of life spontaneously look at objects for familiar words (for instance, hearing the word "cup" and then looking at a picture of a cup versus a picture of another object). This ability increases in efficiency between 15 and 20 months of age, and the oldest children are about as fast as adults at doing this (Fernald et al., 1998). In other words, children in the latter part of their second year are getting faster at understanding the words they hear.

Other research has shown that even children at 12 to 17 months of age are learning new words at a rapid rate, but for their **receptive vocabulary** (words they can recognize) rather than for their **productive vocabularies** (words they can say, or produce) (Schafer & Plunkett, 1998). This all indicates that a toddler's word spurt doesn't appear out of nowhere but has its beginnings in prespeaking processing.

What accounts for children's rapid acquisition of words, specifically nouns, during this time? Some have speculated that children have a set of specific language-processing constraints that kick in at this time to make word learning easy (Carey, 1978; Mervis & Bertrand, 1994). Susan Carey (1978) labeled the process underlying the word spurt as **fast mapping**. Fast mapping refers to the ability to learn new words based on very little input (that is, few opportunities to learn the words), although children's understanding of words acquired through fast mapping is usually fragmented and incomplete. Carolyn Mervis and Jacquelyn Bertrand (1994) demonstrated fast mapping by showing children between the ages of 16 and 20 months a set of objects, one of which was unfamiliar to them (for example, a garlic press). They were asked to pick out the items, one at a time, and were given a nonsense word for the unfamiliar item (for example, "May I have the bliff?"). Only some of the children were able to learn new words for these unfamiliar items after only a few exposures (the fast mappers). These children were found to have larger vocabularies than the children who did not learn words for these novel items. This latter group of children was seen several months later, after they had gone through their word spurts, and now showed the ability to fast map. These results indicate that the word spurt is associated with a special processing ability, reflected by fast mapping, in which children map novel words to novel objects for which they do not yet have a name.

Most of the first 50 or so words that children acquire refer to familiar people, toys, and food (Nelson, 1974), and this is apparently true across different languages (Caselli et al., 1995). Early words also tend to be those relevant in social interaction ("hello," "bye-bye"). Although nouns constitute most of children's first words, verbs begin to increase in frequency following the early "noun spurt" (Nelson, 1973; Snedecker, Geren, & Shafto, 2007).

### Constraints on Word Learning

How do children figure out what the words spoken by others refer to? When a child sees a white, long-eared object hopping across the lawn and her father points and says "See the rabbit," how does the child know what he is referring to? Is it the animal itself, the color of the animal, the long ears, the act of hopping, or perhaps the phenomenon of an object moving across one's lawn? There must be a lot of trial-and-error learning in acquiring the meaning of words, of course, yet once children begin their word spurts, they learn words with great speed, suggesting that some **lexical constraints** on word learning exist such that children do not consider all possibilities each time they hear a new word (Markman, 1994).

One proposed lexical constraint is the **whole-object assumption**, in which children, when hearing a word, assume that it refers to the whole object and not to some part of that object. Thus, the child is not likely to think that "rabbit" refers to color, or long ears, or pattern of movement when her father shouts the word. Another proposed constraint is the **taxonomic assumption**, in which children assume that words refer to things that are similar. For example, after associating the word "rabbit" with the white, long-eared creature that hopped across her backyard, a child should assume that the similar-looking, brown animal sitting in the pet store window also goes by the same name. And finally, the **mutual exclusivity assumption** holds that different words refer to different things, so that the word "rabbit," for example, would not overlap with the word "mouse." For instance, when children are given a novel word and asked to select a referent for that word, they pick the objects for which they do not already have a word, realizing, apparently, that the new word is not a synonym for a word they already know but, instead, must refer to a distinct (mutually exclusive) object. For example, in studies by Ellen Markman and Gwyn Wachtel (1988), 3-year-olds who knew the word for "cup," but not for "tongs," were asked, "Show me the dax." Eighty percent of children selected the tongs, presumably believing that "dax" referred to the novel object rather than being another word for "cup."

Children may also get some idea of what a word means by its grammatical form. For instance, in the sentence "Here is a blicket," the use of the determiner "a" indicates that the word "blicket" must be a proper noun or the name of a discrete object or thing, such as a cat, a cookie, or a wink. In contrast, for the sentence "I want some blicket," the use of the adjective "some" indicates that the word "blicket" cannot be a discrete object but is instead a quantity, such as juice, sugar, or peace and quiet (MacWhinney, 2005). This is referred to as **syntactic bootstrapping** (Gleitman, 1990; Hoff & Naigles, 2002).

In a social species such as ours, however, it would be hard to believe that word learning relied only on these sorts of linguistic constraints, and accordingly, it has been proposed that shared, or joint, attention is an important mechanism that gives rise to word learning (see discussion of the development of shared attention in Chapter 6). For example, children attend to a speaker's gaze and gestures, and they are sensitive to behavioral and emotional cues and to a speaker's intentions when figuring out the referent of an utterance (Baldwin, 1993; Diesendruck & Markson, 2001). Most likely, children use multiple cues, including lexical constraints and social cues, and are also influenced by general mechanisms of memory and attention and by conceptual knowledge in deciding what a novel vocal utterance refers to (Bloom, 2000; Hollich, Hirsh-Pasek, & Golinkoff, 2000).

The point that is most critical for our discussion here is that children are *prepared* to learn words. Whether this preparation comes in the form of lexical constraints or is a by-product of their developing social cognition, children seem *not* to experience language as random noise. Rather, their cognitive systems (or social-cognitive systems) are ready to make sense of the connection between things they hear and things they see, making the process of word learning much easier than it would be in the absence of such constraints.

### Overextensions and Underextensions

Often, the errors children make in using words provide us with a good indication of their level of semantic development. Researchers who have analyzed these early errors find that one common pattern is to use **overextensions**—stretching a familiar word beyond its correct meaning (Thompson & Chapman, 1977). For example, children might use the word "doggie" to describe all four-legged creatures, even Daddy when he is on his hands and knees (whether barking or not). Many developmental psychologists argue against the concept of "error" in children's early language use, pointing out that practices such as use of overextensions result in having adults provide the correct words and, thus, can be very effective learning devices. For example, although children might use the word "doggie" to label a kitten or a horse, they usually perform well when given a set of pictures and asked to choose which one is a doggie (Thompson & Chapman, 1977). By overextending the word "doggie," however, they often get some expansion or clarification from adults (for example, "That's not a doggie, that's a kitty"), thus receiving more information about language than they would have gotten had they remained silent.

At other times, children will make **underextensions**—for example, claiming that only their pet Lucy Starbright is a "cat" and that other felines must go by another name. Underextensions indicate that children's boundary for a category is too restricted. During childhood, children learn to classify words and concepts as adults in their culture do. This process doesn't stop in childhood, however, but continues throughout life. It is likely that none of us has exactly the same meaning for all common concepts used in our native language (Nelson, 1996). That speakers of a language are able to make sense of what others say most of the time, however, suggests that most of us have very similar interpretations for the words we use. Both the number of words we know and our understanding of these words change during development. In fact, most changes in language development beyond the age of about 5 years are not in syntax or phonology but in semantics, in the form of vocabulary growth.

## Pragmatics

How we actually use language in a social context, or the ability to use language to get things done in the world, is termed **pragmatics**. *Pragmatics* refers to knowledge about how language can be used and adjusted to fit different circumstances, such as using different tones when speaking to a teacher versus an agemate. Knowing the phonology, morphology, syntax, and semantics of language does one little good in communicating unless one can use language appropriately in a social context. For example, although babies are not competent at language use, they are able to communicate to adults when they are hungry, uncomfortable, or unhappy. On the other hand, we all know people who are quite capable of forming proper sentences but who are less adept at truly communicating with people. They find it difficult to express their thoughts properly, explain how to do something, or to refrain from saying things that offend people.

Children must learn a number of conversational principles to become effective communicators (Grice, 1975). Children must learn that messages need to have the right *quantity* of information, or be at the proper level of description. For example, a mother might request her son to "put the plates on the table." Such a message is likely at the proper level of abstraction to be understood. It would be unnecessary and inappropriate for the mother to say, "Open the kitchen cupboard door, remove a dish using two hands, take it into the dining room, and place it at the head of the table where your father usually sits. Repeat the procedure for the place where I usually sit, where your sister usually sits, and where you usually sit." At the other extreme, an instruction to "prepare the table for dinner" might not have enough information in it, especially if the job of putting out silverware usually fell to the boy's sister. Not surprisingly, children, when presenting their own messages, are more likely to provide too little rather than too much information.

Good messages should have other characteristics, such as being truthful (except for jokes and sarcasm) and relevant to the present context. Also, speakers need to realize the importance of taking turns. Monologues do not make for good conversation.

Beginning early in life, children learn these various conversation principles. For example, toddlers know to watch their listener for signs that they are being understood (Wilcox & Webster, 1980). They know that they must be close to their listener to be heard and, if they are not close to their listener, that they need to speak louder (Wellman & Lempers, 1977). They also know to clarify their speech when they are being misunderstood (Shwe & Markman, 1997). A responsive listener provides a speaker with nonverbal cues, such as nods, gazes, and smiles, and he or she says "yes" and "uh huh" at appropriate times to make it clear that the message is being understood. These skills increase with age, but even 2-year-olds use many of these tactics when listening to an adult (Miller, Lechner, & Rugs, 1985). Children also learn that, depending on the context, sometimes a question is not really a question. For example, when a father says "How many times do I have to tell you to leave that alone?" and "Why do you insist on carrying that blanket everywhere?", children learn that the question is a rhetorical one and does not require a serious answer. Children learn from the speaker's tone of voice that these are really statements because even young preschoolers seldom mistake them for real questions (de Villiers & de Villiers, 1978). The reverse is also true: Sometimes questions can be hidden in statements, such as asking a babysitter for a bedtime extension by stating, "Mommy always lets me watch *The Simpsons*" (Reeder, 1981).

## Speech Registers: The Case of Black English

One aspect of pragmatics involves using different styles of speech in different situations. For example, children use one style of speech when at home or with their friends and another, more formal style when in school. These different styles are referred to as **speech registers** (Warren & McCloskey, 1997).

When the speech registers, or codes, children use at home and the ones they are expected to use in school differ considerably, there is the potential for educational difficulties. Usually, children from middle-class families speak a "standard" version of the language that is similar to the more formal style used in school. In contrast, children from less affluent homes often speak a nonstandard version of the language that is often appreciably different from the one used in school (see, for example, Bernstein, 1971). In the United States, this distinction between social (or home) language and school language among native speakers is often more obvious for children whose home language is described as **Black English** (or sometimes *Ebonics,* or *African American Vernacular English*) (Green, 2002; Rickford, 1999).

Black English is familiar to most Americans, but the term can be somewhat misleading. Although it is used mostly by African Americans, not all African Americans speak it, and many non-African Americans do. Black English has some special rules of pronunciation and syntax (see Table 9-4), the most obvious to many speakers of standard English being the use of the verb "to be." Unlike standard English, this verb is often not conjugated (for example, "We be" or "She be" rather than "We are" or "She is"), and it sometimes is dropped from a sentence entirely. For instance, the verb "to be" can be left out if the sentence refers to a one-time or unusual occurrence of an event, as in the sentence "He playing tennis" for a person who doesn't usually play tennis. But if the sentence refers to a recurrent event, the verb "to be" is included in the sentence. So, for example, "He be playing tennis" describes a person who regularly plays tennis and is playing tennis at this moment (Warren & McCloskey, 1997). Black English is *not* a simplified or inferior linguistic form of standard English. For the most part, the two share common vocabulary and

TABLE **9-4**

Sample Differences Between Standard English and Black English.

| Pronunciation and word forms | Black English | Standard English |
|---|---|---|
| Consonant Substitutions: | /d/ for initial /th/ | "Dey" for "They" |
| | /f/ or /t/ for final /th/ | "toof" for "tooth" |
| | /v/ for medical /th/ | "muvver" for "mother" |
| Consonant Deletions: | medial /r/ | "doing" for "during" |
| | medial /l/ | "hep" for "help" |
| | final consonants | "doe" for "door" |
| Syllable Contractions: | | "spoze" for "suppose" |
| Stress on First Syllable in (some) Bisyllabic Words: | | "Po'-lice" for "Police" |
| Hypercorrection: | | "Pickted" for "picked" |
| | | "2 childrens" for "2 children" |
| *Sentence structure* | | |
| Multiple Negation: | "I ain't done nothing" | "I have not done anything" |
| Aspect: | "He be crazy" | "He's (usually) crazy" |
| | "He crazy" | "He's crazy (right now)" |
| *Nonmarking or nonmatching of verb with subject* | | |
| | "She do all the work" | "She does all the work" |
| | "Two girl wearing hate" | "Two girls wearing hats" |
| Double Subjects: | "My daddy, he works …" | "My daddy works …" |
| Perfective *Done*: | "You done lost your mind" | "You have (already) lost your mind" |

Source: Warren, A. EL, & McCloskey, L A. Language in social contexts. In J. Berko Gleason (Ed.), *The development of language* (4th ed). Published by Allyn and Bacon. Copyright © 1997 by Pearson Education. Reprinted by permission.

syntax, both are syntactically complex, and both are used to express complicated ideas and emotions (Green, 2002; Heath, 1989).

Despite the linguistic legitimacy and complexity of Black English, it is not the language of the schools, nor of the mainstream American marketplace. This means that teachers, who usually speak standard English, will often not understand children who speak Black English, and vice versa. Such children can have a difficult time reading text or comprehending directions expressed in standard English. As a result, they might be unjustly classified as less bright than children who speak standard English. For instance, the language abilities of children who speak Black English are often underestimated when they are tested using standard English (Adler, 1990; Wheldall & Joseph, 1986).

There has been substantial debate over how best to instruct children whose home language is Black English. Should they be taught using Black English, the dialect they know best, or should they be taught using standard English—the dialect, or register, of the marketplace? Some studies have shown the more familiar 5- to 8-year-old

African American children are with standard English, the better their reading achievement is, making the link between speech register and school success clear (Charity, Scarborough, & Griffin, 2004). Most young speakers of Black English do learn some aspects of standard English and use it in school (DeStefano, 1972). For example, in one study, the classroom speech of 8- to 11-year-old African American children contained more components of standard English than did their speech out of school, indicating that elementary school children are able to switch between social (Black English) and school (standard English) registers (DeStefano, 1972). Yet, many African American adolescents tend to *increase* their use of Black English compared with standard English, as use of Black English becomes an important part of their social identity in this period (Delpit, 1990; Delpit & Dowdy, 2002).

The debate about how to educate children whose home language register is different from the language register used by teachers is a controversial one, involving social and political aspects as well as linguistics and educational ones, and no simple answer can— or will—be offered here. But one important thing to remember is that Black English, or any other dialect, is not a linguistically inferior language relative to standard English, just as modern English is neither inferior nor superior to the Elizabethan English used by Shakespeare. One must also keep in mind that, despite Black English's linguistic equivalence to standard English, its use can hinder educability and the opportunity to partake fully in the American economy. Black English is more than just a different language register; it is also a different dialect with some different syntactic and phonological rules compared with standard English. One's language also identifies its user as a member of a social group, and children and adolescents might be reluctant to give up their language style merely for the sake of doing well in school. Ideally, children would master both dialects, just as children might ideally acquire a second language, and have the flexibility to switch between them as the context demands. In such a situation, different dialects would then truly become different registers, to be used when and where appropriate.

### Communicative Competence

Although children may have acquired the basic structure of language and know enough words to make most of their wants and feelings known by age 5 or 6, their ability to communicate effectively continues to increase with age. All types of language knowledge (phonology, morphology, syntax, semantics, and pragmatics) are combined in a package called **communicative competence** (Hymes, 1972). Generally, as children—or, indeed, adults—participate in varied contexts, they become communicatively more competent.

Despite the seeming communicative sophistication of many preschoolers, effective communication between adult and child, or between child and child, is variable. Many messages within the grammatical competence of a child are simply not understood. Also, young children often have difficulty in conveying exactly the right message and are frequently unaware that their message was inadequate. To some extent, their difficulties in communicating effectively can be attributed to other aspects of their cognitive development, in particular to a tendency to assume that other people understand the world exactly as they do. In fact, communication problems are very common among adults and sometimes require therapeutic assistance, such as learning how to be more assertive in one's speech, claiming one's rights in an appropriate manner, or speaking up appropriately when one disagrees with another person.

Early language development in general, and development of conversational skills in particular, does not take place only in the context of adult-child conversations but often in the context of other children, particularly siblings. First-born children usually surpass later-born children in both the early development of vocabulary and grammar but not in the development of conversational skills (Hoff, 2009). In fact, later-born children tend to be better than first-born children in the production of personal pronouns ("I," "you") (Oshima-Takane, Goodz, & Deverensky, 1996). Although reasons for these differences are far from clear, first-born children's vocabulary and grammar advantages likely stem from getting more of their mothers' exclusive attention. Later-born children, in contrast, seem to take advantage of the richer and more varied speech they hear and of social interactions with both their parents and their older siblings (Hoff, 2009). For example, it has been suggested that later-born children's advantage over first-borns regarding the use of personal pronouns might result from the fact that they are overly exposed to a type of speech between first-borns and mothers that includes more personal pronouns than the speech they each address to them (Oshima-Takane & Robbins, 2003).

### Communication and Egocentrism

For years, research and theory in communicative development followed the interpretation of Jean Piaget (1955), who proposed that young children's speech is *egocentric* and *presocial*. In social situations, young children attempt to communicate with others, but their egocentric view of the world often results in speech that does not get the message across to a listener. This failure often does not bother preschool children, however, because in many cases, they are unaware that the message is not being comprehended. Such egocentric speech can be observed in young children in a variety of contexts. Listen to the phone conversation of a 4-year-old. When the voice on the other end of the receiver asked Alese, "What are you wearing today?", Alese responded, "This," while looking down and pointing at her dress. This apparently is not an atypical phone conversation for a preschooler (see Warren & Tate, 1992, for other examples). The conversation of two 5-year-old boys playing together in a sandbox can be interesting. "I drive my truck over here, and then I drive beside your plane and I fill it up with stuff," says one child. In the meantime, the other is saying, "My plane's coming in for a landing. I drop bombs on your truck and crash into it. Boom!" Such a "conversation" would not be taking place if each child were alone. However, what one child says has little to do with the comments of the other. The two boys are talking "with" each other but not necessarily "to" each other. Piaget labeled such egocentric exchanges **collective monologues**.

### Metacommunication

Do children have any idea that they are sometimes not being understood, or that the message they are receiving from someone else is unclear? Research by John Flavell and his associates (Beal & Flavell, 1982) indicated that children 5 years of age and younger seem to recognize an inadequate or ambiguous message but seldom act on their uncertainty, behaving as if the message had been understood loud and clear. When kindergarten children were provided with ambiguous instructions for making a block building, for instance, they often looked puzzled and hesitated in selecting the appropriate block. Yet, when their building was completed, these children said that it was just like the model (which it was not) and that the instructions had been adequate for reproducing the model (which they had not). Carole Beal and John Flavell (1982) found that children's poor performance on these tasks could not be attributed to memory or attentional failures. Rather, their problems were a result of metacognitive deficits; they had "a poor understanding of message quality and its role in determining the success or failure of a communication" (p. 48).

Another **metacommunication** skill involves children's abilities to monitor their own speech. Again, young children tend to display deficits in this area of metacommunication (for reviews, see Shatz, 1983, and Whitehurst & Sonnenschein, 1985); their speech includes a greater incidence of omissions and ambiguities and requires greater contextual support to be comprehended than does the speech of older children.

One way of assessing children's self-monitoring abilities is to examine the frequency with which they correct their speech by repeating, by including new information, by telling the listener to forget the last thing that was said until later, and so forth. Mary Ann Evans (1985) studied such *verbal repairs* in the speech of kindergarten and second-grade children during classroom show-and-tell sessions. Evans reported that the incidence of verbal repairs was significantly greater for the second-grade children than for the kindergartners, occurring for 19% of all the utterances by the older children compared with only 7% by the younger. The following is an example of a story by a second-grade girl that includes several verbal repairs:

> We went to—uh me and Don went to Aunt Judy's. And … and uh my brother came down on Fri—Friday night, Uh there was a acc—came on the train, And there was an accident. And they thought uh … that uh … the—there was an accident with a—a van, And they thought—there was pig's blood in it. And they thought there was somebody hurt. But it was the pig. (Evans, 1985, p. 370)

Evans proposed that the high incidence of self-repairs for the second-grade children relative to the kindergartners reflected an increased ability by the older children to monitor their speech. Evans suggested that as communication skills increase from this point through childhood, the ability to plan and organize one's thoughts improves, resulting in a reduction of verbal repairs into adolescence (see also Sabin et al., 1979). Thus, the incidence of verbal repairs is low in young children's speech because of poor self-monitoring skills, increases during middle childhood as children become increasingly aware of the effectiveness of their speech in conveying a message, and then decreases as other skills, such as planning, improve.

The verbal repairs discussed above were made during a monologue, but conversation involves two or more people. One important metacommunication skill that develops over childhood is sensitivity to the other people, often reflected in linguistic turn-taking. Some researchers have suggested that such turn-taking may stem from parent-infant interactions, such as when parents and babies take turns making cooing or babbling sounds (see Snow & Ferguson, 1977). Piaget described such interchanges as *mutual imitation*, with infants imitating adults who are imitating them. The parents are the real imitators here, of course, but the result is bouts of turn-taking, with one partner making a sound and the other copying it, until one of them (usually the parent) tires of the routine. Other examples of preverbal turn-taking are games such as peek-a-boo (Bruner, 1983) and exchanges during feeding, with the infant learning to "take turns" with Mom or Dad (it's Mom's turn to put the spoon to my mouth, my turn to eat it and then request more) (see Kaye, 1982). Not surprisingly, children whose mothers are more responsive to their vocalizations speak their first words earlier and have larger vocabularies than children whose mothers are less responsive (Nicely, Tamis-LeMonda, & Bornstein, 1999).

Despite the ample evidence of young children's poor communication skills, preschoolers' language is not as egocentric as Piaget and other early researchers believed. In fact, several researchers have reported clearly nonegocentric use of language in the communication attempts of young children. For example, in Evans' (1985) study of speech repairs cited earlier, many 5-year-olds displayed at least limited self-monitoring abilities. In other research, Marilyn Shatz and Rochel Gelman (1973) observed the speech of 4-year-old children when they talked to adults, to other 4-year-olds, or to 2-year-olds. Shatz and Gelman found that these children modified their speech to the 2-year-olds, using different tones of voice and shorter sentences, much as adults do. Other research has demonstrated that preschool children show greater metacommunicative competence when the messages are embedded in familiar scripts, such as a trip to the grocery store (Furman & Walden, 1990). Findings such as these, among others (Nadig & Sedivy, 2002; Warren-Leubecker & Bohannon, 1989), suggest that young children have substantial metacommunication skills. As with many newly acquired skills, however, communication abilities seem to develop first in highly specific, familiar situations and are easily disrupted. With age, children display their communication skills in increasingly diverse contexts, generalizing what they know to new and unfamiliar settings.

# SOME THEORETICAL PERSPECTIVES OF LANGUAGE DEVELOPMENT

The question central to language acquisition has been the acquisition of syntax. How is it that children make sense of the jumble of sounds that surrounds them to eventually discover the underlying rules of language? Although each of the world's 6000-plus languages might have some unique features to them, they also all have some things in common with one another. That is, they all possess, at some "deep level," some common aspects of syntax (see Maratsos, 1998; Pinker, 1994). In this section, I do not intend to cover the intricacies of theories of syntax development in great detail but merely to describe some of the major points of the dominant perspectives so that the reader can get a general idea of how children approach the seemingly complicated task of learning to talk (see Hoff, 2009; MacWhinney, 2005; Tomasello, 2006).

In very general terms, three major types of theories have been postulated to account for language acquisition: (1) behavioral theories, (2) nativist theories, and (3) social-interactionist theories. Behavioral theories were popular in the early and middle part of the last century and proposed, basically, that children learn language like they learn any other complex behavior, through the principles of classical and operant conditioning (Skinner, 1957). Behaviorists emphasized the role of parents as models of, and reinforcers for, language. The behaviorists actually paid relatively little attention to children, who for generations had been producing perfectly understandable original sentences and phrases they could not have possibly learned through conditioning and imitation, such as "all-gone sticky" to announce that their hands have been washed.

Many claims of the behaviorists have not stood the test of time. For example, although words can be learned through conditioning principles in the laboratory, little evidence suggests that parents use such structured techniques at home; yet, almost all children are fluent in their native language before they reach school age. Other research has shown that parents seldom comment to children about the grammatical correctness of their spoken messages, only the meaningfulness of them (Brown & Hanlon, 1970), and although new words are obviously learned by imitation, new grammatical forms (such as plurals or the past tense) are typically not imitated until children are able to produce them spontaneously (Bloom, Hood, & Lightbown, 1974). In addition, although 2- and 3-year-old children hear between 5000 and 7000 utterances each day, more than 20% of those utterances are incomplete sentence fragments, and only about 15% are in the Subject-Verb-Object form that is standard for English (Cameron-Faulkner, Lieven, & Tomasello, 2003). All this makes it very unlikely that a behavioral theory of language development is adequate. Thus, one way in which children apparently do *not* learn the syntax of their mother tongue is through the conventional rules of classical and operant conditioning.

More recent research, however, has discovered that infants seemingly use a domain-general mechanism of **statistical learning** to discern what is a word and what is not, consistent with some claims of the behavioral position (Aslin, Saffran, & Newport, 1998; Saffran, Aslin, & Newport, 1996). In this context, statistical learning refers to infants essentially keeping track of how often different syllables follow one another and then using this information to determine which sound sequences are meaningful (that is, are "words") and which are not. For example, the phrase "pretty baby" consists of two words, but when spoken, the syllables run together. (If you don't believe this, listen to speakers of a foreign language and see if you can be certain where one word ends and another begins.) How do infants figure out which sound sequences constitute a word? (Why "pretty baby" and not "pre tyba by"?) The answer is statistical learning. The syllable "pre" precedes "ty" not just in "pretty baby" but also in "pretty boy," "pretty good," and "pretty much a lot of things." Similarly, the syllable "ba" precedes "by" in a variety of utterances, such as "Mama's baby," "happy baby," and "cry baby." In contrast, infants rarely hear the syllable "pre" followed by the syllable "ba" or "by." Because of the frequency with which infants hear certain syllables uttered in close proximity to one another, they learn that "pretty" is likely one word and "baby" another.

This is certainly a nice idea, but how does one test it? Jenny Saffran, Richard Aslin, and Elisa Newport (1996) used a preference-for-novelty paradigm (see Chapter 4) in which 8-month-old babies heard a series of nonsense words, such as "golabupabiku-tutibubabupugolabu," repeatedly over a 2-minute period. Given that the same sequence of sounds was repeated, infants, if they engage in statistical learning, should come to recognize that "gol" is always followed by "abu," that "ku" is always followed by "tu," and so on. To test this, after the initial 2-minute exposure, the infants were given a tape consisting of the same syllables but in different orders as well as a tape identical to the one they had heard during the first 2-minute period. Infants preferred to listen to the novel tape, with the same sounds in different orders, indicating that they recognized it was different from the original tape, thus providing evidence for statistical learning of language sounds. Moreover, subsequent research demonstrated that infants' statistical learning is not limited to language sounds but also is found for tones (Saffran et al., 1999). This suggests that statistical learning is a domain-general ability and not one specific to learning language.

Despite evidence of a domain-general language-learning mechanism, most contemporary researchers believe that traditional behavioral accounts of language acquisition are not adequate to account for learning syntax. What are the alternatives? Advocates of **nativist theories** propose that children are biologically prepared to learn language and do so with special, innate learning mechanisms, not through some domain-general set of learning devices as hypothesized by the behaviorists. As Steve Pinker (1994) put it, children are born with a *language instinct*. In contrast, proponents of **social-interactionist theories** blend aspects of the behavioral and nativists perspectives, granting that humans are specially prepared to acquire language but holding that aspects of the environment, especially parents, also might be specially prepared to foster language acquisition, although not to the extent that Skinner and his behaviorist colleagues once believed.

In the following sections, I outline some of the theory and data associated with nativist and social-interactionist theories of language acquisition. This account is admittedly a cursory one, and readers who would like to pursue some of the ideas mentioned are encouraged to seek out some of suggested readings at the end of the chapter.

## Nativist Perspectives on Language Development

Contemporary nativist perspectives on language development can trace their beginnings to the work of Noam Chomsky (1957). In 1959, Chomsky, reviewing B. F. Skinner's (1957) book *Verbal Behavior,* wrote, "I can find no support whatsoever for the doctrine ... that slow and careful shaping of verbal behavior through differential reinforcement is an absolute necessity" (p. 42). Chomsky's ideas were as radical in one direction as Skinner's were in the other. Instead of viewing language as something that is taught, produced by the child's environment, Chomsky insisted that language is something innate, produced by the child's biology. Chomsky believed that language, as we commonly use the term, is only one part of this process—the **surface structure**. Infants hear language being spoken around them and end up being able to speak it themselves within a few years. No simple rules of learning or conditioning account adequately for this acquisition, however, because the language children hear is too complicated, and often too ambiguous, for them to discern the rules. Chomsky suggested that another mechanism is necessary to explain why children have the ability to sample the surface structure of the language being spoken around them and then produce it fully and fluently by the age of 3, even creating sentences that they could not have heard before.

Chomsky believed that a second structure of language exists, the **deep structure**, which refers to the underlying meaning of language. This is a more gut-level understanding of language, a "species-specific characteristic ... latent in the nervous system until kindled by actual language use" (Sacks, 1989, p. 81). According to Chomsky, all human languages share this deep structure, and it is an innate concept in humans, much like the concepts of time and space.

Chomsky believed that humans possess a mental organ, much like a heart or liver, that is dedicated to language use and is located in the brain. This innate neural device (the **language acquisition device**, or **LAD**) imposes order on incoming stimuli. This is not a totally novel concept. As Chomsky points out, a similar function has been found for the visual cortex; it orders incoming visual stimuli into meaningful patterns before passing them on to higher levels of the brain.

Chomsky's ideas about the innateness of language derive from linguistic theory. Other support for the nativism school of thought is less specifically linguistic in nature. For example, more than 40 years ago, Eric Lenneberg (1967) argued that language is a special human ability (that is, not just a result of "learning") that has a strong biological basis. Lenneberg noted several characteristics of language as support for this contention, among them:

1. *Language is species specific.* Humans are the only species to possess it. Apes can be taught simple sign language comparable with that of a 2-year-old child (Savage-Rumbaugh et al., 1993), and other species certainly do communicate complicated ideas (such as bees' ability to communicate the location of pollen-rich flowers). However, at least as human linguists define it, only humans possess language.

2. *Language is species uniform.* All normal members of the species possess language. Moreover, the complexity of a language is not related to the complexity of a culture's technology. That is, the language of "primitive" people is no more or no less complicated, on average, than is the language of people from information-age societies (Pinker, 1994).

3. *Language is difficult to retard.* Except for children raised in closets or in other severely deprived situations, nearly all children learn to speak. This is true even for many severely mentally impaired children, whose language skills are often far in excess of their more general intellectual abilities.

4. *Language develops in a regular sequence.* Children around the world acquire language in about the same way at about the same time. This is similar to the universal sequence of motor development.

5. *There are specific anatomical structures for language.* The structure of the mouth and throat are unique to our species and specially suited for the task of speaking. Equally critical, areas in the brain are dedicated to different aspects of language, and damage to specific areas of the brain can result in very specific types of *aphasia*, or language disability.

6. *There are language disabilities that are genetically based.* Specific language disorders run in families, suggesting that there is a genetic basis for these disorders, with some apparently being controlled by a dominant gene (Gopnik & Crago, 1991).

All this is well and good, but how does it give us a better picture of how children actually learn to talk? What it does is place language in the realm of an important, species-uniform skill that was likely selected in human evolution for its survival value. But saying that language is based in biology doesn't, by itself, tell us a whole lot. We need to look at more specific theories and research to get a better picture of how children acquire language. I do this briefly in the next two sections. First, I examine the neurological basis of language development. I then look at evidence for a universal grammar that all children begin life with and modify until it resembles the language spoken around them. Finally I review research suggesting that there is a critical period for language—a time when the child is biologically prepared to learn language.

### Language and Brain Development

Since the 19th century, scientists have known that certain areas of the brain are associated with aspects of language functioning. Specific areas of the left hemisphere (in right-handed people) are associated with specific language abilities, and damage to these areas produces specific language impairment. For example, damage to **Wernicke's area**, located in the temporal lobe, results in problems comprehending speech, although the ability to produce speech is not usually affected. Damage to **Broca's area**, located in the frontal lobes, usually results in problems with speech production. As I mentioned in Chapter 2, when these areas are damaged in infancy or early in childhood, recovery of language function is often good, and much better than when damage occurs later in life, especially after adolescence (Kolb & Whishaw, 1990; Stiles et al., 2005).

Advances in neuroimaging technologies have permitted scientists to examine how the brain operates when it processes language and, important from our perspective, to look at the neurological basis of language development. For example, Figure 9-5 (from Sakai, 2005) presents two views of the left hemisphere in an adult. Figure 9-5A identifies areas of the brain associated with phonology, semantics, syntax, and sentence comprehension. Other areas of the brain are also involved in language processing, but the areas identified here are domain-specific areas, as hypothesized by nativist theorists, specialized for particular types of language processing. Figure 9-5B shows what Kuniyoshi Sakai (2005) has termed the **grammar center**. The frontal lobe has areas that are specifically related to processing grammatical information. Although these areas are also involved in other types of processing, they appear to represent a domain-specific neural system dedicated to syntactic processing. For instance, Ryuichiro Hashimoto and Sakai (2002) reported that activation of the grammar center was found only when people made syntactic decisions (for example, is a sentence grammatical or not?); activation was not found during tasks involving verbal short-term memory

FIGURE **9-5**

Two views of the left hemisphere. Figure A shows possible networks for various language functions. Figure B shows the grammar center and other areas involved in language, as proposed by Sakai (2005). The green area is selectively involved in comprehending sentences. The red areas are specifically involved in syntactic processing and can be regarded as the grammar center.

Source: Sakai, K. L. (2005). Language acquisition and brain development. *Science, 310,* 815–919. Reprinted with permission from AAAS.

(for example, recalling a list of words in exact order). This and related work led Sakai (2005) to conclude that "the human left frontal cortex is thus uniquely specialized in the syntactic processes of sentence comprehension, without any counterparts in other animals" (p. 817).

Do children or infants display this same neurological specialization for language? Perhaps not surprisingly, there has been much less neuroimaging research with children than with adults, making it difficult to provide any definitive answer to the question of when such hemispheric specialization begins. However, research has shown that even the hemispheres of newborns are different, or *lateralized*. For example, neonates show greater electrical activation to language in the left than in the right hemisphere, while music and other nonlanguage sounds show the opposite pattern (Molfese & Molfese, 1980, 1985). More recent research has shown that children's brains are especially sensitive to language and that different parts of the brain, in addition to those used to process language in adults' brains, are involved in language learning (specifically, the frontal cerebella and occipital regions) (Redcay, Haist, & Courchesne, 2007).

Evidence also indicates that different areas of the brain are involved when a second language is learned in childhood versus in adolescence or adulthood (Kim et al., 1997; Wartenburger et al., 2003). For example, in one study (Wartenburger et al., 2003), brain images were taken of "early" and "late" adult bilinguals while they spoke in either their first or second language. For people who had learned their second language during childhood, the same areas of their brains "lit up" regardless of whether they were using their first or second language. In contrast, different parts of the brains of the "late" bilinguals were activated when using their first versus their second language (see Figure 9-6). Both the "early" and "late" bilinguals in this study reported comparable fluency in their second languages, so differences in language ability between these two groups is not likely to be the cause of this effect. Rather, these results suggest that different parts of the brain and, thus, likely different cognitive processes, are involved when a second language is learned early in childhood rather than later.

Like all complex cognitive abilities, scientists have long known that the brain is the source of our language facility and that developmental differences in children's language skills are associated with age-related differences in brain functioning. New technologies are giving us a glimpse of the relationship between brain development and language development, which will give us greater insight into language acquisition and how we can intervene when children (and adults) have language impairments.

### Universal Grammar and Language Development

Following the nativist ideas of Chomsky, most linguistic theorists today believe that children around the world acquire language so easily because they possess at birth a "mental organ" specially designed to perform the job of learning language. In addition to this mental organ (the language acquisition device), infants also have at birth some primitive "knowledge" about the structure, or syntax, of language. This is referred to as **universal grammar**, which consists of the basic grammatical rules that typify all languages. Having this "theory of syntax" in their heads from the beginning of life, children do not have to learn all the rules of their language. Rather, they have to examine

FIGURE **9-6**

Bilingual speakers made grammatical judgments in their second language. For adults who were highly proficient in both languages (A), different parts of the brain were involved in making grammatical judgments for those who learned their second language late (LAHP) versus those who learned their second language early (EAHP). When considering people only who learned their second language late, different areas of the brain were involved for people with high- versus low-language proficiency in their second language (B).

Source: Reprinted from Neuron, 37, Wartenburger, I., Heekereb, H. R., Abutalebi, J., Cappa, S. F., Villringer, A., & Perani, D., Early setting of grammatical processing in the bilingual brain, 159–170, Copyright (2003), with permission from Elsevier.

the language that surrounds them, see how it fits with the universal grammar that resides in their brains, and make the appropriate modifications so that their innate theory of syntax comes to match the theory that people around them use.

Children, of course, don't actually "know" any language (universal or otherwise) at birth, but, the theory goes, they have a set of *principles* and *parameters* that guide their interpretation of speech. Parameters, as used here, refer to aspects of grammar that vary across languages. For example, although all languages have subjects, some languages require that proper sentences state the subject (as in the English, "I love you"), whereas in other languages, the subject can be expressed as part of the verb, eliminating the necessity of stating the subject (as in the Spanish, "Te amo"). This is a parameter, and children must learn whether their language requires the subject to be explicitly stated (as in English) or not (as in Spanish). One piece of evidence for universal grammar is that English-speaking children's early sentences often resemble those of languages that don't require an explicit subject. This is reflected in children's statements such as "Helping Mommy" or "Make a house" (Bloom, Lightbown, & Hood, 1975).

The many similarities across languages argue for a universal grammar. For example, all languages have extensive vocabularies divided into parts-of-speech categories that include nouns and verbs; words are organized into phrases that follow a similar underlying rule system (called the X-bar system); all permit movement of grammatical categories, such as the subject-auxiliary inversion used to transform declarative sentences in English into questions (for example, "You are going" transformed to "Are you going?"); and all use word prefixes or suffixes for verbs and nouns (for example, adding the *ed* to make a verb past tense) (see Hoff, 2009; Pinker, 1994). The similar way and rate that children around the world acquire many of the same grammatical forms is further evidence for a universal grammar.

One source of evidence that children create a grammatical system based on some universal principles comes from **pidgins** and **creoles** (Bickerton, 1990). When a group of people with a variety of native languages moves to a foreign land where they are not given the opportunity to participate in the majority culture or to learn the language of their new homeland, they develop a communication system termed a *pidgin*. Pidgins combine several languages at a rudimentary level and are used to convey necessary information within the group and between the group and its "hosts." Word order is often highly variable, and there is little in the way of a grammatical system. (Bickerton proposed that pidgins might be similar in form to the protolanguage spoken by our ancient ancestors.) In the hands (or mouths) of children, however, pidgins can quickly transform into true languages. Derek Bickerton documented (based on historical evidence and his own studies of Hawaii creole) how the children of pidgin speakers take the remnants of their parents' language and create a fully developed language in only one generation—a language termed a *creole*. Thus, rather than acquiring language in the typical sense, these children *create* a language. Although there might not be an easy interpretation of this phenomenon, the creation of a creole by children suggests that they possess an innate grammar and use it to "correct" the fragmented pidgin spoken by their parents and convert it into a true (and new) language.

Evidence consistent with this hypothesis comes from a study of several cohorts of children creating Nicaraguan Sign Language (*Idioma de Señas de Nicaragua*) (Senghas & Coppola, 2001; Senghas, Kita, & Ozyürek, 2004). Deaf education in Nicaragua began only in the 1970s, with deaf children before this time having little contact with one another. There was also no recognized form of Nicaraguan Sign Language for children to be taught. Such a language began to emerge in the 1980s, however, in the Managua school for the deaf and was well developed by the late 1990s. Ann Senghas and Marie Coppola (2001) tested deaf Nicaraguan signers who had first been exposed to Nicaraguan Sign Language as early as 1978 (Cohort 1) or as late as 1990 (Cohort 2) and examined changes in early linguistic structures of the newly emerged sign language. They found that Nicaraguan Sign Language was systematically modified from one cohort of children to the next, with children aged 10 years and younger generating most of the changes. In other words, sequences of children created a new sign language from the incomplete forms used by their predecessors.

The evidence of children "inventing" language suggests that they have been especially prepared by natural selection to make sense of vocal and gestural information for the purpose of communicating. Given that language today is acquired most easily by children, it is likely that language first evolved through the mouths of babes. The physician and science writer Lewis Thomas (1993) proposed that our ancient adult ancestors likely used gestures and a few words to express themselves, but that it was children who discovered how to put them together into sentences while playing with other children.

Language has many important functions for adults, of course, but it may have had some particularly important functions for ancestral children. For example, John Locke and Barry Bogin (2006; see also Locke, 2009) proposed that language improved communication between young children and their parents at a time when children are particularly in need of assistance—between the ages of about 3 and 7, when children are no longer nursing, can get around their environment relatively well, but are still highly dependent on adults for support. Facility with language also may have been particularly important in adolescence, being related to same-sex competition and courtship. These ideas must remain speculative, for we may never know with certainty the adaptive roles that language played for our ancestors. However, I think we can be confident that the greatest adaptive pressures for evolving language were placed on children, not on adults, and that it was the structure and functioning of children's brains that afforded the invention of language and its many advantages.

### *Is There a Critical Period for Learning Language?*

Almost without exception, adults learn things more easily than children do. This is hardly surprising, and this truism is apparent in our school system. Children first starting school are not expected to master complicated material. In fact, some schools of thought argue that expecting too much in the way of intellectual mastery from young children is not only foolish but also emotionally harmful (Elkind, 1987). Young children just don't have the mental capacity to acquire and understand information that an older child or adult has.

One major exception to this, however, is language development. Children are better than adults at acquiring both first and second languages. The cognitive system of the child is seemingly not less efficient in any respect than the adult's when it comes to language learning; in fact, it is well suited to the demands, making immaturity highly adaptive for the important human ability of acquiring language. This has suggested to many that there is a *critical period,* or *sensitive period,* for learning language—that children must be exposed to language early in life if they are ever to master it.

Lenneberg (1967) was the first vocal proponent of a critical period for language acquisition. With age, the nervous system loses its flexibility, so by puberty, the organization of the brain is fixed, making language learning difficult.

In support of Lenneberg's claim, John Locke (1993) stated that there are four types of evidence for a sensitive period for language acquisition. The first involves people who were socially deprived or isolated during infancy and early childhood, who typically demonstrate only a tenuous mastery of language (particularly syntax) (Curtiss, 1977).

The second and largest body of evidence for a sensitive period comes from studies involving second-language learning, with eventual proficiency in the foreign tongue being related to the age of first exposure. For example, Jacqueline Johnson and Elissa Newport (1989) tested 46 native Chinese or Korean speakers who had immigrated to the United States and learned English as a second language. These people had arrived in the United States at ages ranging from 3 to 39 years and had lived in the United States for between 3 and 26 years when they were tested (all were educated adults). Johnson and Newport reported that their subjects' proficiency in English was related to the age at which they arrived in the United States, not to the number of years they had been speaking the language or to years of formal instruction. Figure 9-7 graphs average scores on a test of grammatical competency (having people determine whether a sentence is properly grammatical or not) as a function of age of arrival in the United States. As you can see, people who learned their second language early in childhood showed greater proficiency as adults than did people who learned their second language later in childhood. In fact, people who arrived in the United States between the ages of 3 and 7 years had grammatical proficiency comparable with that of native

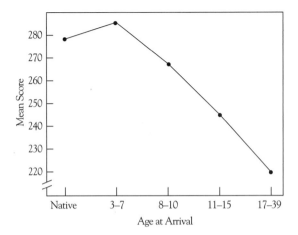

FIGURE **9-7**

The relationship between age at arrival in the United States and total number of correct answers on a test of English grammar (data from Johnson & Newport, 1989, as reported in Newport, 1991).

Source: "Critical Period Effects in Second Language Learning: The influence of maturational state on the acquisition of English as a second language," by J. S. Johnson and E. L. Newport, 1989. *Cognitive Psychology, 21,* 60–99. Copyright © 1989 Academic Press. Reprinted with permission.

speakers. Grammatical proficiency decreased gradually the older people were when they immigrated to the United States and were first exposed to English (see also Hakuta, Bialystok, & Wiley, 2003). Although it might not be surprising that one maintains an accent when the second language is not learned until the teen years, these data demonstrate that the same holds true for syntax.

A third source of evidence for a sensitive period comes from deaf children who are not exposed to any formal language, spoken or signed, until late in childhood or adolescence. Newport (1990) performed studies with such a population, evaluating their proficiency in American Sign Language as a function of when they were first exposed to it. The logic here is similar to that in the Johnson and Newport study (1989), except in this study, American Sign Language is people's first language, not their second. Newport (1990) reports results similar to those she found for second-language learning: Grammatical proficiency is related to age of first exposure to sign language, not to the number of years one has been using the language.

The fourth type of evidence concerns recovery of language function after specific brain damage. I discussed some of this research in Chapter 2. Basically, when the language areas of the left hemisphere are damaged early in life, much plasticity is observed, with other areas of the brain taking over the language function of the destroyed area. This plasticity is reduced with age (see Huttenlocher, 2002; Stiles, 2008; Witelson, 1987).

Although much remains to be learned about the nature of language acquisition, it is clear that the cognitive system of the young child is especially suited to language learning—both of a first and a second language. This ability is gradually lost over childhood, and although adults are able to acquire a second language, they rarely attain the same proficiency as achieved when language is acquired in childhood.

But why is language learning easier early in life compared with later? There has been much speculation over the years, with recent data providing evidence permitting researchers to go beyond interesting speculation to real (if still preliminary) theories. One theory proposes that young children acquire language so easily not so much because of their advanced cognitive abilities for processing language but, somewhat counterintuitively, because of their cognitive limitations. This idea is examined in Box 9-2.

---

**BOX 9-2**     **The "Less Is More" Hypothesis**

When it comes to cognitive abilities, we naturally think that "more is better," but with respect to language development, that may not always be the case. For example, Elisa Newport (1991) has proposed that the cognitive limitations of infants and young children simplify the corpus (the body of language they process), thus making the complicated syntactical system of any human language easier to learn. Newport's **"less is more" hypothesis** is based on the ideas of Gerald Turkewitz and Patricia Kenny (1982), who proposed that perceptual limitations in infancy are adaptive, in that they allow one sensory system to develop (hearing, for example) without having to compete for neural resources with another, usually later-developing system (vision, for example). (See Turkewitz and Kenny's ideas of the advantage of perceptual immaturity in infancy, along with some research examples, in Chapter 2.) The principal application of these ideas to language acquisition is that children's limited information-processing abilities reduce the complexity of what they must master, resulting in easier initial acquisition. With success and time, maturationally paced abilities gradually increase, as does language learning.

Newport (1991) observes that children in the early stages of language learning start out slowly—more slowly, in fact, than adults do when learning a second language. This is partly because children perceive and store only component parts of complex stimuli. Their speech starts with single morphemes (usually a single syllable), and they gradually increase the syntactic complexity and the number of units they can control. This is true not only in spontaneous speech but also in imitation. As a result, children are able to extract only limited pieces of the speech stream. Newport claims that because of their limited cognitive abilities, the simplified language that they deal with makes the job of learning language easier. Adults, in contrast,

begin learning a second language faster than children do, producing more complex words and sentences. This is because adults more readily perceive and remember the whole, complex stimulus. But the advantage is short-lived. Adults extract more of the language input but are then faced with a more difficult problem of analyzing everything all at once. As a result, adult learners often fail to analyze aspects of language they have acquired in a rote-like fashion, limiting the eventual proficiency they are apt to attain.

Newport (1991) presented the result of a simulation in which a computer program was given aspects of language to "learn." The "language-learning" mechanism of the computer program was constant, but the size of the input filter was varied, which effectively limited how much the computer program could keep in memory at any one time. This is essentially equivalent to varying the size of a child's short-term store. In the simulation, the input filter became less restricted over repeated trials, similar to the effect that maturation has on the size of the short-term store in developing children (Dempster, 1981). Newport reported that the restricted filter did result in the loss of data for morphology (the smallest units of word meanings, including word endings that denote pluralization and verb tense), making initial learning worse than when a less restricted input filter was used. However, there was greater loss at the whole-word level than at the morphology level (indicating that prefixes and suffixes were often retained). Importantly, the restricted filter resulted in an improvement in the signal-to-noise ratio (that is, the ratio of relevant linguistic information to irrelevant background information). There was also greater loss of data from accidental cooccurrences than from systematic cooccurrences of form and meaning. This means that with the less restricted filter (reflecting a larger short-term store), many

*(Continues)*

**BOX 9-2**   **The "Less Is More" Hypothesis (Continued)**

language-irrelevant associations were retained, which impeded rather than facilitated language learning. Newport (1991) concluded, "[O]verall, then, a learning mechanism with a restricted input filter more successfully acquired a morphology; the same learning mechanism with a less restricted filter, or with no filter at all, entertains too many alternative analyses and cannot uniquely determine which is the better one" (p. 127). Jeffrey Elman (1994) reached a similar conclusion, using a very different connectionist type of computer simulation. Elman used the metaphor "the importance of starting small" to describe his findings and suggested that the critical period for language acquisition involves the developmental delay of certain abilities rather than the loss of some language-specific capabilities. Preliminary empirical support for the "importance of starting small" position comes from evidence that adults learn an artificial grammar faster when presented with smaller units of the language (Kersten & Earles, 2001).

## Social-Interactionist Perspectives of Language Development

Most contemporary theorists who adhere to a social-interactionist perspective believe that the nativists have much of the story right. There is an overwhelming (though not unanimous) belief that humans are specially prepared to acquire language, that something akin to universal grammar exists, and that there is a critical period for language. Despite this near consensus, some theorists see the social environment as playing a more important role than some of the more vocal proponents of the nativist camp believe. As Michael Tomasello (2006) stated, one of the problems in studying language is "that quite often the study of language acquisition has been cut off from the study of children's other cognitive and social skills" (p. 292).

This interactive perspective is well illustrated in the theorizing of Jerome Bruner (1983). He rejected the idea that language is encountered willy-nilly by the child and that the innate language acquisition device abstracts rules from this shower of spoken language. Instead, Bruner believes that language is carefully presented to children by the people around them. Not only is the content selected for the child's current abilities, but the presentation is executed to provide the best possible chance of learning. According to this *social-pragmatic view* of language acquisition, "children's initial skills of linguistic communication are a natural outgrowth of their emerging understanding of other persons as intentional agents" (Carpenter, Nagell, & Tomasello, 1998, p. 126). Others concur, arguing that language has fewer true universals than the nativists propose, and that the similarities in language and language acquisition around the world result from the constraints of human cognition and cultural-historical factors (Evans & Levinson, 2009). Language is viewed as a powerful social-cognitive tool, used to manipulate other people's attention. It is based on more primitive social processes, such as *shared attention*, which makes language possible. In this section, I first examine some of the underlying social-cognitive abilities that may make language possible, focusing on infants seeing others as *intentional agents*. I then look at the role of gestures in early language acquisition and, finally, review research on the role of child-directed speech and how the way adults talk to infants and young children might contribute to language acquisition.

### The Emergence of Communicative Intentions

By the time toddlers put their first two-word sentence together, around 18 months of age, they have been communicating with their parents for some time. Early communication is sometimes vocal (coos, babbles, cries, and holophrastic phrases) and sometimes physical (gestures). As I described in Chapter 6, beginning around 9 months, babies engage in *shared attention*, sharing experiences with other social beings. For example, an infant, while looking at his mother, may vocalize and simultaneously point to the kitty that has gotten into a flowerbed. Behavior like this implies that the infant sees his mother as an *intentional agent*, someone whose actions are based on what she knows and what she wants and who acts deliberately to achieve her goals.

The connection between seeing others as intentional agents and language acquisition may not seem immediately obvious. However, advocates of the social-interactionist perspective argue that shared-attention activities between children and their mothers (and others) provide the context for effective communication in which language will emerge (see Tomasello, 1999, 2005, 2006). Parents begin treating their infants as if they are intentional agents before they actually are, pointing out objects and events to them, and, beginning around 9 months of age, babies start to catch on and to even initiate such interactions. There is often much language from the parents in these exchanges. For instance, a toddler, while gazing at her mother's eyes, may point to an object on a shelf. Mom in turn may focus on the object, perhaps identifying it ("Oh, those are Mommy's glasses"), explaining something about them ("I need those to read" or "They're blue"), asking the child to name them ("Can you say 'glasses'?), or having it lead to other interactions ("Yes, those are mommy's reading glasses. Do you want to read one of your books?").

Children who engage in shared-attention activities early tend to begin talking early. For example, Malinda Carpenter and her colleagues (Carpenter, Akhtar, & Tomasello, 1998) followed infants from 9 to 15 months of age, observing the social interaction between the infants and their mothers. They found that infants of mothers who engaged them in more shared-attention events and who used language that made some reference to objects that the infants were holding developed better communication skills than infants of less-sharing mothers.

### Gestures and Language Development

One prevalent component of shared attention between parents and their infants and toddlers is pointing (as well as gesturing in general). Whereas a more verbal child would use language, infants often use pointing to request things (for example, pointing to a doll with a plaintive look on her face as if to say, "Please hand me my doll"). Some researchers have argued that, by 12 months of age, infants are deliberately using pointing to influence how other people behave and think (Tomasello, Carpenter, & Liszkowski, 2007) and that pointing and gestures more generally serve as a prelinguistic form of communication and predict children's later language development (Goldin-Meadow, 2007; Iverson & Goldin-Meadow, 2005). For instance, a child who says "play" while pointing to a favorite toy is likely getting his message across loud and clear. In support of the idea that gestures point the way to language, children who produce word-plus-gesture combinations (for example, "play" plus pointing to a toy) produce their first two-word utterances sooner than children who don't produce such combinations (Iverson & Goldin-Meadow, 2005). Children continue to use gestures beyond the one-word stage, of course. For example, children say things like "I like it" while making a drinking gesture several months before they say "I like drinking it" (Ozcaliskan & Goldin-Meadow, 2005).

The relation between gestures and language development was investigated in a longitudinal study that followed children between 10 and 14 months of age (Iverson & Goldin-Meadow, 2005). Jana Iverson and Susan Goldin-Meadow (2005) noted objects that children first identified by speech or gesture and examined whether those items transferred to the other modality. The proportion of items that were initially (1) identified in speech and stayed in speech, (2) identified in gesture and stayed in gesture, (3) identified in speech and transferred to gesture, and (4) identified in gesture and transferred to speech are shown in Figure 9-8. As the figure shows, once an object was identified in gesture it was usually transferred to speech. The authors proposed the *gesture-facilitation hypothesis,* arguing that the use of gestures facilitates the acquisition of spoken language. Evidence in support of this comes from a study that found the more children used gestures at 14 months of age, the larger their vocabularies were at 54 months (Rowe & Goldin-Meadow, 2009). In addition, more affluent parents in this study were more likely to use gestures with their young children than less affluent parents, which in turn affected the gesturing and communication skills of their children, accounting for some of the differences in vocabulary size between children from higher- and lower-socioeconomic-status families.

How do pointing and gestures make language learning easier for children? Susan Goldin-Meadow (2007) suggests at least two possibilities. First, gestures could cause parents to say words and sentences that children need to expand their speaking abilities. For instance, a child may point to a bottle and be told "milk," or she may point to an object in a particular context, say "hat," and be told "Yes, that's grandpa's hat." In this example, a child's word-plus-gesture becomes translated by an adult as a complete sentence. Second, children who use gestures tend to perform better on a host of cognitive task, and this may also be true for language learning. For example, encouraging school-age children to use gestures while solving math problems increases their chances of getting the problems right (Goldin-Meadow, Cook, & Mitchell, 2009; see also Goldin-Meadow, 2009, and the discussion in Chapter 11).

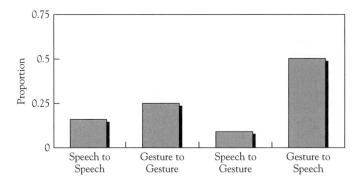

## FIGURE **9-8**

Proportion of objects children learned to identify by speech or gesture that either remained within the original modality (speech to speech or gesture to gesture) or transferred to the other modality (speech to gesture of gesture to speech). Children were much more likely to acquire a new gesture and transfer it to speech than vice versa, supporting the *gesture-facilitation hypothesis*

Source: Iverson, J. M., & Goldin-Meadow, S. (2005). Gesture paves the way for language development. *Psychological Science, 16,* 368–371.

Treating other people as intentional beings does not *cause* children to develop language, of course. Instead, shared attention and seeing others as intentional beings serve as the social-cognitive foundation for language development. However, a social-interactionist perspective also recognizes that parents present language to children not in a random way but, instead, in a form that is packaged just for them (Bruner, 1983). It is not only *what* adults say to children that is carefully selected but also *how* they say it that facilitates the process of language learning.

### Child-Directed Speech

Anyone who has listened to adults, especially mothers, talking to babies knows that this is a special type of speech that is *not* used when talking to other adults. In everyday parlance, this is "baby talk" ("Hi, big girl! How is my baby today? Huh? How is Mama's little angel? Did we just go for a walk? Did you and Mommy just walk around the block? We did, didn't we? Did you see the kitty? Huh? Did we see the little kitty?").

The speech that mothers and others use with infants and young children is special. It is simpler and more redundant than the speech they use with their older children. Such speech was originally termed *motherese* (Snow, 1972), and subsequent research has revealed additional properties, showing that mothers typically talk to their young children using high-pitched tones, exaggerated modulations, simplified forms of adult words, many questions, and many repetitions (see Hoff, 2009). It is done spontaneously and is found in caregivers around the world (Fernald, 1992; Kuhl et al., 1997). In fact, for many people, it is difficult *not* to speak in these exaggerated ways to young children. When "motherese" was found to be used by fathers and 4-year-old children, the new term became **child-directed speech** (or **infant-directed speech** when directed specifically to infants), and it was suggested that this special form of speech is connected with some innate language-transmittal mechanism found in adults—the counterpart to Chomsky's language acquisition device. (Bruner [1983] proposed that adults have a device in their brains that responds to infants and young children by automatically altering speech to a more understandable form, and he even suggested an appropriate name, **language acquisition support system**, or **LASS**.)

**Prosodic features of child-directed speech.** Beginning in the late 1970s and early 1980s, a new phase of research focused on the prosodic features of speech, or prosody, the ups and downs of the tones and the rhythms of the sounds we make. Instead of counting repetitions or comparing words used in infant-directed (I-D) speech versus adult-directed (A-D) speech, researchers used instruments to measure the acoustic features of different types of speech. I-D speech, compared with A-D speech, was found to have a higher mean frequency, a wider range of frequencies, and a greater incidence of rising frequency contours. In other words, when mothers talk to infants, they use higher tones of voice in general, more high and low tones, and more tones that move from low to high (Fernald & Mazzie, 1991).

Using this acoustic comparison method, mothers in other cultures were studied as they interacted with their infants, and these same general prosodic features were found for Latvian, Comanche, Mandarin Chinese, Japanese, Sinhala, Russian, Thai, and Swedish mothers (see Fernald, 1992; Fisher & Tokura, 1996; Kitamura et al., 2002; Kuhl et al., 1997). In a study of French, Italian, German, Japanese, British, and American families, Anne Fernald and her colleagues (1989) demonstrated typical I-D speech versus A-D speech differences for both mothers and fathers. Not all cultures use the same exaggerated style of I-D speech as American mothers (and fathers) frequently do, but as the list of cultures mentioned suggests, some aspects of I-D speech might be universal (Fernald, 1992; Kuhl et al., 1997).

Why do people use I-D speech when talking to babies? One reason seems to be that this is the way babies "want" to be spoken to. They are more attentive to adults who speak to them using I-D rather than A-D speech. For example, 4-month-old infants who have been conditioned to turn their heads to one side or the other to select which of two tapes they will listen to, will turn their heads to hear I-D speech rather than A-D speech. There is even evidence that 1-month-old infants show a preference for I-D speech (Cooper & Aslin, 1990, 1994).

One interesting study examined mothers of deaf infants signing to their babies and to their deaf friends (Masataka, 1996). Similar to the findings for spoken language, these mothers signed more slowly and used more repetitions and greater exaggerations of movements to their deaf infants than to their deaf adult friends. Moreover, like hearing babies, the deaf infants paid greater attention and made more affective responses to I-D signing than to A-D signing. In a follow-up study, Nobuo Masataka (1998) demonstrated that *hearing* babies who had never been exposed to sign language were also more responsive to the greater exaggerations found in I-D sign language than to A-D sign language, suggesting that this effect is not modality specific (see also O'Neill et al., 2005).

Other studies have shown that when I-D speech styles are used, young infants can discriminate between words that have very slight differences in sounds (Moore, Spence, & Katz, 1997). For example, research has shown that 1- to 4-month-old infants can discriminate among three-syllable sequences (such as "ma*ra*na" versus "ma*la*na") if the words are spoken using the exaggerated style of I-D speech (Karzon, 1985). In these examples, the middle syllables would be accented in I-D speech ("ma-**ra**-na" and "ma-**la**-na"), which would not be the case in normal adult-to-adult speech (see Trehub, Trainor, & Unyk, 1993). Babies at this age cannot tell the difference between the two words when they are spoken in normal A-D speech.

In related work, Daniel Stern and his colleagues (1982) found that mothers of 2-, 4-, and 6-month-old babies used rising intonations when they wished to *get* a baby's attention and down-up-down phrasing (as in the "malana" example earlier) when wishing to *maintain* an infant's attention. The results of these and other studies suggest that babies are born ready to process certain types of language, and it is no coincidence that the sing-songy type of speech babies best understand is the same kind of speech that adults and children seem compelled to produce in the presence of an infant.

**The role of child-directed speech.** Earlier theories about child-directed speech centered on mothers' roles as teachers of language for their children (Hoff-Ginsburg, 1985). Individual differences in how mothers converse with their 1- and 2-year-old children have been found to be related to early aspects of language development (see Hoff, 2000). For example, the use of expansions (that is, expanding a statement that a child made), repetitions, and questions, all of which are frequent in child-directed speech, has been shown to be related to children's language development. The relation between mothers' speech and children's language development is not straightforward, however, with different aspects of mothers' speech influencing different aspects of their children's language development at different times. Nevertheless, it seems clear that mothers are, indeed, "teaching" their children something important about the syntactic properties of language, even if that "something" cannot be easily specified.

Infant-directed speech also seems to serve other types of development at much earlier ages. Stern and his colleagues (1983) showed that the prosodic features of mothers' I-D speech peak when the infant is 4 months old, almost half a year before the infant shows any sign of understanding specific words. This has led to the alternative interpretation that I-D speech plays a role not only in syntactic development but also in the emotional relationship between infant and caregiver. Fernald (1992) suggested that by using specific tones, the mother regulates the infant's emotions, behavior, and attention and conveys her own emotional state to her infant. Fernald divided I-D speech into four different acoustical patterns, all of which are used by British, American, German, French, and Italian mothers when talking to their 12-month-old infants. These patterns convey the mother's approval, express prohibition, ask for attention, and provide comfort to the infant. Such nonverbal communication is important in developing secure mother-infant attachment, and according to Locke (1994), "Spoken language piggybacks on this open channel, taking advantage of mother-infant attachment by embedding new information in the same stream of cues" (p. 441). Although children do not need a secure attachment to develop language, evidence suggests that maltreated toddlers have significant delays in language acquisition (Cicchetti, 1989). Fernald's claim is that the evolutionary origins of language may stem from mothers attempting to regulate the emotions of their infants, something that I-D speech continues to do today (see also Trainor, Austin, & Desjardins, 2000). Consistent with Fernald's argument, there is evidence that rhesus-monkey mothers use special vocalizations with their infants that serve to attract and engage their attention, much as human mothers do (Whitham et al., 2007).

In the previous section examining the critical period for language acquisition, the importance of "starting small" was emphasized (see Box 9-2). Children's limited information-processing abilities might constrain the amount of information they can process, which in turn might make the task of acquiring language easier. But if young children acquire language best by "starting small," this is apparently accomplished not only because of their limited cognitive abilities but also because of the help of adults (Bjorklund & Schwartz, 1996). Adults around the world talk to children using highly repetitive and greatly simplified child-directed speech. As children's language competencies increase, so too does the complexity of language addressed to them. Thus, in the early phases of language acquisition, children receive a highly simplified language corpus. As Richard Schwartz and I wrote, "Such modified language, accompanied with young children's limited information-processing abilities, results in children receiving a much reduced body of linguistic evidence from which to extract the phonological, syntactic, and semantic rules of their mother tongue" (p. 26). I should also note that there is large variation in the amount of speech adults in different cultures direct toward infants, yet children from cultures that address little speech directly to children still acquire language pretty much "on schedule," making it unlikely that child-directed speech is necessary for language acquisition.

The significance of using simplified child-directed speech for language acquisition is illustrated by anecdotal evidence that simply being exposed to A-D speech is not sufficient to learn a first or second language. For example, a hearing child of deaf parents who was confined to his home because of poor health learned sign language from his parents but could neither speak nor understand spoken English by the age of 3, despite frequently watching television (Moskowitz, 1978). In another example, Dutch children who regularly watched (and frequently preferred) German television often failed to understand the programs and did not achieve appreciable control of the German language (reported in Snow et al., 1976). Not only does watching and listening to television provide no opportunity for social (and language) give-and-take, but the language heard on television consists almost totally of A-D speech and not the modified (and simplified) child-directed speech that children typically receive from adults.

Research examining the role that child-directed speech plays in development makes it clear that although infants might be biologically prepared to acquire their mother tongue, language development is embedded within the social-emotional context of the family. Parents around the world provide children with an environment that promotes communication, motivates language development, and acts as a model for language (Hoff, 2006). Language development cannot be properly understood unless it is viewed as part of the broader human developmental perspective (see Locke, 1993; Tomasello, 2005).

# BILINGUALISM AND SECOND-LANGUAGE LEARNING

**Bilingualism**—being fluent in two languages—is becoming increasingly common and has long been the norm in some parts of the world. For instance, about 20% of children in the United States do not speak English as a first language, with this figure soaring to between 33% and 43% for some states, such as California, New Mexico, and Texas (U.S. Census Bureau, 2006). In some European countries, such as Switzerland and Luxembourg, it is typical for people to speak three or four languages.

There has been a long debate about the benefits and detriments of bilingualism. Should children be taught a second language early, when they are "primed" to learn language, or will learning a second language before they've mastered their first have long-term negative effects? This question has attracted the attention of psychologists as well as educators, and the conclusion seems to be that bilingualism has both costs and benefits (see Bialystock & Craik, 2010).

There are different ways to become bilingual, and there are different types of bilingualism. For example, in **simultaneous bilingualism**, children are exposed from birth to two languages. By contrast, in **sequential bilingualism**, children learn a second language *after* mastering their first. Simultaneous bilinguals generally acquire the two languages separately and show relatively little interference from either language (see de Houwer, 1995; Hakuta & García, 1989). Children who are learning two languages at the same time do make some temporary mistakes, such as when they apply a rule from one language to their speech in another. For example, in Spanish, the adjective comes after the noun ("flor roja") whereas in English the order is reversed ("red flower"). It would not be unusual to hear a Spanish/English-speaking child say "flower red" or "roja flor" as he or she learns the two languages together. Moreover, simultaneous bilingual children often have smaller vocabularies in both languages and a slight delay in syntactic development compared with monolingual children, but by the age of 8 or so, there are typically no differences between them and monolingual children (Gathercole, 2002). Bilinguals of all ages are also slower than monolinguals at retrieving individual words from their long-term memories (Bialystock, Craik, & Luk, 2008).

Learning two languages, either simultaneously or sequentially, requires more effort than learning one (Pearson et al., 1997; Díaz, 1983). But even with the greater effort and, for sequential bilinguals, the developmental lag in vocabulary and syntactic development, there are many benefits. Bilinguals are able to recognize a wider range of phonemes than monolinguals (Bosch & Sebastián-Gallés, 2001; MacWhinney, 2005), and they often develop a greater sensitivity toward the cultural values and the speakers of both the languages they have mastered (Pérez, 2004; Snow & Yusun Kang, 2006). Bilingual children and adults display higher levels of metalinguistic awareness than monolingual children, which has been linked to greater proficiency in reading and writing.

One interesting area in which bilinguals seem to have an advantage is in terms of executive function, particularly on tasks that demand flexible thinking (Bialystock, 1999, 2001; 2010; Lambert et al., 1993). Bilinguals must manage two languages at the same time, ensuring that one does not interfere with the other one, and this requires significant attentional control. As a result, simultaneous bilingual children display enhanced levels of executive control (see Chapter 7), and such bilingualism postpones the deterioration of executive function in the elderly (Bialystock, 2007; Bialystock, Craik, & Freedman, 2007; Carlson & Meltzoff, 2008). Perhaps related to their greater executive control, 3-year-old bilingual children have been shown to perform better on theory-of-mind tasks compared to monolingual children (Kovács, 2009).

Interestingly, some advantage to executive function has been shown for preverbal infants growing up in bilingual versus monolingual homes (Kovács & Mehler, 2009). In a series of three studies, 7-month-old infants from bilingual and monolingual homes learned to associate either a verbal nonsense word or a visual cue (for instance, ◆◆♣) with the appearance of a reward (dancing puppets) at a specific location (to their left of right). Both groups of infants learned these associations quickly, after which the rules were changed so that infants now had to look toward the *opposite* side than had been previously rewarded. This requires inhibiting a previously rewarded behavior, an important component in executive function. Infants from bilingual homes showed increased performance on these postswitch trials with experience (that is, they increasingly looked in the right direction with practice), unlike the infants from monolingual homes, whose performance never improved with experience. The authors of this study argued that even before children can speak, having to process information from two languages results in enhancements of executive function.

Bilingual children, however, are a large and diverse group, and a number of factors affect the acquisition of a second language, making it difficult to draw too many definite conclusions. For instance, the age when a child is exposed to a second language influences eventual proficiency. As discussed earlier in this chapter, when learning the second language is begun during the preschool years, pronunciation and complex grammatical forms are mastered more easily than if learning the second language is begun later (Johnson & Newport, 1989). How similar the two languages are may also affect the ease of learning the second language. For example, English-speaking children learning Japanese may experience more difficulty than English-speaking children learning German, as Japanese and English are linguistically more different than German and English (Bialystock & Hakuta, 1994; Snow & Yusun Kang, 2006).

Also important in the eventual proficiency of a second language is how well children have mastered the first language before starting on the second. When young children arrive in a country and are exposed to a new language for the first time, their initial exposure to the second language is often in school. Such a scenario presents the possibility of **semilingualism,** or the lack of mastery of either languages. This can influence cognitive development, school achievement, and social adjustment (Crawford, 1997; Ovando & Collier, 1998). However, when children master their first language and the second language is as highly valued as the first in social contexts, as is the case in Canada with French and English, this negative impact is greatly minimized or absent (Genesee, 2003; Turnbull, Hart, & Lapkin, 2003).

## GENDER DIFFERENCES IN LANGUAGE ACQUISITION

There is a persistent belief that females are better than males at language and language-related skills. For example, girls and women are believed to be better readers than boys and men are, with this difference appearing early and lasting into adulthood. Research pertinent to this question will be examined in Chapter 11. Here, I review research concerning possible gender differences in the acquisition of a first language.

Some researchers have reported faster rates of language acquisition for girls (Bornstein & Haynes, 1998; Galsworthy et al., 2000). Other studies have failed to observe any significant gender differences (McCarthy, 1954), and some find a difference favoring young girls for spontaneous speech but not on standardized tests (Morisset, Barnard, & Booth, 1995). In related research, Michael Lewis and his colleagues reported greater vocalization by infant girls than by infant boys. For example, 3-month-old girls were found to vocalize more than boys in response to their mothers' invitations to "talk" (Lewis & Freedle, 1973), and infant girls between the ages of 3 and 13 months vocalized more in response to facial stimuli than did boys of the same age (Lewis, 1969). In a meta-analysis summarizing the effects reported in more than 30 studies looking at differences in how mothers talked with their sons and their daughters, Campbell Leaper, Kristin Anderson, and Paul Sanders (1998) reported moderate gender differences, with mothers talking more and using more supportive speech with their daughters than with their sons. Other research has shown that mothers talk about different things with their sons than with their daughters. For example, examining the emotion talk of women to their 2-, 3-, and 4-year-old children, mothers were more apt to explain emotions to boys rather than just label them, but they showed no difference in the use of explanations and labels with their daughters (Cervantes & Callanan, 1998). Of equal interest, even the youngest girls in this study talked about emotions quite frequently and as often as older girls. In contrast, emotion talk was less frequent for the youngest boys but increased with age.

Others have proposed that the gender differences sometimes found in language acquisition are related to cultural factors. In Greece, for example, where boys are often valued more than girls, there is evidence that boys rather than girls are more vocally responsive (Roe et al., 1985). Perhaps the gender differences favoring girls in the United States can be attributed to different ways in which girls and boys are spoken to rather than to endogenous factors. Recall from Chapter 8 on memory development that parents use a more elaborative conversation style with their daughters than with their sons when prompting them to remember past events (Reese, Haden, & Fivush, 1996). Such differences are related to gender differences in event memory (girls' event memory being better than boys') and are consistent with the hypothesis that differences in cultural practices are responsible, in part, for gender differences in rate of language acquisition (Roe et al., 1985).

Some gender differences in early language that are *not* related to differences in how parents talk to boys and girls, however, are also found. Catherine Haden, Rochel Haine, and Robyn Fivush (1997) reported that girls between 40 and 70 months of age produced longer and more structured narratives than did boys of the same age; however, unlike other aspects of language presented to boys and girls, these authors found no differences in how parents used narratives to talk about past experiences with their sons and daughters. These results indicate that girls are more advanced in their narrative production than boys are and that a simple socialization explanation cannot adequately account for these differences. Similarly, in a behavior-genetics study examining more than 3000 pairs of 2-year-old twins (Galsworthy et al., 2000), gender differences favoring girls in verbal ability were found (although they accounted for only 3% of the variance). Interestingly, the heritability of verbal ability was higher for the boys than for the girls. In other research, 18- and 24-month-old girls had significantly larger vocabularies than boys did, and this difference was related to exposure to fetal testosterone—that is, the greater exposure to testosterone (a male hormone) prenatally, the smaller a child's vocabulary tended to be (Lutchmaya, Baron-Cohen, & Raggatt, 2002).

As of this writing, the question of gender differences in language acquisition is unanswered. Research suggests that girls might be more vocal than boys early in infancy and that this difference leads to a subsequent advantage in learning a first language. However, other research suggests that whatever small advantage in language acquisition girls do hold is a function of cultural practices, with boys in some cultures displaying the typical "feminine" pattern of faster language acquisition we've come to expect in our own.

## LANGUAGE AND THOUGHT

Although most laypeople would agree that language is not only a system of communication but also an important vehicle for thought, most theorists of language would likely disagree. Language is used to *express* thought, both to others and to ourselves, but it is not thought itself (Pinker, 1994). For example, we frequently have a difficult time putting thoughts into words. We often have an image in our head, or understand a problem (perhaps a math problem) intuitively, but have a difficult time expressing it. It was once believed that deaf children who had not been taught sign language were intellectually impaired because they lacked language. What these children truly lacked, however, was a way to communicate their knowledge and intelligence, and when tested in ways that overcame their communication difficulties, they showed typical rates of cognitive development in terms of Piaget's stages (Furth, 1964). Researchers also have demonstrated that 12-month-old infants use pointing to communicate about absent entities, something that is usually handled by language (that is, talking about something that is not in one's immediate perception). Chimpanzees do not use pointing in this way (nor language, of course), suggesting that young children's underlying cognitive abilities, and not language, are what allows them to communicate about absent entities (Liszkowski et al., 2009).

Some developmental psychologists have taken a different perspective. For example, theorists such as Bruner (1966) have argued that the ability to use language as a conceptual tool transforms a child's thinking during early childhood and, moreover, that the use of language in social situations facilitates this transformation. Knowledge of the physical world is imbedded in the social world, and language is a universal mechanism for communicating and, thus, structuring knowledge. Perhaps more to the point, language is used to communicate ideas and thoughts (that is, mental representations) between people, and language structures these mental representations. This perspective is probably best represented by the work of Katherine Nelson (1993, 1996) and was discussed with respect to the development of autobiographical memory in Chapter 8.

Along similar lines, Soviet psychologist Lev Vygotsky (1962) proposed that language directs much of children's intelligent behavior, with the relationship between language and thought changing developmentally. Vygotsky believed that thought and speech have different roots in development, with the two initially being independent. In other words, thought is prelinguistic and speech is preintellectual. In development, however, thought and speech merge, with thought becoming verbal and speech rational. This developmental relationship between language and thought, particularly during the stages in which the two cross, has attracted the interest of psychologists.

Vygotsky was particularly interested in the role of **egocentric speech** in affecting children's thought. Egocentric speech, also known as **private speech**, can be thought of as speech-for-self. This overt language is carried out with apparent satisfaction even though it does not function to communicate. Private speech can be observed both when children are alone and in social settings. Vygotsky believed that private speech plays a specific role in affecting children's thought and problem solving. Language can guide children's behavior (and, thus, their thought), but young children cannot yet use language covertly, "in their heads." To benefit from the self-regulatory function of language, young children must essentially talk to themselves, using their speech to guide thought and behavior. With development, the self-regulatory function of language changes so that children can direct their behavior using **inner speech**. In other words, private speech serves as a **cognitive self-guidance system** and then goes "underground" as covert verbal thought. (Vygotsky contrasted his position with that of Piaget, 1955, who believed that private speech plays no functional role in cognitive development but is merely symptomatic of ongoing mental activity.)

Several studies have assessed aspects of Vygotsky's theory of private speech, and most generally find support for his ideas (Winsler & Naglieri, 2003; Kohlberg, Yaeger, & Hjertholm, 1968; see Winsler, 2009, for a review). In fact, adolescents and adults still sometimes talk to themselves when facing a difficult task, but it is questionable whether such speech actually helps their performance (Duncan & Tarulli, 2009; Winsler, 2003).

Other research has shown that school-age children use private speech to help them solve a host of school-type tasks, such as addition and subtraction problems

**DENNIS THE MENACE**

"I'M GONNA HAVE TO STOP THINKIN' OUT LOUD."

CARTOON **9-1**

Young children have a difficult time keeping their thoughts to themselves.

Source: *Dennis the Menace*®, used by permission of Hank Ketcham and © 1986 by North America Syndicate.

(Berk, 1986). For example, Laura Berk (1986) observed first- and third-grade children during daily math periods for 4 months. Various forms of private speech were recorded (for example, task-irrelevant, self-stimulating speech; task-relevant, externalized speech; and task-relevant, external manifestations of inner speech, such as lip movements), as were other aspects of their overt behavior (movement, pointing to objects to help them add) and measures of their task performance (daily math papers and achievement and IQ tests). Berk reported high levels of private speech in this sample of children that changed with age. The self-guidance function of private speech varied with age and eventually gave way to covert, inner speech. Most of the children's task-relevant, externalized speech was used to guide their problem solving, with third-graders using more internalized forms of speech (for example, inaudible mutterings, lip and tongue movements) to facilitate their performance. The total amount of private speech was positively related to intelligence at grade 1 but not at grade 3, an indication that brighter children not only begin to use private speech to guide their problem solving earlier than less bright children but also stop sooner, as thought goes "underground" in the form of inner speech (see also Berk & Landau, 1993; Kohlberg et al., 1968).

Also consistent with Vygotsky's claims, children rely more heavily on private speech when facing difficult rather than easy tasks and when deciding how to proceed after making errors (Berk, 1992), and their performance often improves after turning to self-instruction (Behrend, Rosengren & Perlmutter, 1989; Berk & Spuhl, 1995). Moreover, private speech does eventually go "underground," progressing from words and phrases to whispers and mutterings and then to inner speech (Bivens & Berk, 1990). Although the use of private speech on problem-solving tasks persists into adolescence, such speech is not associated with improved task performance for these older children (Winsler, 2003). In related research, children who are asked to generate explicit explanations for problems they are solving (for example, "7 + 2 – 2 = 7, because you add 2 and take it away, so you don't really have to add and subtract all the numbers, you just know that it's 7") perform better on a variety of academic-type tasks than children who are not prompted to provide such self-directed speech (Rittle-Johnson, 2006; Siegler, 2002).

The debate about the relationship between language and thought extends far beyond the role of private speech in children's problem solving (see Winsler, Fernyhough, & Montero, 2009). However, the developmental association between the two can be informative. For instance, telling a young reader to "Read quietly to yourself!" may not be worthwhile, as beginning readers may not be able to read quietly "in their heads." In fact, some researchers have suggested that preschool children do not believe that inner speech is possible, believing instead that a person cannot "talk to himself" and think at the same time. When preschool children are prompted to use inner speech (for example, "Silently think about how your name sounds"), they are just as likely to say that they had a *picture* of their name in their heads while thinking as to say that they said their names in their heads (Flavell et al., 1997). Although it seems unlikely that preschool children never engage in inner speech, it is difficult to know when the monologue that seems to run constantly through people's minds begins. However, it appears that the "inner life" of young children is not as (linguistically) rich as that of adults.

Although some general discrepancies from Vygotsky's theory have been reported, the existing research suggests that there is, indeed, a developmental relationship between language and thought, along the lines that Vygotsky and his colleagues hypothesized.

## SUMMARY

Human language has three important components: (1) It is symbolic, (2) it is grammatical, and (3) the particular language children learn to speak varies with culture. Children's language development can be described in terms of several dimensions, including *phonology, semantics, grammar,* and *pragmatics.*

Phonology refers to the sounds of language and is first reflected in infants' babbling, which varies initially as a function of physical anatomy and later as a function of the language infants hear. *Phonemic awareness* becomes important later in learning to read.

Morphology refers to the structure of language, specifically words. *Morphemes* (both *free* and *bound*) are the smallest unit of meaning in a language. Children learn rules and *overregularize* irregular words to fit these rules (forming words such as "goed" and "mouses"). The average number of morphemes used in a sentence, or the *mean length of utterance (MLU),* is one indication of the language complexity of a preschool child. Children use single words, referred to as *holophrases* (or *holophrastic speech*), to convey complex meaning, and early sentences are *telegraphic,* including only high-content words.

Syntactic development progresses quickly during the preschool years and is reflected by regular, age-related changes in forming negatives, asking questions, and using the passive voice.

Semantic development refers to the development of word meaning. Around 18 months of age, children experience a *word spurt,* in which the rate of new word learning (mostly nouns) increases rapidly. Children's *receptive vocabulary* (words they can understand) is greater than their *productive vocabulary* (words they can speak). This has been attributed to *fast mapping,* in which children are able to learn novel words with minimal input. Researchers have proposed the existence of *lexical constraints* to make word learning easier. These include the *whole-word assumption,* the *taxonomic assumption,* the *mutual exclusivity assumption,* and *syntactic bootstrapping.* Infants and young children also likely make use of social cues from speakers, such as gazes, to help them identify the referents to words. Early in development, children often make *overextensions* (applying a word beyond its correct meaning, such as calling all four-legged animals "dog"), but children also sometimes make *underextensions* (incorrectly restricting the use of a term).

*Pragmatics* refers to knowledge about how language can be used and adjusted to fit different circumstances. Even young children are aware of some basic aspects of pragmatics, although substantial improvements occur with age. *Speech registers* refer to a distinct style of speaking that is used only in specific contexts (for instance, when talking to children, when talking in school). As an example, *Black English*—a dialect of American English used mostly (but not exclusively) by members of the African American community—is characterized by some special rules of pronunciation and syntax.

*Communicative competence* refers to the various types of language knowledge (phonology, morphology, syntax, semantics, and pragmatics) that are combined in a package to yield effective communication. Preschool children often display poor communication and *metacommunication* skills, being less aware of factors that influence comprehension of messages than older children are, and they sometimes speak in *collective monologues* (speaking "with" but not necessarily "to" one another).

Behavioral theories of language acquisition have generally been discredited, although evidence suggests that infants engage in *statistical learning* to determine which sound sequences are words. Counter to empiricist theories are nativist and social-interactionist theories. *Nativist theories* follow the theorizing of Noam Chomsky, who proposed language has both a *surface structure* and a *deep structure,* that children are born with a *language acquisition device (LAD),* and that exposure to speech is all that is needed for language acquisition. Nativist theories argue that the brain is specialized for language, as evidenced by the identification of a *grammar center* in the frontal lobe, and propose an innate *universal grammar* that contains the basic syntactic structure of all human languages. Both a first and a second language are learned more easily by younger than by older children, suggesting a critical period for language learning. Some support for the nativist position comes from children creating *creoles* from *pidgins* after only one generation. Newport's *"less is more" hypothesis* suggests that young children's cognitive limitations actually make it easier for them to acquire a first or second language compared with older children or adults.

*Social-interactionist theorists* examine the interplay between language, cognitive, and social development. Young infants are responsive to human speech and are especially responsive to *infant-directed* (or *child-directed*) *speech,* which includes a distinctive type of prosody, or rhythm. Bruner suggested that adults have an innate device, which he called the *Language Acquisition Support System,* or *LASS,* that causes them to respond to infants and young children with child-directed speech.

*Bilingualism* refers to people who speak two languages. *Simultaneous bilingualism* refers to children who are exposed to two languages from birth, whereas *sequential bilingualism* refers to children who learn a second language after mastering the first. For sequential bilinguals, there is generally a developmental lag of 3 to 5 years before children become proficient in their second language. When children immigrate to a country in which the dominant language is different from their native language, there is the possibility of developing *semilingualism,* which refers to the lack of mastery of both languages.

Gender differences in language acquisition favoring girls have occasionally been found. However, evidence suggests that different cultural practices regarding how boys and girls are treated play an important role in possible gender differences in language acquisition.

Vygotsky proposed that *egocentric* (or *private*) *speech* has a special role in guiding children's thinking and behavior. Young children's private speech serves as a *cognitive self-guidance system* and is eventually replaced by covert verbal thought, or *inner speech*. Recent research provides support for Vygotsky's theory.

## KEY TERMS AND CONCEPTS

phonology

phonemic awareness

morphology

morpheme

free morphemes

bound morphemes

mean length of utterance (MLU)

overregularization

holophrases (or holophrastic speech)

telegraphic speech

semantics

word spurt

receptive vocabulary

productive vocabularies

fast mapping

lexical constraints

whole-object assumption

taxonomic assumption

mutual exclusivity assumption

syntactic bootstrapping

overextensions

underextensions

pragmatics

speech registers

Black English

communicative competence

collective monologues

metacommunication

statistical learning

nativist theories

social-interactionist theories

surface structure

deep structure

language acquisition device (or LAD)

Wernicke's area

Broca's area

grammar center

universal grammar

pidgins

creoles

"less is more" hypothesis

child-directed speech (or infant-directed speech)

language acquisition support system (LASS)

bilingualism

simultaneous bilingualism

sequential bilingualism

semilingualism

egocentric speech

private speech

inner speech

cognitive self-guidance system

## SUGGESTED READINGS

### Scholarly Work

Hoff, E. (2009). *Language development (4th edition).* Belmont, CA: Wadsworth. This textbook presents an overview of all aspects of language development, from linguistic theory to brain development.

Senghas, A., & Coppola, M. (2001). Children creating language: How Nicaraguan Sign Language acquired a spatial grammar. *Psychological Science, 12,* 323–326. This is a report of a research project looking at children's "spontaneous" invention of a sign language. In addition to providing fodder for debates about the nature of language development, it is an excellent demonstration of a "naturalistic experiment."

Tomasello, M. (2005). *Constructing a language: A usage-based theory of language acquisition.* Cambridge, MA: Harvard University. Michael Tomasello presents a social-constructivist approach to language as a contrast to the nativist approach advocated by people such as Noam Chomsky and Steven Pinker.

## Reading for Personal Interest

Karmiloff, K., & Karmiloff-Smith, K. (2002). *Pathways to language: From fetus to adolescent.* Cambridge, MA: Harvard University Press. This is a comprehensive, well-grounded, and easy-to-read book about the "state of the art" in children's language development. The book is part of *The Developmental Child Series*, addressed to a general audience.

Pinker, S. (1994). *The language instinct: How the mind creates language.* New York: Morrow. This popular book (but *not* a book of pop psychology) presents the nativist position of language acquisition perhaps more clearly and thoroughly than any other source. Whether you agree with Pinker's arguments or not, it provides an excellent look at the issues and data dealing with the child's acquisition of language.

CHAPTER **10**

# Social Cognition

**Social Learning**
Forms of Social Learning
Age Differences in Social Learning
Social Learning in Chimpanzees
   **BOX 10-1:** Mirror Neurons: The Foundation
   of Social Learning?

**Social Cognitive Theory**
Factors Involved in Observational
   Learning
The Development of Self-Efficacy

**Social Information Processing**

**The Development of a Concept of Self**

**Cognitive Bases of Gender Identity**
Gender Constancy
Gender Schemas
Gender Knowledge and Sex-Typed
   Behavior: Possible Predispositions
Children's Theories of Gender

**How "Special" Is Social Cognition?**

SUMMARY
KEY TERMS AND CONCEPTS
SUGGESTED READINGS

A 4-year-old boy eating at an Italian restaurant with his parents and another couple noticed that his father and the other gentleman had ordered pizza, whereas his mother had ordered lasagna. In the car on the way home, the child announced that he had figured it out: "Men eat pizza and women don't."

What is this child thinking? What does "eating pizza" have to do with being a man or a woman, and why is this topic even important to this child? It is important because being male or female is a distinction made by people in all societies (for some rather obvious reasons), and it is one that is "acquired" over the course of childhood. It is an example of **social cognition**—thinking about one's own thoughts, feelings, motives, and behaviors as well as those of other people (Olson & Dweck, 2009).

As a cognitive psychologist, I tend to believe that most aspects of human behavior are a function, to some significant degree, of one's cognitions. I find this especially easy to believe for the social behavior of children, who can only be as social as their level of cognitive functioning will permit. One cannot expect children to behave in a socially appropriate way if they cannot understand the social relationships among individuals and the ramifications of behaving in one way rather than another.

Many of a child's day-to-day activities involve interactions with people. These interactions require thought. Children must make evaluations of social situations and must understand their relationships with other people in a particular context. This requires an appreciation of who they are as social beings and who their fellow interactants are. It involves anticipating the thoughts and feelings of others and the execution of social "strategies." These strategies can be aimed at facilitating the formation of relationships, such as mother-infant attachment or playground friendships, or the successful completion of some cooperative task, such as jumping rope or playing baseball.

There are few narrow topics in cognitive development. Research into memory, perception, and language involves many subtopics, with numerous facets to each. The number of topics subsumed under the rubric of social cognition, however, is even greater. Any thinking involved in any social setting or about any social phenomenon is a potential area of inquiry. And there is not necessarily a hard line drawn between social and nonsocial cognition. For example, much of the research I reviewed on theory of mind in Chapter 6 could just as easily have been included in a chapter on social cognition (see Flavell & Miller, 1998).

Social cognition represents *folk psychology*, people's intuitive understanding of themselves and other people, as I discussed in Chapter 6. Recall that David Geary (2005) proposed that children are born with *skeletal competencies* within the domain of folk psychology, and that these competencies become fleshed out with experience. He also proposed that folk psychology was organized in a hierarchy, with three major subgroups, or domains (Self, Individual, Group), each having more specific components. For example, the "Self" subgroup includes a component dealing with self-awareness; the "Individual" subgroup has components for reading facial expressions, language, and theory of mind; and the "Group" subgroup has components for relating to kin and for making distinctions between "in groups versus out groups." Although I do not follow Geary's model rigidly here, my focus in this chapter is on how children come to be functional social beings in their culture, based on the development of their intuitive folk psychologies.

As a specific example of children being "prepared" by natural selection to deal with social situations (that is, of children possessing "skeletal competencies," to use Geary's term), consider the proposal of evolutionary psychologists Leda Cosmides and John Tooby (1992), who claimed that one important form of social reasoning involves social exchanges—or "the art of the deal," as Donald Trump might call it. We make social contracts all the time. They are central to normal functioning in everyday life. Some of these contracts are formal, as when we agree to make monthly payments to someone who sells us his car, and some are informal, as when we lend someone our notes for a class she missed and expect that she will reciprocate if the need arises. Sometimes the deals we make "work," but other times they do not. We get cheated when a person defaults on the car payment (or neglects to tell us about the series of accidents the car had been in) or refuses to share her notes when we miss a class. Cosmides and Tooby found that adults were particularly sensitive in identifying when rules were broken in a social contract, much more so than when the same rules were presented in a nonsocial or abstract way.

Forming such contracts and avoiding social cheaters involves complicated cognition and is beyond the abilities of young children. However, social-contract problems reflect a form of *deontic reasoning*, which is reasoning about what one may, should, or ought to do, and this type of reasoning has been found in young children (Cummins, 1996; Keller et al., 2004). For instance, in one study (see Experiment 4 in Harris & Núñez, 1996), 3- and 4-year-old children were told a series of short stories, some of which involved breaking a rule and some of which had the same content but without breaking any rule. For instance, in the deontic condition (or *prescriptive* condition, to use the authors' term), children were told, "One day Carol wants to do some painting. Her Mum says if she does some painting she should put her apron on." In contrast, children in the descriptive condition were told, "One day Carol wants to do some painting. Carol says that if she does some painting she always puts her apron on." Children were then shown four drawings: (1) Carol painting with her apron, (2) Carol painting without her apron, (3) Carol not painting with her apron, and (4) Carol not painting without her apron. Children in the deontic conditions were then told, "Show me the picture where Carol is doing something naughty and not doing what her Mum said." Children in the descriptive condition were told, "Show me the picture where Carol is doing something different and not doing what she said." Both the 3- and 4-year-old children were correct more often in the deontic, or "naughty," condition (72% and 83% for the 3- and 4-year-olds, respectively) than in the descriptive (no-social-rule-breaking) condition (40% for both the 3- and 4-year-olds). Like adults, young children reasoned correctly about a problem in which a social contract was being broken, but not about a problem in which no such social obligation was mentioned (see also Dack & Astington, 2007; Kalish & Lawson, 2008).

Is this ability "innate"? Probably not. Rather, children are biased from early in life to be sensitive to feedback related to social contracts/exchanges, which facilitates the development of deontic reasoning. In other words, children seem specially prepared for developing "the art of the deal," particularly for recognizing when someone is breaking a social rule. These biases, along with children's abilities to see other people as intentional agents and to take the perspective of others, increase the chance that they will not only survive but also thrive in a complex social world.

I will not attempt to provide a representative review of the topics in developmental social cognition. Rather, I have selected several topics to examine, in varying degrees of detail, hoping to provide a flavor of developmental social cognition, how the research is done, and how it relates to nonsocial cognitive development. In the sections to follow, I first define and describe various forms of social learning and their development. I then review briefly two broad theories of developmental social cognition: Albert Bandura's social cognitive theory, and Kenneth Dodge's social information processing model. I then review research on the cognitive bases for the development of self and of gender identification.

---

# SOCIAL LEARNING

Two-year-old Shayne and his father walked hand-in-hand from the car to the supermarket. As they approached the automatic door, Shayne raced into the store and stepped onto the scale in the lobby. Once on the scale, he stood very still, his arms to his side and his head pointed upward, staring at the face of the scale. After a few moments he looked at his father, smiled, and stepped down. His father then repeated the same routine (Bjorklund & Hernández Blasi, 2012, p. 290).

If this were the only observation one had, you may think that Shayne's dad is copying his young son's behavior. In actuality, it's the other way around. Shayne's dad routinely checks to see how his latest diet-and-exercise regime is going by stepping on the grocery-store scale, and Shayne has learned this routine and mimics it perfectly. Young Shayne likely has no idea of the "purpose" behind his actions; but he is a social creature. Copying the repeated behavior of an important person in his life just seems to make sense.

At its most basic, **social learning** refers to acquiring information from other individuals. A narrower definition of social learning refers to "situations in which one individual comes to behave similarly to others" (Boesch & Tomasello, 1998, p. 598). I cannot emphasize enough the significance of social learning in everyday functioning and the emergence of the modern human mind. Although humans are not the only animals that acquire information through social learning, we do this better than any other species on the planet. The ability to learn from others permitted our ancestors to pass knowledge from one generation to another with great fidelity. Like all other animals, ancient humans learned through their own experiences. But by excelling at social learning, each individual no longer had to depend on trial and error to acquire new knowledge. Rather, each generation could begin where the last left one off, which is a tremendous advantage and results in the rapid accumulation of cultural knowledge (Meltzoff et al., 2009; Richerson & Boyd, 2005; Tomasello, 2000).

A number of scholars have proposed the *social brain hypothesis* to account for the evolution of human intelligence and our species' eventual ecological dominance (Alexander, 1989; Bailey & Geary, 2009; Bjorklund, Causey, & Periss, 2010; Dunbar, 1995, 2010; Tomasello & Moll, 2010). Basically, the hypothesis is that humans evolved the ability to better learn from other members of their species, which resulted in enhanced skills at both competing and cooperating with one another as well as the rapid acquisition and transmission of material culture. Some versions of the social brain hypothesis hold that our species' advanced form of social cognition resulted from the confluence of a big brain, living in socially complex groups, and an extended juvenile period (Bjorklund & Bering, 2003; Bjorklund, Cormier, & Rosenberg, 2005). Human social environments are complicated and vary from culture to culture. People need not only a large brain to figure out such environments but also a long time to do so. An extended childhood may also be necessary to acquire some important nonsocial skills, such as tool use (Kaplan et al., 2000); however, the ability to learn how to use tools is greatly afforded by social learning. In support of the social brain hypothesis, there is a significant relationship between brain size and social complexity among primates (correlation between neocortex size and group size = .76; see Dunbar, 1992, 2001), and primate species with larger brains have, on average, the longest juvenile periods (Bonner, 1988) and live in the most socially complex groups (Joffe, 1997).

The important point for our purposes is that social learning develops. More specifically, social learning involves many "basic" cognitive abilities that develop over early childhood, including shared attention and theory of mind, which were discussed in Chapter 6 in the section of Folk Psychology. In this section, I examine various forms of social learning, their development, and finally, social learning in our close genetic cousins, chimpanzees.

## Forms of Social Learning

Until recently, most child developmentalists who studied social learning assumed that, if children acquire some behavior by observation, the mechanism of that learning is imitation. However, imitation is only one rather sophisticated form of social learning, and it is worthwhile distinguishing among the various forms.

Table 10-1 presents several mechanisms by which social learning can occur. Most of these mechanisms have been identified by comparative (animal) psychologists to explain the behavior of their subjects, but the list is equally applicable to human children (see Bjorklund & Pellegrini, 2002; Want & Harris, 2003). **Local enhancement** (or **stimulus enhancement**) occurs when an individual notices activity at a particular location (for instance, some chimpanzees cracking nuts at a spot that has plentiful stones), moves to that location, and in a process of trial and error, discovers a useful behavior (for instance, cracking nuts with stones, although using other techniques than the ones observed). Other mechanisms include **mimicry**, which is the duplication of a behavior without any understanding of the goal of that behavior. The behavior of 2-year-old Shayne in the story that opened this section is an example of mimicry. Shayne would step on the scale, look up at the face of the scale, and then step off, just like his father did, despite not having any understanding of the purpose of such actions. More cognitively sophisticated processes include **emulation** (sometimes called *goal emulation*),

## TABLE **10-1**
### Different Forms of Social Learning.

*Local enhancement:* An individual notices activity at a particular location, moves to that location, and, in a process of trial and error, discovers a useful behavior. *Example:* One chimpanzee notices another chimpanzee cracking nuts with stones at a location, moves to that location, and, in a process of trial and error, learns to crack nuts with stones, although using other techniques than the ones observed.

*Mimicry:* The duplication of a behavior without any understanding of the goal of that behavior. *Example:* A 2-year-old child steps on a scale, looks at the scale face, and steps off, just like Dad does.

*Emulation:* One individual observes another interacting with an object to achieve a specific goal. The first individual then interacts with the object attempting to attain the same end but does not duplicate the same behavior as the model to achieve that goal. *Example:* A child watches someone sifting sand through her fingers to get seashells, then tosses sand in the air to find seashells.

*Imitative learning:* Reproduction of observed behavior to achieve a specific goal. May require an understanding of the goal that the model had in mind, as well as the reproduction of important components of the observed behavior. *Example:* Child watches an adult open a latch and push a button to open a box to get a piece of candy, and repeats same actions with the same result.

*Teaching (Instructed learning):* Actor A modifies his or her behavior only in the presence of another, Actor B, without attaining any immediate benefits. As a result of encouraging or discouraging B's behavior, B acquires a new skill. To be done effectively, teaching requires that both the instructor and student take the perspective of the other. *Example:* An adult shows a child how to make actions to open a box, perhaps making slow and deliberate motions, molding the child's fingers, and the child, not the adult, gets the candy inside.

true imitation, or **imitative learning** (Tomasello, 2000), and **teaching** (or **instructed learning**) (Tomasello, Kruger, & Ratner, 1993).

Emulation refers to understanding the goal of a model and engaging in similar behavior to achieve that goal without necessarily reproducing the exact actions of the model (Horner & Whiten, 2005; Tomasello, 2000). For example, Child A may observe Child B sifting sand through her fingers to search for seashells. Child A may then start searching through sand with his hands, but by tossing handfuls of sand that separates sand from the shells. Unlike in mimicry (or imitative learning), Child A does not reproduce the behaviors of the model (in this case, Child B) but, rather, through a trial-and-error process, achieves the desired goal he had observed Child B attain by using different behaviors. In contrast to emulation, imitative learning, according to Tomasello and his colleagues (Tomasello, 2000; Tomasello, Kruger, & Ratner, 1993), requires that the observer take the perspective of the model, understand the model's goal, and reproduce important portions of the model's behavior.

If imitative learning were the most sophisticated form of learning, then human culture and cognition would be much less complex than we know it to be. A more sophisticated form of cultural learning, requiring more sophisticated perspective taking, is instructed learning, or teaching, with a more accomplished person instructing a less accomplished person. According to Michael Tomasello and his colleagues (1993), not all cases of instruction qualify as instructed learning. Specifically, instructed learning requires that "children learn about the adult, specifically, about the adult's understanding of the task and how that compares with their own understanding" (Tomasello, Kruger, & Ratner, 1993, p. 499). What distinguishes instructed learning from other aspects of "learning from instruction" is that, in the former, children will reproduce the instructed behavior in the appropriate context to regulate their own behavior. That is, as in imitative learning, children must understand the purpose of the behavior—the adult's purpose when he or she initially taught the behavior. Children must internalize the adult's instruction, not just repeat a behavior on demand. Thus, a child who is taught to bounce a ball off the wall and into the wastebasket has learned a complicated trick. However, it is a trick that can be acquired by a monkey, and it is not the same as learning that putting a ball in a basket in certain situations is a goal to a game. Each is learning through instruction, but only the latter is instructed learning.

According to Tomasello, Kruger, and Ratner (1993), *self-regulation* is the best evidence of instructed learning. Self-regulation refers, basically, to self-control—a person's ability to purposefully direct his or her own behavior in the pursuit of some goal. Effective self-regulation requires the monitoring of one's actions and progress toward the goal (forms of metacognition). It is also reflected in children's self-regulated speech—their use of self-produced language to direct their problem-solving behavior (see Chapter 9). Tomasello and his colleagues proposed that such self-regulation and the associated metacognitive competence are not present until about the age of 4, around the time that children can pass false-belief tasks, demonstrating they realize that other people can have different knowledge and a different perspective from their own (see Chapter 6). This last point is critical, for true instructed learning requires that the learner appreciate the perspective of the teacher. According to Tomasello Kruger, and Ratner, "To learn from an instructor culturally—to understand the instruction from something resembling the instructor's point of view—requires that children be able to understand a mental perspective that differs from their own, and then to relate that point of view to their own in an explicit fashion"

(1993, p. 500). The importance of theory of mind in instruction is demonstrated when children serve as teachers. Research with 3.5- to 5.5-year-old children showed that children having higher levels of theory of mind were more effective teachers than children whose theory-of-mind abilities were less well-developed (Davis-Unger & Carlson, 2008).

The more advanced forms of social learning, such as emulation, imitative learning, and teaching are not the mindless matching behavior of an unsophisticated organism, as in mimicry, but reflect rather sophisticated cognitive processing. These underlying abilities develop over infancy and early childhood. In the following section, I examine the development of social learning in children, starting with neonatal imitation.

## Age Differences in Social Learning
### Neonatal Imitation

Social learning is supported by social interaction, which begins in the first hours of life. Over 30 years ago, Andrew Meltzoff and M. Keith Moore (1977) reported that infants, within their first days of life, will copy the facial expressions of an adult, a phenomenon known as **neonatal imitation**. Photo 10-1 shows examples of the facial gestures modeled to infants in this experiment and responses by infants. Following each demonstration, the model continued to look at the newborn but made no facial gestures. The researchers videotaped the infants' faces during this time and later compared the expressions of the babies to those of the model. Did infants make more tongue protrusions when they had just seen the model stick out his tongue at them, or were infants' expressions simply "random"—that is, not related to what they had just seen? Meltzoff and Moore reported that infants' facial gestures were selective: They opened their mouths more often when the model had displayed mouth opening, and they stuck out their tongues more often when the model had demonstrate tongue protrusion. Other researchers have similarly reported imitation of tongue protrusions and other facial gestures in infants during the first 2 months of life (Meltzoff & Moore, 1992; Nagy & Molnar, 2004), with several researchers reporting imitation in newborns (Field et al., 1982; Vinter, 1986; for a review, see Anisfeld, 1991).

The effect is somewhat elusive, however, and several experimenters have failed to replicate early imitation using procedures similar to those Meltzoff and Moore used (Anisfeld et al., 2001; Kaitz et al., 1988). Moreover, imitation of facial gestures actually declines during the first year of life. For the most-studied facial gesture of tongue protrusion, the majority of investigators who have examined infants of different ages report a peak in imitation sometime during the first 2 months, followed by a decline within weeks to chance values (Abravanel & Sigafoos, 1984; Jacobson, 1979; but see Meltzoff & Moore, 1992, for an exception). This is, indeed, perplexing, in that we have what appears to be a sophisticated cognitive phenomenon that actually decreases in frequency over a very brief period.

How can neonatal imitation be explained? Meltzoff and Moore (1977, 1985) have suggested that modeling effects during early infancy could be attributed to (1) learning; (2) selective imitation, guided by the integration of information from one sensory modality (vision) with information from another (proprioception derived from self-initiated movements); or (3) an *innate releasing mechanism*, where reflex-like responses are elicited by a specific set of stimuli.

According to Meltzoff and Moore, the first possibility, learning, is an unlikely candidate to explain early imitation. The most compelling reason for rejecting a

## PHOTO **10-1**

Neonatal imitation in humans and monkeys. Photographs of 2- to 3-day-old infants imitating (*A*) tongue protrusion, (*B*) mouth opening, and (*C*) lip protrusion as demonstrated by an adult experimenter. Newborn rhesus monkeys will also imitate facial expressions.

Source: Meltzoff, A. N., & Moore, M. K. (1977). Imitation of facial and manual gestures by human neonates. *Science, 198*, 75–78. Gross, L. (2006). Evolution of neonatal imitation. *PLoS Biol* 4(9): e311. doi:10.1371/journal.pbio.0040311.

learning or reinforcement interpretation is that infants who are only hours old will match certain facial expressions to those of an adult (Field et al., 1982; Vinter, 1986). It is unlikely that such young infants would have had sufficient experience to "learn" these responses.

The second alternative, selective imitation, is the one Meltzoff and Moore favor. They propose that the matching behavior observed in the early weeks of life is true imitation. Newborns are able to coordinate information from two senses. They can visually observe a stimulus, store an abstract representation of that stimulus, and compare it shortly thereafter with a proprioceptive representation (that is, their own movements). This position holds that newborns possess the ability to integrate information from two senses—in other words, they possess intermodal integration (see Chapter 4). Meltzoff and Moore (1985) referred to this as **active intermodal mapping**. If one accepts this interpretation, it advances the ability to coordinate two sensory modalities to a period many months earlier than that suggested by Piaget. Such an interpretation is not without some additional empirical support. As I discussed in Chapter 4, for example, research has demonstrated tactual-visual transfer of information in 4- to 6-month-olds (Streri & Spelke, 1989), and Meltzoff and Borton (1979) reported visual-tactual integration in infants less than 1 month old.

Yet, babies are not learning anything new during these episodes; the behaviors they are copying are already within their behavioral repertoire. Richard Byrne (2005) described such matching behavior as *social mirroring*, in which one member of a dyad (the newborn) copies the behavior of the other (the mother or, perhaps, Andrew Meltzoff) to stay "in tune" with one another, serving to foster and consolidate the social interaction. This social-mirroring interpretation is supported by research showing that newborns both imitate an adult and provoke imitation from an adult, with different patterns of heart-rate changes accompanying imitation (decreasing heart rate) and provocations (increasing heart rate) (Nagy, 2006; Nagy & Molnar, 2004). This suggests that neonatal imitation may serve a different role than the imitative responses that are seen later in infancy, one better described by Meltzoff and Moore's third alternative explanation. Rather than reflecting active intermodal mapping and "true" imitation, the newborn's matching behavior may reflect an **innate releasing mechanism** (or **fixed-action pattern**), which refers to inherited sets of behaviors elicited by specific sets of stimuli without prior environmental experience (Tinbergen, 1951). Such mechanisms would serve an adaptive role for the young infant and disappear when they are no longer needed.

Consistent with this interpretation, neonatal imitation appears to be under the control of subcortical, rather than cortical, brain areas, unlike the "true" imitation seen in children and adults. For instance, newborns who were later shown to be cortically blind, were still able to orient to objects visually in the first month of life before losing this ability (Dubowitz, et al., 1986), suggesting that early visual processing is done primarily by subcortical regions. Other research has shown that the visual recognition memory displayed by 3-day-old infants is largely controlled by subcortical structures (Pascalis & de Schonen, 1994). Not too long into development, however, these abilities move under the control of cortical circuits (Nagy, 2006).

What adaptive function might neonatal imitation play? One interpretation is that such responses play a specific role in survival of the infant at that time and that time only, and that they disappear when they are no longer needed (Bjorklund, 1987b). R. W. Oppenheim (1981) referred to such phenomena as **ontogenetic adaptations**. He argued that the young organism lives in a very different world from the adult and requires different behavioral or neurological organization to cope with life. Such organization might not be the basis for later development but, rather, might be present only for survival at that time and in that specific environment. Sandra Jacobson (1979), for example, suggested that tongue protrusions might be functional in early nursing. Similar to the argument made by Byrne (2005), I have suggested (Bjorklund,

1987b) that the neonatal imitation might play a role in early social development. The matching of adult facial gestures by the infant might help maintain social interaction between the two, with these reflexes declining when infants are better able to intentionally direct their gaze and control their head and mouth movements in response to social stimulation, somewhere between the second and fourth months of life (Cairns, 1979). In a similar vein, Maria Legerstee (1991) suggested that early imitation serves as a form of prelinguistic communication. Mikael Heimann (1989) provided tentative support for these positions, documenting a relationship between imitation in newborns and mother-infant social interactions at 3 months of age (specifically, infants who showed high levels of neonatal imitation had more social interactions with their mothers 3 months later).

One reason for favoring the "social" as opposed to the "symbolic" interpretation of neonatal imitation is that, as I mentioned earlier, these behaviors decline to chance values over the first 2 months (Abravanel & Sigafoos, 1984). Another reason is that neonatal imitation is also observed in chimpanzees (Bard, 2007; Myowa-Yamakoshi et al., 2004) and monkeys (Ferrai et al., 2006) (see Photo 10-1), and it is questionable whether mother-reared chimpanzees or monkeys ever develop the cognitive abilities that a symbolic interpretation of neonatal imitation implies. Like human babies, the incidence of neonatal imitation declines in chimpanzees around 2 months of age (Myowa-Yamakoshi et al., 2004). These behaviors are also more frequently seen in the context of more "natural" social communication as opposed to more formal (and "unnatural") settings, causing some primate researchers to argue for a communicative and/or affiliative function of neonatal primate imitation (Bard, 2007; Ferreri et al., 2006), similar to what has been argued for human infants (Bjorklund, 1987b; Byrne, 2005).

### Social Learning in Infancy Beyond the Neonatal Period

Jean Piaget (1962) documented in detail the development of social learning over infancy, and his basic observations have generally been replicated (Kaye & Marcus, 1981; McCall, Parke, & Kavanaugh, 1977). Piaget claimed that the earliest form of social learning is **mutual imitation**, in which the baby initiates a behavior that is mimicked by the adult, which in turn activates the baby to continue that behavior (Nagy & Molnar, 2004). Piaget's (1962) description of such interaction with his daughter will help illustrate this phenomenon: "I noted a differentiation in the sounds of her laughter. I imitated them. She reacted by reproducing them quite clearly, but only when she had already uttered them immediately before" (p. 10). As in neonatal imitation, infants are learning nothing new; they are merely engaging in social give-and-take with an adult, involving behaviors that they already possess (and, in fact, that they were the first to emit). Infants apparently enjoy these bouts of mother-infant imitation. For example, 3.5-month-old babies smile and vocalize more during and immediately after being imitated by their mothers than they do for nonimitative behaviors (Field, Guy, & Umbel, 1985).

Mothers and infants continue this reciprocal imitative relationship over the course of infancy. For instance, Elise Frank Masur and Jennifer Rodemaker (1999) observed mothers and their infants during free play or bath time when the babies were 10, 13, 17, and 21 months old. Rates of imitation were about one episode per minute, with mothers imitating infants more than infants imitated mothers. And unlike neonatal imitation or the mutual imitation described by Piaget, infants at this age are learning many new things through social learning. For example, in a study in which parents were asked to keep diaries of their children's imitative behavior, 12-, 15-, and 18-month olds learned, on average, one or two new behaviors a day simply by watching (Barr & Hayne, 2003; see also Masur & Eichorst, 2002).

Piaget did not observe the first signs of true social learning (that is, in which infants acquire some new behavior) until between 8 and 12 months. At this time, infants are now able to copy bodily movements and sounds that they have not produced before, although the new behaviors must be close to what the infants can already produce if they are to be successful. During this time, infants also begin to reproduce behaviors for which they receive no visual or auditory feedback, such as facial gestures. These are the same facial gestures newborns will copy but that drop off around 2 months of age. Piaget referred to these unseen actions as *invisible gestures*. During the next 6 months, infants become increasingly skilled at acquiring new behavior through observation, but according to Piaget, children of this age are limited to imitating a model in the model's presence. They are unable to observe a model and delay imitation for any length of time. More recent research, discussed previously in Chapter 8 in the context of memory development, has shown that infants are capable of *deferred imitation* much earlier than Piaget observed (see Bauer, 2007). Yet, Piaget's overall description of observational learning in infancy has generally been supported, with infants showing no copying of motor behaviors before 6 months of age and then gradually increasing their observational-learning abilities over the next 14 months (Jones, 2007).

### Young Children as Imitators and Emulators

Piaget, like most child developmental psychologists, did not differentiate among the different forms of social learning but used the term *imitation* to describe all forms of learning by observation. As I noted earlier, social learning can take various forms, with imitative learning being the most cognitively sophisticated. In fact, when looking closely at observational learning in infants and young children, the picture gets quite complicated (see Want & Harris, 2003).

For example, toddlers 2 years of age and younger frequently engage in emulation, seemingly understanding the goal of the model but engaging in alternative behaviors to achieve that goal (McGuigan & Whiten, 2009; Nielsen, 2006). However, this soon changes to a tendency to copy faithfully the actions of a model, even if those actions are unnecessary. For instance, several researchers have noted that preschoolers will faithfully reproduce the actions of a model even when those actions are irrelevant to attaining a goal (Gardiner, Greif, & Bjorklund, 2011; Horner & Whiten, 2005; Nagell, Olguin, & Tomasello, 1993). This was illustrated by a study in which an experimenter, using a rake to retrieve an out-of-reach object, displayed one of two sets of actions to 2-year-old children (Nagell et al., 1993). The children copied the actions of the adults even when a more effective way of solving the problem was possible. In contrast, chimpanzees given the same task achieved the goal not by copying the often-inefficient behaviors of the model (that is, by mimicry or imitative learning) but by using often more straightforward and effective actions to attain the goal (that is, by emulation) (see also Horner & Whiten, 2005, for other examples of chimpanzees using emulation rather than imitative learning). Similarly, in a study by Derek Lyons and his colleagues (2007), preschool children watched adults perform a series of actions on an object to open that object and get a toy that had been locked inside. Some of the actions were seemingly irrelevant to opening the object, but even when being warned to avoid "silly," unnecessary actions, the children copied them anyway. Such "overimitation" is not limited to children from Western culture but has also been observed in Kalahari Bushman 2- to 6-year-old children (Nielsen & Tomaselli, 2010).

This and similar research suggest that, unlike chimpanzees, young children are motivated to copy the actions of others to maintain a social interaction. Consistent with this, 2-year-olds are more likely to mimic the actions of a live, socially responsive person than a person in a video, and they are more likely to copy the behavior of a person they could communicate with via a closed circuit-TV system than the behavior of a person on a videotape who could not provide feedback (Nielsen, Simcock, & Jenkins, 2008). Two- and 3-year-old children also learn about the uses of tools during simple problem-solving tasks more readily by watching a model than by actually manipulating the materials themselves (Gardiner, Greif, & Bjorklund, 2009).

Some researchers have suggested that young children's "overimitation" results from their beliefs that all of an adults' actions are causally related to achieving a goal, making imitation (or mimicry) of all those actions the best course to take (Lyons et al., 2007; McGuigan et al., 2007). Their nearly automatic imitation of all the behaviors of a model is typically adaptive, in that it results in children copying key parts of actions that enable them to achieve a goal. Such an approach is not perfect, however, in that it can result in children executing irrelevant actions, even though such actions would seem to be "obviously" unnecessary from the point of view of an objective observer.

These findings seem to suggest that young children are blind mimics (or imitators), copying the exact behaviors of a model with regard to the model's intention (that is, why the model is engaging in the behavior in the first place). Yet, we know that toddlers are more apt to engage in emulation than in imitation (McGuigan & Whiten, 2009) and that even infants can sometimes "read" the intentions of a model and behave accordingly. Recall the experiments described in Chapter 6, in which infants as young as 7 months old copied behavior based on what they inferred the model's *intentions* were (for example, to remove the ends of a dumbbell) (Carpenter, Akhtar, & Tomasello, 1998; Hamlin, Hallinan, & Woodward, 2008; Meltzoff, 1995). These results demonstrate quite clearly that infants can, under some circumstances anyway, display true imitation (imitative learning) and not just mimicry.

Young children's social learning is flexible, and they will engage in emulation (attending to a model's intention but not the exact means of achieving that intention) in certain situations. For example, György Gergely and his colleagues (2002) replicated an earlier experiment by Andrew Meltzoff (1988) in which 14-month-old babies would imitate an adult by using their heads to press a button to turn on a light. This is a novel action (one would usually use one's hand), and it indicates that the babies were reproducing the exact behaviors of the model they had witnessed to achieve a goal. Gergely and his colleagues hypothesized that infants may have believed the model did not use her hands when she could have because using her head may have provided some advantage in turning on the light. In their study, 14-month-old infants watched as a model turned on the light with her head either (1) with her hands free, as in the earlier Meltzoff study, or (2) with her hands wrapped in a blanket (that is, her hands were occupied and thus not available to turn on the light). Figure 10-1 presents the percentage of infants in the "hands free" versus "hands occupied" conditions who turned on the light using their head (reflective of imitation) versus using their hands (reflective of emulation). As you can see, most of the infants in the "hands free" condition used their head to turn on the light, just as Meltzoff had found. But the pattern was reversed in the "hands occupied" condition. Now most of the infants (79%) used their hands to turn on the light. That is, when there was a reason why the model did not use her hands (they were wrapped in a blanket), the babies focused on the goal (turn on the light), not on the means (use your head), and they used their hands as the most efficient way to turn on the light. When no such reason was available, they copied the model's behavior exactly, reflective of imitative learning or perhaps mimicry. Gergely and his colleagues referred to

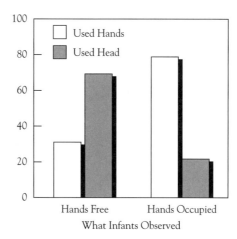

FIGURE **10-1**

Percentage of infants who used their hands or head to turn on the light as a function of whether the model had her hands free or occupied.

Source: Gergely, G., Bekkering, H., & Kiraly, I. (2002). Rational imitation in preverbal infants. *Nature, 415* (14 February), 755.

this behavior as *rational imitation*. Other researchers have similarly shown that young children's social learning is flexible, with children between 12 and 26 months of age displaying both imitative learning (focusing on the means as well as the ends of a model) and emulation (focusing only on the ends), depending on the context (Carpenter, Call, & Tomasello, 2005; Nielson, 2006; Thompson & Russell, 2004).

Most of the social-learning research I've reviewed here involves children imitating adults. But children learn a lot from observing one another, of course, and this has been a focus of much research, most of it from the perspective of Bandura's social cognitive theory (see discussion to follow). Recent research has examined the fidelity with which children learn specific skills from a child model over several different "generations" of children (Hooper et al., 2010; Horner et al., 2006). For example, in *diffusion chain* studies, one child is shown how to operate a novel apparatus. For instance, in research by Lydia Hooper and her colleagues (2010), a preschool child was shown one way to operate the pan-pipes apparatus, shown in Figure 10-2. There are three possible ways to operate the pan-pipes using a stick tool to receive a reward. The stick can be (1) inserted through a hole to lift the T-bar (lift method), (2) inserted through a different hole and used to poke the base of the T-bar (poke method), or (3) used to push and then slide the T-bar (push-lift method). A single child was shown the lift method. This child in turn served as a model for another child, who in turn served as a model for another child, and so on for a total of 20 different children. Hooper and her colleagues reported that all 20 children learned the lift method. In contrast, only 3 of 16 children learned to operate the pan-pipes without observing another child (that is, by "discovering" how to release the reward), and only one of these children used the lift method. These findings make it clear that preschool children are successful social learners and are able to learn a detailed skill from watching one another.

In actuality, of course, children rarely sit down one-on-one, with one child demonstrating a skill to another. In a group setting, several children at a time may play together, with skill transmission being a more complicated affair. This was examined in a study by Andrew Whiten and his colleagues (2011), who taught preschool children one of two ways to operate the pan-pipes (lift or poke), placed the pan-pipes in the

FIGURE **10-2**

Pan-pipes apparatus. (*A*) The stick-tool inserted under the T-bar for the lift method. (*B*) The stick-tool inserted into the top hole for the poke method. (*C*) the push-slide method by using the stick-tool pushing the T-bar back. In (*D*) the Pan-pipes viewed from the child's perspective, inside the clear plastic box with the access holes, with lift being demonstrated.

Source: Hooper, L. M., Flynn, E. G., Wood, L. A. N., & Whiten, A. (2010). Observational learning of tool use in children: Investigating cultural spread through diffusion chains and learning mechanisms through ghost displays. *Journal of Experimental Child Psychology, 106*, 82–97.

classroom, and watched what happened. Many children played with the pan-pipes, most after watching the trained child first successfully operate them, and 83% of children who attempted the task received the reward. Initially, most of the children not only used the method that the trained child had initially used but also stuck with this method over the course of several days. Consistent with the earlier studies, this likely reflects imitation, passing the skill from one child to the next with great fidelity. However, some children in both the lift and poke classrooms discovered other methods to operate the pan-pipes, and these too spread to different members of the groups. This would seem to reflect a form of emulation, with children understanding the goal of a model but achieving that goal through alternative means. Perhaps not surprisingly, in addition to simply demonstrating the method, many children talked about what they were doing, attempting to teach other children how to operate the pan-pipes. This research indicates that preschool children have a variety of social-learning abilities available to them and that a skill learned by one child will, indeed, be transmitted to other children, sometimes exactly as initially demonstrated and sometimes with modifications.

## Social Learning in Chimpanzees

Chimpanzees are impressive social learners, passing on "cultural" information such as forms of greeting, grooming, and foraging from one generation to the next (Whiten,

2010; Whiten et al., 1999). And they are not the only nonhuman animal that possess "culture": Orangutans (van Schaik et al., 2003) and cetaceans (dolphins and killer whales; Bender, Herzing, & Bjorklund, 2009; Rendell & Whitehead, 2001) have also been observed to transmit information across generations, although no species does so with the ease, the fidelity, and to the extent that humans do. Using diffusion studies similar to those with children described earlier, members of a chimpanzee group have been shown to acquire the lift or poke methods for operating the pan-pipes, much as human children do (Horner et al., 2006; Whiten et al, 2005). As I noted earlier, however, chimpanzees seem not to engage in true imitation but, rather, in emulation, focusing on the ends (achieving a goal) and not on the means (the actual behaviors displayed by a model) in their social learning (Call, Carpenter, & Tomasello, 2004; Horner & Whiten, 2005; Nagell et al., 1993).

Some scientists have suggested that the limited social cognitive abilities displayed by chimpanzees can be attributed, in part, to their early experience. Michael Tomasello, Sue Savage-Rumbaugh, and Ann Kruger (1993) speculated that one reason for chimpanzees' impoverished social cognition is that "unlike human children, they do not develop in a social environment in which adult conspecifics are constantly encouraging their attention to objects, intentionally teaching them how to use objects as tools, and rewarding them for imitating actions on objects" (p. 1689). Some chimpanzees, however, do have these experiences, being reared by humans much as children are. The **enculturation hypothesis** proposes that chimpanzees raised this way—with adult humans engaging them in shared attention, teaching, and using language—will develop some social cognitive abilities more similar to those of human children (Bjorklund & Rosenberg, 2005; Call & Tomasello, 1996).

Tomasello and his colleagues (1993) evaluated their idea by testing mother-reared chimpanzees (that is, chimpanzees reared by their own chimpanzee mothers), human-reared (enculturated) chimpanzees, and 18- and 30-month-old human children on a series of object-imitation tasks. They reported that the mother-reared chimpanzees were much poorer at immediate imitation than were either the enculturated chimps or the human children, who did not differ from one another. The findings for *deferred imitation* (imitating actions 2 days after observing the actions) were even more interesting (see Figure 10-3). Somewhat surprisingly, the enculturated chimpanzees actually showed greater deferred imitation than the human children did (see also Bering, Bjorklund, & Ragan, 2000; Bjorklund et al. 2002; Buttelmann et al., 2007). These findings indicate that chimpanzees possess the rudimentary cognitive skills for object imitation but rarely express it in species-typical situations. When provided with a human-typical rearing environment, however, their abilities appear comparable with those observed for 30-month-old children. Such experience does not (nor ever could) make a chimpanzee think like a human, but the rearing conditions of these animals did change their cognitions substantially.

What about teaching? There are a handful of observations of chimpanzee mothers in the wild altering their behavior in such a way to enhance learning of a foraging task by their offspring (Boesch, 1991; Greenfield et al., 2000). For example, Christophe Boesch (1991) observed mother chimpanzees making exaggerated movements while cracking nuts when in the presence of their infants, which he interpreted as teaching. However, the rarity of these observations suggests that this is not the typical way in which knowledge is transmitted across generations in chimpanzees. No well-controlled experiments have demonstrated teaching in enculturated chimpanzees, but Roger Fouts (1997) reported that the language-trained and enculturated chimpanzee Washoe taught about 50 signs to her adopted son Loulis, which he used both with Washoe and with his human caretakers.

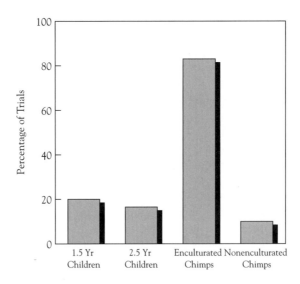

FIGURE **10-3**

Percentage of trials on which children and apes displayed deferred imitation.

Source: Tomasello, M., Savage-Rumbaugh, S., & Kruger, A. C. (1993). Imitative learning of actions and objects by children, chimpanzees, and enculturated chimpanzees. *Child Development, 64*, 1688–1705. Reprinted with permission of the Society for Research in Child Development.

Many aspects of chimpanzees' social cognition seem not to be seriously influenced by human rearing, such as shared attention (Tomasello & Carpenter, 2005) and performing false-belief tasks (Call & Tomasello, 1999; Herrmann et al., 2007). However, the fact that chimpanzees raised in a species-atypical environment can alter aspects of their social-learning ability in a way that resembles that of human children suggests radical environmental changes could have been the impetus for evolutionary change in our ancestors. These findings are consistent with the developmental systems approach discussed in Chapter 2 (Gottlieb, 2000), in that species-atypical environments can produce species-atypical behaviors—in this case, humanlike imitation in chimpanzees. For human cognitive development, these results point to the necessity of considering the role of the social environment when examining the development of intellectual ability. The findings also hint at possible developmental mechanisms for the evolution of human cognition (Bjorklund & Bering, 2003; Bjorklund & Pellegrini, 2002), and they suggest that mothers played an important role in modifying the social cognition of their offspring. Changes in how mothers interact with their infants, prompted perhaps by ecological changes, may have resulted in social cognitive transformations that would have given their offspring a competitive advantage and led to increased reproductive success. Such advanced social cognitive abilities could have resulted in new selection pressures for these animals, setting the stage for evolutionary change (Bjorklund, 2006; Bjorklund, Grotuss, & Csinady, 2009). As my mother often said, "If it wasn't for women, men would still be hanging by their tails from the trees." She may have been more right than she knew.

Social learning has not only caught the attention of developmental and animal-comparative psychologists, but also of neuroscientists. The neurobiology of social learning and its development is complicated and no single brain area is "responsible" for social learning. However, neuroscientists have identified what have been termed *mirror neurons* in the brains of monkeys and humans that may play an important role on social learning, and these are discussed in Box 10-1.

---

**BOX 10-1** | **Mirror Neurons: The Foundation of Social Learning?**

It seems clear that humans are born to learn from others (or at least learn to do so very early in life). As for all other types of learning, the brain mediates social learning, and in recent years, scientists have begun to probe the neurological basis of social learning and cognition, creating the field of *social neuroscience* (Cacioppo, 2002; Decety & Cacioppo, 2010). One phenomenon in social neuroscience of particular relevance for the development of social learning is the discovery of **mirror neurons**. First identified in the frontal lobes of monkeys, mirror neurons responded when a monkey either performed or watched someone else perform a goal-directed act, such as grasping a piece of food (Rizzolatti & Craighero, 2004; Rizzolatti et al., 1996). The neurons did not fire when a monkey watched a hand making grasping movements without something to grasp. In other words, these animals possessed specific neurons that became active when they performed an action *and* when they watched others performing actions the monkey itself could make.

Rizzolatti and his colleagues speculated that these neurons might permit monkeys to perform certain behaviors without having to think about them and to comprehend such behaviors without the need of explicit reasoning. Neurons such as these may play an important role in observational learning. A monkey sees an action, and neurons associated with motor areas of the brain are activated, providing a neurological system underlying social learning. Subsequent research discovered mirror neurons in other parts of the monkey brain associated with the mouth—for example, responding when a monkey sees food being eaten or when another individual makes a species-typical lip-smacking response (see Rizzolatti & Craighero, 2004).

Later research has shown that mirror neurons in monkeys seem not to be involved in reproducing (that is, in imitating) behavior but, rather, are used to recognize when another individual's behavior matches its own. For instance, Annika Paukner and her colleagues (2004) had both monkeys and humans manipulate small cubes with either their hands or their mouths. In some cases, the person produced the exact actions of a monkey, whereas other times, he or she simply engaged in monkey-like actions, just not the same actions that the monkey was currently doing. Paukner and her colleagues reported that the monkeys generally preferred to look at the human who was copying them, seemingly recognizing that another individual was displaying the same or similar behavior as they were. More generally, mirror neurons reflect an individual being "able to recognize when another is doing something that the self can do" (Byrne, 2005, p. R499).

It wasn't long after the discovery of mirror neurons in monkeys that neuroscientists began to search for them in humans, and they found them. Brain-imaging studies, however, showed that the mirror-neuron system in humans is different from that in monkeys. For example, mirror neurons are activated when one person observes another person express an emotion, such as disgust as a result of smelling something foul or pain as a result of being shocked (see Rizzolatti, Fogassi, & Gallese, 2005). Also, mirror neurons in humans become active both for goal-directed behavior (for example, grasping a piece of food) and, unlike monkeys, for "meaningless" actions, such as random finger movements. And human mirror neurons, unlike those of monkeys, seem to code for movements *forming* an action, not only for the action itself (see Rizzolatti & Craighero, 2004). This suggests that mirror neurons are important in imitative learning, where the specific behaviors a model performs (the "means") are as important as the goal the model attains (the "ends"). Giovani Buccino and his colleagues (2004) investigated the possible role of mirror neurons in imitative learning by asking people to watch an expert as he played guitar chords. Mirror neurons were activated when

*(Continues)*

participants watched the expert play chords, and these neurons were even more active when they tried to imitate the movements.

Most research on human mirror neurons has been performed with adults, although evidence of mirror neurons in infants and children has been found in several studies. For example, using EEG recordings, evidence of mirror neurons for children as young as 3 years of age has been documented for the observation and execution of hand movements (Fecteau et al., 2004; Lepage & Théoret, 2006). Similarly, fMRI studies suggest that 10- to 14-year-old children have a mirror-neuron system for emotional expressions (Dapretto et al., 2006). Some have speculated that the mirror-neuron system is functioning at birth (Lepage & Théoret, 2007; Pfeifer et al., 2008), based mainly on the presence of neonatal imitation (Meltzoff & Moore, 1977), discussed earlier in this chapter. To date, however, there is no solid neurological evidence of a mirror-neuron system in newborns of any species (Lepage & Théoret, 2007), but a 2009 study by Victoria Southgate and her colleagues provided evidence of such a system in 9-month-old infants. The researchers measured EEG recordings of infants when they reached for objects and when they observed someone else reach for the same objects. Southgate and her colleagues reported that, like in adults, watching a grasping action activated the motor portion of infants' brains, although only after the infants had observed the action several times. At that point, the neural activity began *before* they observed the behavior, in anticipation of the action. That is, observing someone perform a behavior they too could perform did not directly activate infants' mirror neurons; instead, activation was determined by their knowledge of the forthcoming action.

The presence of a mirror-neuron system may play a central role in social learning. For instance,

V. S. Ramachandran (2000; Ramachandran & Oberman, 2006) proposed that mirror neurons provide the brain-based mechanisms for identifying with others, which is the basis of empathy, perspective taking, imitative learning, and even language (see also Meltzoff et al., 2009). Mirror neurons fire when people observe another person doing something, or even attempting to do something. This may provide the neurological basis for understanding another person's intention. Recall from Chapter 6 our discussion about the important role in folk psychology of infants seeing others as *intentional agents*, individuals who *cause* things to happen and whose behavior is designed to achieve some goal (Tomasello & Carpenter, 2007; Woodward, 2009). Some have speculated that the seeming absence of well-developed theory-of-mind abilities in people with autism spectrum disorder may be associated with defects in the mirror-neuron system (Ramachandran & Oberman, 2006; Williams et al., 2001), and these speculations have been confirmed in research with both children (Dapretto et al., 2006) and adults (Oberman et al., 2005).

Mirror neurons are a hot topic today, but understanding the neurological basis of social learning and its development is still in its infancy. Future research will shed more light on how brain organization and development foster social learning and provide valuable insights into social cognition, the development of social learning, and possibly even the evolution of the human mind. Some have speculated, for example, that changes in the mirror-neuron system over hominid evolution afforded greater social-learning abilities and set the stage for the revolutionary changes in thinking and lifestyle that occurred over relatively brief periods of evolutionary time (Ramachandran & Oberman, 2006; Rizzolatti & Craighero, 2004).

# SOCIAL COGNITIVE THEORY

One of the most influential theories in developmental psychology during the past 40 years has been Albert Bandura's **social learning theory,** which Bandura later renamed **social cognitive theory** to reflect a more mentalistic approach. Initial formulations of social learning theory (Bandura & Walters, 1963) were based on extensions of models of classical and operant conditioning, popular throughout most of the 20th century in American psychology. It became apparent, however, that explicit reinforcement was not necessary for children (and adults) to learn about their social world. Rather, people learn much about their world simply by watching. As the field of cognitive psychology developed during the 1960s and 1970s, Bandura incorporated many cognitive principles, transforming his theory into a cognitive one in which children learn about important social relationships by watching (Bandura, 1986, 1989; Bussey & Bandura, 1999).

There are many similarities between the ideas expressed in social cognitive theory and those expressed by Jean Piaget (as discussed in Chapter 5). For example, similar to Piaget, Bandura believes that children affect their environment as much as their environment affects them, selecting and creating the world in which they live. Bandura refers to this interaction between children and their environment as **reciprocal determinism**, with children determining how others respond toward them as much as they are influenced by others. Bandura proposes complex interactions between children's thoughts, feelings, and behaviors and the external environment. How children feel or think about something will affect their behavior. Likewise, their behavior in certain situations will influence their thought. Each of us tries to make sense of our behavior, and we often change our thinking and beliefs to be in line with our actions. Children's behavior will influence how other people in the environment perceive and act toward them, which will, of course, affect their thinking and behavior. Thus, Bandura proposes a process of causation that gives serious attention to the internal states of children (their thoughts and emotions), to their observable behaviors, and to the perceptions and actions of others.

## Factors Involved in Observational Learning

Bandura proposed five capabilities that contribute to children's learning about their social world and their place in it, each of which develops (see Table 10-2): (1) symbolization, (2) forethought, (3) self-regulation, (4) self-reflection, and (5) vicarious learning. The first capability, **symbolization**, means that we can think about our social behavior in words and images. This is necessary for us to be aware of various aspects of our actions. The capability of **forethought** means that we are able to anticipate the consequences of our actions and the actions of others. This future-time perspective motivates behavior. **Self-regulation** involves adopting standards of acceptable behavior for ourselves. These include aspirational standards (hoped-for levels of accomplishment) as well as social and moral standards. A capacity for **self-reflection** allows us to analyze our thoughts and actions.

The final capability, **vicarious learning**, is the cornerstone of social cognitive theory. Children do not need to receive specific reinforcement for their behavior to learn; rather, they learn much social behavior merely by observing others. This places **observational learning** at the center of Bandura's theory.

Bandura proposed four subprocesses that govern observational learning: (1) attentional processes, (2) retention processes, (3) production processes, and (4) motivational processes. Information must be attended to, coded in memory, stored, and retrieved, and the behavior must be performed at the appropriate time. Each of these processes changes with age, and a failure in any one process (retention, for example) rules out successful observational learning. Children do not need to physically imitate a model to have learned from observing the model. Children might have learned all they need to know from observing but never have the motivation to produce the behavior.

TABLE **10-2**

Capabilities Involved in Bandura's Social Cognitive Theory and the Four Subprocesses of Observational Learning.

| Key Cognitive Capabilities |
| --- |
| *Symbolization:* The ability to think about social behavior in words and images. |
| *Forethought:* The ability to anticipate the consequences of our actions and the actions of others. |
| *Self-regulation:* The ability to adopt standards of acceptable behavior for ourselves. |
| *Self-reflection:* The ability to analyze our thoughts and actions. |
| *Vicarious learning:* The ability to learn new behavior and the consequences of one's actions by observing others. |

| Subprocesses of Observational Learning |
| --- |
| Attentional Processes |
| Retention Processes |
| Production Processes |
| Motivational Processes |

Following Bandura's theory, after children have attended to a model and formed a mental representation of the behavior, they must convert that representation to action. Yet, children observe some things that they do not have the motoric ability to reproduce. For example, a 5-year-old boy may have watched and mentally practiced the behaviors involved in driving a car, but because of his short arms and legs (among other things), he is physically unable to produce the behaviors he has observed. Despite such obvious shortcomings, young children frequently overestimate their imitative abilities. They have watched a behavior being performed and believe that "seeing is knowing." (More than one parent has been shocked to see his or her young child behind the wheel of a moving car.) During a study in which mothers recorded the imitative attempts of their preschoolers, children overestimated their imitative abilities 55.5% of the time—stating that they were capable of imitating a behavior when they were not. Cases of underestimation were rare, occurring on only 4.7% of the observations (Bjorklund, Gaultney, & Green, 1993). As this study reminds us, young children have great confidence in their own abilities. To improve observational learning, children must learn to monitor and compare their actions with their symbolic representations and to correct mismatches. As these production processes improve with age, the difference between what children know and what they can produce declines (Bandura, 1989).

## The Development of Self-Efficacy

The concept of **self-efficacy**, the extent to which a person views him- or herself as an effective individual, plays a central role in Bandura's theory. Self-efficacy develops through experience. Children evaluate the effectiveness of their own actions, compare it with the actions of others, and are told by others how their behavior meets certain standards. Children who believe they are competent (even if they are not) develop feelings of positive self-efficacy. Conversely, when self-efficacy is poor, people tend to behave ineffectually, regardless of their actual abilities (Bandura, 1997). Developing feelings of positive self-efficacy has important consequences for children's social, emotional, and intellectual development (Bandura et al., 1996). One should not, however, think of self-efficacy as a general characteristic of a child. Rather, self-efficacy (and the related concept of self-worth) is specific to a domain and a task (Harter, Waters, & Whitesell, 1998). A child can have a positive sense of self-efficacy for playing baseball, for example, but a poor sense of self-efficacy for doing long division.

The development of self-efficacy begins early, as infants learn that they can exert some control over their environment. Beginning around 3 or 4 months, babies learn that their actions have consequences—for example, if they kick their feet, the mobile over the crib will move, and if they smile and coo, their parents will smile and talk back to them. Infants who have experienced some control over their environments are better able to learn new behaviors (Finkelstein & Ramey, 1977). Mary Ainsworth and her colleagues (1978) proposed that parents' responsiveness to their infants' attempts to communicate their needs gives the infants some sense of control over their parents and is related to later social and cognitive development.

With the development of language and other symbols, children are able to reflect on their new social and intellectual abilities and evaluate what others tell them about their skills. Initially, the family provides children with feedback on their effectiveness. As children approach school age, their peer group becomes a valuable source of information, and school itself is a potent agent in forming children's self-efficacy. Children learn through daily experience with teachers and peers that they are good at some tasks and not so good at others (Bandura, 1997).

Although children learn self-efficacy through experience, developing a positive sense of self-efficacy is facilitated by a generally optimistic (and unrealistic) opinion of their own abilities. Preschool children think that they can remember more items, communicate more effectively, perform tasks better, imitate a model more accurately, and perform a host of tasks better than they actually can (Bjorklund et al., 1993; Lipko, Dunlosky, & Merriman, 2009; Plumert, 1995).

Most of us can likely recall a time from childhood when we overestimated our abilities. I have one especially vivid memory that is now over 50 years old:

> The first grade class was getting fidgety. There were a few minutes left before the bell rang, so the teacher decided to fill the time with some entertainment. "Can anyone sing a song for us?" she asked, and several children gave renditions of their favorite tunes. "Can anyone dance?" she asked. I felt that this was my time to shine. "I can tap dance!" I answered. I walked to the front of the room and proceeded to shuffle my feet, trying my best to imitate the dancers I had seen on TV. Well, the result *was* entertainment, but strictly comedy. My classmates roared with laughter and even the teacher was unable to hide her amusement. Fortunately, the bell rang soon and the children lined up to go home, so my stint in the spotlight was short lived (Bjorklund, 2007a, p. 11).

My false belief in my dancing ability is not uncommon, and although this particular event led to some embarrassment without any obvious benefit (other than having a story to tell many years later), young children's beliefs that they know more than they actually do, and that they can do more than they actually can, provide them with positive perceptions of their own skills. This positive sense of self-efficacy might encourage children to attempt things that they would not try if they had a more realistic idea of their abilities. In other words, their cognitive immaturity, as reflected by their unrealistic assessments of their abilities, can actually facilitate development rather than hinder it (Bjorklund, 1997a; Bjorklund & Green, 1992).

Evidence for the positive effects of an unrealistic belief in one's abilities comes from several sources. For example, in one study, brighter 3-year-olds overestimated their imitation abilities more than less bright 3-year-olds did (Bjorklund et al., 1993). The positive consequences of overestimation are not limited to the preschool years, however. Research has shown, for example, that 8- to 11-year-old children who overestimated their capabilities had better school performance than did less optimistic children (Lopez et al., 1998). These children may not have been quite as good as they thought, but their school performance was better than that of their more accurate peers. In other research, kindergarten, first-grade, and third-grade children who overestimated their memory abilities showed greater subsequent improvement on memory tasks than more accurate children (Shin, Bjorklund, & Beck, 2007).

Children's overly optimistic appraisal of their abilities also poses some problems, however. For example, Jodie Plumert (1995) reported that 6-year-olds who consistently overestimate their physical abilities were more accident prone than less optimistic children were (see also Plumert & Schwebel, 1997). In other research, Plumert and her colleagues (Plumert, Kearney, & Cremer, 2004, 2007) asked 10- and 12-year-old children and adults to determine when it was safe to ride their bikes across a busy street. (They did not actually cross streets. Judgments were made on a "virtual" street.) Plumert and her colleagues reported that the children were less accurate in making safety judgments than the adults. Children took longer to get moving, so the gap between cars that they judged to be safe resulted in more close calls than when adults made judgments.

What is the origin of young children's tendency for overestimation? It does not seem to stem from a general cognitive deficit in evaluating performance. For instance, Deborah Stipek (Stipek, 1984; Stipek & Daniels, 1988) noted that young children can make relatively accurate predictions of how other children are likely to perform on school-like tasks but are overly optimistic in predicting their own future performance. Stipek suggested that this overly optimistic self-perception is the result of **wishful thinking**, a concept originally introduced by Piaget (1930): Children wish for A's on their report cards; therefore, they expect A's. By the third or fourth grade, however, children's assessments of their own abilities move closer to reality, and they are able to tell the difference between what they wish would happen and what they can reasonably expect to happen. Stipek believes that this tendency to overestimate one's own abilities enhances children's self-efficacy and gives them the confidence to attempt things they would not otherwise try. Stipek proposed that rather than trying to make young children's self-assessments more accurate, we should "try harder to design educational environments which maintain their optimism and eagerness" (1984, p. 53).

Bandura's ideas have been applied to many different contents, the majority of which are more social than cognitive in character. As a cognitive psychologist, however, I believe that knowledge, be it of inanimate objects, of other people, or of one's self, is mentally represented and operated on by a set of cognitive mechanisms. Bandura's approach to development acknowledges this, blurring the distinction between what is social and what is cognitive, recognizing that it is all governed by the same nervous system.

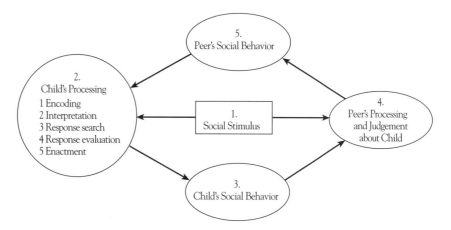

FIGURE **10-4**

Dodge's model of social exchange in children.

Source: From Dodge et al. (1986). Social competence in children. *Monographs of the Society for Research in Child Development, 51* (Serial No. 213). Copyright © 1986 The Society for Research in Child Development, Inc. Reprinted with permission.

## SOCIAL INFORMATION PROCESSING

Social cognitive theorists have adopted many of the tenets of information processing. Social information must be encoded, compared with other pertinent information, and retrieved so that social interactions run smoothly. The more skillfully social information is processed, the more socially competent a child is seen to be. Kenneth Dodge and his colleagues (Crick & Dodge, 1994; Dodge, 1986; Dodge et al., 1986; see also Rubin & Krasnor, 1986) have postulated a theory that describes the mental processes involved in evaluating social information. Dodge's original model of social exchange in children is shown in Figure 10-4.

As can be seen in the figure, the model has five major units of social interaction. The first unit is the social stimulus, or cue. This is the information that a child must process. For example, a shove by another child, a smile, a scowl, a pout, and an invitation to join a game are all social signals that must be interpreted. The second unit of the model is a child's processing of these cues. A child must make sense of the social cues and decide how to respond. More will be said of this unit shortly. Once a child evaluates the information, he or she must emit some social behavior (unit 3). Does the 6-year-old enter the play group by jumping in the middle of an ongoing game and ask if she can play, or does she just stand to the side, waiting to be asked? This behavior serves as a social stimulus for a child's peers, who make some judgment of the child (unit 4), and then act themselves (unit 5). (The model has been reformulated to include a sixth stage between the representation and search processes in which children clarify their goals in the situation [Crick & Dodge, 1994]. The reformulated model refines the theory but does not substantially change it. The basic model has been quite successful in accounting for a wide range of children's social behaviors.)

Of major concern here is the part of Dodge's theory dealing with **social information processing** (unit 2). How do children make sense of social information to select a proper social response? Dodge postulated five sequential steps of information processing that are necessary for competent social functioning:

1. *Encoding.* The child must first encode the social stimulus. This requires that the child be properly attentive and adequately perceive the social signal. The child must know what cues are important to encode. For a child entering an already established group, for example, whether he is greeted by a smile or a frown is an important social cue. Less critical are things such as what the other children are wearing or that Kevin needs a haircut.

2. *Interpretation.* Once encoded, the social information must be interpreted. What does this information mean? To determine meaning, children must compare this information with what they already know. What does it mean if the child is greeted by smiles? This will depend on what this child knows about the smiles of others in similar situations. "When I approach a group of kids I know who are already playing a game, smiles are usually a sign of welcome. But when Marvin smiles at me, it usually means he's going to trip me the first chance he gets." Children develop rules for interpreting social signals. These rules are probably not conscious, and they are executed in a matter of microseconds.

3. *Response search.* Once an interpretation has been made, a child must decide what his or her next move is. Children must generate a variety of response alternatives. Do they join the group? If so, by what means? Do they approach the playground bully, walk around him, think of something clever to say, or run away? With age, children have a greater number of more sophisticated options from which to choose, which should contribute greatly to behaving in a socially competent fashion.

4. *Response evaluation.* Once responses have been generated, they must be evaluated. Does it make sense to approach the bully, hitting him before he hits me, or might one of the other options be wiser? To what extent can children anticipate the consequences of their behavior, selecting the response alternative that will be most successful in the current situation?

5. *Enactment.* Finally, the child must execute the chosen response.

Dodge proposed that these steps are executed in order. However, steps can be skipped, and when they are, socially incompetent behavior will likely result. For example, the first response a child comes up with might not be the ideal response for the situation. If this response is not evaluated and found wanting, the resulting behavior will probably not ingratiate the child to his or her peers. Similarly, a child might make a decision based on misinterpreted information. The quiet manner of a peer while studying may have been interpreted as an invitation to horse around, or the smile of the well-known bully may have been construed erroneously as a peace offering. Also, as mentioned earlier, the wrong information might be encoded. The cues may have been there, but because the child was attending to other more salient environmental or internal cues, they may have been ignored or missed.

Dodge and his colleagues (1986) tested this model with respect to the social skill of peer-group entry—that is, entering an established group of other children. Children in kindergarten and the first and second grades were shown videotapes of two children playing a game and asked a series of questions related to peer-group entry. The questions were selected so that each of the five aspects of Dodge's model of social information processing could be evaluated. After viewing the video, for example, the children were asked to imagine that they wanted to join the group. They were then asked how much the child on the left and how much the child on the right from the video would like to play with them. Answers to these questions reflected the children's interpretation of social cues, or step 2 of the model. The children were then asked the reasons for their decisions. Answers to this question indicated the children's use of specific cues from the videotapes in making their decisions, or step 1 of the model (encoding). Next, the children were asked to think of as many ways as possible to join the group, or step 3 of the model (response search). After this, the children viewed five scenarios consisting of the original video of two children playing followed by the arrival of a third child who attempted to join the group. The new arrival displayed one of five strategies for joining the group (competent, aggressive, self-centered, passive, or authority intervention). After watching these scenarios, the children were asked a series of questions concerning the potential effectiveness of each of the five strategies to assess step 4 of the model (response evaluation). Finally, the children were asked to pretend that they wished to play with the experimenter and were told to "show me how you would ask me if you could play with me." This corresponded to step 5 of the model (enactment).

In a separate session, conducted 1 to 2 weeks later, each child was brought into a room in which two other children were already playing and was told to play with these children. Based on videotapes of these sessions and interviews with the children, each child's actual peer-group entry was evaluated.

The most important aspect of the results of this study concerns the prediction of children's peer-group entry (their actual social behavior) as a function of their skills at social information processing. In general, children who scored higher on the assessment of social information processing were rated as more successful at actual peer-group entry. Children who used presented cues (step 1), who generated competent and nonaggressive strategies in response to a hypothetical entry situation (step 3), who evaluated incompetent responses negatively (step 4), and who demonstrated high skill in enactment of responses (step 5) were relatively likely to perform competently and successfully in actual group entry. Furthermore, Dodge and his colleagues reported that these skills were relatively independent of one another, suggesting that each contributes something unique to social judgment and behavior rather than reflecting different aspects of a single social intelligence. Other researchers have tested the relation between children's competence for each of the five areas of social information processing and subsequent social behavior and, as Dodge and his colleagues (1986), report modest relations (Dodge & Price, 1994; Slaby & Guerra, 1988).

The area in which social information processing theory has been most frequently applied is aggressive behavior (Coie & Dodge, 1998; Crick & Dodge, 1996; Dodge et al., 2006). Research has found characteristic ways in which at least some aggressive children encode, interpret, search, evaluate, and enact social behavior. For example, highly aggressive children are less likely to recall relevant social cues from a videotape (Dodge et al., 1995) and are more attentive to potentially aggressive cues (Gouze, 1987) than less aggressive children. Concerning interpretation, highly aggressive children are more likely to interpret an ambiguous situation (for example, a peer spills water on you) as having an aggressive, rather than an accidental, intent (Graham & Hudley, 1994) and also interpret events with clearly benign intentions as hostile (Dodge et al., 1986) more often than less aggressive children. Concerning response search, aggressive children tend to generate more atypical and socially inappropriate responses than less aggressive children do (see Coie & Dodge, 1998), and they have a difficult time inhibiting aggressive responses (Perry, Perry, & Rasmussen, 1986). Aggressive children perceive aggressive responses as socially appropriate and normative (Guerra, Huesmann, & Hanish, 1995), and they believe that they can engage in aggression relatively easily (Perry et al., 1986). Although such a pattern does not reduce in any way the effect of other, more traditionally "social" factors on aggression, it does point to the conclusion that how children process social information with respect to aggression is related to their own level of aggressive behavior.

The work of Dodge and his colleagues clearly points to the cognitive basis of social behavior. Complex social situations must be evaluated and thought about just as strictly "intellectual" situations must be contemplated. Theories of nonsocial information processing have routines, such as encoding and retrieval, and structures, such as the short-term store and semantic memory, that are specified with relative precision. Although there is still much debate concerning the particulars of nonsocial information processing, there is also much consensus. The field of social information processing is less advanced, however, because it is more complicated. How can one specify the features of a social stimulus? How is social information represented in long-term memory? How is it retrieved? Can the concepts of the short-term store, schemas, and strategies, which are so useful for explaining nonsocial cognition, be successfully applied to social cognition? Social information processing theory is in its infancy. However, the work of Dodge and others (Rubin & Krasnor, 1986) represents an exciting beginning to research that will surely lead to a better understanding of the development of children's social lives.

# THE DEVELOPMENT OF A CONCEPT OF SELF

Few mental concepts are more important to us than the personal sense of self. By **self-concept**, I mean the way a person defines himself or herself. Some theorists have speculated that a conscious awareness of oneself greatly influences cognitive development, particularly the use of goal-directed strategies (Bullock & Lütkenhaus, 1988). Others have stressed the significance of a sense of self for social and emotional development (Brooks-Gunn & Lewis, 1984; Gallup, 1979). Many believe our well-developed sense of self is what makes humans unique as a species. Some people have even speculated that the development of self-awareness vaulted our hominid ancestors to full human cognition and social organization (Alexander, 1989). The significance of the concept of self for the developing person and for the species cannot be overstated.

Although self-awareness may seem self-evident to you, there can be—and has been—great debate among philosophers, psychologists, theologians, and people in general about what exactly it entails. It certainly involves an awareness of one's thoughts (that is, reflecting upon the contents of one's mind). It requires a psychological sense of self, an ability to distinguish oneself from others and to identify one's actions as intentionally motivated ("I" did that for a reason). Having a sense of self permits us to evaluate the causes of our behavior and, importantly, the behavior of others (Bering & Bjorklund, 2007). That is, by becoming self-aware, we also become "other-aware," and this becomes useful when dealing with other members of our species. In fact, we may actually come to see ourselves as others see us. Charles Cooley

(1902) used the term *looking-glass-self* to capture the idea that our self-concept is a reflection of how other people see and respond to us or, according to Philippe Rochat (2009), that "self-consciousness stands for the representation we hold of ourselves through the eyes of others" (p. 3).

How can we know if young children have a concept of self? If they are too young to talk, we cannot ask them and must infer self-awareness from their behavior. Piaget (1952), among others, proposed that infants only gradually come to recognize themselves as distinct from the objects around them, with the distinction becoming fully developed sometime around 18 to 24 months of age (see Chapter 5).

Perhaps one of the earliest indications of a self-concept is infants' ability to differentiate themselves from other people and objects. During the first several months of life, infants should be receiving various forms of proprioceptive, visual, and acoustic feedback from their behavior. This should give them some sense of "who they are," at least with respect to other people.

How can one determine this? One technique is to show infants pictures or videos of themselves along with pictures or videos of other infants or objects and assess their looking time (Bahrick, Moss, & Fadil, 1996; Legerstee, Anderson, & Schaffer, 1998). If infants "recognize" themselves, they should pay less attention (a novelty effect) or, possibly, more attention (a familiarity effect) to these other stimuli than to images of themselves (see the discussion of preference for novelty/familiarity effects in Chapter 4). If they can't tell the difference between images of themselves and those of other people or objects, there should be no differential attention to any of the stimuli. In experiments using variants of this technique, infants as young as 3 months were able to discriminate between images of themselves and same-aged infants (Legerstee et al., 1998; Rochat & Striano, 2002), suggesting a primitive form of self-recognition early in infancy. How do infants this young know what they look like? The most likely source of this self-knowledge is mirrors. Infants as young as 2-months-old often have daily exposure to their image from mirrors (Bahrick, 1995), and so by 3 months of age, they recognize themselves as a familiar sight.

Still, the ability to differentiate one's self from the environment is a far cry from what we typically mean by a sense of self. Theorists have proposed that two types of self-concept develop in the first 2 years of life. The first, which typifies infants from birth to about 15 or 18 months of age, has been referred to as the *I-self* (Lewis, 1991), or the *implicit self* (Case, 1991). The I-self reflects what Lewis (1991) termed the "machinery of the self." There is no self-awareness of the I-self. There is a distinction between the self and others and a realization that "I can cause things to happen." This is contrasted with the *me-self* (Lewis, 1991), or the *explicit self* (Case, 1991). The me-self requires a conscious (explicit) awareness of the self or, as Lewis has stated, the "idea of me."

How can one tell if an infant has an explicit self rather than an implicit self? One technique that some people think captures the idea of an explicit self (or the me-self) is *visual self-recognition*. Children prove that they have a sense of self by recognizing themselves in a mirror. The procedure involves seruptciously placing a mark on a child's nose or forehead and then seeing the child's reaction to his or her image in the mirror. Children's behavior in the marked condition is then compared to their behavior when their faces have no marks or to the behavior of other unmarked children. Beginning around 15 months, children show the first signs of self-recognition by touching the mark on their face rather than touching the mirror (Lewis &

Brooks-Gunn, 1979). Not all studies report mark-directed behavior this early (Schulman & Kaplowitz, 1977), but by 18 to 24 months, this form of self-recognition is found in about 75% of all children tested (Brooks-Gunn & Lewis, 1984; Nielsen, Suddendorf, & Slaughter, 2006). It is also found in the great apes—chimpanzees, orangutans, and a few gorillas (Gallup, 1979)—as well as in dolphins (Reiss & Marino, 2001), elephants (Plotnik, de Waal, & Reiss, 2006), and magpies (Prior, Schwarz, & Güntürkün, 2008), but not in any other animal tested.

Our culture provides more ways than mirrors for children to identify themselves. For example, when do children show a sense of self in pictures or videos? Daniel Povinelli and his colleagues (Povinelli, Landau, & Perilloux, 1996; Povinelli & Simon, 1998) took Polaroid photos or videotaped preschool children while they played. Without the children knowing it, the experimenters placed large stickers on the children. How would children react when they saw themselves in the photos or on the video with stickers on their heads? Most 2- and younger 3-year-old children did not reach for the sticker on their heads, whereas most older preschoolers did. All children, however, removed the sticker when they looked at themselves in a mirror (Povinelli et al., 1996). These results suggest that children's sense of self develops gradually over the preschool years, as their ability to deal with different modes of representation (mirrors, photos, videos) develops (see also Skouteris, Spataro, & Lazarid, 2006; Zelazo, Sommerville, & Nichols, 1999).

The development of a sense of self, as reflected by self-recognition, has important consequences for emotional, social, and cognitive development. Brooks-Gunn and Lewis (1984) make this clear: "The acquisition of the self by the end of the second year not only facilitates the acquisition of social knowledge, but underlies social competence, peer relations, gender identity, and empathy" (p. 234). The change from a helpless newborn, who seemingly cannot distinguish where he or she ends and the world begins, to a self-conscious child is a remarkable and important change indeed.

Mirror recognition is not the only sign of self-awareness that develops late in the second year. In one study, the ability to recognize oneself in a mirror was associated with the tendency to become embarrassed in certain situations, suggesting that both are related to the emergence of a child's concept of self (Lewis et al., 1989). Perhaps the most important indication of a sense of self can be gleaned from children's use of language. Sometime late in the second year or early in the third year, many children begin using the personal pronouns *I*, *me*, *my*, and *mine*, thereby indicating a distinction between themselves and others (Lewis & Brooks-Gunn, 1979; Lewis & Ramsay, 2004). Children also begin to display secondary, or self-conscious, emotions, such as shame, pride, and embarrassment (Lewis et al., 1989). As Piaget (1962) observed, this corresponds to the advent of symbolic, or representational, abilities, and self-concept seems to be one important product of the symbolic function. Neuroscience researchers have reported a connection between the onset of these early signs of self-awareness and brain development. For example, the degree of self-representation that 15- to 30-month-old children display, as reflected by mirror self-recognition, use of personal pronouns, and pretend play, is related to maturation of a portion of the left hemisphere (Lewis & Carmody, 2008).

As was noted in Chapter 8 on memory, the development of a sense of self during the second and third years of life has been proposed as one reason for infantile amnesia—that is, our inability to remember information from infancy and early childhood. What we fail to recall is autobiographical memory, and there can be no such memory (no "auto") unless there is a sense of self (see Bogdan, 2010; Howe & Courage, 1993).

Once children realize they are distinct from other people and objects, what methods can we use to determine how they think about themselves? One way of gaining some insight into children's self-concepts is simply to ask them to describe themselves. Preschool children generally describe themselves in terms of physical characteristics ("I'm strong," "I have brown hair," "I have blue eyes"), by their actions ("I run real fast," "I play baseball," "I walk my dog"), where they live, and who's in their family (Keller, Ford, & Meachum, 1978; Livesley & Bromley, 1973). Rarely do preschool children provide psychological descriptions of themselves (for example, "I'm happy," "I'm smart," "I'm friendly"). This self-definition by physical characteristics is consistent with the Piagetian idea that children's thinking is concrete and tied to specific experiences. This picture does not change substantially during the early school years. As children approach adolescence, their thinking becomes more abstract, and so does the way they view themselves. Children are now more likely to define themselves in terms of psychological qualities—things they like and personality characteristics (Montemayor & Eisen, 1977). (For a more in depth discussion of the development of self-concept over childhood, see Harter, 2006.)

## COGNITIVE BASES OF GENDER IDENTITY

Being male or female is a matter of biology. But behaving in a fashion consistent with societal views of masculinity and femininity and identifying oneself with males or females encompasses more than biology. This process of incorporating the roles and values of one's sex is referred to as **gender identification**. Our identification of ourselves as male or female has implications far beyond reproduction. Unlike other demarcations of social standing, such as age, occupation, or marital status, our gender is one characteristic that remains constant throughout development. All societies make distinctions between the sexes, although outside of reproduction, few (if any) universal roles or behaviors delineate the sexes. What is universal is the significance that gender has in defining who an individual is in society and the striving of children around the world to acquire an appropriate gender role.

Many factors contribute to children's gender identification (see Eagan & Perry, 2001; Martin & Ruble, 2004; Ruble, Martin, & Berenbaum, 2006). One important factor is their ability to understand gender as a concept, and to understand that gender remains stable over time and is consistent over situations. Whether a boy decides to identify with his father is related to what the boy understands about his gender, that of his father, and the continuity of his own gender over time. Children should not be expected to behave as if gender is important if they are not yet aware that differences among males and females exist and that their own gender is constant. Another important factor is children's knowledge of gender stereotypes. What information do they have about how boys and men and girls and women behave, and what consequences does this knowledge have for their own actions and attitudes? In the following sections, I review research on the development of gender constancy and gender schemas and how these cognitive factors relate to the societally important process of gender identification.

## Gender Constancy
### *The Development of Gender Constancy*

One of the first people to postulate a cognitive basis for gender identification was Lawrence Kohlberg (1966). He proposed that children's understanding of gender develops in the same way as their understanding of the physical world. According to Kohlberg, knowledge of gender follows Piaget's model of cognitive development, with children not having a mature notion of gender until the advent of concrete operations, beginning about 7 years of age.

Kohlberg proposed that a key cognitive accomplishment in the understanding of gender is that of **gender constancy**—the knowledge that gender remains the same despite changes in physical appearance. Rheta De Vries (1969) conducted one of the first studies to test this aspect of Kohlberg's theory as part of a larger study of the appearance/reality distinction, discussed in Chapter 5. De Vries reported that 3-year-olds believed a person temporarily changes his or her sex when engaging in opposite-sex behavior or when wearing opposite-sex clothing. That is, boys who wear girls' clothes or play girls' games are, for the time being, girls.

The significance of dress in determining gender for young children is illustrated by an observation that Stone and Church (1973) reported. A new family with a baby had moved into the neighborhood. When a 4-year-old girl was asked whether the baby was a boy or a girl, she responded, "I don't know. It's so hard to tell at that age, especially with their clothes off" (p. 297). Another demonstration of gender being determined by dress came from my daughter, Heidi, when she was about 3. She declared that I could not wear a pink shirt because if I did, I would be a girl. The major difference between boys and girls, she said, is that girls wear pink and boys do not. Always fashion conscious, she added that both boys and girls could wear blue and yellow. Pink, it seemed, is the critical color.

Following De Vries' study, several researchers investigated the development of gender constancy in greater detail (Ruble, Balaban, & Cooper, 1981; Slaby & Frey, 1975). In a pioneering study, Ronald Slaby and Karin Frey (1975) interviewed children aged 2 to 5.5 years about their beliefs in the constancy of gender. In agreement with Kohlberg's theory, Slaby and Frey reported three components in the development of gender constancy: (1) gender identity, (2) gender stability, and (3) gender consistency. As Slaby and Frey defined the term, **gender identity** refers to the ability to identify oneself as male or female and to accurately identify the gender of others. **Gender stability** refers to the knowledge that gender remains stable over time. Thus, at some point, little boys come to believe that they will become fathers when they grow up, and little girls believe that they will become mothers. The questions these researchers asked made it clear that the children were expressing not just a preference but a necessity; for example, they asked boys: "Could you ever be a mommy when you grow up?" **Gender consistency** refers to the knowledge that gender remains the same despite changes in behavior or dress. The researchers tested this knowledge with questions such as "If you wore boys' clothes, would you be a girl or a boy?" and "If you played girls' games, would you be a boy or a girl?" These questions might seem trivial to an adult, but answers by preschool children can be quite revealing (for example, "I can't wear girls' clothes, 'cause then I'd be a girl!").

Slaby and Frey reported an age-related developmental sequence such that gender identity was acquired before gender stability and gender stability was acquired before gender consistency (that is, identity → stability → consistency). Other researchers have confirmed this three-stage sequence, with gender identity being achieved, on average, by 2.5 years, gender stability by 4 or 5 years, and gender consistency by 6 or 7 years (Eaton & Von Bargen, 1981; Ruble et al., 2007; see Ruble et al., 2006, for a review). This sequence of development is not confined to North America or to industrialized countries; it has also been found in traditional communities in Belize, Kenya, Nepal, and American Samoa (Munroe, Shimmin, & Munroe, 1984).

As with many other aspects of cognition in young children, performance can be helped or hindered by subtle changes in the task. For example, Warren Eaton and Donna Von Bargen (1981) asked preschool children gender-constancy questions pertaining to (1) themselves, (2) a same-sex child, and (3) an opposite-sex child. The children answered the questions relating to themselves at a more advanced level than they did the questions relating to a same-sex child, and the questions relating to a same-sex child were answered at a more advanced level than the questions relating to an opposite-sex child. In other words, young children become confident of the stability and consistency of their own gender before that of the gender of other children, particularly children of the opposite sex. These and other research findings (for example, Szkrybalo & Ruble, 1999) indicate that seemingly subtle differences in how the gender-constancy task is administered can result in dramatic changes in children's responses. These findings also indicate that beliefs about the constancy of gender are not well established until middle childhood, but that even preschoolers sometimes believe gender is constant over time and situations. The range of situations in which they believe this, however, is limited and expands with age.

### Consequences of Gender Constancy for Gender Identification

Why should knowing that gender is constant over time and over situations affect children's gender identification? For one thing, it makes little sense to learn the behaviors and roles of one gender if you are not certain that your own gender will remain the same.

Several researchers have compared attention to same-sex models for children who score high on tests of gender constancy (knowing that gender is stable or consistent over time) with children who seem unaware of either the consistency or the stability of gender. In an early study by Slaby and Frey (1975), preschool children were shown a 5.5-minute silent video depicting a man and a woman engaging in simple, separate activities. The man was on one side of the screen and the woman on the other. As children watched the film, an observer recorded the amount of time the children spent attending to the male and female models. Slaby and Frey reported that the high-gender-constancy children spent more time looking at the same-sex model than did the low-gender-constancy children and that this effect was stronger in boys than in girls. That is, the high-gender-constancy boys looked at the male model longer than did the other boys (108.2 seconds versus 63.0 seconds), and the high-gender-constancy girls looked more at the female model than did the other girls (86.8 seconds versus 63.8 seconds).

Other researchers have reported findings similar to those of Slaby and Frey. For example, in one study, 5-year-old boys who scored high on gender constancy spent more time viewing TV programs featuring a greater percentage of men than did boys who scored lower on a test of gender constancy; no such effect, however, was found for girls (Luecke-Aleksa et al., 1995).

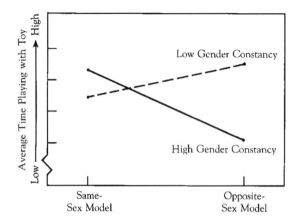

FIGURE **10-5**

Average amount of time spent playing with a toy as a function of stage of gender constancy (high versus low) and sex of model in the commercial (same-sex versus opposite-sex).

Source: Adapted from Ruble, D. N., Balaban, T., & Cooper J., 1981. Gender constancy and the effects of sex-typed television toy commercials. *Child Development, 52*, 667–673. Copyright © 1981 The Society for Research in Child Development, Inc. Adapted with permission.

In other research, Diane Ruble and her colleagues (1981) showed high- and low-gender-constancy children cartoons, complete with commercials of same-sex or opposite-sex children playing with a gender-neutral toy (a movie viewer). Children were later given the opportunity to play with the movie viewer, along with many other toys not shown in the commercial. The results of this study are shown in Figure 10-5. As can be seen, little difference was found between the high- and low-gender-constancy children when viewing a same-sex model. Differences were substantial, however, when the children viewed an opposite-sex model playing with the toy. The low-gender-constancy children showed no differentiation. They actually played with the movie viewer slightly more when they had seen an opposite-sex child in the commercial. Not so for the high-gender-constancy children, however. These children knew that gender remains constant over time and that there are certain things boys do and other, different things that girls do. When these young children thought that a toy was appropriate for an opposite-sex child (as reflected by the commercial), they avoided it. The important point here is that this distinction is not made until children have acquired the cognitive sophistication to know that gender is a stable characteristic.

Despite the impressive effects of some of these studies, not everyone looking for the influence of gender constancy of behavior has found it (see Ruble & Martin, 1998; Ruble et al., 2006). One reason some studies fail to find relations between gender constancy and children's behavior may be attributed to overestimating children's knowledge of constancy. For example, some children may display *pseudoconstancy* (Ruble & Martin, 1998; Szkrybalo & Ruble, 1999), revealing high levels of gender constancy when answering forced-choice questions ("If John wore a dress, would he be a boy or a girl?" "A boy.") but illustrating less-secure knowledge when asked to explain their answers. ("He's still a boy 'cause he has a boy's face," or "I don't know why.") In general, gender constancy does show regular increases with age and is (often) related to important gender-related behaviors.

Certainly, the process of gender identification involves more than strictly cognitive factors, but it is also very likely that cognitive factors other than gender constancy might be involved in the process as well (see Ruble et al., 2006). In recent years, researchers have emphasized the role of knowledge of gender stereotypes as an important factor, with gender schemas playing a central role as the organizing mechanisms underlying children's gender knowledge.

## Gender Schemas

Contemporary cognitive theories of gender identification have been based on the tenets of information processing, particularly the concept of schemas (Bem, 1981; Martin & Halverson, 1981), discussed in Chapter 4. A *schema* is a mentalistic structure consisting of a set of expectations and associations that guide processing with respect to a particular content. According to Diane Ruble and her colleagues (2006), **gender schemas** "are interrelated networks of mental associations representing information about the sexes. Schemas are not passive copies of the environment, but instead they are active constructions, prone to errors and distortions" (p. 908). Carol Martin and Charles Halverson (1981) state that schemas develop primarily from observation. Sex is a salient characteristic in children's worlds, relating both to themselves and to others. Thus, it is used to organize information in place of other, more subtle characteristics of a person or event that older and more knowledgeable children might use. Children use their developing gender schemas to evaluate the appropriateness of some behavior. When children can answer questions such as "Is this OK for boys to do?" positively, they attempt to acquire more information about the activity ("What are the rules of football? How do you throw a pass?").

Martin and Halverson (1987) provide a model of how children might interpret gender-relevant information (see Figure 10-6). Based on observing others, children acquire some idea of sex stereotypes (trucks are for boys, dolls are for girls). Once children have identified themselves as a boy or a girl, they label objects and activities that are "for their gender" as being "for them," and they incorporate those objects, behaviors, or attitudes into their own-sex schemas. Objects or activities they interpret as being "for the other gender" are labeled as "not for me" and are avoided, not attended to, or forgotten.

Although even infants make distinctions between males and females, they do not seem to have any knowledge of gender stereotypes. This knowledge, however, develops early during the preschool years. Most studies assessing children's knowledge of gender stereotypes use concrete objects (for example, a hammer or a doll) or specific activities (for example, playing football or jumping rope) as stimuli (see Ruble et al., 2006). Children are typically shown some objects or pictures of some activities and asked if these objects or activities are usually for girls, for boys, or for both. Not surprisingly, older children generally show greater gender-stereotype knowledge than younger children (for reviews, see Ruble et al., 2006; Signorella, Bigler, & Liben, 1993). Girls are also more likely to say that a toy or activity is appropriate for both sexes, reflecting greater flexibility regarding sex stereotypes in girls than in boys (see Ruble et al., 2006).

Carol Martin and Diane Ruble (2004) proposed that gender stereotyping can be described as involving three phases (see Figure 10-7; see also Trautner et al., 2005).

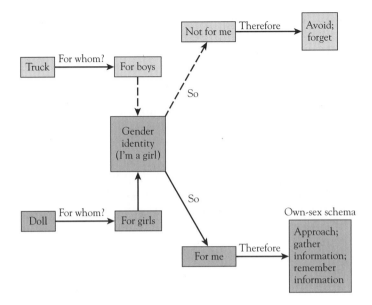

## FIGURE **10-6**

A model of how gender knowledge may be processed beginning in early childhood in agreement with a gender schema theory approach. Once children identify themselves as boys or girls, they label objects, behaviors, and attitudes as being for one gender or the other, and they incorporate the gender-appropriate ones and avoid the gender-inappropriate ones.

Source: Martin, C. L., & Halverson, C.F. (1987). The roles of cognition in sex role acquisition. In D. B. Carter (Ed.), *Current conceptions of sex roles and sex typing: Theory and research*. New York: Praeger.

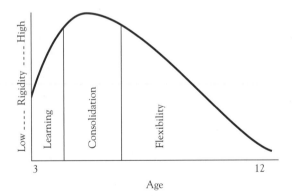

## FIGURE **10-7**

A model of phase changes in the rigidity of children's gender stereotypes as a function of age. As children first learn about gender characteristics as preschoolers, they become increasingly rigid in their stereotypes, with rigidity peaking as their gender knowledge becomes consolidated between 5 and 7 years of age. Children become less rigid in their stereotypes until adolescence, when they increase again (not shown in figure).

Source: Martin, C. L., & Ruble, D. (2004). Children's search for gender cues. *Current Directions in Psychological Science, 13*, 67–70.

The first phase reflects children learning about gender-related characteristics during the first 3 or 4 years of life. The second phase is a period of consolidation, in which gender-related activities are viewed in an inflexible manner, so that children view cross-gender play and activities negatively. Girls and women behave in one way, and boys and men behave in another. Such rigidity of gender stereotypes peaks between 5 and 7 years of age. Children's gender stereotypes become more flexible over the elementary-school years until adolescence, when they become more rigid again. Perhaps not surprisingly, both periods of gender rigidity seem to correspond with milestones in subsequent development of gender identity: the acquisition of gender constancy around 5 to 7 years of age and, in adolescence, awareness of sexual feelings and orientation. Sex-typed behaviors are relatively stable, with children who show the most highly sex-typed behavior between 2.5 and 5 years of age being the most sex-typed at age 8 (Golombok et al., 2008).

This pattern is seen in a study of gender schemas and their relations to sex-stereotypic behavior by Lisa Serbin and Carol Sprafkin (1986). Because sex is a highly salient dimension, Serbin and Sprafkin hypothesized that young children would use gender to classify people and activities to a greater extent than older children would. Older children, whose knowledge of sex roles is greater and whose gender schemas are thus more elaborated, were expected to be more flexible in their classifications, relying less on gender and more on other characteristics of behavior. To assess this hypothesis, 3- to 7-year-old children were administered a gender classification task. In this task, the children were shown photographs of adults engaging in some routine activities. For example, one picture was of a man stirring a pot. The children were then shown three other pictures and were asked to choose the one that "went best" with the standard. One picture was of a man reading (same sex, different activity); children who chose this picture as going with the standard would be making a classification based on gender. A second picture was of a woman rolling dough (different sex, similar activity); children choosing this picture would be making their classification on the basis of type of activity. A third picture was of a woman sweeping (different sex, different activity). This third picture was a control picture, and children who chose this alternative would, presumably, be responding randomly. The children were also administered tests of sex typing. For example, they were shown pictures of objects typically associated with males (hammer, shovel, baseball) and others typically associated with females (iron, needle and thread, baby bottle) and were asked who would use each object—boys, girls, or both. When children said that either boys or girls could use the object, they were later asked which sex would use it most. The extent to which children made sex-stereotypic responses was used as an indication of their knowledge of sex stereotypes.

Following the researchers' predictions, children's classifications of activities on the basis of gender declined with age. Three-year-olds chose the same-sex, different-activity picture 57% of the time. This percentage decreased to 20% for the 7-year-olds. Furthermore, children's gender classifications were significantly related to their knowledge of sex roles. Children who knew more about sex roles tended to make *fewer* classifications based on gender. In other words, as children's knowledge of sex roles expands, so do their gender schemas. The better established children's gender schemas are, the more flexible those children become in interpreting gender differences, and the more tolerant they become of people engaging in cross-sex activities (Stoddart &

Turiel, 1985). Thus, whereas a 4-year-old might be aghast that his sister's teenage boy-friend wears a dangling earring, the 7-year-old codes it only as an exception to the rule and realizes that it does not alter the "maleness" of the person (see also Basne et al., 2010).

As I mentioned previously, in most studies assessing children's knowledge of gender stereotypes, concrete objects or specific activities are used as stimuli. In addition to these objects and activities, however, genders come to have *metaphoric* meanings. Some objects or characteristics, which have no concrete association with either males or females, are nonetheless associated with one gender or the other. For example, most people would tend to associate *bear*, *dog*, and *angry* with males and *heart*, *pink*, and *flower* with females. When do children make such associations? Mary Leinbach, Barbara Hort, and Beverly Fagot (1997) developed a test to assess children's knowledge of metaphorical sex stereotypes. They tested children between the ages of 3 and 7 years and reported that children as young as 4 years consistently classified metaphorical items according to their "appropriate" gender stereotype, although this tendency increased with age. Three-year-olds, in contrast, rarely made such classifications. Also, Leinbach and colleagues reported that 4-year-old children who were high in gender constancy were more likely to classify sex-stereotyped metaphorical items "appropriately" than were 4-year-olds who scored low on a gender-constancy test.

A particular type of gender schema is the **gender script**, which is a temporally organized event sequence related to gender. Knowledge of such scripts should increase with age, with children presumably becoming more familiar with same-sex than with opposite-sex gender scripts. Martha Boston and Gary Levy (1991) investigated this by giving preschool children a series of scrambled pictures that would make a coherent event when placed in order. Some of these events were stereotypically feminine (for example, doing laundry, preparing dinner in the kitchen), and others were stereotypically masculine (for example, building a birdhouse, barbecuing). Children were shown the pictures one set at a time and told to "put these in the order the way they would happen" (p. 424).

First, older preschoolers were better able to sequence the pictures than were younger preschoolers, demonstrating an age-related increase in gender-script knowledge, although even the youngest children (3.5 to 4 years old) performed quite well at sequencing the pictures. Following the researchers' predictions, boys were more accurate at sequencing masculine activities than feminine activities. Contrary to predictions, girls showed no difference in the accuracy of sequencing the feminine and masculine activities.

One primary function of schemas is to organize information, making it more accessible in memory. Several researchers have demonstrated that children remember information that is consistent with their sex stereotypes better than they do information that is inconsistent (Bauer, 1993; Liben & Signorella, 1993). Perhaps the most impressive demonstration of this is Patricia Bauer's (1993) study with a group of 25-month-old toddlers. In her study, children were shown a series of six activities: two stereotypically masculine activities (for example, building a house), two stereotypically feminine activities (for example, putting a diaper on a baby), and two neutral activities (for example, having a birthday party). Children were then encouraged to imitate each activity, both immediately and following a 2-week delay. The results were similar both for immediate and for delayed imitation: Although no difference was found in successful imitation among the three types of activities for the girls, the boys showed greater imitation of the masculine and neutral activities than of the feminine activities. Moreover, the boys spent more time interacting with the props for the masculine and neutral activities than with those for the feminine activities. These results suggest that, at least for boys, gender schemas are operating as early as 2 years of age, with boys avoiding traditionally feminine activities.

Although both boys and girls show a decided preference for same-sex toys and activities, and both boys and girls seem to remember and understand same-sex stereotypes better than opposite-sex stereotypes (Liben & Signorella, 1993; Martin, Wood, & Little, 1990), these effects generally appear earlier (as in the Bauer, 1993, study) and are more extreme (as in the Boston and Levy, 1991, study) in boys than in girls. Consistent with these observations, boys show sex-stereotyped toy preferences earlier than girls do (O'Brien & Huston, 1985), and they avoid opposite-sex toys more than girls do (Fagot, Leinbach, & Hagan, 1986). One interpretation of these findings is that young boys are more strongly sex-stereotyped than are young girls (Bauer, 1993).

There are many levels of gender identification, and even young children who have mastered only the rudiments of gender differences can behave in a more sex-typed fashion than do less knowledgeable children. For example, Beverly Fagot and her colleagues (1986) assessed the relationship between the ability of young children to identify pictures of males and females and their adoption of sex-typed behaviors. Children between the ages of 21 and 40 months were shown pairs of pictures (one of a male, one of a female) and were asked to identify the boys and girls (or men and women). The children were also observed in their preschool classroom to obtain measures of sex-typed behaviors. Differences in aggression, interaction with same-sex peers, and play with sex-stereotyped toys (for example, blocks, trucks, and carpentry tools for boys) were measured. Fagot and her colleagues reasoned that 2- and 3-year-old children with greater knowledge of gender differences (as reflected by their ability to identify males and females) should show greater sex-typed behavior.

The results generally supported the researchers' hypothesis of a relationship between gender knowledge and sex-stereotypic behavior in young children. Children who could correctly apply gender labels to the pictures were more likely to play with same-sex peers, and girls who performed well on this task showed almost no aggression in the classroom. Aggression is more associated with males than with females, so preschool girls who showed low levels of aggression were assumed to be displaying more sex-appropriate behavior than were girls who showed more aggression.

Although most of the research cited so far suggests that children's knowledge of gender and gender stereotypes does not become apparent until into the third year of life, this would be an overstatement. Before their first birthdays, infants are able to discriminate between men and women, and by their second birthdays, infants can identify themselves and other children as boys or girls. Table 10-3 (adapted from Martin, Ruble, & Szkrybalo, 2002) provides some of the gender-based knowledge that children demonstrate between 6 months and about 2 years of age. As can be seen, gender has been a salient category in children's lives from very early on, and it should not be surprising that they are quick to associate different behaviors and expectations from males and females, including themselves (once they identify which they are).

TABLE **10-3**
Time Line for Early Gender Development.

| Age | Gender-Based Knowledge and Perception |
| --- | --- |
| 6–8 months | Discriminate between voices of males and females |
| | Will habituate (reduce looking time) to one category of faces (male or female) |
| 9–11 months | Discriminate between male and female faces |
| | Associate female faces with female voices |
| 12–14 months | Associate female faces with female voices and male faces with male voices |
| 18–20 months | Associate sex-stereotypic objects with "appropriate" gender (that is, associate male faces with male-stereotypic objects and female faces with female-stereotypic objects) |
| | Associate verbal labels (lady, man) with appropriate faces |
| 24–26 months | Correctly identify pictures of boys and girls |
| | Imitate gender-related sequences |
| | Generalize imitation to appropriate gender (for example, using a male doll to imitate a masculine activity) |

Source: Martin, C. L., Ruble, D. N., & Szkrybalo, J. (2002). Cognitive theories of early gender development. *Psychological Bulletin, 128*, 903–933.

## Gender Knowledge and Sex-Typed Behavior: Possible Predispositions

Based on what we've reviewed to this point, one would think that children's toy preferences would be related to their knowledge of gender stereotypes. This certainly seems to be true for older children (Ruble et al., 1981; see also Ruble et al., 2006), but it does not appear to be true for children under 3 years old. For example, in the study by Fagot and her colleagues (1986) discussed earlier, toy preference (that is, which toys the children played with during school) was not related to the ability to identify males and females. Rather, boys and girls generally displayed a preference for sex-typed toys regardless of their level of gender knowledge. This finding is similar to that reported by David Perry, Adam White, and Louise Perry (1984), who found no relationship between young children's toy preferences and their knowledge of sex stereotypes for toys. Rather, children (particularly boys) showed a preference for same-sex toys before showing knowledge of which toys are usually for girls and which are usually for boys. These results suggest that early toy and play preferences are not related to children's understanding of gender. Instead, these patterns might be the result of biological differences in activity and interactional styles between the sexes or of differences in the type of toys and activities adults introduce to children.

Support for a biological rather than an environmental basis for early toy preference comes from studies examining the relation between prenatal exposure to the male hormone androgen and later toy preference (Berenbaum & Hines, 1992; Berenbaum & Snyder, 1995). Children who had been exposed to high levels of androgen before birth (because of overproduction of androgen in the fetus' adrenal glands) were seen when they were between 3 and 8 years old and contrasted in terms of their

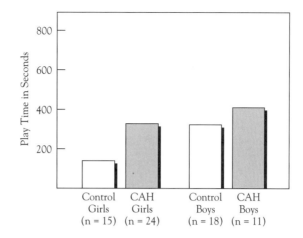

FIGURE **10-8**

Average time spent playing with boys' toys for androgenized (CAH) and control boys and girls.

Source: Adapted from "Early androgens are related to childhood sex-typed toy preferences," by S. A. Berenbaum & M. Hines, 1992, *Psychological Science, 3*, p. 205. Copyright © 1992 Blackwell Publishers. Reprinted with permission.

toy preference with groups of nonaffected boys and girls (Berenbaum & Hines, 1992). (In a nice methodological touch, the control children were sisters, brothers, or cousins of the affected children.) Children were brought into a playroom where stereotypically masculine, feminine, and neutral toys were available. As expected, for the control children, boys played more often with the masculine toys, and girls played more often with the feminine toys. For the androgenized boys, no difference was seen in their toy preferences compared to those of the control boys, although the affected boys spent somewhat more time playing with the masculine toys than did the control boys (see Figure 10-8). In contrast, the androgenized girls demonstrated a strong masculine toy preference. As can be seen in Figure 10-8, the androgenized girls spent much more time playing with the masculine toys than did the control girls, such that their masculine toy preferences were comparable with those of the boys. This pattern of toy preference was replicated in later research (Berenbaum & Snyder, 1995). More recent research has shown that levels of testosterone in pregnant women predicted later gender-role behavior in girls (but not boys) at 3.5 years of age; in contrast, other factors, including the presence of older brothers or sisters in the home, maternal education, and parents' adherence to traditional gender roles, did not predict subsequent gender role behavior (Hines et al., 2002). Along with the findings of Berenbaum and her colleagues, these results suggest that normal variation in levels of prenatal testosterone/androgen exposure contributes significantly to gender-related behavior in girls, at least during the preschool years.

These results, coupled with the findings that young children's toy preferences are not related to their knowledge of gender stereotypes, suggest that early toy preference is influenced more by biological than by cognitive factors. Sheri Berenbaum's studies (Berenbaum & Hines, 1992; Berenbaum & Snyder, 1995) suggest that exposure to prenatal androgen has a defeminizing effect on toy preferences, although extra androgen is apparently not necessary for boys to show this effect. This does not mean, however, that androgen has a direct effect on toy preference. (I seriously doubt there is a part of the brain that causes us to find toy guns attractive and toy dolls unattractive.) One possibility is that the androgen influences activity level, temperament, or motor skills, which in turn leads to a preference for more stereotypically masculine toys (Halverson & Waldrop, 1973; O'Brien & Huston, 1985).

These findings do not imply that children's gender-related behavior is biologically "fixed." Children around the world are exposed to a wide variety of culturally "appropriate" male and females models, and the social setting, more than anything else, determines what behaviors children will adopt for their own. It should not be surprising that biology can predispose male and female children toward certain general types of behavior (males more to manipulation of objects and large-muscle activity, perhaps, and females more to social relations), and it is interesting that boys tend to be more sex-typed (that is, approach and attend to male and avoid female activities/models) than females are. Might this also reflect a biological influence? Biology is not destiny, and as has been made clear throughout this book, there are no pure biological or environmental factors on development. However, acknowledging that some aspects of gender behavior are influenced by biological dispositions in interaction with a child's social environment can help us better understand the developmental process of gender identification.

## Children's Theories of Gender

The process of gender identification is a complex one, involving biological dispositions and culture-appropriate experiences. However, it also seems clear that cognitive differences among children contribute substantially to their developing identification with members of their own sex. Controversy does exist concerning how important cognitive factors are in gender identification (in comparison with environmental and biological factors), as well as about which aspects of cognitive development are most important. Moreover, once cognitive factors are given their due, there is the question of how gender knowledge in its various forms influences children's sex roles and behaviors. But there is little question that children's knowledge of gender roles and their understanding of the concept of gender are important for development.

Children realize early that gender is an important dimension and formulate theories concerning exactly what it is that differentiates the sexes. Many of these theories are wrong. For example, a 6-year-old boy, noticing that my infant daughter had brown hair, just like his, asked if that meant "she will be a boy when she gets older." It's also reflected by the story that opened this chapter, of a 4-year-old old declaring that he had figured it out: "Men eat pizza and women don't."

Once a child starts mingling with peers, what other children do largely determines what is viewed as appropriate male and female behavior, often independent of the wishes of that child's parents. For example, friends of mine refused to buy guns for their 3-year-old son and restricted the number of aggressive programs he watched on television. Nevertheless, the boy learned from his preschool peers that gun play is boys' stuff: He ran around the house pointing sticks, spoons, or fingers at people and saying "bang," despite constant reprimands from his parents. He had learned from other 3-year-olds one special thing that boys do and, over his parents' objections, was making it something that he did as well.

Children continually gain knowledge about what differentiates males and females in society, and with this knowledge, they continually devise and test theories about sex differences (as suggested by "theory theories" of cognitive development; see Chapter 6). Their early theories are simplistic, based on the grossest of characteristics (clothing, for example), and often are not even tangentially related to societal sex stereotypes. However, much like the scientist delving into a new field of inquiry, children discard old theories, try new ones, and eventually acquire the meaning of gender that is implicitly agreed upon by members of their society.

## HOW "SPECIAL" IS SOCIAL COGNITION?

Should social cognition be covered at all in a textbook on cognitive development, or does it more properly belong in books about social development? My opinion on this issue should be obvious, given the inclusion of this topic in this book. People use the same brains that they do to solve analogical-reasoning problems or to compute the cost per ounce of laundry detergent to figure out what other people are thinking and how they themselves should best behave. Whereas people with faulty mathematical or scientific reasoning abilities will likely get along all right in the world, someone who lacks a well-developed sense of self, shows deficits in social learning, or is ineffective at social information processing is in for a tough time.

I mentioned in the introduction to this chapter that some people believe human intelligence evolved in the form that it has chiefly to deal with other members of our species (Alexander, 1989). We are far more intelligent than necessary to eke out an existence on the African savannas. In fact, so are chimpanzees. Nicholas Humphrey (1976) suggested that most of humans' technological genius is absent from our daily lives. If alien anthropologists had observed Albert Einstein during a typical day, they would likely infer that he had a "humdrum mind." But we do use our superior intelligence everyday when dealing with other people. We became the intelligent species not so much to cope with the demands of a hostile physical world but to meet the demands of hostile members of our own species.

Like all others, however, this form of cognition develops. Children are born prepared by evolution for a social world, but they do not have the requisite skills necessary to function effectively in that world. Their social intelligence emerges, in part, following a universal time line, much as Piaget proposed, but also varying as a function of the particular society they are born into. There is much variability among cultures, and children must have the cognitive skills to adapt to the particular environment in which they live. But what is common to all children across the globe is that they are part of a social species, and they develop the requisite intellectual skills necessary to live in such a world.

## SUMMARY

*Social cognition* is cognition about social relations and social phenomena. Many topics can be subsumed under the heading of social cognition. *Social learning* refers to the acquisition of social information and behavior. Different forms of social learning include *local enhancement* (or *stimulus enhancement*), *mimicry*, *emulation*, *imitative learning*, and *teaching*, (or *instructed learning*). Whereas both emulation and imitative learning involve the observer understanding the intention of the model, only imitative learning also includes reproducing many of the same actions of the model.

*Neonatal imitation* has been observed, with Meltzoff and Moore attributing this phenomenon to *active-intermodal* mapping and thus seeing it as a reflection of symbolic functioning. Others observe that neonatal imitation typically disappears by about 2 months and suggest that it reflects an *innate releasing mechanisms* (or *fixed-action pattern*) and an *ontogenetic adaptation*, serving a specific function at a particular time in development, rather than a reflection of symbolic ability. Although even infants display imitative and emulative learning in some contexts, young children tend to mimic the behavior of adults. Most chimpanzees and other great apes display emulation learning, but, following the *enculturation hypothesis*, chimpanzees who are reared as children display evidence of imitative learning. *Mirror neurons*, that may play an important role on social learning, have been identified in the brains of monkeys and humans.

Bandura's *social cognitive theory* is an extension of earlier *social learning theory* and is mainly a theory about how children operate cognitively on their social experiences. Bandura postulated five capabilities that contribute to development, all of which change with age: (1) *symbolization*, (2) *forethought*, (3) *self-regulation*, (4) *self-reflection*, and (5) *vicarious learning*. Bandura believes that children affect their environment as much as their environment affects them, and he referred to such interaction as *reciprocal determinism*. Following social cognitive theory, *observational learning* involves four subprocesses, each of which changes with development: (1) attentional processes, (2) retention processes, (3) production processes, and (4) motivational processes. *Self-efficacy* is the sense of control people have over their lives, beginning in infancy and developing during childhood. Young children tend to overestimate their abilities, which can be attributed in part to *wishful thinking*, in which children fail to differentiate between their wishes and their expectations.

Dodge proposed a model that adopts many of the tenets of contemporary information-processing approaches to explain children's social functioning. Dodge proposed five sequential steps of *social information processing* that are necessary for competent social behavior: (1) encoding of the social stimulus; (2) interpretation of the social information; (3) response search, in which children generate possible response alternatives; (4) response evaluation, in which children evaluate the potential effectiveness of the various alternatives; and (5) enactment, in which children execute the chosen response. Dodge and his colleagues have shown a relationship between the efficacy of children's social information processing and their social behavior, suggesting that how children process social information plays a significant role in their social competence.

A child's *self-concept* begins to develop in infancy, with mirror recognition being observed as early as 15 months for some children. Children's self-concept changes during childhood and is reflected in how they describe themselves.

The process of incorporating the roles and values of one's sex is referred to as *gender identification*. Children's knowledge of *gender constancy* develops during the preschool years, with *gender identity* preceding *gender stability*, which in turn precedes *gender consistency*. *Gender schemas* are mentalistic structures consisting of a set of associations and expectations related to gender. *Gender scripts* are a particular type of gender schema that involves temporally organized event sequences related to gender. Gender schemas influence how children process information related to gender and are related to their knowledge of sex stereotypes and gender-related behavior. As children's knowledge of gender expands, their schemas change, resulting in a more sophisticated use of gender in classifying people and behavior.

## KEY TERMS AND CONCEPTS

social cognition

social learning

local enhancement (stimulus enhancement)

mimicry

emulation

imitative learning

teaching (instructed learning)

neonatal imitation

active intermodal mapping

innate releasing mechanism (fixed-action pattern)

ontogenetic adaptations

mutual imitation

enculturation hypothesis

mirror neurons

social learning theory

social cognitive theory

reciprocal determinism

symbolization

forethought

self-regulation

self-reflection

vicarious learning

observational learning

self-efficacy

wishful thinking

social information processing

self-concept

gender identification

gender constancy

gender identity

gender stability

gender consistency

gender schemas

gender script

## SUGGESTED READINGS

### Scholarly Work

Harter, S. (2006). The self. In W. Damon (Gen Ed.) & N. Eisenberg (Vol. Ed.), *Handbook of child psychology: Vol. 3. Social, emotional, and personality development* (5th edition, pp. 505–570). New York: Wiley. Harter presents a thorough review of research and theory on the development of self-concept from infancy through adolescence.

Ruble, D. N., Martin, C. L., & Berenbaum, S. (2006). Gender development. In W. Damon & R. M. Lerner (Gen. Eds.), *Handbook of Child Psychology* (6th edition), N. Eisenberg (Vol. Ed.), Vol. 3, *Social, emotional, and personality development* (pp. 858–932). New York: Wiley. This is a comprehensive review of gender development and gender differences written by three of the leading experts on these topics.

Tomasello, M. (2000). Culture and cognitive development. *Current Directions in Psychological Science*, 9, 37–40. This paper presents a brief summary of Tomasello's ideas on the social origins of human cognition and a discussion of some of the different forms of social learning. For a more in-depth discussion, read his 1999 book *The Cultural Origins of Human Cognition* (Cambridge, MA: Harvard University Press).

### Reading for Personal Interest

Seligman, M. E. P. (with Reivich, K., Jaycox, L., & Gillham, J.) (1995). *The optimistic child*. Boston: Houghton Mifflin. Martin Seligman describes children as being inherently optimistic and provides some ideas for how to promote such optimism and how to turn optimistic kids into optimistic and psychologically healthy adults.

Tomasello, M. (2009). *Why we cooperate*. Cambridge, MA: MIT Press. In this short book, Michael Tomasello provides a concise and highly readable review of his group's research with both children and great apes, all pointing to the importance of social cognition in the development and evolution of human intelligence.

# Schooling and Cognition

**The Development of Reading Skills**
A Brief Overview of Learning to Read
Emergent Literacy
Cognitive Development and Reading
How to Teach Children to Read
Sex Differences in Reading and Verbal
   Abilities

**Children's Number and Arithmetic Concepts**
Conservation of Number
Learning to Count
Children's Arithmetic Concepts
   **BOX 11-1:** The (Math) Games Children Play
Math Disability
Cultural Differences in Mathematics
Sex Differences in Mathematical Ability

**Schooling and Cognitive Development**
Schooling versus Age Effects on Intelligence
The Effect of Schooling on IQ
The Costs and Benefits of Academic
   Preschools

**Evolutionary Educational Psychology**
Principles of Evolutionary Educational
   Psychology
Physical Activity

SUMMARY
KEY TERMS AND CONCEPTS
SUGGESTED READINGS

Eight-year-old Nicholas was reading a book with his grandmother, who was impressed at how well he was reading and told the young boy so. "It's a trick, Grandma," he said, almost conspiratorially. "I'm not really reading. I just see the word and I know it." Nicholas no longer had to sound out words to "know" them, and to him, this wasn't reading—it was a trick. Nicholas had "broken the code." He was no longer "learning to read" but was on his way to "reading to learn."

Reading is perhaps the single most important technological skill in postindustrial cultures. Children learn to read using universal cognitive skills, but it is unheard of for an unschooled child from an illiterate culture to learn to read. Humans did not evolve to read, and unlike language, reading is rarely acquired "spontaneously." Reading is understandably classified in educational circles as a language skill, but it is a very different language skill, acquired in a very different way, from a child's native tongue. Although all neurologically typical children learn to be proficient speakers of their native language, not all learn to be proficient readers, even with instruction.

Reading is perhaps the clearest example of what David Geary (1995, 2007) calls *biologically secondary abilities*—cognitive skills that must be taught and that are cultural inventions. Geary distinguishes these from *biologically primary abilities.* Recall from Chapter 2 that biologically primary abilities evolved to deal with recurrent problems faced by our ancestors, are universal, develop in a species-typical pattern if children experience a species-typical environment, and children are intrinsically motivated to engage in them. Language is perhaps the prototypical example of a biological primary ability. In contrast, biologically secondary abilities do not have an evolutionary history but, rather, are based on biologically primary abilities; children acquire these secondary skills, such as reading, to deal with ecological problems that were unknown to our forebears. Reading also requires tedious repetition and practice, so it is little wonder that many children have a difficult time learning to read. Nevertheless, it is a skill that most children in schooled cultures do master on their way to adulthood, and success in school, and often in adult life, is related to how well one can read.

If reading is the number-one technological skill in modern society, mathematical abilities must come in second. Verbal and quantitative skills constitute the two major subtests of the Scholastic Assessment Test (SAT), the Graduate Record Exam (GRE), and even most IQ tests (see Gardner, 1983). Although verbal and quantitative abilities involve more than just than reading and mathematics, these are the core abilities. Unlike reading, basic mathematical skills can be acquired without formal schooling. However, beginning in preschool, children in postindustrial societies receive instruction in simple number concepts and arithmetic, and math constitutes one of the primary subject areas in schools.

In this chapter, I review the development of reading and mathematical abilities. Individual, gender, and cultural differences in these topics have been of great interest to educators and the public at large, and I devote considerable space to these issues. In the latter part of the chapter, I look at several issues directly related to cognitive development and schooling. I selected these issues from the many topics that I could have included in this chapter primarily because I believe they are related to issues we have already dealt with in this book, or will deal with in the final two chapters: First, how does the effect of schooling influence cognitive development in comparison with the effect of age? Second, what is the effect of schooling on IQ? I conclude the chapter with a brief section on a new way of thinking about the relation between schooling and cognitive development: *evolutionary educational psychology*, following mainly the ideas of David Geary.

---

# THE DEVELOPMENT OF READING SKILLS

Learning to read takes time. In this section, I describe the typical course of reading development, and then examine (1) what preschool children often know *about* reading before actually learning to read, (2) the cognitive processes involved in reading, (3) some methods used to teach children how to read, and finally (4) sex differences in reading and verbal abilities.

## A Brief Overview of Learning to Read

Learning to read involves acquiring a set of skills that are built on preceding skills. Jeanne Chall (1979) proposed five stages (stages 0 to 4) in the development of proficient reading, ranging from the prereading skills of the preschool child to the highly skilled reading of the adult (see also Ehri, 1995).

In stage 0, covering the years before a child enters first grade, children must master the prerequisites of reading, most notably learning to discriminate the letters of the alphabet. By the time children enter school, many can already "read" some words, such as "Pepsi," "McDonald's," "Pizza Hut," and perhaps their own names. Many also now recognize some of the letters in their name, especially the first letter (Trieman et al., 2007). Their ability to recognize these symbols, flashed at them from the television and seen repeatedly on the roadside or the dinner table, indicates that they can tell the difference between patterns of letters even if they are unable to sound out the words. Children's knowledge of letters and single words is generally better than it was several generations ago, partly because of the influence of children's television shows, such as *Sesame Street*.

Stage 1 covers children's first year of formal reading instruction. In first grade (or perhaps kindergarten), children learn phonological recoding skills, used to translate written symbols into sounds and, thus, into words. This is followed in the second and third grades by stage 2, in which children learn to read fluently. By the end of the third grade, most children have mastered the letter-to-sound correspondence and can read many words and simple sentences. But reading is effortful for these children, in that the process of identifying individual words requires so much of their limited mental resources that they often do not comprehend much of what they read. They are still concentrating on what individual sets of letters mean, and they are not very skilled at putting the words together to abstract the broader meaning of the text.

The change from "learning to read" to "reading to learn" begins in stage 3, usually spanning grades 4 through 8. Children can now more readily acquire information from written material, and this is reflected by the school curriculum. Children in these grades are expected to learn from the books they read. If children have not mastered the "how to's" of reading by the fourth grade, progress in school can be difficult. Stage 4, beginning in the high school years, reflects truly proficient reading, with adolescents becoming increasingly able to comprehend a variety of written material and to draw inferences from what they read.

Not surprisingly, like many other things, children become better readers the more they read. This results in an interesting phenomenon called the **Matthew effect**, in which the difference between good and poor readers increases over time (Stanovich, 1986). The name comes from the New Testament's Book of Matthew, which makes the observation (basically) that the "rich get richer and the poor get poorer." ("For to everyone who has, more shall be given, and he will have an abundance; but from the one who does not have, even what he does have shall be taken away," Matthew 25:29, American Standard Version). Good readers, because they enjoy and are relatively good at reading, read more, so they become increasingly proficient at reading. Poor readers, on the other hand, because they are less skilled and enjoy it less, read less and, although they may be improving in an absolute sense, find themselves falling farther behind their more skilled peers.

## Emergent Literacy

Although most children learn to read in school, most learn *about* reading in the home. They learn that arbitrary written symbols correspond to spoken language and convey meaning. They learn that language is used to communicate with others, as a memory reminder (writing down a phone number to call later), and for pleasure (Bialystok, 1996). In the United States and many other literate cultures around the world, books are written just for adults to read to children. Parents who share storybooks and picture books with their preschool children are teaching them much about reading and are preparing their children for success in a literate culture. For example, mothers and fathers who read to their children have children with better language, cognitive, and reading abilities (Oliver, Dale, & Plomin, 2005), and some research has found a link between being read to and the development of theory of mind (Adrián, Clemente & Villanueva, 2007; Symons et al., 2005).

Most preschool children, however, do not read—not really. They might be able to identify Coca-Cola, Burger King, or Fruit Loops signs when they see them, but this is not really reading. Nevertheless, what children are learning during story times with a parent and in a household where reading is done frequently are skills that set the stage for true reading. The idea of a developmental continuum of reading skills, from those of the preschooler to those of the proficient reader, is referred to as **emergent literacy**.

According to Grover Whitehurst and Christopher Lonigan (1998), emergent literacy "consists of the skills, knowledge and attitudes that are presumed to be developmental precursors to conventional forms of reading and writing ... and the environments that support these developments (for example, shared book reading ...)" (p. 849). Whitehurst and Lonigan list nine components of emergent literacy:

1. *Language:* Reading is obviously a language skill, and children need to be versatile with their spoken language before they can be expected to read it. However, skilled (and even early) reading requires more than just proficiency with spoken language. Reading does *not* seem to be simply a reflection of spoken language, with children who have advanced language skills becoming children who have advanced reading skills. For example, Catherine Crain-Thoreson and Philip Dale (1992) examined a group of early talkers over several years and found virtually no relation between spoken language skills and literacy knowledge at age 4.5 years. Later reading, however, that involves "reading to learn" might be more sensitive to children's background knowledge, their vocabulary, and their familiarity with complex grammar (Mason, 1992).

2. *Conventions of print:* Children exposed to reading in the home know the conventions of print. For example, in English, children learn that reading is done left-to-right, top-to-bottom, and front-to-back.

3. *Knowledge of letters:* Most children can recite their ABCs before entering school and can identify individual letters of the alphabet (although some children think "elemeno" is the name of the letter between "k" and "p"). Knowledge of letters is critical for reading. For example, research has shown that kindergarten children's ability to name letters predicts their later reading achievement scores (Levy et al., 2006; Schneider & Näslund, 1999).

4. *Linguistic awareness:* Children must learn to identify not only letters but also linguistic units, such as phonemes, syllables, and words. Perhaps the most important set of linguistic abilities for reading deals with phonological processing, or the discrimination and making sense of the various sounds of a language.

5. *Phoneme-grapheme correspondence:* Once children have figured out how to segment and discriminate the various sounds of a language, they must learn how these sounds correspond to written letters. Most begin this process during the preschool years, with letter knowledge and phonological sensitivity developing simultaneously and reciprocally (Burgess & Lonigan, 1998).

6. *Emergent reading:* Many children pretend to read. They will take a familiar storybook and "read" one page after another, often "just like Daddy does," or they will take an unfamiliar book and pretend to read, making up a narrative to go along with the pictures on the pages.

7. *Emergent writing:* Similar to pretend reading, children often pretend to write, making squiggles on a page to "write" their name or a story, or stringing together real letters to produce something they think corresponds to a story, a shopping list, or a note to Mom.

8. *Print motivation:* How interested are children in reading and writing? How important is it for them to figure out what the secret code is that permits adults to make sense of a series of marks on a page? Some evidence indicates that young children who are interested in print and reading have greater emergent literacy skills than less motivated children do (Crain-Thoreson & Dale, 1992). Children

who are interested in reading and writing are more likely to notice print, ask questions about print, encourage adults to read to them, and spend more time reading once they are able.

9.  *Other cognitive skills:* A host of individual cognitive skills, in addition to those associated with language and linguistic awareness, influence a child's reading ability. Various aspects of memory are important, and some of these will be discussed.

Relations between any specific component of emergent literacy and later reading are sometimes difficult to establish. However, families that provide "the whole package" of emergent literacy skills to their children have children who are better readers, both early in school and later, than do families that provide less of the package (Bialystok, 1996; Whitehurst & Lonigan, 1998). This has been confirmed by longitudinal studies that report significant relations between emergent literacy skills as assessed during the preschool years and reading ability in elementary school (Lonigan, Burgess, & Anthony, 2000; Storch & Whitehurst, 2002).

As in other aspects of school performance, differences in reading are frequently found as a function of socioeconomic status (SES). Children from poverty homes are much more likely to encounter reading problems in school than are children from middle-income homes. The point I want to make here is that these SES differences do not begin in school but in the home during the years before children start formal reading instructions. Parents from lower-SES families are much less likely to read to their children, have fewer books in the house, and generally do not foster the emergent literacy skills that are so important in learning to read. Reading may be a highly technological skill, but its origins are in everyday family interactions.

Does this mean that children's literacy skills are determined before they enter school? No, but their experiences at home do establish a foundation on which school instruction is based. And the quality of home environments tends to be stable: Children who receive intellectual support for literacy early in life can expect similar support later on (see Chapter 13 for a discussion of the stability of intelligence). This implies that children from homes in which emergent literacy is *not* fostered will likely not receive the kind of support during the elementary school years that is associated with proficient reading. However, it also suggests that if the amount or quality of support in the environment (both home and school) changes for the better, so, too, may children's reading abilities.

## Cognitive Development and Reading

A number of cognitive abilities are related to skilled reading and develop over the preschool and school years (Roman et al., 2009). These include phonemic awareness, phonological recoding, working memory, and knowledge base, among others.

### The Role of Phonological Processing in Identifying Words

**Phonemic awareness.**   One early skill that predicts good reading in later years is **phonemic awareness**, which refers to the knowledge that words consist of separable sounds. Such awareness is generally not available to preschool children. In one early study, 4- and 5-year-olds were taught to tap once for each sound in a short word (Liberman et al., 1974). For instance, children would tap twice for "at" and three times for "cat." Although the children presumably understood the task, their performance was poor, with none of the 4-year olds (and only a few of the 5-year-olds) performing it accurately. Although this task might seem trivial, it predicts children's early reading achievement quite well (Liberman & Shankweiler, 1977). Other aspects of phonological awareness, such as children's abilities to detect rhymes, also develop slowly during the preschool and early school years and predict reasonably well children's early reading skills (Gottardo, Stanovich, & Siegel, 1996; Wagner et al., 1997). This is also true in languages other than English (Lundberg, Frost, & Petersen, 1988; Schneider & Näslund, 1999), including Chinese, which includes a phonetic component in its characters (Chan & Siegel, 2001; McBride-Chang & Kail, 2002).

These are only correlations, of course, and perhaps children who read well acquire good phonemic awareness along the way. But there is also evidence indicating a causal influence of phonemic awareness on reading abilities. For example, some longitudinal studies that measure phonemic awareness well before children learn to read show that children with good phonemic awareness as prereaders become more proficient readers when they start school (Lyytinen et al., 2001). Also, kindergarten and first-grade children who receive instruction in phonemic awareness show enhanced early reading ability relative to children who are not given such instruction (Cunningham, 1990; Schneider et al., 1997). Anne Cunningham (1990) states that the results from her training study argue against the idea that phonemic awareness is a consequence of learning to read. Rather, she proposes, as have others (Bryant et al., 1990), that phonemic awareness is causally related to reading achievement, even in the early stage of learning to read.

Research has shown that children's sensitivity to rhymes leads to awareness of phonemes, which in turn affects reading and also, presumably, makes it easier for children to recognize written words that both sound and look alike (for example, "cat" and "hat") (Bryant et al., 1990). Other research has suggested that children's ability to segment phonemes, not children's sensitivity to rhymes per se, is the critical component to literacy (Muter et al., 1998). Valerie Muter and her colleagues tested a group of preschool children (average age, 4 years, 3 months) on rhyming and phonemic segmentation abilities. Tests of rhyming included asking children to identify pictures and then pick out those that rhyme and to produce words that rhymed with each of two words ("day" and "bell"). For one test of phonemic segmentation, children were shown a picture of an object (a cat, for instance), the interviewer provided the first two phonemes ("ca"), and then children were asked to finish the word (in this case, to say "t"). In another test, children were shown a picture and asked to say the word without the first phoneme (for example, "Bus without the 'b' ... ," with the correct response being "us"). The researchers reported that reading ability at the end of first grade was significantly related to preschool phonemic segmentation ability but not to rhyming ability (see also Hulme et al., 2002).

**Phonological recoding.** The reason that phonological awareness is such a good predictor of early reading is that early reading generally involves sounding out words. This process of **phonological recoding** (Ziegler & Goswami, 2006) is the basis for the majority of reading-instruction programs in the United States today (the phonics method). Children are taught the sound of each letter and how to combine these sounds, blending them into words.

The relation between printed and spoken words is referred to as *grapheme-phoneme correspondence*, and how easy it is for children to learn to read is related to how obvious these relationships are in their language. For example, as speakers and readers of English, you are likely aware that the relationship between letters and sounds is often quite variable, and this represents a difficult task for readers. For instance, the playwright George Bernard Shaw commented that, following the rules of English spelling, "ghoti" should be a perfectly acceptable alternative spelling for the word "fish": "gh" as in "cough," "o" as in "women," and "ti" as in "nation." (Go ahead, sound it out.) English has what is called a *deep orthography*, meaning the spelling system for converting letters into sounds is irregular, with there being multiple ways in which some letter combinations can be sounded out. Other languages, such as Finnish, German, and Italian, have *shallow orthographies*, with a close correspondence between letters and their sounds. For example, Italian uses 25 phonemes, and 33 combinations of letters are used to represent these sounds. In contrast, English uses 40 phonemes, but 1,120 different letter combinations are needed to completely represent these sounds. Because of these differences, language with shallow orthographies, such as Spanish and Italian, are relatively easy to learn to read, whereas languages with deep orthographies, such as English and French, are more difficult.

The relationship between children's reading ability and the degree to which the written language corresponds to the spoken language (that is, the degree to which a language is orthographically regular) is illustrated in Figure 11-1. This figure presents the percentage of children speaking and reading languages with shallow orthographies (Greek, Finish, and Italian) and languages with deep orthographies (French, Danish, and Scottish English) who correctly read familiar real words and pseudowords (Seymour, Aro, & Erskine, 2003; Ziegler & Goswami, 2005). Pseudoword reading

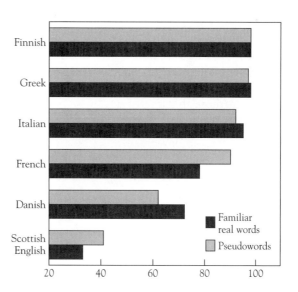

## FIGURE **11-1**

Percentage of correct responses by children reading familiar real words and pseudowords for orthographically regular languages (Finnish, Greek, and Italian) versus orthographically irregular languages (French, Danish, and Scottish English).

Source: Adapted from data in Seymour, P. H. K., Aro, M., & Erskine, J. M. (2003). Foundations of literacy acquisition in European orthographies. *British Journal of Psychology, 94*, 143–174.

requires children to read a sequence of pronounceable letters that do not make up a word (for example, "joak" or "kake" in English). As you can see, performance was nearly perfect for children reading languages with regular (shallow) orthographies but much lower for children reading languages with irregular (deep) orthographies.

The importance of phonological coding to proficient reading can be seen by looking at children with reading disability, often referred to as **dyslexia** (Adams, Trieman, & Pressley, 1998). Children are said to have reading disability if they have great difficulty in learning to read despite an average intelligence. Stated another way, if a child's reading ability is substantially worse than his or her general intellectual ability would predict, that child is said to have a reading disability, or dyslexia. Perhaps the single best predictor of reading difficulty is phonological processing, including phonological recoding (Adams et al., 1998; White et al., 2006). For example, research by Linda Siegel and her colleagues (Siegel, 1993; Siegel & Ryan, 1988) compared the phonological processing of groups of children with and without reading disability between the ages of 7 and 14 years. As one test of phonological processing, children were asked to read pseudowords. As can be seen in Figure 11-2, older children with reading disability were better at pseudoword reading than younger disabled readers were, demonstrating that these skills were developing. However, the performance of 13- and 14-year-old children with reading disability was comparable to that of 7- and 8-year-old nondisabled readers, reflecting a significant delay of this skill. Moreover, longitudinal research suggests that phonological-processing abilities remain relatively stable over childhood (Storch & Whitehurst, 2002; Wagner et al., 1997), making early intervention all the more important.

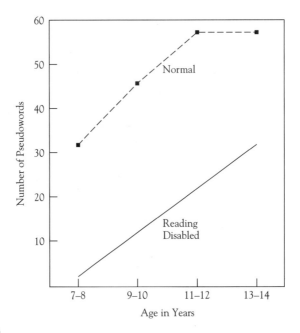

**FIGURE 11-2**

Accuracy of pseudoword reading for children with and without reading disability.

Source: "The Cognitive Basis of Dyslexia," by L. S. Siegel. In R. Pasnak and M. L. Howe (Eds.), *Emerging Themes in Cognitive Development, **Vol. II**: Competencies.* Copyright © 1993 Springer-Verlag. Reprinted with permission.

Research using brain-imaging techniques has supported the interpretation that phonological problems are at the core of many types of reading disability (Shaywitz, Mody, & Shaywitz, 2006; Shaywitz et al., 1998). For example, Sally Shaywitz and her colleagues (1998) gave adults with developmental reading disability and adults without such disability a series of reading-related tasks that varied in the amount of phonological processing required to perform each one. Brain activation patterns, as measured by fMRI (see Chapter 2), were observed between the nondisabled and dyslexic readers. Shaywitz and her colleagues reported different brain-wave patterns for the nondisabled and disabled readers, especially when the tasks required substantial phonological processing. Compared with the nondisabled readers, the dyslexic readers showed underactivation in some portions of the brain (mainly posterior regions) and overactivation in others (mainly anterior regions). Underactive parts of the brain included those areas typically associated with phonological processing and cross-modal integration. In reading, cross-modal integration (see the discussion of cross-modal integration in infancy in Chapter 4) involves the translation of symbols in one modality (in this case, vision, as in the letters and words on a page) into another modality (in this case, audition, as in the sounds of letters and words). Shaywitz and her colleagues concluded that the patterns of brain activity in dyslexic readers "provide evidence of an imperfectly functioning system for segmenting words into their phonological constituents ... and adds neurobiological support for previous cognitive/behavioral data pointing to the critical role of phonological analysis and its impairment in dyslexia" (p. 2640).

Further evidence for the neurological basis of reading disability comes from a study assessing brain activation patterns of those with dyslexia in Great Britain, France, and Italy (Paulesu et al., 2001). Eraldo Paulesu and his colleagues reported similar patterns of brain activity (PET) while reading for groups of university-level English, French, and Italian speakers with dyslexia. Moreover, all three groups showed deficits in tests of phonological short-term memory, pointing, again, to problems in phonological processing as the basis for dyslexia. However, there was an interesting catch in this study. Although the three language-speaking groups with dyslexia did equally poorly in tests of phonological processing, only the English and French speakers showed problems in reading. The Italian group displayed relatively good reading ability. These Italian speakers had been identified as having dyslexia based on impaired reading speed and poor phonological processing, true reading difficulties being rare in Italian university-level adults.

Why should this be so? The reason seems to be related to the specific language people speak and, specifically, the relationship between how a language is spoken and how it is written. As noted earlier, the correspondence between spoken and written Italian is quite close, whereas both English and French have deep orthographies.

What this research indicates is that the neurological basis of dyslexia is universal, likely the result of unknown genetic or prenatal anomalies; however, the likelihood that this particular neurological abnormality will adversely affect reading is a function of how closely the written language of one's culture corresponds to the structure of its spoken language. If you recall from Chapter 3 our discussion about the tools of intellectual adaptation a culture provides to its members, the relationship between the structure of one's spoken and written language is another unexpected (at least to me) way in which one's cultures influences one's thought.

### Working Memory

Efficient reading involves a series of processes, each of which must be integrated with one another for proper comprehension. Individual words must be identified and related to other words in the sentence. One factor that limits children's comprehension is the amount of information they can hold in working memory at any one time. Meredyth Daneman and her colleagues proposed that information needs to be retained in working memory for as long as possible so that each newly read word in a passage can be integrated with the words and concepts that preceded it. Younger or less proficient readers have less available mental capacity to store and maintain information in working memory because it is necessary for them to devote considerable capacity to the processes involved in identifying words and comprehension. Daneman and her colleagues showed that listening span, defined as the number of successive short sentences that can be recalled verbatim, correlates significantly with comprehension for people ranging from preschoolers to college students (Daneman & Blennerhassett, 1984; Daneman & Green, 1986).

The relationship between working memory and reading comprehension was demonstrated in a longitudinal study that followed children between the ages of 8 and 11 years (Cain, Oakhill, & Bryant, 2004). The researchers reported that individual differences in working memory predicted subsequent levels of reading comprehension independent of children's vocabulary and general reading abilities. Moreover, deficits in working memory have been found to be related to the incidence of reading disability (Gathercole et al., 2006; Swanson & Jerman, 2007). For example, Linda Siegel and Ellen Ryan (1989) gave 7- to 13-year-old children with and without reading disability a series of incomplete sentences, requiring them to supply the final word of each sentence. Sentences included the following: "In the summer it is very _____. People go to see monkeys in a _____. With dinner we sometimes eat bread and _____." After being presented two, three, four, or five such sentences, children were asked to repeat the final words, in order, that they had generated for each sentence (in this case, presumably "hot," "zoo," and "butter"). The results of the study are graphed in Figure 11-3. As can be seen, working memory improved with age for both the children with and the children without reading disability, but the children with reading disability had shorter memory spans than the nondisabled readers at each age level.

### Knowledge Base

Another critical factor in proficient reading is the knowledge an individual has of the material being read. As discussed in earlier chapters, having detailed knowledge of a topic permits one to process information about that topic more efficiently (Bjorklund, Muir-Broaddus, & Schneider, 1990). This is especially true in reading comprehension.

Richard Anderson and his colleagues (1984) defined reading as "a process in which information from the text and the knowledge possessed by the readers act together to produce meaning" (p. 8). In other words, "reading is a constructive process" (p. 9), in which the background knowledge that one brings to a text interacts with what is written on the page to produce understanding. Anderson and his associates cited considerable evidence from the research literature to support these claims. In one such study, for example, second-graders who were equated in reading skill were tested for their knowledge of spiders and then given a passage about spiders to read (Pearson, Hansen, & Gordon, 1979). The children who knew more about spiders at

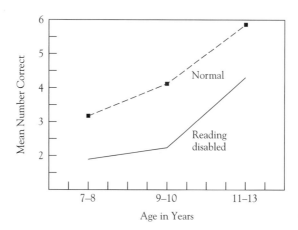

FIGURE **11-3**

Performance on a working-memory task as a function of age for normal (nonreading disabled) children and those with reading disability. Working memory increased with age for both groups of children, but was higher at each age for the normal children than for the children with reading disability.

Source: "The Cognitive Basis of Dyslexia," by L. S. Siegel. In R. Pasnak and M. L. Howe (Eds.), *Emerging Themes in Cognitive Development*, **Vol. II**: *Competencies*. Copyright © 1993 Springer-Verlag. Reprinted with permission.

the outset were better at answering subsequent questions about the passage, especially those questions that involved reasoning. Instructional efforts aimed at increasing background knowledge have also been found to enhance reading comprehension (Hansen & Pearson, 1983; Omanson et al., 1984). The relation between background knowledge and text comprehension will be explored further in Chapter 13.

In other research, the ease with which children could think of a sentence containing a specific word (referred to as *context availability*) predicted several aspects of word processing (word identification, determining whether a set of letters was a word or not) for second-, third-, and fifth-grade children and for high- and low-ability readers in each grade (Schwanenflugel & Noyes, 1996). However, the effect of context availability was greater for younger and low-ability readers than for older and high-ability readers. Paula Schwanenflugel and Caroline Noyes suggested that young and low-ability readers have difficulty connecting low-context available words to their meanings, and the result is many reading errors. Although context availability might not be equivalent to "knowledge" as defined by Anderson and his colleagues (1984), it is, I argue, a function of word knowledge, and this research demonstrates the importance of background knowledge not only for reading comprehension but also for reading individual words.

## How to Teach Children to Read

The focus of this chapter is on children's developing cognitive abilities as they relate to important tasks—here, reading. As such, I have chosen not to get involved in the often-heated debate over how best to teach children to read. The topic should not be totally neglected, however, so I will briefly outline the two major approaches to reading instruction and comment on how the research evidence weighs in on this topic.

Basically (and simplistically), reading instruction can be thought of as either (1) a *bottom-up process,* with children learning the individual components of reading (identifying letters, letter-sound correspondence) and putting them together to achieve meaning, or (2) a *top-down process,* with children's goals, background knowledge, and expectations determining what information they select from text (see Adams et al., 1998). The latter is a constructivist perspective, reminiscent of Piaget's ideas. Surely, skilled reading involves both bottom-up and top-down processes, making any dichotomy artificial. However, reading instruction, particularly in the early grades, often emphasizes one over the other. Thus, the dichotomy has some basis in reality.

Curricula that emphasize bottom-up processes are exemplified by the **phonics** method, in which children are taught specific letter-sound correspondence, often independent of any "meaningful" context. Curricula that emphasize top-down processes are exemplified by the **whole-language approach.** According to Marilyn Adams and her colleagues (1998), "the whole language approach holds that learning is anchored on and motivated by meaning. Further, since meaning and meaningfulness are necessarily defined internally and never by pronouncement, learning can be effective only to the extent that it is cognitively controlled by the learner" (p. 277). Thus, whole-language curricula emphasize reading interesting and meaningful text from the very beginning.

Proponents of the whole-language approach point out that truly proficient reading is not done by sounding out each letter but, rather, by directly retrieving the meaning of the whole word from memory (whole-word, or visually based, retrieval). Think for a while about how you read. Very few college students sound out words, letter by letter; instead, they simply know the meaning of a word when they see it. Adults and older children who read phonetically are not good readers. The amount of mental effort it takes to process a single word by this method is tremendous, making it unlikely that much meaning will be obtained from what is read.

Classrooms where whole language is taught are more apt to be student—rather than teacher—centered, have an integration of reading and writing within the overall curriculum, have an avoidance of drill, and are less likely to have rigid groupings of abilities. All this sounds quite inviting, actually. However, many proponents of the whole-language approach "have steadfastly, adamantly, and sometimes vitriolically denied the value and rejected the practice of skills instruction, including phonics, and this has been a point of heated contention" (Adams et al., 1998, p. 277). Yet, without phonological recoding skills, we would be unable to read novel words (such as "defenestration," defined as the act of throwing something out of a window); we would be limited to reading only words we have learned before. So it seems that phonological skills are necessary if one's reading ability is to advance.

The research evidence reviewed earlier in this chapter should make clear the importance of bottom-up processing in learning to read. Phonological skills are the single best predictor of reading ability (and disability). These abilities do not develop spontaneously; they are acquired only with practice, and usually with explicit instruction. Curricula that ignore phonics, regardless of how "meaningful" they make the experience of reading, are risking the literacy of many of their students. This is not to argue for a curriculum that has children reading only stories about "Dick, Jane, and their dog Spot." But it does argue for including some aspects of phonics in any reading instruction. In fact, it should not be surprising that some combination of phonics and "meaningful reading" is, on average, the most effective approach, and that reading instruction is most effective when it is individualized to a child's learning abilities and styles (Morrison & Connor, 2009).

## Sex Differences in Reading and Verbal Abilities

"Female superiority on verbal tasks has been one of the more solidly established generalizations in the field of gender differences," wrote Eleanor Maccoby and Carol Jacklin (1974, p. 75) in introducing their section on gender differences in verbal ability in their seminal book that set the stage for contemporary investigations of sex differences. In reviewing research on sex differences in verbal abilities more than 20 years after the publication of Maccoby and Jacklin's book, Diane Halpern (1997) concluded that females, on average, perform better than males do on "tasks that require rapid access to and use of phonological and semantic information in long-term memory, [and] production and comprehension of complex prose" (p. 1091). The topic of sex differences in verbal ability has continued to be of interest to contemporary researchers, in part because of the importance reading and verbal ability have for education and economic success in modern society.

One technique that has permitted researchers to better evaluate the extent of sex differences in verbal abilities is **meta-analysis**. Meta-analysis provides an estimate of *effect size,* which is expressed in terms of how large the average differences between males and females are across the various studies, taking into consideration the overall amount of variability. An effect size of 1.0 would mean that the average male-female difference was one standard deviation in magnitude. If this were for IQ, for example, it would be equivalent to saying that the average difference between the sexes was about 15 points, which would be quite substantial. The statistic of effect size is used because it would be meaningless to compute mean performance across the many different studies, which used different measurements and often assessed different verbal tasks. By using the effect size statistic, however, differences in performance among different studies can be meaningfully combined.

The first meta-analysis of verbal sex differences was reported by Janet Hyde (1981), who examined 27 studies of verbal ability included in the original Maccoby and Jacklin review. Hyde reported an effect size of .24 (about one-quarter of a standard deviation), favoring females. Since the publication of Hyde's report, several other meta-analytic studies have been published, and they point to similar conclusions: Although sex differences in verbal abilities favoring females continue to be found, the effect size is small in an absolute sense, and depending on which specific verbal ability is being tested, the effect size is getting smaller (Feingold, 1988; Hyde & Linn, 1988; Marsh, 1989; but for a different interpretation of the data, see Hedges & Nowell, 1995). For example, Hyde and Marcia Linn (1988) reviewed 165 different studies, involving 1,418,899 participants, and reported that the effect size, again favoring females, for studies published after 1973 was .10 (or one-tenth of a standard deviation) compared with .23 for pre-1973 studies. More recent studies typically continue to show a small female advantage on most verbal tests, but the magnitude of the advantage varies with the test, with males actually scoring higher than females on some. For example, after revising the verbal portion of the SAT in the 1970s, males actually had slightly higher scores than females (mean scores = 437 for males and 425 for females, effect size = −.11; Feingold, 1988). The 2006 SAT results for college-bound high-school seniors reported a slight edge for males on the Critical Reading test (505 versus 502), although females showed a more substantial advantage on the writing test (502 versus 491) (reported in Halpern et al., 2007).

Sex differences in reading and verbal abilities are not limited to the United States; they are found worldwide. The results of a 25-nation study assessing the reading/verbal abilities in fourth-grade children in 2001 are presented in Figure 11-4 (from Halpern et al., 2007, and based on data reported in Mullis et al., 2003). The length of each line reflects the magnitude of the sex difference in each country. And in every country, females performed significantly better than males.

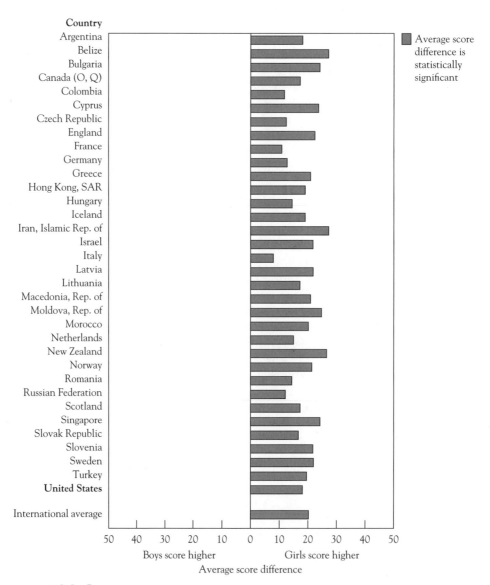

## FIGURE **11-4**

Sex differences in reading/verbal abilities in 25 countries. The longer the line, the greater the sex difference, favoring girls.

Source: Halpern, D. F., Benbow, C. P., Geary, D. C., Gur, R. C., Hyde, J. S., & Gernsbacher, M. A. (2007). The science of sex differences in science and mathematics. *Psychological Science in the Public Interest, 8,* 1–51.

Similarly, in a 2006 study of sex differences in reading ability among secondary school students in more than 40 countries, the average effect size, favoring females, was .19 (Lietz, 2006).

Despite the relatively consistent female advantage in verbal abilities, the absolute difference is small. For example, in her original meta-analysis, Hyde (1981) concluded that the gender of the child alone accounted for approximately 1% of the variance in verbal performance. In other words, the difference, although statistically significant, is small in absolute magnitude. To understand the magnitude of these differences, look at the idealized distribution of verbal skills for males and females graphed in Figure 11-5 (expressed as standard scores). You can see substantial overlap of performance between males and females, and the absolute difference in the means is small. Moreover, the variability within the sexes is even greater than the variability between them. That is, although there is a substantial and consistent average difference in reading ability between boys and girls, many boys are better readers than many girls. In fact, in a review of meta-analyses of sex differences for all domains, Hyde (2005) concluded that the effect sizes in most meta-analyses are in the close-to-zero ($\leq$.10) or small (.11 to .35) range. This includes verbal ability. Based on results summarized in Hyde (2005), I computed an average efffect size for verbal ability of about .10 (favoring females).

There is no single reason for these sex differences, but boys are far more likely to be identified as having reading disability than girls, suggesting a biological basis. Moreover, the fact that many aspects of reading disability can be traced to basic cognitive abilities that are found early and tend to be stable over childhood suggests a substantial biological component to reading disability.

Sex differences in brain structure or function may also be responsible for sex differences in reading and verbal abilities. In Chapter 2, I briefly discussed sex differences in brain development. Females have proportionally more gray matter than males, and their brains are more symmetrical than those of males, in that the proportion of gray and white matter is more similar in the two hemispheres. Also, females are more apt to use language-related areas of their brains in solving complex problems than males (see Halpern et al., 2007). This pattern suggests that females should outperform males on verbal tasks, consistent with the findings.

Experiential factors, however, also likely play a role in sex differences in reading ability. Reading and the expression of feelings (both verbal tasks) are viewed as

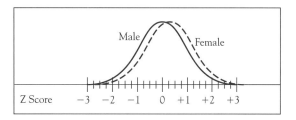

FIGURE **11-5**

The idealized distribution of verbal ability for males and females.

Source: "How Large Are Cognitive Gender Differences? A Meta-Analysis Using v2 and d," by J. S. Hyde (1981). *American Psychologist, 36,* 892–901. Copyright © 1981 American Psychological Association. Reprinted with permission.

stereotypically female activities and might contribute to girls' superior verbal skills. Also, many of the stories in children's reading books are not inherently interesting to children (Blom, Waite, & Zimet, 1968), and evidence suggests that boys are particularly motivated by the interest level of the reading material (Renninger, 1992; Schiefele, Krapp, & Winteler, 1992). For example, Steven Asher and Richard Markel (1974) reported that fifth-grade boys displayed better comprehension for stories of high interest than for those of low interest. This difference in reading level was much smaller for fifth-grade girls (see Figure 11-6).

Book publishers are aware of the importance of interest in getting boys to read and are now publishing books with topics more appealing to boys. The *Harry Potter* series did a lot to get boys (and girls) interested in reading, but recently, publishers have come out with boy-oriented books that are not always welcomed into the elementary school classroom. For example, a 2009 listing of popular books for boys included:

**Nonfiction:**
*Getting to Know Your Toilet: The Disgusting Story Behind Your Home's Strangest Feature*

*Oh, Yuck: The Encyclopedia of Everything Nasty*

*It's Disgusting and We Ate It! True Food Facts From Around the World and Throughout History*

**Fiction:**
*Captain Underpants* (series)

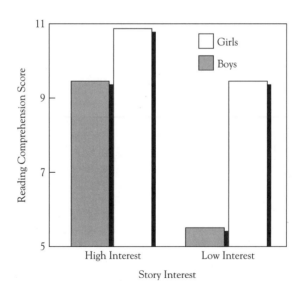

## FIGURE **11-6**

Mean reading comprehension scores for high- and low-interest stories for groups of fifth-grade boys and girls.

Source: Adapted from Asher, S. R., & Markel, R. A. (1974). Sex differences in comprehension of high- and low-interest reading material. *Journal of Educational Psychology, 66,* 680–687. Copyright © 1974 by the American Psychological Association. Adapted with permission.

*Sir Fartsalot Hunts the Booger*

*The Day My Butt Went Psycho* (trilogy; described on Amazon.com as "wisely rated G for Gross" as it "contains immature material not suitable for adults")

The origins of sex differences have long fascinated psychologists. Are differences mainly the result of genes and biology or mainly the product of culture and learning? This led many in academic psychology to use the phrase *sex differences* to refer to differences between males and females that were attributed chiefly to biology and *gender differences* to those that were attributed chiefly to learning and culture. Although well meaning, such a distinction perpetuates a false nature-nurture dichotomy—the belief that the contributions of biology and culture (or genes and environment, or biology and learning) can be neatly separated and packaged (Halpern, 2004). For all practical purposes, the terms *sex differences* and *gender differences* are equivalent. (For simplicity sake, I used the term *sex difference* here, although *gender difference* would have been equally appropriate.) According to Halpern (2004), "Differences in the interests of females and males both derive from differences in the areas in which they have achieved success and lead to further differential success in these areas because of differential knowledge and experience. Learning is both a biological and an environmental variable, and biology and environment are as inseparable as conjoined twins who share a common heart" (p. 138). This does not mean that searching for the origins of sex differences is not useful, only that it is not an "either/or" matter. Rather, all aspects of psychological functioning interact over time to produce the differences between males and females that we observe.

## CHILDREN'S NUMBER AND ARITHMETIC CONCEPTS

Although the quintessential symbols of human cognition are probably found in language, a good case can be made for the primacy of numbers. Our tendency to quantify objects and events in our world is ubiquitous. The bulk of the technological advancements made during the past three centuries—and particularly in this and the last century—can be attributed to our species' quantitative skills. Although children develop a basic sense of number and mathematical relations without explicit instruction, most people's mathematical abilities are acquired through formal instruction. This is true even of simple arithmetic as well as more complicated mathematics.

Arithmetic is one of education's three Rs, and a discussion of its development clearly belongs in a chapter devoted to schooling and cognition. But just as language serves as a basis for reading (and writing), there are "cognitive primitives" that underlie arithmetic and other mathematical skills. Recall from Chapter 2 and earlier in this chapter our discussion of David Geary's (1995, 2005) ideas about biologically primary and biologically secondary abilities. The former represent basic cognitive abilities that were selected during evolution to solve recurrent problems faced by our ancestors, are universal, and are acquired at about the same time and in about the same way by all typically developing children. In contrast, biologically secondary abilities are built on biologically primary abilities, are specific to a particular culture, and often need tedious repetition and external pressure for their mastery. Most mathematics, including simple arithmetic, are examples of biologically secondary abilities, but Geary proposed that the quantitative skills children master in school are based on a set of biologically primary abilities—specifically, numerosity, ordinality, counting, and simple arithmetic. Numerosity, ordinality, and simple arithmetic were discussed in Chapter 4 on infant cognitive development. In this chapter, I examine the role of counting as well as the development of more complicated arithmetic.

I start with a look at the Piagetian phenomenon of conservation of number, followed by a review of the development of counting and the development of basic arithmetic skills. I then look briefly at characteristics of children with math disability, followed by an examination of cross-cultural differences in mathematical achievement. I then explore the controversial topic of sex differences in mathematical ability. Do such differences exist? And if so, how big are they, and what difference do they make?

## Conservation of Number

Piaget (1965) believed that the concept of number is reflected in conservation. Tasks that involve **conservation of number** follow the same basic procedures as all of Piaget's conservation problems (see Chapter 5). Children are first shown a set of items—black jelly beans, for instance. The children are then asked to take white jelly beans from a container so that there are an equal number of black and white beans. Once the appropriate number of white beans has been selected (with assistance from the experimenter, if necessary), the beans are arranged in two rows, one black and one white (see Figure 11-7). While the children are watching, the experimenter spreads out the white jelly beans so that the line of white beans extends beyond the line of

"Select from the jar the same number of white jelly beans as there are black jelly beans."

"Are there the same number of black jelly beans as there are white jelly beans?"

The row of white jelly beans is extended while the child watches.

"Are there the same number of white jelly beans as there are black jelly beans now? Which has more? Why"

FIGURE **11-7**

A conservation-of-number task.

black beans. The children are then asked if the two rows still have the same number of jelly beans. If they answer no, they are asked which row has more, and why.

As with conservation in general, Piaget proposed three stages in the acquisition of conservation of number. In stage 1, children are unable to consistently establish a one-to-one correspondence between the two sets of items. So, for example, children at stage 1 select either too few or too many white jelly beans or fail to arrange them in a one-to-one relationship with the black beans. When two equal sets of beans are established and one is modified, children say that the longer, less dense row now has more beans in it, being unable to ignore the perceptual differences between the two rows. During stage 2, children can establish an "intuitive one-to-one correspondence" between the items in the two sets, but judgments of equivalence between the sets do not last long. Once the beans in one row are extended, the children say that the longer row has more. Only the child in stage 3 (concrete operations) realizes that the number of beans does not change when one of the rows is elongated and that changes in spatial extension of elements are compensated for by equivalent changes in the density of the elements.

Non-Piagetian research, using variants of Piaget's original task, has generally replicated his observations, illustrating that (1) children are able to form a one-to-one correspondence before they can conserve; (2) young children make their evaluations on the basis of relative length, independent of other factors; (3) slightly older children sometimes consider density but do not coordinate the dimensions of length and density, thus failing to conserve in many situations; and (4) not until 7 or 8 years of age do children consistently pass conservation-of-number tasks (see Brainerd, 1978).

According to Piaget, the core ability underlying conservation of number, *inversion reversibility*, is necessary if children are to understand addition and subtraction. For example, if 5 + 3 = 8, then, by the logical rule of inversion, 8 − 3 must equal 5. In one experiment, Piaget (1965) showed children an array of eight objects. The array was then modified; for example, it was first divided into two equal sets of four objects and then divided again into unequal sets (seven objects and one object, for instance). Do children recognize the equivalence of these two groupings? In other words, do they know that 4 + 4 is the same as 7 + 1? As with conservation of number, Piaget reported three stages in children's early arithmetic abilities. In stage 1, characterizing most children under 5 years of age, the children typically relied on the spatial arrangement of the objects, erroneously asserting that there were different numbers of elements in the two combinations. In stage 2, characterizing 5- and 6-year-olds, the children could correctly solve the task, but only after counting the objects or establishing a spatial one-to-one correspondence between the items. In stage 3, children (7-year-olds) solved the problem without resorting to physical counting techniques. Without this understanding, according to Piaget, children cannot have a true comprehension of addition, although they can be taught to memorize certain formulas (for example, 2 + 3 = 5, but will they know what 3 + 2 equals?).

## Learning to Count

Three-year-old Paul was fascinated by the stairs in a neighbor's home, and while climbing and then scooting down them on his backside, he counted them, saying one number word for each step he traversed: "One, two, three, four, five, seven, nine, ten, eleventeen, tweeleveteen, fiveteen, seventeen, nineteen, *twenty*." He usually said the last number word with some authority, often stating, "There are *twenty* of them." Paul used some, but certainly not all, of the number words that adults in his culture use, but he obviously had some things to learn. He also likely did not understand numbers and counting the way he would in just a few more years. But he was motivated to count, realizing, at some level, that this is an important thing to do (Bjorklund & Hernández Blasi, 2012, p. 423).

By the time children can speak, most give the impression of having some concept of number. The 18-month-old might respond with a loud and definitive "Two!" when asked how many cookies he wants, and the 3-year-old might point at her dolls and say, "One, two, three, seven, nine, twelveteen, threeteen, seventeen." Each is displaying some knowledge of number, yet neither is using numbers with the same consistency and meaning that a 7- or 8-year-old can.

How do children's conceptions of numbers develop? One popular non-Piagetian candidate for the precursor of number conservation is counting. Rochel Gelman and C. R. Gallistel (1978) extensively investigated children's early counting and proposed five principles:

1. *The one-one principle:* Each item in an array is associated with one and only one number name, such as "two."
2. *The stable-order principle:* Number names must be in a stable, repeatable order.
3. *The cardinal principle:* The final number in a series represents the quantity of the set.
4. *The abstraction principle:* The first three principles can be applied to any array or collection of entities, physical (for example, chairs, jelly beans) or nonphysical (for example, minds in a room, ideas).
5. *The order-irrelevant principle:* The order in which things are counted is irrelevant.

Gelman and Gallistel (1978) referred to the first three principles as the "how-to" principles of counting, and they proposed that children as young as 2.5 years demonstrate knowledge of them under some circumstances. For example, in a counting experiment where 3-, 4-, and 5-year-old children were asked to discern the number of objects in a series of arrays, all groups of children used the one-one principle (that is, one unique number name per object), although performance deteriorated for the youngest children with arrays of six or greater. Let me provide an example of a 4-year-old child's difficulty applying the one-one rule. Brendan and his grandfather were playing a "catch" game, in which each took a specified number of steps backward before one threw a ball to the other. In playing, Brendan called his numbers aloud, one number per step. This began to break down, however, once the numbers got larger than five. He'd call out "One, two, three, four, five, six, seven, eight, nine," pausing between announcing some of the larger numbers, but although his counting slowed down when he reached six, his stepping didn't. By the time Brendan got to "nine," he'd taken more than a dozen steps, violating the one-one rule of counting.

Gelman and Gallistel (1978) also reported that children who counted items in arrays used the stable-order principle; more than 90% of the 4- and 5-year-olds and 80% of the 3-year-olds used the same list of number words in the same order on all trials. The children sometimes used an idiosyncratic list of number words, as young Paul did on the example that opened this section, but they used this list consistently across arrays of varying size.

Children seem to have mastered the cardinal principle by age 4. For example, Karen Fuson and her colleagues (1985) demonstrated that after counting arrays of objects ranging in number from 2 to 19, children 3 and 4 years of age generally gave the last counting word they had spoken in response to the question "How many things are there?" This was true even for children who counted incorrectly, implying that accurate counting is not a requirement for attainment of the cardinal principle (see also Gelman, Meck, & Merkin, 1986). However, many 2- and 3-year olds seem to have only a tenuous grasp of the cardinality principle (Bermejo, 1996). For example, children might correctly count a set of objects, "One, two, three, four, five," but when asked how many objects are in the set, instead of stating the last number they counted ("five"), they often count again (Fuson, 1988). It's as if the purpose of the first count was independent of determining "how many" objects were in the set. Most of these children can come up with the correct answer, but that they seemed to think a second count was necessary suggests this knowledge is not well established.

In related research, Diane Briars and Robert Siegler (1984) investigated children's knowledge of the counting principles. These researchers asserted that children must induce which features of counting are critical and which are merely optional in enumerating an array, and they speculated that some children might believe that more is required for successful counting than is actually the case. In their experiment, 3-, 4-, and 5-year-old children watched a puppet counting and were asked to determine whether the puppet had counted properly. The puppet demonstrated (sometimes accurately and sometimes inaccurately) five features of counting, one of which was necessary for counting and four of which were optional. The necessary feature was that of word-object correspondence, which encompasses the first two principles of Gelman and Gallistel (one-one correspondence and stable order). The four optional features were that (1) adjacent objects were counted consecutively, (2) counting started from the end rather than the middle, (3) counting progressed from left to right, and (4) each object in an array was pointed to exactly once. Children's knowledge that word-object correspondence was critical in counting increased with age (30%, 90%, and 100% for the 3-, 4-, and 5-year-olds, respectively). However, 60% of the 5-year-olds also viewed other features, such as beginning to count at an end rather than in the middle and pointing to each object only once, as essential. Other research has shown, however, that children as old as 11 years continue to believe that the order in which items are counted (for example, left-to-right or top-to-bottom) is essential for proper counting (Kamawar et al., 2010). In other words, young children learn the critical features of counting by 4 years of age, but from watching others, they infer additional features that are characteristic of, but not necessary for, proper counting. More recent research has shown that children's mastery of counting principles at the end of kindergarten predicted their level of arithmetic abilities at the end of first grade (Stock, Desoete, & Roeyers, 2009).

In summary, young children do possess a limited knowledge of numbers, relations among numbers, and counting, but they are restricted to dealing with small quantities. As children's knowledge of numbers expands, they refine their number concept, discriminating between what is necessary and what is optional in dealing with numbers. In addition, and importantly, their ability to deal with large quantities increases, and their belief in the invariance of number is applied more consistently across a wider range of tasks.

## Children's Arithmetic Concepts

Clearly, young children have some concept of number. They can count, and they can determine which of two quantities is the larger. Moreover, research by Karen Wynn (1992) discussed in Chapter 4 using the violation-of-expectation method suggested that even 5-month-old infants have some appreciation of addition and subtraction of small numbers. But when can children perform tasks of basic arithmetic, such as addition and subtraction? These skills are not formally taught until the first grade in many schools, and from a Piagetian perspective, they require concrete-operational ability.

### The Development of Arithmetic Strategies

Although Piaget believed that addition and subtraction were based on the ability to conserve number and reversibility (that is, if 5 + 3 = 8, then 8 − 5 = 3), more recent research has questioned some of Piaget's interpretations and demonstrated that even preschool children are able to handle simple addition and subtraction problems. These children do so by using strategies. Children's earliest arithmetic strategies involve counting out loud, often using their fingers or other objects. I discussed children's counting strategies briefly in Chapter 7. The simplest strategy consists of counting from the number 1 to the first addend (in 3 + 5 = ?, the first addend is 3), then counting the second, then counting the two together (for example, "1, 2, 3 ... 1, 2, 3, 4, 5 ... 1, 2, 3 ... 4, 5, 6, 7, 8" or, a bit more efficiently using the *short-cut sum strategy*, "1, 2, 3 ... 4, 5, 6, 7, 8"). This has been referred to as the **sum strategy**, and although it usually produces the correct answer, it takes a considerable amount of time to execute and is not very effective when large addends are involved (for example, 23 + 16 = ?). A more economical counting strategy has been called the **min strategy**, which involves starting with the larger addend and then counting up from there— that is, making the *minimum* number of counts. For example, given the problem 3 + 2 = ?, a child would start with the cardinal value of the first number ("3") and continue counting from there ("4, 5"). Preschoolers use a variety of such rules to arrive at correct answers to simple addition and subtraction problems. These rules, however, almost always involve forward counting by ones of concrete objects, including fingers (Carpenter & Moser, 1982). Such addition and subtraction by counting can be successful for unpracticed combinations, such as 14 + 1 = ? and 15 − 1 = ?, which is in violation of Piaget's tenet that true addition cannot be achieved by simple counting. Table 11-1 presents some of the more frequently used arithmetic strategies.

Sometime during the early school years, children's solutions to simple arithmetic problems become covert. They no longer rely on counting objects or their fingers but perform the calculations in their heads. At this point, knowing precisely what children are doing becomes more difficult because the only evidence of the mental processes underlying performance is the answers they give. However, children's arithmetic strategies can be inferred from how quickly they solve the problems. For example, if children are using the min strategy, their reaction times to solve problems will vary as a function of the second, smaller addend. Thus, for any individual child using the min strategy, arriving at an answer for 5 + 4 (thinking "5 ... 6, 7, 8, 9") takes longer than arriving at an answer for 5 + 2 (thinking "5 ... 6, 7").

Based on patterns of reaction times to solve simple addition problems, researchers have demonstrated that children in the early elementary school years frequently use both the sum and the min strategy "in their heads" (Groen & Resnick, 1977). Some time during the elementary school years, children begin to use **fact retrieval** to answer simple arithmetic problems (see Ashcraft, 1990; Siegler, 2006). When adults are given the problem 7 + 5 = ?, for example, they need not start at 7 and mentally increase this by 5 to arrive at the answer. Rather, the knowledge that 7 + 5 = 12 resides in

TABLE **11-1**

Some of the Addition Strategies Children use for the Problem "How Much Is 3 plus 2?"

**Sum strategy:** This is a counting strategy in which young children count, often on their fingers, each addend (for example, saying "1, 2 … 1, 2, 3 … 1, 2, 3, 4, 5": or a bit more efficiently, "1, 2, 3 … 4, 5").

**Min strategy:** This is a more efficient counting strategy than the sum strategy, in which children count from the larger addend (in this case 3), thus making the minimum number of counts (for example, saving "3 … 4, 5"). Slightly older children will use both the sum and min strategy "in their heads," counting covertly.

**Max strategy:** This is like the min strategy but counting from the smaller addend (for example, saying "2 … 3, 4, 5").

**Finger recognition:** Without apparent counting, children hold up five fingers and say "5."

**Fact retrieval:** This is a non-counting strategy, in which children have memorized the answer to a problem (for the problem "How much is 3 plus 2?", they "just know" that 2 plus 3 equals 5), and say the answer quickly without counting either out loud or covertly.

**Decomposition:** Transforming the original problem into two or more simpler problems (for example, saying "2 and 3 is like 3 + 3 minus 1").

**Guessing:** Saying "4" or "8" without apparent counting.

long-term memory, and this fact can be retrieved just like any other fact in memory. Many elementary school-age children eventually will use a **decomposition** strategy for more difficult problems (Lemaire & Callies, 2009). Decomposition consists of transforming the original problem into two or more simpler problems. If the problem were $13 + 3 = ?$, for example, a child might say, "13 is 10 plus 3; 3 and 3 are 6; 10 and 6 are 16; so the answer is 16."

This shift in development from procedural (that is, counting) to retrieval-based techniques for solving simple arithmetic problems reflects changes in the efficiency of information processing. With age, children solve problems more quickly. This increased speed can be attributed to the fact that processes are becoming more automatic, requiring less of one's limited mental capacity for successful execution. In contrast with the fact retrieval of older children, first-graders' use of counting strategies is highly conscious and laborious. However, even 5- and 6-year-olds apparently store and retrieve some arithmetic facts. For small whole-number problems (for example, $2 + 2 = ?$), young children's performance is relatively rapid, indicating fact retrieval (Siegler & Shrager, 1984). With age and experience, more arithmetic facts become stored and can be retrieved with increasing ease, without the need of laborious counting procedures. Although children learn how to multiply later than they learn how to add, much of even third-grade children's multiplication seems to be based on fact retrieval (Koshmider & Ashcraft, 1991), likely as a result of memorizing the multiplication tables.

Arithmetic becomes more complex, of course, and as it does, children must rely again on procedural knowledge. When subtraction involves borrowing (as in $92 - 59 = ?$) or addition involves carrying (as in $92 + 59 = ?$), procedures are at first slow and difficult, but with practice, they become more efficient. In general, the development of arithmetic competence can be described as involving an increase in the efficiency of both procedural knowledge and, most important, information retrieval (Ashcraft, 1990; Geary, 2006). Older children know more facts, can retrieve those facts more easily, and when necessary, can use arithmetic procedures more efficiently than younger children can.

One factor that appears to be important in successful mental arithmetic is working memory (Berg, 2008; LeFevre et al., 2005). To arrive at a correct answer to a simple problem such as $7 + 5 = ?$, children must hold the two addends in mind and execute the addition operation (either by retrieving the "fact" or through some counting method). For example, Marilyn Adams and Graham Hitch (1997) showed that differences in memory span play a critical role in computation for groups of both English- and German-speaking children (ranging in age from about 7.5 to 11.5 years). Adams and Hitch also found a relation between speed of adding the digits and both age and memory span, confirming the role of speed of processing in memory span as discussed in Chapter 7.

Another factor related to children's successful use of arithmetic strategies is metacognition, as reflected by children's knowledge of the effectiveness and appropriateness of different strategies. For example, Martha Carr and Donna Jessup (1995) presented second-grade children with sets of arithmetic problems and metacognitive assessment in April and tested them again in June. Children were asked about the effectiveness of the strategies they used (for example, "Why did you use that way for this problem?") and about the appropriateness of the strategy (for example, "When do you use that way to get the answer?" and "Is there any time it's not a good idea to use that way?"). Carr and Jessup looked at changes in children's use of the min strategy, fact retrieval, and decomposition, and the relation between changes in strategy use and metacognition. Children's use of the decomposition and fact-retrieval strategies increased during the 2-month period (although the accuracy of fact retrieval did not increase during this same time), and the use of the min strategy decreased over time. How did children's metacognitive knowledge in April predict their strategy use in June? Quite well for the decomposition strategy, but not well for the use of fact retrieval. Carr and Jessup reasoned that metacognition is important when strategy use is both effortful and in the early stages of being acquired, something that described the decomposition strategy well. It is less important, however, for highly automated and less effortful strategies, such as fact retrieval (see Carr, 2009).

### Is Children's Acquisition of Arithmetic Strategies Stagelike?

The impression one might get from this research is of a steady improvement in arithmetic strategy use, with children moving from the sum to the min to the fact-retrieval strategy in a regular, stagelike progression. Such a view is not entirely accurate, however. At any given age, children use a variety of strategies to solve arithmetic problems, although the average sophistication of their strategies increases with age (Ashcraft, 1990; Hopkins & Lawson, 2001).

Robert Siegler and his colleagues have demonstrated this in several studies. Recall our discussion in Chapter 7 of Siegler's (1996, 2006) *adaptive strategy choice model*. According to this model, strategies develop in a wavelike fashion, with children using multiple strategies; new strategies never fully displace older ones but become more frequent as a result of experience and the development of underlying cognitive capacities. Sometimes one strategy will win the mental competition (the min strategy, for example), and sometimes another strategy will win (fact-retrieval, for example). For new problems or problems with which children are less familiar, the older, more familiar (or fallback) strategies often come up as the winners.

For example, Siegler and Eric Jenkins (1989) looked at the acquisition of the min strategy using a short-term longitudinal study (or a microgenetic approach, see Chapter 3). In this study, Siegler and Jenkins examined the development of arithmetic strategies in eight children over an 11-week period. Four- and 5-year-old children were selected who could perform simple addition using counting methods but had never used the min strategy. Over 11 weeks, these children were given a series of addition problems to solve.

Siegler and Jenkins reported that all the children used multiple strategies. These included the sum, min, fact-retrieval, and decomposition strategies discussed earlier, plus strategies such as finger recognition (putting up two fingers on one hand and three on the other and saying "five"), shortcut sum (similar to the sum) counting from the first addend (similar to min, but counting the larger addend), and guessing. The percentage of the most frequently used strategies can be seen in Figure 11-8, and there was great variety in strategy use. Moreover, different children used different combinations of the strategies, so that any particular child used a unique mixture of the strategies in his or her solutions. (Similar findings were reported for arithmetic and other strategies in Chapter 7.) Also, during the 11 weeks, the children's strategies tended to become more sophisticated, so that the children who started mainly by guessing or using the sum strategy progressed to using the min or fact-retrieval strategy more frequently.

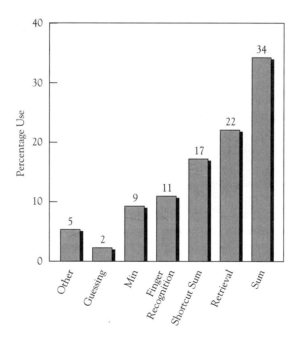

FIGURE **11-8**

Percentage use for each arithmetic strategy.

Source: Adapted from Siegler, R. S., & Jenkins, E. (1989). *How children discover new strategies.* Hillsdale, NJ: Erlbaum.

One major aspect of the Siegler and Jenkins study was children's "discovery" of the min strategy. Remember that none of the children were using the min strategy at the beginning of the study. By the 11th week, however, seven of the eight children were using the min strategy, and six of these children were able to describe how they used it. It is interesting to note that the first time the children used the min strategy, and on the problem immediately before it, they took much longer than average to arrive at a solution. Siegler and Jenkins speculated that the longer times spent on these problems indicated that the children were experiencing conflict, or interference, from alternative strategies and that new strategies require more mental effort than previously established ones. Thus, the children required more time and did some hemming and hawing before arriving at an answer.

### *Gestures and Strategy Development*

In Chapter 9, I discussed research showing that children's use of gestures may play a role in their language development (Goldin-Meadow, 2007). Interestingly, recent research has shown that gestures may also play a role in arithmetic strategy development (Broaders et al., 2007; Goldin-Meadow, Cook, & Mitchell, 2009). In studies by Goldin-Meadow and her colleagues (2009), third- and fourth-grade children were given problems of the type $3 + 5 + 7 =$ _____ $+ 7$. To solve this, children must add together the first two numbers. For the present problem, the correct answer is 8. In one study, children who originally could not solve these problems were given instructions that included either correct gestures, partially correct gestures, or no gestures (see Figure 11-9). For correct gestures, children were taught to point with a V-hand (index and second finger) to the first two numbers in the problem (in this example, $3 + 5$), then to point with their index finger to the blank (see the top photos in Figure 11-9). For the partially correct gestures, children were taught to point with a V-hand to the second two numbers in the equation ($5 + 7$ in the example), then to point with their index finger to the blank (see middle photos in Figure 11-9). In the no-gestures condition, children were given no instructions about gestures. All children were given a verbal lesson about how to solve these types of problems and, later, were given a posttest of six problems to solve.

Children taught to use correct gestures generally used them when solving the problems and, importantly, solved significantly more problems correctly than children taught to use the partially correct gestures, who in turn solved more problems correctly than children who were not instructed to use gestures (see Figure 11-10). Why did the gestures help? Based on children's explanations for how they solved the problems, children who used gestures were more apt to discover the strategy of adding the first two numbers together (Goldin-Meadow et al., 2009).

As for strategy development in general, children's use of arithmetic strategies start simple, but increase in complexity as their basic cognitive abilities improve (for example, working memory, speed of processing, metacognition) and as they practice adding numbers and, perhaps, learn to use their hands to help them discover new strategies. New, more efficient strategies increase in frequency but never fully replace older, simpler strategies that children will sometimes use when the newer strategies fail to produce an easy answer (Siegler, 2006). Children are explicitly taught some of these strategies in schools, but they often learn them in less-formal venues, such as playing number and math games with their parents, siblings, or friends. The math games children play and how they may contribute to children's arithmetic ability is examined in Box 11-1.

**CORRECT GESTURE**

**PARTIALLY CORRECT GESTURE**

**NO GESTURE**

FIGURE **11-9**

Examples of gestures children were taught by Goldin-Meadow and colleagues (2009). Children in the Correct Gesture condition were taught to point with a V-hand (their index and second finger) to the first two numbers in the equation, and then point with their index finger to the blank. This is a "correct" gesture, because the fist two numbers need to be added together, and their sum placed in the blank. Children in the Partially Correct Gesture condition first pointed with a V-hand to the second and third numbers in the equation, and then with their index finger to the blank. This is only partially correct, because the second two numbers do not need to be added together, although pointing to the blank is correct. Children in the No Gesture condition received no instructions about pointing. All children were given verbal instructions about how to solve these problems.

Source: Goldin-Meadow, S., Cook, S. W., & Mitchell, Z. A. (2009). Gesturing gives children new ideas about math. *Psychological Science, 20*, 267–272. Reprinted by Permission of SAGE Publications.

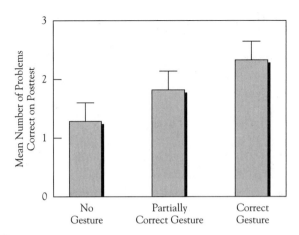

FIGURE **11-10**

Mean number of correct posttest problems (maximum = 6) for children in the No Gesture, Partially Correct Gesture, and Correct Gesture conditions in the study by Goldin-Meadow and colleagues (2009). Children taught to use gestures "correctly" solved more problems than children taught to use the partially correct gestures, who in turn got more correct than children in the No Gesture condition. Apparently, using gestures increased children's awareness of the need to group the first two numbers in the equation together, critical for solving this problem.

Source: Goldin-Meadow, S., Cook, S. W., & Mitchell, Z. A. (2009). Gesturing gives children new ideas about math. *Psychological Science, 20*, 267–272.

## Math Disability

Not all children show regular improvement in mathematical skills over the school years. As with reading, approximately 10% of school-age children display specific disabilities in mathematics (Hulme & Snowling, 2009; Mazzocco & Myers, 2003), or math disability. Children with math disability can be identified early (in kindergarten) and their progress in arithmetic followed.

David Geary and his colleagues have taken this longitudinal approach and report that children with math disability display two types of difficulties (Geary, 1993; Geary, Brown, & Samaranayake, 1991). First, these children show poor procedural skills, in that they use a more immature mix of arithmetic strategies than nondisabled children do. Also, first-grade children with math disability show poorer knowledge of the rules of counting. Using a procedure similar to the one described earlier by Briars and Siegler (1984), in which a puppet counts arrays either correctly or incorrectly, Geary and his associates (1991) found that children with math disability demonstrated an immature understanding of counting. For example, many believed that adjacent items in an array had to be counted consecutively for the count to be correct. However, Geary and his colleagues note that the procedural skills of many kindergarten and first-grade children with math disability approached those of their nondisabled peers by the end of the second grade. That is, with respect to using procedures, they catch up, suggesting that their deficit was a developmental delay. The second source of difficulties for children with math disability is a memory-retrieval deficit. Children with math disability retrieve fewer facts from long-term memory (that is, they use fact retrieval less often), and when they do, they are often wrong. Moreover, simple

## BOX 11-1   The (Math) Games Children Play

Children are explicitly taught basic arithmetic in school, but instruction rarely starts in school. Rather, it begins in the home, often in the context of games, usually with a parent or older sibling. Card games such as Go Fish help young children to identify numbers, and games such as War help them to learn the cardinal value of numbers (the larger number always wins). Children also play board games, in which they have to move their game piece around a board according to the outcome of a roll of the dice or a twirl of a spinner. Sometimes all children have to do is to recognize the number on a single die or that an arrow points to and move their game piece the corresponding number. This is less trivial than it may sound, as children need to learn that each of their counts corresponds to one space on the board. Real arithmetic becomes possible when two dice are used and children must combine their total to arrive at an answer.

In one study, parents and their 5-year-old children played a modified game of Chutes and Ladders®, in which the spinner that is usually used in this game was replaced by a pair of dice (Bjorklund, Hubertz, & Rubens, 2004). Did parents take the opportunity to teach their children some basic addition and, if they did, were they successful? Some children started the game using fact retrieval (that is, they did not count out loud or on their fingers but just "knew" the answer), and parents usually gave such children little assistance or instruction—the children did not need it. Most children, however, used more effortful counting strategies, especially sum. For example, if they rolled a 3 and a 4, they would count the pips on the first die ("one, two, three"), then count the pips on the second die ("four, five, six, seven"), and then move their game piece seven squares. Parents often made an effort to teach their children more effective ways of arriving at an answer. For instance, many parents demonstrated on their moves or instructed on children's moves the min strategy ("Look here, this is a 4,

you know 4. So start here, say 'four,' and count the other ones, 'five, six, seven'"). Some prompted them to use fact retrieval ("See, that's 2 and 2. You know what 2 plus 2 is, right? You don't have to count them. You can just say 'four'"). Many parents were working in what Vygotsky described as the *zone of proximal development*, scaffolding their children's behavior (see Chapter 3).

In other work, 4- and 5-year-old low-income children played a board game with squares on the board having either the numbers 1 through 10 on them or different colors (Ramani & Siegler, 2008; Siegler & Ramani, 2009; see Siegler, 2009). Moves on the game were determined by twirling a spinner that had either numbers or colors to denote the children's moves. Children's numerical knowledge (for example, counting, identifying numerals, judging which of two numbers was larger) was measured both before and after playing these games. Roughly 1 hour of playing the game with numbers resulted in significant improvements in children's numerical knowledge, and the gains were still apparent 9 weeks later. There were no corresponding improvements for children who played the "color game" (see also Whyte & Bull, 2008).

What these studies demonstrate is that young children can learn about numbers, numerical relations, and even arithmetic, all while playing games. The work with low-income children is especially impressive. Low-income children tend to lag behind their middle-class peers in numerical knowledge before ever entering the schoolhouse. The demonstration that playing simple games that merely expose them to numbers can increase their numerical knowledge may result in easy ways for parents, preschool teachers, or day-care workers to enhance low-income children's mathematical understanding. This also reminds us why involving parents in early intervention programs increases their effectiveness by showing parents specific things to do at home.

practice at fact retrieval alone does not appreciably improve performance, and unlike procedural difficulties, these deficits tend not to improve to the level of their agemates with time (see Geary, 1993).

One possible reason for these children's persistent problems with fact retrieval has to do with working-memory capacity (see Hulme & Snowling, 2009). For example,

Geary and his colleagues (1991) reported that the digit spans for children with math disability (4.2 words) were about one word less than the digit spans for children without math disability (5.3 words). This deficit might be the result of faster decay of information (that is, the memory representations might disappear more quickly in working memory for children with math disability), of slower counting speed (recall from Chapter 7 that digit span is related to articulation rate), or of a slower domain-general speed-of-processing capacity (Berg, 2008; Bull & Johnston, 1997). Because these children make computation errors, they arrive at many incorrect answers, and these answers can become part of their long-term memory representations of arithmetic facts. Unfortunately, they are wrong.

The deficits shown by many children with math disability are similar to those shown by many children with reading disability. In fact, there is considerable overlap between the two populations (see Hulme & Snowling, 2009). For example, in a large-scale study, N. A. Badian (1983) reported that 43% of children with math disability were also classified as reading disabled, and that 56% of children with reading disability were similarly classified as math disabled. Both math and reading disabilities seem to share a common problem—the inability to retrieve information efficiently from long-term memory. Math facts are proposed to be represented in a semantic network, much as word definitions are. Geary (1993) proposed that a single deficit underlies many math and reading disabilities: "At the cognitive level, this deficit manifests itself as difficulties in the representation and retrieval of semantic information from long-term memory. This would include fact-retrieval problems in simple arithmetic and, for instance, word-recognition and phonological awareness in reading" (p. 356). In addition, phonological processing, so important in reading, is also implicated in mathematics. Children with better phonological processing skills tend to show better math computation ability (Hecht et al., 2001; Swanson & Sachse-Lee, 2001).

Many children, however, read just fine but have great difficulty in math, and vice versa. It appears that there is no single cause of math disability (or of reading disability, for that matter), and that some of these disabilities are domain specific in nature. However, the substantial overlap between the reading- and math-disabled populations suggests that some domain-general abilities are involved in these important technological skills—namely, working-memory capacity and efficiency of retrieval from semantic memory.

## Cultural Differences in Mathematics

Mathematics is truly the universal language (although many would give that distinction to love, I suppose). Regardless of one's native tongue, the rules of mathematics are the same all over the globe. However, most forms of mathematics beyond arithmetic are explicitly taught, at least in our culture. Yet, people from traditional cultures still have a need for basic arithmetic and other forms of mathematical problem solving. How do people from nonschooled societies acquire mathematics? And how is it similar to and different from what happens in cultures such as ours, where formal schooling is universal?

Differences in mathematical attainment also occur between different information-age cultures. In recent years, this has been brought to the public's attention by reports of substantial differences in mathematics performance between American children and college students and those from other information-age cultures, particularly those in East Asia. How different are Americans from East Asians in mathematical attainment, when do those differences appear, and what factors contribute to them? These issues are discussed in the next section, following a brief examination of arithmetic in unschooled cultures.

### Arithmetic in Unschooled Children

Research examining the arithmetic ability of nonschooled Brazilian children has shown that they possess a high level of computational skill, but only when the problems are tied to real-life situations. For example, Terezinha Carraher, David Carraher, and Analucia Schliemann (1985) gave 9- and 15-year-old unschooled street vendors a series of arithmetic problems to solve. Problems that were imbedded in real-life contexts (for example, "If a large coconut costs 76 cruzeiros, and a small one costs 50, how much do the two cost together?") were solved at a much higher rate than were the same problems presented out of context (for example, "How much is 76 + 50?"). Carraher and her associates reported that the children answered the context-appropriate questions correctly 98% of the time; in contrast, the out-of-context questions were answered correctly only 37% of the time. Reviewing their research on schooled versus nonschooled Brazilian children's mathematical reasoning, Schliemann (1992) stated that these children use mathematics to solve everyday problems where mistakes have real consequences. This is contrasted with school learning, in which children are taught standardized procedures with little or no application. Schliemann concluded that unschooled street vendors (and unschooled people from other professions, such as brick layers and lottery bookies) develop a flexible arithmetic system and apply it appropriately within their work context, and that "unschooled people develop at work not only fixed procedures to solve specific problems but a conceptual and flexible understanding of the mathematical models applied to solve problems" (p. 2).

In other research, Steven Guberman (1996) has shown that Brazilian shantytown children frequently use their knowledge of currency to help them solve school-type arithmetic problems. Also, interviews with children's parents indicated that parents adjusted the complexity of the purchases they asked their children to make depending on the perceived skill of the child. As children grew older and more arithmetically competent, parents presented them with more difficult real-world problems to solve (such as purchases to make). This is consistent with working within the zone of proximal development, a concept developed by Lev Vygotsky (1978) and discussed in some detail in Chapter 3.

### Academic Performance by American and Asian Schoolchildren

Evidence has been accumulating that American school children lag behind children from other industrialized countries in their academic knowledge, including mathematics (Baker, 1992; Stevenson & Lee, 1990). In fact, American children typically fall in the middle of the pack in most international comparisons of mathematics performance, often scoring much below nations with considerably less wealth (Organization for Economic Cooperation and Development, 2004). This is not a new phenomenon, as can be seen in Figure 11-11, which presents percentage correct on tests of mathematics from 1990 for first- and fifth-grade children from the United States (Minneapolis), Japan (Sendai), and Taiwan (Taipei) (Stevenson & Lee, 1990). As you can see, differences favoring the Asian children appear as early as the first grade, and they become larger by the fifth grade.

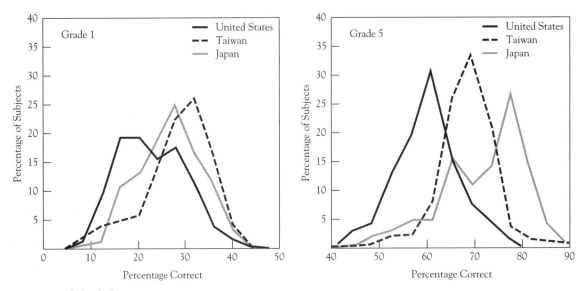

**FIGURE 11-11**

Frequency distributions of mathematics scores for first- and fifth-grade children in the United States, Japan, and Taiwan.

Source: "Context of Achievement," by H. W. Stevenson & S. Y. Lee (1990), *Monographs of the Society for Research in Child Development, 55.* (Serial No. 221). Copyright © 1990 The Society for Research in Child Development, Inc. Reprinted with permission.

One possible reason for the early difference might be the greater digit spans for many East Asian relative to American children because of differences in the rate at which the number words can be articulated in the different languages (Geary et al., 1993; see the discussion in Chapter 7). There are also early differences in the use of arithmetic strategies, however. Geary and his colleagues reported that Chinese first-grade children used a more sophisticated mix of strategies, including decomposition (Geary et al., 1996; Geary, Fan, & Bow-Thomas, 1992). The Chinese children were also faster at retrieving an answer directly from long-term memory (that is, at fact retrieval) than the American children were. But this speed advantage was apparently limited to retrieval of arithmetic facts and did not reflect an overall greater speed-of-processing advantage, for the Chinese and American children were equally fast at counting. (Recall, however, our discussion in Chapter 3 about Chinese preschool children being able to count to 20 before American children could [Miller et al., 1995].) Other research has shown that this advantage in the use of arithmetic strategies for Chinese relative to American children is present even before the start of formal schooling (Geary et al., 1993).

One might ask, "So what?" We're talking about the most basic of arithmetic abilities, which American children clearly master by the end of elementary school. But children's early arithmetical accomplishments set the stage for later achievements. Geary and his colleagues (1992) argue that "if the mastery of basic skills facilitates the acquisition of more complex mathematical concepts and procedures, then the results of the current study suggest that Chinese children will have a consistent 3- to 4-year advantage over their American peers in the development of mathematical cognition" (p. 184).

What is the origin of these differences? One source of the difference is likely practice. Children who practice elementary computation more frequently are able to retrieve math facts more quickly from long-term memory and have greater opportunities to develop arithmetic strategies than do children who practice them less often (Geary et al., 1992). Harold Stevenson and his colleagues reported that Chinese and Japanese children do, indeed, spend more time on mathematics, both in and out of the classroom (Fuligni & Stevenson, 1995; Stevenson & Lee, 1990). This pattern of cultural difference begins in preschool (Siegler & Mu, 2008; Zhou et al., 2006). Thus, we have the very commonsense finding of practice makes perfect (or at least makes for enhanced performance), with children who practice arithmetic more frequently (Chinese and Japanese children) performing better than children who practice it less frequently (American children).

Yet, what causes this cultural difference in time invested in mathematics and the overall greater academic performance? Again, the answer is quite commonsensical: parents' attitudes and behavior regarding education and child-rearing. Although American parents tend to believe that their children's academic performance is due to effort, this tendency to emphasize effort and hard work is even more obvious in Japanese and Chinese parents (Ng, Pomerantz, & Lam, 2007).

Because of Japan's cultural traditions, children also spend more time in school and devote a higher percentage of their school time to academic material than do American children. For example, whereas the average school year in Minneapolis is 174 days, it is 230 days in Taipei and 243 days in Sendai (Stevenson & Lee, 1990). Subsequent research found that American first-grade children show greater improvements in academic subjects as a result of attending an extended-year schooling program (210 to 230 days) rather than a school program of conventional length (180 days) (Frazier & Morrison, 1998).

It's worth noting that American children of recent Asian descent perform better in school, on average, than do White or Black native-born Americans (Chen & Stevenson, 1995). A major reason for this difference is the attitudes that Chinese American and Japanese American parents have toward education. For example, Chin-yau Lin and Victoria Fu (1990) compared the child-rearing practices of Caucasian American parents with those of Chinese parents from Taiwan and immigrant-Chinese parents living in the United States. Lin and Fu reported that both the immigrant-Chinese and the Taiwanese parents rated higher on parental control, encouragement of independence, and emphasis on achievement than Caucasian American parents did. In other research, Chinese American 7- and 8-year-old children spent more time doing homework and taking music lessons, spent less time playing organized sports, and had less free time than comparable European American children (Huntsinger, Jose, & Larson, 1998). The Chinese American parents also used more formal teaching methods for math and reading than did the European American parents. From these findings, we can see how cultural attitudes of Chinese American parents exert an influence on their children's educational attainment, which is likely responsible for the academic edge these children have in American schools.

## Sex Differences in Mathematical Ability

When most people think of sex differences in academic abilities, perhaps the first area to come to mind is mathematics, with males generally being better than females. (The other area is verbal abilities, with the common wisdom being that females are generally more verbal than males, as discussed earlier in this chapter.) Such observations date back in the scientific literature to at least 1894, with Havelock Ellis' comments regarding male superiority on a host of cognitive tasks, and they continue to be much studied today. What is the nature of sex differences in mathematical abilities? When, in development, are they observed? Are they a reflection primarily of biology or of educational opportunities?

On average, and perhaps somewhat surprisingly, given the stereotype, girls get better school grades than boys in mathematics at all academic levels (Halpern et al., 2007). This is related in large part to girls performing better in all school subjects than boys. In a 2-year longitudinal study examining math performance in children starting in fifth grade, girls displayed greater achievement goals (as reflected, for example, by items such as "An important reason I do my math work is because I want to improve my skills") and showed less disruptive behavior than boys, both of which were related to learning strategies and grades in math (Kenney-Benson et al., 2006). However, males score higher on standardized math tests than females (Halpern et al., 2007; Hedges & Nowell, 1995), although the absolute magnitude of the sex difference is small and varies in different countries (Else-Quest, Hyde, & Linn, 2010). As an example, Figure 11-12 presents the average SAT Math scores for males and females between 1967 and 2003 (from Halpern et al., 2007). As can be seen, the gap between males and females has been between 30 and 40 points for most years, with a decided male advantage. In general, females tend to perform better

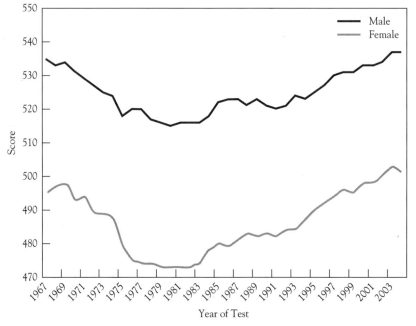

### FIGURE **11-12**

Average SAT Math scores for males and females from 1967 to 2003.

Source: Halpern, D. F., Benbow, C. P., Geary, D. C., Gur, R. C., Hyde, J. S., & Gernsbacher, M. A. (2007). The science of sex differences in science and mathematics. *Psychological Science in the Public Interest, 8*, 1–51.

on familiar material, as reflected by assessments of school learning, whereas males tend to perform better applying mathematical knowledge to new contexts, as reflected by standardized tests.

Yet, a recent report analyzing results of standardized math tests from over 7 million American children in grades 2 through 11 as part of "No Child Left Behind" assessments reported no sex differences in math scores at any grade (Hyde et al., 2008). Males continued to score higher than females on the SAT Math by about 7%, however, suggesting that a small male advantage is still found, although its explanation may not be straightforward.

Similar to what has been done to evaluate sex differences in verbal abilities, researchers have used meta-analysis to evaluate the many studies looking at sex differences in mathematical ability. To reiterate, meta-analysis is a statistical technique that allows an investigator to evaluate the magnitude of a significant effect across a large number of studies. Differences between the sexes across studies are expressed in terms of effect size, with 1.0 corresponding to a difference equivalent to one standard deviation. Hyde (1981) reported the first meta-analysis of sex differences in mathematical ability, but more recent and extensive studies have been published, each reporting similar results (Feingold, 1988; Hedges & Nowell, 1995; Hyde, Fennema, & Lamon, 1990; Marsh, 1989; see Halpern et al., 2007).

Take, for example, the meta-analysis reported by Hyde and her colleagues (1990), which included 100 studies and the data of 3,175,188 participants. Contrasts were made between elementary school children for simple arithmetic computation, high-school students, college students, and adults. Several main conclusions can be stated:

1. Sex differences are small and often nonsignificant for arithmetic computation in elementary school, and what effect there is favors girls.
2. Significant differences in mathematics favoring males are first seen in high school, with this difference increasing somewhat in college and adulthood (effect size = .29, .41, and .59 for high school, college, and adult samples, respectively).
3. The magnitude of the sex differences between males and females has declined since the 1970s (effect size: pre-1973 = .31, post-1973 = .14).
4. Sex differences are greater at the highest ability levels, with males much more likely than females to be represented among the top percentiles of mathematics ability.

Related to this last point are the results of meta-analyses by Alan Feingold (1992) and by Larry Hedges and Amy Nowell (1995) looking at sex differences in *variability*. Both studies reported that males are much more variable than females in their performance. This greater male variability has long been noted (Ellis, 1894), and it is not limited to mathematics (Hedges & Nowell, 1995). These results suggest that, for most of the population, there is much overlap and little real difference in mathematical abilities between males and females. Differences are most apparent at the extremes, particularly at the upper levels of performance.

### Gender Differences at the Extremes

Differential representation of males in the top 5% of mathematics ability was demonstrated most dramatically by Camilla Benbow and Julian Stanley (1980). These researchers examined the verbal and mathematics SAT scores of a group of seventh- and eighth-grade children selected to participate in a study of mathematically skilled youth conducted at Johns Hopkins University. The students were selected in a series of talent searches conducted between 1972 and 1979 and scored in the top 5% of students taking the exam. The data revealed consistent sex differences favoring boys. Further, the students were essentially equivalent in SAT Verbal scores and in math-course background. Benbow and Stanley (1983) reported similar findings in a second investigation with a much larger number of students (nearly 40,000). In this second study, they found that the disparity between the sexes was greater at the higher ability levels. For example, the ratio of boys to girls scoring 420 or more on the SAT Math was 1.5:1. In contrast, this boy-to-girl ratio was 4.1:1 for students scoring 600 or more and 13:1 for the small number of students scoring 700 or more. Since that time, great strides have been made in providing opportunities for girls and young women to take more math classes, and according to Julian Stanley, the male-to-female ratio for scoring 700 and over on the SAT Math has been reduced to only 2.8:1 (quoted in Monastersky, 2005). This is a reflection of a more general trend, as discussed earlier (Hyde et al., 1990, 2008).

### Source of Sex Differences in Mathematics

Although Benbow and Stanley's (1983) results point to substantial sex differences at the highest levels of mathematics performance, their data reveal nothing about the sources of these differences, nor about the source of sex differences in the general population. There is also no compelling reason to conclude that SAT scores reflect innate differences in aptitude or capacity. For example, children's and adolescents' academic performance is influenced by the attitudes of their parents and peers. By adolescence, math and science are viewed as masculine disciplines, and girls may receive less support from their peers for such activities than boys (Stake & Nickens, 2005).

Cindy Raymond and Camilla Benbow (1986) investigated the connection between parental attitudes, gender typing, and mathematical ability for groups of adolescents scoring high on the quantitative and verbal portions of the SAT. Raymond and Benbow reported that mathematically talented students received greater parental encouragement in mathematics than did verbally talented students and that this pattern did not differ with sex. Related to this, the amount of encouragement in mathematics that children received was comparable for boys and girls, regardless of their area or level of talent (that is, high verbal or high math). Finally, mathematically talented girls were no more sex typed as masculine than were verbally talented girls, and no relationship was found between sex typing and SAT scores. Raymond and Benbow concluded that parental socialization practices during adolescence could not account for mathematical ability in this group of mathematically talented children.

One interesting sex difference in mathematics performance concerns **stereotype threat,** in which females perform worse on a mathematics test after simply being reminded that math is typically a masculine activity (Spencer et al., 1999). This effect has been observed in children as young as 5 years (Ambady et al., 2001) and in elementary and middle-school children (Muzzatti & Agnoli, 2007). These findings suggest that females, from an early age, may have the ability to perform as well as males on many mathematics tasks but are highly susceptible to the stereotype threat that identifies excellence in math as a male, and not a female, thing. Consistent with this interpretation, one recent study suggests that first- and second-grade girls who have female teachers with high levels of math anxiety develop the stereotype that "boys are better at math than girls" and score lower on math achievement tests compared to boys or to girls who do not have teachers with math anxiety (Beilock et al., 2010).

We also cannot ignore sex differences in brain development. As mentioned in the discussion of sex differences in reading ability, differences between the brains of males and females may be responsible, at least in part, for sex differences in some cognitive tasks. The male advantage in mathematics may be associated with their brains having more white matter than the brains of females (see Halpern et al., 2007, and Chapter 2).

One fascinating and educationally important finding is the steady reduction of sex differences in mathematics ability since the 1960s. Why are sex differences in mathematics ability decreasing over time? The answer favored by many is that attitudes and curricula are changing, that gender roles are being viewed more flexibly (Hyde & Linn, 1988), and that girls are taking more mathematics courses than before (Marsh, 1989). For example, in Herbert Marsh's (1989) assessment of math performance of 14,825 students in the High School and Beyond project, much smaller sex differences in performance were found than in previous studies. This was associated with evidence that the boys and girls in the study had taken, on average, equal numbers of mathematics courses in high school. However, evidence also suggests that test publishers, during the past 35 years, have been attempting to minimize sex differences in their tests, possibly accounting for the diminished sex differences in performance (Stanley et al., 1992). Whatever the reason, sex differences favoring males in high-school mathematics and beyond are still found, but they are relatively small in magnitude—and are getting smaller. The only exception to this statement concerns performance at the highest levels, where males are disproportionately represented.

### What Do Mathematically Gifted Females Do?

It is perhaps worth looking at the exceptions to the general phenomenon of sex differences at the extreme—the minority of females who fall within the top 5% in mathematics ability. What are these people like? Camilla Benbow, David Lubinski, and their colleagues (Benbow et al., 2000; Lubinski & Benbow, 1992; Lubinski, Benbow, & Sander, 1993) followed a sample of mathematically gifted females (top 1%) from identification in seventh grade to adulthood. Compared with equally mathematically gifted males, the females tended to select different areas of study in college and, later, different professions: The males were two to three times more likely to choose careers in engineering or the physical sciences than the females, who were more likely to pursue careers in biology, the social sciences, or the humanities.

Why this difference? One possibility is that there are still educational or occupational roadblocks for women in these traditionally male-dominated fields. However, Lubinski and Benbow proposed an alternative interpretation. They found that these mathematically gifted women are different from the mathematically gifted men in some noncognitive ways that could influence their choice of careers. For instance, in an assessment of values, gifted males gave higher ratings to theoretical issues than gifted females did; the reverse was true for ratings of social issues. Lubinski and Benbow reported that having strong theoretical values was positively associated with an interest in the physical sciences, whereas an interest in social values was negatively associated with such an interest. Basically, Lubinski and Benbow proposed that, in addition to cognitive abilities, other gender differences—possibly rooted in biology, possibly in socialization—contribute significantly to career choice. People choose a career not only because they think they will be good at it (that is, they think they have the requisite intellectual abilities) but also because it fits their values and interests. This position is consistent with Sandra Scarr and Kathleen McCartney's (1983)

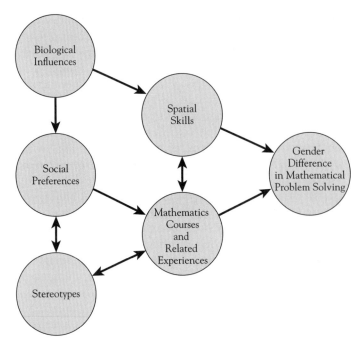

FIGURE **11-13**

Relationships among biological, cognitive, and psychosocial influences on the development of sex differences in mathematics.

Source: Geary, D. C. (1994). *Children's mathematical development: Research and practical applications.* Washington, DC: American Psychological Association.

genotype → environment model, suggesting that people select environments in which they feel comfortable.

Sex differences in mathematical performance are apparently real, but they are not simple. Girls actually get better grades in math than boys at all levels, whereas boys consistently perform better than girls on standardized tests. There seems to be no single reason for this pattern of differences. The gap between the sexes at the highest levels of achievement is declining, a result of increased academic opportunities for girls and young women. But differences in socialization practices and interests are also related to the sex differences we see in mathematics performance. As for nearly all sex differences, biological, cognitive, and psychosocial factors clearly interact over time to produce the pattern. Figure 11-13 shows a representation of the relationships among these various factors that influence sex differences in mathematics (from Geary, 1994).

## SCHOOLING AND COGNITIVE DEVELOPMENT

There should be little question that schooling makes a difference in how a child thinks. In our day-to-day experience, children who attend school are brighter than children who don't, and children in more advanced grades are smarter than children in lower grades. But children in higher grades not only have had more school experience than have children in lower grades, they are also older. Does attending school actually make a difference in cognitive development beyond the effect of age?

## Schooling versus Age Effects on Intelligence

The question of how schooling versus age influences intelligence has been addressed by examining the effects of years of education on intellectual performance while statistically controlling for age (Cahan & Cohen, 1989) or, more frequently, by using the *cut-off method,* in which children who just missed the cut-off date for entering school are compared with children who are close to their age but just made the cut-off date. Thus, the two groups of children are nearly identical in age but differ in that the former group has had one more year of education than the latter group (Morrison, Griffith, & Frazier, 1996). For example, Sorel Cahan and Nora Cohen (1989) compared intelligence test scores and school achievement of fourth-, fifth-, and sixth-grade children. They reported significant effects of schooling; children in the higher grade scored better than children their same age in the lower grade. These findings clearly show that IQ and related cognitive skills are strongly associated with schooling. In this study, effects of both age and schooling were reported (that is, older children did better than younger children, and children with one more year of school did better than children without the extra year), but the effect of schooling was two to three times greater than the effect of age. In related research, kindergarten and first-grade children showed greater gains on tests of cognitive skills during periods when more academic information was presented during school (between October and April) than for comparable time periods when less academic information was provided (between April and October) (Huttenlocher, Levine, & Vevea, 1998).

The results of this line of research may not be surprising. After all, we expect education to produce smarter children. But these findings force us to question the concept of intelligence as measured by IQ tests, which are age-based. In other words, the norms for these tests change as a function of age, not grade. (The logic of the construction behind IQ tests will be discussed in Chapter 12.) The results of the research cited here indicate that not only age but also school experience should be considered in computing an IQ score. Moreover, the idea that some intelligence tests can be "culture fair" (that is, used in any culture without yielding biased results) must be questioned. One of the tests Cahan and Cohen (1989) used was the Ravens' Progressive Matrices Test, which has been proposed to produce "an index of intellectual capacity whatever [a person's] nationality or education" (Raven, Court, & Raven, 1975, p. 1). The effect of 1 year of schooling, however, was found to be twice as large as the effect of 1 year of age on the Ravens' test, seriously challenging the fairness of this test when assessing children from cultures with no formal education (see also Cliffordson & Gustafsson, 2008).

Other researchers, notably Frederick Morrison and his colleagues, have looked at age versus schooling effects for specific cognitive and educational abilities in children just beginning formal education. In Morrison's research, "old kindergarten" children, who just missed the school-entry cut-off date, are compared with "young first-grade" children, with contrasts typically being made at the beginning and end of the school year. Morrison and his colleagues report both schooling and age effects, depending on the particular skill that is being assessed. For example, 1 year of schooling has a greater effect than 1 year of age on (1) phonological awareness (Morrison et al., 1996); (2) free-recall memory, including simple strategy use (Morrison, Smith, & Dow-Ehrensberger, 1995; Morrison et al., 1996); (3) accuracy in mental arithmetic (Bisanz, Morrison, & Dunn, 1995); (4) ability to understand complex sentences with longer subjects (Ferreira & Morrison, 1994); (5) knowledge of the alphabet (Christian et al., 2000); and (6) ability to use causal structure (that is, connections between different pieces in a story) in recalling stories (Varnhagen, Morrison, & Everall, 1994). However, significant *age* effects have also been found for (1) subsyllabic segmentation, or the ability to differentiate between sounds within one-syllable words (for example, for the word "grasp," being able to segment "gr" from "asp") (Morrison et al., 1996); (2) conservation of number (Bisanz et al., 1995); (3) the use of simple arithmetic strategies, such as fact retrieval and various counting methods (Bisanz et al., 1995); (4) gist recall of stories (Varnhagen et al., 1994); (5) ability to understand the use of pronouns in sentences (Ferreira & Morrison, 1994); and (6) vocabulary, cultural knowledge, and general narrative skills (Morrison et al., 1996). Of course, for most academic abilities, significant effects are found for both school experience and age (Morrison, Griffith, & Alberts, 1997). And at least some of these effects are not unique to American schools and children but have been reported for some aspects of arithmetic abilities in Japanese children as well (Naito & Miura, 2001).

The conclusion to draw from this research is that changes in different cognitive skills follow different developmental paths, reflecting a large degree of domain specificity. Some skills, such as phonemic awareness, free-recall memory, accuracy of mental arithmetic, and the abilities that underlie IQ test performance, are greatly affected by schooling experiences. Presumably, the experiences of children in school have a direct impact on these skills (for example, reading instruction affects phonemic awareness). However, other seemingly closely related skills, such as story recall, use of arithmetic strategies, and vocabulary, are more influenced by the presumably maturational and general (versus schooling-specific) experiences associated with age. According to Morrison and his colleagues (1996), this pattern reflects a substantial degree of specificity in the timing, magnitude, and nature of changes in cognitive abilities.

In other research, the effects of schooling on memory were investigated longitudinally by following children enrolled in the academically demanding curriculum of the German Gymnasium (for university-bound students) versus the less demanding curricula of the Hauptschule ("main school") (Schneider, Knopf, & Stefanek, 2002). Wolfgang Schneider and his colleagues hypothesized that differences in memory performance between children in the more rigorous (Gymnasium) versus less rigorous (Hauptschule) programs would increase over time because of the greater demands on memory of the Gymnasium curriculum. The results did not confirm their hypothesis, however. Although the various memory measures were moderately correlated with IQ at all ages, and although children in the higher-achieving schools showed greater performance than did children in the lower-achieving schools for all memory measures (free recall, text recall, and listening span), these differences were present at age 8, *before* children began their different curricula. Average performance for each memory measure increased with age, but the magnitude of the difference between the groups remained relatively constant. That is, memory differences existing among children at age 8 predicted which types of educational programs they would attend but were not subsequently affected by their different educational experiences. Thus, general memory performance, at least from age 8 into adolescence, is influenced by age, not by differences in schooling experience.

## The Effect of Schooling on IQ

The research contrasting the effects of 1 year of schooling versus 1 year of age demonstrates that schooling, indeed, plays a role in cognitive development, at least for some important skills. I suppose that this should not be surprising, given the evidence presented earlier in this and in previous chapters demonstrating substantial differences in mathematics, memory, and classification abilities for children from schooled versus nonschooled cultures. The question of a relationship between schooling and intellectual functioning is not a trivial one, however. For example, to what extent does schooling affect IQ? Cahan and Cohen (1989) found that 1 year of schooling has a substantial effect on IQ—twice the size associated with 1 year of age, in fact. That schooling affects IQ indicates that an IQ score is greatly influenced by experiential factors and is not solely under the influence of genetic or other biological factors that are relatively impervious to societal-level effects. The effects of schooling on IQ have been studied for a number of years, and Stephen Ceci (1991, 1996; Ceci & Williams, 1997) has organized and reviewed this literature, making the point that schooling has a powerful impact on IQ.

In addition to citing Cahan and Cohen's (1989) data as evidence for the influence of schooling on IQ, Ceci examined several additional areas of research pertinent to the schooling-IQ question, some of which I will mention here.

1. Perhaps the most obvious approach to the question would be to compute correlations between years of education and IQ. When this is done, the correlations tend to be very high, usually higher than .60 and often in excess of .80. The effects remain large even after controlling for differences in SES.
2. A small but statistically significant drop in children's IQ occurs over summer vacation. This drop is larger among children from low-income homes, probably because their summer activities have less resemblance to school activities than do those of children from more affluent homes.
3. Children who attend school intermittently, being frequently absent, have lower IQs than do children who attend school regularly. What is typically found in samples of frequently truant children is that IQ scores get lower with age. That is, children lose IQ points as they get older, partly because they increasingly fall behind in school.
4. Children who enter school late show an IQ decrement relative to children who start school on time. In one study, children experienced, on average, a five-point IQ deficit for each year that their schooling was delayed.
5. Just as people who start school late have lower IQs, so, too, do people who drop out of school early. One study of Swedish males (Harnquist, 1968) reported a loss of 1.8 IQ points for each year of school not finished.
6. Evidence suggests that the quality, not just the quantity, of schooling is important for IQ effects. For example, a classic study of African Americans who migrated from segregated and poor school systems in Georgia to better-quality systems in Philadelphia between World Wars I and II showed that children gained about one-half of an IQ point for each year they were enrolled in the Philadelphia schools (Lee, 1951). However, it is difficult to measure quality of schooling, and other investigators question the connection between quality of school and IQ (Bouchard & Segal, 1985).

More recently Heiner Rindermann and Ceci (2010) evaluated international differences in cognitive abilities and concluded that such differences are not due to differences in genes, but to differences in countries' educational systems.

Taken together, the evidence is impressive that attending school influences one's IQ. Again, perhaps this should not be too surprising, in part because IQ tests, although purporting not to assess specific aptitudes, do tap general cultural knowledge (the information and vocabulary subtests on the Wechsler scales, for example), much of which is learned in school. What seems inarguable is that whatever IQ tests measure, it is influenced greatly by the school experience.

## The Costs and Benefits of Academic Preschools

The evidence presented in the preceding sections clearly shows that schooling has a powerful impact on cognitive development. One year of schooling has a greater impact on some components of cognition than does 1 year of age, and schooling influences IQ. All this, along with evidence that a longer school year likely produces cognitive gains, makes a compelling argument for extended education, at least in postindustrial societies. In fact, some people have looked at the evidence and concluded that intellectual gains could be still greater if formal education were to begin even earlier (Doman, 1984). If starting formal education at 5 is good, then surely starting at 4, 3, or even 2 is better.

Evidence indicates that children who attend high-quality child-care programs during the preschool years score higher on measures of cognitive ability during elementary school than do matched groups of children who do not attend preschool programs (Broberg et al., 1997). Quality preschool education may be especially important to children from high-risk environments, as these children may not receive adequate preparation for school in their homes (Vandell et al., 2010; see discussion of preschool intervention programs in Chapter 13). But quality child care and preschool education does not necessarily mean *academically oriented* education. In fact, several researchers and educators have seriously questioned the idea of rigorous academic instruction for preschoolers (Elkind, 1987; Sigel, 1987). David Elkind (1987), for example, stated that academic programs for preschoolers amount to *miseducation*. Young children do not have the cognitive capacity to adequately master the academic skills of these programs, and the overall result is unnecessary stress with no long-term benefits.

Research has assessed the costs and benefits of formal education during the preschool period. Contrasts are often made between preschool programs that take children's "natural" propensities for play and activity into consideration (termed **developmentally appropriate programs**) and those that stress formal instruction (termed **direct-instructional programs**). Concerning academic abilities following a year in these programs, some studies find better performance for children attending developmentally appropriate programs (Stipek et al., 1998), some find better performance for children attending direct-instructional programs (Stipek et al., 1995), and some find no differences (Hirsh-Pasek, Hyson, & Rescorla, 1990). When long-term effects (greater than 1 year) are assessed, more studies find greater benefits for developmentally appropriate programs (Burts et al., 1993; Marcon, 1999). For instance, in one study, children who had attended either a developmentally appropriate or direct-instructional preschool were followed for 6 years (Marcon, 1999). Although there were no differences in academic performance between the two groups of children by the end of third grade, by the end of fourth grade children who had the developmentally appropriate preschool curriculum had higher grades than those who had attended the direct-instructional programs.

Differences between developmentally appropriate and direct-instructional programs are clearer when motivational and psychosocial factors are considered, with most studies finding that children attending developmentally appropriate programs experience less stress, like school better, are more creative, and have less test anxiety than children attending direct-instructional programs (Burts et al., 1993; Stipek et al., 1995, 1998; see also Bjorklund, 2007b). For example, in a study by Deborah Stipek and her colleagues (1995), preschool and kindergarten children from a range of households attended either developmentally appropriate or direct-instructional programs. Although children who attended direct-instructional programs showed greater knowledge of letters and reading achievement than children who attended developmentally appropriate programs, no differences were found on knowledge of numbers, and children in the developmentally appropriate programs rated themselves as having greater intellectual abilities, were less dependent on adults for permission and approval, expressed greater pride in accomplishment, had higher expectations for success on school-like tasks, chose more challenging math problems to perform, and said they worried less about school than children in the direct-instructional programs. In other words, any academic benefits gained from a teacher-directed program had its costs in terms of motivation.

Most of these effects, although statistically significant, are small in magnitude. Nevertheless, the pattern is clear. In general, there are no long-term benefits of an academically oriented preschool program for middle-class children, and some evidence indicates that such programs might actually be detrimental. The authors of one well-done study proposed two alternative interpretations for this pattern of findings (Hyson, Hirsh-Pasek, & Rescorla, 1990; Rescorla, Hyson, & Hirsh-Pasek, 1991). The first points to the small differences between the schools, so that from a practical perspective, the academic orientation of a school likely makes little difference in the long run. The second and stronger interpretation of the data holds that an academic orientation provides no advantage and actually has some small negative consequences. Marion Hyson and her colleagues concluded that whichever interpretation is adopted, there seems to be no defensible reason for encouraging formal academic instruction during the preschool years. Rather, for most children from middle-class homes, cognitive development and creativity can best be fostered in a developmentally appropriate preschool program that considers children's limitations as well as their abilities. In the opinion of these researchers, "it may be developmentally prudent to let children explore the world at their own pace rather than to impose our adult timetables and anxieties on them" (Hyson et al., 1990, p. 421).

## EVOLUTIONARY EDUCATIONAL PSYCHOLOGY

I have highlighted throughout this chapter—in fact, throughout this book—how children's thinking is influenced by evolved psychological biases (Bjorklund & Hernández Blasi, 2005; Geary, 2007). In Chapter 6, for example, I examined the development of folk physics, folk biology, and folk psychology (see also Chapter 10), and we saw that children are motivated to attend to certain aspects of their physical and social worlds. These aspects proved valuable to our ancestors by helping people to predict and control important parts of their environments. People certainly become aware of some of this knowledge, but much of it remains unavailable to consciousness. Moreover, although these processing biases continue to be useful for people today, they sometimes conflict with the demands of modern society. We live in environments that are evolutionarily novel, and children must learn things that could not have been conceived by their ancestors. To do this requires formal education, something that itself is novel for our species.

Humans have always educated their children. The complexity of social groups and the technological skills that even early humans acquired could be not mastered without some form of instruction or sophisticated social learning. For most of our history, cultural knowledge was transmitted by "on the job training," and it remains so today in traditional cultures and for many occupations even in developed societies. Education is informal, accomplished by demonstrations and observations, "through participation with more skilled partners in culturally organized activities" (Rogoff, 1990, p. 39). But unlike other animals, each generation of humans does not start out from square one but begins with the knowledge of the previous generation, permitting the rapid expansion of information over time (Tomasello, 1999). Until relatively recently, humans have been able to transmit this valuable knowledge in social settings, with apprentices learning from masters. But as knowledge has accumulated and culture has moved away from the environments in which we evolved as a species, new skills were required, and these were best learned "out of context." In other words, these skills were best learned not on the job but in classrooms of one form or another. Formal education—teaching the new technological skills of reading, writing, and arithmetic—has only recently become important for economic success, dating back a few hundred years at most, and it is only within the past 100 years that a majority of people in most societies have received formal education. Such education is a necessity today, guiding children in the acquisition of many of the explicit cognitive skills discussed earlier in this chapter, and this presents a serious challenge for human educability. Modern children possess the same brains and minds as did their hunter/gatherer peers dating back at least 60,000 years, and perhaps as far back as 300,000 years. Yet, modern culture necessitates that children learn things unimaginable by their ancient predecessors.

## Principles of Evolutionary Educational Psychology

David Geary (1995, 2007, 2010) has championed the new field of **evolutionary educational psychology** (see also Bjorklund & Bering, 2002, and papers in Carlson & Levin, 2007). Geary proposed six principles of evolutionary educational psychology, which are summarized in Table 11-2.

As we saw in Chapter 6, Geary proposes that children evolved cognitive and motivational systems for dealing with their physical, biological, and social worlds (folk physics, folk biology, and folk psychology, respectively). He referred to these as biologically primary systems, and they are mostly implicit in nature (see discussion in Chapter 2 and earlier in this chapter). These systems helped children and, later, adults to predict and control their world. However, despite facilitating peoples' understanding of their physical and social environments, they were not always scientifically accurate. For example, children assume that a container with a higher level of liquid in it contains "more" of that liquid than a container with a lower level, often ignoring differences in width. This will generally result in correct assessments, in that containers that look like they hold more usually do, in fact, hold more. But this can also result in some problems, such as when the contents are poured from a tall, thin container into a shorter, wider container, causing children to assert that the

## TABLE **11-2**
### Principles of Evolutionary Educational Psychology.

1. Biologically secondary abilities associated with scientific, technological, and academic advances emerged from the biologically primary abilities associated with folk physics, folk biology, and folk psychology. As a society's knowledge increases, the gap between folk knowledge and the skills necessary to acquire the technological skills of society widens.
2. Schools emerged in societies to fill the gap between folk knowledge and needed technological skills.
3. The purpose of schools is to organize the activities of children so they can acquire the biologically secondary abilities that close the gap between folk knowledge and the occupational and social demands of their society.
4. Biologically secondary abilities are built from biologically primary ability and components of general intelligence, evolved to deal with environmental variation and novelty.
5. Children are inherently motivated to engage in activities that promote their folk knowledge, but this sometimes conflicts with the need to engage in activity that will promote secondary learning (for example, reading), because children are not inherently motivated to engage in biologically secondary abilities.
6. There is a need for direct instruction for children to learn most biologically secondary abilities.

Source: (Adapted from Geary, D. C. (2007). *Educating the evolved mind: Conceptual foundations for an evolutionary educational psychology.* In J. S. Carlson & J. R. Levin (Eds.), Educating the evolved mind: Conceptual foundations for an evolutionary educational psychology (pp. 1–99). Charlotte, NC: Information Age Publishing.

amount of liquid has now changed (this is Piaget's conservation-of-liquid task discussed in Chapter 5). Children's intuitive understanding interferes with logical thinking. A more sophisticated example involves understanding the forces on a thrown ball. Most people believe (and before Isaac Newton, nearly all people did) that there are two forces acting on a thrown ball: The first impels it forward and dissipates over time, and the second pulls the ball downward. This second force, of course, is gravity. The first force also has a name, impetus, but in the context of a thrown ball, it does not exist. Once the ball leaves the person's hand, it has no propelling force (that was provided by the thrower), only gravity. Our naïve (nonscientific) understanding is sufficient to let us predict where a thrown object is likely to fall, but our underlying theory, despite permitting us to make relatively accurate predictions, is wrong.

Although folk knowledge works well enough most of the time, the accumulation of knowledge over many generations and the development of new technologies result in a gap between folk knowledge and the skills necessary for success in one's society. Most of these new skills are in the form of biologically secondary abilities, which are available to consciousness (that is, a form of explicit cognition). It is under these situations that schools become necessary. After all, most children are unlikely to learn to read or multiply "on their own," or to acquire the knowledge of biology, government, or world geography without instruction, for example. The job of schools is to organize children's activities so that they acquire the biologically secondary abilities (built upon biologically primary abilities) deemed important by their culture, such as reading and mathematics.

Although children have intrinsic motivation to engage in biologically primary abilities, Geary notes this is not the case for biologically secondary abilities, which often require tedious practice and external pressure to master some of the skills and the strategies that underlie them. Reading is an obvious example. Based upon the biologically primary abilities of language, few children learn to read spontaneously, as they seem to learn how to talk. It is not surprising that many young children fail to see the "big picture" of the importance of reading and, thus, have little intrinsic motivation to learn how to read. Children learn to read because teachers and parents make them (although in several families I have noticed younger children who are motivated to learn to read because they see it as something that an older sibling has mastered). And once a certain level of reading ability is acquired, children's motivation to read to learn new information can increase. In fact, reading instruction can likely be facilitated by having children read content that is related to their biologically primary interests. As Geary (1995) states, "The motivation to read ... is probably driven by the content of what is being read rather than by the process itself. In fact, the content of many stories and other secondary activities (e.g., video games, television) might reflect evolutionary relevant themes that motivate engagement in these activities (e.g., social relationships, competition ...)" (p. 28). As I noted earlier in this chapter, boys are more sensitive to the interest level of what they read than are girls, showing lower levels of reading comprehension for low-interest stories compared to girls (Renninger, 1992). As a result of less motivation for acquiring biologically secondary skills, explicit instruction (as opposed to "discovery learning") is necessary for many children to acquire these skills.

## Physical Activity

It is not just children's cognitive abilities that are sometimes at odds with the demands of formal schools but also aspects of their physical and social development. For instance, in most American schools, children spend the bulk of their day inside, seated in chairs or at tables and attending to instruction from a teacher. They are usually encouraged to perform "seat work" independently, keeping their hands and eyes to themselves. Schools understandably discourage more vigorous activity, such as rough-and-tumble play, a favorite activity of many elementary school-age boys (Pellegrini & Smith, 1998). However, some have argued that physical activity, often in the form of recess, actually facilitates young children's learning and should be incorporated into the daily curriculum (Pellegrini, 2005; Pellegrini & Dupuis, 2010).

For example, a number of studies have shown that elementary-school children show more on-task behavior (Pellegrini & Davis, 1993; Pellegrini, Huberty, & Jones, 1995) and less "fidgeting" (Jarrett et al., 1998) after a recess break than when recess is denied to them. In a series of three studies, Anthony Pellegrini and his colleagues (1995) varied the timing of school recess for kindergarten, second-grade, and fourth-grade children. Some children had recess delayed by 30 minutes for 2 days a week relative to the other days. Children's attention to seat work was assessed both before and after recess. At each grade, children were significantly more attentive after recess than before, and the effects of delaying recess were significantly greater for the younger than for the older children.

Despite this positive effect, the frequency of recess has been steadily declining in schools of the United States and other countries (see Pellegrini, 2005). This seems not to be the case, however, in many Asian schools. For instance, a 1990 study reported that first- and fifth-grade children in Taipei, Taiwan, and in Sendai, Japan, had more recesses than children in Minneapolis (four versus two for first graders, and four or five versus two [or fewer] for the fifth graders) (Stevenson & Lee, 1990). That is, despite having what most people believe is a more rigorous curriculum, the Asian schools recognize the cognitive and behavioral limitations of young children and structure the day to take these limitations into consideration.

Some researchers have gone so far as to speculate that children's natural high rates of activity and exploration of novel environments (especially for boys) may be behind the high rates of diagnosis of ADHD (Panksepp, 1998; Pellegrini & Horvat, 1995). Some cases may reflect active children who are at the high end of a normal distribution but whose propensity for activity gets them in trouble with teachers and some of their more sedentary classmates. The high activity of some children in ancient environments may have been advantageous. For instance, having individuals who constantly scanned the horizon for signs of predators or prey would seem to have obvious benefits, although such off-task behavior is maladaptive in contemporary school classrooms (Jensen et al., 1997). ADHD is a complicated disorder (see Chapter 7), and many individuals with it would fare poorly in any environment. One must keep in mind that schools are an evolutionary novelty and that normal levels of activity and playful behavior, especially as shown by preadolescent boys, although sometimes interfering with ideal educational practices, may not in and of themselves be signs of pathology.

## SUMMARY

Reading is perhaps the most critical technological skill for people in postindustrial societies. Chall proposed five stages of learning to read: (1) the prereading skill of letter identification, (2) phonological recoding in the first grade, (3) fluent but effortful reading in grades 2 and 3, (4) "reading to learn" in grades 4 through 8, and (5) proficient reading in high school and beyond. The difference between good and poor readers tends to increase over time, termed the *Matthew effect*, as good readers read more often than poor readers.

*Emergent literacy* refers to the skills, knowledge, and attitudes that are presumed to be developmental precursors to conventional forms of reading and writing and the environments that support these developments. There are at least nine components to emergent literacy: (1) language, (2) knowledge of the conventions of print, (3) knowledge of letters, (4) linguistic awareness, (5) phoneme-grapheme correspondence, (6) emergent reading, (7) emergent writing, (8) print motivation, and (9) other cognitive abilities, such as memory.

*Phonemic awareness* and *phonological recoding* are important skills for both beginning and later reading, with children who have *dyslexia*, or reading disability, generally exhibiting poor phonological processing skills. Skilled reading also involves working memory and is influenced by one's knowledge base, both of which develop over childhood.

Two broadly defined types of reading instruction have been used: *phonics*, which is a bottom-up system that emphasizes learning letter-sound correspondence, and the *whole-language approach*, which is a top-down system that emphasizes a reader's construction of meaning. Although reading surely involves both top-down and bottom-up processes, research evidence makes it clear that any reading program should include some instruction in phonics.

More boys than girls are classified as dyslexic. *Meta-analyses* have found that females show an overall advantage in verbal abilities relative to males, although the magnitude of this gender difference has diminished during the last several decades.

Children's concept of number has been studied in terms of *conservation of number,* following Piaget. Children appear to acquire knowledge of counting gradually during the preschool years, and this knowledge precedes that necessary for conservation of number.

Research on children's arithmetic has concentrated primarily on the strategies children use to solve problems. Early arithmetic is done out loud, often on fingers. Children's early strategies include the *sum strategy,* in which children count all numbers, and the *min strategy,* in which children begin with the larger addend and count up from there. More sophisticated strategies include retrieving addition and subtraction facts directly from long-term memory (*fact retrieval*) and *decomposition,* in which a problem is decomposed into simpler problems. Children actually use a variety of arithmetic strategies at any one time, including gestures.

Children with math disability typically display procedural deficits early but often catch up to their peers by second grade. Difficulties in storing and retrieving math facts from long-term memory persist, however, with deficits in working-memory capacity being a likely contributor to math disability.

The mathematics performance of unschooled children tends to be good when their familiarity with the test materials and the context of testing are considered. Patterns of cognitive abilities vary as a function of culture even in those societies that require formal education, with different values and educational practices affecting children's academic performance.

Sex differences in mathematics favoring males are not typically found until high school and then increase slightly into college and adulthood. The absolute magnitude of these differences is small, however, and has been decreasing during the past 40 years. The largest sex differences are found among the most mathematically gifted, with males being disproportionately represented. A number of factors have been hypothesized as responsible for sex differences, including *stereotype threat,* in which females perform worse on a mathematics test after simply being reminded that math is typically a masculine activity.

Attending school enhances development of many cognitive skills beyond the effects of age, although age has a greater impact on development of other cognitive abilities. Evidence from a variety of sources suggests that schooling influences IQ. Although the effects are typically small, middle-class children who attend preschool programs that stress academics (*direct-instruction programs*) demonstrate no long-term gains and have less positive attitudes about school than do children who attend nonacademic preschool programs (*developmentally appropriate programs*).

*Evolutionary educational psychology* applies the concepts of evolutionary psychology to education. Geary proposes that children evolved cognitive and motivational mechanisms for dealing with their physical, biological, and social worlds and that an understanding of these mechanisms can facilitate the development of educational systems. For example, physical activity, in the form of recess, may facilitate children's attention to course work and enhance schooling effects.

## KEY TERMS AND CONCEPTS

Matthew effect

emergent literacy

phonemic
   awareness

phonological
   recoding

dyslexia

phonics

whole-language
   approach

meta-analysis

conservation of
   number

sum strategy

min strategy

fact retrieval

decomposition

stereotype threat

developmentally
   appropriate
   programs

direct-instructional
   programs

evolutionary
   educational
   psychology

## SUGGESTED READINGS

### Scholarly Work

Geary, D. C. (2006). Development of mathematical understanding. In D. Kuhn & R. S. Siegler (Vol. Eds.), *Cognition perception, and language* (Vol. 2) (pp. 777–810). In W. Damon & R. M. Lerner (Gen. Eds.), *Handbook of child psychology* (6th edition). New York: Wiley. This chapter reviews research and theory on children's developing mathematical abilities, covering topics of more advanced math as well as the basic number concepts and arithmetic discussed in this chapter.

Geary, D. C. (2007). Educating the evolved mind: Conceptual foundations for an evolutionary educational psychology. In J. S. Carlson & J. R. Levin (Eds.), *Educating the evolved mind: Conceptual foundations for an evolutionary educational psychology* (pp. 1–99). Charlotte, NC: Information Age Publishing. In this lengthy chapter, David Geary sets out his ideas about applying evolutionary psychology to modern education. The article is followed by seven commentaries and a response from the author.

Halpern, D. F., Benbow, C. P., Geary, D. C., Gur, R. C., Hyde, J. S., & Gernsbacher, M. A. (2007). The science of sex differences in science and mathematics. *Psychological Science in the Public Interest*, *8*, 1–51. This paper, written by leading researchers in various aspects of sex differences, examines the controversial topic of sex differences in science and mathematics and their possible origins.

### Reading for Personal Interest

Golinkoff, R. M., Hirsh-Pasek, K., & Eyer, D. (2004). *Einstein never used flashcards: How our children really learn—and why they need to play more and memorize less.* New York: Rodale Books. This trio of developmental psychologists makes the compelling argument that preschool children learn better when they are not pressured to perform academic-type work. Rather, young children acquire problem-solving, social, and attentional skills best through play.

Wolf, M. (2007). *Proust and the squid: The story and science of the reading brain.* New York: Harper. Maryann Wolf provides a fascinating account of how our ancestors taught their brains how to read only a few thousand years ago and, in the process, changed the intellectual evolution of our species.

# Approaches to the Study of Intelligence

**The Psychometric Approach to the Study of Intelligence**
Factors of Intelligence
IQ Tests

**Information-Processing Approaches to the Study of Intelligence**
Basic-Level Processes
Higher-Level Cognitive Abilities

**Sternberg's Triarchic Theory of Intelligence**
The Contextual Subtheory, or Practical Intelligence
The Experiential Subtheory, or Creative Intelligence

The Componential Subtheory, or Analytic Intelligence
**BOX 12-1:** The Triarchic Theory Goes to School

**Gardner's Theory of Multiple Intelligences**
Criteria of an Intelligence
Multiple Intelligences and Education
Assessment of Gardner's Theory

SUMMARY
KEY TERMS AND CONCEPTS
SUGGESTED READINGS

"Look at the fingers of your right hand. No two are alike. That's the way children are." This homily, attributed to a retired elementary school teacher, reflects the individuality of children.

In the previous chapters of this book, I focused on different ways in which cognition changes from infancy through adolescence. Although I occasionally discussed individual differences in children's thinking—for example, how children with ADHD display poor executive function, or how children with autism show an underdeveloped theory of mind—for the most part our attention has been on age-related differences in children's thinking. Yet, we are all aware that some children think better than other children of the same age. Some kids are smarter than others. When psychologists and educators discuss relatively stable individual differences in cognitive functioning between people, they usually use the term *intelligence*. If Ashley gets better grades in school, follows the complicated story lines of movies and TV dramas more easily, and generally solves everyday problems more effectively than Isabella, then despite the two being the same age, we would typically say that Ashley is more intelligent than Isabella.

For psychologists, however, intelligence is more than just a synonym for "smart." Rather, it reflects an important characteristic of individuals that can be measured and used to predict people's performance on a host of social and cognitive tasks. In fact, that is why the study of intelligence is important to child development: Children who score high on tests of intelligence tend to perform better in school, acquire important technological skills more easily, and often display better social adjustment than children who score lower on such tests. Scores on intelligence tests can alert parents, teachers, and other people concerned with a child's welfare to potential problems and their amelioration (or to potential areas of giftedness and their amplification).

I should also say a few words about the connotation that the word "intelligence" has for most people. Although my intention is to focus on the psychological definition of the term, it also has significance from a sociological perspective. We all show different patterns of cognitive skills: Some people have better memories than others; some are more distractible, more verbal, or better with numbers than others; and most of us do not hesitate to comment on our cognitive strong and weak points. However, to say someone is of high or low intelligence means a lot more to most people than to say someone has good or poor memory, high or low mathematical ability, or is more or less attentive. In part, this results from how theorists and educators have defined intelligence as a set of intellectual skills that affect nearly all problems one attempts to solve. We value people of high intelligence, believing that they are more effective at a broad range of tasks, are apt to be more interesting to talk to, and are more economically successful. We likewise tend to undervalue people of low intelligence, thinking they are less skilled at performing the tasks of daily living. One often hears people saying things like people should have to take an IQ test before they have children or before they're allowed to vote. Although I cannot change peoples' connotation for the term, I can alert students to the unconscious bias that most of us have attached to *intelligence*, and I can emphasize that my discussion is limited to the cognitive aspects of the term.

What exactly do psychologists and educators mean when they use the term **intelligence**? Most broadly, it refers to acting or thinking in ways that are goal directed and adaptive. This definition covers a lot of ground, allowing much leeway for theorists to sculpt their own meanings of the concept while still being understood by others. I am in general agreement with Robert Sternberg's (1997) definition of intelligence as "the mental activities necessary for adaptation to, as well as shaping and selecting of, any environmental context ... [I]ntelligence is not just reactive to the environment but also active in forming it. It offers people an opportunity to respond flexibly to challenging situations" (p. 1030). Following this definition, intelligence is obviously a multifaceted phenomenon that no single test can likely tap. Several researchers have produced tools that aim to assess some of the multiple aspects of intelligence described in this definition (Sternberg, Ferrari, & Clinkenbeard, 1996; Wexler-Sherman, Gardner, & Feldman, 1988), but the bulk of data, both historically and in contemporary research, has come from the testing, or *psychometric approach*, with IQ tests being the measure most often associated with intelligence. Much of this chapter concentrates on the theory and practice of IQ testing, but alternatives to the testing approach to intelligence are given even more total space. More specifically, I examine information-processing approaches to intelligence, followed by a detailed look at two popular alternative theories: Robert Sternberg's triarchic theory and Howard Gardner's theory of multiple intelligences. In the next chapter, I continue the discussion of intelligence, focusing on the extent to which intelligence is biologically and environmentally influenced and on the stability of intelligence over time.

---

# THE PSYCHOMETRIC APPROACH TO THE STUDY OF INTELLIGENCE

The major approach to the study of individual differences in intelligence since the turn of the 20th century has been the **psychometric approach** (or the **differential approach**). Psychometric theories of intelligence have as their basis a belief that intelligence can be described in terms of mental **factors** and that tests can be constructed that reveal individual differences in those factors that underlie mental performance. Factors are related mental skills that (presumably) affect thinking in a wide range of situations.

## Factors of Intelligence

What constitutes a factor is determined by a statistical procedure known as **factor analysis**. In factor analysis, numerous test items are administered to people, and the resulting data are examined to see which items fit together well. Tests might show, for example, that the pattern of individual differences among people is very similar on vocabulary, reading comprehension, story completion, and verbal analogies. That is, people who score high on one of these tests usually score high on all of them, whereas people who score low on one usually score low on all. In contrast, performance on these test items might not correlate as highly with performance on items that involve rotating three-dimensional figures, solving maze problems, or quickly placing geometric forms in a form board, although these three tests might all correlate highly with one another. What do the first tests (vocabulary, reading comprehension, story completion, and verbal analogies) have in common? It is not difficult to conclude that all involve some aspect of verbal thinking, whereas the second set (three-dimensional rotation, maze learning, and form-board performance) are all basically nonverbal and involve some form of spatial thinking. Accordingly, based on the results of the statistical analysis, an investigator can assume that two factors that account for individual differences among people are verbal ability and spatial thinking.

Patterns of performance are not always clear-cut, however. The extent to which sets of test items correlate with one another is a matter of degree. Only in textbooks do we find perfect data that can be interpreted in only one way. Thus, how one defines mental factors is influenced not only by the data but also by one's theoretical and statistical perspective.

Determining the number and makeup of factors is a function of the items included on a test (you could not very well have a verbal component if no verbal items were included in your test) and the particular way you perform statistical analyses. Based on variants of the same form of analysis, the number of factors that have been proposed to account for human intelligence has varied considerably. At one extreme is J. P. Guilford's (1988) theory that includes 180 unique intellectual factors. More influential (and older), however, is Charles Spearman's (1927) proposal that intelligence consists of only two kinds of factors. He viewed the most critical kind of factor as a single, general one, labeled *g* (or **general intelligence**), that influences performance on all intellectual tasks. He saw the other kind of factors as specific ones that are not generalizable and that are each pertinent to only a single task. As such, these highly specific abilities are of little interest to psychologists trying to construct theories to explain individual differences among people. In other words, from Spearman's point of view, intelligence exists on a single dimension and is not some multifaceted phenomenon (that is, there is actually only one factor of intelligence, *g*). Intellectual functioning is relatively homogeneous, or even, across different tasks performed by a single person—in other words, it is a domain-general ability. Smart people are smart all the time (or most of the time, anyway), and less bright people are consistently so. (I will have more to say about the concept of *g* later in this and the following chapter.)

Falling between these two extremes is Raymond Cattell's (1971) theory, which recognizes both a general intellectual factor similar to Spearman's *g* and two second-order factors that he called **fluid abilities** and **crystallized abilities**. Basically, Cattell proposed that fluid abilities (or fluid intelligence) are biologically determined and are reflected in memory span and most tests of spatial thinking. In contrast, crystallized abilities are best reflected in tests of verbal comprehension or social relations, skills that depend more highly on cultural context and experience (see Blair, 2006).

The best evidence for the existence of *g* is what has been termed the **positive manifold**, the frequent finding of high correlations among scores on sets of cognitive tests that have little in common with one another in content or types of strategies used (see Daniel, 1997; Jensen, 1998). This is exactly what Spearman proposed earlier in the 20th century, and the finding is still with us.

Research has produced at least one interesting caveat to the positive manifold. Douglas Detterman and Mark Daniel (1989) found much higher correlations among scores on a variety of cognitive and intelligence tasks for low-IQ people than for high-IQ people. For example, in one study, adults with intellectual impairment (mean IQ = 67.5) and college students (mean IQ = 115.5) were given a battery of nine cognitive tasks and an IQ test. Detterman and Daniel correlated performance on the cognitive tasks with IQ and then examined the correlations of the scores on the nine cognitive tasks with each other. The correlations were considerably higher for the low-IQ group (.60 for IQ scores and .44 for the cognitive tasks) than for the high-IQ group (.26 for IQ scores and .23 for the cognitive tasks), which means that the cognitions of high-IQ people (in this case, college students) are more varied than the cognitions of low-IQ people.

There is no single interpretation of this finding, but Detterman (1987) proposed that intelligence is made up of several independent mechanisms, with each of these being influenced by central (domain-general) processes. According to Detterman (1987), intellectual impairment is caused by a deficit in central processes, which in turn affects all other components in the cognitive system, producing relative homogeneity of cognitive function. When there is no central deficit, however, variability is more apt to be found in different components of intelligence, thus producing lower correlations. In other words, a certain level of domain-general central processing resources must exist for individual components of intelligence to operate adequately. Once that level is achieved, there will be substantial variability in cognitive task performance within a given person. If that level is not achieved, as is the case for the people with intellectual impairment, then no individual component will receive enough in the way of processing resources to function well, resulting in relative homogeneity of cognitive functioning and, thus, high correlations.

Some tentative evidence also suggests that the positive manifold develops. Thomas Price and his colleagues (2000) investigated the degree to which verbal and nonverbal cognitive abilities were related in early childhood. As I've just commented, verbal and nonverbal abilities tend to be highly correlated in later childhood and adulthood, suggesting that they are influenced by some general intellectual factor, such as *g*. However, in a sample of nearly 2,000 same-sex 2-year-old twins, Price and his colleagues reported that correlations between verbal and nonverbal abilities were only of moderate magnitude. This suggested to the authors that cognitive abilities are relatively domain-specific in infancy and early childhood and become more domain-general in nature as children get older.

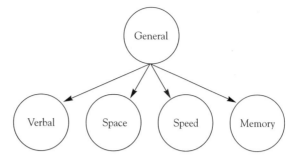

FIGURE **12-1**

Hierarchical model of cognitive abilities. Intelligence is composed of specific cognitive abilities (for example, verbal, spatial, speed of processing, memory) that are intercorrelated and influenced by a higher-order general intellectual factor, *g*.

Most psychometricians today adhere to some form of the **hierarchical model of cognitive abilities** (Carrol, 1993). Basically, this model postulates a series of relatively specific cognitive abilities, such as verbal, spatial, speed of processing, and memory, as shown in Figure 12-1. These abilities, however, are correlated with one another (recall the positive manifold) and are influenced by a second-order general factor, or *g*. Thus, this model suggests that, depending on how one looks at the data, one can find evidence for either domain generality (*g*) or domain specificity (separate verbal and spatial modules, for example), and both could be correct (Petrill, 1997).

In some interesting research using neural imagining techniques, John Duncan and his colleagues (2000) used PET to examine which parts of the brain were most activated when adults performed a variety of cognitive tasks. These researchers compared verbal, spatial, and perceptual-motor tasks with high-*g* involvement (that is, those that loaded heavily on *g*) with low-*g* tasks (that is, those that did not load heavily on *g*). They found that the high-*g* tasks are associated with activation of a particular area of the brain—specifically, the lateral frontal cortex. More recent research has shown that the thickness of cortical areas of the brains in children 6 to 18 years old were positively associated with performance on a set of cognitive tasks that load heavily on *g*, further pointing to a connection between brain structure and function and intelligence (Karama et al., 2009).

As we'll see when we examine some alternative approaches to intelligence, not everyone agrees with the way psychometricians define or measure intelligence. However, regardless of whether you are a fan of psychometric theory or not, it has had great influence on generations of children and society in general by way of its best-known product, the IQ test.

## IQ Tests

Although mental testing has had a profound influence on psychologists' attempts to conceptualize the nature of intelligence, the greatest impact of mental testing has been the **IQ (Intelligent Quotient) test**. Intelligence testing is so widespread in our society that it is virtually impossible for a child to graduate from high school without having been administered at least one IQ test and more than a dozen other tests assessing more specific academic aptitudes.

IQ tests are less the result of psychometric theorizing than they are the instruments that produce the raw data for theory construction. IQ tests were developed at the turn of the 20th century in France by Alfred Binet and Theodore Simon. The original tests—and even modern versions, to a large extent—were not based on explicit theory. Rather, they were constructed to assess school-related abilities and to differentiate among those children who could benefit from standard school instruction and those who would require special education. It would be inappropriate, however, to classify IQ tests as atheoretical. Modern IQ tests are based on certain concepts of what intelligence is (for example, the hierarchical model of cognitive abilities). Nevertheless, pragmatic considerations of which items best differentiate children of a given age are critical in constructing IQ tests, causing some to question their contribution to understanding the underlying mechanisms of intelligence (Sternberg, 1985).

Numerous IQ-type tests are available today. Many are pencil-and-paper tests that can be administered to a group. The standard tests by which most are judged include the Stanford-Binet and the three intelligence scales developed by David Wechsler. These tests have been standardized on large samples and are individually administered by trained examiners using standardized procedures.

The **Stanford-Binet** was developed in 1916 by Lewis Terman, who made extensive revisions to Binet's original scale. The test has gone through revisions from time to time, the most recent one being in 2003 (Roid, 2003). The latest version of the Stanford-Binet has 10 subtests, organized in a three-level hierarchical model of the structure of intelligence. A general reasoning factor (g) is the most inclusive, followed by five second-level abilities (fluid reasoning, knowledge, quantitative processing, visual/spatial processing, and working memory) and then sets of more specific tasks within each of the second-level abilities.

The **Wechsler scales** have similarly been revised periodically since their inception in the 1940s. There are three primary Wechsler scales, developed for people of different ages: (1) the Wechsler Preschool and Primary Scale of Intelligence (WPPSI) for children 2 to 7 years old; (2) the Wechsler Intelligence Scale for Children (WISC), for children 6 through 16 years old; and (3) the Wechsler Adult Intelligence Scale (WAIS) for adults. The latest version of the WISC (the WISC-IV; Wechsler, 2003) provides a Full Scale IQ based on four separate indexes: Verbal Comprehension, Perceptual Reasoning, Working Memory, and Processing Speed. Table 12-1 lists the subtests for each index and provides brief examples of the types of items on these tests.

There are many other IQ tests, some nonverbal measures of visual reasoning (The Ravens Progressive Matrices; Raven, Raven, & Court, 2003; Figure 12-2 for an example), and many paper-and-pencil tests that can be administered to groups of people, such as a classroom of students, with only minimal supervision. Enter "IQ test" in Google and you will find several on-line tests you can take in the comfort of your home. These tests do not have the reliability or validity of the individually administered Stanford-Binet or the Wechsler scales, but the logic in their construction is the pretty much the same. Like the gold-standard tests, most of the easily administered tests will give you a score, with 100 being average, that will tell you where you stand with respect to other people who have taken the test.

Although the youngest children who can be assessed using the Wechsler or Stanford-Binet scales are early preschoolers, psychometricians have not forgotten

TABLE **12-1**

Examples of the Types of Items on Each Subtest of the WISC-IV

**Verbal Comprehension Index**

*Similarities:* Children are read two words in pairs similar to the following and are to tell how they are alike: pear-peach: inch-ounce: snow-sand.

*Vocabulary:* Children are read words and are to tell what each word means, for example, "What is a magazine?" "What does democracy mean?"

*Comprehension:* Children are asked questions assessing their knowledge of societal conventions and of appropriate behavior in a variety of situations: "What are some reasons we need soldiers?" "What are you supposed to do if you find someone's watch in school?" "Why is it important to have speed limits on roads?"

*Information:* Children are asked questions assessing their general world knowledge, similar to the following: "How many pennies make a dime?" "What do the lungs do?" "What is the capital of Italy?" This is an optional test, not included in the index total score.

*Word Reasoning:* Children are given sets of hints and must identify the object that the hints describe. For example, "This has a flat end and a long handle": "You use it to dig holes."

**Perceptual Reasoning Index**

*Block Design:* Children are given nine cubes, colored red on two sides, white on two sides, and red and white on two sides. They are shown designs and are to reproduce them using the nine blocks. Bonus points are given for fast response times.

*Picture Concepts:* Children are shown pictures and must match those that belong together based on common features, for example, things to drink, toys.

*Picture Completion:* Children are shown black-and-white pictures and are to determine what important part of each picture is missing. This is an optional test, not included in the index total score.

**Working Memory Index**

*Digit Span:* Children are read digits at a rate of one per second and are to repeat them back in exact order. This is followed by a test in which children must repeat the numbers in the reverse order from the order the examiner spoke them.

*Letter-Number Sequencing:* The examiner reads children a sequence of letters and numbers (for example, 7, K, 3, P, 8, D) and asks children to recall the numbers in ascending order (3, 7, 8) and the letters in alphabetical order (D, K, P).

*Arithmetic:* Children are given arithmetic problems. The easiest involve counting, addition, and subtraction using physical reminders. A child might be shown a picture of nine trees and asked to cover up all but five. More complex problems are read aloud: for example, "Joyce had six dolls and lost two. How many dolls did she have left?" "Three girls had 48 cookies. They divided them equally among themselves. How many cookies did each girl get?" This is an optional test, not included in the index total score.

**Processing Speed Index**

*Coding:* Children are shown a key associating simple geometric figures (for instance, a triangle, a square, and a circle) with other symbols (a cross, a vertical line, and so on). Children are to mark the associated symbol below a set of randomly arranged figures as quickly as possible without skipping any. Bonus points are given for fast response times.

*Symbol Search:* Children are shown a target symbol (for example, ≠) and beside it a series of three symbols (for example, ∂∝¥, or ¥∂≠). Children must determine if the first (target) symbol is contained in the second (search) set of symbols.

*Cancellation:* Children are shown arrays of objects and asked to mark each object of a certain type (all the trucks, for example) as quickly as possible. This is an optional test, not included in the index total score.

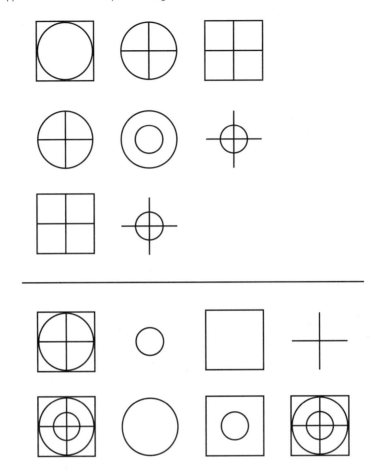

FIGURE **12-2**

An example of a type of item used on the Ravens Progressive Matrices. Which of the eight items below the solid line best completes the pattern in the top of the figure?

Source: Raven, J., Raven, J. C., & Court, J. H. (2003). *Manual for raven's progressive matrices and vocabulary scales. Section 1: general overview.* San Antonio, TX: Harcourt Assessment.

infants. Tests to assess infant intelligence have been developed with the same psychometric properties as IQ tests and yield a **developmental quotient (DQ)**. Tests such as the Bayley Scales of Infant Development (Bayley, 1969, 1993, 2005), the Gesell Developmental Schedules (Gesell & Amatruda, 1954), the Neonatal Behavioral Assessment Scale (Brazelton, 1973), and their precursors are based primarily on evaluations of individual differences in sensory and motor abilities (although the newest version of the Bayley scales [2005] includes more cognitive measures). These tests have been well standardized, are reliable (that is, there is high test-retest and intertester agreement), and describe important differences among infants (McCall, Hogarty, & Hurlburt, 1972). For example, items used to compute a DQ at different age levels in the Bayley scales include:

1 to 3 months: responds to sound of bell; vocalizes once or twice; displays social smile;

5 to 7 months: smiles at mirror image; turns head after fallen spoon; vocalizes four different syllables;

9 to 12 months: responds to verbal requests; stirs with spoon in imitation; attempts to scribble; and

14 to 17 months: says two words; shows shoes or other clothing; builds a tower of three cubes.

Basically, IQ tests (and DQ tests) are standardized on large samples of people, and items that differentiate among people of a given age are retained whereas items that do not (those that are too easy or too difficult) are eliminated. For each age assessed, the number of test items the average child passes is determined. For example, the number of items passed by 50 percent of the 8-year-olds in the standardization sample would reflect the number of items an average 8-year-old should be able to pass.

Historically, the relationship between the number of items passed and the age of the child was expressed as a quotient of one's **mental age** to one's chronological age (thus the term *intelligence quotient*, or *IQ*). A child's mental age corresponds to the number of items he or she passes. If a child passes the number of items equal to the number passed by an average 12-year-old, the child's mental age is 12 years. The child's mental age is then divided by his or her chronological age, and the result is multiplied by 100. Thus, a 10-year-old child with a mental age of 10 years has an IQ of 100 ($10/10 \times 100$). A 10-year-old with the mental age of 9.5 years has an IQ of 95 ($9.5/10 \times 100$), and a 10-year-old with a mental age of 12 has an IQ of 120 ($12/10 \times 100$).

The concept of mental age has received substantial criticism (see Wechsler, 1974). One criticism is that a 7-year-old with a mental age of 10 and a 10-year-old with the same mental age are not, in reality, of comparable intelligence. They may have the same mental age with respect to test performance, but they do not have the same kind of minds. Also, a 5-year-old with a mental age of 6 has an IQ of 120; a 10-year-old with a comparable IQ has a mental age of 12. In the first case, the child's mental age is 1 year ahead of his chronological age; in the second case, there is a difference of 2 years.

These and other problems led test developers to abandon the concept of mental age and develop instead the **deviation IQ**. In this method, children's performance is compared with that of children of their own age and not with the performance of older or younger children. Thus, tests can be constructed so that the statistical characteristics of IQ are the same at each age level. Modern tests are constructed so that IQ scores are distributed according to a normal distribution with specified statistical properties. The theoretical distribution of IQ scores for the WISC is shown in Figure 12-3. As can be seen, children with scores of 100 have IQs equal to or greater than 50% of the population. Children with scores of 115 have IQs equal to or greater than approximately 84% of the population. Thus, by knowing a child's IQ score, one knows where he or she stands with respect to intelligence relative to his or her agemates.

The renouncement of the concept of mental age and the use of the deviation IQ enable a more accurate comparison among children of a specified age. However, using the deviation IQ to express intelligence makes developmental contrasts difficult. IQ

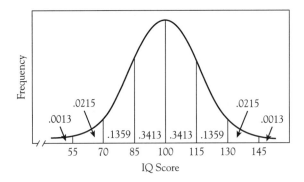

FIGURE **12-3**

Theoretical distribution of WISC-IV scores. The test is constructed so that 50% of all people at a given age will have IQ scores of 100 and below and 50% will have scores of 100 and above.

tests are not constructed to be a mechanism for understanding the development of intelligence. In fact, by using the deviation IQ, we hold developmental differences constant, so that we can make comparisons among agemates in the same way for children of all ages. As I noted earlier, this procedure has obvious advantages for making comparisons of children's intelligence. For the developmentalist, however, difficulties arise when changes in intelligence over time are of interest.

I think few people would argue that IQ tests are the last word in intelligence—that a score on a test accurately reflects one's true intelligence. Yet, I think that most educators and scientists (but not all) who have given the subject serious thought would concur that IQ tests measure some aspect of intelligence, particularly as it relates to academic performance.

### What Does IQ Predict?

Does IQ measure anything "important"? Does it predict how well one will do in school or in life? Many researchers and educators think so, at least to some degree. Research has shown, for example, that IQ predicts reasonably well individual differences in academic performance, occupational status, and longevity.

First, how well does IQ predict academic performance? The simple answer is pretty well. The average correlation between children's IQ scores and current and future grades is about .50 (Neisser et al., 1996; White, 2000). One interpretation of this relatively strong relationship is that the mental abilities tapped by IQ tests reflect general intelligence, or *g*, and that these are the intellectual skills that are needed to perform well in school (Jensen, 1998). Longitudinal studies have found that IQ measures predict subsequent academic achievement better than earlier academic achievement predicts later IQ, suggesting a causal connection between IQ and achievement (Watkins, Lei, & Canivez, 2007). Keep in mind, however, that although the correlation between IQ and academic performance is relatively high, it still only accounts for about 25% of the differences in school performance among children. Clearly, other factors, perhaps some in interaction with IQ, affect how well children do in school (motivation, for example) (Spinath et al., 2006).

How does IQ do in predicting occupational status? Again, pretty well. People with higher-status (and usually higher-paying) jobs have higher IQs than people with lower-status (and usually lower-paying) jobs (Brody, 1997; Neisser et al., 1996). There are many potentially confounding factors for this relationship, with the most obvious being those between IQ and education and between education and occupation. Nonetheless, even when levels of education are controlled, a significant relationship between IQ and occupational status remains (Neisser et al., 1996). Also, there is a positive correlation of about .5 between IQ and job performance for people *within* a profession (among a group of lawyers or accountants, for example). People with higher IQs tend to be rated as better at their jobs than people with lower IQs, although there are obviously many other factors associated with job performance, given that 75% of the variance is left unexplained after considering the effect of IQ.

In addition to its association with academic performance and occupational status, childhood IQ is positively related with longevity (Deary et al., 2008; Hart et al., 2005; Leon et al., 2009) and better health (Batty et al., 2006). There are no easy explanations for these relationships. Are genes associated with high IQ also associated with longevity and health? Might these all be related to prenatal environments, with healthier prenatal environments being associated with higher IQ, longevity, and health, or might the effect of IQ be related to education? Perhaps people with higher IQs are more aware of many health hazards, such as smoking and obesity, and choose to lead healthier lives as a result. As you will see in Chapter 13, there is no simple cause for a high or low IQ. Thus, the many relations that are found between IQ and various other measures of physical, social, and cognitive functioning do not likely have a single and simple explanation.

### *IQ Tests and Minority Children*

Even in the area of predicting academic performance, IQ tests are far from perfect. For example, there has been much controversy about IQ testing of minority children, with critics arguing that the tests and the testing situation do not serve as fair assessments for such children. On average, the IQ scores of African American children are about 10 to 15 points lower than those of European American children (Herrnstein & Murray, 1994). Part of the group difference can be attributed to SES. Children from lower-SES homes score lower on IQ tests than children from middle-SES homes, and African American children are more likely to live in low-SES homes than European American children (Suzuki & Valencia, 1997). This is clearly illustrated by adoption studies in which African American children born of parents from lower-income homes were adopted by middle-class parents. In one study (Scarr & Weinberg, 1976; Weinberg, Scarr, & Waldman, 1992), the average IQ of the adopted African American children was about 110, or 20 points higher than the average IQ of comparable children being reared in the local African American community.

One source of differences in IQ scores between cultural-minority and European American children is related to **stereotype threat** (Steele, 1997). I discussed stereotype threat with respect to females' poorer performance on standardized mathematics tests in Chapter 11. People are aware of negative stereotypes for their particular social group, and when the stereotype is activated, they tend to confirm them. For instance, the cultural stereotype for African Americans is that they perform poorly on IQ tests. When groups of African American and European American college students were administered a test of verbal intelligence (Steele & Aronson, 1995), performance of the

African American students varied, depending on whether they were told it was a test of intelligence or not. The African Americans who were told the test was assessing their intelligence scored significantly lower than those who were not told it was an intelligence test. This suggests that the tests may not be measuring people's intelligence per se but their tendency to choke under situations in which a stereotype threat was activated (see, however, Sackett, Hardison, & Cullen, 2004, who caution that the stereotype threat does not eliminate the White/African American difference in IQ).

Another possibility for racial and ethnic differences in IQ scores is that the tests are biased as a result of being based on skills and knowledge deemed important by the majority culture but perhaps not the minority one. Children from minority homes might not share the same values or even have access to the same knowledge that middle-class children do, making the test culturally biased. Many believe that intelligence can only be meaningfully assessed within the culture in which a child lives (Laboratory of Comparative Human Cognition, 1983; Miller-Jones, 1989; see discussion of Sternberg's theory later in this chapter). Thus, although IQ tests measure accurately some aspects of intelligence for children from the majority culture, they do not assess intelligence adequately for minority children. For example, IQ differences between minority and majority children are reduced when "culture fair" tests, such as the non-verbal Ravens Progressive Matricies test mentioned earlier, are used (Anastasi, 1988). Moreover, the rigorously standardized nature of IQ tests might be a detriment to minority children because the tests must be administered in a constant format. The examiner cannot provide feedback to a child and, usually, cannot probe a child's answers to determine if he or she has more knowledge than is reflected by an initial response. Minority children might have different expectations of what type of answers the examiner is looking for, and children's competencies will be masked by the requirements of standard test administration (Miller-Jones, 1989).

Dalton Miller-Jones (1989) provided several examples of how a 5-year-old Black child's performance on an IQ test could be underestimated because of the standardized nature of the test:

> Tester: "How are wood and coal alike? How are they the same?"
> Child: "They're hard."
> Tester: "An apple and a peach?"
> Child: "They taste good."
> Tester: "A ship and an automobile?"
> Child: "They're hard."
> Tester: "Iron and silver?"
> Child: "They're hard." (p. 362)

These answers all earn a score of zero, but does this mean that the child does not know the conceptual relation between iron and silver or between an apple and a peach? By the rules of the test, no feedback can be provided, and the child must guess what type of answer the examiner wants. There is nothing incorrect about the child's answers to these questions, but they do not fit the test makers' conceptions. They also do not likely exhaust this child's knowledge of the relations between these objects, but the test format precludes finding this out.

Other aspects of test administration also influence minority children's performance on IQ tests. The testing situation, for example, with a child sitting quietly across the table from an adult and answering a series of questions, might be more familiar and comfortable to a middle-class child than to a lower-class or minority child. Also, in most testing situations, the examiner is a member of a different ethnic and social class than the minority child, adding further discomfort and novelty to the testing situation.

Not all agree that there is bias against minority children in mental testing (Jensen, 1998). Despite all the criticism, the tests are cost-efficient and widely (though not universally) accepted by both educational professionals and the public. Yet, most would argue that we could do a better job of assessing minority children's intelligence and achievement, and Miller-Jones (1989) makes five recommendations for improving minority assessment:

1. When assessing any area of intelligence, it is important to specify the cognitive processes that might be involved in the task or elicited by the stimuli.
2. Multiple tasks with different materials should be used with the same individual.
3. Tests must be appropriate for the culture from which the child comes.
4. The connection must be validated between the cognitive operations assessed by a test and the attainment of school-related concepts, such as arithmetic and reading.
5. Procedures must be developed that permit an examiner to probe for the reasoning behind a child's answers.

Miller-Jones's advice is sound and applies to nonminority as well as to minority children.

Teachers also sometimes expect less of minority students in terms of academic performance than they expect of children from the majority culture. Can the expectations of teachers (and perhaps of parents and peers) affect school performance and IQ? The answer seems to be a resounding yes, as illustrated in a classic study by Robert Rosenthal and Lenore Jacobson (1968) titled *Pygmalion in the Classroom*. The title refers to a play by George Bernard Shaw, in which a professor bets that in a short time he can pass off a poor, uneducated flower girl as a proper member of society. (You may know it from the movies as *My Fair Lady*.) The **Pygmalion effect** is a form of *self-fulfilling prophecy*, in which a person internalizes the expectations of an authority figure. In the play, the flower girl internalized the professor's perception of her. In the classroom, children internalize the intellectual expectations teachers have for them (see McGown, Gregory, & Weinstein, 2010).

Rosenthal and Jacobson told elementary school teachers at the beginning of the year that some children in their class were expected to bloom intellectually. In fact, the names of the children were chosen randomly. At the end of the school year, children took an IQ test, and the results were compared to one that had been taken a year earlier. Children identified as bloomers gained significantly more on the IQ tests than the other children, illustrating the effect that teacher expectation can have not only on academic performance but also on IQ scores.

There is nothing magic about the IQ test itself. It does not necessarily measure innate intelligence, nor does it necessarily reflect a constant value that will typify an individual throughout life. However, IQ does predict reasonably well academic performance, occupational status, and even longevity. Yet, the psychometric approach, with its emphasis on a single score, is not the only way to think of individual differences in intelligence. Scientists and educators have developed alternative ways of conceptualizing intelligence, and the remainder of this chapter deals with alternative approaches to the study of intelligence—basically, approaches that don't see IQ tests as the only, or the best, or perhaps even a good measure of intelligence.

# INFORMATION-PROCESSING APPROACHES TO THE STUDY OF INTELLIGENCE

One criticism of the psychometric approach, and of IQ tests specifically, is that test construction is based primarily on pragmatic considerations—which items discriminate reliably among children—and not on theoretical considerations (Sternberg, 1985). The factors that constitute intelligence are determined by statistical analyses and not because of any a priori model of intelligence. As I noted earlier, however, it would be unfair to say that IQ tests are atheoretical. Nevertheless, pragmatic considerations of selecting items that discriminate among children at a given age are still extremely important in choosing which items will be included on the tests. Thus, although IQ tests can assess individual differences in intelligence well, they are less successful at providing insight into the nature of the intelligence that underlies test performance. This is critical not just from the point of view of theory but also for practice. For instance, Douglas Detterman and Lee Ann Thompson (1997) proposed that the key to improving education (particularly special education) is an understanding of the basic cognitive abilities that underlie individual differences in intelligence. With such an understanding, educational interventions can be individualized, and only through such practices will children, especially those whose style of learning differs from that of the majority, reap the benefit of educational research.

Individual differences in cognitive abilities have been extensively studied from the information-processing perspective. In a sense, the same mechanisms used to describe cognitive development from an information-processing perspective can be used to describe individual differences. Thus, for example, differences in how information is encoded, speed of processing, how easily information is categorized, and metacognition are all sources of individual (as well as developmental) differences in thinking and intelligence.

When cognitive psychologists examine individual differences in children's thinking, they often make contrasts between groups known to vary on the basis of IQ (for example, children with and without intellectual impairment or gifted and nongifted children) or between children matched in IQ who differ on the basis of some academic ability (for example, good and poor readers or children with and without learning disabilities). In such studies, researchers attempt to discover the underlying processes responsible for group differences in IQ, task performance, or academic skill. No attempt will be made here to assess the origins of intellectual impairment, learning and reading disabilities, or giftedness. The etiologies of these intellectual exceptionalities are interesting and important, but they would require separate chapters (or books) to investigate properly (although I did discuss possible origins of reading and math disabilities in Chapter 11). Rather, in this section, I examine differences in cognitive processing between exceptional and typical children to elucidate the nature of cognition in general and to discover educationally important differences in thinking among these groups of children. I look at a number of different aspects of cognitive processing that are implicated in intelligence, classified into two broad categories: basic-level processes, including speed of processing as well as working memory and executive function, and higher-level cognitive abilities, including strategies, knowledge base, and metacognition.

## Basic-Level Processes

Basic-level processes include tasks of working memory and memory span (such as the digit-span task, versions of which are included in the Stanford-Binet and Wechsler IQ tests) and laboratory tests designed to measure people's response times as they make presumably simple decisions. These latter tasks include short-term memory scanning, retrieval of familiar words from the long-term store, and simple categorization tasks (see Jensen, 1998). The basic processes measured by these tasks are presumed to be closely related to neurological functioning and, thus, primarily under the influence of endogenous (and inherited) factors. Although a number of basic-level processing abilities have been touted as influencing individual differences in intelligence, including, among others, inhibition (Harnishfeger & Bjorklund, 1994; McCall & Carriger, 1993), resistance to interference (Dempster, 1993), and the ability to process novelty (Bornstein & Sigman, 1986; Sternberg, 1985), most research has focused on two general mechanisms: (1) speed of processing and (2) working memory and executive function. I discuss research on these two topics here.

### *Speed of Information Processing*

Older children perform most, if not all, aspects of information processing faster than younger children do (see Kail, 1991; Kail & Ferrer, 2008). Moreover, both children and adults show similar patterns of reaction times across a large variety of tasks (Kail & Salthouse, 1994). Similar differences in speed of retrieval between gifted and nongifted children (Saccuzzo, Johnson, & Guertin, 1994) and between children with and without learning disabilities (Ceci, 1983) have also been observed. The differences in memory performance between children with and without learning disabilities and between good and poor readers attributed to higher-order cognitive abilities (see later) might be mediated by differences in speed of processing. Some children might require more time to activate relevant concepts used on these memory and problem-solving tasks than other children do, which in turn requires greater expenditure of mental effort. The increased effort associated with the slower retrieval of language terms, for example, might be indirectly responsible for the less strategic approach of these children to the task and, thus, for their overall lower levels of performance.

In addition to distinguishing children with and without learning disabilities and good readers from poor ones, the efficiency of retrieval from long-term memory has been hypothesized to be an important component of individual differences in intelligence in the general population (Fry & Hale, 2000; Jensen, 1998). Most forms of intelligence require retrieving information from memory and acting on that information. Several researchers have reasoned that people who retrieve information quickly and efficiently will display an advantage on cognitive tasks, particularly verbal ones. Earl Hunt and his colleagues (1981) provided support for this position using a variety of experimental tasks. In an early study, Hunt and his colleagues asked adults to verify category statements, such as "A dog is an animal." They found that the time needed to confirm such simple statements correlated significantly with verbal ability.

Several literature reviews of the evidence from both children and adults reported modest correlations (between about −.30 and −.50) between speed of responding and intelligence, with faster responding (and, thus, presumably faster information processing) being associated with higher IQs (Fry & Hale, 2000; Jensen, 1998). Moreover, speed of information processing correlates significantly both with performance on timed tests, when speed is important, and on nontimed tests, when fast responding is irrelevant (Vernon & Kantor, 1986). This pattern of results, along with the evidence from the developmental literature indicating the role of processing speed in cognitive development (Kail, 1991), suggests that speed of processing is an important component of individual differences in intelligence.

Individual differences in speed of processing are reliable but often small, and they point to important differences in intelligence at a microscopic level. Differences are often in milliseconds, and you may wonder what the significance of a 50-millisecond (that is, 1/20th of a second) difference might be with respect to intelligence. Although such differences are small, they can be important indeed. Perhaps one of the most vital cognitive skills for people in technological societies is reading. Small differences in rate of retrieving the meaning of a word or in integrating letters to form words can, over a very short time, result in substantial differences in reading rate and reading comprehension.

### Working Memory and Executive Function

Several researchers have suggested that working memory and executive function may be an important component to intelligence (Alloway & Alloway, 2010; Tillman, Nyberg, & Bohlin, 2008), above and beyond the effects of speed of processing. For example, Linda Miller and Philip Vernon (1996) administered the WISC and batteries of reaction-time and working-memory tasks to children between 4 and 6 years of age. Not surprisingly, children became faster with age, and working-memory span increased with age. Also, when general reaction time and memory factors were computed, the two were found to correlate significantly (−.44; the shorter the reaction time, the greater working memory tended to be). Reaction time was also significantly correlated with IQ at each age (overall correlation = −.42). The correlation between IQ and working memory, however, was even greater (.82), and it remained significant even after the effects of reaction time and age were taken into consideration. Miller and Vernon concluded that, for children between the ages of 4 and 6 years, "memory accounts for significant variability in intelligence" (p. 184). Reaction time, in contrast, has a smaller role in intelligence, at least once individual differences in working memory are taken into consideration.

Working memory is a significant component of executive function (see Chapter 7), which recent research suggests plays an important role in almost all areas of thinking. For example, several studies have shown that children and adults with intellectual impairment have shorter working-memory spans (Henry & MacLean, 2003) and perform more poorly on executive function tasks (Kittler, Krinsky-McHale, & Devenny, 2008) than people without intellectual impairment. Similarly, gifted children have higher levels of executive function than nongifted children do (Arffa, 2007; Mahone et al., 2002). In fact, the only psychological measures that have been found to predict school performance better than IQ are those reflecting executive function. For example, in one study, the effects of self-regulation (or self-discipline, to use the authors' term) on children's academic performance accounted for more than twice as much of the differences in school grades as did IQ (Duckworth & Seligman, 2005). In other research, a measure of working memory at age 5 predicted academic performance at age 11 better than IQ measured either at age 5 or at age 11 (Alloway & Alloway, 2010).

Although the relationship between measures of speed or processing, working memory, and executive function and IQ sometimes differ as a function of the age of the children tested (Fry & Hale, 2000; Miller & Vernon, 1996), it is clear that basic-level processes and intelligence are strongly interrelated, and as pointed out by Fry and Hale (2000), they have nearly the same developmental function, suggesting a single underlying mechanism.

## Higher-Level Cognitive Abilities

Speed of processing, working memory, and executive function are clearly important components of intelligence. Yet, other, more macro processes vary among people and contribute to individual differences in intelligence. Chief among these are *strategies*, *knowledge base*, and *metacognition*.

### *Strategies*

Strategies allow people to plan the course of their cognitive operations, to anticipate the consequences of their acts and the acts of others (see Chapter 7). Given this view, it is not surprising that many researchers have proposed that strategies are a central aspect of intelligence (Bray, Fletcher, & Turner, 1996; Das, 1984). For example, J. P. Das (1984) wrote, "What qualifies as intelligence may be the ability to plan or structure one's behavior with an end in view. The more efficient and parsimonious the plan is, the more intelligent the resulting behavior" (p. 116).

Differences in strategy implementation have been hypothesized to explain the difference in task performance between children with and without intellectual impairment, children with and without learning disabilities, good and poor readers, and gifted and nongifted children. For example, Richard Bauer (1979) gave 9- and 10-year-old children with and without learning disabilities a series of free-recall tasks. No group differences were found for the last several items on the lists. Recall for these last items was characteristically high and was attributed to children's emptying the contents of their short-term store, without the need of any specific strategy, termed a *recency effect*. In contrast, large group differences were noted in the recall of items from the beginning of the list. Recall of items from the beginning of a list has usually been interpreted as reflecting the use of strategies. In other words, the children with learning disabilities differed from the nondisabled children in strategy use but not in nonstrategic functioning. This interpretation was bolstered by the results of two subsequent experiments in which Bauer observed lower levels of categorical clustering (an indication of the memory strategy of organization; see Chapter 7) for the children with learning disabilities. Similar observations have been made for poor readers, who likewise show lower levels of memory performance than do good readers of equal IQ (Dallago & Moely, 1980; Goldstein, Hasher, & Stein, 1983).

In other research, Jane Gaultney (1998) statistically equated the amount of strategy use on memory tasks between third-, fourth-, and fifth-grade children with and without learning disabilities and found that children without learning disabilities benefited more from comparable strategy use than children with learning disabilities did. That is, even when children with learning disabilities were strategic (sometimes as strategic as nondisabled children), they didn't reap the benefits of the strategy in terms of memory performance compared to the children without learning disabilities. This is a utilization deficiency (see Chapter 7), and Gaultney proposed that the children with learning disabilities exerted more mental effort executing the memory strategies than the nondisabled children did and, as a result, had less mental capacity available for holding items in working memory.

Differences in strategy use are sometimes found to be a source of differences in task performance between gifted and nongifted children (Coyle et al., 1998; Gaultney, Bjorklund, & Goldstein, 1996). For example, in a series of free-recall experiments, Gaultney and her colleagues (1996) contrasted gifted and nongifted middle school children for their use of memory strategies and found that gifted children consistently were more likely to be strategic than were their nongifted peers. One interesting finding of their study was that, despite the greater use of strategies by gifted than by nongifted children, it was more important to task performance to be strategic for the nongifted children than for the gifted children. This is illustrated by looking at the average performance of children classified as strategic compared with those classified as nonstrategic for the gifted and nongifted children in this study. Figure 12-4 presents the mean difference in recall between the strategic and nonstrategic children through five trials for the gifted and the nongifted children. The higher the score, the greater advantage to recall there was for being strategic.

The first thing to note is that all the scores are positive (from a little over 1 word to about 3.5 words remembered per trial). This means that, on average, being strategic was always to a child's advantage. But look at the difference between the gifted and nongifted children. Except for the first trial, it made a greater difference in amount recalled for the nongifted children to be strategic than it did for the gifted children. That is, the difference between nongifted children who used a memory strategy and those who did not was quite large. This difference was much smaller for the gifted children.

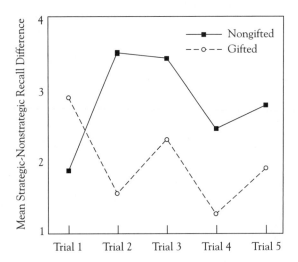

FIGURE **12-4**

Mean strategic minus nonstrategic difference in recall for gifted and nongifted children at each trial in the study by Gaultney and colleagues (1996). The higher the score, the greater the advantage for being strategic.

Source: Gaultney, J. F., Bjorklund, D. F., & Goldstein, D. (1996). To be young, gifted, and strategic: Advantages for memory performance. *Journal of Experimental Child Psychology, 61*, p. 51. Reprinted with permission.

Why should being strategic be more important for nongifted than gifted children? Gaultney and her colleagues (1996) proposed that many gifted children did not need strategies to perform reasonably well on this task. When nonstrategic gifted and nongifted children were compared, the gifted children did significantly better. Thus, according to Gaultney and her colleagues, much of the superior performance of the gifted children was mediated by nonstrategic factors, including, perhaps, faster speed of processing and a more elaborated knowledge base.

Interestingly, the tendency of many gifted children to "just know" an answer can sometimes have a negative side effect. For example, Katherine Kipp Harnishfeger and I (Harnishfeger & Bjorklund, 1990b) speculated that some gifted children have not needed to use deliberate learning and memory strategies during the elementary school years because they have been able to apprehend course material in a relatively automatic fashion. When the cognitive demands become more challenging in middle or high school, however, these children might be at a disadvantage relative to their lower-IQ but more strategic peers, accounting, in part, for some of the academic difficulties some gifted teenagers encounter. I have seen similar difficulties in some bright students making the transition from high school to college or from junior college to university.

In other research, David Geary and Sam Brown (1991) assessed third- and fourth-grade gifted children, nongifted children, and children with math disability for their selection and use of strategies in solving a series of addition problems. All the children used some combination of strategies to solve the problems, but the gifted children used the most mature mix of strategies, followed by the nongifted children and, finally, the children with math disability. Geary and Brown concluded that the principal reason for the group differences in strategy use in this experiment was children's long-term memory organization of basic addition facts. The gifted third- and fourth-grade children knew their basic math facts ($9 + 7 = 16$; $6 + 8 = 14$) better than did the other two groups of children, permitting them to use more efficient strategies. In other words, one of the reasons for gifted children's more effective use of strategies was their greater knowledge base.

### Knowledge Base

One factor that seems to make an important contribution to all other factors in terms of cognitive performance is *knowledge base*. What a person knows about the topic he or she is thinking or reasoning about greatly influences cognitive performance.

Just as developmental differences in cognition can be explained, in part, by differences in knowledge base (see Chapter 7), so can individual differences. For example, some researchers have suggested that memory differences between good and poor readers more likely stem from differences in knowledge base than from differences in strategy use. The semantic memories of poor readers are not as well developed as the semantic memories of good readers, resulting in the inefficient retrieval of word meaning from the long-term store and, thus, less effective processing of verbal information (Bjorklund & Bernholtz, 1986; Vellutino & Scanlon, 1985). Jean Bernholtz and I (Bjorklund & Bernholtz, 1986) illustrated this possibility by giving a series of concept and memory tasks to good and poor readers in junior high school (average age = 13 years) who were matched for IQ. In a first experiment, children were asked to select examples from specified natural language categories (for example, birds, clothes, tools) and to rate each item by how typical it was of its category. In general, differences in judged typicality affect the performance of both children and adults on a variety of tasks, and children's judgments become more adultlike with age. We reported that the judgments of the 13-year-old poor readers resembled those of typical 9-year-olds and were less adultlike than were the ratings of the good readers. In other words, differences in the semantic memory organization of good and poor 13-year-old readers were found with respect to category typicality.

In later experiments (see Experiments 3 and 4 in Bjorklund & Bernholtz, 1986), children were given sets of 12 typical and 12 atypical items to recall in any order they wanted. In one experiment, the typicality of the items was based on norms generated by adults (adult-generated lists). In another experiment, the typicality of the items was based on each child's self-generated norms, obtained from the earlier session (self-generated lists). Significant differences in memory performance were observed only for the adult-generated lists. Recall was comparable between the good and poor readers when typical and atypical category items were selected based on each child's own judgments. Furthermore, measures of strategy use in these experiments (based on amount of clustering and latencies between the recall of words) indicated that the good readers were no more strategic than the poor readers were. Rather, their superior memory performance could best be attributed to differences in knowledge base. These results do not mean that there are no strategic differences between good and poor readers. Rather, they indicate that differences in knowledge base contribute significantly to performance differences observed between these two groups of children and might be partly responsible for any apparent differences noted in strategy use.

One study that demonstrates the importance of knowledge base in learning and memory and its relation to IQ is that of Wolfgang Schneider, Joachim Körkel, and Franz Weinert (1989), discussed in Chapter 1. To reiterate, German children in grades 3, 5, and 7 were classified as either soccer experts or soccer novices and also classified as successful or unsuccessful learners based on IQ tests and their grades in school. The children then heard a story about a boy playing a soccer game and later asked to remember it. As you may recall from Chapter 1 (see Figure 1-8 on page 27), at every age, the soccer experts remembered more than the soccer novices, but, somewhat surprisingly, the academically unsuccessful learners remembered as much as the successful learners. In other words, knowing a lot about soccer was sufficient to produce high levels of recall, regardless of one's IQ or school-learning ability (see also Recht & Leslie, 1988; Walker, 1987). Although IQ might be related to academic performance, such as reading comprehension, what seems especially important for intelligent performance is knowledge. Children with substantial knowledge of a subject act smart when dealing with matter from that subject area, independent of their level of IQ.

This situation is admittedly not typical. In most contexts, successful learners do perform better than unsuccessful learners. One important reason why this is so, however, is that successful learners generally know more about the things they are dealing with than unsuccessful learners do. Successful learners acquire information more readily and, thus, have a more elaborated knowledge base on which to base future learning. The more children know, the more easily they are able to learn and remember new information.

A detailed knowledge base does not always eliminate IQ effects, however. Wolfgang Schneider and I (Schneider & Bjorklund, 1992; Schneider, Bjorklund & Maier-Brückner, 1996) classified high- and low-IQ second- and fourth-grade children as soccer experts or novices and gave them two sort-recall memory tasks. Children were given sets of written words to remember, which they could sort into categories before recalling them (see Chapter 7). On one task, stimuli were sets of soccer-related words in one of four categories (soccer plays, equipment, players, parts of the field); in the second task, sets of words from familiar language categories were used (tools, fruits, mammals, vehicles—the nonsoccer list). As in the study by Schneider and his colleagues (1989) that examined story recall, experts remembered more than novices did from the soccer-related list but not from the nonsoccer-related list. However, the effect of IQ was not eliminated in these studies, with high-IQ children remembering more than low-IQ children on both the soccer and nonsoccer lists, regardless of level of expertise. Schneider and I (Schneider & Bjorklund, 1992) argued that intelligence played a greater role here than in the story-recall experiment because of the more deliberate encoding strategies used on sort-recall tasks. Expertise can reduce or eliminate the impact of intelligence (as measured by IQ) in some situations, but IQ will have a residual effect when explicit strategies, such as those used in sort-recall tasks, are called for.

### *Metacognition*

One higher-level aspect of cognition that has been postulated as being significant to individual differences in intelligence is *metacognition,* a person's understanding of his or her own cognitive abilities. Basically, the brighter individuals of any age are those who possess the ability to monitor their task performance and to apply the techniques they possess to solve a problem. John Borkowski and his colleagues suggested that differences in metacognition are a major cause of differences in strategy use and training effectiveness between children with and without intellectual impairment (Borkowski, Reid, & Kurtz, 1984), between reflective and impulsive children (Borkowski et al., 1983), between gifted and nongifted children (Borkowski & Peck, 1986), and among children within the normal range of intelligence (Carr, Borkowski, & Maxwell, 1991).

This is illustrated in a study by Borkowski and Virginia Peck (1986), who instructed gifted and nongifted 7- and 8-year-olds to use an elaboration strategy or a simpler clustering strategy on a memory task. The children were later tested for transfer of the strategy to other memory problems. Elaboration involves creating a relationship between two items so that the presentation of one item elicits the recall of the other. For example, if I wanted to remember the pair of words *banana-coat,* I might form an image of a bunch of bananas hanging in the closet where I usually find my coat, or I might think that a banana peel covers a banana in a way similar to how a coat covers my body. Although forming such relations may seem like a lot of work, the memory performance of both children and adults is facilitated by the use of an elaboration strategy (see Pressley, 1982). For the children who received the clustering instructions (for example, "Try to remember words from the same category together"), training was less explicit than it was for the children who were trained to use the elaboration strategy. Would both the gifted and nongifted children be able to benefit from the training, and would the extent of training affect the transfer of the strategy differently for the two groups of children?

Both the gifted and the nongifted children who were trained in the elaboration strategy learned it. Differences between the groups for this strategy became apparent only during a generalization task, when the children were given different sets of problems to learn. The gifted children were more likely to generalize the strategy they had learned than were the nongifted children, with the extent of generalization being significantly related to scores on a battery of metacognition questions, specifically questions assessing their metamemory. For the clustering strategy, differences in training as well as transfer between the two groups of children were noted. The gifted children benefited more from the minimal training than did the nongifted children. This difference was extended to the transfer trials. That is, gifted children required less explicit prompting before they learned a strategy and generalized it to new situations, all relative to the nongifted children. According to Borkowski and Peck (1986), because of their greater metamemory awareness, "gifted children realized the effectiveness of the strategy and applied it appropriately even without the aid of complete and explicit instructions" (p. 193). Gifted children apparently do not always show greater metacognitive awareness relative to nongifted children (see Alexander & Schwanenflugel, 1996; Alexander, Schwanenflugel, & Carr, 1995), but when task performance is challenging, gifted children typically show greater metacognitive knowledge than their nongifted peers do (Kurtz & Weinert, 1989).

Although the picture is complex, information-processing models provide researchers with specific aspects of cognition to investigate the source of intellectual differences among people and experimental methods to facilitate the search. One integrated theory of intelligence that takes individual differences in information processing seriously is Robert Sternberg's triarchic theory, which we turn to now.

# STERNBERG'S TRIARCHIC THEORY OF INTELLIGENCE

Robert Sternberg's (1985) **triarchic theory of intelligence** includes three subtheories: (1) the contextual, (2) the experiential, and (3) the componential (see Table 12-2). Sternberg has revised his theory since its original inception (Cianciolo & Sternberg, 2004; Sternberg, 1999; Sternberg & the Rainbow Project Collaborators, 2006) and describes it now as the *triarchic theory of successful intelligence*. Sternberg defines successful intelligence as "the ability to achieve success in life in terms of one's personal standards, within one's sociocultural context" (Sternberg & the Rainbow Project Collaborators, 2006, p. 323). People's abilities to succeed require them to capitalize on their strengths and correct or compensate for their weakness; they need a balance of skills to adapt to, shape, and select environments. Success is attained via a balance of three aspects of intelligence: (1) practical skills, (2) creative skills, and (3) analytic skills. Each of these skills is examined in the following sections.

## The Contextual Subtheory, or Practical Intelligence

The **contextual subtheory** holds that intelligence must be viewed in the context in which it occurs. Intelligent behaviors for the middle-class American school child might not be considered intelligent for the ghetto dropout or the unschooled Guatemalan farm boy. By defining intelligence in terms of real-world environments, Sternberg stresses the importance of the external as well as the internal world to intelligence. Such a definition also avoids the circularity of theories that basically define intelligence as a score on an IQ test (or a test of information processing). In other words, intelligence can only be assessed in terms of the real-world problems that children experience, and it must be evaluated within a cultural context (Sternberg, 2004). Because people who are gifted in this subtheory have "street smarts," making an ideal fit between themselves and whatever context they find themselves in, this subtheory is sometimes called **practical intelligence**. People with practical intelligence may also excel in social intelligence. Most real-world contexts where intelligence is useful in

TABLE **12-2**

The componential (analytic), experiential (creative), and contextual (practical) subtheories/intelligence in Sternberg's triarchic theory of intelligence. Some examples related to a college course psychology are provided for each subtheory.

---

**Contextual (Practical) subtheory/intelligence:** Intelligence must be viewed in the context in which it occurs. This type of intelligence is involved in solving everyday problems, for example, "What would you do about a friend who has a substance-abuse problem," or "What are the implications for Freud's theory of dreaming for your life?" It has three subprocesses:

> *Adapting*: Adjusting one's behavior to obtain a good fit with one's environment.
> *Selecting*: Selecting an environment to obtain a good fit with one's abilities.
> *Shaping*: Modifying the behaviors and reactions of others so that they become more compatible to oneself.

**Experiential (Creative) subtheory/intelligence:** Examines how people deal with novel information and the extent to which they are able to *automatize* certain processes. For example, "Design a study to test a theory of language acquisition."

**Componential (Analytic) subtheory/intelligence:** A set of information-processing mechanisms that can be used in any environmental context or culture. This type of intelligence is involved in tasks requiring the analysis of information. For example, "Compare Piaget's theory of cognitive development to Vygotsky's." It has three components:

> *Metacomponents:* control, monitor, and evaluate task performance and allocate attentional resources.
> *Performance components:* Components that execute strategies assembled by the metacomponents. These include encoding, mental comparison, and retrieval of information.
> *Knowledge-acquisition components:* Components involved in acquiring new knowledge and selectively acting on newly acquired information.

---

Source: (adapted from Sternberg, R. J., Ferrari, M., & Clinkenbeard, P. (1996). Identification, instruction, and assessment of gifted children: A construct validation of a triarchic model. *Gifted Child Quarterly*, 40, 129–137; p. 131)

solving problems involve other people, and being able to deal effectively with other, sometimes contrary members of one's own species can be a sign of substantial practical intelligence.

Sternberg proposes three processes of intelligence within the contextual subtheory: (1) *adaptation,* (2) *selection,* and (3) *shaping.* Adaptation is adjustment of one's behavior to achieve a good fit with one's environment. For example, how effectively do children recognize that their attempts at joining a playgroup are not successful, and are they able to modify their behavior to become included in the games at recess and make new friends? When adaptation is not possible or is not desirable, a person can select an alternative environment in which he or she can adapt well. Failing to adapt to the whims of a new supervisor, for example, a person can choose to quit her job and select another. Or a child might find it difficult to get along with children in the neighborhood and instead become friendly with other children from school who do not live as close by. If for some reason a new environment cannot be selected, a person can attempt to shape the environment. The employee can try to convince her supervisor to change his ways or may go over his head to bring changes from above, and the child can try to alter the behavior of his neighborhood peers by placating them with his mother's cookies or by inviting one child at a time over to play instead of the entire group.

Although these three processes typify intelligence universally, what is required for adaptation, selection, and shaping will vary among different groups of people, so a single set of behaviors cannot be specified as intelligent for all individuals. Also, what is deemed intelligent at one point in life might not be so judged later. For example, because children have less freedom than adults do to select new environments and are often powerless to significantly shape certain aspects of these environments, adapting to their uncomfortable surroundings might be the most intelligent option they have. Thus, whereas the school-phobic adult will select nonacademic environments, the 10-year-old child typically cannot, making adaptation the most intelligent choice.

Basically, the contextual subtheory is one of **cultural relativism.** Intellectual skills that are critical for survival in one culture might not be as important in another. Likewise, important intellectual skills within a culture can undergo some change from one generation to another. For example, arithmetic computation has unquestionably been a vital skill for people in technological societies. Wechsler noted the significance of arithmetic to intelligence in the construction of the WISC and WAIS and in their subsequent revisions: Each has an arithmetic subtest. Yet, with the widespread use of calculators and computers, being able to add and subtract numbers quickly and accurately becomes a little less critical to everyday functioning. Although I would not care to say that arithmetic computation will become unimportant, it will probably be viewed by generations to come as being much less critical to intelligence than it is today, and it will certainly be seen as less important than it was a generation ago.

Sternberg is not the only person to propose a theory of intelligence that is culturally relative (see, for example, Laboratory of Comparative Human Cognition, 1983). Such theories have rightly been criticized, however, for preventing any general conclusions about the universal nature of human intellectual functioning. According to such theories, everything is relative; thus, intelligence can be studied only from the perspective of a particular culture or subculture. Sternberg avoids this problem by combining his contextual subtheory with the experiential and componential subtheories, which propose aspects of intelligence that are universal.

## The Experiential Subtheory, or Creative Intelligence

The **experiential subtheory** is concerned with how prior knowledge influences performance on certain cognitive tasks. More specifically, the subtheory examines the ability to deal with novelty and the degree to which processing is automatized (that is, made to involve relatively little mental effort). Both skills are highly dependent on experience. A stimulus is novel only to the extent that it differs from what is already familiar (Rheingold, 1985). Similarly, newly acquired processing skills are rarely executed effortlessly; rather, they require substantial expenditure of one's limited mental effort for their deployment. Only when a skill has been exercised frequently does it become automatized. Sternberg proposes that how people respond to novelty and the ease with which they can automatize information processing are important and universal aspects of intelligence. Because Sternberg believes that people who are gifted in the mechanisms of this subtheory are especially able to generate new ideas and solve novel problems, this subtheory is sometimes referred to as **creative intelligence**.

The importance of such skills is apparent in any occupation. Good scientists must be able to apprehend quickly the relevant factors that are influencing whatever phenomenon they are concerned with. If scientists are to make major contributions to their field, however, they must also be able to devise clever ways of testing their hypotheses and to appreciate the significance of an unexpected result. These factors are important not only in the "ivory tower" but also in more "worldly" occupations. This importance was made apparent to me by an electrician who installed three ceiling fans in my home after two other electricians had failed. He quickly discerned what approach to take, and after 9 hours of running into more obstacles than I knew existed in my walls and above my ceilings, he finished the task. After I expressed my appreciation for a job well done, the electrician commented: "Any yahoo can lay wire in a straight line. It only takes brains when things don't go as you planned."

The experiential subtheory suggests what tasks are good indicators of intelligence—namely, those that involve dealing with novelty or automatic processing for their successful completion. Many of the laboratory tasks of modern cognitive psychology are good candidates for assessing intelligence because they stress speed of responding, which is a good indicator of the extent to which processing has become automatized. For example, simple letter-identification tasks, in which people must respond as rapidly as possible to signal the presence of a specified letter, measure the degree to which processing for this overlearned code (the alphabet) is automatized. Similarly, word-identification tasks (deciding whether a letter string is a word or not) and category-identification tasks (deciding whether a word is a member of a specified category or not) also test automatic processing. More complex laboratory tasks, such as solving analogies or syllogisms, probably assess aspects of both automatic processing and response to novelty. Similarly, many items on psychometric batteries test the same processes as do laboratory tasks and, Sternberg (1985) asserts, are probably better estimators of intelligence than laboratory tasks. Why? Because these items are usually more difficult than the laboratory tasks, involving, on the average, greater degrees of novelty. Examples of psychometric test items that would fit Sternberg's experiential subtheory include picture arrangement ("Put these pictures together so that they make a story"), similarities ("How are television and education alike?"), and comprehension ("Why might it be important that Supreme Court judges be appointed and not elected?").

## The Componential Subtheory, or Analytic Intelligence

The **componential subtheory** is Sternberg's information-processing model of cognition. Sternberg (1997) argues that intelligence has a common core of mental processes that can be used in any environmental context or culture. These include recognizing the existence and defining the nature of a problem, representing information about the problem, devising a strategy for solving the problem, allocating sufficient mental resources to solve the problem, and monitoring and evaluating one's solution to the problem. How does one go about doing all these things? Basically, they require different aspects of information processing. Because a person gifted in information-processing abilities is able to take apart, or analyze, problems and see solutions that are not seen by less-gifted individuals, Sternberg refers to this type of thinking as **analytic intelligence.**

Briefly, Sternberg proposed three general types of information-processing components: (1) metacomponents, (2) performance components, and (3) knowledge-acquisition components. *Metacomponents* allocate attentional resources and control, monitor, and evaluate task performance. These reflect *metacognition.* Are people aware about their progress on a task? Do they need to slow down, alter a strategy, or attend more to some aspects of a task or situation than to others? *Performance components* execute strategies assembled by the metacomponents and include encoding the to-be-processed information ("The letters l-i-o-n spell a word I know"), retrieving information ("Lions live in Africa and hunt in packs"), and making mental comparison ("A lion is like a cat in some ways"). *Knowledge components* are involved in acquiring new knowledge and in selectively acting on newly acquired information. Individual differences in these three interacting components influence how people process information and, thus, how they solve problems, which is what human intelligence is "for."

What causes people to get smarter with age? The simple answer from Sternberg's theory is knowledge. We saw in Chapter 7 that the more a person knows about a particular topic, the more efficiently he or she can process information within that domain. For example, children who know a great deal about dinosaurs, or dinosaur experts, can incorporate new information about dinosaurs more effectively than a novice. This involves the knowledge-acquisition components in Sternberg's theory. Dinosaur experts know how to categorize a new species and know many details about the extinct beasts (their diets, habitats, and offensive and defensive weapons). This in turn makes it easier for them to acquire new knowledge, further enhancing processing efficiency (via the performance components in Stenberg's theory). New knowledge also serves to enhance the metacomponents, leading to greater self-awareness about the topic ("I'm not really sure if triceratops and stegosaurus lived at the same time, come to think about it"), which in turn results in the increased effectiveness of the metacomponents. This interaction of the subcomponents of the componential subtheory is shown in the bottom portion of Figure 12-5.

The various mechanisms of the different subtheories also interact, as seen in Figure 12-5. The information-processing components are applied differently depending if the task is a highly familiar one (classifying dinosaurs for our dinosaur expert) or an unfamiliar one (learning how to make chocolate-chip cookies). In one setting (classifying dinosaurs), much processing would be automatic, whereas in the other (baking cookies), the novelty of the task would require more deliberate and effortful problem solving. Finally, we must evaluate the context in which these aspects of intelligence are applied (during play, in school, with or without adult help) and how children adapt, select, or shape the contexts in which they live.

Sternberg's theory has been a popular one with psychologists and educators since its inception in the mid-1980s. He has applied it directly to education, developing techniques to assess children's intellectual strengths and weaknesses and school curricula to maximize learning. Some of this research is discussed in Box 12-1. In some sense, Sternberg is arguing for educating "the whole child," instructing children in the use of their analytic intelligence, their creative intelligence, and their practical intelligence, which differs from the one-track emphasis of curricula based on a "general ability" (g) theory of intelligence.

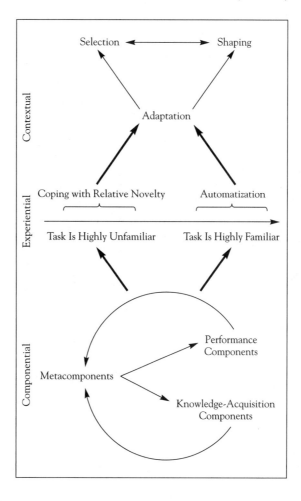

FIGURE **12-5**

Relationships among the various aspects of the triarchic theory of intelligence.

Source: Sternberg, R. J. (1988). *The triarchic mind: A new theory of human intelligence.* New York: Viking. Reprinted with permission of the author.

## GARDNER'S THEORY OF MULTIPLE INTELLIGENCES

Howard Gardner (1983, 1993, 1999) has proposed that intelligence is comprised of separate components, or modules, much like the concept of factors used by the psychometric approach. Gardner's **theory of multiple intelligences** (referred to as *MI* by its practitioners) is different, however, because it relies heavily on neuropsychological evidence for the existence of relatively independent "frames of mind." Gardner originally proposed seven such abilities but has since added one more and has speculated about a ninth (Gardner, 1999): (1) linguistic, (2) logical-mathematical, (3) musical, (4) spatial, (5) bodily-kinesthetic, (6) interpersonal, (7) intrapersonal, (8) naturalist, and (possibly) (9) spiritual/existential. Linguistic and logical-mathematical intelligences are highly valued in technological societies such as ours, and people high in these

| BOX 12-1 | The Triarchic Theory Goes to School |
|---|---|

If people do, indeed, have different intellectual patterns based around Sternberg's three thinking styles (practical, creative, and analytic), then people who receive instruction that matches their preferred style should learn more easily than do people who receive instruction that does not match. To assess this hypothesis, one must first generate a test to assess thinking style, then develop a curriculum tailored to each style of thinking, and finally, adequately assess how much was learned as a result of matched versus mismatched instruction. Sternberg and his colleagues (1996) did just that in a study with 199 gifted high school students.

Gifted high school students attended an intense, 4-week, summer college-level course in introductory psychology. Students' thinking style was evaluated as either practical, creative, analytic, or balanced (that is, similar on all three styles). All students were assigned the same textbook and attended the same morning lecture series. Instruction varied, however, during afternoon sessions, with students receiving instruction that either matched their preferred style (for example, analytic style-analytic instruction) or not (for example, creative style-analytic instruction). Examples of the type of tasks that would exemplify each of the three thinking style types are shown in Table 12-2. Course performance was assessed by multiple-choice exams; homework assignments that evaluated practical, creative, or analytic thinking; and essay exams that asked for either practical, creative, or analytic responses.

Children were administered an abbreviated version of the *Sternberg Triarchic Abilities Test (STAT)*. This test assessed the three basic types of thinking styles (practical, creative, and analytic) for three types of content (verbal, quantitative, and figural), resulting in nine subtests. Examples for each thinking style for the verbal content are:

- *Practical-Verbal:* Students were presented with some everyday problems in the life of an adolescent and asked to come up with a solution (for example, what would you do about a friend who has a substance-abuse problem?).
- *Creative-Verbal:* Students were given verbal analogies preceded by false premises (for

example, money falls off trees) and had to solve the analogies as if the false premises were true.
- *Analytic-Verbal:* Students had to figure out the meaning of artificial words from a natural context. Students would see a novel word used in a paragraph and would have to infer the meaning of the word from the context. (Sternberg et al., 1996, p. 131)

Sternberg and his colleagues reported that the three subsections of the STAT (practical, creative, and analytic) had low to moderate correlations with one another. When factor-analytic techniques were applied to the data, nine factors emerged (one for each thinking-style × content combination). According to Sternberg and his colleagues, these findings indicate that "clearly, the STAT is not just another measure of Spearman's (1927) *g* (general ability)" (Sternberg et al., 1996, p. 134). Most psychometric tests load heavily on *g* likely because of the relatively narrow range of abilities tested—not because it underlies *all* intellectual functioning.

Sternberg and his colleagues next correlated children's STAT scores with their performance in the course and found moderate but significant correlations between scores on each of the three subtests and course performance (correlations ranged from .24 to .42). More critical, however, was the performance of students whose thinking style matched the instruction they received. The results here were quite consistent: Students who received instruction matched to their thinking style performed significantly better than did mismatched students. Moreover, the same pattern of results was found not just for the homework and essay assessments (some of which would have matched children's thinking style) but for the multiple-choice items as well.

In subsequent research, Sternberg, Bruce Torff, and Elena Grigorenko (1998) designed, based on the triarchic theory, a social-studies curriculum for third-grade children (Study 1) and an introductory psychology curriculum for advanced eighth-grade children (Study 2). Unlike their earlier research (Sternberg et al., 1996), the curriculum in each study involved all three aspects of thinking for all students. Course performance was contrasted

*(Continues)*

| **BOX 12-1** | **The Triarchic Theory Goes to School** (*Continued*) |

among students who had the triarchic instructions, those who had special instruction in critical thinking, and those who received a traditional curriculum. The results of the research were consistent across the two studies: Students who received the triarchic instruction performed better on a variety of dependent measures than did children who received either the critical thinking or traditional curricula (although those receiving the critical thinking curriculum usually performed better than did those receiving the traditional one). To top it off, third-grade children given the triarchic instruction enjoyed the course more than the other students did.

More recently, Sternberg and his colleagues have developed an assessment device to serve as a college entrance exam (Sternberg & The Rainbow Project Collaborators, 2006). They administered a modified version of the STAT to nearly 1000 students in their first year of college and evaluated how well it predicted first-year GPA in comparison to high school grades and scores on the SAT. They reported that the triarchic measure doubled the amount of variance in college GPA accounted for by the SAT alone. Moreover, the STAT reduced differences among ethnic groups (who generally score lower on standardized tests, such as the SAT) in predicting GPA, making "a compelling case for furthering the study of the measurement of analytic, creative, and practical skills for predicting success in college" (p. 344).

types of intelligence are generally viewed as smart. Musical intelligence is usually associated with the composition or performance of music, and spatial intelligence involves the ability to perceive form, solve visual problems, and get around effectively in one's environment. Bodily-kinesthetic intelligence is reflected in control of one's body, as epitomized by athletes of exceptional ability. The two forms of personal intelligence involve knowing how to deal with others (interpersonal) and knowledge of one's self (intrapersonal). Naturalistic intelligence concerns knowledge of the natural world (fauna and flora), and spiritual/existential intelligence deals with issues related to the meaning of life (and death) and other aspects of the ultimate human condition. Table 12-3. summarizes the various types of intelligences, lists people who excel in each type, and provides the neurological system hypothesized to underlie each intelligence.

Gardner's claim is not that these are eight (or nine) different components of a single intelligence but, rather, that these represent eight distinct intelligences, each being independent of the others. And there may be more. Gardner's proposal is for different, domain-specific forms of intelligence—the antithesis of *g*-based theories. For Gardner, each form of intelligence represents a modular, brain-based capacity. Gardner asserts that these various forms of intelligence have different degrees of importance in different cultures and at different times in history. For example, in a hunting society, physical dexterity, an ability to locomote effectively, and an understanding of one's natural surroundings are more important than numerical computation skills. In medieval Europe's apprenticeship system, emphasis was placed on bodily, spatial, and interpersonal abilities, whereas in today's Western society, 400 years later, the emphasis is on linguistic and logical-mathematical skills. Thus, Gardner views the cultural aspects of intelligence to be of utmost importance: Different cultures value different types of intelligence. Moreover, Gardner argues that our society's reliance on IQ tests to classify children by intelligence does a great disservice to many of them and to society itself. Because these tests emphasize linguistic and mathematical abilities, children

TABLE **12-3**

A list of multiple intelligences in Gardner's theory: Their definition, people who exemplify them, and their theorized neurological locus.

| Intelligence | Definition | People who exemplify this intelligence | Neurological system hypothesized to be associated with this intelligence |
|---|---|---|---|
| Linguistic | Sensitive to meaning and order of words | Maya Angelou (poet) Stephen King (writer) Martin Luther King (civil rights leaders and orator) | Left hemisphere, temporal and frontal lobes |
| Logical-mathematical | Ability to reason logically and recognize patterns and order | Bill Gates (former CEO of Microsoft) Stephen Hawking (physicist) James Watson (biologist) | Left parietal lobe; left hemisphere for verbal naming; right hemisphere for spatial organization; frontal system for planning |
| Musical | Sensitivity to pitch, melody, rhythm, and tone | Yo Yo Ma (cellist) Mariah Carey (singer) Wolfgang Amadeus Mozart (composer) | Right anterior temporal: frontal lobes |
| Bodily-kinesthetic | Ability to use one's body skillfully and handle objects adroitly | David Copperfield (magician) LeBron James (basketball player) Debbie Allen (dancer) | Cerebral motor strip; thalamus; basal ganglia; cerebellum |
| Spatial | Ability to perceive physical environment accurately and to re-create or transform aspects of that environment | Frank Lloyd Wright (architect) Pablo Picasso (painter) Georgia O'Keefe (painter) | Right hemisphere, parietal occipital lobe |
| Naturalist | Ability to recognize and classify numerous species of flora and fauna | Charles Darwin (biologist) Jane Goodall (primatologist) E. O. Wilson (biologist) | Left parietal lobe (discriminating living from nonliving) |
| Interpersonal | Ability to understand people and relationships | Barack Obama (politician) Ronald Reagan (politician) Hillary Clinton (diplomat) | Frontal lobes |
| Intrapersonal | Access to one's emotional life as a means to understand oneself and others | Oprah Winfrey (talk show host) Bono (singer, philanthropist) | Frontal lobes |
| Spiritual/Existential | Individuals who exhibit the proclivity to pose (and ponder) questions about life, death, and ultimate realities. | Albert Einstein (scientist) Socrates (philosopher) Dalai Lama (monk) | Hypothesized as specific region in the right temporal lobe |

Source: (Adapted from Gardner, H. (1983). *Frames of mind: The theory of multiple intelligences.* New York: Basic; Gardner, H. (1999). Are there additional intelligences? The case for naturalist, spiritual, and existential intelligences. In J. Kane (Ed.), *Education, information and transformation.* Engelwood Cliffs, NJ: Prentice-Hall.)

gifted in other areas, such as working with their hands, are often "thrown on society's scrap heap" instead of receiving the education that could enhance their special abilities.

## Criteria of an Intelligence

On what basis did Gardner select his list of intelligences? To answer this question, Gardner (1983) provides a set of criteria that must be met for an ability to be considered an intelligence. Each of these criteria does not have to be met for an ability to be classified as an intelligence, but these are the criteria that Gardner lists "by which each candidate intelligence can be judged" (p. 66).

### *Potential Isolation by Brain Damage*

Ample evidence indicates that damage to specified areas of the brain can selectively impair language production or comprehension. Similar evidence abounds for mathematical, musical, and spatial abilities. Evidence even suggests that damage to the frontal lobes of the neocortex can leave general intellectual functioning unimpaired but produce a socially tactless individual, affecting interpersonal intelligence. The frontal cortex plays an important role in the inhibition of task-irrelevant and inappropriate responses (see Chapters 2 and 7), and many of those inappropriate responses that are no longer inhibited occur in social situations (Fuster, 1989).

### *The Existence of Savants and Prodigies*

An intelligence is reflected by exceptionalities and, thus, can be exhibited by savants and prodigies. *Savants* (sometimes called *idiot savants*) are people with intellectual impairment but who possess an exceptional talent in a single domain. Savants have been identified for several skills, most notably mathematics and music. For example, the neurologist Oliver Sacks (1985), in his book *The Man Who Mistook His Wife for a Hat*, describes John and Michael, 26-year-old twin brothers who had been in institutions since the age of 7, diagnosed at various times as autistic, psychotic, or intellectually impaired. John and Michael were already well known for their extraordinary facility with the calendar, a skill possessed by many savants, being able to provide quickly the day of the week for any date in history (for example, December 9, 1786, a Saturday). Working with these young men, Sacks discovered several other remarkable abilities. For example, the twins would sometimes play a game in which they said numbers to one another and smile. Sacks wrote: "John would say a number—a six-figure number. Michael would catch the number, nod, smile and seem to savour it. Then he, in turn, would say another six-figure number, and now it was John who received, and appreciated it richly. They looked, at first, like two connoisseurs wine-tasting, sharing rare tastes, rare appreciations. I sat still, unseen by them, mesmerised, bewildered" (pp. 201–202). Although it took some detective work for Sacks to figure out what the twins were doing, it turned out that the numbers that brought smiles were all, and only, prime numbers.

Savants are perhaps most impressive when it comes to musical ability. There have been numerous newspaper articles and television stories about people with severe mental retardation who can play Beethoven piano sonatas after hearing them only once. Although these are impressive abilities, what is customarily lacking in savants is creativity. To my knowledge, there have been no musical savants who also compose great music or who are great improvisers, only those with an outstanding ability to play back accurately what they have heard.

The *prodigy* is on the other side of the coin from the savant. A prodigy is a child with generally normal abilities in all but a small number of areas (usually one). Similar to savants, prodigies are most frequently found in the areas of mathematics and music. Wolfgang Amadeus Mozart was the quintessential musical prodigy. Raised in a musical family, he, while still a preschooler, was playing instruments and composing music at a level few humans ever attain. He was touring the great capitals of Europe by age 8, but aside from his musical prowess, Wolfgang was a normal boy. This is shown in an observation made in 1764 by Daines Barrington (cited in Gould, 1992), who was impressed by the 8-year-old Mozart's musical skill but who also noted that music seemed to be the only area in which Mozart was exceptional:

> I must own that I could not help suspecting his father imposed with regard to the real age of the boy, though he had not only a most childish appearance, but likewise had all the actions of that stage of life. For example, whilst he was playing to me, a favorite cat came in, upon which he immediately left his harpsichord, nor could we bring him back for a considerable time. He would also sometimes run about the room with a stick between his legs by way of horse. (p. 10)

Why do savants and prodigies indicate multiple intelligences? Gardner believes that such exceptionalities reflect modular, brain-based skills. The savant and the prodigy are only extreme examples of unevenness in abilities, but their existence suggests that the special skills they possess are domain-specific and can be found in lesser degrees of development in the vast normal range of the human population.

### An Identifiable Core Operation or Set of Operations

Consistent with modern cognitive science, Gardner believes that each intelligence should have associated with it one or more basic information-processing operations, specialized to deal with a particular type of input (language, music, and so on). For example, sensitivity to pitch relations would be a core operation for musical intelligence, and the ability to imitate movements made by others would be central to bodily intelligence.

### A Distinctive Developmental History, Along with a Definable Set of Expert End-State Performances

An intelligence must develop. Any skill that is present fully formed when it first appears does not qualify as a type of intelligence. Also, it must have an identifiable end-state—that is, a level of performance attainable by mature experts. We can certainly specify a developmental course and an expert end-state for most, if not all, of Gardner's intelligences. The gifted writer or speaker serves as the expert for verbal intelligence, as does the mathematician for logical-mathematical intelligence, the professional athlete or dancer for bodily intelligence, the composer or musician for musical intelligence, the visual artist or trail guide for spatial intelligence, perhaps the skilled politician or therapist for interpersonal intelligence, the philosopher for intrapersonal intelligence, the biologist (or possibly the hunter or farmer) for naturalist intelligence, and religious leaders for spiritual/existential intelligence. Some of these intelligences can have different developmental courses, leading to slightly different expert end-states, with developmental milestones along the way from immature to mature performance.

### An Evolutionary History and Evolutionary Plausibility

Why do humans possess these intelligences? Human intelligence is a significant part of the human condition, and it likely played an important role in the evolution of our species. As such, there should be some evolutionary history of an intelligence (and perhaps evidence of antecedents of these abilities in other species) and a plausible evolutionary explanation of how these intelligences may have been selected. We clearly share social skills and social organization with our primate cousins (see Byrne & Whiten, 1988; Kappeler & Silk, 2010) and spatial and bodily intelligence with most large mammals.

Even abilities that might be unique to humans, such as music (although this is debated), have an evolutionary plausibility. Music is an important part of contemporary humans' lives. We fall in love to music, praise God to music, and go to war to music. (I love Woody Allen's line, directly related to this last point: "Every time I hear Wagner, I get the urge to invade Poland.") Although I find it hard to find phylogenetic antecedents to music (my guess is that it grew out of general language ability), it is easy to see how once the ability evolved, those who had control of music could have an important social (or perhaps sexual) advantage relative to others.

### Support from Experimental Psychological Tasks and from Psychometric Findings

Psychologists from both the psychometric and cognitive-experimental approaches have been studying tasks that assess at least some of the eight intelligences, and findings from these literatures should reveal important individual differences. Psychologists have most often studied tasks assessing language, spatial, and mathematical abilities.

### Susceptibility to Encoding in a System

One of the hallmarks of human cognitive functioning is that it is based on symbols. Ideally, an intelligence should have its own symbol system. This seems to be true for language, mathematics, and music, and perhaps for spatial and bodily intelligence.

## Multiple Intelligences and Education

Gardner argues for the exclusion of intelligence and aptitude tests from our schools because, as currently practiced, they measure only two types of intelligence and ignore other, equally important types. Gardner is not opposed to intellectual assessment in general, however. He advocates the development of measures that would evaluate all types of intelligence. He believes that such assessments should be done early so that intellectual strengths can be discovered and developed through education. Although Gardner believes that each form of intelligence has its origins in biology, he also believes that they are flexible and can be enhanced by education.

Gardner's theory has been perhaps the most widely applied theory of intelligence to education since the advent of the psychometric approach over 100 years ago. The theory has been applied and evaluated in hundreds, if not thousands, of schools in North America and Europe, mostly in kindergarten through 12th grade (see Cuban, 2004; Hoerr, 2004) but also in college and graduate education (Díaz-LeFebvre, 2004;

Shore, 2004) and in special populations, such as second-language learners (Haley, 2004) and children with ADHD (Schirduan & Case, 2004).

Table 12-4 presents some of the distinctions between a traditional classroom and one based on multiple intelligences (from Hoerr, 2004). Typically, curricula based on the theory of multiple intelligences give children substantial freedom to explore a range of topics, with many hands-on opportunities. Although textbooks may be used, teachers are more apt to create their own curricula, working with their students and other teachers. Children, rather than the curriculum, are the center of a multiple-intelligences classroom, with individual differences in intellectual abilities being valued.

## Assessment of Gardner's Theory

Gardner's theory has attracted a lot of attention since its inception in 1983. I find that of all the theories of intelligence I discuss in class, Gardner's is usually my students' favorite. But the merits of a theory are not determined by popular vote. In fact, a claim often made against Gardner's theory is that it is not testable—that it is not really a theory but a framework about what is and what is not an intelligence. Yet, even here there is room for debate. For example, chess performance would fit many of the criteria set by Gardner to qualify as a candidate for an intelligence: There are chess prodigies, chess has a developmental history with an expert end-state, and chess ability perhaps meets other criteria (symbol systems, core set of operations). It does not have a plausible evolutionary explanation, however, and rightly seems not to be an intelligence. Also, Gardner's theory includes abilities that most people have not

TABLE **12-4**

Some Differences Between a Traditional Classroom and one Based on Multiple Intelligences (MI).

| In a Traditional Classroom | In a Multiple Intelligences (MI) Classroom |
|---|---|
| Kids with strong scholastic intelligence are smart, and the other kids aren't | Everyone has a different profile of intelligence: we are all smart in different ways. |
| Teachers create a hierarchy of intellect. | Teachers use all students' intelligences to help them learn. |
| The classroom is curriculum centered. | The classroom is child centered. |
| Teachers help students acquire information and facts. | Teachers help students create meaning in a constructivist way. |
| The focus is on the scholastic intelligences, the three *Rs*. | Personal Intelligences are valued: Who you are is more important than what you know. |
| Teachers work from texts. | Teachers create curriculum-lessons, units, themes. |
| Teachers assess students by paper-and-pencil, "objective" measures. | Teachers create assessment tools—projects, exhibitions, presentations (PEPs)—which incorporate MI. |
| Teachers close the door and work in isolation | Teachers work with colleagues in using MI, developing collegiality. |

Source: (from Hoerr, T. (2004). How MI informs teaching at New City School. *Teachers College Record*, 106, 40–48.)

traditionally considered to be in the realm of intelligence. Musical talent has always been recognized as something special but also usually as something distinct from intelligence. And although athletic ability and bodily control are certainly important human characteristics, they are not typically considered to be mental operations in the way that mathematical computation and verbal comprehension, which have been at the center of the definition of intelligence, are.

In many ways, Gardner's theory is an extension of the domain-specific theories of psychometricians such as Guilford. Gardner's considerable contribution has been getting people to look for evidence beyond psychometric testing, placing intelligence in the realm of both biology and culture, where it belongs. Gardner's ideas have been very influential, particularly in educational circles. Gardner might, indeed, find greater independence of intellectual abilities than *g* theorists typically do, and one reason for this might be that Gardner includes a broader range of abilities than conventional psychometric theorists. Thus, part of Gardner's appeal is his broader definition of intelligence. However, this may also be part of the difficulty in evaluating his theory.

The book is not closed on the nature of intelligence. Sternberg and Gardner make it clear that intelligence is a many-splendored thing—that any theorist who proposes intelligence is a single phenomenon that influences all aspects of intellectual functioning equally is just not looking at the data (see also Ceci, 1996). Yet, the evidence of the positive manifold and the fact that basic cognitive processes such as individual differences in working memory do predict IQ-test performance relatively well, for example, argue that there might be some general, cross-domain mechanisms that influence, to various degrees, most if not all cognitive task performance. I do not plan to provide my own theory of intelligence here. But it is clear to me that intelligence is multifaceted, and that intellectual functioning varies considerably as a function of a person's knowledge and the context in which the cognitive operations were acquired and are assessed. Yet, certain aspects of information processing also appear to be domain general and will influence task performance to a significant degree in a variety of contexts. Factors such as motivation and practice are critically important, and even at their best, measures of basic information processing cannot account for all, or even most, of the variance in intellectual development. The most tenable position from my point of view is that some aspects of human intelligence are domain general in nature, whereas others are domain specific in nature.

# SUMMARY

*Intelligence* is generally understood to reflect goal-directed and adaptive functioning. The primary approach to the study of individual differences in intelligence has been the *psychometric* (or *differential*) *approach.* Intelligence is described in terms of *factors,* or sets of related abilities that can be discerned on tests by the statistical technique of *factor analysis.* The most general factor is called *g,* or *general intelligence,* which describes a domain-general mechanism that influences thinking on all tasks. Others have divided intelligence into two general factors: *fluid abilities,* which are biologically determined and reflected by tests of memory span, speed of processing, and spatial thinking; and *crystallized abilities,* which are more highly dependent on experience and are reflected in tests of verbal comprehension or social relations. The best evidence for the existence of *g* is the *positive manifold,* the fact that a person's performances on a variety of different cognitive tasks tend to be similar. The *hierarchical model of cognitive abilities* proposes four related sets of cognitive skills (verbal, spatial thinking, speed of processing, and memory) that are all influenced by a general intellectual factor. The impact of the psychometric approach has been most strongly expressed in *IQ tests,* which assess intellectual abilities relative to a normative population. Frequently used IQ tests are the *Stanford-Binet* and *Wechsler scales* (WPPSI, WISC, WAIS), both of which are individually administered and highly standardized. Infant intelligence has been expressed in terms of *DQ (developmental quotient) tests.* IQs were originally derived based on a ratio between *mental age* and chronological age. Modern tests abandoned the concept of mental age and developed the *deviation IQ.*

IQ scores predict academic performance, occupational status, and longevity relatively well. The IQ test has been criticized as being inappropriate for minority children, who may misinterpret the testing situation and illustrate *stereotype threat,* in which minority members perform worse on IQ tests after being reminded of the negative stereotype concerning their groups' performance on such tests. Teachers' expectations for their students' academic performance can also influence children's accomplishments and even their IQ scores, which is termed the *Pygmalion effect.*

Information-processing approaches to intelligence provide researchers with well-developed theories and methods for assessing individual differences in intelligence. Differences in speed of processing, working memory, executive function, strategy use, knowledge base, and metacognition have been suggested as the basis for individual differences in children's thinking. Developmental psychologists often use information-processing paradigms to explain differences in the thinking of children of different IQ levels (children with and without intellectual impairment) and children of comparable IQ levels but differential academic abilities (for example, children with and without learning disabilities).

Sternberg's *triarchic theory of intelligence* consists of three subtheories: *contextual, experiential,* and *componential,* each with a characteristic thinking style (*practical, creative,* and *analytic,* respectively). The contextual subtheory states that intelligence must be evaluated in the environment in which the individual lives, which by itself reflects a form of *cultural relativism.* The experiential subtheory proposes that how people deal with novelty and the extent to which they can automatize cognitive functioning are important aspects of intelligence. The componential subtheory describes three universal information-processing mechanisms by which knowledge is acquired and manipulated. The theory is an attempt to go beyond earlier approaches by viewing intelligence from a wider scope, and it has been successfully applied to educational settings.

Gardner's *theory of multiple intelligences* relies heavily on neuropsychological evidence and postulates eight (and possibly nine) distinct forms of intelligence: linguistic, logical-mathematical, musical, spatial, bodily-kinesthetic, interpersonal, intrapersonal, and naturalistic (and possibly spiritual/existential). Gardner lists several criteria of an intelligence, including potential isolation by brain damage, the existence of savants and prodigies, an identifiable set of operations, developmental history, an evolutionary history and plausibility, support from experimental and psychometric tasks, and susceptibility to an encoding system. Like Sternberg's theory, Gardner's theory has frequently been applied to educational settings.

# KEY TERMS AND CONCEPTS

| | | | |
|---|---|---|---|
| intelligence | positive manifold | deviation IQ | experiential subtheory (or creative intelligence) |
| psychometric approach (or differential approach) | hierarchical model of cognitive abilities | stereotype threat | |
| | | Pygmalion effect | componential subtheory (or analytic intelligence) |
| | IQ (Intelligent Quotient) tests | triarchic theory of intelligence | |
| factors | Stanford-Binet | contextual subtheory (or practical intelligence) | |
| factor analysis | Wechsler scales | | theory of multiple intelligences |
| *g* (or general intelligence) | developmental quotient (DQ). | cultural relativism | |
| fluid abilities | mental age | | |
| crystallized abilities | | | |

# SUGGESTED READINGS

## Scholarly Work

Alloway, T. P., & Alloway, R. G. (2010). Investigating the predictive roles of working memory and IQ in academic attainment. *Journal of Experimental Child Psychology*, *106*, 20–29. This study reports research demonstrating the important role of working memory on children's academic performance, predicting school abilities better even than IQ.

Blair, C. (2006). How similar are fluid cognition and general intelligence? A developmental neuroscience perspective on fluid cognition as an aspect of human cognitive ability. *Behavioral and Brain Sciences*, *29*, 109–160. This article examines the relation between fluid intelligence and *g*, examines the cognitive mechanisms involved in intelligence (for example, working memory and executive function), and presents a neurological model to account for the findings. This target article is followed by 19 commentaries, reflecting the controversy that surrounds the concept of general intelligence.

Shearer, B. (2004). Multiple intelligences theory after 20 years. *Teachers College Record*, *106*, 2–16. This is the organizing paper in a special issue the *Teachers College Record* that devotes 10 articles to reviewing aspects of Gardner's theory of multiple intelligences and its application to education. Most authors are staunch supporters of the theory, but several of the articles provide critical evaluation.

Sternberg, R. J., & the Rainbow Project Collaborators (2006). The Rainbow Project: Enhancing the SAT through assessments of analytical, practical, and creative skills. *Intelligence*, *34*, 321–350. This article reviews Sternberg's triarchic theory of successful intelligence and presents the results of a study using the theory to develop an assessment device that improves prediction of success in college.

## Reading for Personal Interest

Nisbett, R. E. (2009). *Intelligence and how to get it: Why schools and cultures count*. New York: Norton. In this highly readable book, social psychologist Richard Nisbett explores the roles of genes, family, schools, and culture on the development of intelligence. He explores many of the issues that I examine in the final three chapters of this book, including the effects of schooling on intelligence, why children from different cultures often seem "smarter" than children from other cultures, and the Flynn effect, among others.

# Origins, Modification, and Stability of Intellectual Differences

**A Transactional Approach to the Study of Intelligence**

**Behavioral Genetics and the Heritability of Intelligence**
The Concept of Heritability
Elementary Cognitive Tasks and Intelligence
Familial Studies of Intelligence
The Role of the Environment in Behavioral Genetics Analyses
How Seriously Should We Take Heritability Studies of IQ?

**Experience and Intelligence**
Establishing Intellectual Competence
Modification and Maintenance of Intellectual Functioning

How Modifiable Is Human Intelligence?

**The Stability of Intelligence**
Defining Stability
Predicting Later Intelligence from Tests in Infancy
The Stability of IQ Scores During Childhood
Patterns of IQ Change During Childhood
    **BOX 13-1:** Are People Getting Smarter? The Flynn Effect

SUMMARY
KEY TERMS AND CONCEPTS
SUGGESTED READINGS

Emily and Alexandra were cousins, born the same month, and had attended the same school since kindergarten. As often as not, they were in the same class. Although they shared many friends and some interests (Emily was more into sports than Alexandra, and beginning in sixth grade, Alexandra was more interested in fashion and boys than Emily was), they differed consistently in their academic performance. Alexandra was usually near the top of her class and, in fact, became upset when she received grades below a B. Emily had always been a bit more laid-back about school. She did well in most of her courses but was generally in the middle of her class in terms of grades, and she rarely got upset when she received a poor grade. (In fact, in third grade, Emily tried to soothe a distressed Alexandra, who had received a C on a major math test, by telling her, "That's OK. A C's not so bad. I get Ds and Fs a lot, and nothing really bad ever happens." Both teachers' assessments and scores on standardized tests indicated that Alexandra was gifted, whereas Emily was average in intelligence. Differences in the girls' intellectual performance and academic abilities had been apparent since they started school, if not before, and remained relatively constant through high school.

Everyone knows that, at any age, some children are smarter than others. The last chapter focused on how such individual differences can be conceptualized and measured. Although the measurement of individual differences in intelligence has fascinated researchers and educators for years, an even more basic question is "What are the origins of individual differences in children's thinking?" Why, for example, does Alexandra seem smarter than Emily? As with many things in psychology, there are two extreme camps. On one side—the *nature* side—individual differences in intelligence are viewed as part of our biological heritage, with experience playing only a minor role. That is, people are born smart or not so smart, and this is a stable characteristic across the life span (Jensen, 1998). On the other side—the *nurture* side—individual differences in intelligence are viewed as being highly influenced by experience. That is, our environments make us smart or not so smart, we can increase (or decrease) our intelligence through experience, and intelligence is not even stable across situations, let alone years (Ceci, 1996). These are socially and educationally important issues. How we view intelligence in terms of its origins (What are the seeds of intelligence?) and its modifiability (Can intelligence be enhanced through education and, if so, how much?) affects real-world decisions, particularly as they relate to education and one's occupation.

As I mentioned in Chapter 1, developmental psychologists long ago abandoned models that pitted "nature" against "nurture" in explaining the course of the life span in favor of models that describe development as resulting from the continuous and bidirectional interaction of multiple factors, from the genetic through the cultural, over time (Gottlieb, 2007; Sameroff, 2010). The proper question here is not *how much* of intelligence is attributable to nature (genes, biology) and *how much* to nurture (experience, environment) but, rather, *how do nature and nurture interact to produce a particular pattern of development or of intelligence?* This can best be accomplished by using models that seriously consider the transaction between biological and environmental factors. I introduced two of those models in Chapter 2 (the developmental systems approach and Scarr and McCartney's genotype → environment theory). Basically, these models propose that a bidirectional interaction occurs between organismic factors (for example, genes and hormones) and environmental factors (for example, physical and social environments) and that the two are intricately entwined, making it impossible to evaluate one without considering the other (that is, a contextualist perspective). Yet, even within these transactional models, there is considerable latitude for interpretation of which factors (genotype versus social environment, for example) play the major role in shaping development and intellect.

In this chapter, I examine some of the research relating to these issues. I first introduce a transactional approach to intelligence, a variant of the developmental systems approach introduced in Chapter 2. I then look at recent work in behavioral genetics that supports a strong role for genetics in intelligence. I follow this with research focusing on the role of environmental factors in influencing intelligence—in the establishment as well as the modification and maintenance of intelligence. Finally, I include a section on the stability of intelligence from infancy to young adulthood. There is no definitive conclusion at the end of this chapter—no bold statement saying what the origin of intelligence is or is not. But I hope the chapter will provide enough theory and data for students to appreciate better what is perhaps the most magnificent quality of our species—our intelligence.

----

# A TRANSACTIONAL APPROACH TO THE STUDY OF INTELLIGENCE

Chapters 1 and 2 introduced a general approach to studying development. This approach emphasized the bidirectionality of structure and function. Bidirectionality can be studied at many levels, of course, from the function of a firing neuron affecting its subsequent growth to the actions of a child influencing how significant others respond to him or her. I want to focus on this latter level now, examining the transaction between a child and people in that child's immediate environment and how this transaction might affect a developing intellect.

It has long been recognized that children play a critical role in their own development. Jean Piaget clearly recognized this, placing the child's mental and physical actions at the center of his theory. Yet, throughout most of the 20th century, theorists who looked at the development of intelligence tended to view children as passive beings who are either constrained by their biology to develop in a certain way or are shaped and molded by their environment (usually their early environment). Little emphasis was given by theorists in either of these extreme camps to children themselves.

This began to change in the 1960s, with Richard Bell (1968) emphasizing the idea that parent and child have equal abilities to contribute to a social exchange and that each affects the other. This viewpoint holds that cognitive influences are transactional (Sameroff, 2009a; Sameroff & Chandler, 1975): Not only do parents act to produce behavior in their children, children also modify their parents' behaviors.

The **transactional model** as proposed by Arnold Sameroff views the child's biological constitution (genotype in Figure 13-1) as having an organizing effect on the development of the child (phenotype in Figure 13-1). However, the child's environment (environtype in Figure 13-1) also has an organizing effect on the child. What is critical in the transactional model are the *bidirectional* effects between the multiple levels of organization (compare this with the developmental systems approach described in Chapter 2 and Figure 2-2). The environment and child have reciprocating effects, which influence that child's biology, and so forth, and these factors continue to transact during development. From this viewpoint, then, *development is seen as the continuous and bidirectional interaction between an active organism with a unique biological constitution and a changing environment.*

The transactional model has been used to understand the nature of differences in intelligence among children as a function of socioeconomic (SES), which is customarily defined in terms of level of family income, parents' occupational status, and years of parental education. Research has consistently shown that a significant portion of the differences in IQ and academic achievement among children can be attributed to SES

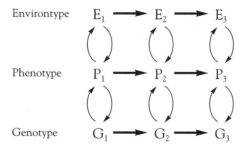

**FIGURE 13-1**

The transactional model of development, reflecting the continuous interaction of the child's constitution and the environment over time.

Source: Sameroff, A. J. (Ed.) (2009). *The transactional model of development: How children and contexts shape each other.* Washington, DC: American Psychological Association, p.15.

factors (Ackerman & Brown, 2006; NICHD Early Child Care Research Network, 2005; see also Ceci, 1996), and children from low-income homes fare worse than children from more advantaged homes.

Variables such as SES do not influence children independently of other factors. Thus, a high correlation exists between SES and home environment, friend selection, neighborhood, academic expectation, and academic opportunities, among other factors. In pioneering research, Arnold Sameroff and Michael Chandler (1975) proposed that some caretaking environments (middle-income homes) are more likely to produce intellectually and socially competent children than are others (lower-income homes). Furthermore, children who experience perinatal trauma (trauma at or around the time of birth) were proposed to be especially susceptible to nonsupportive caretaking, so the negative consequences of early biological impairment are exacerbated in such environments. That is, Sameroff and Chandler proposed a transaction between infants' biological constitutions and their environment, as reflected by differences in SES.

Support for Sameroff and Chandler's model was provided by an examination of the outcomes of children experiencing stress at birth (oxygen deprivation, or anoxia) as a function of their SES level. Although differences in developmental level between normal and biologically impaired infants are obvious at birth in both lower- and middle-income groups, these differences are diminished, or often even eliminated, by age 6 or 7 years in middle-income homes. In contrast, these differences are either maintained or increase with age in lower-income homes. Sameroff and Chandler speculated that distressed infants—characterized by more aversive cries; slower attainment of social-developmental milestones, such as smiling and vocalization; and a sickly appearance—receive different types of treatment in different environments. In reasonably affluent and well-educated families, these distressed children might receive lavish attention and stimulation, facilitating the amelioration of their impaired condition. In deprived, stressed, and poorly educated families, these same infant characteristics result in a pattern of reduced attention and stimulation and, thus, continued cognitive and social deficits. That is, there is a transaction between parent and child, with the particular characteristics of the child interacting with the particular characteristics of the parents, yielding distinct patterns of development.

Philip Sanford Zeskind and Craig Ramey (1978, 1981) experimentally assessed the effects of different caretaking environments as a function of infants' biological status in a series of studies. Infants from poor, rural environments who had been classified as at high risk for intellectual impairment were assigned to one of two caregiving environments. Infants in one group received medical care and nutritional supplements, and they participated in an educationally oriented day-care program beginning at approximately 3 months of age (experimental group). Infants in a control group received the medical care and nutritional supplements but did not participate in the day-care program. Within each group, approximately half of the infants were classified as fetally malnourished at birth, whereas the remaining infants were described as biologically normal. Fetal malnourishment typically produces infants who are developmentally delayed, lethargic, and have aversive cries.

At 3 months of age, fetally malnourished infants in both the control and experimental groups had lower developmental scores on the Bayley Mental Developmental Index than the nonmalnourished (normal) infants did. However, Stanford-Binet IQ scores at 24 and 36 months demonstrated (1) higher IQ scores overall for the experimental than for the control children, (2) no difference in IQ scores between the normal and fetally

TABLE **13-1**

Mean Stanford-Binet Scores at 36 Months for Children
in the Zeskind and Ramey Study.

|  | Biologically Normal | Fetally Malnourished |
|---|---|---|
| Experimental (daycare) group | 98.1 | 96.4 |
| Control group | 84.7 | 70.6 |

Source: Zeskind, P. S., & Ramey, C. T. (1981). Sequelae of fetal malnutrition: A longitudinal, transactional, and synergistic approach. *Child Development, 52,* 213–218. Copyright © 1981 The Society for Research in Child Development, Inc. Adapted with permission.

malnourished infants in the experimental group, and (3) higher IQ scores for the normal than for the fetally malnourished infants in the control group. IQ scores at 36 months are shown for the four groups of this experiment in Table 13-1. In general, the pattern of IQ change observed in this experiment is similar to what Sameroff and Chandler (1975) observed, with the effects of a nonsupportive environment (the control group) being especially deleterious for the biologically distressed children.

Zeskind and Ramey (1978) also measured the degree of mother-child interaction in the home. They reported no difference in the amount of maternal attention received by fetally malnourished and normal infants in the experimental group. In the control group, however, fetally malnourished infants received less maternal attention by age 24 months than the nonmalnourished children did. Consistent with Sameroff's transactional interpretation, Zeskind and Ramey proposed that the increased responsivity of fetally malnourished infants receiving the educational day care resulted in increased attention from their mothers and a generally positive developmental outcome. In contrast, the withdrawn and sickly behavior of the fetally malnourished infants in the control group resulted in less maternal attention, exaggerating the injurious effects of their biological impairment.

Although the patterns reported while children were still participating in the enrichment program are impressive and demonstrate the transaction of children's biology and environment in development, they do not mean that the effects of fetal malnutrition have necessarily disappeared. When environments change (as when children leave the enrichment program), patterns of interaction can also change, and the residual effects of fetal malnutrition might return (Zeskind, 1996). But the pattern demonstrated by Zeskind and Ramey (1978, 1981) provides an elegant demonstration of the dynamic relationship between children's biology and their environment over time, and it indicates that any simple interpretations of "biological causes" or "environmental causes" are likely wrong.

Most of the research I will examine in the remainder of this chapter does not fit together as many pieces of the puzzle as nicely as the Zeskind and Ramey study. Some examine genetic factors, and others examine detailed characteristics of the home environment. It is the unusual study that carefully measures biological and environmental characteristics and has good experimental controls while assessing intelligence in natural contexts. Nonetheless, all the research presented here can be viewed from the perspective of the transactional model. Although the next several sections are roughly divided into accounts of genetic factors and environmental factors, never lose sight of the fact that intelligence (or any other aspect of cognitive development) is always a transaction between an active organism with its own biological dispositions and a changing environment.

# BEHAVIORAL GENETICS AND
# THE HERITABILITY OF INTELLIGENCE

**Behavioral genetics** examines patterns of individual differences in often-complex behaviors as a function of the genetic relationship between individuals. Stated simply, derived statistics provide estimates of the percentage of variance, or differences in a trait, that can be accounted for by genetics, environment, and their interaction.

According to some, we have entered the age of *genomics,* a period when the entire human genome will be known and connections between genotypes and phenotypes will be elucidated (Venter et al., 2001). This is, indeed, an exciting time for biological science, and relationships between genes and behavior are continually being discovered (Plomin & Schalkwyk, 2007), making anyone who claims that genetics are unimportant for explaining individual differences in complex behavior such as intelligence very much out of touch with contemporary science. However, one must be careful not to let this "genomicophelia" cause us to lose track of the fact that genes are only part (albeit a critical part) of a complex developmental system and that their expressions are governed by events surrounding them during development (Gottlieb, 2007; Meany, 2010; Oyama, 2000; see Chapter 2). Genes must be seen as interacting with their local environments; thus, genotype-phenotype relations should vary at different points in development and under different environmental conditions. Moreover, the search for genes "for" intelligence has not been as productive as scientists had originally hoped. In general, many genes are involved in determining general intelligence (in interaction with the environment, of course), but so far, the quest to isolate specific genes has been elusive, likely because the effect of any single gene on general intelligence is very small in magnitude (Plomin, Kennedy, & Craig, 2006). Moreover, when individual genes associated with intelligence have been found, their effect is usually mediated by the environment, as in the version of one gene associated with higher IQ, but only when children were breastfed (Caspi et al., 2007), which was discussed in Chapter 2.

## The Concept of Heritability

Before we delve too deeply into the data of behavioral genetics, some explanation concerning what is meant by the term **heritability** is appropriate here. Heritability is the extent to which differences in any trait within a population can be attributed to inheritance. Heritability is expressed as a statistic that ranges from 0 (none of the differences in a trait are attributed to inheritance) to 1.0 (100% of the differences in a trait are attributed to inheritance). It reflects the proportion of variance in an observed trait that results from genetic variability.

Heritability is a population statistic, in that it describes average differences among people within a population. It does not refer to how much of any one person's intelligence (or height, or personality characteristics) can be attributed to genetic factors, only to what percentage of the difference in a trait within a specific population can be attributed to inheritance, on average.

For the purpose of illustration, assume that individual differences in height are the result of only two factors: inheritance and diet. On an isolated island, every person receives 100% of his or her nutritional needs (no one receives less or more). The average height of men on the island is 6 feet. If you were to meet two men from this island, one being 6 feet 1 inch tall and the other being 5 feet 11 inches tall, 100% of the 2-inch difference in their height would be attributable to inheritance—in other words, heritability would be 1.0. The reason for this is that their environments (diets, in this case) are homogeneous (no differences in environments exist). Thus, any difference in height between people must be attributable to inheritance.

What would happen if a famine hit the island, changing the diet of the people and, thus, the average height (from 6 feet to 5 feet 10 inches, say)? If the change were uniform (if, for example, everyone were getting 75% of his or her nutritional needs), the heritability would still be 1.0. Although the environment would have changed drastically, it would have changed equally for everyone. If the effects of the famine were not uniform, however, the heritability picture would change. If some people still received 100% of their nutritional needs, others 75%, and still others only 50%, now when you meet two men from the island who differed by 2 inches in height you would know that, on average, some proportion of this difference must be attributable to differences in diet—that is, heritability in this latter case would be something less than 1.0. The more heterogeneous, or variable, the environments are, the lower the heritability will be. Heritability is thus relative, varying with the environmental conditions in which people within the population live.

The concept of heritability is the same regardless of whether we are studying height or intelligence. One difference between concepts such as height and intelligence, however, is that of measurement. When we express height in inches or meters, we can be confident that the measure accurately reflects the underlying concept. There is less confidence with intelligence. In most studies examining the heritability of intelligence, IQ or other psychometric tests are used to measure intelligence. Thus, the findings of these studies more accurately pertain to the heritability of IQ (and usually $g$), with IQ being one (popular) index of intelligence.[1]

The statistical models underlying heritability are complicated and beyond the scope of this chapter (see Appendix B of Plomin et al., 2008, for a discussion of the statistical models underlying estimates of heritability). Contemporary models consider not only genetic and environmental effects but also the interaction of these effects (G × E) (Moffitt, Caspi, & Rutter, 2006). For example, a certain characteristic might be more strongly expressed in one environment than in another.

---

[1] Most of the research in behavioral genetics (and in the studies to follow examining the effects of home environment) are correlational, not experimental, in nature. Given the reliance on correlations for interpreting the findings of these studies, let me say a few words about correlations as they are used in the remainder of this chapter. Correlations measure the degree to which two factors vary. Correlations range from 1.0 (a perfect positive relation) to −1.0 (a perfect negative relation), with 0 being chance (no systematic relation). For example, we would expect a positive correlation between height and weight. Taller people, on average, are heavier than shorter people. There are many exceptions, of course, so the correlation will not be perfect. But we would expect a correlation in the magnitude of .60 or .70. The correlation between weight and some measure of intelligence, however, should be close to 0. Among a group of adults, we would not expect heavy people to be more or less smart, on average, than light people.

In familial studies of intelligence, the IQs (or speed of processing, etc.) of people with a known genetic relationship are correlated. For example, the IQs of sets of monozygotic twins might be obtained, and the score of each twin paired with his or her mate's. These scores can be contrasted with the IQs of randomly chosen, genetically unrelated people. In the latter case, the IQ of one person is paired at random with the IQ of another, and the correlation is computed. In the former case, a high correlation is expected, because the twins are genetically identical and grew up in the same home at the same time. In fact, the strong genetic position would predict a correlation of 1.0 even for monozygotic twins reared apart. In the case of the unrelated people, the correlation should be 0; knowing the IQ of one unrelated person does not help predict the IQ of another randomly selected person. Thus, the higher the correlation, the greater the relationship. These statistics are then used to infer the degree to which a characteristic is heritable (see later).

These models also consider the covariation of genetic and environmental effects, or genotype-environment correlations. In fact, Sandra Scarr and Kathleen McCartney's (1983) genotype → environment model, discussed in Chapter 2, reflects such correlations. Thus, although it is not trivial to interpret results from behavioral genetics research in terms of the transactional model discussed earlier (and patterns of correlations might not tell the entire story of genetic and environmental effects), most contemporary behavioral geneticists would agree with the basic tenets of the transactional model presented earlier. This is not to say that behavioral geneticists view the developing nature of intelligence the same way as do people such as Sameroff, discussed in the previous section. However, both groups of scientists see intelligence as developing through a dynamic relationship between one's biological constitution and a changing environment and this relationship as varying during development.

I should comment here that variance associated with genetic and environmental effects cannot be truly identified as if each contributes something unique to the phenotype. As I've argued in earlier chapters, all development should be viewed as the product of the continuous, bidirectional interaction of factors at multiple levels of organization, from the genetic through the cultural. Thus, attributing a certain proportion of differences in IQ to genetics and another proportion to environment has serious limitations (see Moore, 2001). Nonetheless, I believe that this general approach of behavioral genetics provides an estimate of how a particular trait is apt to vary as a function of genetic relatedness in known environments and, thus, provides useful information about the source of individual differences in a trait, including intelligence.

Even though a trait may be highly heritable, this does not mean that the environment cannot have a significant effect. Consider the effects of exercise on the heritability of executive function (see Chapter 7). Recent research has shown that performance on tests of executive function (inhibition, working memory, and cognitive flexibility) is one of the most highly heritable psychological traits ever assessed (Friedman et al., 2008). Yet, performance on executive functioning tasks in children can be modified greatly as a function of experience, including physical exercise (Buck, Hillman, & Castelli, 2008; Hillman et al., 2009). For instance, in one study, one group of 9-year-old children described as physically fit in terms of aerobic capacity (number of laps they could do), muscle strength (doing push-ups and curl-ups), and body mass index and another group described as less fit were given a test of executive function while their brain activity was monitored (Hillman et al., 2009). The physically fit children had significantly greater executive function abilities—specifically, in terms of allocating their attentional resources—as shown both by performance on the cognitive task and by measures of brain functioning (EEG). Thus, although executive function may be highly heritable, it is also affected by physical fitness, which may be one good reason to keep recess and physical education in the school curriculum (see Pellegrini, 2011). Other research has shown that executive function can be trained in young children (Diamond, et al., 2007; Holmes, Gathercole, & Dunning, 2009), again demonstrating that even if a trait is highly heritable, it can be significantly influenced by experience.

## Elementary Cognitive Tasks and Intelligence

Elementary cognitive tasks (ECTs) (or basic-level processes) are simple laboratory tests designed to measure people's response times as they make presumably simple decisions. These include short-term memory scanning, retrieval of familiar words from the long-term store, and simple categorization tasks (Jensen, 1998). Some of these tasks were described in Chapter 12 in the discussion of information-processing approaches to individual differences. The basic processes measured by ECTs are presumed to be closely related to physiological functioning and, thus, primarily under the influence of endogenous (and inherited) factors.

Arthur Jensen, among others, has presented evidence that response times for several ECTs are significantly related to g-factor scores obtained from conventional psychometric tests (see Jensen, 1993, 1998). As noted in Chapter 12, significant relations have been found between basic-level processes and verbal ability for both adults (Hunt, Davidson, & Lansman, 1981) and children (Fry & Hale, 2000). Following Jensen's argument, variations in these basic cognitive processes are probably inherited and are the basis for individual differences in intelligence. To bolster this contention, several researchers have demonstrated significant relationships between aspects of evoked brain potentials measured via EEG patterns and psychometrically measured intelligence (see Jensen, 1998).

Stephen Petrill, Lee Ann Thompson, and Douglas Detterman (1995) assessed the genetic basis of performance on ECTs by administering a series of timed cognitive tasks to 287 monozygotic (genetically identical) and dizygotic (genetically nonidentical) twin pairs between 6 and 13 years of age. The correlation between decision times on the information-processing tasks and psychometrically measured intelligence had previously been found to be significant (correlation = –.42). Decision times also proved to be highly heritable. The correlation of decision times for the identical twins was .61, but the correlation was only .39 for the nonidentical twins. This resulted in a heritability of about 45% (see also McGue et al., 1984). Heritability for other cognitive tasks was lower, with the heritability of simple reaction times being zero. Nevertheless, the findings clearly reflect a strong genetic basis for overall speed of processing (decision time) on experimental cognitive tasks, and this speed component was strongly related to a general intellectual factor (that is, g).

Even if speed of information processing is highly heritable, why should it correlate so strongly with psychometric measures of intelligence? Jensen (1993) states the dilemma: "It seems almost incredible that individual differences in reaction time (RT) in simple tasks that involve no intellectual content and are so easy as to be performed by most persons in less than 1 second should be correlated with scores on nonspeeded, complex tests of reasoning ability, vocabulary, and general knowledge—the kinds of content that compose IQ tests" (p. 53). Jensen (1993) proposed three possible brain-based reasons for the high correlations of reaction times with measures of g. First, speed of information processing might reflect speed of nerve transmission. Speed is important because of the brain's limited capacity to process information. Only so much can be done at once; faster processing will permit more to be done, and this will be true across domains. Second, evidence suggests that people whose reaction times are more variable across trials have lower psychometrically measured intelligence (Eysenck, 1987). Third, the longer neurally encoded information can be maintained in immediate consciousness, the more efficient cognition will be. Thus, more durable memory traces, with information being retained longer in short-term memory, result in more effective information processing. Jensen acknowledges that the neurological aspects of his theory remain speculative, but he states that the theory is consistent with the empirical evidence showing a strong relation between speed of information processing and g.

Although the findings and theories regarding ECTs are intriguing and applauded by many, not all researchers are ready to accept them as conclusive or as representative of functioning on higher-level cognitive tasks. For example, Stephen Ceci (1996) argues that other important cognitive skills, such as strategic and metacognitive processes, are ignored in this research. Also, it is well established that response times on simple cognitive tasks can vary greatly as a function of a person's knowledge base. Response times are fast when decisions are made concerning very familiar information but are slower when dealing with less familiar information (Case, Kurland, & Goldberg, 1982; Chi, 1977). Differences in knowledge base might be indirectly responsible for many of the group and individual differences observed in some of these experiments, and such differences might well be more a function of education and general experience than they are of genetics (see Ceci, 1996; see also Chapter 11 for a compelling argument of this).

## Familial Studies of Intelligence

Most researchers in behavioral genetics take the position that the primary influence of genes on intelligence is indirect. Genes do not necessarily make someone intelligent but, rather, influence the behavior and the experiences an individual will have. For example, the genes of a child's parents influence how those parents behave toward the child, affecting a substantial part of that child's experiences, especially early in life. And children's own genotypes determine which situations they find comfortable and pleasing, which causes them to seek out some environments and to avoid others (Bouchard et al., 1990; Sameroff, 2009a; Scarr, 1993). Thus, although genes surely influence things such as the rate of neural transmission or the durability of memory traces, which might have a direct effect on cognitive functioning (Jensen, 1998), their *indirect* effect, through the behavior of parents and of the children themselves, can have even greater consequences for the development of intellect. (Review Scarr and McCartney's genotype → environment theory in Chapter 2.)

The preponderance of research examining the heritability of intelligence has dealt with comparisons of IQ scores among people of varying genetic relationships (or **familial studies of intelligence**). If one holds a genetic theory of intelligence, then the greater the genetic similarity between two groups of individuals, the higher the correlations of their IQs should be. One of two general approaches has usually been taken: *adoption studies*, in which the parents who rear the children are genetically unrelated to them (Plomin, Fulker et al., 1997; Weinberg, Scarr, & Waldman, 1992), and *twin studies*, in which monozygotic twins separated early in life are contrasted with dizygotic (nonidentical) twins and with people of varying genetic relationships (Bouchard et al., 1990; Wilson, 1983).

Many large-scale and tightly controlled adoption and twin studies have been conducted over the past half-century, and their findings are relatively consistent. Thomas Bouchard and Matt McGue (1981) reviewed 111 familial studies of intelligence, including only studies that met strict methodological and statistical criteria. Some of the average correlations from this investigation are summarized in Figure 13-2. The results of several dozen additional studies during the past several decades have not altered the patterns shown in this figure (Plomin et al., 2008; Plomin & Petrill, 1997).

Generally, the correlations increase as genetic similarity increases, implying a significant role for genetics in patterns of individual differences in intelligence. From

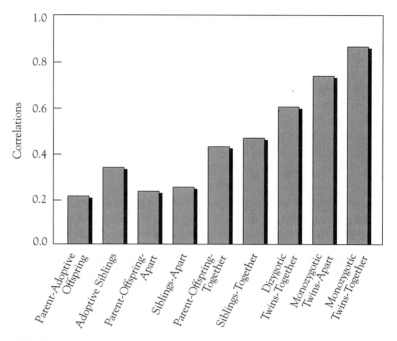

FIGURE **13-2**

Average correlations of familial studies of intelligence.

Source: Bouchard, T. J., Jr., & McGue, M. (1981). Familial studies of intelligence:
A review. *Science, 212*, 1055–1059.

these correlations, heritability estimates are derived. The easiest way to compute a heritability coefficient (*H*) is by using data from twin studies. The correlation (denoted as *r*) based on data from nonidentical twins is subtracted from the correlation based on data from identical twins, and the difference is doubled; that is,

$$H = (r \; identical \; twins - r \; nonidentical \; twins) \times 2$$

If you take the correlations for the IQs of identical twins reared together shown in Figure 13-2 (.86) and those of nonidentical twins reared together (.60), the resulting computation is $H = (.86 - .60) \times 2 = .52$ This means that the heritability of intelligence (at least based on this data set) is .52, or that 52% of the differences in intelligence between people is attributed to genetics.

Based on the dozens of studies that have been conducted during the past 30 years or so, a somewhat conservative conclusion would be that the heritability of IQ is approximately .50, meaning that, on average, 50% of the difference in intelligence between people in a population can be attributed to genetics (Plomin et al., 2008; Plomin & Petrill, 1997). However, recall that heritability is a population statistic and, thus, is subject to change across time and populations. So, for example, research has indicated that IQ has a higher heritability in middle childhood than in early childhood (Davis, Haworth, & Plomin, 2009), is higher in North American Whites than in North American Blacks, and is higher in Whites living in Great Britain than in Whites living in America (see Ceci, 1993).

## The Role of the Environment in Behavioral Genetics Analyses

If we accept the .50 heritability figure, this means that about 50% of the differences in IQ between people are attributable to *nongenetic* effects—namely, environment (Plomin et al., 2008; Plomin & Petrill, 1997). In family comparisons, behavioral geneticists typically consider the environmental effects of shared and nonshared environments. A **shared environment** is a home environment shared by different family members. A **nonshared environment** is an environment unique to an individual (not shared by a sibling, for instance). Thus, twins growing up in the same home at the same time, for example, would share the same family environment. Nontwin siblings growing up in the same family at different times would not share the same environment to the extent that twins do. As noted in Chapter 2, research has consistently shown that siblings become less alike the older they get and that this reflects the contribution of nonshared environments (McCartney, Harris, & Bernieri, 1990). Following the arguments of Scarr and McCartney (1983; Scarr, 1992, 1993), with increasing age, children's genotypes influence them to select their own environments, and the experiences they have in those environments affect their intelligence. Thus, some portion of the nonshared environmental effects can likely be attributed to indirect genetic effects (active genotype → environment effects in Scarr and McCartney's model).

Research has consistently found that the effects of shared environment on IQ are modest. In fact, in most behavioral genetics models, nonshared environmental effects account for the greatest amount of nongenetic variance (Harris, 1995; McCartney et al., 1990; Turkheimer & Waldron, 2000). Nancy Segal (2000) developed the *virtual twin* method to illustrate this. Segal defined virtual twins as unrelated siblings of about the same age who grew up in the same family from early infancy. For example, two adopted siblings, or a biological child and an adopted child, separated by fewer than 9 months in age, would be virtual twins. In such cases, they share the same family environment, similar to that shared by monozygotic or dizygotic twins, but they are not genetically related. Segal reported a significant correlation between the IQs of the virtual twins (.26), but consistent with the argument that shared environments have only small effects on intellectual development, this correlation was substantially less than that found between monozygotic twins (.86), dizygotic twins (.60), or full siblings (.50).

It is too early to conclude, however, that shared environments have little impact on the development of intelligence. For example, Mike Stoolmiller (1999) proposed that the lack of effects of shared environment in adoption studies can be attributed to statistical anomalies, associated with the restricted range of family environmental qualities in such studies. Adoptive parents are a selective group, and although they may differ in measures such as SES, few provide inadequate environments for their children. As a result, these studies greatly underestimate the degree of shared-family environment, and when this is taken into consideration, the amount of variance accounted for by shared-family environment increases substantially.

Behavioral geneticists have also been criticized for simplifying the notion of "the environment," in part by not explicitly acknowledging the role that self-produced function may play in early development, by failing to objectively define specific aspects of children's environments that contribute to the characteristics under study, and by measuring only postnatal and not prenatal environments (Gottlieb, 1995). When prenatal environments are evaluated, the effects of shared environments increase. B. Devlin, Michael Daniels, and Kathryn Roeder (1997) illustrated this in a meta-analysis of IQ studies. Devlin and his colleagues demonstrated that a mathematical model that included shared maternal (that is, prenatal) environment as a separate factor explained the variance in IQ performance significantly better than did traditional models that excluded this factor. In this model, 20% of IQ differences among twins was accounted for by shared-maternal environment, whereas shared-maternal environment accounted for only 5% of IQ differences among nontwin siblings. This pattern makes sense, given that twins share the womb concurrently whereas siblings share it consecutively. Although a woman may maintain a common physiology and personal habits (in terms of diet, for example) from one pregnancy to another, both the temporal separation between offspring and the (presumed) differences through time in the physiological status of the mother contribute to a lessening of the similarities of IQ among nontwin siblings.

It is easy to imagine many of the factors that may contribute to the maternal effects Devlin and his colleagues reported. The brain grows rapidly during the prenatal period, and although there is substantial cognitive plasticity in postnatal intelligence, it should not be surprising that patterns of neural organization can be affected prenatally by factors impinging on the fetus. Individual differences in childhood intelligence have been reported as a function of prenatal malnutrition (Lukas & Campbell, 2000), prenatal exposure to drugs and other potential teratogens (Reinisch et al., 1995), alcohol and cigarette consumption (Olds, Henderson, & Tatelbaum, 1994; Wakschlag et al., 2006), lead poisoning (Baghurst et al., 1992), and air pollution (Perera et al., 2009), among others. Research has also shown the degree of bodily symmetry correlates positively with adult IQ (Furlow et al., 1997); bodily asymmetry is believed to be caused principally by prenatal stressors. Thus, more symmetrical (and higher-IQ) people likely experienced less stress in the womb than did less symmetrical (and lower-IQ) people, providing another source of nongenetic, environmental variation in IQ.

These findings suggest that when behavioral geneticists broaden their definition of environment, as with the inclusion of a very general measure of prenatal environment in the study by Devlin and colleagues, estimates of heritability decline as the contribution of experiential factors increases. This pattern is predicted by the developmental systems approach, with its emphasis on the continuing interaction of structure and function at all levels of organization, beginning not with birth but with conception. Contemporary behavioral geneticists are also recognizing such effects (Molenaar, Boomsma, & Dolan, 1993; Turkheimer, 2000).

The behavioral genetics research I've reported here looks at correlations of IQs (or other tests of cognitive ability) as a function of the degree of genetic similarity, and the conclusion is clear: The more similar two groups of people are genetically, the higher the correlation. But remember that correlations are independent of means—in this case, average levels of IQ scores. When looking at average levels of IQ, environment (as reflected, for example, by the average level of IQ in the parental home) can have a greater effect than biology. How can this be? How can there be such an overpowering genetic relation when looking at correlations and a strong environmental effect when looking at means?

Sandra Scarr and Richard Weinberg (1976; Weinberg et al., 1992) illustrated the combined impact of environment and genetics on intelligence in a transracial adoption study, mentioned briefly in Chapter 12. African American children born primarily of parents from lower-income homes were adopted by White, primarily upper-middle-class parents. The average IQ of the adopted children who were placed in middle-income homes as infants was found to be 110, or 20 points higher than the average IQ of comparable children being reared in the local African American community and comparable with the estimated IQs of their adopted parents. This effect demonstrates the potent influence of environment on IQ. However, the correlation between the children's IQs and their biological mothers' educational level (IQ scores were not available for the biological mothers) was significantly higher (.43) than was a similar correlation with the educational level of the children's adoptive parents (.29).

The findings of this study appear paradoxical at first. How could the level of the children's IQs be more similar to that of their adopted parents yet the correlation of their IQs be higher with the educational level of their biological mothers? To help understand this difference, keep in mind that correlations in this type of research reflect the degree to which knowing a parent's IQ (or equivalent) score will predict where a child's IQ will fall relative to other children in his or her particular group. Correlations are independent of level of IQ; that is, correlations predict rank order and not level of IQ. In fact, the 20-point IQ difference between the children and their biological mothers could, theoretically, have been accompanied by a perfect correlation (1.0). In such a hypothetical situation, the child with the highest IQ of all the children (125, let's say) would have the biological mother with the highest IQ of all the mothers (105, let's say), and the child with the next highest IQ (119, for instance) would have the biological mother with the next highest IQ (101, for example), and so on, until the child with the lowest IQ (82, say), who would have the biological mother with the lowest IQ (65, perhaps). The correlation would be perfect, yet there would be, on average, a 20-point IQ difference between the children and their biological mothers.

In Scarr and Weinberg's study, the adopted children had all been placed in intellectually stimulating homes and had received similar treatment at the hands of their academically accelerating, adoptive parents. Such stimulation was responsible for their relatively high levels of IQ in comparison with those of their biological mothers. Furthermore, given the similar patterns of experience that these children had, individual differences among the children were best predicted by genetics. When environmental conditions are relatively homogeneous, as they presumably were for the adopted children in Scarr and Weinberg's study, the best predictor of individual differences in intelligence is genetics. Prediction here refers to knowing a child's relative rank in a specified group of children (that is, where the child stands compared with his or her peers); it does not refer to the actual level of IQ. When environments vary considerably (that is, are heterogeneous), differences in environments will play a more substantial role in affecting individual differences in intelligence (see later discussion). Thus, had the environments of the adopted families been more varied, chances are the correlations between the IQs of the children and the educational level (and IQ, presumably) of their adoptive parents would have been greater. In other words, the heritability of intelligence is not constant but varies as a function of the similarity of environments among the people under study. As I noted earlier, however, nonshared-environmental factors increase in influence as children get older, and these factors serve, essentially, to make the environments experienced by children more dissimilar to one another. Because these nonshared environments are influenced by their genetics (active genotype → environment effects), however, one would still expect the correlations of children's IQs with their biological parents to be high relative to those of adoptive parents during adolescence.

Several studies have explicitly assessed the interaction of genetics and environment on IQ using patterns of correlations derived from sets of siblings (Rowe, Jacobson, & van der Oord, 1999; Turkheimer et al., 2003). For example, David Rowe and his colleagues (1999) obtained verbal IQ scores from 3139 sibling pairs, including sets of monozygotic and dizygotic twins as well as adopted siblings. The siblings, all adolescents, were White, African American, and Hispanic, and they came from economically diverse backgrounds. Of particular interest to Rowe and his colleagues was the relation between education level of the children's parents and the heritability of IQ. The range of education of the parents was from no school to graduate or professional training. Rowe and his colleagues first computed correlations of IQs between siblings as a function of genetic relationship and found, similar to other research, that correlations increased as the degree of genetic similarity increased. For example, the correlation of the monozygotic twins was .73, the correlation of full siblings was .39, and the correlation of unrelated siblings was .07. The researchers next computed estimates of heritability and shared-environmental effects as a function of parental education. For the overall sample, the researchers reported a heritability of .57 and an effect of shared environment of .13, which is similar to results reported by others. The patterns differed, however, when education level of the parents was considered. For adolescents in the low-education group (high school education or less), Rowe and his colleagues reported a heritability of .26 and an effect of shared environment of .23. In other words, both genetics and shared environment accounted for about one-quarter of the variability of differences in verbal IQ for the low-education group. In contrast, for the high-education group (greater than high-school education), the researchers reported a heritability of .74 and an effect of shared environment of 0. That is, heritability increased from about 25% for offspring of parents with less than a high-school education to about 75% for offspring of parents with greater than a high-school education, with a corresponding decrease in the effects of shared environment (from about 25% to about 0%) (see Turkheimer et al., 2003, for similar findings).

These findings indicate, consistent with the theorizing of others (Bronfenbrenner & Ceci, 1994; Scarr, 1992), that heritability increases with improved environmental conditions (reflected here by level of parental education). This is because harmful environments might have a particularly strong influence on the development of certain traits, whereas according to Scarr (1992), average or above-average environments will have little impact beyond that contributed by genetics (recall Scarr's "good enough parents" from Chapter 2). Although we need not adopt Scarr's ideas of "good enough" parents to make sense of these data, the findings of Rowe and his colleagues indicate that environment and genetics do, indeed, interact and that these interactions can be found by using the methods of behavioral genetics.

## How Seriously Should We Take Heritability Studies of IQ?

At one level, the behavioral genetics of intelligence is a highly esoteric topic, steeped in statistical models that most people don't even bother trying to understand. At a second level, however, it is the study of down-to-earth issues that most people have some opinions about and that affect social, economic, and educational policies. How much of one's intelligence is "in the genes"? And if the answer to that question is "quite a lot," what does it mean about educability and the modification of intelligence during development?

I am convinced that IQ tests assess something important for people from information-age societies, that the .50 heritability of IQ reported by behavioral geneticists is real, and that this tells us something important about intelligence. However, I also believe that this is only part of the "intelligence" picture. Intelligence is a multifaceted thing, and I believe that a highly heritable general factor ($g$) can coexist with other aspects of intelligence (a position not all theorists of intelligence would agree with). Recall our earlier discussion of the transactional model. Biologically based abilities (or disabilities) transact with the environment over time, yielding patterns of behavior and development that cannot be neatly described as "50% of the variance can be attributed to genetics."

# EXPERIENCE AND INTELLIGENCE

Undoubtedly, one's intellect is greatly influenced by experience. Even proponents of a strong genetic perspective, such as Scarr (1993), argue that one's genotype has its greatest influence in terms of which environments a child explores and experiences. Others, however, argue that the environments in which children are reared and the experiences they have during childhood mold intellect far more than genetic influences do (see Ceci, 1996).

In discussing experience and intelligence, it is useful to distinguish among the establishment, the modification, and the maintenance of intelligence. What factors are responsible for establishing intellectual competence? Once a certain level of intellectual functioning has been achieved, what is necessary to maintain that level? Finally, to what extent can an established level of intelligence be modified, either positively or negatively? Factors that influence the establishment of intelligence most certainly also exert an influence on its maintenance and modification. But it is important to recognize that these three aspects of the intelligence-experience relationship can be distinct. Once intellectual competence is established, the child will not necessarily maintain that same relative level of intelligence independent of his or her surroundings. That is, establishing some level of intellectual ability does not guarantee that it will be maintained or that it cannot be modified.

## Establishing Intellectual Competence

Extremes in environments can have drastic effects on intelligence. Studies with laboratory animals clearly show that social, emotional, and intellectual functioning is greatly impaired when animals are raised in restricted environments (Greenough, Black, & Wallace, 1987). Although these lab experiments cannot be done with children, some naturalistic studies have been done in institutions and homes to assess the consequences of growing up in impoverished environments.

### *Institutionalization Studies*

In the early decades of the 20th century, there were numerous institutions in Europe and North America for infants and children who could not be cared for by their parents. These institutions tended to be understaffed, with children getting little in the way of social stimulation (Dennis, 1973; Spitz, 1945). The results of such early living conditions were increased susceptibility to illness; delayed physical, mental, and social development (Provence & Lipton, 1962; Skeels, 1966); and in some cases, death (Spitz, 1945).

For example, Wayne Dennis (1973) contrasted the outcomes of children reared in an orphanage in Beirut, Lebanon, called the Crèche, with those of infants placed in adoptive homes. The Crèche was a charity-run institution for illegitimate children. Infants received little direct stimulation in the form of play or other social interactions. The infants spent much of their day in small cribs without toys and with sheets covering the sides, limiting substantially what they could see. Life was more varied for older children, but opportunities for intellectual stimulation and the development of normal patterns of adult-child interaction were minimal. Furthermore, many of the primary caretakers were "graduates" of the Crèche themselves and were characterized by low IQ scores and a general unresponsiveness toward their young wards. Dennis reported that infants who remained institutionalized displayed signs of severe intellectual impairment within their first year and that their average IQs by age 16 ranged between 50 and 80. In contrast, infants leaving the Crèche for adoptive homes before the age of 2 years regained normal intellectual functioning, having average IQ scores by age 16 of about 100. Children adopted following their second birthday also demonstrated gains in intellectual performance, but they typically performed several years below their age level on all subsequent testings.

The effects of social deprivation appear early, within the first 2 or 3 months of life, and are reflected in infants' responses to simply being held. For example, Sally Provence and Rose Lipton (1962) describe 2- and 3-month-old institutionalized infants as feeling "something like sawdust dolls; they moved, they bent easily at the proper joints, but they felt stiff or wooden" (p. 56). Signs of intellectual impairment and inappropriate social reactions to adults increased during the first 2 years, although these signs declined somewhat as children became able to move around on their own and were moved from nurseries to wards for older children (Provence & Lipton, 1962; Skeels, 1966).

The influence of spending their early years in institutions persisted years after children were removed from the foundling homes and placed in adoptive or foster homes. For example, Provence and Lipton (1962) followed into the preschool years a small group of institutionalized infants who had been placed in foster homes, most between 18 and 24 months of age. Provence and Lipton commented on the considerable resilience and capacity for improvement that these children showed but also noted that early institutionalization still caused long-term problems. These children, although relating to other toddlers, did not form strong personal attachments, either to other children or to adults. Their emotional behavior was described as "increasingly impoverished and predominantly bland.... One gained the impression on watching them that they had largely given up on their efforts to initiate a contact with the adult" (p. 145). These children continued to improve, socially and intellectually, during the preschool years so that many looked, on casual observation, like normal children. Closer examination, however, revealed problems in forming emotional relationships, controlling impulses, developing language, and solving problems flexibly. In testing situations with adults, the children rarely sought assistance from their mothers and only infrequently turned to their mothers for comfort when distressed.

Although we would like to think that such institutions are a thing of the past, they are not. Many children in some poorer countries today are abandoned and spend significant parts of their lives as wards of the state, sometimes receiving care not much better than institutionalized children early in the last century. With the fall of communism in Eastern Europe in the 1990s, one heart-wrenching discovery was institutions in Romania for infants and young children that were at least as horrendous as any that existed during the Great Depression. (The Romanian government encouraged its citizens to have many children as a way to increase economic production. In fact, families with fewer than five children were punished with increased taxes. As a result, many parents could not support all of their children, and the State developed a network of institutions to handle the increase in abandoned children [Nelson et al., 2009].) UNICEF estimates that approximately 1.5 million children in Central and Eastern Europe live in public institutions, and many children in parts of Asia, South America, and Africa are abandoned, orphaned, or live in abject poverty (Nelson, 2007).

The effect on cognition of children living in these modern-day institutions was similar to that found for children growing up in orphanages earlier in the last century. Children who spend their first 2 years in such institutions display impaired levels of basic cognitive abilities, such as visual memory, attention, and inhibitory control (Beckett et al., 2010; Pollak et al., 2010), and have lower IQs, often within the intellectually disabled range, than similar children who are adopted or placed in foster care (van Ijzendoorn & Juffer, 2005).

Modern researchers examining the effects of institutionalization have some tools that researchers of earlier generations did not. Brain-imaging techniques can provide scientists with a look at how early deprivation can affect the structure and functioning of children's brains (Chugani et al., 2001; Eluvathingal et al., 2006; Tottenham et al., 2010). For example, in one study, researchers compared the PET scans of 10 adopted children who had formerly lived in a Romanian institution from birth to an average of 38 months of age with a group of age-matched children having epilepsy (Chugani et al., 2001). The adopted orphans were between 7 and 11 years old when tested and had an average Wechsler IQ of 81. Figure 13-3 shows images reflecting areas of the brain (marked in red and yellow) where the Romanian orphan group showed lower glucose metabolism relative to the control children. Some of the greatest differences were in the prefrontal cortex and the temporal lobe, both of which are associated with higher cognitive functions. The hippocampus and amygdala, areas involved in memory and emotion, also showed differences. Subsequent research showed that former Romanian orphans have less white matter (mainly myelinated axons) in parts of the brain that serve as pathways between the amygdala and frontal lobes (Eluvathingal et al., 2006) and

## FIGURE **13-3**

Brain images of Romanian orphan children. Areas in red and yellow show parts of the brain where Romanian orphan children showed significantly less glucose metabolism than control children. Most of the areas where there were significant differences are in the prefrontal cortex and temporal lobe, both associated with higher cognitive functions.

Source: Reprinted from NeuroImage, 14, Chugani, H.T., Behen, M.E.; Muzik, O., Juhasz, C., Nagy, F., & Chugani, D. C., Local brain functional activity following early deprivation: A study of postinstitutionalized Romanian orphans, 1290–1301, Copyright (2001), with permission from Elsevier.

display less cortical activity (using EEG recordings) than noninstitutionalized control children (Moulson et al., 2009a; 2009b).

The negative consequences of institutionalization on brain development are substantial, if not surprising. According to Charles Nelson (2007), "[I]nstitutionalization appears to lead to a reduction in cortical brain activity (both metabolically and electrophysiologically) and to dysregulation of neuroendocrine systems that mediate social behavior" (p. 16). Nelson proposed that such children do not receive the stimulation that developing brains have evolved to "expect," thus hampering brain development. As Nelson writes, "[M]any forms of institutional rearing lack most elements of a mental-health-promoting environment. As a result, the young nervous system, which actively awaits and seeks out environmental input, is robbed of such input" (p. 16). Looking at data from Romanian institutionalized children, Nelson proposes that too many neurons and synapses are lost in the deprived children, most of which can never be replaced, suggesting a sensitive period from which these children cannot fully recover.

Institutionalization studies are natural experiments and demonstrate how extremes in early environment can affect children's intellectual development. But such studies, although informative, lack the experimental rigor that psychologists like. Furthermore, such early deprived environments probably represent an extreme of child-rearing and might not apply to the vast majority of parent-child interaction styles.

### The Home Environment: Naturalistic Studies of Parent-Child Interaction

Many studies have examined aspects of children's home environments and related them to IQ and other measures of intellectual performance (Melhuish et al., 2008; NICHD Early Child Care Research Network, 2005). One of the more impressive longitudinal projects evaluating the quality of parent-child interactions and later intelligence was begun in the 1970s by Betty Caldwell, Richard Bradley, and their colleagues. They developed an inventory for assessing the quality of the home environment, called the Home Observation for Measurement of the Environment (HOME) scale (Caldwell & Bradley, 1978; Bradley, Caldwell, & Elardo, 1977). The **HOME scale** is divided into six subscales and is used to code aspects of a child's home environment that relate to intellectual development. Following are some sample items from the six subscales:

1. *Emotional and Verbal Responsivity of the Mother*
   a. Mother spontaneously vocalizes to child at least twice during visit (excluding scolding).
   b. Mother responds to child's vocalizations with a vocal or verbal response.
   c. Mother caresses or kisses child at least once during visit.
2. *Avoidance of Restriction and Punishment*
   a. Mother does not shout at child during visit.
   b. Mother neither slaps nor spanks child during visit.
   c. Mother does not interfere with child's actions or restrict child's movement more than three times during visit.
3. *Organization of the Physical and Temporal Environment*
   a. Someone takes the child to the grocery store at least once a week.
   b. When Mother is away, care is provided by *one* of three regular substitutes.
   c. The child's environment appears safe and free of hazards.

4. *Provision of Appropriate Play Materials*
   a. Child has a pull or push toy.
   b. Mother provides toys or interesting activities for child during interview.
   c. Mother provides toys involving literature and music (books, records).
5. *Maternal Involvement with the Child*
   a. Mother tends to keep child within visual range and to look at him or her often.
   b. Mother "talks" to child while doing her work.
   c. Mother structures child's play period.
6. *Opportunities for Variety in Daily Stimulation*
   a. Father provides some caregiving every day.
   b. Mother reads stories to child at least three times a week.
   c. Child has at least three or more books of his or her own.

Subsequent studies revealed moderate correlations (.30 to .60) between HOME scores and IQ measures (Bradley & Caldwell, 1976; Bradley et al., 1989; Espy, Molfese, & DiLalla, 2001). More specifically, mothers who were emotionally and verbally responsive to their infants, who provided more play materials for their children, and who were generally more involved with their children during observations when infants were 6 and 24 months of age had children with higher Stanford-Binet IQ scores at 54 months of age than did mothers who provided less stimulation for their youngsters (Bradley & Caldwell, 1976). Table 13-2 presents the correlations between 6- and 24-month HOME scores and 54-month IQ scores for children in this study. Subsequent research using the HOME scale demonstrated that descriptions of the home environment during the first 2 years of life predict academic performance at age 11 reasonably well (Bradley, 1989).

TABLE **13-2**

Correlations Between 54-month Stanford-Binet Performance and Scores on the HOME Scale at 6 and 24 Months.

|  | Correlations | |
| --- | --- | --- |
| HOME Subscale | 6 months | 24 months |
| 1. Emotional and Verbal Responsibility of Mother | .27 | .50** |
| 2. Avoidance of Restriction and Punishment | .10 | .28* |
| 3. Organization of Physical and Temporal Environment | .31* | .33* |
| 4. Provision of Appropriate Play Materials | .44** | .56** |
| 5. Maternal Involvement with Child | .28* | .55** |
| 6. Opportunities for Variety in Daily Stimulation | .30* | .39** |
| Total score | .44** | .57** |
| Multiple correlation[a] | .50* | .63** |

[a]This represents the correlation of all HOME subscales with Binet scores.

*p < .05

**p < .01

Source: R. H. Bradley and B. M. Caldwell (1976). The relation of infants' home environment to mental test performance at fifty-four months: A followup study. *Child Development, 47,* 1172–1174. Copyright © 1976 The Society for Research in Child Development, Inc. Adapted with permission.

More recent research has essentially confirmed the findings of Caldwell, Bradley, and their colleagues: Children who grow up in emotionally supportive homes and receive cognitively rich experiences tend to have higher IQs than children who grow up in homes with less intellectual stimulation (Brooks-Gunn, Linver, & Fauth, 2005; NICHD Early Child Care Research Network, 2002). However, the picture is complicated. A beneficial early environment, for example, is not apt to have long-term consequences if later environments are less supportive. That is, when the childhood environment is stable, patterns of development are usually stable, but when the childhood environment is constantly changing, patterns of intellectual development are also apt to change (Bradley, 1989). Thus, not only is a beneficial early environment important for sound intellectual development, but so is its stability—the beneficial environment needs to be continuous.

### Children at Risk

The adverse effects of a nonstimulating environment are often exaggerated for children with early health problems (Caughy, 1996). Early biological risk makes infants especially susceptible to the effects of poor parenting. Unfortunately, their biological impairments contribute to their problems by causing their often highly stressed parents to be less responsive to them. This in turn results in their slower intellectual development, which may further promote less intellectual stimulation from their parents. The result is a transaction that is less than conducive to good intellectual functioning.

Biological risks are only some of the factors that can adversely affect a child's intellectual development. Although far from the deprivation experienced by institutionalized children mentioned previously, children in many homes receive little direct attention, are talked to only minimally, and live in environments that are not conducive to developing intellectual skills suited for academic learning. Few children live in perfect homes, but as the risk factors mount, so do the negative effects on intelligence. This is known as the **cumulative deficit effect**. Multiple risks persisting over many years add up, and as a result, children who do not receive intervention display deficits in social, emotional, and cognitive functioning.

The cumulative effects of multiple risk factors was illustrated in a longitudinal study conducted by Sameroff and his colleagues (1993). Children from mainly lower-SES homes were administered IQ tests at 4 and 13 years of age. Children's home environments were also evaluated for risk factors (for example, family size, father absence, maternal education, maternal stress, maternal anxiety). First, Sameroff and his colleagues reported that a composite score of risk factors associated with each child's home life accounted for 34% of the variance in IQ scores at 4 years of age and for 37% at 13 years of age. (This percentage increased to 50% at both ages when researchers used a more liberal measure of risk factors.) This relation is clearly seen in Figure 13-4, which shows IQ scores of 4-year-old children as a function of number of risk factors. Thus, environmental risk contributed significantly to children's IQ; this remained true even after SES and mothers' IQ scores were taken into consideration. Second, the researchers reported that children's IQ scores at age 4 were significantly related with their IQ scores at age 13 (correlation = .72). However, environmental risk scores were also highly correlated between 4 and 13 years (correlation = .76). Thus, children living in nonsupportive and high-risk environments at age 4 were likely to be living in similar environments at age 13. It is exactly under such conditions that high correlations in IQs over time are expected. It is also worth remembering that cumulated risks affect the whole child and not just intelligence. For example, in one study, cumulative risk exposure over

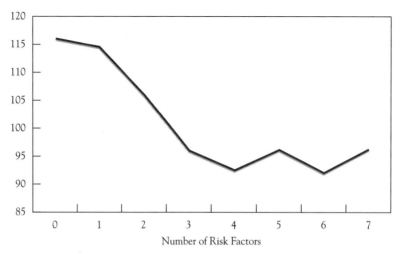

FIGURE **13-4**

Cumulative effect. The relationship between the number of risk factors and IQ for a group of 4-year-old children. The greater the number of risk factors, such as low family income and father absence, the lower children's IQs tended to be.

Source: Sameroff, A. J., Seifer, R., Baldwin, A., & Baldwin, C. (1993). Stability of intelligence from preschool to adolescence: The influence of social risk factors. *Child Development, 64*, 80–97.

childhood associated with poverty (for example, substandard housing, family turmoil) was associated with dysregulated cardiovascular responses and elevated cortisol levels (a measure of stress) at age 13 (Evans & Kim, 2007).

A number of other longitudinal studies have examined the effects of combined biological and environmental risk on children's intellectual performance (Caughy, 1996; Landry et al., 1997). For example, Margaret Caughy (1996) examined the relation between several biological risk factors (low birth weight, length of hospitalization, re-hospitalization during first year), environmental risk factors (low income, low maternal education, quality of the home environment as measured by a version of HOME scale), and tests of mathematical and reading readiness in a group of 867 children (ages 5 and 6 years). Caughy reported a strong relation between maternal education and HOME scores with both reading and mathematics performance. Not surprisingly, children from more intellectually supportive homes performed better on these tests. Also, biological risks (for example, low birth weight) adversely affected children's academic scores, although the impact of biological risk was not as great overall as that of environmental risk. And importantly, the children who were most adversely affected were those who experienced early health problems *and* who lived in intellectually nonstimulating environments, as reflected primarily by low HOME scores. For example, children who were re-hospitalized during their first year of life and came from homes with low HOME scores (indicating a nonsupportive intellectual environment) had significantly lower mathematics scores than did children who came from similar homes (that is, also having low HOME scores) but who were not re-hospitalized. In contrast, re-hospitalization did not affect academic scores for those children who came from homes with higher HOME scores (that is, a supportive intellectual environment). These findings are consistent with the transactional model described earlier, and they indicate that children living in nonsupportive homes are especially affected by biological risk.

### Experience Counts

More than 40 years of research makes it clear that experiences during the preschool years set the stage for later intellectual accomplishments. Supportive and responsive environments tend to produce intelligent and competent children. Other research has extended beyond the family and shown that the quality of early child care outside the home predicts subsequent intellectual attainment. For example, a study of more than 1300 children examined the relationship between quality of nonrelative preschool child care and functioning at age 15 (Vandell et al., 2010). The researchers reported that quality child care was associated with greater cognitive-academic achievement in adolescence as well as with better emotional functioning (less externalizing behavior).

It is impossible to specify when, during childhood, these experiences are most important. Rather, from the available literature one can conclude that early experience is important, but so is later experience. From a transactional perspective, we cannot put any numbers or percentages on how much of intellectual growth is influenced by nature versus nurture. From the current perspective, in fact, *how much* is the wrong question. The better question concerns how nature and nurture interact to yield a particular pattern of development.

## Modification and Maintenance of Intellectual Functioning

It seems clear from the preceding discussion that individual differences in intelligence can be influenced by a child's early environment. A related series of questions concerns the modification of intelligence. Will the elevated or depressed IQ levels that are found in some populations still be present decades later, or can people's level of intellectual functioning be modified by subsequent experiences? In this section, the modification and maintenance of intellectual functioning are considered for two related sets of conditions. First, to what extent are the intellectual deficits resulting from an impoverished early environment permanent? That is, can the deleterious effects of deprivation be ameliorated? And second, to what extent are the intellectual benefits resulting from enriched early environments permanent? In other words, are intellectual skills that have been acquired during the preschool years maintained into later childhood?

### Modification of Intellectual Impairment Caused by Early Experience

As I noted earlier, an impoverished environment often results in reduced mental functioning. Based on the results of institutionalization studies of the type described earlier (Dennis, 1973; Spitz, 1945), it was once assumed that the deleterious effects of stimulus and social deprivation were permanent. Nevertheless, evidence suggesting the reversibility of the negative consequences of early deprivation has surfaced from time to time. Observations of children reared in relative isolation, for example, have indicated some plasticity of intellectual functioning with rehabilitation.

One of the best-documented studies concerning the mental growth of isolated children is that of Jarmila Koluchova (1976). A set of monozygotic twins who were physically and psychologically normal at 11 months experienced abuse, neglect, and malnutrition until discovered at 7 years 2 months of age. The children had no language and an estimated mental age of about 3 years. They were placed in foster care and provided with an educational program in the hope that they would attain some semblance of intellectual normalcy. The program was far more successful than originally expected; the twins had WISC scores of 93 and 95 by 11 years of age and 101 and 100 by 14 years. Several other studies have similarly reported normal intellectual or language functioning following educational intervention for children initially classified as intellectually impaired because of neglect or isolation during the preschool years (see Clarke & Clarke, 1976). Related to these findings are reports of drastic changes in the intellectual performance of children from war-torn Southeast Asia in the 1970s who were adopted into American homes (Clark & Hanisee, 1982; Winick, Meyer, & Harris, 1975), which I discussed briefly in Chapter 2. It must be noted, however, that these are exceptions. Not all children who experience severe deprivation early in life show such reversibility as a result of later education (Curtiss, 1977).

Harold Skeels (1966) reported one controversial study concerning the reversibility of the negative effects of early experience. He studied infants who were wards of an orphanage. The orphanage was similar to many other Depression-era institutions, overcrowded and understaffed, and it was the type of institution that had been associated with reduced mental functioning by as early as 4 months of age (Spitz, 1945). During the course of several years, 13 children (10 girls and 3 boys) were transferred to a school for the intellectually impaired and placed on the wards of the brighter women inmates. These infants all showed signs of intellectual impairment at the time of placement. Their IQ scores ranged from 35 to 89, with an average of 64.3. The average age at placement was 19 months, with a range from 7 to 36 months. These 13 children made up the experimental group. A contrast group (eight boys and four girls) was chosen from children who remained in the orphanage until at least the age of 4. The mean IQ score of the children in this group was 86.7 when first tested (mean age at first test = 16 months), with a range from 50 to 101.

The children in the experimental group received loving attention from the intellectually impaired women. There was competition between wards to see who would have the first baby to walk or to talk. The attendants also spent much time with the youngsters. In almost every case, a single adult (inmate or attendant) became closely attached to a child, resulting in an intense, one-to-one relationship that was supplemented by other adults. The experimental children remained in the institution for an average of 19 months and were then returned to the orphanage, with most being subsequently placed in adoptive homes. On their removal from the school for the intellectually impaired, each child was administered an IQ test; the average score was 91.8, an increase of 27.5 points. The children in the contrast group were tested at approximately 4 years of age and had an average IQ score of 60.5 points, a decline of 26.2 points. Both groups of children were retested approximately 2.5 years later, with the experimental group having an average score of 95.9 and the contrast group an average of 66.1 (see Figure 13-5).

The results of this study are very impressive, and they demonstrate that toddlers characterized as severely impaired can realize significant gains in intelligence when placed in certain environments. Skeels extended his study by following these people into adulthood when they were between 25 and 35 years old. IQ tests were not given, but information was obtained concerning the occupational and educational levels of the participants, as was information pertaining to their social adjustment. All 13 people in the experimental group had married, whereas only 2 of the 11 surviving members of the contrast group had married. The median number of years of formal education completed by the experimental group was 12 (that is, high school education), whereas the contrast group had completed a median of only 2.75 years. Most experimental participants or their spouses were employed in skilled or semiskilled jobs. The range of SES, based on income and occupation, was comparable with regional norms. In contrast, and with one exception, people in the contrast group were in the lowest two socioeconomic levels. Four of the people in the contrast group

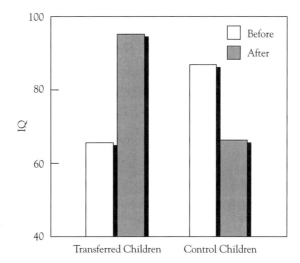

FIGURE **13-5**

Average IQ scores before placement and 2.5 years after completion of program for children in the experimental and control groups.

Source: Skeels, H. M. (1966). Adult status of children with contrasting early life experiences. *Monographs of the Society for Research in Child Development, 31* (Serial No. 105).

remained institutional inmates; five held menial jobs, such as dishwashers or cafeteria help; and only one had a skilled occupation (compositor and typesetter). IQ scores were available for some of the 28 children of the experimental participants and ranged from 86 to 125, with an average of 103.9. In general, people in the experimental group, who started life with a severe disadvantage, were normal by a variety of intellectual, occupational, and social standards.

The Skeels study demonstrates the potential plasticity of human intelligence. However, the study is not without its detractors. As an experiment, it leaves much to be desired. Skeels took advantage of a naturally occurring situation and assessed the effects of early environments within the constraints imposed on him by ethical and institutional considerations. As a result, there is much to fault with the methodology of the study, and although the study has been widely praised, its serious shortcomings have also been noted (see Longstreth, 1981).

One interpretation of the Skeel's study consistent with the transactional view of development is that the cognitive immaturity of the intellectually impaired women might actually have facilitated social interaction with the children, providing those children with stimulation they would not normally have received in the orphanage. In most situations, the characteristics of the severely impaired children in the experimental group would not produce lavish attention from adults. Most well-intending adults who direct their attention to a child expect some response in return. Children who are nonresponsive and generally lethargic tend not to elicit continued stimulation from adults, particularly adults from highly stressed homes (Sameroff & Chandler, 1975). This presumably would be especially true of overburdened members of an institution's staff. Because of the limited mental capacity of the inmates, however, their attention might have been repeatedly directed to the children even in the absence of appropriate responses. After prolonged stimulation, the children might have become more responsive and begun the climb back to normal intellectual functioning. That is, the intellectual immaturity of the institutionalized women in the Skeels study may have matched the needs of the children.

Of course, highly responsive people of normal or above-normal intelligence could also have served as appropriate "therapists" for these children, as was apparently the case in the Asian adoption studies cited earlier (Clark & Hanisee, 1982). But this is not the type of experience that these children could have expected from the orphanage staff. Moreover, had the children remained in the institution for the intellectually impaired for considerably longer, their intellectual gains would surely have been lost. As their intelligence increased, so would their needs for intellectual stimulation, quickly exceeding the boundaries of what the intellectually impaired women could have provided.

As I noted earlier, deprived environments for young children are not ancient history. Such environments were prevalent in Romania and other countries in the 1990s and are still found in parts of Europe, Asia, and Africa today. Many infants discovered in these orphanages were adopted into advantaged homes across the globe. Some were adopted very early in life (0 to 6 months), whereas others were not adopted until after 2 or 3 years of age (Beckett et al., 2006; Rutter et al., 1998). What happened to these children, all of whom were suffering from the effects of malnutrition and emotional neglect when adopted? Were they able to catch up, and if so, by how much? What effect did age of adoption (or, stated another way, time spent institutionalized) have on their eventual recovery? Research examining the course of development for Romanian children adopted in the United Kingdom (UK) provides some preliminary answers to these questions (Beckett et al., 2006; O'Connor et al., 2000). Romanian children left their institutions for adoptive UK homes at ages ranging from a few months to 42 months of age. For comparison purposes, they were classified into one of three groups: (1) those adopted between 0 and 6 months, (2) those adopted between 6 and 24 months, and (3) those adopted at more than 24 months. These children were compared with a group of infants born in the UK and adopted by other UK parents. All the UK-born children were adopted between 0 and 6 months of age. All children were administered the McCarthy scale at 6 and 11 years of age; this scale produces a Global Cognitive Index (GCI) that has a population mean of 100 (like an IQ test).

Figure 13-6 shows the average IQs of adopted Romanian children at ages 6 and 11 years as a function of their age of placement in UK homes. As you can see, despite the early deprivation experience by these children, those who were adopted within their first 6 months of life showed no long-term effects of their deprivation, having IQ scores comparable to those of the UK sample. IQs were lower for children adopted at later ages, particularly those adopted after 24 months. However, note that the 11-year IQs were higher than the 6-year IQs for these late-adopted children, suggesting a catch-up effect for the children who experienced the longest deprivation.

As I mentioned previously, there are methodological problems with these studies. For instance, children from these institutions who are adopted or selected for foster care may be brighter or more maturationally advanced than children who remain institutionalized. One study was able to overcome this problem by randomly assigning Romanian infants who had been abandoned at birth to either foster care or continued institutional care. These infants were then tested at 54 months of age and compared to a group of never-institutionalized infants being reared by their biological families in Bucharest, Romania (Nelson et al., 2007). (To conduct such a random-assignment

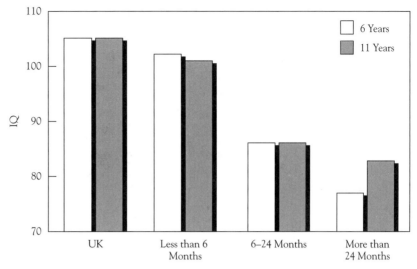

FIGURE **13-6**

IQ scores for adopted Romanian children at 6- and 11-years of age as a function of their age of placement in adoptive homes. Also shown are the IQs for a group of UK adopted children.

Source: Beckett, C., Maughan, B., Rutter, M., Castle, J., Colvert, E., Groothues, C., Kreppner, J., Stevens, S., O'Connor, T. G., & Sonuga-Barke, E. J. S. (2006). Do the effects of early severe deprivation on cognition persist into early adolescence? Findings from the English and Romanian Adoptee Study. *Child Development, 77*, 696–711.

study raises certain ethical issues, which the authors of this study considered carefully and discussed in some detail.)

The effects of institutionalization on IQ were significant, with the institutionalized group having an average IQ at 54 months of 73, compared to average IQs of 81 for the foster Care group and of 109 for the never-institutionalized group. Perhaps of greater interest were differences in the IQs of children in the foster care group as a function of their age at placement (see Figure 13-7). Children who were placed in foster care by 2 years of age had significantly higher IQs than children who were placed in foster care after age 2. In fact, as you can see from the figure, children placed in foster care after 30 months of age had IQs similar to those of children in the institutionalized group (72 vs. 73).

Collectively, these findings indicate not only the remarkable resilience of children to the effects of early deprivation but also the long-term consequences of prolonged nutritional, social, and emotional neglect. One should not be surprised that children who experienced more than 2 years of extreme privation demonstrated some long-term effects. However, that many of these children were functioning above normal at 6 years of age is impressive, and we must wait for future research before we know if this group will show any subsequent gains.

Along similar lines, the short-term effectiveness of **compensatory education programs** has been well documented by several projects designed to provide preschool children from low-income homes with the intellectual skills necessary to do well in school. It has long been recognized that poverty is associated with lower academic and educational attainment. Parents from poor families typically fail to provide the

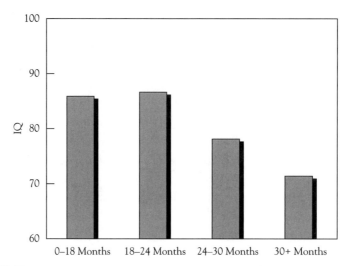

FIGURE **13-7**

IQs at 54 months for children in the foster care groups by age of placement in the study by Nelson and colleagues (2007). Children placed in foster care before 2 years of age had significantly higher IQs than children placed in foster care after 2 years of age.

Source: Nelson, C. A. III, Zeanah, C. H., Fox, N. A., Marshall, P. J., Smuke, A. T., & Guthrie, D. (2007). Cognitive recovery in socially deprived young children: The Bucharest Early Intervention Program. *Science, 318* (21 December), 1937–1940.

type of child-rearing environments associated with academic attainment, and as a result, children from impoverished homes start school behind their middle-class peers, usually stay behind, and often lose even more ground the longer they stay in school (Ackerman & Brown, 2006; NICHD Early Child Care Research Network, 2005). Beginning in the 1960s, compensatory education programs were established in the United States that aimed to provide preschool children at high risk for intellectual impairment and academic failure with the intellectual skills to do well in school (Klaus & Gray, 1968; Ramey, Campbell, & Finkelstein, 1984). Such programs have raised the IQ scores of high-risk children by 10 to 15 points during the program.

Generally, children in the more rigorous, highly structured programs demonstrated the greatest gains. In some studies, large gains in IQ level were noted relative to control children and to the children's performance before they entered the programs (see Barnett, 1995). In others, intervention began shortly after birth, with children demonstrating high IQ scores relative to control children at every age tested, thus never needing compensation for below-average intellectual achievement (Garber, 1988; Ramey et al., 1984).

Before we move on, let us consider a final question relating to the reversibility of deleterious effects of early experience: At what age is plasticity lost? Unfortunately, we are not able to answer this question. We do know from animal research that plasticity is reduced with age and that we are most malleable as infants (see Chapter 2). Human development has been proposed to be highly *canalized* during the first 18 or 24 months of life, meaning that all children follow the species-typical path "under a wide range of diverse environments and exhibit strong self-righting tendencies following exposure to severely atypical environments" (McCall, 1981, p. 5). In other words, although early maladaptive environments might adversely affect infants, there is a strong tendency to return to a course of normalcy given an appropriate environment. This plasticity is progressively reduced later in life, beginning as early as 18 or 24 months of age. In general, the earlier intervention is begun, the greater its chance of reversing an established behavior pattern, if for no other reason than older children and adults are more reluctant than younger children to accept the imposition of a drastically changed environment.

### Maintenance of the Beneficial Effects of Early Experience on Intelligence

If the effects of a negative early environment can be reversed, what about the effects of a beneficial early environment? If intelligence can be modified for the better by experiences later in childhood, can a later-childhood environment also modify a child's intellectual functioning for the worse? For the most part, evidence of the long-term effects of positive early environments comes from follow-up studies of preschool compensatory education programs. Although the initial reports of these programs were favorable, doubts concerning their long-term effectiveness began to surface shortly thereafter. The initial gains in IQ and academic performance shown by program graduates were slowly lost, and by the end of the fourth grade, levels of intellectual attainment were comparable between children who had participated in the programs and those who had not (Bradley, Burchinal, & Casey, 2001; Klaus & Gray, 1968). Figure 13-8 shows the typical pattern of IQ changes for graduates of preschool intervention programs.

Despite these findings, researchers were not ready to dismiss the influence of early compensatory education on the later intellectual functioning of high-risk children, and several investigators inquired into the long-term (middle school and beyond) consequences of the preschool experience. Two of the more comprehensive investigations of the long-term effects of preschool compensatory education programs were reported by

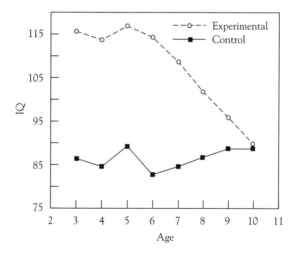

FIGURE **13-8**

Typical pattern of IQ changes for experimental and control children during preschool program (2 to 6 years) and after.

Irving Lazar and his colleagues (1982), who evaluated the effects of 11 experimental programs, and by W. Steven Barnett (1995), who examined the effects of 36 model demonstration projects and large-scale public programs, such as Head Start. The findings of the two studies were similar. Compensatory preschool programs had minimal long-term effects on IQ and academic achievement. Although the programs had an initial impact on children's IQ scores, few reliable differences were found between experimental and control participants by 10 years of age. Preschool graduates did score higher on some achievement tests than control children did, but this effect was not widespread.

More encouraging findings were found for school competence. For example, Lazar and his colleagues (1982) reported the median rate of assignment to special education classes was 13.8% for children who had participated in preschool programs and 28.6% for control children. Although less dramatic, there were also significant group differences in the percentage of children who were held back in grade. The median grade-retention rate was 30.5% for children in the control group and 25.8% for children who had participated in the preschool programs. Differences were also found in children's attitudes toward achievement. Program graduates were more likely to give achievement-related reasons for being proud of themselves, and the mothers of the experimental children felt more positively about their children and their likelihood of success than did the mothers of the control subjects.

There have been some important exceptions to this general pattern, including the North Carolina Abecedarian Program (Campbell & Ramey, 1994; Campbell et al., 2001, 2002; Ramey et al., 2000). Children from rural North Carolina who were identified as at-risk for intellectual impairment attended an educationally oriented day-care program beginning shortly after birth and continuing until they entered first grade. When tested at age 12, children who had attended the preschool program had significantly higher IQ scores (94) than did control children (88). Also, children in the preschool group scored consistently higher on a battery of academic tests (Woodcock-Johnson Psychoeducational Battery; see Figure 13-9). Many of these differences were maintained when participants were tested at age 21 (Campbell et al., 2002), although the effects were greater for women than for men. As adults, members of the experimental group continued to score higher on measures of math and reading, were more likely to attend college (36% versus 14%), were more likely to have a skilled job (47% versus 27%), were less likely to have had their first child at age 18 or younger (36% versus 45%), and were less likely to smoke (39% versus 55%) or to use marijuana (18% versus 39%) than were members of the control group (Zimmerman, 2007). Similar effects of greater sixth-grade reading and math achievement for high-risk children who attended an urban preschool program relative to control children have also been reported (Reynolds et al., 1996).

What about Head Start? Head Start, a nationwide, publically funded program, was not set up as an experiment, making it difficult to evaluate the long-term benefits in a scientific way. However, several studies have shown that children who attended Head Start were more likely to complete high school (Ludwig & Miller, 2007) and, for African Americans, were less likely to be charged with or convicted of a crime (Graces, Thomas, & Currie, 2002). This has caused some analysts to conclude that the Head Start Program, as it is currently operated, is worth the public expense from a strictly economic perspective (Ludwig & Phillips, 2008).

The findings of the long-term benefits of preschool intervention are somewhat mixed. On the one hand, most (but not all) studies found that the intellectual benefits

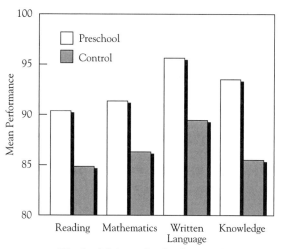

FIGURE **13-9**

Mean scores on Woodcock-Johnson Psychoeducational Battery at age 12 for children who participated in the Abecedarian preschool program and control children.

Source: Adapted from data presented in Campbell, F. A., & Ramey, C. T. (1994). Effects of early intervention on intellectual and academic achievement: A follow-up study of children from low-income families. *Child Development, 65*, 684–698.

realized during the preschool years were lost when the program responsible for those gains was discontinued. Once intellectual competence is attained, it must be maintained. Apparently, the intellectual environment for most of the low-income children after leaving the program was not sufficiently supportive to maintain the level of intelligence established during the preschool years. On the other hand, several studies have reported long-term intellectual effects, and taken together, several significant and important noncognitive benefits of compensatory education have been found. The difference in assignment to special education classes alone represents a significant savings in tax dollars, justifying the cost of the preschool programs (Karoly et al., 1998). Furthermore, differences in grade retention (and presumably the probability of completing high school) and in personal and maternal attitudes suggest that program graduates will be more likely to succeed economically in the years to come than will children in the control conditions. In an extensive review of the literature, economist Flavio Cunha and his colleagues (2006) reported that early interventions have long-term effects on motivation, which in turn affects achievement-test scores, school participation, delinquency, and teenage pregnancy rates, and concluded that "Early interventions have a substantial effect on adult performance and have a high economic return" (p. 801).

What if the compensatory preschool program had been extended into the early elementary school years? Might there then have been long-term effects of early education? Wesley Becker and Russell Gersten (1982) examined the academic performance of fifth- and sixth-grade children who had participated in Project Follow Through, a program designed to take over where the Head Start left off. In Project Follow

Through, low-income children are provided with compensatory education through the third grade. Becker and Gersten evaluated the effectiveness of five different Follow Through programs, comparing children's performance with that of control groups and with national norms on a series of achievement tests.

Children in the study had been administered portions of the Wide Range Achievement Test (WRAT) or the Metropolitan Achievement Test (MAT). Significant differences were found between the Follow Through and control children in both the fifth and sixth grades. Most striking were differences in reading level on the WRAT and differences on the spelling and math-problem-solving subscales of the MAT—all of which were in favor of the Follow Through children. In fact, of the 180 statistical comparisons made between the control and Follow Through children from the five different programs, 76 (42%) favored the Follow Through children, whereas only 2 (1%) favored the control subjects. Thus, compensatory education programs that are continued beyond the preschool years have beneficial effects on academic achievement.

As I mentioned, Becker and Gersten also compared the performance of the Follow Through children on the WRAT and MAT with national norms. Mean percentile ranks for the Follow Through children for tests given in the third, fifth, and sixth grades are presented in Table 13-3. The percentiles are based on national averages for the WRAT and the MAT, with a score of 50 representing average performance. Tests given in the third grade reflect the children's performance while they were still participating in Project Follow Through, whereas scores in the fifth and sixth grades reflect their performance 2 and 3 years after termination of the program.

The most striking aspect of these data is the steady decline in percentile standing as a function of grade. These high-risk children were performing close to or above the national average on three of the four tests in the third grade (the exception being MAT reading, 38th percentile). Two years after they had left Project Follow Through, only their WRAT reading scores were comparable to the national average, and by the sixth grade, their performance had declined to the 38th percentile. These results indicate that although the Follow Through children maintained an academic advantage relative to matched sets of control children, they showed a decrement relative to national averages after leaving the program. Again, the social and educational benefits

## TABLE **13-3**
Mean Percentile Ranks for Children in Project Follow Through for Subtests of the WRAT and the MAT.

| Time of Test | WRAT Reading | MAT Reading | MAT Math | MAT Spelling |
|---|---|---|---|---|
| Last year of Follow Through: | | | | |
| Grade 3 | 63rd | 38th | 62nd | 47th |
| After completion of Follow Through: | | | | |
| Grade 5 | 53rd | 22nd | 29th | 37th |
| Grade 6 | 38th | 20th | 27th | 37th |

Source: W. C. Becker & R. Gersten, (1982). A Follow-up of Follow-Through: The Later Effects of the Direct Instruction Model for Children in Fifth and Sixth Grades. *American Educational Research Journal, 19*, 75–92. Copyright © 1982 American Educational Research Association.

of the program are significant, but as with the findings of Lazar and his associates (1982) and Barnett (1995), intellectual gains diminished once the children left the program.

## How Modifiable Is Human Intelligence?

In general, the results of the studies reviewed in the previous sections indicate that the negative effects of early experience can be reversed and that the beneficial effects of an early stimulating environment can be altered by experiences that follow. Human intelligence is modifiable in both positive and negative directions. Intelligence is not something that, once gotten, is necessarily kept. Intelligence, as measured by IQ tests, reflects a person's intellectual functioning at a given time. Once established, intelligence (or any other complex behavior, for that matter) must be maintained. If the environmental supports responsible for establishing cognitive competence are removed, we should not be surprised that intelligence suffers.

The results of these studies reflect a flexible cognitive system that can be greatly modified by changes in the environment during childhood. However, the research cited can be criticized for not being representative of the way the world is structured for most children. Fortunately, few children spend their early years restricted to closets, and most children who are provided stimulating environments as preschoolers can expect comparably stimulating environments in the years to come. These studies indicate what *can* happen to levels of intelligence during childhood, not necessarily what actually *does* happen. Children's environments do change normally over time, such as the transition from home to school and a related shift from a family-centered to a peer-centered lifestyle. To the extent that these changes in environments do not represent major shifts in intellectual emphasis, levels of intelligence can be expected to be maintained. The more diverse the changing environments are, the greater the change in level of intelligence that can be expected.

# THE STABILITY OF INTELLIGENCE

We like to believe that the world we live in is relatively stable and predictable. This predilection includes some implicit beliefs concerning the stability of mental functioning. We looked briefly at the issue of stability in earlier chapters of this book. For example, certain aspects of memory performance remain stable over time, whereas other aspects do not. But the primary arena for studying the stability of mental functioning has been the topic of intelligence. To what extent is intellectual functioning, as measured by IQ or other general assessments of intelligence, stable over time? Will a bright 5-year-old turn out to be an intelligent teenager, or is a prediction of adolescent and adult intelligence from early childhood intelligence no more reliable than tossing a coin? And what about infancy? Is there any way that we can predict what level of intellectual functioning a child will attain from assessments during infancy?

## Defining Stability

Before looking at any evidence, let me define again what is meant by **stability**. Obviously, stability does not mean that intelligence stays the same over time. Of course, children get smarter as they get older. Rather, stability refers to the relative constancy of individual differences—the extent to which different children maintain their rank order over time in comparison with their peers. Is the valedictorian of her kindergarten class likely to be among the top students when her high school class graduates? Is the highly attentive 4-month-old likely to be a better reader than his less attentive peer? Stability in this sense is measured by correlations of rank order. If a group of children is given IQ tests at age 5, for example, they can be ranked in IQ score from highest to lowest. If that same group is tested again at age 10, we can compare the rankings of the children's IQ scores at the two ages. If the rankings are similar, the correlation will be positive and high. If there is no stability of individual differences in IQ scores between ages 5 and 10, the correlation will be close to 0. It is also possible, although unlikely, that the brightest children at age 5 will be, on the average, the least bright children at age 10, resulting in a negative correlation. Note that the correlations used to assess stability are unrelated to the actual level of performance. Correlations may be high, implying stability, even though the average level of performance might have systematically increased (or decreased) for most members of the sample.

In the following sections, I examine research on the stability of individual differences in intelligence over time. For the most part, IQ data are used as a measure of intellectual functioning, although several studies that used other measures of cognition are also reported. In addition to investigating stability of intelligence via cross-age correlations, I also examine patterns of change. That is, although there might be high correlations between measures of intelligence at two ages, it does not mean that intelligence has not changed during that period. In other words, the relationship between developmental function—patterns of change over time and the stability of individual differences will be evaluated.

## Predicting Later Intelligence from Tests in Infancy

One research topic in cognitive development that received much attention in the recent past has been that of predicting childhood IQ from measures taken in infancy. Before presenting this new research, let me provide a little necessary history.

Psychometricians have generally believed that intelligence is stable across time, including from infancy into childhood. In part, this prediction is based on the assumption that human intelligence can be described most accurately as a unitary construct that varies in a continuous fashion over time. From a psychometric perspective, this is best described as a single general factor of intelligence, *g*. When developmental function is continuous and quantitative in nature, there is every reason to expect that individual differences will be stable (**continuity with stability**).

Testing this hypothesis is relatively straightforward: Tests given in infancy are correlated with IQ tests given in childhood. The problem, of course, is developing tests that assess intelligence in infancy. Such tests have been around for nearly 70 years in the form of infant psychometric scales that produce a DQ (developmental quotient) with the same psychometric properties as IQ tests. Examples from one of these tests, the first edition of the Bayley Scale, were presented in Chapter 12. However, when babies who were given the Bayley and other scales are later administered IQ tests in early childhood, the correlations are disappointingly low. Prediction is only slightly greater for high-risk infants. Table 13-4 summarizes the results of studies examining the relationship between sensorimotor tests of development (that is, DQ tests) and later IQ scores for both typically developing and high-risk samples as a function of age at testing (both in infancy and in childhood). As can be seen, the correlations are

TABLE **13-4**

Median Correlations Between DQ Test Scores and Later IQ Test Scores for Typically Developing and High-Risk Samples.

| Infant Test (Months) | Typically Developing Sample | | | | High-Risk Sample | | | |
|---|---|---|---|---|---|---|---|---|
| | Age at Follow-up Test (Years) | | | | Age at Follow-up Test (Years) | | | |
| | 3 | 4–5 | 6+ | Mean | 3 | 4–5 | 6+ | Mean |
| 3–4 | .04 | .06 | .07 | .06 | .14 | .08 | .07 | .10 |
| | (4)* | (2) | (3) | | (2) | (4) | (2) | |
| 5–7 | .25 | .20 | .06 | .15 | .27 | .24 | .28 | .26 |
| | (14) | (5) | (6) | | (5) | (13) | (3) | |
| 8–11 | .20 | .23 | .21 | .21 | .29 | .23 | .29 | .27 |
| | (8) | (5) | (3) | | (6) | (10) | (6) | |
| Mean | .16 | .16 | .11 | | .23 | .18 | .21 | |

*Numbers in parentheses represent number of studies in each median correlation.

Sources: Fagan, J. F., III & Singer, J. T. (1983). Infant recognition memory as a measure of intelligence. In L. P. Lipsitt & C. K. Rovee-Collier (Eds.), *Advances in infancy research* (Vol. 2). Norwood, NJ: Ablex. Reprinted with permission.

uniformly low; the average correlation between infant tests and IQ scores at 6 years of age is only
.11 for typically developing infants. Prediction is often considerably higher for infants scoring very low on the tests (for example, below 80), suggesting some power of these tests to predict pathology in limited situations (see McCall, Hogarty, & Hurlburt, 1972).

This should be very discouraging for people who believe the continuity-with-stability theory of intelligence, yet there is always the argument that the infant DQ tests are not sensitive enough and that new tests will eventually find the relationship. Others looked at these data, however, and were not surprised. The reason for the low correlations is that development varies in a discontinuous way between infancy and childhood, with qualitative differences in the nature of intelligence. When developmental function is discontinuous (that is, relatively abrupt and qualitative in nature), there is no reason to expect stability. The bright sensorimotor child might become a bright preoperational child, for example, but because of the substantial difference in the nature of cognition between the infant and the preschool child, such stability should not be expected.

This **discontinuity-with-instability** position was best articulated by Robert McCall and his colleagues (McCall, Eichorn, & Hogarty, 1977), who demonstrated, using longitudinal data, little stability of individual differences in cognitive performance even across different stages in infancy, to say nothing of between infancy and later childhood. For example, McCall and his associates were able to identify five stages in cognitive development between birth and 3 years of age: (1) birth to 2 months, (2) 2 to 8 months, (3) 8 to 13 months, (4) 13 to 21 months, and (5) 21 to between 31 and 36 months. These stage correspond roughly to Piaget's stages of sensorimotor development, as outlined in Chapter 5. McCall and his colleagues found substantial stability of individual differences (that is, high cross-age correlations) when comparing performance *within* a stage (for example, between 8 and 12 months) but much less stability (that is, low cross-age correlations) when comparisons were made *between* stages (for example, between 10 and 14 months). These data very nicely demonstrate continuity with stability for contrasts *within* a cognitive stage and discontinuity with instability for contrasts *between* cognitive stages.

This, basically, is where the argument stood until the 1980s, when new research reported evidence for stability of intelligence from infancy to childhood. The evidence came from what to many was an unlikely source—measures of infant memory and attention. Recall the habituation/dishabituation paradigm from our discussions of infant perception and attention in Chapter 4. Infants are presented a stimulus (a picture, for example), and their attention to that stimulus is noted (in this case, looking time). The same stimulus is presented repeatedly, with the typical finding that infant attention to the stimulus decreases. When attention to the stimulus decreases sufficiently (usually to 50% of what it was on the initial trials), the infant is said to have habituated to the stimulus.

This same technique has been used to assess recognition memory. Some time after habituation (minutes, hours, or even days), the infant is shown two stimuli, usually simultaneously. One stimulus is the same picture the infant had been habituated to earlier. The other stimulus is a new one. Memory is indicated if infants look at the novel stimulus more than at the habituated stimulus. They remember the old stimulus and are still tired of looking at it. This *preference-for-novelty* measure has been used extensively and has revealed much about infant memory capacity. (See further discussion in Chapter 8.)

Psychologists began to look for relationships between individual differences in measures of infant attention/memory and childhood IQ. Joseph Fagan was the first person to systematically examine this relationship, which is fitting, given that he was a pioneer of the preference-for-novelty technique in assessing infant recognition memory.

In an early review, Fagan and Lynn Singer (1983) examined the results of previously published experiments concerning the prediction of childhood intelligence from infants' references for novelty by means of visual recognition, and they also reported the results of their own longitudinal study. The ages of the infants assessed ranged from 3 to 7 months, and assessments of later childhood IQ for 12 sets of data ranged from 2 to 7.5 years. The range of correlations between infants' preferences for novelty and later IQ was .33 to .66, with a mean value of .44. That is, the stronger an infants' preference for novelty was (the more they looked at the novel versus the familiar stimulus), the higher their IQ during early childhood was apt to be. Compare this with the values given in Table 13-4, where average correlations between sensorimotor tests and IQ scores for developmentally typical infants ranged from .16 (for IQ tests given between the ages of 3 and 5 years) to .11 (for IQ tests given at age 6 and beyond). Similar results were later reported using habituation measures, with infants who habituate faster having higher childhood IQs (see Bornstein, 1989; Bornstein et al., 2006; Bornstein & Sigman, 1986).

Habituation and preference-for-novelty tasks have been used with hearing and touch as well as vision, and researchers have reported comparable correlations with childhood IQ when infants are tested in these other modalities (for hearing, see O'Connor, Cohen, & Parmelee, 1984; for touch, see Rose et al., 1991). Results are found both for full-term infants (Rose, Feldman, & Wallace, 1992; Slater et al.,

1989) and for preterm infants (Rose et al., 1989; Sigman et al., 1986). More recent reviews of the literature have demonstrated the reliability of these findings (Bornstein et al., 2006; McCall & Carriger, 1993). Average correlations between infant measures of habituation or preference for novelty and childhood IQ are about .40 or higher. This compares with correlations of about .15 between tests like the Bayley Scales and later IQ. (The latest version of the Bayley Scales [2005] includes items to assess some of the basic cognitive abilities believed to underlie infant intelligence. To my knowledge, no published studies have assessed the new Bayley Scales' ability to predict childhood IQ.)

The evidence just cited indicates a moderate degree of continuity of developmental function and stability of individual differences from infancy to early childhood. Given these findings, how might continuity of developmental function be interpreted? Marc Bornstein and Marian Sigman (1986) examined several possibilities and concluded that the high correlations can best be explained by the continuity of an underlying process. This model proposes that a constant process underlies individual differences in both the allocation of infant attention and later performance on tests of intelligence. The question is, what might that process be?

Most researchers have assumed that habituation and preference for novelty involve information-processing mechanisms and that such mechanisms are stable in form during infancy and into childhood (Bornstein & Sigman, 1986; Fagan, 1992; McCall & Carriger, 1993). Recall from our discussion of executive function in Chapter 7 that there are age-related differences in memory span, working memory, speed of processing, ability to inhibit thoughts and behaviors, ability to resist interference, and cognitive flexibility. Individual differences in these basic-level abilities are first seen in infancy and may be at the core of intelligence (Reznick, 2009; Rose et al., 2005). For example, habituation and recognition memory involve encoding a stimulus, storing it, categorizing it, comparing a present stimulus with a memory representation, and discriminating the old from the new stimulus. McCall and Carriger (1993) further suggested that the information-processing mechanisms underlying performance might be "the disposition to inhibit responding to familiar stimuli and to stimuli of minor prominence (e.g., low energy, static, etc.)" (p. 77). Such a position is consistent with the evidence presented in Chapter 7 of age-related differences in sensitivity to interference and the ability to inhibit prepotent responses.

Another related aspect of information processing that might underlie both infant and childhood measures is the ability to process novelty. In particular, the preference-for-novelty paradigm used for assessing recognition memory involves the handling of novel information. Unlike many of the sensorimotor skills assessed on infant scales of intelligence, these abilities are also characteristic of cognition in later life and, thus, might serve as a basis for the continuity of intelligence. Along similar lines, Robert Sternberg (1985) argues that response to novelty is a major element of individual differences in intelligence that is constant across the life span (recall Sternberg's theory from Chapter 12). He proposes that how people react to novel situations is central to most definitions of intelligence. Even what Piaget called assimilation and accommodation, for example, are essentially means for dealing with novel environmental events. In a similar vein, Harriet Rheingold (1985) stressed the importance of novelty in development. She asserted that the development of behavior, including mental processes, can be viewed as a process of becoming familiar with our world (both internal and external). The child's task in development is essentially to render the novel familiar. Thus, like Sternberg, Rheingold sees the process of acquiring new knowledge—that is, of rendering the novel familiar—to be a central aspect of development that is continuous throughout life.

Does this new evidence of continuity with stability from infancy to childhood mean that there is a general factor of intelligence, or *g*? The data certainly seem to point in that direction. Fagan (1992) believes that the origins of intelligence can be found in the infant's ability to process information and that such processing is tapped by habituation and recognition memory procedures. These basic-level information-processing abilities have a high heritability. This all suggests that there is a strong biological (genetic and possibly prenatal) basis for individual differences in intelligence. Fagan (1992) proposes that what underlies intelligence is best thought of as information-processing mechanisms rather than as a mental factor; nevertheless, the relatively high prediction of later intelligence from infant measures is consistent with the continuity-with-stability position advocated by *g* theorists.

Some evidence supports the idea of the stability of information-processing mechanisms that underlie tests in both infancy and childhood. For example, Susan Rose and Judith Feldman (1995) reported that visual-recognition memory tests given at 7 months correlated significantly at age 11 years not only with IQ scores (correlation = .41) but also with perceptual speed (correlation = .38). In other work, Thomas Dougherty and Marshall Haith (1997) found infant visual reaction time (the time it took infants to begin an eye movement toward a picture after it appeared) measured at 3.5 months of age correlated significantly both with childhood IQ (correlation = .44) and with childhood (age 4) visual reaction times (measured similarly as they were in infancy; correlation = .51). These studies argue for cognitive continuity from infancy through childhood and for speed of processing as a likely component that underlies intellectual performance and that is responsible, at least in part, for the stability observed.

Yet, the correlations, although substantially higher than those found with infant DQ tests, are far from perfect, and Fagan and others point out that individual differences in infant information processing do not constitute the whole picture. For example, reliable differences in IQ scores are found between children of different races and different parental educational backgrounds in the United States. But no differences are found between children of different races or with different parental educational backgrounds on measures of recognition memory (Fagan, 1984). This suggests that experiential factors play a separate role in the establishment of intelligence.

Catherine Tamis-LeMonda and Marc Bornstein (1989; see also Bornstein, 1989) nicely illustrated the combined influence of basic information-processing abilities and environmental factors. They demonstrated that the quality of mother-child interaction predicted childhood intelligence at age 4 independent of infant habituation rates. In other words, how parents interact with their babies has an important influence on their children's intelligence beyond that measured by habituation rate. This means that intelligence is a multifaceted thing, and we must interpret any global pronouncements concerning its development very cautiously.

Intelligence is not a single, well-defined dimension. If a *g* factor does exist, it reflects only part of the picture. The work of Fagan, Bornstein, and others suggests that at least some aspects of intelligence vary continuously during infancy and childhood and are stable over time. Yet, the earlier claim by McCall and his colleagues—that intelligence during infancy changes in a discontinuous manner and is not stable over time—is also likely true. The difference is that the various investigators are measuring different aspects of infant intelligence, with some aspects changing continuously and showing stability and others changing discontinuously and showing instability.

## The Stability of IQ Scores During Childhood

Although infant psychometric measures do not predict later IQ scores well, the stability of individual differences in intelligence as measured by IQ tests increases dramatically by age 2. Table 13-5 summarizes the findings of longitudinal studies by Nancy Bayley (1949) and by M. P. Honzik, J. W. MacFarlane, and L. Allen (1948), and it presents the correlations between scores on IQ tests given at various times during childhood and IQ scores as young adults (17 or 18 years of age). Whereas the correlations between intelligence tests given at 12 months and at 18 years are approximately 0, the correlations rise quickly by the beginning of the third year and are relatively stable from age 8 or so on. Claire Kopp and Robert McCall (1982) stated, "[F]ollowing age 5, IQ is perhaps the most stable, important behavioral characteristic yet measured" (p. 39).

Why should there be such a high degree of stability in IQ scores during childhood, especially when predictions from infant psychometric tests are so poor? In all likelihood, the reason for the increased stability of IQ scores beginning around age 2 is the increasing similarity both of the test items and of the nature of intelligence for children 2 years of age and beyond. Following Piaget, a qualitative change in intelligence occurs sometime between 18 and 30 months of age. Children become adept symbol users during this period, and they will remain symbol users throughout their lives. IQ tests are constructed to reflect meaningful dimensions of intelligence for people of a given age, and accordingly, the ability to retrieve and manipulate symbols is a central aspect of most (if not all) intelligence tests from the 2-year level onward. There is thus a continuity of developmental function to the extent that symbolic functioning is involved in measuring intelligence at all ages. Although continuity of developmental function does not necessitate stability of individual differences, it can be seen from the earlier discussion of IQ prediction based on infancy data that such a relationship probably exists.

## TABLE **13-5**
Cross-age Correlations between IQ Tests Given in Childhood and Adult IQ Scores.

| Age of First Testing | Honzik, MacFarlane, and Alien (1948) | Bayley (1949) |
|---|---|---|
| 1 year | — | −.14 |
| 2–3 years | .33 | .40 |
| 4–5 years | .42 | .52 |
| 6–7 years | .67 | .68 |
| 8–9 years | .71 | .80 |
| 10–11 years | .73 | .87 |
| 12–13 years | .79 | — |
| 14–15 years | .76 | .84 |

Source: Honzik et al., 1948 and Bayley, 1949.

## Patterns of IQ Change During Childhood

Despite the impressive stability of the rank order of IQ scores from the early school years, there is still room for change, particularly change in the level of IQ. Recall that correlations of rank order are statistically independent of average values. So, for example, the average level of IQ scores could vary substantially for a particular sample of children and affect the correlations of rank order only minimally.

Robert McCall, Mark Appelbaum, and Pamela Hogarty (1973) examined patterns of IQ change during childhood based on data from the Fels Longitudinal Study. In their study, the data of 80 people (38 males and 42 females) who had been administered a Stanford-Binet IQ test at 17 points in development (ages 2.5, 3, 3.5, 4, 4.5, 5, 5.5, 6, 7, 8, 9, 10, 11, 12, 14, 15, and 17 years) were examined for changes in level and pattern of IQ scores over time.

First, how much change, in IQ points, was observed? The range of IQ scores for a given child was obtained, and the difference between a child's highest score during the 17 testing sessions and his or her lowest score was computed. Note that this is *not* the difference between a child's IQ score at 17 years and his or her score at 2.5 years, but the difference between the highest and lowest scores a child received, independent of age. The average shift in IQ score for children in this sample was 28.5 points. The range for 21% of the children in this sample was 20 points or less, and 43% of the children shifted between 21 and 30 points sometime between 2.5 and 17 years of age. Slightly more than one-third of the sample (36%) showed shifts of more than 30 points, with one child displaying an amazing increase of 74 points! Although such a drastic change is rare, other researchers have reported shifts of more than 50 points (Honzik et al., 1948; Moore, 1967). In general, it's fair to say that, on average, IQ scores changed substantially during the 15-year period.

One potential problem with longitudinal studies is that children can become "test wise" because of repeated testings. It is possible that the large shifts in IQ scores observed in this study were the result of practice effects, with the children getting better at taking the tests with experience, and that this resulted in elevated levels of performance as they grew older. This explanation, although reasonable, was not supported by the data. McCall and his colleagues subjected the IQ scores to cluster analysis, a statistical technique that discerns common patterns among sets of data. Thus, children showing similar patterns of IQ change over time would be grouped together in a single cluster. The cluster analysis yielded five distinct patterns of IQ change, graphed in Figure 13-10. The first thing to note is that the general trend is *not* consistently increasing IQ scores with each subsequent testing, making unlikely the hypothesis that the large IQ shifts observed for this sample were caused by practice effects.

The largest group was Cluster 1 (45% of the sample), with children displaying minimal systematic variation from a slightly rising pattern during childhood. Cluster 2 (11%) showed a sharp decline in IQ between the ages of 4 and 6 years, with a slight recovery in middle childhood, followed by a decrease in adolescence. Cluster 3 (13%) also showed a decline in IQ scores during the preschool years, followed by relatively stable performance from 6 to 14 years and an increase to age 17. Cluster 4 (9%) demonstrated a rapid rise in IQ scores, peaking between 8 and 10 years, followed by a comparably sharp decline. Cluster 5 (6%) showed a steady rise in IQ scores until age 8 or 10 years, much like the pattern for children in Cluster 4, but displayed less of a subsequent drop in scores. The data for 16% of the sample followed no consistent pattern.

FIGURE **13-10**

Mean IQ scores over time for five clusters of children in the study by McCall and colleagues (1973).

Source: R. B. McCall, M. I. Appelbaum, and P. S. Hogarty (1973). Developmental changes in mental performance: *Monographs of the Society for Research in Child Development, 38* (Serial No. 150). Copyright © 1973 The Society for Research in Child Development, Inc. Reprinted with permission.

Note in Figure 13-10 that the children having the highest IQ scores (Cluster 4) also displayed the greatest amount of IQ change. This result is consistent with the findings of other investigators, who have similarly reported that very bright children tend to change more in test scores over time than do children with lower scores (Terman & Merrill, 1937). Along these same lines, it is interesting to observe that for the two groups of children showing the overall highest levels of IQ (Clusters 4 and 5), scores increased until 8 or 10 years of age and then declined. One speculative interpretation of this pattern is that a transition in cognitive functioning (concrete to formal operations, for example) occurs at 8 to 10 years and that bright concrete operational thinkers, although making the transition to formal operations sooner than less bright children, do not maintain their high level of performance for this qualitatively different style of thought. McCall and his colleagues also suggested that children's intellectual performance during the early school years is under the direct influence of their parents, who emphasize acquiring basic skills in math and reading. As children grow older and develop interests outside the home, parents' influence on their intellectual functioning wanes, and IQ scores drop accordingly (compare with Scarr & McCartney, 1983).

McCall and his colleagues obtained some support for this latter position. As part of the Fels Longitudinal Study, children and their parents were evaluated on a variety of behavioral and attitudinal factors. McCall and his associates examined aspects of parents' child-rearing, including their attitudes toward discipline and academic achievement. The children having the highest overall IQ scores and showing the most change in test scores during childhood (Clusters 4 and 5) were characterized by having parents who were classified as accelerating, in that they strove to increase their children's mental or motor development. These parents also tended to have clear household policies, were rewarding, and had medium to severe penalties for children's transgressions. The researchers described these parents as providing an encouraging and rewarding environment with some structure and enforcement of the rules. These findings are consistent with the researchers' view that the children's increase in IQ scores during the early school years resulted from the influence of their academically oriented parents. Children in the two clusters showing decreasing preschool IQ scores (Clusters 2 and 3) tended to have parents who were minimally accelerating. Children in Cluster 2 were the least severely penalized, whereas children in Cluster 3 were the most severely punished of any group. The parents of children in Cluster 1 showed a wide range of attitudes and behaviors.

This study by McCall and his colleagues (1973) indicates that substantial changes in IQ scores occur during childhood for some children. These findings should be considered relative to the very high stability of individual differences reported in the literature. How can rank order of individual differences be so high, yet actual levels of IQ vary so drastically for some children? One clue to this paradox can be found by again examining Figure 13-10. Note that the lines depicting IQ change for the five clusters remain relatively distinct during the 15-year period. After age 7, there are only two points at which any line crosses another. Thus, despite the substantial variability in IQ scores that these lines reflect, the rank order of the various clusters remained essentially unchanged for most testings. Moreover, recall again that the children who showed the greatest amount of change were high-IQ children. Because of the way IQ tests are constructed, a change in IQ score from 130 to 160 is not the same as a 30-point shift from 75 to 105. In the former case, a child's relative rank order changes from approximately the 97th to the 99th+ percentile. In both cases, a child would be brighter than all but a small minority of his of her agemates. In contrast, a change in IQ from 75 to 105 represents a change in relative rank order from about the 5th to the 63rd percentile, a change from borderline intellectually impaired to slightly above normal! As the data indicate, changes of the former type are more common than are changes of the latter type, leaving the impression, both statistically and intuitively, that intelligence is relatively stable over time (McCall et al., 1973).

In discussing the stability and consistency of IQ scores over time, I have necessarily made use of longitudinal data, in which the same people are tested at different points in their development. But a related question about changes in IQ over time can be asked: Has the absolute level of intelligence, as measured by IQ, changed during the past century? And if so, are we getting smarter or dumber? This question is examined in Box 13-1.

---

| **BOX 13-1** | **Are People Getting Smarter? The Flynn Effect** |

As I mentioned in Chapter 12, IQ tests are routinely re-standardized. One reason for this is to keep the tests relevant for contemporary populations. Questions that might have been appropriate for people in 1930 can be meaningless for people in the year 2010. Perhaps more critically, however, tests are re-standardized so that the average remains at or about 100. If people start scoring higher or lower, on average, than 100, the test loses some of the statistical properties that make it such a valuable assessment tool. There are several ways of evaluating whether average IQ scores have changed over historical time. One is to examine the scores of many people who take the same test at different times (for example, in 1960 versus 1980). Another is to give people today versions of earlier IQ tests, standardized on samples decades before.

*(Continued)*

## BOX 13-1    Are People Getting Smarter? The Flynn Effect (*Continued*)

What prediction would you make? On the one hand, scores on standardized tests, such as the SAT, have been reported to decline during the past 40 years, and there has been much lament in the popular press about the "dumbing of America." Perhaps, then, IQ scores have gone down through the decades. On the other hand, more people are receiving both primary and secondary education than in decades past, and public health has improved considerably since the early years of the 20th century. So perhaps we're getting smarter.

The answer is that we're getting smarter, and that this phenomenon is not limited to the United States but is worldwide. The average increase in IQ is about 5 to 9 points per decade, which corresponds to more than a full standard deviation since 1940. This has been termed the **Flynn effect**, after James Flynn (1987, 1997, 2007), the first person to describe the phenomenon systematically. The increase appears to be larger for people on the low end of the IQ range (Teasdale & Owen, 1989), and the effect seems to be slowing down or to have stopped (or even reversed) in recent decades (Teasdale & Owen, 2008). Moreover, the effect is not limited to the developed world but has been observed in rural areas of Kenya as well (Daley et al., 2003). Interestingly, a similar gain in Piagetian formal operational abilities among adolescents has also been observed between the late 1960s to the mid-1990s (Flieller, 1999).

How can this be explained? One possibility concerns more education for more people, which surely is a contributor to the change (Blair et al., 2005). However, the largest changes in performance are for *fluid abilities,* which are supposedly less influenced by education and cultural differences than are crystallized abilities, such as vocabulary (see Chapter 12). That is, the type of cognitions that have changed the most are those *least* influenced by education and culture. Another explanation relates to better nutrition and health care (Daley et al., 2003; see Neisser, 1998). More people are healthy; thus, fewer people score very low on IQ tests. A third speculation is that life has gotten more complex. Today, we are constantly bombarded with visual messages not only from television but also from photographs and billboards (Greenfield, 1998). The 20th century saw the advent of movies, VCRs, DVDs, computers, and now video games. Children grow up inundated with visual information that must be organized and comprehended, and, the argument goes, these experiences may directly affect fluid intelligence. Flynn (2007) argues that improvements in education, greater use of technology, and more people being engaged in intellectually demanding work have lead to a greater number of people dealing with abstract concepts than was the case in decades past, which in turn is responsible for elevated IQ scores.

The flexibility of fluid intelligence is demonstrated in a study examining cognitive abilities in 8- to 14-year-old Greek and Chinese children (Demetriou et al., 2005). Although no differences were found in measures of general intelligence between the two groups, the Chinese children outperformed the Greek children on all measures involving visual/spatial processing. The researchers attributed these substantial differences to the Chinese children's extensive practice with their logographic (pictorial symbols) writing system, in contrast to the phonetic system used by Greek children.

If these gains reflect true increases in intelligence, they would indicate cultural changes of enormous magnitude. Flynn (1987, 2007), however, thinks otherwise. Surely, some aspects of intellectual functioning have changed. But the absurdity of a 30-point or more IQ increase since 1900 must cause one to ponder what the IQ test is actually measuring. The IQ test is a good measure of intelligence and permits us to know where a person stands relative to other people in his or her cohort. But the fact that IQ can change so substantially over historical time emphasizes the relative nature of the measure. This does not diminish its usefulness, but it does suggest that an IQ score is not "the" measure of a permanent and stable intelligence.

# SUMMARY

Most contemporary theorists adopt some variant of a *transactional model* for studying the development of intelligence, emphasizing the interactive and bidirectional relations of children and their environments.

*Behavioral genetics* examines patterns of individual differences in often-complex behaviors as a function of the genetic relationship between individuals. *Heritability* is a statistic that refers to the extent to which differences in a trait within a population are the result of inheritance. One approach to the heritability of intelligence has been to examine *elementary cognitive tasks (ECTs)*. Research has shown that response times on ECTs are related to psychometrically measured *g*, suggesting to some that these simple, and presumably highly heritable, cognitive operations are the basis for higher-order intelligence.

*Familial studies of intelligence,* comparing the IQs of people with varying degrees of genetic relations (monozygotic twins, adopted siblings), have been a major tool for assessing the heritability of intelligence. Studies show that the correlations of IQ between groups of people increase as genetic similarity increases. The current estimate for the heritability of IQ is about .50, meaning that, on average, 50% of the difference in IQ scores among people in a population can be attributed to inheritance. The heritability of IQ increases with age, which is attributed, in part, to a lessening of the effect of *shared environment,* and a greater impact of *nonshared environment,* on intelligence.

Early approaches to assessing the effects of experience on intelligence used human institutionalization studies, demonstrating that intellectual functioning can be seriously impaired under conditions of physical and social deprivation. Naturalistic studies of parent-child interaction, often assessing the quality of the environment using the *HOME scale,* generally find that mothers who provide their children with a variety of objects to play with and who are responsive have brighter children than do mothers who provide less intellectual stimulation. The effects of a nonstimulating environment tend to be especially detrimental for children with early medical problems. The *cumulative deficit effect* refers to multiple risks that persist over many years adding up and contributing to deficits in social, emotional, and cognitive functioning.

Early environmentally induced intellectual impairment can be reversed under certain conditions. Similarly, children from intellectually impoverished, low-income homes who receive cognitively enriched early experience through intensive *compensatory education programs* display immediate gains in IQ scores. However, follow-up data indicate that many of the gains manifested by these children are lost after the program ends. Once intellectual accomplishments are established, they must be maintained by subsequent environments. If the contexts of early, middle, and later childhood are highly similar, the relative level of intelligence is likely to be comparable across these years. Modifications in environment and experience, however, can foster modifications in intellectual attainments, for better or for worse.

*Stability* of intelligence is the degree to which the rank order of individual differences remains constant over time. Stability is evaluated by cross-age correlations, with high correlations reflecting stability of individual differences. Evidence from the psychometric literature indicates that the correlation between scores on sensorimotor tests given in infancy and IQ scores later in childhood is low. However, other research has shown significant correlations between measures of infants' preference for novelty and rate of habituation and later IQ scores. The findings suggest that infant intelligence is multifaceted, with some aspects presumably developing in a continuous fashion (*continuity with stability*) and others developing in a discontinuous fashion (*discontinuity with instability*).

Stability of individual differences in intelligence over the course of childhood increases with age. These increases are attributed to age-related increases in the similarity of cognitive functioning between children and adults. Despite the high cross-age correlations, however, there are significant changes in the level and pattern of IQ over age.

The *Flynn effect* refers to the systematic increase in IQ scores during the 20th century. Although speculative, changes in nutrition, health, and education, as well as a generally more complex visual environment, have been hypothesized to account for this effect.

## KEY TERMS AND CONCEPTS

transactional model

behavioral genetics

heritability

elementary cognitive tasks (ECTs)

familial studies of intelligence

shared environment

nonshared environment

HOME scale

cumulative deficit effect

compensatory education programs

stability

continuity with stability

discontinuity with instability

Flynn effect

## SUGGESTED READINGS

### Scholarly Work

Flynn, J. R. (2007). *What is intelligence?: Beyond the Flynn Effect*. New York: Cambridge University Press. In this book, the discoverer of the Flynn Effect speculates about the rising IQ over the past century and presents the view that intelligence is a dynamic phenomenon, involving the interaction of genetics, neurology, and experience at multiple levels.

Nelson, C. A., III, Zeanah, C. H., Fox, N. A., Marshall, P. J., Smuke, A. T., & Guthrie, D. (2007). Cognitive recovery in socially deprived young children: The Bucharest Early Intervention Program. *Science, 318* (21 December), 1937–1940. This study examines the effect on IQ of social deprivation and its reversal in a group of abandoned Romanian children who were randomly assigned either to foster care or to an institution. Not only are the findings of great interest, the study raises and addresses the ethical issues of doing this type of research.

Sameroff, A. (Ed.) (2009). *The transactional model of development: How children and contexts shape each other*. Washington, DC: American Psychological Association. This edited volume includes chapters written by experts in various areas of developmental psychology, showing how the transactional model can be applied to understanding children and their development. Of particular interest for issues of cognitive development is the opening chapter by Sameroff himself ("The transactional model") and the chapter by Mary Gauvain ("Social and cultural transactions in cognitive development: A cross-generational view").

### Reading for Personal Interest

Nelson, C. A., Furtado, E. A., Fox, N. A., & Zeanah, Jr., C. H. (2009). The deprived human brain. *American Scientist, 97* (May–June), 222–229. In this article, Charles Nelson and his colleagues describe the many effects of institutionalization as well as children's ability to recover from such effects, as illustrated in the Bucharest Early Intervention Project.

Rutter, M. (2006). *Genes and behavior: Nature-nurture interplay explained*. Malden, MA: Blackwell. This book provides a highly readable and up-to-date account of research in behavioral genetics, written by one of the leaders of the field who also knows a thing or two about development. I was tempted to include this in the category *Scholarly Work* because it is so thorough, but it is written so that it can be easily understood by the educated layperson.

# GLOSSARY

**A-not-B task** Object permanence task in which the infant has to retrieve a hidden object at one location (B) after having retrieved it several times previously from another one (A). (Chapter 4)

**accommodation** In Piaget's theory, the process of changing a mental structure to incorporate new information; contrast with *assimilation*. (Chapter 5)

**accommodation (of the lens)** In vision, the process of adjusting the lens of the eye to focus on objects at different distances. (Chapter 4)

**active intermodal mapping** In Meltzoff and Moore's account of neonatal cognitive abilities, the ability to integrate information from two senses. (Chapter 10)

**active rehearsal** See *cumulative rehearsal*.

**adaptation** In Piaget's theory, the process of adjusting one's cognitive structures to meet environmental demands; includes the complementary processes of assimilation and accommodation. (Chapter 5)

**adaptive strategy choice model** Siegler's model to describe how strategies change over time; the view that multiple strategies exist within a child's cognitive repertoire at any one time, with these strategies competing with one another for use. (Chapter 7)

**analogical reasoning** Reasoning that involves using something one already knows to help reason about something not known yet. (Chapter 7)

**animism** Attributing human properties, like hopes, feelings, and thoughts, to inanimate things. (Chapter 6)

**appearance/reality distinction** The knowledge that the appearance of an object does not necessarily correspond to its reality. (Chapter 5)

**arbitrariness** The fact that a word is not inherently related to the concept it represents. (Chapter 9)

**architectural constraints (or architectural innateness)** Ways in which the architecture of the brain is organized at birth; the type and manner in which information can be processed by the brain. (Chapter 1)

**articulatory loop** In Baddeley and Hitch's model of the short-term store, a phonological system that stores phonological information. (Chapter 7)

**artificialism** The belief that everything that exists was constructed by people (or God) for specific purposes, much as artifacts (for example, tools, tables, automobiles) are constructed. (Chapter 6)

**assimilation** In Piaget's theory, the process of incorporating information into already existing cognitive structures; contrast with *accommodation*. (Chapter 5)

**attention deficit hyperactivity disorder (ADHD)** An inability to sustain attention, believed to be caused by deficits in behavioral inhibition. People with ADHD display hyperactivity, impulsiveness, show great difficulty sustaining attention, and are at high risk for academic difficulties. (Chapter 7)

**autobiographical memory** Personal and long-lasting memories that are the basis for one's personal life history. (Chapter 8)

**automatic processes** Cognitive processes that require no mental effort (or mental space) for their execution, and are hypothesized (1) to occur without intention and without conscious awareness, (2) not to interfere with the execution of other processes, (3) not to improve with practice, and (4) not to be influenced by individual differences in intelligence, motivation, or education; contrast with *effortful processes*. (Chapter 7)

**axon** The long fiber of a neuron that carries messages from that cell to another. (Chapter 2)

**behavioral genetics** The study of genetic effects on behavior and on complex psychological characteristics such as intelligence and personality. (Chapter 2, 13)

**belief-desire reasoning** The process whereby we explain and predict what people do based on what we understand their desires and beliefs to be. (Chapter 5)

**bidirectionality of structure and function (structure ↔ function)** The reciprocal interaction of structure and function to produce a pattern of development. (Chapter 1)

**bilingualism** Speaking two languages proficiently. (Chapter 9)

**biologically primary abilities** Cognitive abilities that have been selected for in evolution, are acquired universally, and children typically have high motivation to perform tasks involving them, such as language. (Chapter 2)

**biologically secondary abilities** Cognitive abilities that build upon biologically primary abilities but are principally cultural inventions, and often-tedious repetition and external motivation are necessary for their mastery, such as reading. (Chapter 2)

**Black English** A dialect of American English used mostly (but not exclusively) by members of the African American community, which is characterized by some special rules of pronunciation and syntax. (Chapter 9)

**bound morphemes** Morphemes that cannot stand alone but are attached to free morphemes, such as the word endings "ed" and "ing" in English. (Chapter 9)

**category prototype** An abstract representation of a category, reflecting the central tendency, or "best example," of a category. (Chapters 4)

**centration** In Piaget's theory, the tendency of preoperational children to attend to one aspect of a situation to the exclusion of others; contrast with *decentration*. (Chapter 5)

**cerebral cortex** See *neocortex*.

**child-directed speech** The specialized register of speech adults and older children use when talking to infants and young children. (Chapter 9)

**chronotopic constraints (or chronotopic innateness)** Neural limitations on the developmental timing of events. (Chapter 1)

**cognition** The processes or faculties by which knowledge is acquired and manipulated. (Chapter 1)

**cognitive flexibility** The ability to shift between sets of tasks or rules. (Chapter 7)

**cognitive self-guidance system** In Vygotsky's theory, the use of private speech to guide problem-solving behavior. (Chapter 9)

**collaborative learning** See *cooperative learning*.

**collective monologues** Egocentric exchanges between two or more children with participants talking "with" one another, but not necessarily "to" one another, such that what one child says has little to do with the comments of the other. (Chapter 9)

**communicative competence** Mastery of five aspects of language: semantics, syntax, morphology, phonology, and pragmatics. (Chapter 9)

**compensatory education programs** Programs designed to provide preschool children from low-income homes with the intellectual skills necessary to do well in school. (Chapter 13)

**componential subtheory** In Sternberg's triarchic theory, an information-processing model of intelligence that includes three types of components: knowledge acquisition, performance, and metacomponents. (Chapter 12)

**concrete operations** In Piaget's theory, the third major stage of cognitive development, in which children can decenter their perception, are less egocentric, and can think logically about concrete objects. (Chapter 5)

**conjugate-reinforcement procedure** Conditioning procedure used in memory research with infants, in which children's behaviors control aspects of a visual display. (Chapter 8)

**conservation** In Piaget's theory, the knowledge that the quantity of a substance remains the same despite changes in its form. (Chapter 5)

**conservation of number** In Piaget's theory, the knowledge that the number of items in an array remains the same despite changes in the form of the array. (Chapter 11)

**contextual subtheory** In Sternberg's triarchic theory, the idea that

intelligence must be viewed in terms of the context in which it occurs. (Chapter 12)

**continuity with stability** The expectation and research finding that there is stability of individual differences in cognitive performance over time when the developmental function underlying performance is continuous and quantitative in nature; see also *continuity versus discontinuity of development; stability*; contrast with *discontinuity with instability*. (Chapter 13)

**convergence (of the eyes)** Both eyes looking at the same object. (Chapter 4)

**cooperative (collaborative) learning** Exercises in which students are encouraged to assist each other so that the less competent members of the team are likely to benefit from the instruction they receive from their more skillful peers, who also benefit by playing the role of teacher. (Chapter 3)

**coordination (of the eyes)** Both eyes following a moving stimulus in a coordinated fashion. (Chapter 4)

**core knowledge** Expression used by some infant researchers to refer to the set of knowledge that young infants possess in certain domains, including objects, people and social relations, numbers and quantities, and geometry. (Chapter 4)

**corpus callosum** A thick mass of nerves that connects the right and left hemispheres of the neocortex. (Chapter 2)

**creoles** Languages that develop when children transform the pidgin of their parents to a grammatically more complex "true" language. (Chapter 9)

**critical period** See *sensitive period*.

**cross-modal matching** See *intermodal matching*.

**crystallized abilities** In Cattell's theory of intelligence, intellectual abilities that develop from cultural context and learning experience; contrast with *fluid abilities*. (Chapter 12)

**cultural relativism** The idea that intellectual skills critical for survival in one's culture may not be important in another. (Chapter 12)

**cumulative (active) rehearsal** In memory research, type of rehearsal in which a person repeats the most recently presented word and then rehearses it with as many other different words as possible; contrast with *passive rehearsal*. (Chapter 6)

**cumulative deficit effect** The phenomenon by which multiple risks

persisting over many years add up, resulting in children who display deficits in social, emotional, and cognitive functioning. (Chapter 13)

**decentration** In Piaget's theory, the ability of concrete operational children to consider multiple aspects of a stimulus or situation; contrast with *centration*. (Chapter 5)

**declarative memory** Facts and events stored in the long-term memory, which come in two types: episodic and semantic memory; see also *explicit memory*; contrast with *nondeclarative memory*. (Chapter 8)

**declarative metacognition** The explicit, conscious, and factual knowledge a person has about the characteristics of the task he or she is performing, one's own weak and strong points with respect to performing the task, and the possible strategies that could be used on the task; contrast with *procedural metacognition*. (Chapter 7)

**decomposition** An arithmetic strategy in which children transform the original problem into two or more simpler problems. (Chapter 11)

**deep structure** In Chomsky's theory, the grammatical organization and meaning that underlies all language; contrast with *surface structure*. (Chapter 9)

**deferred imitation** Imitation of a modeled act sometime after viewing the behavior. (Chapter 8)

**dendrites** The numerous fibers of a neuron that receive messages from other neurons. (Chapter 2)

**dentate gyrus** Part of the hippocampus that continues to develop after birth and plays an important role in memory. (Chapter 8)

**design stance** The assumption that tools are designed for an intended function. (Chapter 6)

**development** Predictable changes that occur in structure or function over the life span. (Chapter 1)

**developmental cognitive neuroscience** The perspective that takes data from a variety of sources—molecular biology, cell biology, artificial intelligence, evolutionary theory, as well as conventional cognitive development—to create a picture of how the mind/brain develops. (Chapter 2)

**developmental contextual model** Model that proposes that all parts of the organism (such as genes, cells, tissues, and organs), as well as the whole organism itself, interact dynamically with the contexts within which the organism is embedded. See also *developmental systems approach*. (Chapter 1)

**developmental function** The form that development takes over time. (Chapter 1)

**Development quotient tests (DQ)** See *DQ*.

**developmental systems approach (developmental contextual model)** Perspective that views development as the result of bidirectional interaction between all levels of biological and experiential variables. (Chapters 1, 2)

**developmentally appropriate programs** Preschool programs that take children's "natural" propensities for play and activity into consideration. (Chapter 11 )

**deviation IQ** Method of constructing IQ scores that compares a child's performance to that of other children the same age; contrast with *mental age*. (Chapter 12)

**differential approach;** see *psychometric approach.*

**differentiation (of neurons)** The final stage of neuronal development, in which neurons gain in size, produce more dendrites, and extend their axons farther away from the cell body. (Chapter 2)

**direct-instructional programs** Preschool programs that stress formal instruction. (Chapter 11)

**discontinuity with instability** The expectation and research finding that there is instability of individual differences in cognitive performance over time when the developmental function underlying performance is discontinuous and qualitative in nature; see also *continuity versus discontinuity of development; stability;* contrast with *continuity with stability.* (Chapter 13)

**discrepancy principle** The idea that infants are most attentive to slightly novel stimuli. (Chapter 4)

**dishabituation** The tendency to show renewed interest in a stimulus when some features of it have been changed; contrast with *habituation.* (Chapter 4)

**domain-general abilities** General, underlying cognitive abilities that influence performance over a wide range of situations (or domains); contrast with *domain-specific abilities.* (Chapter 1)

**domain-specific abilities** Cognitive abilities specific to one cognitive domain

under control of a specific mind/brain function; contrast with *domain-general abilities.* (Chapter 1)

**DQ (developmental quotient) tests** A test of infant abilities, such as the Bayley Scales of Infant Development. (Chapter 12)

**dual encoding** See *dual representation.*

**dual orientation** See *dual representation.*

**dual representation (dual encoding, dual orientation)** The ability to represent an object simultaneously as the object itself and as a representation of something else. (Chapter 5)

**dynamic systems** A set of elements that undergoes change over time as a result of interactions among the elements. Dynamic systems theories propose that developmental differences emerge as a result of the self-organization of lower-level elements. See *self-organization.* (Chapter 1)

**dyslexia** Reading disability, such that a person has difficulty in learning to read despite an average intelligence. (Chapter 11)

**effortful processes** Cognitive processes that consume some of the information-processing system's limited capacity and are hypothesized to (1) be available to conscious awareness, (2) interfere with the execution of other processes, (3) improve with practice, and (4) be influenced by individual differences in intelligence, motivation, or education; contrast with *automatic processes.* (Chapter 7)

**egocentricity** In Piaget's theory, the tendency to interpret objects and events from one's own perspective. (Chapter 5)

**egocentric (or private) speech** Children's speech that is apparently produced for the self and not directed to others. (Chapter 9)

**elementary cognitive tasks (ECTs)** Simple laboratory tests designed to measure subjects' response times as they make presumably simple decisions; the low-level, or basic, processes measured by ECTs are presumed to be closely related to physiological functioning and thus primarily under the influence of endogenous (and inherited) factors. (Chapter 13)

**emergent literacy** The skills, knowledge, and attitudes that are presumed to be developmental precursors to conventional forms of reading and writing and the environments that support these developments. (Chapter 11)

**empiricism** Philosophical perspective that nature provides only species-general learning mechanisms, with cognition arising as a result of experience. (Chapter 1)

**emulation** A form of social learning that refers to understanding the goal of a model and engaging in similar behavior to achieve that goal, without necessarily reproducing the exact actions of the model. (Chapter 10)

**encephalization quotient** A measurement to evaluate the expected brain weight/body weight ratio for animals. (Chapter 2)

**enculturation hypothesis** With respect to great apes, the hypothesis that apes that are raised much as human children are raised will develop some social-cognitive abilities more similar to those of human children than of mother-raised apes (Chapter 10)

**epigenesis** The emergence of new structures and functions during the course of development. (Chapter 2)

**episodic memory** Long-term memory of events or episodes; contrast with *semantic memory;* see also *autobiographical memory; event memory.* (Chapter 8)

**equilibration** In Piaget's theory, the process by which balance is restored to the cognitive structures through assimilation and accommodation. (Chapter 5)

**event memory** Memory for everyday events, a form of episodic memory. (Chapter 8)

**evolution** The process of change in gene frequencies in populations over many generations that in time produces new species. (Chapter 2)

**evolutionary developmental psychology** The application of the principles of modern evolutionary biology to explain human development. (Chapter 2)

**evolutionary educational psychology** Principles of evolution applied to educational psychology. (Chapter 11)

**executive function** The processes involved in regulating attention and in determining what to do with information just gathered or retrieved from long-term memory. (Chapters 1, 7)

**experience-dependent processes (or experience-dependent synaptogenesis)** Processes whereby synapses are formed and maintained as a result of the unique experiences of an individual; contrast with *experience-expectant processes.* (Chapter 2)

**experience-expectant processes (or experience-expectant synaptogenesis)** Processes whereby synapses are formed and maintained when an organism has species-typical experiences; as a result, functions (such as vision) will develop for all members of a species, given a species-typical environment; contrast with *experience-dependent processes.* (Chapter 2)

**experiential subtheory** In Sternberg's triarchic theory, the subtheory concerned with how prior knowledge influences performance, specifically with the individual's ability to deal with novelty and the degree to which processing is automatized. (Chapter 12)

**explicit memory** See *declarative memory.*

**externality effect** The tendency of young infants (1-month-olds) to direct their attention primarily to the outside of a figure and to spend little time inspecting internal features. (Chapter 4)

**fact retrieval** In information-processing approaches to cognition, the retrieval of a fact directly from long-term memory without using effortful procedures. (Chapter 11)

**factor analysis** A statistical technique used to define mental factors by analyzing results from intelligence tests. (Chapter 12)

**factors** In psychometric approaches to intelligence, a set of related mental skills (such as verbal or spatial skills) that underlies intellectual functioning. (Chapter 12)

**false-belief task** A type of task used in theory-of-mind studies, in which the child must infer that another person does not possess knowledge that he or she possesses (that is, that other person holds a belief that is false). (Chapter 6)

**familial studies of intelligence** Studies in which some measure or measures of intelligence among people of a known genetic relationship are correlated; the extent to which performance varies as a function of genetic similarity is used as an indication of the heritability of that measure; see also *heritability.* (Chapter 13)

**fast mapping** The ability to learn new words based on very little input. (Chapter 9)

**finalism** Young children's tendency to attribute human causes to natural events. (Chapter 6)

**fixed-action patterns** See *innate releasing mechanisms.*

**fluid abilities** In Cattell's theory of intelligence, intellectual abilities that are biologically determined and reflected in tests of memory span and spatial thinking; contrast with *crystallized abilities.* (Chapter 12)

**Flynn effect** The systematic increase in IQ scores (between 5 and 9 points per decade) observed over the 20th century. (Chapter 13)

**folk biology** How people "naturally" come to understand the biological world. (Chapter 6)

**folk knowledge** How people "naturally" come to understand aspects of their world. Folk knowledge is differentiated from scientific knowledge. (Chapter 6)

**folk physics** How people "naturally" come to understand aspects of the physical world. (Chapter 6)

**folk psychology** How people "naturally" come to understand the psychological world. (Chapter 6)

**forethought** In Bandura's social cognitive theory, the ability to anticipate the consequences of one's actions and the actions of others. (Chapter 10)

**formal operations** In Piaget's theory, the final stage of cognitive development, in which children are able to apply abstract logical rules. (Chapter 5)

**free morphemes** Morphemes that can stand alone as a word, such as "dog," "chase," or "happy." (Chapter 9)

**function** In developmental psychology, action related to a structure, such as movement of a muscle, firing of a nerve, or activation of a mental representation; contrast with *structure*; see also *bidirectionality of structure and function.* (Chapter 1)

**functional invariants** In Piaget's theory, the processes of organization and adaptation that characterize all biological systems and operate throughout the life span. (Chapter 5)

**fuzzy traces** In fuzzy-trace theory, imprecise memory representations that are more easily accessed, generally require less effort to use, and are less susceptible to interference and forgetting than verbatim traces. (Chapter 5)

**fuzzy-trace theory** Brainerd and Reyna's theory that proposes that information is encoded on a continuum from verbatim to fuzzy, gistlike traces, and that developmental differences in many

aspects of cognition can be attributed to age differences in encoding and in differences in sensitivity to output interference. (Chapter 5)

**g (Spearman's g, general intelligence)** In psychometric theory, the idea that intelligence can be expressed in terms of a single factor, general intelligence or g, first formulated by Spearman in the early 1900s. (Chapter 12)

**Gardner's theory of multiple intelligences** See *theory of multiple intelligences.*

**gender consistency** The concept that gender remains the same despite changes in behavior. (Chapter 10)

**gender constancy** The concept that gender remains the same despite changes in physical appearance, time, and behavior; includes gender identity, gender stability, and gender consistency. (Chapter 10)

**gender identification** The process of identifying oneself as male or female and adopting the roles and values of that gender. (Chapter 10)

**gender identity** The ability of children to identify themselves as either boys or girls. (Chapter 10)

**gender schema** A mentalistic structure consisting of a set of expectations and associations that guide processing with respect to gender. (Chapter 10)

**gender script** A particular type of gender schema that is a temporally organized event sequence related to gender. (Chapter 10)

**gender stability** The concept that gender remains the same over time. (Chapter 10)

**general genetic law of cultural development** The idea that cognition occurs on two planes, first the social, between individuals, and later the psychological, as it is internalized by the child. (Chapter 3)

**general intelligence** See *g.*

**genetic determinism** The idea that one's genes determine one's behavior. (Chapter 1)

**genotype → environment effects** In Scarr and McCartney's theory, the proposal that one's genotype (genetic constitution) influences which environments one encounters and the type of experiences one has, or that genes drive experience. Three types of genotype → environment effects are proposed: passive, evocative, and active. (Chapter 2)

**goal-directed behavior** Means-end problem solving, seen first in the latter part of the first year. (Chapter 5, 7)

**"good enough" parents** The controversial proposal by Scarr that individual differences in parenting have little consequence for children's development and that "good enough" parents are adequate for proper development. (Chapter 2)

**grammar center** An area in the frontal lobe that is specifically related to processing grammatical information. (Chapter 9)

**guided participation** Adult-child interactions, not only during explicit instruction but also during the more routine activities and communication of everyday life; the process and system of involvement of individuals with others as they communicate and engage in shared activities; contrast with *zone of proximal development*; see also *sociocultural perspective*. (Chapter 3)

**habituation** The tendency to decrease responding to a stimulus that has been presented repeatedly; contrast with *dishabituation*. (Chapter 4)

**heritability** The extent to which differences in any trait within a population can be attributed to inheritance. (Chapter 13)

**hierarchical model of cognitive abilities** The model that proposes that intelligence is composed of specific cognitive abilities (for example, verbal, spatial, speed of processing, memory) that are intercorrelated and influenced by a higher-order general intellectual factor, *g*. (Chapter 12)

**HOME scale** The Home Observation for Measurement of the Environment scale, a scale developed by Bradley, Caldwell, and Elardo that provides a detailed analysis of parental behavior and characteristics of the home environment that are hypothesized to be associated with intelligence. (Chapter 13)

**holophrases (holophrastic speech)** Children's use of one-word sentences. (Chapter 9)

**hypothetico-deductive reasoning** In Piaget's theory, a formal operational ability to think hypothetically. (Chapter 5)

**imaginary audience** Expression of adolescent egocentrism, with adolescents feeling that they are constantly "on stage," or playing to an imaginary audience. (Chapter 5)

**imaginary friends** Make-believe friends. (Chapter 5)

**imitative learning** Reproduction of observed behavior to achieve a specific goal. May require an understanding of the goal that the model had in mind, as well as the reproduction of important components of the observed behavior. (Chapter 10)

**implicit memory** See *nondeclarative memory*.

**individual differences** Differences in patterns of intellectual aptitudes among people of a given age. (Chapter 1)

**inductive reasoning** The type of thinking that goes from specific observations to broad generalizations and, in Piaget's theory, is characteristic of formal operational thought. (Chapter 5)

**infant-directed speech** The specialized register of speech adults and older children use when talking specifically to infants. (Chapter 9)

**infantile amnesia** The inability to remember events from infancy and early childhood. (Chapter 8)

**inhibition** The ability to prevent from making some cognitive or behavioral response. (Chapter 7)

**innate releasing mechanisms** Inherited sets of behaviors elicited by specific sets of stimuli without the need of prior environmental experience. (Chapter 10)

**inner speech** In Vygotsky's theory, the covert language used to guide thought. (Chapter 9)

**intelligence** Acting or thinking in ways that are goal-directed and adaptive. (Chapter 12)

**intentional agents** Beings whose behavior is based on what they know and what they want, and who act deliberately to achieve their goals. (Chapter 6)

**intermodal (cross-modal) integration** The coordination or integration of information from two or more senses. (Chapter 4)

**intermodal (cross-modal) matching** The ability to recognize an object initially inspected in one modality (touch, for example) via another modality (vision, for example). (Chapter 4)

**intersensory integration** See *intermodal integration*.

**intersensory redundancy hypothesis** Redundant information from two or more sources (for example, vision and

audition) causes infants to explore *amodal* properties of those stimuli, that is, properties that are not specific to one modality (vision or audition) but cut across modalities, such as, for example, rhythm, temporal synchrony, tempo, and changing intensity (Chapter 4)

**IQ (intelligence quotient) tests** Aptitude tests, such as the Stanford-Binet and Wechsler scales, that are intended to measure aspects of intellectual functioning. (Chapter 12)

**knowledge base** The general background knowledge a person possesses, which influences most cognitive task performance. (Chapter 7)

**language acquisition device (LAD)** In Chomsky's theory, the hypothetical construct possessed by all humans at birth enabling them to acquire language. (Chapter 9)

**language acquisition support system (LASS)** The idea proposed by Bruner that adults and older children have learning devices that interact with children's language acquisition devices (LAD). (Chapter 9)

**legitimate peripheral participation** From sociocultural theory, the idea that children acquire mature, culturally appropriate behaviors simply by observation of skilled members of their community (Chapter 3)

**"less is more" hypothesis** Newport's hypothesis that the cognitive limitations of infants and young children may serve to simplify the body of language they process, thus making it easier to learn the complicated syntactical system of any human language. (Chapter 9)

**lexical constraints** Constraints that facilitate word learning in young children by limiting the possible interpretations that an utterance is likely to have. See *whole-object assumption, taxonomic assumption,* and *mutual exclusivity assumption*. (Chapter 9)

**limited capacity** The concept that one's information processing ability is restricted (that people can only do so many things at any single time). Metaphors for capacity include mental space, mental energy or effort, and time. (Chapter 7)

**long-term store** In information-processing approaches to cognition, the large and presumably permanent repository of information in the brain. (Chapter 7)

**mean length of utterance (MLU)** A measure of language development defined by the average number of meaningful language units (root words and endings) a child uses at any one time. (Chapter 9)

**memory span** The number of items a person can hold in the short-term store, assessed by testing the number of (usually) unrelated items that can be recalled in exact order. (Chapter 7)

**memory strategies** See *mnemonics*.

**mental age** Level of mental functioning (in years) as measured by the number of items passed on an intelligence test, formerly used in determining IQ scores; contrast with *deviation IQ*. (Chapter 12)

**mental rotation** Form of spatial visualization in which a person must mentally rotate a visual stimulus to determine if it matches another stimulus (Chapter 6)

**meta-analysis** A statistical technique that allows an investigator to evaluate the magnitude of a significant effect across a large number of studies, by providing an estimate of effect size, expressed in terms of how large average differences between targeted groups are across the various studies, taking into consideration the overall amount of variability. (Chapter 11)

**meta-attention** Knowledge of factors that influence one's attention. (Chapter 7)

**metacognition** Knowledge about one's own thoughts and the factors that influence thinking. (Chapter 7)

**metacommunication** Knowledge of the adequacy of one's own communication abilities. (Chapter 9)

**metamemory** Knowledge of one's own memory abilities and the factors that influence memory. (Chapter 7)

**microgenetic development** In Vygotsky's sociocultural theory, changes that occur over relatively brief periods of time, in seconds, minutes, or days, as opposed to larger-scale changes, as conventionally studied in ontogenetic development. (Chapter 3)

**migration (of neurons)** The movement of neurons to their permanent positions in the brain, most of which is completed during the prenatal period. (Chapter 2)

**mimicry** A form of social learning that involves the duplication of a behavior without any understanding of the goal of that behavior. (Chapter 10)

**mindblindness** A deficit in theory of mind, characteristic of people with

autism, in which a person cannot read the minds of others. (Chapter 6)

**min strategy** An arithmetic strategy in which children faced with an addition problem start with the largest addend and count up from there. (Chapter 11)

**mnemonics (memory strategies)** Effortful techniques used to improve memory, including rehearsal, organization, and elaboration. (Chapter 7)

**modularity** Concept that certain areas of the brain are dedicated to performing specific cognitive tasks. (Chapter 1)

**morphemes** Meaningful language units. See *bound morphemes*, *free morphemes* (Chapter 9)

**morphology** In the study of language development, the knowledge of word formation. (Chapter 9)

**motherese** See *child-directed speech*.

**multiple intelligences** See *theory of multiple intelligences*.

**mutual exclusivity assumption** A type of lexical constraint in which children believe that different words refer to different things. (Chapter 9)

**mutual imitation** Imitative-like behavior in which the adult imitates a behavior that is first emitted by the baby, which in turn activates the baby to continue that behavior (Chapter 10)

**myelin** A sheet of fatty substance that develops around the neurons to promote faster transmission of electrical signals through the nervous system. (Chapter 2)

**myelination** The development of myelin around neurons, which proceeds at different rates in different areas of the brain. (Chapter 2)

**nativism** Philosophical perspective that human intellectual abilities are innate. (Chapter 1)

**nativist theories (of language acquisition)** Theories that propose that children are born with a broad theory of language that they modify in accordance with the speech they hear growing up; contrast with *social-interactionist perspective*. (Chapter 9)

**natural selection** In Darwin's theory of evolution, the idea that more individuals are produced in a generation than can usually survive, and that variations in individuals make some members of a species more fit than others and thus more likely to survive to reproduce; according to Darwin, natural selection is the primary mechanism for evolution. (Chapter 2)

**neocortex** The outer layer of the brain, which gives humans their highly developed intelligence. (Chapter 2)

**neonatal imitation** The ability of newborns to reproduce some behavior, such as a facial expression, that they have seen in others. (Chapter 10)

**neural Darwinism** Edelman's theory that groups of neurons are in constant competition with one another, each attempting to recruit adjacent neurons to their group and thus perform a particular function. (Chapter 2)

**neuroimaging techniques** New technologies that permit imaging of brain activities, including high-density event-related potentials, positron emission tomography (PET), and functional magnetic resonance imaging (fMRI). (Chapter 2)

**neurogenesis (proliferation)** The process of nerve-cell division by mitosis. (Chapter 2)

**neuron** Nervous system cell through which electrical and chemical signals are transmitted. (Chapter 2)

**neurotransmitters** Chemicals in synapses that serve to transmit electrical impulses between neurons. (Chapter 2)

**nondeclarative (or procedural or implicit) memory** Knowledge in the long-term store of procedures that are unconscious; contrast with *declarative memory*. (Chapter 8)

**nonshared environment** A home environment that is unique to an individual, not shared by a sibling, for instance. (Chapter 13)

**numerosity** The ability to determine quickly the number of items in a set without counting. (Chapter 4)

**object and location memory** A form of spatial cognition that involves locating and remembering objects in arrays. Unlike other forms of spatial cognition, object and location memory tends to be better in females than in males and shows relatively little improvement over development. (Chapters 6)

**object constancy** The knowledge that an object remains the same despite changes in the how it is viewed (Chapter 4)

**object permanence** The knowledge that objects have an existence in time and space independent of one's own perception or action on those objects. (Chapters 4, 8)

**observational learning** The ability to learn about the world simply by watching, central to Bandura's social cognitive theory; according to Bandura, observational learning includes four subprocesses: attentional processes, retention processes, production processes, and motivational processes. (Chapter 10)

**ontogenetic adaptations** Behaviors that play a specific role in survival for an individual at one time only and then disappear when they are no longer needed. (Chapter 10)

**ontogenetic development** Development of the individual over his or her lifetime. (Chapter 3)

**operations** In Piaget's theory, particular types of cognitive schemes that are mental (that is, require symbols), derive from action, exist in organized systems (structures of the whole), and follow a set of logical rules, most importantly that of reversibility. (Chapter 5)

**ordinality** A basic understanding of *more than* and *less than* relationships. (Chapter 4)

**organization (in memory research)** The structure discovered or imposed upon a set of items that is used to guide memory performance. (Chapter 7)

**organization (in Piaget's theory)** The idea that every intellectual operation is related to all other acts of intelligence. (Chapter 5)

**overextensions** In the study of language development, the stretching of a familiar word beyond its correct meaning; for example, calling all four-legged mammals "doggie." (Chapter 9)

**overregularization** In the study of language development, the tendency to apply rules to words when they are not appropriate, for example, runned, foots, mices. (Chapter 9)

**passive rehearsal** Style of rehearsing in which a person includes few (usually one) unique items per rehearsal set; contrast with *cumulative rehearsal*. (Chapter 7)

**perceptual centration** See *centration*.

**perceptual decentration** See *decentration*.

**personal fable** A belief in one's uniqueness and invulnerability, which is an expression of adolescent egocentrism. (Chapter 5)

**phonemes** Individual sounds that are used to make up words. (Chapters 4, 11)

**phonemic awareness** The knowledge that words consist of separable sounds;

contrast with *phonological recoding*. (Chapter 9, 11)

**phonics** Reading instruction method based on learning letter-sound correspondence; see also *phonological recoding*. (Chapter 11)

**phonological recoding** Reading skills used to translate written symbols into sounds and words; contrast with *phonemic awareness*. (Chapter 11)

**phonology** In language acquisition, the knowledge of how words are pronounced. (Chapter 9)

**phylogenetic development** Development over evolutionary time. (Chapter 3)

**pidgins** Structurally simple communication systems that arise when people who share no common language come into constant contact. (Chapter 9)

**plasticity** The extent to which behavior or brain functioning can be changed. (Chapters 1, 2)

**positive manifold** In psychometric approaches to intelligence, the high correlations among scores on sets of cognitive tests that have little in common with one another in terms of content or types of strategies used. (Chapter 12)

**pragmatics** In the study of language development, knowledge about how language can be adjusted to fit different circumstances. (Chapter 9)

**preference for novelty paradigms** Tasks in which an infant's preference, usually measured in looking time, for a novel as opposed to a familiar stimulus is used as an indication of memory for the familiar stimulus. (Chapter 8)

**preoperations** In Piaget's theory, the second major stage of cognitive development (approximately ages 2 to 7), characterized by prelogical, intuitive thought. (Chapter 5)

**private (egocentric) speech** Children's speech apparently for self and not directed to others. (Chapter 9)

**problem solving** Process in which someone has a specific goal in mind that cannot be attained immediately because of the presence of one or more obstacles; problem solving involves a goal, obstacles to that goal, strategies for overcoming the obstacles, and an evaluation of the results. (Chapter 7)

**procedural memory** See *nondeclarative memory*.

**procedural metacognition** The knowledge about when strategies are necessary as well as monitoring how

well one is performing on a task; contrast with *declarative metacognition*. (Chapter 7)

**production deficiency** Children's tendency not to use spontaneously a strategy that they are capable of using when instructed; contrast with *utilization deficiency*. (Chapters 7)

**productive vocabulary** The language a child can actually produce, or speak; contrast with *receptive language*. (Chapter 9)

**proliferation (of neurons; neurogenesis)** The process of nerve-cell division by mitosis. (Chapter 2)

**promiscuous teleology** Children's tendency to reason about events and objects in terms of purpose. (Chapter 6)

**psychometric (differential) approach** The theory that intelligence can be described in terms of mental factors and that tests can be constructed that reveal individual differences in the factors underlying mental performance. (Chapter 12)

**Pygmalion effect** A form of self-fulfilling prophecy, in which a person internalizes the expectations of an authority figure. (Chapter 12)

**reasoning** A particular type of problem solving that involves making inferences. (Chapter 7)

**receptive vocabulary** The language that a child can understand; contrast with *productive language*. (Chapter 9)

**reciprocal determinism** In Bandura's theory, the belief that children have as much of an effect on their environment as their environment has on them. (Chapter 10)

**reflective abstraction** In Piaget's theory, the ability to reflect upon knowledge one already possesses, and without the need of additional information from the external environment, to arrive at new knowledge; characteristic of adolescent thought. (Chapter 5)

**rehearsal** A memory strategy in which target information is repeated; see also *cumulative rehearsal, passive rehearsal*. (Chapter 7)

**relational mapping** The application of what one knows about one set of elements (the relation of A to B) to relations about different elements (the relation of C to D). (Chapter 7)

**relational shift** In analogical reasoning, the proposal that there is in development a shift from focusing on perceptual similarity to relational similarity to solve problems. (Chapter 7)

**representation** The mental encoding of information. (Chapters 1, 5)

**representational constraints (or representational innateness)** Representations that are hard-wired into the brain so that some types of "knowledge" are innate. (Chapter 1)

**representational insight** The knowledge that an entity can stand for something other than itself. (Chapter 5)

**resistance to interference** The ability to ignore irrelevant information so that it does not impede task performance; its inverse is interference sensitivity. (Chapter 7)

**reversibility** In Piaget's theory, the knowledge that an operation can be reversed, characteristic of the concrete operational period; see also *compensation, negation.* (Chapter 5)

**scaffolding** An expert, when instructing a novice, responding contingently to the novice's responses in a learning situation, so that the novice gradually increases his or her understanding of a problem. (Chapter 3)

**schema** An abstract representation of an object or event. (Chapter 4)

**scheme** An abstract representation of an object or event. (Chapter 5)

**scientific reasoning** A type of reasoning that involves the generation of hypotheses and the systematic testing of those hypotheses. (Chapter 7)

**scripts** A form of schematic organization, with real-world events organized in terms of temporal and causal relations between component acts. (Chapter 8)

**selective attention** Concentration on chosen stimuli without distraction by nontarget stimuli. (Chapter 7)

**selective cell death** Early developmental process in which neurons that are not activated by sensory and motor experience die. (Chapter 2)

**self-concept** The way a person defines himself or herself. (Chapter 10)

**self-efficacy** The belief that one can influence one's own thoughts and behavior. (Chapter 10)

**self-organization** In dynamic systems theories, the process whereby patterns emerge from interactions of the components of a complex system without explicit instructions either in the organism itself or from the environment. (Chapter 1)

**self-reflection** In Bandura's social cognitive theory, the ability to analyze one's thoughts and actions. (Chapter 10)

**self-regulation** The process of adopting standards of acceptable behavior, including aspirational standards (hoped-for levels of accomplishment) as well as social and moral standards. (Chapter 10)

**semantic memory** Long-term memory representation of definitions and relations among language terms; contrast with *episodic memory.* (Chapter 8)

**semantics** In language acquisition, knowledge of the meaning of words and sentences. (Chapter 9)

**sensitive period** The time in development (usually early in life) when a certain skill or ability is most easily acquired. (Chapter 2)

**sensorimotor stage** In Piaget's theory, the first major stage of cognitive development (birth to approximately 2 years), in which children understand their world through sensory and motor experiences. (Chapter 5)

**sequential bilingualism** The situation in which children learn a second language after mastering the first (Chapter 9)

**shared attention (joint attention)** Two people both attending to the same thing or event and sharing that experience. (Chapter 6)

**shared environment** A home environment shared by different family members. (Chapter 13)

**short-term store (primary memory, contents of consciousness)** Memory store that can hold a limited amount of information for a matter of seconds; cognitive operations are executed in the short-term store and information can be maintained indefinitely in the short-term store through operations such as rehearsal; see also *working memory.* (Chapter 7)

**simultaneous bilingualism** The situation in which children are exposed from birth to two languages. (Chapter 9)

**social cognition** Thinking about the self, other people, and social relationships. (Chapter 10)

**social cognitive theory** Bandura's theory of how individuals operate cognitively on their social experiences and how these cognitive operations influence behavior and development. (Chapter 10)

**social information processing** As exemplified by Dodge's theory, the view that social information must be encoded, compared with other pertinent information, and retrieved so that social interactions run smoothly. (Chapter 10)

**social-interactionist theories (of language acquisition)** The position that children's domain-general social-cognitive abilities and the social environment play a central role in language development; contrast with *nativist perspective.* (Chapter 9)

**social learning** The acquisition of social information and behavior; situations in which one individual comes to behave similarly to others. (Chapter 10)

**social learning theory** An earlier version of Bandura's social cognitive theory. (Chapter 10)

**sociocultural perspective** A perspective of cognitive development that emphasizes that development is guided by adults interacting with children, with the cultural context determining to a large extent how, where, and when these interactions take place; see also *guided participation; zone of proximal development.* (Chapters 1, 3)

**sociohistorical development** Changes that have occurred in one's culture and the values, norms, and technologies such a history has generated (Chapter 3)

**source monitoring** The awareness of the origins of one's memories, knowledge, or beliefs. (Chapter 8)

**span of apprehension** The number of items that people can keep in mind at any one time, or the amount of information that people can attend to at a single time (Chapter 7)

**spatial cognition** The type of cognition that involves processing visual information in terms of spatial relationships, including spatial orientation, spatial visualization, and object and location memory. (Chapter 6)

**spatial orientation** How people understand the placement of objects in space with themselves as the reference point. (Chapter 6)

**spatial visualization** An aspect of spatial cognition that involves the mental manipulations of visual stimuli, such as performing mental rotation or solving embedded-figures problems. (Chapter 6)

**Spearman's g** See *g (general intelligence).*

**speech register** A distinct style of speaking, which is used only is specific contexts (for example, when talking to children; when talking in school). (Chapter 9)

**stability** In developmental psychology, the degree to which a person maintains over time the same rank order in comparison with peers for a particular characteristic. (Chapters 1, 13)

**Stanford-Binet** An individually administered IQ test. (Chapter 12)

**statistical learning** In language learning, a domain-general mechanism in which infants essentially keep track of how often different syllables follow one another and using this information to determine which sound sequences are meaningful (that is, are "words"), and which are not. (Chapter 9)

**stereotype threat** Phenomenon in which minority members perform worse on IQ or other tests after being reminded of the negative stereotype concerning their groups' performance on such tests (Chapters 11, 12)

**Sternberg's triarchic theory** See *triarchic theory.*

**strategies** Goal-directed and deliberately implemented mental operations used to facilitate task performance; see also *mnemonics.* (Chapters 1, 6)

**structure** In developmental psychology, a substrate of the organism that develops, such as muscle, nervous tissue, or mental knowledge; contrast with *function*; see *bidirectionality of structure and function.* (Chapter 1)

**sum strategy** A simple addition strategy used by young children that involves counting together the two addends of a problem. (Chapter 11)

**surface structure** In Chomsky's theory, the actual words of a sentence, derived from the deep structure. (Chapter 9)

**symbolization** In Bandura's social cognitive theory, the ability to think about one's social behavior in terms of words and images. (Chapter 10)

**synapse** The tiny space between the dendrite of one neuron and the axon of another through which chemical messages are passed. (Chapter 2)

**synaptogenesis** The process of synapse formation. (Chapter 2)

**syntax** In language acquisition, the knowledge of how words are put together to form grammatical sentences. (Chapter 9)

**syntactic bootstrapping** In learning the meaning of words, the idea that the grammatical form of speech may give children important clues for guessing what a word means. (Chapter 9)

**taxonomic assumption** A type of lexical constraint in which children assume that words refer to things that are similar. (Chapter 9)

**teaching** A form of social learning in which a more accomplished person intentionally conveys his or her knowledge and/or skills to a less accomplished person. (Chapter 10)

**telegraphic speech** Children's economical use of words, including only high-information words that are most important in conveying meaning. (Chapter 9)

**theory of mind** A person's concepts of mental activity; used to refer to how children conceptualize mental activity and how they attribute intention to and predict the behavior of others; see also *belief-desire reasoning.* (Chapter 6)

**theory of multiple intelligences** Gardner's theory postulating eight components, or modules, of intelligence (1) linguistic, (2) logical-mathematical, (3) musical, (4) spatial, (5) bodily-kinesthetic, (6) interpersonal, (7) intrapersonal, and (8) naturalistic. (Chapter 12)

**theory theories** Theories of cognitive development that combine neo-nativism and constructivism, proposing that cognitive development progresses by children generating, testing, and changing theories about the physical and social world. (Chapter 6)

**tools of intellectual adaptation** Vygotsky's term for methods of thinking and problem-solving strategies that children internalize from their interactions with more competent members of society. (Chapter 3)

**transactional model** A framework that views development as the continuous and bidirectional interchange between an active organism with a unique biological constitution, and a changing environment. (Chapter 13)

**triarchic theory of intelligence** Sternberg's theory that describes intelligence in terms of three subtheories: contextual, experiential, and componential. (Chapter 12)

**underextensions** Incorrectly restricting the use of a term (for example, believing that only one's pet, Fido, deserves the label "dog"). (Chapter 9)

**universal grammar** In nativist theories of language acquisition, the innate grammar that characterizes all human languages. (Chapter 9)

**utilization deficiency** The inability of children to benefit from strategies they

are able to implement; contrast with *production deficiency.* (Chapter 7)

**verbatim traces** In fuzzy-trace theory, precise, literal memory representations that are less easily accessed, generally require more effort to use, and are more susceptible to interference and forgetting than fuzzy traces. (Chapter 5)

**vicarious learning** In Bandura's social cognitive theory, learning without the need to receive specific reinforcement for one's behavior; rather, learning by observing others. (Chapter 10)

**violation-of-expectation method** Based on habituation/dishabituation procedures, techniques in which increases in infants' looking time are interpreted as reflecting a violation of an expected outcome. (Chapter 4)

**visual preference paradigm** In research with infants, observing the amount of time infants spend looking at different visual stimuli to determine which one they prefer (that is, look at more often); such preferences indicate an ability to discriminate between stimuli. (Chapter 4)

**Wechsler scales** Individually administered IQ tests, including the "WPPSI, WISC, and WAIS". (Chapter 12)

**whole-language approach** A top-down approach to teaching reading that emphasizes the readers' active construction of meaning; often excludes the use of phonics. (Chapter 11)

**whole-object assumption** A type of lexical constraint in which children assume when hearing a word that it refers to the whole object and not to some part of that object. (Chapter 9)

**wishful thinking** A characteristic of preschool thought such that children often do not differentiate between their wishes and their expectations. (Chapter 10)

**word spurt** The rapid increase in word (mostly noun) learning, occurring at about 18 months of age. (Chapter 9)

**working memory** The capacity to store and transform information being held in the short-term system. See *short-term store.* (Chapter 7)

**zone of proximal development** In Vygotsky's theory, the difference between a child's actual level of ability and the level of ability that he or she can achieve when working under the guidance of an instructor; contrast with *guided participation*; see *sociocultural perspective.* (Chapter 3)

# REFERENCES

ABRAVANEL, E., & SIGAFOOS, A. D. (1984). Explaining the presence of imitation during early infancy. *Child Development, 55,* 381–392.

ACKERMAN, B. P., & BROWN, E. D. (2006). Income poverty, poverty co-factors, and the adjustment of children in school. In R. V. Kail (Ed.), *Advances in child development and behavior,* Vol. 34 (pp. 91–129). Oxford: Elsevier.

ACKIL, J. K., VAN ABBEMA, D. L., & BAUER, P. J. (2003). After the storm: Enduring differences in mother-child recollections of traumatic and nontraumatic events. *Journal of Experimental Child Psychology, 84,* 286–309.

ACKIL, J. K., & ZARAGOZA, M. S. (1995). Developmental differences in eyewitness suggestibility and memory for source. *Journal of Experimental Child Psychology, 60,* 57–83.

ADAMS, J. W., & HITCH, G. J. (1997). Working memory and children's mental addition. *Journal of Experimental Child Psychology, 67,* 21–38.

ADAMS, M. J., TREIMAN, R., & PRESSLEY, M. (1998). Reading, writing, and literacy. In K. A. Renninger & I. E. Sigel (Vol. Eds.), *Child psychology in practice,* Vol. 4, in W. Damon (Gen. Ed.), *Handbook of child psychology* (5th ed.). New York: Wiley.

ADAMS, R. J., & COURAGE, M. L. (1998). Human newborn color vision: Measurement with chromatic stimuli varying in excitation purity. *Journal of Experimental Child Psychology, 68,* 22–34.

ADAMS, R. J., COURAGE, M. L., & MERCER, M. E. (1994). Systematic measurement of human neonatal color vision. *Vision Research, 34,* 1691–1701.

ADEY, P. S., & SHAYER, M. (1992). Accelerating the development of formal thinking in middle and high school students: II. Postproject effects on science achievement. *Journal of Research in Science Teaching, 29,* 81–92.

ADLER, S. (1990). Multicultural clients: Implications for the SLP. *Language, Speech, and Hearing in the Schools, 21,* 135–139.

ADRIÁN, J. E., CLEMENTE, R. A., & VILLANUEVA, L. (2007). Mothers use of cognitive state verbs in picture-book reading and the development of children's understanding of mind: A longitudinal study. *Child Development, 78,* 1052–1067.

AGUIAR, A., & BAILLARGEON, R. (1998). Eight-and-a-half-month-old infants' reasoning about containment events. *Child Development, 69,* 636–653.

AGUIAR, A., & BAILLARGEON, R. (1999). 2.5-month-old infants' reasoning about when objects should and should not be occluded. *Cognitive Psychology, 39,* 116–157.

AINSWORTH, M. D. S., BLEHAR, M. C., WATERS, E., & WALL, S. (1978). *Patterns of attachment: A psychological study of the strange situation.* Hillsdale, NJ: Erlbaum.

AITCHINSON, J. (1994). *Words in the mind: An introduction to the mental lexicon* (2nd ed.). Oxford: Blackwell.

AKHTAR, N. (1999). Acquiring basic word order: Evidence for data-driven learning of syntactic structure. *Journal of Child Language, 26,* 339–356.

ALEXANDER, J. M., & SCHWANENFLUGEL, P. J. (1996). Development of metacognitive concepts about thinking in gifted and nongifted children: Recent research. *Learning and Individual Differences, 8,* 305–325.

ALEXANDER, J. M., SCHWANENFLUGEL, P. J., & CARR, M. (1995). Development of metacognition in gifted children: Directions for future research. *Developmental Review, 15,* 1–37.

ALEXANDER, R. D. (1989). Evolution of the human psyche. In P. Mellers & C. Stringer (Eds.), *The human revolution: Behavioral and biological perspectives on the origins of modern humans* (pp. 455–513). Princeton, NJ: Princeton University Press.

ALIBALI, M. W. (1999). How children change their minds: Strategy change can be gradual or abrupt. *Developmental Psychology, 35,* 127–145.

ALLEN, D., BANKS, M. S., & SCHEFRIN, B. (1988). Chromatic discrimination in human infants. *Investigative Ophthalmology and Visual Science, 29* (Suppl.), 25.

ALLOWAY, T. P., & ALLOWAY, R. G. (2010). Investigating the predictive roles of working memory and IQ in academic attainment. *Journal of Experimental Child Psychology, 106,* 20–29.

ALLOWAY, T. P., GATHERCOLE, S. E., & PICKERING, S. J. (2006). Verbal and visuospatial short-term and working memory in children: Are they separable? *Child Development, 77,* 1698–1716.

ALS, H. (1995). The preterm infant: A model for the study of fetal brain expectation. In J.-P. Lecanuet, W. Fifer, N. Krasnegor, & W. Smotherman (Eds.), *Fetal development: A psychobiological perspective.* Hillsdale, NJ: Erlbaum.

AMBADY, N., SHIH, M., KIM, A., & PITTINSKY, T. L. (2001). Stereotype susceptibility in children: Effects of identity activation on quantitative performance. *Psychological Science, 12,* 385–390.

AMOS, D., & CASEY, B. J. (2006). Beyond what develops when: Neuroimaging may inform how cognition changes with development. *Current Directions in Psychological Science, 15,* 24–29.

ANASTASI, A. (1988). *Psychological testing* (6th ed.). New York: Macmillan.

ANDERSON, R. C., HIEBERT, E. H., SCOTT, J. A., & WILKINSON, I. A. G. (1984). *Becoming a nation of readers: The report of the Commission on Reading.* Washington, DC: U.S. Department of Education.

ANGLIN, J. M. (1977). *Word, object, and conceptual development.* New York: Norton.

ANISFELD, M., (1991). Neonatal imitation: A review. *Developmental Review,* 11, 60–97.

ANISFELD, M., TURKEWITZ, G., ROSE, S. A., ROSENBERG, F. R., SHEIBER, F. J., COUTURIER-FAGAN, D. A., GER, J. S., & SOMMER, I. (2001). No compelling evidence that newborns imitate oral gestures. *Infancy,* 2, 111–122.

ANNETT, M. (1973). Laterality of childhood hemiplegia and the growth of speech and intelligence. *Cortex,* 9, 4–33.

ANOOSHIAN, L. J., & YOUNG, D. (1981). Developmental changes in cognitive maps of a familiar neighborhood. *Child Development,* 52, 341–348.

ANTELL, S. E., & KEATING, D. P. (1983). Perception of numerical invariance in neonates. *Child Development,* 54, 695–701.

ARFFA, S. (2007). The relationship of intelligence to executive function and nonexecutive function measures in a sample of average, above average, and gifted youth. *Archives of Clinical Neuropsychology,* 22, 969–978.

ARNETT, J. (1992). Reckless behavior in adolescence: A developmental perspective. *Developmental Review,* 12, 339–373.

ARTERBERRY, M. E., & BORNSTEIN, M. H. (2001). Three-month-old infants' categorization of animals and vehicles based on static and dynamic attributes. *Journal of Experimental Child Psychology,* 80, 333–346.

ASHCRAFT, M. H. (1990). Strategic processing in children's mental arithmetic: A review and proposal. In D. F. Bjorklund (Ed.), *Children's strategies: Contemporary views of cognitive development.* Hillsdale, NJ: Erlbaum.

ASHER, S. R., & MARKEL, R. A. (1974). Sex differences in comprehension of high- and low-interest reading material. *Journal of Educational Psychology,* 66, 680–687.

ASLIN, R. N. (2007). What's in a look? *Developmental Science,* 10, 48–53.

ASLIN, R. N., & JACKSON, R. W. (1979). Accommodative-convergence in young infants: Development of a synergistic sensory-motor system. *Canadian Journal of Psychology,* 33, 222–231.

ASLIN, R. N., JUSCZYK, P. W., & PISONI, D. B. (1998). Speech and auditory processing during infancy. In D. Kuhn & R. S. Siegler (Eds.), *Cognitive, language, and perceptual development,* Vol. 2, in W. Damon (Gen. Ed.), *Handbook of child psychology* (5th ed.). New York: Wiley.

ASLIN, R. N., SAFFRAN, J. R., & NEWPORT, E. L. (1998). Computation of conditional probability statistics by 8-month-old infants. *Psychological Science,* 9, 321–324.

ASTINGTON, J. W., & JENKINS, J. M. (1995). Theory of mind development and social understanding. *Cognition and Emotion,* 9, 151–165.

ASTUTI, R. (2001). Are we all natural dualists? A cognitive developmental approach. The 2000 Malinowski Memorial Lecture. *Journal of the Royal Anthropological Institute,* 7, 429–447.

ASTUTI, R., SOLOMON, G. E. A., & CAREY, S. (2004). Constraints on conceptual development: A case study of the acquisition of folk biological and folk sociological knowledge in Madagascar. *Monographs of the Society for Research in Child Development,* 69 (Serial No. 277).

ATANCE, C. M. (2008). Future thinking in young children. *Current Directions in Psychological Science,* 17, 295–298.

ATKINSON, R. C., & SHIFFRIN, R. M. (1968). Human memory: A proposed system and its control processes. In K. W. Spence & J. T. Spence (Eds.), *The psychology of learning and motivation: Advances in research and theory,* Vol. 2. New York: Academic.

ATRAN, S. (2002). *In gods we trust: The evolutionary landscape of religion.* New York: Oxford University Press.

AUGUST, G. J. (1987). Production deficiencies in free recall: A comparison of hyperactive, learning-disabled, and normal children. *Journal of Abnormal Child Psychology,* 15, 429–440.

AUSLEY, J. A., & GUTTENTAG, R. E. (1993). Direct and indirect assessments of memory: Implications for the study of memory development. In M. L. Howe & R. Pasnak (Eds.), *Emerging themes in cognitive development:* Vol. 1. *Foundations.* New York: Springer-Verlag.

AVIS, J., & HARRIS, P. L. (1991). Belief-desire reasoning among Baka children: Evidence for a universal conception of mind. *Child Development,* 62, 460–467.

AYLWARD, G. P. (1997). *Infant and early childhood neuropsychology.* New York: Plenum.

AZMITIA, M. (1992). Expertise, private speech, and the development of self-regulation. In R. M. Diaz & L. E. Berk (Eds.), *Private speech: From social interaction to self-regulation.* Hillsdale, NJ: Erlbaum.

BADDELEY, A. D. (1986). *Working memory.* Oxford: Clarendon.

BADDELEY, A. D., & HITCH, G. J. (1974). Working memory. In G. Bower (Ed.), *The psychology of learning and motivation: Advances in research and theory,* Vol. 8. New York: Academic.

BADIAN, N. A. (1983). Dyscalculia and nonverbal disorders of learning. In H. R. Myklebust (Ed.), *Progress in learning disabilities.* New York: Stratton.

BAENNINGER, M., & NEWCOMBE, N. (1995). Environmental input to the development of sex-related differences in spatial and mathematical ability. *Learning and Individual Differences,* 7, 363–379.

BAGHURST, P. A., MCMICHAEL, A. J., WIGG, N. R., VIMPANI, G. V., ROBERTSON, E. F., ROBERTS, R. J., & TONG, S.-L. (1992). Environmental exposure to lead and children's intelligence at the age of seven years. *New England Journal of Medicine,* 327, 1279–1284.

BAHRICK, L. E. (1995). Intermodal origins of self-perception. In P. Rochat (Ed.), *The self in infancy: Theory and research.* New York: Elsevier Science.

BAHRICK, L. E. (2002). Generalization of learning in three-and-a-half-month-old infants on the basis of amodal relations. *Child Development,* 73, 667–681.

BAHRICK, L. E., HERNANDEZ-REIF, M., & PICKENS, J. N. (1997). The effect of retrieval cues on visual preferences and memory in infancy: Evidence for a four-phase attention function. *Journal of Experimental Child Psychology,* 67, 1–20.

BAHRICK, L. E., & LICKLITER, R. (2002). Intersensory redundancy guides early perceptual and cognitive development. *Advances in Child Development and Behavior,* 30, 153–187.

BAHRICK, L. E., LICKLITER, R., & FLOM, R. (2004). Intersensory redundancy guides the development of selective attention, perception, and cognition in infancy. *Current Directions in Psychological Science,* 13, 99–102.

BAHRICK, L. E., MOSS, L., & FADIL, C. (1996). The development of self recognition in infancy. *Ecological Psychology,* 8, 189–208.

BAHRICK, L. E., PARKER, J. F., FIVUSH, R., & LEVITT, M. (1998). The effects of stress on young children's memory for a natural disaster. *Journal of Experimental Psychology: Applied,* 4, 308–331.

BAHRICK, L. E., & PICKENS, J. N. (1995). Infant memory for object motion across a period of three months: Implications for a four-phase attention function. *Journal of Experimental Child Psychology,* 59, 343–371.

BAHRICK, L. E., & WATSON, J. S. (1985). Detection of intermodal proprioceptive-visual contingency as a potential basis of self-perception in infancy. *Developmental Psychology,* 21, 963–973.

BAILEY, D. H., & GEARY, D. C. (2009). Hominid brain evolution: Testing climatic, ecological, and social competition models. *Human Nature,* 20, 67–79.

BAILEY, U. L., LORCH, E. P., MILICH, R., & CHARNIGO, R. (2009). Developmental changes in attention and comprehension among children with attention deficit hyperactivity disorder. *Child Development,* 80, 1842–1855.

BAILLARGEON, R. (1987). Object permanence in 3½- and 4½-month-old infants. *Developmental Psychology,* 23, 655–664.

BAILLARGEON, R. (2004). Infants' reasoning about hidden objects: Evidence for event-general and event-specific expectations. *Developmental Science,* 7, 391–424.

BAILLARGEON, R. (2008). Innate ideas revisited: For a principle of persistence in infants' physical reasoning. *Perspectives on Psychological Science,* 3, 2–13.

BAILLARGEON, R., & DE VOS, J. (1991). Object permanence in young infants: Further evidence. *Child Development,* 62, 1227–1246.

BAILLARGEON, R., KOTOVSKY, L., & NEEDHAM, A. (1995). The acquisition of physical knowledge in infancy. In G. Lewis, D. Premack, & D. Sperber (Eds.), *Casual understandings in cognition and culture.* Oxford: Oxford University Press.

BAIRD, A. A., KAGAN, J., GAUDETTE, T., WALZ, K. A., HERSHLAG, N., & BOAS, D. A. (2002). Frontal lobe activation during object permanence: Data from near-infrared spectroscopy. *NeuroImage,* 16, 120–126.

BAKEMAN, R., ADAMSON, L. B., KONNER, M., & BARR, R. G. (1990). !Kung infancy: The social context of object exploration. *Child Development,* 61, 794–809.

BAKER, D. P. (1992). Compared to Japan the U. S. is a low achiever—Really. *Educational Research,* 22, 18–20.

BAKER, S. T., FRIEDMAN, O., & LESLIE, A. M. (2010). The opposites task: Using general rules to test cognitive flexibility in preschoolers. *Journal of Cognition and Development,* 11, 240–254.

BAKER-WARD, L., GORDON, B. N., ORNSTEIN, P. A., LARUS, D. M., & CLUBB, P. A. (1993). Young children's long-term retention of a pediatric visit. *Child Development,* 64, 1519–1533.

BAKER-WARD, L., & ORNSTEIN, P. A. (1988). Age differences in visual-spatial memory performance: Do children really out-perform adults when playing Concentration? *Bulletin of the Psychonomic Society,* 26, 331–332.

BALDWIN, D. A. (1993). Infant's ability to consult the speaker for clues to word reference. *Journal of Child Language,* 20, 395–418.

BANDURA, A. (1986). *Social foundations of thought and action: A social cognitive theory.* Englewood Cliffs, NJ: Prentice Hall.

BANDURA, A. (1989). Social cognitive theory. In R. Vasta (Ed.), *Annals of child development: Six theories of child development,* Vol. 6. Greenwich, CT: JAI Press.

BANDURA, A. (1997). *Self-efficacy: The exercise of control.* New York: Freeman.

BANDURA, A. (2006). Toward a psychology of human agency. *Perspectives on Psychological Science,* 1, 164–180.

BANDURA A., BARBARANELLI, C., CAPRARA, G. V., & PASTORELLI, C. (1996). Multifaceted impact of self-efficacy beliefs on academic functioning. *Child Development,* 67, 1206–1222.

BANDURA, A., & WALTERS, R. H. (1963). *Social learning and personality development.* New York: Holt, Rinehart & Winston.

BANKS, M. S. (1980). The development of visual accommodation during early infancy. *Child Development,* 51, 646–666.

BARD, K. (2007). Neonatal imitation in chimpanzees (*Pan troglodytes*). *Animal Cognition,* 10, 233–242.

BARKLEY, R. A. (1990). Attention deficit disorders: History, definition, and diagnosis. In M. Lewis & S. M. Lewis (Eds.), *Handbook of developmental psychopathology: Perspectives in developmental psychology.* New York: Plenum.

BARKLEY, R. A. (1997). Behavioral inhibition, sustained attention, and executive functions. Constructing a unifying theory of ADHD. *Psychological Bulletin,* 121, 65–94.

BARKLEY, R. A. (1998). *Attention deficit hyperactivity disorder: A handbook for diagnosis and treatment.* New York: Guilford.

BARKLEY, R. A., KOPLOWITZ, S., ANDERSON, T., & MCMURRAY, M. B. (1997). Sense of time in children with ADHD: Effects of duration, distraction, and stimulant medication. *Journal of the International Neuropsychological Society,* 3, 359–369.

BARNES, M. A., DENNIS, M., & HAEFELE-KALVAITIS, J. (1996). The effects of knowledge availability and knowledge accessibility on coherence and elaborative inferencing in children six to fifteen years of age. *Journal of Experimental Child Psychology,* 61, 216–241.

BARNETT, W. S. (1995). Long-term effects of early childhood programs on cognitive and school outcomes. *The Future of Children,* 5 (No. 3, Winter).

BARON-COHEN, S. (1995). *Mindblindness: An essay on autism and theory of mind.* Cambridge, MA: MIT Press.

BARON-COHEN, S. (2005). The Empathizing System: A revision of the 1994 model of the Mindreading System. In B. J. Ellis & D. F. Bjorklund (Eds.), *Origins of the social mind: Evolutionary psychology and child development* (pp. 468–492). New York: Guilford.

BARON-COHEN, S., LESLIE, A. M., & FRITH, U. (1985). Does the autistic child have a 'theory of mind'? *Cognition,* 21, 37–46.

BARR, R., & HAYNE, H. (2003). It's not what you know, it's who you know: Older siblings facilitate imitation during infancy. *International Journal of Early Years Education, 11,* 7–21.

BARRETT, H. C. (2004). Descent versus design in Shuar children's reasoning about animals. *Journal of Cognition and Culture, 4,* 25–50.

BARRETT, H. C. (2005). Cognitive development and the understanding of animal behavior. In B. J. Ellis & D. F. Bjorklund (Eds.), *Origins of the social mind: Evolutionary psychology and child development* (pp. 438–467). New York: Guilford.

BARRETT, H. C., & BEHNE, T. (2005). Children's understanding of death as the cessation of agency: A test using sleep vs. death. *Cognition, 96,* 93–108.

BARRETT, T. M., DAVIS, E. F., & NEEDHAM, A. (2007). Learning about tools in infancy. *Developmental Psychology, 43,* 352–368.

BARTLETT, F. C. (1932). *Remembering: A study in experimental and social psychology.* Cambridge, UK: Cambridge University Press.

BARTON, R. A., & HARVEY, P. H. (2000). Mosaic evolution of brain structure in mammals. *Nature, 405,* 1055–1058.

BASNE, R., GAWRONSKI, B., REBETEZ, C., GUTT, H., & MORTON, B. (2010). The development of spontaneous gender stereotyping in childhood: Relations to stereotype knowledge and stereotype flexibility. *Developmental Science, 13,* 298–306.

BATES, E., CARLSON-LUDEN, V., & BRETHERTON, I. (1980). Perceptual aspects of tool use in infancy. *Infant Behavior and Development, 3,* 127–140.

BATESON, P. (2002). The corpse of a wearisome debate. *Science, 297,* 2212–2213.

BATKI, A., BARON-COHEN, S., WHEELWRIGHT, S., CONNELLAN, J., & AHLUWALIA, J. (2000). Is there an innate gaze module? Evidence from human neonates. *Infant Behavior and Development, 23,* 223–229.

BATTY, G. D., DER, G., MACINTYRE, S., & DEARY, I. J. (2006). Does IQ explain socioeconomic inequalities in health? Evidence from a population based cohort study in the west of Scotland. *British Medical Journal, 332,* 580–584.

BAUER, P. J. (1993). Memory for gender-consistent and gender-inconsistent event sequences by twenty-five-month-old children. *Child Development, 64,* 285–297.

BAUER, P. J. (2002). Long-term recall memory: Behavioral and neurodevelopmental changes in the first 2 years of life. *Current Directions in Psychological Science, 11,* 137–141.

BAUER, P. J. (2007). *Remembering the times of our lives: Memory in infancy and beyond.* Mahwah, NJ: Erlbaum.

BAUER, P. J. (2009). The cognitive neuroscience of the development of memory. In M. L. Courage & N. Cowan (Eds.), *The development of memory in infancy and childhood* (pp. 115–144). New York: Psychology Press.

BAUER, P. J., & MANDLER, J. M. (1989). One thing follows another: Effects of temporal structure on 1- to 2-year-olds' recall of events. *Developmental Psychology, 25,* 197–206.

BAUER, P. J., & MANDLER, J. M. (1992). Putting the horse before the cart: The use of temporal order in recall of events by one-year-old children. *Developmental Psychology, 28,* 441–452.

BAUER, P. J., WENNER, J. A., DROPIK, P. L., & WEWERKA, S. S. (2000). Parameters of remembering and forgetting in the transition from infancy to early childhood. *Monographs of the Society for Research in Child Development, 65* (Serial No. 263).

BAUER, P. J., WENNER, J. A., & KROUPINA, M. G. (2002). Making the past present: Later verbal accessibility of early memories. *Journal of Cognition and Development, 3,* 21–47.

BAUER, P. J., WIEBE, S. A., WATERS, J. M., & BANGSTON, S. K. (2001). Reexposure breeds recall: Effects of experience on 9-month-olds' ordered recall. *Journal of Experimental Child Psychology, 80,* 174–200.

BAUER, R. H. (1979). Memory, acquisition, and category clustering in learning-disabled children. *Journal of Experimental Child Psychology, 27,* 365–383.

BAUMRIND, D. (1993). The average expectable environment is not good enough: A response to Scarr. *Child Development, 64,* 1299–1317.

BAYLEY, N. (1949). Consistency and variability in the growth of intelligence from birth to eighteen years. *Journal of Genetic Psychology, 75,* 165–196.

BAYLEY, N. (1969). *The Bayley Scales of Infant Development.* New York: Psychological Corporation.

BAYLEY, N. (1993). *The Bayley Scales of Infant Development* (2nd ed.) (BSID-II). New York: Psychological Corporation.

BAYLEY, N. (2005). *Bayley Scales of Infant and Toddler Development®* (3rd ed.) (Bayley-III®). San Antonio, TX: Harcourt Assessment.

BEAL, C. R., & FLAVELL, J. H. (1982). Effects of increasing salience of message ambiguities on kindergarteners' evaluations of communicative success and message adequacy. *Developmental Psychology, 10,* 43–48.

BECKER, W. C., & GERSTEN, R. (1982). A follow-up of Follow Through: The later effects of the direct instruction model for children in fifth and sixth grades. *American Educational Research Journal, 19,* 75–92.

BECKETT, C., CASTLE, J., RUTTER, M., & SONUGA-BARKE, E. J. (2010). Institutional deprivation, specific cognitive functions, and scholastic achievement: English and Romanian adoptees (ERA) study findings (pp. 125–142). In M. Rutter, E. J. Sonuga-Barke, C. Beckett, J. Castle, J. Kreppner, R. Kumsta, W. Scholtz, S. Stevens, & C. A. Bell (Eds.), Deprivation-specific psychological patterns: Effects of institutional deprivation. *Monographs of the Society for Research in Child Development, 75* (Serial No. 295).

BECKETT, C., MAUGHAN, B., RUTTER, M., CASTLE, J., COLVERT, E., GROOTHUES, C., KREPPNER, J., STEVENS, S., O-CONNOR, T. G., & SONUGA-BARKE, E. J. S. (2006). Do the effects of early severe deprivation on cognition persist into early adolescence? Findings from the English and Romanian Adoptee Study. *Child Development, 77,* 696–711.

BEHREND, D. A., ROSENGREN, K., & PERLMUTTER, M. (1989). A new look at children's private speech: The effects of age, task difficulty, and parent presence. *International Journal of Behavioral Development, 12,* 305–320.

BEILIN, H. (1992). Piaget's enduring contribution to developmental psychology. *Developmental Psychology, 28,* 191–204.

BEILOCK, S. L., GUNDERSON, E. A., RAMIREZ, G., & LEVINE, S. C. (2010). Female teachers' math anxiety impacts girls' math achievement. *Proceedings of the National Academy of Sciences of the United States of America, 107,* 1860–1863.

BELL, M. A., & FOX, N. A. (1992). The relations between frontal brain electrical activity and cognitive development during infancy. *Child Development, 63,* 1142–1163.

BELL, R. Q. (1968). A reinterpretation of the direction of effects in studies of socialization. *Psychological Review, 75,* 81–95.

BELL, M. A., WOLFE, C. D., & ADKINS, D. R. (2007). Frontal lobe development during infancy and childhood: Contributions of brain electrical activity temperament, and language to individual differences in working memory and inhibition control. In D. Coch, K. W. Fischer, & G. Dawson (Eds.), *Human behavior, learning, and the developing brain: Typical development* (pp. 247–276). New York: Guilford.

BELSKY, J., & MOST, R. K. (1981). From exploration to play: A cross-sectional study of infant free play behavior. *Developmental Psychology, 17,* 630–639.

BEM, S. (1981). Gender schema theory: A cognitive account of sex-typing. *Psychological Review, 88,* 354–364.

BENBOW, C. P., LUBINSKI, D., SHEA, D. L., & EFTEKHARI-SANJANI, H. (2000). Sex differences in mathematical reasoning ability at age 13: Their status 20 years later. *Psychological Science, 11,* 474–480.

BENBOW, C. P., & STANLEY, J. C. (1980). Sex differences in mathematical ability: Fact or artifact? *Science, 210,* 1262–1264.

BENBOW, C. P., & STANLEY, J. C. (1983). Sex differences in mathematical reasoning: More facts. *Science, 222,* 1029–1031.

BENDER, C. E., HERZING, D. L., & BJORKLUND, D. F. (2009). Evidence of teaching in Atlantic spotted dolphins (*Stenella frontalis*) by mother dolphins foraging in the presence of their calves. *Animal Cognition, 12,* 43–53.

BENEDICT, H. (1979). Early lexical development: Comprehension and production. *Journal of Child Language, 6,* 183–200.

BERENBAUM, S. A., & HINES, M. (1992). Early androgens are related to childhood sex-typed toy preferences. *Psychological Science, 3,* 203–206.

BERENBAUM, S. A., & SNYDER, E. (1995). Early hormonal influences on childhood sex-types activity and playmate preferences: Implications for the development of sexual orientation. *Developmental Psychology, 31,* 31–42.

BERG, D. H. (2008). Working memory and arithmetic calculation in children: The contributory roles of processing speed, short-term memory, and reading. *Journal of Experimental Child Psychology, 99,* 288–308.

BERING, J. M. (2002). Intuitive conceptions of dead agents' minds: The natural foundations of afterlife beliefs as phenomenological boundary. *Journal of Cognition and Culture, 2,* 263–308.

BERING, J. M. (2006). The folk psychology of souls. *Behavioral and Brain Sciences, 29,* 453–498.

BERING, J. M., & BJORKLUND, D. F. (2004). The natural emergence of afterlife reasoning as a developmental regularity. *Developmental Psychology, 40,* 217–233.

BERING, J. M., & BJORKLUND, D. F. (2007). The serpent's gift: Evolutionary psychology and consciousness. In P. D. Zelazo, M. Moscovitch, & E. Thompson (Eds.), *Cambridge Handbook of Consciousness.* New York: Cambridge University Press.

BERING, J. M., BJORKLUND, D. F., & RAGAN, P. (2000). Deferred imitation of object-related actions in human-reared juvenile chimpanzees and orangutans. *Developmental Psychobiology, 36,* 218–232.

BERING, J. M., HERNÁNDEZ BLASI, C., & BJORKLUND, D. F. (2005). The development of "afterlife" beliefs in religiously and secularly schooled children. *British Journal of Developmental Psychology, 23,* 587–607.

BERING, J. M., & PARKER, B. D. (2006). Children's attributions of intentions to an invisible agent. *Developmental Psychology, 42,* 253–262.

BERK, L. E. (1986). Relationship of elementary school children's private speech to behavioral accompaniment to task, attention, and task performance. *Developmental Psychology, 22,* 671–680.

BERK, L. E. (1992). Children's private speech: An overview of theory and the status of research. In R. M. Diaz & L. E. Berk (Eds.), *Private speech: From social interaction to self-regulation.* Hillsdale, NJ: Erlbaum.

BERK, L. E., & LANDAU, S. (1993). Private speech of learning disabled and normally achieving children in classroom academic and laboratory contexts. *Child Development, 64,* 556–571.

BERK, L. E., & SPUHL, S. T. (1995). Maternal intervention, private speech, and task performance in preschool children. *Early Childhood Research Quarterly, 10,* 145–169.

BERKO, J. (1958). The child's learning of English morphology. *Word, 14,* 150–177.

BERMEJO, V. (1996). Cardinality development and counting. *Developmental Psychology, 32,* 263–268.

BERNSTEIN, A. C., & COWAN, P. A. (1975). Children's concepts of how people get babies. *Child Development, 46,* 77–91.

BERNSTEIN, B. (1971). *Class codes and control,* Vol. 1. London: Routledge & Kegan Paul.

BERTENTHAL, B. I. (1996). Origins and early development of perception, action, and representation. *Annual Review of Psychology, 47,* 431–435.

BERTENTHAL, B. I., & CAMPOS, J. J. (1987). New directions in the study of early experience. *Child Development, 58,* 560–567.

BERTENTHAL, B. I., PROFFITT, D. R., & CUTTING, J. E. (1984). Infant sensitivity to figural coherence in biomechanical motions. *Journal of Experimental Child Psychology, 37,* 213–230.

BERTENTHAL, B. I., PROFFITT, D. R., & KRAMER, S. J. (1987). Perception of biomechanical motions by infants: Implementation of various processing constraints. *Journal of Experimental Psychology: Human Perception & Performance, 13,* 577–585.

BERTHIER, N. E., DEBOIS, S., POIRIER, C. R., NOVAK, M. A., & CLIFTON, R. K. (2000). Where's the ball? Two- and three-year-olds reason about unseen events. *Developmental Psychology, 36,* 384–401.

BEST, D. L. (1993). Inducing children to generate mnemonic organizational strategies: An examination of long-term retention and materials. *Developmental Psychology, 29,* 324–336.

BEST, D. L., & ORNSTEIN, P. A. (1986). Children's generation and communication of mnemonic organizational strategies. *Developmental Psychology, 22,* 845–853.

BHATT, R. S., BERTIN, E., HAYDEN, A., & REED, A. (2005). Face processing in infancy: Developmental changes in the use of different kinds of relational information. *Child Development, 76,* 169–181.

BHATT, R. S., ROVEE-COLLIER, C., & SHYI, C.-W. G. (1994). Perception and 24-hour retention of feature relations in infancy. *Developmental Psychology, 30,* 142–150.

BIALYSTOK, E. (1996). Preparing to read: The foundations of literacy. In H. W. Reese (Ed.), *Advances in child development and behavior,* Vol. 26. San Diego, CA: Academic.

BIALYSTOK, E. (1999). Cognitive complexity and attentional control in the bilingual mind. *Child Development, 70,* 636–644.

BIALYSTOK, E. (2001). *Bilingualism in development: Language, literacy, and cognition.* New York: Cambridge University Press.

BIALYSTOK, E. (2007). Language acquisition and bilingualism: Consequences for a multilingual society. *Applied Psycholinguistics, 28,* 393–397.

BIALYSTOK, E. (2010). Global-local and trail-making tasks by monolingual and bilingual children: Beyond inhibition. *Developmental Psychology, 46,* 93–105.

BIALYSTOK, E., & CRAIK, F. I. M. (2010). Cognitive and linguistic processing in the bilingual mind. *Current Directions in Psychological Science, 19,* 19–23.

BIALYSTOK, E., CRAIK, F. I. M., & FREEDMAN, M. (2007). Bilingualism as a protection against the onset of symptoms of dementia. *Neuropsychologia, 45,* 459–464.

BIALYSTOK, E., CRAIK, F., & LUK, G. (2008). Cognitive control and lexical access in younger and older individuals. *Journal of Experimental Psychology: Learning, Memory, and Cognition, 34,* 859–873.

BIALYSTOK, E., & HAKUTA, K. (1994). *In other words.* New York: Basic Books.

BICKERTON, D. (1990). *Language and species.* Chicago: University of Chicago Press.

BILLINGSLEY, R. L., SMITH, M. L., & MCANDREWS, M. P. (2002). Developmental patterns on priming and familiarity in explicit recollection.

*Journal of Experimental Child Psychology, 82,* 251–277.

BISANZ, J., MORRISON, F. J., & DUNN, M. (1995). The effects of age and schooling on the acquisition of elementary quantitative skills. *Developmental Psychology, 31,* 221–236.

BIVENS, J. A., & BERK, L. E. (1990). A longitudinal study of the development of elementary school children's private speech. *Merrill-Palmer Quarterly, 36,* 443–463.

BJORKLUND, D. F. (1980). Developmental differences in the timing of children's awareness of category relations in free recall. *International Journal of Behavioral Development, 3,* 61–70.

BJORKLUND, D. F. (1987a). A note on neonatal imitation. *Developmental Review, 7,* 86–92.

BJORKLUND, D. F. (1987b). How age changes in knowledge base contribute to the development of children's memory: An interpretive review. *Developmental Review, 7,* 93–130.

BJORKLUND, D. F. (1997a). The role of immaturity in human development. *Psychological Bulletin, 122,* 153–169.

BJORKLUND, D. F. (1997b). In search of a metatheory for cognitive development (or, Piaget's dead and I don't feel so good myself). *Child Development, 68,* 142–146.

BJORKLUND, D. F. (2006). Mother knows best: Epigenetic inheritance, maternal effects, and the evolution of human intelligence. *Developmental Review, 26,* 213–242.

BJORKLUND, D. F. (2007a). *Why youth is not wasted on the young: Immaturity in human development.* Oxford: Blackwell.

BJORKLUND, D. F. (2007b). The most educable of species. In J. S. Carlson & J. R. Levin (Eds.), *Psychological perspectives on contemporary educational issues* (pp. 119–129). Greenwich, CT: Information Age Publishing.

BJORKLUND, D. F. (2011). Cognitive development: An overview. In P. D. Zelazo (Ed.), *Oxford handbook of developmental psychology.* Oxford, UK: Oxford University Press.

BJORKLUND, D. F., & BERING, J. M. (2002). The evolved child: Applying evolutionary developmental psychology to modern schooling. *Learning and Individual Differences, 12,* 1–27.

BJORKLUND, D. F., & BERING, J. M. (2003). Big brains, slow development, and social complexity: The developmental and evolutionary origins of social cognition. In M. Brüne, H. Ribbert, & W. Schiefenhövel (Eds.), *The social brain: Evolutionary aspects of development and pathology* (pp. 133–151). New York: Wiley.

BJORKLUND, D. F., & BERNHOLTZ, J. F. (1986). The role of knowledge base in the memory performance of good and poor readers. *Journal of Experimental Child Psychology, 41,* 367–373.

BJORKLUND, D. F., BJORKLUND, B. R., BROWN, R. D., & CASSEL, W. S. (1998). Children's susceptibility to repeated questions: How misinformation changes children's answers and their minds. *Applied Developmental Science, 2,* 99–111.

BJORKLUND, D. F., BROWN, R. D., & BJORKLUND, B. R. (2002). Children's eyewitness memory: Changing reports and changing representations. In P. Graf & N. Ohta (Eds.), *Lifespan memory development.* Cambridge, MA: MIT Press.

BJORKLUND, D. F., CAUSEY, K., & PERISS, V. (2010). The evolution and development of human social cognition. In P. Kappeler & J. Silk (Eds.), *Mind the gap: Tracing the origins of human universals* (pp. 351–371). Berlin: Springer-Verlag.

BJORKLUND, D. F., CORMIER, C., & ROSENBERG, J. S. (2005). The evolution of theory of mind: Big brains, social complexity, and inhibition. In W. Schneider, R. Schumann-Hengsteler, & B. Sodian (Eds.), *Young children's cognitive development: Interrelationships among executive functioning, working memory, verbal ability and theory of mind* (pp. 147–174). Mahwah, NJ: Erlbaum.

BJORKLUND, D. F., COYLE, T. R., & GAULTNEY, J. F. (1992). Developmental differences in the acquisition of an organizational strategy: Evidence for the utilization deficiency hypothesis. *Journal of Experimental Child Psychology, 54,* 434–448.

BJORKLUND, D. F., DUKES, C., & BROWN, R. D. (2009). The development of memory strategies. In M. L. Courage & N. Cowan (Eds.), *The development of memory in infancy and childhood* (pp. 145–175). New York: Psychology Press.

BJORKLUND, D. F., ELLIS, B. J., & ROSENBERG, J. S. (2007). Evolved probabilistic cognitive mechanisms. In R. V. Kail (Ed.), *Advances in child development and behavior,* Vol. 35 (pp. 1–39). Oxford: Elsevier.

BJORKLUND, D. F., & GARDINER, A. K. (2010). Object play and tool use: Developmental and evolutionary perspectives. In A. D. Pellegrini (Ed.), *Oxford handbook of the development of play.* Oxford: Oxford University Press.

BJORKLUND, D. F., GAULTNEY, J. F., & GREEN, B. L. (1993). "I watch, therefore I can do": The development of meta-imitation over the preschool years and the advantage of optimism in one's imitative skills. In R. Pasnak & M. L. Howe (Eds.), *Emerging themes in cognitive development,* Vol. 1 (pp. 79–102). New York: Springer-Verlag.

BJORKLUND, D. F., & GREEN, B. L. (1992). The adaptive nature of cognitive immaturity. *American Psychologist, 47,* 46–54.

BJORKLUND, D. F., GROTUSS, J., & CSINADY, A. (2009). Maternal effects, social cognitive development, and the evolution of human intelligence. In D. Maestripieri & J. Mateo (Eds.), *Maternal effects in mammals* (pp. 292–321). Chicago: University of Chicago Press.

BJORKLUND, D. F., & HARNISHFEGER, K. K. (1987). Developmental differences in the mental effort requirements for the use of an organizational strategy in free recall. *Journal of Experimental Child Psychology, 44,* 109–125.

BJORKLUND, D. F., & HARNISHFEGER, K. K. (1995). The role of inhibition mechanisms in the evolution of human cognition and behavior. In F. N. Dempster & C. J. Brainerd (Eds.), *New perspectives on interference and inhibition in cognition* (pp. 141–173). New York: Academic.

BJORKLUND, D. F., & HERNÁNDEZ BLASI, C. (2005). Evolutionary developmental psychology. In D. Buss (Ed.), *Evolutionary psychology handbook* (pp. 828–850). New York: Wiley.

BJORKLUND, D. F., & HERNÁNDEZ BLASI, C. (2012). *Child and adolescent development: An integrative approach.* Belmont, CA: Wadsworth.

BJORKLUND, D. F., HUBERTZ, M. J., & REUBENS, A. C. (2004). Young children's arithmetic strategies in social context: How parents contribute to children's strategy development while playing games. *International Journal of Behavioral Development, 28,* 347–357.

BJORKLUND, D. F., & JACOBS, J. W. (1985). Associative and categorical processes in children's memory: The role of automaticity in the development of organization in free recall. *Journal of Experimental Child Psychology, 39,* 599–617.

BJORKLUND, D. F., & KIPP, K. (2002). Social cognition, inhibition, and theory of mind: The evolution of human intelligence. In R. J. Sternberg & J. C. Kaufman (Eds.), *The evolution of intelligence* (pp. 27–53). Mahwah, NJ: Erlbaum.

BJORKLUND, D. F., MILLER, P. H., COYLE, T. R., & SLAWINSKI, J. L. (1997). Instructing children to use memory strategies: Evidence of utilization deficiencies in memory training studies. *Developmental Review, 17,* 411–442.

BJORKLUND, D. F., MUIR-BROADDUS, J. E., & SCHNEIDER, W. (1990). The role of knowledge in the development of strategies. In D. F. Bjorklund (Ed.), *Children's strategies: Contemporary views of cognitive development.* Hillsdale, NJ: Erlbaum.

BJORKLUND, D. F., & PELLEGRINI, A. D. (2002). *The origins of human nature: Evolutionary developmental psychology.* Washington, DC: American Psychological Association.

BJORKLUND, D. F., PERISS, V., & CAUSEY, K. (2009). The benefits of youth. *European Journal of Developmental Psychology, 6,* 120–137.

BJORKLUND, D. F., & ROSENBERG, J. S. (2005). The role of developmental plasticity in the evolution of human cognition. In B. J. Ellis & D. F. Bjorklund (Eds.), *Origins of the social mind: Evolutionary psychology and child development* (pp. 45–75). New York: Guilford.

BJORKLUND, D. F., & ROSENBLUM, K. E. (2002). Context effects in children's selection and use of simple arithmetic strategies. *Journal of Cognition and Development, 3,* 225–242.

BJORKLUND, D. F., & SCHWARTZ, R. (1996). The adaptive nature of developmental immaturity: Implications for language acquisition and language disabilities. In M. Smith & J. Damico (Eds.), *Childhood language disorders.* New York: Thieme Medical.

BJORKLUND, D. F., YUNGER, J. L., BERING, J. M., & RAGAN, P. (2002). The generalization of deferred imitation in enculturated chimpanzees (*Pan troglodytes*). *Animal Cognition, 5,* 49–58.

BJORKLUND, D. F., & ZEMAN, B. R. (1982). Children's organization and metamemory awareness in the recall of familiar information. *Child Development, 53,* 799–810.

BLACK, J. E., JONES, T. A., NELSON, C. A., & GREENOUGH, W. T. (1998). Neuronal plasticity and the developing brain. In N. E. Alessi, J. T. Coyle, S. I. Harrison, & S. Eth (Eds.), *Handbook of child and adolescent psychiatry,* Vol. 6 (pp. 31–53). New York: Wiley.

BLAIR, C. (2006). How similar are fluid cognition and general intelligence? A developmental neuroscience perspective on fluid cognition as an aspect of human cognitive ability. *Behavioral and Brain Sciences, 29,* 109–160.

BLAIR, C., GAMSON, D., THORNE, S., & BAK, D. (2005). Rising mean IQ: Cognitive demand of mathematics education for young children, population exposure to formal schooling, and the neurobiology of the prefrontal cortex. *Intelligence, 33,* 93–106.

BLAKEMORE, C., & VAN SLUYTERS, R. C. (1975). Innate and environmental factors in the development of the kitten's visual cortex. *Journal of Physiology, 248,* 663–716.

BLOM, G. E., WAITE, R. R., & ZIMET, S. (1968). Content of first-grade reading books. *The Reading Teacher, 21,* 317–323.

BLOOM, L. (1993). *Language development form two to three.* Cambridge, UK: Cambridge University Press.

BLOOM, L. (1998). Language acquisition in developmental contexts. In D. Kuhn & R. S. Siegler (Eds.), *Cognitive, language, and perceptual development,* Vol. 2, in W. Damon (Gen. Ed.), *Handbook of child psychology* (5th ed.). New York: Wiley.

BLOOM, L., HOOD, L., & LIGHTBOWN, P. (1974). Imitation in language development: If, when and why. *Cognitive Psychology, 6,* 380–420.

BLOOM, L., LIGHTBOWN, P., & HOOD, L. (1975). Structure and variation in child language. *Monographs of the Society for Research in Child Development*, 40 (Serial No. 160).

BLOOM, P. (2000). *How children learn the meanings of words*. Cambridge, MA: MIT Press.

BLOOM, P. (2004). *Descartes' baby: How the science of child development explains what makes us human.* New York: Basic Books.

BLOOM, P., & MARKSON, L. (1998). Capacities underlying word learning. *Trends in Cognitive Science*, 2, 67–73.

BLUMBERG, F. C., & TORENBERG, M. (2005). The effects of spatial configuration on preschoolers' attention strategies, selective attention, and incidental learning. *Infant and Child Development*, 14, 243–258.

BLUMBERG, F. C., TORENBERG, M., & RANDALL, J. D. (2005). The relationship between preschoolers' selective attention and memory for location strategies. *Cognitive Development*, 20, 242–255.

BOCK, J. (2005). Farming, foraging, and children's play in the Okavango Delta, Botswana. In A. D. Pellegrini, & P. K. Smith (Eds.), *The nature of play: Great apes and humans* (pp. 254–281). New York: Guilford.

BOESCH, C. (1991). Teaching among wild chimpanzees. *Animal Behavior*, 41, 530–532.

BOESCH, C., & TOMASELLO, M. (1998). Chimpanzee and human culture. *Current Anthropology*, 39, 591–604.

BOGARTZ, R. S., & SHINSKEY, J. L. (1998). On perception of a partially occluded object in 6-month-olds. *Cognitive Development*, 13, 141–163.

BOGARTZ, R. S., SHINSKEY, J. L., & SPEAKER, C. (1997). Interpreting infant looking: The event set × event set design. *Developmental Psychology*, 33, 408–422.

BOGDAN, R. J. (2010). *Our own minds: Sociocultural grounds for self-consciousness*. Cambridge, MA: MIT Press.

BONNER, J. T. (1988). *The evolution of complexity by means of natural selection*. Princeton, NJ: Princeton University Press.

BORKE, H. (1975). Piaget's mountains revisited: Changes in the egocentric landscape. *Developmental Psychology*, 11, 240–243.

BORKOWSKI, J. G., & PECK, V. A. (1986). Causes and consequences of

metamemory in gifted children. In R. J. Sternberg & J. C. Davidson (Eds.), *Conceptions of giftedness.* Cambridge, UK: Cambridge University Press.

BORKOWSKI, J. G., PECK, V., REID, M. K., & KURTZ, B. (1983). Impulsivity and strategy transfer: Metamemory as mediator. *Child Development*, 54, 459–473.

BORKOWSKI, J. G., REID, M. K., & KURTZ, B. E. (1984). Metacognition and retardation: Pragmatic, theoretical and applied perspectives. In P. H. Brooks, R. Sperber, & C. McCauley (Eds.), *Learning and cognition in the mentally retarded.* Hillsdale, NJ: Erlbaum.

BORNSTEIN, M. H. (1989). Stability in early mental development: From attention and information processing in infancy to language and cognition in childhood. In M. H. Bornstein & N. A. Krasnegor (Eds.), *Stability and continuity in mental development: Behavioral and biological perspectives.* Hillsdale, NJ: Erlbaum.

BORNSTEIN, M. H., FERDINANDSEN, K., & GROSS, C. G. (1981). Perception of symmetry in infancy. *Developmental Psychology,* 17, 82–86.

BORNSTEIN, M. H., HAHN, C.-S., BELL, C., HAYNES, O. M., SLATER, A., GOLDING, J., WOLKE, D., & THE ALSPAC STUDY TEAM (2006). Stability in cognition across childhood. *Psychological Science*, 17, 151–158.

BORNSTEIN, M. H., & HAYNES, O. M. (1998). Vocabulary competence in early childhood: Measurement, latent construct, and predictive validity. *Child Development*, 69, 654–671.

BORNSTEIN, M. H., HAYNES, O. M., O'REILLY, A. W., & PAINTER, K. M. (1996). Solitary and collaborative pretense play in early childhood: Sources of individual variation in the development of representational competence. *Child Development*, 67, 2910–2929.

BORNSTEIN, M. H., & SIGMAN, M. D. (1986). Continuity in mental development from infancy. *Child Development*, 57, 251–274.

BOSCH, L., & SEBASTIÁN-GALLÉS. (2001). Evidence of early language discrimination abilities in infants from bilingual environments. *Infancy*, 2, 29–49.

BRONSON, G. W. (1990). Changes in infants' visual scanning across the

2–14-week age period. *Journal of Experimental Child Psychology*, 49, 101–125.

BOSTON, M. B., & LEVY, G. D. (1991). Changes and differences in preschoolers' understanding of gender scripts. *Cognitive Development*, 6, 417–432.

BOUCHARD, T. J., JR., LYKKEN, D. T., MCGUE, M., SEGAL, N. L., & TELLEGEN, A. (1990). Sources of human psychological differences: The Minnesota study of twins reared apart. *Science*, 250, 223–228.

BOUCHARD, T. J., JR., & MCGUE, M. (1981). Familial studies of intelligence: A review. *Science*, 212, 1055–1059.

BOUCHARD, T. J., JR., & SEGAL, N. (1985). Environment and IQ. In B. Wolman (Ed.), *Handbook of intelligence.* New York: Wiley.

BOWERMAN, M. (1979). The acquisition of complex sentences. In P. Fletcher & M. Garman (Eds.), *Language acquisition* (pp. 285–306). Cambridge, UK: Cambridge University Press.

BOYER, P. (2001). *Religion explained: The evolutionary origins of religious thought.* New York: Basic Books.

BRADLEY, B. S. (1989). *Visions of infancy. A critical introduction to child psychology.* Oxford: Basil Blackwell Ltd.

BRADLEY, R. H., BURCHINAL, M. R., & CASEY, P. H. (2001). Early intervention: The moderating role of the home environment. *Applied Developmental Science*, 5, 2–8.

BRADLEY, R. H., & CALDWELL, B. M. (1976). The relation of infants' home environment to mental test performance at fifty-four months: A follow-up study. *Child Development*, 47, 1172–1174.

BRADLEY, R. H., CALDWELL, B. M., & ELARDO, R. (1977). Home environment, social status, and mental test performance. *Journal of Educational Psychology*, 69, 697–701.

BRADLEY, R. H., CALDWELL, B. M., ROCK, S. L., RAMEY, C. T., BARNARD, K. E., GRAY C., HAMMOND, M. A., MITCHELL, S., GOTTFRIED, A. W., SIEGEL, L., & JOHNSON, D. L. (1989). Home environments and cognitive development in the first 3 years of life: A collaborative study including six sites and three ethnic groups in

North America. *Developmental Psychology, 25*, 217–235.

BRAINERD, C. F. (1996). Piaget: A centennial celebration. *Psychological Science, 7*, 191–195.

BRAINERD, C. J. (1978). *Piaget's theory of intelligence.* Englewood Cliffs, NJ: Prentice Hall.

BRAINERD, C. J., & ALLEN, T. W. (1971). Training and generalization of density conservation: Effects of feedback and consecutive similar stimuli. *Child Development, 42*, 693–704.

BRAINERD, C. J., & BRAINERD, S. H. (1972). Order of acquisition of number and liquid quantity conservation. *Child Development, 43*, 1401–1405.

BRAINERD, C. J., & GORDON, L. L. (1994). Development of verbatim and gist memory for numbers. *Developmental Psychology, 30*, 163–177.

BRAINERD, C. J., & MOJARDIN, A. H. (1999). Children's and adults' spontaneous false memories for sentences: Long-term persistence and mere-testing effects. *Child Development, 69*, 1361–1377.

BRAINERD, C. J., & POOLE, D. A. (1997). Long-term survival of children's false memories: A review. *Learning and Individual Differences, 9*, 125–152.

BRAINERD, C. J., & REYNA, V. F. (1990). Gist is the grist: Fuzzy-trace theory and the new intuitionism. *Developmental Review, 10*, 3–47.

BRAINERD, C. J., & REYNA, V. F. (1993). Domains of fuzzy trace theory. In M. L. Howe & R. Pasnak (Eds.), *Emerging themes in cognitive development*, Vol. 1. New York: Springer-Verlag.

BRAINERD, C. J., & REYNA, V. F. (1996). Mere memory testing creates false memories in children. *Developmental Psychology, 32*, 467–478.

BRAINERD, C. J., & REYNA, V. F. (2002). Fuzzy-trace theory and false memory. *Current Directions on Psychological Science, 11*, 164–169.

BRAINERD, C. J., & REYNA, V. F. (2005). *The science of false memory.* Oxford: Oxford University Press.

BRAINERD, C. J., REYNA, V. F., & BRANDSE, E. (1995). Are children's false memories more persistent than their true memories? *Psychological Science, 6*, 359–364.

BRAINERD, C. J., REYNA, V. F., & CECI, S. J. (2008). Developmental reversals in false memory: A review of data

and theory. *Psychological Review, 134*, 343–382.

BRAINERD, C. J., REYNA, V. F., & ZEMBER, E. (2011). Theoretical and forensic implications of developmental studies of the DRM illusion. *Memory & Cognition*.

BRÄUER J., CALL J., & TOMASELLO, M. (2005). All great ape species follow gaze to distant locations and around barriers. *Journal of Comparative Psychology, 119*, 145–154.

BRAY, N. W., FLETCHER, K. L., & TURNER, L. A. (1996). Cognitive competencies and strategy use in individuals with mild retardation. In W. E. MacLean, Jr. (Ed.), *Handbook of mental deficiency, psychological theory and research* (3rd ed.). Hillsdale, NJ: Lawrence Erlbaum.

BRAZELTON, T. B. (1973). *Neonatal Behavioral Assessment Scale* (Clinics in Developmental Medicine, No. 50). Philadelphia: Lippincott.

BREMNER, A. J., & MARESCHAL, D. (2004). Reasoning . . . what reasoning? *Developmental Science, 7*, 419–421.

BRIARS, D., & SIEGLER, R. S. (1984). A featural analysis of preschoolers' counting knowledge. *Developmental Psychology, 20*, 607–618.

BROADERS, S., COOK, S. W., MITCHELL, Z., GOLDIN-MEADOW, S. (2007). Making children gesture brings out implicit knowledge and leads to learning. *Journal of Experimental Psychology: General, 136*, 539–550.

BROBERG, A. G., WESSELS, H., LAMB, M. E., & HWANG, C. P. (1997). Effects of day care on the development of cognitive abilities in 8-year-olds: A longitudinal study. *Developmental Psychology, 33*, 62–69.

BRODY, N. (1997). Intelligence, schooling, and society. *American Psychologist, 52*, 1046–1050.

BRONFENBRENNER, U., & CECI, S. J. (1994). Nature-nurture reconceptualized in developmental perspective: A bioecological model. *Psychological Review, 101*, 568–586.

BRONFENBRENNER, U., & MORRIS, P. A. (2006). The bioecological model of human development. In R. M. Lerner (Ed.), *Theoretical models of human development* (pp. 793–828), in W. Damon & R. M. Lerner (Gen. Eds.),

*Handbook of Child Psychology* (6th ed.). New York: Wiley.

BROOKS-GUNN, J., LINVER, M. R., & FAUTH, R. C. (2005). *Children's competence and socioeconomic status in the family and neighborhood.* New York: Guilford.

BROOKS-GUNN, J., & LEWIS, M. (1984). The development of early self-recognition. *Developmental Review, 4*, 215–239.

BROOKS, R., & MELTZOFF, A. N. (2002). The importance of eyes: How infants interpret adult looking behavior. *Developmental Psychology, 38*, 958–966.

BROWN, A. L., & KANE, M. J. (1988). Preschool children can learn to transfer: Learning to learn and learning by example. *Cognitive Psychology, 20*, 493–523.

BROWN, A. L., KANE, M. J., & LONG, C. (1989). Analogical transfer in young children: Analogies as tools for communication and exposition. *Applied Cognitive Psychology, 3*, 275–293.

BROWN, R. (1973). *A first language: The early stages.* Cambridge, MA: Harvard University Press.

BROWN, R., & HANLON, C. (1970). Derivational complexity and the order of acquisition in child speech. In R. Brown (Ed.), *Psycholinguistics.* New York: Free Press.

BRUCK, M., CECI, S. K., FRANCOEUR, E., & BARR, R. (1995). "I hardly cried when I got my shot!" Influencing children's reports about a visit to their pediatrician. *Child Development, 66*, 193–208.

BRUCK, M., CECI, S. J., & PRINCIPE, G. F. (2006). The child and the law. In K. A. Renninger & I. E. Sigel (Vol. Eds.), *Child psychology in practice*, Vol. 4 (pp. 776–816), in W. Damon & R. M. Lerner (Gen. Eds.), *Handbook of Child Psychology* (6th ed.). New York: Wiley.

BRUNER, J. S. (1966). On cognitive growth. In J. S. Bruner, R. R. Olver, & P. M. Greenfield (Eds.), *Studies in cognitive growth.* New York: Wiley.

BRUNER, J. S. (1972). The nature and uses of immaturity. *American Psychologist, 27*, 687–708.

BRUNER, J. S. (1983). *Child's talk: Learning to use language.* New York: Norton.

BRYANT, P. E., MACLEAN, M., BRADLEY, L. L., & CROSSLAND, J. (1990). Rhyme and alliteration, phoneme detection, and learning to read.

*Developmental Psychology, 26,* 429–438.

BUCCINO, G., VOGT, G. S., RITZL, A., FINK, G. R., ZILLES, K., FREUND, H.-J., & RIZZOLATTI, G. (2004). Neural circuits underlying imitation learning of hand actions: An event-related fMRI study. *Neuron, 42,* 323–334.

BUCK, S. M., HILLMAN, C. H., & CASTELLI, D. M. (2008). Aerobic fitness influences Stroop task performance in preadolescent children. *Medicine & Science in Sports & Exercise, 40,* 166–172.

BUDGWIG, N. (1990). The linguistic marking of nonprototypical agency: An exploration into children's use of passives. *Linguistics, 28,* 1221–1252.

BULL, R., & JOHNSTON, R. S. (1997). Children's arithmetical difficulties: Contributions from processing speed, item identification, and short-term memory. *Journal of Experimental Child Psychology, 65,* 1–24.

BULLOCK, M., & LÜTKENHAUS, P. (1988). The development of volitional behavior in the toddler years. *Child Development, 59,* 664–674.

BULLOCK, M., SODIAN, B., & KOERBER, S. (2009). Doing experiments and understanding science: Development of scientific reasoning from childhood to adulthood. In W. Schneider & M. Bullock (Eds.), *Human development from early childhood to early adulthood: Findings from a 20-year longitudinal study* (pp. 173–197). New York: Psychology Press.

BUNGE, S. A., & ZELAZO, P. D. (2006). A brain-based account of the development of rule use in childhood. *Current Directions in Psychological Science, 15,* 118–121.

BURGESS, S. R., & LONIGAN, C. J. (1998). Bidirectional relations of phonological sensitivity and prereading abilities: Evidence from a preschool sample. *Journal of Experimental Child Psychology, 70,* 114–141.

BURTS, D. C., HART, C. H., CHARLESWORTH, R., DEWOLF, D. M., RAY, J., MANUEL, K., & FLEEGE, P. O. (1993). Developmental appropriateness of kindergarten programs and academic outcomes in first grade. *Journal of Research in Childhood Education, 8,* 23–31.

BUSHNELL, I. W. R., SAI, F., & MULLIN, J. T. (1989). Neonatal recognition of the mother's face. *British Journal of Developmental Psychology, 7,* 3–15.

BUSS, D. M. (2009). The great struggles of life: Darwin and the emergence of evolutionary psychology. *American Psychologist, 64,* 140–148.

BUSSEY, K., & BANDURA, A. (1999). Social-cognitive theory of gender development and differentiation. *Psychological Review, 106,* 676–713.

BUTTELMANN, D., CARPENTER, M., CALL, J., & TOMASELLO, M. (2007). Enculturated chimpanzees imitate rationally. *Developmental Science, 10,* F31–F38.

BUTTELMANN, D., CARPENTER, M., CALL, J., & TOMASELLO, M. (2008). Rational tool use and tool choice in human infants and great apes. *Child Development, 79,* 609–626.

BYRNES, J. P., & FOX, N. A. (1998). The educational relevance of research in cognitive neuroscience. *Educational Psychology Review, 10,* 297–342.

BYRNE, R. W. (2005). Social cognition: Imitation, imitation, imitation. *Current Biology, 15,* R489–R500.

BYRNE, R., & WHITEN, A. (EDS.). (1988). *Machiavellian intelligence: Social expertise and the evolution of intellect in monkeys, apes, and humans.* Oxford: Clarendon.

CACIOPPO, J. T. (2002). Social neuroscience: Understanding the pieces fosters understanding the whole and vice versa. *American Psychologist, 57,* 819–831.

CAHAN, S., & COHEN, N. (1989). Age versus schooling effects on intelligence development. *Child Development, 60,* 1239–1249.

CAIN, K., OAKHILL, J., & BRYANT, P. (2004). Children's reading comprehension ability: Concurrent prediction by working memory, verbal ability, and component skills. *Journal of Educational Psychology, 96,* 31–42.

CAIRNS, R. B. (1979). *Social development: The origins and plasticity of interchanges.* San Francisco: W. H. Freeman.

CALDERA, Y. M., O'BRIEN, M., TRUGLIO, R. T., ALVAREZ, M., & HUSTON, A. C. (1999). Children's play preferences, construction play with blocks, and visual-spatial skills: Are they related? *International Journal of Behavioral Development, 23,* 855–872.

CALDWELL, B. M., & BRADLEY, R. H. (1978). *Home observation for measurement of the environment.* Little Rock: University of Arkansas at Little Rock.

CALL, J., CARPENTER, M., & TOMASELLO, M. (2004). Copying results and copying actions in the process of social learning: Chimpanzees (*Pan troglodytes*) and human children (*Homo sapiens*). *Animal Cognition, 8,* 151–163.

CALL, J., & TOMASELLO, M. (1996). The effects of humans on the cognitive development of apes. In A. E. Russon, K. A. Bard, & S. T. Parker (Eds.), *Reaching into thought: The minds of the great apes* (pp. 371–403). New York: Cambridge University Press.

CALVERT, S. L., MAHLER, B. A., ZEHNDER, S. M., JENKINS, A., & LEE, M. (2003). Sex differences in preadolescent children's online interactions. Symbolic modes of self-presentation and self-expression. *Journal of Applied Developmental Psychology, 24,* 627–644.

CAMERON-FAULKNER, T., LIEVEN, T., & TOMASELLO (2003). A construction-based analysis of child-directed speech. *Cognitive Science, 27,* 843–873.

CAMPBELL, F. A., PUNGELLO, E. P., MILLER-JOHNSON, S., BURCHINAL, M., & RAMEY, C. T. (2001). The development of cognitive and academic abilities: Growth curves from an early childhood educational experiment. *Developmental Psychology, 37,* 231–242.

CAMPBELL, F. A., & RAMEY, C. T. (1994). Effects of early intervention on intellectual and academic achievement: A follow-up study of children from low-income families. *Child Development, 65,* 684–698.

CAMPBELL, F. A., RAMEY, C. T., PUNGELLO, E., SPARLING, J., & MILLER-JOHNSON, S. (2002). Early childhood education: Young adult outcomes from the Abecedarian project. *Applied Developmental Science, 6,* 42–57.

CANFIELD, R. L., SMITH, E. G., BREZSNYAK, M. P., & SNOW, K. L. (1997). Information processing through the first year of life. *Monographs of the Society for Research in Child Development, 62* (Serial No. 250).

CAPON, N., & KUHN, D. (1979). Logical reasoning in the supermarket: Adult females' use of a proportional reasoning strategy in an everyday context. *Developmental Psychology, 15,* 450–452.

CAREY, S. (1978). The child as a word learner. In M. Halle, J. Bresnan, &

G. A. Miller (Eds.), *Linguistic theory and psychological reality* (pp. 264–293). Cambridge, MA: MIT Press.

CAREY, S. (1985). Are children fundamentally different kinds of thinkers and learners than adults? In S. F. Chapman, J. W. Segal, & R. Glaser (Eds.), *Thinking and learning skills,* Vol. 2. Hillsdale, NJ: Erlbaum.

CAREY, S. (1999). Sources of conceptual change. In E. K. Scholnick, K. Nelson, S. A. Gelman, & P. Miller (Eds.), *Conceptual development: Piaget's legacy* (pp. 293–326). Hillsdale, NJ: Erlbaum.

CARLSON, J. S., & LEVIN, J. R. (EDS.). (2007). *Educating the evolved mind: Conceptual foundations for an evolutionary educational psychology.* Charlotte, NC: Information Age Publishing.

CARLSON, S. M., & MELTZOFF, A. N. (2008). Bilingual experience and executive functioning in young children. *Developmental Science,* 11, 282–298.

CARLSON, S. M., & MOSES, L. J. (2001). Individual differences in inhibitory control and children's theory of mind. *Child Development,* 72, 1032–1053.

CARLSON, S. M., MOSES, L. J., & HIX, H. R. (1998). The role of inhibitory processes in young children's difficulties with deception and false belief. *Child Development,* 69, 672–691.

CARON, A. J. (2009). Comprehension of the representational mind in infancy. *Developmental Review,* 29, 69–95.

CARPENDALE, J. I. M., & LEWIS, C. (2004). Constructing an understanding of mind: The development of children's social understanding within social interaction. *Behavioral and Brain Sciences,* 27, 79–151.

CARPENTER, M., AKHTAR, N., & TOMASELLO, M. (1998). 14- through 18-month-old infants differentially imitate intentional and accidental actions. *Infant Behavior and Development,* 21, 315–330.

CARPENTER, M., CALL, J., & TOMASELLO, M. (2005). Twelve- and 18-month-olds copy actions in terms of goals. *Developmental Science,* 8, F13–F20.

CARPENTER, M., NAGELL, K., & TOMASELLO, M. (1998). Social cognition, joint attention, and communicative competence from 9 to 15 months of age. *Monographs of the Society for Research in Child Development,* 63 (Serial No. 255).

CARPENTER, T. P., & MOSER, J. M. (1982). The development of addition and subtraction problem-solving skills. In T. P. Carpenter, J. M. Moser, & T. A. Romberg (Eds.), *Addition and subtraction: A cognitive perspective.* Hillsdale, NJ: Erlbaum.

CARR, M. (2009). The importance of metacognition for conceptual change and strategy use in mathematics. In H. S. Waters & W. Schneider (Eds.), *Metacognition, strategy use, and instruction* (pp. 176–199). New York: Guilford.

CARR, M., BORKOWSKI, J. G., & MAXWELL, S. E. (1991). Motivational components of underachievement. *Developmental Psychology,* 27, 108–118.

CARR, M., & JESSUP, D. L. (1995). Cognitive and metacognitive predictors of mathematics strategy use. *Learning and Individual Differences,* 7, 235–247.

CARR, M., KURTZ, B. E., SCHNEIDER, W., TURNER, L. A., & BORKOWSKI, J. G. (1989). Strategy acquisition and transfer among American and German children: Environmental influences on metacognitive development. *Developmental Psychology,* 25, 765–771.

CARRAHER, T. N., CARRAHER, D., & SCHLIEMANN, A. D. (1985). Mathematics in the streets and in the schools. *British Journal of Developmental Psychology,* 3, 21–29.

CARROL, J. B. (1993). *Human cognitive abilities.* New York: Cambridge University Press.

CARROLL, J. M., SNOWLING, M. J., HULME, C., & STEVENSON, J. (2003). The development of phonological awareness in preschool children. *Developmental Psychology,* 39, 913–923.

CARVER, L. J., & BAUER, P. J. (1999). When the event is more than the sum of its parts: Individual differences in 9-month-olds long-term ordered recall. *Memory,* 2, 147–174.

CASE, R. (1985). *Intellectual development: Birth to adulthood.* New York: Academic.

CASE, R. (1991). Stages in the development of the young child's first sense of self. *Developmental Review,* 11, 210–230.

CASE, R. (1992). *The mind's staircase: Exploring the conceptual underpinnings of children's thought and knowledge.* Hillsdale, NJ: Erlbaum.

CASE, R., KURLAND, M., & GOLDBERG, J. (1982). Operational efficiency and the growth of short-term memory span. *Journal of Experimental Child Psychology,* 33, 386–404.

CASELLI, M. C., BATES, E., CASADIO, P., FENSON, J., FENSON, L., SANDERS, L., & WEIR, J. (1995). A cross-linguistic study of early lexical development. *Cognitive Development,* 10, 159–199.

CASLER, K., & KELEMEN, D. (2005). Young children's rapid learning about artifacts. *Developmental Science,* 8, 472–480.

CASPI, A., WILLIAMS, B., KIM-COHEN, J., CRAIG, I. W., MILNE, B. J., POULTON, R., SCHALKWYK, L. C., TAYLOR, A., WERTS, H., & MOFFITT, T. E. (2007). Moderation of breastfeeding effects on the IQ by genetic variation in fatty acid metabolism. *Proceeding of the National Academy of Sciences of the United States of America,* 104, 18860–18865.

CASSEL, W. S., & BJORKLUND, D. F. (1995). Developmental patterns of eyewitness memory and suggestibility: An ecologically based short-term longitudinal study. *Law & Human Behavior,* 19, 507–532.

CASSEL, W. S., ROEBERS, C. E. M., & BJORKLUND, D. F. (1996). Developmental patterns of eyewitness responses to increasingly suggestive questions. *Journal of Experimental Child Psychology,* 61, 116–133.

CATTELL, R. B. (1971). *Abilities: Their structure, growth and action.* Boston: Houghton Mifflin.

CAUGHY, M. O. (1996). Health and environmental effects on the academic readiness of school-age children. *Developmental Psychology,* 32, 515–522.

CAUSEY, K., & BJORKLUND, D. F. (October, 2009). *Individual differences in children's prospective memory performance: Qualitative change matters.* Poster presented at meeting of the Cognitive Development Society, San Antonio, TX.

CAVANAUGH, J. C., & BORKOWSKI, J. G. (1980). Searching for metamemory-memory connections: A developmental study. *Developmental Psychology,* 16, 441–453.

CECI, S. J. (1983). Automatic and purposive semantic processing characteristics of normal and language/ learning disabled (L/LD) children. *Developmental Psychology, 19,* 427–439.

CECI, S. J. (1991). How much does schooling influence general intelligence and its cognitive components? A reassessment of the evidence. *Developmental Psychology, 27,* 703–722.

CECI, S. J. (1993). Contextual trends in intellectual development. *Developmental Review, 13,* 403–435.

CECI, S. J. (1996). *On intelligence: A bio-ecological treatise on intellectual development* (2nd ed.). Cambridge, MA: Harvard University Press.

CECI, S. J., & BRUCK, M. (1993). Suggestibility of the child witness: A historical review and synthesis. *Psychological Bulletin, 113,* 403–439.

CECI, S. J., & BRUCK, M. (1995). *Jeopardy in the courtroom: A scientific analysis of children's testimony.* Washington, DC: American Psychological Association.

CECI, S. J., & BRUCK, M. (1998). Children's testimony: Applied and basic issues. In I. E. Sigel & K. A. Renninger (Vol. Eds.) *Child psychology in practice* (Vol. 4), in W. Damon (Gen. Ed.), *Handbook of child psychology.* New York: Wiley.

CECI, S. J., BRUCK, M., & BATTIN, D. (2000). The suggestibility of children's testimony. In D. F. Bjorklund (Ed.), *False-memory creation in children and adults: Theory, research, and implications.* Mahwah, NJ: Erlbaum

CECI, S. J., LOFTUS, E. F., LEICHTMAN, M., & BRUCK, M. (1994). The role of source misattributions in the creation of false beliefs among preschoolers. *International Journal of Clinical and Experimental Hypnosis, 62,* 304–320.

CECI, S. J., ROSS, D. F., & TOGLIA, M. P. (1987). Age differences in suggestibility: Psycholegal implications. *Journal of Experimental Psychology: General, 117,* 38–49.

CECI, S. J., & WILLIAMS, W. M. (1997). Schooling, intelligence, and income. *American Psychologist, 52,* 1051–1058.

CERVANTES, C. A., & CALLANAN, M. A. (1998). Labels and explanations in mother-child emotion talk: Age and gender differentiation. *Developmental Psychology, 34,* 88–98.

CHALL, J. S. (1979). The great debate: Ten years later, with a modest proposal for reading stages. In L. B. Resnick & P. A. Weaver (Eds.), *Theory and practice of early reading.* Hillsdale, NJ: Erlbaum.

CHAN, C. K. K., & SIEGEL, L. S. (2001). Phonological processing in reading Chinese among normally achieving and poor readers. *Journal of Experimental Child Psychology, 80,* 23–43.

CHANDLER, M., FRITZ, A. S., & HALA, S. (1989). Small-scale deceit: Deception as a marker of two-, three-, and four-year-olds' early theories of mind. *Child Development, 60,* 1263–1277.

CHANGEUX, J. P., & DEHAENE, S. (1989). Neural models of cognitive function. *Cognition, 33,* 63–109.

CHARITY, A. H., SCARBOROUGH, H. S., & GRIFFIN, D. M. (2004). Familiarity with school English in African American children and its relation to early reading achievement. *Child Development, 75,* 1340–1356.

CHECHILE, R. A., & RICHMAN, C. L. (1982). The interaction of semantic memory with storage and retrieval processes. *Developmental Review, 2,* 237–250.

CHELUNE, G. J., & BAER, R. A. (1986). Developmental norms for the Wisconsin Card Sorting Test. *Journal of Clinical and Experimental Neuropsychology, 8,* 219–228.

CHEN, C., & STEVENSON, H. W. (1988). Cross-linguistic differences in digit span of preschool children. *Journal of Experimental Child Psychology, 46,* 150–158.

CHEN, C., & STEVENSON, H. W. (1995). Motivation and mathematics achievement: A comparative study of Asian-American, Caucasian-American, and East Asian high school students. *Child Development, 66,* 1215–1234.

CHEN, Z., & KLAHR, D. (1999). All other things being equal: Acquisition and transfer of the control of variables strategy. *Child Development, 70,* 1098–1120.

CHEN, Z., SANCHEZ, R. P., & CAMPBELL, T. (1997). From beyond to within their grasp: The rudiments of analogical problem solving in 10- and 13-month olds. *Developmental Psychology, 33,* 790–801.

CHEN, Z., & SIEGLER, R. S. (2000). Across the great divide: Bridging the gap between understanding of

toddlers' and older children's thinking. *Monographs of the Society for Research in Child Development, 65* (Serial No. 261).

CHENEY, D. F., & SEYFARTH, R. M. (1990). *How monkeys see the world: Inside the mind of another species.* Chicago: University of Chicago Press.

CHEYNE, J. A., & RUBIN, K. H. (1983). Playful precursors of problem solving in preschoolers. *Developmental Psychology, 19,* 577–584.

CHI, M. T. H. (1977). Age differences in memory span. *Journal of Experimental Child Psychology, 23,* 266–281.

CHI, M. T. H. (1978). Knowledge structure and memory development. In R. Siegler (Ed.), *Children's thinking: What develops?* Hillsdale, NJ: Erlbaum.

CHI, M. T. H., FELTOVICH, P. J., & GLASER, R. (1981). Categorization and representation of physics problems by experts and novices. *Cognitive Science, 5,* 121–152.

CHOMSKY, N. (1957). *Syntactic structures.* The Hague: Mouton.

CHOMSKY, N. (1959). Review of B. F. Skinner's *Verbal Behavior. Language, 35,* 26–129.

CHRISTIAN, K., MORRISON, F. J., FRAZIER, J. A., & MASSETTI, G. (2000). Specificity in the nature and timing of cognitive growth in kindergarten and first grade. *Journal of Cognition and Development, 1,* 429–448.

CHUAH, Y. M. L., & MAYBERY, M. T. (1999). Verbal and spatial short-term memory: Common sources of developmental change? *Journal of Experimental Child Psychology, 73,* 7–44.

CHUGANI, H. T., BEHEN, M. E., MUZIK, O., JUHÁSZ, C., NAGY, F., & CHUGANI, D. C. (2001). Local brain functional activity following early deprivation: A study of postinstitutionalized Romanian orphans. *NeuroImage, 117,* 1290–1301.

CHUGANI, H. T., PHELPS, M. E., & MAZZIOTTA, J. C. (1987). Positron emission tomography study of human brain functional development. *Annals of Neurology, 22,* 487–497.

CHURCH, R. B., & GOLDIN-MEADOW, S. (1986). The mismatch between gesture and speech as an index of transitional knowledge. *Cognition, 23,* 43–71.

CIANCIOLO, A. T., & STERNBERG, R. S. (2004). *A brief history of intelligence.* Malden, MA: Blackwell.

CICCHETTI, D. (1989). How research on child maltreatment has informed the study of child development: Perspectives from developmental psychopathology. In D. Cicchetti & V. Carlson (Eds.), *Child maltreatment: Theory and research on causes and consequences of child abuse and neglect.* New York: Cambridge University Press.

CLARK, E. A., & HANISEE, J. (1982). Intellectual and adaptive performance of Asian children in adoptive American settings. *Developmental Psychology, 18,* 595–599.

CLARKE, A. D. B., & CLARKE, A. M. (1976). Formerly isolated children. In A. M. Clarke & A. D. B. Clarke (Eds.), *Early experience: Myth and evidence.* London: Open Books.

CLEARFIELD, M. W., & WESTFAHL, S. M.-C. (2006). Familiarization in infants' perception of addition problems. *Journal of Cognition and Development, 7,* 27–43.

CLEMENTS, W. A., & PERNER, J. (1994). Implicit understanding of belief. *Cognitive Development, 9,* 377–395.

CLEMENTS, W. A., RUSTIN, C. L., & MCCALLUM, S. (2000). Promoting the transition from implicit to explicit understanding: A training study of false belief. *Developmental Science, 3,* 81–92.

CLEVELAND, E. S., & REESE, E. (2005). Maternal structure and autonomy support in conversations about the past: Contributions to children's autobiographical memory. *Developmental Psychology, 41,* 376–388.

CLIFFORDSON, C., & GUSTAFSSON, J.-E. (2008). Effects of age and schooling on intellectual performance: Estimates obtained from analysis of continuous variation in age and length of schooling. *Intelligence, 36,* 143–152.

CLUBB, P. A., NIDA, R. E., MERRITT, K., & ORNSTEIN, P. A. (1993). Visiting the doctor: Children's knowledge and memory. *Cognitive Development, 8,* 361–372.

COFFMAN, J. L., ORNSTEIN, P. A., MCCALL, L. E., & CURRAN, P. J. (2008). Linking teachers' memory-relevant language and the development of children's memory skills. *Developmental Psychology, 44,* 1640–1654.

COHEN, L. B., & CASHON, C. H. (2006). Infant cognition. In D. Kuhn & R. S. Siegler (Vol. Eds.), *Cognition, perception, and language,* Vol. 2 (pp. 214–251), in W. Damon & R. M. Lerner (Gen. Eds.), *Handbook of child psychology* (6th ed.). New York: Wiley.

COHEN, L. B., & STRAUSS, M. S. (1979). Concept acquisition in the human infant. *Child Development, 50,* 419–424.

COHEN, M. (1996). Preschooler's practical thinking and problem solving: The acquisition of an optimal solution. *Cognitive Development, 11,* 357–373.

COIE, J. D., & DODGE, K. A. (1998). Aggression and antisocial behavior. In N. Eisenberg (Vol. Ed.), *Social, emotional, and personality development,* Vol. 3, in W. Damon (Gen. Ed.), *Handbook of child psychology* (5th ed.). New York: Wiley.

COLE, M. (1990). Cognitive development and formal schooling: The evidence from cross-cultural research. In L. C. Moll (Ed.), *Vygotsky and education.* New York: Cambridge University Press.

COLE, M. (2006). Culture and cognitive development in phylogenetic, historical, and ontogenetic perspective. In D. Kuhn & R. S. Siegler (Vol. Eds.), *Cognition, perception, and language,* Vol. 2 (pp. 636–683), in W. Damon & R. M. Lerner (Gen. Eds.), *Handbook of Child Psychology* (6th ed.). New York: Wiley.

COLE, M., & SCRIBNER, S. (1977). Cross-cultural studies of memory and cognition. In R. V. Kail, Jr., & J. W. Hagen (Eds.), *Perspectives on the development of memory and cognition.* Hillsdale, NJ: Erlbaum.

COLLAER, M. L., & HINES, M. (1995). Human behavioral sex differences: A role for gonadal hormones during early development? *Psychological Bulletin, 118,* 55–107.

COLLIE, R., & HAYNE, R. (1999). Deferred imitation by 6- and 9-month-old infants: More evidence for declarative memory. *Developmental Psychobiology, 35,* 83–90.

CONNOR, J. M., & SERBIN, L. A. (1977). Behaviorally based masculine and feminine-activity-preference scales for preschoolers: Correlates with other classroom behaviors and cognitive tests. *Child Development, 48,* 1411–1416.

COOLEY, C. H. (1902). *Human nature and the social order.* New York: Scribner's.

COOPER, R. P., & ASLIN, R. N. (1990). Preference for infant-directed speech in the first month after birth. *Child Development, 61,* 1584–1595.

COOPER, R. P., & ASLIN, R. N. (1994). Developmental differences in infant attention to the spectral properties of infant-directed speech. *Child Development, 65,* 1663–1677.

CORDES, S., & BRANNON, E. M. (2009). Crossing the divide: Infants discriminate small from large numerosities. *Developmental Psychology, 45,* 1583–1594.

COSMIDES, L., & TOOBY, J. (1987). From evolution to behavior: Evolutionary psychology as the missing link. In J. Dupre (Ed.), *The latest and the best essays on evolution and optimality.* Cambridge, MA: MIT Press.

COSMIDES, L., & TOOBY, J. (1992). Cognitive adaptations for social exchange. In J. H. Barkow, L. Cosmides, & J. Tooby (Eds.), *The adapted mind: Evolutionary psychology and the generation of culture* (pp. 163–228). New York: Oxford University Press.

COSMIDES, L., TOOBY, J., & BARKOW, J. H. (1992). Introduction: Evolutionary psychology and conceptual integration. In J. H. Barkow, L. Cosmides, & J. Tooby (Eds.), *The adapted mind: Evolutionary psychology and the generation of culture.* New York: Oxford University Press.

COURAGE, M. L., & HOWE, M. L. (1998). The ebb and flow of infant attentional preferences: Evidence for long-term recognition memory in 3-month-olds. *Journal of Experimental Child Psychology, 70,* 26–53.

COURAGE, M. L., & HOWE, M. L. (2001). Long-term retention in 3.5-month-olds: Familiarization time and individual differences in attentional style. *Journal of Experimental Child Psychology, 79,* 271–293.

COURAGE, M. L., & HOWE, M. L. (2002). From infant to child: The dynamics of cognitive change in the second year of life. *Psychological Bulletin, 128,* 250–277.

COURAGE, M. L., MURPHY, A. N., GOULDING, S., & SETLIFF, A. E. (2010). When television is on: The impact of infant-directed video on 6- and 18-month-olds' toy play and on parent-infant interaction. *Infant*

*Behavior and Development, 33,* 176–188.

COURAGE, M. L., & SETLIFF, A. E. (2010). When babies watch television: Attention-getting, attention holding, and the implications for learning from video material. *Developmental Review, 30,* 220–238.

COWAN, N., & ALLOWAY, T. (2009). Development of working memory in childhood. In M. L. Courage & N. Cowan (Eds.), *The development of memory in infancy and childhood* (pp. 304–342). New York: Psychology Press.

COWAN, N., ELLIOTT, E. M., SAULTS, J. S., MOREY, C. C., MATTOX, S., HISMJATULLI, A., & CONWAY, A. R. A. (2005). On the capacity of attention: Its estimation and its role in working memory and cognitive aptitudes. *Cognitive Psychology, 51,* 42–100.

COWAN, N., NUGENT, L. D., ELLIOTT, E. M., PONOMAREV, I., & SAULTS, J. S. (1999). The role of attention in the development of short-term memory: Age differences in the verbal span of apprehension. *Child Development, 70,* 1082–1097.

COX, B. C., ORNSTEIN, P. A., NAUS, M. J., MAXFIELD, D., & ZIMLER, J. (1989). Children's concurrent use of rehearsal and organizational strategies. *Developmental Psychology, 25,* 619–627.

COX, D., & WATERS, H. S. (1986). Sex differences in the use of organization strategies: A developmental analysis. *Journal of Experimental Child Psychology, 41,* 18–37.

COYLE, T. R., & BJORKLUND, D. F. (1997). Age differences in, and consequences of, multiple- and variable strategy use on a multitrial sort-recall task. *Developmental Psychology, 33,* 372–380.

COYLE, T. R., READ, L. E., GAULTNEY, J. F., & BJORKLUND, D. F. (1998). Giftedness and variability in strategic processing on a multitrial memory task: Evidence for stability in gifted cognition. *Learning and Individual Differences, 10,* 273–290.

CRABTREE, J. W., & RIESEN, A. H. (1979). Effects of the duration of dark rearing on visually guided behavior in the kitten. *Developmental Psychobiology, 12,* 291–303.

CRAIN-THORESON, C., & DALE, P. S. (1992). Do early talkers become early readers? Linguistic precocity, preschool language, and emergent literacy. *Developmental Psychology, 28,* 421–429.

CRAWFORD, J. (1997). The campaign against Proposition 227: A postmortem. *Bilingual Research Journal, 21,* 1–23.

CRICK, N. R., & DODGE, K. A. (1994). A review and reformulation of social information-processing mechanisms in children's social adjustment. *Psychological Bulletin, 115,* 74–101.

CRICK, N. R., & DODGE, K. A. (1996). Social-information-processing mechanisms in reactive and proactive aggression. *Child Development, 67,* 993–1002.

CRONBACH, L. J. (1957). The two disciplines of scientific psychology. *American Psychologist, 12,* 671–684.

CSIBRA, G., BÍRÓ, S., KOÓS, O., & GERGELY, G. (2003). One-year-old infants use teleological representations of actions productively. *Cognitive Science, 27,* 111–133.

CUBAN, L. (2004). Assessing the 20-year impact of Multiple Intelligences on schooling. *Teachers College Record, 106,* 140–146.

CUMMINS, D. D. (1996). Evidence of deontic reasoning in 3- and 4-year-old children. *Memory and Cognition, 24,* 823–829.

CUMMINS, D. D. (1998). Social norms and other minds: The evolutionary roots of higher cognition. In D. D. Cummins & C. Allen (Eds.), *The evolution of mind.* New York: Oxford University Press.

CUMMINS-SEBREE, S. W., & FRAGASZY, D. M. (2005). Choosing and using tools: Capuchins (*Cebus apella*) use a different metric than tamarins (*Saguinus oedipus*). *Journal of Comparative Psychology, 119,* 210–219.

CUNHA, F., HECKMAN, J. J., LOCHNER, L. J., & MASTEROV, D. V. (2006). Interpreting the evidence on life cycle skill formation. In E. A. -Hanushek, & F. Welch (Eds.), *Handbook of the economics of education* (pp. 607–812) Amsterdam: North-Holland.

CUNNINGHAM, A. E. (1990). Explicit versus implicit instruction in phonemic awareness. *Journal of Experimental Child Psychology, 50,* 429–444.

CURTISS, S. (1977). *Genie: A psycholinguistic study of a modern day "wild child."* New York: Academic.

CYNADER, M., BERMAN, N. M., & HEIN, A. (1976). Recovery of function in cat visual cortex following prolonged deprivation. *Experimental Brain Research, 25,* 139–156.

DACK, L. A., & ASTINGTON, J. W. (October, 2007). *Children's deontic reasoning: Effects of context and language.* Poster presented at meeting of the Cognitive Development Society, Santa Fe, NM.

DAEHLER, M., & CHEN, Z. (1993). Protagonist, theme and goal objects: Effects of surface features on analogical transfer. *Cognitive Development, 8,* 211–229.

DAEHLER, M. W., LONARDO, R., & BUKATKO, D. (1979). Matching and equivalence judgments in very young children. *Child Development, 50,* 170–179.

DALEY, T. C., WHALEY, S. E., SIGMAN, M. D., ESPINOSA, M. P., & NEUMANN, C. (2003). IQ on the rise: The Flynn Effect in rural Kenyan children. *Psychological Science, 14,* 215–210.

DALLAGO, M. L. P., & MOELY, B. E. (1980). Free recall in boys of normal and poor reading levels as a function of task manipulations. *Journal of Experimental Child Psychology, 30,* 62–78.

DAMAST, A. M., TAMIS-LEMONDA, C. S., & BORNSTEIN, M. H. (1996). Mother-child play: Sequential interactions and the relation between maternal beliefs and behaviors. *Child Development, 67,* 1752–1766.

DANEMAN, M., & BLENNERHASSETT, A. (1984). How to assess the listening comprehension skills of prereaders. *Journal of Educational Psychology, 76,* 1372–1381.

DANEMAN, M., & GREEN, I. (1986). Individual differences in comprehending and producing words in context. *Journal of Memory and Language, 25,* 1–18.

DANIEL, M. H. (1997). Intelligence testing: Status and trends. *American Psychologist, 52,* 1038–1045.

DAPRETTO, M., DAVIES, M. S., PFEIFER, J. H., SCOTT, A. A., SIGMAN, M., BOOKHEIMER, S. Y., & IACOBONI, M. (2006). Understanding emotions in others: Mirror neuron dysfunction in children with autism spectrum disorders. *Nature Neuroscience, 9,* 28–30.

DARWIN, C. (1859). *On the origin of species.* New York: Modern Library.

DARWIN, C. (1871). *The descent of man, and selection in relation to sex.* London: John Murray.

DAS, J. P. (1984). Cognitive deficits in mental retardation. A process approach. In P. H. Brooks, R. Sperber, & C. McCauley (Eds.), *Learning and cognition in the mentally retarded.* Hillsdale, NJ: Erlbaum.

DASEN, P. R. (ED.). (1977). *Piagetian psychology: Cross cultural contributions.* New York: Gardner.

DAVIS, O. S., HAWORTH, C. M., & PLOMIN, R. (2009). Dramatic increase in heritability of cognitive development from early to middle childhood: An 8-year longitudinal study of 8,700 pairs of twins. *Psychological Science, 20,* 1301–1308.

DAVIS-UNGER, A. C., & CARLSON, S. M. (2008). Development of teaching skills and relations to theory of mind in preschoolers. *Journal of Cognition and Development, 9,* 26–45.

DAWSON, G., TOTH, K., ABBOTT, R., OSTERLING, J., MUNSON, J., ESTES, A., & LIAW, J. (2004). Early social attention impairments in autism: Social orienting, joint attention, and attention to distress. *Developmental Psychology, 40,* 271–283.

DE HAAN, M., BAUER, P. J., GEORGIEFF, M. K., & NELSON, C. A. (2000). Explicit memory in low-risk infants aged 19 months born between 27 and 42 weeks gestation. *Developmental Medicine and Child Neurology, 42,* 304–312.

DE HAAN, M., & JOHNSON, M. (EDS.). (2003). *The cognitive neuroscience of development.* Hove, UK: Psychology Press.

DE HAAN, M., OLIVER, A., & JOHNSON, M. H. (1998). Electrophysiological correlates of face processing by adults and 6-month-old infants. *Journal of Cognitive Neural Science, 36* (Annual Meeting Supplement).

DE HOUWER, A. (1995). Bilingual language acquisition. In P. Fletcher & B. MacWhinney (Eds.), *The handbook of child language* (pp. 219–250). Oxford: Blackwell.

DE LISI, R., & STAUDT, J. (1980). Individual differences in college students' performance on formal operations tasks. *Journal of Applied Developmental Psychology, 1,* 163–174.

DE VILLIERS, J. G., & DE VILLIERS, P. A. (1973). A cross sectional study of the acquisition of grammatical morphemes in child speech. *Journal of Psycholinguistic Research, 2,* 267–278.

DE VILLIERS, J. G., & DE VILLIERS, P. A. (1978). *Language acquisition.* Cambridge, MA: Harvard University Press.

DE VRIES, R. (1969). Constancy of generic identity in the years three to six. *Monographs of the Society for Research in Child Development, 34* (Serial No. 127).

DEACON, T. W. (1997). *The symbolic species: The co-evolution of language and the brain.* New York: Norton.

DEÁK, G. O., RAY, S. D., & BRENNEMAN, K. (2003). Children's perseverative appearance/reality errors are related to emerging language skills. *Child Development, 74,* 944–964.

DEARY, I. J., BATTY, G. D., PATTIE, A., & GALE, C. R. (2008). More intelligent, more dependable children live longer: A 55-year longitudinal study of a representative sample of the Scottish nation. *Psychological Science, 19,* 874–880.

DEBELL, M., & CHAPMAN, C. (2003). *Computer and Internet use by children and adolescents in 2001* (National Center for Education Statistics). Washington, DC: U.S. Department of Education.

DECASPER, A. J., & FIFER, W. P. (1980). Of human bonding: Newborns prefer their mother's voice. *Science, 208,* 1174–1176.

DECASPER, A. J., & SPENCE, M. J. (1986). Prenatal maternal speech influences newborns' perception of speech sounds. *Infant Behavior and Development, 9,* 133–150.

DECASPER, A. J., LECANUET, J.-P., BUSNEL, M.-C., GRANIER-DEFERRE, C., & MAUGEAIS, R. (1994). Fetal reactions to recurrent maternal speech. *Infant Behavior and Development, 17,* 159–164.

DECETY, J., & CACIOPPO, J. T. (2010). (Eds.) *Handbook of social neuroscience.* New York: Oxford University Press.

DELEVATI, N. M., & BERGAMASCO, N. H. P. (1999). Pain in the neonate: An analysis of facial movements and crying in response to nociceptive stimuli. *Infant Behavior and Development, 22,* 137–143.

DELOACHE, J. S. (1987). Rapid change in the symbolic functioning of very young children. *Science, 238,* 1556–1557.

DELOACHE, J. S. (1991). Symbolic functioning in very young children: Understanding of pictures and models. *Child Development, 62,* 736–752.

DELOACHE, J. S. (2000). Dual representation and young children's use of scale models. *Child Development, 71,* 329–338.

DELOACHE, J. S., & BROWN, A. L. (1983). Very young children's memory for the location of objects in a large scale environment. *Child Development, 54,* 888–897.

DELOACHE, J. S., CASSIDY, D. J., & BROWN, A. L. (1985). Precursors of mnemonic strategies in very young children's memory for the location of hidden objects. *Child Development, 56,* 125–137.

DELOACHE, J. S., & DEMENDOZA, O. A. P. (1987). Joint picturebook reading of mothers and one-year-old children. *British Journal of Developmental Psychology, 5,* 111–123.

DELOACHE, J. S., & MARZOLF, D. P. (1992). When a picture is not worth a thousand words: Young children's understanding of pictures and models. *Cognitive Development, 7,* 317–329.

DELOACHE, J. S., MILLER, K. F., & PIERROUTSAKOS, S. L. (1998). Reasoning and problem solving. In D. Kuhn & R. S. Siegler (Vol. Eds.), *Cognitive, language, and perceptual development,* Vol. 2, in W. Damon (Gen. Ed.), *Handbook of child psychology* (5th ed.). New York: Wiley.

DELOACHE, J. S., MILLER, K. F., & ROSENGREN, K. S. (1997). The credible shrinking room: Very young children's performance with symbolic and nonsymbolic relations. *Psychological Science, 8,* 308–313.

Deloitte's State of the Media Democracy Survey, Third Edition: Rethink what you know. (2009). Retrieved November 10, 2010, from http://www.deloitte.com/dtt/article/0,1002,sid%253D108581%2526cid%253D235500,00.html.

DELPIT, L. D. (1990). Language diversity and learning. In S. Hynds & D. L. Rubin (Eds.), *Perspectives on talk and learning.* Urbana, IL: National Council of Teachers of English.

DELPIT, L. D., & DOWDY, J. K. (2002). *The skin that we speak: Thoughts on language and culture in the classroom.* New York: New Press.

DEMARIE, D., & FERRON, J. (2003). Capacity, strategies, and metamemory: Tests of a three-factor model of memory development. *Journal of Experimental Child Psychology, 84,* 167–193.

DEMARIE, D., MILLER, P. H., FERRON, J., & CUNNINGHAM, W. R. (2004). Path analysis tests for theoretical models of children's memory performance. *Journal of Cognition and Development, 5,* 461–492.

DEMARIE-DREBLOW, D., & MILLER, P. H. (1988). The development of children's strategies for selective attention: Evidence for a transitional period. *Child Development, 59,* 1504–1513.

DEMETRIOU, A., XIANG KUI, Z., SPANOUDIS, G., CHRISTOU, C., KYRIAKIDES, L., & PLATSIDOU, M. (2005). The architecture, dynamics, and development of mental processing: Greek, Chinese, or universal? *Intelligence, 33,* 109–141.

DEMPSTER, F. N. (1981). Memory span: Sources of individual and developmental differences. *Psychological Bulletin, 89,* 63–100.

DEMPSTER, F. N. (1993). Resistance to interference: Developmental changes in a basic processing mechanisms. In M. L. Howe & R. Pasnak (Eds.), *Emerging themes in cognitive development*: Vol. 1. *Foundations.* New York: Springer-Verlag.

DENNETT, D. (1990). The interpretation of texts, people, and other artifacts. *Philosophy and Phenomenological Quarterly, 1* (Suppl.), 177–194.

DENNIS, W. (1973). *Children of the Crèche.* New York: Appleton-Century-Crofts.

DESTEFANO, J. (1972). Social variation in language: Implications for teaching reading to Black ghetto children. In J. A. Figurel (Ed.), *Better reading in urban schools.* Newark, DE: International Reading Association.

DETTERMAN, D. K. (1987). What does reaction time tell us about intelligence? In P. E. Vernon (Ed.), *Speed of information processing and intelligence.* Norwood, NJ: Ablex.

DETTERMAN, D. K., & DANIEL, M. H. (1989). Correlations of mental tests with each other and with cognitive variables are highest for low IQ groups. *Intelligence, 13,* 340–359.

DETTERMAN, D. K., & THOMPSON, L. A. (1997). What is so special about special education? *American Psychologist, 52,* 1082–1090.

DEVLIN, B., DANIELS, M., & ROEDER, K. (1997). The heritability of IQ. *Nature, 388,* 468–471.

DEWHURST, S. A., PURSGLOVE, R. C., & LEWIS, C. (2007). Story contexts increase susceptibility to the DRM illusion in 5-year-olds. *Developmental Science, 10,* 274–278.

DIAMOND, A. (1985). Development of the ability to use recall to guide action as indicated by infants' performance on AB. *Child Development, 56,* 868–883.

DIAMOND, A. (1991). Frontal lobe involvement in cognitive changes during the first year of life. In K. R. Gibson & A. C. Petersen (Eds.), *Brain maturation and cognitive development: Comparative and cross-cultural perspectives.* New York: Aldine de Gruyter.

DIAMOND, A., & AMSO, D. (2008). Contributions of neuroscience to our understanding of cognitive development. *Current Directions in Psychological Science, 17,* 136–141.

DIAMOND, A., BARNETT, W. S., THOMAS, J., & MUNRO, S. (2007). Preschool program improves cognitive control. *Science, 318,* 1387–1388.

DIAMOND, A., CRUTTENDEN, L., & NEIDERMAN, D. (1994). AB with multiple wells: 1. Why are multiple wells sometimes easier than two wells? 2. Memory or memory + inhibition? *Developmental Psychology, 30,* 192–205.

DIAMOND, A., KIRKHAM, N., & AMSO, D. (2002). Conditions under which young children can hold two rules in mind and inhibit a prepotent response. *Developmental Psychology, 38,* 352–362.

DIAMOND, A., & TAYLOR, C. (1996). Development of an aspect of executive control: Development of the abilities to remember what I said and to "Do as I say, not as I do." *Developmental Psychobiology, 29,* 315–324.

DIAZ, R. M. (1983). Thought and two languages: The impact of bilingualism on cognitive development. *Review of Research in Education, 10,* 23–54.

DIAZ, R. M., NEAL, C. J., & VACHIO, A. (1991). Maternal teaching in the zone of proximal development: A comparison of low- and high-risk dyads. *Merrill-Palmer Quarterly, 37,* 83–108.

DÍAZ-LEFEBVRE, R. (2004). Multiple intelligences, learning for understanding, and creative assessment: Some pieces to the puzzle of learning. *Teachers College Record, 106,* 49–57.

DIESENDRUCK, G., & MARKSON, L. (2001). Children's avoidance of lexical overlap: A pragmatic account. *Developmental Psychology, 37,* 630–641.

DIRIX, C. E. H., NIJHUIS, J. G., JONGSMA, H. W., & HORNSTRA, C. (2009). Aspects of fetal learning and memory. *Child Development, 80,* 1251–1258.

DOBZHANSKY, T. (1964). Biology, molecular and organismic. *American Zoologist, 4,* 443–452.

DODGE, K. A. (1986). A social information processing model of social competence in children. In M. Perlmutter (Ed.), *Minnesota symposium on child psychology,* Vol. 18. Hillsdale, NJ: Erlbaum.

DODGE, K. A., COIE, J. D., & LYNAM, D. (2006). Aggression and antisocial behavior in youth. In N. Eisenberg (Vol. Ed.), *Social, emotional, and personality development,* Vol. 3 (pp. 719–788), in W. Damon & R. M. Lerner (Gen. Eds.), *Handbook of Child Psychology* (6th ed.). New York: Wiley.

DODGE, K. A., PETTIT, G. S., BATES, J. E., & VALENTE, E. (1995). Social information processing patterns partially mediate the effect of early physical abuse on later conduct problems. *Journal of Abnormal Psychology, 104,* 632–643.

DODGE, K. A., PETTIT, G. S., McCLASKEY, C. L., & BROWN, M. M. (1986). Social competence in children. *Monographs of the Society for Research in Child Development, 51* (Serial No. 213).

DODGE, K. A., & PRICE, J. M. (1994). On the relation between social information processing and socially competent behavior in early school-age children. *Child Development, 65,* 1385–1397.

DOMAN, G. (1984). *How to multiply your baby's intelligence.* Garden City, NY: Doubleday.

DORE, F. Y., & DUMAS, C. (1987). Psychology of animal cognition:

Piagetian studies. *Psychological Bulletin, 102,* 219–233.

DOUGHTERTY, T. M., & HAITH, M. M. (1997). Infant expectations and reaction time as predictors of childhood speed of processing and IQ. *Developmental Psychology, 33,* 146–155.

DRACHMAN, D. B., & COULOMBRE, A. J. (1962). Experimental clubfoot and arthrogryposis multiplex congenita. *Lancet, 7255,* 523–526.

DRUMMEY, A. B., & NEWCOMBE, N. (1995). Remembering versus knowing the past: Children's explicit and implicit memory. *Journal of Experimental Child Psychology, 59,* 549–565.

DUCKWORTH, A. L., & SELIGMAN, M. E. P. (2005). Self-discipline outdoes IQ in predicting academic performance of adolescence. *Psychological Science, 16,* 939–944.

DUBOWITZ, L. M., MUSHIN, J., DE-VRIES, L., & ARDEN, G. B. (1986). Visual function in the newborn infant: Is it cortically mediated? *Lancet, 8490,* 1139–1141.

DUFFY, S., HUTTENLOCHER, J., & LEVINE, S. (2005). It's all relative: How young children encode extent. *Journal of Cognition and Development, 6,* 51–63.

DUFFY, S., & KITAYAMA, S. (2007). Mnemonic context effect in two cultures: Attention to memory representations? *Cognitive Science, 31,* 1–12.

DUFFY, S., TORIYAMA, R., ITAKURA, S., & KITAYAMA, S. (2009). Development of cultural strategies of attention in North American and Japanese children. *Journal of Experimental Child Psychology, 102,* 351–359.

DUNBAR, R. I. M. (1992). Neocortex size as a constraint on group size in primates. *Journal of Human Evolution, 20,* 469–493.

DUNBAR, R. I. M. (1995). Neocortex size and group size in primates: A test of the hypothesis. *Journal of Human Evolution, 28,* 287–296.

DUNBAR, R. I. M. (2001). Brains on two legs: Group size and the evolution of intelligence. In F. B. M. de Waal (Ed.), *Tree of origins: What primate behavior can tell us about human social evolution* (pp. 173–191). Cambridge, MA: Harvard University Press.

DUNBAR, R. I. M. (2010). Brain and behavior in primate evolution. In P. M. Kappler & J. B. Silk (Eds.),

*Mind the gap: Tracing the origins of human universals* (pp. 315–330). New York: Springer.

DUNCAN, J., SEITZ, R. J., KOLODNY, J., BOR, D., HERZOG, H., AHMED, A., NEWELL, F. N., & EMSLIE, H. (2000). A neural basis for general intelligence. *Science, 289,* 457–460.

DUNCAN, R., & TARULLI, D. (2009). On the persistence of private speech: Empirical and theoretical considerations. In A. Winsler, C. Fernyhough, & I. Montero (Eds.), *Private speech, executive functioning, and the development of verbal self-regulation* (pp. 176–187). Cambridge, UK: Cambridge University Press.

EAGAN, S. K., & PERRY, D. G. (2001). Gender identity: A multidimensional analysis with implications for psychological adjustment. *Developmental Psychology, 37,* 451–463.

EASTERBROOK, M. A., KISILEVSKY, B. S., HAINS, S. M. J., & MUIR, D. W. (1999). Faceness or complexity: Evidence from newborn visual tracking of facelike stimuli. *Infant Behavior and Development, 22,* 17–35.

EATON, W. O., & VON BARGEN, D. (1981). Asynchronous development of gender understanding in preschool children. *Child Development, 52,* 1020–1027.

EDELMAN, G. M. (1987). *Neural Darwinism: The theory of neuronal group selection.* New York: Basic Books.

EHRI, L. C. (1995). Phases of development in learning to read words by sight. *Journal of Research in Reading, 18,* 116–125.

EILERS, R. W., GAVIN, W. J., & WILSON, W. R. (1979). Linguistic experience and phonemic perception in infancy: A cross-linguistic study. *Child Development, 50,* 14–18.

EIMAS, P. D., & QUINN, P. C. (1994). Studies on the formation of perceptually based basic-level categories in young infants. *Child Development, 65,* 903–917.

EIMAS, P. D., SIQUELAND, E. R., JUSCZYK, P., & VIGORITO, J. (1971). Speech perception in infants. *Science, 71,* 303–306.

EINSTEIN, G. O., & MCDANIEL, M. A. (2005). Prospective memory: Multiple retrieval processes. *Current Directions in Psychological Science, 14,* 286–290.

EIZENMAN, D. R., & BERTENTHAL, B. I. (1998). Infants' perception of object unity in translating and rotating displays. *Developmental Psychology, 34,* 426–434.

ELISCHBERGER, H. B. (2005). The effects of prior knowledge on children's memory and suggestibility. *Journal of Experimental Child Psychology, 92,* 247–275.

ELKIND, D. (1967). Egocentrism in adolescence. *Child Development, 38,* 1025–1033.

ELKIND, D. (1987). *Miseducation: Preschoolers at risk.* New York: Knopf.

ELKIND, D. (1996). Inhelder and Piaget on adolescence and adulthood: A postmodern appraisal. *Psychological Science, 7,* 216–220.

ELKIND, D., & BOWEN, R. (1979). Imaginary audience behavior in children and adolescents. *Developmental Psychology, 15,* 38–44.

ELLIS, H. (1894). *Man and woman: A study of human secondary sexual characters.* London: Walter Scott.

ELLIS, N. C., & HENNELLEY, R. A. (1980). A bilingual word-length effect: Implications for intelligence testing and the relative ease of mental calculation in Welsh and English. *British Journal of Psychology, 71,* 43–52.

ELLIS, S., & ROGOFF, B. (1986). Problem solving in children's management of instruction. In E. Mueller & C. Cooper (Eds.), *Process and outcome in peer relationships.* Orlando, FL: Academic.

ELMAN, J. (1994). Implicit learning in neural networks: The importance of starting small. In C. Umilta & M. Moscovitch (Eds.), *Attention and performance XV: Conscious and nonconscious information processing.* Cambridge, MA: MIT Press.

ELMAN, J. L., BATES, E. A., JOHNSON, M. H., KARMILOFF-SMITH, A., PARISI, D., & PLUNKET, K. (1996). *Rethinking innateness: A connectionist perspective on development.* Cambridge, MA: MIT Press.

ELSE-QUEST, N. M., HYDE, J. S., & KINN, M. C. (2010). Cross-national patterns of gender differences in mathematics: A meta-analysis. *Psychological Bulletin, 136,* 103–127.

ELUVATHINGAL, T. J., CHUGANI, H. T., BEHEN, M. E., JUHÁSZ, C., MUZIK, O., MAQBOOL, M., CHUGANI, D. C., & MAKKI, M. (2006). Abnormal brain connectivity in children after early severe socioemotional deprivation: A diffusion tensor imaging study. *Pediatrics, 117,* 2093–2100.

ERDELYI, M. (1994). Hypnotic hypermnesia: The empty set of hypermnesia. *International Journal of Clinical and Experimental Hypnosis, 42,* 379–390.

ERIKSSON, P. S., PERFILIEVA, E., BJOERK-ERIKSSON, T., ALBORN, A.-M., NORDBORG, C., PETERSON, D. A., & GAGE, F. H. (1998). Neurogenesis in the adult human hippocampus. *Nature Medicine, 4,* 1313–1317.

ESPY, K. A., MOLFESE, V. J., & DiLALLA, L. F. (2001). Effects of environmental measures on intelligence in young children: Growth curve modeling of longitudinal data. *Merrill-Palmer Quarterly, 47,* 42–73.

EVANS, G. W., & KIM, P. (2007). Childhood poverty and health: Cumulative risk exposure and stress dysregulation. *Psychological Science, 18,* 953–957.

EVANS, M. A. (1985). Self-initiated speech repairs: A reflection of communicative monitoring in young children. *Developmental Psychology, 21,* 365–371.

EVANS, M. E. (2001). Cognitive and contextual factors in the emergence of diverse belief systems: Creation versus evolution. *Cognitive Psychology, 42,* 217–266.

EVANS, N., & LEVINSON, S. (2009). The myth of language universals: Language diversity and its importance for cognitive science. *Behavioral and Brain Science, 32,* 429–492.

EVANS, P. D., GILBERT, S. L., MEKEL-BOBROV, N., VALLENDER, E. J., ANDERSON, J. R., VAEZ-AZIZI, L. M., TISHKOFF, S. A., JUDSON, R. R., & LAHN, B. T. (2005). *Microcephalin,* a gene regulating brain size, continues to evolve adaptively in humans. *Science, 309,* 1717–1720.

EYSENCK, H. J. (1987). Speed of information processing, reaction time, and the theory of intelligence. In P. E. Vernon (Ed.), *Speed of information processing and intelligence.* Norwood, NJ: Ablex.

FABRICIUS, W. V., BOYER, T., WEIMER, A. A., & CARROLL, K. (2010). True or False: Do five-year-olds understand belief? *Developmental Psychology, 46,* 1402–1416.

FABRICIUS, W. V., & IMBENS-BAILEY, A. L. (2000). False beliefs about false beliefs. In P. Mitchell & K. Riggs (Eds.), *Children's reasoning about the mind* (pp. 267–280). Hove, UK: Psychology Press.

FABRICIUS, W. V., & KHALIL, S. L. (2003). False beliefs or false positives? Limits on children's understanding of mental representation. *Journal of Cognition and Development, 4,* 239–262.

FAGAN, J. F., III. (1973). Infants' delayed recognition memory and forgetting. *Journal of Experimental Child Psychology, 16,* 424–450.

FAGAN, J. F., III. (1974). Infant recognition memory: The effects of length of familiarization and type of discrimination task. *Child Development, 45,* 351–356.

FAGAN, J. F., III. (1984). The relationship of novelty preferences during infancy to later intelligence and recognition memory. *Intelligence, 8,* 339–346.

FAGAN, J. F., III. (1992). Intelligence: A theoretical viewpoint. *Current Directions in Psychological Science, 1,* 82–86.

FAGAN, J. F., III, & SINGER, J. T. (1983). Infant recognition memory as a measure of intelligence. In L. P. Lipsitt & C. K. Rovee-Collier (Eds.), *Advances in infancy research,* Vol. 2. Norwood, NJ: Ablex.

FAGAN, J., PRIGOT, J., CARROLL, M., PIOLO, L., STEIN, A., & FRANCO, A. (1997). Auditory context and memory retrieval in young infants. *Developmental Psychology, 68,* 1057–1066.

FAGOT, B. I., LEINBACH, M. D., & HAGAN, R. (1986). Gender labeling and the adoption of sex-typed behaviors. *Developmental Psychology, 22,* 440–443.

FANTZ, R. L. (1958). Pattern vision in young infants. *Psychological Record, 8,* 43–47.

FANTZ, R. L. (1961). The origin of form perception. *Scientific American, 204,* 66–72.

FANTZ, R. L., & MIRANDA, S. B. (1975). Newborn attention to form of contour. *Child Development, 46,* 224–228.

FARRONI, T., CSIBRA, G., SIMION, F., & JOHNSON, M. H. (2002). Eye contact detection in humans from birth. *Proceedings of the National Academy of Sciences of the United States of America, 99,* 9602–9605.

FECTEAU, S., CARMANT, L., TREMBLAY, C., ROBERT, M., BOUTHILLIER, A., & THÉORET, H. (2004). A motor resonance mechanism in children? Evidence from subdural electrodes in a 36-month-old child. *Neuroreport, 15,* 2625–2627.

FEIGENSON, L., CAREY, S., & HAUSER, M. (2002). The representations underlying infants' choice of more: Object-files versus analog magnitudes. *Psychological Science, 13,* 150–156.

FEIN, G. (1981). Pretend play: An integrative review. *Child Development, 52,* 1095–1118.

FEINBERG, I. (1982/1983). Schizophrenia: Caused by a fault in programmed synaptic elimination during adolescence? *Journal of Psychiatric Research, 4,* 319–334.

FEINGOLD, A. (1988). Cognitive gender differences are disappearing. *American Psychologist, 43,* 95–103.

FEINGOLD, A. (1992). Sex differences in variability in intellectual abilities: A new look at an old controversy. *Review of Educational Research, 62,* 61–84.

FELDMAN, R., & EIDELMAN, A. I. (2004). Parent–infant synchrony and the social–emotional development of triplets. *Developmental Psychology, 40,* 1133–1147.

FERNALD, A. (1992). Human maternal vocalizations to infants as biologically relevant signals: An evolutionary perspective. In J. H. Barkow, L. Cosmides, & J. Tooby (Eds.), *The adaptive mind: Evolutionary psychology and the generation of culture* (pp. 391–428). New York: Oxford University Press.

FERNALD, A., & MAZZIE, C. (1991). Prosody and focus in speech to infants and adults. *Developmental Psychology, 27,* 209–221.

FERNALD, A., PINTO, J. P., SWINGLEY, D., WEINBERG, A., & McROBERTS, G. W. (1998). Rapid gains in speed of verbal processing by infants in the 2nd year. *Psychological Science, 9,* 228–231.

FERNALD, A., TAESCHNER, T., DUNN, J., PAPOUSEK, M., FUKUI, I., & BOYSSON-BARDIES, B. DE. (1989). A cross-language study of prosodic modifications in mothers' and fathers' speech to infants. *Journal of Child Language, 16,* 477–501.

FERRARI, P. F., VISALBERGHI, E., PAUKNER, A., FOGASSI, L., RUGGIERO, A., SUOMI, S. J. (2006). Neonatal imitation in rhesus macaques. *PLoS Biol, 4*(9), e302. DOI: 10.1371/journal. pbio.0040302.

FERREIRA, F., & MORRISON, F. J. (1994). Children's knowledge of syntactic constituents: Effects of age and schooling. *Developmental Psychology, 30,* 663–678.

FIELD, T. M., WOODSON, R., GREENBERG, R., & COHEN, D. (1982). Discrimination and imitation of facial expression by neonates. *Science, 218,* 179–181.

FIELD, T., GUY, L., & UMBEL, V. (1985). Infants' responses to mothers' imitative behaviors. *Infant Mental Health Journal, 6,* 40–44.

FINKELSTEIN, N. W., & RAMEY, C. T. (1977). Learning to control the environment in infancy. *Child Development, 48,* 806–819.

FISCHER, K. W. (1980). A theory of cognitive development: The control and construction of hierarchies of skills. *Psychological Review, 87,* 477–531.

FISCHER, K. W., & BIDELL, T. (1998). Dynamic development of psychological structures in action and thought. In R. M. Lerner (Vol. Ed.), *Theoretical models of human development,* Vol. 1, in W. Damon (Gen. Ed.), *Handbook of child psychology* (5th ed.). New York: Wiley.

FISCHER, K. W., & BIDELL, T. (1991). Constraining nativist inferences about cognitive capacities. In S. Carey & R. Gelman (Eds.), *The epigenesis of mind: Essays on biology and cognition.* Hillsdale, NJ: Erlbaum.

FISCHER, K. W., & HENCKE, R. W. (1996). Infants' construction of actions in context: Piaget's contribution to research on early development. *Psychological Science, 7,* 204–211.

FISHER, C., & TOKURA, H. (1996). Acoustic cues to grammatical structure in infant-directed speech: Cross-linguistic evidence. *Child Development, 67,* 3192–3218.

FIVUSH, R. (1988). The functions of event memory: Some comments on Nelson and Barsalou. In U. Neisser & E. Winograd (Eds.), *Remembering reconsidered: Ecological and traditional approaches to the study of memory.* New York: Cambridge University Press.

FIVUSH, R. (2008). Remembering and reminiscing: How individual lives are constructed in family narratives. *Memory Studies, 1,* 49–58.

FIVUSH, R. (2009). Sociocultural perspectives on autobiographical memory. In M. L. Courage & N. Cowan (Eds.), *The development of memory in infancy and childhood* (pp. 283–301). New York: Psychology Press.

FIVUSH, R., HADEN, C. A., & REESE, E. (2006). Elaborating on elaborations: Role of maternal reminiscing style in cognitive and socioemotional development. *Child Development, 77,* 1568–1588.

FIVUSH, R., & HAMOND, N. R. (1990). Autobiographical memory across the preschool years: Toward reconceptualizing childhood amnesia. In R. Fivush & J. A. Hudson (Eds.), *Knowing and remembering in young children.* Cambridge, UK: Cambridge University Press.

FIVUSH, R., & HUDSON, J. A. (EDS.). (1990). *Knowing and remembering in young children.* Cambridge, UK: Cambridge University Press.

FIVUSH, R., KUEBLI, J., & CLUBB, P. A. (1992). The structure of events and event representations: A developmental analysis. *Child Development, 63,* 188–201.

FIVUSH, R., MARIN, K., McWILLIAMS, K., & BOHANEK, J. G. (2009). Family reminiscing style: Parent gender and emotional focus in relation to child well-being. *Journal of Cognition and Development, 10,* 210–235.

FIVUSH, R., McDERMOTT SALES, J., GOLDBERG, A., BAHRICK, L., & PARKER, J. (2004). Weathering the storm: Children's long-term recall of Hurricane Andrew. *Memory, 12,* 104–118.

FLANNAGAN, D., BAKER-WARD, L., & GRAHAM, L. (1995). Talk about preschool: Patterns of topic discussion and elaboration related to gender and ethnicity. *Sex Roles, 32,* 1–15.

FLAVELL, J. H. (1970). Developmental studies of mediated memory. In H. W. Reese & L. P. (Eds.), *Advances in child development and child behavior,* Vol. 5. New York: Academic.

FLAVELL, J. H. (1978). Developmental stage: Explanans or explanandum? *Behavioral and Brain Sciences, 2,* 187.

FLAVELL, J. H. (1996). Piaget's legacy. *Psychological Science, 7,* 200–203.

FLAVELL, J. H., BEACH, D. R., & CHINSKY, J. H. (1966). Spontaneous verbal rehearsal in a memory task as a function of age. *Child Development, 37,* 283–299.

FLAVELL, J. H., GREEN, F. L., & FLAVELL, E. R. (1986). Development of knowledge about the appearance-reality distinction. *Monographs of the Society for Research in Child Development, 51* (Serial No. 212).

FLAVELL, J. H., GREEN, F. L., & FLAVELL, R. R. (1995). The development of children's knowledge about attentional focus. *Developmental Psychology, 31,* 706–712.

FLAVELL, J. H., GREEN, F. L., FLAVELL, E. R., & GROSSMAN, J. B. (1997). The development of children's knowledge about inner speech. *Developmental Psychology, 68,* 39–47.

FLAVELL, J. H., & MILLER, P. H. (1998). Social cognition. In D. Kuhn & R. S. Siegler (Vol. Eds.), *Cognition, perception, and language,* Vol. 2, in W. Damon (Gen. Ed.), *Handbook of child psychology* (5th ed.). New York: Wiley.

FLIELLER, A. (1999). Comparison of the development of formal thought in adolescent cohorts aged 10 to 15 years (1967–1996 and 1972–1993). *Developmental Psychology, 35,* 1048–1058.

FLEMING, V. M., & ALEXANDER, J. M. (2001). The benefits of peer collaboration: A replication with a delayed posttest. *Contemporary Educational Psychology, 26,* 588–601.

FLIN, R., BOON, J., KNOX, A., & BULL, R. (1992). The effect of a five-month delay on children's and adult's eyewitness memory. *British Journal of Psychology, 83,* 323–336.

FLINN, M., & WARD, C. (2005). Evolution of the human child. In B. J. Ellis & D. F. Bjorklund (Eds.), *Origins of the social mind: Evolutionary psychology and child development* (pp. 19–44). New York: Guilford.

FLYNN, E., O'MALLEY, C., & WOOD, D. (2004). A longitudinal, microgenetic study of the emergence of false belief understanding and inhibition skills. *Developmental Science, 7,* 103–115.

FLYNN, J. R. (1987). Massive IQ gains in 14 nations: What IQ tests really measure. *Psychological Bulletin, 101,* 171–191.

FLYNN, J. R. (1999), Searching for justice: The discovery of IQ gains over time. *American Psychologist, 54,* 5–20.

FLYNN, J. R. (2007). *What is intelligence? Beyond the Flynn Effect.* New York: Cambridge University Press.

FODOR, J. A. (1983). *The modularity of mind.* Cambridge, MA: MIT Press.

FODOR, J. (2000). *The mind doesn't work that way: The scope and limits of computational psychology.* Cambridge, MA: MIT Press.

FOLDS, T. H., FOOTO, M., GUTTENTAG, R. E., & ORNSTEIN, P. A. (1990). When children mean to remember: Issues of context specificity, strategy effectiveness, and intentionality in the development of memory. In D. F. Bjorklund (Ed.), *Children's strategies: Contemporary views of cognitive development.* Hillsdale, NJ: Erlbaum.

FOLEY, M. A., & RATNER, H. H. (1998). Distinguishing between memories for thoughts and deeds: The role of prospective processing in children's source monitoring. *British Journal of Developmental Psychology, 16,* 465–484.

FOLEY, M. A., RATNER, H. H., & GENTES, E. (2010). Helping children enter into another's experiences: The look and feel of it. *Journal of Cognition and Development, 11,* 217–239.

FOLEY, M. A., RATNER, H. H., & PASSALACQUA, C. (1993). Appropriating the actions of another: Implications for children's memory and learning. *Cognitive Development, 8,* 373–401.

FOLEY, M. A., SANTINI, C., & SOPASAKIS, M. (1989). Discriminating between memories: Evidence for children's spontaneous elaborations. *Journal of Experimental Child Psychology, 48,* 146–169.

FOUTS, R. (1997). *Next of kin: My conversations with chimpanzees.* New York: William Morrow and Company.

FOUTS, R. S., & FOUTS, D. H. (1989). Loulis in conversation with cross-fostered chimpanzees. In R. A. Gardner, B. T. Gardner, & T. E. van Cantfort (Eds.), *Teaching sign language to chimpanzees* (pp. 293–307). Albany, NY: State University of New York Press.

FOX, S. E., LEVITT, P., & NELSON, C. A., III (2010). How timing and quality of early experience influence the development of brain architecture. *Child Development, 81,* 28–40.

FRAZIER, J. A., & MORRISON, F. J. (1998). The influence of extended-year schooling on growth of achievement and perceived competence in early elementary school. *Child Development, 69,* 495–517.

FREUD, S. (1963). Three essays on the theory of sexuality. In J. Strachey (Ed. and Trans.), *The standard edition of the complete psychological works of Sigmund Freud,* Vol. 7. London: Hogarth.

FREUND, L. S. (1990). Maternal regulation of children's problem-solving behavior and its impact on children's performance. *Child Development, 61,* 113–126.

FRIEDMAN, N. P., MIYAKE, A., YOUNG, S. E., DeFRIES, J. C., CORLEY, R. P., & HEWITT, J. K. (2008). Individual differences in executive functions are almost entirely genetic in origin. *Journal of Experimental Psychology: General, 137,* 201–225.

FRIEDMAN, S. (1972). Habituation and recovery of visual response in the alert human newborn. *Journal of Experimental Child Psychology, 13,* 339–349.

FRIEDMAN, W. J. (1986). The development of children's knowledge of temporal structure. *Child Development, 57,* 1386–1400.

FRIEDMAN, W. J. (1991). The development of children's memory for the time of past events. *Child Development, 62,* 139–155.

FRIEDMAN, W. J. (2000). The development of children's knowledge of the times of future events. *Child Development, 71,* 913–932.

FRIEDMAN, W. J. (2003). The development of a differentiated sense of the past and the future. In R. Kail (Ed.), *Advances in child development and behavior,* Vol. 31 (pp. 229–269). San Diego, CA: Academic.

FRIEDMAN, W. J. (2008). Developmental perspectives on the psychology of time. In S. Grondin (Ed.), *The psychology of time.* Bingley, UK: Emerald Publishing Group.

FRIEDMAN, W. J., GARDNER, A. G., & ZUBIN, N. R. E. (1995). Children's comparisons of the recency of two events from the past year. *Child Development, 66,* 44–66.

FRY, A., & HALE, S. (2000). Relationships among processing speed, working memory and fluid intelligence in children. *Biological Psychology, 54,* 1–34.

FULIGNI, A. J., & STEVENSON, H. W. (1995). Time use and mathematics achievement among American, Chinese, and Japanese high school students. *Child Development, 66,* 830–842.

FURLOW, F. B., ARMIJO-PREWITT, T., GANGSTEAD, S. W., & THORNHILL, R. (1997). Fluctuating asymmetry and psychometric intelligence. *Proceedings of the Royal Society of London, Series B, 264,* 823–829.

FURMAN, L. N., & WALDEN, T. A. (1990). Effects of script knowledge on preschool children's communicative interactions. *Developmental Psychology, 26,* 227–233.

FURTH, H. G. (1964). Research with the deaf: Implications for language and cognition. *Psychological Bulletin, 62,* 251–267.

FUSON, K. C. (1988). *Children's counting and concepts of number.* New York: Springer-Verlag.

FUSON, K. C., PERGAMENT, G. G., LYONS, B. G., & HALL, J. W. (1985). Children's conformity to the cardinality rule as a function of set size and counting accuracy. *Child Development, 56,* 1429–1436.

FUSTER, J. M. (1989). *The prefrontal cortex: Anatomy, physiology, and neuropsychology of the frontal lobe.* New York: Raven.

GALLAY, M., BAUDOUIN, J.-Y., DURAND, K., LEMOINE, C., & LÉCUYER, R. (2006). Qualitative difference in the exploration of upright and upside-down faces in four-month-old infants: An eye-movement study. *Child Development, 77,* 984–996.

GALLUP, G. G., JR. (1979). Self-recognition in chimpanzees and man: A developmental and comparative perspective. In M. Lewis & L. A. Rosenblum (Eds.), *Genesis of behavior: Vol. 2. The child and its family.* New York: Plenum.

GALSWORTHY, M. J., DIONNE, G., DALE, P. S., & PLOMIN, R. (2000). Sex differences in early verbal and nonverbal cognitive development. *Developmental Science, 3,* 206–215.

GANEA, P. A., ALLEN, M. L., BUTLER, L., CAREY, S., & DeLOACHE, J. S. (2009). Toddler's referential understanding of pictures. *Journal of Experimental Child Psychology, 104,* 283–295.

GANGER, J., & BRENT, M. R. (2004). Reexamining the vocabulary spurt. *Developmental Psychology, 40,* 621–632.

GANGESTAD, S. W., & THORNHILL, R. (1997). Human sexual selection and developmental stability. In J. A. Simpson & D. T. Kenrick (Eds.), *Evolutionary social psychology* (pp. 169–195). Mahwah, NJ: Erlbaum.

GARBER, H. L. (1988). *The Milwaukee Project: Preventing mental retardation in children at risk.* Washington, DC: American Association on Mental Retardation.

GARDINER, A. K., GRAY, S. K., & BJORKLUND, D. F. (April, 2009). *Two- and three-year-olds judge tool functionality more accurately after tool-use observation than haptic experience.* Poster presented at the biannual meeting of the Society for Research in Child Development, Denver, CO.

GARDINER, A., GREIF, M., & BJORKLUND, D. F. (2011). Guided by intention: Preschoolers' imitation reflects inferences of causation. *Journal of Cognition and Development.*

GARDNER, H. (1983). *Frames of mind: The theory of multiple intelligences.* New York: Basic.

GARDNER, H. (1999). Are there additional intelligences? The case for naturalist, spiritual, and existential intelligences. In J. Kane (Ed.), *Education, information and transformation.* Englewood Cliffs, NJ: Prentice Hall.

Gardner, H. (ED.). (1993). *Multiple intelligences: The theory in practice.* New York: Basic.

GARDNER, R. A., & GARDNER, B. T. (1969). Teaching sign language to a chimpanzee. *Science, 165,* 244–267.

GAREIL, J. D. (1998). Cognitive neuroscience of human memory. *Annual Review of Psychology, 49,* 87–115.

GARNHAM, W. A., & RUFFMAN, T. (2001). Doesn't see, doesn't know: Is anticipatory looking really related to understanding belief? *Developmental Science, 4,* 94–100.

GARON, N., BRYSON, S. E., & SMITH, I. M. (2008). Executive function in preschoolers: A review using an integrative framework. *Psychological Bulletin, 134,* 31–60.

GASKINS, S. (2000). Children's daily lives in a Mayan village: A culturally grounded description. *Cross-Cultural Research, 34,* 375–389.

GATHERCOLE, S. E., ALLOWAY, T. P., WILLIS, C., & ADAMS, A.-M. (2006). Working memory in children with reading disabilities. *Journal of Experimental Child Psychology, 93,* 265–281.

GATHERCOLE, V. C. M. (2002). Grammatical gender in bilingual and monolingual children: A Spanish morphosyntactic distinction. In D. Kimbrough Oller & R. E. Eilers (Eds.), *Language and literacy in bilingual children. Multilingual matters* (pp. 207–219). Cleveland, OH: Multilingual Matters Limited.

GAULTNEY, J. F. (1995). The effect of prior knowledge and metacognition on the acquisition of a reading comprehension strategy. *Journal of Experimental Child Psychology, 59,* 142–163.

GAULTNEY, J. F. (1998). Utilization deficiencies among children with learning disabilities. *Learning and Individual Differences, 10,* 13–28.

GAULTNEY, J. F., BJORKLUND, D. F., & GOLDSTEIN, D. (1996). To be young, gifted, and strategic: Advantages for memory performance. *Journal of Experimental Child Psychology, 61,* 43–66.

GAUVAIN, M. (2001). *The social context of cognitive development.* New York: Guilford.

GAUVAIN, M. (2009). Social and cultural transactions in cognitive development: A cross-generational view. In A. Sameroff (Ed.), *The transactional model of development: How children and contexts shape each other* (pp. 163–182). Washington, DC: American Psychological Association.

GAUVAIN, M. (2011). Sociocultural contexts of development. In P. D. -Zelazo (Ed.), *Oxford handbook of developmental psychology.* Oxford, UK: Oxford University Press.

GAUVAIN, M., & MUNROE, R. L. (2009). Contributions of societal modernity to cognitive development: A comparison of four cultures. *Child Development, 80,* 1628–1642.

GAVA, L., VALENZA, E., TURATI, C., & DE SCHONEN, S. (2008). Effect of partial occlusion on newborns' face preference and recognition. *Developmental Science, 11,* 563–574.

GEARY, D. C. (1993). Mathematical disabilities: Cognitive, neuropsychological, and genetic components. *Psychological Bulletin, 114,* 345–362.

GEARY, D. C. (1994). *Children's mathematical development: Research and practical applications.* Washington, DC: American Psychological Association.

GEARY, D. C. (1995). Reflections of evolution and culture in children's cognition: Implications for mathematical development and instruction. *American Psychologist, 50,* 24–37.

GEARY, D. C. (2005). *The origin of mind: Evolution of brain, cognition, and general intelligence.* Washington, DC: American Psychological Association.

GEARY, D. C. (2006). Development of mathematical understanding. In D. Kuhn & R. S. Siegler (Vol. Eds.), *Cognition perception, and language,* Vol. 2 (pp. 777–810), in W. Damon & R. M. Lerner (Gen. Eds.), *Handbook of child psychology* (6th ed.). New York: Wiley.

GEARY, D. C. (2007). Educating the evolved mind: Conceptual foundations for an evolutionary educational psychology. In J. S. Carlson & J. R. Levin (Eds.), *Educating the evolved mind: Conceptual foundations for an evolutionary educational psychology* (pp. 1–99). Charlotte, NC: Information Age Publishing.

GEARY, D. C. (2009). *Male, female: The evolution of human sex differences* (2nd ed.). Washington, DC: American Psychological Association.

GEARY, D. C. (2010). Evolution and education. *Psicothema, 22,* 35–40.

GEARY, D. C., & BJORKLUND, D. F. (2000). Evolutionary developmental psychology. *Child Development, 71,* 57–65.

GEARY, D. C., BOW-THOMAS, C. C., FAN, L., & SIEGLER, R. S. (1993). Even before formal instructions, Chinese children outperform American children in mental arithmetic. *Cognitive Development, 8,* 517–529.

GEARY, D. C., BOW-THOMAS, C. C., LIU, F., & SIEGLER, R. S. (1996). Development of arithmetic competencies in Chinese and American children: Influence of age, language, and schooling. *Child Development, 67,* 2022–2044.

GEARY, D. C., & BROWN, S. C. (1991). Cognitive addition: Strategy choice and speed-of-processing differences in gifted, normal and mathematically disabled children. *Developmental Psychology, 27,* 398–406.

GEARY, D. C., BROWN, S. C., & SAMARANAYAKE, V. A. (1991). Cognitive addition: A short longitudinal study of strategy choice and speed of processing differences in normal and mathematically disabled children. *Developmental Psychology, 27,* 787–797.

GEARY, D. C., FAN, L., & BOW-THOMAS, C. C. (1992). Numerical cognition: Loci of ability differences comparing children from China and the United States. *Psychological Science, 3,* 180–185.

GEARY, D. C., & HUFFMAN, K. (2002). Brain and cognitive evolution: Forms of modularity and functions of mind. *Psychological Bulletin, 128,* 667–698.

GEISER, C., LEHMANN, W., & EID, M. (2008). A note on sex differences in mental rotation in different age groups. *Intelligence, 36,* 556–563.

GELMAN, R. (1969). Conservation acquisition: A problem of learning to attend to relevant attributes. *Journal of Experimental Child Psychology, 7,* 167–187.

GELMAN, R., & GALLISTEL, R. (1978). *The child's understanding of number.* Cambridge, MA: Harvard University Press.

GELMAN, R., MECK, E., & MERKIN, S. (1986). Young children's numerical competence. *Cognitive Development, 1,* 1–30.

GELMAN, R., & WILLIAMS, E. M. (1998). Enabling constraints for cognitive development and learning: Domain-specificity and epigenesis. In D. Kuhn & R. S. Siegler (Vol. Eds.), *Cognition, perception, and language,* Vol. 2 (pp. 575–630), in W. Damon (Gen. Ed.), *Handbook of child psychology* (5th ed.). New York: Wiley.

GELMAN, S. A., & KREMER, K. E. (1991). Understanding natural cause: Children's explanations of how objects and their properties originate. *Child Development, 62,* 396–414.

GENESEE, F. (2003). Rethinking bilingual acquisition. In J. M. deWaele (Ed.). *Bilingualism: Challenges and directions for future research* (pp. 158–182). Clevedon, UK: Multilingual Matters.

GENTNER, D. (1989). The mechanisms of analogical learning. In S. Vosniadou & A. Ortony (Eds.), *Similarity and analogical reasoning.* London: Cambridge University Press.

GERGELY, G., BEKKERING, H., & KIRALY, I. (2002). Rational imitation in preverbal infants. *Nature, 415,* 755.

GERGELY, G., NÁDASDY, Z., CSIBRA, G., & BÍRÓ, S. (1995). Taking the intentional stance. *Cognition, 56,* 165–193.

GERMAN, T., & JOHNSON, S. (2002). Function and the origins of the design stance. *Journal of Cognition and Development, 3,* 279–300.

GESELL, A., & AMATRUDA, C. (1954). *Developmental diagnosis.* New York: Paul B. Holber.

GHATALA, E. S. (1984). Developmental changes in incidental memory as a function of meaningfulness and encoding condition. *Developmental Psychology, 20,* 208–211.

GHATALA, E. S., LEVIN, J. R., PRESSLEY, M., & GOODWIN, D. (1986). A componential analysis of the effects of derived and supplied strategy-utility information on children's strategy selection. *Journal of Experimental Child Psychology, 41,* 76–92.

GIBSON, E. J., & WALKER, A. S. (1984). Development of knowledge of visual-tactual affordances of substance. *Child Development, 55,* 453–460.

GIEDD, J. N., BLUENTHAL, J., JEFFRIES, N. O., CASTELLANOS, F. X., LIU, H., ZIJDENBOS, A., PAUÀS, A., EVANS, A. C., & RAPOPORT, J. L. (1999). Brain development during childhood and adolescence: A longitudinal MRI study. *Nature Neuroscience, 2,* 861–863.

GLADWELL, M. (2008). *Outliers: The story of success.* New York: Little, Brown, & Company.

GLEITMAN, L. R. (1990). The structural sources of verb meanings. *Language Acquisition, 1,* 3–55.

GOLDBERG, R. F., & THOMPSON-SCHILL, S. L. (2009). Developmental "roots" in mature biological knowledge. *Psychological Science, 20,* 480–487.

GOLDBERG, S., & LEWIS, M. (1969). Play behavior in the year-old infant: Early sex differences. *Child Development, 40,* 21–32.

GOLDFIELD, B. A., & REZNICK, J. S. (1990). Early lexical acquisition: Rate, content, and the vocabulary spurt. *Journal of Child Language, 17,* 171–184.

GOLDIN-MEADOW, S. (2007). Pointing sets the stage for learning language— and creating language. *Child Development, 78,* 741–745.

GOLDIN-MEADOW, S. (2009). How gesture promotes learning throughout childhood. *Child Development Perspectives, 3,* 106–111.

GOLDIN-MEADOW, S., COOK, S. W., & MITCHELL, Z. A. (2009). Gesturing gives children new ideas about math. *Psychological Science, 20,* 267–272.

GOLDMAN, R., & GOLDMAN, J. (1982). *Children's sexual thinking: A comparative study of children aged 5 to 15 years in Australia, North America, Britain, and Sweden.* London: Routledge & Kegan Paul.

GOLDSTEIN, D., HASHER, L., & STEIN, D. K. (1983). Processing of occurrence-rate and item information by children of different ages and abilities. *American Journal of Psychology, 96,* 220–241.

GOLDSTEIN, S., & BARKLEY, R. A. (1998). ADHD, hunting, and evolution: "Just so stories." *ADHD Report,* Vol. 6, No. 5.

GOLOMB, C., & GALASSO, L. (1995). Make believe and reality: Explorations of the imaginary realm. *Developmental Psychology, 31,* 800–810.

GOLOMBOK, S., RUST, J., ZERVOULIS, K., CROUDACE, T., GOLDING, J., & HINES, M. (2008). Developmental trajectories of sex-typed behavior in boys and girls: A longitudinal general population study of children aged 2.5-8 years. *Child Development, 79,* 1583–1593.

GÓMEZ, J. C. (2005). Species comparative studies and cognitive development. *Trends in Cognitive Sciences, 9,* 118–125.

GOODMAN, G. S., AMAN, C. J., & HIRSCHMAN, J. (1987). Child sexual and physical abuse: Children's testimony. In C. J. Ceci, M. P. Toglia, & D. F. Ross (Eds.), *Children's eyewitness memory.* New York: Springer-Verlag.

GOODMAN, G. S., & CLARKE-STEWART, A. (1991). Suggestibility in children's testimony: Implications for sexual abuse investigations. In J. Doris (Ed.), *The suggestibility of children's recollections: Implications for eyewitness testimony.* Washington, DC: American Psychological Association.

GOODMAN, G. S., QUAS, J. A., BATTERMAN-FAUNCE, J. M., RIDDLESBERGER, M. M., & KUHN, J. (1994). Predictors of accurate and inaccurate memories of traumatic events experienced in childhood.

*Consciousness and Cognition, 3,* 269–294.

GOODMAN, G. S., QUAS, J. A., BATTERMAN-FAUNCE, J. M., RIDDLESBERGER, M. M., & KUHN, J. (1997). Children's reactions to and memory for a stressful event: Influences of age, anatomical dolls, knowledge, and parental attachment. *Applied Developmental Science, 1,* 54–75.

GOODMAN, J. F. (1992). *When slow is fast enough: Educating the delayed preschool child.* New York: Guilford.

GOODZ, N. S. (1982). Is before really easier to understand than after? *Child Development, 53,* 822–825.

GOPNIK, A. (1996). The post-Piaget era. *Psychological Science, 7,* 221–225.

GOPNIK, A. (2009). *The philosophical baby: What children's minds tell us about truth, love, and the meaning of life.* New York: Farber, Straus, and Giroux.

GOPNIK, A., & ASTINGTON, J. W. (1988). Children's understanding of representational change and its relation to the understanding of false belief and the appearance-reality distinction. *Child Development, 59,* 26–37.

GOPNIK, A., & MELTZOFF, A. N. (1997). *Words, thoughts, and theories.* Cambridge, MA: MIT Press.

GOPNIK, A., & SLAUGHTER, V. (1991). Young children's understanding of changes in their mental states. *Child Development, 62,* 98–110.

GOPNIK, M., & CRAGO, M. D. (1991). Familial aggregation of a developmental language disorder. *Cognition, 39,* 1–50.

GORDON, B. N., ORNSTEIN, P. A., NIDA, R. E., FOLLMER, A., CRENSHAW, M. C., & ALBERT, G. F. (1993). Does the use of dolls facilitate children's memory of visits to the doctor? *Applied Cognitive Psychology, 7,* 459–474.

GORDON, P. (2004). Numerical cognition without words: Evidence from Amazonia. *Science, 306,* 496–499.

GOSSO, Y., OTTA, E., DE LIMA SALUM E MORAIS, M., LEITE RIBEIRO, F. J., & RAAD BUSSAB, V. S. (2005). Play in hunter-gatherer society. In A. D. Pellegrini & P. K. Smith (Eds.), *Play in humans and great apes* (pp. 213–253). Mahwah, NJ: Erlbaum.

GOSWAMI, U. (1995). Transitive relational mapping in three- and four-year-olds: The analogy of Goldilocks and the Three Bears. *Child Development, 66,* 877–892.

GOSWAMI, U. (1996). Analogical reasoning and cognitive development. In H. W. Reese (Ed.), *Advances in child development and behavior,* Vol. 26. San Diego, CA: Academic.

GOSWAMI, U., & BROWN, A. L. (1990). Higher-order structure and relational reasoning: Contrasting analogical and thematic relations. *Cognition, 36,* 207–226.

GOTTARDO, A., STANOVICH, K. E., & SIEGEL, L. S. (1996). The relationships between phonological sensitivity, syntactic processing, and verbal working memory in the reading performance of third-grade children. *Journal of Experimental Child Psychology, 63,* 563–582.

GOTTLIEB, G. (1971). Ontogenesis of sensory functioning in birds and mammals. In E. Tobach, L. R. Aronson, & E. Shaw (Eds.), *The biopsychology of development.* New York: Academic.

GOTTLIEB, G. (1991a). Experiential canalization of behavioral development: Theory. *Developmental Psychology, 27,* 4–13.

GOTTLIEB, G. (1991b). Experiential canalization of behavioral development: Results. *Developmental Psychology, 27,* 35–39.

GOTTLIEB, G. (1995). Some conceptual deficiencies in "developmental" behavior genetics. *Human Development, 38,* 131–141.

GOTTLIEB, G. (2000). Environmental and behavioral influences on gene activity. *Current Directions in Psychological Science, 9,* 93–102.

GOTTLIEB, G. (2007). Probabilistic epigenesis. *Developmental Science, 10,* 1–11.

GOTTLIEB, G., WAHLSTEN, D., & LICKLITER, R. (2006). The significance of biology for human development: A developmental psychobiological systems view. In R. M. Lerner (Vol. Ed.), *Theoretical models of human development,* Vol. 1 (pp. 210–257), in W. Damon & R. M. Lerner (Gen. Eds.), *Handbook of Child Psychology* (6th ed.). New York: Wiley.

GOULD, E., BEYLIN, A., TANAPAT, P., REEVES, A., & SHORS, T. J. (1999). Learning enhances adult neurogenesis in the hippocampal formation. *Nature Neuroscience, 2,* 260–265.

GOULD, S. J. (1992). Mozart and modularity. *Natural History, 101,* 8–14.

GOULD, S. J. (2002). *The structure of evolutionary theory.* Cambridge, MA: Harvard University Press.

GOUZE, K. R. (1987). Attention and social problem-solving as correlates of aggression in preschool males. *Journal of Abnormal Child Psychology, 15,* 181–197.

GRACES, E., THOMAS, D., & CURRIE, J. (2002). Longer term effects of Head Start. *American Economic Review, 92,* 999–1012.

GRAHAM, S., & HUDLEY, C. (1994). Attributions of aggressive and nonaggressive African-American early adolescent boys: A study of construct accessibility. *Developmental Psychology, 30,* 365–373.

GRAY, W. M., & HUDSON, L. M. (1984). Formal operations and the imaginary audience. *Developmental Psychology, 20,* 619–627.

GREDLEIN, J. M., & BJORKLUND, D. F. (2005). Sex differences in young children's use of tools in a problem-solving task: The role of object-oriented play. *Human Nature, 16,* 211–232.

GREEN, L. J. (2002). *African American English: A linguistic introduction.* Cambridge, UK: Cambridge University Press.

GREENFIELD, P. M. (1998). The cultural evolution of IQ. In U. Neisser (Ed.), *The rising cure: Long-term gains in IQ and related measures* (pp. 81–123). Washington, DC: American Psychological Association.

GREENFIELD, P. M. (2009). Linking social change and developmental change: Shifting pathways of human development. *Developmental Psychology, 45,* 401–418.

GREENFIELD, P., MAYNARD, A., BOEHM, C., & SCHMIDTLING, E. Y. (2000). Cultural apprenticeship and cultural change: Tool learning and imitation in chimpanzees and humans. In S. T. Parker, J. Langer, & M. L. McKinney (Eds.), *Biology, brains, and behavior: The evolution of human development* (pp. 237–277). Santa Fe, NM: School of American Research Press.

GREENOUGH, W. T., BLACK, J. E., & WALLACE, C. S. (1987). Experience and brain development. *Child Development, 58,* 539–559.

GREENOUGH, W. T., MCDONALD, J., PARNISARI, R., & CAMEL, J. E.

(1986). Environmental conditions modulate degeneration and new dendrite growth in cerebellum of senescent rats. *Brain Research,* 380, 136–143.

GREIF, M. L., KEMLER NELSON, D., KEIL, F., & GUTIERREZ, F. (2006). What do children want to know about animals and artifacts? *Psychological Science,* 17, 455–459.

GRICE, H. P. (1975). Logic and conversation. In P. Cole & J. Morgan (Eds.), *Speech acts: Syntax and semantics,* Vol. 3. New York: Academic.

GROEN, G. J., & RESNICK, L. B. (1977). Can preschool children invent addition algorithms? *Journal of Educational Psychology,* 69, 645–652.

GRUNAU, R. E., OBERLANDER, T. F., WHITFIELD, M. F., FITZGERALD, C., MORISON, S. J., & SAUL, J. P. (2001). Pain reactivity in former extremely low birth weight infants at corrected age 8 months compared with term born controls. *Infant Behavior and Development,* 24, 41–55.

GUBERMAN, S. R. (1996). The development of everyday mathematics in Brazilian children with limited formal education. *Child Development,* 67, 1609–1623.

GUERRA, N. G., HUESMANN, L. R., & HANISH, L. (1995). The role of normative beliefs in children's social behavior. In N. Eisenberg (Ed.), *Review of personality and social psychology: Vol. 15. Social development* (pp. 140–158). Thousand Oaks, CA: Sage.

GUILFORD, J. P. (1988). Some changes in the structure-of-the-intellect model. *Educational and Psychological Measurement,* 48, 1–4.

GÜLER, O. E., LARKINA, M., KLEINKNECHT, E. E., & BAUER, P. J. (2010). Memory strategies and retrieval success in preschool children: Relations to maternal behavior over time. *Journal of Cognition and Development,* 11, 159–184.

GUTTENTAG, R. E. (1984). The mental effort requirement of cumulative rehearsal: A developmental study. *Journal of Experimental Child Psychology,* 37, 92–106.

GUTTENTAG, R. E., ORNSTEIN, P. A., & SEIMENS, L. (1987). Children's spontaneous rehearsal: Transitions in strategy acquisition. *Cognitive Development,* 2, 307–326.

HADEN, C. A., HAINE, R. A., & FIVUSH, R. (1997). Developing narrative structure in parent-child reminiscing across the preschool years. *Developmental Psychology,* 33, 295–307.

HADEN, C. A., & ORNSTEIN, P. A. (2009). Research on talking about the past: The past, present, and future. *Journal of Cognition and Development,* 10, 135–142.

HADEN, C. A., ORNSTEIN, P. A., ECKERMAN, C. O., & DIDOW, S. M. (2001). Mother-child conversational interactions as event unfold: Linkages to subsequent remembering. *Child Development,* 72, 1016–1031.

HAIER, R. J., SIEGEL, B. V., NUECHTERLEIN, K. H., HAZLETT, E., WU, J. C., PAEK, J., BROWNING, H. L., & BUCHSBAUM, M. S. (1988). Cortical glucose metabolic rate correlates of abstract reasoning and attention studies with positron emission tomography. *Intelligence,* 12, 199–217.

HAIGHT, W. L., & MILLER, P. J. (1993). *Pretending at home: Early development in a sociocultural context.* Albany, NY: State University of New York Press.

HAITH, M. M. (1966). The response of the human newborn to visual movement. *Journal of Experimental Child Psychology,* 3, 235–243.

HAITH, M. M. (1993). Preparing for the 21st century: Some goals and challenges for studies of infant sensory and perceptual development. *Developmental Review,* 13, 354–371.

HAKUTA, K., BIALYSTOK, E., & WILEY, E. (2003). Critical evidence: A test of the critical period hypothesis for second-language acquisition. *Psychological Science,* 14, 31–38.

HAKUTA, K., & GARCIA, E. E. (1989). Bilingualism and education. *American Psychologist,* 44, 374–379.

HALA, S., & CHANDLER, M. (1996). The role of strategic planning in accessing false-belief understanding. *Child Development,* 67, 2948–2966.

HALA, S., CHANDLER, M., & FRITZ, A. S. (1991). Fledgling theories of mind: Deception as a marker of three-year-olds' understanding of false belief. *Child Development,* 62, 83–97.

HALBERSTADT, J., & RHODES, G. (2000). The attractiveness of nonface averages: Implications for an evolutionary explanation of the attractiveness of average faces. *Psychological Science,* 11, 285–289.

HALE, S., FRY, A. F., & JESSIE, K. A. (1993). Effects of practice on speed of information processing in children and adults: Age sensitivity and age invariants. *Developmental Psychology,* 29, 880–892.

HALEY, M. H. (2004). Learner-centered instruction and the theory of multiple intelligences with second language learners. *Teachers College Record,* 106, 163–180.

HALFORD, G. S. (1993). *Children's understanding: The development of mental models.* Hillsdale, NJ: Erlbaum.

HALLIDAY, M. A. K. (1973). *Explorations in the functions of language.* London: Edward Arnold.

HALPERN, D. F. (1992). *Sex difference in cognitive abilities* (2nd ed.). Hillsdale, NJ: Erlbaum.

HALPERN, D. F. (ED.). (1995). Special issue: Psychological and psychobiological perspectives on sex differences in cognition. I. Theory and research. *Learning and Individual Differences,* 7.

HALPERN, D. F. (1997). Sex differences in intelligence. *American Psychologist,* 52, 1091–1102.

HALPERN, D. F. (2000). *Sex differences in cognitive abilities* (3rd ed.). Mahwah, NJ: Erlbaum.

HALPERN, D. F. (2004). A cognitive-process taxonomy for sex differences in cognitive abilities. *Current Directions in Psychological Science,* 13, 135–139.

HALPERN, D. F., BENBOW, C. P., GEARY, D. C., GUR, R. C., HYDE, J. S., & GERNSBACHER, M. A. (2007). The science of sex differences in science and mathematics. *Psychological Science in the Public Interest,* 8, 1–51.

HALVERSON, C. F., & WALDROP, M. F. (1973). The relations of mechanically recorded activity level to varieties of preschool play behavior. *Child Development,* 44, 678–681.

HAMLIN, J. K., HALLINAN, E. V., & WOODWARD, A. L. (2008). Do as I do: 7-month-old infants selectively reproduce others' goals. *Developmental Science,* 11, 487–494.

HAMOND, N. R., & FIVUSH, R. (1991). Memories of Mickey Mouse: Young children recount their trip to Disneyworld. *Cognitive Development,* 6, 433–448.

HAN, J. J., LEITCHMAN, M. D., & WANG, Q. (1998). Autobiographical memory in Korean, Chinese, and

American children. *Developmental Psychology, 34,* 701–713.

HANANIA, R., & SMITH, L. B. (2009). Selective attention and attention switching: Toward a unified developmental approach. *Developmental Science, 12,* 1–14.

HANSEN, J., & PEARSON, P. D. (1983). An instructional study: Improving the inferential comprehension of good and poor readers. *Journal of Educational Psychology, 75,* 821–829.

HARE, B., CALL, J., AGENTTA, B., & TOMASELLO, M. (2000). Chimpanzees know what conspecifics do and do not see. *Animal Behaviour, 59,* 771–785.

HARE, B., CALL, J., & TOMASELLO, M. (2001). Do chimpanzees know what conspecifics know? *Animal Behaviour, 61,* 139–151.

HARLOW, H. (1959). The development of learning in the rhesus monkey. *American Scientist,* 459–479.

HARLOW, H. F., DODSWORTH, R. O., & HARLOW, M. K. (1965). Total isolation in monkeys. *Proceedings of the National Academy of Sciences of the United States of America, 54,* 90–97.

HARNISHFEGER, K. K. (1995). The development of cognitive inhibition: Theories, definitions, and research evidence. In F. Dempster & C. Brainerd (Eds.), *New perspectives on interference and inhibition in cognition.* New York: Academic.

HARNISHFEGER, K. K., & BJORKLUND, D. F. (1990a). Children's strategies: A brief history. In D. F. Bjorklund (Ed.), *Children's strategies: Contemporary views of cognitive development.* Hillsdale, NJ: Erlbaum.

HARNISHFEGER, K. K., & BJORKLUND, D. F. (1990b). Memory functioning of gifted and nongifted middle school children. *Contemporary Educational Psychology, 15,* 346–363.

HARNISHFEGER, K. K., & BJORKLUND, D. F. (1994). Individual differences in inhibition: Implications for children's cognitive development. *Learning and Individual Differences, 6,* 331–355.

HARNISHFEGER, K. K., & POPE, R. S. (1996). Intending to forget: The development of cognitive inhibition in directed forgetting. *Journal of Experimental Child Psychology, 62,* 292–315.

HARNQUIST, K. (1968). Relative changes in intelligence from 13 to 18.

*Scandinavian Journal of Psychology, 9,* 50–64.

HARRIS, J. R. (1995). Where is the child's environment? A group socialization theory of development. *Psychological Review, 102,* 458–489.

HARRIS, P. (2006). Social cognition. In D. Kuhn & R. S. Siegler (Vol. Eds.), *Cognition, perception, and language,* Vol. 2 (pp. 811–858), in W. Damon & R. M. Lerner (Gen. Eds.), *Handbook of Child Psychology* (6th ed.). New York: Wiley.

HARRIS, P. L., BROWN, E., MARRIOTT, C., WHITTALL, S., & HARMER, S. (1991). Monsters, ghosts and witches: Testing the limits of fantasy-reality distinction in young children. *British Journal of Developmental Psychology, 9,* 105–123.

HARRIS, P. L., & NÚÑEZ, M. (1996). Understanding of permission rules by preschool children. *Child Development, 67,* 1572–1591.

HART, C. L., TAYLOR, M. D., SMITH, G. D., WHALLEY, L. J., STARR, J. M., HOLE, D. J., WILSON, V., & DEARY, I. J. (2005). Childhood IQ and all-cause mortality before and after age 65: Prospective observational study linking the Scottish Mental Survey 1932 and the Midspan studies. *British Journal of Health Psychology, 10,* 153–165.

HARTER, S. (2006). The self. In N. Eisenberg (Vol. Ed.), *Social, emotional and personality development,* Vol. 3 (pp. 505–570), in W. Damon & R. M. Lerner (Gen. Eds.), *Handbook of child psychology* (6th ed.). New York: Wiley.

HARTER, S., WATERS, P., & WHITESELL, N. R. (1998). Relational self-worth: Differences in perceived worth as a person across interpersonal contexts among adolescents. *Child Development, 69,* 756–766.

HASHER, L., & ZACKS, R. T. (1979). Automatic and effortful processes in memory. *Journal of Experimental Psychology: General, 108,* 356–388.

HASHIMOTO, R., & SAKAI, K. L. (2002). Specialization in the left prefrontal cortex for sentence comprehension. *Neuron, 35,* 589–597.

HASSELHORN, M. (1992). Task dependency and the role of category typicality and metamemory in the development of an organizational strategy. *Child Development, 63,* 202–214.

HATANO, G., & INAGAKI, K. (1992). Desituating cognition through the construction of conceptual knowledge. In P. Light & G. Butterworth (Eds.), *Context and cognition: Ways of knowing and learning* (pp. 115–133). New York: Harvester.

HATANO, G., SIEGLER, R., RICHARDS, D., INAGAKI, K., STAVY, R., & WAX, N. (1993). The development of biological knowledge: A multinational study. *Cognitive Development, 8,* 47–62.

HAUSER, M. D., CAREY, S., & HAUSER, L. B. (2000). Spontaneous number representation in semi-free-ranging rhesus monkeys. *Proceedings of the Royal Society of London, Series B, 267,* 829–833.

HAYES, B. K., & HENNESSY, R. (1996). The nature and development of nonverbal implicit memory. *Journal of Experimental Child Psychology, 63,* 22–43.

HAYES, C. (1951). *The ape in our house.* New York: Harper.

HAYNE, H., & SIMCOCK, G. (2009). Memory development in toddlers. In M. L. Courage & N. Cowan (Eds.), *The development of memory in infancy and childhood* (pp. 43–68). New York: Psychology Press.

HEATH, S. B. (1989). Oral and literate traditions among Black Americans living in poverty. *American Psychologist, 44,* 367–373.

HEBB, D. O. (1949). *The organization of behavior.* New York: Wiley.

HECHT, S. A., TORGESEN, J. K., WAGNER, R. K., & RASHOTTE, C. A. (2001). The relationship between phonological processing abilities and emerging individual differences in mathematical computation skills: A longitudinal study from second to fifth grades. *Journal of Experimental Child Psychology, 79,* 192–227.

HEDGES, L. V., & NOWELL, A. (1995). Sex differences in mental test scores, variability, and numbers of high scoring individuals. *Science, 269,* 41–45.

HEDRICK, A. M., SAN SOUCI, P., HADEN, C. A., & ORNSTEIN, P. A. (2009). Mother-child joint conversational exchanges during events: Linkages to children's memory reports over time. *Journal of Cognition and Development, 10,* 143–161.

HEIMANN, M. (1989). Neonatal imitation gaze aversion and mother-infant interaction. *Infant Behavior and Development, 12*, 495–505.

HENRY, L. A., & MacLEAN, M. (2003). Relationships between working memory, expressive vocabulary and arithmetic reasoning in children with and without intellectual disabilities. *Educational and Child Psychology, 20*, 51–63.

HERMAN, J. F., SHIRAKI, J. H., & MILLER, B. S. (1985). Young children's ability to infer spatial relationships: Evidence from a large, familiar environment. *Child Development, 36*, 1195–1203.

HERMAN, J. F., & SIEGEL, A. W. (1978). The development of cognitive mapping of the large-scale environment. *Journal of Experimental Child Psychology, 26*, 389–406.

HERNÁNDEZ BLASI, C. (1996). Vygotsky y la escuela socio-histórica. In R. A. Clemente & C. Hernández Blasi (Eds.), *Contextos de desarrollo psicoilógico y educación.* Málaga, Spain: Aljibe.

HERRMANN, E., CALL, J., HERNÁNDEZ-LLOREDA, M. V., HARE, B., & TOMASELLO, M. (2007). Humans have evolved specialized skills of social cognition: The cultural intelligence hypothesis. *Science, 317*, 1360–1366.

HERRNSTEIN, R. J., & MURRAY, C. (1994). *The bell curve: Intelligence and class structure in American life.* New York: Simon & Schuster.

HESPOS, S. J., & BAILLARGEON, R. (2001). Reasoning about containment events in very young infants. *Cognition, 78*, 207–245.

HICKLING, A. K., & GELMAN, S. A. (1994). How does your garden grow? Early conceptualization of seeds and their place in the plant growth cycle. *Child Development, 66*, 856–876.

HILLMAN, C. H., BUCK, S. M., THEMANSON, J. R., PONTIFEX, M. B., & CASTELLI, D. M. (2009). Aerobic fitness and cognitive development: Event-related brain potential and task performance indices of executive control in preadolescent children. *Developmental Psychology, 45*, 114–129.

HINES, M., GOLOMBOK, S., RUST, J., JOHNSTON, K. J., GOLDING, J., & THE AVON LONGITUDINAL STUDY OF PARENTS AND CHILDREN STUDY TEAM (2002). Testosterone during pregnancy and gender role behavior of preschool children: A longitudinal, population

study. *Child Development, 73*, 1678–1687.

HIRSH-PASEK, K., HYSON, M. C., & RESCORLA, L. (1990). Academic environments in preschool: Challenge or pressure? *Early Education and Development, 1*, 401–423.

HOBSON, R. P., CHIDAMBI, G., LEE, A., & MEYER, J. (2006). Foundations for self-awareness: An exploration through autism. *Monographs of the Society for Research in Child Development, 71* (Serial No. 284).

HOERR, T. (2004). How MI informs teaching at New City School. *Teachers College Record, 106*, 40–48.

HOFF, E. (2000). Soziale umwelt und sprachlernen (The social environment and language learning). In H. Grimm (Hrsg), *Enzyklopadie der Psychologie, Vol. C3/3, Sprachentwicklung (Encyclopedia, Vol. 3, Language Development)* (pp. 463–494). Gottingen: Hogrefe.

HOFF, E. (2006). How social contexts support and shape language development. *Developmental Review, 26*, 55–88.

HOFF, E. (2009). *Language development* (4th ed.). Belmont, CA: Wadsworth.

HOFF, E., & NAIGLES, L. (2002). How children use input to acquire a lexicon. *Child Development, 73*, 418–433.

HOFF-GINSBURG, E. (1985). Some contributions of mothers' speech to their children's syntactic growth. *Journal of Child Language, 12*, 367–385.

HOFFMAN, M. L. (1975). Altruistic behavior and the parent-child relationship. *Journal of Personality and Social Psychology, 31*, 937–943.

HOGREFE, G.-J., WIMMER, H., & PERNER, J. (1986). Ignorance versus false belief: A developmental lag in attribution of epistemic states. *Child Development, 57*, 567–582.

HOLLICH, G., HIRSH-PASEK, K., & GOLINKOFF, R. M. (2000). Breaking the language barrier: An emergentist coalition model of word learning. *Monographs of the Society for Research in Child Development, 65* (Serial No. 262).

HOLMBOE, K., PASCO FEARON, R. M., CSIBRA, G., TUCKER, L., & JOHNSON, M. H. (2008). "Freeze-Frame": A new infant inhibition task and its relation to frontal cortex tasks in infancy and early childhood. *Journal of Experimental Child Psychology, 100*, 89–114.

HOLMES, J., GATHERCOLE, S. E., & DUNNING, D. L. (2009). Adaptive training leads to sustained enhancement of poor working memory in children. *Developmental Science, 12*, F9–F15.

HOLOWKA, S., & PETITTO, L. A. (2002). Left hemisphere cerebral specialization for babies while babbling. *Science, 297*, 1515.

HOLYOAK, K. J., JUNN, E. N., & BILLMAN, D. O. (1984). Development of analogical problem-solving skills. *Child Development, 55*, 2042–2055.

HONZIK, M. P., MacFARLANE, J. W., & ALLEN, L. (1948). Stability of mental test performance between 2 and 18 years. *Journal of Experimental Education, 17*, 309–324.

HOOD, B. M. (2004). Is looking good enough or does it beggar belief? *Developmental Science, 7*, 415–417.

HOOD, B., CAREY, S., & PRASADA, S. (2000). Predicting the outcomes of physical events: Two-year-olds fail to reveal knowledge of solidity and support. *Child Development, 71*, 1540–1554.

HOOPER, L. M., FLYNN, E. G., WOOD, L. A. N., & WHITEN, A. (2010). Observational learning of tool use in children: Investigating cultural spread through diffusion chains and learning mechanisms through ghost displays. *Journal of Experimental Child Psychology, 106*, 82–97.

HOPKINS, S. L., & LAWSON, M. J. (2001). Explaining the acquisition of a complex skill: Methodological and theoretical considerations uncovered in the study of simple addition and the moving-on process. *Educational Psychology Review, 14*, 121–154.

HORNER, V., & WHITEN, A. (2005). Causal knowledge and imitation/emulation switching in chimpanzees (*Pan troglodytes*) and children (*Homo Sapiens*). *Animal Cognition, 8*, 164–181.

HORNER, V., WHITEN, A., FLYNN, E., & DE WAAL, F. B. M. (2006). Faithful replication of foraging techniques along cultural transmission chains by chimpanzees and children. *Proceedings of the National Academy of Sciences of the United States of America, 103*, 13878–13883.

HOWE, M. L. (2000). *The fate of early memories: Developmental science and the retention of childhood experiences.* Washington, DC: American Psychological Press.

Howe, M. L., & Courage, M. L. (1993). On resolving the enigma of infantile amnesia. *Psychological Bulletin,* 113, 305–326.

Howe, M. L., Courage, M. L., & Rooksby, M. (2009). The genesis and development of autobiographical memory. In M. L. Courage & N. Cowan (Eds.), *The development of memory in infancy and childhood* (pp. 178–196). New York: Psychology Press.

Hudson, J. A. (1990). The emergence of autobiographical memory in mother-child conversation. In R. Fivush & J. A. Hudson (Eds.), *Knowing and remembering in young children.* Cambridge, UK: Cambridge University Press.

Hudson, J. A., & Mayhew, E. M. (2009). The development of memory for recurring events. In M. L. Courage & N. Cowan (Eds.), *The development of memory in infancy and childhood* (pp. 69–91). New York: Psychology Press.

Hughes, C., & Ensor, R. (2007). Executive function and theory of mind: Predictive relations from ages 2 to 4. *Developmental Psychology,* 43, 1447–1459.

Hulme, C., Hatcher, P. J., Nation, K., Brown, A., Adams, J., & Stuart, G. (2002). Phoneme awareness is a better predictor of early reading skill than onset-rime awareness. *Journal of Experimental Child Psychology,* 82, 2–28.

Hulme, C., & Snowling, M. J. (2009). *Developmental disorders of language learning and cognition.* Chichester, UK: Wiley.

Hulme, C., Thomson, N., Muir, C., & Lawrence, A. (1984). Speech rate and the development of spoken words: The role of rehearsal and item identification processes. *Journal of Experimental Child Psychology,* 38, 241–253.

Humphrey, N. K. (1976). The social function of intellect. In P. P. G. Bateson & R. A. Hinde (Eds.), *Growing points in ethology* (pp. 303–317). Cambridge, UK: Cambridge University Press.

Hunt, E., Davidson, J., & Lansman, M. (1981). Individual difference in long-term memory access. *Memory and Cognition,* 9, 599–608.

Huntsinger, C. S., Jose, P. E., & Larson, S. L. (1998). Do parent practices to encourage academic competence influence the social adjustment of young European American and Chinese American children? *Developmental Psychology,* 34, 747–756.

Hutt, C. (1966). Exploration and play in children. *Symposia of the Zoological Society of London,* 18, 61–81.

Huttenlocher, J., Levine, S., & Vevea, J. (1998). Environmental input and cognitive growth: A study using time-period comparisons. *Child Development,* 69, 1012–1029.

Huttenlocher, J., & Vasileya, M. (2003). How toddlers represent enclosed spaces. *Cognitive Sciences,* 27, 749–766.

Huttenlocher, P. (1979). Synaptic density in human frontal cortex: Developmental changes and effects of aging. *Brain Research,* 163, 195–205.

Huttenlocher, P. (2002). *Neural plasticity: The effects of environment on the development of the cerebral cortex.* Cambridge, MA: Harvard University Press.

Huttenlocher, P. R. (1994). Synaptogenesis, synapse elimination, and neural plasticity in human cerebral cortex. In C. A. Nelson (Ed.), Threats to optimal development. *The Minnesota symposium on child psychology,* Vol. 27. Hillsdale, NJ: Erlbaum.

Huttenlocher, P., & Dabholkar, A. S. (1997). Regional differences in synaptogenesis in human cerebral cortex. *Journal of Comparative Neurology,* 387, 167–178.

Hyde, J. S. (1981). How large are cognitive gender differences? A meta-analysis using $\omega^2$ and d. *American Psychologist,* 36, 892–901.

Hyde, J. S. (2005). Gender similarity hypothesis. *American Psychologist,* 60, 581–592.

Hyde, J. S., Fennema, E., & Lamon, S. J. (1990). Gender differences in mathematics performance: A meta-analysis. *Psychological Bulletin,* 107, 139–155.

Hyde, J. S., Lindberg, S. M., Linn, M. C., Ellis, A. B., & Williams, C. C. (2008). Gender similarities characterize math performance. *Science,* 321, 494–495.

Hyde, J. S., & Linn, M. C. (1988). Gender differences in verbal ability: A meta-analysis. *Psychological Bulletin,* 194, 53–69.

Hymes, D. (1972). On communicative competence. In J. B. Pride & J. Holmes (Eds.), *Sociolinguistics.* Harmondsworth, UK: Penguin.

Hymovitch, B. (1952). The effects of experimental variations on problem solving in the rat. *Journal of Comparative and Physiological Psychology,* 45, 313–321.

Hyson, M. C., Hirsh-Pasek, K., & Rescorla, L. (1990). Academic environments in preschool: Challenge or pressure? *Early Education and Development,* 1, 401–423.

Inagaki, K. (1990). The effects of raising animals on children's biological knowledge. *British Journal of Developmental Psychology,* 8, 119–129.

Inagaki, K., & Hatano, G. (1991). Constrained person analogy in young children's biological inference. *Cognitive Development,* 6, 219–231.

Inagaki, K., & Hatano, G. (1993). Young children's understanding of the mind-body distinction. *Child Development,* 64, 1534–1549.

Inagaki, K., & Hatano, G. (2002). *Young children's naive thinking about the biological world.* New York: Psychology Press.

Inagaki, K., & Hatano, G. (2006). Young children's conception of the biological world. *Current Directions in Psychological Science,* 15, 177–181.

Inhelder, B., & Piaget, J. (1958). *The growth of logical thinking from childhood to adolescence.* New York: Basic.

Istomina, Z. M. (1975). The development of voluntary memory in preschool-age children. *Soviet Psychology,* 13, 5–64.

Iverson, J. M., & Goldin-Meadow, S. (2005). Gesture paves the way for language development. *Psychological Science,* 16, 368–371.

Jack, F., MacDonald, S., Reese, E., & Hayne, H. (2009). Maternal reminiscing style during early childhood predicts the age of adolescents' earliest memories. *Child Development,* 80, 496–505.

Jackson, J. F. (1993). Human behavioral genetics, Scarr's theory, and her views on intervention: A critical review and commentary on their implications for African American children. *Child Development,* 64, 1318–1332.

Jacobson, S. W. (1979). Matching behavior in the young infant. *Child Development,* 50, 425–430.

JACOBY, L. L. (1991). A process dissociation framework: Separating automatic from intentional uses of memory. *Journal of Memory and Language, 30,* 513–541.

JARRETT, O. S., MAXWELL, D. M., DICKERSON, C., HOGE, P., DAVIES, G., & YETLEY, A. (1998). The impact of recess on classroom behavior: Group effects and individual differences. *Journal of Educational Research, 92,* 121–126.

JENKINS, J. M., & ASTINGTON, J. W. (1996). Cognitive factors and family structure associated with theory of mind development in young children. *Developmental Psychology, 32,* 70–78.

JENSEN, A. R. (1993). Why is reaction time correlated with psychometric *g? Current Directions in Psychological Science, 2,* 53–56.

JENSEN, A. R. (1998). *The g factor: The science of mental ability.* Westport, CT: Praeger.

JENSEN, P. S., MRAZEK, D., KNAPP, P. K., STEINBERG, L., PFEFFER, C., SCHWALTER, J., & SHAPIRO, T. (1997). Evolution and revolution in child psychiatry: ADHD as a disorder of adaptation. *Journal of the American Academy of Child & Adolescent Psychiatry, 36,* 1672–1681.

JERISON, H. J. (1973). *Evolution of the brain and intelligence.* New York: Academic.

JERISON, H. J. (2002). On theory in comparative psychology. In R. J. Sternberg & J. C. Kaufman (Eds.), *The evolution of intelligence* (pp. 251–288). Mahwah, NJ: Erlbaum.

JOFFE, T. H. (1997). Social pressures have selected for an extended juvenile period in primates. *Journal of Human Evolution, 32,* 593–605.

JOHNSON, D. W., & JOHNSON, R. T. (1987). *Learning together and alone: Cooperative, competitive, and individualistic learning* (2nd ed.). Englewood Cliffs, NJ: Prentice Hall.

JOHNSON, D. W., & JOHNSON, R. T. (1989). *Cooperation and competition: Theory and research.* Edina, MN: Interaction.

JOHNSON, J. S., & NEWPORT, E. L. (1989). Critical period effects in second language learning: The influence of maturational state on the acquisition of English as a second language. *Cognitive Psychology, 21,* 60–99.

JOHNSON, M. H. (1998). The neural basis of cognitive development. In D. Kuhn & R. S. Siegler (Vol. Eds.), *Cognition, perception, and language,* Vol. 2, in W. Damon (Gen. Ed.), *Handbook of child psychology* (5th ed.). New York: Wiley.

JOHNSON, M. H. (2000). Functional brain development in infants: Elements of an interactive specialization framework. *Child Development, 71,* 75–81.

JOHNSON, M. H. (2007). The social brain in infancy: A developmental cognitive neuroscience approach. In D. Coch, K. W. Fischer, & G. Dawson (Eds.), *Human behavior, learning, and the developing brain: Typical development* (pp. 115–137). New York: Guilford.

JOHNSON, M. H., & DE HAAN, M. (2001). Developing cortical specialization for visual-cognitive function: The case of face recognition. In J. L. McClelland & R. S. Siegler (Eds.), *Mechanisms of cognitive development: Behavioral and neural perspectives.* Mahwah, NJ: Erlbaum.

JOHNSON, M. H., DZIURAWIEC, S., ELLIS, H. D., & MORTON, J. (1991). Newborns' preferential tracking of faces and its subsequent decline. *Cognition, 40,* 1–19.

JOHNSON, S. P., & ASLIN, R. N. (1995). Perception of object unity in 2-month-old infants. *Developmental Psychology, 31,* 739–745.

JOHNSON, S. P., & ASLIN, R. N. (1996). Perception of object unity in young infants: The roles of motion, depth, and orientation. *Cognitive Development, 11,* 161–180.

JOHNSON, S. P., HANNON, E. E., & AMSO, D. (2005). Perceptual development. In B. Hopkins (Ed.), *Cambridge encyclopedia of child development* (pp. 210–216). Cambridge, UK: Cambridge University Press.

JONES, L. B., ROTHBART, M. K., & POSNER, M. I. (2003). Development of executive attention in preschool children. *Developmental Science, 6,* 498–504.

JONES, S. (2007). Imitation in infancy: The development of mimicry. *Psychological Science, 18,* 593–599.

JUSCZYK, P. W. (1997). *The discovery of spoken language.* Cambridge, MA: MIT Press.

JUSTICE, E. M., BAKER-WARD, L., GUPTA, S., & JANNINGS, L. R. (1997). Means to the goal of remembering: Developmental changes in awareness of strategy use-performance relations. *Journal of Experimental Child Psychology, 65,* 293–314.

KAGAN, J. (1971). *Change and continuity in infancy.* New York: Wiley.

KAGAN, J. (1976). New views on cognitive development. *Journal of Youth and Adolescence, 5,* 113–129.

KAIL, R. (1991). Development of processing speed in childhood and adolescence. In H. W. Reese (Ed.), *Advances in child development and behavior,* Vol. 23. San Diego, CA: Academic.

KAIL, R. (1997). Processing time, imagery, and spatial memory. *Journal of Experimental Child Psychology, 64,* 67–78.

KAIL, R. V., & FERRER, E. (2008). Processing speed in childhood and adolescence: Longitudinal models for examining developmental change. *Child Development, 78,* 1760–1770.

KAIL, R. V., & LEVINE, L. E. (1976). Encoding processes and sex-role preferences. *Journal of Experimental Child Psychology, 21,* 256–263.

KAIL, R. V., & SALTHOUSE, T. A. (1994). Processing speed as a mental capacity. *Acta Psychologica, 86,* 199–225.

KAITZ, M., MESCHULACH-SARFATY, O., AUERBACH, J., & EIDELMAN, A. (1988). A reexamination of newborns' ability to imitate facial expressions. *Developmental Psychology, 24,* 3–7.

KALICHMAN, S. C. (1988). Individual differences in water-level task performance: A component-skill analysis. *Developmental Review, 8,* 273–295.

KALISH, C. W., & LAWSON, C. A. (2008). Development of social category representation: Early appreciation of roles and deontic relations. *Child Development, 79,* 577–593.

KAMAWAR, D., LEFEVRE, J.-A., BISANZ, J., FAST, L., SKWARCHUK, S.-L., SMITH-CHANT, B., & PENNER-WILGER, M. (2010). Knowledge of counting principles: How relevant is order irrelevance? *Journal of Experimental Child Psychology, 105,* 138–145.

KAPLAN, H., HILL, K., LANCASTER, J., & HURTADO, A. M. (2000). A theory of human life history evolution: Diet intelligence, and longevity.

*Evolutionary Anthropology, 9,* 156–185.

Kappeler, P., & Silk, J. (Eds.). (2010). *Mind the gap: Tracing the origins of human universals.* Berlin: Springer-Verlag.

Karama, S., Ad-Dab'bagh, Y., Haier, R. J., Deary, I. J., Lyttelton, O. C., Lepage, C., Evans, A. C., & the Brain Development Cooperative Group (2009). Positive association between cognitive ability and cortical thickness in a representative U.S. sample of healthy 6- to 18-year-olds. *Intelligence, 37,* 145–155.

Karmiloff-Smith, A. (1992). *Beyond modularity: A developmental perspective on cognitive science.* Cambridge, MA: MIT Press.

Karoly, L. A., Greenwood, P. W., Everingham, S. S., Houbé, J., Kilburn, M. R., Rydell, C. P., Sanders, M., & Chiesa, J. (1998). *Investing in our children: What we know and don't know about the costs and benefits of early childhood interventions.* Santa Monica, CA: RAND Distribution Services.

Karzon, R. G. (1985). Discrimination of polysyllabic sequences by one- to four-month-old infants. *Journal of Experimental Child Psychology, 39,* 326–342.

Kaye, K. (1982). *The mental and social life of babies: How parents create persons.* Chicago: University of Chicago Press.

Kaye, K., & Marcus, J. (1981). Infant imitation: The sensory-motor agenda. *Developmental Psychology, 17,* 258–265.

Kee, D. W. (1994). Developmental differences in associative memory: Strategy use, mental effort, and knowledge-access interactions. In H. W. Reese (Ed.), *Advances in child development and behavior,* Vol. 25. New York: Academic.

Keen, R. (2003). Representation of objects and events: Why do infants look so smart and toddlers look so dumb? *Current Directions in Psychological Science, 12,* 79–83.

Kelemen, D. (1999a). Why are rocks pointy? Children's preferences for teleological explanations of the natural world. *Developmental Psychology, 35,* 1440–1453.

Kelemen, D. (1999b). The scope of teleological thinking in preschool children. *Cognition, 70,* 241–272.

Kelemen, D. (2004). Are children "intuitive theists"? Reasoning about

purpose and design in nature. *Psychological Science, 15,* 295–301.

Keller, A., Ford, L. H., Jr., & Meachum, J. A. (1978). Dimensions of self-concept in preschool children. *Developmental Psychology, 14,* 483–489.

Keller, H., Lohaus, A., Kuensemueller, P., Abels, M., Yovsi, R., Voelker, S., Jensen, H., Papaligoura, Z., Rosabal-Coto, M., Kulks, D., & Mohite, P. (2004). The bio-culture of parenting: Evidence from five cultural communities. *Parenting: Science and Practice, 4,* 25–50.

Kellman, P. J., & Arterberry, M. E. (2006). Perceptual development. In D. Kuhn & R. Siegler (Vol. Eds.), *Cognition, perception, and language,* Vol. 2 (pp. 109–160), in W. Damon & R. M. Lerner (Gen. Eds.), *Handbook of child psychology* (6th ed.). New York: Wiley.

Kellman, P. J., & Banks, M. S. (1998). Infant visual perception. In D. Kuhn & R. S. Siegler (Vol. Eds.), *Cognitive, language, and perceptual development,* Vol. 2, in W. Damon (Gen. Ed.), *Handbook of child psychology* (5th ed.). New York: Wiley.

Kellman, P. J., & Spelke, E. S. (1983). Perception of partly occluded objects in infancy. *Cognitive Development, 15,* 483–524.

Kellogg, W. N., Kellogg, L. A. (1933). *The ape and the child.* New York: Hafner Publishing Company.

Kelly, D. J., Liu, S., Lee, K., Quinn, P. C., Pascalis, O., Slater, A. M., & Ge, L. (2009). Development of the other-race effect in infancy: Evidence toward universality? *Journal of Experimental Child Psychology, 104,* 105–114.

Kelly, D. J., Quinn, P. C., Slater, A. M., Lee, K., Ge, L., & Pascalis, O. (2007). The other-race effect develops during infancy. *Psychological Science, 18,* 1084–1089.

Kelly, M. K., Miller, K. F., Fend, G., & Feng, G. (1999). When days are numbered: Calendar structure and the development of calendar processing in English and Chinese. *Journal of Experimental Child Psychology, 73,* 289–314.

Kenney-Benson, G. A., Pomerantz, E. M., Ryan, A. M., & Patrick, H. (2006). Sex differences in math performance: The role of children's approach to schoolwork. *Developmental Psychology, 42,* 11–26.

Kent, R. (2005). Speech development. In B. Hopkins (Ed.), *The Cambridge encyclopedia of child development* (pp. 257–264). New York: Cambridge University Press.

Kerns, K. A. (2000). The CyberCruiser: An investigation of development of prospective memory in children. *Journal of the International Neuropsychological Society, 6,* 62–70.

Kersten, A. W., & Earles, J. L. (2001). Less really is more for adults learning a miniature artificial language. *Journal of Memory and Language, 44,* 250–273.

Kessen, W. (1996). American psychology just before Piaget. *Psychological Science, 7,* 196–199.

Khaitovich, P., Hellman, I., Enard, W., Nowick, K., Leinweber, M., Franz, H., Weiss, G., Lachmann, M., & Pääbo, S. (2005). Parallel patterns of evolution in the genomes and transcriptomes of humans and chimpanzees. *Science, 309,* 1850–1854.

Kikuchi, Y., Senju, A., Tojo, Y., Osanai, H., & Hasegawa, T. (2009). Faces do not capture special attention in children with autism spectrum disorder: A change blindness study. *Child Development, 80,* 1421–1433.

Kim, K. H. S., Relkin, N. R., Lee, K.-M., & Hirsch, J. (1997). Distinct cortical areas associated with native and second languages. *Nature, 388,* 171–174.

Kim-Cohen, J., Moffitt, T. E., Caspi, A., & Taylor, A. (2004). Genetic and environmental processes in young children's resilience and vulnerability to socioeconomic deprivation. *Child Development, 75,* 651–668.

Kipp, K., & Pope, S. (1997). The development of cognitive inhibition in stream-of-consciousness and directed speech. *Cognitive Development, 12,* 239–260.

Kirschner, S., & Tomasello, M. (2009). Joint drumming: Social context facilitates synchronization in preschool children. *Journal of Experimental Child Psychology, 102,* 299–314.

Kitamura, C., Thanavishuth, C., Burnham, D., & Luksaneeyanawin, S. (2002). Universality and specificity in infant-directed speech: Pitch modifications as a function of infant age and sex in a tonal and nontonal language. *Infant Behavior and Development, 24,* 372–392.

KITAYAMA, S., DUFFY, S., KAWAMURA, T., & LARSEN, J. T. (2003). Perceiving an object and its context in different cultures: A cultural look at new look. *Psychological Science, 14,* 201–206.

KITTLER, P. M., KRINSKY-MCHALE, S. J., & DEVENNY, D. A. (2008). Dual-task processing as a measure of executive function: A comparison between adults with Williams and Down syndromes. *American Journal on Mental Retardation, 113,* 117–132.

KLACZYNSKI, P. A. (1997). Bias in adolescents' everyday reasoning and its relationship with intellectual ability, personal theories, and self-serving motivation. *Developmental Psychology, 33,* 273–283.

KLACZYNSKI, P. A., & NARASIMHAM, G. (1998). Development of scientific reasoning biases: Cognitive versus ego-protective explanations. *Developmental Psychology, 34,* 175–187.

KLAUS, R. A., & GRAY, S. (1968). The early training project for disadvantaged children: A report after five years. *Monographs of the Society for Research in Child Development, 33* (Serial No. 120).

KLIBANOFF, R. S., LEVINE, C., HUTTENLOCHER, J., VASILYEVE, M., & HEDGES, L. V. (2006). Preschool children's mathematical knowledge: The effect of teacher "math talk." *Developmental Psychology, 32,* 59–69.

KLIEGEL, M., & JÄGER, T. (2007). The effects of age and cue-action reminders on event-based prospective memory performance in preschoolers. *Cognitive Development, 22,* 33–46.

KOCHANSKA, G., MURRAY, K. T., JACQUES, T. Y., KOENIG, A. L., & VANDEGEEST, K. A. (1996). Inhibitory control in young children and its role in emerging internalization. *Child Development, 67,* 490–507.

KOHLBERG, L. (1966). A cognitive-developmental analysis of children's sex-role concepts and attitudes. In E. E. Maccoby (Ed.), *The development of sex differences.* Stanford, CA: Stanford University Press.

KOHLBERG, L., YAEGER, J., & HJERTHOLM, E. (1968). Private speech: Four studies and a review of theories. *Child Development, 39,* 691–736.

KÖHLER, W. (1925). *The mentality of apes.* New York: Harcourt & Brace.

KOLB, B. (1989). Brain development, plasticity and behavior. In M. Johnson (Ed.), *Brain development and cognition* (pp. 338–357). Oxford, UK: Blackwell.

KOLB, B., GIBB, R., & ROBINSON, T. E. (2003). Brain plasticity and behavior. *Current Directions in Psychological Sciences, 12,* 1–5.

KOLB, B., & WHISHAW, I. Q. (1981). Neonatal frontal lesions in the rat: Sparing of learned but not species-typical behavior in the presence of reduced brain weight and critical thickness. *Journal of Comparative and Physiological Psychology, 95,* 235–276.

KOLB, B., & WHISHAW, I. Q. (1990). *Fundamentals of human neuropsychology* (3rd ed.). San Francisco: W. H. Freeman.

KOLUCHOVA, J. (1976). A report on the further development of twins after severe and prolonged deprivation. In A. M. Clarke & A. D. B. Clarke (Eds.), *Early experience: Myth and evidence.* London: Open Books.

KOPP, C. B., & MCCALL, R. B. (1982). Predicting later mental performance for normal, at-risk, and handicapped infants. In P. Baltes & O. G. Brim (Eds.), *Life-span development and behavior,* Vol. 4. New York: Academic.

KOPP, C. B., SIGMAN, M., & PARMELEE, A. H. (1974). Longitudinal study of sensorimotor development. *Developmental Psychology, 10,* 687–695.

KORNHUBER, H. H., BECHINGER, D., JUNG, H., & SAUER, E. (1985). A quantitative relationship between the extent of localized cerebral lesions and the intellectual and behavioral deficiency in children. *European Archives of Psychiatry and Neurological Science, 235,* 125–133.

KOSHMIDER, J. W., & ASHCRAFT, M. H. (1991). The development of children's mental multiplication skills. *Journal of Experimental Child Psychology, 51,* 53–89.

KOTOVSKY, L., & BAILLARGEON, R. (1994). Calibration-based reasoning about collision events in 11-month-old infants. *Cognition, 51,* 107–129.

KOTOVSKY, L., & BAILLARGEON, R. (2000). Reasoning about collisions involving inert objects in 7.5-month-old infants. *Developmental Science, 3,* 344–359.

KOVÁCS, A. M. (2009). Early bilingualism enhances mechanisms of false-belief reasoning. *Developmental Science, 12,* 48–54.

KOVÁCS, A. M., & MEHLER, J. (2009). Cognitive gains in 7-month-old bilingual infants. *Proceedings of the National Academy of Sciences of the United States of America, 106,* 6556–6560.

KRACHUN, C., CARPENTER, M., CALL, J., & TOMASELLO, M. (2009). A competitive nonverbal false belief task for children and apes. *Developmental Science, 12,* 521–535.

KREUTZER, M. A., LEONARD, C., & FLAVELL, J. H. (1975). An interview study of children's knowledge about memory. *Monographs of the Society for Research in Child Development, 40* (Serial No. 159).

KROUPINA, M. G., BAUER, P. J., GUNNAR, M. R., & JOHNSON, D. E. (2010). Institutional care as a risk for declarative memory development. In P. J. Bauer (Ed.), Varieties of early experience: Implications for the development of declarative memory in infancy. *Advances in Child Development and Behavior, 38.* London, UK: Elsevier.

KRUMHANSL, C. L., & JUSCZYK, P. W. (1990). Infants' perception of phrase structure in music. *Psychological Science, 1,* 70–73.

KUHL, P. (April, 2007). *Language and the infant brain: How children learn.* Plenary talk presented at meeting of the Cognitive Development Society, Santa Fe, NM.

KUHL, P. K., ANDRUSKI, J. E., CHRISTOVICH, I. A., CHRISTOVICH, L. A., KOZHEVNIKOVA, E. V., RYSKINA, V. L., STOLYAROVA, E. I., SUNDBERG, U., & LACERDA, F. (1997). Cross-language analysis of phonetic units in language addressed to infants. *Science, 277,* 684–686.

KUHL, P. K., & MELTZOFF, A. N. (1982). The bimodal perception of speech in infancy. *Science, 218,* 1138–1141.

KUHL, P. K., STEVENS, E., HAYASHI, A., DEGUCHI, T., KIRITANI, S., & IVERSON, P. (2006). Infants show a facilitation effect for native language phonetic perception between 6 and 12 months. *Developmental Science, 9,* F13–F21.

KUHLMEIER, V. (2005). Symbolic insight and inhibitory control: Two problems facing young children on symbolic retrieval tasks. *Journal of*

*Cognition and Development, 6,* 365–380.

KUHN, D. (1989). Children and adults as intuitive scientists. *Psychological Review, 96,* 674–689.

KUHN, D. (2000). Does memory development belong on an endangered topic list? *Child Development, 71,* 21–25.

KUHN, D. (2006). Do cognitive changes accompany developments in the adolescent brain? *Perspectives on Psychological Science, 1,* 59–67.

KUHN, D., AMSEL, E., & O'LOUGHLIN, M. (1988). *The development of scientific thinking skills.* San Diego, CA: Academic.

KUHN, D., PEASE, M., & WIRKALA, C. (2009). Coordinating the effects of multiple variables: A skill fundamental to scientific thinking. *Journal of Experimental Child Psychology, 103,* 268–284.

KURTZ, B. E. (1990). Cultural differences in children's cognitive and metacognitive development. In W. Schneider & F. E. Weinert (Eds.), *Interactions among aptitudes, strategies, and knowledge in cognitive performance.* New York: Springer-Verlag.

KURTZ, B. E., SCHNEIDER, W., CARR, M., BORKOWSKI, J. G., & RELLINGER, E. (1990). Strategy instruction and attributional beliefs in West Germany and the United States: Do teachers foster metacognitive development? *Contemporary Educational Psychology, 15,* 268–283.

KURTZ-COSTES, B., SCHNEIDER, W., & RUPP, S. (1995). Is there evidence for intraindividual consistency in performance across memory tasks? New evidence on an old question. In F. E. Weinert & W. Schneider (Eds.), *Memory performance and competencies: Issues in growth and development.* Hillsdale, NJ: Erlbaum.

KURTZ, B. E., & WEINERT, F. E. (1989). Metamemory, memory performance, and causal attributions in gifted and average children. *Journal of Experimental Child Psychology, 48,* 45–61.

KVAVILASHVILI, L., KYLE, F., & MESSER, D. J. (2008). The development of prospective memory in children: Methodological issues, empirical findings and future directions. In M. Kliegel, M. A. McDaniel, & G. O. Einstein (Eds.), *Prospective memory: Cognitive, neuroscience, developmental, and applied*

*perspectives* (pp. 115–140). Mahwah, NJ: Erlbaum.

LABORATORY OF COMPARATIVE HUMAN COGNITION. (1983). Culture and cognitive development. In W. Kessen (Ed.), *History, theory, and methods,* Vol. 1, in P. H. Mussen (Ed.), *Handbook of child psychology* (4th ed.). New York: Wiley.

LAMB, M. E., STERNBERG, K. J., & ESPLIN, P. W. (1998). Conducting investigative interviews of alleged sexual abuse victims. *Child Abuse & Neglect, 22,* 813–823.

LAMB, M. E., & THIERRY, K. L. (2005). Understanding children's testimony regarding their alleged abuse: Contributions of field and laboratory analog research. In D. M. Teti (Ed.), *Handbook of research methods in developmental psychology.* Malden, MA: Blackwell Publishers.

LAMBERT, W. E., GENESEE, F., HOLOBOW, N. E., & CHARTRAND, L. (1993). Bilingual education for majority English-speaking children. *European Journal of Psychology of Education, 8,* 3–22.

LANDRY, D. J., KAESER, L., & RICHARDS, C. L. (1999). Abstinence promotion and the provision of information about contraception in public school district sexuality education policies. *Family Planning Perspective, 31,* 280–286.

LANDRY, S. H., SMITH, K. E., MILLER-LONCAR, C. L., & SWANK, P. R. (1997). Predicting cognitive-language and social growth curves from early maternal behaviors in children at varying degrees of biological risk. *Developmental Psychology, 33,* 1040–1053.

LANE, D. M., & PEARSON, D. A. (1982). The development of selective attention. *Merrill-Palmer Quarterly, 28,* 317–337.

LANGE, G., & JACKSON, P. (1974). Personal organization in children's free recall. *Child Development, 45,* 1060–1067.

LANGE, G., & PIERCE, S. H. (1992). Memory-strategy learning and maintenance in preschool children. *Developmental Psychology, 28,* 453–462.

LANGLOIS, J. H., RITTER, J. M., ROGGMAN, L. A., & VAUGHN, L. S. (1991). Facial diversity and infant preferences for attractive faces. *Developmental Psychology, 27,* 79–84.

LANGLOIS, J. H., & ROGGMAN, L. A. (1990). Attractive faces are only average. *Psychological Science, 1,* 115–121.

LANGLOIS, J. H., ROGGMAN, L. A., CASEY, R. J., RITTER, J. M., RIESER-DANNER, L. A., & JENKINS, V. Y. (1987). Infant preferences for attractive faces: Rudiments of a stereotype? *Developmental Psychology, 23,* 363–369.

LARKINA, M., GÜLER, O. E., KLEINKNECHT, E. E., & BAUER, P. J. (2008). Maternal provision of structure in a deliberate memory task in relation to their preschool children's recall. *Journal of Experimental Child Psychology, 100,* 235–251.

LARSSON, A., & LAMB, M. E. (2009). Making the most of information-gathering interviews with children. *Infant and Child Development, 18,* 1–16.

LAVE, J., & WENGER, E. (1991). *Situated learning: Legitimate peripheral participation.* Cambridge, UK: Cambridge University Press.

LAZAR, I., DARLINGTON, R., MURRAY, H., ROYCE, J., & SNIPPER, A. (1982). Lasting effects of early education: A report from the Consortium for Longitudinal Studies. *Monographs of the Society for Research in Child Development, 47* (Serial No. 195).

Le GRAND, R., MONDLOCH, C. J., MAURER, D., & BRENT, H. P. (2001). Early visual experience and face processing. *Nature, 410,* 890.

LEAPER, C., ANDERSON, K. J., & SANDERS, P. (1998). Moderators of gender effects on parents' talk to their children: A meta-analysis. *Developmental Psychology, 34,* 3–27.

LEE, E. S. (1951). Migration: A Philadelphia test of the Klineberg hypothesis. *American Journal of Sociology, 16,* 227–232.

LEFEVRE, J., DESTEFANO, D., COLEMAN, B., & SHANAHAN, T. (2005). Mathematical cognition and working memory. In J. I. D. Campbell (Ed.), *Handbook of mathematical cognition* (pp. 361–378). New York: Psychology Press.

LEGERSTEE, M. (1991). The role of person and object in eliciting early imitation. *Journal of Experimental Child Psychology, 51,* 423–433.

LEGERSTEE, M., ANDERSON, D., & SCHAFFER, A. (1998). Five- and eight-month-old infants recognize their faces and voices as familiar social stimuli. *Child Development, 69,* 37–50.

LEHMAN, E. B., MCKINLEY-PACE, M. J., WILSON, J. A., SAVSKY, M. D., & WOODSON, M. E. (1997). Direct and indirect measures of intentional forgetting in children and adults: Evidence for retrieval inhibition and reinstatement. *Journal of Experimental Child Psychology, 64,* 295–316.

LEHMANN, M., & HASSELHORN, M. (2007). Variable memory strategy use in children's adaptive intratask learning behavior: Developmental changes and working memory influences in free recall. *Child Development, 78,* 1068–1082.

LEICHTMAN, M. D., & CECI, S. J. (1993). The problem of infantile amnesia: Lessons from fuzzy-trace theory. In M. L. Howe & R. Pasnak (Eds.), *Emerging themes in cognitive development: Vol. 1. Foundations.* New York: Springer-Verlag.

LEICHTMAN, M. D., & CECI, S. J. (1995). The effect of stereotypes and suggestion on preschoolers' reports. *Developmental Psychology, 31,* 568–578.

LEINBACH, M. D., HORT, B. E., & FAGOT, B. I. (1997). Bears are for boys: Metaphorical associations in young children's gender stereotypes. *Cognitive Development, 12,* 107–130.

LEMAIRE, P., & CALLIES, S. (2009). Children's strategies in complex arithmetic. *Journal of Experimental Child Psychology, 103,* 49–65.

LENHART, A., KAHNE, J., MIDDAUGH, E., MACGILL, A. R., EVANS, C., & VITAK, J. (September, 2008). Teens, video games and civics: Teens' gaming experiences are diverse and include significant social interaction and civic engagement. *Pew Internet and American Life Project.* www.pewinternet.org/PPF/r/263/report_display.asp (September 18, 2008) Downloaded July 30, 2010.

LENNEBERG, E. H. (1967). *Biological foundations of language.* New York: Wiley.

LENROOT, R. K., & GIEDD, J. N. (2007). The structural development of the human brain as measured longitudinally with magnetic resonance imaging. In D. Coch, K. W. Fischer, & G. Dawson (Eds.), *Human behavior, learning, and the developing brain: Typical development* (pp. 50–73). New York: Guilford.

LEON, D. A., LAWLOR, D. A., CLARK, H., BATTY, G. D., & MACINTYRE, S. (2009). The association of childhood intelligence with mortality risk from adolescence to middle age: Findings from the Aberdeen children of the 1950s cohort study. *Intelligence, 37,* 520–528.

LEPAGE, J. F., & THEORET, H. (2006). EEG evidence for the presence of an action observation-execution matching system in children. *European Journal of Neuroscience, 23,* 2505–2510.

LEPAGE, J. F., & THEORET, H. (2007). The mirror neuron system: Grasping others' actions from birth? *Developmental Science, 10,* 513–529.

LERNER, R. M. (1991). Changing organism-context relations as the basic process of development: A developmental contextual perspective. *Developmental Psychology, 27,* 27–32.

LERNER, R. M. (2006). Developmental science, developmental systems, and contemporary theories of human development. In R. M. Lerner (Vol. Ed.), *Theoretical models of human development*, Vol. 1 (pp. 1–17), in W. Damon & R. M. Lerner (Gen. Eds.), *Handbook of child psychology* (6th ed.). New York: Wiley.

LESLIE, A. (1994). ToMM, ToBy, and agency: Core architecture and domain specificity. In L. Hirschfeld & S. Gelman (Eds.), *Mapping the mind: Domain specificity in cognition and culture.* Cambridge, UK: Cambridge University Press.

LESLIE, A. M., & KEEBLE, S. (1987). Do six-month-old infants perceive causality? *Cognition, 25,* 265–288.

LESTER, D., ALDRIDGE, M., ASPENBERG, C., BOYLE, K., RADSNIAK, P., & WALDON, C. (2002). What is the afterlife like? Undergraduate beliefs about the afterlife. *Omega: Journal of Death and Dying, 44,* 113–126.

LEVINE, S. C., HUTTENLOCHER, J., TAYLOR, A., & LANGROCK, A. (1999). Early sex differences in spatial skills. *Developmental Psychology, 35,* 940–949.

LEVY, B. A., GONG, Z., HESSELS, S., EVANS, M. A., & JARED, D. (2006). Understanding print: Early reading development and the contributions of home literacy experiences. *Journal of Experimental Child Psychology, 93,* 63–93.

LEWIS C., FREEMAN, N. H., KYRIAKIDOU, C., MARIDAKI-KASSOTAKI, K., & BERRIDGE, D. M. (1996). Social influence on false belief access: Specific sibling influences or general apprenticeship? *Child Development, 67,* 2930–2947.

LEWIS, M. (1969). Infants' responses to facial stimuli during the first year of life. *Developmental Psychology, 1,* 75–86.

LEWIS, M. (1991). Ways of knowing: Objective self-awareness of consciousness? *Developmental Review, 11,* 231–243.

LEWIS, M. (1993). The emergence of human emotions. In M. Lewis & J. M. Haviland (Eds.), *Handbook of emotions* (pp. 223–235). New York: Guilford.

LEWIS, M., & BROOKS-GUNN, J. (1979). *Social cognition and the acquisition of self.* New York: Plenum.

LEWIS, M., & CARMODY, D. P. (2008). Self-representation and brain development, *Developmental Psychology, 44,* 1329–1334.

LEWIS, M., & FREEDLE, R. O. (1973). Mother-infant dyad: The cradle of meaning. In P. Pilner, L. Krames, & T. Alloway (Eds.), *Communication and affect: Language and thought.* New York: Academic.

LEWIS, M., & RAMSAY, D. (2004). Development of self-recognition, personal pronoun use, and pretend play during the 2nd year. *Child Development, 75,* 1821–1831.

LEWIS, M., SULLIVAN, M. W., STANGER, C., & WEISS, M. (1989). Self development and self-conscious emotions. *Child Development, 60,* 146–156.

LEWIS, M. D. (2000). The promise of dynamic systems approaches for an integrated account of human development. *Child Development, 71,* 36–43.

LEWIS, C., KOYASU, M., OH, S., OGAWA, A., SHORT, B., & HUANG, Z. (2009). Culture, executive function, and social understanding. *New Directions in Child and Adolescent Development,* Spring (Issue 123), 69–85.

LEWIS, K. D. (1999). Maternal style in reminiscing: Relations to child individual differences. *Cognitive Development, 14,* 381–399.

LEWKOWICZ, D. J. (1992). Infants' response to temporally based intersensory equivalence: The effect of synchronous sounds on visual preferences for moving stimuli. *Infant Behavior and Development, 15,* 297–324.

LEWKOWICZ, D. J. (2000). The development of intersensory temporal perception: An epigenetic systems/limitations view. *Psychological Bulletin, 126,* 281–308.

LEWKOWICZ, D. J. (2004). Perception of serial order in infant. *Developmental Science, 7,* 175–184.

LEWKOWICZ, D. J., & GHAZANFAR, A. A. (2006). The decline of cross-species intersensory perception in human infants. *Proceedings of the National Academy of Sciences of the United States of America, 103,* 6771–6774.

LEWKOWICZ, D. J., & GHAZANFAR, A. A. (2009). The emergence of multisensory systems through perceptual narrowing. *Trends in Cognitive Sciences, 13,* 470–478.

LEWKOWICZ, D. J., LEO, I., & SIMION, F. (2010). Intersensory perception at birth: Newborns match nonhuman primate faces and voices. *Infancy, 15,* 46–60.

LEWKOWICZ, D. J., & TURKEWITZ, G. (1980). Cross-modal equivalence in early infancy: Auditory-visual intensity matching. *Developmental Psychology, 16,* 597–607.

LI, S.-C. (2003). Biocultural orchestration of developmental plasticity across levels: The interplay of biology and culture in shaping the mind throughout the lifespan. *Psychological Bulletin, 129,* 171–194.

LIBEN, L. S. (2009). The road to understanding maps. *Current Directions in Psychological Science, 18,* 310–315.

LIBEN, L. S., & SIGNORELLA, M. L. (1993). Gender-schematic processing in children: The role of initial interpretations of stimuli. *Developmental Psychology, 29,* 141–149.

LIBEN, L., & YEKEL, C. A. (1996). Preschoolers understanding of plan and oblique maps: The role of geometric and representational correspondence. *Child Development, 67,* 2780–2796.

LIBERMAN, I. Y., & SHANKWEILER, D. (1977). Speech, the alphabet, and teaching to read. In L. B. Resnick & P. A. Weaver (Eds.), *Theory and practice of early reading.* Hillsdale, NJ: Erlbaum.

LIBERMAN, I. Y., SHANKWEILER, D., FISCHER, R. N., & CARTER, B. (1974). Explicit syllable and phoneme segmentation in the young child. *Journal of Experimental Child Psychology, 18,* 201–212.

LICKLITER, R. (1990). Premature visual stimulation accelerates intersensory functioning in bobwhite quail neonates. *Developmental Psychobiology, 23,* 15–27.

LICKLITER, R. (1996). Structured organisms and structured environments: Development systems and the construction of learning capacities. In J. Valsiner & H. Voss (Eds.), *The structure of learning processes.* Norwood, NJ: Ablex.

LICKLITER, R. (2000). The role of sensory stimulation in perinatal development: Insights from comparative research for care of the high-risk infant. *Developmental and Behavioral Pediatrics, 21,* 437–447.

LICKLITER, R. (2011). Biological development: Theoretical approaches, techniques, and key findings. In P. D. Zelazo (Ed.), *Oxford handbook of developmental psychology.* Oxford, UK: Oxford University Press.

LICKLITER, R., & BAHRICK, L. E. (2000). The development of infant intersensory perception: Advantages of a comparative convergent-operations approach. *Psychological Bulletin, 126,* 260–280.

LIE, E., & NEWCOMBE, N. S. (1999). Elementary school children's explicit and implicit memory for faces of preschool classmates. *Developmental Psychology, 35,* 102–112.

LIEBERMAN, P. (1967). *Intonations, perception, and language.* Cambridge, MA: MIT Press.

LIETZ, P. (2006). A meta-analysis of gender differences in reading achievement at the secondary school level. *Studies in Educational Evaluation, 32,* 317–344.

LILLARD, A. (1998). Ethnopsychologies: Cultural variations in theories of mind. *Psychological Bulletin, 123,* 3–32.

LILLARD, A. S. (2001). Pretend play as Twin Earth: A social-cognitive analysis. *Developmental Review, 21,* 495–531.

LIN, C.-Y. C., & FU, V. R. (1990). A comparison of child-rearing practices among Chinese, immigrant Chinese, and Caucasian-American parents. *Child Development, 61,* 429–433.

LINDBERG, M. (1980). The role of knowledge structures in the ontogeny of learning. *Journal of Experimental Child Psychology, 30,* 401–410.

LINDBERG, M. A. (1991). An interactive approach to assessing the suggestibility and testimony of eyewitnesses. In J. Doris (Ed.), *The suggestibility of children's recollections: Implications for eyewitness testimony* (pp. 47–55). Washington, DC: American Psychological Association.

LINDBERG, M. A., KEIFFER, J., & THOMAS, S. W. (2000). Eyewitness testimony for physical abuse as a function of personal experience, development, and focus of study. *Journal of Applied Developmental Psychology, 21,* 555–591.

LINN, M. C., & PETERSEN, A. C. (1985). Emergence and characterization of sex differences in spatial ability: A meta-analysis. *Child Development, 56,* 1479–1498.

LIPKO, A. R., DUNLOSKY, J., & MERRIMAN, W. E. (2009). Persistent overconfidence despite practice: The roles of task experience in preschooler's recall predications. *Journal of Experimental Child Psychology, 103,* 152–166.

LIPTON, J. S., & SPELKE, E. (2000). Origins of number sense: Large-number discrimination in human infants. *Psychological Science, 15,* 396–401.

LISTON, C., & KAGAN, J. (2002). Brain development: Memory enhancement in early childhood. *Nature, 419,* 896.

LISZKOWSKI, U., CARPENTER, M., & TOMASELLO, M. (2007). Pointing out new news, old news, and absent referents at 12 months of age. *Developmental Science, 10,* F1–F7.

LISZKOWSKI, U., SCHÄFER, M., CARPENTER, M., & TOMASELLO M. (2009). Prelinguistic infants, not chimpanzees, communicate about absent entities. *Psychological Science, 20,* 654–660.

LIU, D., WELLMAN, H. M., TARDIF, T., & SABBAGH, M. A. (2008). Theory of mind development in Chinese children: A meta-analysis of false-belief understanding across cultures and languages. *Developmental Psychology, 44,* 523–531.

LIVESLEY, W., & BROMLEY, D. (1973). *Person perception in childhood and adolescence.* New York: Wiley.

LLOYD, M. E., & NEWCOMBE, N. S. (2009). Implicit memory in childhood: Reassessing developmental invariance. In M. L. Courage & N. Cowan (Eds.), *The development of memory in infancy and childhood* (pp. 92–113). New York: Psychology Press.

LOCKE, J. L. (1993). *The child's path to spoken language.* Cambridge, MA: Harvard University Press.

LOCKE, J. L. (1994). Phases in the child's development of language. *American Scientist, 82,* 436–445.

LOCKE, J. L. (2009). Evolutionary developmental linguistics: Naturalization of the faculty of language. *Language Sciences, 31,* 33–59.

LOCKE, J. L., & BOGIN, B. (2006). Language and life history: A new perspective on the development and evolution of human language. *Behavioral and Brain Sciences, 29,* 259–280.

LOCKL, K., & SCHNEIDER, W. (2007). Knowledge about the mind: Links between theory of mind and later metamemory. *Child Development, 78,* 148–167.

LOCKMAN, J. J. (2000). A perception-action perspective on tool use development. *Child Development, 71,* 137–144.

LOE, I. M., BALESTRINO, M. D., PHELPS, R. A., KURS-LASKY, M., CHAVES-GNECCO, D., PARADISE, J. L., & FELDMAN, H. M. (2008). Early histories of school-aged children with attention-deficit/hyperactivity disorder. *Child Development, 79,* 1853–1868.

LOFTUS, E. F., & PICKRELL, J. E. (1995). The formation of false memories. *Psychiatric Annals, 25,* 720–725.

LONGSTRETH, L. E. (1981). Revisiting Skeels' final study: A critique. *Developmental Psychology, 17,* 620–625.

LONIGAN, C. J., BURGESS, S. R., & ANTHONY, J. L. (2000). Development of emergent literacy and early reading skills in preschool children: Evidence from a latent-variable longitudinal study. *Developmental Psychology, 36,* 596–613.

LOOFT, W. R., & BARTZ, W. H. (1969). Animism revived. *Psychological Bulletin, 71,* 1–19.

LOPEZ, D. F., LITTLE, T. D., OETTINGEN, G., & BALTES, P. B. (1998). Self-regulation and school performance: Is there optimal level of action-control? *Journal of Experimental Child Psychology, 70,* 54–74.

LUBINSKI, D., & BENBOW, C. P. (1992). Gender differences in abilities and preferences among the gifted: Implications for the math-science pipeline. *Current Directions in Psychological Science, 1,* 61–66.

LUBINSKI, D., BENBOW, C. P., & SANDER, C. (1993). Reconceptualizing gender differences in achievement among the gifted. In K. A. Keller, F. J. Monks, & A. H. Passow (Eds.), *International handbook of research on and development of giftedness and talent.* New York: Pergamon.

LUDWIG, J., & MILLER, D. L. (2007). Does Head Start improve children's life chances? Evidence from a regression discontinuity design. *Quarterly Journal of Economics, 122,* 159–208.

LUDWIG, J., & PHILLIPS, D. A. (2008). Long-term effects of Head Start on low-income children. *Annals of the New York Academy of Science, 113,* 257–286.

LUECKE-ALESKA, D., ANDERSON, D. R., COLLINS, P. A., & SCHMITT, K. L. (1995). Gender constancy and television viewing. *Developmental Psychology, 31,* 773–780.

LUKAS, W. D., & CAMPBELL, B. C. (2000). Evolutionary and ecological aspects of early brain malnutrition in humans, *Human Nature, 11,* 1–26.

LUM, J. A., KIDD, E., DAVIES, S., & CONTI-RAMSDEN, G. (2009). A longitudinal study of declarative and procedural memory in primary school aged children. *Australian Journal of Psychology.* DOI: 10.1080/00049530903150547. http://www.informaworld.com/smpp/content~content=a914255555~db=all~jumptype=rss.

LUNA, B., THULBORN, K. R., MONOZ, D. P., MERRIAM, E. P., GARVER, K. E., MINSHEW, N. J., KESHAVAN, M. S., GENOVESE, C. R., EDDY, W. F., & SWEENEY, J. A. (2001). Maturation of widely distributed brain function subserves cognitive development. *NeuroImage, 13,* 786–793.

LUNDBERG, I., FROST, J., & PETERSON, O.-P. (1988). Effects of an extensive program for stimulating phonological awareness in preschool children. *Reading Research Quarterly, 23,* 264–284.

LURIA, A. R. (1973). *The working brain.* New York: Basic Books.

LURIA, A. R. (1976). *Cognitive development: Its cultural and social foundations.* Cambridge, MA: Harvard University Press.

LUTCHMAYA, S., BARON-COHEN, S., & RAGGATT, P. (2002). Foetal testosterone and vocabulary size in 18- and 24-month-old infants. *Infant Behavior and Development, 24,* 418–424.

LYNCH, M. P., EILERS, R. E., OLLER, K., & URBANO, R. C. (1990). Innateness, experience, and music perception. *Psychological Science, 1,* 272–276.

LYNN, S. J., LOCK, T. G., MYERS, B., & PAYNE, D. G. (1997). Recalling the unrecallable: Should hypnosis be used to recover memories in psychotherapy? *Current Directions in Psychological Science, 6,* 79–83.

LYONS, D. E., YOUNG, A. G., & KEIL, F. C. (2007). The hidden structure of overimitation. *Proceedings of the National Academy of Sciences of the United States of America, 104,* 19751–19756.

LYYINEN, H., AHONEN, T., EKLUND, K., GUTTORM, T. K., LAAKSO, M. L., LEINONEN, S., LEPPÄNEN, P. H. T., LYYTINEN, P., POIKKEUW, A.-M., PUOLAKANAHO, A., RICHARDSON, U., & VIHOLAINEN, H. (2001). Developmental pathways of children with and without familial risk for dyslexia during the first years of life. *Developmental Neuropsychology, 20,* 535–554.

MACCOBY, E. E., & JACKLIN, C. N. (1974). *The psychology of sex differences.* Stanford, CA: Stanford University Press.

MACFARLANE, A. (1975). Olfaction in the development of social preferences in the humane neonate. *CIBA Foundation Symposium 33: Parent-infant interaction.* Amsterdam, The Netherlands: Elsevier.

MACKINLAY, R., KLIEGEL, M., & MÄNTYLÄ, T. (2009). Predictors of time-based prospective memory in children. *Journal of Experimental Child Psychology, 102,* 251–264.

MACLEAN, P. D. (1990). *The triune brain in evolution: Role in paleocerebral functions.* New York: Plenum.

MACWHINNEY, B. (2005). Language evolution and human development. In B. J. Ellis & D. F. Bjorklund (Eds.), *Origins of the social mind: Evolutionary psychology and child development* (pp. 383–410). New York: Guilford.

MAHONE, E. M., HAGELTHORN, K. M., CUTTING, L. E., SCHUERHOLZ, L. J., PELLETIER, S. F., RAWLINS, C., SINGER, H. S., &. DENCKLA, M. B. (2002). Effects of IQ on executive function measures in children with ADHD. *Child Neuropsychology, 8,* 52–65.

MAKIN, J. W., & PORTER, R. H. (1989). Attractiveness of lactating females' breast odors to neonates. *Child Development, 60,* 803–810.

MALLOY, P. (1987). Frontal lobe dysfunction in obsessive-compulsive disorder. In E. Perecman (Ed.), *The frontal lobes revisited.* New York: IRBN.

MANDEL, D. R., JUSCZYK, P. W., & PISONI, D. B. (1995). Infants' recognition of sound patterns of their own names. *Psychological Science, 5,* 314–317.

MANDEL, D. R., KEMLER NELSON, D. G., & JUSCZYK, P. W. (1996). Infants remember the order of words in a spoken sentence. *Cognitive Development, 11,* 181–196.

MANDLER, J. M. (1992). How to build a baby: II. Conceptual primitives. *Psychological Review, 99,* 587–604.

MANDLER, J. M. (2000). Perceptual and conceptual processes in infancy. *Journal of Cognition and Development, 1,* 3–36.

MANION, V., & ALEXANDER, J. M. (1997). The benefits of peer collaboration on strategy use, metacognitive causal attribution, and recall. *Journal of Experimental Child Psychology, 67,* 268–289.

MÄNTYLÄ, T., CARELLI, M. G., & FORMAN, H. (2007). Time monitoring and executive functioning in children and adults. *Journal of Experimental Child Psychology, 96,* 1–19.

MARATSOS, M. (1998). The acquisition of grammar. In D. Kuhn & R. S. Siegler (Eds.), *Cognitive, language, and perceptual development,* Vol. 2, in W. Damon (Gen. Ed.), *Handbook of child psychology* (5th ed.). New York: Wiley.

MARCON, R. A. (1999). Differential impact of preschool models on development and early learning of inner-city children: A three cohort study. *Developmental Psychology, 35,* 358–375.

MARCOVTICH, S., & ZELAZO, P. D. (1999). The A-not-B error: Results from a logistic meta-analysis. *Child Development, 70,* 1297–1313.

MARCOVTICH, S., ZELAZO, P. D., & SCHMUCKLER, M. A. (2002). The effect of the number of A trials on performance on the A-not-B task. *Infancy, 3,* 519–529.

MARCUS, G. F. (1995). Children's overregularization of English plurals: A quantitative analysis. *Journal of Child Language, 22,* 447–460.

MARCUS, G. F., PINKER, S., ULLMAN, M., HOLLANDER, M., ROSEN, T. J., & XU, F. (1992). Overregularization in language acquisition. *Monographs of the Society for Research in Child Development, 57* (Serial No. 228).

MAREAN, G. C., WERNER, L. A., & KUHL, P. K. (1992). Vowel categorization by very young infants. *Developmental Psychology, 28,* 396–405.

MARIANI, M. A., & BARKLEY, R. A. (1997). Neuropsychological and academic functioning in preschool boys with attention deficit hyperactivity disorder. *Developmental Neuropsychology, 13,* 111–129.

MARKMAN, E. M. (1994). Constraints on word meaning in early language acquisition. In L. Gleitman & B. Landau (Eds.), The acquisition of the lexicon. Cambridge, MA: MIT Press.

MARKMAN, E. M., & WACHTEL, G. A. (1988). Children's use of mutual exclusivity to constrain the meaning of words. *Cognitive Psychology, 20,* 121–157.

MARLIER, L., SCHAAL, B., & SOUSSIGNAN, R. (1998). Neonatal responsiveness to the odor of amniotic and lacteal fluids: A test of perinatal chemosensory continuity. *Child Development, 69,* 611–623.

MARSH, H. W. (1989). Sex differences in the development of verbal and mathematics constructs: The High School and Beyond Study. *American Educational Research Journal, 26,* 191–225.

MARSHALL, N. L. (2004). The quality of early child care and children's development. *Current Directions in Psychological Science, 13,* 165–168.

MARTIN, C. L., & HALVERSON, C. F. (1981). A schematic processing model of sex-typing and stereotyping in children. *Child Development, 49,* 1119–1134.

MARTIN, C. L., & HALVERSON, C. F. (1987). The roles of cognition in sex role acquisition. In D. B. Carter (Ed.), *Current conceptions of sex roles and sex typing: Theory and research.* New York: Praeger.

MARTIN, C. L., & RUBLE, D. (2004). Children's search for gender cues. *Current Directions in Psychological Science, 13,* 67–70.

MARTIN, C. L., RUBLE, D. N., & SZKRYBALO, J. (2002). Cognitive theories of early gender development. *Psychological Bulletin, 128,* 903–933.

MARTIN, C. L., WOOD, C. H., & LITTLE, J. K. (1990). The development of gender stereotype components. *Child Development, 61,* 1891–1904.

MASATAKA, N. (1996). Perception of motherese in a signed language by 6-month-old deaf infants. *Developmental Psychology, 32,* 874–879.

MASATAKA, N. (1998). Perception of motherese in Japanese sign language by 6-month-old hearing infants. *Developmental Psychology, 34,* 241–246.

MASATAKA, N. (1999). Preferences for infant-directed signing in 2-day old hearing infants of deaf parents. *Developmental Psychology, 35,* 1001–1005.

MASON, J. M. (1992). Reading stories to preliterate children: A proposed connection to reading. In P. B. Gough, L. C. Ehri, & R. Treiman (Eds.), Reading acquisition. Hillsdale, NJ: Erlbaum.

MASTEN, A. S., & COATSWORTH, J. D. (1998). The development of competence in favorable and unfavorable environments. *American Psychologist, 53,* 205–220.

MASTERS, S., & SOARES, M. (1993). Is the gender difference in mental rotation disappearing? *Behavioral Genetics, 23,* 337–341.

MASTROPIERI, M. A., & SCRUGGS, T. E. (1991). *Teaching students ways to remember: Strategies for learning mnemonically.* Cambridge, MA: Brookline Books.

MASUR, E. F., & EICHORST, D. L. (2002). Infants' spontaneous imitation of novel vs. familiar words: Relations to observational and maternal report measures of their lexicons. *Merrill- Palmer Quarterly, 48,* 405–426.

MASUR, E. F., & RODEMAKER, J. E. (1999). Mothers' and infants' spontaneous vocal, verbal, and action imitation during the second year. *Merrill-Palmer Quarterly, 45,* 392–412.

MATHENY, A. P., JR., WILSON, R. S., DOLAN, A. B., & KRANTZ, J. Z. (1981). Behavioral contrasts in twinships: Stability and patterns of differences in childhood. *Child Development, 52,* 579–598.

MAURER, D., LEWIS, T. L., BRENT, H. P., & LEVIN, A. V. (1999). Rapid improvement in the acuity of infants after visual input. *Science, 286,* 108–110.

MAURER, D., MONDLOCH, C. J., & LEWIS, T. L. (2007). Effects of early visual deprivation on perceptual and cognitive development. *Progress in Brain Research, 164,* 87–104.

MAURER, D., & SALAPATEK, P. (1976). Developmental changes in the scanning of faces by young infants. *Child Development, 47,* 523–527.

MAURER, D., STAGER, C., & MONDLOCH, C. (1999). Cross-modal transfer of shape is difficult to demonstrate in 1-month-olds. *Child Development, 70,* 1047–1057.

MAZZOCCO, M. M. M., & MYERS, G. F. (2003). Complexities in identifying and defining mathematics learning disability in the primary school-age years. *Annals of Dyslexia, 53,* 218–253.

MAZZONI, G. (1998). Memory suggestibility and metacognition in child eyewitness testimony: The roles of source monitoring and self-efficacy. *European Journal of Psychology of Education, 13,* 43–60.

MCBRIDE-CHANG, C., & KAIL, R. V. (2002). Cross-cultural similarities in the predictors of reading acquisition. *Child Development, 73,* 1392–1407.

MCCALL, R. B. (1981). Nature-nurture and the two realms of development: A proposed integration with respect to mental development. *Child Development, 52,* 1–12.

MCCALL, R. B., APPELBAUM, M. I., & HOGARTY, P. S. (1973). Developmental changes in mental performance. *Monographs of the Society for Research in Child Development, 38* (Serial No. 150).

MCCALL, R. B., & CARRIGER, M. S. (1993). A meta-analysis of infant habituation and recognition memory performance as predictors of later IQ. *Child Development, 64,* 57–79.

MCCALL, R. B., EICHORN, D. H., & HOGARTY, P. S. (1977). Transitions in early mental development. *Monographs of the Society for Research in Child Development, 42* (Serial No. 171).

MCCALL, R. B., HOGARTY, P. S., & HURLBURT, N. (1972). Transitions in infant sensori-motor development and the prediction of childhood IQ. *American Psychologist, 27,* 728–748.

MCCALL, R. B., KENNEDY, C. B., & APPELBAUM, M. I. (1977). Magnitude of discrepancy and the distribution of attention in infants. *Child Development, 48,* 772–785.

MCCALL, R. B., PARKE, R. D., & KAVANAUGH, R. D. (1977). Imitation of live and televised models by children one to three years of age. *Monographs of the Society for Research in Child Development, 42* (Serial No. 173).

MCCARTHY, D. (1954). Language development in children. In L. Carmichael (Ed.), *A manual of child psychology* (2nd ed.). New York: Wiley.

MCCARTNEY, K., HARRIS, M. J., & BERNIERI, F. (1990). Growing up and growing apart: A development meta-analysis of twin studies. *Psychological Bulletin, 107,* 226–237.

MCDONOUGH, L., MANDLER, J. M., MCKEE, R. D., & SQUIRE, L. R. (1995). The deferred imitation task as a nonverbal measure of declarative memory. *Proceedings of the National Academy of Sciences of the United States of America, 92,* 7580–7584.

MCGILLY, K., & SIEGLER, R. S. (1990). The influence of encoding strategic knowledge on children's choices among serial recall strategies. *Developmental Psychology, 26,* 931–941.

MCGOWN, C., GREGORY, A., & WEINSTEIN, R. S. (2010). Expectations, stereotypes, and self-fulfilling prophecies in classroom and school life. In J. L. Meece & J. S. Eccles (Eds.), *Handbook of research on schools, schooling, and human development* (pp. 256–274). New York: Routledge.

MCGUE, M., BOUCHARD, T. J., JR., LYKKEN, D. T., & FEUER, D. (1984). Information processing abilities in twins reared apart. *Intelligence, 8,* 239–258.

MCGUIGAN, N., & WHITEN, A. (2009). Emulation and "overemulation" in the social learning of causally opaque versus causally transparent tool use by 23 and 30-month-old children. *Journal of Experimental Child Psychology, 104,* 367–381.

MCGUIGAN, N., WHITEN, A., FLYNN, E. F., & HORNER, V. (2007). Imitation of casually necessary versus unnecessary tool use by 3- and 5-year-old children. *Cognitive Development, 22,* 356–364.

MEANY, M. J. (2010). Epigenetics and the biological definition of gene × environment interactions. *Child Development, 81,* 41–79.

MEJIA-ARAUZ, R., ROGOFF, B., & PARADISE, R. (2005). Cultural variation in children's observation during a demonstration. *International Journal of Behavioral Development, 29,* 282–291.

MEKEL-BOBROV, N., GILBERT, S. L., EVANS, P. D., VALLENDER, E. J., ANDERSON, J. R., HUDSON, R. R., TISHKOFF, S. A., & LAHN, B. T. (2005). Ongoing adaptive evolution of ASPM, a brain size determinant in Homo sapiens. *Science, 309,* 1720–1722.

MELHUISH, E. C., SYLVA, K., SAMMONS, P., SIRAJ-BLATCHFORD, I., TAGGART, B., PHAN, M. B., & MALIN, A. (2008). Preschool influences on mathematics achievement. *Science, 321,* 1161–1162.

MELINDER, A. M., KRISTEN, W., ALEXANDER, K. W., CHO, Y., GOODMAN, G. S., THORESEN, C., LONNUM, C. K., & MAGNUSSEN, S. (2010). Children's eyewitness memory: A comparison of two interviewing strategies. *Journal of Experimental Child Psychology, 105,* 155–177.

MELIS, A. P., CALL, J., & TOMASELLO, M. (2006). Chimpanzees conceal visual and auditory information from others. *Journal of Comparative Psychology, 120,* 154–162.

MELOT, A.-M. (1998). The relationship between metacognitive knowledge and metacognitive experiences: Acquisition and re-elaboration. *European Journal of Psychology of Education, 13,* 75–89.

MELTZOFF, A. N. (1988). Infant imitation after a 1-week delay: Long-term memory for novel acts and multiple stimuli. *Developmental Psychology, 24,* 470–476.

MELTZOFF, A. N. (1990). Towards a developmental cognitive science: The implications of cross-modal matching and imitation for the development of memory in infancy. *Annals of the New York Academy of Sciences, 608,* 1–31.

MELTZOFF, A. N. (1995). Understanding the intentions of others: Reenactment of intended acts by 18-month-old children. *Developmental Psychology, 31,* 838–850.

MELTZOFF, A. N., & BORTON, R. W. (1979). Intermodal matching by human neonates. *Nature, 282,* 403–404.

MELTZOFF, A. N., KUHL, P. K., MOVELLAN, J., & SEJNOWSKI, T. J. (2009). Foundations for a new science of learning. *Science, 325,* 284–288.

MELTZOFF, A. N., & MOORE, M. K. (1977). Imitation of facial and manual gestures by human neonates. *Science, 198,* 75–78.

MELTZOFF, A. N., & MOORE, M. K. (1985). Cognitive foundations and social functions of imitation and intermodal representation in infancy. In J. Mehler & R. Fox (Eds.), *Neonate cognition: Beyond the booming buzzing confusion.* Hillsdale, NJ: Erlbaum.

MELTZOFF, A. N., & MOORE, M. K. (1992). Early imitation within a functional framework: The importance of person identity, movement, and development. *Infant Behavior and Development, 15,* 479–505.

MENDELSON, M. J., & HAITH, M. M. (1976). The relation between audition and vision in the human newborn. *Monographs of the Society for Research in Child Development,* 41 (Serial No. 167).

MENZEL, E. W., JR. (1974). A group of young chimpanzees in a 1-acre field: Leadership and communication. In A. M. Schrier & F. Stollnitz (Eds.), *Behavior of nonhuman primates,* Vol. 5 (pp. 83–153). New York: Academic.

MERRITT, K. A., ORNSTEIN, P. A., & SPICKER, B. (1994). Children's memory for a salient medical procedure: Implications for testimony. *Pediatrics, 94,* 12–23.

MERVIS, C. B., & BERTRAND, J. (1994). Acquisition of the novel name-nameless category (N3C) principle. *Child Development, 65,* 1646–1662.

MICHOTTE, A. (1963). *The perception of causality.* London: Methuen.

MILES, H. L. (1990). The cognitive foundations for reference in a signing orangutan. In S. T. Parker & K. K. Gibson (Eds.), *"Language" and intelligence in monkeys and apes* (pp. 511–539). Cambridge, UK: Cambridge University Press.

MILLER-JONES, D. (1989). Culture and testing. *American Psychologist, 44,* 360–366.

MILLER, K. F., SMITH, C. M., ZHU, J., & ZHANG, H. (1995). Preschool origins of cross-national differences in mathematical competence. *Psychological Science, 6,* 56–60.

MILLER, L. C., LECHNER, R. E., & RUGS, D. (1985). Development of conversational responsiveness: Preschoolers' use of responsive listener cues and relevant comments. *Developmental Psychology, 21,* 473–480.

MILLER, L. T., & VERNON, P. A. (1996). Intelligence, reaction time, and working memory in 4- to 6-year-old children. *Intelligence, 22,* 155–190.

MILLER, L. T., & VERNON, P. A. (1997). Developmental changes in speed of information processing in young children. *Developmental Psychology, 33,* 549–554.

MILLER, P. H. (1990). The development of strategies of selective attention. In D. F. Bjorklund (Ed.), *Children's strategies: Contemporary views of cognitive development.* Hillsdale, NJ: Erlbaum.

MILLER, P. H., & COYLE, T. R. (1999). Developmental changes: Lessons from microgenesis. In E. K. Scholnick, K. Nelson, S. A. Gelman, & P. H. Miller (Eds.), *Conceptual development: Piaget's legacy* (pp. 209–239). Mahwah, NJ: Erlbaum.

MILLER, P. H., HAYNES, V. F., DeMARIE-DREBLOW, D., & WOODY-RAMSEY, J. (1986). Children's strategies for gathering information in three tasks. *Child Development, 57,* 1429–1439.

MILLER, P. H., & SEIER, W. L. (1994). Strategy utilization deficiencies in children: When, where, and why. In H. W. Reese (Ed.), *Advances in child development and behavior,* Vol. 25. New York: Academic.

MILLER, P. H., SEIER, W. L., PROBERT, J. S., & ALOISE, P. A. (1991). Age differences in the capacity demands of a strategy among spontaneously strategic children. *Journal of Experimental Child Psychology, 52,* 149–165.

MILLER, P. H., & WEISS, M. G. (1982). Children's and adults' knowledge about what variables affect selective attention. *Child Development, 53,* 543–549.

MILLER, S. A. (2009). Children's understanding of second-order mental states. *Psychological Bulletin, 135,* 749–773.

MILLIGAN, K., ASTINGTON, J. W., & DACK, L. A. (2007). Language and theory of mind: Meta-analysis of the relationship between language ability and false-belief understanding. *Child Development, 78,* 622–646.

MILNER, B. (1964). Some effects of frontal lobectomy in man. In J. M. Warren & K. Akert (Eds.), *The frontal granular cortex and behavior.* New York: McGraw-Hill.

MISTRY, J. (1997). The development of remembering in cultural context. In N. Cowan (Ed.), *The development of memory in childhood.* Hove, UK: Psychology Press.

MIX, K. S., HUTTENLOCHER, J., & LEVINE, S. C. (2002). Multiple cues for quantification in infancy: Is number one of them? *Psychological Bulletin, 128,* 278–294.

MOELY, B. E., HART, S. S., LEAL, L., SANTULLI, K. A., RAO, N., JOHNSON, T., & HAMILTON, L. B. (1992). The teacher's role in facilitating memory and study strategy development in the elementary school classroom. *Child Development, 63,* 653–672.

MOELY, B. E., SANTULLI, K. A., & OBACH, M. S. (1995). Strategy instruction, metacognition, and motivation in the elementary school classroom. In F. Weinert & W. Schneider (Eds.), *Memory performance and competencies: Issues in growth and development.* Hillsdale, NJ: Erlbaum.

MOFFITT, T. W., CASPI, A., & RUTTER, M. (2006). Measured gene-environment interactions in psychology: Concepts, research strategies, and implications for research, intervention, and public understanding of genetics. *Perspective on Psychological Science, 1,* 5–27.

MOLENAAR, P. C. M., BOOMSMA, D. I., & DOLAN, C. V. (1993). A third source of developmental differences. *Behavior Genetics, 23,* 519–524.

MOLFESE, D. L., & MOLFESE, V. J. (1980). Cortical responses of preterm infants to phonetic and nonphonetic speech stimuli. *Developmental Psychology, 16,* 574–581.

MOLFESE, D. L., & MOLFESE, V. J. (1985). Electrophysiological indices of auditory discrimination in newborn infants: The bases for predicting later language development? *Infant Behavior and Development, 8,* 197–211.

MONASTERSKY, R. (2005). Women and science: The debate goes on. *Chronicle of Higher Education, 51.* Retrieved March 3, 2008, from http://chronicle.com/free/v51/i26/26a00102.htm.

MONDLOCH, C. J., LEWIS, T. L., BUDREAU, D. R., MAURER, D., DANNEMILLER, J. L., STEPHENS, B. R., & KLEINER-GATHERCOAL, K. A. (1999). Face perception during early infancy. *Psychological Science, 10,* 419–422.

MONEY, J. (1988). *Gay, straight, and in-between: The sexology of erotic orientation.* New York: Oxford University Press.

MONK, C. S., WEBB, S. J., & NELSON, C. A. (2001). Prenatal neurobiological development: Molecular mechanisms and anatomical change. *Developmental Neuropsychology, 19,* 211–236.

MONTEMAYOR, R., & EISEN, M. (1977). The development of self-conceptions from childhood to adolescence. *Developmental Psychology, 13,* 314–319.

MOOD, D. W. (1979). Sentence comprehension in preschool children: Testing an adaptive egocentrism hypothesis. *Child Development, 50,* 247–250.

MOORE, D. S. (2001). *The dependent gene: The fallacy of "nature vs. nurture."* New York: Freeman Books.

MOORE, D. S., & COCAS, L. A. (2006). Perception precedes computation: Can familiarity preferences explain apparent calculation by human babies? *Developmental Psychology, 42,* 666–678.

MOORE, D. S., & JOHNSON, S. P. (2009). Mental rotation in human infants: A sex difference. *Psychological Science, 19,* 1063–1066.

MOORE, D. S., SPENCE, M. J., & KATZ, G. S. (1997). Six-month-olds' categorization of natural infant-directed utterances. *Developmental Psychology, 33,* 980–989.

MOORE, T. (1967). Language and intelligence: A longitudinal study of the first eight years. Part I. Patterns of development in boys and girls. *Human Development, 10,* 88–106.

MORELLI, G. A., ROGOFF, B., & ANGELILLO, C. (2003). Cultural variation in young children's access to work or involvement in specialized child-focused activities. *International Journal of Behavioral Development, 27,* 264–274.

MORGANTE, J. D., & KEEN, R. (2008). Vision and action: The effect of visual feedback on infants' exploratory behaviors. *Infant Behavior and Development, 31,* 729–733.

MORIGUCHI, Y., & HIRAKI, K. (2009). Neural origin of cognitive shifting in young children. *Proceeding of the National Academy of Sciences, USA, 106,* 6017–6021.

MORISSET, C. E., BARNARD, K. E., & BOOTH, C. L. (1995). Toddlers' language development: Sex differences within social risk. *Developmental Psychology, 31,* 851–865.

MORRISON, F. J., & CONNOR, C. M. (2009). The transition to school: Child-instruction transactions in learning to read. In A. Sameroff (Ed.), *The transactional model of development: How children and contexts shape each other* (pp. 183–201). Washington, DC: American Psychological Association.

MORRISON, F. J., GRIFFITH, E. M., & ALBERTS, D. M. (1997). Nature-nurture in the classroom: Entrance age, school readiness, and learning in children. *Developmental Psychology, 33,* 254–262.

MORRISON, F. J., GRIFFITH, E. M., & FRAZIER, J. A. (1996). Schooling and the 5–7 shift: A natural experiment. In A. Sameroff & M. M. Haith (Eds.), *Reason and responsibility: The passage through childhood.* Chicago: University of Chicago Press.

MORRISON, F. J., SMITH, L., & DOW-EHRENSBERGER, M. (1995). Education and cognitive development: A natural experiment. *Developmental Psychology, 31,* 789–799.

MORRONGIELLO, B. A., FENWICK, K. D., HILLIER, L., & CHANCE, G. (1994). Sound localization in newborn human infants. *Developmental Psychobiology, 27,* 519–538.

MORTENSEN, E. L., MICHAELSEN K. F., SANDERS S. A., & REINISCH, J. M. (2002). The association between duration of breastfeeding and adult intelligence. *Journal of the American Medical Association, 287,* 2365–2371.

MORTON, J., & JOHNSON, M. H. (1991). CONSPEC and CONLEARN: a two-process theory of infant face recognition. *Psychological Review, 98,* 164–181.

MOSKOWITZ, B. A. (1978). The acquisition of language. *Scientific American, 239,* 92–108.

MOULSON, M. C., FOX, N. A., ZEANAH, C. H., & NELSON, C. A. (2009). Early adverse experiences and the neurobiology of facial processing. *Developmental Psychology, 45,* 17–30.

MOULSON, M. C., WESTERLUND, A., FOX, N. A., ZEANAH, C. H., & NELSON, C. A. (2009). The effects of early experience on face recognition: An event-related potential study of institutionalized children in Romania. *Child Development, 80,* 1039–1056.

MUIR-BROADDUS, J. E. (1995). Gifted underachievers: Insights from the characteristics of strategic functioning associated with giftedness and achievement. *Learning and Individual Differences, 7,* 189–206.

MULLEN, M. K. (1994). Earliest recollections of childhood: A demographic analysis. *Cognition, 52,* 55–79.

MULLEN, M. K., & YI, S. (1995). The cultural context of talk about the past: Implications for the development of autobiographical memory. *Cognitive Development, 10,* 407–419.

MÜLLER, G. B. (2003). Embryonic motility: Environmental influences and evolutionary innovation. *Evolution & Development, 5,* 56–60.

MULLIS, I. V. S., MARTIN, M. O., GONZALEZ, E. J., & KENNEDY, A. M. (2003). PIRLS 2001 international report: IEA's study of reading literacy achievement in primary schools. Chestnut Hill, MA: Boston College. Retrieved May 31, 2010, from http://timss.bc.edu/pirls2001.html.

MUNROE, R. H., SHIMMIN, H. S., & MUNROE, R. L. (1984). Gender understanding and sex role preference in four cultures. *Developmental Psychology, 20,* 673–682.

MUTER, V., HULME, C., SNOWLING, M., & TAYLOR, S. (1998). Segmentation, not rhyming, predicts early progress in learning to read. *Journal of Experimental Child Psychology, 71,* 3–27.

MUZZATTI, B., & AGNOLI, F. (2007). Gender and mathematics: Attitudes and stereotype threat susceptibility in Italian children. *Developmental Psychology, 43,* 747–759.

MYOWA-YAMAKOSHI, M., & TOMONAGA, M. (2001). Development of face recognition in an infant gibbon (*Hylobates agilis*). *Infant Behavior and Development, 24,* 215–227.

MYOWA-YAMAKOSHI, M., TOMONAGA, M., TANAKA, M., & MATSUZAWA, T. (2004). Imitation in neonatal chimpanzees (*Pan troglodytes*). *Developmental Science, 7,* 437–442.

NADIG, A. S., & SEDIVY, J. C. (2002). Evidence of perspective-taking constraints in children's on-line reference resolution. *Psychological Science, 13,* 329–336.

NAGELL, K., OLGUIN, K., & TOMASELLO, M. (1993). Processes of social learning in the tool use of chimpanzees (*Pan troglodytes*) and human children (*Homo sapiens*). *Journal of Comparative Psychology, 107,* 174–186.

NAGY, E. (2006). From imitation to conversation: The first dialogues with human neonates. *Infant and Child Development, 15,* 223–232.

NAGY, E., & MOLNAR, P. (2004). Homo imitans or homo provocans? Human imprinting model of neonatal imitation. *Infant Behavior and Development, 27,* 54–63.

NAITO, M., & MIURA, H. (2001). Japanese children's numerical competencies: Age- and schooling-related influences in the development of number concepts and addition skills. *Developmental Psychology, 37,* 217–230.

NASH, M. R. (1987). What, if anything, is age regressed about hypnotic age regression? A review of the empirical literature. *Psychological Bulletin, 102,* 42–52.

NASH, M. R., DRAKE, M., WILEY, R., KHALSA, S., & LYNN, S. J. (1986). The accuracy of recall of hypnotically age regressed subjects. *Journal of Abnormal Psychology, 95,* 298–300.

Neisser, U. (ED.). (1998). *The rising curve: Long-term gains in IQ and related measures.* Washington, DC: American Psychological Association.

NEISSER, U., BOODOO, G., BOUCHARD, T. J., BOYKIN, A. W., BRODY, N., CECI, S. J., HALPERN, D. F., LOEHLIN, J. C., PERLOFF, R., STERNBERG, R. J., & URBINA, S. (1996). Intelligence: Knowns and unknowns. *American Psychologist, 51,* 77–101.

NELSON, C. A. (1997). The neurobiological basis of early memory development. In N. Cowan (Ed.), *The development of memory in childhood* (pp. 41–82). Hove, UK: Psychology Press.

NELSON, C. A. (2001). Neural plasticity and human development: The role of experience in sculpting memory systems. *Developmental Science, 3,* 115–130.

NELSON, C. A. (2007). A neurobiological perspective on early human deprivation. *Child Development Perspectives, 1,* 13–18.

NELSON, C. A., FURTADO, E. A., FOX, N. A., & ZEANAH, JR., C. H. (2009). The deprived human brain. *American Scientist, 97,* 222–229.

NELSON, C. A., THOMAS, K. M., & DE HAAN, M. (2006). Neural bases of cognitive development. In D. Kuhn & R. S. Siegler (Vol. Eds.), *Cognition, perception, and language,* Vol. 2 (pp. 3–57), in W. Damon & R. M. Lerner (Gen. Eds.), *Handbook of Child Psychology* (6th ed.). New York: Wiley.

NELSON, C. A., III, ZEANAH, C. H., FOX, N. A., MARSHALL, P. J., SMYKE, A. T., & GUTHRIE, D. (2007). Cognitive recovery in socially deprived young children: The Bucharest Early Intervention Program. *Science, 318,* 1937–1940.

NELSON, K. (1973). Structure and strategy in learning to talk. *Monographs of the Society for Research in Child Development, 38* (Serial No. 149).

NELSON, K. (1974). Variations in children's concepts by age and category. *Child Development, 45,* 577–584.

NELSON, K. (1993). The psychological and social origins of autobiographical memory. *Psychological Science, 4,* 7–14.

NELSON, K. (1996). *Language in cognitive development: The emergence of the mediated mind.* New York: Cambridge University Press.

NELSON, K. (2005). Evolution and development of human memory systems. In B. J. Ellis & D. F. Bjorklund (Eds.), *Origins of the social mind: Evolutionary psychology and child development* (pp. 354–382). New York: Guilford.

NESSE, R. M., & WILLIAMS, G. C. (1994). *Why we get sick: The new science of Darwinian medicine.* New York: Times Books.

NEWCOMBE, N. S. (2002). The nativist-empiricist controversy in the context of recent research on spatial and quantitative development. *Psychological Science, 13,* 395–401.

NEWCOMBE, N. S., BANDURA, M. M., & TAYLOR, D. C. (1983). Sex differences in spatial ability and spatial activities. *Sex Roles, 9,* 377–386.

NEWCOMBE, N. S., DRUMMEY, A. B., FOX, N. A., LIE, E., & OTTINGER-ALBERTS, W. (2000). Remembering early childhood: How much, how, and why (or why not). *Current Directions in Psychological Science, 9,* 55–58.

NEWCOMBE, N., & DUBAS, J. S. (1992). A longitudinal study of predictors of spatial ability in adolescent females. *Child Development, 63,* 37–46.

NEWCOMBE, N., & FOX, N. A. (1994). Infantile amnesia: Through a glass darkly. *Child Development, 65,* 31–40.

NEWCOMBE, N. S., & HUTTENLOCHER, J. (2006). Development of spatial cognition. In D. Kuhn & R. S. Siegler (Vol. Eds.), *Cognition, perception, and language,* Vol. 2 (pp. 734–776), in W. Damon & R. Lerner (Gen. Eds.), *Handbook of child psychology* (6th ed.). New York: Wiley.

NEWCOMBE, N., HUTTENLOCHER, J., DRUMMEY, A. B., & WILEY, J. (1998). The development of spatial location coding: Use of external frames of reference and dead reckoning. *Cognitive Development, 13,* 185–200.

NEWCOMBE, N., HUTTENLOCHER, J., & LEARMONTH, A. (1999). Infants' coding of location in continuous space. *Infant Behavior and Development, 22,* 483–510.

NEWPORT, E. L. (1990). Maturational constraints on language learning. *Cognitive Science, 14,* 11–28.

NEWPORT, E. L. (1991). Contrasting concepts of the critical period for language. In S. Carey & R. Gelman (Eds.), *Epigenesis of mind: Essays in biology and knowledge.* Hillsdale, NJ: Erlbaum.

NG, F. F.-Y., POMERANTZ, E. M., & LAM, S.-F. (2007). European American and Chinese parents' responses to children's success and failure: Implications for children's responses. *Developmental Psychology, 43,* 1239–1255.

NICELY, P., TAMIS-LEMONDA, C. S., & BORNSTEIN, M. H. (1999). Mothers' attuned responses to infant affect expressivity promote earlier achievement of language milestones. *Infant Behavior and Development, 22,* 557–568.

NICHD EARLY CHILD CARE RESEARCH NETWORK. (2002). Child-care structure → process → outcome: Direct and indirect effects of child-care quality on young children's development. *Psychological Science, 13,* 199–206.

NICHD EARLY CHILD CARE RESEARCH NETWORK. (2005). Duration and developmental timing of poverty and children's cognitive and social development from birth through third grade. *Child Development, 76,* 795–810.

NIELSEN, M. (2006). Copying actions and copying outcomes: Social learning through the second year. *Developmental Psychology, 42,* 555–565.

NIELSEN, M., SIMCOCK, G., & JENKINS, L. (2008). The effect of social engagement on 24-month-olds' imitation from live and televised models. *Developmental Science, 11,* 722–731.

NIELSEN, M., SUDDENDORF, T., & SLAUGHTER, V. (2006). Mirror self-recognition beyond the face. *Child Development, 77,* 176–185.

NIELSEN, M., & TOMASELLI, K. (2010). Overimitation in Kalahari Bushman children and the origins of human cultural cognition. *Psychological Science, 21,* 729–736.

NISBETT, R. E., PENG, K., CHOI, I., & NORENZAYAN, A. (2001). Culture and systems of thought: Holistic vs. analytic cognition. *Psychological Review, 108,* 291–310.

NYITI, R. M. (1982). The validity of "cultural differences explanation" in the rate of Piagetian cognitive development. In D. A. Wagner & H. W. Stevenson (Eds.), *Cultural perspectives on child development.* San Francisco: W. H. Freeman.

O'BRIEN, M., & HUSTON, A. C. (1985). Development of sex-typed play behavior in toddlers. *Developmental Psychology, 21,* 866–871.

O'CONNOR, J. J., COHEN, S., & PARMELEE, A. H. (1984). Infant auditory discrimination in preterm and full-term infants as a predictor of 5 year intelligence. The effects of global severe privation on cognitive competence: Extension and longitudinal follow-up. *Developmental Psychology, 20,* 159–165.

O'CONNOR, T. G., RUTTER, M., BECKETT, C., KEAVENEY, L., & KREPPNER, J. M., & THE ENGLISH AND ROMANIAN ADOPTEES STUDY TEAM (2000). The effects of global severe privation on cognitive competence: Extension and longitudinal follow-up. *Child Development, 71,* 376–390.

O'NEILL, M., BARD, K. A., LINNELL, M., & FLUCK, M. (2005). Maternal gestures with 20-month-old infants in two contexts. *Developmental Science, 8,* 352–359.

O'SULLIVAN, J. T., HOWE, M. L., & MARCHE, T. A. (1996). Children's beliefs about long-term retention. *Child Development, 67,* 2989–3009.

OAKES, L. M. (1994). Development of infants' use of continuity cues in their perception of causality. *Developmental Psychology, 30,* 869–879.

OAKES, L. M., & MADOLE, K. L. (2000). The future of infant categorization research: A process-oriented approach. *Child Development, 71,* 119–126.

OAKES, M. A., & HYMAN, I. E., JR. (2000). The changing face of memory and self. In D. F. Bjorklund (Ed.), *False-memory creation in children and adults: Theory, research, and implications.* Mahwah, NJ: Erlbaum.

OBERMAN, L. M., HUBBARD, E. M., MCCLEERY, J. P., ALTSCHULER, E. L., & PINEDA, J. A., & RAMACHANDRAN, V. S. (2005). EEG evidence for mirror neuron dysfunction in autism spectrum disorder. *Cognitive Brain Research, 24,* 190–198.

ODEGARD, T. M., COOPER, C. M., LAMPINEN, J. M., REYNA, V. F., & BRAINERD, C. J. (2009). Children's eyewitness memory for multiple real-life events. *Child Development, 80,* 1877–1890.

OLDS, D. L., HENDERSON, C. R., & TATELBAUM, R. (1994). Intellectual impairment in children of women who smoke cigarettes during pregnancy. *Pediatrics, 93,* 221–227.

OLIVER, B. R., DALE, P. S., & PLOMIN, R. (2005). Predicting literacy at age 7 from preliteracy at age 4: A longitudinal genetic analysis. *Psychological Science, 16,* 861–865.

OLLER, D. K., & EILERS, R. (1988). The role of audition in babbling. *Child Development, 59,* 441–449.

OLSON, K. R., & DWECK, C. S. (2009). Social cognitive development: A new look. *Child Development Perspectives, 3,* 60–65.

OMANSON, R. C., BECK, I. L., VOSS, J. F., & MCKEOWN, M. G. (1984). The effects of reading lessons on comprehension: A processing description. *Cognition and Instruction, 1,* 45–67.

ONISHI, K. H., & BAILLARGEON, R. (2005). Do 15-month-old infants understand false belief? *Science, 308,* 255–258.

OPFER, J. E., & GELMAN, S. A. (2001). Children's and adults' models for predicting teleological action: The development of a biology-based model. *Child Development, 72,* 1367–1381.

OPPENHEIM, R. W. (1981). Ontogenetic adaptations and retrogressive processes in the development of the nervous system and behavior. In K. J. Connolly & H. F. R. Prechtl (Eds.), *Maturation and development: Biological and psychological perspectives* (pp. 73–108). Philadelphia: International Medical Publications.

ORBACH, Y., & LAMB, M. E. (2007). Young children's references to temporal attributed of allegedly experienced events in the course of forensic interviews. *Child Development, 78,* 1100–1120.

ORGANIZATION FOR ECONOMIC CO-OPERATION AND DEVELOPMENT. (OECD). (2004). *Learning for tomorrow's world: First results from PISA 2003.* Paris: OECD.

ORNSTEIN, P. A. (1999). Comments: Toward an understanding of the development of memory. In F. E. Weinert & W. Schneider (Eds.), *Individual development from 3 to 12: Findings from the Munich Longitudinal Study* (pp. 94–105). Cambridge, UK: Cambridge University Press.

ORNSTEIN, P. A., BAKER-WARD, L., GORDON, B. N., & MERRITT, K. A. (1997). Children's memory for medical experiences: Implications for testimony. *Applied Cognitive Psychology, 11,* 87–104.

ORNSTEIN, P. A., BAKER-WARD, L., GORDON, B. N., PELPHREY, K. A., TYLER, C. S., & GRAMZOW, E. (2006). The influence of prior knowledge and repeated questioning on children's long-term retention of the details of a pediatric examination, *Developmental Psychology, 42,* 332–344.

ORNSTEIN, P. A., BAKER-WARD, L., & NAUS, M. J. (1988). The development of mnemonic skill. In M. Weinert & M. Perlmutter (Eds.), *Memory development.* Hillsdale, NJ: Erlbaum.

ORNSTEIN, P. A., COFFMAN, J., GRAMMAR, J., SAN SOUCI, P., & MCCALL, L.

(2010). Linking the classroom context and the development of children's memory skills. In J. L. Meece & J. S. Eccles (Eds.), *Handbook of research on schools, schooling, and human development* (pp. 42–59). New York: Routledge.

ORNSTEIN, P. A., GORDON, B. N., & LARUS, D. M. (1992). Children's memory for a personally experienced event: Implications for testimony. *Applied Developmental Psychology, 6,* 49–60.

ORNSTEIN, P. A., GRAMMAR, J. K., & COFFMAN, J. L. (2009). Teachers' "mnemonic style" and the development of skilled memory. In H. S. Waters & W. Schneider (Eds.), *Metacognition, strategy use, and instruction.* New York: Guilford.

ORNSTEIN, P. A., & GREENHOOT, A. F. (2000). Remembering the distant past: Implications of research on children's memory for the recovered memory debate. In D. F. Bjorklund (Ed.), *False-memory creation in children and adults: Theory, research, and implications.* Mahwah, NJ: Erlbaum.

ORNSTEIN, P. A., & HADEN, C. A. (2001). Memory development or the development of memory? *Current Directions in Psychological Science, 10,* 202–209.

ORNSTEIN, P. A., HALE, G. A., & MORGAN, J. S. (1977). Developmental differences in recall and output organization. *Bulletin of the Psychonomic Society, 9,* 29–32.

ORNSTEIN, P. A., & LIGHT, L. L. (2010). Memory development across the lifespan. In W. F. Overton (Ed.), *Biology, cognition and methods across the life-span,* Vol. 1., in R. M. Lerner (Gen. Ed.), *Handbook of life-span development.* Hoboken, NJ: Wiley.

ORNSTEIN, P. A., MERRITT, K. A., BAKER-WARD, L., FURTADO, E., GORDON, B. N., & PRINCIPE, G. F. (1998). Children's knowledge, expectation, and long-term retention. *Applied Cognitive Psychology, 12,* 387–405.

ORNSTEIN, P. A., & NAUS, M. J. (1978). Rehearsal processes in children's memory. In P. A. Ornstein (Ed.), *Memory development in children.* Hillsdale, NJ: Erlbaum.

ORNSTEIN, P. A., NAUS, M. J., & LIBERTY, C. (1975). Rehearsal and organizational processes in children's memory. *Child Development, 46,* 818–830.

ORNSTEIN, P. A., NAUS, M. J., & STONE, B. P. (1977). Rehearsal training and developmental differences in memory. *Developmental Psychology, 13,* 15–24.

OSHIMA-TAKANE, Y., GOODZ, E., & DEREVENSKY, J. L. (1996). Birth order effects on early language development: Do secondborn children learn from overheard speech? *Child Development, 67,* 621–634.

OSHIMA-TAKANE, Y., & ROBBINS, M. (2003). Linguistic environment of secondborn children. *First Language, 23,* 21–40.

OSTROVSKY, Y., ANDALMAN, A., & SINHA, P. (2006). Vision following extended congenital blindness. *Psychological Science, 12,* 1009–1014.

OVANDO, C. J., & COLLIER, V. P. (1998). *Bilingual and ESL classrooms: Teaching in multicultural contexts.* Boston: McGraw-Hill.

OYAMA, S. (2000). *The ontogeny of information: Developmental systems and evolution* (2nd ed.). Durham, NC: Duke University Press.

OZCALISKAN, S., & GOLDEN-MEADOW, S. (2005). Gesture is at the cutting edge of early language development. *Cognition, 96,* B101–B113.

PALINCSAR, A. S., & BROWN, A. L. (1984). Reciprocal teaching of comprehension-monitoring activities. *Cognition and Instruction, 1,* 117–175.

PALINCSAR, A. S., BROWN, A. L., & CAMPIONE, J. C. (1993). First-grade dialogues for knowledge acquisition and use. In E. A. Forman, N. Minilk, & C. A. Stone (Eds.), *Contexts for learning.* New York: Oxford University Press.

PANKSEPP, J. (1998). Attention deficit hyperactivity disorders, psychostimulants, and intolerance of childhood playfulness: A tragedy in the making? *Current Directions in Psychological Science, 7,* 91–98.

PAPOUSEK, H. (1977). Entwicklung der Lernfähigkeit im Säuglingsalter (The development of learning ability in infancy). In G. Nissen (Ed.), *Intelligenz, Lernen und Lernstörungen (Intelligence, learning, and learning disabilities).* Berlin: Springer-Verlag.

PARKER, J. F. (1995). Age differences in source monitoring of performed and imagined actions on immediate and delayed tests. *Journal of Experimental Child Psychology, 60,* 84–101.

PASCALIS, O., DE HAAN, M., & NELSON, C. A. (2002). Is face processing species-specific during the first year of life? *Science, 296,* 1321–1323.

PASCALIS, O., & DE SCHONEN, S. (1994). Recognition memory in 3- to 4-day-old human neonates. *NeuroReport: Learning and Memory, 5,* 14.

PASCALIS, O., & KELLY, D. J. (2009). The origins of face processing in humans. *Perspectives on Psychological Science, 4,* 200–209.

PATTERSON, F. (1978). Linguistic capabilities of a lowland gorilla. In F. Peng (Ed.), *Sign language and language acquisition in man and ape* (pp. 161–201). Boulder, CO: Westview Press.

PATTERSON, M. L., & WERKER, J. F. (2003). Two-month-old infants match phonetic information in lips and voice. *Developmental Science, 6,* 191–196.

PAUKNER, A., ANDERSON, J. R., BORELLE, E., VISALBERGHI, E., & FERRARI, P. F. (2004). Macaques (*Macaca nemestrina*) recognize when they are being imitated. *Biology Letters, 1,* 219–222.

PAULESU, E., DÉMONET, J.-F., FAZIO, F., MCCRORY, E., CHANOINE, V., BRUNSWICK, N., CAPPA, S. F., COSSU, G., HABIB, M., FRITH, C. D., & FRITH, U. (2001). Dyslexia: Cultural diversity and biological unity. *Science, 291,* 2165–2167.

PAZ-ALONSO, P. M., LARSON, R. P., CASTELLI, P., ALLEY, D., & GOODMAN, G. S. (2009). Memory development: Emotion, stress, and trauma. In M. L. Courage & N. Cowan (Eds.), *The development of memory in infancy and childhood* (pp. 197–239). Hove, UK: Psychology Press.

PEARSON, B. Z., FERNÁNDEZ, S. C., LEWEDAG, V., & OLLER, D. K. (1997). The relation of input factors to lexical learning by bilingual infants (ages 10 to 30 months). *Applied Psycholinguistics, 18,* 41–58.

PEARSON, P. D., HANSEN, J., & GORDON, C. (1979). The effect of background knowledge on young children's comprehension of explicit and implicit information. *Journal of Reading Behavior, 11,* 201–209.

PELLEGRINI, A. D. (2005). *Recess: Its role in education and development.* Mahwah, NJ: Erlbaum.

PELLEGRINI, A. D. (2011). Play. In P. Zelazo (Ed.), *Oxford handbook of developmental psychology.* New York: Oxford University Press.

PELLEGRINI, A. D., & BJORKLUND, D. F. (2004). The ontogeny and phylogeny of children's object and fantasy play. *Human Nature, 15,* 23–43.

PELLEGRINI, A. D., & DAVIS, P. (1993). Confinement effects on playground and classroom behavior. *British Journal of Educational Psychology, 63,* 88–95.

PELLEGRINI, A., & DUPUIS, D. (2010). Developmental and educational role of recess in school. In J. L. Meece & J. S. Eccles (Eds.), *Handbook of research on schools, schooling, and human development* (pp. 356–365). New York: Routledge.

PELLEGRINI, A. D., & HORVAT, M. (1995). A developmental contextual critique of attention deficit hyperactivity disorder. *Educational Researcher, 24,* 13–20.

PELLEGRINI, A. D., HUBERTY, P. D., & JONES, I. (1995). The effects of play deprivation on children's recess and classroom behaviors. *American Educational Research Journal, 32,* 845–864.

PELLEGRINI, A. D., & SMITH, P. K. (1998). Physical activity play: The nature and function of neglected aspect of play. *Child Development, 69,* 577–598.

PENNISI, E. (2001). Behind the scenes of gene expression. *Science, 293,* 1064–1067.

PERERA, F. P., LI, Z., WHYATT, R., HOEPNER, L., WANG, S., CAMANN, D., & RAUH, V. (2009). Prenatal airborne polycyclic aromatic hydrocarbon exposure and child IQ at age 5 years. *Pediatrics. 124,* e195-e202.

PÉREZ, B. (2004). *Becoming biliterate: A study of two-way bilingual immersion education.* Mahwah, NJ: Erlbaum.

PERNER, J. (1991). *Understanding the representational mind.* Cambridge, MA: MIT Press.

PERNER, J., & LANG, B. (2000). Theory of mind and executive function: Is there a developmental relationship? In S. Baron-Cohen, H. Tager-Flusberg, & D. Cohen (Eds.), *Understanding other minds: Perspectives from autism and developmental cognitive neuroscience* (2nd ed.). Oxford: Oxford University Press.

PERNER, J., RUFFMAN, T., & LEEKAM, S. R. (1994). Theory of mind is contagious: You catch it from your sibs.

*Child Development, 67,* 1228–1238.

PERRY, D. G., PERRY, L. C., & RASMUSSEN, P. (1986). Cognitive learning mediators of aggression. *Child Development, 57,* 700–711.

PERRY, D. G., WHITE, A. J., & PERRY, L. C. (1984). Does early sex typing result from children's attempts to match their behavior to sex role stereotypes? *Child Development, 55,* 2114–2121.

PESKIN, J. (1992). Ruse and representations: On children's ability to conceal information. *Developmental Psychology, 28,* 84–89.

PETERSON, C., WANG, Q., & HOU, Y. (2009). "When I was little": Childhood recollections in Chinese and European Canadian grade school children. *Child Development, 80,* 506–518.

PETERSON, C. C., WELLMAN, H. M., & LIU, D. (2005). Steps in theory-of-mind development for children with deafness or autism. *Child Development, 76,* 502–517.

PETITTO, L. A. (2000). On the biological foundations of human language. In K. Emmorey & H. Lane (Eds.), *The signs of language revisited: An anthology in honor of Ursula Bellugi and Edward Klima.* Mahwah, NJ: Lawrence Erlbaum.

PETITTO, L. A., & MARENTETTE, P. F. (1991). Babbling in the manual mode: Evidence for the ontogeny of language. *Science, 251,* 1483–1496.

PETRILL, S. A. (1997). Molarity versus modularity of cognitive functioning? A behavioral genetic perspective. *Current Directions in Psychological Science, 6,* 96–99.

PETRILL, S. A., THOMPSON, L. A., & DETTERMAN, D. K. (1995). The genetic and environmental variance underlying elementary cognitive tasks. *Behavioral Genetics, 25,* 199–209.

PEZDEK, K., & HODGE, D. (1999). Planting false childhood memories in children. The role of event plausibility. *Child Development, 70,* 887–895.

PFEIFER, J. H., IACOBONI, M., MAZZIOTTA, J. C., & DAPRETTO, M. (2008). Mirroring others' emotions relates to empathy and interpersonal competence in children. *NeuroImage, 39,* 2076–2085.

PHILLIPS, S., KING, S., & DUBOIS, L. C. (1978). Spontaneous activity of female versus male newborns. *Child Development, 49,* 590–597.

PIAGET, J. (1929/1969). *The child's conception of the world.* Lanham, MD: Rowman & Littlefield.

PIAGET, J. (1930). *The child's conception of physical causality.* London: Routledge & Kegan Paul.

PIAGET, J. (1946). *Le développement de la notion de temps chez l'enfant.* Paris: PUF.

PIAGET, J. (1952). *The origins of intelligence in children.* New York: Norton.

PIAGET, J. (1954). *The construction of reality in the child.* New York: Basic.

PIAGET, J. (1955). *The language and thought of the child.* New York: World.

PIAGET, J. (1962). *Play, dreams, and imitation in childhood.* New York: Norton.

PIAGET, J. (1965/1932). *The moral judgment of the child.* New York: Free Press.

PIAGET, J. (1971). *Biology and knowledge.* Chicago: University of Chicago Press.

PIAGET, J., & INHELDER, B. (1967). *The child's conception of space.* New York: Norton.

PIAGET, J., & INHELDER, B. (1969). *The psychology of the child.* New York: Basic.

PIAGET, J., & INHELDER, B. (1973). *Memory and intelligence.* New York: Basic.

PICA, P., LEMER, C., IZARD, V., DEHAENE, S. (2004). Exact and approximate arithmetic in an Amazonian indigene group. *Science, 306,* 499–503.

PIERCE, K. A., & GHOLSON, B. (1994). Surface similarity and relational similarity in the development of analogical problem solving: Isomorphic and nonisomorphic transfer. *Developmental Psychology, 30,* 724–737.

PILLEMER, D. B., & WHITE, S. H. (1989). Childhood events recalled by children and adults. In H. W. Reese (Ed.), *Advances in child development and behavior,* Vol. 21. New York: Academic.

PILLOW, B. H. (1988). Young children's understanding of attentional limits. *Child Development, 59,* 31–46.

PINE, K. J., & MESSER, D. J. (1998). Group collaboration effects and the explicitness of children's knowledge. *Cognitive Development, 13,* 109–126.

PINKER, S. (1994). *The language instinct: How the mind creates language.* New York: Morrow.

PINKER, S. (1997). *How the mind works.* New York: Norton.

PIPE, M. E., GOODMAN, G. S., QUAS, J., BIDROSE, S., ABLIN, D., & CRAW, S. (1997). Remembering early experiences during childhood: Are traumatic events special? In D. J. Read & D. S. Lindsay (Eds.), *Recollections of trauma: Scientific evidence and clinical practice* (pp. 417–423). New York: Plenum Press.

PIPE, M.-E., & SALMON, K. (2009). Memory development and the forensic context. In M. L. Courage & N. Cowan (Eds.), *The development of memory in infancy and childhood* (pp. 241–282). Hove, UK: Psychology Press.

PITMAN, C. A., & SHUMAKER, R. W. (2009). Does early care affect joint attention in great apes (*Pan troglodytes, Pan paniscus, Pongo abelii, Pongo pygmaeus, Gorilla gorilla*)? *Journal of Comparative Psychology, 123,* 334–341.

Plomin, R., DeFries, J. C., McClearn, G. E., & McGuffin, P. (2008). Behavioral genetics (5th edition.). New York: Worth Publishers.

PLOMIN, R., FULKER, D. W., CORLEY, R., & DEFRIES, J. C. (1997). Nature, nurture, and cognitive development from 1 to 6 years: A parent-offspring adoption study. *Psychological Science, 8,* 442–447.

PLOMIN, R., KENNEDY, J. K. J., & CRAIG, I. W. (2006). The quest for quantitative trait loci associated with intelligence. *Intelligence, 34,* 513–526.

PLOMIN, R., & PETRILL, S. A. (1997). Genetics and intelligence: What's new? *Intelligence, 24,* 53–77.

PLOMIN, R., & SCHALKWYK, L. C. (2007). Microarrays. *Developmental Science, 10,* 19–23.

PLOTKIN, H. (2001). Some elements of a science of culture. In E. Whitehouse (Ed.), *The debated mind: Evolutionary psychology versus ethnography* (pp. 91–109). New York: Berg.

PLOTNIK, J. M., DE WAAL, F. B. M., & REISS, D. (2006). Self-recognition in an Asian elephant. *Proceedings of the National Academy of Sciences of the United States of America, 103,* 17053–17057.

PLUMERT, J. M. (1995). Relation between children's overestimation of their physical abilities and accident proneness. *Developmental Psychology, 31,* 866–876.

PLUMERT, J. M., & HUND, A. M. (2001). The development of memory for location: What role do spatial prototypes play? *Child Development, 72,* 370–384.

PLUMERT, J. M., KEARNEY, J. K., & CREMER, J. F. (2004). Children's perception of gap avoidances: Bicycling across traffic-filled intersections in an immersive virtual environment. *Child Development, 75,* 1243–1253.

PLUMERT, J. M., KEARNEY, J. K., & CREMER, J. F. (2007). Children's road crossing: A widow into perceptual-motor development. *Current Directions in Psychological Science, 16,* 255–258.

PLUMERT, J. M., & NICHOLS-WHITEHEAD, P. (1996). Parental scaffolding of young children's spatial communication. *Developmental Psychology, 32,* 523–532.

PLUMERT, J. M., & SCHWEBEL, D. C. (1997). Social and temperamental influences on children's overestimation of their physical abilities: Links to accidental injuries. *Journal of Experimental Child Psychology, 67,* 317–337.

POLLAK, S. D., NELSON, C. A., SCHLAAK, M. F., ROEBER, B. J., WEWERKA, S. S., WIIK, K. L., FRENN, K. A., LOMAN, M. M., & GUNNAR, M. R. (2010). Neurodevelopmental effects of early deprivation in postinstitutionalized children. *Child Development, 81,* 224–236.

POLLARD, K. S., SALAMA, S. R., LAMBERT, N., LAMBOT, M. A., COPPENS, S., PEDERSEN, J. S., KATZMAN, S., KING, B., ONODERA, C., SIEPEL, A., KERN, A. D., DEHAY, C., IGEL, H., ARES, M., JR., VANDERHAEGHEN, P., & HAUSSLER D. (2006). An RNA gene expressed during cortical development evolved rapidly in humans. *Nature, 443,* 167–172.

PONS, F., LEWKOWICZ, D. J., SOTO-FARACO, S., & SEBASTIÁN-GALLÉS, N. (2009). Narrowing of intersensory speech perception in infancy. *Proceedings of the National Academy of Science, 106,* 10598–10602.

POOLE, D. A. (1995). Strolling fuzzy-trace theory through eyewitness testimony (or vice versa). *Learning and Individual Differences, 7,* 87–93.

POOLE, D. A., & LAMB, M. E. (1998). *Investigative interviews of children: A guide of helping professionals.*

Washington, DC: American Psychological Association.

POOLE, D. A., & LINDSAY, D. S. (2002). Reducing child witnesses' false reports of misinformation from parents. *Journal of Experimental child Psychology, 81,* 117–140.

POOLE, D. A., & WHITE, L. T. (1993). Two years later. Effects of question repetition and retention interval on the eyewitness testimony of children and adults. *Developmental Psychology, 29,* 844–853.

POOLE, D., & WHITE, L. (1995). Tell me again and again: Stability and change in the repeated testimonies of children and adults. In. M. S. Zaragoza, J. R. Graham, C. N. Gordon, R. Hirschman, & Y. S. Ben Porath (Eds.), *Memory and testimony in the child witness.* Newbury Park, CA: Sage.

PORTER, R., H., & WINBERG, J. (1999). Unique salience of maternal breast odors for newborn infants. *Neuroscience and Biobehavioral Reviews, 23,* 439–449.

POULIN-DUBOIS, D., & FORBES, J. N. (2002). Toddlers' attention to intentions–in–action in learning novel action words. *Developmental Psychology, 38,* 104–114.

POULIN-DUBOIS, D., SERBIN, L. A., KENYON, B., & DERBYSHIRE, A. (1994). Infants' intermodal knowledge about gender. *Developmental Psychology, 30,* 436–442.

POVINELLI, D. J., & EDDY, T. J. (1996). What young chimpanzees know about seeing. *Monograph of the Society for Research in Child Development, 61* (Serial No. 247).

POVINELLI, D. J., LANDAU, K. R., & PERILLOUX, H. K. (1996). Self-recognition in young children using delayed versus live feedback: Evidence of a developmental asynchrony. *Child Development, 67,* 1540–1554.

POVINELLI, D. J., & SIMON, B. B. (1998). Young children's understanding of briefly versus extremely delayed images of the self: Emergence of the autobiographical stance. *Developmental Psychology, 34,* 188–194.

POWELL, M. B., ROBERTS, K. P., CECI, S. J., & HEMBROOKE, H. (1999). The effects of repeated experience on children's suggestibility. *Developmental Psychology, 35,* 1462–1477.

PREISSLER, M. A., & BLOOM, P. (2007). Two-year-olds appreciate the dual nature of pictures. *Psychological Science, 18*, 1–2.

PREMACK, D., & WOODRUFF, G. (1978). Does the chimpanzee have a theory of mind? *Behavioral and Brain Sciences, 1*, 515–526.

PRESSLEY, M. (1982). Elaboration and memory development. *Child Development, 53*, 296–309.

PRESSLEY, M., BORKOWSKI, J. G., & SCHNEIDER, W. (1989). Good information processing: What is it and what education can do to promote it. *International Journal of Educational Research, 13*, 857–867.

PRESSLEY, M., & HILDEN, K. R. (2006). Cognitive strategies. In D. Kuhn & R. S. Siegler (Vol. Eds.), *Cognition, perception, and language,* Vol. 2 (pp. 511–556), in W. Damon & R. M. Lerner (Gen. Eds.), *Handbook of Child Psychology* (6th ed.). New York: Wiley.

PRESSLEY, M., & WOLOSHYN, V. (1995). *Cognitive strategy instruction that really improves children's academic performance* (2nd ed.). Cambridge, MA: Brookline Books.

PRICE, T. S., ELEU, T. C., DALE, P. S., STEVENSON, J., SAUDINO, K., & PLOMIN, R. (2000). Genetic and environmental covariation between verbal and nonverbal cognitive development in infancy. *Child Development, 71*, 948–959.

PRINCIPE, G. F., HAINES, B., ADKINS, A., & GUILIANO, S. (2010). False rumors and true belief: Memory processes underlying children's errant reports of rumored events. *Journal of Experimental Child Psychology, 107*, 407– 422.

PRINCIPE, G. F., KANAYA, T., CECI, S. J., & SINGH, M. (2006). Believing is seeing: How rumors can engender false memories in preschoolers. *Psychological Science, 17*, 243–248.

PRINCIPE, G. F., & SMITH, E. (2008). Seeing things unseen: Fantasy beliefs and false reports. *Journal of Cognition and Development, 9*, 89–111.

PRIOR, H., SCHWARZ, A., & GÜNTÜRKÜN, O. (2008). Mirror-induced behavior in the magpie (*Pica pica*): Evidence of self-recognition. *PLoS Biol 6(8)*, e202. DOI: 10.1371/journal. pbio.0060202.

PROVENCE, S., & LIPTON, R. C. (1962). *Infants in institutions: A comparison of their development with family-reared infants during the first year of life.* New York: International Universities Press.

QUAS, J. A., BAUER, A., & BOYCE, W. T. (2004). Physiological reactivity, social support, and memory in early childhood. *Child Development, 75*, 797–814.

QUAS, J. A., MALLOY, L. C., MELINDER, A., GOODMAN, G. S., & D'MELLO, M. (2007). Developmental differences in the effects of repeated interviews and interviewer bias on young children's event memory and false reports. *Developmental Psychology, 43*, 823–837.

QUINN, P. C. (1994). The categorization of above and below spatial relations by young infants. *Child Development, 65*, 58–69.

QUINN, P. C. (2002). Category representation in young infants. *Current Directions in Psychological Science, 11*, 66–70.

QUINN, P. C., & EIMAS, P. D. (1996). Perceptual cues that permit categorical differentiation of animal species by infants. *Journal of Experimental Child Psychology, 63*, 189–211.

QUINN, P. C., KELLY, D. J., LEE, K., PASCALIS, O., & SLATER, A. M. (2008). Preference for attractive faces in human infants extends beyond conspecifics. *Developmental Science, 11*, 76–83.

QUINN, P. C., & LIBEN, L. S. (2009). A sex difference in mental rotation in young infants. *Psychological Science, 19*, 1067–1070.

QUINN, P. C., YAHR, J., KUHN, A., SLATER, A. M., & PASCALIS, O. (2002). Representation of the gender of human faces by infants: A preference for female. *Perception, 31*, 1109–1121.

QUON, E., & ATANCE, C. M. (2010). A comparison of preschoolers' memory, knowledge, and anticipation of events. *Journal of Cognition and Development, 11*, 37–60.

RABINOWITZ, M., & KEE, D. (1994). A framework for understanding individual differences in memory: Strategy-knowledge interactions. In P. A. Vernon (Ed.), *Handbook of the neuropsychology of individual differences.* New York: Academic.

RAKOCZY, H. (2010). Executive function and the development of belief-desire psychology. *Developmental Science, 13*, 648–661.

RADZISZEWSKA, B., & ROGOFF, B. (1988). Influence of adult and peer collaborators on children's planning skills. *Developmental Psychology, 24*, 840–848.

RAMACHANDRAN, V. S. (2000). Mirror neurons and imitation learning as the driving force behind "the great leap forward" in human evolution. *The Third Culture.* Retrieved November 9, 2010 from http://www.edge.org/3rd_culture/ramachandran/ramachandran_index.html.

RAMACHANDRAN, V. S., & OBERMAN, L. M. (2006). Broken mirrors: A theory of autism. *Scientific American, 295*, 62–69.

RAMAN, L., & GELMAN, S. A. (2008). Do children endorse psychosocial factors in the transmission of illness and disgust? *Developmental Psychology, 44*, 801–813.

RAMANI, G. B., & SIEGLER, R. S. (2008). Promoting broad and stable improvements in low-income children's numerical knowledge through playing number board games. *Child Development, 79*, 375–394.

RAMEY, C. T., CAMPBELL, F. A., BURCHINAL, M., SKINNER, M. L., GARDNER, D. M., & RAMEY, S. L. (2000). Persistent effects of early childhood education on high-risk children and their mothers. *Applied Developmental Science, 4*, 2–14.

RAMEY, C. T., CAMPBELL, F. A., & FINKELSTEIN, N. W. (1984). Course and structure of intellectual development in children at risk for developmental retardation. In P. H. Brooks, R. Sperber, & C. McCauley (Eds.), *Learning and cognition in the mentally retarded.* Hillsdale, NJ: Erlbaum.

RAMSEY, J. L., LANGLOIS, J., & MART, N. C. (2005). Infant categorization of faces: Ladies first. *Developmental Review, 25*, 212–246.

RAMSEY-RENNELS, J. L., & LANGLOIS, J. H. (2006). Infants' differential processing of female and male faces. *Current Directions in Psychological Science, 15*, 59–62.

RATNER, H. H. (1984). Memory demands and the development of young children's memory. *Child Development, 55*, 2173–2191.

RATNER, H. H., FOLEY, M. A., & GIMPERT, N. (2002). The role of collaborative planning in children's source-monitoring errors and learning. *Journal of Experimental Child Psychology, 81*, 44–73.

RAVEN, J., RAVEN, J. C., & COURT, J. H. (2003). *Manual for Raven's Progressive Matrices and Vocabulary Scales. Section 1: General overview.* San Antonio, TX: Harcourt Assessment.

RAVEN, J. C., COURT, J. H., & RAVEN, J. (1975). *Manual for Raven's Progressive Matrices and Vocabulary Scales.* London: Lewis.

RAYMOND, C. L., & BENBOW, C. P. (1986). Gender differences in mathematics: A function of parental support and student sex typing? *Development Psychology, 22,* 808–819.

RECHT, D. R., & LESLIE, L. (1988). Effect of prior knowledge on good and poor readers' memory of text. *Journal of Educational Psychology, 80,* 16–20.

REDCAY, E., HAIST, F., & COURCHESNE, E. (2008). Functional neuroimaging of speech perception during a pivotal period in language acquisition. *Developmental Science, 11,* 237–252.

REEDER, K. (1981). How young children learn to do things with words. In P. S. Dale & D. Ingram (Eds.), *Child language—An international perspective.* Baltimore: University Park.

REESE, E. (1995). Predicting children's literacy from mother-child conversations. *Cognitive Development, 10,* 381–405.

REESE, E., HADEN, C., & FIVUSH, R. (1993). Mother-child conversations about the past: Relationships of style and memory over time. *Cognitive Development, 8,* 403–430.

REESE, E., HADEN, C. A., & FIVUSH, R. (1996). Mothers, fathers, daughters and sons: Gender differences in autobiographical reminiscing. *Research on Language and Social Interaction, 29,* 27–56.

REINISCH, J. M., SANDERS, S. A., MORTENSEN, E. L., & RUBIN, D. B. (1995). In utero exposure to phenobarbital and intelligence deficits in adult men. *Journal of the American Medical Association, 274,* 1518–1525.

REISS, D., & MARINO, L. (2001). Mirror self-recognition in the bottlenose dolphin: A case of cognitive convergence. *Proceedings of the National Academy of Sciences of the United States of America, 98,* 5937–5942.

RENDELL, L., & WHITEHEAD, H. (2001). Culture in whales and dolphins. *Behavioral and Brain Science, 24,* 309–382.

RENNINGER, K. A. (1992). Individual interest and development: Implications for theory and practice. In K. A. Renninger, S. Hidi, & A. Krapp (Eds.), *The role of interest in learning and development.* Hillsdale, NJ: Erlbaum.

REPACHOLI, B. M., & GOPNIK, A. (1997). Early reasoning about desires: Evidence from 14- and 18-month-olds. *Developmental Psychology, 33,* 12–21.

Rescorla, L., Hyson, M. C., & Hirsh-Pasek, K. (EDS.). (1991). *Academic instruction in early childhood: Challenge or pressure?* San Francisco: Jossey-Bass.

REUVEN, B., SEKAL, R., & STAVY, R. (2010). Persistence of the intuitive conception of living things in adolescence. *Journal of Science Education and Technology, 19,* 20–26.

REYNOLDS, A. J., MAVROGENES, N. A., BEZUCZKO, N., & HAGEMANN, M. (1996). Cognitive and family-support mediators of preschool effectiveness: A confirmatory analysis. *Child Development, 67,* 1119–1140.

REZNICK, J. S. (2009). Working memory in infants and toddlers. In M. L. Courage & N. Cowan (Eds.), *The development of memory in infancy and childhood* (pp. 343–365). New York: Psychology Press.

RHEINGOLD, H. L. (1985). Development as the acquisition of familiarity. *Annual Review of Psychology, 36,* 1–17.

RICHARDSON, R., & HAYNE, H. (2007). You can't take it with you: The translation of memory across development. *Current Directions in Psychological Science, 16,* 223–227.

RICHERSON, P., & BOYD, R. (2005). *Not by genes alone: How culture transformed human evolution.* Chicago: Chicago University Press.

RICHERT, R., ROBB, M. B., FENDER, J. G., & WARTELLA, E. (2010). Word learning from baby videos. *Achieves of Pediatric and Adolescent Medicine, 164,* 432–437.

RICHLAND, L. E., CHAN, T.-K., MORRISON, R. G., & AU, T. (2010). Young children's analogical reasoning across cultures: Similarities and differences. *Journal of Experimental Child Psychology, 105,* 146–153.

RICHLAND, L. E., MORRISON, R. G., & HOLYOKE, K. J. (2006). Children's development of analogical reasoning: Insights from scene analogy problems. *Journal of Experimental Child Psychology, 94,* 249–273.

RICHMOND, J., & NELSON, C. A. (2007). Accounting for changes in declarative memory: A cognitive neuroscience perspective. *Developmental Review, 27,* 349–373.

RICKFORD, J. R. (1999). *African American vernacular English.* Malden, MA: Blackwell.

RIDDERINKHOF, K. R., & VAN DER MOLEN, M. (1995). A psychophysiological analysis of developmental differences in the ability to resist interference. *Child Development, 66,* 1040–1056.

RIDDERINKHOF, K. R., VAN DER MOLEN, M., & BAND, G. P. H. (1997). Sources of interference from irrelevant information: A developmental study. *Journal of Experimental Child Psychology, 65,* 315–341.

RILLING, J. K., & INSEL, T. R. (1999). The primate neocortex in comparative perspective using magnetic resonance imaging. *Journal of Human Evolution, 37,* 191–223.

RINDERMANN, H., & CECI, S. J. (2010). Educational policy and country outcomes in international cognitive competence studies. *Perspectives on Psychological Science, 4,* 551–577.

RINGEL, B. A., & SPRINGER, C. J. (1980). On knowing how well one is remembering: The persistence of strategy use during transfer. *Journal of Experimental Child Psychology, 29,* 322–333.

RITTLE-JOHNSON, B. (2006). Promoting transfer: Effects of self-explanation and direct instruction. *Child Development, 77,* 1–29.

RITTLE-JOHNSON, B., & SIEGLER, R. S. (1999). Learning to spell: Variability, choice, and change in children's strategy use. *Child Development, 70,* 332–348.

RIVA, D., & CAZZANIGA, L. (1986). Late effects of unilateral brain lesions sustained before and after age one. *Neuropsychology, 24,* 423–428.

RIZZOLATTI, G., & CRAIGHERO, L. (2004). The mirror neuron system. *Annual Review of Neuroscience, 27,* 169–192.

RIZZOLATTI, G., FADIGA, L., FOGASSI, L., GALLESE, V. (1996). Premotor cortex and the recognition of motor actions. *Cognitive Brain Research,* 3, 131–141.

RIZZOLATTI, G., FOGASSI, L., & GALLESE, V. (2005). Mirrors in the mind. *Scientific American, 295,* 54–61.

ROBERTS, K. (1988). Retrieval of a basic-level category in prelinguistic children. *Developmental Psychology,* 24, 21–27.

ROBERTS, K., & HOROWITZ, F. D. (1986). Basic level categorization in seven-and nine-month-old infants. *Journal of Child Language, 13,* 191–208.

ROCHAT, P. (2009). *Other minds: Social origins of self-consciousness.* New York: Cambridge University Press.

ROCHAT, P., & MORGAN, R. (1995). Spatial determinants in the perception of self-produced leg movements by 3- to 5-month-old infants. *Developmental Psychology, 31,* 626–636.

ROCHAT, P., & STRIANO, T. (2002). Who's in the mirror? Self-other discrimination in specular images by four- and nine-month-old infants. *Child Development, 73,* 35–46.

ROE, K. V., DRIVAS, A., KARAGELLIS, A., & ROE, A. (1985). Sex differences in vocal interaction with mother and stranger in Greek infants: Some cognitive implications. *Developmental Psychology, 21,* 372–377.

Roebers, C. M. (2002). Confidence judgments in children's and adults' event recall and suggestibility. *Developmental Psychology, 38,* 1052–1067.

ROEBERS, C. M., MOGA, N., & SCHNEIDER, W. (2001). The role of accuracy motivation on children's and adults' event recall. *Journal of Experimental Child Psychology, 78,* 313–329.

ROEBERS, C. M., & SCHNEIDER, W. (2001). Individual differences in children's eyewitness recall: The influence of intelligence and shyness. *Applied Developmental Science, 5,* 9–20.

ROGOFF, B. (1990). *Apprenticeship in thinking: Cognitive development in social context.* New York: Oxford University Press.

ROGOFF, B. (1998). Cognition as a collaborative process. In D. Kuhn & R. S. Siegler (Vol. Eds.), *Cognition language, and perceptual development,* Vol. 2, in W. Damon (Gen. Ed.), *Handbook of child psychology* (5th ed.). New York: Wiley.

ROGOFF, B. (2003). *The cultural nature of human development.* New York: Oxford University Press.

ROGOFF, B., MISTRY, J., GÖNCÜ, A., & MOSIER, C. (1993). Guided participation in cultural activity by toddlers and caregivers. *Monographs of the Society for Research in Child Development, 58* (Serial No. 236).

ROGOFF, B., & WADDELL, K. J. (1982). Memory for information organized in a scene by children from two cultures. *Child Development, 53,* 1224–1228.

ROHWER, W. D., JR., & LITROWNIK, J. (1983). Age and individual differences in the learning of a memorization procedure. *Journal of Educational Psychology, 75,* 799–810.

ROID, G. (2003). *Stanford-Binet Intelligence Scales* (5th ed.). Scarborough, Canada: Nelson Education.

ROMAN, A. A., KIRBY, J. R., PARRILA, P. K., WADE-WOOLLEY, L., & DEACON, S. H. (2009). Toward a comprehensive view of the skills involved in word reading in grades 4, 6, and 8. *Journal of Experimental Child Psychology, 102,* 96–113.

ROSCH, E. (1975). Cognitive representations of semantic categories. *Journal of Experimental Psychology: General, 7,* 192–233.

ROSE, S. A., & FELDMAN, J. F. (1995). Prediction of IQ and specific cognitive abilities at 11 years from infancy measures. *Developmental Psychology, 31,* 685–696.

ROSE, S. A., FELDMAN, J. F., JANKOWSKI, J. J., & CARO, D. M. (2002). A longitudinal study of visual expectation and reaction time in the first year of life. *Child Development, 73,* 47–61.

ROSE, S. A., FELDMAN, J. F., JANKOWSKI, J. J., & ROSSEM, R. V. (2005). Pathways from prematurity and infant abilities to later cognition. *Child Development, 76,* 1172–1184.

ROSE, S. A., FELDMAN, J. F., & WALLACE, I. F. (1992). Infant information processing in relation to six-year cognitive outcomes. *Child Development, 63,* 1126–1141.

ROSE, S. A., FELDMAN, J. F., WALLACE, I. F., & MCCARTON, C. (1989). Infant visual attention: Relation to birth status and developmental outcome during the first 5 years. *Developmental Psychology, 25,* 560–576.

ROSE, S. A., FELDMAN, J. F., WALLACE, I. F., & MCCARTON, C. (1991). Information processing at 1 year: Relation to birth status and developmental outcome during the

first 5 years. *Developmental Psychology, 27,* 723–737.

ROSE, S. A., GOTTFRIED, A. W., & BRIDGER, W. H. (1981). Cross-modal transfer in 6-month-old infants. *Developmental Psychology, 17,* 661–669.

ROSE, S., GOTTFRIED, A. W., MELLOY-CARMINAR, P., & BRIDGER, W. H. (1982). Familiarity and novelty preferences in infant recognition memory: Implications for information processing. *Developmental Psychology, 18,* 704–713.

ROSENGREN, K. S., & HICKLING, A. K. (1994). Seeing is believing: Children's explanations of commonplace, magical, and extraordinary transformations. *Child Development, 65,* 1605–1626.

ROSENTHAL, R., & JACOBSON, L. (1968). *Pygmalion in the classroom: Teacher expectation and pupils' intellectual development.* New York: Rinehart and Winston.

ROSENTHAL, R., & RUBIN, D. B. (1982). Further meta-analytic procedures for assessing cognitive gender differences. *Journal of Educational Psychology, 74,* 708–712.

ROTH, G., & DICKE, U. (2005). Evolution of the brain and intelligence. *Trends in Cognitive Sciences, 9,* 249–257.

ROVEE-COLLIER, C. (1999). The development of infant memory. *Current Directions in Psychological Science, 8,* 80–85.

ROVEE-COLLIER, C., & CUEVAS, K. (2009). The development of infant memory. In M. L. Courage & N. Cowan (Eds.), *The development of memory in infancy and childhood* (pp. 11–41). New York: Psychology Press.

ROVEE-COLLIER, C., SCHECHTER, A., SHYI, C.-W. G., & SHIELDS, P. (1992). Perceptual identification of contextual attributes and infant memory retrieval. *Developmental Psychology, 28,* 307–318.

ROVEE-COLLIER, C., & SHYI, C.-W. G. (1992). A functional and cognitive analysis of infant long-term retention. In M. L. Howe, C. J. Brainerd, & V. F. Reyna (Eds.), *Development of long-term retention.* New York: Springer-Verlag.

ROWE, D. C., JACOBSON, K. C., & VAN DER OORD, E. J. C. G. (1999). Genetic and environmental influences on vocabulary IQ: Parental education level as a moderator. *Child Development, 70,* 1151–1162.

Rowe, M. L., & Goldin-Meadow, S. (2009). Differences in early gesture explain SES disparities in child vocabulary size at school entry. *Science, 323*, 951–953.

Rubenstein, A. J., Kalakanis, L., & Langlois, J. H. (1999). Infant preferences for attractive faces: A cognitive explanation. *Developmental Psychology, 35*, 848–855.

Rubin, D. C. (2000). The distribution of early childhood memories. *Memory, 8*, 265–269.

Rubin, K. H., Fein, G., & Vandenberg, B. (1983). Play. In E. M. Hetherington (Ed.), *Handbook of child psychology*, Vol. 4, *Socialization, personality and social development*, (4th ed., pp. 693–774). New York: Wiley.

Rubin, K. H., & Krasnor, L. R. (1986). Social cognitive and social behavior perspectives on problem solving. In M. Perlmutter (Ed.), *Minnesota Symposium on Child Psychology*, Vol. 18. Hillsdale, NJ: Erlbaum.

Ruble, D. N., Balaban, T., & Cooper, J. (1981). Gender constancy and the effects of sex-typed televised toy commercials. *Child Development, 52*, 667–673.

Ruble, D. N., & Martin, C. L. (1998). Gender development. In N. Eisenberg (Vol. Ed.), *Social, emotional, and personality development*, Vol. 3, in W. Damon (Gen. Ed.), *Handbook of child psychology* (5th ed.). New York: Wiley.

Ruble, D. N., Martin, C. L., & Berenbaum, S. A. (2006). Gender development. In N. Eisenberg (Vol. Ed.), *Social, emotional, and personality development*, Vol. 3 (pp. 858–932), in W. Damon & R. M. Lerner (Gen. Eds.), *Handbook of child psychology* (6th ed.). Hoboken, NJ: Wiley.

Ruble, D. N., Taylor, L. J., Cyphers, L., Greulich, F. K., Lurye, L. E., & Shrout, P. E. (2007). The role of gender constancy in early gender development. *Child Development, 78*, 1121–1136.

Ruda, M. A., Ling, Q-D., Hohmann, A. G., Bo Peng, Y., & Tachibana, T. (2000). Altered nociceptive neuronal circuits after neonatal peripheral inflammation. *Science, 289*, (28 July), 628–630.

Ruff, H. A., & Birch, H. G. (1974). Infant visual fixation: The effect of concentricity, curvilinearity, and number of directions. *Journal of Experimental Child Psychology, 17*, 460–473.

Ruff, H. A., Capozzoli, M., & Weisberg, R. (1998). Age, individuality, and context as factors in sustained visual attention during the preschool years. *Developmental Psychology, 34*, 454–464.

Ruff, H. A., & Lawson, K. R. (1990). Development of sustained, focused attention in young children during free play. *Developmental Psychology, 26*, 85–93.

Ruff, H. A., Lawson, K. R., Parrinello, R., & Weissberg, R. (1990). Long-term stability of individual differences in sustained attention in the early years. *Child Development, 61*, 60–75.

Ruffman, T., Perner, J., Naito, M., Parkin, L., & Clements, W. A. (1998). Older (but not younger) siblings facilitate false belief understanding. *Developmental Psychology, 34*, 161–174.

Ruffman, T., Rustin, C., Garnham, W., & Parkin, A. (2001). Source monitoring and false memories in children: Relation to certainty and executive functioning. *Journal of Experimental Child Psychology, 80*, 95–111.

Ruffman, T., Slade, L., Devitt, K., & Crowe, E. (2006). What mothers say and what they do: The relation between parenting, theory of mind, language and conflict/cooperation. *British Journal of Developmental Psychology, 24*, 105–124.

Rugani, R., Fontanari, L., Simoni, E., Regolin, L., & Giorgio Vallortigara, G. (2009). Arithmetic in newborn chicks. *Proceedings of the Royal Society of London, Series B, 276*, 2451–2460.

Rumbaugh, D. M. (Ed.), (1977). *Language learning by a chimpanzee: The Lana project*. New York: Academic.

Rumbaugh, D. M., Beran, M. J., & Savage-Rumbaugh, E. S. (2003). Language. In D. Maestripieri (Ed.), *Primate psychology* (pp. 395–423). Cambridge, MA: Harvard University Press.

Russell, J., Mauthner, N., Sharpe, S., & Tidswell, T. (1991). The "windows tasks" as a measure of strategic deception in preschoolers and autistic subjects. *British Journal of Developmental Psychology, 9*, 331–349.

Rutter, M. (2006). *Genes and behavior: Nature-nurture interplay explained*. Malden, MA: Blackwell.

Rutter, M., & the English and Romanian Adoptees Study Team (1998). Developmental catch-up and deficit following adoptions after severe global and early deprivation. *Journal of Child Psychology and Psychiatry, 39*, 465–476.

Sabbagh, M. A., Xu, F., Carlson, S. M., Moses, L. J., & Lee, K. (2006). The development of executive functioning and theory of mind. *Psychological Science, 17*, 74–81.

Sabin, E. J., Clemmer, E. J., O'Connell, D. C., & Kowal, S. (1979). A pausological approach to speech development. In A. W. Siegman & S. Feldstein (Eds.), *Of speech and time: Temporal speech patterns in interpersonal contexts*. Hillsdale, NJ: Erlbaum.

Saccuzzo, D. P., Johnson, N. E., & Guertin, T. L. (1994). Information processing in gifted versus nongifted African American, Latino, Filipino, and white children: Speeded versus nonspeeded paradigms. *Intelligence, 19*, 219–243.

Sachs, J. (1977). The adaptive significance of linguistic input to prelinguistic infants. In C. E. Snow & C. A. Ferguson (Eds.), *Talking to children: Language input and acquisition*. Cambridge, UK: Cambridge University Press.

Sackett, P. R., Hardison, C. M., Cullen, M. J. (2004). On interpreting stereotype threat as accounting for African American-White differences on cognitive tests. *American Psychologist, 59*, 7–13.

Sacks, O. (1985). *The man who mistook his wife for a hat*. New York: Touchstone Books.

Sacks, O. (1989). *Seeing voices: A journey into the world of the deaf*. New York: Harper Perennial.

Saffran, J. R., & Aslin, R. N., & Newport, E. L. (1996). Statistical learning by 8-month-old infants. *Science, 274*, 1926–1928.

Saffran, J. R., & Griepentrog, G. J. (2001). Absolute pitch in infant auditory learning: Evidence for developmental reorganization. *Developmental Psychology, 37*, 74–85.

Saffran, J. R., Johnson, E. K., Aslin, R. N., & Newport, E. L. (1999). Statistical learning of tone sequences by human infants and adults. *Cognition, 70*, 27–52.

SAFFRAN, J., WERKER, J., & WERNER, L. A. (2006). The infant's auditory world: Hearing, speech and the beginnings of language. In D. Kuhn, & R. Siegler (Vol. Eds.), *Cognition, perception, and language,* Vol. 2, in W. Damon & R. M. Lerner (Gen. Eds.), *Handbook of child psychology* (6th ed.). New York: Wiley.

SAKAI, K. L. (2005). Language acquisition and brain development. *Science, 310,* 815–919.

SALAPATEK, P. (1975). Pattern perception in early infancy. In L. B. Cohen & P. Salapatek (Eds.), *Infant perception: From sensation to cognition,* Vol. 1. New York: Academic.

SALAPATEK, P., & KESSEN, W. (1966). Visual scanning of triangles by the human newborn. *Journal of Experimental Child Psychology, 3,* 155–167.

SALATAS, H., & FLAVELL, J. H. (1976). Behavioral and metamnemonic indicators of strategic behaviors under remember instructions in first grade. *Child Development, 47,* 81–89.

SALMON, K., CHAMPION, F., PIPE, M., MEWTON, L., & MCDONALD, S. (2008). The child in time: The influence of parent-child discussion about a future experience on how it is remembered. *Memory, 16,* 485–499.

SALMON, K., & PIPE, M.-E. (1997). Props and children's event reports: The impact of a 1-year delay. *Journal of Experimental Child Psychology, 65,* 261–292.

SAMEROFF, A. (2009a). The transactional model. In A. Sameroff (Ed.), *The transactional model of development: How children and contexts shape each other.* Washington, DC: American Psychological Association.

Sameroff, A. (ED.). (2009b). *The transactional model of development: How children and contexts shape each other.* Washington, DC: American Psychological Association.

SAMEROFF, A. (2010). A unified theory of development: A dialectic integration of nature and nurture. *Child Development, 81,* 6–22.

SAMEROFF, A. J., & CHANDLER, M. J. (1975). Reproductive risk and the continuum of caretaking causality. In F. D. Horowitz (Ed.), *Review of child development research,* Vol. 4. Chicago: University of Chicago Press.

SAMEROFF, A. J., SEIFER, R., BALDWIN, A., & BALDWIN, C. (1993). Stability of intelligence from preschool to adolescence: The influence of social risk factors. *Child Development, 64,* 80–97.

SANDBERG, E. H., & HUTTENLOCHER, J. (2001). Advanced spatial skills and advanced planning: Components of 6-year-olds navigational map use. *Journal of Cognition and Development, 2,* 51–70.

SANDMAN, C. A., WASHWA, P., HETRICK, W., PORTO, M., & PEEKE, H. V. S. (1997). Human fetal heart rate dishabituation between thirty and thirty-two weeks gestation. *Developmental Psychology, 68,* 1031–1040.

SAVAGE-RUMBAUGH, E. S. (1986). *Ape language: From conditioned response to symbol.* New York: Columbia University Press.

SAVAGE-RUMBAUGH, E. S., MURPHY, J., SEVCIK, R. A., BRAKKE, K. E., WILLIAMS, S. L., & RUMBAUGH, D. M. (1993). Language comprehension in ape and child. *Monographs of the Society for Research in Child Development, 58* (Serial No. 233).

SCARR, S. (1992). Developmental theories for the 1990s: Development and individual differences. *Child Development, 63,* 1–19.

SCARR, S. (1993). Biological and cultural diversity: The legacy of Darwin for development. *Child Development, 64,* 1333–1353.

SCARR, S., & MCCARTNEY, K. (1983). How people make their own environments: A theory of genotype-environment effects. *Child Development, 54,* 424–435.

SCARR, S., & WEINBERG, R. A. (1976). IQ test performance of black children adopted by white families. *American Psychologist, 31,* 726–739.

SCARR, S., & WEINBERG, R. A. (1978). The influence of "family background" on intellectual attainment. *American Sociological Review, 43,* 674–692.

SCHAAL, B., MARLIER, L., & SOUSSIGNAN, R. (2000). Human fetuses learn odors from their pregnant mother's diet. *Chemical Senses, 25,* 729–737.

SCHACTER, D. L. (1992). Understanding implicit memory. *American Psychologist, 47,* 559–569.

SCHACTER, D. L., NORMAN, K. A., & KOUTSTAAL, W. (2000). The cognitive neuroscience of constructive memory. In D. F. Bjorklund (Ed.), *False-memory creation in children and adults: Theory, research, and implications* (pp. 129–168). Mahwah, NJ: Erlbaum.

SCHAFER, G., & PLUNKETT, K. (1998). Rapid word learning by fifteen-month-olds under tightly controlled conditions. *Child Development, 69,* 309–320.

SCHANBERG, S. M., & FIELD, T. M. (1987). Sensory deprivation stress and supplemental stimulation in the rat pup and preterm human. *Child Development, 58,* 1431–1447.

SCHAUBLE, L. (1990). Belief revision in children: The role of prior knowledge and strategies for generating evidence. *Journal of Experimental Child Psychology, 49,* 31–57.

SCHAUBLE, L. (1996). The development of scientific reasoning in knowledge-rich context. *Developmental Psychology, 32,* 102–119.

SCHELLENBERG, E. G., & TREHUB, S. E. (1996). Natural musical intervals: Evidence from infant listeners. *Psychological Science, 5,* 272–277.

SCHELLENBERG, E. G., & TREHUB, S. E. (1999). Culture-general and culture-specific factors in the discrimination of melodies. *Journal of Experimental Child Psychology, 74,* 107–127.

SCHIEFELE, U., KRAPP, A., & WINTELER, A. (1992). Interest as a predictor of academic achievement: A meta-analysis of research. In K. A. Renninger, S. Hidi, & A. Krapp (Eds.), *The role of interest in learning and development.* Hillsdale, NJ: Erlbaum.

SCHIRDUAN, V., & CASE, K. S. (2004). Mindful curriculum leadership for students with attention deficit hyperactivity disorder: Leading in elementary schools by using Multiple Intelligences Theory (SUMIT). *Teachers College Record, 106,* 87–95.

SCHLAGMÜLLER, M., & SCHNEIDER, W. (2002). The development of organizational strategies in children: Evidence from a microgenetic longitudinal study. *Journal of Experimental Child Psychology, 81,* 298–319.

SCHLIEMANN, A. D. (1992). Mathematical concepts in and out of school in Brazil: From developmental psychology to better teaching. *Newsletter of the International Society for the Study of Behavioural*

*Development* (Serial No. 22, No. 2), 1–3.

SCHLOTTMANN, A., & RAY, E. (2010). Goal attribution to schematic animals: Do 6-month-old perceive biological motion as animate? *Developmental Science,* 13, 1–10.

SCHMIDT, M. E., PEMPEK, T. A., KIRKORIAN, H. L., LUND, A. F., & ANDERSON, D. R. (2008). The effects of background television on the toy play behavior of very young children. *Child Development,* 79, 1137–1151.

SCHNEIDER, W. (1986). The role of conceptual knowledge and metamemory in the development of organizational processes in memory. *Journal of Experimental Child Psychology,* 42, 218–236.

SCHNEIDER, W. (2009). Metacognition and metamemory development in childhood and adolescence. In H. S. Waters & W. Schneider (Eds.), *Metacognition, strategy use, and instruction* (pp. 54–83). New York: Guilford.

SCHNEIDER, W. (2010). Memory development in childhood. In U. Goswami (Ed.), *Blackwell handbook of childhood cognitive development* (2nd ed.). London, UK: Blackwell.

SCHNEIDER, W., & BJORKLUND, D. F. (1992). Expertise, aptitude, and strategic remembering. *Child Development,* 63, 461–473.

SCHNEIDER, W., & BJORKLUND, D. F. (1998). Memory. In R. S. Siegler & D. Kuhn (Eds.), *Cognitive, language, and perceptual development,* Vol. 2 (pp. 467–521), in W. Damon (Gen. Ed.), *Handbook of child psychology* (5th ed.). New York: Wiley.

SCHNEIDER, W., & BJORKLUND, D. F. (2003). Memory and knowledge development. In J. Valsiner & K. Connolly (Eds.), *Handbook of developmental psychology* (pp. 370–403). London: Sage.

SCHNEIDER, W., BJORKLUND, D. F., & MAIER-BRÜCKNER, W. (1996). The effects of expertise and IQ on children's memory: When knowledge is, and when it is not enough. *International Journal of Behavioral Development,* 19, 773–796.

Schneider, W., & Bullock, M. (EDS.). (2009). *Human development from early childhood to early adulthood: Findings from a 20-year longitudinal study.* New York: Psychology Press.

SCHNEIDER, W., GRUBER, H., GOLD, A., & OPWIS, K. (1993). Chess expertise and memory for chess positions in children and adults. *Journal of Experimental Child Psychology,* 56, 328–349.

SCHNEIDER, W., KNOPF, M., & SODIAN, B. (2009). Verbal memory development from early childhood to early adulthood. In W. Schneider & M. Bullock (Eds.), *Human development from early childhood to early adulthood: Findings from a 20-year longitudinal study* (pp. 63–90). New York, NY: Psychology Press.

SCHNEIDER, W., KNOPF, M., & STEFANEK, J. (2002). The development of verbal memory in childhood and adolescence: Findings from the Munich Longitudinal Study. *Journal of Educational Psychology,* 94, 751–761.

SCHNEIDER, W., KÖRKEL, J., & WEINERT, F. E. (1989). Domain-specific knowledge and memory performance: A comparison of high- and low-aptitude children. *Journal of Educational Psychology,* 81, 306–312.

SCHNEIDER, W., KRON-SPERL, V., & HÜNNERKOPF, M. (2009). The development of young children's memory strategies: Evidence from the Würzburg Longitudinal Memory Study. *European Journal of Developmental Psychology,* 6, 70–99.

SCHNEIDER, W., KRON, V., HÜNNERKOPF, M., & KRAJEWSKI, K. (2004). The development of young children's memory strategies: Findings from the Würzburg Longitudinal Memory Study. *Journal of Experimental Child Psychology,* 88, 193–209.

SCHNEIDER, W., KÜSPERT, P., ROTH, E., & VISÉ, M. (1997). Short- and long-term effects of training phonological awareness in kindergarten: Evidence from two German studies. *Journal of Experimental Child Psychology,* 66, 311–340.

SCHNEIDER, W., & LOCKL, K. (2002). The development of metacognitive knowledge in children and adolescents. In T. Perfect & B. Schwartz (Eds.), *Applied metacognition* (pp. 224–257). Cambridge, UK: Cambridge University Press.

SCHNEIDER, W., & NÄSLUND, J. C. (1999). The impact of early phonological processing skills on reading and spelling in school: Evidence from the Munich Longitudinal Study.

In F. E. Weinert & W. Schneider (Eds.), *The Munich Longitudinal Study on the Genesis of Individual Competencies (LOGIC).* Cambridge, UK: Cambridge University Press.

SCHNEIDER, W., & PRESSLEY, M. (1997). *Memory development between 2 and 20* (2nd ed.). Mahwah, NJ: Erlbaum.

SCHNEIDER, W., SCHLAGMÜLLER, M., & VISÉ, M. (1998). The impact of metamemory and domain-specific knowledge on memory performance. *European Journal of Psychology of Education,* 13, 91–103.

SCHNEIDER, W., & WEINERT, F. E. (1995). Memory development during early and middle childhood: Findings from the Munich Longitudinal Study (LOGIC). In F. E. Weinert & W. Schneider (Eds.), *Memory performance and competencies: Issues in growth and development.* Hillsdale, NJ: Erlbaum.

SCHULMAN, A. H., & KAPLOWITZ, C. (1977). Mirror-image response during the first two years of life. *Developmental Psychobiology,* 10, 133–142.

SCHUMANN-HENGSTELER, R. (1992). The development of visuo-spatial memory: How to remember location. *International Journal of Behavioral Development,* 15, 445–471.

SCHWANENFLUGEL, P. J., & NOYES, C. R. (1996). Context availability and the development of word reading skills. *Journal of Literary Research,* 28, 35–54.

SCHWENCK, C., BJORKLUND, D. F., & SCHNEIDER, W. (2007). Factors influencing the incidence of utilization deficiencies and other patterns of recall/strategy-use relations in a strategic memory task. *Child Development,* 78, 1771–1787.

SCHWENCK, C., BJORKLUND, D. F., & SCHNEIDER, W. (2009). Developmental and individual differences in young children's use and maintenance of a selective memory strategy. *Developmental Psychology,* 45, 1034–1050.

SCOTT, L. S., PASCALIS, O., & NELSON, C. A. (2007). A domain general theory of the development of perceptual discrimination. *Current Directions in Psychological Science,* 16, 197–201.

SEARLE, J. R. (1992). *The rediscovery of the mind.* Cambridge, MA: MIT Press.

SEGAL, N. (2000). Virtual twins: New findings on within-family environmental influences on intelligence. *Journal of Educational Psychology, 92*, 442–448.

SEGALOWITZ, S. J., & HISCOCK, M. (2002). The neuropsychology of normal development: Developmental neuroscience and a new constructivism. In S. J. Segalowitz & I. Rapin, (Eds.), *Handbook of neuropsychology* (2nd ed.), *Vol. 8, Part I: Child neuropsychology*. Amsterdam: Elsevier.

SENDEN, M. VON (1960). *Space and sight: The perception of space and shape in the congenitally blind before and after operation*. Glencoe, IL: Free Press.

SÉNÉCHAL, M., & LEFEVRE, J. (2002). Parental involvement in the development of children's reading skill: A five-year longitudinal study. *Child Development, 73*, 445–460.

SENGHAS, A., & COPPOLA, M. (2001). Children creating language: How Nicaraguan Sign Language acquired a spatial grammar. *Psychological Science, 12*, 323–326.

SENGHAS, A., KITA, S., & OZYÜREK, A. (2004). Children creating core properties of language: Evidence from an emerging sign language in Nicaragua. *Science, 305*, 1179–1782.

SERBIN, L. A., & SPRAFKIN, C. (1986). The saliency of gender and the process of sex typing in three- to seven-year-old children. *Child Development, 57*, 1188–1199.

SERESS, L. (2001). Morphological changes of the human hippocampal formation from midgestation to early childhood. In C. A. Nelson & M. Luciana (Eds.), *Handbook of developmental cognitive neuroscience* (pp. 45–58). Cambridge, MA: MIT Press.

SEYMOUR, P. H. K., ARO, M., & ERSKINE, J. M. (2003). Foundations of literacy acquisition in European orthographies. *British Journal of Psychology, 94*, 143–174.

SHACKELFORD, T. K., & LARSEN, R. J. (1997). Facial asymmetry as an indicator of psychological, emotional, and physiological distress. *Journal of Personality and Social Psychology, 72*, 456–466.

SHATZ, M. (1983). Communication. In J. H. Flavell & E. M. Markman (Eds.), *Cognitive development,* Vol. 3, in P. H. Mussen, *Handbook of child psychology* (4th ed.). New York: Wiley.

SHATZ, M., & GELMAN, R. (1973). The development of communication skills. *Monographs of the Society for Research in Child Development, 38* (Serial No. 152).

SHAW, P., ECKSTRAND, K., SHARP, W., BLUMENTHAL, J., LERCH, J. P., GREENSTEIN, D., CLASEN, L., EVANS, A., GIEDD, J., & RAPOPORT, J. L. (2007). Attention-deficit/hyperactivity disorder is characterized by a delay in cortical maturation. *Proceedings of the National Academy of Sciences of the United Sates of America, 104*, 19649–19654.

SHAW, P., GREENSTEIN, D., LERCH, J., CLASEN, L., LENROOT, R., GOGTAY, N., EVANS, A., RAPOPORT, J., & GIEDD, J. (2006). Intellectual ability and cortical development in children and adolescents. *Nature, 440*, 676–679.

SHAYWITZ, S. E., MODY, M., & SHAYWITZ, B. A. (2006). Neural mechanisms in dyslexia. *Current Directions on Psychological Science, 15*, 278–281.

SHAYWITZ, S. E., SHAYWITZ, B. A., PUGH, K. R., FULBRIGHT, R. K., CONSTABLE, R. T., MENCL, W. E., SHANKWEILER, D. P., LIBERMAN, A. M., SKUDLARSKI, P., FLETCHER, J. M., KATZ, L., MARCHIONE, K. E., LACADIE, C., GATENBY, C., & GORE, J. C. (1998). Functional disruption in the organization of the brain for reading in dyslexia. *Proceedings of the National Academy of Sciences of the United States of America, 95*, 2636–2641.

SHIN, H.-E., BJORKLUND, D. F., & BECK, E. F. (2007). The adaptive nature of children's overestimation in a strategic memory task. *Cognitive Development, 22*, 197–212.

SHINSKEY, J. L., & MUNAKATA, Y. (2005). Familiarity breeds searching: Infants reverse their novelty preferences when reaching for hidden objects. *Psychological Science, 16*, 596–600.

SHORE, J. R. (2004). Teacher education and Multiple Intelligences: A case study of multiple intelligences and teacher efficacy in two teacher preparation courses. *Teachers College Record, 106*, 112–139.

SHWE, H. I., & MARKMAN, E. M. (1997). Young children's appreciation of the mental impact of their communicative signals. *Developmental Psychology, 33*, 630–636.

SIEGAL, M. (2008). *Marvelous minds: The discovery of what children know*. Oxford, UK: Oxford University Press.

SIEGAL, M., & SHARE D. L. (1990). Contamination sensitivity in young children. *Developmental Psychology, 26*, 455–458.

SIEGEL, L. S. (1993). The cognitive basis of dyslexia. In R. Pasnak & M. L. Howe (Eds.), *Emerging themes in cognitive development: Vol. 2., Competencies*. New York: Springer-Verlag.

SIEGEL, L. S., & RYAN, E. B. (1988). Development of grammatical-sensitivity, phonological, and short-term memory skills in normally achieving and learning disabled children. *Developmental Psychology, 24*, 28–37.

SIEGEL, L. S., & RYAN, E. B. (1989). The development of working memory in normally achieving and subtypes of learning disabled children. *Child Development, 60*, 973–980.

SIEGLER, R. S. (1996). *Emerging minds: The process of change in children's thinking*. New York: Oxford University Press.

SIEGLER, R. S. (2000). The rebirth of children's learning. *Child Development, 71*, 26–35.

SIEGLER, R. S. (2002). Microgenetic studies of self-explanation. In N. Garnott & J. Parziale (Eds.), *Microdevelopment: A process-oriented perspective for studying development and learning* (pp. 31–58). Cambridge, MA: Cambridge University Press.

SIEGLER, R. S. (2006). Microgenetic analyses of learning. In D. Kuhn & R. S. Siegler (Vol. Eds.), *Cognition, perception, and language,* Vol. 2 (pp. 464–510), in W. Damon & R. M. Lerner (Gen. Eds.), *Handbook of Child Psychology* (6th ed.). New York: Wiley.

SIEGLER, R. S. (2009). Improving the numerical understanding of children from low-income families. *Child Development Perspectives, 3*, 118–124.

SIEGLER, R. S., & ELLIS, S. (1996). Piaget on childhood. *Psychological Science, 7*, 211–215.

SIEGLER, R. S., & JENKINS. E. (1989). *How children discover strategies*. Hillsdale, NJ: Erlbaum.

SIEGLER, R. S., & MU, Y. (2008). Chinese children excel on novel mathematics problems even before elementary school. *Psychological Science, 19,* 759–763.

SIEGLER, R. S., & RAMANI, G. B. (2009). Playing linear number board games—but not circular one—simproves low-income preschoolers' numerical understanding. *Journal of Educational Psychology, 101,* 545–560.

SIEGLER, R. S., & SHRAGER, J. (1984). Strategy choices in addition and subtraction: How do children know what to do? In C. Sophian (Ed.), *Origins of cognitive skills.* Hillsdale, NJ: Erlbaum.

SIEGLER, R. S., & SVETINA, M. (2002). A microgenetic/cross-sectional study of matrix completion: Comparing short-term and long-term change. *Child Development, 73,* 793–809.

SIGEL, I. E. (1987). Does hothousing rob children of their childhood? *Early Childhood Research Quarterly, 2,* 211–225.

SIGMAN, M., COHEN, S. E., BECKWITH, L., & PARMELEE, A. H. (1986). Infant attention in relation to intellectual abilities in childhood. *Developmental Psychology, 22,* 788–792.

SIGMAN, M., NEWMANN, C., CARTER, E., CATTLE, D., D'SOUZA, S., & BWIDO, N. (1988). Home interactions and the development of Embu toddlers in Kenya. *Child Development, 59,* 1251–1261.

SIGNORELLA, M. L., BIGLER, R. S., & LIBEN, L. S. (1993). Developmental differences in children's gender schemata about others: A meta-analytic review. *Developmental Review, 13,* 147–183.

SIGNORELLA, M. L., JAMISON, W., & KRUPA, M. H. (1989). Predicting spatial performance from gender stereotyping in activity preferences and in self-concept. *Developmental Psychology, 25,* 89–95.

SILVERMAN, I., & EALS, M. (1992). Sex differences in spatial abilities: Evolutionary theory and data. In J. H. Barkow, L. Cosmides, & J. Tooby (Eds.), *The adapted mind: Evolutionary psychology and the generation of culture.* New York: Oxford.

SIMCOCK, G., & DELOACHE, J. (2006). Get the picture? The effects of iconicity on toddlers' re-enactment from picture books. *Developmental Psychology, 42,* 1352–1357.

SIMCOCK, G., & HAYNE, H. (2002). Breaking the barrier? Children fail to translate their preverbal memories into language. *Psychological Science, 13,* 225–231.

SIMON, T. J., HESPOS, S. J., & ROCHAT, P. (1995). Do infants understand simple arithmetic? A replication of Wynn (1992). *Cognitive Development, 10,* 253–269.

SKEELS, H. M. (1966). Adult status of children with contrasting early life experiences. *Monographs of the Society for Research in Child Development, 31* (Serial No. 105).

SKINNER, B. F. (1957). *Verbal behavior.* New York: Appleton-Century-Crofts.

SKOCZENSKI, A. M., & NORCIA, A. M. (2002). Late maturation of visual hyperacuity. *Psychological Science, 13,* 537–541.

SKOUTERIS, H., SPATARO, J., & LAZARIDS, M. (2006). Young children's use of a delayed video representation to solve a retrieval problem pertaining to self. *Developmental Science, 9,* 505–517.

SLABY, R. G., & FREY, K. S. (1975). Development of gender constancy and selective attention to same-sex models. *Child Development, 46,* 849–856.

SLABY, R. G., & GUERRA, N. G. (1988). Cognitive mediators of aggression in adolescent offenders: 1. Assessment. *Developmental Psychology, 24,* 580–588.

SLATER, A. (1995). Visual perception and memory at birth. In C. Rovee-Collier & L. P. Lipsitt (Eds.), *Advances in infancy research,* Vol. 9. Norwood, NJ: Ablex.

SLATER, A., COOPER, R., ROSE, D., & MORISON, V. (1989). Prediction of cognitive performance from infancy to early childhood. *Human Development, 32,* 137–147.

SLATER, A., MATTOCK, A., & BROWN, E. (1990). Size constancy at birth: Newborn infants' responses to retinal and real size. *Journal of Experimental Child Psychology, 49,* 314–322.

SLATER, A. M., MATTOCK, A., BROWN, E., & BREMNER, G. J. (1991). Form perception at birth: Cohen and Younger (1984) revisited. *Journal of Experimental Child Psychology, 51,* 395–406.

SLATER, A. M., QUINN, P. C., HAYES, R., & BROWN, E. (2000). The role of facial orientation in newborn infants' preference for attractive faces. *Developmental Science, 3,* 181–185.

SLATER, A. M., VON DER SCHULENBURGB, C., BROWN, E., BADENOCHB, M., BUTTERWORTH, G., & PARSONS, S. (1998). Newborn infants prefer attractive faces. *Infant Behavior and Development, 21,* 345–354.

SLAUGHTER, V., JAAKKOLA, K., & CAREY, S. (1999). Constructing a coherent theory: Children's biological understanding of life and death. In M. Siegel & C. Peterson (Eds.), *Children's understanding of biology and health* (pp. 71–98). Cambridge, UK: Cambridge University Press.

SLOBIN, D. I. (1970). Universals of grammatical development in children. In G. B. Flores, J. Arcais, & W. J. M. Levelt (Eds.), *Advances in psycholinguistics.* Amsterdam, The Netherlands: North-Holland.

SMITH, P. K. (1982). Does play matter? Functional and evolutionary aspects of animal and human play. *Behavioral and Brain Sciences, 5,* 139–184.

SMITH, P. K. (2005). Social and pretend play in children. In A. D. Pellegrini & P. K. Smith (Eds.), *Play in humans and great apes* (pp. 173–209). Mahwah, NJ: Erlbaum.

SMITH, P. K., & CONNOLLY, K. (1980). *The ecology of preschool behavior.* London: Cambridge University Press.

SMITH, P. K., & DUTTON, S. (1979). Play and training in direct and innovative problem solving. *Child Development, 50,* 830–836.

SMITH, R. E., BAYEN, U. J., & MARTIN, C. (2010). The cognitive processes underlying event-based prospective memory in school age children and young adults: A formal model-based study. *Developmental Psychology, 46,* 230–244.

SMITSMAN, A. W., & BONGERS, R. M. (2002). Tool use and tool making: A developmental action perspective. In J. Valsiner & K. J. Connolly (Ed.), *Handbook of developmental psychology* (pp. 172–193). London: Sage.

SNEDECKER, J., GEREN, J., & SHAFTO, C. L. (2007). Starting over: International adoption as a natural experiment in language development. *Psychological Science, 18,* 79–87.

SNOW, C. (1972). Mother's speech to children learning language. *Child Development, 43,* 549–565.

SNOW, C. E., ARLMAN-RUPP, A., HASSING, Y., JOBSE, J., JOOSTEN, J., & VORSTER, J. (1976). Mothers' speech in three social classes. *Journal of Psycholinguistic Research, 5,* 1–20.

SNOW, C. E., & FERGUSON C. A. (EDS.). (1977). *Talking to children: Language input and acquisition.* Cambridge, UK: Cambridge University Press.

SNOW, C. E., & YUSUN KANG, J. (2006). Becoming bilingual, biliterate, and bicultural. In K. A. Renninger & I. E. Sigel (Vol. Eds.), *Child psychology in practice,* Vol. 4, in W. Damon (Gen. Ed.), *Handbook of child psychology* (6th ed.). New York: Wiley.

SOCHA, T. J., & SOCHA, D. M. (1994). Children's task-group communication. In L. R. Frey (Ed.), *Group communication in context: Studies of natural groups.* Hillsdale, NJ: Erlbaum.

SODIAN, B., & SCHNEIDER, W. (1999). Memory strategy development: Gradual increase, sudden insight, or roller coaster? In F. E. Weinert & W. Schneider (Eds.), *Individual development from 3 to 12: Findings from the Munich longitudinal study.* Cambridge, UK: Cambridge University Press.

SODIAN, B., SCHNEIDER, W., & PERLMUTTER, M. (1986). Recall, clustering, and metamemory in young children. *Journal of Experimental Child Psychology, 41,* 395–410.

SODIAN, B., TAYLOR, C., HARRIS, P. L., & PERNER, J. (1991). Early deception and the child's theory of mind: False trails and genuine markers. *Child Development, 62,* 468–483.

SOLEY, G., & HANNON, E. E. (2010). Infants prefer the musical meter of their own culture: A cross-cultural comparison. *Developmental Psychology, 46,* 286–292.

SOMEL, M., FRANZ, H., YAN, Z., LOREC, A., GUO, S., GIGER, T., KELSO, J., NICKEL, B., DANNEMANN, M., BAHN, S., WEBSTER, M. J., WEICKERT, C., LACHMANN, M., PÄÄBO, S., & KHAITOVICH, P. (2009). Transcriptional neoteny in the human brain. *Proceedings of the National Academy of Sciences, USA, 106,* 5743–5748.

SOMERVILLE, S. C., WELLMAN, H. M., & CULTICE, J. C. (1983). Young children's deliberate reminding. *Journal of Genetic Psychology, 143,* 87–96.

SONG, H., & BAILLARGEON, R. (2008). Infants' reasoning about others'

false perceptions. *Developmental Psychology, 44,* 1789–1795.

SONGUA-BARKE, E. J. S., TAYLOR, E., SEMBI, S., & SMITH, J. (1992). Hyperactivity and delay aversion—I. The effect of delay on choice. *Journal of Child Psychology and Psychiatry, 33,* 399–409.

SOPHIAN, C. (1997). Beyond competence: The significance of performance for conceptual development. *Cognitive Development, 12,* 281–303.

SOUTHGATE, V., JOHNSON, M. H., OSBORNE, T., & CSIBRA, G. (2009). Predictive motor activation during action observation in human infants. *Biology Letters, 5,* 769–772.

SOWELL, E. R., THOMPSON, P. M., HOLMES, C. J., JERNIGAN, T. L., & TOGA, A. W. (1999). In vivo evidence for postadolescent brain maturation in frontal and striatal regions. *Nature Neuroscience, 1,* 859–861.

SPEAR, L. P. (2000). Neurobehavioral changes in adolescence. *Current Directions in Psychological Science, 9,* 111–114.

SPEAR, L. P. (2007). Brain development and adolescent behavior. In D. Coch, K. W. Fischer, & G. - Dawson (Eds.), *Human behavior, learning, and the developing brain: Typical development* (pp. 362–396). New York: Guilford.

SPEARMAN, C. (1927). *The abilities of man.* New York: Macmillan.

SPELKE, E. S. (1976). Infants' intermodal perception of events. *Cognitive Psychology, 5,* 553–560.

SPELKE, E. S. (1985). Perception of unity, persistence and identity: Thoughts on infants' conceptions of objects. In J. Mehler & R. Fox (Eds.), NJ: Erlbaum *Neonate cognition.* Hillsdale, NJ: Erlbaum.

SPELKE, E. S. (1991). Physical knowledge in infancy: Reflections on Piaget's theory. In S. Carey & R. Gelman (Eds.), *Epigenesis of mind: Essays in biology and knowledge.* Hillsdale, NJ: Erlbaum.

SPELKE, E. S. (2000). Core knowledge. *American Psychologist, 55,* 1233–1243.

SPELKE, E. S., & CORTELYOU, A. (1981). Perceptual aspects of social knowing: Looking and listening in infancy. In M. E. Lamb & L. R. Sherrod (Eds.), *Infant social cognition: Empirical and theoretical considerations.* Hillsdale, NJ: Erlbaum.

SPELKE, E. S., & KINZLER, K. D. (2007). Core knowledge. *Developmental Science, 10,* 89–96.

SPELKE, E. S., & NEWPORT, E. L. (1998). Nativism, empiricism, and the development of knowledge. In R. Learner (Vol. Ed.), *Theories of theoretical models of human development,* Vol. 1 (pp. 275–340), in W. Damon (Gen. Ed.), *Handbook of child psychology* (5th ed.). New York: Wiley.

SPENCE, M. J. (1996). Young infants' long-term auditory memory: Evidence for changes in preference as a function of delay. *Developmental Psychobiology, 29,* 685–695.

SPENCE, M. J., & FREEMAN, M. S. (1996). Newborn infants prefer the maternal low-pass filtered voice, but not the maternal whispered voice. *Infant Behavior and Development, 19,* 199–212.

SPENCER, J. P., BLUMBERG, M. S., McMURRAY, B., ROBINSON, S. R., SAMUELSON, L. K., & TOMBLIN, J. B. (2009). Short arms and talking legs: Why we should no longer abide the nativist-empiricist debate. *Child Development Perspectives, 3,* 79–87.

SPENCER, S. J., STEELE, C. M., & QUINN, D. M. (1999). Stereotype threat and women's math performance. *Journal of Experimental Social Psychology, 35,* 4–28.

SPINATH, B., PINATH, F. M., HARLAAR, N., & PLOMIN, R. (2006). Predicting school achievement from general cognitive ability, self-perceived ability, and intrinsic value. *Intelligence, 34,* 363–374.

SPITZ, R. (1945). Hospitalism: An inquiry into the genesis of psychiatric conditions in early childhood. *Psychoanalytic Study of the Child, 1,* 53–74.

SPREEN, O., RISSER, A., & EDGELL, D. (1995). *Developmental neuropsychiatry.* New York: Oxford University Press.

SPRINGER, K. (1999). How a naïve theory of biology is acquired. In M. Siegal & C. C. Peterson (Eds.), *Children's understanding of biology and health* (pp. 45–70). Cambridge, UK: Cambridge University Press.

STAKE, J. E., & NICKENS, S. D. (2005). Adolescent girls' and boys' science peer relationship and perceptions of the possible self as scientist. *Sex Roles, 52,* 1–12.

STANLEY, J. C., BENBOW, C. P., BRODY, L. E., DAUBER, S., & LUPKOWSKI, A. E. (1992). Gender differences on eighty-six nationally standardized aptitude and achievement tests. In N. Coangelo, S. G. Assouline, & D. L. Ambroson (Eds.), *Talent development*. Unionville, NY: Trillium.

STANOVICH, K. E. (1986). Matthew effects in reading: Some consequences of individual differences in the acquisition of literacy. *Reading Research Quarterly, 21,* 360–406.

STEELE, C. M. (1997). A threat in the air: How stereotypes shape intellectual identity and performance. *American Psychologist, 52,* 613–629.

STEELE, C. M., & ARONSON, J. (1995). Stereotype threat and the intellectual test performance of African Americans. *Journal of Social and Personality Psychology, 69,* 797–811.

STEINER, J. E. (1979). Human facial expressions in response to taste and smell stimulation. In H. W. Reese & L. P. Lipsitt (Eds.), *Advances in child development and behavior,* Vol. 13 (pp. 257–295). New York: Academic.

STERN, D. N., SPIEKER, S., BARNETT, R. K., & MACKAIN, K. (1983). The prosody of maternal speech: Infant age and context related changes. *Journal of Child Language, 10,* 1–15.

STERN, D. N., SPIEKER, S., & MACKAIN, K. (1982). Intonation contours as signals in maternal speech to prelinguistic infants. *Developmental Psychology, 18,* 727–735.

STERNBERG, K. J., LAMB, M. E., ORBACH, Y., ESPLIN, P. W., & MITCHELL, S. (2001). Use of a structured investigative protocol enhances young children's responses to free recall prompts in the course of forensic interviews. *Journal of Applied Psychology, 86,* 997–1005.

STERNBERG, R. J. (1985). *Beyond IQ: A triarchic theory of human intelligence.* Cambridge, UK: Cambridge University Press.

STERNBERG, R. J. (1997). The concept of intelligence and its role in lifelong learning and success. *American Psychologist, 52,* 1030–1037.

STERNBERG, R. S. (1999). The theory of successful intelligence. *Review of General Psychology, 3,* 292–316.

STERNBERG, R. J. (2004). Culture and intelligence. *American Psychologist, 59,* 325–338.

STERNBERG, R. J., FERRARI, M., & CLINKENBEARD, P. (1996). Identification, instruction, and assessment of gifted children: A construct validation of a triarchic model. *Gifted Child Quarterly, 40,* 129–137.

STERNBERG, R. J., & THE RAINBOW PROJECT COLLABORATORS (2006). The Rainbow Project: Enhancing the SAT through assessments of analytical, practical, and creative skills. *Intelligence, 34,* 321–350.

STERNBERG, R. J., TORFF, B., & GRIGORENKO, E. L. (1998). Teaching triachically improves school achievement. *Journal of Educational Psychology, 90,* 374–384.

STEVENSON, H. W., & LEE, S. Y. (1990). Context of achievement. *Monographs of the Society for Research in Child Development, 55* (Serial No. 221).

STILES, J. (2008). *The fundamentals of brain development.* Cambridge, MA: Harvard University Press.

STILES, J. (2009). On genes, brains, and behavior: Why should developmental psychologists care about brain development? *Child Development Perspectives, 3,* 196–202.

STILES, J., REILLY, J., PAUL, B., & MOSES, P. (2005). Cognitive development following early brain injury: Evidence for neural adaptation. *Trends in Cognitive Sciences, 9,* 136–143.

STIPEK, D. (1984). Young children's performance expectations: Logical analysis or wishful thinking? In J. G. Nicholls (Ed.), *Advances in motivation and achievement: Vol. 3. The development of achievement motivation.* Greenwich, CT: JAI.

STIPEK, D., & DANIELS, D. (1988). Declining perceptions of competence: A consequence of changes in the child or the educational environment? *Journal of Educational Psychology, 80,* 352–356.

STIPEK, D., FEILER, R., BLYER, P., RYAN, R., MILBURN, S., & SALMON, J. M. (1998). Good beginnings: What difference does the program make in preparing children for school. *Journal of Applied Developmental Psychology, 19,* 41–46.

STIPEK, D., FEILER, R., DANIELS, D., & MILBURN, S. (1995). Effects of different instructional approaches on young children's achievement and motivation. *Child Development, 66,* 209–223.

STOCK, R., DESOETE, A., & ROEYERS, H. (2009). Mastery of the counting principles in toddlers: A crucial step in the development of budding arithmetic abilities? *Learning and Individual Differences, 19,* 419–422.

STODDART, T., & TURIEL, E. (1985). Children's concepts of cross-gender activities. *Child Development, 56,* 1241–1252.

STOEL-GAMMON, C., & MENN, L. (1997). Phonological development: Learning sounds and sound patterns. In J. Berko Gleason (Ed.), *The development of language* (4th ed.). Boston: Allyn & Bacon.

STONE, C. A., & DAY, M. C. (1978). Levels of availability of a formal operational strategy. *Child Development, 49,* 1054–1065.

STONE, L. J., & CHURCH, J. (1973). *Childhood and adolescence: A psychology of the growing person.* New York: Random House.

STOOLMILLER, M. (1999). Implications of the restricted range of family environments for estimates of heritability and nonshared environment in behavior genetic adoption studies. *Psychological Bulletin, 125,* 393–407.

STORCH, S. A., & WHITEHURST, G. J. (2002). Oral language and code-related precursors to reading: Evidence from a longitudinal structural model. *Developmental Psychology, 38,* 934–947.

STRERI, A., LHOTE, M., & DUTILLEUL, S. (2000). Haptic perception in newborns. *Developmental Science, 3,* 319–327.

STRERI, A., & SPELKE, E. S. (1989). Effects of motion and figural goodness on haptic object perception in infancy. *Child Development, 60,* 1111–1125.

STRIANO, T., TOMASELLO, M., & ROCHAT, P. (2001). Social and object support for early symbolic play. *Developmental Science, 4,* 442–455.

SUDDENDORF, T. (2003). Early representational insight: Twenty-four-month-olds can use a photo to find an object in the world. *Child Development, 74,* 896–904.

SUDDENDORF, T., & CORBALLIS, M. C. (2007). The evolution of foresight: What is mental time travel, and is it unique to humans? *Behavioral and Brain Sciences, 30,* 299–313.

SULLIVAN, K., & WINNER, E. (1991). When 3-year-olds understand ignorance, false belief and representational change. *British Journal of*

*Developmental Psychology, 9,* 159–171.

SULLIVAN, K., & WINNER, E. (1993). Three-year-olds' understanding of mental states: The influence of trickery. *Journal of Experimental Child Psychology, 56,* 135–148.

SULLIVAN, M. W., ROVEE-COLLIER, C. K., & TYNES, D. M. (1979). A conditioning analysis of infant long-term memory. *Child Development, 50,* 152–162.

SUNDET, J. M., ERIKSEN, W., & TAMBS, K. (2008). Intelligence correlations between brothers decrease with increasing age differences: Evidence for shared environmental effects in young adults. *Psychological Science, 19,* 843–847.

SUOMI, S., & HARLOW, H. (1972). Social rehabilitation of isolate-reared monkeys. *Developmental Psychology, 6,* 487–496.

SUSSMAN, A. L. (2001). Reality monitoring of performed and imagined interactive events: Developmental and contextual effects. *Journal of Experimental Child Psychology, 79,* 115–138.

SUZUKI, L. A., & VALENCIA, R. R. (1997). Race-ethnicity and measured intelligence: Educational implications. *American Psychologist, 52,* 1103–1114.

SWANSON, H. L., & JERMAN, O. (2007). The influence of working-memory on reading growth in subgroups of children with reading disabilities. *Journal of Experimental Child Psychology, 96,* 249–283.

SWANSON, H. L., & SACHSE-LEE, C. (2001). Mathematical problem solving and working memory in children with learning disabilities: Both executive and phonological processes are important. *Journal of Experimental Child Psychology, 79,* 294–321.

SYMONS, D. K., PETERSON, C. C., SLAUGHTER, V., ROCHE, J., & DOYLE, E. (2005). Theory of mind and mental state discourse during book reading and story-telling tasks. *British Journal of Developmental Psychology, 23,* 81–102.

SZKRYBALO, J., & RUBLE, D. N. (1999). "God made me a girl": Sex-category constancy judgments and explanations revisited. *Developmental Psychology, 35,* 393–402.

SZPUNAR, K. K. (2010). Episodic future thought: An emerging concept. *Perspectives on Psychological Science, 5,* 142–162.

TALWAR, V., & LEE, K. (2002). Development of lying to conceal a transgression: Children's control of expressive behavior during verbal deception. *International Journal of Behavioral Development, 26,* 436–444.

TAMIS-LEMONDA, C. S., & BORNSTEIN, M. H. (1989). Habituation and maternal encouragement of attention in infancy as predictors of toddler language, play, and representational competence. *Child Development, 60,* 738–751.

TANNER, J. M. (1978). *Fetus into man: Physical growth from conception to maturity.* Cambridge, MA: Harvard University Press.

TARDIF, T., & WELLMAN, H. M. (2000). Acquisition of mental state language in Mandarin- and Cantonese-speaking children. *Developmental Psychology, 36,* 25–43.

TAUMOEPEAU, M., & RUFFMAN, T. (2006). Mother and infant talk about mental states relates to desire language and emotion understanding. *Child Development, 77,* 465–481.

TAUMOEPEAU, M., & RUFFMAN, T. (2008). Stepping stones to others' minds: Maternal talk relates to child mental state language and emotion understanding at 15, 24 and 33 months. *Child Development, 79,* 284–302.

TAYLOR, M. (1999). *Imaginary companions and the children who create them.* New York: Oxford University Press.

TAYLOR, M. J., BATTY, M., & ITIER, R. J. (2004). The faces of development: A review of early face processing over childhood. *Journal of Cognitive Neuroscience, 16,* 1426–1442.

TAYLOR, M., & FLAVELL, J. H. (1984). Seeing and believing: Children's understanding of the distinction between appearance and reality. *Child Development, 55,* 1710–1720.

TEASDALE, T. W., & OWEN, D. R. (1989). Continuing secular increases in intelligence and a stable prevalence of high intelligence levels. *Intelligence, 13,* 255–262.

TEASDALE, T. W., & OWEN, D. R. (2008). Secular declines in cognitive test scores: A reversal of the Flynn effect. *Intelligence, 36,* 121–126.

TEASLEY, S. D. (1995). The role of talk in children's peer collaborations. *Developmental Psychology, 31,* 207–220.

TERMAN, L. M., & MERRILL, M. A. (1937). *Measuring intelligence.* Boston: Houghton Mifflin.

TERRANCE, H. S., PETITTO, L. A., SANDERS, R. J., & BEVER, T. G. (1979). Can an ape create a sentence? *Science, 206,* 891–900.

THELEN, E., & SMITH, L. B. (1994). *A dynamic systems approach to the development of cognition and action.* Cambridge, MA: MIT Press.

THELEN, E., & SMITH, L. B. (1998). Dynamic systems theories. In R. M. Lerner (Vol. Ed.), *Theoretical models of human development,* Vol. 1, in W. Damon (Gen. Ed.), *Handbook of child psychology* (5th ed.). New York: Wiley.

THELEN, E., & SMITH, L. B. (2006). Dynamic systems theories. In R. M. Lerner (Vol. Ed.), *Theoretical models of human development,* Vol. 1 (pp. 258–312), in W. Damon & R. M. Lerner (Gen. Eds.), *Handbook of Child Psychology* (6th ed.). New York: Wiley.

THIBAUT, J.-P., FRENCH, R. M., & VEZNEVA, M. (2010). The development of analogy-making in children: Cognitive load and executive function. *Journal of Experimental Child Psychology, 106,* 1–19.

THIERRY, K. L., & SPENCE, M. J. (2002). Source-monitoring training facilitates preschoolers' eyewitness memory performance. *Developmental Psychology, 38,* 428–437.

THOMAS, L. (1993). *The fragile species.* New York: Charles Scribner's Sons.

THOMAS, S. C., & JOHNSON, M. H. (2008). New advances in understanding sensitive periods in brain development. *Current Directions in Psychology Science, 17,* 1–5.

THOMPSON, D. E., & RUSSELL, J. (2004). The ghost condition: Imitation versus emulation in young children's observational learning. *Developmental Psychology, 40,* 882–889.

THOMPSON, J. R., & CHAPMAN, R. S. (1977). Who is "Daddy" revisited? The status of two-year-olds' overextended words in use and comprehension. *Journal of Child Language, 4,* 359–375.

TILLMAN, C. M., NYBERG, L., & BOHLIN, G. (2008). Working memory components and intelligence in children. *Intelligence, 36,* 394–402.

TIMNEY, B., MITCHELL, D. E., & CYNADER, M. (1980). Behavioral evidence for prolonged sensitivity to effects of monocular deprivation in dark-reared cats. *Journal of Neurophysiology, 43,* 1041–1054.

TINBERGEN, N. (1951). *The study of instinct.* New York: Oxford University Press.

TOMASELLO, M. (1999). *The cultural origins of human cognition.* Cambridge, MA: Harvard University Press.

TOMASELLO, M. (2000). Culture and cognitive development. *Current Directions in Psychological Science, 9,* 37–40.

TOMASELLO, M. (2005). *Constructing a language: A usage-based theory of language acquisition.* Cambridge, MA: Harvard University Press.

TOMASELLO, M. (2006). Acquiring linguistic constructions. In D. Kuhn, & R. Siegler (Vol. Eds.), *Cognition, perception, and language,* Vol. 2 (pp. 255–298), in W. Damon & R. M. Lerner (Gen. Eds.), *Handbook of child psychology* (6th ed.). New York: Wiley.

TOMASELLO, M. (2008). *Origins of human communication.* Cambridge, MA: MIT Press.

TOMASELLO, M., & CALL, J. (1997). *Primate cognition.* New York: Oxford University Press.

TOMASELLO, M., CALL, J., & HARE, B. (2005). Chimpanzees understand psychological states—the question is which ones and to what extent. *Trends in Cognitive Science, 7,* 153–156.

TOMASELLO, M., & CARPENTER, M. (2005). The emergence of social cognition in three young chimpanzees. *Monographs of the Society for Research in Child Development, 70* (Serial No. 279).

TOMASELLO, M., & CARPENTER, M. (2007). Shared intentionality. *Developmental Science, 10,* 121–125.

TOMASELLO, M., CARPENTER, M., & LISZKOWSKI, U. (2007). A new look at infant pointing. *Child Development, 78,* 705–722.

TOMASELLO, M., KRUGER, A. C., & RATNER, H. H. (1993). Cultural learning. *Behavioral and Brain Sciences, 16,* 495–511.

TOMASELLO, M., & MOLL, H. (2010). The gap is social: Human shared intentionality and culture. *Mind the gap: Tracing the origins of human universals* (pp. 331–350). New York: Springer.

TOMASELLO, M., SAVAGE-RUMBAUGH, S., & KRUGER, A. C. (1993). Imitative learning of actions on objects by children, chimpanzees, and enculturated chimpanzees. *Child Development, 64,* 1688–1705.

TONDEL, G. M., & CANDY, T. R. (2008). Accommodation and vergence latencies in human infants. *Vision Research, 48,* 564–576.

TONKOVA-YOMPOL'SKAYA, R. V. (1969). Development of speech intonation in infants during the first two years of life. *Soviet Psychology, 7,* 48–54.

TOOBY, J., & COSMIDES, L. (1992). The psychological foundations of culture. In J. H. Barkow, L. Cosmides, & J. Tooby (Eds.), *The adapted mind: Evolutionary psychology and the generation of culture.* New York: Oxford University Press.

TOOBY, J., & COSMIDES, L. (2005). Conceptual foundations of evolutionary psychology. In D. M. Buss (Ed.), *Handbook of evolutionary psychology* (pp. 5–67). Hoboken, NJ: Wiley.

TOTTENHAM, N., HARE, T. A., QUINN, B. T., MCCARRY, T. W., NURSE, M., GILHOOLY, T., GALVAN, A., DAVIDSON, M. C., EIGSTI, I-M., THOMAS, K. M., FREED, P., BOOMA, E. S., GUNNAR, M., ALTEMUS, M., ARONSON, J., & CASEY, B. J. (2010). Prolonged institutional rearing is associated with atypically large amygdala volume and difficulties in emotional regulation. *Developmental Science, 13,* 46–61.

TRAINOR, L. J. (1996). Infant preferences for infant-directed versus noninfant-directed playsongs and lullabies. *Infant Behavior and Development, 19,* 83–92.

TRAINOR, L. J., AUSTIN, C. M., & DESJARDINS, R. N. (2000). Is infant-directed speech prosody a result of the vocal expression of emotion? *Psychological Science, 11,* 188–195.

TRAINOR, L. J., & HEINMILLER, B. M. (1998). The development of evaluative responses to music: Infants prefer to listen to consonance over dissonance. *Infant Behavior and Development, 21,* 77–88.

TRAUTNER, H. M., RUBLE, D. N., CYPHERS, L., KIRSTEN, B., BEHRENDT, R., & HARTMANN, P. (2005). Rigidity and flexibility of gender stereotypes in children: Developmental or differential? *Infant and Child Development, 14,* 365–380.

TREHUB, S. E. (1976). The discrimination of foreign speech contrasts by infants and adults. *Child Development, 47,* 466–472.

TREHUB, S. E. (2003). The developmental origins of musicality. *Nature Neuroscience, 6,* 669–673.

TREHUB, S. E., & NAKATA, T. (2001–2002). Emotion and music in infancy. *Musicae Scientiae* (special issue), 37–61.

TREHUB, S. E., & SCHELLENBERG, E. G. (1995). Music: Its relevance to infants. *Annals of Child Development, 11,* 1–24.

TREHUB, S. E., TRAINOR, L. J., & UNYK, A. M. (1993). Music and speech processing in the first year of life. In H. W. Reese (Ed.), *Advances in child development and behavior,* Vol. 24. San Diego, CA: Academic.

TRIEMAN, R., COHEN, J., MULQUEENY, K., KESSLER, B., & SCHECHTMAN, S. (2007). Young children's knowledge about printed names. *Child Development, 78,* 1458–1471.

TRIONFI, G., & REESE, E. (2009). A good story: Children with imaginary companions create richer narratives. *Child Development, 80,* 1301–1313.

TROSETH, G. L. (2003). TV guide: Two-year-old children learn to use video as a source of information. *Developmental Psychology, 39,* 140–150.

TSAO, F.-M., LUI, H.-M., & KUHL, P. K. (2004). Speech perception in infancy predicts language development in the second year of life: A longitudinal study. *Child Development, 75,* 1067–1084.

TUDGE, J. R. H. (1992). Processes and consequences of peer collaboration: A Vygotskian analysis. *Child Development, 63,* 1364–1379.

TUDGE, J., PUTNAM, S., & VALSINER, J. (1996). Culture and cognition in developmental perspective. In R. B. Cairns, G. H. Elder, Jr., & E. J. Costello (Eds.), *Developmental science.* New York: Cambridge University Press.

TULKIN, S. R., & KONNER, M. J. (1973). Alternative conceptions of intellectual functioning. *Human Development, 16,* 33–52.

TULVING, E. (1987). Multiple memory systems and consciousness. *Human Neurobiology, 6,* 67–80.

TULVING, E. (2005). Episodic memory and autonoesis: Uniquely human? In H. S. Terrace & J. Metcalfe (Eds.), *The missing link in cognition: Origins of self-reflective consciousness* (pp. 3–56). New York: Oxford University Press.

TURATI, C. (2004). Why faces are not special to newborns: An alternative account of the face preference. *Current Directions in Psychological Science,* 13, 5–8.

TURKEWITZ, G. (1993). The influence of timing on the nature of cognition. In G. Turkewitz & D. A. Devenny (Eds.), *Developmental time and timing.* Hillsdale, NJ: Erlbaum.

TURKEWITZ, G., & KENNY, P. (1982). Limitations on input as a basis for neural organization and perceptual development: A preliminary theoretical statement. *Developmental Psychobiology,* 15, 357–368.

TURKHEIMER, E. (2000). Three laws of behavior genetics and what they mean. *Current Directions in Psychological Science,* 9, 160–164.

TURKHEIMER, E., HALEY, A., WALDRON, M., D'ONOFRIO, B., & GOTTESMAN, I. I. (2003). Sociometric status modifies heritability of IQ in young children. *Psychological Science,* 14, 623–628.

TURKHEIMER, E., & WALDRON, M. (2000). Nonshared environment: A theoretical, methodological, and quantitative review. *Psychological Bulletin,* 126, 78–108.

TURNBULL, M., HART, D., & LAPKIN, S. (2003). Grade 6 French immersion students' performance on large-scale literacy and mathematics: Exploring two hypotheses. *Alberta Journal of Educational Research,* 49, 6–23.

TURNER, A. M., & GREENOUGH, W. T. (1985). Differential rearing effects on rat visual cortex synapses. I. Synaptic and neuronal density and synapses per neuron. *Brain Research,* 329, 195–203.

U. S. CENSUS BUREAU (2006). *Language spoken at home.* Retrieved February 3, 2009, from http://factfinder.census.gov/servlet/STTable?_bm=y&geo_id=01000US&-qr_name=AC-S_2006_EST_G00_S1601&-ds_name=ACS_2006_EST_G00_.

ULLER, C., CAREY, S., HUNTLEY-FENNER, G., & KLATT, L. (1999). What representations might underlie infant numerical knowledge? *Cognitive Development,* 14, 1–36.

UNGERER, J. A., ZELAZO, P. R., KEARSLEY, R. B., & O'LEARY, K. (1981). Developmental changes in the representation of objects in symbolic play from 18 to 34 months of age. *Child Development,* 52, 186–195.

USHER, J. A., & NEISSER, U. (1993). Childhood amnesia and the beginnings of memory for four early life events. *Journal of Experimental Psychology: General,* 122, 155–165.

UTTAL, D. H. (2000). Seeing the big picture: Map use and the development of spatial cognition. *Developmental Science,* 3, 247–286.

UTTAL, D. H., FISHER, J. A., & TAYLOR, H. A. (2006). Words and maps: Developmental changes in mental models of spatial information acquired from descriptions and depictions. *Developmental Science,* 9, 221–235.

UTTAL, D. H., GREGG, V. H., TAN, L. S., CHAMBERLIN, M. H., & SINES, A. (2001). Connecting the dots: Children's use of a systematic figure to facilitate mapping and search. *Developmental Psychology,* 37, 338–350.

UTTAL, D. H., & WELLMAN, H. M. (1989). Young children's representation of spatial information acquired from maps. *Developmental Psychology,* 25, 128–138.

UZGIRIS, I. C. (1964). Situational generality of conservation. *Child Development,* 35, 831–841.

UZGIRIS, I. C., & HUNT, J. McV. (1975). *Assessment in infancy: Ordinal scales of psychological development.* Urbana, IL: University of Illinois Press.

VALDEZ-MENCHACA, M. C., & WHITEHURST, G. J. (1992). Accelerating language development through picture book reading: A systematic extension to Mexican day care. *Developmental Psychology,* 28, 1106–1114.

VAN DER MAAS, H. L. J., & MOLENAAR, P. C. M. (1992). Stage-wise cognitive development: An application of catastrophe theory. *Psychological Review,* 99, 395–417.

VAN IJZENDOORN, M. H., & JUFFER, F. (2005). Adoption is a successful natural intervention enhancing adopted children's IQ and school performance. *Current Directions in Psychological Science,* 14, 326–330.

VAN LOOSBROEK, E., & SMITSMAN, A. W. (1990). Visual perception of numerosity in infancy. *Developmental Psychology,* 26, 916–922.

VAN SCHAIK, C. P., ANCRENAZ, M., BORGEN, G., GALDIKAS, B., KNOTT, C. D., Singleton, I., SUZUKI, A., UTAMI, S. S., & MERRILL, M. (2003). Orangutan cultures and the evolution of material culture. *Science,* 299, 102–105.

VAN VALIN, R. D. (2002). The development of subject-auxiliary inversion in English wh-questions: An alternative analysis. *Journal of Child Language,* 29, 161–175.

VANDELL, D. L., BELSKY, J., BURCHINAL, M., STEINBERG, L., VANDERGRIFT, N., & AND THE NICHD EARLY CHILD CARE RESEARCH NETWORK (2010). Do effects of early child care extend to age 15 Years? Results from the NICHD Study of Early Child Care and Youth Development. *Child Development,* 81, 737–756.

VANDER LINDE, E., MORRONGIELLO, B. A., & ROVEE-COLLIER, C. (1985). Determinants of retention in 8-week-old infants. *Developmental Psychology,* 21, 601–613.

VARNHAGEN, C. K., MORRISON, F. J., & EVERALL, R. (1994). Age and schooling effects in story recall and story production. *Developmental Psychology,* 30, 969–979.

VARNUM, M. E., GROSSMANN, I., KITAYAMA, S., & NISBETT, R. E. (2010). The origin of cultural differences in cognition: The social orientation hypothesis. *Current Directions in Psychological Science,* 19, 9–13.

VASILYEVA, M., DUFFY, S., & HUTTENLOCHER, J. (2007). Developmental changes in the use of absolute and relative information: The case of spatial extent. *Journal of Cognition and Development,* 8, 455–471.

VASTA, R., & LIBEN, L. S. (1996). The water-level task: An intriguing puzzle. *Current Directions in Psychological Science,* 5, 171–177.

VELLUTINO, F. R., & SCANLON, D. M. (1985). Free recall of concrete and abstract words in poor and normal readers. *Journal of Experimental Child Psychology,* 39, 363–380.

VENTER, J. C. ET AL. (2001). The sequence of the human genome. *Science,* 291 (16 February), 1304–1351.

VERNON, P. E., & KANTOR, L. (1986). Reaction time correlations with intelligence test scores obtained under either timed or untimed conditions. *Intelligence,* 10, 315–330.

VINTER, A. (1986). The role of movement in eliciting early imitations. *Child Development,* 57, 66–71.

VOLBERT, R. (2000). Sexual knowledge of preschool children. *Journal of Psychology and Human Sexuality,* 12, 22–48.

VOLKOW, N. (April, 2007). *Drug addiction: A brain developmental disorder: Adolescence-typical alcohol sensitivities and intake.* Invited address presented at meeting of the Society for Research in Child Development, Boston, MA.

VOULOUMANOS, A., & WERKER, J. F. (2007). Listening to language at birth: Evidence for a bias for speech in neonates. *Developmental Science,* 10, 159–171.

VYGOTSKY, L. S. (1962). *Thought and language.* Cambridge, MA: MIT Press.

VYGOTSKY, L. S. (1978). *Mind in society: The development of higher psychological processes.* Cambridge, MA: Harvard University Press.

VYGOTSKY, L. S. (1981). The genesis of higher mental functions. In J. V. Wertsch (Ed.), *The concept of activity in Soviet psychology.* Armonk, NY: Sharpe.

WAGNER, R. K., TORGESEN, J. K., RASHOTTE, C. A., HECHT, S. A., BARKER, T. A., BURGESS, S. R., DONAHUE, J., & GARON, T. (1997). Changing relations between phonological processing abilities and word level reading as children develop from beginning to skilled readers: A 5-year longitudinal study. *Developmental Psychology,* 33, 468–479.

WAKSCHLAG, L. S., LEVENTHAL, B. L., PINE, D. S., PICKETT, K. E., & CARTER, A. S. (2006). Elucidating early mechanisms of developmental psychopathology: The case of prenatal smoking and disruptive behavior. *Child Development,* 77, 893–906.

WALKER, C. H. (1987). Relative importance of domain knowledge and overall aptitude on acquisition of domain-related information. *Cognition and Instruction,* 2, 25–42.

WALTON, G. E., BOWER, N. J. A., & BOWER, T. G. R. (1992). Recognition of familiar faces by newborns. *Infant Behavior and Development,* 15, 265–269.

WANG, Q. (2001). Culture effects on adults' earliest childhood recollection and self-description: Implications for the relation between memory and the self. *Journal of Personality and Social Psychology,* 81, 220–233.

WANG, Q. (2006). Earliest recollections of self and others in European American and Taiwanese young adults. *Psychological Science,* 17, 708–714.

WANG, S., BAILLARGEON, R., & PATERSON, S. (2005). Detecting continuity violations in infancy: A new account and new evidence from covering and tube events. *Cognition, 95,* 129–173.

WANG, S., KAUFMAN, L., & BAILLARGEON, R. (2003). Should all stationary objects move when hit? Developments in infants' causal and statistical expectations about collision events. *Infant Behavior and Development,* 26, 529–567.

WANT, S. C., & HARRIS, P. L. (2001). Learning from other peoples' mistakes: Causal understanding in learning to use a tool. *Child Development,* 72, 431–443.

WARNEKEN, F., & TOMASELLO, M. (2006). Altruistic helping in human infants and young chimpanzees. *Science,* 311, 1301–1303.

WARREN, A. R., & McCLOSKEY, L. A. (1997). Language in social contexts. In J. Berko Gleason (Ed.), *The development of language* (4th ed.). Boston, MA: Allyn & Bacon.

WARREN, A. R., & TATE, C. S. (1992). Egocentrism in children's telephone conversations: Recent evidence regarding Piaget's position. In R. Diaz & L. Berk (Eds.), *From social interaction to self-regulation.* Hillsdale, NJ: Erlbaum.

WARREN-LEUBECKER, A., & BOHANNON, J. N. (1989). Pragmatics: Language in social context. In J. B. Berko Gleason (Ed.), *The development of language* (2nd ed.). Columbus, OH: Charles E. Merrill.

WARTENBURGER, I., HEEKEREB, H. R., ABUTALEBI, J., CAPPA, S. F., VILLRINGER, A., & PERANI, D. (2003). Early setting of grammatical processing in the bilingual brain. *Neuron,* 37, 159–170.

WASON, P., & JOHNSON-LAIRD, P. (1972). *Psychology of reasoning: Structure and content.* Cambridge, MA: Harvard University Press.

WATERS, H. S., & KUNNMAN, T. W. (2009). Metacognition and strategy discovery in early childhood. In H. S. Waters & W. Schneider (Eds.), *Metacognition, strategy use, and instruction* (pp. 3–22). New York: Guilford.

WATKINS, M. W., LEI, P., & CANIVEZ, G. L. (2007). Psychometric intelligence and achievement: A cross-lagged panel analysis. *Intelligence,* 35, 59–68.

WEBER, A., & STRUBE, G. (1999). Memory for events experienced and events observed. In F. E. Weinert & W. Schneider (Eds.), *The Munich Longitudinal Study on the Genesis of Individual Competencies (LOGIC).* Cambridge: Cambridge University Press.

WECHSLER, D. (1974). *Manual for the Wechsler Intelligence Scale for Children–Revised.* New York: Psychological Corporation.

WECHSLER, D. (2003). *Wechsler Intelligence Scale for Children, Fourth Edition (WISC-IV).* Toronto: The Psychological Corporation.

WEIKUM, W. M., VOULOUMANOS, A., NAVARRA, J., SOTO-FARACO, S., SEBASTIÁN-GALLÉS, N., &. WERKER, J. F. (2007). Visual language discrimination in infancy. *Science,* 316, 1159.

WEINBERG, R. A., SCARR, S., & WALDMAN, I. D. (1992). The Minnesota Transracial Adoption Study: A follow-up of IQ test performance at adolescence. *Intelligence,* 16, 117–135.

WELCH-ROSS, M. K. (1995). An integrative model of the development of autobiographical memory. *Developmental Review,* 15, 338–365.

WELCH, M. K. (1999). Preschoolers' understanding of mind: Implications for suggestibility. *Cognitive Development,* 14, 101–131.

WELLMAN, H. M. (1988). The early development of memory strategies. In F. Weinert & M. Perlmutter (Eds.), *Memory development: Universal changes and individual differences.* Hillsdale, NJ: Erlbaum.

WELLMAN, H. M. (1990). *The child's theory of mind.* Cambridge, MA: MIT Press.

WELLMAN, H. M., CROSS, D., & WATSON, J. (2001). Meta-analysis of theory-of-mind development: The truth about false belief. *Child Development,* 72, 655–684.

WELLMAN, H. M., FANG, F., LIU, D., ZHU, L., & LIU, G. (2006). Scaling theory-of-mind understanding in Chinese children. *Psychological Science,* 17, 1075–1081.

WELLMAN, H. M., & LEMPERS, J. D. (1977). The naturalistic communicative and organismic points of view. In D. B. Harris (Ed.), *The concept of development.*

Minneapolis: University of Minnesota Press.

WENNER, J. A., BURCH, M. M., LYNCH, J. S., & BAUER, P. J. (2008). Becoming a teller of tales: Associations between children's fictional narratives and parent-child reminiscence narratives. *Journal of Experimental Child Psychology, 101,* 1–19.

WERTSCH, J. V., & TULVISTE, P. (1992). L. S. Vygotsky and contemporary developmental psychology. *Developmental Psychology, 28,* 548–557.

WEST, T. A., & BAUER, P. J. (1999). Assumptions of infantile amnesia: Are there differences between early and later memories? *Memory, 7,* 257–278.

WEXLER-SHERMAN, C., GARDNER, H., & FELDMAN, D. H. (1988). A pluralistic view of early assessment: The Project Spectrum approach. *Theory Into Practice, 27,* 77–83.

WHELDALL, K., & JOSEPH, R. (1986). Young black children's sentence comprehension skills: A comparison of performance in standard English and Jamaican Creole. *First Language, 6,* 149–154.

WHITE, S. H. (2000). Conceptual foundations of IQ testing. *Psychology, Public Policy, and Law, 6,* 33–43.

WHITE, S., MILNE, E., ROSEN, S., HANSEN, P., SWETTENHAM, J., FRITH, U., & RAMUS, F. (2006). The role of sensorimotor impairments in dyslexia: A multiple case stuffy of dyslexic children. *Developmental Science, 9,* 237–269.

WHITEHURST, G. J., FALCO, F., LONIGAN, C. J., FISCHAL, J. E., DeBARYSHE, B. D., VALDEZ-MANCHACA, M. C., & CAUFIELD, M. (1988). Accelerating language development through picture book reading. *Developmental Psychology, 24,* 552–559.

WHITEHURST, G. J., & LONIGAN, C. J. (1998). Child development and emergent literacy. *Child Development, 69,* 848–872.

WHITEHURST, G. J., & SONNENSCHEIN, S. (1985). The development of communication: A functional analysis. In G. J. Whitehurst (Ed.), *Annals of child development,* Vol. 2. Greenwich, CT: JAI.

WHITEN, A. (2010). Ape behavior and the origins of human culture. *Mind the gap: Tracing the origins of human universals* (pp. 429–450). New York: Springer.

WHITEN, A., & FLYNN, E. G. (2010). The transmission and evolution of experimental 'microcultures' in groups of young children. *Developmental Psychology, 46,* 1694–1709.

WHITEN, A., GOODALL, J., McGREW, W. C., NISHIDA, T., REYNOLDS, V., SUGIYAMA, Y., TUTIN, C. E. G., WRANGHAM, R. W., & BOESCH, C. (1999). Cultures in chimpanzees. *Nature, 399,* 682–685.

WHITEN, A., HORNER, V., & DE WAAL, F. B. M. (2005). Conformity to cultural norms of tool use in chimpanzees. *Nature, 437,* 737–740.

WHITHAM, J. C., GERALD, M. S., SANTIAGO, C., & MAESTRIPIERI, D. (2007). Intended receivers and functional significance of grunt and girney vocalizations in free-ranging female rhesus macaques, *Ethology, 113,* 862–874.

WHYTE, J. C., & BULL, R. (2008). Number games, magnitude representation, and basic number skills in preschoolers. *Developmental Psychology, 44,* 588–596.

WICKELGREN, L. (1967). Convergence in the human newborn. *Journal of Experimental Child Psychology, 5,* 74–85.

WIEBE, S. A., ESPY, K. A., & CHARAK, D. (2008). Using confirmatory factor analysis to understand executive control in preschool children: I. Latent structure. *Developmental Psychology, 44,* 575–587.

WILCOX, J., & WEBSTER, E. (1980). Early discourse behavior: An analysis of children's responses to listener feedback. *Child Development, 51,* 1120–1125.

WILCOX, T., & CHAPA, C. (2004). Priming infants to use color and pattern information in an individuation task. *Cognition, 90,* 265–302.

WILLATTS, P. (1990). Development of problem-solving strategies in infancy. In D. F. Bjorklund (Ed.), *Children's strategies: Contemporary views of cognitive development.* Hillsdale, NJ: Erlbaum.

WILLIAMS, J. H., WHITEN, A., SUDDENDORF, T., & PERRETT, D. I. (2001). Imitation, mirror neurons and autism. *Neuroscience & Biobehavioral Review, 25,* 287–295.

WILSON, R. S. (1983). The Louisville Twin Study: Developmental synchronies in behavior. *Child Development, 54,* 298–316.

WILSON, S. P., & KIPP, K. (1998). The development of efficient inhibition: Evidence from directed-forgetting tasks. *Developmental Review, 18,* 86–123.

WIMMER, M. C., & HOWE, M. L. (2010). Are children's memory illusions created differently than adults'? Evidence from levels-of-processing and divided attention paradigms. *Journal of Experimental Child Psychology, 107,* 31–49.

WIMMER, H., & PERNER, J. (1983). Beliefs about beliefs: Representation and constraining function of wrong beliefs in young children's understanding of deception. *Cognition, 13,* 103–128.

WINER, G. A. (1980). Class-inclusion reasoning in children: A review of the empirical literature. *Child Development, 51,* 309–328.

WINICK, M., MEYER, K. K., & HARRIS, R. C. (1975). Malnutrition and environmental enrichment by early adoption. *Science, 190,* 1173–1175.

WINSLER, A. (2003). Overt and covert verbal problem-solving strategies: Developmental trends in use, awareness, and relations with task performance in children age 5 to 17. *Child Development, 74,* 659–678.

WINSLER, A. (2009). Still talking to ourselves after all these years: A review of current research on private speech. In A. Winsler, C. Fernyhough, & I. Montero (Eds.), *Private speech, executive functioning, and the development of verbal self-regulation* (pp. 3–41). Cambridge, UK: Cambridge University Press.

Winsler, A., Fernyhough, C., Montero, I. (EDS.). (2009). *Private speech, executive functioning, and the development of verbal self-regulation.* Cambridge, UK: Cambridge University Press.

WINSLER, A., & NAGLIERI, J. (2003). Overt and covert verbal problem-solving strategies: Developmental trends in use, awareness, and the relations with task performance in children aged 5 to 17. *Child Development, 74,* 659–678.

WITELSON, S. F. (1985). On hemisphere specialization and cerebral plasticity from birth: Mark II. In C. Best (Ed.), *Hemispheric function and collaboration in the child.* New York: Academic.

WITELSON, S. F. (1987). Neurobiological aspects of language in children. *Child Development, 58,* 653–688.

Wood, D., Bruner, J. S., & Ross, G. (1976). The role of tutoring in problem-solving. *Journal of Child Psychology and Psychiatry, 17,* 89–100.

Wood, J. N., & Spelke, E. S. (2005). Infants' enumeration of actions: Numerical discrimination and its signature limits. *Developmental Science, 8,* 173–181.

Woods, B. T., & Carey, S. (1979). Language deficits after apparent clinical recovery from childhood aphasia. *Annals of Neurology, 6,* 405–409.

Woodward, A. L. (2009). Infants' grasp of others' intentions. *Current Directions in Psychological Science, 18,* 53–57.

Woody-Dorning, J., & Miller, P. H. (2001). Children's individual differences in capacity: Effects on strategy production and utilization. *British Journal of Developmental Psychology, 19,* 543–557.

Woolley, J. D. (1997). Thinking about fantasy: Are children fundamentally different thinkers and believers from adults? *Child Development, 68,* 991–1011.

Woolley, J. D., & Boerger, E. A. (2002). Development of beliefs about the origins of controllability of dreams. *Developmental Psychology, 38,* 24–41.

Woolley, J. D., Boerger, E. A., & Markman, A. B. (2004). A visit from the Candy Witch: Factors influencing young children's belief in a novel fantastical being. *Developmental Science, 7,* 456–468.

Woolley, J. D., & Wellman, H. M. (1992). Children's conceptions of dreams. *Cognitive Development, 7,* 365–380.

Wynn, K. (1992). Addition and subtraction by human infants. *Nature, 358,* 749–750.

Xu, F., & Spelke, E. S. (2000). Large number discrimination in 6-month-old infants. *Cognition, 74,* B1–B11.

Xu, F., Spelke, E. S., & Goddad, S. (2005). Number sense in infants. *Developmental Science, 8,* 88–101.

Yeats, K. O., & Taylor, G. H. (2005). Neurobehavioral outcomes of mild head injury in children and adolescents. *Pediatric Rehabilitation, 8,* 5–16.

Yoon, J. M. D., & Johnson, S. C. (2009). Biological motion displays elicit social behavior in 12-month-olds. *Child Development, 80,* 1069–1075.

Youngblade, L. M., & Dunn, J. (1995). Individual differences in young children's pretend play with mother and sibling: Links to relationships and understanding of other people's feelings and beliefs. *Child Development, 66,* 1472–1492.

Younger, B., & Gotlieb, S. (1988). Development of categorization skills: Changes in the nature or structure of infant form categories? *Developmental Psychology, 24,* 611–619.

Zelazo, P. D. (2000). Self-reflection and the development of consciously controlled processing. In P. Mitchell & K. Rigg (Eds.), *Children's reasoning and the mind.* New York: Psychology Press.

Zelazo, P. D., & Boseovski, J. J. (2001). Video reminders in a representational change task: Memory for cues but not beliefs or statements. *Journal of Experimental Child Psychology, 78,* 107–129.

Zelazo, P. D., Carlson, S. M., & Kesek, A. (2008). The development of executive function in childhood. In C. A. Nelson & M. Luciana (Eds.), *Handbook of cognitive devleopmental neuroscience* (2nd ed., pp. 553–574). Cambridge, MA: MIT Press.

Zelazo, P. D., Carter, A., Reznick, J. S., & Frye, D. (1997). Early development of executive function: A problem-solving framework. *Review of General Psychology, 1,* 198–226.

Zelazo, P. D., & Frye, D. (1997). Cognitive complexity and control: A theory of the development of deliberate reasoning and intentional action. In M. Stamenov (Ed.), *Language structure, discourse, and the access to consciousness.* Amsterdam & Philadelphia: John Benjamins.

Zelazo, P. D., Frye, D., & Rapus, T. (1996). An age-related dissociation between knowing rules and using them. *Cognitive Development, 11,* 37–63.

Zelazo, P. D., Kearsley, R. B., & Stack, D. M. (1995). Mental representation for visual sequences: Increased speed of central processing from 22 to 32 months. *Intelligence, 20,* 41–63.

Zelazo, P. D., Müller, U., Frye, D., & Marcovitch, S. (2003). The development of executive function in early childhood. *Monographs of the Society for Research in Child Development, 68* (Serial No. 274).

Zelazo, P. D., Sommerville, J. A., & Nichols, S. (1999). Age-related changes in children's use of external representation. *Developmental Psychology, 35,* 1059–1071.

Zeskind, P. S. (April, 1996). *Infant crying: A biobehavioral synchrony between infants and caregivers.* Paper presented at the Conference on Human Development, Birmingham, AL.

Zeskind, P. S., & Ramey, C. T. (1978). Fetal malnutrition: An experimental study of its consequences on infant development in two caregiver environments. *Child Development, 49,* 1155–1162.

Zeskind, P. S., & Ramey, C. T. (1981). Sequelae of fetal malnutrition: A longitudinal, transactional, and synergistic approach. *Child Development, 52,* 213–218.

Zhou, X., Huang, J., Wang, B., Zhao, Z., Yang, L., & Zhengzheng, Y. (2006). Parent-child interaction and children's number learning. *Early Child Development and Care, 176,* 763–775.

Ziegler, J. C., & Goswami, U. (2005). Reading acquisition, developmental dyslexia, and skilled reading across languages: A psycholinguistic grain size theory. *Psychological Bulletin, 131,* 3–29.

Ziegler, J. C., & Goswami, U. (2006). Becoming literate in different languages: Similar problems, different solutions. *Developmental Science, 9,* 429–453.

Zimmerman, F. J., Christakis, D. A., & Meltzoff, A. N. (2007). Associations between media viewing and language development in children under age 2 years. *The Journal of Pediatrics, 151,* 364–368.

Zimmerman, T. (Ed.). (2007). *Poverty and early childhood intervention.* Chapel Hill, NC: The Carolina Abecedarian Program.

Zuber, J., Pixner, S., Moeller, K., & Nuerk, H.-C. (2009). On the language-specificity of basic number processing: Transcoding in a language with inversion and its relation to working memory capacity. *Journal of Experimental Child Psychology, 102,* 60–77.

# CREDITS

This page constitutes an extension of the copyright page. We have made every effort to trace the ownership of all copyrighted material and to secure permission from copyright holders. In the event of any question arising as to the use of any material, we will be pleased to make the necessary corrections in future printings. Thanks are due to the following authors, publishers, and agents for permission to use the material indicated.

## Chapter 1.

12: From R. M. Lerner, "Changing Organism-Context Relations as the Basic Process of Development: A Developmental Contextual Perspective", *Developmental Psychology*, 27, pp. 27–32. Copyright © 1991 American Psychological Association. Reprinted with permission. 15: From Siegler, R. S., & Svetina, M. (2002). "A microgenetic/cross-sectional study of matrix completion: Comparing short-term and long-term change." *Child Development*, 73, pp. 793–809. Copyright © 2002 The Society for Research in Child Development, Inc. Reprinted by permission. 22: "Addition and Subtraction by Human Infants," by K. Wynn, 1992, Nature, 358, 749–750. Copyright © 1992 Macmillan Magazines Ltd. Reprinted with permission from Nature.

## Chapter 2.

41: From Individual development and evolution: The genesis of novel behavior by Gilbert Gottlieb, copyright © 1991 by Oxford University Press, Inc. Used by permission of Oxford University Press, Inc. 48: Adapted with permission from S. Scarr and K. McCartney "How People Make Their Own Environments: A Theory of Genotype à Effects", *Child Development*, 54, pp. 424–435. Copyright © 1983 The Society for Research in Child Development, Inc. 63: Source: D. F. Bjorklund and B. R. Bjorklund, 1992. Looking at children: An introduction to child development. Belmont, CA: Wadsworth, p. 129. 67: Adapted with permission from S. F. Witelson, "Neurobiological Aspects of Language in Children", *Child Development*, 58, pp. 653–688. Copyright © 1987 The Society for Research in Child Development, Inc.

## Chapter 3.

90: From "Guided participation in cultural activity by toddlers and caregivers," by B. Rogoff, J. Mistry, A. Goncu, C. Moiser, 1993, *Monographs of the Society for Research in Child Development*, 58 (Serial No. 236, No. 8). Copyright © 1993 The Society for Research in Child Development, Inc. Reprinted with permission. 91: From "Guided participation in cultural activity by toddlers and caregivers," by B. Rogoff, J. Mistry, A. Goncu, C. Moiser, 1993, *Monographs of the Society for Research in Child Development*, 58 (Serial No. 236, No. 8). Copyright © 1993 The Society for Research in Child Development, Inc. Reprinted with permission. 91: From

"Guided participation in cultural activity by toddlers and caregivers," by B. Rogoff, J. Mistry, A. Goncu, C. Moiser, 1993, *Monographs of the Society for Research in Child Development*, 58 (Serial No. 236, No. 8). Copyright © 1993 The Society for Research in Child Development, Inc. Reprinted with permission.

## Chapter 4.

104: From R. L. Fantz, "The Origin of Form Perception", *Scientific American*, 204, pp. 66–72. Copyright © 1961 Scientific American, Inc. All rights reserved. Reprinted with permission. 109: Photo by Barbara Bjorklund. 110: From P. Salapatek and W. Kessen, "Visual Scanning of Triangles by the Human Newborn", *Journal of Experimental Child Psychology*, 3, pp. 155–167. Copyright © 1966 Academic Press. Reprinted with permission. 111: From H. A. Ruff and H. G. Birch, "Infant Visual Fixation: The Effect of Concentricity, Curvilinearity, and Number of Directions", *Journal of Experimental Child Psychology*, 17, pp. 460–473. Copyright © 1974 Academic Press. Reprinted with permission. 113: From R. B. McCall, C. B. Kennedy, and M. I. Appelbaum, "Magnitude of Discrepancy and the Distribution of Attention in Infants", *Child Development*, 48, pp. 772–785. Copyright © 1977 The Society for Research in Child Development, Inc. Reprinted with permission. 114: From M. H. Johnson, S. Dziurawiec, H. D. Ellis, and J. Morton, "Newborns' Preferential Tracking of Faces and Its Subsequent Decline", *Cognition*, 40, pp. 1–19. Copyright © 1991 Elsevier Science Publishing Co., Inc. Reprinted with permission. 118: Gava, L., Valenza, E., Turati, C., & de Schonen, S. (2008). Effect of partial occlusion on newborns' face preference and recognition. Developmental Science, 11, 563–574. 127: Lewkowicz, D. J. & Ghazanfar, A. A. 2006. The decline of cross-species intersensory perception in human infants. Proceedings of the National Academy of Sciences, USA,103, 6771–6774. 132: Adapted from Slater, A. M., Mattock, A., Brown, E., & Bremner, G. J. (1991). "Form perception at birth: Cohen and Younger (1984) revisited." *Journal of Experimental Child Psychology*, 51, pp. 395–406. Reprinted by permission. 140: From R. Baillargeon, "Object Performance in 3 1/2- and 4 1/2-month-old infants", *Developmental Psychology*, 23, pp. 655–664. Copyright © 1987 American Psychological Association. Reprinted with permission. 141: From R. Baillargeon, "Object Performance in 3 1/2- and 4 1/2-month-old infants", *Developmental Psychology*, 23, pp. 655-664. Copyright © 1987 American Psychological Association. Reprinted with permission. 149: Robert Blanchard/iStockphoto.com. Ken Hewitt/iStockphoto.com. Jim Zipp / Photo Researchers, Inc. Robert Hardholt, 2010/Shutterstock.com. Mike Neale, 2010/Shutterstock.com. William Ju, 2010/Shutterstock.com.

## Chapter 5.

**157:** From J. S. DeLoache, "Rapid Change in the Symbolic Functioning of Very Young Children", *Science*, 238, pp. 1556–1557. Copyright © 1987 American Association for the Advancement of Science. Reprinted with permission. **191:** From Brainerd, C. J., & Gordon, L. L., "Development of verbatim and gist memory for numbers." *Developmental Psychology*, 30, pp.163–177. Copyright © 1994 by the American Psychological Association. Reprinted with permission.

## Chapter 6.

**201:** From H. M. Wellman, *The Child's Theory of Mind.* Copyright © 1990 Massachusetts Institute of Technology Press. Reprinted with permission. DENNIS THE MENACE® used by permission of Hank Ketcham and © 1990 by North America Syndicate **204:** From A. Gopnik & J. W. Astington, "Children's Understanding of the Representational Change and Its Relation to the Understanding of False Belief and the Appearance-Reality Distinction", *Child Development*, 59, pp. 26–37. Copyright © 1988 The Society for Research in Child Development. Reprinted with permission. **210:** From M. Chandler, A. S. Fritz, and S. Hala, "Small-Scale Deceit: Deception as a Marker of Two-, Three-, and Four-Year-Olds' Early Theories of Mind," *Child Development*, 60, pp. 1263–1277. Copyright © 1989 The Society for Research in Child Development. Reprinted with permission. **233:** From *Sex Differences in Cognitive Abilities*, 3rd ed. (p. 18), by D. F. Halpern, 2000, Mahwah, NJ: Erlbaum. Copyright 2000 by Lawrence Erlbaum Associates. Reprinted with permission.

## Chapter 7.

**253:** From R. Kail, "Development of Processing Speed in Childhood and Adolescence," in H. W. Reese (Ed.), *Advances in Child Development and Behavior*, 23, pp. 151–187. Copyright © 1991. Reprinted with permission from Elsevier.Academic Press. Reprinted with permission. **256:** Adapted from M. T. H. Chi, "Knowledge Structures and Memory Development," in R. Siegler (Ed.), *Children's Thinking: What Develops?* Copyright © 1978 Lawrence Erlbaum Associates, Inc. Reprinted with permission. **258:** From C. Hulme, N. Thomson, C. Muir, and A. Lawrence, "Speech Rate and the Development of Spoken Words: the Role of rehearsal and Item Identification Processes", *Journal of Experimental Child Psychology*, 38, pp. 241–253. Copyright (c) 1984 Academic Press. Reprinted with permission. **262:** © Baby Blue Partnership. Reprinted with special permission of King Features Syndicate **269:** Courtesy of Patricia Miller **288:** From Chen, Z., Sanchez, R. P., & Campbell, T., "From beyond to within their grasp: The rudiments of analogical problem solving in 10- and 13-month-olds." *Developmental Psychology*, 33, pp. 790–801. Copyright © 1997 by the American Psychological Association. Reprinted with permission. **289:** From Chen, Z., Sanchez, R. P., & Campbell, T., "From beyond to within their grasp: The rudiments of analogical problem solving in 10- and 13-month-olds." *Developmental Psychology*, 33, pp. 790–801. Copyright © 1997 by the American Psychological Association. Reprinted with permission. **292:** Goswami, U., & Brown, A. L., "Higher-order structure and relational reasoning: Contrasting analogical and thematic relations," *Cognition*, 36, pp. 207–226. Reprinted with permission of Elsevier Science.

## Chapter 8.

**308:** CALVIN AND HOBBES © Watterson. Reprinted with permission of UNIVERSAL PRESS SYNDICATE. All rights reserved. Thanks to Carolyn Rovee-Collier. Thanks to Patricia Bauer. Thanks to Patricia Bauer. Thanks to Patricia Bauer. Thanks to Patricia Bauer. **327:** In J. Doris (Ed.), *The Suggestibility of Children's Recollections: Implications for Eyewitness Testimony* (pp. 47–55). Washington, DC: American Psychological Association. Reprinted by permission. **338:** From Ceci, S. J., Loftus, E. F., Leichtman, M., & Bruck, M., "The role of source misattributions in the creation of false beliefs among preschoolers," *International Journal of Clinical and Experimental Hypnosis*, 62, pp. 304–320. © 1994 by Sage Publications, Inc. Reprinted by permission.

## Chapter 9.

**358:** From Berko, J. (1958). "The Child's Learning of English Morphology," *Word*, 14, pp. 150–177. Reprinted with permission. **375:** Sakai, K. L. (2005). Language acquisition and brain development. Science, 310, 815–919, p. 817. Reprinted with permission from AAAS. **377:** Reprinted from Neuron, 37, Wartenburger, I., Heekereb, H. R., Abutalebi, J., Cappa, S. F., Villringer, A., & Perani, D., Early setting of grammatical processing in the bilingual brain, 159–170, Copyright (2003), with permission from Elsevier. **380:** From J. S. Johnson and E. L. Newport, "Critical Period Effects in Second Language Learning: The Influence of Maturational State on the Acquisition of English as a Second Language", *Cognitive Psychology*, 21, pp. 60–99. Copyright © 1989 Academic Press. Reprinted with permission. **393:** Dennis the Menace®, used by permission of Hank Ketcham and © 1986 by North America Syndicate

## Chapter 10.

**406:** Meltzoff, A. N., & Moore, M. K. (1977). Imitation of facial and manual gestures by human neonates. Science, 198, 75–78. Pier Ferrari. **412:** From Hooper, L. M., Flynn, E. G.,Wood, L.A. N,, & Whiten, A., "Observational learning of tool use in children: Investigating cultural spread through diffusion chains and learning mechanisms through ghost displays," *Journal of Experimental Child Psychology*, 106, pp. 82–97. Reprinted by permission. **414:** From Tomasello, M., Savage-Rumbaugh, S., & Kruger, A. C., "Imitative learning of actions and objects by children, chimpanzees, and enculturated chimpanzees," *Child Development*, 64, pp. 1688–1705. Reprinted with permission of the Society for Research in Child Development. **421:** Adapted from Dodge et al., "Social Competence in Children", *Monographs of the Society for Research in Child Development*, 51, (Serial No. 213). Copyright © 1986 The Society for Research in Child Development, Inc. Reprinted with permission. **430:** Adapted from Ruble, D. N., Balaban, T., & Cooper J., "Gender Constancy and the Effects of Sex-Typed Television Toy Commercials," *Child Development*, 52, pp. 667–673. Copyright © 1981 The Society for Research in Child Development, Inc. Adapted with permission.

## Chapter 11.

**450:** "The Cognitive Basis of Dyslexia," by L. S. Siegel. In R. Pasnak and M. L. Howe (Eds.), Emerging Themes in Cognitive Development, Vol. II: Competencies. Copyright © 1993 Springer-Verlag New York, Inc. Reprinted by permission. **453:** "The Cognitive Basis of Dyslexia," by L. S. Siegel. In R. Pasnak and M. L. Howe (Eds.), Emerging

Themes in Cognitive Development, Vol. II: Competencies. Copyright © 1993 Springer-Verlag New York, Inc. Reprinted with permission. **457:** From J. S. Hyde, "How Large Are Cognitive Gender Differences? A Meta-Analysis Using w2 and d," *American Psychologist*, 36, pp. 892–901. Copyright © 1981 American Psychological Association. Reprinted with permission. **458:** Adapted with permission from Asher, S. R., & Markel, R. A. (1974). "Sex differences in comprehension of high- and low-interest reading material." *Journal of Educational Psychology*, 66, pp. 680–687. **469:** Goldin-Meadow, S., Cook, S. W., & Mitchell, Z. A., Gesturing gives children new ideas about math. Psychological Science, 20, 267–272, 2009, Reprinted by Permission of SAGE Publications. **474:** From H. W. Stevenson & S. Y. Lee, "Context of Achievement," *Monographs of the Society for Research in Child Development*, 55, (Serial No. 221). Copyright © 1990 The Society for Research in Child Development, Inc. Reprinted with permission. **480:** From Geary, D. C. (1994). "Children's mathematical development: Research and practical applications." Washington, DC: American Psychological Association. Reprinted by permission

## Chapter 12.

**510:** From Gaultney, J. F., Bjorklund, D. F., & Goldstein, D. (1996). "To be young, gifted, and strategic: Advantages for memory performance." *Journal of Experimental Child Psychology*, 61, p. 51. Reprinted with permission.

## Chapter 13.

**533:** From A. Sameroff, (Ed.) "The transactional model of development: How children and contexts shape each other." Washington, DC: American Psychological Association, p.15. Reprinted by permission. **541:** Adapted with permission from R. H. Bradley and B. M. Caldwell, *Child Development*, 47, pp. 1172–1174. Copyright © 1976 The Society for Research in Child Development, Inc. **548:** Adapted with permission from W. C. Becker and R. Gersten, "A Follow-up of Follow-Through: The Later Effects of the Direct Instruction Model for children in Fifth and Sixth Grades," *American Educational Research Journal*, 19, pp. 75–92. Copyright © 1982 American Educational Research Association. Reprinted from Neuro-Image, 14, Chugani, H.T., Behen, M.E.; Muzik, O., Juhasz, C., Nagy, F., & Chugani, D. C., Local brain functional activity following early deprivation: A study of postinstitutionalized Romanian orphans, 1290–1301, Copyright (2001), with permission from Elsevier. **552:** From Fagan, J. F., III & Singer, J. T., "Infant recognition memory as a measure of intelligence," in L. P. Lipsitt & C. K. Rovee-Collier (Eds.), *Advances in infancy research (Vol. 2)*. Norwood, NJ: Ablex. Reprinted with permission. **571:** From R. B. McCall, M. I. Appelbaum, and P. S. Hogarty, "Developmental Changes in Mental Performance," *Monographs of the Society for Research in Child Development*, 38, (Serial No. 150). Copyright © 1973 The Society for Research in Child Development, Inc. Reprinted with permission.

# AUTHOR INDEX

## A

Abravanel, E., 405, 407
Abutalebi, J., 376–377
Ackerman, B. P., 534, 558
Ackil, J. K., 333, 337, 340
Adams, J. W., 466
Adams, M. J., 88, 450, 454
Adams, R. J., 108
Adey, P. S., 182
Adkins, D. R., 63, 267
Adler, S., 367
Adrián, J. E., 445
Agnoli, F., 478
Aguiar, A., 129, 134
Ainsworth, M. D. S., 419
Aitchinson, 362
Akert, K., 266
Akhtar, N., 202, 359–360, 383, 410
Alberts, D. M., 481
Alexander, J. M., 95, 514
Alexander, R. D., 402, 424, 439
Alibali, M. W., 270
Allen, D., 108
Allen, L., 569
Allen, T. W., 182
Alloway, R. G., 508, 529
Alloway, T. P., 256, 508, 529
Als, H., 46
Aman, C. J., 328
Amatruda, C., 500
Ambady, N., 478
Amsel, E., 281, 295–297
Amso, D., 33, 52, 69, 118, 261
Anastasi, A., 504
Andalman, A., 61
Anderson, D., 425
Anderson, K. J., 390
Anderson, R. C., 452, 453
Angelillo, C., 17, 83
Anglin, J. M., 149
Anisfeld, M., 405
Annett, M., 66
Anooshian, L. J., 231
Antell, S. E., 143
Anthony, J. L., 447
Appelbaum, M. I., 112–113, 570–571
Arffa, S., 508
Arnett, J., 178
Aro, M., 449
Aronson, J., 503
Arterberry, M. E., 108, 148, 153
Ashcraft, M. H., 278, 464–466

Asher, S. R., 458
Aslin, R. N., 107, 120, 121, 129, 133, 372, 386
Astington, J. W., 90, 204, 205–206, 401
Astuti, R., 223
Atance, C. M., 343
Atkinson, R. C., 250
Atran, S., 216
August, G. J., 263
Ausley, J. A., 320
Austin, C. M., 387
Avis, J., 203
Aylward, G. P., 56
Azmitia, M., 95

## B

Baddeley, A. D., 256–257
Badian, N. A., 471
Baenninger, M., 232
Baer, R. A., 267
Bahrick, L. E., 112–113, 124, 125, 128, 330, 340, 425
Bailey, D. H., 402
Baillargeon, R., 129–130, 134–136, 153, 206, 242
Baird, A. A., 64
Bakeman, R., 235
Baker, D. P., 473
Baker, S. T., 261
Baker-Ward, L., 230, 278, 325, 329
Balaban, T., 428
Baldwin, A., 552
Baldwin, C., 552
Baldwin, D. A., 364
Band, G. P. H., 262
Bandura, A., 200, 416–419
Banks, M. S., 107–108
Bard, K., 407
Barhrick, L. E., 306
Barki, A., 116
Barkley, R. A., 63, 262–263
Barkow, J. H., 33
Barnard, K. E., 390
Barnes, M. A., 278
Barnett, W. S., 560
Baron-Cohen, S., 213–215, 391
Barr, R., 408
Barrett, H. C., 221, 223
Barrett, T. M., 238
Bartlett, F. C., 321
Barton, R. A., 54
Bartz, W. H., 221–222

Basne, R., 433
Bates, E., 236, 238
Bates, E. A., 30
Bateson, P., 9
Battin, D., 330
Batty, G. D., 186, 503
Bauer, A., 333
Bauer, P. J., 182, 310–316, 321–322, 340, 347, 408, 434–435
Bauer, R. H., 509
Baumrind, D., 50
Bayen, U. J., 343
Bayley, N., 500, 569
Beach, D. R., 272
Beal, C. R., 369–370
Beck, E. F., 19, 270, 420
Becker, W. C., 561–562
Beckett, C., 68, 548, 556–557
Behen, M. E., 548
Behne, T., 223
Behrend, D. A., 394
Beilin, H., 181
Beilock, S. L., 478
Bekkering, H., 410–411
Bell, M. A., 63, 64, 267
Belsky, J., 234–235
Bem, S., 431
Benbow, C. P., 476–479, 491
Bender, C. E., 412
Benedict, H., 362
Bengbow, C. P., 456
Beran, M. J., 350
Berenbaum, S. A., 235, 427, 436, 441
Berg, D. H., 466, 471
Bergamasco, N. H. P., 102
Bering, J. M., 187, 195, 216–219, 224, 402, 413–414, 424, 486
Berk, L. E., 392–393
Berko, J., 357–358
Berman, N. M., 61
Bermejo, V., 463
Bernholtz, J. F., 511–513
Bernieri, F., 49, 542
Bernstein, A. C., 224–225
Bernstein, B., 366
Bertenthal, B. I., 61, 133, 221, 222
Berthier, N. E., 136
Bertrand, J., 362–363
Best, D. L., 25, 274, 278
Bhatt, R. S., 119, 309
Bialystok, E., 380, 388–390, 445, 447
Bickerton, D., 349, 378
Bidell, T., 86, 150–151

Billingsley, R. L., 319
Billman, D. O., 291
Birch, H. G., 111
Bisanz, J., 481
Bivens, J. A., 394
Bjorklund, B. R., 19, 20, 46, 62, 221, 335
Bjorklund, D. F., 7, 18, 24–25, 27, 30, 33, 35–38, 47, 62, 68–69, 72, 84–85, 97, 151, 175, 178, 184, 205, 209, 217–219, 224–225, 230, 234–238, 241, 265, 267–272, 274, 276–280, 284, 300, 312, 328–329, 333–336, 343, 387, 401–403, 407, 409, 412–414, 418–420, 424, 452, 462, 470, 484–486, 507, 510–512
Black, J. E., 60, 546
Blair, C., 496, 529, 573
Blakemore, C., 61
Blennerhassett, A., 452
Blom, G. E., 458
Bloom, L., 359–360, 362, 372, 377
Bloom, P., 158, 216–217, 238, 364
Blumberg, F. C., 268
Blumberg, M., 73
Bock, J., 235
Boerger, E. A., 185, 186
Boesch, C., 402, 413
Bogartz, R. S., 113, 146, 306
Bogin, B., 378
Bohannon, J. N., 371
Bohlin, G., 508
Boners, R. M., 240
Bonner, J. T., 402
Boomsma, D. I., 543
Booth, C. L., 390
Borke, H., 182
Borkowski, J. G., 286, 344, 513–514
Bornstein, M. H., 44, 89, 110, 148, 184, 235, 370, 390, 507, 566–568
Borton, R. W., 125–126, 406
Bosch, L., 122, 389
Boseovski, J. J., 203
Boston, M. B., 434–435
Bouchard, T. J., Jr., 483, 540
Bowen, R., 178
Bowerman, M., 359
Bow-Thomas, C. C., 474
Boyce, W. T., 333
Boyd, R., 402
Boyer, P., 216
Boyer, T., 209
Bradley, R. H., 549–551, 559
Brainerd, C. J., 175, 181–183, 189–192, 195, 280, 316, 321, 327–329, 333, 336, 339, 347, 461
Brainerd, S. H., 182
Brandse, E., 329
Brannon, E. M., 145
Bräuer, J., 220
Bray, N. W., 509
Brazelton, T. B., 500
Bremner, A. J., 142

Brenneman, K., 160
Brenner, G. J., 132
Brent, M. R., 362
Bretherton, I., 236
Briars, D., 463, 471
Bridger, W. H., 126
Broaders, S., 468
Brody, N., 503
Bromley, D., 427
Bronfenbrenner, U., 16, 545
Bronson, G. W., 109–110
Brooks, R., 202
Brooks-Gunn, J., 424–426, 551
Brown, A., 268
Brown, A. L., 95, 292–293, 295
Brown, E., 131–132
Brown, E. D., 534, 558
Brown, R., 356–357, 372
Brown, R. D., 267–268, 274, 278, 300, 333–336
Brown, S. C., 471, 511
Bruck, M., 328, 330–333, 337, 339, 347
Bruner, J. S., 84, 240, 370, 382, 385, 392
Bryant, P. E., 448, 452
Bryson, S. E., 252
Buccino, G., 415
Buck, S. M., 538
Budgwig, N., 361
Bukatko, D., 157
Bull, R., 470, 471
Bullock, M., 275, 289, 295, 424
Bunge, S. A., 266
Burchinal, M. R., 559
Burgess, S. R., 446–447
Burts, D. C., 484
Bushnell, I. W. R., 115
Buss, D. M., 37
Buttelmann, D., 240, 413
Byrne, R., 220, 525
Byrne, R. W., 406–407, 415
Byrnes, J. P., 69

**C**

Cacioppo, J. T., 415
Cahan, S., 480–482
Cain, K., 452
Cairns, R. B., 407
Caldera, Y. M., 235
Caldwell, B. M., 549–551
Call, J., 220, 410, 413
Callanan, M. A., 390
Callies, S., 465
Calvert, S. L., 81
Cameron-Faulkner, T., 372
Campbell, B. C., 543
Campbell, F. A., 558, 560–561
Campbell, T., 288–289
Campione, J. C., 95
Campos, J. J., 61

Candy, 107
Canfield, R. L., 252
Canivez, G. L., 502
Capon, N., 178, 182
Capozzoli, M., 259
Cappa, S. F., 376–377
Carelli, M. G., 343
Carey, S., 66, 136–137, 143–144, 222–223, 362–363
Carlson, J. S., 486
Carlson, S. M., 205, 212, 252, 262, 300, 389
Carlson-Luden, V., 236
Carmody, D. P., 426
Caron, A. J., 206
Carpendale, J. I. M, 205
Carpenter, M., 182, 200, 202, 220, 382–383, 410, 413, 416
Carpenter, T. P., 464
Carr, M., 281, 285, 466, 513, 514
Carraher, D., 472
Carraher, T. N., 472
Carriger, M. S., 507, 567
Carrol, J. B., 497
Carroll, J. M., 356
Carroll, K., 209
Carver, L. J., 310
Case, K. S., 526
Case, R., 26, 68, 181, 183, 256, 276, 425, 540
Caselli, M. C., 363
Casey, B. J., 52
Casey, P. H., 559
Casler, K., 239–240
Caspi, A., 41–42, 536, 537
Cassel, W. S., 328–329, 333–334
Cassidy, D. J., 268
Castelli, D. M., 538
Castle, J., 557
Cattell, R. B., 496
Caughy, M. O., 550, 552
Causey, K., 19, 38, 343, 402
Cavanaugh, J. C., 344
Cazzaniga, L., 67
Ceci, S. J., 44, 280, 290–291, 316–317, 328–331, 333, 335–340, 347, 482–483, 507, 527, 531, 540, 541, 545–546
Cervantes, C. A., 390
Chall, J. S., 444
Chamberlin, M. H., 228
Chan, C. K. K., 448
Chandler, M., 210–211
Chandler, M. J., 533–534, 555
Changeux, J. P., 61
Chapa, C., 136
Chapman, C., 81
Chapman, R. S., 364–365
Charak, D., 251
Charity, A. H., 368
Chechile, R. A., 278
Chelune, G. J., 267

Chen, C., 257–258, 475
Chen, Z., 236–238, 241, 288–289, 294–297
Cheney, D. F., 350
Cheyne, J. A., 240
Chi, M. T. H., 255–256, 278, 540
Chinsky, J. H., 272
Chomsky, N., 373
Christakis, D. A., 20
Christian, K., 481
Chuah, Y. M. L., 257
Chugani, D. C., 548
Chugani, H. T., 57, 548
Church, J., 428
Church, R. B., 270
Cianciolo, A. T., 514
Cicchetti, D., 387
Clark, E. A., 68, 554, 556
Clarke, A. D. B., 554
Clarke, A. M., 554
Clarke-Stewart, A., 335
Clearfield, M. W., 23, 145
Clemente, R. A., 445
Clements, W. A., 206–207
Cleveland, E. S., 324
Cliffordson, C., 481
Clinkenbeard, P., 494
Clubb, P. A., 321, 330
Coatsworth, J. D., 51
Cocas, L. A., 23, 145
Coffman, J. L., 286
Cohen, L., 147
Cohen, L. B., 132
Cohen, M., 268
Cohen, N., 480–482
Cohen, S., 566
Coie, J. D., 423
Cole, M., 16–17, 76–77, 98, 178–179, 285
Collaer, M. L., 235
Collie, R., 312–313
Collier, V. P., 390
Colvert, E,, 557
Conner, J. M., 232
Connolly, K., 235
Connor, C. M., 454
Cook, S. W., 385, 468–469
Cooley, C., 424
Cooper, J., 428
Cooper, R. P., 386
Copopola, M., 378
Corballis, M. C., 342
Cordes, S., 145
Cormier, C., 402
Cortelyou, 126
Cosmides, L., 32–33, 35–36, 37, 400
Coulombre, A. J., 5
Courage, M. L., 20, 108, 112, 183, 280, 306–307, 315–317, 347, 426
Courchesne, E., 376
Court, J. H., 481, 498, 500
Cowan, N., 252, 256, 276, 347
Cowan, P. A,, 224–225

Cox, B. C., 274
Cox, D., 274
Coyle, T. R., 270, 272
Crabtree, J. W., 60
Crago, M. D., 374
Craig, I. W., 41–42, 536
Craighero, L., 415–416
Craik, F. I. M., 388–389
Crain-Thoreson, C., 446
Crawford, J., 390
Cremer, J. F., 420
Crick, N. R., 421, 423
Cronbach, L. J., 7
Cross, D., 200, 212
Cruttenden, L., 305
Csibra, G., 117, 214
Csinady, A., 414
Cuban, L., 526
Cuevas, K., 306
Cullen, M. J., 504
Cultice, J. C., 342
Cummins, D. D., 206, 400
Cummins-Sebree, S. W., 240
Cunha, F., 561
Cunningham, A. E., 448
Cunningham, W. R., 284
Currie, J., 560
Curtiss, S., 378–379, 554
Cutting, J. E., 221–222
Cynader, M., 60, 61

**D**

Dabholkar, A. S., 57–58
Dack, L. A., 205, 401
Daehler, M., 294–295
Daehler, M. W., 157
Dale, P. S., 445–446
Daley, T. C., 573
Dallago, M. L. P., 509
Daneman, M., 452
Daniel, M. H., 496
Daniels, D., 420
Daniels, M., 542
Dapretto, M., 416
Darwin, C., 34–35, 123
Das, J. P., 509
Dasen, P. R., 178–179
Davidson, J., 539
Davis, E. F., 238
Davis, O. S., 541
Davis, P., 488
Dawson, G., 215
Day, M. C., 182
Deacon, T. W., 54
Deák, G. O., 160
Deary, I. J., 503
DeBell, M., 81
DeCasper, A. J., 103, 119–120
Decety, J., 415
de Haan, M., 10, 57, 62, 67, 113, 119, 313
Dehaene, S., 61

De Houwer, A., 388
Delevati, N. M., 102
De Lisi, R., 178, 180, 182
DeLoache, J. S., 88, 156–158, 160, 195, 268, 287, 290, 293, 294, 298
Deloitte's State of the Media Democracy Survey, Third Edition, 81
Delpit, L. D., 368
DeMarie, D., 278, 284
DeMarie-Dreblow, D, 269
DeMendoza, O. A. P., 88
Demetriou, A., 92, 573
Dempster, F. N., 68, 252, 254–255, 267, 381, 507
Dennett, D., 238
Dennis, M., 278
Dennis, W., 546, 553
de Schonen, S., 117–118
Desjardins, R. N., 387
Desoete, A., 463
DeStefano, J., 368
Detterman, D. K., 496, 506, 539
Devenny, D. A., 508
Deverensky, J. L., 369
de Villiers, J. G., 356, 361, 366
de Villiers, P. A., 356, 361, 366
Devlin, B., 542
De Vos, J., 134, 139–140
De Vries, R., 159, 428
de Waal, F. B. M., 425
Dewhurst, S. A., 280
Diamond, A., 33, 63–64, 69, 142, 261, 305, 538
Diaz, R. M., 95
Díaz, R. M., 390
Díaz-LeFebvre, R., 526
Dicke, U., 54
Diesendruck, G., 364
DiLalla, L. F., 550
Dirix, C. E. H., 106
Dobbs, D., 153
Dobzhansky, T., 17
Dodge, K. A., 421–423
Dolan, C. V., 543
Doman, G., 483
Dore, F. Y., 130
Dougherty, T. M., 568
Dowdy, J. K., 368
Dow-Ehrensberger, M., 481
Drachman, D. B., 5
Dropik, P. L., 312
Drummey, A. B., 319
Dubas, J. S., 232
DuBois, L. C., 6
Duffy, S., 259–260
Dukes, C., 267–268, 274, 278, 300
Dumas, C., 130
Dunbar, R. I. M., 402
Duncan, J., 497
Duncan, R., 392
Dunlosky, J., 419
Dunn, J., 89, 90
Dunn, M., 481

Dunning, D. L., 538
Dupuis, D., 488
Dutilleul, S., 106
Dutton, S., 240
Dweck, C. S., 399

**E**

Eagan, S. K., 427
Eals, M., 231–232
Earles, J. L., 382
Easterbrook, M. A., 114
Eaton, W. O., 428–429
Eddy, T. J., 220
Edelman, G. M., 61
Ehri, L. C., 444
Eichorn, D. H., 565
Eichorst, D. L., 408
Eidelman, A., 200
Eilers, R., 121, 354
Eimas, P. D., 120–121,
    147–148, 356
Einstein, G. O., 341
Eisen, M., 427
Elardo, R., 549
Elischberger, H. B., 330
Elkind, D., 178, 182, 378–379, 484
Ellis, B. J., 47
Ellis, H., 477
Ellis, N. C., 258
Ellis, S., 96, 182
Elman, J., 382
Elman, J. L., 9, 26, 30, 47, 58
Else-Quest, N. M., 475
Eluvathingal, T. J., 548
English and Romanian Adoptee Study,
    557
Ensor, R., 205, 252
Erdelyi, M., 317
Eriksen, W., 49
Eriksson, P. S., 56
Erlbaum, L., 233
Erskine, J. M., 449
Esplin, P. W., 341, 347
Espy, K. A., 251, 550
Evans, G. W., 552
Evans, M. A., 370–371
Evans, M. E., 216
Evans, N., 382
Evans, P. D., 53
Everall, R., 481
Eyer, D., 491
Eysenck, H. J., 539

**F**

Fabricius, W. V., 208–209
Fadil, C., 425
Fagan, J. F., III, 306, 309, 565–566,
    567–568
Fagot, B. I., 434–435
Fan, L., 474
Fantz, R. L., 104, 108, 110–112

Farroni, T., 116–117
Fauth, R. C., 550
Fecteau, S., 415
Feigenson, L., 143
Fein, G., 183–184, 234
Feinberg, I., 58
Feingold, A., 455, 476, 477
Feldman, D. H., 494
Feldman, J. F., 566, 568
Feldman, R., 200
Feltovich, P. J., 278
Fennema, E., 476
Ferdinandsen, K., 110
Ferguson, C. A., 355, 370
Fernald, A., 362, 385–387
Fernyhough, C., 394
Ferrari, M., 494
Ferrari, P. F., 407
Ferreira, F., 481
Ferrer, E., 68, 252, 507
Ferron, J., 284
Field, T. M., 102, 405–406, 408
Fifer, W. P., 119
Finkelstein, N. W., 419, 558
Fischer, K. W., 86, 150–151, 181–182
Fisher, C., 385
Fisher, J. A., 227
Fivush, R., 316, 321–325, 340, 391
Flannagan, D., 325
Flavell, E. R., 159–160, 200, 282
Flavell, J. H., 159–160, 182–183, 200,
    204, 267, 272, 274, 282, 369–370,
    394, 399
Fleming, V. M., 95
Fletcher, K. L., 509
Flieller, A., 573
Flin, R., 329
Flinn, M., 38
Flom, R., 124, 128
Flynn, E., 205
Flynn, E. G., 410–412
Flynn, J. R., 573, 575
Fodor, J. A., 26
Fogassi, L., 415
Folds, T. H., 280
Foley, M. A., 96–97, 185, 337
Forbes, J. N., 202
Ford, L. H., 427
Forman, H., 343
Fouts, D. H., 350
Fouts, R. S., 350, 413
Fox, N. A., 64, 69, 319, 558, 575
Fox, S. E., 59
Fragaszy, D. M., 240
Frazier, J. A., 475, 480
Freedle, R. O., 390
Freedman, M., 389
Freeman, W. P., 119–120
French, R. M., 293
Freud, S., 315
Freund, L. S., 95, 97
Frey, K. S., 428–429
Friedman, N. P., 252

Friedman, O., 261
Friedman, S., 106, 305
Friedman, W. J., 241, 243–244
Fritz, A. S., 210–211
Frost, J., 448
Fry, A., 507–509, 539
Fry, A. F., 252
Frye, D., 263–264
Fu, V. R., 475
Fuligni, A. J., 474
Fulker, D., 540
Furlow, F. B., 543
Furman, L. N., 278, 371
Furtado, E. A., 575
Furth, H. G., 391
Fuson, K. C., 462–463
Fuster, J. M., 62, 66, 523

**G**

Galasso, L., 185
Gallay, M., 119
Gallese, V., 415
Gallistel, C. R., 462
Gallup, G. G., Jr., 424
Galsworthy, M. J., 391
Ganea, P. A., 158–159
Ganger, J., 362
Gangestad, S. W., 116
Garber, H. L., 558
Garcia, E. E., 388
Gardiner, A., 409
Gardiner, A. K., 225, 234–236
Gardner, A. G., 243
Gardner, B., 350
Gardner, H., 122, 443, 494, 521–523
Gardner, R. A., 350
Gareil, J. D., 319
Garnham, W. A., 206
Garon, N,, 252
Garon, N., 263
Gaskins, S., 17
Gathercole, S. E., 256, 538
Gathercole V. C. M, 389, 452
Gaultney, J. F., 270, 286, 418, 509–511
Gauvain, M., 16, 77–78, 82, 87–88, 93,
    96–99, 323
Gava, L., 117–118
Ge, L., 119, 153
Geary, D. C., 35–39, 72, 130, 143–144,
    151, 197–198, 221, 225, 231, 234–
    235, 240–241, 246, 257, 265, 352,
    399–400, 402, 443, 456, 459, 466,
    471, 474, 476, 479–480, 485–487,
    490–491, 511
Gelman, R., 23, 36, 130, 150, 182, 199,
    371, 462–463
Gelman, S. A., 216, 221–224
Genesee, F., 390
Genter, D., 293
Gentes, E., 337
Geren, J., 363
Gergely, G., 410–411

German, T., 238
Gernsbacher, M. A., 456, 476, 491
Gersten, R., 561–562
Gesell, A., 500
Ghatala, E. S., 279, 283
Ghazanfar, A. A., 10, 119, 127
Gholson, B., 294
Gibb, R., 54
Gibson, E. J., 126
Giedd, J. N., 51–52, 56–57, 72, 254, 319
Gimpert, N., 96–97
Gladwell, M., 93, 99
Glaser, R., 278
Gleitman, L. R., 364
Goddard, 145
Godfield, B. A., 362
Goldberg, J., 540
Goldberg, R. F., 222
Goldberg, S., 235
Goldin-Meadow, S., 270, 383–385, 468–469
Goldman, J., 224–225
Goldman, R., 224–225
Goldstein, D., 509, 510
Goldstein, S., 263
Golinkoff, R. M., 364, 491
Golomb, C., 185
Golombok, S., 433
Gómez, J. C., 351
Göncü, A., 90–92
Goodman, G. S., 328, 330, 335
Goodman, J. F., 20
Goodz, E., 369
Goodz, N. S., 361
Gopnik, A., 182, 195, 198–199, 203–204, 207, 246, 325
Gopnik, M., 374
Gordon, B. N., 328, 332
Gordon, C., 452
Gordon, L. L., 191–192
Gordon, P., 79
Gosso, Y., 185
Goswami, U., 291–293, 294, 448–449
Gotlieb, S., 147
Gottardo, A., 448
Gottfried, A. W., 126
Gottlieb, G., 11, 39, 40–42, 45, 72, 413, 532, 536, 542
Gould, E., 56
Gould, S. J., 35, 524
Gouze 1987, 423
Graces, E., 560
Graham, L., 325
Graham, S., 423
Grammar, J., 286
Gray, S., 558–559
Gray, W. M., 178
Gredlein, J. M., 235, 237–238, 241
Green, B. L., 19, 69, 175, 178, 418
Green, F. L., 159–160, 200, 282
Green, I., 452

Green, L. J., 366
Greenfield, P., 413
Greenfield, P. M., 93, 573
Greenhoot, A. F., 330–332
Greenough, W. T., 60–61, 65, 546
Gregg, V. H., 228
Gregory, A., 505
Greif, M., 409
Greif, M. L., 223
Grice, H. P., 365
Griepentrog, G. J., 118
Griffin, D. M., 368
Griffith, E. M., 480, 481
Grigorenko, E. L., 520
Groen, G. J., 464
Groothues, c., 557
Gross, C. G., 110
Grotuss, J., 414
Grunau, R. E., 102
Guberman, S. R., 473
Guerra, N. G., 423
Guertin, T. L., 507
Guilford, J. P., 495
Güler, O. E., 285
Güntürkün, O, 425
Gur, R. C., 456, 476, 491
Gustafsson, J.-E., 481
Guthrie, D., 558, 575
Guttentag, R. E., 273, 277, 320
Guy, L., 408

**H**

Haden, C. A., 303, 323–325, 391
Haefele-Kalvaitis, J., 278
Hagan, R., 435
Haier, R. J., 251
Haight, W. L., 184
Haine, R. A., 391
Haist, F., 376
Haith, M. M., 109, 124, 128, 151, 320, 568
Hakuta, K., 380, 388, 390
Hala, S., 210–212
Halberstadt, J., 116
Hale, G. A., 278
Hale, S., 252, 507–509, 539
Haley, M. H., 526
Halford, G. S., 291, 293
Halliday, M. A. K., 352
Hallinan, E. V, 202, 410
Halpern, D. F., 229, 231, 233–234, 455–457, 459, 475–476, 478, 491
Halverson, C. F., 431–432, 437
Hamlin, J. K., 202, 410
Hamond, N. R., 316, 321–322
Han, J. J., 325
Hanania, R., 263
Hanisee, J., 68, 554, 556
Hanish, L., 423
Hanlon, C., 372

Hannon, E. E., 118, 123
Hansen, J., 452–453
Hardison, C. M., 504
Hare, B., 220
Harlow, H. F., 19, 21, 68
Harnishfeger, K. K., 24, 209, 261–262, 265, 270, 276–277, 507, 511
Harnquist, K., 483
Harris, J. R., 542
Harris, M. J., 49, 542
Harris, P. L., 185–186, 200, 203, 400, 403, 409
Harris, R. C., 68, 554
Hart, C. L., 503
Hart, D., 390
Harter, S., 418–419, 441
Harvey, P. H., 54
Hasher, L., 68–69, 251, 320, 509
Hashimoto, R., 375
Hasselhorn, M., 274, 276, 343
Hatano, G., 221, 223
Hauser, L. B., 144
Hauser, M., 143
Hauser, M. D., 144
Haworth, C. M., 541
Hayes, B. K., 319
Hayes, C., 350
Hayne, H., 315–316, 408
Hayne, R., 312–313
Haynes, O. M, 390
Healy, J., 73
Heath, S. B., 367
Hebb, D. O., 65
Hecht, S. A., 471
Hedges, L. V., 455, 475–476
Hedrick, A. M., 324
Heekereb, H. R., 376–377
Heimann, M., 407
Hein, A., 61
Heinmiller, B. M., 123
Hencke, R. W., 182
Henderson, C. R., 543
Henelley, R. A., 258
Hennessy, R., 319
Henry, L. A., 508
Herman, J. F., 227
Hernández Blasi, C., 18, 35, 78, 217, 401, 462, 485
Hernandez-Reif, 113
Herrmann, E., 220, 413
Herrnstein, R. J., 503
Hershkowitz, L., 347
Herzing, D. L., 412
Hespos, S. J., 134–135, 145
Hickling, A. K., 188, 223
Hilden, K. R., 24, 25, 265
Hillman, C. H., 252, 538
Hines, M., 235, 436–437
Hiraki, K., 266
Hirschman, J., 328

Hirsh-Pasek, K., 364, 484–485, 491
Hiscock, M., 64
Hitch, G. J., 256–257, 466
Hix, H. R., 212, 262
Hjertholm, E., 392–393
Hobson, R. P., 215
Hodge, D., 338
Hoerr, T., 526
Hoff, E., 88, 351, 353, 361, 364, 369, 371, 378, 385, 386, 388, 396
Hoff-Ginsberg, E., 386
Hoffman, M. L., 182
Hogarty, P. S., 500, 565, 570–571
Hogrefe, G.-J., 203
Hollich, G., 364
Holmboe, K., 64, 267
Holmes, J., 538
Holowka, S., 355
Holyoak, K. J., 291, 293, 294, 295
Honzik, M. P., 569–570
Hood, B., 136–137
Hood, B. M., 128, 142
Hood, L., 372, 377
Hooper, L. M., 410–412
Hopkins, S. L., 466
Horner, V., 404, 409–410, 412–413
Horowitz, F. D., 149
Hort, B. E., 434
Horvat, M., 488
Hou, Y., 317
Howe, M. L., 112, 183, 280, 306–307, 315–318, 322, 337, 426
Huberty, P. D., 488
Hubertz, M. J., 84–85, 470
Hude, J. S., 476
Hudley, C., 423
Hudson, J. A., 321, 323
Hudson, L. M., 178
Huesmann, L. R., 423
Huffman, K., 36, 151
Hughes, C., 205, 252
Hulme, C., 257–258, 448, 470–471
Humphrey, N. K., 209, 439
Hund, A. M., 230
Hünnerkopf, M., 275–276
Hunt, E., 507, 539
Hunt, J. McV., 139, 166
Huntsinger, C. S., 475
Hurlburt, N., 500
Huston, A. C., 435, 437
Hutt, C., 234
Huttenlocher, J., 145, 226–227, 229, 247, 260, 481
Huttenlocher, P., 57, 58, 227, 380
Hyde, J. S., 231, 455–457, 475–478, 491
Hyman. I. E., Jr., 338
Hymes, D, 368

Hymovitch, B., 65
Hyson, M. C., 484–485

**I**

Imbens-Bailey, A. L., 208
Inagaki, K., 221, 223
Inhelder, B., 169, 176–177, 229–230, 291, 295, 298, 320
Insel, T. R., 53
Istomina, Z. M., 320
Itier, R. J., 186
Iverson, J. M., 383–384

**J**

Jaakkola, K., 222
Jack, F., 324
Jacklin, C. N., 231, 455
Jackson, J. F., 50
Jackson, P., 274
Jackson, R. S., 107
Jacobs, J. W., 279
Jacobson, K. C., 544
Jacobson, L., 505
Jacobson, S. W., 405, 407
Jacoby, L. L., 320
Jager, T., 343
Jamison, W., 232
Jarrett, O. S., 488
Jenkins, E., 78, 285, 467
Jenkins, J. M., 90, 205–206
Jenkins, L., 409
Jensen, A. R., 496, 502, 505, 507–508, 531, 539, 540
Jensen, P. S., 263, 488
Jerison, H. J., 53
Jerman, O., 452
Jessie, K. A., 252
Jessup, D. L., 281, 466
Joffe, T. H., 402
Johnson, D. W., 95, 96
Johnson, J. S., 378–380, 389
Johnson, M. H., 10, 30, 33, 40, 52, 56–60, 65, 67, 69, 113–115, 117, 119
Johnson, N. E., 507
Johnson, R. T., 95
Johnson, S., 238
Johnson, S. C., 221
Johnson, S. P., 133, 231
Johnston, R. S., 471
Jones, I., 488
Jones, L. B., 251
Jones, S., 408
Jose, P. E., 475
Joseph, R., 367
Juffer, F., 548
Juhász, C., 548
Junn, E. N., 291
Jusczyk, P., 122
Jusczyk, P. W., 118, 120, 242
Justice, E. M., 283

**K**

Kagan, J., 21–22, 112, 313
Kail, R. V., 68, 175, 252–253, 448, 507–550
Kaitz, M., 405
Kalakanis, 149
Kalichman, S. C., 230
Kalish, C. W., 401
Kamawar, D., 463
Kane, M. J., 295
Kantor, L., 508
Kaplan, H., 38, 402
Kaplowitz, C., 425
Kappeler, P., 525
Karama, S., 497
Karmiloff, K., 397
Karmiloff-Smith, A., 27, 30, 142, 150
Karmiloff-Smith, K., 397
Karoly, L. A., 561
Karzon, R. G., 386
Katz, G. S., 386
Kaufman, L., 134, 242
Kavanaugh, R. D., 408
Kawamura, T., 260
Kaye, K., 370, 408
Kearney, J. K., 420
Kearsley, R. B., 252
Keating, D. P., 143
Kee, D. W., 278
Keeble, S., 242
Keen, R., 137
Keiffer, J., 326
Kelemen, D., 216–217, 239–240, 246
Keller, A., 427
Keller, H., 400
Kellman, P. J., 107–108, 133, 153
Kellogg, A., 350
Kellogg, W. N., 350
Kelly, D., 119, 153
Kelly, M. K., 243
Kemler Nelson, D. G., 242
Kennedy, C. B., 112–113
Kennedy, J. K. J., 536
Kenney-Benson, G. A., 475
Kenny, P., 19, 30, 36, 45, 381
Kent, R., 355
Kerns, K. A., 343
Kersten, A. W., 382
Kesek, A., 252, 300
Kessen, W., 109–110, 182
Khaitovich, P., 53
Khalil, S. L., 208
Kikuchi, Y., 215
Kim, K. H. S., 376
Kim, P., 552
Kim-Cohen, J., 41–42, 51
King, S., 6
Kinzler, K. D., 9, 23, 36, 130, 134, 153, 182, 197, 199
Kipp, K., 36, 205, 261, 262

Kiraly, I., 410–411
Kirkham, N., 261
Kirschner, S,, 123
Kita, S., 378
Kitamura, C., 385
Kitayama, S., 259–260
Kittler, P. M., 508
Klaczynski, P. A., 189, 298
Klahr, D., 296–297
Klaus, R. A., 558–559
Klibanoff, R. S., 286
Kliegel, M., 343
Knopf, M., 254, 275, 344–345, 482
Kochanska, G., 261
Koerber, S., 295
Kohlberg, L., 392–393, 427
Köhler, W., 236
Kolb, B., 54, 67, 375
Koluchova, J., 553
Konner, M. J., 179
Kopp, C. B., 139, 166, 569
Körkel, J., 26–27, 278, 512–514
Kornhuber, H. H., 67
Koshmider, J. W., 465
Kotovsky, L., 134
Kotovsky, L, 242
Koustaal, W., 318
Kovács, A. M., 389
Krachun, C., 220
Kramer, S. J., 221
Krapp, A., 458
Krasnor, L. R., 421, 424
Kremer, K. E., 216
Kreppner, J., 557
Kreutzer, M. A., 282
Krinsky-McHale, S. J., 508
Kron-Sperl, V., 275–276
Kroupina, M. G., 313, 315
Kruger, A. C., 351, 403–404,
    413–414
Krumhansl, C., 122
Krupa, M. H., 232
Kuebli, J., 321
Kuhl, P., 120–121, 126–127
Kuhl, P. K., 356, 385–386
Kuhlmeier, 156
Kuhn, D., 64, 178, 182, 267, 281,
    295–297, 303
Kurland, M., 540
Kurtz, B. E., 284, 285
Kurtz-Costes, B., 344
Kvavilashvili, L, 342
Kyle, F., 342


**L**

Laboratory of Comparative Human
    Cognition, 86, 504, 516
Lam, S.-F., 474
Lamb, M. E., 340–341, 345, 347
Lambert, W. E., 390
Lamon, S. J., 476
Landau, K. R., 426

Landau, S., 392
Landry, S. H., 552
Lane, D. M., 259
Lang, B., 205
Lange, G., 274
Langlois, J., 115–116, 119, 149
Langlois, J. H., 116, 126
Lansman, M., 539
Lapkin, S., 390
Larkina, M., 285
Larsen, J. T., 260
Larsen, R. J., 116
Larson, S. L., 475
Larsson, A., 341
Larus, D. M., 328
Lave, J., 92
Lawrence, A., 258
Lawson, C. A., 401
Lawson, K. R., 259
Lawson, M. J., 466
Lazar, I., 560
Lazarids, M., 426
Leaper, C., 390
Learmonth, A., 227
Lechner, R. E., 366
Lee, E. S., 483, 488
Lee, K., 119, 153, 212
Lee, S. Y., 473–474
Leekam, S. R., 205
LeFevre, J., 89, 466
Legerstee, M., 407, 425
Le Grand, R., 61
Lehman, E. B., 262
Lehmann, M., 276, 343
Lei, P., 502
Leichtman, M. D., 316–317, 325, 329,
    336
Leinbach, M. D., 434–435
Lemaire, P., 465
Lempers, J. D., 366
Lenhart, A., 81
Lenneberg, E. H., 44, 373, 378–379
Lenroot, R. K., 51–52, 56–57, 72, 254,
    319
Leo, I., 127
Leon, D. A., 503
Leonard, C., 282
Lepage, J. F., 415–416
Lerner, R. M., 11–12, 30, 39, 40
Leslie, A., 213
Leslie, A. M., 242, 261
Leslie, L., 27, 512
Lester, D., 218
Levin, J. R., 486
Levine, L. E., 175
Levine, S., 260, 481
Levine, S. C., 145, 231
Levinson, S., 382
Levitt, P., 59
Levy, B. A., 446
Levy, G. D., 434–435
Lewis, C., 205, 252, 280
Lewis, K. D., 325

Lewis, M., 215, 235, 390, 424, 425, 426
Lewis, M. D., 11, 13, 30
Lewis, T. L., 61
Lewkowicz, D. J., 10, 119, 124–125,
    127, 242
Lhote, M., 106
Li, S.-C., 39
Liben, L. S., 227, 230–231,
    434–435
Liberman, I. Y., 447–448
Liberty, C., 273
Lickliter, R., 39, 42, 45–47, 124–125,
    128
Lie, E., 319
Lieberman, P., 355
Lietz, P., 457
Lieven, T., 372
Light, L. L., 267–268, 303
Lightbrown, P., 372, 377
Lillard, A., 184, 203
Lin, C.-Y. C., 475
Lindberg, M., 279
Lindberg, M. A., 326–328
Lindsay, D. S., 337
Linn, M. C., 231, 455, 475, 478
Linver, M. R., 550
Lipko, A. R., 419
Lipton, J. S., 145
Lipton, R. C., 546–547
Liston, C., 313
Liszkowski, U., 202, 383, 392
Litrownik, J., 278
Little, J. K., 435
Liu, D., 203
Liu, H.-M., 120, 356
Livesley, W., 427
Lloyd, M. E., 319
Locke, J. L., 378–379, 387–388
Lockl, K., 205, 281
Lockman, J. J., 235
Loe, I. M., 262
Loftus, E. F., 337–338
LOGIC study, 275–276
Lonardo, R., 157
Long, C., 295
Longstreth, L. E., 555
Lonigan, C. J., 446
Lonigan, C. J., 446–447
Looft, W. R., 221–222
Lopez, D. F., 420
Lubinski, D., 479
Ludwig, J., 560
Luecke-Aleska, D., 429
Luk, G., 389
Lukas, W. D., 543
Lum, J., 319
Luna, B., 63, 64, 267
Lundberg, I., 448
Luria, A. R., 179–180, 267
Lutchmaya, S., 391
Lütkenhaus, P., 289, 424
Lynch, M. P., 123
Lynn, S. J., 317

Lyons, D. E., 409
Lyytinen, H., 448

**M**

Maccoby, E., 231
Maccoby, E. E., 455
Macfarlane, A., 102–103
MacFarlane, J. W., 569
MacKinlay, R., 343
MacLean, M., 508
MacLean, P. D., 52
MacWhinney, B., 122, 364, 371, 389
Madole, K. L., 148
Mahone, E. M., 508
Maier-Brückner, W., 284, 512
Makin, J. W., 103
Malloy, P., 266
Mandel, D. R., 242
Mandler, J. M., 146, 150, 321
Manion, V., 95
Mäntylä, T., 343
Manwah, NJ, 233
Maratsos, M., 371
Marche, T. A., 337
Marcon, R. A., 484
Marcovitch, S., 139, 142
Marcus, G. F., 357–358
Marcus, J., 408
Marean, G. C., 121
Marentette, P. F., 355
Mareschal, D., 142
Mariani, M. A., 263
Marino, L., 425
Markel, R. A., 458
Markman, E. M., 186, 363–364, 366
Markson, L., 238, 364
Marlier, L., 102–103
Marsh, H. W., 478
Marshall, P. J., 558, 575
Martin, C., 343
Martin, C. L., 427, 430, 431–432, 435, 441
Marzolf, D. P., 156, 158, 160
Masataka, N., 123, 386
Mason, J. M., 446
Masten, A. S., 51
Mastropieri, M. A., 286
Masur, E. F., 408
Matheny, A. P., Jr., 49
Mattock, A., 131–132
Maughan, B., 557
Maurer, D., 61, 110, 126
Maxwell. S. E., 513
Maybery, M. T., 257
Mayhew, E. M., 321
Mazzie, C., 385
Mazziotta, J. C., 57
Mazzocco, M. M. M., 470
Mazzoni, G., 337
McAndrews, M. P., 319
McBride-Chang, C., 448

McCall, R. B., 112–113, 408, 500, 507, 559, 565, 567, 569–572
McCallum, S., 206
McCarthy, D., 390
McCartney, K., 39, 48–50, 479, 538, 542, 571
McCloskey, L. A., 366–367
McDaniel, M. A., 341
McDounough, L., 312
McGilly, K., 272
McGown, C., 505
McGue, M., 539–540
McGuigan, N., 409–410
Meachum, J. A., 427
Meany, M. J., 536
Meck, E., 463
Mehler, J., 389
Mejia-Arauz, R., 17
Mekel-Bobrov, N., 53
Melhuish, E. C., 549
Melinder, A. M., 333
Melis, A. P., 220
Melot, A.-M., 283
Meltzoff, A. N., 20, 23, 125–127, 150, 198–199, 202, 246, 315, 389, 402, 405–406, 410, 416
Mendelson, M., 124
Menn, L., 353–354
Menzel, E. W., Jr., 220
Mercer, M. E., 108
Merkin, S., 463
Merrill, M. A., 571
Merriman, W. E., 419
Merritt, K. A., 340
Mervis, C. B., 362–363
Messer, D. J., 96, 342
Meyer, K. K., 68, 554
Michotte, A., 242
Miles, H. L., 350
Miller, B. S., 227
Miller, D., 560
Miller, K., 99
Miller, K. F., 79–80, 92, 158, 287, 290, 293, 294, 298
Miller, L. C., 366, 474
Miller, L. T., 252, 508–509
Miller, P., 268–270, 276–277
Miller, P. H., 200, 281–282, 284, 399
Miller, P. J., 184
Miller, S. A., 219
Miller-Jones, D., 504–505
Milligan, K., 205
Milne, B. J., 41–42
Milner, B., 266, 318
Miranda, S. B., 111–112
Mistry, J., 90–92, 284
Mitchell, D. E., 60
Mitchell, Z. A., 385, 468–469
Miura, H., 481
Mix, K. S., 145
Mody, M., 451

Moely, B. E., 285–286, 509
Moffitt, T. E., 41–42
Moffitt, T. W., 537
Moga, N., 330
Mojardin, A. H., 329
Molenaar, P. C. M., 14, 543
Molfese, D. L., 376
Molfese, V. J., 376, 550
Moll, H., 200, 402
Molnar, P., 405, 407–408
Mondloch, C. J., 61, 114, 126
Money, J., 70
Monk, C. S., 313
Montemayor, R., 427
Montero, I., 394
Mood, D. W., 175
Moore, D. S., 23, 39, 145, 231, 386, 538
Moore, M. K., 23, 405–406, 416
Moore, T., 570
Morelli, G. A., 17, 82–83
Morgan, J. S., 278
Morgan, R., 125
Moriguchi, Y., 266
Morisset, C. E., 390
Morris, P. A., 16
Morrison, F., 481–482
Morrison, F. J., 454, 475, 480
Morrison, R. G., 293
Morrongiello, B. A., 307
Mortensen, E. L., 41
Morton, J., 114–115
Moser, J. M., 464
Moses, L. J., 205, 212, 262
Mosier, C., 90–92
Moskowitz, B. A., 388
Moss, L., 425
Most, R. K., 234–235
Moulson, M. C., 549
Mu, Y., 474
Muir, C., 258
Muir-Broaddus, J. E., 278, 291, 452
Mullen, M. K., 317, 325
Müller, G. B., 5
Mullin, J. T., 115
Mullis, I. V. S., 456
Munakata, Y., 142
Munroe, R. H., 428
Munroe, R. L., 93
Murray, C., 503
Muter, V., 448
Muzik, O., 548
Muzzatti, B., 478
Myers, G. F., 471
Myowa-Yamakoshi, M., 115, 407

**N**

Nadig, A. S., 371
Nagell, K., 200, 382, 409, 413
Naglieri, J., 392
Nagy, E., 405, 407–408

Nagy, F., 548
Naigles, L., 364
Naito, M., 481
Nakata, T., 123
Narasimham, G., 298
Nash, M. R., 318
Näslund, J. C., 446, 448
Naus, M. J., 267, 273–274, 278
Neal, C. J., 95
Needham, A., 133, 238
Neiderman, D., 305
Neisser, U., 315, 502, 503, 573
Nelson, C. A., III, 10, 33, 56–57, 59–60, 62, 65, 113, 119, 313, 547, 549, 556, 558, 575
Nelson, K., 77, 314, 316–317, 321–322, 325, 349, 363, 365, 392
Nesse, R. M., 35
Newcombe, N. S., 141–142, 226–227, 229, 232, 247, 319, 320
Newport, E. L., 44, 121, 349, 372, 378–382, 389
Ng, F. F.-Y., 474
Nicely, P., 370
NICHD Early Child Care Research Network, 341, 345, 534, 549, 551, 558
Nichols, S., 426
Nichols-Whitehead, P., 85
Nickens, S. D., 478
Nielsen, M., 409–410, 425
Nisbett, R. E., 259, 529
Norcia, A. M., 108
Norman, K. A., 318
Nowell, A., 455, 475–476
Noyes, C. R., 453
Núñez, M., 400
Nyberg, L., 508
Nyiti, R. M., 179

**O**

Oakes, L. M., 148, 242
Oakes, M. A., 338
Oakhill, J., 452
Obach, M. S., 286
Oberman, L. M., 416
O'Brien, M., 435, 437
O'Connor, J. J., 566
O'Connor, T. G., 556
Odegard, T. M., 191
Olds, D. L., 543
Olguin, K., 409
Oliver, A., 113, 119
Oliver, B. R., 445
Oller, D. K., 354
O'Loughlin, M., 281, 295–297
Olson, K. R., 399
Omanson, R. C., 453
O'Neill, M., 386

Onishi, K. H., 206
Opfer, J. E, 221
Oppenheim, R. W., 19, 407
Orbach, Y., 340, 347
Ornstein, P. A., 230, 267–268, 273–275, 278, 280, 286, 303, 323, 328, 330–332, 336, 340
Oshima-Takane, Y., 369
Ostrovsky, Y., 61
O'Sullivan, J. T., 337
Ovando, C. J., 390
Owen, D. R., 573
Oyama, S., 39, 40, 536
Ozcaliskan, S., 383
Ozyürek, A., 378

**P**

Paley, V. G., 195
Palincsar, A. S., 95
Panksepp, J., 263, 488
Paradise, R., 17
Parisi, D., 30
Parke, R. D., 408
Parker, B. D., 187, 195
Parker, J. F., 185
Parmelee, A. H., 139, 166, 566
Pascalis, D., 113
Pascalis, O., 10, 62, 119, 153
Passalacqua, C., 96, 337
Patterson, F., 350
Patterson, M. L., 127
Paukner, A., 415
Paulesu, E., 451
Paz-Alonso, P. M., 329
Pearson, B. Z., 390
Pearson, D. A., 259
Pearson, P. D., 452
Pease, M., 296
Peck, V. A., 513–514
Pellegrini, A. D., 35, 38, 68, 151, 184, 234–235, 241, 403, 414, 488, 538
Pennisi, E., 40
Perani, D., 376–377
Perera, F. P., 543
Pérez, B., 389
Perilloux, H. K., 426
Periss, V., 19, 38, 402
Perlmutter, M., 274, 394
Perner, J., 200, 203–207
Perry, D. G., 423, 427, 436
Perry, L. C., 423, 436
Peskin, J., 205, 212
Petersen, A., 231
Peterson, C., 317
Peterson, O.-P., 448
Petitto, L. A., 354–355
Petrill, S. A., 497, 540–542
Pezdek, K., 338
Phelps, M. E., 56, 57
Phillips, D. A., 560
Phillips, S., 6

Piaget, J., 138–139, 166, 168–169, 170–171, 174, 176–177, 182, 184, 195, 216, 221, 229–230, 236, 241, 291, 295, 298, 320, 369, 392, 408, 420, 424, 460–461
Pica, P., 79
Pickens, J. N., 112, 113, 306
Pickering, S. J., 256
Pickrell, J. E., 337–338
Pierce, K. A., 294
Pierce, S. H., 274
Pierroutsakos, S. L., 287, 290, 293, 294, 298
Pilemer, D. B., 314
Pillow, B. H., 282
Pine, K. J., 96
Pinker, S., 9, 371, 373–374, 378, 391, 397
Pipe, M.-E., 329, 340
Pisoni, D. B., 120, 122
Pitman, P. A., 220
Plomin, R., 47, 70, 445, 536–537, 540–542
Plotkin, H., 76
Plotnik, J. M., 425
Plumert, J. M., 85, 230, 419–420
Plunkett, K., 30, 363
Pollak, S. D., 548
Pollard, K. S., 53
Pomerantz, E. M., 474
Pons, F., 127
Poole, D. A., 328–329, 336, 337, 340–341, 345
Pope, S., 261, 262
Porter, R. H., 103
Posner, M. I., 251
Poulin-Dubois, D., 126, 202
Poulton, R., 41–42
Povinelli, D. J., 426
Powell, M. B., 336
Prasada, S., 136–137
Preissler, M. A., 158
Premack, D., 203
Pressley, M., 24, 25, 88, 256, 265, 281, 285–287, 450, 514
Price, J. M., 423
Price, T. S., 496
Principe, G. F., 185, 328, 339, 347
Prior, H., 425
Proffitt, D. R., 221–222
Provence, S., 546–547
Pursglove, R. C., 280
Putnam, S., 78, 88, 93–94

**Q**

Quas, J. A., 333
Quinn, P. C., 116, 119, 147–148, 149, 153, 231
Quon, E., 343

# R

Rabinowitz, M., 278
Ragan, P., 413
Raggatt, P., 391
Rainbow Project Collaborators, 514–515, 521, 529
Rakoczy, H., 205
Ramachandran, V. S., 416
Raman, L., 224
Ramani. G. B., 470
Ramey, C. T., 419, 534–535, 558, 560–561
Ramsey, J. L., 149
Ramsey-Rennels, J. L., 119, 126
Randall, J. D., 268
Rapus, T., 263–264
Rasmussen, P., 423
Ratner, H. H., 96, 185, 324, 337, 351, 403–404
Raven, J., 481, 498, 500
Raven, J. C., 481, 498, 500
Ray, E., 221
Ray, S. D., 160
Raymond, C. L., 478
Recht, D. R., 27, 512
Redcay, E., 376
Reeder, K., 366
Reese, E., 89, 186, 324–325, 391
Reid, M. K., 513
Reinisch, J. M., 543
Reiss, D., 425
Rendell, L., 412
Renninger, K. A., 458, 488
Repacholi, B. M., 207
Rescorla, L., 484–485
Resnick, L. B., 464
Reubens, A. C., 84–85
Reyna, V. F., 189–191, 280, 316, 321, 327–329, 333, 336, 347
Reynolds, A. J., 560
Reznick, J. S., 362, 567
Rheingold, H. L., 112, 517, 567
Rhodes, G., 116
Richardson, R., 315
Richerson, P., 402
Richert, R., 20
Richland, L. E., 260, 293
Richman, C. L., 279
Richmond, J., 313
Rickford, J. R., 366
Ridderinkhof, K. R., 192, 262
Riesen, A. H., 60
Rilling, J. K., 53
Rindermann, H., 483
Ringel, B. A., 270, 283
Rittle-Johnson, B., 270, 394
Riva, D., 67
Rizzolatti, G., 415–416
Robbins, M., 369
Roberts, K., 149
Robinson, T. E., 54
Rochat, P., 90, 125, 148, 153, 424, 425

Rodemaker, J. E., 408
Roe, K. B., 391
Roebers, C. E. M., 328
Roebers, C. M., 330, 336–337
Roeder, K., 542
Roeyers, H., 463
Roggman, L. A., 116
Rogoff, B., 16–17, 76–77, 86–88, 90–92, 95–97, 285, 485
Rohwer, W. D., Jr., 278
Roid, G., 498, 500
Roman, A. A., 447
Rooksby M., 280, 315–317
Rosch, E., 148
Rose, S. A., 112, 125, 126, 252, 566–568
Rosenberg, J. S., 47, 402, 413
Rosenblum, K. E., 271
Rosengren,K., 394
Rosengren, K. S., 158
Rosenthal, R., 231, 505
Ross, D. F., 336
Ross, G., 84
Roth, G., 54
Rothbart, M. K., 251
Rovee-Collier, C., 306–310, 318
Rowe, D. C., 544
Rubens, A. C., 470
Rubenstein, 149
Rubin, D. B., 231
Rubin, D. C., 314
Rubin, K. H., 183–184, 234, 240, 421, 424
Ruble, D. N., 427, 428–432, 435, 441
Ruda, M. A., 44, 102
Ruff, H. A., 111, 259
Ruffman, T., 205–206, 336
Rugani, R., 145
Rugoff, B., 83
Rugs, D., 366
Rumbaugh, D. M., 350–351
Rupp, S., 344
Russell, J., 205, 410
Rustin, C. L., 206
Rutter, M., 30, 47, 70, 537, 556–557, 575
Ryan, E. B., 256, 450, 452

# S

Sabbagh, M. A., 203, 261
Sabin, E. J., 370
Saccuzzo, D. P., 507
Sachs, J., 355
Sachse-Lee, C., 471
Sackett, P. R., 504
Sacks, O., 373, 523
Saffran, J. R, 118, 356, 372
Sakai, K. L., 375–376
Salapatek, P., 109–110
Salatas, H., 274
Salmon, K., 323, 329, 340

Salthouse, T. A., 253, 507
Samaranayake, V. A., 471
Sameroff, A. J., 11, 532–534, 540, 551–552, 555, 575
Sanchez, R. P., 288–289
Sandberg, E. H., 227
Sander, C., 479
Sanders, P., 390
Sandman, C. A., 106
Santini, C., 337
Santulli, K. A., 286
Savage-Rumbaugh, E. S., 169, 349–350, 374, 413–414
Scammon, R. E., 52
Scanlon, D. M., 511
Scarborough, H. S., 368
Scarr, S., 39, 48–51, 72–73, 503, 538, 540, 543, 545–546, 571
Schaal, B., 102–103
Schacter, D. L., 304, 318
Schafer, G., 363
Schaffer, A., 425
Schalkwyk, L. C., 41–42, 536
Schanberg, S. M., 102
Schauble, L., 270, 296
Schechter, A., 309
Schefrin, B., 108
Scheider, W., 448
Schellenberg, E. G., 118, 122, 123
Schiefele, U., 458
Schirduan, V., 526
Schlagmüller, M., 275, 284
Schliemann, A..D., 472
Schlottmann, A., 221
Schmidt, M. E., 20
Schmuckler, M. A., 142
Schneider, W., 25–27, 205, 230, 254–256, 267, 272, 274–275, 278–279, 281–282, 284, 286, 312, 319, 330, 344–345, 446, 448, 452, 482, 512–513
Schulman, A. H., 425
Schumann-Hengsteler, R., 230
Schwanenflugel, P. J., 453, 514
Schwartz, R., 387
Schwarz, A., 425
Schwebel, D. C., 420
Schwenck, C., 25, 267, 270, 272, 274, 278
Scott, L. S., 119
Scribner, S., 285
Scruggs, T. E., 286
Searle, J. P., 33
Sebastián-Gallés, N., 122, 389
Sedivy, J. C., 371
Segal, N., 483, 542
Segalowitz, S. J., 64
Seier, W., 268
Seifer, R., 552
Seimes, L., 273
Seligman, M. E. P., 441
Senden, M. Von, 60

Sénéchal, M., 89
Senghas, A., 378
Seplke, E. S., 406
Serbin, L. A., 232, 433
Seress, L., 313
Setliff, A. E., 20
Seyfarth, M., 350
Seymour, P. H. K., 449
Shackelford, T. K., 116
Shaffer, D. R., 111, 250
Shafto, C. L., 363
Shankweiler, D., 448
Share D. L., 223
Shatz, M., 371
Shaw, P., 57, 267
Shayer, M., 182
Shaywitz, B. A., 451
Shaywitz, S. E., 451
Shearer, B., 529
Shields, P., 309
Shiffrin, R. M., 250
Shimmin, H. S., 428
Shin, H.-E., 19, 270, 420
Shinskey, J. L., 113, 142, 146, 306
Shiraki, J. H., 227
Shore, J. R., 526
Shrager, J., 465
Shumaker, R. W., 220
Shwe, H. I., 366
Shyi, C.-W. G., 309
Siegal, M., 199, 223
Siegel, A. W., 227
Siegel, L. S., 256, 448, 450, 452–453
Siegler, R. S., 14–15, 78, 182,
    236–238, 241, 256, 270–272, 285,
    300, 394, 463–467, 469–470, 471,
    474
Sigafoos, A. D., 405, 407
Sigman, M., 139, 166, 235,
    566–567
Sigman, M. D., 507
Signorella, M. L., 232, 434–435
Silk, J., 525
Silverman, I., 231–232
Simcock, G., 88, 315–316, 409
Simion, F., 117
Simon, B. B., 426
Simon, T. J., 127, 145
Sines, A., 228
Singer, J. T., 565–566
Sinha, P., 61
Skeels, H. M., 21–22, 547, 554
Skinner, B. F., 371, 373
Skoczenski, A. M., 108
Skouteris, H., 426
Slaby, R. G., 423, 428–429
Slater, A. M., 107–108, 115–116,
    131–132, 133–134, 153, 566
Slaughter, V., 203–204, 222, 224, 425
Slobin, D. I., 357
Smith, C. M., 78–80, 92, 99
Smith, E., 185
Smith, I. M., 252

Smith, L., 481
Smith, L. B., 11–13, 263
Smith, M. L., 319
Smith, P. K., 184, 225, 235, 240,
    488
Smith, R. E., 343
Smitsman, A. W., 143, 240
Smuke, A. T., 558, 575
Snedecker, J., 363
Snow, C. E., 355, 370, 385,
    388–390
Snowling, M. J., 470–471
Snyder, E., 436–437
Soares, M., 231
Socha, D. M., 96
Socha, T. J., 96
Sodian, B., 212, 274–275, 295,
    344–345
Soley, G., 123
Solomon, G. E. A., 223
Somel, M., 54
Somerville, S. C., 342
Sommerville, J. A., 426
Song, H., 206
Songua-Barke, E. J. S., 263
Sonnenschein, S., 370
Sonuga-Barke, E. J. S., 557
Sopasakis, M., 337
Sophian, C., 150
Soussignan, R., 102–103
Sowell, E. R., 56
Spataro, J., 426
Speaker, C., 113, 146
Spear, L. P., 57, 64
Spearman, C., 495, 520
Spelke, E. S., 9, 21, 23, 36,
    124–126, 130, 133–134,
    145, 153, 182, 197, 199,
    349
Spence, M. J., 103, 119, 120, 306, 337,
    386
Spencer, J. P., 146
Spencer, S. J., 478
Spicker, B., 340
Spinath, B., 502
Spitz, R., 21, 546, 553–554
Sprafkin, C., 433
Springer, C. J., 270, 283
Springer, K., 223
Spuhl, S. T., 394
Stack, D. M., 252
Stager, C. L., 126
Stake, J. E., 478
Stanley, J. C., 477, 478
Stanovich, K. E., 445, 448
Stark, R., 354
Staudt, J., 178, 180, 182
Steele, C. M., 503
Stefanek, J., 254, 482
Stein, D. K., 509
Steiner, J. E., 102
Stern, D. N., 386–387
Sternberg, K. J., 340–341

Sternberg, R. J., 291, 494, 498,
    506–507, 514–515, 517–519,
    529, 567
Stevens, S., 557
Stevenson, H. W., 257–258, 473–475,
    488
Stiles, J., 59–60, 67, 380
Stipek, D., 420, 484
Stock, R., 463
Stoddart, T., 433
Stoel-Gammon, C., 353–354
Stone, B. P., 267, 274
Stone, C. A., 182
Stone, L. J., 428
Stoolmiller, M., 542
Storch, S. A., 447, 450
Strauss, M. S., 147
Streri, A., 106, 125, 126, 406
Striano, T., 90, 425
Strube. G., 325
Suddendorf, T., 156–157, 158, 342, 425
Sullivan, K., 210, 211–212
Sullivan, M. W., 307
Sundet, J. M., 49
Suomi, S., 21, 68
Sussman, A. L., 185
Suzuki, L. A., 503
Svetina, M., 14–15
Swanson, H. L., 452, 471
Symons, D. K., 445
Szkrybalo, J., 429–430, 435
Szpunar, K. K., 343

### T

Talwar, V., 212
Tambs, K., 49
Tamis-LeMonda, C. S., 89, 370, 568
Tan, L. S., 228
Tanner, J. M., 51
Tardif, T., 203
Tarulli, D., 392
Tate, C. S., 369
Tatelbaum, R., 543
Taumoepeau, M., 205
Taylor, A., 41–42
Taylor, C., 261
Taylor, G. H., 66
Taylor, H. A., 227
Taylor, M., 159, 186
Teasdale, T. W., 573
Teasley, S. D., 95
Terman, L. M., 571
Terrance, H. S., 351
Thelen, E., 11–13
Théoret, H., 415–416
Thibaut, J.-P., 293
Thierry, K. L., 337, 340
Thomas, D., 560
Thomas, L., 378
Thomas, S. C., 10
Thomas, S. W., 326
Thompson, D. E., 410

Thompson, J. R., 364
Thompson, L. A., 506, 539
Thompson-Schill, S. L., 222
Thomson, N., 258
Thornhill, R., 116
Tillman, C. M., 508
Timney, B., 60
Toglia, M. P., 336
Tokura, H., 385
Tomasello, M., 90, 123, 131, 182, 200,
     202, 214, 220, 240, 351, 359, 361,
     371–372, 382–383, 388, 397,
     402–404, 409–410, 413–414, 416,
     441, 485
Tomonaga, M., 115
Tondel, G. M., 107
Tonkova-Yompol'skaya, R. V., 355
Tooby, J., 32–33, 35–36, 37, 400
Torenberg, M., 268
Torff, B., 520
Tottenham, N., 548
Trainor, L. J., 122–123, 386, 387
Trehub, S. E., 118, 121–122, 123, 386
Trieman, R., 88, 444, 450
Trionfi, G., 186
Troseth, G. L., 158
Tsao, F.-M., 120, 356
Tudge, J., 78, 88, 93–94, 96
Tudge, J. R. H., 95
Tulkin, S. R., 179
Tulving, E., 303, 320, 342
Tulviste, P., 77, 82
Turati, C., 117–118
Turiel, E., 433
Turkewitz, G., 19, 30, 36, 43–45, 125,
     381
Turkheimer, E., 542–545
Turnbull, M., 390
Turner, A. M., 65
Turner, L. A., 509
Tynes, D. M., 307

**U**

Uller, C., 146
Umbel, V., 408
Ungerer, J. A., 184
Unyk, A. M., 122, 386
Usher, J., 315
Uttal, D. H., 221–222, 227–228, 287,
     290, 293, 294, 298
Uzgiris, I. C., 139, 166

**V**

Vachio, A., 95
Valdez-Manchaca, M. C., 88
Valencia, R. R., 503
Valenza, E., 117–118
Valsiner, J., 78, 88, 93–94
Van Abbema, D. L., 340
Vandell, D. L., 484, 553
Vandenberg, B., 183–184, 234

Vander Linde, E., 307
van der Maas, H. L. J., 14
van der Molen, M., 192, 262
van der Oord, E.J.C.G., 544
Van Ijzendoorn, M. H., 548
Van Loosbroek, E., 143
van Schaik, C. P., 412
Van Sluyters, N. M., 61
Van Valin, R. D., 359–360
Varnhagen, C. K., 481
Varnum, M. E., 259
Vasilyeva, M., 227, 260
Vasta, R., 230
Vellutino, F. R., 511
Venter, J.C., 536
Vernon, P. A., 252, 508–509
Vernon, P. E., 508
Vevea, J., 481
Vezneva, M., 293
Villaneuva, L., 445
Villringer, A., 376–377
Vinter, A., 405–406
Visé, M., 284
Volbert, R., 225
Volkow, N., 267
Von Bargen, D., 428–429
Vouloumanos, A., 120
Vygotsky, L. S., 16, 77–78, 81–82, 84,
     227, 243, 323, 392, 473

**W**

Wachtel, G. A., 364
Waddell, K. J., 285
Wagner, R. K., 448, 450
Wahlsten, D., 39
Waite, R. R., 458
Wakschlag, L S., 543
Walden, T. A., 278, 371
Waldman, I. D., 503
Waldman, J. D., 540
Waldron, M., 542
Waldrop, M. F., 437
Walker, A. S., 126
Walker, C. H., 27, 512
Wallace, C. S., 60, 546
Wallace, I. F., 566
Walters, R. H., 416–417
Walton, G., 115
Wang, Q., 317, 325
Wang, S., 134, 135, 242
Want, S. C., 403, 409
Ward, C., 38
Warneken, F., 202
Warren, A. R., 366–367, 369
Warren, J. M., 266
Warren-Leubecker, Q., 371
Wartenburger, I., 376–377
Wason, P., 180
Waters, H. S., 274
Waters, P., 418–419
Watkins, M. W., 502
Watson, J., 200, 212

Watson, J. S., 124
Webb, S. J., 313
Weber, A., 325
Webster, E., 366
Wechsler, D., 501
Weikum, W. M., 121, 127
Weimer, A. A., 209
Weinberg, R. A., 49, 503, 540, 543
Weinert, F. E., 26–27, 275, 278,
     344–345, 512–514
Weinstein, R. S., 505
Weiss, M. G., 281–282
Weissberg, R., 259
Welch, M. K., 336–337
Welch-Ross, M. K., 185
Wellman, H. M., 185, 199–201, 203,
     212, 228, 268, 342, 366
Wenger, E., 92
Wenner, J. A., 312, 315, 324
Werker, J., 356
Werker, J. F., 118, 120, 127
Werner, L. A., 118, 121, 356
Werts, H., 41–42
Wertsch, J. V., 77, 82
West, T. A., 314
Westfahl, S. M.-C., 23, 145
Wewerka, S. S., 312
Wexler-Sherman, C., 494
Wheldall, K., 367
Whishaw, I. Q., 67, 375
White, A. J., 436
White, L., 328, 329
White, S., 450
White, S. H., 314, 502
Whitehead, H., 412
Whitehurst, G. J., 88, 370, 446–447,
     450
Whiten, A., 219–220, 235, 404,
     409–413
Whiten. A., 525
Whitesell, N. R., 418–419
Whitham, J. C., 387
Whyte, J. C., 470
Wickelgren, L., 107
Wiebe, S. A.,, 251
Wilcox, J., 366
Wilcox, T., 136
Wiley, E., 380
Willats, P., 288
Williams, B., 41–42
Williams, E. M., 23, 36, 130, 150,
     199
Williams, G. C., 35
Williams, J. H., 416
Williams, W. M., 482
Wilson, R. S., 540
Wilson, S. P., 262
Wimmer, H., 203–204
Wimmer, M. C., 280
Winberg, J., 103
Winick, M., 68, 554
Winner, E., 210–212
Winsler, A., 392, 394

Winteler, A., 458
Wirkala, C., 296
Witelson, S. F., 66–67, 380
Wolf, M., 491
Wolfe, C. D., 63, 267
Woloshyn, V., 285–287
Wood, C. H., 435
Wood, D., 84
Wood, J. N., 145
Wood, L. A. N., 410–412
Woodruff, G., 203
Woods, B. T., 66
Woodward, A. L, 200, 202, 410, 416
Woody-Dorning, J., 276, 284
Woolley, J. D., 185–186, 188
Wynn, K., 23–24, 148, 464

## X

Xu, F., 145

## Y

Yaeger, J., 392–393
Yeats, K. O., 66
Yekel, C. A., 227
Yi, S., 317, 325
Yoon, J. M. D, 221
Young, D., 231
Youngblood, L. M., 89–90
Younger, B., 132, 147
Yusun Kang, J., 389–390

## Z

Zacks, R. T., 68–69, 251, 320
Zaragoza, M. S., 333, 337
Zeanah, C. H., 558

Zeanah, C. H., Jr., 575
Zelazo, P. D., 139, 142, 203, 252, 263–264, 266, 300, 426
Zeman, B. R., 279
Zember, E., 280
Zeskind, P. S., 534–535
Zhang, H., 78–80, 92, 99
Zhou, S., 474
Zhu, J., 78–80, 92, 99
Ziegler, J. C., 448–449
Zimet, S., 458
Zimmerman, T., 20, 560
Zuber, J., 81
Zubin, N. R. E., 243

# SUBJECT INDEX

## A

Academic performance
  academic preschools and, 484
  ADHD and, 262
  cultural differences in, 473–475
  gender differences in, 477–478
  HOME scale and, 550
  IQ and, 502
  positive early environments and,
    559, 561–562
  Pygmalion effect and, 505
  self-regulation and, 508
  working memory and, 508
Academic preschools, costs and benefits
  of, 483–485
Accommodation
  of the eye lens, 107
  imitation and, 163
  in Piaget's theory, 163–165, 166
Action schemes, 162
Active intermodal mapping, 406
Active rehearsal, 273, 274
Acuity, visual, in infants, 107
Adaptation, 162–163, 515–516
Adaptationist reasoning, 35
Adaptive strategy choice model,
  270–272
ADD/ADHD, 262–263
Adolescents
  brain changes in, 64
  egocentricity in, 177–181
Affordances of objects, 235
Altruistic behavior, in infants, 202
Amnesia, 304
Amodal properties, 128
Analogical reasoning
  familiarity and, 294
  metacognition and, 294
  reasoning, 291–295
  relational mapping and, 291
  relational shift and, 293–294
Analogical-reasoning, 294
Analytic subtheory of intelligence, 515,
  518–519
Androgens, prenatal
  influence on gender differences in
    thinking, 70
  influence on gender-typed behavior,
    436–437
  influence on object-oriented
    play, 235
  influence on sexual orientation, 70
Animism, 221–222

A-not-B object permanence task, 62–64,
  138–139, 142–143
Anterograde amnesia, 304
Apes, language and, 350–351
Apoptosis, 57
Appearance/reality distinction,
  159–160
Apprenticeship in thinking. 86, 92. *See
  also* Guided participation
Architectural constraints, 9–10
Arithmetic. *See also* Number and
    arithmetic concepts
  concepts in, 463–470
  simple arithmetic, 144–146
  unschooled children and, 472–473
Articulatory loop, 256
Artificialism, 216
Assessing cognitive development, 93–94
Assimilation, 163–165
Asymmetries, in neocortex, 43–44
Attention, 258–260
Attention deficit hyperactivity disorder
  (ADHD), 262–263
Auditory development, 118–123
Autism, 215
Autobiographical memories, 314
Automatic processes, 251
Axons, 54

## B

Babbling, of infants, 353–355
Ba/pa continuum, 120
Basic reflexes, 166
Bayley Scales of Infant Development,
  500
Behavioral genetics
  defined, 47
  elementary cognitive tasks, 538–540
  environment and, 542–545
  expanded role of, 70
  familial studies of intelligence,
    540–541
  heritability and, 536–538
  IQ and, 545–546
Belief-desire reasoning, 199–201
Bidirectionality of structure and
  function, 5–6
Bilingual abilities, 122
Bilingualism, 388–390
Biological basis of cognition, 32–72
  brain development. *See* Brain
    development

developmental cognitive neuroscience
  and, 69–70
evolutionary theory and, 34–38
folk knowledge and, 36–37
gene-environment interaction
  and. *See* Gene-environment
  interactions
overview, 32–34
summary, 70–72
Biological factors, role in
  development, 11
Biologically primary abilities, 38
Biologically secondary abilities, 38, 443
Biology
  developmental, 69–70
  folk, 221–225
Black English, 366–368
Bound morphemes, 356
Brain
  changes, in adolescents, 64
  damage. *See* Brain damage.
  early development of, 62
  hemispheres, development of, 43–44
  plasticity of, 65–69
Brain damage
  impact on brain function, 66–68
  impact on intelligence, 523
  IQ and, 67
Brain development, 51–69
  behavioral development and,
    59–62, 64
  brain plasticity and, 65–69
  evolution of human brain, 53–54
  executive function and, 266–267
  impact of deprivation on, 68–69
  IQ and, 57
  language and, 374–376
  mechanisms involved in, 59–62
  neocortex development, 62–64
  neuronal development, 54–59
  overview, 51–52
  rate of brain growth, 68–69

## C

Calendar systems, 243–244
Casual perception, 242
Category prototype, 148–150
Category representation, 147–150
Cause and effect thinking, 287–289
Centration, 173
Cerebral cortex, 62. *See also* Neocortex
Chemical senses, 102

Child-directed speech, 385–388
Chimpanzees
    language and, 350–351
    social learning in, 412–416
    theory of mind and, 219–220
Chronotopic constraints, 10. *See also*
    Innateness
Class inclusion, 173
Cognition
    as constructive process, 161–162
    defined, 3
    measuring, 4
    overview, 3–4
Cognitive development
    academic preschools, costs and
        benefits of, 483–485
    basic concepts, 3–7
    biological bases of. *See* Biological
        basis of cognition
    developmental biology, 69–70
    domain-general/domain-specific
        abilities in, 25–27
    dynamic systems approaches,
        11–16
    evolutionary theory and, 34–38
    intelligence, schooling vs. age,
        480–483
    issues in, 7
    nature/nurture, 8–11
    Piaget's theory of. *See* Piaget's theory
    problem solving, 24–25
    representation and, 22–24
    research goals in, 28
    schooling and, 479–485
    social context for, 16–17
    sociocultural perspectives and, 93–94
    sociocultural theory and, 97
    sociohistorical influences on, 92–93
    stability and plasticity in, 18–22
    theory theories of, 198–199
Cognitive flexibility, 263–264
Cognitive immaturity, 19–20
Cognitive inhibition, 205
Cognitive self-guidance system, 392
Collaborative learning, 95–97
Collective monologues, 369
Collision, 134
Color vision, in infants, 108
Communicative competence, 368–369
Communicative intentions, 382–383
Compensatory education programs,
    557–558
Competencies, social origins of, 81–84
Componential subtheory of intelligence,
    515, 518–519
Concentration, 258–260
Concrete operations, 169, 175–177
Cones, of the eyes, 108
Conjugate-reinforcement procedures,
    306–310
Conservation, in operational thought,
    170–173
Conservation of number, 460–461

Constraints
    architectural, 9–10
    chronotopic, 10
    on learning, 35
    lexical, 363–364
Contents of consciousness, 250
Context, role in development, 11
Context availability, 153
Contextual subtheory of intelligence,
    515–516
Continuity with stability, 564
Convergence, of the eyes, 107
Cooperative learning, 95–97
Coordination, of the eyes, 107
Coordination of secondary circular
    reactions, 168
Core knowledge, 129–146
    arguments against, 146
    infant cognition. *See* Infant cognition
    numerosity and ordinality,
        143–145
    object constancy, 131–133
    object continuity and cohesion,
        133–137
    object permanence, 137–143
    simple arithmetic, 144–146
    systems of, 129–131
    theory theories and, 199
Core operations, 524
Corpus callosum, 62
Counting, 144, 461–463
Creative subtheory of intelligence,
    515, 517
Creoles, 378
Cross-modal matching, 125–127
Crystallized abilities, 496
Cultural context, 78. *See also* Sociocul-
    tural perspectives
Cultural differences, in mathematical
    ability, 472–475
Cultural relativism, 516
Culture and symbolic development,
    179–180
Cumulative deficit effect, 551
Cumulative rehearsal, 273, 274
Curvature, 110–111
Curvilinearity, 110–112
Cut-off method, for entering school, 480
Cytodifferentiation, 56

**D**

Decentration, 173
Deception, 209–212
Declarative memory, 303
Declarative metacognition, 281
Decomposition strategy, 465
Deductive reasoning. *See*
    Hypothetico-deductive reasoning
Deep structure, 373
Deferred imitation, 310–312
Dendrites, 54
Dentate gyrus, 313

Deprivation, impact on brain
    development, 68–69
Design stance, 238–240
Development
    defined, 3
    developmental contextual models,
        11, 12, 17
    evolutionary theory and, 17
    fuzzy vs. verbatim trace processing in,
        191–192
    of infant memory, 304–314
    of neocortex, 62–64
    neuronal, 54–59
    overview, 4–6
    role of context in, 11
    sociocultural perspective of.
        *See* Sociocultural perspectives
Developmental biology, 69–70
Developmental cognitive neuroscience,
    33–34, 69–70
Developmental contextual models
    development and, 17
    nature/nurture and, 11
    person-context interactions, 12
Developmental function, 3, 6–7
Developmental quotient (DQ), 500–501
Developmental systems approach
    epigenesis and, 40–44
    timing and, 44–47
Developmental timing, 44–47
Developmentally appropriate
    programs, 484
Deviation IQ (Intelligent Qotient), 501
Differential approach, 494–506
Differentiation, of neurons, 56–57
Digital natives, 81
Direct-instructional programs, 484
Discontinuity-with-instability, 565–566
Discrepancy principle, 112–113
Discriminating differences, in language,
    121–122
Dishabituation, 105–106, 147
Domain-general abilities, 25–27,
    36, 161
Domain-general vs. domain specific,
    memory as, 343–344
Domain-specific abilities, 25–27, 36–37
Dominance theory, theory of mind, 206
Dual encoding. *See* Dual representation
Dual orientation, 157–158
Dual representation, 157–158, 204
Dual-processing theories, 189
Dynamic systems approaches, 11–16
Dyslexia, 450–451

**E**

Early number concepts and
    numerosity and ordinality, 143–145
    simple arithmetic, 144–146
Education
    Evolutionary educational psychology
        and, 485–489

multiple intelligences and, 525–527
sociocultural perspectives and, 94–97
Effortful processes, 251
Egocentric speech, 369, 392
Egocentricity
  in adolescents, 177–181
  in language development, 369, 392
  in young children, 174–177
Electroencephalography (EEG), 52
Elementary cognitive tasks (ECTs), 538–540
Elementary mental functions, 78
Emergent literacy, 445–447
Emotion Detector (TED), 214
Empathizing System (TESS), 214
Empiricism, 8
Emulation, 403–405, 412
Encephalization quotient, 53
Enculturation hypothesis, 413–414
Epigenesis
  defined, 40
  developmental systems approach and, 40–44
  gene-environment interactions and, 40–44
  Piaget's theory and, 165
Episodic memory, 303
Equilibration, 163–165
Event memory, 320–326. *See also* Eyewitness memory
Evidence, in scientific reasoning, 296–298
Evolution
  defined, 34
  of human brain, 53–54
Evolutionary developmental psychology, 35–38
Evolutionary educational psychology, 485–489
Evolutionary plausibility of intelligence, 525
Evolutionary theory
  cognitive development and, 34–38
  development and, 17
Executive control. *See* Executive function
Executive function, 251–265. *See also* Information processing
  attention, 258–260
  brain development and, 266–267
  cognitive flexibility, 263–264
  defined, 25
  false belief and, 205
  inhibition, 260–263
  memory span, 254–256
  overview, 251–252
  processing speed, 252–254
  resistance to interference, 261
  summary, 264–265
  working memory, 252, 256–258
Experience-dependent processes, 61, 71

Experience-expectant processes, 60, 71
Experiential subtheory of intelligence, 515, 517
Explicit tasks, 206
Exploration, 234
Externality effect, 110
Eye gaze, 116–117
Eye-Direction Detector (EDD), 214
Eyewitness memory, 326–341
  accuracy of, 328–329
  age differences in, 327–333
  assessing, 340–341
  false memories in, 337–339
  influences on, 330
  leading questions in, 333–337
  overview, 326–327
  participant factors in, 327
  recall of, 329–330
  stress and, 330, 333
  suggestibility and, 333–339
  summary, 339–341

**F**

Face perception, 10, 62
Face processing, 113–119
Fact retrieval, 464–465
Factor analysis, 495
Factors of intelligence, 495–497
False belief
  dual representation and, 204
  executive function and, 205
  mind reading, 203–209
  in problem solving, 203–209
  theory of mind and, 203–209
False memory, 328–329, 337–339
Familial studies of intelligence, 540–541
Familiarity, analogical-reasoning and, 294
Family size, theory of mind and, 205–206
Fantasy, 185–188
Fantasy play, 89–90, 183–185
Fast mapping, 363
Feedback effects, 190
Finalism, 216
Fixed-action pattern, 407
Fluid abilities, 496
Flynn effect, 572–573
Focusing, of the eye lens, 107
Folk biology, 221–225
Folk knowledge, 197–246
  folk biology, 221–225
  folk physics. *See* Folk physics 225–245
  folk psychology. *See* Theory of mind
  overview, 197–198
  summary, 245–246
  theory theories, 198–199
Folk physics, 225–245
  calendar systems, 243–244

casual perception, 242
children's understanding of, 245
design stance and, 238–240
future events and, 243
gender differences in spatial cognition, 230–234
object and location memory, 230
object-oriented play, 234–235, 240–241
overview, 225
problem solving and, 235–238
spatial cognition, 226
spatial orientation, 226–229
spatial visualization, 229–230
temporal order, 241–242
temporal terms, 242–243
time, 241
timing of events, 243
tools, 235–241
Folk psychology. *See* Theory of mind
Forethought, 417
Formal operational thought, 175–180
Formal operations, 169
Forward strategy, 237
Foveas, 108
Free morphemes, 356
Frontal lobes, 62–63
Function, 5
Functional invariants, 162–163
Functional magnetic resonance imaging (fMRI), 52
Functional relationships, 235
Future, in time, 243
Fuzzy trace theory, 188–192
Fuzzy traces, 188–192
Fuzzy vs. verbatim trace processing, 191–192
Fuzzy-trace theory, 188–192

**G**

*g* intelligence factor, 495
Gardner's Theory of Multiple Intelligences, 521–527
Gender differences
  in language, 390–391
  in mathematical ability, 475–479
  in reading and verbal abilities, 455–457
  in spatial cognition, 230–234
Gender identity, 427–438
  children's gender theories, 438
  defined, 428
  gender consistency, 428
  gender constancy, 427–430
  gender identification, 427
  gender schemas, 431–435
  gender scripts, 434
  gender stability, 428
  gender-typed behavior, 435–438

Gene-environment interactions, 38–51
  biological basis of cognition and, 38–51
  developmental timing and, 44–47
  early brain development, 62
  epigenesis and, 40–44
  genotype → environment theory, 47–50
  "good enough" parents and, 50–51
  IQ and, 41–42, 49
  overview, 38–39
General genetic law of cultural development, 82
General intelligence, 495
Genetic determinism, 8. *See also* Innateness
Genetics, behavior and. *See* Behavioral genetics
Genotype → environment theory, 47–51
Genotype of child, 50–51
Gesell Developmental Schedules, 500
Gestalt concept of continuation, 133
Gestures, language development and, 383–385
Gist extraction, 189, 190
Goal emulation, 403
Goal-directed behavior, 166–168, 287–290
Goals, inferred, 202
"Good enough" parents, 50–51
Grammatical nature of language, 352
Grapheme-phoneme correspondence, 448–449
Grasping scheme, 162
Gray matter, 56
Guided participation
  cultural influences on, 90–92
  reading to children as, 88–89
  sociocultural perspectives, 86–92
  in symbolic play, 89–90
  talking to children as, 88–89
  types of, 86–90
  zone of proximal development and, 84–87

**H**

Habituation, 105–106
Habituation/dishabituation paradigm, 105–106, 147
Hearing development, 118–123
Heritability, *See also* Behavioral genetics
  concept of, 536–538
  IQ and, 545–546
Hierarchical model of cognitive abilities, 497
High-density event-related potentials, 52
Higher mental functions, 78
Holophrases, 359
Home Observation for Measurement of the Environment (HOME) scale, 549–551

Hormones, prenatal
  cognition and, 69–70
  influence on gender differences in thinking, 70
  influence on gender-typed behavior, 436–437
  influence on object-oriented play and, 235
  influence on sexual orientation, 70
  influence on vocabulary size, 391
Human intelligence, 563
Human social functioning, 219
Humans as symbolic species, 192
Hypermetabolism, 58
Hypnotic age regression, 318
Hypothetico-deductive reasoning, 175

**I**

Imaginary audience, 178
Imaginary friends, 186
Imitation
  accommodation and, 163
  of intentional agents, 202
  as social learning, 408–412
Imitative learning, 403–405
Implicit memory, 318–320
Implicit understanding, 206
Impossible occlusion events, 129
Indirect strategy, 237
Individual differences, 531–575. *See also* intelligence
  behavioral genetics and, 536–546
  defined, 3
  experience and, 546–563
  Flynn effect, 572–573
  heritability and, 536–546
  overview, 7, 531–532
  stability of intelligence and, 563–573
  summary, 574–575
  transactional model, 532–536
Inductive reasoning, 176
Infant cognition
  category representation and, 147–150
  complexity of, 150–151
  core knowledge and, 129–131, 146
  lower-level abilities, 128
  object constancy and, 131–133
  object continuity and cohesion and, 133–137
  object permanence and, 137–143
  object representation and, 131
  violation-of-expectation method, 129
Infant memory
  conditioning techniques and, 306–310
  deferred imitation, 310–312
  neurological basis of, 313–314
  novelty, preference for, 305–306
  overview, 304–305
Infant perception, 101–151
  assessing infant perception, 103–106

auditory development, 118–123
cognition and. *See* Infant cognition
combining senses, 124–128
overview, 101–103
summary, 151–153
visual perception, 107–108
Infant-directed speech, 385–388
Infantile amnesia, 314–318
Inference, in infants, 202
Information processing
  approaches to study of intelligence, 506–514
  basic level processes, 507–509
  executive function and, 508–509. *See also* Executive function
  higher level cognitive abilities, 509–514
  knowledge base and, 511–513
  metacognition and, 513–514
  overview, 249–251
  problem solving. *See* Problem solving
  speed of, 507–508
  strategies. *See* Strategies
  strategies for, 509–511
  summary, 298–299
  working memory and, 508–509
Inhibition
  ADHD and, 262–263
  cognitive, 205
  developmental differences and, 261–262
  executive function and, 260–263
Innate releasing mechanism, 407
Innateness, 8–10
Inner speech, 392–394
Instinctive behavior, 42–43
Institutionalization studies, 546–549
Instructed learning, 403–405
Intellectual competence, 546–553
Intellectual functioning
  impact of compensatory education programs on, 557–558
  impact of positive early experience on, 559–563
  intellectual impairment from early experience and, 553–557
Intelligence
  approaches to study of, 493–528
  approaches to study of, overview, 493–494
  approaches to study of, summary, 527–528
  behavioral genetics and, 536–546
  brain damage and, 523
  criteria of, 523–525
  defined, 493
  experience and, 546–563
  Flynn effect, 572–573
  heritability and, 536–546
  individual differences in. *See* Individual differences
  information processing approach, 506–514

nature/nurture, 18–21
overview, 2
patterns of IQ change during childhood, 570–573
predicting later intelligence from infancy tests, 564–569
psychometric approach, 494–506
schooling vs. age, effects on, 480–482
stability of, defined, 563–564
stability of intelligence and, 563–573
stability of IQ scores during childhood, 569
summary, 574–575
theory of multiple intelligences, 521–527
transactional model, 532–536
triarchic theory of, 514–521
types of, 522
Intelligent Quotient. See IQ (Intelligent Quotient)
Intent, 200, 202–203
Intentional agents, 200, 202
Intentional reasoning, 215–216, 221–224
Intentionality Detector (ID), 213–214
Interaction, of nature and nurture, 8
Interference, resistance to, 261
Intermodal integration, 124–125
Intermodal matching, 125–127
Interpreting pictures and models, 156–159
Intersensory integration, 124–125
Intersensory redundancy hypothesis, 127–128
Intrinsic activity in children, 161
Intuitionism, 189
Intuitive theism, 216–219
Intuitive theories, 198–199
Invention of new means through mental combinations, 169
Invisible displacements, 138–139
IQ (Intelligent Quotient)
age, impact on test scores, 480–481
brain damage and, 67
brain development and, 57
childhood stability of, 569
deviation IQ, 501
gene-environment interaction and, 41–42, 49
heritability and, 545–546
IQ tests, 497–506
longevity and, 503
minority children and, 503–506
patterns of change during childhood, 570–573
as performance predictor, 502–503
predicting later intelligence from infancy tests, 564–569
school experience and, 480–481
schooling effects on, 480–483
stereotype threat and, 503–504
tests, 497–506

**J**
Joint attention, 200, 202–203

**K**
Kennard effect, 66
Knowledge, 294
Knowledge base, 278–281, 284, 452–453
Knowledge-acquisition components, 515

**L**
Language, 349–396
apes and, 350–351
bilingualism, 388–390
Black English, 366–368
brain development and, 374–376
child-directed speech, 385–388
communicative competence, 368–369
defined, 351–352
development of. See Language development
discriminating differences in, 121–122
egocentrism, 369
functions of, 352
gender differences in, 390–391
gestures and, 383–385
learning, 379–381
metacommunication, 369–371
morphological development, 356–358
overview, 349–351
phonological development, 353–356
pragmatics, 365–366
semantic development, 361–365
summary, 394–396
syntactic development, 358–361
thought and, 391–394
uniqueness of, 350–351
universal grammar, 376–377
Language acquisition device (LAD), 373
Language acquisition support system (LASS), 385
Language development, 352–371
Black English, 366–368
communicative competence, 368–369
early development, 353
egocentrism, 369
gestures and, 383–385
"less is more" hypothesis, 381–382
metacommunication, 369–371
morphological development, 356–358
nativist theory of, 373–379
overview, 352–353
phonological development, 353–356
pragmatics, 365–366
semantic development, 361–365
social-interactionist theory, 382–388
syntactic development, 358–361
Leading questions, in eyewitness memory, 333–337

Learning
constraints on, 35
hypermetabolism and, 58
language, 379–381
problem solving, 286–287
tool usage, 235–238
Legitimate peripheral participation, 92
"Less is more" hypothesis, 381–382
Lexical constraints, 363
Life after death, 217–219
Limbic system, 52
Limited capacity, 250–251
Linear change, 13
Local enhancement, 403
Longevity, 503
Longitudinal assessments of memory strategies, 274–275
Long-term store, 250
Lure-retrieval task, 236
Lying, 212

**M**
Macromechanisms, 4
Magical thinking, 186, 188, 221
Male hormones, prenatal
influence on gender differences in thinking, 70
influence on gender-typed behavior, 436–437
influence on object-oriented play, 235
influence on sexual orientation, 70
influence on vocabulary size, 391
Math ability
cultural differences in, 473–475
gender differences in, 475–479
Math disability, 470–472
Math games, 470
Math performance, stereotype threat and, 478
Mathematically gifted females, 479
Matthew effect, 445
Maturation, Piaget's theory and, 163
Mean length of utterance (MLU), 356
Means-end thinking, 287–289
Memory, 302–346
development in infancy, 304–314
domain-general vs. domain specific, 343–344
episodic, 303
event memory, 320–326
eyewitness. See Eyewitness memory
false memory, 328–329, 337–339
habituation/dishabituation paradigm and, 105–106
hypnotic age regression, 318
implicit memory, 318–320
infantile amnesia, 314–318
in infants, 304–314
memory span, 254–256
overview, 302–303
procedural memory, 304

Memory, (continued)
  prospective memory, 341–343
  representation of knowledge, 303–304
  retrospective memory, 341
  script-based memory, 321–322
  semantic, 303
  shared remembering, 87–88
  stability of, 344–345
  summary, 346
  tools of intellectual adaptation and,
    78–79
Memory span, 254–256
Mental age, 501
Mental capacity, 276–278, 284
Mental rotation, 229
Meta-analysis, 231, 455–457
Meta-attention, 281–282
Metacognition, 281–284, 294
Metacommunication, 369–371
Metacomponents, 515
Metamemory, 282–283, 284
Microgenetic development, 78
Micromechanisms, 4
Migration, of neurons, 56
Mimicry, 403–405
Min strategy, 464–466
Mind reading
  autism and, 215
  deception, 209–212
  Empathizing system, 214–215
  false belief, 203–209
  Mindreading System, 213–214
Mindblindness, 215
Mindreading System, 214–215
Minority children, IQ and, 503–506
Mirror neurons, 414–416
Misleading questions, 333–337
Mnemonics, 272–275
Mobile task, 305–309
Models, interpreting, 156–159
Modularity, 26–27
Monkeys, social learning and, 415–416
Monolingual abilities, 122
Morphemes, 356–357
Morphological development, 356–358
Morphology, 356–358
Movement, as visual stimulus, 108–109
Multiple classification, 173
Multiple intelligences theory, 521–527
Music perception, 122–123
Mutual exclusivity assumption, 364
Mutual imitation, 408
Myelin, 55–56

**N**

Name recognition, 122
Naming numbers, 79–81
Nativism, 8–10, 373–379
Natural selection, 34
Nature/nurture
  cognitive development, 8–11
  developmental contextualism and, 11

intelligence and, 18–21
  interaction of, 8
Negatives, 360
Neocortex
  asymmetries in, 43–44
  defined, 62
  development of, 62–64
Neonatal Behavioral Assessment Scale,
    500
Neonatal imitation, 405–408
Neural Darwinism, 61
Neurogenesis, 56
Neuroimaging techniques, 52
Neuronal development, 54–59
Neuronal plasticity, 65–66
Neurons
  development of, 56–59
  differentiation of, 56–57
  migration of, 56
  neural Darwinism, 61
  plasticity of, 65–66
  proliferation of, 56
  structure of, 54–56
Neurotransmitters, 55–56
Newborns. See also Infants
  hearing in, 118
  visual perception in, 107–108
Nondeclarative memory, 304
Nonlinear change, 13
Number and arithmetic concepts,
    459–479
  arithmetic concepts, 145–146
  conservation of number, 460–461
  core knowledge and, 143–145
  counting, 461–463
  cultural differences in, 472–475
  gender differences in ability in,
    475–479
  math disability, 470–472
  math games, 470
  numerosity and ordinality, 143–145
Number names, 79–80
Number representation, 130
Numerosity, 143–145
Nurture. See Nature/nurture

**O**

Object and location memory, 230
Object cohesion and continuity,
    133–137
Object constancy, 131–133
Object permanence, 138–143
Object play, 234–235, 240–241
Object representation
  defined, 131
  object constancy, 131–133
  object continuity and cohesion,
    133–137
  object permanence, 137–143
Object-oriented play, 234–235, 240–241
Observational learning, 417–418
Olfaction, 102

Ontogenetic adaptations, 407
Ontogenetic development, 78
Ontogeny, 4, 78
Operational thought
  in adolescents, 177–181
  centration vs. decentration, 173–174
  characteristics of, 169–170
  conservation in, 170–173
  egocentricity in, 174–175, 177–181
  formal operational, 175–180
  transitioning from concrete to formal,
    175–177
  transitioning from preoperational to
    concrete, 170–173
  in young children, 174–175
Operations
  defined, 170
  Piaget's theory and, 162
Ordinality, 143–145
Organization
  in Piaget's theory, 162
  as memory strategy, 274
Other-race effect, 119
Output interference, 190
Overextensions, 364–365

**P**

Pain response, in infants, 102
Parenting
  genotype of child and, 50–51
  "good enough" parents, 50–51
  teaching children to remember,
    323–326
Passive rehearsal, 273
Passive sentences, 361
Perception
  casual perception, 242
  centration vs. decentration,
    173–174
  face perception, 10, 62
  face processing and, 113–119
  infants and. See Infant perception
  music perception, 122–123
  speech perception, 120–122
  sucking behavior and, 103
  visual, in newborns, 107–108
Performance components, 515
Performance predictor, IQ as,
    502–503
Personal fable, 178
Person-context interactions, 12
Perspective taking, 200
Phase transitions, 14–16
Phonemes, 120–122
Phonemic awareness, 356, 447–448
Phonics, 454
Phonological development,
    353–356
Phonological recoding, 448–451
Phonology, 353–356
Phylogenetic development, 78
Phylogeny, 78

Physical activity, schooling and, 488–489
Physical environment, Piaget's theory and, 163
Physical stimuli, for visual preferences, 108–112
Physical world. *See* Folk physics
Physics, folk. *See* Folk physics
Piaget's theory, 160–183
　action schemes, 162
　A-not-B object permanence task, 62–64, 138–139, 142–143
　cognition as constructive process, 161–162
　current state of, 181–183
　domain general abilities, 161
　epigenesis and, 165
　equilibration, 163–165
　functional invariants, 162–163
　intrinsic activity in in children, 161
　maturation, 163
　operations. *See* Operational thought
　operations, 162
　overview, 160–161
　sensorimotor. *See* Sensorimotor stage
　stages in cognitive development, 161
　underlying continuity of functions, 161
Pictures, interpreting, 156–159
Pidgins, 378
Plasticity
　of brain, 65–69
　defined, 18
　of neurons, 65–66
Play
　assimilation and, 163
　guided participation in, 88–89
　symbolic, 89–90, 158, 169, 184–185
Positive early experience, 559–563
Positive manifold, 496
Positron emission tomography (PET), 52
Practical intelligence, 515–516
Pragmatics, 365–366
Preference-for-novelty paradigms, 305–306
Prefrontal lobes, 62–63
Prenatal hormones
　influence on cognition, 69–70
　influence on gender differences in thinking, 70
　influence on gender-typed behavior, 436–437
　influence on object-oriented play and, 235
　influence on sexual orientation, 70
　influence on vocabulary size, 391
Preoperational thought, transitioning to concrete operational, 170–173
Preoperations, 169
Presocial speech, 369
Pretending, 89–90, 183–185
Primary circular reactions, 166–167

Primary memory, 250
Primary regions of neocortex, 62
Principle of persistence, 135–136
Private speech, 392–394
Problem solving
　cognitive development, 24–25
　development of, 287–290
　false belief in, 203–209
　goal-directed behavior and, 287–290
　learning, 286–287
　reasoning, 290–298
　strategies and, 24–25
　using tools for, 235–238
Procedural memory, 304
Procedural metacognition, 281
Processing speed, executive function, 252–254
Prodigies, 523–524
Productive vocabularies, 363
Proliferation, of neurons, 56
Promiscuous teleology, 216
Proprioception, 124–125
Prosody, 385–386
Prospective memory, 341–343
Psychological stimuli, for visual preferences, 112–113
Psychological world. *See* Theory of mind
Psychology, folk. *See* Theory of mind
Psychometric theories of intelligence, 494–506
Pupillary reflex, 107
Purposeful intent, 200
Pygmalion effect, 505

**Q**

Questions, 360–361

**R**

Reading disability, 450–453, 471
Reading skills, 444–459
　cognitive development and, 445–447
　emergent literacy and, 445–447
　gender differences in, 455–459
　knowledge base and, 452–453
　learning to read, 444–445
　phonemic awareness and, 447–448
　phonological recoding and, 448–451
　teaching children to read, 453–454
　verbal abilities and, 455–459
　working memory and, 452
Reading to children, as guided participation, 88–89
Reality, fantasy vs., 185–188
Reasoning
　analogical reasoning, 291–295
　overview, 290
　problem solving, 290–298
　scientific reasoning, 295–298
Recalling false memories, 328–329
Receptive vocabularies, 363

Reciprocal determinism, 417
Reduction to essence rule, 190
Referential communication, 200–201
Reflection, 264
Reflective abstraction, 177
Rehearsal, 272–274
Relational mapping, 291
Relational shift, 293–294
Release from habituation, 105–106, 147
Religious beliefs, social cognition and, 216–219
Remembering
　parents teaching children, 323–326
　remembering to remember, 341–343
Representation, 155–194
　appearance/reality distinction, 159–160
　cognitive development and, 22–24
　culture and symbolic development, 179–180
　defined, 22, 155
　fantasy vs. reality, 185–188
　fuzzy trace theory, 188–192
　humans as symbolic species, 192
　interpreting pictures and models, 156–159
　of knowledge, 303–304
　overview, 22–24
　Piaget's theory. *See* Piaget's theory
　representational insight and, 156–157, 158
　summary, 192–194
　symbolic play, 183–185
Representational change, 203–204
Representational constraints, 9
Representational deficit, 204
Representational insight, 156–158
Reproduction, children's understanding of of, 224–225
Reproductive fitness, 34
Research goals, in cognitive development, 28
Resistance to interference, 261
Retrograde amnesia, 304
Retrospective memory, 341
Reversibility, 170

**S**

Savants, 523–524
Scaffolding, 84–86
Scanning, 109–110, 111
Scheduling effects, 190
Schemas, 112
Schemes, 162
Schooling, 443–490
　age vs., effects on intelligence, 480–481
　cognitive development and, 479–485
　evolutionary educational psychology and, 485–489
　IQ, effects on, 480–483

Schooling, (continued)
number and arithmetic concepts. See Number and arithmetic concepts
overview, 443–444
physical activity and, 488–489
reading skills. See Reading skills
summary, 489–490
Scientific reasoning, 295–298
evidence in, 296–298
Script-based memory, 321–322
Secondary circular reactions, 167–168
Secondary regions of neocortex, 62
Second-language learning, 388–390
Selection, 515
Selectionist models of neural development, 61
Selective attention, 259
Selective cell death, 57
Self-concept, 424–427
Self-control, 404
Self-efficacy, 418–420
Self-fulfilling prophecies, 505
Self-organization, 12–16
Self-reflection, 417
Self-regulation
instructed learning and, 404
observational learning and, 417
Semantic development, 361–365
Semantic memory, 303
Semilingualism, 390
Sensitive period, 44
Sensorimotor stage, 165–169
basic reflexes, 166
coordination of secondary circular reactions, 168
invention of new means through mental combinations, 169
primary circular reactions, 166–167
secondary circular reactions, 167–168
tertiary circular reactions, 168–169
Sensory deprivation, 60
Sensory registers, 250
Sensory representations, 112
Sensory stores, 250
Sequential bilingualism, 388–389
Seriation, 173
Sex differences. See Gender differences
Shape constancy, 131–133
Shaping, in Sternberg's theory, 515
Shared attention, 200, 202–203
Shared remembering, 86–88
Shared-Attention Mechanism (SAM), 214
Short-term store, 250
Siblings, theory of mind and, 205–206
Siegler's adaptive strategy choice model, 270–272
Simple arithmetic, 144–146. See also Number and arithmetic concepts
Simultaneous bilingualism, 388–389
Single-photon emission computed tomography (SPECT), 52
Size constancy, 131–133

"Smarties" task, 203
Social cognition, 399–440
children's gender theories, 438
defined, 399
gender constancy, 427–430
gender schemas, 431–435
gender-typed behavior, 435–438
overview, 399–401
religious beliefs and, 216–219
self-concept, 424–427
self-efficacy, 418–420
social cognitive theory, 416–420
social learning. See Social learning
summary, 438–440
Social cognitive skills, 200–203
Social cognitive theory
observational learning, 417–418
self-efficacy, 418–420
Social environment, 16–18
Social information processing, 420–424
Social learning, 401–416
age differences in, 405–412
in chimpanzees, 412–416
defined, 402
emulation as form of, 412
forms of, 403–405
imitation as, 408–412
mirror neurons and, 415–416
monkeys and, 415–416
overview, 401–403
Social learning theory. See Social cognitive theory
Social origins of cognitive competencies, 81–84
Social transmission and, 163
Social-interactionist theories of language development, 382–388
Socially constituted cognitive activity, 82
Sociocultural perspectives, 75–97
apprenticeship in thinking, 86–92
assessing cognitive development and, 93–94
guided participation, 86–92
implications for education, 94–97
overview, 75–78
social context for cognitive development, 16–17
social origins of cognitive competencies, 81–84
sociocultural theory, 97
sociohistorical influences on cognitive development, 92–93
summary, 97–98
tools of intellectual adaptation, 78–81
zone of proximal development, 84–86
Sociocultural theory, 97
cognitive development, 97
sociocultural perspectives, 97
Sociodramatic play, 184–185. See also Symbolic play
Socioeconomic status (SES)

differences in intelligence and, 533–534
effect on reading skills, 447
Sociohistorical development, 78
Sociohistorical influences on cognitive development, 92–93
Solidity, 136–137
Source monitoring, 185
Span of apprehension, 254
Spatial cognition
gender differences in, 230–234
object and location memory, 230
overview, 226
spatial orientation, 226–229
spatial visualization, 229–230
Spatial orientation, 226–229
Spatial visualization, 229–230
Speech perception, 120–122
Speech registers, 366–368
Stability defined, 18
Stability, of memory, 344–345
Stability and plasticity, in cognitive development, 18–22
Stability of intelligence
defined, 563–564
Flynn effect, 572–573
individual differences and, 563–573
patterns of IQ change during childhood, 570–573
predicting later intelligence from infancy tests, 564–569
stability of IQ scores during childhood, 569
Stages in cognitive development, 161
Stanford-Binet IQ test, 498
Statistical learning, 372
Stereotype threat
IQ scores and, 503–504
mathematics performance and, 478
Sternberg's triarchic theory of intelligence, 514–521
Strategies, 265–286. See also Problem solving
adaptive strategy choice model, 270–272
in classrooms, 285–286
culture and, 284–285
decomposition strategy, 465
defined, 24–25
forward strategy, 237
increase in use of, 265–268
indirect strategy, 237
influences on, 275–284
memory strategies, 272–275
overview, 265
production deficiencies, 267
tool strategy, 237–238
utilization deficiencies, 268–270
Structure
defined, 4–5
of neurons, 54–56
Structure ↔ function, 5–6
Sucking behavior, 103

Sucking scheme, 162
Suggestibility, in eyewitness memory, 333–339
Support, concept of, 134, 136–137
Surface structure, 373
Switch trials, 264
Symbolic function, 183–188
Symbolic nature of language, 351–352
Symbolic play, 89–90, 158, 169, 183–185
Symbolic species, 192
Symbolization, 417
Symbols. *See* Representation
Symmetrical forms, 110
Synapses, 54–55, 65
Synaptic plasticity, 65–66
Synaptogenesis, 57
Syntactic bootstrapping, 364
Syntactic development, 358–361
Syntax, 358–361

**T**

Tactile stimulation, 102
Talking to children, as guided participation, 88–89
Tape recorder model, 21–22
Taste, 102
Taxonomic assumption, 363–364
Teaching, 403–405
Teaching children to remember, 323–326
TED (The Emotion Detector), 214
Telegraphic speech, 359
Temporal order, 241–242
Temporal terms, 242–243
Tertiary circular reactions, 168–169
TESS (The Empathizing SyStem), 214
Testosterone, prenatal
   influence on gender-typed behavior, 437
   influence on vocabulary size, 391
Theory of mind
   belief-desire reasoning, 199–200
   chimpanzees and, 219–220
   deception and, 209–212
   dominance theory and, 206
   false belief and, 203–209

family size and, 205–206
folk psychology defined, 198
human social functioning and, 219
mind reading. *See* Mind reading
mind structure and, 36–37
overview, 199–200
skeletal competencies and, 130
social cognition and, 200–203, 399–400
three-year-olds and, 212
Theory theories
   of cognitive development, 198–199
   core knowledge and, 199
   folk knowledge, 198–199
Theory-of-Mind Module (ToMM), 214–215
Thought, language and, 391–394
Time
   calendar systems, 243–244
   casual perception, 242
   children's understanding of, 245
   future, 243
   overview, 241
   temporal order, 241–242
   temporal terms, 242–243
   timing of events, 243
Timing, developmental systems approach and, 44–47
Tools
   design stance and, 238–240
   of intellectual adaptation, 78–81
   learning to use, 235–238
   object-oriented play and, 240–241
   strategies for use for problem solving, 235–238
Touch, 102
Train task, 309
Transactional model, 532–536
Transitive inference, 173, 190
Triarchic theory of intelligence, 514–521
True imitation, 403
True-belief tasks, 208–209

**U**

Underextensions, 365
Underlying continuity of functions, 161

Uniqueness, of language, 350–351
Universal grammar, 376–377

**V**

Verbatim traces, 189–190
Vertical symmetry, 110
Vicarious learning, 417
Violation-of-expectation method, 128–129
Vision. *See* Visual perception
Visual discrimination, 104
Visual perception
   face processing, 113–119
   in newborns, 107–108
Visual preferences
   paradigm for, 104
   physical stimuli for, 108–112
   psychological stimuli for, 112–113
Visual stimulus, movement as, 108–109
Vocabulary development, 361–363, 391

**W**

Wechsler scales, 498
White matter, 56
Whole-language approach, 454
Whole-object assumption, 363
Wishful thinking, 420
Word spurt, 362
Word-learning constraints, 363–364
Working memory. *See also* Executive function
   defined, 252
   executive function, 256–258
   math disability and, 471
   reading skills and, 452

**Y**

Young children, egocentricity in, 174–177

**Z**

Zone of proximal development, 84–87